# WOMEN
## IMAGES AND REALITIES

## A Multicultural Anthology

### *Second Edition*

Amy Kesselman

*State University of New York, New Paltz*

Lily D. McNair

*The University of Georgia*

Nancy Schniedewind

*State University of New York, New Paltz*

Mayfield Publishing Company
Mountain View, California
London • Toronto

D1445253

**Library of Congress Cataloging-in-Publication Data**

Women : images and realities : a multicultural anthology / [edited by]
   Amy Kesselman, Lily D. McNair, Nancy Schniedewind. — 2nd ed.
      p.    cm.
   Includes bibliographical references.
   ISBN 1-55934-978-6
   1. Feminism—United States.  2. Women—United States—Social
conditions.  3. Women's studies—United States.  I. Kesselman, Amy
Vita.  II. McNair, Lily D.  III. Schniedewind, Nancy.
HQ1421.W653  1998
305.42'0973—dc21                    98-39649
                                      CIP

Manufactured in the United States of America
10  9  8  7  6  5  4  3  2  1

Mayfield Publishing Company
1280 Villa Street
Mountain View, California 94041

Sponsoring editor, Serina Beauparlant; production, Michael Bass & Associates; manuscript editor, Helen Walden; design manager, Jean Mailander; text designer, Joan Greenfield; cover designer, Diana Coe; illustrations, The Asterisk Group; manufacturing manager, Randy Hurst. The text was set in 9.5/12 Plantin Light by G & S Typesetters, Inc., and printed on 50# Chromatone Matte Light by The Banta Book Group.

Cover image: Gunta Stölzl, *Schlitzgobelin Rot-Grün*, 1926/27. Kette Leinen, Schuss vorw. Baumwolle, 195 x 113 cm. © Bauhaus Archiv, Berlin. Photo by Hans-Joachim Bartsch. © Artists Rights Society (ARS), New York/Beeldrecht, Amsterdam. Photographs: Parts I–IV and VI–VII, Virginia Blaisdell; Part V, © 1993 Illene Perlman/Impact Visuals. Text credits continue at the back of the book on pages 574–578, which constitute an extension of the copyright page.

*Dedicated to our students,*

*our sisters:  Laura Kesselman Devlin (1938–1981)*
*Naomi McNair Vliet*
*Carol Schniedewind*

*and to:  Virginia Blaisdell*
*George, Randall, and Marguerite Roberts*
*Dave Porter and Jesse and Daniel Schniedewind*

# Preface

This second edition of *Women: Images and Realities* has emerged from a process of reflective teaching and research that builds on our experiences in writing the first edition. That book grew out of our experiences as teachers of introductory women's studies and psychology of women courses. Dissatisfied with the available texts, we spent many years foraging among journals and anthologies to bring our students a view of feminism that reflected their diverse experience and spoke in a language that was accessible and compelling. Although we wanted to include some of the fruits of feminist research, we felt it most important that students' first encounter with women's studies be one that engaged them and evoked the flash of recognition and connection that has drawn women to feminism. To this end, *Women: Images and Realities* includes a great many first-person and fictional accounts of women's experiences. To address issues that emerge from discussions of the lives of women with diverse backgrounds, we not only present pieces about a variety of female experiences but also, in Part V, directly address some of the systems of domination that interact with gender in women's lives.

The introductory women's studies course at State University of New York (SUNY) at New Paltz, called Women: Images and Realities, provided both the inspiration and structure for this anthology. Since it was first offered in 1974, the course has developed to reflect the responses of the thousands of students who have taken it. Instructors found that students were more adept at analyzing social structures after they had discussed ideas about gender and its effect on individual women's lives. We have therefore structured the book to move from the more visible manifestations of sexism in our culture to the forms of discrimination that are embedded in social institutions.

This second edition reflects the experiences of students and faculty who have used this book in the past four years. In our classrooms we have engaged students with the material and each other, reflected on what we have learned, and reconceived the book anew. We have benefited from the feedback of others who also have shared what they have learned from this process.

We are all academics: a historian, a clinical psychologist, and an educator. Amy has written about women workers during World War II and is currently researching the history of women's liberation. Lily's research focuses on women's issues in addictive behaviors and African-American women's experiences in psychotherapy. Nancy's work is in the areas of multicultural education, feminist pedagogy, and cooperative learning.

Our interest in women's studies and feminism, however, is not merely academic; we are all deeply committed to feminist social change. We have tried, in *Women: Images and Realities,* to stimulate an intellectual interest in women's studies by presenting a wide variety of women's studies topics. In addition, by demonstrating the ways that women have been able to make significant changes in our society and culture, we hope to encourage a political commitment to creating a just and generous world.

## ACKNOWLEDGMENTS

The second edition of this book, like the first, has truly been a collaborative effort. Our cooperative working arrangements and consensual decision-making process, characteristic of feminist process, have been both stimulating and arduous. We appreciate each other's patience and commitment.

Many people have made invaluable contributions to this second edition. Sarah Ellis and Ellenbeth Kaiser have been resourceful, able, and dedicated research assistants. Chris Fox, Shalom Palacio, and Kellie-Ann Ffrench have also provided valuable research support. Thanks for the ongoing contributions of Virginia Blaisdell, Dave Porter, and George Roberts.

Pat Clarke, the program assistant at the Women's Studies Program at SUNY–New Paltz, has helped in innumerable and invaluable ways over the years. We also appreciate the clerical assistance of Lynn Johnson, Ceal Donato, Lorraine Fazio, Cathy Ragsdale, Becky Walters, Michelle Rice, and Michelle Ayers. The State University of New York–New Paltz has supported this project through several grants under its program for research and creative projects.

The work of many who contributed to the first edition was also essential to the completion of this collection. Candace Watson, Lisa DeBoer, Lorie Gross, Lena Hatchett, and Stephanie Brown were able and dedicated research assistants. We appreciate the ideas and perspectives that Johnella Butler and Elisa Dávila contributed to the early stages of this project. Stacey Yap offered many valuable resources on Asian American women. Rayna Green and Paula Gunn Allen provided helpful suggestions regarding a number of pieces included here. Alison Nash, Eudora Chikwendu, Lee Ann Bell, and Rickie Solinger also gave useful feedback. Virginia Blaisdell's thoughtful editorial assistance improved several parts of this manuscript.

The thoughtful feedback of reviewers who read earlier drafts of the manuscript has been incorporated into the text.

Serina Beauparlant, sponsoring editor at Mayfield Publishing Company, has been encouraging throughout the process of completing the second edition of this book. April Wells-Hayes of Mayfield and Tobi Giannone of Michael Bass & Associates shepherded the book through the final stages of production with consistent resourcefulness and good humor. Finally, we especially thank all the contributors to this volume, some of whom rewrote pieces they had written earlier.

# Contents

## PART III
## GENDER AND WOMEN'S BODIES   107

### Female Beauty   111

# Introduction

Inspired by the very positive responses to the first edition of *Women: Images and Realities: A Multicultural Anthology,* we are pleased to bring even more diverse women's voices, additional feminist issues, and updated information and resources to this second edition. We have tried to gather into this book, once again, readings that will challenge your thinking and be meaningful to your life experiences.

In *Women: Images and Realities: A Multicultural Anthology* you will enter the lives of many different women. By exploring their experiences and ideas, you will learn more about yourself and what it means to be female in the United States today. You will hear the voices of women of different racial, cultural, and socioeconomic backgrounds who have made various choices in their lives. Because the selections reflect a wide variety of female experience, some parts of this book will resonate with your experience while others will not. We hope the book will enable you to understand what women have in common as well as the different ways that the experience of being female is shaped by race, class, and culture.

The structure of this book is inspired by the consciousness-raising process that has been a central part of contemporary feminism. The goal of consciousness-raising is to use insights from personal experience to enhance a political critique of the position of women in society. Echoing this process, the book moves back and forth between personal experience and social realities, illuminating the way sexism in society affects women's lives. We hope the selections in this book will stimulate your thinking about your own life.

## ORGANIZATION AND USE OF THIS BOOK

The second edition of *Women: Images and Realities* is organized somewhat differently from the first edition. In the previous edition we addressed in the first six parts of the book ways women have been constrained by our society and culture and saved until the last two parts of the book methods for improving women's lives. In this second edition we have included in all parts examples of the ways women have challenged the constraints that they face.

*Women: Images and Realities* is divided into seven parts. We begin by introducing the subject of women's studies, an approach to knowledge that emerged as part of the contemporary feminist movement. Because a feminist perspective provides the groundwork for women's studies, Part I explores the meaning of feminism and women's studies for different groups of women and, to a lesser extent, for men. It examines the impact of women's studies and feminist scholarship on other academic disciplines.

Part II presents prevailing ideas about what it means to be female in our society and describes the way we learn and internalize these ideas. Part III explores the effects of these ideas on women's attitudes toward our bodies and sexuality. Because this anthology is designed to enable you to make connections between your personal life and social realities, it moves from a focus on individual experience in Parts II and III to an examination of the social institutions that shape women's lives in Part IV. Articles in this part demonstrate the ways that the subordination of women is deeply embedded in social institutions such as the legal system, the workplace, the family, the health care system, and religion.

While all the parts in *Women: Images and Realities* include accounts of female experience in a variety of cultural contexts, Part V directly addresses the ways women have been divided from each other. It examines the ways that racial and class inequities in our society have often separated women and explores the interplay between institutional discrimination and the relationships among different groups of women. Part VI discusses several issues that women in the United States face today. Although these issues have always been a part of women's lives, they have only recently been publicly discussed as a result of the efforts of the feminist movement. Part VII explores ways that women have worked together to make social and political change. By reminding us of the rich tradition of female resistance both within and outside an organized feminist movement, the selections in Parts VII provide inspiration and hope.

We have tried to create a rich brew—a mixture of short stories, poems, autobiographical accounts, and journal excerpts as well as analytical and descriptive essays from a variety of disciplines. We hope this mixture will engage you intellectually and emotionally. Introductions to sections provide a framework that places the selections in the broader context of the part. While most of the material is current, some articles provide a historical perspective. Those written in the earlier years of the contemporary feminist movement are important because they laid the conceptual groundwork for future research and analysis.

Although there are theoretical insights in *Women: Images and Realities*, this book does not provide a theoretical introduction to women's studies in all the various disciplines. Theory is discussed in those women's studies courses that explore feminist issues and particular disciplines in depth. Here, you will hear the words of a wide variety of writers, some prominent feminist writers and some students like yourself. Because the emotions provoked by this material can sometimes be unsettling, you may find it useful to discuss your responses outside class as well as in the classroom. These discussions might take place with friends, family members, or a counselor, depending on the intensity of the personal connection with the issues.

This book may raise specific questions for African-American, Asian-American, Latina, American Indian, and Jewish women. Women of color are struggling against both the sexism in minority communities and the particular ways that sexism and racism interact in their lives. The different priorities and emphases that emerge from various cultural and racial contexts enrich and deepen a feminist perspective. The focus of *Women: Images and Realities* is on the struggle of women in the United States for freedom. The U.S. feminist movement, however, is part of a global women's movement that has raised significant questions for women in the United States. Although some of the issues raised by the global feminist movement are touched on in this book, they are explored more fully in other women's studies courses.

Men who have taken women's studies courses have often found it intellectually and emotionally challenging to be in a course that is focused on women, taught by women, and that usually includes a majority of female students. By listening to women's experiences and sharing the experience of being male in a sexist society, men can both benefit from and contribute to a women's studies course.

Many students will use this book—in the introductory women's studies course, an interdisciplinary course that familiarizes students with the field of women's studies and the feminist perspective that shapes women's studies scholarship. In such a course, you may also read *Our Bodies, Our Selves for the New Century* written by the Boston Women's Health Book Collective (Simon & Schuster, 1998). Even if the book is not assigned in your course, it is an excellent complement to *Women: Images and Realities,* and we recommend it.

## HOW WE SEE FEMINISM

Because *Women: Images and Realities* is informed by a feminist perspective, we want to describe what feminism means to us. We see sexism as a central fact of all women's lives, even though it wears many different faces. The life of a single mother struggling to support her family on the wages she earns doing domestic work is very different from the life of a woman struggling to succeed in a scientific establishment dominated by men. But both survive in a world where women are paid less than men on all levels, both live in a society in which one woman is raped every three minutes, and both face the possibility of losing their jobs if they resist their employer's sexual advances. Feminism is a social movement whose goal is to eliminate the oppression of women in all its forms. This means making major social, economic, political, and cultural changes in our society—changes so fundamental and numerous that the task sometimes seems overwhelming. Yet feminists have succeeded in making changes that would have appeared unthinkable 50 years ago—and such accomplishments give us hope and courage.

One of the most important ideas that contemporary feminism has generated is that "the personal is political"—what happens in our private lives reflects the power relations in our society. This book examines the inequities in both women's personal lives and the world. The belief in our right to determine our lives empowers us to expand our choices: to develop relationships based on equality and mutual respect, to choose when and whether to have children, to work toward career goals that are meaningful to us.

Because of the connection between personal and political life, our ability to control our own lives is limited by the environment in which we live. We cannot, for example, choose when and whether we have children unless safe, effective, and legal birth control and abortion are available. Feminism is more than an individual lifestyle. It involves a commitment to social change, which can take a variety of forms. It might mean working to make your campus safer for women; forming a support group for women in your school, department, or office to discuss the conditions of your lives and ways to improve them; organizing a forum about sexual harassment at your workplace or on your campus; or organizing a cooperative child-care center in your community. Feminism means making changes wherever you are.

## THE AUTHORS: THREE FEMINIST JOURNEYS

Because this book affirms the differences among us, we want to tell you who we are and what feminism means to each of us.

*Amy*   Growing up Jewish in New York City in the 1950s, I always felt different from the boys and girls whose images I confronted in grade school textbooks. The blond children and white picket fences represented normalcy to me, while my apartment building and multiethnic neighborhood seemed deviant. I went to a large city college in which men dominated the intellectual and cultural life, and I struggled to be taken seriously in and out of the classroom. The movements of the 1960s for civil rights and peace in Vietnam gave direction and meaning to my life, but I found that even as we worked toward a fairer world, women were treated in demeaning ways. In the late 1960s when *feminism* was a foreign word to most people, I began talking with other women about my experiences and participated in the birth of the women's liberation movement.

Feminism saved my life. It replaced the self-hatred of being female in a woman-hating culture with the power of anger at injustice. It replaced isolation with a sense of connection and identification with other women. It replaced despair with a vision of a world in which everyone is able to develop fully in loving connection with one another. But feminism did not liberate me. I am still subject to rape, sexual harassment, discrimination, and the unremitting degradation by the media and other woman-hating institutions. Ultimately, I see feminism as a political movement. Its power to change the world depends on its ability to mobilize women to challenge the power relations of the institutions in our society.

*Lily*   I grew up in a rural community on the outskirts of a major military installation in New Jersey. My childhood memories are filled with images of other children who, like me, were of mixed racial backgrounds. Most had mothers who were Asian (Japanese, Korean, or Filipino) and fathers who were African American. This setting made it impossible for me to ignore the effects of race and class on the lives of people around me. I began to realize that the world was unfair and that this unfairness shaped the lives of most of the people I knew.

My parents taught me, very early, that I was a black child in a racist society. At times I didn't quite understand why they attached so much significance to this fact, but I gradually learned about the world from their history. My mother talked about her experiences as a Japanese girl-child during World War II and as a "war bride" in the Deep South of the 1950s. Bitter toward a society that treated him as less than a person because of his black skin, my father promised me that one day I would understand what he meant.

When I went away to an Ivy League college, I saw inequity both within the structure of the institution (such as hiring and tenure practices) and within the student body. Blacks and women were still viewed as unwanted, unqualified newcomers to this formerly all-white, all-male bastion. Fortunately, the African-American community provided me with peers and a black, female mentor who helped to strengthen my commitment to fighting racial, sexual, and class oppression.

For me, feminism is a natural extension of my experiences as an African-American-Asian woman. Feminism provides me with a framework for looking at and understanding power relationships in our society. I recognize that I must be aware of the realities of oppression because this knowledge forces me to challenge racism and sexism. A feminist perspective is consistent with my view of a more just society—one in which differences among people can be appreciated and celebrated, not dismissed. Feminism is a positive force in my personal life as well. It enables me to develop relationships that are based on equality, cooperation, and an affirmation of the strengths of women and men.

*Nancy*   Growing up as a white female in a semirural New England community, I was not aware of the price I was paying for being female. I did not wonder why I hated science. No one called my attention to how few females appeared in my textbooks or discussed the ways that the absence of role models inhibits learning and stunts expectations. I never wondered why no one encouraged me to become a scientist despite my aptitude for science. Though I knew I loved sports, I never connected my failure to take myself seriously as an athlete with the fact that the high school athletic budget and programs for boys' sports were extensive, while those for girls were nonexistent.

I was also unaware of the privileges I received by being white. I didn't realize that because we were white, my family was able to move to our town and to find housing, thereby benefiting from better public schools. I didn't wonder why there were only two African-American families in our town. I never thought about the comfort of being in the racial majority in my school and how my sense of being "normal" enhanced my ability to learn. I didn't ask why I had the privilege of going home to play when my African-American classmates went home to help their mothers do the laundry they took in to support their families.

I saw my life as my own. Even throughout my master's degree program, I failed to see patterns of discrimination and privilege. I thought the sexual harassment I experienced was my own problem, not part of a pattern experienced by millions of women. There were no women's studies courses in the late 1960s, and it was only through long talks with friends and coworkers that I opened my eyes to sexism. Subsequently, I read much of what the burgeoning women's movement was producing. Reflecting on my life, I saw how I had been affected by gender, race, and class and look to the future with a renewed commitment to work for change.

Feminism offers me the support, values, and ideas for living an authentic life. It provides me a way to understand women's experiences and a vision of a more just and humane future. Feminism contributes to my role as an educator by helping me understand how sexism limits both men's and women's educational potential. Feminist values inspire a more equitable and empowering educational vision and practice. Feminism reaffirms for me the values of cooperation and care, strengthening my female friendships. Feminism gives me the consciousness and strength to make family relationships more equitable. Finally, feminism sustains my faith in women's collective power to transform individual lives and social institutions.

As our own stories demonstrate, the experience of integrating feminism into one's life can be challenging and exhilarating. We hope this book makes you feel stronger and better able to both make choices in your own life and participate in the process of creating a more just and generous world.

## PART I

# What Is Women's Studies?

The evolution and growth of women's studies over the past 30 years reflect dramatic changes in not only our educational system but also the way students' learning can be personally and politically relevant. However, despite the increase in numbers of women's studies courses, programs, and departments in U.S. colleges and universities, many student still ask, "What is women's studies?" You will probably hear this question often when you tell people you are taking a women's studies course.

What *is* women's studies? The question itself tells you something about the answer; some faculty members and students still view women's studies as marginal to the main business of the university. Yet to countless others, women's studies is an important and exciting experience that introduces new ways of seeing both the world and oneself. Women's studies scholars and teachers place women at center stage in the learning process, challenging both the content and form of education. A basic premise of women's studies is that women's experiences and contributions are integral to understanding our world. A women's studies approach to education emphasizes an interactive learning process in which all students are intellectually and emotionally challenged.

The realities of schooling in the United States contradict these goals of women's studies. Education has often been a bittersweet experience for women. We expect that knowledge of our world can be empowering, enabling us to change our lives and communities. For many women, particularly those who have experienced racial or ethnic discrimination, education achievement assures greater access to resources and opportunities. But the educational institutions of our society have too often been limiting, rather than empowering, for women. The practices of educational institutions frequently encourage girls and women to pursue occupations in traditionally "female" areas rather than in traditionally "male" domains, such as math and the sciences. Schools and teachers tend to reinforce girls' compliance and passivity rather than their assertiveness and inquisitiveness. Men have historically exercised authority in institutions of higher learning, determining "valid" areas of inquiry and "legitimate" methods of analysis and research. In sum, the world that students encounter in college classrooms can be one in which women play marginal roles, while men occupy center stage. The dominant message is that human experience equals male experience.

Women's studies was born out of the conviction that women are worth learning about and that understanding women's experiences helps us to change the condition of women. Women's studies courses first appeared in the late 1960s and quickly spread across the country. By 1989, over 500 colleges in the United States had women's studies programs. In the past 20 years, thousands of books and articles about women have been published, challenging old assumptions and charting new territory. Today, women's studies conferences, workshops, journals, and research institutes addressing the concerns of diverse groups of women flourish.

A women's studies perspective contests the male-centered bias so prominent in scholarship across academic disciplines. The nature of this challenge, however, has changed as the field of women's studies has developed. Initially, women scholars endeavored to address the absence of women in the literature of various academic areas by uncovering women's achievements. For example, psychology has benefited from the work of scholars who focused on the important contributions of women such as Mamie Phipps Clark, Carolyn Sherif, and Margaret Harlow to psychological research. It quickly became apparent, however, that the central concepts of many academic disciplines excluded women or assumed women's inferiority to men. Even the language used to describe these concepts and ideas can be laden with assumptions about female inferiority. As Emily Martin points out, for example, "scientific" descriptions of the egg and sperm rely on stereotyped notions of male and female gender roles and reinforce widely held beliefs about female passivity and male power.[1] Thus, even scientists examining seemingly objective events can imbue their observations with gendered meaning. A women's studies perspective allows us to critique these interpretations, thereby challenging some of the basic tenets that structure academic knowledge. In this way, women's experiences can be at center stage rather than an anomalous footnote.

In the field of history, for example, historical subject matter was traditionally limited to the public arena such as political parties, wars, and the economy. The domestic world, where many women spent a great deal of their time, was considered trivial or irrelevant; and the relationship between the domestic and public worlds was ignored. In literature, the very definition of great literature, or "the canon," was based on standards that white male authors generated. By emphasizing the contributions of women, critically challenging the conceptual frameworks underlying traditional scholarship, and presenting theory and research focusing on women's experiences, women's studies research is transforming the terrain of human knowledge. When women are placed at the center of inquiry, everything dramatically changes, as if a kaleidoscope has been turned. Even the boundaries that separate the disciplines begin to blur and appear arbitrary when we seek to answer questions about women's lives.

The word *sexism* appeared because the available term *sex discrimination* did not adequately describe the pervasive bias against women in our culture. Sexism has therefore come to mean behaviors, attitudes, and institutions based on the assumption of male superiority. *Patriarchy* refers to "power of the fathers" and is used by feminists in two ways: to describe a society in which older men are in positions of power and authority and to describe a male-dominated society. This new vocabulary has been instrumental in shaping the ways in which we now think about the experiences of women and girls in our society.

The ideas of feminism have inspired the development of women's studies theory and courses. *Feminism* refers to the belief that women have been historically subordinate to men, as well as to the commitment to working for freedom for women in all aspects of social life. Although feminist beliefs, values, and practices are continually evolving, reflecting new ideas, movements, and historical research, it is clear that similar values have informed the lives and work of many different groups of women,

---

[1] Emily Martin, "The Egg and the Sperm: How Science Has Constructed a Romance Based on Stereotypical Male-Female Roles," *Signs, 16* (1991), 485–501.

even when they may not have identified their beliefs as "feminist." Paula Gunn Allen, a Native American writer, pointed out that roots of contemporary feminism can be found in many Native American cultures.[2] Some of these societies were gynarchies (governed by women) that were egalitarian, pacifist, and spiritually based. These values and practices are comparable to those of present-day feminism such as cooperation and respect for human freedom. As we understand the varied ways that women have worked toward self-determination in different contexts and cultures throughout history, the definition of feminism becomes broader and richer.

By making gender visible feminist scholarship has also paved the way for increased attention to "gender studies," the examination of issues related to the social construction of gender. As stated earlier, by placing women at center stage, the entire landscape of intellectual inquiry changes. Not only do women's studies scholars focus on women's and girl's experiences, they also examine the relations between men and women, and the influence of *gender* on a variety of attitudes and behaviors. Thus, examining gender is more than examining women's lives; it also includes acknowledging the enormous influence of gender on *all* of our lives. Boys' and men's experience is powerfully affected by ideas about masculinity and femininity. Gender studies examines the ways that ideas about the social relations of women and men structure our politics and culture and the way we all experience our world. By reaffirming the significance of gender in our lives, gender studies is very much related to women's studies in its content, though distinct in its goals and process. Elizabeth Minnich aptly describes this complementary relationship: "Gender Studies requires Women's Studies, just as Women's Studies requires the study of gender. One does not substitute for the other; they are mutually enriching."[3]

As feminist scholars began to chart women's experiences, they sometimes found the available vocabulary confusing and inadequate for describing the realities of women's lives. As a result, feminist scholarship has generated several new words and has endowed some familiar words with new meaning. The word *gender,* for example, once pertained only to the grammatical grouping of nouns but has come to refer to the socially constructed behaviors and characteristics associated with each sex. Whereas "gender" is a social category, the word *sex* describes the physiological identities of women and men. The distinction between sex and gender allows us to see that the particular expectations for women and men in our culture are neither immutable nor universal. Rather, these expectations are predicated on assumed differences between women and men as a function of the social rules ascribed to us.

The word *feminism* originated in France and was introduced into this country in the early 1900s after efforts to expand women's political rights had been flourishing throughout the world for many decades.[4] The women who first identified themselves as feminist in the early twentieth century believed that the "emancipation of women"

---

[2] Paula Gunn Allen, *The Sacred Hoop: Recovering the Feminine in American Indian Traditions* (Boston: Beacon Press, 1986), p. 213.

[3] Elizabeth Minnich, *Transforming Knowledge* (Philadelphia: Temple University Press, 1990), p. 139.

[4] Nancy Cott, *The Grounding of Modern Feminism* (New Haven, CT: Yale University Press, 1987), p. 14.

required changes in the relations between women and men and between women and the family, as well as between women and the state. At a 1914 meeting entitled "What Is Feminism?" Mary Jenny Howe stated, "We want simply to be ourselves, . . . not just our little female selves but our whole big human selves." [5]

For many women, the goal of freedom for women was inextricably linked with the end of all forms of domination. Women of color in particular saw the connections between sexual and racial oppression. Anna Cooper, an African-American woman, pointed out in her address to the World's Congress of Representative Women in 1896:

> Not till . . . race, color, sex and condition are seen as accidents, and not the substance of life . . . not till then is woman's lesson taught and woman's cause won—not the white woman's, nor the black woman's nor the red woman's but the cause of every man and every woman who has writhed silently under a mighty wrong. Woman's wrongs are thus indissolubly linked with all undefended woe, and the acquirement of her "rights" will mean the final triumph of all right over might.[6]

U.S. historians often refer to the movement that began in the nineteenth century and culminated with the Nineteenth Amendment, granting women the right to vote, as the first wave of feminism. The legal, educational, and political achievements of the movement were considerable, despite the fact that it faced enormous opposition to every demand. Yet the organizations that led the movement did not speak for all women and often refused to seriously consider the concerns of African-American and immigrant women. The history of the suffrage movement demonstrates how race and class divisions can prevent a movement from working effectively to achieve freedom for all women.

In the decades after women won the right to vote in 1920, the organized women's rights movement dissipated, and the word *feminism* fell into disuse and ill repute. In the 1960s, a new generation revived the fight for what they now called "women's liberation" and a vision of a world free of domination and subordination. This movement struck a responsive chord in thousands of women. The feminist movement grew rapidly throughout the 1970s, permeating every aspect of social, political, and cultural life. The new feminist movement has argued that reproductive rights are essential for women's freedom. It has criticized the disadvantaged position of women in the workplace and the subordination of women in the family, pointing out the connection between the place of women in the labor force and the family. By declaring that "the personal is political," contemporary feminists have brought into the open subjects that had only previously been discussed in whispers, such as sexuality, rape, incestuous sexual abuse, and domestic violence. For feminists, all of these struggles are inextricably connected, and changes in all of them are necessary to attain freedom for women.

---

[5] Quoted in Cott, p. 39.

[6] Anna Cooper in May Wright Sewell, *World's Congress of Representative Women* (Chicago, 1983), quoted in Elsa Barkley Brown, "Womanist Consciousness: Maggie Lena Walker and the Independent Order of St. Luke," *Signs, 14*(3), 614.

Feminism is continually developing a more multicultural and inclusive perspective, mirroring the lives of women in all races, ethnic groups, and classes. Feminists of varied races and ethnicities are generating theory and practice that address their particular experiences and consciousness, broadening and deepening the scope of feminist analysis.

Black feminist thought, for example, reflects the unique position of African-American women in American society. As eloquently expressed by Alice Walker, black feminism, or "womanism," draws on the historical strength of black women in their families and communities and the rich African-American tradition of resistance, persistence, and survival. By describing a "womanist" with a broad brush that celebrates the everyday lives of black girls and women, as well as the political implications of their activism, Walker's definition resonates with the experiences of many black women. Black feminists have also emphasized the concept of "multiple consciousness": that the distinct systems of racism, sexism, and class oppression interact simultaneously in the lives of women of color in the United States. They have also suggested an African-centered rather than a Eurocentric perspective on the history of women, allowing for an appreciation of the powerful roles that women have played in some African societies.

Jewish feminists have also reclaimed their tradition of Jewish female resistance and have reexamined insulting stereotypes such as the "pushy Jewish mother" and "Jewish American Princess" to express the legitimacy of female assertiveness. They have revived Rabbi Hillel's question "If I am not for myself, who will be? If I am only for myself, what am I?" to explore both the meaning of anti-Semitism for Jewish women and the importance of the connections between different groups of suppressed people. Reflecting on this project, Melanie Kaye/Kantrowitz has pointed out, "What is best in people is a sturdy connection between respect for the self and respect for the other: reaching in and out at the same time."[7]

Asian and Latina feminists have pointed out the tensions between immigrant and U.S. cultures and the concurrent need to affirm their cultural heritage and reject its sexism. Traditional Japanese culture, for instance, expects women to be docile and to put family honor ahead of their own needs. One's self is inextricably tied to one's family; to break away is often viewed as an act of betrayal. Asian-American feminists have also confronted the myths about Asian women's sexuality, myths that have emerged from an interplay between Western stereotypes and the expectations of women in Asian cultures. Latina feminists have demonstrated the need to negotiate a path between the sometimes conflicting demands of the Latino community's expectations and female self-determination. Feminism for Latina women, and women of other oppressed groups, means simultaneously working with Latino men against their common oppression and challenging sexist or "macho" attitudes and behavior.

Contemporary American Indian feminists carry many of the traditional values and practices of woman-centered Native American cultures into the present. In ad-

---

[7] Melanie Kaye/Kantrowitz, "To Be a Radical Jew in the Late Twentieth Century," *Sinister Wisdom, 29–30* (1986), 280.

dition, Native American women's history and their vision of connectedness to the earth and spiritual world, along with a legacy of responsibility toward the environment, are emerging as important concerns for many feminists. For example, ecofeminism addresses the connection between women's oppression and the exploitation of the earth's natural resources, emphasizing women's role in confronting these environmental issues.

The ideas and concerns of different groups of women are expanding the boundaries of feminism, contributing to multicultural feminist theory and practice aimed at liberating all people. As this feminism continues to develop, we acknowledge and incorporate the struggles of women who have worked for equality and freedom for women, though they may not have called themselves "feminists."

The atmosphere of a women's studies classroom is often different from that of most academic classrooms. Women's studies emerged as an academic discipline from women asking questions about their own experiences, and this process remains a central part of a women's studies education. Women's studies instructors usually encourage students to critically ask questions of the material and to bring their own experiences to bear. The values of feminism, including a critique of all forms of domination, an emphasis on cooperation, and a belief in the integration of theory and practice, have shaped an approach to teaching called "feminist pedagogy," which makes the women's studies classroom a stimulating and interactive learning environment.

Speaking up for ourselves is an essential first step for women in taking an active role in their education. In the first selection, bell hooks writes from the context of the Southern black community in which she grew up, where "talking back" as a girl was an act of daring. It often takes courage for women to speak up for themselves in educational settings, where male-oriented norms, curricula, and classroom processes often silence women's voices. Mai Kao Thao echoes this message in her essay, "Sins of Silence," as she describes the pain she and other "good Hmong women" have endured when they kept silent about the realities of their lives.

Adrienne Rich, feminist author and poet, wrote the next selection as an address to a primarily white, female graduating class in 1977. Its message, about the importance of women "claiming an education" that is meaningful to them, continues to be relevant today in any educational setting. Rich provides a personal context for understanding the role of women's studies courses in shaping such an education.

Just as feminism has become more inclusive of women from diverse backgrounds, so too has the content of women's studies expanded over the years, embodying the experiences of women from varying racial, ethnic, and class groups. In their classic essay, Akasha (Gloria T.) Hull and Barbara Smith place the development of black women's studies in a political and historical context. By highlighting the legacy of black women's struggles to obtain an education during and after slavery, Hull and Smith show us the connection between black women's studies and the politics of oppression.

The next essay focuses on men and women's studies. Originally delivered as a lecture by Michael Kimmel at an anniversary of the women's studies program at a major university, the essay points out that by illuminating the workings of gender in culture and society, women's studies has opened new ways of looking at men, who, though they may not have been conscious of it, have also been affected by the social relations of women and men and ideas about masculinity. Convinced that men, too, need to challenge the destructive effects of sexism, Kimmel has unearthed a historical legacy of male support for women's struggle for equality and independence.

The next six selections in this part are voices of a women's studies teacher and former students. These students are women and a man of varied racial and ethnic backgrounds who explore the meaning and value of a women's studies education for their own lives, both personally and politically.

We end this section with an essay examining the influence of women's studies on a variety of disciplines within American colleges and universities. By documenting the changes that have been prompted by the evolution of women's studies, Carol Christ highlights the far-reaching impact of a feminist perspective in research and teaching, and she celebrates the movement of a women's studies perspective from the margin to the center of academic research.

 1

# Talking Back

BELL HOOKS

In the world of the southern black community I grew up in, "back talk" and "talking back" meant speaking as an equal to an authority figure. It meant daring to disagree and sometimes it just meant having an opinion. In the "old school," children were meant to be seen and not heard. My great-grandparents, grandparents, and parents were all from the old school. To make yourself heard if you were a child was to invite punishment, the back-hand lick, the slap across the face that would catch you unaware, or the feel of switches stinging your arms and legs.

To speak then when one was not spoken to was a courageous act—an act of risk and daring. And yet it was hard not to speak in warm rooms where heated discussions began at the crack of dawn, women's voices filling the air, giving orders, making threats, fussing. Black men may have excelled in the art of poetic preaching in the male-dominated church, but in the church of the home, where the everyday rules of how to live and how to act were established, it was black women who preached.

There, black women spoke in a language so rich, so poetic, that it felt to me like being shut off from life, smothered to death if one were not allowed to participate.

It was in that world of woman talk (the men were often silent, often absent) that was born in me the craving to speak, to have a voice, and not just any voice but one that could be identified as belonging to me. To make my voice, I had to speak, to hear myself talk—and talk I did—darting in and out of grown folks' conversations and dialogues, answering questions that were not directed at me, endlessly asking questions, making speeches. Needless to say, the punishments for these acts of speech seemed endless. They were intended to silence me—the child—and more particularly the girl child. Had I been a boy, they might have encouraged me to speak believing that I might someday be called to preach. There was no "calling" for talking girls, no legitimized rewarded speech. The punishments I received for "talking back" were intended to suppress all possibility that I would create my own speech. That speech was to be suppressed so that the "right speech of womanhood" would emerge.

Within feminist circles, silence is often seen as the sexist "right speech of womanhood"—the sign of woman's submission to patriarchal authority. This emphasis on woman's silence may be an accurate remembering of what has taken place in the households of women from WASP backgrounds in the United States, but in black communities (and diverse ethnic communities), women have not been silent. Their voices can be heard. Certainly for black women, our struggle has not been to emerge from silence into speech but to change the nature and direction of our speech, to make a speech that compels listeners, one that is heard.

Our speech, "the right speech of womanhood," was often the soliloquy, the talking into thin air, the talking to ears that do not hear you—the talk that is simply not listened to. Unlike the black male preacher whose speech was to be heard, who was to be listened to, whose words were to be remembered, the voices of black women—giving orders, making threats, fussing—could be tuned out, could become a kind of background music, audible but not acknowledged as significant speech. Dialogue—the sharing of speech and recognition—took place not between mother and child or mother and male authority figure but among black women. I can remember watching fascinated as our mother talked with her mother, sisters, and women friends. The intimacy and intensity of their speech—the satisfaction they received from talking to one another, the pleasure, the joy. It was in this world of woman speech, loud talk, angry words, women with tongues quick and sharp, tender sweet tongues, touching our world with their words, that I made speech my birthright—and the right to voice, to authorship, a privilege I would not be denied. It was in that world and because of it that I came to dream of writing, to write.

Writing was a way to capture speech, to hold onto it, keep it close. And so I wrote down bits and pieces of conversations, confessing in cheap diaries that soon fell apart from too much handling, expressing the intensity of my sorrow, the anguish of speech—for I was always saying the wrong thing, asking the wrong questions. I could not confine my speech to the necessary corners and concerns of life. I hid these writings under my bed, in pillow stuffings, among faded underwear. When my sisters found and read them, they ridiculed and mocked me—poking fun. I felt violated, ashamed, as if the secret parts of my self had been exposed, brought into the open, and hung like newly clean laundry,

out in the air for everyone to see. The fear of exposure, the fear that one's deepest emotions and innermost thoughts will be dismissed as mere nonsense, felt by so many young girls keeping diaries, holding and hiding speech, seems to me now one of the barriers that women have always needed and still need to destroy so that we are no longer pushed into secrecy or silence.

Despite my feelings of violation, of exposure, I continued to speak and write, choosing my hiding places well, learning to destroy work when no safe place could be found. I was never taught absolute silence, I was taught that it was important to speak but to talk a talk that was in itself a silence. Taught to speak and yet beware of the betrayal of too much heard speech, I experienced intense confusion and deep anxiety in my efforts to speak and write. Reciting poems at Sunday afternoon church service might be rewarded. Writing a poem (when one's time could be "better" spent sweeping, ironing, learning to cook) was luxurious activity, indulged in at the expense of others. Questioning authority, raising issues that were not deemed appropriate subjects brought pain, punishments—like telling mama I wanted to die before her because I could not live without her—that was crazy talk, crazy speech, the kind that would lead you to end up in a mental institution. "Little girl," I would be told, "if you don't stop all this crazy talk and crazy acting you are going to end up right out there at Western State."

Madness, not just physical abuse, was the punishment for too much talk if you were female. Yet even as this fear of madness haunted me, hanging over my writing like a monstrous shadow, I could not stop the words, making thought, writing speech. For this terrible madness which I feared, which I was sure was the destiny of daring women born to intense speech (after all, the authorities emphasized this point daily), was not as threatening as imposed silence, as suppressed speech.

Safety and sanity were to be sacrificed if I was to experience defiant speech. Though I risked them both, deep-seated fears and anxieties characterized my childhood days. I would speak but I would not ride a bike, play hardball, or hold the gray kitten. Writing about the ways we are traumatized in our growing-up years, psychoanalyst Alice Miller makes the point in *For Your Own Good* that it is not clear why childhood wounds become for some folk an opportunity to grow, to move forward rather than backward in the process of self-realization. Certainly, when I reflect on the trials of my growing-up years, the many punishments, I can see now that in resistance I learned to be vigilant in the nourishment of my spirit, to be tough, to courageously protect that spirit from forces that would break it.

While punishing me, my parents often spoke about the necessity of breaking my spirit. Now when I ponder the silences, the voices that are not heard, the voices of those wounded and/or oppressed individuals who do not speak or write, I contemplate the acts of persecution, torture—the terrorism that breaks spirits, that makes creativity impossible. I write these words to bear witness to the primacy of resistance struggle in any situation of domination (even within family life); to the strength and power that emerges from sustained resistance and the profound conviction that these forces can be healing, can protect us from dehumanization and despair.

These early trials, wherein I learned to stand my ground, to keep my spirit intact, came vividly to mind after I published *Ain't I A Woman* and the book was sharply and harshly criticized. While I had expected a climate of critical dialogue, I was not expecting a critical avalanche that had the power in its intensity to crush the spirit, to push one into silence. Since that time, I have heard stories about black women, about women of color, who write and publish (even when the work is quite successful) having nervous breakdowns, being made mad because they cannot bear the harsh responses of family, friends, and unknown critics, or becoming silent, unproductive. Surely, the absence of a humane critical response has tremendous impact on the writer from any oppressed, colonized group who endeavors to speak. For us, true speaking is not solely an expression of creative power; it is an act of resistance, a political gesture that challenges politics of domination that would render us nameless and voiceless. As such, it is a courageous act—as such, it represents a threat. To those who wield oppressive power, that which is threatening must necessarily be wiped out, annihilated, silenced.

Recently, efforts by black women writers to call attention to our work serve to highlight both our presence and absence. Whenever I peruse women's bookstores, I am struck not by the rapidly growing body of feminist writing by black women, but by the paucity of available published material. Those of us who write and are published remain few in number. The context of silence is varied and multidimensional. Most obvious are the ways racism, sexism, and class exploitation act to suppress and silence. Less obvious are the inner struggles, the efforts made to gain the necessary confidence to write, to re-write, to fully develop craft and skill—and the extent to which such efforts fail.

Although I have wanted writing to be my life-work since childhood, it has been difficult for me to claim "writer" as part of that which identifies and shapes my everyday reality. Even after publishing books, I would often speak of wanting to be a writer as though these works did not exist. And though I would be told, "you are a writer," I was not yet ready to fully affirm this truth. Part of myself was still held captive by domineering forces of history, of familial life that had charted a map of silence, of right speech. I had not completely let go of the fear of saying the wrong thing, of being punished. Somewhere in the deep recesses of my mind, I believed I could avoid both responsibility and punishment if I did not declare myself a writer.

One of the many reasons I chose to write using the pseudonym bell hooks, a family name (mother to Sarah Oldham, grandmother to Rosa Bell Oldham, great-grandmother to me), was to construct a writer-identity that would challenge and subdue all impulses leading me away from speech into silence. I was a young girl buying bubble gum at the corner store when I first really heard the full name bell hooks. I had just "talked back" to a grown person. Even now I can recall the surprised look, the mocking tones that informed me I must be kin to bell hooks—a sharp-tongued woman, a woman who spoke her mind, a woman who was not afraid to talk back. I claimed this legacy of defiance, of will, of courage, affirming my link to female ancestors who were bold and daring in their speech. Unlike my bold and daring mother and grandmother, who were not supportive of talking back, even though they were assertive and powerful in their speech, bell hooks as I discovered, claimed, and invented her was my ally, my support.

That initial act of talking back outside the home was empowering. It was the first of many acts of defiant speech that would make it possible for me to emerge as an independent thinker and writer. In retrospect, "talking back" became for me a rite of initiation, testing my courage, strengthening my commitment, preparing me for the days ahead—the days when writing, rejection notices, periods of silence, publication, ongoing development seem impossible but necessary.

Moving from silence into speech is for the oppressed, the colonized, the exploited, and those who stand and struggle side by side a gesture of defiance that heals, that makes new life and new growth possible. It is that act of speech, of "talking back," that is no mere gesture of empty words, that is the expression of our movement from object to subject—the liberated voice.                    [1989]

 2

## Sins of Silence

MAI KAO THAO

My mother used to tell me that I should always be a good, obedient woman, and smile silently as I swallow the bitterness that others give me. "Nod your head and say yes even if you don't agree. It's much easier. No trouble," she would say. Through these words, I heard, "Silence is power! It is a woman's strength." I remember hearing my father criticize my mother, even about the smallest things. "The rice doesn't taste good enough! Now the meat is too hard! You are a bad woman, a stupid woman! No good." And all the while, my mother would go about fixing what she did "wrong" without uttering a word, just wearing her usual, invisible mask of sadness. Oh well. At least there was no trouble.

I was trained to avoid conflict. When my brother lectured me, I'd reply "uh" and shake my head in agreement. I was punished with harsh reprimands and scorching displeasure if I talked back or offered an opinion, so I was silent. I was declared insolent if I spoke a little louder than I should have, so I learned to whisper. My voice was soft, sweet, and so delicious to the ear of authority. Yes. I was a good girl. Wordless. Humble. Obedient. A perfect Hmong woman.

Sexism laid comfortably on top of my silent submission. I smiled politely when older men gave me kisses on my cheek, more like wet, slow licks that made my innocent skin crawl. Hands grappled my body. Was that a bad touch or a good touch? Must have been a good touch. Relieved. No one will say that I was wrong in thinking that it was a bad touch, because it wasn't, and no one will call me stupid girl. There will be no trouble. Yes, it must be a good touch! Racism grinned at my passivity, while I, the "damned chink," gave it my pride, tears, and forgiveness. But no matter! I was stone. Silent. Hard. Emotionless. Nothing was going to hurt me!

In reality, I wasn't stone. I was flesh and blood. I was a cup, continuously filled, half with anger, dissatisfaction, and anxiety, and the other half with emptiness. My silence had killed my Self, the essence which holds and molds an individual together in order to form one complete organism. Without it, I was but an empty shell; a bird without the courage to fly. I suppressed my ideas of independence and ignored my innate disposition to feel and need. I had not learned to listen to the voice within, and so I did not know how to express these feelings or needs to others. Sadly, not only did I alone deprive my Self of its necessary nutrients, but I also allowed others to do it. And I wondered why no one understood me or gave me the respect I hungered for.

With love, my mother gave me her legacy, a shield of silence to protect me from pain and to prevent me from troubles. It gave me a source of inner strength, but it also barred inner peace from reaching the premises of my soul. Although my mother's words are wise, they are in some cases unsuitable to deal with problems which I faced in the context of my experiences in this new country. Back in Laos, my mother's life consisted of devotion to others, her parents, her husband, her children, because she was never expected to go beyond the role of the traditional Hmong woman. Here in America, opportunities are more plentiful. Education delivers knowledge. Employment offers financial independence. Women's support groups give an dentity not solely in relation to men, but within the boundaries of our own person. And I can possess all of this!

In addition, I realized that I could not avoid every dragon or retreat from every problem. I was tired of running, of being voiceless, of being afraid, and I no longer wanted to be stepped on, suppressed, or taken for granted. I couldn't continue pretending that I was less than others. I craved to belong in the world, not as a silent observer, but as a human being; shaping, creating, questioning, reforming, or advocating. I wanted to exist!

Silence is power? In my silence, I was the sacrificial lamb. I was the martyr, like my mother. We suffered pain in the name of obedience just so no one will accuse us of being insolent or naughty, and in the struggle for harmony, loving the people around us. These can be good causes, but when we are silent even in the face of injustice, then I cannot in all fairness pronounce them good ones. As a Hmong woman, I am expected to perfect the art of hiding the painful reality of sexual, physical, or mental abuse. These conflicts cannot be resolved with silence, only deepened and catalyzed through it. If to be a good Hmong woman means to ignore my identity, to swallow my pride so others can abuse me, or to shut my eyes in the face of injustice by turning the other cheek, I do not want to be a good Hmong woman.

 3

# *Claiming an Education*

ADRIENNE RICH

For this convocation, I planned to separate my remarks into two parts: some thoughts about you, the women students here, and some thoughts about us who teach in a women's college. But ultimately, those two parts are indivisible. If university education means anything beyond the processing of human beings into expected roles, through credit hours, tests, and grades (and I believe that in a women's college especially it *might* mean much more), it implies an ethical and intellectual contract between teacher and students. This contract must remain intuitive, dynamic, unwritten; but we must turn to it again and again if learning is to be reclaimed from the depersonalizing and cheapening pressures of the present-day academic scene.

The first thing I want to say to you who are students is that you cannot afford to think of yourselves as being here to *receive* an education; you will do much better to think of yourselves as being here to *claim* one. One of the dictionary definitions of the verb "to claim" is: to take as the rightful owner; to assert in the face of possible contradiction. "To receive" is to come into possession of; to act as receptacle or container for; to accept as authoritative or true. The difference is that between acting and being acted-upon, and for women it can literally mean the difference between life and death.

One of the devastating weaknesses of university learning, of the store of knowledge and opinion that has been handed down through academic training, has been its almost total erasure of women's experience and thought from the curriculum, and its exclusion of women as members of the academic community. Today, with increasing numbers of women students in nearly every branch of higher learning, we still see very few women students in nearly every branch of higher learning, we still see very few women in the upper levels of faculty and administration in most institutions. Douglass College itself is a women's college in a university administered overwhelmingly by men, who in turn are answerable to the state legislature, again composed predominantly of men. But the most significant fact for you is that what you learn here (and I mean not only at Douglass but any college in any university) is how *men* have perceived and organized their experience, their history, their ideas of social relationships, good and evil, sickness and health, etc. When you read or hear about "great issues," "major texts," "the mainstream of Western thought," you are hearing about what men, above all white men, in their male subjectivity, have decided is important.

Black and other minority peoples have for some time recognized that their racial and ethnic experience was not accounted for in the studies broadly labeled human; and that even the sciences can be racist. For many reasons, it has been more difficult for women to comprehend our exclusion, and to realize that even the sciences can be sexist. For one thing, it is only within the last hundred years that higher education has grudgingly been opened up to women at all, even to white, middle-class women. And many of us have found ourselves pouring eagerly over books with titles like: *The Descent of Man; Man and His Symbols; Irrational Man; The Phenomenon of Man; The Future of Man; Man and the Machine; From Man to Man; May Man Prevail?; Man, Science and Society; One-Dimensional Man*— books to describe a "human" reality that does not include over one-half the human species.

Less than a decade ago, with the rebirth of a feminist movement in this country, women students and teachers in a number of universities, began to demand and set up women's studies courses—to *claim* a woman-directed education. And, despite the inevitable accusations of "unscholarly," "group therapy," "faddism," etc., despite backlash and budget cuts, women's studies are still growing, offering to more and more women a new intellectual grasp on their lives, new understanding of our history, a fresh vision of the human experience, and also a critical basis for evaluating what they hear and read in other courses, and in the society at large.

But my talk is not really about women's studies, much as I believe in their scholarly, scientific, and human necessity. While I think that any Douglass student has everything to gain by investigating and enrolling in women's studies courses, I want to suggest that there is a more essential experience that you owe yourselves, one which courses in women's studies can greatly enrich, but which finally depends on you, in all your interactions with yourself and your world. This is the experience of *taking responsibility toward yourselves*. Our upbringing as women has so often told us that this should come second to our relationships and responsibilities to other people. We have been offered ethical models of the self-denying wife and mother; intellectual models of the brilliant but slapdash dilettante who never commits herself to anything the whole way, or the intelligent woman who denies her intelligence in order to seem more "feminine," or who sits in passive silence

even when she disagrees inwardly with everything that is being said around her.

Responsibility to yourself means refusing to let others do your thinking, talking, and naming for you; it means learning to respect and use your own brains and instincts, hence, grappling with hard work. It means that you do not treat your body as a commodity with which to purchase superficial intimacy or economic security; for our bodies and minds are inseparable in this life, and when we allow our bodies to be treated as objects, our minds are in mortal danger. It means insisting that those to whom you give your friendship and love are able to respect your mind. It means being able to say, with Charlotte Bronte's Jane Eyre: "I have an inward treasure born with me, which can keep me alive if all the extraneous delights should be withheld or offered only at a price I cannot afford to give."

Responsibility to yourself means that you don't fall for shallow and easy solutions—predigested books and ideas, weekend encounters guaranteed to change your life, taking "gut" courses instead of ones you know will challenge you, bluffing at school and life instead of doing solid work, marrying early as an escape from real decisions, getting pregnant as an evasion of already existing problems. It means that you refuse to sell your talents and aspirations short, simply to avoid conflict and confrontation. And this, in turn, means resisting the forces in society which say that women should be nice, play safe, have low professional expectations, drown in love and forget about work, live through others, and stay in the places assigned to us. It means that we insist on a life of meaningful work, insist that work be as meaningful as love and friendship in our lives. It means, therefore, the courage to be "different"; not to be continuously available to others when we need time for ourselves and our work; to be able to demand of others—parents, friends, roommates, teachers, lovers, husbands, children—that they respect our sense of purpose and our integrity as persons. Women everywhere are finding the courage to do this, more and more, and we are finding that courage both in our study of women in the past who possessed it, and in each other as we look to other women for comradeship, community, and challenge. The difference between a life lived actively, and a life of passive drifting and dispersal of energies, is an immense difference. Once we begin to feel committed to our lives, responsible to ourselves, we can never again be satisfied with the old, passive way.

I have said that the contract on the student's part involves that you demand to be taken seriously so that you can also go on taking yourself seriously. This means seeking out criticism, recognizing that the most affirming thing anyone can do for you is demand that you push yourself further, show you the range of what you *can* do. It means rejecting attitudes of "take-it-easy," "why-be-so-serious," "why-worry-you'll-probably-get-married-anyway." It means assuming your share of responsibility for what happens in the classroom, because that affects the quality of your daily life here. It means that the student sees herself engaged with her teachers in an active, ongoing struggle for a real education. But for her to do this, her teachers must be committed to the belief that women's minds and experience are intrinsically valuable and indispensable to any civilization worthy of the name; that there is no more exhilarating and intellectually fertile place in the academic world today than a women's college—*if* both students and teachers in large enough numbers are trying to fulfill this contract. The contract is really a pledge of mutual seriousness about women, about language, ideas, methods, and values. It is our shared commitment toward a world in which the inborn potentialities of so many women's minds will no longer be wasted, raveled-away, paralyzed, or denied.                                    [1977]

 4

# The Politics of Black Women's Studies

AKASHA (GLORIA T.) HULL AND
BARBARA SMITH

Merely to use the term "Black women's studies" is an act charged with political significance. At the very least, the combining of these words to name a discipline means taking the stance that Black women exist—and exist positively—a stance that is in direct opposition to most of what passes for culture and thought on the North American continent. To use the term and to act on it in a white-male world is an act of political courage.

Like any politically disenfranchised group, Black women could not exist consciously until we began to name ourselves. The growth of Black women's studies is an essential aspect of that process of naming. The very fact that Black women's studies describes something that is really happening, a burgeoning field of study, indicates that there are political changes afoot which have made possible that growth. To examine the politics of Black women's studies means to consider not only what it is, but why it is and what it can be. Politics is used here in its widest sense to mean any situation/relationship of differential power between groups or individuals.

Four issues seem important for a consideration of the politics of Black women's studies: (1) the general political situation of Afro-American women and the bearing this has had upon the implementation of Black women's studies; (2) the relationship of Black women's studies to Black feminist politics and the Black feminist movement; (3) the necessity for Black women's studies to be feminist, radical, and analytical; and (4) the need for teachers of Black women's studies to be aware of our problematic political positions in the academy and of the potentially antagonistic conditions under which we must work.

The political position of Black women in America has been, in a single word, embattled. The extremity of our oppression has been determined by our very biological identity. The horrors we have faced historically and continue to face as Black women in a white-male-dominated society have implications for every aspect of our lives, including what white men have termed "the life of the mind." That our oppression as Black women can take forms specifically aimed at discrediting our intellectual power is best illustrated through the words of a "classic" American writer.

In 1932 William Faulkner saw fit to include this sentence in a description of a painted sign in his novel *Light in August*. He wrote:

But now and then a negro nursemaid with her white charges would loiter there and spell them [the letters on the sign] aloud with *that vacuous idiocy of her idle and illiterate kind.*[1] [Italics ours]

Faulkner's white-male assessment of Black female intellect and character, stated as a mere aside, has fundamental and painful implications for a consideration of the whole question of Black women's studies and the politics that shape its existence. Not only does his remark typify the extremely negative ways in which Afro-American women have been portrayed in literature, scholarship, and the popular media, but it also points to the destructive white-male habit of categorizing all who are not like themselves as their intellectual and moral inferiors. The fact that the works in which such oppressive images appear are nevertheless considered American "masterpieces" indicates the cultural-political value system in which Afro-American women have been forced to operate and which, when possible, they have actively opposed.

The politics of Black women's studies are totally connected to the politics of Black women's lives in this country. The opportunities for Black women to carry out autonomously defined investigations of self in a society which through racial, sexual, and class oppression systematically denies our existence have been by definition limited.

As a major result of the historical realities which brought us enslaved to this continent, we have been kept separated in every way possible from recognized intellectual work. Our legacy as chattel, as sexual slaves as well as forced laborers, would adequately explain why most Black women are, to this day, far away from the centers of academic power and why Black women's studies has just begun to surface in the latter part of the 1970s. What our multilayered oppression does not explain are the ways in which we have created and maintained our own intellectual traditions as Black women, without either the recognition or the support of white-male society.

The entry entitled "A Slave Woman Runs a Midnight School" in Gerda Lerner's *Black Women in White America: A Documentary History* embodies this creative, intellectual spirit, coupled with a practical ability to make something out of nothing.

[In Natchez, Louisiana, there were] two schools taught by colored teachers. One of these was a slave woman who had taught a midnight school for a year. It was opened at eleven or twelve o'clock at night, and closed at two o'clock a.m. . . . Milla Granson, the teacher, learned to read and write from the children of her indulgent master in her old Kentucky home. Her number of scholars was twelve at a time and when she had taught these to read and write she dismissed them, and again took her apostolic number and brought them up to the extent of her ability, until she had graduated hundreds. A number of them wrote their own passes and started for Canada. . . .

At length her night-school project leaked out, and was a for a time suspended; but it was not known that seven of the twelve years subsequent to leaving Kentucky had been spent in this work. Much excitement over her night-school was produced. The subject was discussed in their legislature, and a bill was passed, that it should not be held illegal for a slave to teach a slave. . . . She not only [re]opened her night-school, but a Sabbath-school. . . . Milla Granson used as good language as any of the white people.[2]

This document illuminates much about Black women educators and thinkers in America. Milla Granson learned to read and write through the exceptional indulgence of her white masters. She used her skills not to advance her own status, but to help her fellow slaves, and this under the most difficult circumstances. The act of a Black person teaching and sharing knowledge was viewed as naturally threatening to the power structure. The knowledge she conveyed had a politically and materially transforming function, that is, it empowered people to gain freedom.

Milla Granson and her pupils, like Black people throughout our history here, made the greatest sacrifices for the sake of learning. As opposed to "lowering" educational standards, we have had to create our own. In a totally antagonistic setting we have tried to keep our own visions clear and have passed on the most essential kind of knowledge, that which enabled us to survive. As Alice Walker writes of our artist-thinker foremothers:

They dreamed dreams that no one knew—not even themselves, in any coherent fashion—and saw visions no one could understand. . . . They waited for a day when the unknown thing that was in them would be made known; but guessed, somehow in their darkness, that on the day of their revelation they would be long dead.[3]

The birth of Black women's studies is perhaps the day of revelation these women wished for. Again, this beginning is not unconnected to political events in the world outside university walls.

The inception of Black women's studies can be directly traced to three significant political movements of the twentieth century. These are the struggles for Black liberation and women's liberation, which themselves fostered the growth of Black and women's studies, and the more recent Black feminist movement, which is just beginning to show its strength. Black feminism has made a space for Black women's studies to exist and, through its commitment to all Black women, will provide the basis for its survival.

The history of all these movements is unique, yet interconnected. The Black movements of the 1950s, '60s, and '70s brought about unprecedented social and political change, not only in the lives of Black people, but for all Americans. The early women's movement gained inspiration from the Black movement as well as an impetus to organize autonomously both as a result of the demands for all-Black organizations and in response to sexual hierarchies in Black- and white-male political groupings. Black women were a part of that early women's movement, as were working-class women of all races. However, for many reasons—including the increasing involvement of single, middle-class white women (who often had the most time to devote to political work), the divisive campaigns of the white-male media, and the movement's serious inability to deal with racism—the women's movement became largely and apparently white.

The effect that this had upon the nascent field of women's studies was predictably disastrous. Women's studies courses, usually taught in universities, which could be considered elite institutions just by virtue of the populations they served, focused almost exclusively upon the lives of white women. Black studies, which was much too often male-dominated, also ignored Black women. Here is what a Black woman wrote about her independent efforts to study Black women writers in the early 1970s:

. . . At this point I am doing a lot of reading on my own of Black women writers ever since I discovered Zora Neale Hurston. *I've had two Black Lit courses and in neither were any women writers discussed.* So now I'm doing a lot of independent research since the Schomburg Collection is so close.[4] [Italics ours.]

Because of white women's racism and Black men's sexism, there was no room in either area for a serious consideration of the lives of Black women. And even when they have considered Black women, white women usually have not had the capacity to analyze racial politics and Black culture, and Black men have remained blind or resistant to the implications of sexual politics in Black women's lives.

Only a Black *and* feminist analysis can sufficiently comprehend the materials of Black women's studies; and only a creative Black feminist perspective will enable the field to expand. A viable Black feminist movement will also lend its political strength to the development of Black women's studies courses, programs, and research, and to the funding they require. Black feminism's total commitment to the liberation of Black women and its recognition of Black women as valuable and complex human beings will provide the analysis and spirit for the incisive work on Black women. Only a feminist, pro-woman perspective that acknowledges the reality of sexual oppression in the lives of Black women, as well as the oppression of race and class, will make Black women's studies the transformer of consciousness it needs to be.

Women's studies began as a radical response to feminists' realization that knowledge of ourselves has been deliberately kept from us by institutions of patriarchal "learning." Unfortunately, as women's studies has become both more institutionalized and at the same time more precarious within traditional academic structures, the radical life-changing vision of what women's studies can accomplish has constantly been diminished in exchange for acceptance, respectability, and the career advancement of individuals. This trend in women's studies is a trap that Black women's studies cannot afford to fall into. Because we are so oppressed as Black women, every aspect of our fight for freedom, including teaching and writing about ourselves, must in some way further our liberation. Because of the particular history of Black feminism in relation to Black women's studies, especially the fact that the two movements are still new and have evolved nearly simultaneously, much of the current teaching, research, and writing about Black women is not feminist, is not radical, and unfortunately is not always even analytical. Naming and describing our experience are important initial steps, but not alone sufficient to get us where we need to go. A descriptive approach to the lives of Black women, a "great Black women" in history or literature approach, or any traditional male-identified approach will not result in intellectually groundbreaking or politically transforming work. We cannot change our lives by teaching solely about "exceptions" to the ravages of white-male oppression. Only through exploring the experience of supposedly "ordinary" Black women whose "unexceptional" actions enabled us and the race to survive, will we be able to begin to develop an overview and an analytical framework for understanding the lives of Afro-American women.

### NOTES

1. William Faulkner, *Light in August* (New York: Modern Library 1932), p. 53.
2. Laura S. Haviland, *A Woman's Life-Work, Labors and Experience* (Chicago: Publishing Association of Friends, 1889; copyright 1881), pp. 300–301; reprinted in Gerda Lerner, ed., *Black Women in White America: A Documentary History* (New York: Vintage, 1973), pp. 32–33.
3. Alice Walker, "In Search of Our Mother's Gardens," *Ms.* (Magazine 1974): 64–70. 105.
4. Bernette Golden, Personal letter, April 1, 1974.

 5

# Men and Women's Studies: Premises, Perils, and Promise

MICHAEL KIMMEL

What does women's studies have to do with men? For one thing, it clears an intellectual space for talking about gender. I am not suggesting that among all the other things women's studies has to do, it must now also drop everything and take care of men in some vaguely academic version of the second shift. (I have heard arguments from men suggesting that women's studies must provide us with "a room of our own" within the curriculum, to appropriate the words of Virginia Woolf—and make sure that room has a rather commanding view of the traditional campus!)

When I say women's studies is about men, I mean that *women's studies has made men visible.* Before women's studies, men were invisible—especially to themselves. By making women visible, women's studies also made men visible both to women and to men themselves. If men are now taking up the issue of gender, it is probably less accurate to say, "Thank goodness they've arrived," the way one might when the cavalry appears in a western film, than to say, "It's about time."

Of course, making men visible has not been the primary task of women's studies. But it has been one of its signal successes. The major achievement of women's studies, acting independently and as a force within traditional disciplines, has been making *women* visible through the rediscovery of long-neglected, undervalued, and understudied women who were accomplished leaders, artists, composers, and writers and placing them in the pantheons of significance where they rightly belong. In addition, women's studies has rediscovered the voices of ordinary women—the laundresses and the salesgirls, the union maids and the union organizers, the workers and the wives—who have struggled to scratch out lives of meaning and dignity. For this—whether they know it or not, whether they acknowledge it or not—women all over the world owe a debt.

But in making women visible, women's studies has been at the epicenter of a seismic shift in the university as we know it. Women's studies has made *gender* visible. Women's studies has demonstrated that gender is one of the axes around which social life is organized, one of the most crucial building blocks of our identities. Before women's studies, we didn't know that gender mattered. Twenty-five years ago, there were no women's studies courses in colleges or universities, no women's studies lists at university presses across the country. In my field of sociology, there were no gender courses, no specialty area called the Sociology of Gender. We had, instead, a field called Marriage and the Family—to my mind the Ladies' Auxiliary of Sociology. By making women visible, women's studies decentered men as the unexamined, disembodied authorial voice of the academic canon and showed that men, as well as women, are utterly embodied, their identities are socially constructed as those of women. When the voice of the canon speaks, we can no longer *assume* that voice is going to sound masculine or that the speaker is going to look like a man.

The problem is that many men do not yet know this. Though ubiquitous in positions of power, many men remain invisible to themselves as gendered beings. Courses on gender in the universities are populated largely by women, as if the term applied only to them. "Woman alone seems to have 'gender' since the category itself is defined as that aspect of social relations based on difference between the sexes in which the standard has always been man," writes historian Thomas Lacquer.[1] Or, as the Chinese proverb has it, the fish are the last to discover the ocean.

I know this from my own experience: women's studies made gender visible to me. In the early 1980s I participated in a graduate-level women's studies seminar in which I was the only man among about a dozen participants. During one meeting, a white woman and a black woman were discussing whether all women were, by definition, "sisters" because they all had essentially the same experiences and because all women faced a common oppression by all men. The white women asserted that the fact that they were both women bonded them, in spite of racial differences. The black woman disagreed.

"When you wake up in the morning and look in the mirror, what do you see?" she asked.

"I see a woman," replied the white woman.

"That's precisely the problem," responded the black woman. "I see a *black* woman. To me, race is visible every day, because race is how I am *not* privileged in our culture. Race is invisible to you, because it's how you are privileged. It's why there will always be differences in our experience."

As I witnessed this exchange, I was startled, and groaned—more audibly, perhaps, than I had intended. Someone asked what my response meant. "Well," I said, "when I look in the mirror, I see a human being. I'm universally generalizable. As a middle-class white man, I have no class, no race, no gender. I'm the generic person!"

Sometimes, I like to think it was on that day that I *became* a middle-class white man. Sure, I had been all those before, but they had not meant much to me. Since then, I have begun to understand that race, class, and gender do not refer only to other people, who are marginalized by race, class, or gender privilege. Those terms also describe me. I enjoy the privilege of invisibility. The very processes that confer privilege to one group and not another group are often invisible to those upon whom that privilege is conferred. American men have come to think of ourselves as genderless, in part because gender privilege affords us the luxury of ignoring the centrality of gender. But women's studies offers the possibility of making gender visible to men as well and, in so doing, creating the possibilities of alliances between women and men to collaboratively investigate what gender means, how it works, and what its consequences are.

In *Fire with Fire*, Naomi Wolf returns often to her book's epigraph, that famous line of Audre Lorde, "the Master's tools cannot dismantle the Master's house." Wolf believes that her book is a refutation of that position, and when one considers the impact of women's studies on the university and the culture at large, it seems that on this score at least, Wolf is quite right—that passionate, disciplined scholarship, inspired and dedicated teaching, and committed, engaged inquiry can contribute to the reorientation of the university as an institution. All over the country, schools are integrating "gender awareness" into their first-year curricula, even orienting the entire curriculum around gender awareness. Within the professional organization of my discipline, sociology, the Sex and Gender section is now the largest section of the entire profession. Gender has moved from the margins—Marriage and the Family—to the center and is the largest single constituency within the field.

Most commentators laud the accomplishments of women's studies programs in transforming women's lives, but it is obvious that women's studies programs have also been transformative for men. The Duke case is a particularly successful one: the popular house course "Men and Gender Issues" has been offered under the umbrella of Women's Studies for five years. Men Acting for Change (MAC), the campus group for pro-feminist men that has become a model for similar groups on campuses around the country, found a supportive harbor in the Women's Studies Program. The first time I came to lecture at Duke three years ago, my lecture was jointly sponsored by the Women's Studies Program and the Inter-Fraternity Council—the first time, I'm told, that those two organizations had cooperated on anything. Women's studies can—and does—forge creative alliances!

Essentially, however, the program at Duke and women's studies in general has centered around the same two projects as any other discipline: teaching and research. And to speak personally, the perspectives of women's studies have transformed both my research and my teaching. Women's studies made it *possible* for me to do the work I do. And for that I am grateful. Inspired by the way women's studies made gender visible, I offered a course called "Sociology of the Male Experience" in 1983 at Rutgers University, where I was then a young assistant professor. This was the first such course on men and masculinity in the state of New Jersey, and I received enormous support both from my own department and from the Women's Studies Program at Rutgers, then chaired by Catharine Stimpson. Today, I teach that course as well as a course entitled "Sex and Society" at Stony Brook to over 350 students each semester. Now, as then, the course is cross-listed with women's studies. But I also teach our department's classical sociological theory course, the course on the historical development of social and political theory. In that course, students traditionally read works by Hobbes, Locke, Rousseau, Smith, Marx, Durkheim, Tocqueville, Weber, and Freud. This is probably the most intractably canonical "Dead White European Men" course we offer in the social sciences. But it has become impossible for me to teach the works of those "great men" without reference to gender—without noting, for example, the gendered creation myths that characterize the move from the state of nature to civil society in the thought of Locke or Hobbes, or the chronic anxiety and loss of control attendant upon modern society documented by Tocqueville, Marx, Weber, or Freud. Moreover, I find that I cannot teach about the rise of nineteenth-century liberal individualism without including Frederick Douglass or Mary Wollstonecraft; nor can I teach about the late nineteenth-century critiques of individualism without references to W. E. B. Du Bois or to Charlotte Perkins Gilman.

If women's studies has made gender, and hence *men,* visible, then it has also raised a question about men: where are they? where have they been in women's struggles for equality? Taking my cues from women's history, I began to research men's responses to feminism. *Against the Tide* tries to provide part of the answer, a missing chapter from women's history: the chapter about the men who supported women's equality.[2] When I began *Against the Tide,* I mentioned to Catharine Stimpson, then dean of the Graduate School at Rutgers, what I intended to do. "A book about men who supported feminism?" she asked. "Now that will surely be the world's shortest book!" she joked. Of course, she knew better, but I did not really know what I would find. It turns out that in every arena in which women have struggled for equal rights—education (the right to go to college or professional school, the right to go to college with men), economic life (the right to work, join unions, receive equal wages), social life (the right to own property, have access to birth control, get a divorce), or political life (the right to vote, to hold elective office, to serve on juries)—there have been American men, some prominent, many unheralded, who have supported them: men such as Thomas Paine, who sat before the Declaration of Independence in 1776 and recognized that women would not be included under its provisions, although women had, as he put it, an "equal right to virtue." Men such as famed abolitionists William Lloyd Garrison and Frederick Douglass, who campaigned tirelessly for women's rights from Seneca Falls onward. Men such as Matthew Vassar, William Alan Neilson, and Henry Durant, founders of Vassar, Smith, and Wellesley colleges. It was Durant, founder of Wellesley, who in 1877 called the higher education of women a "revolt": "We revolt against the slavery in which women are held by the customs of society—the broken health, the aimless lives, the subordinate position, the helpless dependence, the dishonesties and shams of so-called education. The Higher Education of Women is one of the great world battle cries for freedom; for right against might. It is the cry of the oppressed slave. It is the assertion of absolute equality."[3]

Pro-feminist men have included educators such as John Dewey, who urged that women be admitted to the University of Chicago and was one of the founders of the Men's League for Woman Suffrage, the nation's first pro-feminist men's organization. The group of pro-feminist men included W. E. B. Du Bois, Ralph Waldo Emerson, and Eugene Debs among the most vigorous supporters of woman suffrage. And there have been academic men such as Lester Ward and George Herbert Mead, to name but two, who pointed toward the scholarly study of women and opposed gender inequality. In one of his major treatises, *Applied Sociology*, Ward provided an epigraph for the advent of women's studies, arguing that "the universal prevalence of the androcentric worldview acts as a wet blanket on all the genial fire of the female sex."[4] Pro-feminist men are also policymakers such as Robert Reich, secretary of labor in the Clinton administration, who wrote a furious letter (reprinted in *Ms.* magazine) to a college president when his wife was denied tenure, and Representative Don Edwards of California, who has introduced the ERA in every session of Congress since 1974, as well as former Supreme Court justice Harry Blackmun, that vigilant defender of women's right to control their own bodies.

Supporters of women's equality have also included the less-celebrated men who simply lived out their principles of equality without fanfare. Men such as James Mott (married to Lucretia), Theodore Weld (married to Angelina Grimké), and Wendell Phillips, ardent abolitionist and suffrage supporter. In 1856, Lucy Stone called her husband, Henry Brown Blackwell, "the best husband in the world. In the midst of all the extra care, hurry and perplexity of business, you stop and look after all my little affairs," she wrote, "doing everything you can to save me trouble."[5] More than a half a century later, Margaret Sanger quotes her husband, William, as telling her to "go ahead and finish your writing, and I'll get dinner and wash the dishes."[6] (She also comments that she drew the curtains in the kitchen of their first-floor Greenwich Village apartment, lest passersby see her husband wearing an apron.) It appears that long before Ted Kramer and Mr. Mom, real men did housework!

Men *have* been there supporting women's equality every step of the way. And if men have been there, it means that men *can* be there and that they *will* be there. This legacy of men who supported women's equality allows contemporary men to join what I like to think of as the Gentlemen's Auxiliary of the Women's Movement. Neither passive bystanders nor the front-line forces—and especially not the leaders of those troops—men still have a pivotal role to play. Men can join this epochal struggle and provide support both individually and collectively. This strikes me as an utterly honorable relationship to feminism, quite different from an impulse I've encountered among newly enlightened men that goes something like, "Thanks for bringing all this to my attention, ladies. We'll take it from here." It also serves as an important corrective to many men's fears, which often boil down to "How can I support feminism without feeling like—or being seen as—a wimp?" To be a member of the Auxiliary is to know that the cental actors in the struggle for gender equality will be, as they always have been, women.

But women's studies has done more than make the study of gender possible; it has made it *necessary*. The issues raised by women in the university and outside it have not "gone away" or subsided now that women have been offered a few resources and an academic room of their own. Women's studies has not been content with one room while the rest of the university goes about its androcentric business, any more than the women's movement has been convinced of its political victory because 100 percent of the U.S. senators from California in 1993 are women. Think about the shockwaves that rippled outward from Clarence Thomas's confirmation hearings over two years ago. Remember how the media responded to that event; recall the shameful way Anita Hill was treated by the Senate Judiciary Committee. The phrase the media used, as if with one voice, was that Thomas's confirmation would have a "chilling effect" on American women—that women would be less likely to come forward to describe their experiences of sexual harassment in the workplace, that women would be less likely to speak of the inequities and humiliations that permeated their working lives. Have the media ever been more wrong? Not only was there no "chilling effect," there was a national thaw. Women have been coming forward in unprecedented numbers to talk about their working lives. And they have not gone away. On campuses and off all across the country, women's studies students and faculty have joined in this virtual national seminar about men, masculinity, and power.

Gender as a power relation is the "it" that men "just don't get" in the current discussion. Women's studies scholars have demonstrated that masculinity and femininity are identities that are socially constructed in a field of power. Gender, like race and class, is not simply a mode of classification by which biological creatures are sorted into their respective and appropriate niches. Gender is about power. Just because both masculinity and femininity are socially constructed does not mean that they are equivalent, that there are no dynamics of power and privilege in operation. The problem with bringing men into this discussion about gender and power is that these issues are invisible to men.           [1996]

*NOTES*

1.  Thomas Lacquer, *Making Sex: Body and Gender from the Greeks to Freud* (Cambridge: Harvard University Press, 1990), 22.
2.  Michael S. Kimmel and Thomas Mosmiller, eds., *Against the Tide: Pro-Feminist Men in the United States, 1776–1990. A Documentary History* (Boston: Beacon Press, 1992).
3.  Thomas Paine, "An Occasional Letter on the Female Sex," 1775, and Henry Fowle Durant, "The Spirit of the College," 1877, in *Against the Tide,* ed. Kimmel and Mosmiller, 63–66, 132.
4.  Lester Frank Ward, *Applied Sociology: A Treatise on the Conscious Improvement of Society by Society* (Boston: Ginn and Company, 1906), 232.

 6

# Have You Ever Heard of Asian-American Feminists?

STACEY G. H. YAP

I can say that I stumbled into women's studies accidentally. I had no intention in my younger days to choose this area. It's true that there were few to no courses offered in women's studies in the early 1970s when I first arrived at college on the East Coast, and it's also true that I stereotyped women's liberation as a group of white women gone mad! I didn't see myself identifying with "them" even if I had seen courses offered in the women's studies area then. It was only when I went to graduate school and unintentionally selected a course about "men and women in corporations" that I was first introduced to the research in women's studies without ever knowing it. And from then on, my life was transformed.

Today I am a faculty member and chair of the women's studies (minor) program in my college, and teaching a course in women's studies, I cannot help thinking how much my life has changed from an undergraduate business major to a women's studies/sociology college teacher. My students must wonder about the irony of any Asian (American) teacher teaching them about women's studies and the American women's movement. The unexpected role that I play in influencing my students' lives will probably help them remember how much common ground we share even though we are ethnically different. What will transform my life and my students' lives is the complete element of surprise that women's studies can offer. It is the story of our lives, our mothers' and our grandmothers' lives, and the conditions and experiences we women have gone through and are going through now. Feminist scholars have researched experiences in great detail and told stories of our lives that have never been told before in colorful and powerful language.

What is more surprising are the uncharted territories women's studies offers, and what is not documented. Particularly, since I look and speak differently from my students, women's studies presents an opportunity for my women students to ask me more questions about me: How do I feel about American white men? What do I think about American black women? Do I think that the socialization process they learn is different in the Asian context? What is different about mother-daughter relationships among whites and those that are written by Chinese Americans like Amy Tan and Maxine Hong Kingston? The fact that Asian-American women are not represented in the mainstream of women's studies literature made my students and myself more intense in our search to wonder about their absence. As a feminist, I acknowledge their absence but do not feel upset nor angry by their lack of recognition. This neglected treatment by white American women who dominated this field in producing women's anthologies for women's studies courses is understandable. I try to remedy this by teaching my students and my friends about Asian-American women and their experiences. I center my research in the "unearthing" of Asian women's experiences. Whether they are Asian-born women or American-born Asian women, I recognize that their experiences have helped shape the history, politics, and literature of this country.

Women's studies has taught me that women must be studied on their own terms and not judged by male-defined standards. Similarly, Asian women must be allowed to speak for themselves because, while we share a great deal with other women, our experiences are unique, and women of other backgrounds can't speak for us. Asian women come to feminism in a variety of ways. Some of us stumbled into politics through fighting against unfair wage practices, and others protested against the Vietnam war. Including Asian women's experiences in women's studies courses is important, for we, like most women around the world, do not passively or silently accept the oppression we share with all women.                                   [1992]

 7

## Women's Studies as a Growth Process

DANISTA HUNTE

I remember trying to fit Introduction to Women's Studies into my schedule for five semesters and feeling frustrated each time that chemistry or some other requirement took precedence. Finally, first semester senior year, I was able to fit it into my schedule. After three years at Vassar College, I thought

my feminist development was far beyond the introductory level and there would not be much for me to learn from the class. I was wrong. My politics were challenged daily. It seemed that everything that was changing and developing could be linked to a reading or discussion in women's studies. I learned life lessons that take some people all of their lives to learn. The most important lesson was that the many parts of myself—black, female, feminist, Caribbean, pro-choice, working class, etc.—could co-exist as one healthy individual. I gained a better understanding of how our society consistently seeks to "divide and conquer" or to squash any possible coalition among oppressed individuals. I confronted a lot of the anger I felt toward white society. I do not know whether I will ever resolve that anger, but identifying its source and understanding the way in which it can stifle my own growth and development are valuable lessons. I gained a better understanding of the environment and the culture in which my mother was raised and in turn how she raised me. I realized how difficult it is to be someone's mother, and I appreciate my mother even more. Although I left some class sessions feeling confused and schizophrenic, by the end of first semester I felt empowered and confident that I could handle anything.

On the first day of class, I counted the number of women of color in the class. There were two of us. I had a reputation of being a vocal student, and nothing less was expected of me in this class. I also knew that I would be the official spokeswoman of color and the voice of all black women on campus. Initially I resented having to occupy the "speaker" role, and I was even angry at the other sister in class who never spoke in concert with me. As a matter of fact she never spoke at all, which may tell another tale altogether. There was no support or comfort upon which to depend.

These feelings were not new. For the three years prior to women's studies, my being was fueled by anger and the thrill of battle. I craved the opportunities for combat with the administration of the college. I enjoyed sitting on committees with faculty and feeling confident about what I had to contribute or debating with a white man who presumed to know "who I was and what my life was about" based upon his proficiency in two Africana studies courses! These encounters excited me and made me feel powerful; however, by the time I had reached senior year, I was *tired* and did not want to fight anymore. After reading Audre Lorde's "The Uses of Anger: Women Responding to Racism" in *Sister Outsider,* those feelings of anger and resentment began to subside. Through Lorde's writings I identified some of the reasons for the anger I was feeling about the class, my experiences at Vassar College, and toward myself. Lorde warns black women not to let our justified anger eat away at our compassion to love ourselves and others. She advocates that black women must find ways in which to channel their anger into *healthy* and *productive* actions that will hopefully transform our situations. Anger should not be denied, but explored and used to produce something positive that will move the individual forward.

Introduction to Women's Studies was painful, but I learned a lot. There is *much* work to be done on the part of all women, and especially by women of color. The class offered very little feminist theory by African-American women, Hispanic women, Asian women, or Native American women, which angered me. From my own personal readings I had found a wealth of writings by women of color on issues of motherhood and parenting, male domination, and the portrayal of women in film, etc. There are time constraints when developing a syllabus. However, when the theoretical and critical analyses that comprise the syllabus are written by white feminists, this conveys only one perspective. This imbalance facilitates the myth that black women do not theorize or are not capable of critically analyzing their own situations or of offering criticism of their society. We as black women need to pursue fields in which we can create and command our own destinies and have an impact upon our lives and the lives of our sisters.

Lorde says that, "for survival, Black children in america must be raised to be warriors."[1] Unfor-

tunately, that often means we grow up justifiably paranoid and untrusting of anyone who is not like us. Women's studies rejuvenated my spirit and reassured me that people can grow and things can change. As a result of the class, I try not to build walls around myself and I want to be more inclusive in my politics. Each new experience, whether categorized as "good" or "bad," facilitates growth. I look upon my experience in Introduction to Women's Studies as a growth process—and, for the record, it was "good." [1991]

 8

# *Finding My Latina Identity Through Women's Studies*

LUANA FERREIRA

Taking a women's studies course entitled Women: Images and Realities helped me to become the person that I am today. It enabled me share both my experience as a woman and my experience of Latino culture with other women and understand more fully the position of women in society.

When I lived in the Dominican Republic, I'd see the same scene over and over, especially around the holidays: women were in the kitchen cooking and setting the table while the men were in the living room discussing sports or politics. My grandmother always told me that once a woman learned how to do house chores, she was ready for marriage, and that a woman should always depend on a man because a woman will always need the *strength* of a man. At this point in my life I was beginning to feel frustrated and anxious. I asked myself why at the age of 17 I still was not engaged, or in a relationship, and what would happen if I never got married.

Once I arrived in the United States and enrolled in college, I began to see male-female relationships differently. I saw that women were indeed more career-oriented and independent. However, as a college student, I thought that the women's

---

[1] Audre Lorde, "Man Child: A Black Lesbian Feminist's Response," *Sister Outsider* (Freedom, CA: The Crossing Press, 1984), p. 75.

movement, womanism, and feminism were a little too radical for me. The word "feminist" to me meant "man hater."

The course taught me a great deal about women in the United States and around the world. I could not believe how much I had been missing out! I must admit that I was biased in choosing the teacher. Looking in the catalogue, I saw three different names, but one stood out: Delgado. Since I am Latina, the idea of having a teacher I can relate to pleased me. Professor Linda Delgado, a proud Puerto Rican woman, taught me how to detach myself from traditional ideas about women without losing my cultural values and awareness. At the same time, having a Latina teacher for this course has helped me to become more involved in my community. I learned about sexism in religion and in the labor force, and I became more aware of issues such as rape, abortion, and sexual harassment.

In my traditional family, my parents always taught me "where a woman's place in society is." According to them, rape victims deserve to get raped because of the way they were dressed, pregnancy is a punishment for the irresponsibility of a woman, virginity is a proof of purity and decency and is the best wedding gift to a man, a spouse can be found through one's cooking, and so forth. I can go on forever with these myths and taboos.

The course made me realize that clothing should not determine the reputation of a woman, that women have the right to make their own decisions about sex, and that both men and women should be concerned about pregnancy. I also learned that one should learn to do chores for survival, not to please someone else. I have become more secure about myself. I am able to make my own decisions because I am using my own judgment, *not* doing what my parents expect or what society dictates. I am also more firm in my decisions. Before, if I were involved in a discussion with a male, I always worried that if I opened my mouth he would lose interest in me. I cannot believe that I used to think this way! I operated on the assumption that if I were too articulate or too much of an activist, I would lose the relationship of my dreams. I thank my teacher and the course for making me understand that standing up for your rights and for what you believe in will raise your self-confidence and self-esteem. Now I find myself having interesting discussions with many colleagues, males and females, and I am more open with my female friends.

Today I am happy to say that I am a woman striving for a career. I am very involved in my community, and I am not afraid to state my beliefs and ideas. Now I know that being a feminist, far from being a man hater, is rather fighting for equal rights, struggling against discrimination, and educating one's self and others about women's issues.

[1992]

 9

# What Women's Studies Has Meant to Me

LUCITA WOODIS

I had no understanding of what women's studies meant when I first looked through the spring catalogue at the University of New Mexico, but it sounded intriguing. So I went to the Women's Studies Center on campus and asked lots of questions: What is women's studies? What can I gain from a course like this? Can I use the information from women's studies courses outside the university? Can I use this for a certain area of my life?

Well, my questions were answered in such a positive way that the very same day, I stepped into the Women's Center and signed up as a women's studies minor.

Now that I've been introduced to the curriculum, I believe that women's studies means empowerment for women. We as women want equality in our lives—in areas such as the workplace, where we want to have acknowledged that people should be paid on the basis of their experience, not their sex; that regardless of sex, we are human. As women, we need respect for making our choices and decisions. We need power and control—not power over others, but shared power with other human beings who work together cooperatively. This is especially meaningful to me as a woman of color, a Native American artist who grew up on the Navajo Reservation.

I have never experienced a more close, supportive, nurturing, and expressive multicultural group of women as I did in the Women in Contemporary Society class at the University of New Mexico. Our bond as women enabled us to break through the barriers of race, creed, and color to interact as human beings and discover a common ground. In our class discussions, we were able to express our intolerance at being victims of pornography and sexual abuse, knowing that with every issue there has been some change for the better. We saw how we as women have bonded together through self-help groups, have opened up shelters for battered women, and in a sense have been saying that we do have power—power to overcome these intolerable abuses and survive as powerful women into the 1990s.

The knowledge I gained through the course came from the classroom, my classmates, and my professor, Deborah Klein. Ms. Klein was very avid in our discussions and presentations, as we bonded together through our openness. She helped the class evolve to an intimate level. With no remorse or self-consciousness, we created an atmosphere of acceptance, shared a great deal of ourselves, and enhanced each other's lives. As a sister to women of color, I experienced support, nurturing, and the embrace of other women as we expressed our experiences openly and individually.

I used part of my class experience to take the group on a journey about the meaning of sexual abuse in a woman's life, particularly in mine. I chose to present my journey as a narrative. I told my story with the visual images of my artwork, as well as with my words. My goal was to convey to others that confronting one's self can be a positive path toward strength, confidence, and the ability to be true to one's self.

Exploring women's issues has truly been a journey for me, a spiritual journey filled with healing and cleansing and enlightenment. My explorations have lead me toward harmony and balance and enable me to feel peaceful, calm, and serene.

As a Native American (Navajo), I can only stress that women are powerful. We are a maternal society, the bearers of children. We are patient yet very strong in our decision making. I can say I have benefited from the women's studies program and won't be silent long. I will be verbally expressive as well as visually expressive, because that is who I am—an artist. I share a very intimate part of myself through my art. I will always be a Native first, as I am from a traditional family, and I'm proud to know my clan through my ancestors. Yet I can also say that I'm from the Navajo Nation *and* part of the larger women's experience in our society.

Today, I understand that I am not alone. I am important. I am not a second-class citizen, I am a capable, strong, and independent Native American Navajo woman. I will always carry my culture and traditions in my heart whether on the Reservation or in the outside world. Through my spirit, I will carry a message visually and verbally that to survive and heal from abuse is to come full-circle to contentment, that we are all part of a larger whole.

Nishtįnígíí shit beehozin   (Navajo)
I know who I am   (English)          [1992]

## ✣ 10

# *Why Women's Studies?*

DEBORAH HALSTEAD LENNON

Whenever I tell people I am majoring in women's studies, the response is usually along the lines of, "Whatever are you going to *do* with *that?*" I know they are expecting me to respond by specifying some kind of practical job application for the degree. I could say, "I'm going to be a personnel consultant, increasing morale and productivity through understanding and meeting the needs of the work force." But that's not why I enrolled in the program.

I returned to school as a women's studies major

at the age of 31. My intended purpose was to validate the perspective I had developed from my life experiences. I have found that—and so much more. Women's studies shows us women's lives and their art of living, how women's contributions to society are so intricately woven into the fabric of their daily lives that they go unrecognized because they are so familiar. It has ended my isolation by showing me that other women have had similar experiences. Through nurturing my growth and self-esteem, I have regained my voice and learned how to use it. Women's studies has united me with women and oppressed peoples from all over the world.

Women's studies has enabled me to discuss issues such as birth control, abortion, rape, and domestic violence with my children. Addressing these and other issues as part of my coursework greatly decreased the apprehension parents and children often experience when approaching these topics. My daughter is now a year younger than I was when these became issues in my life. I am now able to look forward to her teenage years with confidence that when these things touch her life, as they almost surely will in some form, she will not feel the confusion and devastation that I endured. The reason for this confidence is twofold: She has an awareness and understanding that precede her experience, enabling her to avoid some situations that ignorance may have otherwise drawn her into; and she knows how to network and form a supportive community with other women.

Women's studies has been, for me, a metamorphosis; it teaches a way of being, a different mode of perception that pervades our very essence. Now when I hear of a woman in an abusive situation, I can see the factors that keep her trapped: housing, earning potential, child care, fear. I also see how our society perpetuates women's fears through promoting the idea that women are defenseless without a male companion. Women's studies teaches us to crack the shell of fear so that we may spread our wings and fly. What do I *do* with *that?* I help other women (and men) be strong and secure in who they are, in following their dreams. Some of us will do this as lawyers, as teachers, as wives and mothers . . . the possibilities are endless.

Welcome to the beginning of *your* journey. You will find your beauty in your strength, and your wings will take you wherever you want to go.

[1992]

## 11

# *Women's Studies: A Man's Perspective*

EVAN WEISSMAN

Bob Marley once sang, "Don't forget, no way, who you are and where you stand in your struggles." Because I was interested in examining my role in society as a young man and exploring what I could do for women's struggles for freedom and equality, I registered for the course "Women: Images and Realities." I have always been aware of the feminist fight for equality; I grew up surrounded by feminists, but I never had the opportunity to take a class focused on women and was eager to learn more about the struggle today.

Although most of the reactions of my friends and family were positive and encouraging, some men ridiculed me for taking a women's studies class. I remember one individual who constantly challenged my "manliness" by saying things like "My, Evan, you look very feminine today; is that class rubbing off on you?" I often felt hopeless in the face of such ridicule, but I realized the mockery came from ignorance. Rather than becoming defensive, I would ask him whether he was insecure about his manhood, since anyone secure in themselves could easily take a women's studies class. Men are often unfamiliar with the facts of women's subordination, the extent to which it is practiced, and the role we can play in changing it. From my experience, it is often easier for people to joke about things they are scared to face or know nothing about. It is much easier for a man to criticize women's studies than to take a critical look at one's self and the advantages given to men in a society based on gender hierarchy.

Because the media portray feminists as "dykes who hate men," I brought into my first women's studies class a fear that my female classmates would hate me because I was a man, I was the oppressor. I learned in the course the difference between acting against men and acting against the actions of men. My classmates judged me by my beliefs and actions, not by what I have between my legs. Feminism, I learned, does not call for men's subordination but for the fair and equal treatment of women.

I learned in "Women: Images and Realities" that sexism is far deeper than I had previously thought. I also came to realize that I have many privileges as a white man. I learned that my skin color and gender give me an unfair advantage in American society, a realization that was extremely difficult to deal with. These privileges make life easier for me than for those who do not benefit from their skin color or sex. Without these privileges, my life goals and dreams would be more distant and difficult to achieve. Once I acknowledged this fact, I had to figure out what I could do with this information. It is not possible for me to divest myself individually of these privileges simply because I now recognize them. But I can work to change the system while being conscious of what these privileges have done for me.

Through "Women: Images and Realities," I became more aware of the prevalence of sexism in everyday life and the many small, seemingly insignificant ways in which men keep women in subordinate roles. I decided to stand up for my beliefs at all times, even when they were not popular. I wanted to contribute to women's struggles by dissenting from sexism in groups of men, but I soon learned that men don't always welcome such intervention.

A few months after the class ended, I was at a party and got into an argument with an acquaintance, who I'll call Bill, who was talking about how "pussy" needed to be "fucked." None of the other guys around had anything to say, so I asked him to clarify himself. When he repeated his statement, I asked him whether his mom had a "pussy" that needed a good "fuck." He replied, "Yeah, for someone else." I was disgusted and tried to explain to him how disrespectful his comment was. I argued that he could never make that comment to a woman's face. After a while I walked off, realizing that I could not make him take his comment back, especially with all

of his friends around. I went up to my cousin and told her about what Bill had said. She immediately went over to him and said "I don't have a pussy that needs to be fucked." In a few minutes Bill approached me ready for a fistfight. "Why did you do that?" he asked. "I was making the point that you couldn't make your comment to a woman's face because it is disrespectful," I responded and walked off.

To this day Bill holds a grudge against me, but I don't regret my action. It was important to me to let Bill know that I would not tolerate sexist behavior. I have to be true to myself and stand for what I believe in. I must fight against injustice whenever possible, even when it is difficult. My male friends seldom say insulting things about women in my presence, and I feel good about this even though they probably continue to say these things when I'm not around. At least I've made them think. I now see myself as a feminist, making the struggle for women's equality my own, and I will not forget who I am and where I stand in this struggle. [1998]

 12

# *The American University and Women's Studies*

CAROL T. CHRIST

The institutionalization of women's studies has been so rapid and so powerful that it prompts us to ask why. The most important cause of the development of women's studies is the feminist movement. Indeed, in the early years of women's studies, it was hard to separate the two. Early discussions of the field forthrightly asserted that one of the principal goals of women's studies courses was consciousness raising. Women's studies conferences in the early 1970s often focused on the relationship of women's studies to a feminist political agenda. Women's studies took its inspiration, its energy, and many of its issues from the women's movement. The women's movement in turn found a model and an analogue in the civil rights movement, and found energy and license from the various rebellions of the '60s. Black studies, ethnic studies, and women's studies developed together and evolved conceptual frameworks that borrowed from one another.

Although the women's movement clearly stimulated the development of women's studies, I don't think it offers a sufficient explanation for its academic institutionalization. Essential to the emergence of women's studies as an academic field has been the increasing representation of women on the faculty of colleges and universities. When I joined the Berkeley faculty in 1970, I became the fourth woman faculty member in an English Department of about eighty tenure-track faculty. In 1970, 3% of the entire Berkeley faculty were women. Now, 23% of the faculty are women. Of this 23%, the largest proportion is in the social sciences and humanities. In the English Department, for example, twenty-eight out of sixty faculty are now women.

If you think for a moment of what the historical experience of the cohort of women currently on the faculty of colleges and universities is likely to be, you will realize that many, like me, will have matured as scholars and teachers during the women's movement and will have experienced the growth in their numbers on the faculties on which they teach. In many fields this increase in the proportion of women on the faculty seems a simple equity issue. In English, for example, women for decades earned a substantial portion of the Ph.D.s yet held few faculty positions in major universities. For many women academics, the increased hiring of women faculty was immediate evidence of the changes the women's movement had brought. The increased hiring of women faculty facilitated the growth of women's studies because it created a cohort of women in colleges and universities throughout the country who had reason to feel that the women's movement had changed their professional world.

Thus far I have identified political factors that facilitated the growth of women's studies—the women's movement, the civil rights movement, the increased presence of women on college and university faculties. There are intellectual factors as well that facilitated the growth of women's studies. A number of disciplines in which women's studies took strongest root experienced paradigm shifts in the '70s that were particularly hospitable to work on gender. Indeed, one of the most interesting issues in the history of women's studies has been the way in which it has developed and located itself in different disciplines. As I was writing this talk, I sent an e-mail to a number of colleagues of mine in different departments asking them the following question: have there been paradigm shifts in your discipline in the past twenty-five years that have facilitated the development of women's studies? I got back a fascinating set of stories that showed how differently women's studies had developed from discipline to discipline. I will spend the next portion of my talk describing how dominant and emerging paradigms in different disciplines have affected the positions of women's studies.

I will begin with my own discipline, English. English is a field in which women's studies emerged as an early and powerful force. In *Female Studies II*, thirty of its sixty-six syllabi were courses in literature. Kate Millett's *Sexual Politics* was developed from a doctoral dissertation in English. Germaine Greer earned her doctorate as a Shakespear scholar. A number of factors contributed to the early emergence of women's studies in the field of English. First, English is a large field and has always attracted a large number of women graduate students. Women's studies moved quickly into the curriculum in the field of English in part because English departments had a substantial number of women faculty. Secondly, literature is necessarily gendered. Authors, obviously, are male or female; furthermore, any story or drama is likely to represent relationships between men and women. It therefore will make assumptions about gender or display conceptions of it. Finally, English literature contains many extraordinary women writers.

Because literature so obviously concerns gender, work in women's studies did not necessarily need to challenge critical paradigms. Scholars focusing on gender issues could and did use traditional critical methods. Although interpretations of individual literary works could be radically revisionary, they often used standard critical procedures. Take, for example, the feminist reinterpretation of *Jane Eyre*, which gives Sandra Gilbert and Susan Gubar's seminal book, *The Madwoman in the Attic,* its name. Although the arguments that a number of women critics made, that *Jane Eyre* concerns women's anger at the restrictions of their lives, entailed a radical re-seeing of the novel, the critical methodologies they used were often traditional—analysis of character, analysis of theme, placement of a work in its historical context. Likewise, the work on women writers that emerged in the '70s and '80s, was not necessarily revisionary in its methodology. The fact that women's studies in literature did not associate itself with a single methodology and did not for the most part attack traditional critical procedures helped its early and rapid institutionalization.

If one turns to other fields, one can see how the development of women's studies has been shaped and situated by the paradigms of those fields. In history, for example, another field in which women's studies has established an early and powerful presence, the development of women's studies has gone hand in hand with the increased attention to social history. In the first chapter of her book, *Disorderly Conduct: Visions of Gender in Victorian America,* the historian Carroll Smith-Rosenberg reflects on both her own development as a historian and on the development of women's history within the field of history. She locates the motivation for women's history in the feminist movement. "Aroused by feminist charges of economic and political discrimination, angered at the sexualization of women by contemporary society and at the psychological ramifications of that sexualization, we turned to our history to trace the origins of women's second-class status." But, Smith-Rosenberg goes on to argue:

> while a sense of personal oppression and of revolt against marginality and invisibility shaped the questions women's historians first addressed, those questions in turn pushed the methodological approaches and conceptual framework of traditional history to new frontiers. They revolutionized historians' understanding of the family, of the processes of economic change, and of the distribution of power within both traditional and industrial societies.[1]

The work of women's historians both built upon the new social history and transformed its conceptual framework. It did this in part by making women visible, not just in the words of men but in the words of women, in diaries and letters in which women gave voice to their experience.

The location of women's studies in the different fields of the social sciences shows some fascinating contrasts. Women's studies established itself fastest and most easily in psychology and in anthropology. In both fields, a focus on gender is central to the discipline, but in both fields women's studies motivated important shifts in how gender was understood.

Professor Christina Maslach, of Berkeley's Psychology Department, answered my e-mail inquiry about the institutionalization of women's studies in a particularly interesting way. She begins by recognizing that psychology was no stranger to issues of sex and gender before the 1960s. Freud's conception of sex roles, the focus of developmental psychologists on sex differences in children's behavior, research on the biological side of the field on the role of sex hormones on sexual behavior, and the use by personality psychologists of masculinity/femininity as a core set of traits all depended upon a bipolar model of masculinity and femininity as opposites that are linked to biological sex. In the late 1960s and early 1970s many scholars questioned the biological determinism of this model and placed increasing emphasis on the social context of behavior and development. Masculinity and feminity were conceptualized as two independent dimensions rather than opposite poles of one dimension, and they were unlinked from sex. Thus a crucial distinction was made between biological sex and social/psychological gender. At the same time, the emergence of new paradigms in cognitive psychology entailed a greater focus on processes of thinking, reasoning, perceiving, and judging. Work on social cognition in particular underscored the notion that gender is a constructed category rather than the expression of innate qualities.

In the 1970s, when feminist work in psychology first emerged, it focused upon the psychology of women, and this focus helped contribute to the legitimacy of women's studies. More recently, emphasis has shifted to include the psychology of men. Across the entire range of psychological research, gender is now understood as a fundamental category. As in the field of history, an interest in women that was at first motivated by the women's movement has broadened and deepened research in the field.

Anthropology, like psychology, seemed to have a natural fit with the concerns of women's studies. As Judy Stacey and Barrie Thorne observe in their article on "The Missing Feminist Revolution in Sociology," the traditional subject matter of anthropology—preliterate tribal cultures in which kinship is central to social life—has always encouraged anthropologists, even those concerned with law, religion, politics, and the economy, to attend to the sexual division of labor and structural and symbolic dimensions of gender relationships. As in literature and psychology, women were a visible subject of study in the discipline. However, placing women at the center of inquiry, as Stacey and Thorne observe, created dramatic conceptual shifts in anthropologists' understanding of the relationship of nature and culture, of the connection between gender and power, and of the connection between public and private life.[2] Furthermore, the fact that social and cultural anthropology were very much involved in the theoretical ferment in the humanities facilitated work on gender. The challenge to the idea of an objective anthropology, in which the anthropologist can describe a society without considering the perspective created by his or her own culture; the argument that all discourse must be understood as text, with a text's instabilities; the absorption of social anthropology into cultureal studies—all reinforced the legitimacy of women's studies in anthropology.

Sociology and political science offer interesting contrasts to psychology and anthropology. In neither field has the influence of women's studies been as powerful as it has been in the fields I have described. The reasons reflect the methodologies and the sociology of the disciplines. In an e-mail in response to my question, Professor David Leonard of Berkeley's Political Science Department observed that in political science women's studies was picked up by the most humanistic part of the discipline—political theory—at the same time that political scientists from other subfields were questioning the explanatory force of theory. Women's studies helped

political theory maintain some credibility, at the same time that the alliance of women's studies with political theory marginalized it within the rest of the discipline. The position of women's studies within the discipline distanced it from orientations that were more quantitative and scientific. This was not a necessary result. Women's studies could influence the study of social movements or political behavior, particularly the behavior of voters. (Remember the soccer Moms.) However, women's studies within political science took on a position that was critical of power, and this position put it at odds with the center of the discipline.

Women's studies, of course, is only one of a number of different kinds of studies that have become current in the last two decades. All of the subfields of ethnic studies, international and area studies, urban studies, American studies are interdisciplinary concentrations that, like women's studies, bring together the subjects of inquiry and methodologies of a number of disciplines in the humanities and social sciences in order to understand a specific population. In considering the allocation of faculty positions across departments, university administrators are now used to thinking not only about the ideal composition of a political science department or a history department but about the range of scholars on a campus studying Latin America, for example, or East Asia. In general, universities have become more alert to the fact that traditional departments do not represent the only organization of knowledge, that there is a horizontal axis in the social sciences and the humanities that represents populations as well as a vertical axis that represents traditional disciplines. Women's studies has been an important participant in this interdisciplinary reorganization of knowledge.

I would like now to turn to the question of what have been the fundamental contributions of women's studies. The most important has been the renewed recognition that social position necessarily shapes experience and perspective. Scholars now understand gender, race, and class as socially constructed categories that shape experience not only for women and for ethnic minorities but for everyone in society. This change has been important both in the humanities and in the social sciences. No

*This segment of a longer piece by Emily Martin (Signs, 16, 1991) provides an example from the discipline of biology of how gender bias can subtly be reinforced in academic disciplines, Martin examined major scientific textbooks and research articles that discuss reproduction and found significant evidence of gender stereotyping in the scientific language.*

# The Egg and the Sperm: How Science Has Constructed a Romance Based on Stereotypical Male-Female Roles

EMILY MARTIN

How is it that positive images are denied to the bodies of women? A look at language—in this case, scientific language—provides the first clue. Take the egg and the sperm. It is remarkable how "femininely" the egg behaves and how "masculinely" the sperm. The egg is seen as large and passive. It does not *move* or journey, but passively "is transported," "is swept," or even "drifts" along the fallopian tube. In utter contrast, sperm are small, "streamlined," and invariably active. They "deliver" their genes to the egg, "activate the developmental program of the egg," and have a "velocity" that is often remarked upon. Their tails are "strong" and efficiently powered. Together with the forces of ejaculation, they can "propel the semen into the deepest recesses of the vagina." For this they need "energy," "fuel," so that with a "whiplashlike motion and strong lurches" they can "burrow through the egg coat" and "penetrate" it.

At its extreme, the age-old relationship of the egg and the sperm takes on a royal or religious patina. The egg coat, its protective barrier, is sometimes called its "vestments," a term usually reserved for sacred, religious dress. The egg is said to have a "corona," a crown, and to be accompanied by "attendant cells." It is holy, set apart and above, the queen to the sperm's king. The egg is also passive, which means it must depend on the sperm for rescue. Gerald Schatten and Helen Schatten liken the egg's role to that of Sleeping Beauty: "a dormant bride awaiting her mate's magic kiss, which instills the spirit that brings her to life." Sperm, by contrast, have a "mission," which is to "move through the female genital tract in quest of the ovum." One popular account has it that the sperm carry out a "perilous journey" into the "warm darkness," where some fall away "exhausted." "Survivors" "assault" the egg, the successful candidates "surrounding the prize." Part of the urgency of this journey, in more scientific terms, is that "once released from the supportive environment of the ovary, an egg will die within hours unless rescued by a sperm." The wording stresses the fragility and dependency of the egg, even though the same text acknowledges elsewhere that sperm also live for only a few hours.

critic can provide a fully adequate account of a text without taking gender into account; similarly, social science research must consider how gender shapes its data.

Secondly, women's studies has contributed a new sensitivity to the metaphoric and figurative use of gendered terms. For example, we cannot any longer read work that uses gendered metaphors without being alert to their implications. In *Thinking About Women*, Ellman makes this point by quoting the following paragraph by Balzac, describing the art of writing:

> To pass from conception to execution, to produce, to bring the idea to birth, to raise the child laboriously from infancy, to put it nightly to sleep surfeited, to kiss it in the mornings with the hungry heart of a mother, to clean it, to clothe it fifty times over in new garments which it tears and casts away, and yet not revolt against the trials of this agitated life—this unwearying maternal love, this habit of creation—this is execution and its toils.[3]

Similarly, women's studies has created a self-consciousness of the gendered terms in everyday language. We now say chair and not chairman, police officer and not policeman, and we do not use "he" as a generic pronoun. This change sometimes has its awkwardnesses—waitperson for waiter, or, as a colleague of mine insists, person-person for mailman. Nonetheless, there is a stratum of assumptions about gender in language to which we are sensitive.

Finally, women's studies has contributed the discovery of an extraordinary body of women's writing and of women's history. Women's studies has brought a new attention to women's lives, experiences, and achievements. Critics have discovered the work of many women writers and have shown rich new dimensions in the work of those already well known. The canon has changed. And the way in which critics construct literary history has changed as well, as we understand increasingly more about the role of women writers in the production of literature.

What is in the future for women's studies? In the early days of women's studies, its first proponents imagined it as always on the margin of the academy, as always in opposition, using its place on the edge to critique the center. Although one can still find this view of women's studies, I do not think it is accurate nor do I think it is very fruitful. As I have shown today, women's studies has profoundly affected work in a range of core disciplines to such an extent that questions about gender are at the center of those fields. In the early days of women's studies, women often debated the question of whether women's studies should be located in the various departments that it could hope to transform. That form of the question no longer makes sense. Whether or not a college or university chooses to have a women's studies program, women's studies is represented across the disciplines of the humanities and social sciences. I believe that women's studies will become an increasingly prominent part of our intellectual landscape. Indeed, the use of gender as a focus for analysis has become so pervasive throughout the humanities and social sciences that I occasionally wonder whether the idea of a discipline that bounds the study of women is adequate to the wealth and variety of work being done.    [1997]

*NOTES*

1. Carroll Smith-Rosenberg, *Disorderly Conduct: Visions of Gender in Victorian America* (New York: Oxford University Press, 1985), pp. 12, 11.
2. Judy Stacey and Barrie Thorne, "The Missing Feminist Revolution in Sociology," *Social Problems*, 32, No. 4 (1985), 305.
3. Honoré de Balzac, quoted in Ellman, *Thinking About Women* (New York: Harcourt Brace Jovanovich, 1968), p. 17.

## PART II

# Becoming a Woman in Our Society

### DOMINANT IDEAS ABOUT WOMEN AND HOW THEY ARE LEARNED

Images of women convey powerful beliefs about what is considered appropriate behavior for girls and women. Regardless of the context of these images, they tend to illustrate prevailing norms. From the notion of the adorable and delicate baby girl, to the depiction of the seductively attractive young woman, such images are part and parcel of our culture's portrayal of females.

What *does* it mean to be a woman? Ideas about what it means to be a woman permeate all cultures, powerfully shaping the way that women are perceived and treated. These ideas vary from culture to culture, yet they are presented as if they were ordained by either God or nature. In this chapter we explore the notion of "femininity" as a social construct: a prevailing set of ideas, myths, stereotypes, norms, and standards that affect the lives of all women in a variety of ways. Disentangling "nature" from "culture" has been a central task of women throughout history as we struggle to free ourselves from constricting myths, stereotypes, and standards.

Western concepts of femininity include a combination of ideas about female good and evil that feminists have identified as the madonna/whore dichotomy. Female virtue has traditionally been presented as pure, selfless, and maternal, whereas female evil has been presented as deceitful, dangerous, and sinful. In a society that is racist as well as sexist, it is frequently the white woman who appears as pure and selfless, whereas women of racial and ethnic minorities are seen as deviant. Thus, we often hear of the African-American woman's "domineering" nature; the exotic sensuality of the Asian-American woman; the Latina woman's stereotype as evil, sexually uncontrollable, and betrayer of her race; and the status-conscious Jewish American woman.

Though specific to different racial and ethnic groups, these images of women reflect the negative half of the madonna/whore and good girl/bad girl stereotypes that have historically defined standards of behavior for all women. One learns very early—from peers, family, educational institutions, and the media—what are acceptable behavior, attitudes, and values. For females, this means that from infancy on, young girls are bombarded with messages about what "good" girls do and, even more insistently, what they do not do.

In the United States, ideas about feminity have been inextricably linked with ideas about race and class. In the nineteenth century, for example, urban, white middle-class women were told it was "woman's nature" to be frail and demure while slave women worked alongside men in the fields. For these reasons, women's studies scholars often describe gender norms as *racialized.*

Consider the many ways in which American society communicates expectations of females and males from the moment of birth. Gender markers in the form of color of clothing immediately differentiate female infants from male infants: pink gowns with frills and bows convey a feminine gentleness, purity, and fragility; blue sleepers decorated with animals, trains, and sports scenes portray boys as strong, active, and vigorous. Additionally, from the family outward to the community, children are continuously exposed to direct and subtle messages regarding appropriate sex-role behavior. For example, different chores are typically assigned to boys and girls at home: dishwashing and housecleaning for girls, washing cars and taking out garbage for boys.

As we explore the experience of being female, we call attention to the ways in which society has limited and trapped women through myths and stereotypes. We see that our self-perceptions are often distorted, reflecting cultural values about women rather than realistic appraisals of our worth. All too often, these self-images take the form of diminished notions of ability and strength, and exaggerated ideas of inferiority and weakness. Ultimately, many girls and women begin to question themselves and feel powerless, whether they are in the classroom, at work, or in relationships with others. To begin to value oneself beyond these limiting boundaries and expectations can be an arduous task when the majority of society's messages are saying otherwise.

Stereotypes about girls and women serve a powerful function in our society: they make it easier for individuals to predict women's behavior, allowing a quick evaluation and categorization of behavior. For example, adhering to stereotypes leads people to (erroneously) evaluate attractive, blonde women as unintelligent. Stereotypes of women's mental capability give rise to snap judgments that women are not as qualified as men for certain positions requiring what are presumed to be masculine attributes (e.g., intelligence, decisiveness, logical reasoning skills). In general, stereotypes are tightly woven into the social fabric of this culture, and reinforce dichotomous notions of "femininity" and "masculinity."

Prevailing norms of behavior also influence how the behavior of women is judged. Women have traditionally been defined in relation to male standards and needs. Man is seen as strong, woman weak, and this type of dichotomy is essential for perpetuating the superiority of males. Woman has historically been viewed as man's subordinate, someone different from and inferior to him. "Masculine" traits are socially desirable and valued, whereas "feminine" ones are not—setting up another dichotomy that influences the ways in which the behavior of women and men is judged. In her classic work in psychology, Naomi Weisstein[1] details the ways in which psychologists have created a mantle of scientific "authority" to these ideas by promoting the concept of a "female essence" and ignoring the powerful influence of the social context on behavior. Weisstein exposes the ways that scientists, rather than pursuing evidence, have created theories on the basis of the ideas of femininity they inherited from the culture. A more effective way of understanding the behavior of both women and men, she argues, would be to study the power of social expectations to influence behavior.

Few cultural institutions and practices do not promote and reinforce the stereotyping of women. Through language, for example, maleness is often the standard (consider the terms "mankind," "chairman," "policeman," "postman," and so on). From subtle uses of language to more overt messages transmitted through the media,

---

[1] Naomi Weisstein, "Psychology Constructs the Female" in *Kinder, Kirche, Kuche as Scientific Law: Psychology Constructs the Female* (Boston: New England Free Press, 1968).

advertisements, and classroom setting, girls are bombarded with sexist views of the world and of themselves. The dynamics of the classroom, for example, reinforce existing power relationships between males and females. These patterns are so pervasive that we don't usually notice then. However, studies of the elementary school classroom reveal teachers calling on female students less frequently than on male students, discouraging females' classroom participation and eroding their confidence in their intellectual capabilities. Ultimately, we see females and males literally tracked into "feminine" and "masculine" fields of study and careers.

In the second section of this part, selections focus on family and cultural norms, educational experiences, nonverbal communication, and the media, which have all had powerful effects on the way women and girls see themselves and their world. One important example of media influences on the socialization process is music. The lyrics of many mainstream contemporary songs, as well as the images in the music videos accompanying them, promote sexist notions of women that emphasize women's sexuality and insubordination to men. When girls and women are constantly exposed to messages of male superiority, we inevitably feel powerless and insignificant. By becoming more conscious of this process of becoming a woman, we can begin to challenge and change those norms, practices, and institutions that have restricted girls' and women's fullest expressions of ourselves. Only then will ideas of "what it means to be a woman" truly reflect women's experiences.

# Dominant Ideas About Women

Images of femininity, while powerful in our culture, vary according to class, ethnic group, and race and have been manipulated to serve the needs of those in power. Precisely because these portrayals of women interact with specific stereotypes, it is critical to examine the ways they affect the experiences of different groups of women. Betty Friedan exposed the myths and realities of the "happy middle-class housewife" of the 1960s in her book *The Feminine Mystique.* This book represented a pivotal point in the consciousness of many white middle-class women, who identified with Friedan's characterization of the discontent and frustration that many women felt with the decorative supportive roles glorified in the popular culture of the 1950s and 1960s. Marge Piercy echoes this theme in her poem "A Work of Artifice," as she equates the fragile beauty of the bonsai tree with traditional expectations of femininity. Piercy suggests that all women pay a price for complying with these social norms, as does the bonsai tree, which is artificially stunted for ornamental purposes.

Often when girls enter puberty we encounter our culture's ideas of femininity. We find we are suddenly treated differently and face restrictions we don't understand. In "Purification," gracepoore describes a rite of passage from southern India that acknowledges a girl's first menstruation. This ritual traditionally signals a girl's readiness for the "wife-mother" role and includes a cleansing ceremony that is meant to "purify" her of her blood. While the ritual functions as a way of bringing family and community together, it can also render individual girls invisible.

Danzy Senna shares her experiences as an adolescent "growing up mixed in the racial battlefield of Boston," when she struggles to become clear about her identity— what kind of women she wanted to be. Torn between her observation of the real-life power dynamics between men and women and her desire to conform to the racialized gender norms of popular culture, Senna shows us that young women with multiple racial and ethnic backgrounds negotiate a complex path as they consider conflicting messages of what they "should" be.

Susan Schnur confronts myths and stereotypes about Jewish women, highlighting the antisemitism and sexism inherent in the term "JAP." Another widely held misconception is that women with physical disabilities do not have sexual lives. Debra Kent challenges this assumption by illustrating how images of disability and women's sexuality give rise to this stereotype.

Like the ceremony in "Purification," the ritual surrounding weddings preserves traditional notions of femininity, even while increasing numbers of women see themselves as independent individuals who are not becoming their husbands' property. This section concludes with an essay in which Elisa Dávila describes how she learned to be a "good girl" in a patriarchal and sexist society. Developing an understanding of the separate standards imposed for men's and women's behavior, Dávila challenged them, creating a life in the United States that resonates with her own needs for self-fulfillment. However, she reminds us that regardless of where she is or what she does, she is still subject to being judged by artificial ideals of womanhood.

---

## 🌿 13

## *The Problem That Has No Name*

BETTY FRIEDAN

Gradually I came to realize that the problem that has no name was shared by countless women in America. As a magazine writer I often interviewed women about problems with their children, or their marriages, or their houses, or their communities. But after a while I began to recognize the telltale signs of this other problem. I saw the same signs in suburban ranchhouses and split-levels on Long Island and in New Jersey and Westchester County; in colonial houses in a small Massachusetts town; on patios in Memphis; in suburban and city apartments; in living rooms in the Midwest. Sometimes I sensed the problem, not as a reporter, but as a suburban housewife, for during this time I was also bringing up my own three children in Rockland County, New York. I heard echoes of the problem in college dormitories and semi-private maternity wards, at PTA meetings and luncheons of the League of Women Voters, at suburban cocktail parties, in station wagons waiting for trains, and in snatches of conversation overheard at Schrafft's. The groping words I heard from other women, on quiet afternoons when children were at school or on quiet evenings when husbands worked late, I think I understood first as a woman long before I understood their larger social and psychological implications.

Just what was this problem that has no name? What were the words women used when they tried to express it? Sometimes a woman would say "I feel empty somehow . . . incomplete." Or she would say, "I feel as if I don't exist." Sometimes she blotted out the feeling with a tranquilizer. Sometimes she thought the problem was with her husband, or her children, or that what she really needed was to redecorate her house, or move to a better neighborhood, or have an affair, or another baby. Sometimes, she went to a doctor with symptoms she could hardly describe: "A tired feeling. . . . I get so angry with the children it scares me. . . . I feel like crying without any reason." (A Cleveland doctor called it "the housewife's syndrome.") A number of women told me about great bleeding blisters that break out on their hands and arms. "I call it the housewife's blight," said a family doctor in Pennsylvania. "I see it so often lately in these young women with four, five and six children who bury themselves in their dishpans. But it isn't caused by detergent and it isn't cured by cortisone."

Sometimes a woman would tell me that the feeling gets so strong she runs out of the house and walks through the streets. Or she stays inside her house and cries. Or her children tell her a joke, and she doesn't laugh because she doesn't hear it. I talked to women who had spent years on the analyst's couch, working out their "adjustment to the feminine role," their blocks to "fulfillment as a wife and mother." But the desperate tone in these women's voices, and the look in their eyes, was the same as the tone and the look of other women, who were sure they had no problem, even though they did have a strange feeling of desperation.

A mother of four who left college at nineteen to get married told me:

I've tried everything women are supposed to do—hobbies, gardening, pickling, canning, being very social with my neighbors, joining committees, running PTA teas. I can do it all, and I like it, but it doesn't leave you anything to think about—any feeling of who you are. I never had any career ambitions. All I wanted was to get married and have four children. I love the kids and Bob and my home. There's no problem you can even put a name to.

But I'm desperate. I begin to feel I have no personality. I'm a server of food and putter-on of pants and a bedmaker, somebody who can be called on when you want something. But who am I?

A twenty-three-year-old mother in blue jeans said:

I ask myself why I'm so dissatisfied. I've got my health, fine children, a lovely new home, enough money. My husband has a real future as an electronics engineer. He doesn't have any of these feelings. He says maybe I need a vacation, let's go to New York for a weekend. But that isn't it. I always had this idea we should do everything together. I can't sit down and read a book alone. If the children are napping and I have one hour to myself I just walk through the house waiting for them to wake up. I don't make a move until I know where the rest of the crowd is going. It's as if ever since you were a little girl, there's always been somebody or something that will take care of your life: your parents, or college, or falling in love, or having a child, or moving to a new house. Then you wake up one morning and there's nothing to look forward to.

A young wife in a Long Island development said:

I seem to sleep so much. I don't know why I should be so tired. This house isn't nearly so hard to clean as the cold-water flat we had when I was working. The children are at school all day. It's not the work. I just don't feel alive."

In 1960, the problem that has no name burst like a boil through the image of the happy American housewife. In the television commercials the pretty housewives still beamed over their foaming dishpans and *Time*'s cover story on "The Suburban Wife, an American Phenomenon" protested: "Having too good a time . . . to believe that they should be unhappy." But the actual unhappiness of the American housewife was suddenly being reported—from the *New York Times* and *Newsweek* to *Good Housekeeping* and CBS Television ("The Trapped Housewife"), although almost everybody who talked about it found some superficial reason to dismiss it. It was attributed to incompetent appliance repairmen (*New York Times*), or the distances children must be chauffeured in the suburbs (*Time*), or too much PTA (*Redbook*). Some said it was the old problem—education: more and more women had educated, which naturally made them unhappy in their role as housewives. "The road from Freud to Frigidaire, from Sophocles to Spock, has turned out to be a bumpy one," reported the *New York Times* (June 28, 1960). "Many young women—certainly not all—whose education plunged them into a world of ideas feel stifled in their homes. They find their routine lives out of joint with their training. Like shut-ins, they feel left out. In the last year, the problem of the educated housewife has provided the meat of dozens of speeches made by troubled presidents of women's colleges who maintain, in the face of complaints, that sixteen years of academic training is realistic preparation for wifehood and motherhood."

There was much sympathy for the educated housewife. ("Like a two-headed schizophrenic . . . once she wrote a paper on the Graveyard poets; now she writes notes to the milkman. Once she determined the boiling point of sulfuric acid; now she determines her boiling point with the overdue repairman. . . . The housewife often is reduced to screams and tears. . . . No one, it seems, is appreciative, least of all herself, of the kind of person she becomes in the process of turning from poetess into shrew.")

Home economists suggested more realistic preparation for housewives, such as high-school workshops in home appliances. College educators suggested more discussion groups on home management and the family, to prepare women for the adjustment to domestic life. A spate of articles appeared in the mass magazines offering "Fifty-eight Ways to Make Your Marriage More Exciting." No month went by without a new book by a psychiatrist or sexologist offering technical advice on finding greater fulfillment through sex.

A male humorist joked in *Harper's Bazaar* (July, 1960) that the problem could be solved by taking away women's right to vote. ("In the pre-19th Amendment era, the American woman was placid, sheltered and sure of her role in American society. She left all the political decisions to her husband and he, in turn, left all the family decisions to her. Today a woman has to make both the family *and* the political decisions, and it's too much for her.")

A number of educators suggested seriously that women no longer be admitted to the four-year colleges and universities: in the growing college crisis, the education which girls could not use as housewives was more urgently needed than ever by boys to do the work of the atomic age.

The problem was also dismissed with drastic solutions no one could take seriously. (A woman writer proposed in *Harper's* that women be drafted for compulsory service as nurses' aides and baby-sitters.) And it was smoothed over with the age-old panaceas: "love is their answer," "the only answer is inner help," "the secret of completeness—children," "a private means of intellectual fulfillment," "to cure this toothache of the spirit—the simple formula of handing one's self and one's will over to God."

The problem was dismissed by telling the housewife she doesn't realize how lucky she is—her own boss, no time clock, no junior executive gunning for her job. What if she isn't happy—does she think men are happy in this world? Does she really, secretly, still want to be a man? Doesn't she know yet how lucky she is to be a woman?

The problem was also, and finally, dismissed by shrugging that there are no solutions: this is what being a woman means, and what is wrong with American women that they can't accept their role gracefully? As *Newsweek* put it (March 7, 1960):

> She is dissatisfied with a lot that women of other lands can only dream of. Her discontent is deep, pervasive, and impervious to the superficial remedies which are offered at every hand. . . . An army of professional explorers have already charted the major sources of trouble. . . . From the beginning of time, the female cycle has defined and confined woman's role. As Freud was credited with saying: "Anatomy is destiny." Though no group of women has ever pushed these natural restrictions as far as the American wife, it seems that she still cannot accept them with good grace. . . . A young mother with a beautiful family, charm, talent and brains is apt to dismiss her role apologetically. "What do I do?" you hear her say. "Why nothing. I'm just a housewife." A good education, it seems, has given this paragon among women an understanding of the value of everything except her own worth. . . .

And so she must accept the fact that "American women's unhappiness is merely the most recently won of women's rights," and adjust and say with the happy housewife found by *Newsweek:* "We ought to salute the wonderful freedom we all have and be proud of our lives today. I have had college and I've worked, but being a housewife is the most rewarding and satisfying role. . . . My mother was never included in my father's business affairs . . . she couldn't get out of the house and away from us children. But I am an equal to my husband; I can go along with him on business trips and to social business affairs."

The alternative offered was a choice that few women would contemplate. In the sympathetic words of the *New York Times:* "All admit to being deeply frustrated at times by the lack of privacy, the physical burden, the routine of family life, the confinement of it. However, none would give up her home and family if she had the choice to make again." *Redbook* commented: "Few women would want to thumb their noses at husbands, children and community and go off on their own. Those who do may be talented individuals, but they rarely are successful women."

The year American women's discontent boiled over, it was also reported (*Look*) that the more than 21,000,000 American women who are single, widowed, or divorced do not cease even after fifty their frenzied, desperate search for a man. And the search begins early—for seventy per cent of all American women now marry before they are twenty-four. A pretty twenty-five-year-old secretary took thirty-five different jobs in six months in the futile hope of finding a husband. Women are moving from one political club to another, taking evening courses in accounting or sailing, learning to play golf or ski, joining a number of churches in succession, going to bars alone, in their ceaseless search for a man.

Of the growing thousands of women currently getting private psychiatric help in the United States, the married ones were reported dissatisfied with their marriages, the unmarried ones suffering from anxiety and, finally, depression. Strangely, a number of psychiatrists stated that, in their experience, unmarried women patients were happier than married ones. So the door of all those pretty suburban houses opened a crack to permit a glimpse of uncounted thousands of American housewives who suffered alone from a problem that suddenly everyone was talking about, and beginning to take for granted, as one of those unreal problems in American life that can never be solved—like the hydrogen bomb. By 1962 the plight of the trapped American housewife had become a national parlor game. Whole issues of magazines, newspaper columns, books learned and frivolous, educational conferences and television panels were devoted to the problem.

Even so, most men, and some women, still did not know that this problem was real. But those who had faced it honestly knew that all the superficial remedies, the sympathetic advice, the scolding words and the cheering words were somehow drowning the problem in unreality. A bitter laugh was beginning to be heard from American women. They were admired, envied, pitied, theorized over until they were sick of it, offered drastic solutions or silly choices that no one could take seriously. They got all kinds of advice from the growing armies of marriage and child-guidance counselors, psychotherapists, and armchair psychologists, on how to adjust to their role as housewives. No other road to fulfillment was offered to American women in the middle of the twentieth century. Most adjusted to their role and suffered or ignored the problem that has no name. It can be less painful, for a woman, not to hear the strange, dissatisfied voice stirring within her.                                    [1964]

# 𝒴 14

## *A Work of Artifice*

MARGE PIERCY

The bonsai tree
in the attractive pot
could have grown eighty feet tall
on the side of a mountain
till split by lightning.
But a gardener
carefully pruned it.
It is nine inches high.

Every day as he
whittles back the branches
the gardener croons,
It is your nature
to be small and cozy,
domestic and weak;
how lucky, little tree,
to have a pot to grow in.
With living creatures
one must begin very early
to dwarf their growth:
the bound feet,
the crippled brain,
the hair in curlers,
the hands you
love to touch.                                    [1973]

# 𝒴 15

## *Purification*

gracepoore

The Tamil custom of observing a girl's first menstruation through ritual and ceremony is an acknowledgement of her rite of passage to womanhood. While this custom can serve as a powerful and positive affirmation of her femaleness, in practice it evolved as a means for the girl's family to publicize their daughter's availability for marriage. Hence, the ceremony is more for the family than for the girl herself.

In time, as more and more middle-class urban Tamil families like mine encouraged education first, marriage later, women put off marriage until their mid or late twenties, even early thirties. With this development, it seemed as if the custom of celebrating a girl's first period would become an actual honoring of her rite of passage rather than a mechanism for placing her on the marriage market. Yet it hasn't. For while a Tamil girl may no longer need to marry when she is an adolescent or young teenager, her puberty marks the point at which she is ready to produce children via the institution of marriage. Hence, everything, from her dietary changes during her period to her ceremonial clothes, inform her and others around her that she has inherited the role and responsibility of being a potential wife-mother.

In my family, the menstruation ritual took on an added dimension due to their Christian belief that menstrual blood is impure. Not only was the girl to be "celebrated" for coming of age but she was also to be "cleansed."

The use of milk to purify is a Tamil and Hindu custom. However, as with many immigrants living in the South Asian diaspora, cultural practices persist in co-opted forms irrespective of religious affiliation or belief systems. Hence, cleansing with milk became simply a Tamil, no longer a Hindu, custom while serving a Tamil Christian function.

No doubt, exposing one's culture to a foreign audience is like sharing a family secret that discredits family honor. Yet there are practices in all cultures that need to be revised, re-interpreted, and/or eventually discarded because they disempower individuals. There was great hesitation in writing this story, an even greater hesitation in submitting it for publication, but it was a necessary act—to give voice to anger and to transform experience into narrative.

"Purification" is written for several reasons: to expose a custom that is meant to celebrate but in fact humiliates girls and women; to defy the silence that all cultures impose on those who question and challenge repressive customs; to protest forced participation of children in rituals that have no meaning to them, that frighten and strip them of their dignity as people; and to confront those who practice the very customs that disempowered them at some time in their lives, but who perpetuate them in exchange for social status, who pass on these traditions to the generations after them in the name of preserving a cultural heritage.

I write this story for my nieces so they will not have to go through what Geeta went through for growing up female in a christianized Tamil family.

It was there one afternoon—a stain on my panties, the color of dried plantain juice. "Amma, I have a brown patch on my pants," I said at the lunch table.

Mother dropped the ball of curried rice she was about to pop in her mouth, and stared at me. "What patch? Where?" she rapped.

"I dunno. It just came. On my knickers." I noticed a strange look on her face. In silence she kept her eyes on me, then tossed the ball of rice into her mouth and chewed.

I bit into a piece of chicken. Of all the chicken curries I had tasted at other people's homes on Deepavali, Mother's was the best. She made it so her chicken was tender without falling apart in shreds inside the gravy. Her spices blended just right so the hotness didn't stick in your throat. I picked another piece of chicken off my plate, curry collecting in the creases of my palm and soaking into my finger tips. Long after I had eaten, the scent would remain as it always did with the curries that my mother made.

"Ma, can I ride Peter's bike after I finish my homework?" Jeevan's voice crashed through the silence. He was my nine-year-old brother. Dad did not like him riding bicycles since the time he fell and grazed his knee so badly, he had a purple scab for two months.

Mother ignored Jeevan. She went on shaping another ball of rice in her plate while he sat licking his fingers. Jeevan tried again, "Ma, can I . . ."

"How many times have I told you not to lick your fingers. If you've finished eating, go and wash your hands," Mother scolded even before he could complete his sentence.

"But I haven't finished eating," Jeevan complained.

"Then hurry up and finish," Mother snapped and poured a glass of water.

Jeevan was not ready to give up on the bicycle and went on pestering her. "So, can I ride Peter's . . ."

"Take your food into the hall, Jeevan," Mother jerked her head sideways and turned to him. I looked at her.

"But you're the one who told us not to eat in the hall," Jeevan argued.

"Take your food and eat it in the hall. I want to talk to Geeta."

"But why?" Jeevan whined.

"Will you stop asking bloody questions and just

---

*Deepavali*   the Hindu Festival of Lights, to celebrate the return of the mythical hero Rama to Ayodha.

do what I tell you? Take your plate and get out there!" Mother yelled, her hands furiously mixing curry and rice.

Jeevan knew he was in for trouble if he stayed one minute longer. He picked up his plate and walked out of the kitchen. Mother thrust back her chair, went to the sink, washed her hands and disappeared into the bedroom. I followed her, my lunch and hers half-eaten on the table.

Behind closed doors, she thrust a soft white object at me and said in a cold voice, "Put this between your legs." I stared at what she held out to me, a large slice of bread with a loop on each end. "Put it in your panties," she ordered.

I took the bread from her. One side felt smooth like one of Mother's saris, the other side a little rough, with a fine net-like surface and a blue line running up and down the middle.

"Go on. What are you waiting for? Adjust that between your thighs," Mother broke into my thoughts.

I had no idea what to do. "How, Amma?" I asked.

"Can't you do a simple thing?" she bristled and snatched the pad from me. Then she picked up her sari, lifted it halfway up, and held the pad between her thighs. I had never seen anything above mother's knees, so the sight of her thighs made me forget the pad. There she stood, exposed, green lines snaking under her light brown skin. Instantly, Mother noticed and pulled her sari down. In her eyes I saw what I felt in my heart, and I wished I had never seen my mother's thighs. Then it was my turn.

I kept trying to hold my skirt down while fumbling with the pad inside my panties, unable to see what I was doing, yet unwilling to expose myself like she had. Then I heard her say, "This evening, when Dad comes home, he'll get a belt for the pad." I wondered where the belt would go. Mother went on, "You put the loops into the belt hooks so the pad won't move."

"How long do I wear this?"

"Till your period is over. Every time it gets dirty, you change it. There's newspaper under the sink. Wrap the pads in that and throw them in the front dustbin, not the one in the kitchen. Take it to the front, understand?" I pulled the panties up over the pad. "Tomorrow, you stay home. I'll write a note to your teacher."

But I had a netball game. I had to go. "Ma, Mrs. Koh told us not to be absent. I'm playing netball."

"I'll write a note," she silenced me.

"But Mrs. Koh said not to be absent."

"I'm telling you, you can't go."

"But I'm not sick, why can't I go?"

"When did you get such a big mouth? You aren't going and that's final."

"But Mrs. Koh . . ."

"Who the hell is Mrs. Koh? Is she feeding you or am I? If Dad hears you talking like this, you'll get a bloody lashing." I felt the pad lodged between my thighs. I remembered Dad's terrible temper; I thought about the brown stain, and held my breath.

Mother opened the door and walked out. I sat on the bed and cried quietly. How would I explain to my teammates? What would Mrs. Koh think? Through the open door, I watched Mother clearing away the lunch dishes and felt tears roll down the bridge of my nose.

The next five days were a mystery. Mother gave rules she had never given me before. "Don't take the dog out, don't let Jeevan sit on your bed, don't you dare wash your hair today, you'll get black circles under your eyes. Wait another three days."

Then she screamed, "How many times have I got to tell you, throw the pads in the front dustbin!"

When I yelled back, "I forgot, Ma," she got angry and screamed even louder, "I've told you before, that's girls' stuff and you have to be careful not to let Jeevan see it."

Jeevan never knew why I stayed home from school. Dad told him to mind his own business when he asked about me. I never said a word because Mother said not to. So Jeevan told the neighborhood boys that I had chicken pox.

Twice a day, Mother made me eat a stiff sweet paste of crushed green peas mixed with brown sugar. In the mornings, she forced me to swallow raw egg yolks and drink ginger oil to strengthen my womb. Meanwhile, a tight pink elastic belt girdled my waist and cut into my flesh. My brown stain became a sticky red liquid which Mother called "menses." My stomach ached right below my belly button and all through my lower back.

For a week I missed school. I thought about the netball games and wondered if I would ever play again. Once or twice, I asked Dad if I could go to school. At first, he just said no. The second time, he threatened to smack me so I stopped asking. Most of the week I stayed in bed and read Enid Blyton's mystery books. This part was fun, the only part that was fun.

Soon the pain in my stomach stopped and the blood started to go away. Mother told me I could soak my clothes with the others' again, and I did not have to hang my panties at the far end of the clothes line where spiders built cobwebs to catch beetles.

Just when my sickness was nearly gone, Mother gave me something I had only seen in Tamil movies, a costume that women wore when they danced before a king or some rich man who turned out to be a villain. She gave me a satin, yellow midriff blouse and a sweeping, yellow sequined skirt made from one of her new georgette saris. The skirt came down to the ankles and the blouse had press studs down the front and little eared sleeves.

"Tomorrow you wear this," she said, "Uncles and aunts are coming here and pastor is doing a prayer service for you."

"Why are they praying?" I asked.

"It's our custom. Every girl must go through it," she answered, ending the conversation.

All day that day, Mother stood over the kerosene stove, cooking Indian sweets. She grumbled about the price of cardamom and worried about not having enough food to feed the guests. When I asked her again why people were coming to our house, she said it was a celebration. When I asked what we were celebrating, she scolded me for wasting her time and told me to leave the kitchen.

At three o'clock the next afternoon relatives poured into our small terrace house, invading every room except mine. Mother said I had to stay in the room till she called. I lay in bed, listening to the laughter and chatter around me. Two aunts came in to ask how I felt. My cousins peeked through open window louvres. Uncles stood at the door, glancing at me occasionally, but never venturing close.

After awhile, they all left me alone. I tried to read *The Mystery of The Missing Red Coat*, but my mind kept wandering outside. Soon, only my eyes were in the book. My ears pulled my head outside, to the stories floating around behind the closed door. Uncle Arthur was having a cataract operation. Aunt Esther was going to marry an engineer. Mrs. Dorai's daughter failed Oxford. Cousin Joshua's son was coming back with a Jaffna bride.

From the kitchen, smells of mother's cooking wafted through the house. I had watched her pile our special rose-colored plates with gulab jamuns glistening with thick sugar syrup. She had unwrapped fish-shaped steel trays from tissue paper and arranged golden ladhus next to creamy white burfi. This morning, she filled Pyrex bowls with chicken curry and yellow rice spiked with cloves and cinnamon sticks. I lay on the bed and tasted her food on the back of my tongue, wondering when we would eat.

As the sun turned a bright orange outside, Mother came into my room. "Grandcousin Ivy is going to bathe you now," she said and left. I sat on the edge of the bed, terrified. I didn't know grandcousin Ivy.

"Geeta, come. Your bath is waiting." I heard Mother call. I waited by the door. Someone knocked and said, "Geeta, your amma is calling," but I did not move. Maybe if I stayed in the room, Mother would come in again and I'd ask her about grandcousin Ivy. But Mother did not come in. Instead Dad tapped on the louvres. "Oi! Geeta. Amma is calling you. Are you deaf?"

I turned the door knob and stepped out. The uncles stopped talking. The aunts smiled. I suddenly felt trapped and ashamed. Why were they looking at me? What had I done?

The hallway leading to the bathroom seemed to go on forever. I kept walking, my eyes to the floor. Something gripped the middle of my stomach and I felt my legs grow weak.

When I reached the bathroom, grandcousin Ivy was waiting. I had never seen her before. I looked down at her feet and saw a covered pot. I entered the bathroom.

"Come, take off your clothes," she said. I had never undressed before another human being. Not since I was seven and knew the meaning of shame, knew that Jeevan was no longer my brother but a boy, that uncles were no longer uncles but men, and girls were girls who must hide their bodies.

I looked shyly at grandcousin and tried to catch her eye, but she fussed with the towels and pretended not to see me. I shifted from one foot to the other, all the time looking at her face.

Suddenly, she snapped, "Tcheh! Come on, come on. Hurry up. I haven't got all day." I tried to unfasten the buttons on my dress but my fingers were frozen.

"I say, what's this nonsense? Don't stand there like a statue, child. I've seen dozens of crotches before." I winced at her vulgarity. Who was this woman with a hard, proud face? Why did Mother invite her?

Grandcousin bent down and took the cover off the pot. A powerful smell of warm milk rose up and filled the air. Then she straightened up and looked at me, hands on her hips, waiting.

My hands shook as they passed over each button. Finally, the last one was undone. I stood naked against the cool tiles of the bathroom wall. Grandcousin signalled for me to come forward. I moved towards her and squatted on the floor. Mumbling a prayer in Tamil, she picked up the pot and tipped it over my head. Warm milk streamed lazily down my eyes, soaked into my hair and clung to my eyelashes.

"Okay, everything is done!" she announced. I saw the whiteness of the milk against my skin and remembered the time when we had moved into this house. Dad had boiled milk on a charcoal stove in the middle of the living room floor so that our house would be protected from evil spirits. Mother said the milk would purify the air.

I remembered that time, six years ago, and suddenly I understood everything. The milk was purifying me. It was taking away the pollution of my blood.

Grandcousin left the bathroom. I stayed to wash up, to scrub away the sickening liquid, drying quickly on my body. I soaped and scratched at the milk, hating it, hating her, hating them . . . most of all, hating my blood.

When the bath was over, I dressed in the sequinned skirt and shiny blouse. Mother led me out

in front of the relatives and made me sit next to her. The Reverend Thangaraj read a prayer and offered a blessing. A hymn was sung, the benediction received. Then, all eyes fell on me. They studied my face, my hair, the color of my skin. They looked carefully to see if I would make a suitable daughter-in-law someday. Finally, done with their scrutiny, they came over and shook my hand.

At the other end of the room, Dad stood up and invited the guests to begin eating. Soon, one by one, they swarmed over the feast Mother had laid out for them and forgot my presence. I sat in my chair and watched them. Amidst the smells of ladhus and gulab jamuns, chicken curry and spiced rice, I became invisible again.

# 16

## To Be Real

DANZY SENNA

Growing up mixed in the racial battlefield of Boston, I yearned for something just out of my reach—an "authentic" identity to make me real. Everyone but me, it seemed at the time, fit into a neat cultural box, had a label to call their own. Being the daughter of both feminist and integrationist movements, a white socialist mother and a black intellectual father, it seemed that everyone and everything had come together for my conception, only to break apart in time for my birth. I was left with only questions. To Be or Not to Be: black, Negro, African-American, feminist, femme, mulatto, quadroon, lesbian, straight, bisexual, lipstick, butch bottom, femme top, vegetarian, carnivore? These potential identities led me into the maze of American identity politics, and hopefully out the other side.

When I was eleven years old, an awkward child with knobby knees and a perpetually flat chest, I was preoccupied with questions of womanhood and what kind of woman I would become. Even then, I was aware of two kinds of power I could access as a female. There was the kind of power women got from being sexually desired, and the kind women got from being sexually invisible—that is, the power in attracting men and the power in being free of men. I also noticed that women fought one another for the first kind and came together for the second. Even as a child, I knew people craved power. I just wasn't sure which kind I wanted.

I liked the power of looking pretty, but wasn't certain men were worth attracting. I didn't like the effect they had on the women around me. Like most of my friends, I lived in a female-headed household. My mother raised us with the help of other women, a series of sidekick moms who moved in and out of our lives. In the evenings, we all converged in the kitchen, an orange-painted room on the second floor of our house. In the kitchen, laughter, food, and talk formed a safe space of women and children. On those occasions when men did enter the picture—for dinner parties or coffee—the fun of wild, unabashed laughter and fluid gossip seemed to float out the window. In walked huge, serious, booming creatures who quickly became the focus of attention. The energy of the room shifted from the finely choreographed dance of womentalk, where everyone participated in but no one dominated the conversation, to a room made up of margins and centers. The relative kindness of men didn't change the dynamic of their presence. From my perspective, it appeared that they immediately became the center of the kitchen, while the women were transformed into fluttering, doting frames around them. The women who had a moment before seemed strong, impenetrable heroines, became, in the presence of men, soft and powerless girls.

My confusion about which kind of power I wanted to have—which kind of woman I wanted to be—is reflected in a diary entry from that year. In round, flowery script I wrote vows. "Always wear lipstick. Never get married." The prospect of being able to turn heads, to be asked out on dates—to be desired—was an aspect of my impending adolescence which looked thrilling. Lipstick became the symbol of this power in my mind. At the same time, I noticed that once Lipstick Women had attracted men, often they became old and beaten, pathetic, desperate creatures, while the men remained virile and energized. At ten, I hoped there was a space in between the two extremes—a place where I could have both kinds of power—a place where I could wear lipstick and still be free.

My mother and her friends seemed to have settled for only one of these forms of power—the power of feminism—and their brazen rejection of the "lipstick world" insulted and embarrassed my burgeoning adolescent consciousness. I rememeber one dusky evening in particular, when a group of women from the local food cooperative came banging on our door. They wanted my mother's support in a march protesting violence against women. She liked these tough, working-class women and what they stood for, so while other mothers called their kids into dinner, ours dragged us into the streets. My sister, brother, and I were mortified as we ran alongside the march, giggling and pointing at the marching women chanting "Women Unite—Take Back the Night!" The throngs were letting it all hang out: their breasts hung low, their leg hair grew wild, their thighs were wide in their faded blue jeans. Some of them donned Earth shoes and T-shirts with slogans like "A Woman Needs a Man Like a Fish Needs a Bicycle." They weren't in the least bit ashamed. But I was. I remember thinking, "I will never let myself look like that."

Shortly after the march, I began to tease my mother. "Why can't you be a *real* mother?" I asked. It became a running joke between us. She'd say, "Look, a real mother!" pointing at prim women in matching clothes and frosted lipstick at the shopping mall. We'd laugh together, but there was a serious side to it all. I wanted my sixties mother to grow up, to stop protesting and acting out—to be "normal." I loved her, but at the same time craved conformity. In my mind, real mothers wore crisp floral dresses and diamond engagement rings; my mother wore blue jeans and a Russian wedding ring given to her from a high-school boyfriend. (She had lost the ring my father gave to her.) Real mothers got married in white frills before a church; my mother wed my father in a silver lamé mini-dress which she later donated to us kids for Barbie doll clothes. Real mothers painted their nails and colored their hair; my mother used henna. And while real mothers polished the house with lemon-scented Pledge, our house had dog hair stuck to everything.

My mother scolded me, saying I wanted her to be more "bourgeois." Bourgeois or not, to me, *real* equaled what I saw on television and in the movies, whether it was the sensible blond Carol Brady or the Stephen Spielberg suburban landscape—a world so utterly normal that the surreal could occur within it. At night, visions of white picket fences and mothers in housedresses danced in my head. I dreamed of station wagons, golden retrievers, and brief-case-toting fathers who came home at five o'clock to the smell of meat loaf wafting from the kitchen. But *real* was something I could never achieve with my white socialist mother, my black intellectual father who visited on Sundays, and our spotted mongrel from the dog pound, because most of all, real was a white girl—and that was something I could never, ever be.

I was fourteen when I first sat perched on a kitchen stool and allowed a friend to put an iron to my head—a curling iron, that is. She wasn't pressing my hair straight. Just the opposite. She was trying to give my straight, chestnut-brown hair some curl, and I wasn't taking no for an answer. So far, I had been mistaken for almost everything—Italian, Greek, Jewish, Pakistani—but never for black. My features and hair brought me forever short of Negritude. In a 1980s twist on the classic tragic mulatta, I was determined to pass as black. And if that wasn't possible, at least with my hair-sprayed "crunchy curls" I could pass as Puerto Rican. I remember lying in bed at night and smelling Spanish cooking from the apartment downstairs; I would close my eyes and fantasize that I was actually Puerto Rican, that everything else had been just a bad dream, that my name was Yolanda Rivera, and that I lived in the barrio.

I had dropped my quest for a "real mother" and yearned for something within my reach: a real ethnicity, something other than the half-caste purgatory to which I had been condemned. Now I yearned for Blackness, which, like femininity, was defined by the visible signifiers of the times. In my father's era, these had been a daishiki, an Afro, a fisted pik. No longer. This was still Boston in the 1980s and to be authentically black meant something quite different. Now you had to wear processed hair and Puma sneakers. I remember gazing at my best friend's straightened black hair, at the sheen of the chemicals and the way it never moved, and thinking it was the most beautiful hair I had ever seen. I believed the answer to that ubiquitous question "How can I be down?" lay in cultural artifacts: a Louis Vuitton purse, a Kangol, a stolen Ralph Lauren parka.

On my first day of high school, I went decked out in two-toned jeans, Adidas sneakers, and a red bomber with a fur-lined collar. My hair was frozen in hard curls all over my head and I wore frosty pink lipstick. I snapped my bubblegum and trailed after my sister. She is a year older than me and like most firstborn children, had inherited what I saw as the riches: kinky hair and visible blackness. We sauntered into the cafeteria where everyone hung out before class began. Doug E. Fresh beats boomed from someone's radio. Old friends greeted my sister with hugs; she introduced me and, to my relief, everyone smiled and commented on how much we looked alike. A dark-skinned boy with a shaved-bald head asked my sister where she had been hiding me, and I blushed and glanced away from his steady brown-eyed stare. There, across the cafeteria, my gaze fell on a girl, and we stared at each other with that intensity that could only mean love or hate.

She looked a little like me, but right away I knew she was more authentic than I would ever be. With an olive complexion, loose dark curls, and sad brown eyes, she sat in a cluster of pretty brown-skinned girls. She was smoking and squinting at me from across the hazy cafeteria.

I whispered to my sister: "Who's that girl?"

"That's Sophia."

Sophia whispered something just then to the girls at her table and they giggled. My cheeks began to burn.

I nudged my sister. "Why's she staring at me?"

"Cause David, her boyfriend, has been eyeing you ever since you came in here."

The bald-headed boy—David—winked at me when our eyes met and I heard my sister's voice beside me warn: "Just keep your distance and it'll be okay."

It wasn't. As the year progressed, the tension between me and Sophia escalated. It was as if we took one look at each other and said, "There ain't room in this school for both of us." From her point of view, I threatened her position not only with David, who had a fetish for light-almost-white girls, but also her position in the school. She, like me, had gotten used to her role as "the only one." Her "whiteness" had brought her status within the black world, and she didn't want that threatened by anyone, and certainly not by me with my crunchy-curls.

In a strange way I idolized Sophia, though I would have never admitted it at the time. To me, she was a role model, something to aspire to. She represented what I had spent my whole life searching for: she was the genuine article. While I lived with my white mother in a rambling brown-shingled house, Sophia lived with her black mother in an inner-city townhouse. While my curls were painstakingly acquired, Sophia's were natural. While I was soft, Sophia was hard-core. And of course, while I was the tragedy trying to walk-the-walk and talk-the-talk, Sophia didn't need to try.

David became our battleground. I told my friends and family that I was in love with him and that I despised Sophia. The truth is that Sophia was the real object of my desire. I wanted to be her. But it was just dawning on me that certain things could not be manufactured. By curling my hair, wearing heavy gold hoop earrings, and a bomber jacket, I could not recreate her experience. My imitation of her life could only go skin deep. So my desire for her was transformed into an obsessive envy. If I couldn't be her, I would beat her.

One day I discovered obscenities about me splattered on the girls' room wall—just the regular catty slander, nothing too creative, saying I was a bitch and a ho. But there was a particular violence to the way it had been written, in thick red marker around the bathroom mirrors. In tears, I went to find my big sister. Always my protector, she dragged me to the girls' room after lunch period to set things straight with Sophia once and for all. We found her in there with her girls, skipping class and preening in front of a mirror.

Sister: "Did you write this about my sister?"

Sophia: "She been trying to get with my man all year. That bitch had it comin' to her."

Sister: "I asked you a question. Did you write this about my sister?"

Sophia: "Yeah, I did. And what are you gonna do about it?"

Soon, in the bright spring sunshine, my sister and Sophia came to blows while I stood on the sidelines with the rest of the black population of our school. I had been warned by Sophia's rather hefty cousin that if I jumped in the fight, she would whip my ass. I didn't jump in. And after all was said and done, my sister ended up with a broken nose, Sophia with two black eyes and a scratched up face. The war was over and I got out without a scar. My sister had protected me, and I knew I was a coward, a fake. And as I sat holding my sister's hand in the hospital waiting room, I knew it wasn't blackness I had failed in. It was sisterhood.

## 🦎 17

## *Blazes of Truth*

SUSAN SCHNUR

When I was 12 years old, my parents sent me off to Camp Ramah in the Poconos. That June, I was a dull kid in an undershirt from Trenton, New Jersey, outfitted in lime-green, mix-and-match irregulars from E. J. Korvette's. By the end of August, though—exposed as I was, for two months, to suburban Philadelphia's finest pre-adolescent fashion cognoscenti—I had contracted that dread disease: "*JAP*itis."

Symptoms included not only the perfection of an elaborate, all-day triple-sink procedure for dyeing white-wool bobby socks to the requisite shade of dirty white (we called it oyster), but also my sudden, ignominious realization that the discount "Beatlemania" record my mother had bought for me the previous spring was not, after all, sung by the real group.

I'm not even sure that the term *JAP* existed yet back then (I don't think it did), but, in any case, by October I was—more or less—cured. I put the general themes of entitlement, of materialism, of canonized motifs (in those days, Lord and Taylor was the label of choice rather than Bloomingdale's) at the back of my mental medicine chest for the next two decades.

It wasn't until six months ago, actually—while teaching a course at Colgate University called "Contemporary Issues of Jewish Existence"—that I again gave the subject of *JAP*s a moment's pause.

A unit on *JAP*s was decidedly *not* on my course syllabus (I taught the standards: Holocaust—Faith—Immigration—Assimilation—Varieties of Religious Experience—Humor—Israel—Women). But my students, as it turned out, were obsessed with *JAP*s.

Week after week, in personal journals that they were keeping for me, they talked *JAP*s: the stereotypes, dating them, hating them, not *being* them, *JAP* graffiti, *JAP* competitiveness, *JAP*s who gave them the willies back home in Scarsdale over spring break.

I had been raised on moron jokes; *they* had been raised on *JAP* jokes. ("What does a *JAP* do with her asshole in the morning? Dresses him up and sends him to work.")

Little by little, I came to realize that the *JAP* theme was by no means a one-note samba. It was kaleidoscopic and self-revealing; the students plugged it into a whole range of Jewish issues. I began to encourage them to look at their throwaway *JAP* comments with a measure of scrutiny.

The first, and most striking, ostinato in the students' journals was the dissociative one. As one Jewish student framed it, "There are so many *JAP*s in this class, it makes me sick." (An astonishing number of students were desperate to let me know this.)

Since over one-third of the class was not Jewish (the enrollment was 30), and since there was no one in the class that I would have identified sartorially as a *JAP*, this was an interesting fillip.

"That's funny," I started commenting back in these students' journals. "The other students think *you're* a *JAP*."

Eventually, one Jewish student wrote, "Maybe when I talk about *JAP*s and that whole negative thing, it's a way for me to get 'permission' to assimilate."

Another wondered why he feels "like every *JAP* on campus somehow implicates me. That's a very

'minority culture' reflex, isn't it? Why am I so hung up on how everyone else perceives Jews?"

Some students perceived the *JAP* phenomenon, interestingly, as a developmental phase in American Judaism—a phase in which one parades both one's success and one's entitlement. "When my best girlfriend from childhood was bat mitzvahed," wrote one student after reading *A Bintel Brief* and *World of Our Fathers*, "her grandmother gave her a '*JAP*-in-training' diamond-chip necklace. It's like the grandmother was saying, 'When I was your age, I had to sew plackets in a Lower East Side sweatshop. So you girls be *JAP*s. Take whatever you can and be proud of it.'"

A Black student mentioned—during a talk about the socialization of Jewish women—that Jewish women, like their Black counterparts, are encouraged to be extremely competent, but then are double-bound with the message that their competence must *only* be used for frivolous purposes. (Like Goldie Hawn, in *Private Benjamin*, scolding her upholsterer with impressive assertiveness: "I specifically said—the ottoman in mushroom!", or informing her superior officer that she refused to go to Guam because "my hair will frizz.") "Minority women are warned not to be a real threat to anyone," the student explained, "That's how *JAP*s evolve."

Another theme of the students touched on their perception that Jews are sometimes discriminated against not because they are *less* endowed than others, but because they are more endowed (smarter, richer, more "connected"). *JAP*s, then, become, in the words of an Irish Catholic student who was doing readings on theology and the theme of chosenness, "the 'chosen of the chosen.' Unlike Irish Catholics who have been discriminated against because we seem 'un-chosen'," she mused, "people hate *JAP*s because they seem to have everything: money, confidence, style."

Of course, it's probably unnecessary for me to point out that the most prolific *JAP* references had to do with that venerable old feud—the Jewish War-Between-The-Sexes.

One pre-law Jewish male in the class (who was under a lot of pressure and had developed colitis during that semester) stated point-blank that he did not date Jewish women. I was shocked by the number of 20-year-old, seemingly fully-assimilated Jewish males who were right up there with Alexander Portnoy on this subject.

Several students responded to his comment in their journals. "He's angry at *JAP*s," one woman wrote, "because they get to be needy and dependent, whereas the expectations on him are really high."

Another student related the experience of two friends of hers at SUNY Binghamton: "Someone spray-painted the word *JAP* on their dormitory door," she recounted. "But now I wonder—which one of the girls was being called a *JAP*? The one with the dozen Benetton sweaters, or the one who'd gotten 750 on her L-SATs?" The question being, of course, which is ultimately more threatening: the demanding woman or the self-sufficient one?

An Hispanic woman in the class talked about what she called "the dialectic of prejudice"—that is, the contradictory nature of racist or sexist slurs as being, in itself, a diagnostic of irrational bias. "A *JAP* is portrayed as both frigid and nymphomaniacal," she wrote. "She's put down both because of her haughty strut that says, 'I'm independent,' and because of her *kvetching* that says, 'I'm dependent.'"

A twist on this theme was provided by a Jewish woman who commented, "Whatever Jewish men call us—cold, hot, leech, bitch—it's all the same thing: They're afraid they can't live up to our standards."

# JAP: The New Antisemitic Code Word

FRANCINE KLAGSBRUN

Isn't it odd that the term *JAP*, referring to a spoiled, self-indulgent woman, should be so widely used at a time when women are working outside their homes in unprecedented numbers, struggling to balance their home lives and their work lives to give as much of themselves as they can to everybody—their husbands, their kids, their bosses?

Jewish women, like women throughout society, are trying to find their own paths, their own voices. And, along with other changes that have taken place, they have been finding themselves Jewishly. And yet we hear the term *JAP* being used, perhaps almost more now than ever before. Why?

The new-found, or rather newly-accepted, drive of women for achievement in many arenas threatens many men. What better put-down of the strong woman than to label her a "Princess"? She is not being attacked as a competitor—that would be too close to home. No—she's called a princess, and that label diminishes her, negating her ambition and her success.

One may note, and rightly so, that there *are* materialistic Jewish women—and men too. But are Jews the only people guilty of excesses in spending? Why should the word "Jewish" be used pejoratively to describe behavior we don't approve of?

I think the answer is that there is an underlying antisemitic message in that label. Loudness is somehow "Jewish." Vulgarity is somehow "Jewish." All the old stereotypes of Jews come into play in the use of the term *JAP*. In this day, polite Christian society would not *openly* make anti-Jewish slurs. But *JAP* is O.K. *JAP* is a kind of code word. It's a way of symbolically winking, poking with an elbow, and saying, "well you know how Jews are—so materialistic and pushy."

What is interesting is that this code word can be used in connection with *women*—the Jewish American *Princess*—and nobody protests its intrinsic antisemitism.          [1980]

A psych major in the class took a different tack. "It's not that the Jewish male really believes Jewish women are terrible, rather that he simply wants majority culture males to believe it. It's like when territorial animals urinate on a tree," she explained. "It's a minority male's possessive instinct. Like a sign that says, 'Robert Redfords—stay away!'"

Finally, several Jewish students framed their relations with one another in the context of Jewish family systems. "Lashing out at Jewish women—calling them all *JAP*s or refusing to marry them—is a way to get back at the entire high-expectation, high-pressure Jewish family," stated one student in response to a film I showed in class called "Parenting and Ethnicity." "You can lash out by becoming an academic failure," he went on, "or you can become a doctor—which is less self-destructive—and then simply refuse to marry a Jewish woman."

Towards the end of the term, a feminist friend pointed out to me something I had not considered: that the characterizations of *JAP*s and Yuppies are often identical—the difference being, of course, that a Yuppie designation is still generally taken as neutral or even positive, whereas there is hardly one of us left—I don't think—who would compete for the label of *JAP*.

All in all, I trust that the larger lessons in all of these *JAP* ruminations have not been lost on my students. For example: Why has it become socially sanctioned to use a *Jewish* designation (*JAP*) for a description that fits as many Christians as Jews? Or why—along the same lines—is it okay to use a *female* designation (again, *JAP*) for a description that fits as many men as women? Or, sensing what we now sense, shouldn't we refuse any truck altogether with the term *JAP*? [1987]

## 🌿 18

# *In Search of Liberation*

DEBRA KENT

When I joined a women's consciousness-raising group a few years ago, I'm not quite sure what I expected—to discover some bond of understanding with other women, perhaps, to feel myself part of the growing sisterhood of the liberation movement. But through session after session, I listened in amazement and awe as the others delivered outraged accounts of their exploitation at the hands of bosses, boyfriends, and passersby. They were tired of being regarded as sex objects by male chauvinist pigs. All their lives, they lamented, they had been programmed for the confining roles of wife and mother, roles in which their own needs were submerged by those of the men they served.

I had to admit that their indignation was justified. But it was impossible for me to confess my own reaction to their tales of horror, which was a very real sense of envy. Society had provided a place for them as women, however restricting that place might be, and they knew it.

Totally blind since birth, I was seldom encouraged to say, "When I grow up I'll get married and have babies." Instead, my intellectual growth was nurtured. I very definitely received the unspoken message that I would need the independence of a profession, as I could not count on having the support of a husband.

For myself and for other disabled women, sex discrimination is a secondary issue—in life and in the job market. To the prospective employer, a visible handicap may immediately connote incompetence, and whether the applicant is male or female may never come under consideration at all. In fact, the connotations that disability holds for the public seem, in many ways, to negate sexuality altogether. In a culture where men are expected to demonstrate strength and dominance, the disabled man is regarded as weak and ineffectual. But in social situations he may have an advantage over the disabled woman.

Our culture allows the man to be the aggressor. If he can bolster himself against the fear of rejection, he can make overtures toward starting a relationship. At least he doesn't have to sit home waiting for the telephone to ring.

According to the stereotype, women are helpless creatures to be cuddled and protected. The disabled woman, however, is often merely seen as helpless. A man may fear that she will be so oppressively dependent upon him that a relationship with her may strike him as a terrifying prospect. To prove him wrong she may strive for self-sufficiency, only to have him say that she's too aggressive and unfeminine.

People may pity the disabled woman for her handicap, or admire her for her strength in overcoming it, but she is too unlike other females to be whistled at on the street. Somehow she is perceived as a nonsexual being. If men don't make passes at girls who wear glasses, what chance does a blind girl have, or one in a wheelchair, or a woman with spastic hands?

American culture still pictures the ideal woman: slender, blonde, blue-eyed, and physically perfect. Of course, there is plenty of leeway, and not every man is worried about these cultural stereotypes when choosing a mate. But as long as a woman remains a status symbol to the man who "possesses" her, the living proof of his prowess, the woman with a disability will be at a severe disadvantage. The man who is not completely secure will be afraid to show her off with pride because she is too different.

The worst period for most disabled men and women is probably adolescence, when conformity to the group's norms is all-important. Then, even overweight or a bad case of acne is enough to brand one as a pariah. Things may become easier later on, as emphasis on outward appearances gradually yields to concern with qualities as well. But it is hard to shake off the sense of being an outcast.

Even when she establishes a healthy relationship with a man, the disabled woman may sometimes find herself wondering, "Why does he want me unless there is something wrong with him? If someone else comes along, won't he leave me for her?"

But why, I ask myself, should it ever make a difference to society whether people with disabilities are ever accepted intact—as human beings with minds, feelings, and sexuality? Though we have become more vocal in recent years, we still constitute a very small minority.

Yet the Beautiful People—the slender, fair, and perfect ones—form a minority that may be even smaller. Between these two groups are the average, ordinary citizens: Men who are too short, women who are too tall, people who are too fat or too thin, people with big noses, protruding ears, receding hairlines, and bad complexions. Millions of people go through life feeling self-conscious or downright inadequate, fearing that others will reject them for these physical flaws. Perhaps the struggle of disabled people is really everyone's battle against the binding rules of conformity, the struggle for the right to be an individual.

As I sat in that consciousness-raising group, I realized that disabled women have a long and arduous fight ahead. Somehow we must learn to perceive ourselves as attractive and desirable. Our struggle is not unlike the striving for self-acceptance of the millions of nonhandicapped who also fall short of the Beautiful People image.

Our liberation will be a victory for everyone.

[1987]

# 🌿 19

# *Brideland*

NAOMI WOLF

Brideland exists primarily in the bridal magazines, which conjure up a fantastic, anachronistic world that really exists nowhere beyond itself. It is a nineteenth-century world, in which major late-twentieth-century events, like the sexual revolution and the rise of the financially self-supporting woman, seem to have transpired only glancingly, to be swept away by a dimity flounce like so much unsightly grit. It is a theme park of upward mobility; in Brideland, in the events surrounding The Event, everyone is temporarily upper middle class: everyone routinely throws catered events and hires musicians and sends engraved invitations and keeps carriages or vintage cars awaiting. At the ceremony itself, things become downright feudal: the bride is treated like a very queen with her court of "maids." She has, perhaps, a child to lift her train, a child to bear her ring, and a sparkling tiara upon her hair. Cinderella is revealed in her true aristocratic radiance at last, and, in the magazines, she is perpetually arriving at the ball.

Brideland has very little to do with the relationship or even the marriage: it is, like any theme park, eternally transient: you enter, you are transformed completely, and then, presumably, you depart. It is a world of lush feminine fantasy, eerily devoid of men, who appear, if at all, as shadow figures retrieving luggage or kneeling before the bride in a state of speechless awe. Brideland has an awful lot to say about what women want that they are not getting, and it taught me a thing or two about myself.

My own initiation was abrupt. Shortly after we made our announcement, I picked up one of those magazines, mostly to find out what the rules were that I was bound to be breaking. As I turned page after page, I started to change. Long-buried yearnings surfaced, a reminder, which little else gives me, that until I was six, I inhabited a world unchanged by the 1970s' women's movement. Somehow, I had picked up atavistic feelings about The Bride that I would never have recognized in my conscious, feminist, and more skeptical mind.

By page 16 my capacity for irony was totally paralyzed. I tried hard to activate it but, as in a dream, I was powerless; it wouldn't budge. By page 32 I was hypnotized; by the time I reached the end, the honeymoon section—for the magazines are structured chronologically, as if they want to be sure you know what comes first—I had acquired new needs; blind, overwhelming, undeniable needs. The fantasies I had put away in 1966 with Bridal Barbie resurfaced with a vengeance. I needed . . . garters! And engraved stationery—engraved, not printed! And fetching little lace mitts; and a bouquet that trailed sprays of stephanotis! And heavens, maybe a veil or mantilla of some kind—down my back, of course, not over my face—would not be as unthinkable as I had thought.

You must understand: this is coming from a woman who had viewed all traditional wedding appurtenances as if they represented death by cuteness. While I am the product of an egalitarian marriage, and fervently believe in the possible goodness of life partnership, I have had such a strong resistance to all things matrimonial that when I pass Tiffany's I break out in a cold sweat. I could imagine eloping; or a civil ceremony; or even an alternative ceremony, so creatively subversive that it would be virtually unrecognizable for what it is. But not—never—a wedding.

Part of my aversion comes from my ambivalence, not about the man—about whom I have no doubts—but about the institution. How can I justify sealing such a private, precious relationship with a legal bond that lets a man rape his wife in fourteen states? How can I endorse an institution that, in the not-too-distant past, essentially conveyed the woman over to her husband as property, denying her even the right to her own property? How can I support a system that allows me to flaunt my heterosexual relationship brazenly, but forbids deeply committed gay and lesbian friends of mine to declare their bonds in the same way? How can I ask my love to be sanctioned by a legal order that leaves divorcing women to struggle in a desperately unevenly matched battle in sexist courts for money and custody of children? And, less profoundly, but no less urgently, if I were to do it, what on earth would I wear?

Brideland lulls the reader into a haze of romantic acquisitiveness that leaves most such political considerations firmly outside the threshold. The magazines' articles about the origins of different rituals leave no doubt as to the naked patriarchalism of the ceremony's origins. Bridesmaids were originally dressed similarly to the bride so as to confuse marauders who would wish to abduct the woman. Groomsmen were warriors whose role was to help the bridegroom fight off the would-be kidnapers. The cedar chest and mother-of-the-bride embroidered handkerchiefs—even the beading and faux-pearling and glitter down the bodices of many dresses—are all vestigial reminders that brides and their trousseaus were essentially chattel to be bartered, bearing a specific value. Even the word *honeymoon* derives from the Old English custom of sending the couple off for a month to drink honeyed ale, as a way to relax sexual inhibitions and, presumably, ease the anxieties of virginal teenage brides who most likely had had little contact with their mates, and whose attraction to them was generally considered an irrelevance. But in the glossy pages, these fairly unnerving details fade into quaintness.

The centerpiece of Brideland is, of course, the dress, and it is this that has elicited my deepest buried fantasies. For a reason that for a long time was mysterious, I felt that I had to, but absolutely had to, create a wedding dress that had an eighteenth-century bodice, three-quarter-length sleeves, and an ankle-length skirt with voluminous panniers. I have since homed in on the trace-memory, and realize that the transcendentally important look of my dress on the critical day was predetermined by a drawing of a milkmaid in the A. A. Milne (creator of Pooh) children's book, *Now We Are Six*.          [1995]

 20

# On Being a "Good Girl": Implications for Latinas in the United States

ELISA DÁVILA

I am an immigrant Latina. My gender, my ethnicity, and my status as an "émigré," shape and define my life and the work I do. I was born in Colombia, a beautiful but violent country. The early years of my life were marked by the horrors of civil war.[1] I grew up witnessing not only the desolation left by civil war but also experiencing the inner devastation forced upon women by the socially constructed demands of *good-girlism*.[2] As a woman, I have had a major struggle to overcome the senseless impositions of a patriarchal and sexist society, which has established different standards of behavior for men and women. This is particularly relevant for Latina women living in a *machista* society and having to conform to the dictates of *marianismo*.

The origins and ideology of *marianismo* and how it affects women was first discussed by Evelyn Stevens in 1973. In the essay "Marianismo: The Other Face of Machismo in Latin America," she writes:

Latin American mestizo cultures—from the Rio Grande to the Tierra del Fuego—exhibit a well-

defined pattern of beliefs and behavior centered on popular acceptance of a stereotype of the ideal woman. This stereotype, like its *macho* counterpart, is ubiquitous in every social class. There is near universal agreement on what a "real woman" is like and how she should act. Among the characteristics of this ideal are semidivinity, moral superiority, and spiritual strength. This spiritual strength engenders abnegation, that is, an infinite capacity for humility and sacrifice. No self-denial is too great for the Latin American woman, no limit can be divined to her vast store of patience with the men of her world. Although she may be sharp with her daughters—and even cruel to her daughter-in-law—she is and must be complaisant toward her own mother and her mother-in-law for they, too, are reincarnations of the great mother. She is also submissive to the demands of the men: husbands, sons, fathers, brothers.[3]

Stevens's definitions of *machismo* and *marianismo* have been criticized and, at times, dismissed by some Latin American feminists who consider them as an exaggerated portrayal of gender relations in Latin America.[4] But the basic premises of *marianismo* have been accepted by therapists, counselors, and other health practitioners working with Hispanic/Latina women in the United States. In a recent book, Rosa María Gil and Carmen Inoa Vazquez explain:

But there is another side to the coin of *machismo*, which is equally rigidly enforced and deeply woven into the fabric of Latino/a life. It is called *marianismo*; it is the mortar holding antiquated cultural structures firmly in place, and it forms the core of the Maria Paradox. While discussed in academic literature—first in a ground-breaking essay by Evelyn P. Stevens in 1973, and subsequently by such eminent academicians as Sally E. Romero, Julia M. Ramos McKay, Lillian Comas-Diaz, and Luis Romero—as far as we know, it has never before presented to the general reader.[5]

As a young woman, I realized that I did not like being what was considered a *good girl* in my culture. I was aware of the different treatment given to the males in the family (brothers, cousins, friends). While men were allowed the freedom to go alone into town, to stay up late, to party all night long, and particularly to wait around to be served by the women around them, my sisters and I were held to different standards. The *Manual de urbanidad y buenas maneras (The Manual of Urbanity and Good Manners)* by Manuel Antonio Carreño[6] was constantly enforced on my sisters and me.

Carreño's book was (still is) the catechism of the do's and dont's for children, but particularly for young women. It covered everything including how to be a good Catholic and a good patriot; how to pray, how to dress, to socialize, to sit at the table and how to eat; how to respond to adults, how to look or not to look at people, particularly at boys; and so on. The topics discussed had to do with the conduct and behavior women should exhibit in order to gain social acceptance. Many of the prescriptions would help females keep appearances, thereby reinforcing the oppressive notions of Catholic morality, race, and class. Compulsory heterosexuality was emphasized, but sexual education was taboo, except for the absolute commandment of no premarital sex and virginity for unmarried women. If one learned to behave according to these rules, one would be praised as a good and adorable girl who would be able to get married and have a family.

Being a *good girl* meant denying big chunks of myself such as the freedom to choose a career over a husband, to work and live away from home, or the basic right to know my feelings and to experience my own body. In a patriarchal society like Colombia's, a woman is expected to conform to a set of rules that dictate the manner by which she can act, dress, talk, have sex, even think. A woman is supposed to accept domesticity and motherhood as the two guiding forces of her life.

> Home. Family. Honor. These are the guiding principles of female-male relations that have remained constant from 1492 to the present. The typical Latin American family is portrayed as patriarchal in structure with an authoritarian male head, bilateral kinship, and a submissive mother and wife concerned with the domestic sphere.[7]

To survive under *goodgirlism*, a woman undergoes a major displacement or disconnection inside her own self. Caught between the expectations of family and community and her individual needs and desires, a Latina is at war with herself. The rewards given to her by society for conforming—protection, security, relationships, alliances, and all the other status-related goods and benefits of a good woman—do not serve to end the war. For in the long process of adjustment to the imperatives of *machismo and marianismo*, a woman suffers from emotional alienation from her own feelings, physical and aesthetic estrangement from her body, social isolation, betrayal of her own gender, and silencing of her own voice.

As an adolescent, I also realized that in order to be other than the ideal subservient, suffering, and chaste woman, destined for motherhood and domesticity, I had to be different from the women in my family, from the women in the large household where I grew up, and from the women around me at school, at church, in the neighborhood. It was a painful realization, for I had to reconcile the expectations of my family and community that were at odds with my own inner imperatives.

It is in the process of reconciling these contradictory messages that a Latina may find the roots of her inner strength and the driving impetus for change. I did not come to these realizations alone or in a vacuum, nor did I arrive at the place where I am now without the example and encouragement of other women, many of them ignored by the recorders of history. Since the early days of European colonization, women's presence in the larger social structure and their universe have been ignored. Historians have traditionally excluded such experience from their writings, except for some notable examples (mostly notorious ones), such as queens, courtesans, mistresses, and nuns. The norm has been to ignore women (women as absence) or to portray them as obstacle, as the other, as atavism, or as foible.

In my own life, I have been inspired by teachers, union organizers, women fighting for human rights in Argentina, Chile, Guatemala, El Salvador, and immigrant women working in sweat shops and maquiladoras in New York City and the Mexican-American border to understand their strength and to emulate their courage to change. These women have some character traits in common: they all have aspired to be *other than* the externally imposed cultural model of the *good woman,* and they do it with unabashed dignity and great courage.

To become *other than*, which means, unlike many of the women in my household, or in my neighborhood, or in my school, I had to cross many borders: educational, sexual, national, linguistic, cultural. With each crossing, I was breaking familiar, many times, psychological bonds that tethered me to the extended family structure and the community.

As I wandered into new inner and outer spaces and geographies, I entered new worlds where there were no female roles to emulate. In the pursuit of my own individuality and my own voice, I went abroad to college, and later I went to teach away from home. In doing so my life became a difficult experiment in overcoming loneliness and fear. Not having received as a child and as a young woman the skills to be anything else but a *good girl*, I did not know how to survive away from *marianismo* and from a class system that determined my place in the social organization. It seemed that my identity was directly linked to being a "señora [casada] de," a married woman, which in Spanish literally means *the woman of* so-and-so.[8] The future depended not so much on my intelligence but on having a home of my own, with a husband, children, and all the other status-related goods, relationships, alliances, and cultural identifiers of an upper-middle-class woman.[9]

After crossing national and linguistic borders and immigrating to the United States, I began living away from the expectations and demands of the family core and the extended family of friends and acquaintances. I entered the realm of being the *alien/other*. A major displacement took place. In a *machista* society, like Colombia where I was born and raised, a woman is the *other* in terms of intergender and class relations. As the *other* she is the object of sexual and sexist oppression and dominance on the part of the males of the society, condoned, of course, by the *marianista* female culture. But, as a Latina immigrant in the United States, one becomes the *other* in terms of ethnic and linguistic categorizations. Also, within the prejudicial male chauvinism of Anglo culture, a Latina becomes either a desirable *other*, objectivized and used as a sensuous and passionate being, or an undesirable "illegal" with no rights.[10]

Married to an Anglo man who brought into my life a new set of expectations and ideas of the concept of a "good American wife" and striving to acculturate and function in the new environment, I began to feel at the margins of society, and on the edge of disintegration. With my hyphenated name that caused a severe rift with my mother-in-law, I became no more than a hyphen to the new family.[11] This *otherness* made me long for what I had left behind. In this new environment, lacking recognition from the family I had married into and not quite understanding its cultural norms and social transactions, I began to idealize my past and my background (family, traditions, friends, etc.). I needed my "cultural security blanket." In *The Maria Paradox*, Rosa María Gil and Carmen Inoa Vazquez explain this syndrome:

> In our new life in the United States, there is so much that is unfamiliar and frightening, even to the best-adjusted among us. When we are adusting to the new culture, or acculturating, some Latinas might feel extremely vulnerable and especially terrified of losing the affection and esteem of loved ones, whose presence helps to anchor our sense of self. Too often, out of that fear, they regress rather than move on.[12]

Patriarchy offers some rewards to the women who conform. Among others, there is social recognition, stability, financial security, and "machista gallantry." There is some attraction to the discourse of family unity and support, motherhood and domestic security. Being a *good girl* seemed attractive to the lonely, newly married woman walking the empty streets of a suburban American neighborhood. Homesickness and silence fueled the desire to return, to give up, to find refuge under the normative system of male oppression and Catholic patriarchy I had left. After all, cultural and familiar oppression and gallant machismo seemed better than the cultural exile I was experiencing in the new country.

To survive, I plunged into working and learning English, as well as the language of acculturation. Alongside my new skills came a divorce, different jobs, other lovers, and a new identity. One family rejected me, the other wanted me to go back to Colombia and be protected by the extended family. I refused to go back with the excuse of finishing my

Ph.D., which I could not have done in Colombia. But guilt and solitude made me doubt my decision to stay in the United States. Was I becoming a *bad girl*? The dualistic and manichean worldview that Western culture imposes on us did not give me anything but a set of oppositions to characterize my new reality: good/bad, male/female, decent/prostitute, mother/spinster. New labels and new categories were superimposed on the old ones: divorced, immigrant, Hispanic, alien, "mojada" (wet back). They did not replace the identity of the young woman who came; they just covered the rupture of separation, of not belonging to either one of the two cultures. As time passed, I abandoned the idea of going back home, and the security of a tenured academic job sealed the impossibility of return.

In the eyes of the society where I grew up, I am successful and, perhaps, secretly admired. But I am also the object of pity and compassion for being a failure as a woman, for not having procreated, and particularly for not having a male at my side. When I travel home or to other Latin American countries, invariably men and women ask me not about my work, or the articles and poems I write, but about husband and children. My responses usually elicit some pitiful comments by women that go more or less like the following:

- "Y no te sientes solita, mi hijita?" (And, don't you feel very alone, my child?)
- "Y dónde está tu familia?" (And where is your family?)
- "Pero, de verdad, no piensas volver donde tu familia?" (But, tell me the truth, don't you want to go back to your family?)
- "Si, mi hija, está bien estudiar, pero también hay que hacer la casa." (Yes, my dearest, it is good to study, but it is also important to make a home.)
- "Y, eso del Ph.D., te va a cuidar cuando estés viejita?" (And that thing called the Ph.D., is it going to take care of you when you are old?)

Men's responses can be very aggressive because they interpret my divorced status either as an invitation to sexual advances or they feel some unstated discomfort about my sexuality that does not include them.

No matter how far I have traveled, the powerful ideological force of sexism that determines the behavior of men and women, and the ways in which girls are raised, or the manner in which women are expected to act, dress, talk, have sex, continues to haunt me. The basic and culturally constructed definers of the female condition are still the parameters by which I am judged and accepted.          [1998]

### NOTES

1. Colombia's history, like that of so many Latin American countries, can be described as a relentless unsuccessful attempt to define and practice democracy. For almost two decades, beginning in the mid-1940s, the traditional conservative forces, supported by the Catholic church and the military, unleashed a bloody period of civil strife in Colombia. Liberal forces made up primarily of intellectuals, union workers, students, poor farm laborers, and the disenfranchised masses of urban centers fought against the military and the police. As in the case of the Mexican Revolution of 1910, the Bolivian and Guatemalan Revolutions of the 1950s, and many other revolutionary movements in Latin America, a popular uprising with political overtones and civil rights goals resulted in indiscriminate killing and devastation. A military coup and dictatorship ended the civil war, but not the abuse of the poor by the rich or the poverty and illiteracy ofthe masses. The dream of equality and freedom was crushed.

2. In 1995, for about eight months, a group of college professors at SUNY–New Paltz (Drs. Sue Books, Ann V. Dean, and Elaine Kolitch), a pastoral counselor (Rev. Kathy Brady), and I worked on trying to understand what it meant to be a *good girl* in different cultures. We presented a panel discussion on this topic at the April 1996 American Educational Research Association (AERA) Conference in New York, "A Cross-Cultural Autobiographical Excavation of *Good-Girlism*." The following was the group's definition of *good-girlism*.

   > *Good-girlism*
   > . . . is a powerful ideology, often invisible to us in our everyday practices and relations, that can be used to monitor female identity in private and public spheres.
   > . . . is a historical, cross-cultural phenomenon, constantly reified by institutions (family, school, church, state, etc.) that benefit from having oppressed members.
   > . . . thrives in discursive practices that mediate moral selfhood.
   > . . . is bred and nurtured in the moral/emotional tyranny that threatens to render us illegitimate should we opt out of the unspoken agreement: protect me and I will legitimate/love/protect you."

3. Evelyn P. Stevens. "Marianismo: The Other Face of Machismo in Latin America," in Ann Pescatello (ed.), *Female and Male in Latin America* (Pittsburgh, PA: University of Pittsburgh Press, 1973), pp. 94–95.

4. See, for example, Josefina Zoraida Vásquez, "Women's Liberation in Latin America: Toward a History of the Present," in Gertrude M. Yeager (ed.), *Confronting*

*Change, Challenging Tradition. Women in Latin American History* (Wilmington, DE: Scholarly Resources Books, 1994), pp. 18–25.

5. Rosa Maria Gil and Carmen Inoa Vazquez, *The Maria Paradox* (New York: Putnam's, 1996), p. 6.

6. Manual Antonio Carreño, *Compendio manual de urbanidad y buenas maneras,* Unica edición completa (Colombia, 1994). *Urbanidad* is a Spanish noun that means how to behave in an urban manner, exhibiting the characteristics of a person living in a city. Carreño, like many other Spanish and Latin American male educators, believes that education consists of a set of norms and rules of behavior that will teach children how to act in a decent, patriotic, and moral manner inspired by European tradition. The oppositions—civilization versus barbarism, urban versus rural, Christian versus non-Christian—emphasized a hierarchical order based on gender and class differences. The education of girls, and of members of the "weaker sex" in Latin America, was traditionally influenced by the dictates of the Catholic church and the state. See Zoraida Vásquez's, op. cit., pp. 18–25. Carreño's book has influenced generations of Latin American men and women all over the continent.

7. Yeager, "Introduction," op. cit. p. xi.

8. "In Spanish the verb "to marry," *casarse,* literally means "to put oneself into a house." A married woman is referred as *casada* (housed in) not only because of a perceived biological tie to children or because she may not be physically or mentally suited for other labor but also because, under the patriarchal system, family honor resides with her." Yeager, op. cit., p. xi.

9. Hispanic culture limits us "by defining us first and foremost as mothers [and wives], and because it refuses to accept families headed by lesbian or gay couples." Ana Maria Isasi-Díaz, *En la lucha. In the Struggle: Elaborating a mujerista Theology* (Minneapolis: Fortress Press, 1993), p. 20.

10. I recommend the film *Carmen Miranda: Bananas Is My Business* by Helena Solberg (New York: Noon Pictures, 1994) to understand some of the issues of exploitation, discrimination, and stereotyping of Latin American women in the United States.

11. My former mother-in-law could never understand why I did not want to be just Mrs. Smith and preferred to be called Mrs. Dávila-Smith.

12. Gil and Inoa Vazquez, op. cit., p. 24.

# Learning Sexism

We learn about sexism in a variety of overt and subtle ways. Images of women are communicated through the language we use—media depictions of women, direct messages from family, friends and teachers, and many other sources. In this section, we begin exploring this process through three women's descriptions of how family expectations, peer norms, and cultural traditions affected them and their ideas of what it meant to be a girl. Murielle Minard's poem, "The Gift," describes a doll given to a girl on her seventh birthday. Beautiful and perfect, the fragile doll symbolizes the essence of femininity. The doll is to be admired for her beauty, never played with lest she be damaged. In "Allegra Maud Goldman" by Edith Konecky, a young girl becomes aware of her family's expectations that she be graceful in dance class and nurturing and protective of her older brother. Allegra astutely realizes that her brother enjoys privileges that she does not. In Helena María Viramontes's "Growing," Naomi, an adolescent Chicana, reflects on the ways girls are treated in her neighborhood. During a rousing game of stickball, she breaks away from the stultifying expectations of "being a girl" and, in doing so, realizes just how limiting being a woman will be for her and Lucia, her younger sister. Each of these girls, who are ethnically different, experiences similar messages about girls' value and worth in our society.

School experiences are another powerful socializing force. In a variety of ways, female students learn more than academic material in the classroom. Here, they also learn about the norms for appropriate behavior in our culture and begin to consider how well they will measure up to those standards. Myra Sadker, David Sadker, and colleagues describe a series of classroom practices and dynamics prevalent in today's schools that perpetuate a bias against girls' educational achievement.

Accepted patterns of interpersonal and nonverbal communication reinforce traditional power relationships between men and women. The ways in which women and men address one another, disclose personal information, and even look at each other during conversations communicate messages about differences in status and power. Nancy Henley and Jo Freeman's piece, written in 1979, was instrumental in calling attention to subtle but powerful patterns of sexism in male-female communication.

One of the most influential purveyors of social norms is the media. From television to print and electronic media, norms projected through these avenues shape our views of what it means to be female. Anastasia Higginbotham addresses the impact of fashion and beauty magazines on teenage girls. Through both advertising and editorial materials, these magazines encourage their readers to pursue strategies for "getting a guy, and dropping 20 pounds." Similarly, much attention has been directed at the negative portrayal of women in music. The lyrics of many contemporary songs depict women in demeaning ways, often reducing us to sex objects and caricatures of passivity and dependency. Venise Berry and Naomi Weisstein approach this issue from two vantage points. Berry traces the shift from degrading images of women in rap music dominated by male singers, to the current efforts of African-American women rap artists who challenge these images by rapping about women taking control in their lives. Recalling an earlier time when she was a member of a women's band that "challenged all the demeaning imperatives for women in music," Weisstein celebrates the emerging voices of women whom she dubs "mutineers." These women depart from the tradition of singing "endless litanies of Suffering Abject Devotion to men." Instead, they represent a new breed of women who are angry about women's position in society. Berry and Weisstein show us that despite the pervasive sexist images of women in our culture, young women are finding new and exciting avenues for creatively expressing themselves in a positive and empowering way.

This part closes with a fictional exploration of what might happen if society abandoned all traditional sex-role stereotypes and expectations of girls and boys. In "X, A Fabulous Child's Story," Lois Gould tells the story of Baby X, a child whose gender is unspecified as a part of a social experiment. This engaging account highlights the many seemingly insignificant ways children and adults learn sexism, giving us a glimpse of what might occur if we risked changing our ideas about traditional sex roles.

---

## 🌿 21

## *The Gift*

MURIELLE MINARD

On my seventh birthday
A beloved uncle
Gave me a doll.
She was a beautiful creature
With blue eyes
That opened and shut,
Golden curls
And a blue velvet dress.

Once a week,
On Sunday afternoon,

My mother would sit me
In a chair
And place the doll in my arms.
I was not to disturb its perfection
In any way,
I would sit there
Transfixed
By its loveliness
And mindful
Of my mother's wishes.

After a time
She would take the doll from me,
Rewrap it carefully
In tissue,
Put it back into its own
Long, gray box

And place it
High on the closet shelf,
Safe from harm.

To this doll
Nothing must happen.                    [1984]

## 22

## *Allegra Maud Goldman*

EDITH KONECKY

"What are you going to be when you grow up?"

My favorite question. Everyone over a certain height asked it. You'd think the whole world turned on what Allegra Maud Goldman was going to *be* when she grew up. I never gave the same answer twice.

"A gentleman farmer," I said to Mrs. Oxfelder, who was helping me into a blue butterfly dress with big gauze wings. She was about to give me my first dancing lesson.

"Ha, ha," said Mrs. Oxfelder, not unkindly. "You can't be a gentleman farmer, Allegra. You're a girl."

"I'm going to change," I said. A girl was something else I was beginning to learn I might be stuck with, and it was not the best thing to be. I had an older brother, David, and he was something it was better to be. He was a boy. He had a bicycle.

"Wouldn't you like to be a dancer?" Mrs. Oxfelder said. "A lovely, graceful vision, music for the eye, making all the people sigh and dream and weep and cry *bravo*?"

"No."

"Using your body to say all the magical, miracle things music says? And love says?"

"No."

"Perhaps you'll change your mind," she said, leading me by the hand into a large room where I stood shivering among a lot of other butterflies, some of them fat.

"This is Allegra, girls, our newest *danseuse*." She sat down at the piano and played a few arpeggios. "Now, girls, I am going to play some airy spring mu-sic and I want you to listen to it. Then I want you to think of yourselves as lovely butterflies, free and joyous in the beautiful sunlit sky. And remember, the delicious flowers are blooming everywhere."

She played and the girls started to flit about, flapping their arms and sucking on imaginary flowers. I couldn't believe my eyes. I clamped them shut and threw myself onto the floor, where I lay spread-eagled. The music abruptly ceased.

"Allegra! What kind of butterfly is that?"

"A dead one in a glass case in the Museum of Natural History," I muttered.

"This is the *dance*," Mrs. Oxfelder said, her voice shrill. "It is not science. Get up off the floor."

It was a long hour, and when my mother came to get me at the end of it, she was wearing her brave face. Where I was concerned, she was usually filled with forebodings.

"Twinkletoes she's not," Mrs. Oxfelder said, handing me over.

"That's why she's here," my mother said.

On the way home in the car I sulked. "I'm not ever going back there again," I said.

"Yes you are."

"David doesn't have to."

"David is a boy."

"I'll kill myself," I said. "I don't see why I have to be some crummy bug."

"You're learning to dance."

"The main thing I'm not going to be when I grow up," I said, "is a dancer."

"You have to learn to be graceful and feminine. You walk like a lumberjack."

The rest of that day I made it a point to flit and leap, waving my hands above my head and giving off whirring sounds. Grandma, my mother's mother, was living with us. She was a widow. She had run away from an arranged marriage and also from something called pogroms (I thought Pogroms was the name of a place) in Russia when she was sixteen, a long time ago, but her English still left something to be desired. Though she spoke Russian, German, Hebrew and Yiddish, and knew a little Polish and Rumanian, her English had obviously been grudgingly acquired out of necessity rather than inclination. She had gone to night school for a term to learn the English alphabet so we could identify her preserves, thereafter labeled phoneti-cally in Grandma's voice: "Blegber," "Agelber" and "Crebebl."

"St. Vita's dance she's got?" Grandma said to my mother after watching me for a while.

"Ignore her," my mother said.

"Your underwear itches?" she said to me.

"Whirr, whirr," I said.

"Meshugenah," she said, shrugging and return-ing to her labors. It was the cook's night out and Grandma's night in. She was making kreplach. If it hadn't been for Grandma, we'd have had no ethnic tone at all. For a while, I hovered about, flapping my wings and watching her. These were not your ordi-nary kreplach. In fact, I've never had any like them since. I've had the meat kind, boiled in soup. I've had ravioli. I've had empanadas and Chinese won-tons. But these were dainty, thin-skinned pockets filled with cottage cheese, or pot cheese, or maybe both, sautéed like blintzes in sweet butter until they were slightly crisp, golden, and delicious. I wish I could find them again.

I drifted upstairs to see what David was doing, though I had a pretty good idea what it would be. I was right. He was making one of his transatlantic liners, an elaborate construction using a number of cardboard boxes of different sizes, paper cut into various shapes and colored with crayons, and a lot of paste. David was chiefly concerned with the interiors of his ships. Our father, a dress manu-facturer, went to Paris once every year and some-times twice, and occasionally we would go with our mother to see him off. He always went first-class on a deluxe ship like the *Ile de France* and had a party in his stateroom with champagne and caviar, and while the grown-ups were dealing with these, David and I would trot around exploring the ship. We never re-ally got to see the outside of it, as it was huddled against a pier and we made our entrance through a kind of canopied and carpeted gangplank, so that we could hardly tell where shore ended and ship began. But the inside, we thought, was gorgeous, and we never really believed that all of that endless luxury would actually float. It was like a fairy tale.

So what David was intent on fabricating, in painstaking detail, was the ship's innards, and only

the first-class parts. We'd never seen the parts of the ship that made it work. He'd make three or four levels, but the top one was open until the very end, cross-sectioned and fitted with cubicles represent-ing the staterooms, the dining salons, the bar, night-club, gym, swimming pool and movie theater. He even had little bathrooms with carefully cut out toi-lets. I had to admire the detail. It was an achieve-ment that took him hours, and sometimes the project spanned a whole weekend. When it was fin-ished, he'd put a top on it with smokestacks, fill the bathtub with water, and sink the ship.

Much later I realized that what he was doing was killing our father, though I don't recall that he ever put any people in the ship. I didn't know about Oe-dipus then, though I was beginning to learn about other complexes. At the time I thought that David was simply doing one of those dopey destructive things boys did. Sometimes he didn't even wait to watch the ship go down. He'd leave it floating in the tub and some time later he'd come back and fish out the soggy, disintegrated mess and throw it away.

This particular day, he was working on the swim-ming pool when I fluttered up to watch. He had a mirror from one of our mother's handbags and was carefully fitting it into a square of cardboard.

"How was the dancing lesson?"

"I'd rather not talk about it."

"What'd they make you do?"

I flopped onto the floor and scrutinized his handiwork. He had outdone himself with the movie theater. There was even a screen with a cowboy riding a horse on it, a picture cut out of *The Satur-day Evening Post*. Black and white. That was before Technicolor.

"You walked in your sleep again last night," I said. "You peed on the bathroom chair instead of in the toilet."

He looked up, interested, a pale, thin boy with a lot of curly brown hair and greenish eyes, not quite a year and a half older than me. Though we fought a lot, we were close. He didn't have any friends because he was shy and also because he didn't like to do any of the things the kids on the block did, punchball and stickball and territory. The other boys called him a sissy and shunned him. He was taking piano lessons and he was already up to "The Turkish March."

"What I'd like to know," I said, "is why you have to come wake me up and tell me you have to go to the bathroom. I can understand it when you come to tell me the house is on fire or there's a robber looking in the window. But why when you have to go to the bathroom? You know where it is."

"I really peed on the chair?"

"Why do you?"

"Pee on the chair?"

"Wake me up."

"How should I know? I'm asleep, aren't I?"

One of the things I was learning about who I was was that I was sometimes expected to be an older sister to my older brother. With none of the privileges. Because, as my mother explained from time to time, "David is so sensitive. He's not like other boys. He has a lot of fears and an inferiority complex."

"What's an inferiority complex?"

"He doesn't know his own worth."

This was a new idea, and one that surprised me, for David was always lording it over me and telling me how stupid I was.

"We have to help him gain self-confidence."

"What's that?"

"Knowing his own worth."

I thought about this for a while.

"How much *is* David worth?" I said.

It was one of my jobs when he sleepwalked into my room to unburden himself of whatever was on his mind, to fix it somehow and then see him back to his bed. If the house was on fire, I'd say, "I'll go look." Then I'd go look and tell him, "It's okay, the house isn't on fire." Or, "There's nobody at the window. If there was, he's gone away." The night before I'd led him to the toilet and gone out into the hall to wait for him. Then, when I went back in, he was standing at the chair fixing his pajama pants. The chair was at the other end of the bathroom, a white chair with a cane bottom, and there was a puddle underneath it. He must have done it on purpose, even in his sleep. But I didn't say anything; I couldn't see much point in making unnecessary conversation with a sleepwalker. I took his arm and

led him back to his bed and waited for him to get into it and said, "Go to sleep," which he was anyhow the whole time, and "Good night." In the morning I got blamed.

"You'd think *I* did it," I protested.

"You shouldn't have let him," my mother said and then added, irrelevantly, "Thank God you'll be starting school soon." [1987]

## 🌿 23

# *Growing*

HELENA MARÍA VIRAMONTES

The two walked down First Street hand in reluctant hand. The smaller of the two wore a thick, red sweater with a desperately loose button swinging like a pendulum. She carried her crayons, swinging her arm while humming *Jesus loves little boys and girls* to the speeding echo of the Saturday morning traffic and was totally oblivious to her older sister's wrath.

"My eye!" Naomi ground out the words from between her teeth. She turned to her youngest sister who seemed unconcerned and quite delighted at the prospect of another adventure. "Chaperone," she said with great disdain. "My EYE!" Lucía was chosen by Apá to be Naomi's chaperone and this infuriated her so much that she dragged her along impatiently, pulling and jerking at almost every step. She was 14, almost going on 15 and she thought the idea of having to be watched by a young snot like Lucía was insulting to her maturity. She flicked her hair over her shoulder. "Goddamnit," she said finally, making sure that the words were low enough so that neither God nor Lucía would hear them.

There seemed to be no way out of this custom either. Her arguments were always the same and always turned into pleas. This morning was no different. Amá, Naomi said, exasperated but determined not to back out of this one, Amá, América is different. Here girls don't need chaperones. Mothers trust their daughters. As usual Amá turned to the kitchen sink or the ice box, shrugged her shoulders and said: You have to ask your father. Naomi's nostrils flexed in fury as she said, But Amá, it's so embarrassing. I'm too old for that; I am an adult. And as usual, Apá felt different and in his house, she had absolutely no other choice but to drag Lucía to a sock hop or church carnival or anywhere Apá was sure she would be found around boys. Lucía came along as a spy, a gnat, a pain in the neck.

Well, Naomi debated with herself; it wasn't Lucía's fault, really. She suddenly felt sympathy for the humming little girl who scrambled to keep up with her as they crossed the freeway overpass. She stopped and tugged Lucía's shorts up, and although her shoelaces were tied, Naomi retied them. No, it wasn't her fault after all, Naomi thought, and she patted her sister's soft light brown and almost blondish hair, it was Apá's. She slowed her pace as they continued their journey to Fierro's house. It was Apá who refused to trust her and she could not understand what she had done to make him so distrustful. *Tú eres mujer,* he thundered, and that was the end of any argument, any questions, and the matter was closed because he said those three words as if they were a condemnation from the heavens and so she couldn't be trusted. Naomi tightened her grasp with the thought, shaking her head in disbelief.

"Really," she said out loud.

"Wait up. Wait," Lucía said, rushing behind her. "Well would you hurry. Would you?" Naomi reconsidered: Lucía did have some fault in the matter after all, and she became irritated at once at Lucía's smile and the way her chaperone had of taking and holding her hand. As they passed El Gallo, Lucía began fussing, grabbing onto her older sister's waist for reassurance and hung onto it.

"Stop it. Would you stop it?" She unglued her sister's grasp and continued pulling her along. "What's wrong with you?" she asked Lucía. I'll tell you what's wrong with you, she thought, as they waited at the corner of an intersection for the light to change: You have a big mouth. That's it. If it wasn't for Lucía's willingness to provide information, she would not have been grounded for three months. Three months, 12 Saturday nights, and

two church bazaars later, Naomi still hadn't forgiven her youngest sister. When they crossed the street, a homely young man with a face full of acne honked at her tight purple pedal pushers. The two were startled by the honk.

"Go to hell," she yelled at the man in the blue and white chevy. She indignantly continued her walk.

"Don't be mad, baby," he said, his car crawling across the street, then speeding off leaving tracks on the pavement, "You make me ache," he yelled, and he was gone.

"GO TO HELL, Goddamn you!" she screamed at the top of her lungs forgetting for a moment that Lucía told everything to Apá. What a big mouth her youngest sister had, for christsakes. Three months.

Naomi stewed in anger when she thought of the Salesian Carnival and how she first made eye contact with a Letterman Senior whose eyes, she remembered with a soft smile, sparkled like crystals of brown sugar. She sighed as she recalled the excitement she experienced when she first became aware that he was following them from booth to booth. Joe's hair was greased back to a perfect sculptured ducktail and his dimples were deep. When he finally handed her a stuffed rabbit he had won pitching dimes, she knew she wanted him.

As they continued walking, Lucía waved to the Fruit Man. He slipped his teeth off and again, she was bewildered.

"Would you hurry up!" Naomi ordered Lucía as she had the night at the Carnival. Joe walked beside them and he took out a whole roll of tickets, trying to convince her to leave her youngest sister on the ferris wheel. "You could watch her from behind the gym," he had told her, and his eyes smiled pleasure. "Come on," he said, "have a little fun." They waited in the ferris wheel line of people. Finally:

"Stay on the ride," she instructed Lucía, making sure her sweater was buttoned. "And when it stops again, just give the man another ticket, okay?" Lucía said okay, excited at the prospect of highs and lows and her stomach wheezing in between. After Naomi saw her go up for the first time, she waved to her, then slipped away into the darkness and joined the other hungry couples behind the gym. Occasionally, she would open her eyes to see the lights of the ferris wheel spinning in the air with dizzy speed.

When Naomi returned to the ferris wheel, her hair undone, her lips still tingling from his newly stubbled cheeks, Lucía walked off and vomited. Lucía vomited the popcorn, a hot dog, some chocolate raisins, and a candied apple, and all Naomi knew was that she was definitely in trouble.

"It was the ferris wheel," Lucía said to Apá. "The wheel going like this over and over again." She circled her arms in the air and vomited again at the thought of it.

"Where was your sister?" Apá had asked, his voice rising.

"I don't know," Lucía replied, and Naomi knew she had just committed a major offense, and that Joe would never wait until her prison sentence was completed.

"Owww," Lucía said. "You're pulling too hard."

"You're a slow poke, that's why," Naomi snarled back. They crossed the street and passed the rows of junk yards and the shells of cars which looked like abandoned skull heads. They passed Señora Nuñez's neat, wooden house and Naomi saw her peeking through the curtains of her window. They passed the "TU y YO," the one-room dirt pit of a liquor store where the men bought their beers and sat outside on the curb drinking quietly. When they reached Fourth Street, Naomi spotted the neighborhood kids playing stickball with a broomstick and a ball. Naomi recognized them right away and Tina waved to her from the pitcher's mound.

"Wanna play?" Lourdes yelled from center field. "Come on, have some fun."

"Can't." Naomi replied. "I can't." Kids, kids, she thought. My, my. It wasn't more than a few years ago that she played baseball with Eloy and the rest of them. But she was in high school now, too old now, and it was unbecoming of her. She was an adult.

"I'm tired," Lucía said. "I wanna ice cream."

"You got money?"

"No."

"Then shut up."

Lucía sat on the curb, hot and tired, and she began removing her sweater. Naomi decided to sit down next to her for a few minutes and watch the game. Anyway, she wasn't really in that much of a hurry to get to Fierro's. A few minutes wouldn't make much of a difference to someone who spent most of his time listening to the radio.

She counted them by names. They were all there. Fifteen of them and their ages varied just as much as their clothes. Pants, skirts, shorts were always too big and had to be tugged up constantly, and shirt sleeves rolled and unrolled, or socks mismatched with shoes that didn't fit. But the way they dressed presented no obstacle for scoring or yelling foul and she enjoyed the zealous abandonment with which they played. She knew that the only decision these kids possibly made was what to play next, and she wished to be younger.

Chano's team was up. The teams were oddly numbered. Chano had nine on his team because everybody wanted to be in a winning team. It was an unwritten law of stickball that anyone who wanted to play joined whatever team they preferred. Tina's team had the family faithful 6. Of course numbers determined nothing. Naomi remembered once playing with Eloy and three of her cousins against ten kids, and still winning by three points.

Chano was at bat and everybody fanned out far and wide. He was a power hitter and Tina's team prepared for him. They couldn't afford a homerun now because Piri was on second, legs apart, waiting to rush home and score a crucial point. And Piri wanted to score it at all costs. It was important for him because his father sat outside the liquor store with a couple of his uncles and a couple of malt liquors watching the game.

"Steal the base!" his father yelled, "Run, menso!" But Piri hesitated. He was too afraid to take the risk. Tina pitched and Chano swung, missed, strike one.

"Batter, batter, swing!" Naomi yelled from the curb. She stood up to watch the action better.

"I wanna ice cream," Lucía said.

"Come on, Chano!" Piri yelled, bending his knees and resting his hands on them like a true baseball player. He spat, clapped his hands. "Come on."

"Ah, shut up, sissy." This came from Lourdes, Tina's younger sister. Naomi smiled at the rivals. "Can't you see you're making the pitcher nervous?" and she pushed him hard between the shoulder blades, then returned to her position in the outfield, holding her hand over her eyes to shield them from the sun. "Strike the batter out," she screamed at the top of her lungs. "Come on, strike the menso out!"

Tina delivered another pitch, but not before going through the motions of a professional preparing for the perfect pitch. Naomi knew she was a much better pitcher than Tina. Strike two. Maybe not, and Lourdes let out such a taunting grito of joy that Piri's father called her a dog.

Chano was angry now, nervous and upset. He put his bat down, spat in his hands and rubbed them together, wiped the sides of his jeans, kicked the dirt for perfect footing.

"Get on with the game!" Naomi shouted impatiently. Chano swung a couple of times to test his swing. He swung so hard he caused Juan, Tina's brother and devoted catcher, to jump back.

"Hey baboso, watch out," he said. "You almost hit my coco." And he pointed to his forehead.

"Well, don't be so stupid," Chano replied, positioning himself once again. "Next time back off when I come to bat."

"Baboso," Juan repeated.

"Say it to my face," Chano said, breaking his stand and turning to Juan "say it again so I could break this bat over your head."

"Ah, come on, Kiki," the shortstop yelled, "I gotta go home pretty soon."

"Let up," Tina demanded.

"Shut up marrana," Piri said, turning to his father to make sure he heard. "Tinasana, cola de marrana, Tinasana, cola de marrano." Tina became so infuriated that she threw the ball directly to his stomach. Piri folded over in pain.

"No! No!" Sylvia yelled. "Don't get off the base or she'll tag you out!"

"It's a trick!" Miguel yelled from behind home plate.

"That's what you get!" This came from Lourdes. Piri did not move, and for a moment Naomi felt sorry for him, but giggled at the scene anyway.

"I heard the ice cream man." Lucía said.

"You're all right, Tina," Naomi yelled, laughing, "You're A-O-K." And with that compliment, Tina bowed, proud of her performance until everyone began shouting, "STOP WASTING TIME!" Tina was prepared. She pitched and Chano made the connection quick, hard, the ball rising high and flying over her head, Piri's, Lourdes', Naomi's and Lu-

cía's, and landed inside the Chinese Cemetery.

"DON'T JUST STAND THERE!" Tina screamed at Lourdes, "Go get it, stupid!" After Lourdes broke out of her trance, she ran to the tall, chain-link fence which surrounded the cemetery, jumped on the fence and crawled up like a scrambling spider, her dress tearing with a rip roar.

"We saw your calzones, we saw your calzones," Lucía sang.

"Go! Lourdes, go!" Naomi jumped up and down in excitement, feeling like a player who although benched in the sidelines, was dying to get out there and help her team win. The kids blended into one huge noise, like an untuned orchestra, screaming and shouting Get the Ball, Run in Piri, Go Lourdes, Go throw the ball Chano pick up your feet throw the ballrunrunrunthrow the ball. "THROW the ball to me!!" Naomi waved and waved her arms. For that moment she forgot all about "growing up," her period, her breasts that bounced with glee. All she wanted was an out on home base. To hell with being benched. "Throw it to me," she yelled.

In the meantime, Lourdes searched frantically for the ball, tip-toeing across the graves saying Excuse me, please excuse me, excuse me, until she found the ball peacefully buried behind a huge gray marble stone, and she yelled to no one in particular, CATCH IT, SOMEONE CATCH IT! She threw the ball up and over the fence and it landed near Lucía. Lucía was about to reach for the ball when Naomi picked it off the ground and threw it straight to Tina. Tina caught the ball, dropped it, picked it up, and was about to throw the ball to Juan at homeplate, when she realized that Juan had picked up the homeplate and ran, zig-zagging across the street while Piri and Chano ran after him. Chano was a much faster runner, but Piri insisted that he be the first to touch the base.

"I gotta touch it first," he kept repeating between pantings, "I gotta."

The kids on both teams grew wild with anger and encouragement. Seeing an opportunity, Tina ran as fast as her stocky legs could take her. Because Chano slowed down to let Piri touch the base first, Tina was able to reach him, and with one quick blow, she thundered OUT! She threw one last desperate throw to Juan so that he could tag Piri out, but she threw it so hard that it struck Piri right in the back of his head, and the blow forced him to stumble just within reach of Juan and homeplate.

"You're out!" Tina said, out of breath. "O-U-T, out."

"No fair!" Piri immediately screamed. "NO FAIR!!" He stomped his feet in rage like Rumpelestiltskin. "You marrana, you marrana."

"Don't be such a baby," Piri's father said. "Take it like a man," he said as he opened another malt liquor with a can opener. But Piri continued stomping and screaming until his shouts were buried by the honk of an oncoming car and the kids obediently opened up like the red sea to let the car pass.

Naomi felt like a victor. She had helped, once again. Delighted, she giggled, laughed, laughed harder, suppressed her laughter into chuckles, then laughed again. Lucía sat quietly, to her surprise, and her eyes were heavy with sleep. She wiped them, looked at Naomi. "Vamos" Naomi said, offering her hand. By the end of the block, she lifted Lucía and laid her head on her shoulder. As Lucía fell asleep, Naomi wondered why things were always so complicated when you became older. Funny how the old want to be young and the young want to be old. Now that she was older, her obligations became heavier both at home and at school. There were too many demands on her, and no one showed her how to fulfill them, and wasn't it crazy? She cradled Lucía gently, kissed her cheek. They were almost at Fierro's now, and reading to him was just one more thing she dreaded doing, and one more thing she had no control over: it was another one of Apá's thunderous commands.

When she was Lucía's age, she hunted for lizards and played stickball with her cousins until her body began to bleed at 12, and Eloy saw her in a different light. Under the house, he sucked her swelling nipples and became jealous. He no longer wanted to throw rocks at the cars on the freeway with her and she began to act different because everyone began treating her different and wasn't it crazy? She could no longer be herself and her father could no longer trust her because she was a woman. Fierro's gate hung on a hinge and she was almost afraid it would

fall off when she opened it. She felt Lucía's warm, deep, breath on her neck and it tickled her momentarily. Enjoy, she whispered to Lucía, enjoy being a young girl, because you will never enjoy being a woman. [1983]

 24

# Gender Equity in the Classroom: The Unfinished Agenda

MYRA SADKER, DAVID SADKER, LYNN FOX, AND MELINDA SALATA

*"In my science class the teacher never calls on me, and I feel like I don't exist. The other night I had a dream that I vanished."*[1]

Our interviews with female students have taught us that it is not just in science class that girls report the "disappearing syndrome" referred to above. Female voices are also less likely to be heard in history and math classes, girls' names are less likely to be seen on lists of national merit finalists, and women's contributions infrequently appear in school textbooks. Twenty years after the passage of Title IX, the law prohibiting gender discrimination in U.S. schools, it is clear that most girls continue to receive a second-class education.

The very notion that women should be educated at all is a relatively recent development in U.S. history. It was not until late in the last century that the concept of educating girls beyond elementary school took hold. Even as women were gradually allowed to enter high school and college, the guiding principle in education was separate and unequal. Well into the twentieth century, boys and girls were assigned to sex-segregated classes and prepared for very different roles in life.

In 1833 Oberlin became the first college in the United States to admit women; but these early female college students were offered less rigorous courses and required to wait on male students and wash their clothes. Over the next several decades, only a few colleges followed suit in opening their doors to women. During the nineteenth century, a number of forward-thinking philanthropists and educators founded postsecondary schools for women—Mount Holyoke, Vassar, and the other seven-sister colleges. It was only in the aftermath of the Civil War that coeducation became more prevalent on campuses across the country, but even here economics and not equity was the driving force. Since the casualties of war meant the loss of male students and their tuition dollars, many universities turned to women to fill classrooms and replace lost revenues. In 1870 two-thirds of all universities still barred women. By 1900 more than two-thirds admitted them. But the spread of coeducation did not occur without a struggle. Consider that as late as the 1970s the all-male Ivy League colleges did not admit women, and even now state-supported Virginia Military Institute fights to maintain both its all-male status and its state funding.

## CYCLE OF LOSS

Today, most female and male students attend the same schools, sit in the same classrooms, and read the same books; but the legacy of inequity continues beneath the veneer of equal access. Although the school door is finally open and girls are inside the building, they remain second-class citizens.

In the early elementary school years, girls are ahead of boys academically, achieving higher standardized test scores in every area but science. By middle school, however, the test scores of female students begin a downward spiral that continues through high school, college, and even graduate school. Women consistently score lower than men on the Graduate Record Exams as well as on entrance tests for law, business, and medical schools. As a group, women are the only students who actually lose ground the longer they stay in school.

Ironically, falling female performance on tests is not mirrored by lower grades. Some have argued that women's grade-point averages are inflated because they tend not to take the allegedly more rigorous courses, such as advanced mathematics and physics. Another hypothesis suggests that female students get better grades in secondary school and college as a reward for effort and better behavior rather than a mastery of the material. Another possibility is that the standardized tests do not adequately measure that female students know and what they are really able to do. Whatever the reason, course grades and test grades paint very different academic pictures.

Lower test scores handicap girls in the competition for places at elite colleges. On average, girls score 50 to 60 points less than boys on the Scholastic Aptitude Test (SAT), recently renamed the Scholastic Assessment Test, which is required for admission to most colleges. Test scores also unlock scholarship money at 85 percent of private colleges and 90 percent of the public ones. For example, in 1991, boys scored so much higher on the Preliminary SAT/National Merit Scholarship Qualifying Test (PSAT/NMSQT) that they were nominated for two-thirds of the Merit Scholarships—18 thousand boys compared to 8 thousand girls in 1991.[2]

The drop in test scores begins around the same time that another deeply troubling loss occurs in the lives of girls: self-esteem. There is a precipitous decline from elementary school to high school. Entering middle school, girls begin what is often the most turbulent period in their young lives. According to a national survey sponsored by the American Association of University Women, 60 percent of elementary school girls agreed with the statement "I'm happy the way I am," while only 37 percent still agreed in middle school. By high school, the level had dropped an astonishing 31 points to 29 percent, with fewer than three out of every 10 girls feeling good about themselves. According to the survey, the decline is far less dramatic for boys: 67 percent report being happy with themselves in elementary school, and this drops to 46 percent in high school.[3]

Recent research points to the relationship between academic achievement and self-esteem. Students who do well in school feel better about themselves; and in turn, they then feel more capable. For most female students, this connection has a negative twist and a cycle of loss is put into motion. As girls feel less good about themselves, their academic performance declines, and this poor performance further erodes their confidence. This pattern is particularly powerful in math and science classes, with only 18 percent of middle school girls describing themselves as good in these subjects, down from 31 percent in elementary school. It is not surprising that

## Gender Bias in the SAT Math Exams

Several studies of large student groups and individual institutions such as MIT, Rutgers, and Princeton demonstrate that although young women typically earn the same or higher grades as their male counterparts in math and other college courses, their SAT scores were 30 to 50 points lower. Researchers Kathy Kessel and Marcia Lynn of the University of California suggest that the disparity is caused by the SAT exam's emphasis on speed and multiple-choice questions. Tests require students to solve 25 to 35 short problems in 30 minutes. Studies show that males do better on speeded tests because they are more self-confident and therefore spend less time checking their answers and reflecting on problems. In countries such as the Netherlands, England, and Australia where exams require solutions to several long problems, there is less disparity between the scores of male and female students. College courses in the United States are increasingly emphasizing the solution of the complex problems. The ability to engage in the sustained reasoning required to solve such problems is not adequately measured by the college entrance examinations.

As a result of these factors, young women receive lower SAT math scores and lose out on college admissions, scholarships, placement into advanced courses, and various career opportunities. Yet given a chance, they are likely to outperform their male counterparts. Kessel and Linn endorse new forms of assessments that use portfolios and projects and applaud those schools where test scores are optional in the admission process.

Adapted from "Fair Test Examiner," National Center for Fair and Open Testing, Winter 1996–97.

## Race, Ethnicity, and Self-Confidence

Research by the American Association of University Women and Peggy Orenstein, author of *Schoolgirls,* indicates that race and ethnicity as well as gender affect girls' experience of self-confidence. While all girls' self-esteem declines during adolescence, African-American girls retain a stronger sense of self, feel more entitled to speak out, and are more satisfied with their appearance than other groups of girls. They are, however, less confident about school than other girls and often feel undermined and stigmatized by the low expectations and racism of their teachers. Latinas experience the most radical decline in both personal and academic self-confidence during adolescence. According to the American Association of University Women, the number of Latina girls who are "happy with the way I am" plunges by 38 percentage points, compared with a 33 percent drop for white girls and a 7 percent drop for black girls.

AAUW Report, Executive Summary, Washington, D.C., 1991, p. 27.

the testing gap between boys and girls is particularly wide in math and science.[3]

## INEQUITY IN INSTRUCTION

During the past decade, Myra and David Sadker have investigated verbal interaction patterns in elementary, secondary, and college classrooms in a variety of settings and subject areas. In addition, they have interviewed students and teachers across the country. In their new book, *Failing at Fairness: How America's Schools Cheat Girls*, they expose the microinequities that occur daily in classrooms across the United States—and they show how this imbalance in attention results in the lowering of girls' achievement and self-esteem.[1] Consider the following:

• From grade school to graduate school, girls receive less teacher attention and less useful teacher feedback.

• Girls talk significantly less than boys do in class. In elementary and secondary school, they are eight times less likely to call out comments. When they do, they are often reminded to raise their hands while similar behavior by boys is accepted.

• Girls rarely see mention of the contributions of women in the curricula; most textbooks continue to report male worlds.

• Too frequently female students become targets of unwanted sexual attention from male peers and sometimes even from administrators and teachers.

From omission in textbooks to inappropriate sexual comments to bias in teacher behavior, girls experience a powerful and often disabling education climate. A high school student from an affluent Northeastern high school describes her own painful experience:

My English teacher asks the class, "What is the purpose of the visit to Johannesburg?" . . . I know the answer, but I contemplate whether I should answer the question. The boys in the back are going to tease me like they harass all the other girls in our class . . . I want to tell them to shut up. But I stand alone. All of the other girls don't even let themselves be bold. Perhaps they are all content to be molded into society's image of what a girl should be like—submis-

sive, sweet, feminine . . . In my ninth period class, I am actually afraid—of what [the boys] might say . . . As my frustration builds, I promise myself that I will yell back at them. I say that everyday . . . and I never do it.[4]

Teachers not only call on male students more frequently than on females; they also allow boys to call out more often. This imbalance in instructional attention is greatest at the college level. Our research shows that approximately one-half of the students in college classrooms are silent, having no interaction whatsoever with the professor. Two-thirds of these silent students are women. This verbal domination is further heightened by the gender segregation of many of today's classes. Sometimes teachers seat girls and boys in different sections of the room, but more often students segregate themselves. Approximately one-half of the elementary and high school classrooms and one-third of the coeducational college classrooms that the Sadkers visited are sex-segregated. As male students talk and call out more, teachers are drawn to the noisier male sections of the class, a development that further silences girls.

Not only do male students interact more with the teacher but at all levels of schooling they receive a higher quality of interaction. Using four categories of teacher responses to student participation—praise, acceptance, remediation, and criticism—the Sadkers' studies found that more than 50 percent of all teacher responses are mere acceptances, such as "O.K." and "uh huh." These nonspecific reactions offer little instructional feedback. Teachers use remediation more than 30 percent of the time, helping students correct or improve answers by asking probing questions or by phrases such as "Try again." Only 10 percent of the time do teachers actually praise students, and they criticize them even less. Although praise, remediation, and criticism provide more useful information to students than the neutral acknowledgment of an "O.K." these clearer, more precise teacher comments are more often directed to boys.

Who gets taught—and how—has profound consequences. Student participation in the classroom enhances learning and self-esteem. Thus, boys gain an educational advantage over girls by claiming a greater share of the teacher's time and attention.

This is particularly noteworthy in science classes, where, according to the AAUW report, *How Schools Shortchange Girls,* boys perform 79 percent of all student-assisted demonstrations. When girls talk less and do less, it is little wonder that they learn less.[5] Even when directing their attention to girls, teachers sometimes short-circuit the learning process. For example, teachers frequently explain how to focus a microscope to boys but simply adjust the microscope for the girls. Boys learn the skill; girls learn to ask for assistance.

When female students do speak in class, they often preface their statements with self-deprecating remarks such as, "I'm not sure this is right," or "This probably isn't what you're looking for." Even when offering excellent responses, female students may begin with this self-criticism. Such tentative forms of speech project a sense of academic uncertainty and self-doubt—almost a tacit admission of lesser status in the classroom.

Women are not only quiet in classrooms; they are also missing from the pages of textbooks. For example, history textbooks currently in use at middle and high schools offer little more than 2 percent of their space to women. Studies of music textbooks have found that 70 percent of the figures shown are male. A recent content analysis of five secondary school science textbooks revealed that more than two-thirds of all drawings were of male figures and that not a single female scientist was depicted. Furthermore, all five books used the male body as the model for the human body, a practice that continues even in medical school texts.[6] At the college level, too, women rarely see themselves reflected in what they study. For example, the two-volume *Norton Anthology of English Literature* devotes less than 15 percent of its pages to the works of women. Interestingly, there was greater representation of women in the first edition of the anthology in 1962 than in the fifth edition published in 1986.[7]

## PRESENCE AND POWER

Not only are women hidden in the curriculum and quiet in the classroom, they are also less visible in other school locations. Even as early as the elementary grades, considered by some to be a distinctly feminine environment, boys tend to take over the territory. At recess time on playgrounds across the country, boys grab bats and balls as they fan out over the school yard for their games. Girls are likely to be left on the sideline—watching. In secondary school, male students become an even more powerful presence. In *Failing at Fairness,* high school teachers and students tell these stories:

> A rural school district in Wisconsin still has the practice of having the cheerleaders (all girls, of course) clean the mats for the wrestling team before each meet. They are called the "Mat Maidens."

> In our local high school, boys' sports teams received much more support from the school system and the community. The boys' team got shoes, jackets, and played on the best-maintained grounds. The girls' softball team received no clothes and nobody took care of our fields. Cheerleaders did not cheer for us. When we played, the bleachers were mostly empty.

Sports are not the only fields where women lose ground. In many secondary schools, mathematics, science, and computer technology remain male domains. In the past, girls were actively discouraged or even prohibited from taking the advanced courses in these fields. One woman, now a college professor, recalls her high school physics class:

> I was the only girl in the class. The teacher often told off-color jokes and when he did he would tell me to the leave the room. My great regret today is that I actually did it.

Today, we hope such explicitly offensive behavior is rare, yet counselors and teachers continue to harbor lower expectations for girls and are less likely to encourage them to take advanced classes in math and science. It is only later in life that women realize the price they paid for avoiding these courses as they are screened out of lucrative careers in science and technology.

By the time they reach college, male students' control of the environment is visible. Male students are more likely to hold positions of student leadership on campus and to play in heavily funded sports programs. College presidents and deans are usually men, as are most tenured professors. In a sense, a "glass wall" divides today's college campus. On one side of the glass wall are men, comprising 70 percent of all students majoring in chemistry,

*Sexism and racism are so embedded in curriculum material that it requires a conscious effort to create a classroom climate that is truly inclusive. The questions below have been helpful to instructors in examining their texts and lectures. How have teachers' choices of materials and patterns of classroom interaction affected you?*

# Checklist for Inclusive Teaching

MERCILEE JENKINS

### TEXTS, LECTURES, AND COURSE CONTENT

1. Are you and your texts' language sex-neutral, using words with relation to both sexes whenever this is the author's intent? If your texts use the masculine generic, do you point this out in the classroom?
2. Is content addressed equitably to men, to women, people of color?
3. Do you and your texts portray equitably the activities, achievements, concerns, and experiences of women and people of color? If your texts do not, do you provide supplemental materials? Do you bring omissions to the attention of your students?
4. Do your and your texts present the careers, roles, interests, and abilities of women and people of color without stereotyping? If there are stereotypes in your texts, do you point this out?
5. Do you and your texts' examples and illustrations (both verbal and graphic) represent an equitable balance in terms of gender and race? If your texts do not, do you point this out?
6. Do your texts and lectures reflect values that are free of sex and race bias, and if not, do you discuss your/their biases and values with your students?
7. Do your texts incorporate new research and theory generated by feminist and ethnic scholarship? If not, do you point out areas in which feminist and ethnic studies are modifying perceived ideas? Do you provide additional bibliographic references for

physics, and computer science. The percentage is even higher in engineering. While the "hard sciences" flourish on the men's side of the campus, the women's side of the glass wall is where education, psychology, and foreign languages are taught. These gender walls not only separate programs, they also indicate social standing. Departments with higher male enrollment carry greater campus prestige and their faculty are often paid higher salaries.

These gender differences can be seen outside academic programs, in peer relationships both at college and in high school. In 1993 a national survey sponsored by the AAUW and reported in *Hostile Hallways* found that 76 percent of male students and 85 percent of female students in the typical high school had experienced sexual harassment.[8] What differed dramatically for girls and boys was not the occurrence of unwanted touching or profane remarks but their reaction to them. Only 28 percent of the boys, compared to 70 percent of the girls, said they were upset by these experiences. For 33 percent of the girls, the encounters were so troubling that they did not want to talk in class or even go to school. On college campuses problems range from sexist comments and sexual propositions to physical assault. Consider the following incidents:

students who want to pursue these issues? When you order books for the library, do they reflect these issues?

8. Do your exams and assignments for papers, projects, etc. allow and encourage students to explore the nature, roles, status, contributions and experience of women and people of color?

9. Do your texts and materials make it clear that not everyone is heterosexual?

### CLASSROOM INTERACTIONS

1. Are you conscious of sex- or race-related expectations you may hold about student performance?

2. How do you react to uses of language (accent, dialect, etc.) that depart from standard English or that are different from your own? Do you discount the speaker's intelligence and information?

3. What is the number of males versus females or of various cultural and racial groups called on to answer questions? Which students do you call by name? Why?

4. Which of these categories of students participate in class more frequently through answering questions or making comments? Is the number disproportional enough that you should encourage some students to participate more frequently?

5. Do interruptions occur when an individual is talking? If so, who does the interrupting? If one group of students is dominating classroom interaction, what do you do about it?

6. Is your verbal response to students positive? Aversive? Encouraging? Is it the same for all students? If not, what is the reason? (Valid reasons occur from time to time for reacting or responding to a particular student in a highly specific manner.)

7. Do you tend to face or address one section of the classroom more than others? Do you establish eye contact with certain students more than others? What are the gestures, postures, facial expressions, etc. used and are they different for men, women, people of color?

---

• A UCLA fraternity manual found its way into a campus magazine. Along with the history and bylaws were songs the pledges were supposed to memorize. The lyrics described sexual scenes that were bizarre, graphic, and sadistic.[9]

• One fraternity on a New England campus hosted "pig parties" where the man bringing the female date voted the ugliest wins.[1]

• A toga party on the campus of another elite liberal arts college used for decoration the torso of a female mannequin hung from the balcony and splattered with paint to look like blood. A sign below suggested the female body was available for sex.[10]

When one gender is consistently treated as less important and less valuable, the seeds of contempt take root and violence can be the result.

### STRATEGIES FOR CHANGE

One of the ironies of gender bias in schools is that so much of its goes unnoticed by educators. While personally committed to fairness, many are unable to see the microinequities that surround them. The research on student-teacher interactions led the Sadkers to develop training programs to enable teachers and administrators to detect this bias and create equitable teaching methods. Program evaluations indicate that biased teaching patterns can be changed, and teachers can achieve equity in verbal interactions with their students. Research shows that for elementary and secondary school teachers, as well as college professors, this training leads not only to more equitable teaching but to more effective teaching as well.

During the 1970s, content analysis research showed women missing from schoolbooks. Publishers issued guidelines for equity and vowed to reform. But recent studies show that not all publishing companies have lived up to the promise of their guidelines. The curriculum continues to present a predominately male model of the world. Once again publishers and authors must be urged to incorporate women into school texts. Teachers and students need to become aware of the vast amount of excellent children's literature, including biographies that feature resourceful girls and strong women. *Failing at Fairness*[1] includes an extensive list of these resources for both elementary and secondary schools.

In postsecondary education, faculty members typically select instructional materials on the basis of individual preference. Many instructors would benefit from programs that alert them to well-written, gender-fair books in their academic fields. And individual professors can enhance their own lectures and discussions by including works by and about women.

Education institutions at every level have a responsibility for students in and beyond the classroom. Harassing and intimidating behaviors that formerly might have been excused with the comment "boys will be boys" are now often seen as less excusable and less acceptable. Many schools offer workshops for students and faculty to help eliminate sexual harassment. While controversy surrounds the exact definition of sexual harassment, the education community must take this issue seriously and devise strategies to keep the learning environment open to all.

After centuries of struggle, women have finally made their way into our colleges and graduate schools, only to discover that access does not guarantee equity. Walls of subtle bias continue to create different education environments, channeling women and men toward separate and unequal futures. To complete the agenda for equity, we must transform our education institutions and empower female students for full participation in society.

[1994]

### REFERENCES

1. M. Sadker and D. Sadker, *Failing at Fairness: How America's Schools Cheat Girls* (New York: Charles Scribner's Sons, 1994). The research for this article as well as the anecdotes are drawn from this book.
2. Test data were obtained from Educational Testing Service.
3. The Analysis Group, Greenberg-Lake. *Shortchanging Girls, Shortchanging America* (Washington, D.C.: American Association of University Women, 1990).
4. L. Kim, "Boys Will Be Boys . . . Right?" *The Lance*, Livingston High School (June 1993), 32:5.
5. The Wellesley College Center for Research on Women. *How Schools Shortchange Girls: The AAUW Report* (Washington, D.C.: American Association of University Women Educational Foundation, 1992).
6. J. Bazler and D. Simonis, "Are Women Out of the Picture?" *Science Teacher 57* (December 1990):9.
7. W. Sullivan, "*The Norton Anthology* and the Canon of English Literature." Paper presented at the Annual Meeting of the College English Association, San Antonio, Texas, 1991.
8. Louis Harris and Associates. *Hostile Hallways: The AAUW Survey on Sexual Harassment in America's Schools* (Washington, D.C.: American Association of University Women, 1993).
9. J. O'Gorman and B. Sandler, *Peer Harassment: Hassles for Women on Campus* (Washington, D.C.: Project on the Status and Education of Women. Association of American Colleges, 1988).
10. B. A. Crier, "Frat Row," *Los Angeles Times* (February 9, 1990).

 25

# The Sexual Politics of Interpersonal Behavior

NANCY HENLEY AND JO FREEMAN

Social interaction is the battlefield where the daily war between the sexes is fought. It is here that women are constantly reminded where their "place" is and that they are put back in their place, should they venture out. Thus, social interaction serves as the most common means of social control employed against women. By being continually reminded of their inferior status in their interactions with others, and continually compelled to acknowledge that status in their own patterns of behavior, women learn to internalize society's definition of them as inferior so thoroughly that they are often unaware of what their status is. Inferiority becomes habitual, and the inferior place assumes the familiarity—and even desirability—of home.

Different sorts of cues in social interaction aid this enforcement of one's social definition, particularly the verbal message, the nonverbal message transmitted within a social relationship, and the nonverbal message transmitted by the environment. Our educational system emphasizes the verbal messages and teaches us next to nothing about how we interpret and react to the nonverbal ones. Just how important nonverbal messages are, however, is shown by the finding of Argyle et al.[1] that nonverbal cues have over four times the impact of verbal ones when both verbal and nonverbal cues are used. Even more important for women, Argyle found that female subjects were more responsive to nonverbal cues (compared with verbal ones) than male subjects. If women are to understand how the subtle forces of social control work in their lives, they must learn as much as possible about how nonverbal cues affect people, and particularly about how they perpetuate the power and superior status enjoyed by men.

Even if a woman encounters no one else directly in her day, visual status reminders are a ubiquitous part of her environment. As she moves through the day, she absorbs many variations of the same status theme, whether or not she is aware of it: male bosses dictate while female secretaries bend over their steno pads; male doctors operate while female nurses assist; restaurants are populated with waitresses serving men; magazine and billboard ads remind the woman that home maintenance and child care are her foremost responsibilities and that being a sex object for male voyeurs is her greatest asset. If she is married, her mail reminds her that she is a mere "Mrs." appended to her husband's name. When she

is introduced to others or fills out a form, the first thing she must do is divulge her marital status acknowledging the social rule that the most important information anyone can know about her is her legal relationship to a man.

These environmental cues set the stage on which the power relationships of the sexes are acted out, and the assigned status of each sex is reinforced. Though studies have been made of the several means by which status inequalities are communicated in interpersonal behavior, they do not usually deal with power relationships between men and women. Goffman has pointed to many characteristics associated with status:

> Between status equals we may expect to find interaction guided by symmetrical familiarity. Between superordinate and subordinate we may expect to find asymmetrical relations, the superordinate having the right to exercise certain familiarities which the subordinate is not allowed to reciprocate. Thus, in the research hospital, doctors tended to call nurses by their first names, while nurses responded with "polite" or "formal" address. Similarly, in American business organizations the boss may thoughtfully ask the elevator man how his children are, but this entrance into another's life may be blocked to the elevator man, who can appreciate the concern but not return it. Perhaps the clearest form of this is found in the psychiatrist-patient relation, where the psychiatrist has a right to touch on aspects of the patient's life that the patient might not even allow himself to touch upon, while of course this privilege is not reciprocated.
>
> Rules of demeanor, like rules of deference, can be symmetrical or asymmetrical. Between social equals, symmetrical rules of demeanor seem often to be prescribed. Between unequals many variations can be found. For example, at staff meetings on the psychiatric units of the hospital, medical doctors had the privilege of swearing, changing the topic of conversation, and sitting in undignified positions; attendants, on the other hand, had the right to attend staff meetings and to ask questions during them . . . but were implicitly expected to conduct themselves with greater circumspection than was required of doctors. . . . Similarly, doctors had the right to saunter into the nurses' station, lounge on the station's dispensing counter, and engage in

joking with the nurses; other ranks participated in this informal interaction with doctors, but only after doctors had initiated it.[2]

A status variable widely studied by Brown and others[3] is the use of terms of address. In languages that have both familiar and polite forms of the second person singular ("you"), asymmetrical use of the two forms invariably indicates a status difference, and it always follows the same pattern. The person using the familiar form is always the superior to the person using the polite form. In English, the only major European language not to have dual forms of address, status differences are similarly indicated by the right of first-naming; the status superior can first-name the inferior in situations where the inferior must use the superior's title and last name. An inferior who breaks this rule by inappropriately using a superior's first name is considered insolent.[4]

According to Brown, the pattern evident in the use of forms of address applies to a very wide range of interpersonal behavior and invariably has two other components: (1) whatever form is used by a superior in situations of status inequality can be used reciprocally by intimates, and whatever form is used by an inferior is the socially prescribed usage for nonintimates; (2) initiation or increase of intimacy is the right of the superior. To use the example of naming again to illustrate the first component, friends use first names with each other, while strangers use titles and last names (though "instant" intimacy is considered proper in some cultures, such as our own, among status equals in informal settings). As an example of the second component, status superiors, such as professors, specifically tell status inferiors, such as students, when they can use the first name, and often rebuff them if they assume such a right unilaterally.

Although Brown did not apply these patterns to status differences between the sexes, their relevance is readily seen. The social rules say that all moves to greater intimacy are a male prerogative: It is boys who are supposed to call girls for dates, men who are supposed to propose marriage to women, and males who are supposed to initiate sexual activity with females. Females who make "advances" are considered improper, forward, aggressive, brassy, or otherwise "unladylike." By initiating intimacy they have stepped out of their place and usurped a status prerogative. The value of such a prerogative is that it is a form of power. Between the sexes, as in other human interaction, the one who has the right to initiate greater intimacy has more control over the relationship. Superior status brings with it not only greater prestige and greater privileges, but greater power.

These advantages are exemplified in many of the various means of communicating status. Like the doctors in Goffman's research hospital, men are allowed such privileges as swearing and sitting in undignified positions, but women are denied them. Though the male privilege of swearing is curtailed in mixed company, the body movement permitted to women is circumscribed even in all-women groups. It is considered unladylike for a woman to use her body too forcefully, to sprawl, to stand with her legs widely spread, to sit with her feet up, or to cross the ankle of one leg over the knee of the other. Many of these positions are ones of strength or dominance. The more "feminine" a woman's clothes are, the more circumscribed the use of her body. Depending on her clothes, she may be expected to sit with her knees together, not to sit cross-legged, or not even to bend over. Though these taboos seem to have lessened in recent years, how much so is unknown, and there are recurring social pressures for a "return to femininity," while etiquette arbiters assert that women must retain feminine posture no matter what their clothing.

Prior to the 1920s women's clothes were designed to be confining and cumbersome. The dress reform movement, which disposed of corsets and long skirts, was considered by many to have more significance for female emancipation than women's suffrage.[5] Today women's clothes are designed to be revealing, but women are expected to restrict their body movements to avoid revealing too much. Furthermore, because women's clothes are contrived to reveal women's physical features, rather than being loose like men's, women must resort to purses instead of pockets to carry their belongings. These "conveniences" have become, in a time of blurred sex distinctions, one of the surest signs of sex, and thus have developed the character of stigma, a sign of woman's shame, as when they are used by comics to ridicule both women and transvestites.

Women in our society are expected to reveal not only more of their bodies than men but also more of themselves. Female socialization encourages greater expression of emotion than does that of the male. Whereas men are expected to be stolid and impassive, and not to disclose their feelings beyond certain limits, women are expected to express their *selves*. Such self-expression can disclose a lot of oneself, and, as Jourard and Lasakow[6] found, females are more self-disclosing to others than males are. This puts them at an immediate disadvantage.

The inverse relationship between disclosure and power has been reported by other studies in addition to Goffman's earlier cited investigation into a research hospital. Slobin, Miller, and Porter[7] stated that individuals in a business organization are "more self-disclosing to their immediate superior than to their immediate subordinates." Self-disclosure is a means of enhancing another's power. When one has greater access to information about another person, one has a resource the other person does not have. Thus not only does power give status, but status gives power. And those possessing neither must contribute to the power and status of others continuously.

Another factor adding to women's vulnerability is that they are socialized to *care* more than men—especially about personal relationships. This puts them at a disadvantage, as Ross articulated in what he called the "Law of Personal Exploitation": "In any sentimental relation the one who cares less can exploit the one who cares more."[8] The same idea was put more broadly by Waller and Hill as the "Principle of Least Interest": "That person is able to dictate the conditions of association whose interest in the continuation of the affair is least."[9] In other words, women's caring, like their openness, gives them less power in a relationship.

One way of indicating acceptance of one's place and deference to those of superior status is by following the rules of "personal space." Sommer has observed that dominant animals and human beings have a larger envelope of inviolability surrounding them—i.e., are approached less closely—than those of a lower status.[10] Willis made a study of the initial speaking distance set by an approaching person as a function of the speaker's relationship.[11] His finding that women were approached more closely

than men—i.e., their personal space was smaller or more likely to be breached—is consistent with their lower status.

Touching is one of the closer invasions of one's personal space, and in our low-contact culture it implies privileged access to another person. People who accidently touch other people generally take great pains to apologize; people forced into close proximity, as in a crowded elevator, often go to extreme lengths to avoid touching. Even the figurative meanings of the word convey a notion of access to privileged areas—e.g., to one's emotions (one is "touched" by a sad story), or to one's purse (one is "touched" for ten dollars). In addition, the act of touching can be a subtle physical threat.

Remembering the patterns that Brown found in terms of address, consider the interactions between pairs of persons of different status, and picture who would be more likely to touch the other (put an arm around the shoulder or a hand on the back, tap the chest, hold the arm, or the like: teacher and student; master and servant; policeman and accused; doctor and patient; minister and parishioner; adviser and advisee; foreman and worker; businessman and secretary. As with first-naming, it is considered presumptuous for a person of low status to initiate touch with a person of higher status.

There has been little investigation of touching by social scientists, but the few studies made so far indicate that females are touched more than males are. Goldberg and Lewis[12] and Lewis[13] report that from six months on, girl babies are touched more than boy babies. The data reported in Jourard[14] and Jourard and Rubin[15] show that sons and fathers tend to refrain from touching each other and that "when it comes to physical contact within the family, it is the daughters who are the favored ones."[16] An examination of the number of different regions in which subjects were touched showed that mothers and fathers touch their daughters in more regions than they do their sons; that daughters touch their fathers in more regions than sons do; that males touch their opposite-sex friends in more regions than females do. Overall, women's mean total "being-touched" score was higher than men's.

Jourard and Rubin take the view that "touching is equated with sexual interest, either consciously, or at a less-conscious level," [17] but it would seem that there is a sex difference in the interpretation of touch. Lewis reflects this when he writes, "In general, for men in our culture, proximity (touching) is restricted to the opposite sex and its function is primarily sexual in nature." [18] Waitresses, secretaries, and women students are quite used to being touched by their male superordinates, but they are expected not to "misinterpret" such gestures. However, women who touch men are often interpreted as conveying sexual intent, as they have often found out when their intentions were quite otherwise. Such different interpretations are consistent with the status patterns found earlier. If touching indicates either power or intimacy, and women are deemed by men to be status inferiors, touching by women will be perceived as a gesture of intimacy, since it would be inconceivable for them to be exercising power.

A study by Henley puts forward this hypothesis. [19] Observations of incidents of touch in public urban places were made by a white male research assistant, naive to the uses of his data. Age, sex, and approximate socioeconomic status were recorded, and the results indicated that higher-status persons do touch lower-status persons significantly more. In particular, men touched women more, even when all other variables were held constant. When the settings of the observations were differentially examined, the pattern showed up primarily in the outdoor setting, with indoor interaction being more evenly spread over sex combinations. Henley has also reported observations of greater touching by higher status persons (including males) in the popular culture media; and a questionnaire study in which both females and males indicated greater expectancies of being touched by higher status persons, and of touching lower status and female ones, than vice versa. [20]

The other nonverbal cues by which status is indicated have likewise not been adequately researched—for humans. But O'Connor argues that many of the gestures of dominance and submission that have been noted in the primates are equally present in humans. [21] They are used to maintain and reinforce the status hierarchy by reassuring those of higher status that those of lower status accept their place in the human pecking order.

The most studied nonverbal communication among humans is probably eye contact, and here too one finds a sex difference. It has repeatedly been found that women look more at another in a dyad than men do. [22] Exline, Gray, and Schuette suggest that "willingness to engage in mutual visual interaction is more characteristic of those who are oriented towards inclusive and affectionate interpersonal relations," [23] but Rubin concludes that while "gazing may serve as a vehicle of emotional expression for women, [it] in addition may allow women to obtain cues from their male partners concerning the appropriateness of their behavior." [24] This interpretation is supported by Efran and Broughton's data showing that even male subjects "maintain more eye contact with individuals toward whom they have developed higher expectancies for social approval." [25]

Another possible reason why women gaze more at men is that men talk more, [26] and there is a tendency for the listener to look more at the speaker than vice versa. [27]

It is especially illuminating to look at the power relationships established and maintained by the manipulation of eye contact. The mutual glance can be seen as a sign of union, but when intensified into a stare it may become a way of doing battle. [28] Research reported by Ellsworth, Carlsmith, and Henson supports the notion that the stare can be interpreted as an aggressive gesture. These authors write, "Staring at humans can elicit the same sort of responses that are common in primates; that is, staring can act like a primate threat display." [29]

Though women engage in mutual visual interaction in its intimate form to a high degree, they may back down when looking becomes a gesture of dominance. O'Connor [30] points out, "The direct stare or glare is a common human gesture of dominance. Women use the gesture as well as men, but often in modified form. While looking directly at a man, a woman usually has her head slightly tilted, implying the beginning of a presenting gesture or enough submission to render the stare ambivalent if not actually submissive." *

---

* "Presenting" is the term for the submissive gesture seen in primates, of presenting the rump to a dominant animal; O'Connor also points out that it is a human female submissive gesture as well, seen, for example, in the can-can.

The idea that the averted glance is a gesture of submission is supported by the research of Hutt and Ounsted into the characteristic gaze aversion of autistic children. They remark that "these children were never attacked [by peers] despite the fact that to a naive observer they appeared to be easy targets; this indicated that their gaze aversion had some signalling function similar to 'facing away' in the kittiwake or 'head-flagging' in the herring gull—behavior patterns which Tinbergen has termed 'appeasement postures.' In other words, gaze aversion inhibited any aggressive or threat behavior on the part of other conspecifics." [31]

Gestures of dominance and submission can be verbal as well as nonverbal. In fact, the sheer use of verbalization is a form of dominance because it can quite literally render someone speechless by preventing one from "getting a word in edgewise." As noted earlier, contrary to popular myth, men do talk more than women, both in single-sex and in mixed-sex groups. Within a group a major means of asserting dominance is to interrupt. Those who want to dominate others interrupt more; those speaking will not permit themselves to be interrupted by their inferiors, but they will give way to those they consider their superiors. Zimmerman and West found in a sample of 11 natural conversations between women and men that 46 of the 48 interruptions were by males. [32]

Other characteristics of persons in inferior status positions are the tendencies to hesitate and apologize, often offered as submissive gestures in the face of threats or potential threats. If staring directly, pointing, and touching can be subtle nonverbal threats, the corresponding gestures of submission seem to be lowering the eyes from another's gaze, falling silent (or not speaking at all) when interrupted or pointed at, and cuddling to the touch. Many of these nonverbal gestures of submission are familiar. They are the traits our society assigns as desirable secondary characteristics of the female role. Girls who have properly learned to be "feminine" have learned to lower their eyes, remain silent, back down, and cuddle at the appropriate times. There is even a word for this syndrome that is applied only to females: coy.

In verbal communication one finds a similar pattern of differences between the sexes. As mentioned earlier, men have the privilege of swearing, and hence access to a vocabulary not customarily available to women. On the surface this seems like an innocuous limitation, until one realizes the psychological function of swearing: it is one of the most harmless and effective ways of expressing anger. The alternatives are to express one's feelings with physical violence or to suppress them and by so doing turn one's anger in on oneself. The former is prohibited to both sexes (to different degrees) but the latter is decisively encouraged in women. The result is that women are "intropunitive"; they punish themselves for their own anger rather than somehow dissipating it. Since anger turned inward is commonly viewed as the basis for depression, we should not be surprised that depression is considerably more common in women than in men, and in fact is the most prevalent form of "mental illness" among women. Obviously, the causes of female depression are complex. [33]

Swearing is only the most obvious sex difference in language. Key has noted that sex differences are to be found in phonological, semantic, and grammatical aspects of language as well as in word use. [34] In one example, Austin has commented that "in our culture little boys tend to be nasal . . . and little girls, oral," but that in the "final stages" of courtship the voices of both men and women are low and nasal. [35] The pattern cited by Brown, [36] in which the form appropriately used by status superiors is used between status equals in intimate situations, is again visible: in the intimate situation the female adopts the vocal style of the male.

In situations where intimacy is not a possible interpretation, it is not power but abnormality that is the usual interpretation. Female voices are expected to be soft and quiet—even when men are using loud voices. Yet it is only the "lady" whose speech is refined. Women who do not fit this stereotype are often called loud—a word commonly applied derogatorily to other minority groups or out-groups. [37] One of the most popular derogatory terms for women is "shrill," which, after all, simply means loud (out of place) and high-pitched (female).

In language, as in touch and most other aspects of interpersonal behavior, status differences between the sexes mean that the same traits are differently interpreted when displayed by each sex. A man's behavior toward a woman might be interpreted as an expression of either power or intimacy, depending on the situation. When the same behavior is engaged in by a woman and directed toward a man, it is interpreted only as a gesture of intimacy — and intimacy between the sexes is always seen as sexual in nature. Because our society's values say that women should not have power over men, women's nonverbal communication is rarely interpreted as an expression of power. If the situation precludes a sexual interpretation, women's assumption of the male prerogative is dismissed as deviant (castrating, domineering, unfeminine, or the like).*

Of course, if women do not wish to be classified either as deviant or as perpetually sexy, then they must persist in playing the proper role by following the interpersonal behavior pattern prescribed for them. Followed repeatedly, these patterns function as a means of control. What is merely habitual is often seen as desirable. The more men and women interact in the way they have been trained to from birth without considering the meaning of what they do, the more they become dulled to the significance of their actions. Just as outsiders observing a new society are more aware of the status differences of that society than its members are, so those who play the sexual politics of interpersonal behavior are usually not conscious of what they do. Instead they continue to wonder that feminists make such a mountain out of such a "trivial" molehill.          [1979]

### NOTES

1. M. Argyle, V. Salter, H. Nicholson, M. Williams, and P. Burgess, "The Communication of Inferior and Superior Attitudes by Verbal and Non-verbal Signals," *British Journal of Social and Clinical Psychology,* 9 (1970), 222–31.
2. Goffman, "The Nature of Deference and Demeanor," *American Anthropologist,* 58 (1956), 473–502.

---

*We are not suggesting that just because certain gestures associated with males are responded to as powerful, women should automatically adopt them. Rather than accepting male values without question, individual women will want to consider what they wish to express and how, and will determine whether to adopt particular gestures or to insist that their own be responded to appropriately meanwhile.

3. R. Brown, *Social Psychology* (Glencoe, Ill.: Free Press, 1965). See also R. Brown and M. Ford, "Address in American English," *Journal of Abnormal and Social Psychology,* 62 (1961), 375–85; R. Brown and A. Gilman, "The Pronouns of Power and Solidarity," in T. A. Sebeak, ed., *Style in Language* (Cambridge, Mass.: M.I.T. Press, 1960).
4. Brown, *Social Psychology,* pp. 92–97.
5. W. L. O'Neill, *Everyone Was Brave: The Rise and Fall of Feminism* (Chicago: Quadrangle, 1969), p. 270.
6. S. M. Jourard and P. Lasakow, "Some Factors in Self-Disclosure," *Journal of Abnormal and Social Psychology,* 56 (1958), 91–98.
7. D. I. Slobin, S. H. Miller, and L. W. Porter, "Forms of Address and Social Relations in a Business Organization," *Journal of Personality and Social Psychology,* 8 (1968), 289–93.
8. E. A. Ross, *Principles of Sociology* (New York: Century, 1921), p. 136.
9. W. W. Waller and R. Hill, *The Family: A Dynamic Interpretation* (New York: Dryden, 1951), p. 191.
10. R. Sommer, *Personal Space* (Englewood Cliffs, N.J.: Prentice-Hall, 1969), Chap. 2.
11. F. N. Willis, Jr., "Initial Speaking Distance as a Function of the Speakers' Relationship," *Psychonomic Science,* 5 (1966), 221–22.
12. S. Goldberg and M. Lewis, "Play Behavior in the Year-old Infant: Early Sex Differences," *Child Development,* 40 (1969), 21–31.
13. M. Lewis, "Parents and Children: Sex-role Development," *School Review,* 80 (1972), 229–40.
14. S. M. Jourard, "An Exploratory Study of Body Accessibility," *British Journal of Social and Clinical Psychology,* 5 (1966), 221–31.
15. S. M. Jourard and J. E. Rubin, "Self-Disclosure and Touching: A Study of Two Modes of Interpersonal Encounter and Their Interrelation," *Journal of Humanistic Psychology,* 8 (1968), 39–48.
16. Jourard, "Exploratory Study," p. 224.
17. Jourard and Rubin, "Self-Disclosure and Touching," p. 47.
18. Lewis, "Parents and Children," p. 237.
19. N. Henley, "The Politics of Touch," American Psychological Association, 1970. In P. Brown ed., *Radical Psychology* (New York: Harper & Row, 1973).
20. N. Henley, *Body Politics: Sex, Power and Nonverbal Communication* (Englewood Cliffs, N.J.: Prentice-Hall, 1977).
21. L. O'Connor, "Male Dominance: The Nitty Gritty of Oppression," *It Ain't Me Babe,* 1 (1970), 9.
22. R. Exline, "Explorations in the Process of Person Perception: Visual Interaction in Relation to Competition, Sex, and Need for Affiliation," *Journal of Personality,* 31 (1963), 1–20; R. Exline, D. Gray, and D. Schutte, "Visual Behavior in a Dyad as Affected by Interview Control and Sex of Respondent," *Journal of Personality and Social Psychology,* 1, (1965), 201–09; and Z. Rubin, "Measurement of Romantic Love," *Journal of Personality and Social Psychology,* 16 (1970), 265–73.
23. Exline, Gray, and Schuette, "Visual Behavior in a Dyad," p. 207.

24. Rubin, "Measurement of Romantic Love," p. 272.
25. J. S. Efran and A. Broughton, "Effect of Expectancies for Social Approval on Visual Behavior," *Journal of Personality and Social Psychology,* 4 (1966), p. 103.
26. M. Argyle, M. Lalljee, and M. Cook, "The Effects of Visibility on Interaction in a Dyad," *Human Relations,* 21 (1968), 3–17.
27. Exline, Gray, and Schuette, "Visual Behavior in a Dyad."
28. Exline, "Explorations in the Process of Person Perception."
29. P. C. Ellsworth, J. M. Carlsmith, and A. Henson, "The Stare as a Stimulus to Flight in Human Subjects: A Series of Field Experiments," *Journal of Personality and Social Psychology,* 21 (1972), p. 310.
30. O'Connor, "Male Dominance."
31. C. Hutt and C. Ounsted, "The Biological Significance of Gaze Aversion with Particular Reference to the Syndrome of Infantile Autism," *Behavioral Science,* 11 (1966), p. 154.
32. D. Zimmerman and C. West, "Sex Roles, Interruptions and Silences in Conversation," in B. Thorne and N. Henley, *Language and Sex* (Rowley, Mass.: Newbury House, 1975).
33. For more on this see P. B. Bart, "Depression in Middle-aged Women," in V. Gornick and B. K. Moran, *Woman in Sexist Society* (New York: Basic Books, 1971); and P. Chesler, *Women and Madness* (New York: Doubleday, 1972).
34. See also M. R. Key, *Male/Female Language* (Metuchen, N.J.: Scarecrow, 1975); R. Lakoff, *Language and Woman's Place* (New York: Harper & Row, 1975); C. Miller and K. Swift, *Words and Women* (New York: Doubleday, 1976); B. Thorne and N. Henley, *Language and Sex: Difference and Dominance* (Rowley, Mass.: Newbury House, 1975).
35. W. M. Austin, "Some Social Aspects of Paralanguage," *Canadian Journal of Linguistics,* 11 (1965), pp. 34, 37.
36. Brown, *Social Psychology.*
37. Austin, "Some Social Aspects of Paralanguage," p. 38.

## 🦎 26

# *Teen Mags: How to Get a Guy, Drop 20 Pounds, and Lose Your Self-Esteem*

ANASTASIA HIGGINBOTHAM

I used to be the teen magazine market's ideal consumer: vain, terribly insecure, white, and middle class. I craved affection and approval from boys (often at the expense of meaningful relationships with girls), spent far too much time staring at myself in the mirror, and trusted the magazines' advice on all sorts of really, really important issues, like lip gloss and *luv.*

I plastered my family's refrigerator with pictures of models I'd torn out of *YM, Seventeen, Sassy,* and *'Teen,* and also *Vogue, Cosmopolitan,* and *Mademoiselle*—a strategy I used to remind me not to eat. I hoped they would inspire me to do great things, like be in a David Lee Roth video. I wish I were kidding.

Though this characterization might lead you to believe I was kind of a doorknob, I assure you I was merely acting like most girls my age at whom these magazines are directed, aspiring to an ideal that I knew would bring me much success in the social world. In my first 14 years, I learned that the pretty girl who knows how to play the game wins the prize. The "prize" being older, cooler, all-star boyfriends, multiple mentions and pictures throughout the school yearbook, and seasonal dubbings as makeshift teen royalty (Homecoming Queen, May Queen, blow-job queen, and so on). And so I absorbed the rules of the game, with teen magazines serving as a reliable source of that information.

Ten years later, I pore over these magazines to see what they're telling girls today. As I flip through the pages of *YM, Seventeen, Sassy,* and *'Teen,* my blood begins to boil and my eyes cloud with anger: teen magazines make millions off of girls by assuming that girls need improving, and then telling girls how to make themselves prettier, cooler, and better. Has anything changed?

As horrified as I am by these magazines, I cannot deny their raging success. *Seventeen* and *YM* (which used to stand for *Young Miss* and now stands for *Young and Modern*) rake in nearly two million subscriptions each from their teen-to-early-twenties market. *'Teen* and *Sassy,* with readerships of 1.3 million and 800,000 respectively, cater to the younger end of the spectrum.

In each of the magazines, cover lines offer the girls "Model hair: how to get it," "Boy-magnet beauty," "Your looks: what they say about you," and "Mega makeovers: go from so-so to supersexy." Their image of the ideal girl is evidenced by the cover models: white, usually blond, and invariably skinny.

When I asked why this is, Caroline Miller, editor in chief of *Seventeen,* explained, "There's a traditional expectation that African Americans don't sell magazines." *Seventeen* has recently tested this proposition (which, by the way, fails to address the invisibility of Asian and Native American models) by featuring pop star Brandy on its April cover and another African American model on October's cover (both months' are normally hot sellers). October sold just as well as the typical white-model cover, while the Brandy cover was possibly *Seventeen*'s best-selling April issue ever. Despite *Seventeen*'s success, rather than jeopardize newsstand sales and advertising dollars, well-intentioned editors at other magazines like *'Teen* and *Sassy* compromise by featuring some white-looking black model in a month that typically has the worst sales. Meanwhile, *YM* would probably be satisfied with a different shot of Drew Barrymore each month.

In the wake of *Sassy*'s transmogrification from bold, feminist teen mag into dumbed-down, superficial teen rag (*Sassy* was sold to Peterson Publishing, the same company that owns *'Teen*, in December 1994 after years of controversy with advertisers and parents over its content), *Seventeen,* under Miller, has taken up the *Sassy* mantle with smart stories about interracial dating, student activists, and African American girls' body image. *YM*, on the other hand, offers nothing more than bullshit and bad advice, and *'Teen* is not much better. The new *Sassy* lacks much of the brains, courage, and wit of the old *Sassy;* something that its editors, tragically, see as a good thing.

Just what are the messages in the teen magazines? A series of catch-22s—ugliness is next to nothingness and a girl with insufficient interest in boys is referred to as a "deserted island," yet one who is too sexy is also in trouble. For instance, April 1995 *Sassy* warns girls to watch who they flirt with because men cannot distinguish between harmless flirting and a full-on pass. According to *Sassy*, while a girl is flirting, "there's always a chance [men are] wondering what you look like without your clothes on." This mentality is used to justify the behavior of grown men who "get a little carried away sometimes" and harass, insult, and assault young women. A girl who bears the responsibility of attracting every "hottie" (hot guy) on the beach, but if one of them jumps her, well then, it sucks to be her. Using *Sassy*'s logic, that girl should have known she was dealing with a potential psychopath.

*YM* echoes this sentiment in the July 1995 episode of "Love Crisis," a column in which Editor in Chief Sally Lee solves "agonizing love problems." A girl reveals that she was invited by her boyfriend to a party that turned out to be just him and his two male friends. They got her really drunk and she "ended up . . . having sex with all of them!" She writes, "I feel so dirty. . . . How could I have been so stupid?" The letter is signed "Mortified." *YM* apparently wonders the same thing: a caption on the page with her letter reads "Wake up and face the facts: you made a pretty big mistake." Lee then chastises the girl for underage drinking and not asserting herself.

Even if the girl has not actually been gang-raped, Lee's complete disregard for a girl who was tricked and humiliated by her boyfriend and his friends is unforgivable. *YM* shamelessly promotes boy-catching tactics with articles like "the ultimate get-a-guy guide," then acts surprised, even judgmental, when the tricks actually work. Girls are bombarded with messages about the thrill of catching boys, so why is it shocking when a girl's pursuit includes a little creative compromise, like forgiving her boyfriend for lying about the party, drinking when he tells her to drink, and being too drunk to care (or too drunk to resist) when he and his friends fuck her? *YM* shows girls 100 asinine ways to be supersexy and then provides them with no follow-up skills, self-defense, or self-esteem—as if ignorance will keep them from going all the way. If *YM* ever changes its name again, I suggest *Dicktease*.

Likewise, when it comes to body image, teen magazines send a convoluted message. Girls are encouraged to love their bodies, no matter what they look like, by magazines with fashion spreads featuring only stick-thin, flawless-faced white models in expensive outfits. Granted, there is that one light-skinned black girl in every fashion layout. But she's just as thin as the white girl standing next to her, and that white girl is *always* there—like a chaperone. Like it's the white girl's responsibility to keep the black girl in line, make sure she doesn't mingle with other black folks, start a riot or something. The black model doesn't have any black girlfriends; she's lucky if she gets a similarly nonthreatening black boyfriend for the prom. Maybe they think if they surround her with enough white people no one will even notice she's black.

The thin factor is equally dismaying. While the old *Sassy* strictly enforced a no-diet policy, forbidding publication of any and all diet advice (including the kind masquerading as a fitness article), the new *Sassy* eats it up. Catherine Ettlinger, until recently the editorial director of the new *Sassy*, rejects the connection between articles offering diet tips and girls' obsession with thinness: "We present them with options. 'If you want to eat more low-fat stuff, here's some information; if you don't, fine.'"

If it were that simple, girls would not be getting sick. In a culture that all but demands that a women weigh no more than 120 pounds, girls do not want for diet advice. Girls do not need more low-fat options, nor do they need to learn how to shed or hide "excess fat." Similarly, when *'Teen, YM,* and *Seventeen* take a turn on the self-love/body-pride trip, they tend to fall flat on their faces. Photos that accompany the stories typically depict a model—who isn't the least bit fat. Readers are supposed to empathize with girls who weigh 125 pounds but who are afraid to put on a bathing suit, exposing what they perceive to be huge thighs and bulging stomachs. Girls are reminded that because of their "low self-esteem" (certainly not because of patriarchy), they imagine their bodies to be much larger than they actually are. So, if they can get over that self-esteem thing and realize that they're not fat, they have nothing to worry about.

While body hatred of this type is epidemic, presenting body image as being about thin girls who think they're fat does nothing to undermine the essential prejudice against fatness, especially fat women. Is a fat girl beautiful? Should she worry? If she relies on these magazines for affirmation of her self-worth, yes, she should. And so should we.

Teen magazines' glorification of boy-focused, looks-based, prom-obsessed idiocy reinforces every negative stereotype that has ever been used to justify—and ensure—women's second-class status. But as a woman with very clear memories of high school, I understand the trauma associated with fitting in and finding love. I was not prepared for a feminist revolution at 16; I could barely deal with what the humidity did to my hair.

I wanted to find out what girls think about teen magazines nowadays, so I staged an informal survey with a group of teenagers and showed them issues of *'Teen, Sassy, Seventeen,* and *YM.* Some girls criticized the magazines for being too white, too into skinny, and too superficial, but readily admitted to delighting in them anyway.

Kate Stroup from Philadelphia subscribes to *Seventeen,* as well as to various "adult" fashion magazines. "I like the ads," she says. Stroup and her friends can spend hours looking at the pictures, talking about the articles, "even talking about how bad it is." She explains, "It gives us something to bond over."

Girls looking for something easy and entertaining are sure to find it within the pages of teen magazines. Just as I lapped up celebrity gossip while researching this story, the girls I spoke with see no harm in learning a stupid hair trick.

Some girls read them for tips on navigating the social scene and dealing with relationships. "Sometimes I like to read about what guys say, not saying that I would actually follow their advice," says Kenya Hooks of Memphis.

But Roshanda Betts from Dallas no longer reads teen magazines. "I can't relate to them and I don't really think that they're made for me," she says, referring to the unrealistic size requirements for girls, racist definitions of beauty, and what she sees as the magazines' self-contradictions. "They have articles talking about, 'You should love yourself for who you are,' and then they have the seven-day diet."

The girls all like *Seventeen*'s "School Zone," which each month features six pages of photos and quotes from a different high school and which, according to Betts, "shows the spectrum of what's really happening." It's the only place in any of the magazines where kids from various racial and ethnic backgrounds, with "imperfect" shapes and "flawed" complexions, are portrayed in all their splendor. "School Zone" puts the rest of the images in the magazine to shame merely by providing a glimpse of truth.

In the articles, reality often comes in the form of "real-life stories" injected into each magazine, it seems, to scare the hell out of the girl reading it. We can choose from "one girl's battle with depression," another's physically abusive relationship, the story of a woman who sank to 55 pounds, a girl who was "raped, shot, and left for dead," and many more. Without some analysis or a context in which to place these stories (Why did she starve herself? How can we avert these tragedies?), they are nothing more than tales of tabloid horror.

Several months' worth of 'Teen, Seventeen, YM and Sassy left me with a blur of contradictory messages about how to navigate life as an adolescent girl. The sum of it is this: be pretty, but not so pretty that you intimidate boys, threaten other girls, or attract inappropriate suitors, such as teachers, bosses, fathers, and rapists; be smart, but not so smart that you intimidate boys or that, god forbid, you miss the prom to study for finals; be athletic, but no so athletic that you intimidate boys or lead people to believe that you are aggressive, asexual, or (gasp!) a lesbian or bisexual; be happy with yourself, but not if you're fat, ugly, poor, gay, disabled, antisocial, or can't at least pass as white.

The creators of teen magazines claim to reflect the reality of girls' lives; they say that they're giving girls what the girls say they want and, I'm sure that sometimes what girls want is, in fact, a new hairstyle and a prom date. But filling girls full of fluff and garbage—under the pretense that this is their reality—is patronizing, cowardly, and just plain lazy. Magazines that pride themselves on teaching girls beauty tips to "hide what they hate" ought to stop reflecting a reality marred by heterosexist double standards and racist ignorance and start changing it.

I understand the tremendous pressures that editors deal with from parents and advertisers who hold pristine ideas about teendom and girlhood and impose those ideas backed by the mighty dollar. But it's very clear where these editors and advertisers draw their lines. If they really wanted girls to love their bodies, they'd give them a few more shapes and colors to choose from, they'd provide articles exploring some of the real reasons why a girl might plow through a box of Oreos one moment, yak her guts out the next, and then zone in front of the television for sixteen hours a day. If they can be so brazen about teaching a girl how to kiss the boy of her dreams, they can teach her how to kiss a girl. They just won't.                                                    [1996]

 27

# Media Images, Feminist Issues

DEBORAH L. RHODE

For those committed to feminism, a central concern has always been how the media reflect and recast feminist issues. For those committed to feminist research, media studies offer a particularly useful perspective on the social construction of a political movement. Indeed, even formulating this topic as a research question yields unexpected insights. In the *Readers' Guide to Periodical Literature*, "feminism" traditionally has not been significant enough to warrant a separate entry. In the listings for the 1950s, the feminist heading has only a cross-reference to "Women, social and moral questions." This entry lists a handful of articles and a "see also" reference to alcoholism, divorce, harem, and prostitution. Over the next two decades, these cross-references expand and eventually come to include "Women, equal rights." But it is not until the early eighties that feminism becomes a topic heading in its own right.

The following discussion chronicles this evolution and certain persistent limitations in media texts and subtexts. The basic story is one of partial progress. Over the last quarter century, much has improved in press portraits of feminism, feminists, and gender-related issues. Yet much still needs improvement. This article suggests what and why. At issue is what the media choose to present (or not to present) as news about women and how they characterize (or caricature) the women's movement. This issue deserves greater attention from those interested in social movements in general and the women's movement in particular. The press is increasingly responsible for supplying the information and images through which we understand our lives (Hall 1977, 340–42). For any social movement, the media play a crucial role in shaping public consciousness and public policy. Journalists' standard framing devices of selection, exclusion, emphasis, and tone can profoundly affect cultural perceptions (Gitlin 1980, 3–7; Goffman 1974, 10–11).

For the contemporary women's movement, mass communications networks have done much both to frustrate and to advance feminist objectives. As subsequent discussion suggests, the mainstream press appeared largely uninterested or unsympathetic during the movement's early years. And female journalists often lacked the critical mass and professional leverage to ensure systematic, even-handed treatment of gender-related issues. That has changed dramatically in recent years, in part because of women's increasing involvement in the media and in part because of broader cultural changes in gender roles. As media theorists remind us, audiences always exert some control over the message they receive, and the public's growing concern about women's issues has reshaped popular discourse (Rapping 1993; 1994, 10–12, 284). The press is increasingly an ally in making those issues into political priorities.

However, despite substantial improvements, we still remain stuck in some familiar places. The discussion that follows identifies persistent feminist concerns. Analysis focuses on the absence of women: their underrepresentation in positions of influence; and the not-so-benign neglect of women's issues. By gaining a better understanding of how media images construct and constrain feminist objectives, we may come closer to realizing them.

## NEGLECT

### Underrepresentation of Women

The frequent absence of women in, on, and behind the news has been chronicled at length elsewhere and does not require extended treatment here. A few illustrative statistics reveal the gaps in women's

representation and in the coverage of women's issues, as well as the relationship between the two. In the late 1940s, only one female journalist appeared on any television news. By 1960, the number had increased to one per network. These female reporters handled "women's" stories, such as those involving political wives, and sometimes filled in as weather girls (Marzolf 1993, 33, 36–44). In the print media, the small group of female journalists generally had a separate, and anything but equal, status. Most were relegated to work as researchers rather than writers or to positions on the women's page, traditionally limited to food, fashion, furnishings, and society "dots and doings" (Ross 1974; Davis 1991, 110–11; Robertson 1992; Beasley and Gibbons, 1993; 16; Mills 1993; Quindlen 1993a, 2). The absence of women on news staffs typified broader patterns from prime-time drama to children's cartoons (Tuchman 1978, 8–10; Robertson 1992, 7, 181).

During the 1960s, the situation began to improve, in response both to the feminist movement and to the broader socioeconomic changes that the movement reflected and reinforced. Between the mid-1960s and the early 1990s, women's representation among television network news reporters rose from under 5 percent to over 15 percent, and among print journalists it increased from under 20 percent to almost 40 percent (Marzolf 1993, 43). Female representation also grew to some 68 percent of journalism school graduates (Marzolf 1993, 43). Yet women in the media continue to be grossly underrepresented in positions of greatest status and power and dramatically overrepresented in the lowest. Women account for less than 10 percent of editors-in-chief, news publishers, and deans or directors of journalism programs (Mills 1993, 19, 25; Otto 1993, 157–58). A recent survey of newspapers and network news programs found that men wrote about two-thirds of the front-page stories and provided 85 percent of the television reporting (Bridge 1993). Women of color are even less visible. They account for only about 7 percent of the newspaper workforce and 3 percent of its executives and managers. In the broadcast media, representative studies from the early 1990s found that women of color filed only 2 percent of the total surveyed stories and that no nonwhite women figured in an annual survey of the fifty most prominent reporters (Beasley and Gibbons 1993, 307, 317).

Once again, these gender imbalances in journalism are symptomatic of broader media patterns. Men hold 90 percent of upper-level Hollywood executive positions, play two-thirds of the leads in prime-time television, supply 90 percent of the narrator's voices in television commercials, and monopolize 90 percent of televised sporting events (Lovdal 1989, 716; Dutka 1990, 8; Carmody 1993, B12; Messner, Duncan, and Jensen 1993). Rarely do women of color exceed what is commonly described as a "sprinkling of minorities" (Edwards 1993, 215–18); Minnesota Advisory committee 1993, 5–7; Women, Men and the Media 1993).

## Inattention to Women and "Women's Issues"

The inadequate representation of women in media decision making is mirrored in the media's inadequate representation of women's perspectives and concerns. In recent surveys, men provided 85 percent of newspaper quotes or references, accounted for 75 percent of the television interviewees, and constituted 90 percent of the most frequently cited pundits (Bridge 1993; O'Reilly 1993, 127, 129). This proportionality, or lack thereof, held up across subject matter areas, even on issues that centrally involved women, such as breast implants (Douglas 1992; Bridge 1993; O'Reilly 1993, 125, 127). During the much-fabled "Year of the Woman" in politics, not one representative of a major women's policy organization appeared on any leading TV talk show (Wolf 1993, 80). Despite increased efforts at token representation, all-male talk shows persist even on topics like single motherhood (Pollitt 1994). When women commentators do appear, it is often on explicitly "women's issues." How often, asks Katha Pollitt, do women show up on *Nightline* or *Crossfire* when the subject is not "Hillary Clinton: Does Whitewater Stigmatize All Women?" or "Is the Wonderbra Sexist?" (quoted in Pollitt 1994, 409). Female commentators who write on general topics often remain in the Rolodex under "F"; "as St. Augustine put it, men need women only for the

things they can't get from a man" (Pollitt 1993, 409). The result is much as Kirk Anderson portrays it in his cartoon of a talk show anchor stating that, "in the next half-hour, my wealthy white conservative male friends and I will discuss the annoyingly persistent black underclass, and why women get so emotional about abortion" (Ward, 1993, 192).

Women's issues are also underrepresented in the mainstream media (Kahn and Goldenberg 1991, 105–7). To be sure, the situation has improved dramatically since the 1960s and early 1970s, when leading papers rarely discussed matters such as child care and domestic violence or did so only in the "style" section (Quindlen 1993a, 3). Coverage has steadily increased, and dramatic events like the Hill-Thomas hearings or the Tailhook scandal can create a sudden cottage industry of commentary on issues that for centuries had gone unchallenged and unchanged. But on a day-to-day basis, gender biases remain. Subjects that are of greater interest to male than female readers have greater priority among largely male editors. Topics with the most appeal to men but the least to women, such as local sports, obtain substantially greater newspaper resources than topics for which the relative interest levels are reversed, such as fashion or lifestyle issues (Miller 1993, 167–68).

Issues of particular concern to women of color are often ignored, as are the women themselves. For example, despite the prominent role that black female politicians played during the 1992 Democratic National Convention, few appeared in media coverage (Women, Men, and the Media 1993). "How Can 29 Million People Be Invisible to Democrats?" asked a recent *Los Angeles Times* headline, referring to the Latino population. The same question could have been asked about the author's own profession, which rarely focuses on that constituency (Rogovin 1992, 51, 55–58; Minnesota Advisory Committee 1993, 5–7; Women, Men and the Media 1993).

What coverage does occur often presents biased images. The mainstream media prefer to center stories on deviance rather than on achievements or victimization among people of color and to explain such deviance in terms of race rather than other, more complicated factors (Minnesota Advisory Committee 1993, 5–7). For example, rapes of white women by black men receive a grossly disproportionate amount of media attention, although they account for only a small minority of reported rapes. Sexual assaults against black women are largely overlooked, even though this is the group likeliest to be victims of such brutality (Benedict 1992, 9). During the week of the highly publicized rape of a white investment banker in Central Park by a nonwhite gang, twenty-eight other women in New York also reported rapes. Nearly all of these were women of color, and their assaults, including at least one of comparable brutality, went largely unreported by the press (Benedict 1992, 219; Terry 1993, 160).

Moreover, despite the enormous volume of commentary attempting to account for the Central Park rape, the most obvious gender-related explanations were notable for their absence. Almost all the coverage focused on race and poverty; almost none surveyed the research on gang rape, which reveals that such crimes are frequently committed by white middle-class athletes and fraternity members. As sociologist Jane Hood put it, "Like the proverbial fish who cannot describe water, Americans see everything but gender at work in the [New York] assault. Given more than 30 years of research on rape, that myopia is hard to explain" (quoted in Benedict 1992, 210).

Any adequate explanation would have to include the media's own selective vision. In Helen Benedict's recent survey, only one of some thirty reporters who routinely covered sex crimes had ever read a book on rape and few had made any effort to consult experts (Benedict, in press, 7). Indeed, many defended their inattention. According to one *Newsday* editor, attempts to analyze sexual brutality are "thumbsucking journalism. . . . Once you write a piece about rape experts talking about why people do a gang rape, there's no follow-up" (quoted in Benedict, in press, 3). In explaining the *New York Times*'s selective coverage of the Central Park rape, the metropolitan editor acknowledged, "I can't imagine the range of reaction to the sexual aspect of the crime would be very strong. I may be wrong but I can't think right off what questions one ought to ask about that" (quoted in Benedict, in press, 3).

Efforts to increase the coverage of women's perspectives are often met with confession and avoidance. The standard response, reflected in one recent interview with a *New Republic* editor, is that "it's really hard to get women; regrettably, writers of opinion pieces tend to be men" (quoted in Wolf 1993, 84). If so, the media are in part responsible. Female journalists frequently bump up against what Anna Quindlen describes as the "quota of one" (Quindlen 1993a, 12). In explaining their unwillingness to carry a column by a woman who writes about women, editors will note that they "already have one" (O'Reilly 1993, 125; Quindlen 1993a, 12). This somehow turns out not to be a problem for columns by and about white men. It is the notion of women pontificating, and not just about women, that seems to be the problem (O'Reilly 1993, 125–26).

The marginalization of women occurs not only through failure to represent their perspectives but also through failure to recognize them as independent agents, apart from their relation to men. This symbolic erasure was apparent in television descriptions of ethnic cleansing in Bosnia, in which the subjects of gang rape figured as wives and daughters (Ward 1993, 190). Like early English common law, which treated rape as a crime against men's property interest, some contemporary media accounts carry similar subtexts: "Five [males] broke into the home of a . . . school teacher, beat him, raped his wife, and looted everything they could find" (Beasley and Gibbons 1993, 34). Similarly, a recent newspaper headline—"Widow, 70, Dies after Beating by Intruder"—reflects the significance of women's marital status even after death (Ward 1993, 191). Other information, such as the victim's work as a crime prevention volunteer, is of less apparent importance. Such persistent value hierarchies are aptly captured in a recent Cath Jackson cartoon. It features a male editor lecturing a female staffer on the obvious problems with an article titled "Wheelchair Woman Climbs Mt. Everest": "You've missed the main points: WHO is her husband? WHAT does he do? WHERE would she be without him and WHY isn't she at home looking after the kids?" (Jackson 1993, 4).                                          [1995]

## REFERENCES

Beasley, Maurine H., and Shiela J. Gibbons. 1993. *Taking Their Place: A Documentary History of Women and Journalism.* Washington, D.C.: American University Press.

Benedict, Helen. 1992. *Virgin or Vamp: How the Press Covers Sex Crimes.* New York: Oxford University Press.

———. In press. "Covering Rape without Feminism." In *Women and Law in the Media,* ed. Martha Fineman. New York: Routledge.

Bridge, M. Junior. 1993. "The News: Looking Like America? Not Yet. . . ." In *Women, Men and Media.* Los Angeles: Center for Women, Men, and the Media.

Carmody, John. 1993. "Minorities Still Shut Out Survey Reports." *Washington Post,* June 16, B12.

Davis, Flora. 1991. *Moving the Mountain: The Women's Movement in America since 1960.* New York: Simon & Schuster.

Douglas, Susan J. 1992. "Missing Voices: Women and the U.S. News Media." *Fairness and Accuracy in Reporting Extra* (Special Issue), 4.

Dutka, Elaine. 1990. "Women and Hollywood: It's Still a Lousy Relationship." *Los Angeles Times,* November 11, Calendar, 8.

Edwards, Audrey. 1993. "From Aunt Jemima to Anita Hill: Media's Split Image of Black Women." *Media Studies Journal,* vol. 7.

Gitlin, Tod. 1980. *The Whole World Is Watching.* Berkeley and Los Angeles: University of California Press.

Goffman, Irving. 1974. *Frame Analysis: An Essay on the Organization of Experience.* New York: Harper & Row.

Hall, Stuart. 1977. "Culture, Media, and the Ideological Effect." In *Mass Communication and Society,* ed. James Curran, Michael Gurevitch, and Janet Woollacott. London: Edward Arnold.

Jackson, Cath. 1993. "Trouble and Strife" (cartoon). In Caryl Rivers, "Bandwagons, Women and Cultural Mythology." *Media Studies Journal,* vol. 7.

Kahn, Kim Fridkin, and Edie N. Goldenberg. 1991. "The Media, Obstacle or Ally of Feminists." *Annals of the American Academy of Political and Social Science,* vol. 515.

Lovdal, Lynn T. 1989. "Sex-Role Messages in Televison Commercials: An Update." *Sex Roles* 21 (11–12): 715.

Marzolf, Marion Tuttle. 1993. "Deciding What's Women's News." *Media Studies Journal,* vol. 7.

Messner, Michael A., Margaret Carlisle Duncan, and Kerry Jensen. 1993. "Separating the Men from the Girls: The Gendered Language of Televised Sports." *Gender and Society,* vol. 7.

Miller, Susan. 1993. "Opportunity Squandered—Newspapers and Women's News." *Media Studies Journal,* vol. 7.

Mills, Kay. 1993. "The Media and the Year of the Woman." *Media Studies Journal,* vol. 7.

Minnesota Advisory Committee to the U.S. Commission on Civil Rights. 1993. *Stereotyping of Minorities by the News Media in Minnesota.* Washington, D.C.: Government Printing Office.

O'Reilly, Jane. 1993. "The Pale Males of Punditry." *Media Studies Journal,* vol. 7.

Otto, Jean. 1993. "A Matter of Opinion." *Media Studies Journal,* vol. 7.

*People.* 1994. "Hillary Pillary." *People,* June 20, 42.

Pollitt, Katha. 1993. "Not Just Bad Sex." *New Yorker,* October 4, 220.

———. 1994. "Subject to Debate." *The Nation,* October 17, 409.

Quindlen, Anna. (1992) 1993. "The Two Faces of Eve." In her *Thinking Out Loud,* 197. New York: Random House.

Rapping, Elayne. 1993. "Gender and Media Theory: A Critique of the 'Backlash Model.'" Unpublished manuscript, Adelphi University, Garden City, N.Y.

———. 1994. *Media-tions: Forays into the Culture and Gender Wars.* Boston: South End.

Robertson, Nan. 1992. *The Girls in the Balcony.* New York: Fawcett Columbine.

Rogovin, Wendy M. 1992. "The Regulation of Television in the Public Interest: On Creating a Parallel Universe in Which Minorities Speak and Are Heard." *Catholic Law Review,* vol. 92.

Ross, Ishbel. 1974. *The Ladies of the Press.* New York: Arno.

Terry, Don. 1993. "In the Week of an Infamous Rape, 28 Other Victims Suffer." In *Gender and Public Policy,* ed. Kenneth Winston and Mary Jo Bane. Boulder, Colo.: Westview.

Tuchman, Gaye. 1978. "Introduction: The Symbolic Annihilation of Women by the Mass Media." In *Hearth and Home: Images of Women in the Mass Media,* ed. Arlene Kaplan Daniels and Jane Benet. New York: Oxford University Press.

Ward, Jean. 1993. "Talking (Fairly) about the World: A Reprieve on Journalistic Language." *Media Studies Journal,* vol. 7.

Wolf, Naomi. 1993. *Fire with Fire.* New York: Random House.

Women, Men and the Media. 1993. "The News, As If All People Mattered." New York: Women, Men and the Media, New York University.

## 28

# Female Images and Roles in Music

VENISE T. BERRY

Music is a business. It is the business of marketing a product for profit, and research has shown that sex can sell.[1] A study by Larry Lance and Christina Berry found a significant increase between 1968 and 1977 in the number of popular songs with implications of sexual intercourse and in the number of females initiating those sexual encounters.[2]

Negative sexual images of females in the male-dominated music industry is a prominent topic of criticism. Men dominate the pop music arena, defining sex role standards from a patriarchal perspective.[3] Research indicates that in country music a woman's role and status is usually related to her ability to get and hold a man.[4] Colleen Hyden and N. Jane McCandless have found that women are typically portrayed as youthful, passive, and childlike in contemporary popular music.[5] Susan Butruille and Anita Taylor have identified three prominent female images in popular music: the ideal woman or saint; the evil/fickle witch, sinner, or whore, and the victim (usually dead). In the same study women were most often shown as sex objects, possessions, or providers in black music culture.[6]

Rock music and music videos have come under intense scrutiny. Barry Sherman and Joseph Dominick examined 366 rock music videos and found a significant amount of violence, sex, and other aggressive acts directed at women.[7] Women were also portrayed in a condescending manner in an overwhelming number of music videos examined by Richard Vincent, Dennis Davis, and Lilly Boruszkowski.[8] Christine Hansen and Ronald Hansen found in their studies that images in rock music videos suggest women are considered more nonthreatening, submissive, sexual, and sympathetic when they return the man's advances.[9] Finally, Jane Brown and Kenneth Campbell report that females, both black and white, are rarely portrayed on MTV or Video Soul as professionals; however, black women in their study were least likely to be found in roles projecting antisocial behavior or victimization.[10]

Research on the acceptance and perpetuation of stereotypical images of women in American culture is prominent and has shown that the application of gender labels and other stereotypical attributes are learned as early as the age of three.[11] Sex role stereotypes are linked to specific gender-related activities and domains, such as girls playing inside with dolls and boys outside playing with guns.[12] Many studies have illustrated the importance of gender rela-

tions and appropriate activity selection in the United States, suggesting that children are taught these roles through peer interaction, socialization, and cultural experience.[13]

Many critics have acknowledged that other music, such as the blues, reflects the sexual exploitation of women. Themes that emerged in a 1988 book about the blues by Daphne Harrison included infidelity, sexual exploitation, and mistreatment. Harrison argued that women in blues usually do not joke about lost love but instead sing of grief, while men brag about their conquests and exploits with women.[14] Mary Ellison, in her book *Lyrical Protests: Black Music's Struggle against Discrimination*, agreed. She discussed such female blues singers as Ma Rainey, Bessie Smith, and Victoria Spivey, who often sang about inadequate men, but she also found the music of female blues reflects black women's strong determination to lead their own lives.[15] Hazel Carby's analysis of the sexual politics of women's blues explained how important "classic blues" were for women: "What has been called 'Classic Blues,' is the women's blues of the twenties and early thirties. It is a discourse that articulates a cultural and political struggle over sexual relations; a struggle that is directed against the objectification of female sexuality within a patriarchal order, but which also tries to reclaim women's bodies as the sexual and sensual subjects of women's songs."[16]

The struggle for independence, equality, and freedom among black women, Ellison also pointed out, has been a part of black music styles from slavery to the present: "There is an explosive dynamism coursing through the songs that black women write specifically about themselves—a tension that springs from the determination to free themselves from male domination and misuse, conflicting with a strong resolution to stand with black men in the fight for the liberation of all black people."[17]

This spirit of rebellion and independence was a major part of music in the 1960s. Ellison observed that Aretha Franklin's popular hit "Respect," insisting that respect be given to black women and men, became a banner for the civil rights movement.[18] She also discussed other contemporary black women, like Millie Jackson and Grace Jones, who sang of independence and individuality through female role reversals.[19]

## EVOLVING RAP MUSIC STYLE

The negative images and messages concerning women in rap music have spawned tremendous publicity. As Reebee Garofalo explained, it is the frankness of rap that creates many of its problems. While making no excuses for rap stars, he suggests that the sexism in rap is a product of all genres of popular music and life in the United States.[20] Music has long been a powerful form of expression in black culture, with rap music stretching and redefining previous boundaries. Born in the New York streets of Harlem and the South Bronx, rap evolved as part of the privileged black male urban street culture, popularizing black dialect, street fashion, style, attitude, and mannerisms.

David Toop in *The Rap Attack* related the evolution of rap music to the griot in West Africa, who was a great singing storyteller and served as a living history book. He went on to link this oral genre to other powerful black traditions, like oral preaching, rhyming stories called toasts, and verbal rhyming word games, such as the "dozens" and "signifying," all popular in urban black neighborhoods and resembling the rhythmic talking style of rap. These cultural legacies were specifically black male traditions. They were a prominent part of the black male experience carried out wherever black men gathered—on street corners or in bars, the armed forces, and prisons.[21]

Male-privileged space is a primary issue for Lisa Lewis in her evaluation of female images on MTV. She explains that the street is traditionally a place for males to explore freedom, rebellious practice, male bonding, and female pursuit. For women, however, the streets are dangerous, feared, and inappropriate. Women on the street are considered prostitutes, or whores, objects of male desire and dominance.[22]

Rap music, a product of black male tradition and experience, has defined the images of women from that limited perspective. Many male rap groups tend to view women with a common lack of respect, but controversial groups like the 2 Live Crew, The Ghetto Boys, Easy E, and Too Short perpetuate extreme negatives. In many male rap videos, the female body is presented as a product of male sexual pleasure; candid shots of breasts, crotches, and buttocks are the norm. Women in these raps are called "skeezers," "hoes," "sluts," "whores," and "bitches." They are described as objects to be sexually used, physically and verbally abused.

The most controversial example is 2 Live Crew, a group whose music has killed love and romance and has taken sex into the realm of perversion, violence, and pain. Many of their song titles can serve as examples of their sexist ideology: "We Want Some Pussy," "Me So Horny," "Head, Booty, and Cock," "Bad Ass Bitch," "Face Down, Ass Up," and "Dick Almighty." The cover of their album "As Nasty as They Wanna Be" flaunts the well-endowed buttocks of four black women in G-strings standing on a table with their backs turned and legs spread. Members of the 2 Live Crew position themselves in front of the women, each centered between a pair of legs, facing the camera. Luther Campbell, leader of the group, argues that his music is no worse than the work of Eddie Murphy or Andrew Dice Clay. In his defense he explains that "bitch" is an endearing term: "We're talking about a hell of a woman who ain't gonna take shit—one of those Dynasty, Alexis type motherfuckers. That's what I like in a woman. I want me a real Bitch, not some pushover."[23]

The hearings of Parents Music Resource Center (PMRC) have led to questions of censorship; however, it must again be noted that music is a business and that sex sells. Major record companies are currently dealing with the controversy of labeling sexually explicit and violent albums as they see fit. Geffen, for example, chose to drop The Ghetto Boys because of their obscenity, while Atlantic Records, in the midst of the media controversy, purchased an interest in the 2 Live Crew's Luke Records.[24]

In the profit-oriented music industry the success of sexually explicit acts is fantastic, considering the lack of radio and television airplay. The 2 Live Crew's album *Nasty as They Wanna Be*, with no video or other major advertising, made the *Rolling Stone* top fifty album chart. Because of the controversy created in their obscenity trials, the album leaped from number forty-four to sixteen in a two-week period.[25] It also outsold the clean version, *As Clean as They Wanna Be*, by nine to one.[26]

In all fairness it should be noted there is a significant number of male rap groups that do not advocate misogyny or violence toward women. Rappers like KRS One, A Tribe Called Quest, Jungle Brothers, and De La Soul are attempting to unify rappers and rap fans through positive information and education. Positive rap efforts are bringing male and female rap stars together to speak against gang violence and black-on-black crime, while empowering the black rap community as a whole.

While it is crucial to confront the perpetuation of sexism in rap music, Lewis suggests moving away from an emphasis on male attitude and behavior and instead focusing on the powerful messages and images of today's popular female stars.[27] Women as contrasting voices, "others," have created a new dialogue in rap music, challenging those negative, male-oriented perspectives. Their music reflects the same macho style and aggressive delivery, but it includes black feminist ideology that tests the line between socially accepted male and female roles.

According to Toop, male rappers were willing to accept female rappers but considered them lacking in the competitiveness necessary to survive and succeed in rap.[28] To compete in the male-dominated music industry, women are serious and hard-hitting in their lyrics and delivery style. The stereotypical portrayals of women as weak, stupid, and sexually out of control conflict with the new identity projected by female rappers. Their lyrical story line and performance style demonstrate an unyielding intelligence and strength.

The popularity of black female rappers comes as no surprise in light of the cultural experience of black women in the United States. The foundation of black music as a spoken song has always included women. Toop describes African women who also developed cultural legacies, such as lampoons and galla abusive poems. These expressions of hostility or hate were usually sung. In this tradition the hostile words of Yoruba women became lyrical poetry. Toop also mentions other prominent black women singers who serve as evolutionary examples of the black feminine voice in African American music: Dorothy Norwood, a prominent gospel storyteller; the sermonette singer Edna Gallman Cooke; the pioneer soul rappers Laura Lee and Irma Thomas; and finally, Millie Jackson, who was dubbed the mistress of musical raps. These women have all played a crucial role in the development of the rap music genre.[29]                                       [1994]

*NOTES*

1. See, for example, Lance and Berry, "Has There Been a Sexual Revolution?"; Zillman and Mundorf, "Image Effects"; and Abramson and Mechanic, "Sex and the Media."
2. Lance and Berry, "Has There Been a Sexual Revolution?" 162.
3. Endres, "Sex Role Standards."
4. Saucier, "Healers and Heartbreakers."
5. Hyden and McCandless, "Lyrics of Contemporary Music."
6. Butruille and Taylor, "Women in American Popular Song."
7. Sherman and Dominick, "Violence and Sex in Music Videos."
8. Vincent, Davis, and Boruszkowski, "Sexism on MTV."
9. Hansen and Hansen, "Influence of Sex and Violence."
10. Brown and Campbell, "Race and Gender in Music Videos."
11. See, for example, Thompson, "Gender Labels"; Weinraub, Clemens, and Sockloff, "Development of Sex Role Stereotypes"; and Masters and Wilkerson, "Consensual and Discrimination Stereotypy."
12. See, for example, Blakemore, Larve, and Olejnik, "Sex Appropriate Toy Preference"; Eisenberg, Murray, and Hite, "Children's Reasoning"; and Ruble, Balaban, and Cooper, "Gender Constancy."
13. See, for example, Masters and Furman, "Friendship Selection"; Lamb and Roopnarine, "Peer Influences on Sex Role Development"; and Langlois and Downs, "Mothers, Fathers, and Peers as Socialization Agents."
14. Harrison, *Black Pearls*, 63–113.
15. Ellison, *Lyrical Protest*, 111.
16. Carby, "'It Jus Be's Dat Way Sometime,'" 241.
17. Ellison, *Lyrical Protest*. 107.
18. Ibid., 115.
19. Ibid., 113.
20. Garofalo, "Crossing Over," 115.
21. Toop, *Rap Attack*, 47, 94.
22. Lewis, "Female Address in Music Video," 75.
23. Quoted in Ressner, "On the Road," 20, 24.
24. See, for example, Dimartino and Rosen, "Labeling Albums," 6; and Newman, Lichtman, and Haring, "Atlantic Invests in Crew Label."
25. "Top Fifty Albums," 74.
26. Roberts-Thomas, "Say It Loud," 30.
27. Lewis, "Form and Female Authorship," 356.
28. Toop, *Rap Attack*, 94.
29. Ibid., 47–48.

🌿 **29**

# Mutineers in Mainstream Music: Heralds of a New Feminist Wave?

NAOMI WEISSTEIN

"He punched out my dog/ he totalled my van/ he beat me up/ I love my man," roared The Chicago Women's Liberation Rock Band 25 years ago, parodying the masochistic lyrics expected of girl vocalists in rock. We challenged all the demeaning imperatives for women in music. We performed at the hurricane-high of the radical second wave of feminism, and audiences danced, shouted, and sang along with our insurrection, mobbing the stage afterward, hugging us and our instruments—even our amplifiers.

In 1973 the band dissolved, and, for a long time afterward (with the splendid but marginalized exception of folkie "women's music"), female vocalists sang endless litanies of Suffering Abject Devotion to men. I despaired of the music and mourned for the politically energized audience that had resonated with our mutinous performance.

And then I could not listen at all. A catastrophic neurological illness attacked me, and for years I have lain supine in a bed without sound or light, the detritus of mass misogynist culture humming in my head.

Recently, a new anti-seizure medication has enabled me to listen again, in tiny bytes over many months—not recommended for music lovers, but it gives you plenty of time to ponder the material. What I hear astonishes me! By turns joyful, angry, moving, original, and hilarious, a cadre of folkateers, funkateers, punkateers, pop stars, rockers, and rappers have left gender church and are rebelling against the frenzied worship of men that defined female popular song for so long.

Many of the new lyrics are marvelously angry. "Did you forget about me, Mr. Duplicity?" asks Alanis Morissette in a tone-perfect shriek, ". . . I'm not gonna fade." "You thought I was a little mouse, . . . but now I'm here, burning down your house," growls Shirley Manson of Garbage. "I'm packing a rod and it's all for you," grunts mock-tough L7. ". . . fucking Napoleon," sneers Ani DiFranco. "Keep him on a leash cuz he's a D-O-G," snarl the usually amiable Salt 'n Pepa.

In these new lyrics, if men are allowed to stick around, it's on *terms:* "I need my car waxed and my floor shellac/I need my back rubbed and da bubbles in the tub," instructs hip-hopper M. C. Lyte. Lil Kim puts in her order: "No dick tonight, eat my pussy right." Even the bubblegum-feminist Spice Girls warn, "If you can't dance, . . . you can't do nothing for me."

While few musical mutineers—as I'll call them —would out themselves as "feminist" (a currently tainted word), protest against women's subjugation pervades the songs. Anti-rape: "Did she ask you for it? Did she ask you nice?" laments Courtney Love of Hole. Anti-harassment: "Who you calling bitch?" demands Queen Latifah. "Who you calling ho?" Anti-beauty traps: "You made me crazy," Kathleen Hanna of Bikini Kill shouts at her mirror. "Ugly girl . . . do you hate her?" rails Jewel.

The new lyrics do more than burn down the man's mission: they build mansions above the ruins. Defying the women-must-love-men injunction, mutineers celebrate lesbian love. "If you must dance, dance for me," funkateer Me'shell Ndegeocello begs Mary Magdalene. "I am your passion, your promise, your end," hard-rocking Melissa Etheridge resoundingly reassures her female partner.

In a stunning departure from anything that has ever gone before, female songwriters also empathically illuminate the lives of other women—clearly not themselves. Joan Osborne elegizes a homeless mother in "St. Theresa." "Lolita, go on home," Suzanne Vega advises a love-hungry teenager. In "Ordinary Morning," Sheryl Crow, the virtuoso of such empathic character sketches, imagines herself a runaway housewife-turned-hooker who is becoming psychotic: "Just an ordinary day . . . Just an ordinary woman . . . slipping away."

The phenomenon-manipulators have not ignored these feminist developments in pop music.

All year long they've been hype-ranting about "girl power," a mindless cheer that rises up equally for sales of battery-powered brassieres, lawsuits against high school dress codes, and adoration of *Titanic*'s Leonardo DiCaprio.

But what really *is* happening? Have the six megacorporations that virtually own entertainment only *now* realized that transgression is the cash crop of rock and rap and that, to reverse the current disastrous sag in music sales, they should start encouraging women to be *bad*? (Followed, of course, in five minutes, by a campaign to dress women musicians in little see-through slave uniforms and encourage them to be *good*?) Or is there such widespread resistance to the old minification that the industry is helpless to contain it?

Blind and bedridden and unable to answer this question myself, I enlisted a few pop-culture junkie friends and some old band members to help me figure this out. Their report was that *it's both*. Some mutineer women are being heavily promoted. But a new energy is also present—an explosion of youthful anti-sexist consciousness. This market empowers female rebels to kick out.

Indeed, the story of the interaction between women's musical mutiny and the passionate audience that is supporting it is almost a feminist fantasy of how political change can work.

Here is a brief history. It has always been difficult to break into rock and rap, but for women it approached impossibility. Performance tours did not include women and (except for last summer's more-timid-than mutinous but nevertheless wildly successful Lilith Fair, they still do not); labels would not sign them; and the radio would air only one woman per playlist.

Recalls Rana Ross, the bassist for Phantom Blue and Vixen (easily the decade's two tightest hard-rock girl bands), "A few years ago, a rock superstar was auditioning players. I sent in my bio and tape, but no picture. I got an excited call, but when they found out I was female, they wouldn't even let me audition. My tape was good enough, but my gender wasn't."

American history professor Rachel Devlin recounts that about ten years ago a tornado of militant feminist musicians blew away anti-woman business-as-usual. Riot Grrrls, Foxcore groups, and others organized showstring production companies and friends-of-friends distribution networks, spreading their openly confrontational music from city to city.

These independents, with their zines and punk bars, might just have ended up as another exercise in the marginality of "women's music," but—mirabile dictu!—the acts got hot. To give an example of how hot, Ani DiFranco, the most successful Indie yet, male or female, played to a sold-out crowd at Jones Beach with—zowie!—*Bob Dylan*! "[She is] One of the decade's defining voices," raved *Rolling Stone* magazine.

Mainstream mutineers followed on the heels of the Indies. "The Indies . . . influenced and set the stage for Alanis, Sheryl, and Melissa," says Devlin. Minimally, Indies influenced *some* labels to record *some* women, if only as weirdo novelty acts to revive dying revenues. Maximally, they struck forked terror into the hearts of Megalopolated Entertainment.

Ultimately, insurrection marched into mainstream music because the fans devoured it. Receipts soared. Alanis Morissette's debut album sold *15 million* units. (Platinum is a million.) Jewel's debut sold 5 million units. Erykah Badu's goodbye rap to the boyfriend ("Tyrone") got so popular with women that some black radio stations started calling it "the female national anthem." The *New York Times*, I'm told, reports that the slump in record sales was over last summer due primarily to mutineer albums.

People who have been there tell me that audiences for mutineers act more like they are at a political rally than at a mere concert. Overwhelmingly female (the ratio of girls to boys at Lilith Fair was 3 : 1), they are wildly participatory and proprietary. Fans admonish Ani DeFranco when her *attitude* decompresses.

Indeed, these audiences *are* at a political rally. Female rebels are singing to the anger, confusion, and aspirations of a generation of young women now coming of age. Despite the relentless attempt by the rest of the media to ridicule feminist ideas and raise victim blaming to religion, these young women suspect, or know already, that they live in a violent, often woman-hating world. They cannot count on lovers to love them or husbands to honor them.

Romance lies bleeding in a battered women's shelter. They seek feminist truths and female heroes, and they are finding them on the soundstages (and on the women's pro-basketball courts and at countless other female venues) across America.

My observers' reports of the intensity of the crowds reminds me—happily—of the ecstatic performance of my rock band a quarter century ago. People might call it "girl power" this time—or some other cute phrase that simultaneously trivializes, commodifies and distances it from feminism, but I believe that we are poised for a renewed surge of women's militance in the world. From what I hear, some restless folks are gathering at the gates.

## MUST-HEAR MUTINEERS

### Rap

| | |
|---|---|
| Queen Latifa: *Black Reign.* | Moving, politically savvy, dramatic |
| M. C. Lyte: *bad as i wanna b.* | Sexually graphic, hilarious |
| Salt 'n Pepa: *Very Necessary.* | Amiable, sexy, playful, comic theater |
| Missy Eliot: *Supadupa Fly.* | Breathtakingly rhythmic mumbling that defies the gotta-be-sexy conventions |

### Rock

| | |
|---|---|
| Sheryl Crow: *Sheryl Crow.* | Sophisticated, novelistic, sixties-legatee |
| Joan Osborne: *Relish.* | Bluesy, gritty-voiced, complex poetry |
| Alanis Morissette: *Jagged Little Pill.* | Rousingly angry, breakneck tempoed, tone-perfect shrieking |

### Funk/Jazz/R&B

| | |
|---|---|
| Me'shell Ndegeocello: *Peace Beyond Passion.* | Many-layered personal/political |
| Erykah Badu: *Baduizm.* | Smooth Jazz from a most imperious presence |

### Funk

| | |
|---|---|
| L7: *Smell the Magic.* | Tough, hip, observant, girls-only band |

### Indies

| | |
|---|---|
| Bikini Kill: *Reject American.* | Swiftian satire from the original riot grrrls |
| Ani DiFranco: *Living in Clip.* | The angriest, most vulnerable, toughest, softest, outest feminist |

[1998]

## ACKNOWLEDGEMENTS

Grateful thanks to rock critics Robert Christgau and Ben Kim; to Rana Ross, John Ross, Rachel Devlin, Anne Snitow, Virginia Blaisdell, and Amy Kesselman; and to Carmen Balkaran, Aleatha Carter, and Maureen Josephs.

## 🦎 30

# X: A Fabulous Child's Story

LOIS GOULD

Once upon a time, a baby named X was born. This baby was named X so that nobody could tell whether it was a boy or a girl. Its parents could tell, of course, but they couldn't tell anybody else. They couldn't even tell Baby X, at first.

You see, it was all part of a very important Secret Scientific Xperiment, known officially as Project Baby X. The smartest scientists had set up this Xperiment at a cost of Xactly 23 billion dollars and 72 cents, which might seem like a lot for just one baby, even a very important Xperimental baby. But when you remember the prices of things like strained carrots and stuffed bunnies, and popcorn for the movies and booster shots for camp, let alone 28 shiny quarters from the tooth fairy, you begin to see how it adds up.

Also, long before Baby X was born, all those scientists had to be paid to work out the details of the Xperiment, and to write the *Official Instruction*

*Manual* for Baby X's parents and, most important of all, to find the right set of parents to bring up Baby X. These parents had to be selected very carefully. Thousands of volunteers had to take thousands of tests and answer thousands of tricky questions. Almost everybody failed because, it turned out, almost everybody really wanted either a baby boy or a baby girl, and not Baby X at all. Also, almost everybody was afraid that a Baby X would be a lot more trouble than a boy or a girl. (They were probably right, the scientists admitted, but Baby X needed parents who wouldn't *mind* the Xtra trouble.)

There were families with grandparents named Milton and Agatha, who didn't see why the baby couldn't be named Milton or Agatha instead of X, even if it *was* an X. There were families with aunts who insisted on knitting tiny dresses and uncles who insisted on sending tiny baseball mitts. Worst of all, there were families that already had other children who couldn't be trusted to keep the secret. Certainly not if they knew the secret was worth 23 billion dollars and 72 cents—and all you had to do was take one little peek at Baby X in the bathtub to know if it was a boy or a girl.

But, finally, the scientists found the Joneses, who really wanted to raise an X more than any other kind of baby—no matter how much trouble it would be. Ms. and Mr. Jones had to promise they would take equal turns caring for X, and feeding it, and singing it lullabies. And they had to promise never to hire any baby-sitters. The government scientists knew perfectly well that a baby-sitter would probably peek at X in the bathtub, too.

The day the Joneses brought their baby home, lots of friends and relatives came over to see it. None of them knew about the secret Xperiment, though. So the first thing they asked was what kind of a baby X was. When the Joneses smiled and said, "It's an X!" nobody knew what to say. They couldn't say, "Look at her cute little dimples!" And they couldn't say, "Look at his husky little biceps!" And they couldn't even say just plain "kitchy-coo." In fact, they all thought the Joneses were playing some kind of rude joke.

But, of course, the Joneses were not joking. "It's an X" was absolutely all they would say. And that made the friends and relatives very angry. The relatives all felt embarrassed about having an X in the family. "People will think there's something wrong with it!" some of them whispered. "There *is* something wrong with it!" others whispered back.

"Nonsense!" the Joneses told them all cheerfully. "What could possibly be wrong with this perfectly adorable X?"

Nobody could answer that, except Baby X, who had just finished its bottle. Baby X's answer was a loud, satisfied burp.

Clearly, nothing at all was wrong. Nevertheless, none of the relatives felt comfortable about buying a present for a Baby X. The cousins who sent the baby a tiny football helmet would not come and visit any more. And the neighbors who sent a pink-flowered romper suit pulled their shades down when the Joneses passed their house.

The *Official Instruction Manual* had warned the new parents that this would happen, so they didn't fret about it. Besides, they were too busy with Baby X and the hundreds of different Xercises for treating it properly.

Ms. and Mr. Jones had to be Xtra careful about how they played with little X. They knew that if they kept bouncing it up in the air and saying how *strong* and *active* it was, they'd be treating it more like a boy than an X. But if all they did was cuddle it and kiss it and tell it how *sweet* and *dainty* it was, they'd be treating it more like a girl than an X.

On page 1,654 of the *Official Instruction Manual*, the scientists prescribed: "plenty of bouncing and plenty of cuddling, *both*. X ought to be strong and sweet and active. Forget about *dainty* altogether."

Meanwhile, the Joneses were worrying about other problems. Toys, for instance. And clothes. On his first shopping trip, Mr. Jones told the store clerk, "I need some clothes and toys for my new baby." The clerk smiled and said, "Well, now, is it a boy or a girl?" "It's an X," Mr. Jones said, smiling back. But the clerk got all red in the face and said huffily, "In *that* case, I'm afraid I can't help you, sir." So Mr. Jones wandered helplessly up and down the aisles trying to find what X needed. But everything in the store was piled up in sections marked "Boys" or "Girls." There were "Boys' Pajamas" and "Girls'

Underwear" and "Boys' Fire Engines" and "Girls' Housekeeping Sets." Mr. Jones went home without buying anything for X. That night he and Ms. Jones consulted page 2,326 of the *Official Instruction Manual.* "Buy plenty of everything!" it said firmly.

So they bought plenty of sturdy blue pajamas in the Boys' Department and cheerful flowered underwear in the Girls' Department. And they bought all kinds of toys. A boy doll that made pee-pee and cried, "Pa-pa." And a girl doll that talked in three languages and said, "I am the Pres-i-dent of Gen-er-al Mo-tors." They also bought a storybook about a brave princess who rescued a handsome prince from his ivory tower, and another one about a sister and brother who grew up to be a baseball star and a ballet star, and you had to guess which was which.

The head scientists of Project Baby X checked all their purchases and told them to keep up the good work. They also reminded the Joneses to see page 4,629 of the *Manual,* where it said, "Never make Baby X feel *embarrassed* or *ashamed* about what it wants to play with. And if X gets dirty climbing rocks, never say 'Nice little Xes don't get dirty climbing rocks.'"

Likewise, it said, "If X falls down and cries, never say 'Brave little Xes don't cry.' Because, of course, nice little Xes *do* get dirty, and brave little Xes *do* cry. No matter how dirty X gets, or how hard it cries, don't worry. It's all part of the Xperiment."

Whenever the Joneses pushed Baby X's stroller in the park, smiling strangers would come over and coo: "Is that a boy or a girl?" The Joneses would smile back and say, "It's an X." The strangers would stop smiling then, and often snarl something nasty—as if the Joneses had snarled at *them.*

By the time X grew big enough to play with other children, the Joneses' troubles had grown bigger, too. Once a little girl grabbed X's shovel in the sandbox, and zonked X on the head with it. "Now, now, Tracy," the little girl's mother began to scold, "little girls mustn't hit little—" and she turned to ask X, "Are you a little boy or a little girl, dear?"

Mr. Jones, who was sitting near the sandbox, held his breath and crossed his fingers.

X smiled politely at the lady, even though X's head had never been zonked so hard in its life. "I'm a little X," X replied.

"You're a *what?*" the lady exclaimed angrily. "You're a little b-r-a-t, you mean!"

"But little girls mustn't hit little Xes, either!" said X, retrieving the shovel with another polite smile. "What good does hitting do, anyway?"

X's father, who was still holding his breath, finally let it out, uncrossed his fingers, and grinned back at X.

And at their next secret Project Baby X meeting, the scientists grinned, too. Baby X was doing fine.

But then it was time for X to start school. The Joneses were really worried about this, because school was even more full of rules for boys and girls, and there were no rules for Xes. The teacher would tell boys to form one line, and girls to form another line. There would be boys' games and girls' games, and boys' secrets and girls' secrets. The school library would have a list of recommended books for girls, and a different list of recommended books for boys. There would even be a bathroom marked BOYS and another one marked GIRLS. Pretty soon boys and girls would hardly talk to each other. What would happen to poor little X?

The Joneses spent weeks consulting their *Instruction Manual* (there were 249½ pages of advice under "First Day of School"), and attending urgent special conferences with the smart scientists of Project Baby X.

The scientists had to make sure that X's mother had taught X how to throw and catch a ball properly, and that X's father had been sure to teach X what to serve at a doll's tea party. X had to know how to shoot marbles and how to jump rope and, most of all, what to say when the Other Children asked whether X was a Boy or a Girl.

Finally, X was ready. The Joneses helped X button on a nice new pair of red-and-white checked overalls, and sharpened six pencils for X's nice new pencilbox, and marked X's name clearly on all the books in its nice new bookbag. X brushed its teeth and combed its hair, which just about covered its ears, and remembered to put a napkin in its lunchbox.

The Joneses had asked X's teacher if the class could line up alphabetically, instead of forming separate lines for boys and girls. And they had asked if X could use the principal's bathroom, because it wasn't marked anything except BATHROOM. X's teacher promised to take care of all those problems. But nobody could help X with the biggest problem of all—Other Children.

Nobody in X's class had ever known an X before. What would they think? How would X make friends?

You couldn't tell what X was by studying its clothes—overalls don't even button right-to-left, like girls' clothes, or left-to-right, like boys' clothes. And you couldn't guess whether X had a girl's short haircut or a boy's long haircut. And it was very hard to tell by the games X liked to play. Either X played ball very well for a girl or played house very well for a boy.

Some of the children tried to find out by asking X tricky questions, like "Who's your favorite sports star?" That was easy. X had two favorite sports stars: a girl jockey named Robyn Smith and a boy archery champion named Robin Hood. Then they asked, "What's your favorite TV program?" And that was even easier. X's favorite TV program was "Lassie," which stars a girl dog played by a boy dog.

When X said that its favorite toy was a doll, everyone decided that X must be a girl. But then X said that the doll was really a robot, and that X had computerized it, and that it was programmed to bake fudge brownies and then clean up the kitchen. After X told them that, the other children gave up guessing what X was. All they knew was they'd sure like to see X's doll.

After school, X wanted to play with the other children. "How about shooting some baskets in the gym?" X asked the girls. But all they did was make faces and giggle behind X's back.

"How about weaving some baskets in the arts and crafts room?" X asked the boys. But they all made faces and giggled behind X's back, too.

That night, Ms. and Mr. Jones asked X how things had gone at school. X told them sadly that the lessons were okay, but otherwise school was a horrible place for an X. It seemed as if the Other Children would never want an X for a friend.

Once more, the Joneses reached for the *Instruction Manual*. Under "Other Children," they found the following message: "What did you Xpect? *Other Children* have to obey all the silly boy-girl rules, be-cause their parents taught them to. Lucky X—you don't have to stick to the rules at all! All you have to do is be yourself. P.S. We're not saying it'll be easy."

X liked being itself. But X cried a lot that night, partly because it felt afraid. So X's father held X tight, and cuddled it, and couldn't help crying a little, too. And X's mother cheered them both up by reading an Xciting story about an enchanted prince called Sleeping Handsome, who woke up when Princess Charming kissed him.

The next morning, they all felt much better, and little X went back to school with a brave smile and a clean pair of red-and-white checked overalls.

There was a seven-letter-word spelling bee in class that day. And a seven-lap boys' relay race in the gym. And a seven-layer-cake baking contest in the girls' kitchen corner. X won the spelling bee. X also won the relay race. And X almost won the baking contest, except it forgot to light the oven. Which only proves that nobody's perfect.

One of the Other Children noticed something else, too. He said: "Winning or losing doesn't seem to count to X. X seems to have fun being good at boys' skills *and* girls' skills."

"Come to think of it," said another one of the Other Children, "maybe X is having twice as much fun as we are!"

So after school that day, the girl who beat X at the baking contest gave X a big slice of her prizewinning cake. And the boy X beat in the relay race asked X to race him home.

From then on, some really funny things began to happen. Susie, who sat next to X in class, suddenly refused to wear pink dresses to school any more. She insisted on wearing red-and-white checked overalls—just like X's. Overalls, she told her parents, were much better for climbing monkey bars.

Then Jim, the class football nut, started wheeling his little sister's doll carriage around the football field. He'd put on his entire football uniform, except for the helmet. Then he'd put the helmet *in* the carriage, lovingly tucked under an old set of shoulder pads. Then he'd start jogging around the field, pushing the carriage and singing "Rockabye Baby" to his football helmet. He told his family that X did the same thing, so it must be okay. After all, X was now the team's star quarterback.

Susie's parents were horrified by her behavior, and Jim's parents were worried sick about him. But the worst came when the twins, Joe and Peggy, decided to share everything with each other. Peggy used Joe's hockey skates, and his microscope, and took half his newspaper route. Joe used Peggy's needlepoint kit, and her cookbooks, and took two of her three baby-sitting jobs. Peggy started running the lawn mower, and Joe started running the vacuum cleaner.

Their parents weren't one bit pleased with Peggy's wonderful biology experiments, or with Joe's terrific needlepoint pillows. They didn't care that Peggy mowed the lawn better, and that Joe vacuumed the carpet better. In fact, they were furious. It's all that little X's fault, they agreed. Just because X doesn't know what it is, or what it's supposed to be, it wants to get everybody *else* mixed up, too!

Peggy and Joe were forbidden to play with X any more. So was Susie, and then Jim, and then *all* the Other Children. But it was too late; the Other Children stayed mixed up and happy and free, and refused to go back to the way they'd been before X.

Finally, Joe and Peggy's parents decided to call an emergency meeting of the school's Parents' Association, to discuss "The X Problem." They sent a report to the principal stating that X was a "disruptive influence." They demanded immediate action. The Joneses, they said, should be *forced* to tell whether X was a boy or a girl. And then X should be *forced* to behave like whichever it was. If the Joneses refused to tell, the Parents' Association said, then X must take an Xamination. The school psychiatrist must Xamine it physically and mentally, and issue a full report. If X's test showed it was a boy, it would have to obey all the boys' rules. If it proved to be a girl, X would have to obey all the girls' rules.

And if X turned out to be some kind of mixed-up misfit, then X should be Xpelled from the school. Immediately!

The principal was very upset. Disruptive influence? Mixed-up misfit? But X was an Xcellent student. All the teachers said it was a delight to have X in their classes. X was president of the student council. X had won first prize in the talent show, and second prize in the art show, and honorable mention in the science fair, and six athletic events on field day, including the potato race.

*Nevertheless,* insisted the Parents' Association, X is a Problem Child. X is the Biggest Problem Child we have ever seen!

So the principal reluctantly notified X's parents that numerous complaints about X's behavior had come to the school's attention. And that after the psychiatrist's Xamination, the school would decide what to do about X.

The Joneses reported this at once to the scientists, who referred them to page 85,759 of the *Instruction Manual.* "Sooner or later," it said, "X will have to be Xamined by a psychiatrist. This may be the only way any of us will know for sure whether X is mixed up—or whether everyone else is."

The night before X was to be Xamined, the Joneses tried not to let X see how worried they were. "What if—?" Mr. Jones would say. And Ms. Jones would reply, "No use worrying." Then a few minutes later, Ms. Jones would say, "What if—?" and Mr. Jones would reply, "No use worrying."

X just smiled at them both, and hugged them hard and didn't say much of anything. X was thinking, What if—? And then X thought: No use worrying.

At Xactly 9 o'clock the next day, X reported to the school psychiatrist's office. The principal, along with a committee from the Parents' Association, X's teacher, X's classmates, and Ms. and Mr. Jones, waited in the hall outside. Nobody knew the details of the tests X was to be given, but everybody knew they'd be *very* hard, and that they'd reveal Xactly what everyone wanted to know about X, but were afraid to ask.

It was terribly quiet in the hall. Almost spooky. Once in a while, they would hear a strange noise inside the room. There were buzzes. And a beep or two. And several bells. An occasional light would flash under the door. The Joneses thought it was a white light, but the principal thought it was blue. Two or three children swore it was either yellow or green. And the Parents' Committee missed it completely.

Through it all, you could hear the psychiatrist's

low voice, asking hundreds of questions, and X's higher voice, answering hundreds of answers.

The whole thing took so long that everyone knew it must be the most complete Xamination anyone had ever had to take. Poor X, the Joneses thought. Serves X right, the Parents' Committee thought. I wouldn't like to be in X's overalls right now, the children thought.

At last, the door opened. Everyone crowded around to hear the results. X didn't look any different; in fact, X was smiling. But the psychiatrist looked terrible. He looked as if he was crying! "What happened?" everyone began shouting. Had X done something disgraceful? "I wouldn't be a bit surprised!" muttered Peggy and Joe's parents. "Did X flunk the *whole* test?" cried Susie's parents. "Or just the most important part?" yelled Jim's parents.

"Oh, dear," sighed Mr. Jones.

"Oh, dear," sighed Ms. Jones.

"*Sssh,*" ssshed the principal. "The psychiatrist is trying to speak."

Wiping his eyes and clearing his throat, the psychiatrist began, in a hoarse whisper. "In my opinion," he whispered—you could tell he must be very upset—"in my opinion, young X here—"

"Yes? Yes?" shouted a parent impatiently.

"*Sssh!*" ssshed the principal.

"Young *Sssh* here, I mean young X," said the doctor, frowning, "is just about—"

"Just about *what?* Let's have it!" shouted another parent. " . . . just about the *least* mixed-up child I've ever Xamined!" said the psychiatrist.

"Yay for X!" yelled one of the children. And then the others began yelling, too. Clapping and cheering and jumping up and down.

"*SSSH!*" SSShed the principal, but nobody did.

The Parents' Committee was angry and bewildered. How *could* X have passed the whole Xamination? Didn't X have an *identity* problem? Wasn't X mixed up at *all?* Wasn't X *any* kind of a misfit? How could it *not* be, when it didn't even *know* what it was? And why was the psychiatrist crying?

Actually, he had stopped crying and was smiling politely through his tears. "Don't you see?" he said.

"I'm crying because it's wonderful! X has absolutely no identity problem! X isn't one bit mixed-up! As for being a misfit—ridiculous! X knows perfectly well what it is! Don't you, X?" The doctor winked. X winked back.

"But what *is* X?" shrieked Peggy and Joe's parents. "*We* still want to know what it is!"

"Ah, yes," said the doctor, winking again. "Well, don't worry. You'll all know one of these days. And you won't need me to tell you."

"What? What does he mean?" some of the parents grumbled suspiciously.

Susie and Peggy and Joe all answered at once. "He means that by the time X's sex matters, it won't be a secret any more!"

With that, the doctor began to push through the crowd toward X's parents. "How do you do," he said, somewhat stiffly. And then he reached out to hug them both. "If I ever have an X of my own," he whispered, "I sure hope you'll lend me your instruction manual."

Needless to say, the Joneses were very happy. The Project Baby X scientists were rather pleased, too. So were Susie, Jim, Peggy, Joe, and all the Other Children. The Parents' Association wasn't, but they had promised to accept the psychiatrist's report, and not make any more trouble. They even invited Ms. and Mr. Jones to become honorary members, which they did.

Later that day, all X's friends put on their red-and-white checked overalls and went over to see X. They found X in the back yard, playing with a very tiny baby that none of them had ever seen before. The baby was wearing very tiny red-and-white checked overalls.

"How do you like our new baby?" X asked the Other Children proudly.

"It's got cute dimples," said Jim.

"It's got husky biceps, too," said Susie.

"What kind of baby is it?" asked Joe and Peggy.

X frowned at them. "Can't you tell?" Then X broke into a big, mischievous grin. *"It's a Y!"*

[1972]

## PART III

# Gender and Women's Bodies

In many ways, women's worth in our culture has been defined by our bodies. Girls quickly learn that their worth is evaluated by their appearance; more attention is directed to girls' beauty, clothes, and hair than to their intelligence and skills. As Rhoda Under and Mary Crawford state, "Learning to care about looks is a lifelong process."[1]

Just as the psychological experience of being female affects women's self-perceptions, it also shapes our perception of our bodies and sexuality. Although women's attitudes about women's bodies are changing, reflecting a greater appreciation of athleticism, strength, and health, most still find fault with our bodies and appearance. For all too many adolescent girls and women, negative body image is related to lowered self-esteem. Bombarded with messages of ideal beauty and body size, many adolescent girls who are physically maturing struggle with meeting these unrealistic standards. The greater incidence of eating disorders among females than males reflects the extreme pressures placed on girls and women to achieve impossible weight standards. For most anorexic and bulimic women, a common belief is "If only I were thin everything would be fine. I would be happier, people would like me more, I would feel better about myself." For these women, concern about weight and appearance becomes the guiding focus of their lives. Organizing their daily activities around when and what they eat, women with eating disorders are caught up in a distressing cycle that includes trying to manage their feelings about themselves by controlling their food intake. These women use their bodies as focal points for achieving control, social acceptance, and self-worth. The experiences of women dealing with eating disorders reminds us that these messages about body weight and attractiveness can have devastating psychological and physical effects.

The advertising world generates standards of beauty that exclude most women, particularly women of color and women who deviate from the white, Anglo-Saxon, thin model. When women strive to fit these standards, we often neglect and devalue our own uniqueness. Along the way, we compare ourselves harshly and critically with "classic beauties" and subject ourselves to beauty aids, unnecessary cosmetic surgeries, unhealthy diets, and dangerous appetite-suppressing drugs to achieve the "right look." More frequently than not these attempts do not succeed, and women end up feeling dissatisfied, often blaming ourselves for our perceived imperfections.

For women of color, white definitions of female beauty are less powerful now than they were 20 years ago. As an example, the shift to celebrating African roots of African-American culture in fashion, hairstyle, and the arts has introduced new concepts of African-American women's beauty. Similarly, a resurgence in ethnic and urban pop culture reminds us that alternatives to traditional norms for beauty are being presented to young people, particularly in urban areas. However, despite these changes, the unrealistic standards of beauty that focus on unbearably thin, waiflike white women remain the dominant images of female beauty promoted in the media.

---

[1] Rhoda Unger and Mary Crawford, *Women and Gender: A Feminist Psychology,* 2nd ed. (New York: McGraw-Hill, 1996), p. 317.

Expressions of women's sexuality are closely related to how we view ourselves and our bodies. Male-defined attitudes about women's sexuality have created myths and stereotypes that have harmed women. These myths and stereotypes have historically defined women's sexuality and set the stage for prescribing certain behaviors and expressions of sexuality as appropriate for women.

Attitudes about female sexuality have changed radically over the years, reflecting shifts in social and cultural norms about sexuality and the role of women in society. In Europe from the 1400s to the 1700s, women were seen as sexually insatiable. Female sexuality was viewed as dangerous, evil, and in need of control. The embodiment of this uncontrollable sexuality was the "witch," who was thought to consort with the devil to satisfy her lust. During the 1800s, these attitudes changed dramatically, reflecting the Victorian values of nineteenth-century Europe. White women were regarded as pure, genteel, and passionless, while darker-skinned women were cast as sexual potentates. During the years of slavery in the United States, this double standard for white and black women was played out in the continued sexual exploitation and rape of slave women by the very same white slaveowners who viewed their own wives as sexually pure.

Prevailing stereotypes reflect the interaction of racism and sexism in our culture. Viewed as "other" relative to white women, Latinas are cast as "hot-blooded" and Asian women as exotic and geisha-like. Their sexuality takes on the added dimension of being unfeminine: to be hot-blooded, seductive, and erotic is at odds with being pure and genteel.

The sexual revolution of the 1960s signaled for many a loosening of restrictions on sexual behavior for men and women. However, the double standard for male and female sexuality has persisted throughout history. The cultural climate of the United States is now more conducive to accepting women's sexuality, and we see greater acceptance among college students of people's exploration of their sexual identities. However, we continue to see men's sexuality described in positive terms, whereas the descriptors for women's sexuality are decidedly negative. According to this double standard, a sexually active man who has several partners is "virile," but a woman who has several partners is described as "easy" and "promiscuous." Prevailing notions of the "appropriate" expressions of women's sexuality continue to affect women's sexual behavior.

Sexual scripts are messages about expected behavior in sexual interactions that derive from stereotypes about men's and women's sexuality. In our culture, these scripts refer to heterosexual behavior, totally excluding the sexual expressions of lesbian and bisexual women. In fact, when these women's sexuality is considered, it is often in the context of being compared with the heterosexual "norm." For example, the definition of "sex" that is often used to survey couples' sexual behavior typically assumes heterosexual behavior, that is, penile-vaginal intercourse. For lesbian couples, this definition is meaningless and fails to capture the range of emotional and physical aspects of "sex" between two women. As Marilyn Frye asserts, "The suspicion arises that what 85% of heterosexual couples are doing more than once a month and what 47% of what lesbian couples are doing less than once a month is not the same thing."[2]

A common sexual script for heterosexuals in our culture contains the following do's and don'ts: The man initiates sex, and therefore the woman should not appear too interested at first; good sex is spontaneous and "just happens"; women should not appear to enjoy sex "too much"; and women should not desire sex "too much." Sexual scripts often place women in the position of being the "gatekeeper"—the partner who is responsible for saying no to sexual advances. College students tend to describe men and women as having opposing goals in sexual interactions: men attempt to have sex, while women's goal is to avoid sex.[3] This portrayal of women's sexuality reaffirms the images of the pure, sexually reticent woman and sexually uncontrollable man.

Taboos about women's sexuality, shaped by cultural ideology and mythology, directly affect a woman's experience of her own sexuality. It is not unusual to hear women discuss ambivalent feelings about their sexual desires and relationships or to question whether "something is wrong" because they do not experience sex the way they think they "should." Again, we see the influence of sexual scripting on women's perceptions of their own behavior. As we explore these different issues, we introduce the feminist perspective, which asserts that for women living in a sexist culture, sexuality encompasses both pleasure and danger. Previously, women's rights to sexual pleasure were denied or restricted. In some cultures they still are, especially regarding practices such as masturbation. A feminist approach to sexuality acknowledges sexual expression as one way in which we can experience ourselves, as an avenue through which we have a right to explore our own feelings, needs and desires. Feminists believe that women should make their own sexual choices. On the other hand, because of the danger of AIDS and other sexually transmitted infections, along with the possibility of unwanted pregnancy, our rights to sexual pleasure must be balanced with the responsibility of taking care of ourselves. Thus, it is important for women to take control of their sexual behavior, making decisions that decrease our risk for HIV/AIDS, sexually transmitted infections, and unwanted pregnancy. By doing so, women can more fully experience and enjoy the aspects of sexual intimacy that are pleasurable and fulfilling.

Our attitudes about beauty, our bodies, and sexuality begin developing early in life. The unrealistic expectations created by a society that objectifies women can restrict our choices and limit our growth. As the selections that follow reveal, understanding how gender socialization and sexism create harmful stereotypes and expectations can help us claim and act on our own standards for personal beauty and sexuality.

---

[2] Marilyn Frye, "Lesbian Sex," *Sinister Wisdom*, 35 (1988), reprinted in Amy Kesselman, Lily McNair, and Nancy Schniedewind, *Women: Images and Realities* (Mountain View CA: Mayfield Press (1995), p. 122.
[3] M. N. LaPlante, N. McCormick, & G. G. Brannigan, "Living the Sexual Script: College Students' Views of Influence in Sexual Encounters," *Journal of Sex Research*, 16 (1980), 338–55.

# Female Beauty

"The beauty myth," as Naomi Wolf calls it in her book by that name, is omnipotent and far-reaching. It consists of the belief that women must possess an immutable quality, "beauty," in order to be successful and attractive to men. In essence, femininity is equated with beauty. Our culture is permeated by the conviction that beauty is the central measure of women's worth. In fact, standards of beauty vary greatly from culture to culture and have changed radically over time. In our culture, prevailing notions of beauty emphasize being young, thin, white, and Anglo-Saxon. Rita Freedman shows us that the beauty myth is a corollary of images of female inferiority; by demanding that women's worth be measured by this superficial quality, society negates the potential equality that can exist between women and men. In fact, Freedman suggests that in a society that equally values men and women, women will gain power and "shift beauty off the back of femininity."

Images of beauty vary across ethnic groups, demonstrating how racism and sexism interact to shape expectations of women. Nellie Wong, Inés Hernandez-Avila, Aishe Berger, and Lucille Clifton describe the effects of stereotyped notions of beauty on Asian-American, Latina, Jewish, and African-American women. As these selections demonstrate, such standards create anguish and confusion for most women, and particularly for women of color, who are outside the prevailing "norms" of beauty.

In addition to affecting a woman's sense of self-worth, ideals of physical beauty often have destructive effects on a woman's physical health. The increasing rates of eating disorders in the United States are just one example of the unhealthy consequences of rigid standards of beauty. In "One Spring," Lesléa Newman recounts the events that propelled her into a journey toward "disappearing" so that she would not receive attention for her emerging physical maturity. Although many other factors contribute to the development of eating disorders, her account reveals the cultural pressures that make it difficult for many girls to be comfortable with their physical selves and the sexuality they often represent. Donna Marquardt captures the intensity of a woman's experience of anorexia, underscoring the ever-present connection between beauty norms and the pressure to conform to them. The obsession with thinness has devastating effects on many women, as shown by July Siebecker. As Linda Delgado points out, however, such notions of female beauty are not universal; Latino/Latina culture, she argues, prizes women of fuller proportions.

When women begin to defy social scripts for physical beauty, we can begin to see the beauty within ourselves and define beauty in a more meaningful way. This section concludes with two pieces reflecting contemporary women's new personal standards of beauty. Written by African-American women, both of these selections convey important messages for women of all racial and ethnic backgrounds who are freeing themselves from restrictive standards of personal beauty.

## 🌿 31

# *The Myth in the Mirror*

RITA FREEDMAN

When a sixteen-year-old blonde was crowned in 1921, she launched America's longest running, most popular beauty contest. Nearly half a century later, demonstrators gathered on the Boardwalk of Atlantic City in what many consider the public birth of the current women's movement.

Why was the Miss America Contest chosen for the site of the first contemporary feminist demonstration? A group of women had discovered that while they outwardly denounced the pageant, they somehow ended up watching it. They chose to picket the contest because it seemed to epitomize woman's role as a passive, decorative object. The message was that all women are hurt by such contests in a culture that substitutes the worship of female beauty for the recognition of women as human beings.

When questioned about the meaning of beauty, some women say they enjoy its challenge; others say they resent its domination. Most find it hard to admit just how much they value beauty and how much they fear its loss. The triumphs and tragedies of their daily beauty quest are shrouded in silence.

This is why beauty reform remains part of the feminist agenda. How *does* beauty influence self-esteem and independence? Is adornment an asset or a liability in achieving equality? Questions of equal pay or equal rights seem clearer and safer. Equal looks are harder to define.

When demonstrators tossed their bras into a trash can in Atlantic City, the response of outrage was disproportionate to the sight of a few sagging bosoms. Bras were correctly identified as part of a crucial support system, as props for a much larger social issue. At stake was not the shape of the breast but the shape of the myth that women are specially endowed with beauty. The unbound liberated breast (like the unbound foot) was quickly recognized as a threat to the idea that feminine beauty should be cultivated and displayed within certain bounds.

At risk was the belief that women are objects of visual pleasure, that their breasts ought to be contained and reshaped to look pleasing, that they are unaesthetic and unacceptable as they are. When great attention is paid to preserving such customs as opening doors, putting on makeup, or wearing bras, it is because these simple acts symbolize more important values. If bras, as symbols, are allowed to be stripped away, then woman's role as a beautiful object may come undone as well.

Beauty is not a gender-neutral trait. There are no televised pageants in which men parade in bikinis to be crowned Mr. America on the basis of their shapely legs and congenial smiles. Because beauty is asymmetrically assigned to the feminine role, women are defined more by their looks than by their deeds. Good looks are prerequisite for femininity but incidental to masculinity. This asymmetry produces different social expectations and different psychological consequences for each sex.

Appearance is important and it will continue to be. Beauty is not the enemy. Rather we are all, men and women, bound by a system that encourages obsessive preoccupation with the female body. By calculating the power of beauty to both enhance and undermine human relations, we may achieve a more realistic view of it. Through greater awareness, reform becomes possible.

As women strive to break free of constricting stereotypes of who they are and what they want, idealized feminine beauty must be identified as part of that challenge. It is not merely a decorative diversion. The sense of self resides within the body. False beauty images generate false body parts—remodeled torsos, remade faces—reconstructions that are worn like acquired accessories. As long as women remain hidden behind these distortions, they will be controlled by them, no matter how safe they feel.

## *DEFINING BEAUTY*

Beauty is many things—an external radiance, an inner tranquillity, a sexual allure, a fact of social exchange. Contradictory definitions of the nature of beauty abound, indicating widespread ambivalence about its meaning. On the one hand, beauty is dismissed as mere facade, a superficial trait of little consequence. On the other hand, it is infused with supernatural power; a spellbinding, dazzling, irresistible princess can capture hearts and control kingdoms.

Beauty norms are in constant flux as new standards are adopted and abandoned. Worship of curves gives way to straight hair; legs replace breasts, and vice versa, as the fashion focus moves down or up. When beauty images change, bodies are expected to change as well, for nature cannot satisfy culture's ideal. Lashes must be longer, hair silkier, cheeks rosier.

As a psychological experience, beauty is an interactive process. It derives as much from the beliefs and perceptions of the beholder as from the face of the beheld. This is why its definition is so elusive and its influence so hard to determine. We can never be sure where it comes from or who possesses it. Does it depend on physical dimensions or on psychological ones? Is it housed in the flesh or created through fantasy? Who owns and controls it, the beholder or the beheld?

One popular misconception about beauty is that it counts most at initial encounters and becomes less important with familiarity. In fact, evidence suggests just the opposite (Berscheid & Walster, 1974). Appearance continues to have a significant influence even on long-standing relationships. Another common misconception is that beauty is democratically distributed so that every person is considered attractive by someone or other. Again the data suggest the opposite conclusion. Certain faces are consistently admired, while others are consistently rejected. Appearance therefore makes a real difference over the course of hundreds of daily encounters (Wooley, 1994). Herein lies the power of beauty to define us.

It is clearly untrue that we regard beauty as merely skin-deep. There is a strong belief that what is beautiful is also good. We may give lip service to so-called higher moral values and dutifully insist that beauty lies within, that looks are superficial, and that character is what counts. But such sanctimonious maxims only cover up a strong unconscious worship of appearance. Furthermore, research indicates that attitudes about attractiveness are applied differently to each sex. Beauty counts for everyone, but more so for women (Garner, 1997).

From the moment of birth, beauty is sought, perceived, and projected onto girls. When parents were asked within twenty-four hours after delivery to rate their first-born infants on a variety of characteristics, daughters were described as beautiful, soft, pretty, cute, delicate, and little. Sons were rated as firm, strong, large-featured, well coordinated, and hardy. The baby boys and girls in this study had been carefully matched for equivalent length, weight, and level of responsiveness. Despite the physical similarities of these infants, their parents nevertheless brought home "beautiful" daughters and "strong" sons. A baby dressed in blue was described in another study as bouncy, strong, active; the same baby dressed in pink was called sweet and lovely. Studies confirm that throughout childhood girls receive more attention for their appearance than do boys.

A growing body of evidence confirms that beauty is a gender-related trait. At every age, appearance is emphasized and valued more highly in females than in males. Women are more critically judged for attractiveness and more severely rejected when they lack it. A woman's beauty is constantly anticipated, encouraged, sought, and rewarded in a wide range of situations, including the romantic arena (Pliner et al., 1990).

Analysis of personal advertisements, for example, shows that women are more likely to offer physical attractiveness, while men are more likely to seek it. The reverse holds true for financial security, which men are more likely to offer and women are more likely to seek. Clearly, the link between beauty and femininity influences dating and mating preferences. It is not merely an abstract concept but a reality that has social importance.

Because beauty is linked with femininity, the influence of body image on self-concept is greater for females than for males. A woman is more likely than a man to equate herself with what she looks like, or what she thinks she looks like, or what she believes others think she looks like. Studies show that women's self-concepts are correlated with their own perceptions of their attractiveness, whereas men's self-concepts relate more closely to perceptions of their effectiveness and their physical fitness (Freedman, 1989).

## THE ROLE OF MYTHS

There are as many contradictory myths about the nature of women as there are about the nature of beauty. Like beauty, women are viewed as both good and evil. Both beauty and women are considered dangerous and seductive. Both are seen as a mysterious enigma, feared as powerful but dismissed as ineffectual.

Myths about beauty alter its impact. They are used as yardsticks for self-evaluation. People measure themselves against a mythical ideal and then remodel themselves to fit that pattern, becoming what they believe they should be. If, for example, women are taught that feminine beauty means having full, softly rounded breasts, they judge themselves against this standard. Missing the mark, they put on padded bras or suffer silicone implants. As flat chests disappear, reality is replaced with a replica, and the truth of the myth is confirmed. Myths thus function as self-fulfilling prophecy and are therefore dangerously self-perpetuating.

How can a myth that equates woman with beauty survive alongside a myth that brands woman as deficient? How can woman be glorified as the fair sex while at the same time be demeaned as "the other sex"? In fact, myths about gender, like myths about beauty, are often linked in just such counterbalanced pairs. Together, contrary myths create an equilibrium that helps preserve them both.

Women are crowned with beauty precisely because they are cloaked in difference. The idealization of female appearance camouflages an underlying belief in female inferiority. Just as excessive narcissism has its roots in self-loathing, the myth of female beauty grows from the myth of female deviance. Beauty helps to balance woman as a misbegotten person. It disguises her inadequacies and justifies her presence.

At the same time, beauty clearly distinguishes woman as different, as a member of the other half of humanity. But beauty is only a temporary equalizer. Ultimately, it exposes the fair sex once again as the other sex. For the symbols of contrived beauty—the lacquered nails, the crimson lips—exaggerate gender differences. They elevate woman onto a pedestal while paradoxically defining her separate role. In lieu of equality, beauty serves as a kind of prop, or consolation prize. In the end, props and pedestals make poor equalizers. They cannot substitute for full personhood.

The myth of woman as the fair sex perpetuates the feminine mystique. Petticoats and veils, padded bras and packaged bodies, everything that accentuates difference confirms woman as the "other." Recall the scene when Cinderella arrives at the ball. Even her stepsisters fail to know her, so blinding is her beauty. Camouflaged as a lovely enigma, she becomes unrecognizable. Unknown and unknowable, she is all the more desirable. Like Venus, a goddess of beauty but also a planet wrapped in steamy clouds, her core is hidden in a romantic mist. Beauty maintains the erotic mystery of a woman by concealing the human being beneath.

## LOOKING GOOD AND FEELING BAD

Belief in one's own attractiveness can be as hard to achieve as physical beauty itself. Members of the fair sex tend to view themselves unfairly. Ashamed of cellulite, limp hair, and age spots, plagued by self-consciousness, distorted body image, and appearance anxiety, women judge their bodies as unworthy of self-love. Many equate what they look like with who they are.

In an interview a woman is asked to "please describe yourself in some way that would give a good sense of who and what you are." She sits for a moment in silent confusion and then says tentatively, "Do you mean physically, or what?" When told that she is free to choose, she begins her response with a list of physical characteristics: "I'm short and blond, a bit overweight." Sociologist Lillian Rubin conducted dozens of these interviews and found again and again that women started by describing their bodies. Although more than half of that sample worked outside the home, some in high-paying professional jobs, not even one began by discussing herself in relation to her career.

Although females have long been stereotyped, like Narcissus, as being enchanted with their own reflections, just the opposite seems true. Asked to evaluate photographs of themselves, more women voice criticism than satisfaction. When psychologist Marcia Hutchinson (1982) selected over one hundred subjects for a project on body image, she carefully chose women who were of normal weight, with no history of eating disorders or of mental illness. Further assessment, however, showed that only one out of the entire sample was not "actively waging war against fat." None of the women was seriously overweight, none was emotionally disturbed, yet all were dieting, all were self-rejecting, and all suffered from poor body image. Hutchinson was forced to conclude that "flesh loathing exists in epidemic proportions among women."

The problem is quite evident by adolescence, when teenage girls say they feel relatively less attractive in comparison to their peers than do boys. More women than men describe persistent feelings of physical inferiority. One out of three report feeling anxious, depressed, or repulsed when they look at their nude bodies in the mirror.

The mind does not remain a blank slate for very long. An idealized image of feminine beauty is soon etched upon it. In our culture, this image is built on a Caucasian model. Fairy-tale princesses and Miss Americas have traditionally been white. This fair image weighs most heavily on the brown shoulders of women of color who bear a special beauty burden. They too are taught that beauty is a feminine imperative.

Even those who are born with the "right" look discover that beauty can be problematic. Positive pleasures are confounded by negative pitfalls. In fact, one complaint voiced by pretty women is that no one takes the problems of being pretty very seriously. Since beauty is associated with goodness, its advantages are assumed to outweigh its disadvantages. But this is not always the case.

"Beautiful" women do attract more attention, but some of it is unwelcome and some of it is quite destructive. They are more likely to become targets for the anger of men who fear the power of their beauty. "They say it's worse to be ugly. I think it must only be different. If you're pretty, you are subject to one set of assaults; if you're plain, you are subject to another," writes Alix Kates Shulman in her novel *Memoirs of an Ex-Prom Queen*.

Film stars and pageant winners who personify the myth also suffer, for they too are worshipped from inside someone else's head. They too remain vulnerable as they strive for a permanent state that is impossible to preserve.

While many roles are denied to females, that of beauty object is subtly as well as overtly encouraged. To enact femininity is to become a kind of exhibitionist, to display oneself as a decorative object. Few women are consciously aware of their objectification. Even fewer are concerned about it. After all, adornment is fun. Dressing up and showing off are ways of pleasing oneself and others. It seems a lot easier to be a sex object than a surgeon; certainly better to be looked at than overlooked. Attention, admiration, and compliments all feel good.

As people watch women, women become preoccupied with being watched. Many become obsessed with some body part they think needs correction. Nancy Henley (1977) concluded that:

> In society in which women's clothing is designed explicitly to reveal the body and its contours; in which women are ogled, whistled at, pinched while simply going about their business; in which they see ads . . . showing revealingly clad women . . . their bodies accessible to touch like community property . . . in such a society it is little wonder that women feel observed. They are. (p. 167)

A mere whistle can insert a wedge between mind and body, reducing a person to an object. Street hassling is generally not intended to make women feel good about themselves but to make them uneasy. Those males who hassle are not motivated simply to compliment, but to assert their right to judge a women, to invade her awareness, to make her self-conscious, to force her to see herself as an object in their eyes. Girl-watching and street hassling perpetuate the belief that female appearance is public property and that female objectification is legitimate.

The everyday objectification of women on Main Street, in the media, and in the mind supports the multimillion-dollar pornography industry. Pornography is a mixture of objectification and sexual hostility. Like the myth of female beauty, pornography also masquerades under the pretense of admiration. It too displays woman as vision while disguising woman as victim. In both cases, the victim in the vision is hidden behind her makeup and her seductive smile.

The centerfold figure is held out like a ripe fruit ready to be plucked and devoured. Her cheeks are luscious, her cleavage is compelling, and she seems powerful in her airbrushed beauty. By infusing woman's body with a mystical element, the myth of female beauty enhances the power of pornography. Without the beauty mask, there would be less mystique to strip away. A centerfold model, a Miss America, and an everyday woman all share a similar role. A woman who is ogled on the street is being visually "had," much like a pornographic model. She too is split off from herself, reduced to a facade, seen as prettier but less human than she really is.

A fine line divides the legitimate display of beauty from the illegitimate display of pornography. Those who seek admiration as a beauty object but fear exploitation as a sex object must be careful not to cross the line. The demands of beauty and the taboos of pornography require a balancing act that often throws women off balance. Vanessa Williams, Miss America 1984, was loudly applauded on the pageant runway but promptly censured when someone discovered that she had once strayed across the border into pornographic territory. Miss America must be provocative but wholesome. Her message is, "Look, but don't touch."

Feminists have actively protested against pornographic and commercial images that degrade women. But paradoxically the women's movement may have increased appearance anxiety even while trying to combat it. Feminism encourages reexamination of one's identity. It fosters an active approach to problem solving and teaches personal control through assertive behavior. Yet this message can easily be misconstrued as a new mandate for physical makeover.

Eager to reshape their lives, some women focus excessively on reshaping their bodies. Ultimately, they become trapped in a cycle of narcissistic self-absorption and masochistic self-rejection. These dynamics are evident in such disorders as anorexia, weight obsession, and compulsive exercising, disorders which have all increased in a climate of feminist reform. Women describe feeling tossed

between traditional feminine images and liberated feminist models. As one observed, "It's scarier to be a woman these days . . . because we are still expected to be svelte, beautiful, and downright delicate while we're running huge corporations with an iron hand. It's a schizophrenic kind of existence."

## PROPS AND PAINT

Women are not really fairer than men. Their special beauty is not innate but an acquired disguise. To act out a myth is to impersonate a caricature. And so the ladies' room becomes the powder room, where the costumes of femininity are applied.

Props and paint are essential elements of the female role, as basic to the culture as to the economy. Though a woman may feel powerless in many ways, her body is an arena she can try to control. Cosmetic rituals serve as a source of salvation. They can change the person as well as her image.

What motivates females to transform themselves? The answer is a strong human need to conform to social norms. A personal decision—to have a perm or a face-lift for example—is dictated partly by group pressure. Women enact the popular image for the pleasure of being like others and of being liked by others. Beauty transformations produce the security of group acceptance while they reduce the fear of social rejection.

Cosmetic strategies do help to normalize women. But they insidiously confirm female deviance even while counterbalancing it. Paradoxically, the more attractive a woman makes herself, the more deviant she often looks in her feminine drag.

Body beautification is a universal social gesture apparently stemming from a deep human need. Practiced by both males and females in virtually every culture, it traces back to ancient civilizations. A staggering variety of decorative rituals are found worldwide. To the western eye, some of them—such as the stretched necks of the Burmese or the elongated heads of the Senegalese—seem quite grotesque.

None of these cosmetic transformations are inherently more pleasing than others. Their aesthetic value depends on their social context. Black teeth or red nails seem attractive to someone conditioned to appreciate them as such. Who can say whether scarring one's face is elegant or hideous? Whether stretching one's lips with bone or implanting one's breasts with silicone is an aesthetic improvement or a monstrous mutilation?

Remember that beauty is defined as a unique and unusual quality—something beyond the ordinary. The distortions fashioned through cosmetic transformations produce an unnatural extreme. Redder lips, longer necks, blonder hair, flatter heads are loud signals that go beyond the boundaries of nature. And pain is often part of the decorative process. Pain signals an extreme commitment; the greater the pain, the more unique the product.

It is only a short step from deceiving others to deceiving oneself. Beauty rituals, initially used to disguise a defect, eventually screen us from self-scrutiny. As the real face becomes fused with fantasy and myth gives the illusion of truth, women end up feeling ashamed when caught unadorned. They learn their parts so well that they forget they are impersonating the role of fairy princess.

This works in several ways. First, props and paint accentuate gender differences, creating some that have no basis in nature (blue eyelids) and exaggerating others that are minimal (hairless legs). Shape of brows, contour of feet, style of hair become potent substitutes for natural sex differences. Lacquered nails and frosted lips flash like neon signs instantly advertising femininity. They transform abstract notions of beauty into something tangible, something we can see and feel. Once grounded in anatomy, these beauty symbols acquire the illusion of biological truth, and we start to think of them as fixed and permanent gender differences. While blue eyelids are pretty and feminine, they are peculiar distortions that affirm female otherness in the flesh.

Finally, beauty transformations maintain female deviance by associating femininity with phoniness. Props and paint may undermine credibiility, evoking suspicion and mistrust. Cellophane nails, silicone breasts, bottled blush, all link women with the false and the trivial. When a woman resembles a mannequin, she is not taken very seriously. Nietzsche associated deception with the feminine nature and wrote, "What is truth to woman? . . . her great art is the lie, her highest concern is mere appearance and beauty."

The artifice inherent in cosmetic rituals has been used as proof of female inferiority. For example, with the revival of corsets in the nineteenth century, critics labeled women not only deceptive but also stupid. Anyone who would subject herself to the senseless torment of corsets was considered "brainless and inferior."

What's a woman to do? If she ignores the demands of the beauty myth, she feels like an outsider, for unadorned means unattractive. If she capitalizes on cosmetics to normalize herself, she only exaggerates her caricature as the other sex. A sense of balance is hard to achieve.

New beauty images are needed—comfortable and potent images that will permit uncorseted movement on unbound feet, and that can lead toward unrestricted goals. By peeling off the beauty mystique, like yesterday's makeup mask, we may uncover faint traces beneath, closer to the skin, closer to reality. By cleansing the surface we can reveal hidden images. Who knows? We may even like what we find there.

If the myth of female beauty is a by-product of female deviance and subordination, as I have tried to show, then the pretty postures of oppression will diminish as sex roles are equalized. "The more women assert themselves as human beings, the more the marvelous quality of the Other will die out in them," predicts Simone de Beauvoir (1953). Giving birth to a new self-image entails work, risk, and commitment. Undoubtedly, independence is woman's greatest asset. An economically, emotionally, and sexually independent woman is armed to be a myth slayer. She is less likely to embrace the static image of a mannequin; less likely to use her body as a gesture of appeasement; less likely to depend on appearance as her primary source of power. As women gain access to the institutions that control society, they gain the means to shift beauty off the back of femininity and onto the gender-neutral position where it belongs. We will be released from the bonds of the beauty myth when women can look as ordinary as men, and still be valued as normal, lovable human beings.     [1998]

**REFERENCES**

de Beauvoir, S. (1953). *The Second Sex*. New York: Bantam.
Berscheid, E., & Walster, E. (1974). "Physical Attractiveness." In L. Berkowitz (ed.), *Advances in Experimental*

*Social Psychology,* vol. 7 (pp. 158–216). New York: Academic Press.

Freedman, R. (1986). *Beauty Bound.* Lexington, MA: Lexington Books.

Freedman, R. (1989). *Bodylove.* New York: HarperCollins.

Garner, D. M. (1997, Jan.). "The 1997 Body Image Survey Results," *Psychology Today,* 30–84.

Henley, N. (1977). *Body Politics: Power, Sex and Nonverbal Communication.* Englewood Cliffs, N.J.: Prentice-Hall.

Hutchinson, M. (1982). "Transforming Body Image: Your Body, Friend or Foe?" *Woman and Therapy,* 1(3), 59–67.

Pliner, P., Chaiken, S., & Flett, G. (1990). "Gender Differences in Concern with Body Weight and Physical Appearance over the Life Span," *Personality and Social Psychology Bulletin,* 16, 263–73.

Wooley, O. W. (1994). "And Man Created: 'Woman': Representation of Women's Bodies in Western Culture." In P. Fallon, M. Katzman, and S. Wooley (eds.), *Feminist Perspectives on Eating Disorders* (pp. 17–52). New York: Guilford Press.

## 🦎 32

# *When I Was Growing Up*

NELLIE WONG

I know now that once I longed to be white.
How? you ask.
Let me tell you the ways.

when I was growing up, people told me
I was dark and I believed my own darkness
in the mirror, in my soul, my own narrow vision

when I was growing up, my sisters
with fair skin got praised
for their beauty, and in the dark
I fell further, crushed between high walls

when I was growing up, I read magazines
and saw movies, blonde movie stars, white
skin,
sensuous lips and to be elevated, to become
a woman, a desirable woman, I began to wear
imaginary pale skin

when I was growing up, I was proud
of my English, my grammar, my spelling
fitting into the group of smart children
smart Chinese children, fitting in,
belonging, getting in line

when I was growing up and went to high
school,
I discovered the rich white girls, a few yellow
girls,
their imported cotton dresses, their cashmere
sweaters,
their curly hair and I thought that I too should
have
what these lucky girls had

when I was growing up, I hungered
for American food, American styles,
coded: white and even to me, a child
born of Chinese parents, being Chinese
was feeling foreign, was limiting,
was unAmerican

when I was growing up and a white man
wanted
to take me out, I thought I was special,
an exotic gardenia, anxious to fit
the stereotype of an oriental chick

when I was growing up, I felt ashamed
of some yellow men, their small bones,
their frail bodies, their spitting
on the streets, their coughing,
their lying in sunless rooms,
shooting themselves in the arms

when I was growing up, people would ask
if I were Filipino, Polynesian, Portuguese.
They named all colors except white, the shell
of my soul, but not my dark, rough skin

when I was growing up, I felt
dirty. I thought that god
made white people clean
and no matter how much I bathed,
I could not change, I could not shed
my skin in the gray water

when I was growing up, I swore
I would run away to purple mountains,
houses by the sea with nothing over
my head, with space to breathe,
uncongested with yellow people in an area
called Chinatown, in an area I later learned
was a ghetto, one of many hearts
of Asian America

I know now that once I longed to be white.
How many more ways? you ask.
Haven't I told you enough?                    [1981]

## 🌿 33

# To Other Women
# Who Were Ugly Once

INÉS HERNANDEZ-AVILA

Do you remember how we used to panic
when Cosmo, Vogue and Mademoiselle
        ladies
            would Glamour-us
            out of existence
                        so ultra bright
                        would be their smile
                        so lovely their
                        complexion
            their confianza[a] based on
            someone else's fashion
            and their mascara'd mascaras[b]
                hiding the cascaras[c]
                that hide their ser?[d]

I would always become cold inside
                    mata*onda*[e] to compete
            to need
            to dress right
            speak right
            laugh in just the
            right places
            dance in just
            the right way

My resistance to this type of
            existence
            grows stronger every day
Y al cabo ahora se
        que se vale
        preferir natural luz[f]
                    to neon.          [1980]

---

[a]Confidence. [b]Masks. [c]Shells. [d]Being. [e]Dampener: *onda* is a
"trip" in the positive sense—to *matar onda* is to kill, to frustrate the "trip"—to dishearten. [f]And now anyway I know that
it is worthy to prefer natural light.

## 🌿 34

# Nose Is a Country . . . I Am
# the Second Generation

AISHE BERGER

*for Emma Eckstein*

---

Emma Eckstein was a socialist and a writer before she became
a patient of Freud's. He diagnosed her as an hysteric because
she was prone to emotional outbursts and masturbated frequently. Freud turned Emma over to his colleague Dr. Fleiss,
who believed operating on the nose would inhibit sexual desire. Fleiss broke Emma's nose and left a large wad of gauze
inside her nasal passage. This "error" wasn't discovered until
years later, long after Emma's physical and emotional health
was ruined and she was left an invalid.

---

*"Such a nice girl, you have the map of Israel all over
your face."*
                    —Woman in fruitstore when I was thirteen

### I. Rhinoplasty

Nose that hangs on my face like a locket
with a history inside    you kiss
on our once a week date like lovers
in their mid forties
or maybe just my mother who is a lover
in her mid forties who had a nose job
in her mid twenties
the bump
the bumpy roads that troubled my father
the trouble with my father
who liked *zoftig*[1] women
all sides moldable
no bumps on the nose
map of Israel    on the face
map of Israel    on the map
a place on the edge of a deep blue
romantic sea    on the map
a place that keeps shuffling its feet
backward    shrinking
like her nose under gauze
under wraps

---

[1]Plump.

under hemorrhage that accidentally
happened when the doctor left
the operating room and didn't
return till the anesthesia was already
loosening to sound
like an avalanche
in preparation
her nose bleeding under that
temporary wrap
a change in the landscape
my mother passes me down
this nation
this unruly semitic landmass on my face

My teeth were always
complimented for their four years
of braces
the rumblings of my jaw as my face
continentally drifted and my nose
grew
not like my mother's which is
like a border with its bone gates
levelled neutral
a passive face my mother's
bumpless smile

## II. Hemorrhage

I think of Emma Eckstein
whose cartilage
was hammered out of her    the ancient
steppes on her face    the long view
of the world flooded
with large quantities of blood

Emma Eckstein who took her hands lovingly
inside her
who perhaps merely rubbed her legs together
in her seat and orgasmed
told she is hysterical
she wants too much in the final analysis
in the final analysis
the nose is inextricably linked
to the clitoris and the need to take hands
to yourself lovingly
is abnormal

Which was then a fresh new word
*abnormal*
the desire to treat oneself with kindness

*Take your hands and put them on your lap*

*Take your nose and put it on inside out*

On the ancient steps
up Emma Eckstein's nose
a man named Fleiss committed

strange unnatural acts in the name of
Psycho therapy
which was then a fresh new word

Emma
Levelled
Neutral
a passive face
a bumpless smile
her hands
jerk
at the thought
of herself
the hammer
reinforced
the hammer

## III. Assimilation into the modern world

and the gauze
under my own eyes
black and blue staying
in my house for a week
like sitting *shiva*[2]
fourteen years old
the most important days of my life

My mother promises me
a profile
like Greta Garbo

She used to tell me
my best friend Hilary
was prettier than me

---

[2] Practice of mourning the death of a relative by sitting in the
house for a week.

The little Yeshiva boys yelled
that I took all their air up
when I walked down the hall
Then the boys at camp said
they'd kiss me if they could
ever find my lips

My dermatologist pierces
my ears
when I'm ten and advises me
to wear big earrings
it will distract people away
from my face

At eight I learn the word *rhinoplasty*
and it becomes a goal in my future
like becoming the first woman president
or flying to the moon

I am the second generation

Nose is a country where little wooden puppets
tell lies
where paintings of Shylock
are in every hotel lobby
Nose is a country where women have to
walk with their heads down
Where I await my new
modern look
assimilated
deconstructed

*IV. Bridges*

The body doesn't let go
of bridges

they expose me to the world after seven days
I expect to be noseless  erased
but I am there    long and sloped
like a mountain after a fierce rain

I am there
the body knows

Mine stopped breathing at the crucial moment
the moment where they smash
bridges
the moment where the enemy
takes over

This time they couldn't finish
what they started
a part of me  revolted
against the gas    they had to
revive me before the last
bone was broken

The suspension of my long
winding bridge where my Jewish soul
still wanders over
the slightly altered terrain

the body knows

My desert nose  my sweet ripe nose
    my kosher nose
my zoftig nose my mountain nose
    my gentle nose
my moon of nose my sea of nose
    my heart pumping
lungs stretching fire of nose
    my full bodied
wine of nose    my acres of *sheyne*
    *sheyne  meydele*[3]
nose

that you kiss at night

Nose that I put my loving hands on.      [1986]

 35

## *Homage to My Hair*

LUCILLE CLIFTON

when i feel her jump up and dance
i hear the music! my God
i'm talking about my nappy hair!
she is a challenge to your hand
black man,
she is as tasty on your tongue as good greens
black man,
she can touch your mind

_____
[3] Pretty, pretty girl.

with her electric fingers and
the grayer she do get, good God,
the blacker she do be!                    [1976]

 36

# One Spring

LESLÉA NEWMAN

The air was thick with the promise
of lilacs and rain that evening
and the clouds hovered about my shoulders
like the mink stole in my mother's closet
I tried on from time to time.
I was sixteen and I knew it.
I tossed my head like a proud pony
my hair rippling down my back in one black wave
as I walked down the sultry street
my bare feet barely touching the ground
past the sounds of a television
a dog barking
a mother calling her child,
my body slicing through the heavy air
like a sailboat gliding on lazy water.

When the blue car slowed alongside me
I took no notice
until two faces leaned out the open window.
"Nice tits you got there, honey."
"Hey sweetheart, shine those headlights over here."
"Wanna go for a ride?"
I stopped,
dazed as a fish thrust out of water
into sunlight so bright it burns my eyes.
I turn and walk away fast
head down, arms folded,
feet slapping the ground.
I hear, "Nice ass, too,"
then laughter
the screech of tires
silence.

All at once I am ashamed of my new breasts
round as May apples,
I want to slice them off with a knife
sharp as a guillotine.

All at once I am mortified by my widening hips,
I want to pare them down with a vegetable peeler
until they are slim and boyish.
All at once I want to yank out my hair by the roots
like persistent weeds that must not grow wild.
But I am a sensible girl.
I do none of these things.

Instead I go home, watch TV with my parents,
brush my teeth and braid my hair for the night.
And the next day I skip breakfast,
eat only an apple for lunch
and buy a calorie counter,
vowing to get thinner and thinner
until I am so slim I can slip
through the cracks in the sidewalk
and disappear. And I do.                    [1993]

 37

# Time to Eat

DONNA MARQUARDT

*I*

Moving with a speed I cannot check,
the car hurtles down the black deserted road
towards an unfamiliar destination.
Immense cautioning roadsigns appear at every
    curve,
warnings that I am too close to turn back.
In school bathroom toilet stalls girls
smoke their first illegal cigarettes,
rites of passage to the world.
They major in beauty, and makeup,
a *Seventeen* magazine their textbook,
taking care to master the tools
of a trade necessary for survival.
Hungry, groping adolescent male hands
touch virgin bodies as clandestine kisses
are stolen in corners of dim high school hallways.
Mother says "sex is dirty."
"Boys are out for one thing."
Maybe she's right;
I don't know.
She tells me nothing;
I am so afraid;

she wants me to be perfect.
I am her firstborn daughter.
Brown-eyed, blond, curly-haired cooing baby,
I grow in her image and have her face.
She pinned her lost dreams on me
like crisp cotton diapers and pink lacy dresses.
Immortalized in bronze,
my baby shoes were placed atop the piano
harbingers of the greatness
I am expected to achieve.
I grew learning the lesson that legends
are hard to live by.
With budding breasts and spreading hips
bursting the protective garment of childhood,
I am left naked and exposed.
I soon will arrive
at this strange place for which I am not ready.
Stomping the brakes to no avail,
feeling powerless and out of control, I cannot stop.
From somewhere deep inside me a voice speaks
    softly.
"To stall the car, simply let it run out of fuel."

## II

Refusing food, my flesh falls away.
Day by day I grow smaller and thinner,
Alice in a carnival funhouse wonderland.
My world becomes narrower.
Daily devotions of arduous exercise, weights and
    scales
assure my redemption through perfection and
    control.
Reborn, emerging purged and purified
under the light of eternal childhood,
I am my own power; I am my own strength.
Only once have I surrendered to temptation
gorging for a week on the forbidden fruit.
The tape measure showed the evidence
of the fall from grace.
Like Hester Prynne I am sentenced to wear
my sins on my body for everyone to see,
two days penance of fasting becoming
the only hope of absolution.

## III

At the dinner table battleground,
Mother and I face each other in endless daily combat.

Like a military general she orders me to eat.
Stabbing at the enemy food on my plate,
raising it to my mouth in surrender,
the sour taste of defeat poisons my lips and tongue.
Rebellious prisoner of war on a hunger strike
I have become a problem to the victor.
Helpless she takes me to a Haitian shrink.
Tap, tap, tap,
he knocks on my brain with his witch doctor chants
of hypnotic incantations.
"Go away; you cannot come into my body temple
or perfection religion."

## IV

Shivering in the cold wind, no flesh to warm me
I walk on the deserted playground
under an overcast, forbidding sky.
Lonely and sad I do not want to play here
    anymore.
All of my friends have grown-up and gone home.
Like castles in the sandbox pelted by
a torrent of sudden summer rain,
I have watched my idols crumble.
Like a broken seesaw off center,
my life is unbalanced and askew.
It is time to stop the games and put away the toys.
They are for children.
I too must go home.
I am hungry.
It is time to eat.                                    [1982]

 38

# Women's Oppression and the Obsession with Thinness

JULY SIEBECKER

Large numbers of women in the U.S. are engaged in a constant battle against our own flesh. Our society tells most of us that we need to change our physical selves in order to be happy, healthy, successful, accepted, and loved. We are too fat, we're told, and when shown the images of beautiful young women on fashion magazine covers, we must agree because all but 5% of us will never have the body shape of those fashion models. We feel immense pressure to conform, to remodel our bodies with an endless string of diet plans and exercise regimens, or hide ourselves in shame and self-loathing. Most of us would see this war against our bodies as a personal issue, but in fact it is a social problem with distinct political ramifications. It affects more than our self-esteem. It helps keep women in an inferior place in our society and is harmful to us socially, psychologically, and physically.

The American obsession with thinness is an issue I have had personal cause to study, as I grew up fat and suffered from a compulsive eating disorder for which I began treatment in my second year of college. While in therapy, I started questioning the directives I got from society, telling me that my success in life was greatly influenced by the size of my hips. I also began to suspect that my problem was not as uncommon as I had thought. I discovered that while not every woman had an eating disorder, *no* woman I knew was happy with her body or appearance. I spoke with many women about this issue and found that those whose backgrounds were similar to mine—white, middle-class, urban or suburban—were most likely to have had similar experiences. The Latina and African-American women I spoke with had the benefit of countervailing norms of beauty in their cultures, but all heard messages telling them they should look a different way than they do and could relate to what I was dealing with on some level.

My experience served as an entry point into feminism for me because I began to see that there is a tremendous gap between the myths and the realities of women's lives. We are all being told that this image is available to all if only we work hard enough and are "good" enough (meaning self-deprivational enough), but rarely do any of us achieve this image. The disparity between what we look like and how we are supposed to look erodes our self-esteem, as we try unsuccessfully to gain approval from our male-dominated society and feel unable to live the lives we want to until we reduce ourselves.

We are assured by the media and the diet indus-

try that anyone can have the perfect body if she tries hard enough. This is a false and deceptive message because it is, in fact, not normal for most women's body types.[1] Millions of women are so caught up in the mythology of the perfect woman that we don't even know what is normal for our bodies. The phenomenon of the flat stomach is simply not anatomically appropriate for most women. In reality, we're not all meant to be one size. According to the research of Dr. David Garner, a specialist in eating disorders at the Clark Institute of Psychiatry, Toronto, each of us has a genetically predetermined "set point" of weight, just as we all have different heights, and our bodies will work to keep us at that size. The reason that 95–98% of all dieters gain back the weight we lose is because our bodies are trying to get back to our set points.[2] So the idea that one's size is a matter of willpower, which contributes to the negative stereotype of fat people as lazy and gluttonous, simply isn't true. If we all had the same rate of exercise and type of diet, some of us would be smaller and some of us would be larger—and very few of us would look the way society presently tells us that we should.

A look at the way we speak about weight makes clear the disapproval society feels for fat people. We categorize people who are not thin as deviant rather than simply being at different places in a continuum of body sizes. We use the words "overweight" or "out of shape" in our kinder moods; "fat" or "obese" in our more blunt moments. All are laden with value judgments. "Obese" is supposedly a bit more objective (though there is a distressingly wide range of definitions for it in the literature on health and size issues), but "fat" has such negative connotations that it is almost impossible to use without conferring an insult upon its recipient. We use "overweight" to talk about someone who isn't thin, but not "overheight" to refer to someone who is tall. Which weight is it that we're talking about, then, when we declare that we are over it? We have an ideal image for the adult female that is so deeply en-

---

[1] Garner and Garfinkel, *Handbook for the Treatment of Eating Disorders* (New York: The Guilford Press, 1985), p. 516.
[2] K. Chernin, *The Obsession: Reflections on the Tyranny of Slenderness* (New York: Harper & Row, 1981), p. 30.

graved in our minds that we see any deviation from it as unattractive and bad.

It is my observation that while both men and women suffer from discrimination because of body size, it is much more severe for women because in our culture a woman's worth is more tied to appearance. When we see that our bodies and sexuality are viewed and treated as commodities, we begin in subtle ways to think of ourselves as objects. Our role models in the media are often shown in pieces; a set of legs here, a torso or just a pair of lips there, implying that we are the sum of our body parts and must be prepared to withstand intense scrutiny part by part for approval, rather than whole, unique individuals, complete with flaws. This leads us to believe that in order to have a successful life, we must fashion ourselves into perfect objects; only then will we be capable of earning the approval and affection of men. We are encouraged to think that if we don't end up in monogamous, heterosexual relationships, we will lead loveless, lonely, sad lives. And we know that if we are fat, we will be scorned and punished by society.

Women pursue the image of beauty for two reasons: because we are told that we need to for our health, and to avoid being social outcasts. While the first reason is what we speak openly about and hear the most public arguments for, I would assert that it is the second that more often truly compels us. Hence, we can be in fine health but miserable if we don't look the way we think we should in a bathing suit, but are delighted when an illness has caused us to temporarily lose a few pounds. We feel that if we fail to conform to the ectomorphic image, we will suffer both personally and socially. We are absolutely right in this assumption.

Fat women's lives are plagued by discrimination and derision because of their "deviance." We are viewed as unfeminine and are treated with a distinct lack of respect, as if we were animals or things rather than human beings with thoughts, feelings, and abilities. We experience ridicule in public and are shown only in negative or "character" roles in the media. Our sexuality is considered a humorous subject by definition at best, and perverse or disgusting at worst. We are told endlessly by well-meaning friends and relatives that we would be pretty if only we took off some weight, thus communicating that we are not and cannot be pretty now, and that until we become thin we are not entitled to participate in many facets of ordinary life. When applying to colleges that require interviews, we are turned away more often than thin women with lower SAT scores. When entering the work force, it is harder for us to get jobs or be promoted. Both socially and economically, fat women are punished and discriminated against for looking different; we are robbed of our personhood, our dignity, our sexuality, our opportunities, our self-esteem, and our power.[3]

The stigma against fat women is reinforced by the pronouncement of the medical world that it is impossible to be both heavy and healthy. In fact, scientific findings about the relationship between health and weight are by no means clear, but until very recently, the media focused exclusively on studies that support the condemnation against fleshiness. For example, we have heard much about the strain put on the heart by gaining weight, but not that losing weight can present the same health risk. An American Cancer Society study showed that a 10% gain *or loss* of body weight puts a strain on the heart.[4] We are not adequately informed that it is yo-yo dieting (a series of unhealthy crash or "fad" diets in which the dieter loses and regains weight a number of times) that is the major cause of permanent weight gain. The body interprets the act of dieting as starvation and will put on more weight—and specifically more fat—than was originally lost in an attempt to defend itself.[5]

We are also not informed about the positive medical facts about fat. For instance, the findings of the 30-year Framingham Study indicated that "life expectancy was worst among the leanest in the populations, and in many instances best among the fattest."[6] In another study, Dr. Reubin Andres, Clinical Director of the National Institute on Aging,

[3] M. Millman, *Such a Pretty Face: Being Fat in America* (New York: W. W. Norton, 1980). See Millman for a comprehensive and moving study of what it is like to be a large woman in a size-biased society.

[4] K. Chernin, *The Obsession: Reflections on the Tyranny of Slenderness,* p. 41.

[5] Garner and Garfinkel, *Handbook for the Treatment of Eating Disorders,* pp. 532–33.

[6] R. Seid, *Never Too Thin: Why Women Are at War with Their Bodies* (New York: Prentice-Hall, 1989), p. 1.

reviewed the mortality data on cancer, diabetes, and hypertension, all of which are supposed to be caused by obesity. He logically assumed that if this was the truth, then the mortality data would show fatter people dying earlier of these conditions. However, he found the *opposite* to be true; thinner people were the ones with higher mortality rates due to these illnesses.[7] These are just a few examples showing that we are not receiving the whole picture when it comes to health and fat.

The other side of this coin is that we are not adequately informed of the health risks of dieting or being underweight. These include "chronic fatigue, irritability, tension, inability to concentrate" as well as symptoms we may know more of, such as anemia and other vitamin deficiencies, dizziness, and headaches.[8] Rapid weight loss can actually release toxins into the body, instead of flushing them out.[9] While the medical industry is now beginning to warn about the dangers of yo-yo dieting, these warnings go unheeded by the majority of American women, who hear a louder and more wish-fulfilling message from the $32 billion diet industry telling us that physical perfection *is* quickly and easily attainable.[10] Clearly, the bias against fat women cannot be accounted for by health concerns; it is a socially induced fear. It must be understood as a product of our society's inability to accept diversity and as a manifestation of sexism.

Eating disorders, which involve both physical and mental health issues, are on the rise in our country. Thirty years ago, they were almost entirely unheard of, while today, they are being called "the sociocultural epidemic of our time."[11] There are three documented forms of eating disorders: bulimia, characterized by bouts of binge eating followed by purging through means such as vomiting or laxative abuse; compulsive eating, which involves binges but not purges; and anorexia nervosa, which involves binges, purges, self-starvation, and often compulsive exercising. All three share a similar fear and loathing of fat, involve similar obsessions with weight, appearance, and control, and afflict mainly women. These disorders have been regarded as bizarre psychological phenomena that affect a minority of emotionally disturbed young women. The problem has thus been isolated from the experiences of other women and marginalized into a psychological category. This has in effect thrown up a smokescreen between the clinically diagnosed eating disorder sufferer and the rest of women in society. If this smokescreen came down, what women would see is that, while we do not all actually have eating disorders, we are not so different from those sufferers. As psychologist Noelle Caskey comments: "In taking their fear of fat to life-threatening extremes, anorexics are simply obeying society's dictates in a more drastic manner than the rest of us."[12]

Symptoms associated with eating disorders are common in less severe forms in the general female population. Studies show, for example, that, like anorexics, large numbers of women whose weight was normal or were underweight, according to the Metropolitan Life Insurance Company tables, consider themselves overweight.[13] If the thriving businesses in liposuction, intestinal bypass surgery, gastric stapling, and jaw-wiring weren't enough to convince us that women are intensely afraid of being overweight (another eating disorder symptom), we should also note the 1980 *Cosmopolitan* survey that found that women are more afraid of becoming fat than they are of *dying*.[14] Eating disorders can be seen as part of a continuum of obsession that affects the vast majority of American women on some level. Even if a woman feels happy with her body as she is, if she is large, she will still be discriminated against in subtle or overt ways, and if she is thin, she will hear urgent messages to stay that way.

[7] Ibid.

[8] K. Chernin, *The Obsession: Reflections on the Tyranny of Slenderness*, p. 41.

[9] C. Solimini, "Body Pollution (Toxins Caused By Rapid Weight Loss)," *Weight Watchers Magazine*, v. 18 (April 1985), p. 62.

[10] C. Hemenway, "The Weighty Issue of Size," *Smith Commentary* (Northampton, MA: Smith College).

[11] E. Szekely, *Never Too Thin* (Toronto: The Women's Press, 1988), p. 12.

[12] N. Caskey, "Interpreting Anorexia Nervosa" in *The Female Body in Western Culture*, ed. S. Suleiman (Cambridge: Harvard University Press, 1986), p. 178.

[13] Garner and Garfinkel, *Handbook for the Treatment of Eating Disorders*, p. 392.

[14] M. MacKenzie, "The Politics of Body Size: Fear of Fat" (Berkeley: The Pacifica Tape Library, 1980).

Besides eating disorders, there is an even more direct way in which the obsession with thinness hurts women psychologically. Women are socialized to be other-oriented, and deprivation of self is seen as virtuous for us. In her traditional (and encouraged) role as wife and mother, a woman becomes the caretaker of others and is considered good for not giving to herself, for being self-sacrificing, for spending all her time in the service of others. This trait of self-abnegation is a staple for the sex-role stereotype of the good woman and also figures strongly into women's conflicts with food, size, and power. For example, when a woman is dieting and announces she was "good," she means she has deprived herself of something she wanted in order to be more appealing. In this way, we surrender the right to have our own needs and desires, and to have them seen as valid as those of men.

These issues demonstrate the pervasiveness of the complex knot of size, power, and sexism. The power relations between women and men are critical to understanding the fear of fat women. Today, in an age and a society where women are beginning to assert our right to equal power, the kind of body that we are told pleases men is a thin one. The womanly qualities of the adult female anatomy are discouraged in favor of the adolescent male's. Lithe, lean, and narrow-hipped, this image says more than androgyny; it says that power and acceptability don't come in overtly female packaging. Women are made to feel guilty for taking up a lot of space with our bodies, for being large, expansive, mature-looking, and for giving to ourselves and nurturing ourselves. These two ideologies are ultimately aimed at keeping women from getting figuratively and literally "too big for our britches." The bottom line is this: If a woman wants to succeed in a man's world, she must not threaten his hold on the power, and that means not appearing too mature, strong, powerful—sticking to little britches, to put it metaphorically. Ultimately, our bodies are a feminist battleground.

One would think that such a wide-reaching problem would be at the forefront of feminist concern over the position of women; after all, how much more basic an issue is there than how we relate to our bodies, and how they are perceived by society? Yet women do not band together to put an end to this situation. Instead, we accept the judgment against our flesh and are often the harshest judges of ourselves and each other. Why would we do this? Why, when faced with a situation of oppression that should be obvious to us, would we continue to condone and internalize it, continue to argue for our own oppression behind cries of concern for health?

I believe some reasons for this are: the strength of the stigma against large women, the power of the messages equating femininity with thinness, the climate of competition for male approval that is fostered within many different areas of society, and the absence of positive alternatives to conforming to the image of thinness. Having been instilled with the belief that we are not good enough as we are, women do not want to hear that diets don't work well and that our fear of fat oppresses us because it would mean having to accept the idea that we aren't able to solve our problems by losing weight. This would be giving up the dream of perfection that we are told is within our reach and is our true road to happiness. We have been sold a package, paid for in confidence and self-esteem, and we want to see our investment turn a profit.

So what alternatives are there to selling ourselves out? Comprehensive answers to such a complex problem would require at least another article, but some general ideas for personal and political action can at least get us started. If this issue were added to the feminist agenda, there are a number of possible ways to organize for change. We could petition the National Institutes of Health to include the obsession with thinness in its Women's Health Initiative project, and in particular press for a critical examination of the diet industry. We could also charge that more responsible research on women and issues of weight and diet be done. We can also challenge the diet industry itself, denounce its messages and tactics as harmful to women. We could put pressure on the fashion industry to create more clothing for women of all sizes and to have their models reflect the diversity of women who might be buying those fashions. We could organize campaigns to demand that a greater number of fat women be portrayed in positive roles in the media.

On the personal level, we need to stop fixating on weight. As Rita Freedman says in *Beauty Bound,* we need to "get off the scales and get on with our lives."[15] We need to educate ourselves and others that our current standards of beauty are inappropriate for 95% of the women trying to achieve them, and that these standards are unhealthy and ultimately oppress us. We should accept more diverse standards of beauty that are inclusive of many ages, shapes, races, and ethnicities. We mustn't let fashion run our lives. If our clothes don't fit, we should change *them,* not ourselves. We need to reject the idea of self-deprivation as a virtue, to recognize that it is unhealthy to our physical and mental well-being and is a way to keep us complicitous in our own oppression. We should recognize and accept the idea that we are entitled to the things we want and not be ashamed of taking up space. We need to recognize that trying to be healthy and trying to be happy are two different projects. We should eat well, exercise, try to eliminate stress, and accept the size that our bodies are when we're following this lifestyle.

Most of all, we must recognize that we have a right to be treated as equals, a right not to spend all our lives worrying about approval from men, a right to feed and nurture ourselves, a right to all the power that comes with our mature women's bodies, whatever size they are. These are rights worth fighting for.                                    [1993]

 **39**

## *Arroz Con Pollo* vs. Slim-Fast

LINDA DELGADO

To many white American women, thinness and tallness are essential parts of beauty. Yet in Spanish, the words *delgada* and *flaca* have a different connotation. Both words mean thin. *Delgada* connotes thin and weak, while *flaca* connotes thin as in skinny.

---

[15] R. Freedman, *Beauty Bound* (Lexington, MA: D.C. Heath, 1986), p. 170.

Neither is very flattering. In fact, the question that usually follows after someone notices you are looking rather *delgada* is whether you have been ill.

Weight problems, aside from their health implications, are not seen as important in Latino culture as they are in mainstream American culture. There is a ceremonial importance to food and many rituals assigned to the sharing of food with others. Recently during a warm-up exercise in a new class, students were asked to introduce themselves by identifying with a particular food. A young Dominican woman said she was like *arroz con pollo* (rice with chicken). Her reason for picking this dish was that rice with chicken symbolized warmth, love, and acceptance. It is a dish made for new neighbors, new in-laws, and new friends to celebrate important events. It means welcome and good luck.

The breaking of bread with family, friends, and strangers is part of Latino hospitality. "*Mi casa, su casa*" is an unaltered tradition. When you visit my aunt's house, for example, go there hungry! The variety and amounts of food are quite extraordinary. I get full just looking at the table! Not only must you partake of everything there, you must also keep in mind that there are at least three or four desserts to follow. On special occasions, such as Easter, Christmas, and Mother's Day, everyone has a signature dish, and part of the celebration is sharing these delicacies. Failure to eat the right amount will cause personal distress to the hostess. What did she do wrong? At my aunt's house, usually my grandmother will ask if you have been sick or if your children have been giving you a hard time. There must be some explanation why you have not eaten your share of food. By "your share of food" they mean enough to feed a small army! The word "diet" or "calories" is never mentioned. For the current generations, these messages can be confusing.

Putting weight on your bones, as my grandmother explains it, is necessary for many reasons. First of all, how else can you carry the burdens of being a woman? You have to eat in order to have the strength to deal with a husband and/or children (regardless of the fact that, at present, you may be 11 years old). You have to eat to have the strength to deal with *lo que Dios te mande,* whatever God sends you because *uno nunca sabe lo de mañana, so uno ti-ene que aprobechar lo de hoy,* we never know what tomorrow may bring, so we have to enjoy what we have today. Living in New York, you also have to eat in order to deal with the cold, wintry weather. There is always a good reason for a second or third helping of food. In the film *Acting Our Age,* an African-American woman about the age of 65 expresses her concern for the next generation of young women. She says, "Now that black women are being used as models and thought of as beautiful, they will pick up the same false notions about beauty as white women." I think this is also true for Latinas in the United States.

One of my childhood memories was an episode involving my grandmother when I was in the fifth grade. She picked me up at school and told my mother we were going shopping. Well, we did, but first she had someplace to take me. For as long as I could remember, I was a tall and very skinny child. That day, my grandmother and I took a bus ride into Manhattan to a nutrition clinic. She swore I was undernourished and that something was wrong. The doctor said I was healthy and of a good weight. My grandmother was quite surprised and, in fact, didn't believe him.

Having a "good set of hips" means not only that you can carry a child well but also that you can manage whatever your husband has in store for you. "You have to eat in order to have strength." So, from the time you are an infant, chubbiness is applauded as healthy. As you grow older, mental and physical well-being are assessed by your outer appearance. Thin is not sexy. It is unhealthy, unappealing, and sad. My grandmother told me that I didn't look strong enough to carry my bookbag and asked how was I going to carry whatever God sent my way. I learned early in life to expect to bear something! That was part of the gender-role experience.

Interestingly, flabbiness is not acceptable, either. Flabbiness is a sign of laziness and overindulgence. Formal exercise is not part of the Latino culture for women, while men often play softball, handball, or paddle ball. It is generally accepted that women who are flabby and out of shape must not be taking care of their homes, themselves, or their children. They must be watching *novelas.* Women's exercise happens in the course of cleaning, cooking, and caring for children.

In the dating game, life gets really confusing for young Latinas. If women look too much like the models, they will be considered the kind of women men play with but don't necessarily marry. A man brings a woman who is a size 10 or 12 home to mother and a family dinner, but a woman who is size 5 or 6, you have to keep away from your brother! A 16-year-old Puerto Rican student recently told me that her boyfriend wanted her to put on some weight before the summer. She said that he was not pleased at the fact that other men were watching her on the beach last summer. The other side of the problem was that her mother had taught her that if she gained weight, she would not have any boyfriends. When I heard this story, it reminded me of the African-American woman in the film and her description of "false notions about beauty."

Some of my fondest memories are wrapped in the warmth of mealtimes. Special foods are part of special holidays. Watching generations of women cook and exchange recipes, taking in all the wonderful aromas and feeling their sense of pride and accomplishment as they fulfilled their understood role, was positive for me. Although their place of power was in the kitchen, I learned how that power worked. Being in the kitchen did not mean being passive or subservient. It meant doing your share of the business of parenting and partnering, since the kitchen is the center of family activity. It is a place of importance in the Latino household. Feeding those whom you care about is nurturing the entire unit, and eating all of your *arroz con pollo* means you are loved for your efforts in return.

There are many mixed messages to negotiate in a cross-cultural environment. Immigrants, like everyone else, want to belong. They find themselves trapped somewhere between the cultural values of their home and their host country. Although some can negotiate the conflict better than others, it nevertheless distorts views of the self. Reconciliation of different cultural repertoires is quite a challenge, especially for young Latinas who are trying to "fit in."

[1992]

**40**

# Homage to My Hips

LUCILLE CLIFTON

these hips are big hips
they need space to
move around in.
they don't fit into little
petty places. these hips
are free hips.
they don't like to be held back.
these hips have never been enslaved,
they go where they want to go
they do what they want to do.
these hips are mighty hips.
these hips are magic hips.
i have known them
to put a spell on a man and
spin him like a top!                    [1976]

 **41**

# Beauty: When the Other Dancer Is the Self

ALICE WALKER

It is a bright summer day in 1947. My father, a fat, funny man with beautiful eyes and a subversive wit, is trying to decide which of his eight children he will take with him to the county fair. My mother, of course, will not go. She is knocked out from getting most of us ready: I hold my neck stiff against the pressure of her knuckles as she hastily completes the braiding and then beribboning of my hair.

My father is the driver for the rich old white lady up the road. Her name is Miss Mey. She owns all the land for miles around, as well as the house in which we live. All I remember about her is that she once offered to pay my mother thirty-five cents for cleaning her house, raking up piles of her magnolia leaves, and washing her family's clothes, and that my mother—she of no money, eight children, and a chronic earache—refused it. But I do not think of this in 1947. I am two and a half years old. I want to go everywhere my daddy goes. I am excited at the prospect of riding in a car. Someone has told me fairs are fun. That there is room in the car for only three of us doesn't faze me at all. Whirling happily in my starchy frock, showing off my biscuit-polished patent-leather shoes and lavender socks, tossing my head in a way that makes my ribbons bounce, I stand, hands on hips, before my father. "Take me, Daddy," I say with assurance; "I'm the prettiest!"

Later, it does not surprise me to find myself in Miss Mey's shiny black car, sharing the back seat with the other lucky ones. Does not surprise me that I thoroughly enjoy the fair. At home that night I tell the unlucky ones all I can remember about the merry-go-round, the man who eats live chickens, and the teddy bears, until they say: that's enough, baby Alice. Shut up now, and go to sleep.

It is Easter Sunday, 1950. I am dressed in a green, flocked, scalloped-hem dress (handmade by my adoring sister, Ruth) that has its own smooth satin petticoat and tiny hot-pink roses tucked into each scallop. My shoes, new T-strap patent leather, again highly biscuit-polished. I am six years old and have learned one of the longest Easter speeches to be heard that day, totally unlike the speech I said when I was two: "Easter lilies/ pure and white/ blossom in/ the morning light." When I rise to give my speech I do so on a great wave of love and pride and expectation. People in the church stop rustling their new crinolines. They seem to hold their breath. I can tell they admire my dress, but it is my spirit, bordering on sassiness (womanishness), they secretly applaud.

"That girl's a little *mess*," they whisper to each other, pleased.

Naturally I say my speech without stammer or pause, unlike those who stutter, stammer, or, worst of all, forget. This is before the word "beautiful" exists in people's vocabulary, but "Oh, isn't she the *cutest* thing!" frequently floats my way. "And got so much sense!" they gratefully add . . . for which thoughtful addition I thank them to this day.

*It was great fun being cute. But then, one day, it ended.*

I am eight years old and a tomboy. I have a cowboy hat, cowboy boots, checkered shirt and pants, all red. My playmates are my brothers, two and four years older than I. Their colors are black and green, the only difference in the way we are dressed. On Saturday nights we all go to the picture show, even my mother; Westerns are her favorite kind of movie. Back home, "on the ranch," we pretend we are Tom Mix, Hopalong Cassidy, Lash LaRue (we've even named one of our dogs Lash LaRue); we chase each other for hours rustling cattle, being outlaws, delivering damsels from distress. Then my parents decide to buy my brothers guns. These are not "real" guns. They shoot "BBs," copper pellets my brothers say will kill birds. Because I am a girl, I do not get a gun. Instantly I am relegated to the position of Indian. Now there appears a great distance between us. They shoot and shoot at everything with their new guns. I try to keep up with my bow and arrows.

One day while I am standing on top of our make-shift "garage"—pieces of tin nailed across some poles—holding my bow and arrow and looking out toward the fields, I feel an incredible blow in my right eye. I look down just in time to see my brother lower his gun.

Both brothers rush to my side. My eye stings, and I cover it with my hand. "If you tell," they say, "we will get a whipping. You don't want that to happen, do you?" I do not. "Here is a piece of wire," says the older brother, picking it up from the roof; "say you stepped on one end of it and the other flew up and hit you." The pain is beginning to start. "Yes," I say. "Yes, I will say that is what happened." If I do not say this is what happened, I know my brothers will find ways to make me wish I had. But now I will say anything that gets me to my mother.

Confronted by our parents we stick to the lie agreed upon. They place me on a bench on the porch and I close my left eye while they examine the right. There is a tree growing from underneath the porch that climbs past the railing to the roof. It is the last thing my right eye sees. I watch as its trunk, its branches, and then its leaves are blotted out by the rising blood.

I am in shock. First there is intense fever, which my father tries to break using lily leaves bound around my head. Then there are chills: my mother tries to get me to eat soup. Eventually, I do not know how, my parents learn what has happened. A week after the "accident" they take me to see a doctor. "Why did you wait so long to come?" he asks, looking into my eye and shaking his head. "Eyes are sympathetic," he says. "If one is blind, the other will likely become blind too."

This comment of the doctor's terrifies me. But it is really how I look that bothers me most. Where the BB pellet struck there is a glob of whitish scar tissue, a hideous cataract, on my eye. Now when I stare at people—a favorite pastime, up to now—they will stare back. Not at the "cute" little girl, but at her scar. For six years I do not stare at anyone, because I do not raise my head.

Years later, in the throes of a mid-life crisis, I ask my mother and sister whether I changed after the "accident." "No," they say, puzzled. "What do you mean?"

*What do I mean?*

I am eight, and, for the first time, doing poorly in school, where I have been something of a whiz since I was four. We have just moved to the place where the "accident" occurred. We do not know any of the people around us because this is a different county. The only time I see the friends I knew is when we go back to our old church. The new school is the former state penitentiary. It is a large stone building, cold and drafty, crammed to overflowing with boisterous, ill-disciplined children. On the third floor there is a huge circular imprint of some partition that has been torn out.

"What used to be here?" I ask a sullen girl next to me on our way past it to lunch.

"The electric chair," says she.

At night I have nightmares about the electric chair, and about all the people reputedly "fried" in it. I am afraid of the school, where all the students seem to be budding criminals.

"What's the matter with your eye?" they ask, critically.

When I don't answer (I cannot decide whether it was an "accident" or not), they shove me, insist on a fight.

My brother, the one who created the story about the wire, comes to my rescue. But then brags so much about "protecting" me, I become sick.

After months of torture at the school, my parents decide to send me back to our old community, to my old school. I live with my grandparents and the teacher they board. But there is no room for Phoebe, my cat. By the time my grandparents decide there *is* room, and I ask for my cat, she cannot be found. Miss Yarborough, the boarding teacher, takes me under her wing, and begins to teach me to play the piano. But soon she marries an African— a "prince," she says—and is whisked away to his continent.

At my old school there is at least one teacher who loves me. She is the teacher who "knew me before I was born" and bought my first baby clothes. It is she who makes life bearable. It is her presence that finally helps me turn on the one child at the school who continually calls me "one-eyed bitch." One day I simply grab him by his coat and beat him until I am satisfied. It is my teacher who tells me my mother is ill.

My mother is lying in bed in the middle of the day, something I have never seen. She is in too much pain to speak. She has an abscess in her ear. I stand looking down on her, knowing that if she dies, I cannot live. She is being treated with warm oils and hot bricks held against her cheek. Finally a doctor comes. But I must go back to my grandparents' house. The weeks pass but I am hardly aware of it. All I know is that my mother might die, my father is not so jolly, my brothers still have their guns, and I am the one sent away from home.

"You did not change," they say.

*Did I imagine the anguish of never looking up?*

I am twelve. When relatives come to visit I hide in my room. My cousin Brenda, just my age, whose father works in the post office and whose mother is a nurse, comes to find me. "Hello," she says. And then she asks, looking at my recent school picture, which I did not want taken, and on which the "glob," as I think of it, is clearly visible, "You still can't see out of that eye?"

"No," I say, and flop back on the bed over my book.

That night, as I do almost every night, I abuse my eye. I rant and rave at it, in front of the mirror. I plead with it to clear up before morning. I tell it I hate and despise it. I do not pray for sight. I pray for beauty.

"You did not change," they say.

I am fourteen and baby-sitting for my brother Bill, who lives in Boston. He is my favorite brother and there is a strong bond between us. Understanding my feelings of shame and ugliness, he and his wife take me to a local hospital, where the "glob" is removed by a doctor named O. Henry. There is still a small bluish crater where the scar tissue was, but the ugly white stuff is gone. Almost immediately I became a different person from the girl who does not raise her head. Or so I think. Now that I've raised my head I win the boyfriend of my dreams. Now that I've raised my head I have plenty of friends. Now that I've raised my head classwork comes from my lips as faultlessly as Easter speeches did, and I leave high school as valedictorian, most popular student, and *queen*, hardly believing my luck. Ironically, the girl who was voted most beautiful in our class (and was) was later shot twice through the chest by a male companion, using a "real" gun, while she was pregnant. But that's another story in itself. Or is it?

"You did not change," they say.

It is now thirty years since the "accident." A beautiful journalist comes to visit and to interview me. She is going to write a cover story for her magazine that focuses on my latest book. "Decide how you want to look on the cover," she says. "Glamorous, or whatever."

Never mind "glamorous," it is the "whatever" that I hear. Suddenly all I can think of is whether I will get enough sleep the night before the photography session: if I don't, my eye will be tired and wander, as blind eyes will.

At night in bed with my lover I think up reasons why I should not appear on the cover of a magazine. "My meanest critics will say I've sold out," I say. "My family will now realize I write scandalous books."

"But what's the real reason you don't want to do this?" he asks.

"Because in all probability," I say in a rush, "my eye won't be straight."

"It will be straight enough," he says. Then, "Besides, I thought you'd made your peace with that."

And I suddenly remember that I have.

*I remember:*

I am talking to my brother Jimmy, asking if he remembers anything unusual about the day I was shot. He does not know I consider that day the last time my father, with his sweet home remedy of cool lily leaves, chose me, and that I suffered and raged inside because of this. "Well," he says, "all I remember is standing by the side of the highway with Daddy, trying to flag down a car. A white man stopped, but when Daddy said he needed somebody to take his little girl to the doctor, he drove off."

*I remember:*

I am in the desert for the first time. I fall totally in love with it. I am so overwhelmed by its beauty, I confront for the first time, consciously, the meaning of the doctor's words years ago: "Eyes are sympathetic. If one is blind, the other will likely become blind too." I realize I have dashed about the world madly, looking at this, looking at that, storing up images against the fading of the light. *But I might have missed seeing the desert!* The shock of that possibility—and gratitude for over twenty-five years of sight—sends me literally to my knees. Poem after poem comes—which is perhaps how poets pray.

### On Sight

I am so thankful I have seen
The Desert
And the creatures in the desert
And the desert itself.

The desert has its own moon
Which I have seen
With my own eye.
There is no flag on it.

Trees of the desert have arms
All of which are always up

That is because the moon is up
The sun is up
Also the sky
The stars
Clouds
None with flags.

If there *were* flags, I doubt
the trees would point.
Would you?

*But mostly, I remember this:*

I am twenty-seven, and my baby daughter is almost three. Since her birth I have worried about her discovery that her mother's eyes are different from other people's. Will she be embarrassed? I think. What will she say? Every day she watches a television program called "Big Blue Marble." It begins with a picture of the earth as it appears from the moon. It is bluish, a little battered-looking, but full of light, with whitish clouds swirling around it. Every time I see it I weep with love, as if it is a picture of Grandma's house. One day when I am putting Rebecca down for her nap, she suddenly focuses on my eye. Something inside me cringes, gets ready to try to protect myself. All children are cruel about physical differences, I know from experience, and that they don't always mean to be is another matter. I assume Rebecca will be the same.

But no-o-o-o. She studies my face intently as we stand, her inside and me outside her crib. She even holds my face maternally between her dimpled little hands. Then, looking every bit as serious and lawyerlike as her father, she says, as if it may just possibly have slipped my attention: "Mommy, there's a *world* in your eye." (As in, "Don't be alarmed, or do anything crazy.") And then, gently but with great interest: "Mommy, where did you *get* that world in your eye?"

For the most part, the pain left then. (So what, if my brothers grew up to buy even more powerful pellet guns for their sons and to carry real guns themselves. So what, if a young "Morehouse man" once nearly fell off the steps of Trevor Arnett Library because he thought my eyes were blue.) Crying and laughing I ran to the bathroom, while

Rebecca mumbled and sang herself off to sleep. Yes indeed, I realized, looking into the mirror. There *was* a world in my eye. And I saw that it was possible to love it: that in fact, for all it had taught me of shame and anger and inner vision, I *did* love it. Even to see it drifting out of orbit in boredom, or rolling up out of fatigue, not to mention floating back at attention in excitement (bearing witness, a friend has called it), deeply suitable to my personality, and even characteristic of me.

That night I dream I am dancing to Stevie Wonder's song "Always" (the name of the song is really "As," but I hear it as "Always"). As I dance, whirling and joyous, happier than I've ever been in my life, another bright-faced dancer joins me. We dance and kiss each other and hold each other through the night. The other dancer has obviously come through all right, as I have done. She is beautiful, whole and free. And she is also me.        [1983]

# Sexuality and Relationships

$O$ur sexual experiences, on both emotional and physical levels, are closely tied to what we learn about the meaning of sexuality and its relationship to other dimensions of our lives. As Rebecca Walker points out, experiencing our sexuality allows us to explore what it means to be a woman, discover our erotic power, and learn about love and intimacy, among other things. For many young women, however, emerging sexuality is shrouded in shame and fear—the shame associated with being a "bad girl" and the fear of pregnancy, sexually transmitted infections, and AIDS. Walker proclaims the importance of young women knowing that "my body is not my enemy and pleasure is my friend and my right." Through acquiring this knowledge, women can become empowered to more fully experience the many dimensions of our lives.

Social scripts about sexuality also shape the ways we think about our sexual identity. In U.S. society, the heterosexual "norm" creates a dichotomy of "right" versus "wrong" in terms of sexual orientation. The experiences of lesbians and bisexuals are frequently ignored and/or dismissed, reinforcing this heterosexual bias. In the context of such restrictive options of sexuality, Lisa DeBoer shares her experience of the complex process of defining one's sexual identity.

No discussion of contemporary sexuality, especially among young adults, would be complete without attending to the effects of AIDS on sexual attitudes and behaviors. Adolescents and young adults, who often consider themselves invulnerable to disease and mortality, continue to be at high risk for contracting HIV. In "Safer Sex Is Real Sex," Zoe Leonard explores some of the ways that having an HIV-positive partner has affected not only her sexual behavior but her emotional relationship with her partner. As she deals with the necessity of practicing safer sex, she presents strategies she has adopted that allow her to explore and enjoy her sexuality, as well as protect her health. Her essay reminds us how pleasure and safety can and must be compatible as we develop new ways of relating sexually in the age of AIDS.

What happens when women are able to move beyond the limited stereotypes of "acceptable" sexuality? The next three selections relate the experiences of women from different walks of life: two lesbians, one of whom is disabled, and an older African-American woman. The portrayal of these women as sexually active and sensual challenges the confining norms that our society prescribes for women's sexual behavior and offers a vision of the many possibilities that exist for women's sexual expression.

This section concludes with two essays that integrate many of the issues related to sexuality and relationships that we have addressed. In "The Turn On," Marge Piercy contemplates the meaning of sex and sensuality in her relationships, going beyond prevailing conceptions of sexual arousal to appreciate relationship qualities and experiences that are exciting and intimate. Robin Ochs shares her exploration of the relation between her feminist ideals and beliefs, her sexual experiences with women and men, and what she has learned about herself in the process. Ochs's essay conveys the subtle ways in which heterosexuals take their privilege for granted as they move through the world of male-female couples. Both of these selections help us see that women can grow beyond the stereotyped images of female sexuality to claim sexual relationships that are truly gratifying.

---

## 42

# *Lusting for Freedom*

REBECCA WALKER

I had sex young and, after the initial awkwardness, loved it. For days and nights, I rolled around in a big bed with my first boyfriend, trying out every possible way to feel good body to body. I was able to carry that pleasure and confidence into my everyday life working at the hair salon, raising my hand in English class, hanging out with my best girlfriend, and flirting with boys. I never felt any great loss of innocence, only great rushes of the kind of power that comes with self-knowledge and shared intimacy.

But experiences like mine are all too rare. There are forces that subvert girls' access to freeing and empowering sex—forces like AIDS, limited access to health care, and parental notification laws that force thousands of young women to seek out illegal and sometimes fatal abortions. The way we experience, speak about and envision sex and sexuality can either kill us or help us to know and protect ourselves better. The responsibility is enormous. Unfortunately, moral codes and legal demarcations complicate rather than regulate desire. And judgments like "right" and "wrong" only build barriers between people and encourage shame within individuals. I personally have learned much more from examining my own life for signs of what was empowering for me and what was not, and from listening to and asking questions of my friends: What did you feel then, what did you learn from that?

When I look back at having sex during my teenage years, I find myself asking: What was it in my own life that created the impulse and the safety; the wanting that led me and the knowing that kept me from harm?

If you are a girl, sex marks you, and I was marked young. I am ashamed to tell people how young I was, but I am too proud to lie. Eleven. I was eleven, and my mother was away working. One autumn night Kevin, a boy I had met in the neighborhood, called and said he had a sore throat. I told him I would make him some tea if he wanted to come over. He said he was on his way. I had told him that I was sixteen, so I ran around for a few minutes, panicking about what to wear. I settled on a satin leopard-print camisole from my mother's bureau and hid it beneath a big red terry-cloth robe.

I have a few vivid memories of that night: I remember being cold and my teeth chattering. I remember his black Nike high tops and red-and-gray football jersey, and the smell of him, male and musky, as he passed me coming through the front door. I remember sitting on our green sofa and telling him rather indignantly that I was not a virgin. I remember faking a fear that I might get pregnant (I didn't have my period yet). I remember his dry penis, both of us looking elsewhere as he pushed it inside of me. I remember that I wanted him to stay with me through the night, but that instead he had to rush home to make a curfew imposed upon him by his football coach.

Shocking, right? Not really. Sex begins much earlier than most people think, and it is far more extensive. It is more than the act of intercourse, much more than penis and vagina. Sex can look like love if you don't know what love looks like. It gives you someone to hold on to when you can't feel yourself. It is heat on your body when the coldness is inside of you. It is trying out trusting and being trusted. Sex can also be power because knowledge is power, and because yeah, as a girl, you can make it do different things. I can give it to you, and I can take it away. This sex is me, you can say. It is mine, take it. Take me. Please keep me.

By the time I was eighteen I was fluent in the language of sex and found myself in restaurants with men twice my age, drinking red wine and artfully playing Woman. By then I had learned about the limitations of male tenderness, men's expectations about black female desire, the taboo of loving other women, the violence of rape. And, like women all over the world, I had mastered the art of transforming myself into what I thought each man would fall in love with. Not at all in control of each affair, but very much in control of the mask I put on for each man, I tried on a dozen personas, played out a dozen roles, decided not to be a dozen people. When Bryan said I was too black, I straightened my hair. When Ray said I was too young, I added four years. For Miles I was a young virgin, nervous and giggly. For Jacob I was a self-assured student of modern art. For Robbie I was a club girl. I was Kevin's steady.

When I think of what determined my chameleonlike identity then, I think of the movie *Grease*, with the dolled-up Olivia Newton-John getting the guy and popularity too after she put on pumps and a push-up bra and became "sexy." I also think about my best girlfriend in the fourth grade who stopped speaking to me and "stole" my boyfriend over Christmas break. It was a tricky world of alliances in those younger years. You could never be sure of who was going to like you and why, so I tried my best to control what parts I could. That explains my attempts to be cool and sexy, my pretending to know everything, my smoking cigarettes, and of course, my doing it with boys. I did what I thought had to be done.

But there were also other elements, other factors.

Like curiosity, desire and my body. These are the urges that account for the wet, tonguey ten-minute kiss outside the laundry room that I remembered with a quivering belly for weeks afterwards. Ditto for my desire to bury my face in my boyfriend's armpits in order to learn his smell well enough to recognize it anywhere. This very same desire to know also made me reach down and feel a penis for the first time, checking almost methodically for shape, sensitivity and any strange aberrations on the skin. My quest was not simply a search for popularity, but a definite assertion of my own nascent erotic power. This strange force, not always pleasurable but always mine, nudged me toward physical exploration and self-definition, risk taking and intimacy building, twisting each element into an inextricable whole.

Because my mother was often away, leaving me with a safe and private space to bring my boyfriends, and because my common sense and experience of nonabusive love led me to decent men, my relationships consisted of relatively safe explorations of sex that were, at the time, fulfilling physically and emotionally. I also began to play with different kinds of strength. While I learned about my partners' bodies, I learned that I had the power to make them need me. While I learned how much of myself to reveal, I learned how to draw them out. While I learned that they were not "right" for me, I learned that I was more than what they saw.

Did I know then that I was learning to negotiate the world around me and answering important questions about the woman I would become? Probably not, but looking back, it seems obvious: I peeled back endless layers of contorted faces, checking out fully the possibilities of the roles I took on. I left them again and again when I felt I could not bring all of myself to the script. I couldn't just be the football player's cheerleader girlfriend, or the club girl friend of a bartender. I wasn't happy faking orgasm (self-deceit for male ego) or worrying about getting pregnant (unprotected ignorance) or having urinary tract infections (victim of pleasure) or sneaking around (living in fear). Instinctively I knew I wanted more pleasure and more freedom, and I intuitively knew I deserved and could get both.

When I think back, it is that impulse I am most proud of. The impulse that told me that I deserve to live free of shame, that my body is not my enemy and that pleasure is my friend and my right. Without this core, not even fully jelled in my teenage mind but powerful nonetheless, how else would I have learned to follow and cultivate my own desire? How else would I have learned to listen to and develop the language of my own body? How else would I have learned to initiate, sustain and develop healthy intimacy, that most valuable of human essences? I am proud that I did not stay in relationships when I couldn't grow. I moved on when the rest of me would emerge physically or intellectually and say, Enough! There isn't enough room in this outfit for all of us.

It is important to consider what happens when this kind of self-exploration is blocked by cultural taboo, government control or religious mandate. What happens when we are not allowed to know our own bodies, when we cannot safely respond to and explore our own desire? As evinced by the worldwide rape epidemic, the incredible number of teenage pregnancies, and the ever-increasing number of sexually transmitted diseases, sex can be an instrument of torture, the usher of unwanted responsibility or the carrier of fatal illness.

It is obvious that the suppression of sexual agency and exploration, from within or from without, is often used as a method of social control and domination. Witness widespread genital mutilation and the homophobia that dictatorially mandates heterosexuality; imagine the stolen power of the millions affected by just these two global murderers of self-authorization and determination. Without being able to respond to and honor the desires of our bodies and our selves, we become cut off from our instincts for pleasure, dissatisfied living under rules and thoughts that are not our own. When we deny ourselves safe and shameless exploration and access to reliable information, we damage our ability to even know what sexual pleasure feels or looks like.

Sex in silence and filled with shame is sex where our agency is denied. This is sex where we, young women, are powerless and at the mercy of our own desires. For giving our bodies what they want and crave, for exploring ourselves and others, we are punished like Eve reaching for more knowledge. We are called sluts and whores. We are considered impure or psychotic. Information about birth control is kept from us. Laws denying our right to control our bodies are enacted. We learn much of what we know from television, which debases sex and humiliates women.

We must decide that this is no longer acceptable, for sex is one of the places where we do our learning solo. Pried away from our parents and other authority figures, we look for answers about ourselves and how the world relates to us. We search for proper boundaries and create our very own slippery moral codes. We can begin to take control of this process and show responsibility only if we are encouraged to own our right to have a safe and self-created sexuality. The question is not whether young women are going to have sex, for this is far beyond any parental or societal control. The question is rather, what do young women need to make sex a dynamic, affirming, safe and pleasurable part of our lives? How do we build the bridge between sex and sexuality, between the isolated act and the powerful element that, when honed, can be an important tool for self-actualization?

Fortunately, there is no magic recipe for a healthy sexuality; each person comes into her or his own sexual power through a different route and at her or his own pace. There are, however, some basic requirements for sexual awareness and safe sexual practice. To begin with, young women need a safe space in which to explore our own bodies. A woman needs to be able to feel the soft smoothness of her belly, the exquisite softness of her inner thigh, the full roundness of her breasts. We need to learn that bodily pleasure belongs to us; it is our birthright.

Sex could also stand to be liberated from pussy and dick and fucking, as well as from marriage and procreation. It can be more: more sensual, more spiritual, more about communication and healing. Women and men both must learn to explore sexuality by making love in ways that are different from what we see on television and in the movies. If sex is about communicating, let us think about what we want to say and how will we say it. We need more words, images, ideas.

Finally, young women are more than inexperienced minors, more than property of the state or legal guardians. We are growing, thinking, inquisitive, self-possessed beings who need information about sex and access to birth control and abortion. We deserve to have our self-esteem nurtured and our personal agency encouraged. We need "protection" only from poverty and violence.

And even beyond all of the many things that will have to change in the outside world to help people in general and young women in particular grow more in touch with their sexual power, we also need to have the courage to look closely and lovingly at our sexual history and practice. Where is the meaning? What dynamics have we created or participated in? Why did we do that? How did we feel? How much of the way we think about ourselves is based in someone else's perception or label of our sexual experiences?

It has meant a lot to me to affirm and acknowledge my experiences and to integrate them into an empowering understanding of where I have been and where I am going. Hiding in shame or running fast to keep from looking is a waste of what is most precious about life: its infinite ability to expand and give us more knowledge, more insight and more complexity. [1995]

## 🌿 43

# *Living My Life: Thoughts on Sexual Identity*

LISA DEBOER

"When we define ourselves, when I define myself, the place in which I am like you and the place in which I am not like you, I'm not excluding you from the joining—I'm broadening the joining."[1] In this quotation, Audre Lorde speaks about the existence of difference among people, and the meaning of

self-definition. Although her statement seems obvious to me now, I couldn't fully understand it until I experienced the process of defining my own sexual identity. I've spent a lot of time thinking about sexual identity, and my thoughts have developed over the years as I've been exposed to various theories, ideas, and experiences.

All of my life I've had sexual feelings and attraction to women and to men. It never seemed strange, or felt like a problem. I joined my friends in heterosexual talk about boys, and read books about teenage girls and their boyfriends. I also read books about girls having deep friendships with other girls, and even crushes on them. I had crushes on female friends and teachers, the Beatles, and Adam Ant. As I grew older, my high school friends were people who accepted differences in sexual orientation. Within my group we were bisexual, straight, and gay: my first boyfriend told me he was bisexual, and later announced he was gay. In this supportive atmosphere, I began coming out publicly as bisexual. I felt that people's sex didn't matter to me; I was interested in them as people. I felt very comfortable with myself and my identity.

One day one of my friends told me she thought she was a lesbian. She was apprehensive and unsure, but willing to accept it. Because she had few lesbian or bisexual role models, she had difficulty interpreting her feelings towards women. She thought that if she had *any* interest in women, she must be a lesbian. In the ensuing months, she alternated between periods of being single and having boyfriends. When she was single, she called herself lesbian. When she had boyfriends, she stopped talking about it. As she became more aware of her own feelings and desires, she accepted the fact that she was attracted to both men and women. She realized that her anxiety came from trying to make herself fit into a label that wasn't right for her. Through self-awareness, she succeeded in finding a way of expressing her sexual identity. She is presently a blissful bisexual activist.

Leaving my supportive environment behind, I ventured into the realm of college life. At my predominantly conservative midwestern state university, I lived a double life, with separate gay and straight worlds. For the first time in my life I met *lots* of lesbians and became involved with a thriving lesbian community. There were few other bisexuals around. During this time, I was often afraid to come out as bisexual. Rather than announce my identity, I allowed each community to assume I was just like them. Prejudices against bisexuals and fear of exclusion from both communities influenced my decision to remain silent. Eventually I did come out to people close to me, and though I was not ostracized, I found little open support for bisexuality.

As a bisexual, I came across most of the current stereotypes and misconceptions in both the straight and gay communities. While there is a multitude of ways these ideas are expressed, they fall into two main categories. The first consists of the denial of bisexual existence. People who spend part of their lives as bisexuals and then change to another orientation are often cited as proof that bisexuality is a transition phase or a denial of one's "true" identity. The second type of misconception is the belief that bisexuals do exist, but are dangerous, unhealthy, untrustworthy, perverse, desperate, and so on. Many people say they would never date a bisexual, because they assume all bisexuals have an inherent need to have someone of each sex all the time, and are therefore unfaithful.

While these stereotypes may be true for certain individuals, they hardly represent all bisexual people. Because bisexuality is not a polar opposite, like heterosexuality and homosexuality, it's harder to define. Bisexuals have fewer role models and less visibility than homosexuals and heterosexuals. In reality, there are many ways that people are bisexual, and for many people it is the healthiest, happiest, and most comfortable way for them to live.

As I encountered these prejudices, I discovered just how hard it is to maintain a bisexual identity in our society. The constant distortion, trivialization, and invalidation of bisexual existence can really wear a person down. One of the clearest societal messages is "Why don't you just choose? Why do you have to have both?" As I struggled against such restrictions, I wished everyone were bisexual—it would make everything so much easier! I fought for bisexual rights, advocated my bisexual identity, and promoted bisexual visibility.

Meanwhile, I studied feminist theory in my classes, and began to see sexual identity not as an innate trait that one discovers, but as socially constructed. Adrienne Rich's essay "Compulsory Heterosexuality and Lesbian Existence" had a particularly powerful effect on my thinking. Rich suggests that heterosexuality, rather than being an inevitable, natural form of sexual behavior, is taught and reinforced by a social structure in which bonding between women represents a threat to male power. I began to think about actively resisting the social pressure to be heterosexual. The idea of consciously shaping my own sexual identity fascinated me. If sexual identity is not biologically predetermined, it is fluid and changeable. We might change from heterosexual to lesbian to bisexual, or bisexual to lesbian, or any other possibility, as we move through our lives.

By my senior year, several major changes had occurred in my life. I had transferred college twice, and chosen a major in Women's Studies. I had relationships with both men and women that led me to look more closely at my sexual identity. The possibility of becoming a lesbian became all the more real. I realized that I felt a strong commitment to women, and felt myself to be women-identified. I began to shift from seeing myself as a person attracted to people regardless of gender, to someone who preferred women but was also attracted to men. I felt like I wanted to be a lesbian, and I felt like I *was* a lesbian—even though I was still sleeping with a man. The contradiction was almost too much for me, and I would stay up late ranting to my roommate about the disadvantages and limitations of these labels. Throughout this time I grappled with my sexual identity, and the thought of being both lesbian and heterosexual at the same time.

So why confine ourselves to terms like lesbian, straight, and bisexual? Why not be comfortable with broader definitions and concepts of sexuality? In an ideal world, each individual would choose lovers based on their own individual preference, and there would be no need for labels. But in this world, people are judged by their sexual orientation. Lesbians, gays, and bisexuals suffer from many forms of discrimination; they are denied jobs, housing, and child custody, are beaten and sometimes even killed. We need to be able to organize politically and fight for our rights as lesbian, gay, and bisexual people. Labels can be personally and politically liberating, as a way for someone to publicly say, "This is who I am and who I love," despite society's hatred. As individuals openly speak about homosexuality and bisexuality, they challenge bigotry and homophobia by making others aware of our existence and our need for society to acknowledge and defend our civil and human rights. Labels also serve social and personal functions, by giving people a shorthand method of communicating preferences and potential availability. We can recognize each other and form communities more easily by using standard terms to describe our sexual orientation.

As I analyzed the functions of labels, I struggled to see what it could do for me in my own life. I still felt uneasy with the labels, despite my understanding of why they exist and why they are useful. I felt as if I didn't fit any of the labels, but I still wanted to find a way to describe my sexual identity to others. Then one night, while raving to my patient and understanding roommate, I experienced a revelation. The problem was in my perception of the relationship between identity and labels. In order to find a label that worked for me, I had to understand that labels serve many functions, but they do not define a person's entire identity. Identity is complex, and exists independently from terms used to describe it. Labels are the beginning of communication, not the end.

My bisexuality has changed into something quite different from my high school days, so now I call myself and identify as a lesbian. My primary interest is in women; men will always be my close friends, but it's extremely unlikely that any of them will be my lovers. However, I have not always been a lesbian, and the future is always uncertain. Bisexuality is an important part of my life that I don't want to forget, and I want others to know of it as well. So although I use the word lesbian to describe myself, I am aware that bisexuality remains an integral part of me.

Describing a self-defined sexual identity to other people can be difficult. While I have a clear understanding of who I am, it's not always easy to express it to others. It can be threatening enough to come out to someone else when you have a label to use and be understood; it's especially difficult when you have to come out and at the same time build a vocabulary with them in order to explain where you're coming from. It takes more energy and effort, and there's no guarantee that people will be able to understand. But it's worth it: through speaking the truth of our lives, we break the silences that keep us separated from each other.

While my story describes my experience and viewpoint, other people have different experiences of sexual orientation. Some people have the same sexual identity for their entire lives. For many people, claiming an identity as lesbian, gay, or bisexual is a positive experience that strengthens their sense of self. I hope to convey the idea that we each can come to our own understanding of our sexual identity, and that the discoveries we make based on our own experience are what matter most for our own happiness.

Living a self-defined life is challenging, as other people and society at large try to pigeonhole us all. But despite the problems, it's the most satisfying way for me to live. I've given up letting other people tell me who I am and what I'm allowed to do. I owe it to myself to be as fully me as I can, and not let other people's fears and insecurities limit me. I'm much happier now, and I feel in control of my life and more aware than ever of my possibilities. My horizons are broader, as I no longer feel limited by labels for my sexual identity. And my future options are all open; like my high school friends, my sexual orientation is something that can change and grow with me. I've realized I can continue to define my own life, and be true to the voice within me that strives to speak independently while living my life.

[1993]

*NOTES*

1. From an interview in *The Feminist Renaissance. Sister Outsider, Essays and Speeches* by Audre Lorde. (Trumansburg, NY: The Crossing Press, 1984.)

Many thanks and hugs and kisses to Dawne Moon, Jerome O'Neill, Erin Clark, Kelly Scanlan, and Joel Greenberg for their support and assistance in writing this paper.

44

# Safer Sex Is Real Sex

ZOE LEONARD

I have a lover who is HIV positive.

I am HIV negative.

I want to talk about my experience with safer sex and loving someone who is HIV positive.

Safer sex is often spoken about as a major drag . . . necessary, but fundamentally unerotic. People never seem to say, "Yeah, I do this with my lover and it's really hot."

Well, I do it with my lover and it's really hot.

I knew he was HIV positive before I slept with him. I had felt surprised when I found out; he just looked so damned healthy. I didn't envision having a sexual relationship with him, mainly because I've been an out and happy lesbian for years. So, when we realized we had crushes on each other, it was a big shock and really scary. I was doing AIDS activism and supposedly I knew all about safer sex, but suddenly I couldn't remember what I knew. All the grey areas of "low-risk" and "safer" sex seemed unclear and menacing; was kissing really OK? Secret fears snuck in. What if everyone is wrong about safer sex, about saliva? I felt I couldn't ask about these scary thoughts, like I should know the answers and had no right to feel so threatened. I didn't want to reinforce the stigma that he fights: feeling infectious, reading about himself as an "AIDS carrier." It had been relatively easy to be supportive and accepting of my friends with AIDS, to be sex positive, to talk about safer sex, but now it was in my bedroom, and I'm wondering: can he put his finger inside me without a glove, can he go down on me, can I touch his penis? Safer sex is different when you know your partner is infected. I don't want to appear frightened. I don't want to make him feel bad by talking about it, but I really, really don't want to get infected. (I tested negative for HIV about two years ago, and swore that I would never again place myself at any risk whatsoever.) And, here I was, a dyke at that, kissing this man goodnight after our first date.

In the beginning I was overwhelmed, terrified after that first kiss. So, we didn't dive right into bed and "do the nasty." We took our time and messed around for months, figuring out what we were comfortable with. It was great, all that sex building up. I always came, but we never did anything outside the strictest confines of "no risk" sex without talking about it first. We talked a lot about limits and seeing each other's points of view: my understanding that he doesn't want to feel like a pariah, or like he represents disease, his understanding that I had a right to be frightened, cautious, curious. It is important that I never do anything out of pressure, out of a need to prove that I'm not prejudiced. I realize that, as much as he cares about my health, I have to decide for myself what is safer, and stick to it. I knew I would resent him if we did something I wasn't sure about, and I would fly into a panic the next day.

I also realize that he is at risk for any infection that I might be carrying, and that safer sex is to protect him, too. A mild infection that might be harmless to me could be devastating to him.

I'm afraid of making him sick. I had hepatitis this summer, and we were worried that I might give it to him. Hepatitis can be very dangerous to anyone with an impaired immune system. I felt frightened and guilty. Later on I got angry that my *being* sick was somewhat overlooked in the panic surrounding the possibility of his *getting* sick. I found myself anxious and worried about his health at a time when I needed comfort and care. Sometimes I don't feel legitimate in feeling sorry for myself or being concerned about my own health.

A great thing about safer sex is that we . . . don't have intercourse all the time. We get off a lot of different ways, so our sex is varied and we don't just fall into one pattern.

The main thing is not to form a hierarchy of what "real sex" is, or equate "real sex" with high-risk practices. We can't think that humping is fake and intercourse is real.

Condoms are great. They are really sexy to me now, like lingerie or the perfume of a lover. Maybe I'm just immature, or particularly responsive to Pavlovian training, but the mere sight of condoms, lube, or dental dams sends a sexy feeling through me. The tools of safer sex become as significant and fetishized as other toys for pleasure. I'm always hearing about how condoms and other latex barriers take away all the spontaneity, as if sex before AIDS was always spontaneous and perfect. There are many barriers to good sex, like being too anxious, too busy, or too tired, or the *phone ringing*, or not finding someone you want to have sex with in the first place.

You can use safer sex to tease each other, waiting until you want something really badly before you screw up the courage to ask for it (or beg for it). Then you stop, and hang in this state of anticipation, feeling like a teenager, waiting while he (for instance) gets the first condom out, squirts the lube in it, and gets it on. Then he gets the second condom out and on. It's tense and full of anticipation, and I rarely feel either of us cooling off. It can be exciting to admit what you want, to articulate it, and to know what your partner wants, and to use the confines of safer sex to create tension and escalate desire.

Also, it can be a gift, like the time we went away for the weekend and he showed up with a shopping bag full of every form of latex known to humankind. It's a way of showing that you care about someone's health, and that you want him or her to be considerate and romantic at the same time.

We've had to negotiate so many aspects of our relationship that otherwise might have remained mute, but this has given us the context to discuss other things: what feels good, what we want, what freaks us out. The need to figure all those things out has built trust between us; it's made us honest.

But divisions do occur between the sick and the well. My lover is asymptomatic, so HIV often seems like an abstract issue to me. When I'm talking about something in the future, he blurts out, "I don't know if I'll be alive in five years." Can I understand the depression? I feel guilty sometimes and cut off other times.

It's one thing to learn to [have safer sex] and quite another to feel committed to someone that you are afraid might get really sick or die. I think: can I do it? Will I have the patience, will I be adequate? What if he really does get sick, what then? . . . can I handle feeling this responsible? Do I want to take care of him? And what if he really does die? What about that?

I've had friends die of AIDS. I have visceral memories of Dan in the hospital just before he died, massaging his feet, feeling the thick lumps of KS lesions through his sweat socks. I remember him semiconscious, making noises, responding to the pressure of my hands, his lover saying yes, he likes that.

I was once very much in love with a woman who got cancer. For a year my whole world telescoped into just her room, her health. My life was filled with nightmares and worrying, cooking, obsessing. My days were spent in the hospital, knowing the staff, being a regular. I knew every detail of her treatment, read all the articles, took notes. Running into friends, everyone would ask, "How's Simone?" People stopped asking, "How are you?" There was a certain relief in turning myself over to this greater cause, where everything was always about her—humidifiers, macrobiotic food, appointments. Even now, we are friends, and still there is a subtext: will she get sick again, will she die?

I wonder, do I just thrive on drama? Do I have a martyr complex, or a death wish? Did I fall for him because of his status? Do I want to get infected; is this my most recent and subtle form of self-destruction? Friends and family are anxious, ask me about *it*. They tell me I'm crazy, and speak of illness and health in hushed tones.

And I have to admit, after all these months, sometimes I'm still scared. I see an article and I think, could I be the first case of saliva transmission? Why am I still scared? I forget for weeks, and then when I get sick, feverish, peaked, HIV is there like a threat. I worry secretly, and when I tell him, he's angry, defensive.

All around us, his friends, my friends, into the hospital, out of the hospital, dying. When will it start with him? He gets a cold, the flu. He's tired, glands swollen.

I hate this virus.

This started out to be about the joys of safer sex, but I guess it's complicated.

I am HIV negative, as of my last test. I've learned a lot and had some really hot sex and lots of flirty, sexy stuff, and there's been a lot of love and happiness in this relationship. There's a difference between rational fears and irrational ones. I try to act on the rational ones. I try to protect myself and my lover from real threats, and try to overcome the irrational fears.

## Demanding a Condom

KAT DOUD

Before I understood AIDS, who got it, and how it could be prevented, I was scared, really scared. I felt at risk but for the wrong reasons. I was afraid of casual contact with people instead of being afraid of having unsafe sex with a man I was seeing at the time. Max (not his real name) was putting a lot of pressure on me to get birth control pills for protection, [but] the only protection pills would offer would be for pregnancy—not AIDS. During this time, my fear of AIDS was growing. I was getting really paranoid, so I called the hotline. They talked a lot about condoms and safer sex. I went immediately to Max to tell him how I was feeling and that I wouldn't have sex with him without condoms. His reaction was horrible. He got very angry and full of contempt and accused me of having AIDS, and angry that I insinuated that he did. I began to try to explain, then realized he wasn't worth my time. Why would I want to sleep with this creature who didn't care about my life? I never saw him again after that night.          [1990]

You *can* make decisions about your life and love based on what you want, and not let illness, or fear of illness, make all the decisions for you.          [1990]

 45

## Pleasures

DIANE HUGS

We both sat there, two disabled lesbians in our wheelchairs, each on opposite sides of the bed. Sudden feelings of fear and timidness came over us. But once we finished the transferring, lifting of legs, undressing and arranging of blankets, we finally touched. Softly and slowly we began to explore each other, our minds and bodies. Neither could make assumptions about the sensations or pleasures of the other. It was wonderful to sense that this woman felt that my body was worth the time it took to explore, that she was as interested in discovering my pleasure as I was in discovering hers.

From the first touch it was a stream of sensations; to listen to every breath, each sigh, and to feel every movement of our love intermingling. It was so intense, so mutual that I must say this beginning was

one of the deepest and most fulfilling that I have ever experienced.

When I was an able-bodied lesbian, my approach to relating sexually had been to find out what moves turned someone on and go from there. Never before have I taken the time or had the opportunity to begin a relationship with such a beautiful feeling of pleasure, not only from the pot of gold at the end of the rainbow, but also from the exploration itself.

[1985]

 46

## My Man Bovanne

TONI CADE BAMBARA

Blind people got a hummin jones if you notice. Which is understandable completely once you been around one and notice what no eyes will force you into to see people, and you get past the first time, which seems to come out of nowhere, and it's like you in church again with fat-chest ladies and old gents gruntin a hum low in the throat to whatever the preacher be saying. Shakey Bee bottom lip all swole up with Sweet Peach and me explainin how come the sweet-potato bread was a dollar-quarter this time stead of dollar regular and he say un hunh he understand, then he break into this *thizzin* kind of hum which is quiet, but fiercesome just the same, if you ain't ready for it. Which I wasn't. But I got used to it and the onliest time I had to say somethin bout it was when he was playin checkers on the stoop one time and he commenst to hummin quite churchy seem to me. So I says, "Look here Shakey Bee, I can't beat you and Jesus too." He stop.

So that's how come I asked My Man Bovanne to dance. He ain't my man mind you, just a nice ole gent from the block that we all know cause he fixes things and the kids like him. Or used to fore Black Power got hold their minds and mess em around till they can't be civil to ole folks. So we at this benefit for my niece's cousin who's runnin for somethin with this Black party somethin or other behind her. And I press up close to dance with Bovanne who blind and I'm hummin and he hummin, chest to chest like talkin. Not jammin my breasts into the man. Wasn't bout tits. Was bout vibrations. And he dug it and asked me what color dress I had on and how my hair was fixed and how I was doin without a man, not nosy but nice-like, and who was at this affair and was the canapés dainty-stingy or healthy enough to get hold of proper. Comfy and cheery is what I'm tryin to get across. Touch talkin like the heel of the hand on the tambourine or on a drum.

But right away Joe Lee come up on us and frown for dancin so close to the man. My own son who knows what kind of warm I am about; and don't grown men call me long distance and in the middle of the night for a little Mama comfort? But he frown. Which ain't right since Bovanne can't see and defend himself. Just a nice old man who fixes toasters and busted irons and bicycles and things and changes the lock on my door when my men friends get messy. Nice man. Which is not why they invited him. Grass roots you see. Me and Sister Taylor and the woman who does heads at Mamies and the man from the barber shop, we all there on account of we grass roots. And I ain't never been souther than Brooklyn Battery and no more country than the window box on my fire escape. And just yesterday my kids tellin me to take them countrified rags off my head and be cool. And now can't get Black

enough to suit em. So everybody passin sayin My Man Bovanne. Big deal, keep steppin and don't even stop a minute to get the man a drink or one of them cute sandwiches or tell him what's goin on. And him standin there with a smile ready case someone do speak he want to be ready. So that's how come I pull him on the dance floor and we dance squeezin past the tables and chairs and all them coats and people standin round up in each other face talkin bout this and that but got no use for this blind man who mostly fixed skates and skooters for all these folks when they was just kids. So I'm pressed up close and we touch talkin with the hum. And here come my daughter cuttin her eye at me like she do when she tell me about my "apolitical" self like I got hoof and mouf disease and there ain't no hope at all. And I don't pay her no mind and just look up in Bovanne shadow face and tell him his stomach like a drum and he laugh. Laugh real loud. And here come my youngest, Task, with a tap on my elbow like he the third grade monitor and I'm cuttin up on the line to assembly.

"I was just talkin on the drums," I explained when they hauled me into the kitchen. I figured drums was my best defense. They can get ready for drums what with all this heritage business. And Bovanne stomach just like that drum Task give me when he come back from Africa. You just touch it and it hum thizzm, thizzm. So I stuck to the drum story. "Just drummin that's all."

"Mama, what are you talkin about?"

"She had too much to drink," say Elo to Task cause she don't hardly say nuthin to me direct no more since that ugly argument about my wigs.

"Look here Mama," say Task, the gentle one. "We just tryin to pull your coat. You were makin a spectacle of yourself out there dancing like that."

"Dancin like what?"

Task run a hand over his left ear like his father for the world and his father before that.

"Like a bitch in heat," say Elo.

"Well uhh, I was goin to say like one of them sex-starved ladies gettin on in years and not too dis-criminating. Know what I mean?"

I don't answer cause I'll cry. Terrible thing when your own children talk to you like that. Pullin me out the party and hustlin me into some stranger's kitchen in the back of a bar just like the damn police. And ain't like I'm old old. I can still wear me some sleeveless dresses without the meat hangin off my arm. And I keep up with some thangs through my kids. Who ain't kids no more. To hear them tell it. So I don't say nuthin.

"Dancin with that tom," say Elo to Joe Lee, who leanin on the folks' freezer. "His feet can smell a cracker a mile away and go into their shuffle number post haste. And them eyes. He could be a little considerate and put on some shades. Who wants to look into them blown-out fuses that—"

"Is this what they call the generation gap?" I say.

"Generation gap," spits Elo, like I suggested castor oil and fricassee possum in the milk-shakes or somethin. "That's a white concept for a white phenomenon. There's no generation gap among Black people. We are a col—"

"Yeh, well never mind," says Joe Lee. "The point is Mama . . . well, it's pride. You embarrass yourself and us too dancin like that."

"I wasn't shame." Then nobody say nuthin. Them standin there in they pretty clothes with drinks in they hands and gangin up on me, and me in the third-degree chair and nary a olive to my name. Felt just like the police got hold to me.

"First of all," Task say, holdin up his hand and tickin off the offenses, "the dress. Now that dress is too short, Mama, and too low-cut for a woman your age. And Tamu's going to make a speech tonight to kick off the campaign and will be introducin you and expecting you to organize the council of elders—"

"Me? Didn nobody ask me nuthin. You mean Nisi? She change her name?"

"Well, Norton was supposed to tell you about it. Nisi wants to introduce you and then encourage the older folks to form a Council of the Elders to act as an advisory—"

"And you going to be standing there with your boobs out and that wig on your head and that hem up to your ass. And people'll say, 'Ain't that the horny bitch that was grindin with the blind dude?'"

"Elo, be cool a minute," say Task, gettin to the next finger. "And then there's the drinkin. Mama, you know you can't drink cause next thing you know you be laughin loud and carryin on," and he grab another finger for the loudness. "And then there's

the dancin. You been tattooed on the man for four records straight and slow draggin even on the fast numbers. How you think that look for a woman your age?"

"What's my age?"

"What?"

"I'm axin you all a simple question. You keep talkin bout what's proper for a woman my age. How old am I anyhow?" And Joe Lee slams his eyes shut and squinches up his face to figure. And Task run a hand over his ear and stare into his glass like the ice cubes goin calculate for him. And Elo just starin at the top of my head like she goin rip the wig off any minute now.

"Is your hair braided up under that thing? If so, why don't you take it off? You always did do a neat cornroll."

"Uh huh," cause I'm thinkin how she couldn't undo her hair fast enough talking bout cornroll so countrified. None of which was the subject. "How old, I say?"

"Sixtee-one or—"

"You a damn lie Joe Lee Peoples."

"And that's another thing," say Task on the fingers.

"You know what you all can kiss," I say, gettin up and brushin the wrinkles out my lap.

"Oh, Mama," Elo say, puttin a hand on my shoulder like she hasn't done since she left home and the hand landin light and not sure it supposed to be there. Which hurt me to my heart. Cause this was the child in our happiness fore Mr. Peoples die. And I carried that child strapped to my chest till she was nearly two. We was close is what I'm tryin to tell you. Cause it was more me in the child than the others. And even after Task it was the girlchild I covered in the night and wept over for no reason at all less it was she was a chub-chub like me and not very pretty, but a warm child. And how did things get to this, that she can't put a sure hand on me and say Mama we love you and care about you and you entitled to enjoy yourself cause you a good woman?

"And then there's Reverend Trent," say Task, glancin from left to right like they hatchin a plot and just now lettin me in on it. "You were suppose to be talking with him tonight, Mama, about giving us his basement for campaign headquarters and—"

"Didn nobody tell me nuthin. If grass roots mean you kept in the dark I can't use it. I really can't. And Reven Trent a fool anyway the way he tore into the widow man up there on Edgecomb cause he wouldn't take in three of them foster children and the woman not even comfy in the ground yet and the man's mind messed up and—"

"Look here," say Task. "What we need is a family conference so we can get all this stuff cleared up and laid out on the table. In the meantime I think we better get back into the other room and tend to business. And in the meantime, Mama, see if you can't get to Reverend Trent and—"

"You want me to belly rub with the Reven, that it?"

"Oh damn," Elo say and go through the swingin door.

"We'll talk about all this at dinner. How's tomorrow night, Joe Lee?" While Joe Lee being self-important I'm wonderin who's doing the cookin and how come no body ax me if I'm free and do I get a corsage and things like that. Then Joe nod that it's O.K. and he go through the swingin door and just a little hubbub come through from the other room. Then Task smile his smile, lookin just like his daddy and he leave. And it just me in this stranger's kitchen, which was a mess I wouldn't never let my kitchen look like. Poison you just to look at the pots. Then the door swing the other way and it's My Man Bovanne standin there sayin Miss Hazel but lookin at the deep fry and then at the steam table, and most surprised when I come up on him from the other direction and take him on out of there. Pass the folks pushin up towards the stage where Nisi and some other people settin and ready to talk, and folks gettin to the last of the sandwiches and the booze fore they settle down in one spot and listen serious. And I'm thinkin bout tellin Bovanne what a lovely long dress Nisi got on and the earrings and her hair piled up in a cone and the people bout to hear how we all gettin screwed and gotta form our own party and everybody there listenin and lookin. But instead I just haul the man on out of there, and Joe Lee and his wife look at me like I'm terrible, but they ain't said boo to the man yet. Cause he blind and old and don't nobody there need him since they grown up and don't need they skates fixed no more.

"Where we goin, Miss Hazel?" Him knowin all the time.

"First we gonna buy you some dark sunglasses. Then you comin with me to the supermarket so I can pick up tomorrow's dinner, which is going to be a grand thing proper and you invited. Then we goin to my house."

"That be fine. I surely would like to rest my feet." Bein cute, but you got to let men play out they little show, blind or not. So he chat on bout how tired he is and how he appreciate me takin him in hand this way. And I'm thinkin I'll have him change the lock on my door first thing. Then I'll give the man a nice warm bath with jasmine leaves in the water and a little Epsom salt on the sponge to do his back. And then a good rubdown with rose water and olive oil. Then a cup of lemon tea with a taste in it. And a little talcum, some of that fancy stuff Nisi mother sent over last Christmas. And then a massage, a good face massage round the forehead which is the worryin part. Cause you gots to take care of the older folks. And let them know they still needed to run the mimeo machine and keep the spark plugs clean and fix the mailboxes for folks who might help us get the breakfast program goin, and the school for the little kids and the campaign and all. Cause old folks is the nation. That what Nisi was sayin and I mean to do my part.

"I imagine you are a very pretty woman, Miss Hazel."

"I surely am," I say just like the hussy my daughter always say I was.                    [1972]

 **47**

# *Loving Another Woman*

ANNE KOEDT

*The following is from a taped interview with a woman who talked about her love relationship with another woman. Both of these women, who requested anonymity, had previously had only heterosexual relationships; both are feminists. The interview was conducted by Anne Koedt.*

*Question:* You said you had been friends for a while before you realized you were attracted to each other. How did you become aware of it?

*Answer:* I wasn't conscious of it until one evening when we were together and it all just sort of exploded. But, looking back, there are always signs, only one represses seeing them.

For example, I remember one evening—we are in the same feminist group together—and we were all talking very abstractly about love. All of a sudden, even though the group was carrying on the conversation in a theoretical way, we were having a personal conversation. We were starting to tell each other that we liked each other. Of course one of the things we discussed was: What is the thin line between friendship and love?

Or, there were times when we were very aware of having "accidentally" touched each other. And Jennie told me later that when we first met she remembered thinking, "abstractly" again, that if she were ever to get involved with a woman, she'd like to get involved with someone like me.

The mind-blowing thing is that you aren't at all conscious of what you are feeling; rather, you subconsciously, and systematically, refuse to deal with the implications of what's coming out. You just let it hang there because you're too scared to let it continue and see what it means.

*Q:* What did you do when you became aware of your mutual attraction?

*A:* We'd been seeing a lot of each other, and I was at her house for dinner. During the evening—we were having a nice time, but I remember also feeling uncomfortable—I became very aware of her as we were sitting together looking at something. There was an unusual kind of tension throughout the whole evening.

It was quite late by the time we broke up, so she asked me whether I wanted to stay over and sleep on her couch. And I remember really being very uptight—something I certainly wouldn't have felt in any other situation with a friend. Yet, even when I was uptight and felt that in some way by staying I would get myself into something, I wasn't quite sure what—something new and dangerous—I decided to stay anyway.

It wasn't really until I tried to fall asleep, and couldn't, that all of a sudden I became very, very aware. I was flooded with a tremendous attraction for her. And I wanted to tell her, I wanted to sleep with her, I wanted to let her know what I was feeling. At the same time I was totally bewildered, because here I was—not only did I want to tell her, but I was having a hard time just facing up to what was coming out in myself. My mind was working overtime trying to deal with this new thing.

She was awake too, and so we sat and talked. It took me about two hours to build up the courage to even bring up the subject. I think it is probably one of the most difficult things I ever had to do. To say—to in any way whatsoever open up the subject—to say anything was just so hard.

When I did bring it up in an oblique way and told her that I was attracted to her, she replied somewhat generally that she felt the same way. You see, she was as scared as I was, but I didn't know it. I thought she seemed very cool, so I wasn't even sure if she was interested. Although I think subconsciously I knew, because otherwise I wouldn't have asked her—I think I would have been too scared of rejection.

But when I finally did bring it up, and she said she felt the same way, well, at that point there was really no space left for anything in your mind. So we agreed to just drop it and let things happen as they would at a later time. My main, immediate worry was that maybe I had blown a good friendship which I really valued. Also, even if she did feel the same way, would we know what to do with it?

*Q:* When you first realized that you were possibly getting involved with a woman, were you afraid or upset?

*A:* No. The strange thing is that the next morning, after I left, I felt a fantastic high. I was bouncing down the street and the sun was shining and I felt tremendously good. My mind was on a super high.

When I got home I couldn't do any kind of work. My mind kept operating on this emergency speed, trying to deal with my new feelings for her. So I sat down and wrote a letter to myself. Just wrote it free association—didn't try to work it out in any kind of theory—and as I was writing I was learning from myself what I was feeling. Unexpectedly I wasn't feeling guilty or worried. I felt great.

*Q:* When did you start sleeping with each other?

*A:* The next time we were together. Again, we really wanted each other, but to finally make the move, the same move that with a man would have been automatic, was tremendously difficult . . . and exhilarating. Although we did sleep together, it wasn't sexual; just affectionate and very sensual. After that evening we started sleeping together sexually as well.

I guess it was also a surprise to find that you weren't struck down by God in a final shaft of lightning. That once you fight through that initial wall of undefined fears (built to protect those taboos), they wither rapidly, and leave you to operate freely in a new self-defined circle of what's natural. You have a new sense of boldness, of daring, about yourself.

*Q:* Was it different from what you had thought a relationship with a woman would be like?

*A:* Generally, no. Most of the things that I had thought intellectually in fact turned out to be true in my experience. One thing, however, was different. Like, I'd really felt that very possibly a relationship with a woman might not be terribly physical. That it would be for the most part warm and affectionate. I think I probably thought this because with men sex is so frequently confused with conquest. Men have applied a symbolic value to sex, where the penis equals dominance and the vagina equals submission. Since sensuality has no specific sex and is rather a general expression of mutual affection, its symbolic value, power-wise, is nil. So sex with a man is usually genitally oriented.

Perhaps I wasn't quite sure what would happen to sexuality once it was removed from its conventional context. But one of the things I discovered was that when you really like somebody, there's a perfectly natural connection between affection and love and sensuality and sexuality. That sexuality is a natural part of sensuality.

*Q:* How is sex different with a woman?

*A:* One of the really mind-blowing things about all this has been that it added a whole new dimension to my own sexuality. You can have good sex, technically, with a woman or a man. But at this point in time I think women have a much broader sense of sensuality. Since she and I both brought our experiences as women to sexuality, it was quite something.

Another aspect of sexuality is your feelings. Again, this is of course an area that has been delegated to women; we are supposed to provide the love and affection. It is one of our duties in a male-female relationship. Though it has been very oppressive in the context that we've been allowed it, the *ability* to show affection and love for someone else is, I think, a fine thing—which men should develop more in themselves, as a matter of fact. Love and affection are a necessary aspect of full sexuality. And one of the things I really enjoy with Jennie is this uninhibited ability to show our feelings.

*Q:* Is the physical aspect of loving women really as satisfying as sex with a man?

*A:* Yes.

*Q:* You've been together a while now. What's your relationship like?

*A:* Once we got over the initial week or so of just getting used to this entirely new thing, it very quickly became natural—natural is really the word I'd use for it. It was like adding another dimension to what we'd already been feeling for each other. It is quite a combination to fall in love with your friend.

We don't have any plans, any desire, to live together, although we do see a great deal of each other. We both like our own apartments, our own space.

I think one of the good things we did in the beginning was to say: Let's just see where it will go. We didn't say that we loved each other, just that we liked each other. We didn't immediately proclaim it a "relationship," as one is accustomed to do with a man—you know, making mental plans for the next ten years. So each new feeling was often surprising, and very intensely experienced.

*Q:* What would you say is the difference between this relationship and those you have had with men?

*A:* Well, one of the biggest differences is that for the first time I haven't felt those knots-in-the-stomach undercurrents of trying to figure out what's *really* happening under what you *think* is happening.

I think it all boils down to an absence of role-playing; I haven't felt with Jen that we've fallen into that. Both of us are equally strong persons. I mean, you can ask yourself the question, if there were going to be roles, who'd play what? Well, I certainly won't play "the female," and I won't play "the male," and it's just as absurd to imagine her in either one of them. So in fact what we have is much more like what one gets in a friendship, which is more equalized. It's a more above-board feeling.

I don't find the traditional contradictions. If I do something strong and self-assertive, she doesn't find that a conflict with her having a relationship with me. I don't get reminded that I might be making myself "less womanly." And along with that there's less *self*-censorship, too. There's a mutual, unqualified, support for daring to try new things that I have never quite known before.

As a result, my old sense of limits is changing. For example, for the first time in my life I'm beginning to feel that I don't have a weak body, that my body isn't some kind of passive baggage. The other day I gritted my teeth and slid down a fireman's pole at a park playground. It may sound ordinary, but it was something I had never dared before, and I felt a very private victory.

*Q:* Given the social disapproval and legal restrictions against lesbianism, what are some of the external problems you have faced?

*A:* One thing is that I hesitate to show my affection for her in public. If you're walking down the street and you want to put your arm around someone or give them a kiss—the kind of thing you do without thinking if it is a man—well, that's hardly considered romantic by most people if it's done with someone of your own sex. I know that if I were to express my feelings in public with Jennie, there would be a lot of social intrusion that I would have to deal with. Somehow, people would assume a license to intrude upon your privacy in public; their hostile comments, hostile attitudes, would ruin the whole experience. So

you're sort of caught in a bind. But we have in fact begun to do it more and more, because it bothers me that I can't express my feeling as I see fit, without hostile interference.

*Q:* What made you fall in love with a woman?

*A:* Well, that's a hard question. I think maybe it's even a bit misleading the way you phrased it. Because I didn't fall in love with "a woman," I fell in love with Jen—which is not exactly the same thing. A better way to ask the question is: How were you able to *overcome* the fact that it was a woman? In other words, how was I able to overcome my heterosexual training and allow my feelings for her to come out?

Certainly in my case it would never have happened without the existence of the women's movement. My own awareness of "maleness" and "femaleness" had become acute, and I was really probing what it meant. You see, I think in a sense I never wanted to be either male *or* female. Even when I was quite little and in many ways seemed feminine and "passive"—deep down, I never felt at home with the kinds of things women were supposed to be. On the other hand, I didn't particularly want to be a man either, so I didn't develop a male identity. Before I even got involved with the women's movement, I was already wanting something new. But the movement brought it out into the open for me.

Another thing the movement helped me with was shedding the notion that, however independent my life was, I must have a man; that somehow, no matter what I did myself, there was something that needed that magical element of male approval. Without confronting this I could never have allowed myself to fall in love with Jennie. In a way, I am like an addict who has kicked the habit.

But most important of all, I like her. In fact I think she's the healthiest person I have ever been involved with. See, I think we were lucky, because it happened spontaneously and unexpectedly from both sides. We didn't do it because we felt compelled to put our ideological beliefs into reality.

Many feminists are now beginning to at least theoretically consider the fact that there's no reason why one shouldn't love a woman. But I think that a certain kind of experimentation going on now with lesbianism can be really bad. Because even if you do ideologically think that it is perfectly fine—well, that's a *political* position; but being able to love somebody is a very personal and private thing as well, and even if you remove political barriers, well, then you are left with finding an individual who particularly fits *you*.

So I guess I'm saying that I don't think women who are beginning to think about lesbianism should get involved with anyone until they are really attracted to somebody. And that includes refusing to be seduced by lesbians who play the male seduction game and tell you, "you don't love women," and "you are oppressing us" if you don't jump into bed with them. It's terrible to try to seduce someone on ideological grounds.

*Q:* Do you now look at women in a more sexual way?

*A:* You mean, do I now eye all women as potential bed partners? No. Nor did I ever see men that way. As a matter of fact, I've never found myself being attracted to a man just because, for example, he had a good physique. I had a sexual relationship with whatever boyfriend I had, but I related to most other men pretty asexually. It's no different with women. My female friends—well, I still see them as friends, because that's what they are. I don't sit around and have secret fantasies of being in bed with them.

But there's a real question here: What is the source, the impetus, for one's sexuality? Is it affection and love, or is it essentially conquest in bed? If it's sex as conquest in bed, then the question you just asked is relevant, for adding the category of women to those you sleep with would mean that every woman—who's attractive enough to be a prize worth conquering, of course—could arouse your sexuality. But if the sexual source lies in affection and love, then the question becomes absurd. For one obviously does not immediately fall in love with every woman one meets simply because one is *able* to sleep with women.

Also, one thing that really turns me off about this whole business of viewing women as potential bedmates is the implied possessiveness of it.

It has taken me this long just to figure out how men are treating women sexually; now when I see some lesbians doing precisely the same kinds of things, I'm supposed to have instant amnesia in the name of sisterhood. I have heard some lesbians say things like, "I see all men as my rivals," or have heard them proudly discuss how they intimidated a heterosexual couple publicly to "teach the woman a political lesson." This brings out in me the same kind of intense rage that I get when, for example, I hear white men discussing how black men are "taking their women" (or vice versa). Who the hell says we belong to anyone?

*Q:* Do you think that you would have difficulty relating to a man again if this relationship broke up? That is, can you "go back" to men after having had a relationship with a woman?

*A:* It's an interesting thing that when people ask that question, most often what they're really asking is, are you "lost" to the world of what's "natural"? Sometimes I find myself not wanting to answer the question at all just because they're starting out by assuming that something's wrong with having a relationship with a woman. That's usually what's meant by "go back to men"—like you've been off someplace wild and crazy and, most of all, unsafe, and can you find your way home to papa, or something. So first of all it wouldn't be "going back."

And since I didn't become involved with a woman in order to make a political statement, by the same token I wouldn't make the converse statement. So, sure I could have a relationship with a man if he were the right kind of person and if he had rejected playing "the man" with me—that leaves out a lot of men here, I must add. But if a man had the right combination of qualities, I see no reason why I shouldn't be able to love him as much as I now love her.

At a certain point, I think, you realize that the final qualification is not being male or female, but whether they've joined the middle. That is—whether they have started from the male or the female side—they've gone toward the center where they are working toward combining the healthy aspects of so-called male and female characteristics. That's where I want to go and that's what I'm beginning to realize I respond to in other people.

Q: Now that you've gotten involved with a woman, what is your attitude toward gay and lesbian groups?

A: I have really mixed feelings about them. To some extent, for example, there has been a healthy interplay between the gay movement and the feminist movement. Feminists have had a very good influence on the gay movement because women's liberation challenges the very nature of the sex role system, not just whether one may be allowed to make transfers within it. On the other hand, the gay movement has helped open up the question of women loving other women. Though some of this was beginning to happen by itself, lesbians made a point of pressing the issue and therefore speeded up the process.

But there is a problem to me with focusing on sexual choice, as the gay movement does. Sleeping with another woman is not *necessarily* a healthy thing by itself. It does not mean—or prove, for that matter—that you therefore love women. It doesn't mean that you have avoided bad "male" or "female" behavior. It doesn't guarantee you anything. If you think about it, it can be the same game with new partners: On the one hand, male roles are learned, not genetic; women can ape them too. On the other, the feminine role can be comfortably carried into lesbianism, except now instead of a woman being passive with a man, she's passive with another woman. Which is all very familiar and is all going nowhere.

The confusing of sexual *partners* with sexual *roles* has also led to a really bizarre situation where some lesbians insist that you aren't really a radical feminist if you are not in bed with a woman. Which is wrong politically and outrageous personally.

Q: Did the fact that lesbians pushed the issue in the women's movement have a major effect upon your own decision to have a relationship with a woman?

A: It's hard to know. I think that the lesbian movement has escalated the thinking in the women's movement, and to that extent it probably escalated mine.

But at the same time I know I was slowly getting there myself anyway. I'd been thinking about it for a long time. Because it is a natural question; if you want to remove sexual roles, and if you say that men and women are equal human beings, well, the next question is: Why should you only love men? I remember asking myself that question, and I remember it being discussed in many workshops I was in—what is it that makes us assume that you can only receive and give love to a man?                                    [1973]

## 🌿 48

# *The Turn On*

MARGE PIERCY

Fantasies are sex in the head. I have often observed that what turns me on in thinking about sex is not at all what turns me on in real time. My erotic fantasies and my sexual reality are quite distinct. My fantasies run to the exotic: a great many of them occur in other times and even in other worlds.

When I was younger, this distinction was not so sharp to me as it is now. In my blue and spiky youth, I was under the spell of various literary incubi; what attracted me was what had been programmed into me as attractive, for purposes far from my own. I was taught to choose men who tried to reduce my autonomy and who attempted to control me in ways that would have prevented me from doing any useful work of my own. Very negative human qualities had been programmed into me by literary and popular culture as triggers to sexual response: male self-pity, sullenness, posing, narcissism, self-dramatization, being or pretending to be violent. I responded to several sorts of men, none of them suitable—but I am not at all persuaded there existed then the sort of men I find attractive now.

Besides the Heathcliff mood-monsters, I was sometimes attracted to men who told me they were geniuses, generally scientists, since that was one field in which I could in no way contest their assertions. I was moved by these contorted, bright types who seemed to yearn for the land of the emotions as for some lush jungle that they could not penetrate. I would of course be their guide.

I imagined that some store of warmth was hidden in these oysters, a pearl of great price and a love that would be worth the incredible work of trying to open a shell not by force but by persuasion and passion. I believe this tendency could probably be better satisfied by that fad of a few years ago, the Pet Rock.

What turns me on not in the head, not in theory, not on paper, but in daily life? Truthfully, my most passionate moments have never been brief encounters. I have given a lot of rope to my sexual curiosity over the years and it has led me into many adventures and strange encounters; but none of them offered the pure sexual pleasure of being in my own bed with someone I trust and love. In my adventures, my omnivorous curiosity was always far better satisfied than my sexuality.

I do not find orgasm easy with a new sexual partner. A woman never quite knows what she is going to find when someone takes off his clothes. Often the polite social mask falls with the pants and she may find a passionate animal, or a four-year-old who wants to make mud pies and scream at mommy, or a machine freak who wants to program her the way he programs his personal computer.

A woman is never quite sure what she has got herself into, and she is generally committed to it, no matter how rough the ride, at least for the duration of the evening or night. Sex with someone new is exciting in the head, but to me tense with anxiety in reality. Even if the new partner's manner is wholly benign, there is anxiety over whether your own body will please. Unless you are plastic perfect, your body reflects the life you have lived. It has its scars, its stretch marks, its wounds of pleasure or pain, its signs of hard use or soft living. You are offering up your skin, your flesh, and there is always that element of suffering oneself to be judged.

There is also the awkwardness of finding out what each other likes and dislikes once the relationship has been established. Our sexual preference may be quite different with different partners. Some men are never any good at oral sex so it is pointless

to try to tell them how you like to be eaten. They approach the vagina with such fear and loathing you might as well give up. Hardly any man nowadays goes about saying how sex disgusts him, so you only find out that cold naysaying hatred after you've already climbed into bed. Some men with the best will in the world are simply incompetent. I have never been able to decide if this is real or feigned incompetence. It reminds me of the old trick of volunteering to do the dishes and being sure to do them so badly that you will not be asked to do them again.

Unless you are overprogrammed in your pleasures, clearly what you enjoy most with one partner may be different from what you enjoy most with another. All those small adjustments and explanations and verbal or nonverbal requests occur over a period of time. In a good sexual relationship you don't ever quite stop making them, but they occur after a while in a context of permission and ease.

Once that ease is created, often I find situations of working together on a common household project or job erotic. I don't necessarily mean something intellectual. That doesn't seem to work nearly as well as something physical. It could be planting beans or building a grape arbor or laying flagstones. The context of working together for a common good that is tangible acts directly on my sexual center.

I do not respond to the skinny icons of our culture. They speak of me of control, anxiety, mistrust of the flesh and of our animal natures. I like a fair amount of flesh and I also appreciate muscles: the kind that ordinary women and men develop when they do physical work. I do not like bodies that appear carved out of plastic resin. I like some belly and some bounce to snuggle against. My partner working outside with me looks good to me, in filthy jeans and an old shirt, as we carry around bags of bone meal and manure. In warmer weather, working in the garden tends to turn us both on, but in truth there is little fine sensual pleasure in attempting to copulate among the rows of cabbages while trying not to crush any, and the bugs do bite bare flesh. It is nicer to take the turned-on feeling inside. I am a great one for enjoying the out-of-doors and then going in for good food, good wine, and a comfortable bed.

Shared laughter is erotic too. Sometimes we are passionate and grunty in our sex, but sometimes we are silly, and silliness can be just as delightful. The permission to play in bed is something that perhaps only people who are fully at ease with each other can signal. It is permission to take on roles, to make noises, to try out spontaneous gestures and notions.

My sexuality is close to my sensuality. I find the common link in our culture between sex and violence peculiar, as if others around me were whipped into a frenzy of desire by the sight of a traffic light or the smell of wet wool. The difference between pleasure and pain is a sharply marked boundary to me. Whatever pleases me tends to express itself in sex eventually.

Sex is one of the few times, at its best, when the conscious mind ceases to be aware of its own machinations. We become our feelings, our sensations, our appetite, without all the quibbling and second-guessing and motive-scouring that normally goes on. While I value, perhaps even overvalue, my own intellect and honed consciousness, I seek those moments of respite from the constant chatter of evaluation. My cats soothe me by their animal presence; my garden soothes me as it requires my hard work and my attention. Sex is the ultimate cave, short of sleep and the sinking of the mind into the body. Sleep and sex are connected as animal functions: when I have trouble with one, I may well have trouble with the other. Insomnia and difficulty in orgasm are both warning signs of something wrong at the core, a problem that has to be dealt with.

When I have good sex with someone, I put up with more and am infinitely more motivated to work out problems. When someone withdraws sexually —a great way to manipulate a partner who likes sex—then already part of the motivation for getting through the muck is diminished. It's all part of the same whole. If you feel closer, the sex tends to be better; if you feel more distant, then the sex tends to be weaker.

I am not someone who is turned on by jealousy. That kind of competition and insecurity makes me ill at ease with my own sexuality. One of my prerequisites for sexual response is that I have a sense that the other person also finds me attractive— though our relationship doesn't have to be sexually exclusive.

That may seem contradictory, but it isn't. I require being able to trust my sexual partner, to feel sure that my partner is willing to offer real intimacy and love. Without that trust, I can never approach full sexual response. Women have such a range of pleasure, anyhow, from little bitty orgasms that are like buzzes and blips to orgasms that pick you up and carry you off and drop you after what feels like miles and years of intensity. I like sex pretty often and have never required that ecstasy be presented to me. I figure it's a mutual responsibility. But there are prerequisites to letting go that have to be there.

To be afraid of a partner, unable to speak my mind or lose my temper or express my will, would dampen my sexuality. Under the gross inequality that has existed between almost all men and women, I think few women can flourish sexually. To be defined as a sexual receptacle for someone else means to be negated as the one who desires.

For some in our culture, sex is possessing. For some, sex is conquering. For some, sex is doing something to someone before they can do it to you. For me, it is primarily knowing, both the other and oneself. In sex I know my body in an immediate way, from deep within it.

In good sex, my partner opens to me his full vulnerability, his capacity for pleasure, tenderness, and passion. We are communicating directly skin on skin. We are communicating through pressure and smell and taste and little sounds, far more than in the occasional words that may be spoken.

If I say that talk is erotic to me, I don't mean spatting and I don't mean those where-were-you-last-night? ordeals. I have had lovers who seemed turned on by fighting, and relationships in which a kind of tearing and gouging and screaming seemed essential, and might end up with fairly heated sex; but those relationships were with basically inarticulate men who needed a fair amount of shouting and banging around to feel in touch. I find I often do want to make love after a fight, but not because I am aroused. It is simply to affirm that the relationship continues.

No, the talking that is most erotic to me is simply

conversation at its own pace, a combination of the intense and the casual, the free association of two people who know each other well but who always have something new to report, to question, to discuss. When we are talking that way, I feel caressed.

Since my partner and I both write at home computers and raise much of our food organically, we are always sharing new skills—whether about the construction of a pitched roof or the recovery of some inadvertently erased data. Bringing to each other new glittering bits of knowledge in our hot beaks is surely part of our mating dance. We like to admire each other, as I think most people in egalitarian couples do.

On such occasions, we often feel especially close. I think it is feeling intimate that produces the best sex—not a great surprise, finally. The more trips we take together, whether by car or by computer or by walking in the dunes, the more opportunities we give each other to explore the rich variables of each other's mind and body. The best sex for me arises out of such an intimacy, constantly stimulated and renewed.                    [1984]

## 🌿 49

# *Bisexuality, Feminism, Men and Me*

ROBYN OCHS

Where does feminist consciousness come from? Why do some women begin to question what has been presented to us as given and, as a result of that questioning, come to understand the ways in which women have been systemically limited? Each of us takes a different road to feminism. Many of our journeys begin with a pivotal event or transition that forces us to question our assumed reality.

My own route to feminism was long, convoluted and closely connected with my developing bisexual consciousness. In my early twenties I realized that my emotional and sexual attractions toward women

as well as men were not going to go away, and I began to address those feelings. Forced off-balance by the turbulence of these emotions and their implications for my future, I began for the first time to consciously question the assumptions I had made about my life. I began to understand that many of my choices had not been freely made, but rather had been made within the context of a system that Adrienne Rich calls "compulsory heterosexuality," a system that posits heterosexuality as the only way to be.[1] In this essay I describe my own journey: what I learned and what I unlearned, and how these changes in my thinking have fundamentally changed my relationships with men.

I grew up believing that women deserved equal pay for equal work and that we had the right not to be raped or battered and the right to control our own reproduction. These beliefs were firmly held by my mother and grandmothers. In the kitchen of the house I grew up in, a cartoon showing two toddlers looking into their diapers was tacked to the bulletin board next to the telephone. One of the toddlers was saying to the other, "So *that* explains the difference in our salaries." Had I been asked as a young person whether I was a feminist I would have answered in the affirmative. To me, these issues were the essence of feminism.

But despite adopting the feminist label for external causes, I did not escape female socialization. I learned some "basic truths": that as a woman my value was in my body, and that mine was not "good enough": that sooner or later every woman needs a man; and that I would have to behave in certain ways in order to get myself one. These truths, which very much shaped my behavior for many years, I'll describe in greater detail below.

### MY BODY AND ME

Like many women, I grew up hating my body. I remember wearing shorts over my bathing suit as a preteen to hide my "ugly" fat thighs. As a teenager, I spent a lot of time worrying whether I was attractive enough. Of course, I was never quite up to standard. I wanted very much to have the kind of exterior that would cause scouting agents from pinup magazines or from modeling agencies to approach me on the street to recruit me. Needless to say, this never happened, reinforcing my belief that physically I was a total failure as a woman. I fantasized about being a dancer but knew I did not have the requisite "dancer's body." I thought my size 7½ feet were enormous. For the record, I have always been more or less average in weight. But average was not good enough. As long as I didn't look like one of those women in *Playboy,* I wasn't pretty enough.

*Too big too short too stocky too busty too round too many zits blackheads disgusting pinch an inch fail the pencil test cellulite don't go out without makeup don't let them see what you* really *look like they'll run away in terror but if you are really lucky and have a few beers and do it in the dark he might not notice so make sure to turn off the light before . . .*

I never questioned my standards of measurement, never realized that these standards are determined by a male-dominated culture and reinforced by a multibillion-dollar "femininity" industry that sells women cosmetics, diet aids, plastic surgery, fashion magazines, liposuction, creams and girdles. I took my inability to live up to these standards as personal failure and never drew any connections between my experience and that of other women.

## MEN AND ME

Men, you can't live without 'em. Sooner or later I would end up with one. My grandfather used to tell me that it was good that I was short, as that way I would have the option of marrying either a tall man or a short one. There aren't enough men to go around and it gets harder and harder to find one as you get older. Men aren't comfortable with women who are more educated/smarter/earn more than they. My fifty-year-old aunt never married. She waited *too long,* and by then it was *too late* because she was *too old, poor dear.* It's just as easy to fall in love with a rich man as a poor man. Men lead.

I always had a boyfriend. From age thirteen until after college, I don't remember going for more than a month without being in a relationship or at least having a crush. Having a boyfriend was a measure of my worth. I would select the boy and flirt with him until he asked me out. Most times, like the Mounties, I got my man. In dance, this is called

backleading, directing the action from the follower's position. It allows the man to look like he is in control.

I learned that there's a man shortage. There are more women than men. And "good men" are extremely rare. Therefore, if you manage to get hold of a good one, you'd better hang on to him. This message got louder as I moved into my twenties. I saw older women in their thirties and beyond searching frantically for a suitable partner with whom to reproduce the human species and make their lives meaningful. I learned that you'd better pay attention to your "biological clock."

## THE UNLEARNING

These messages had a powerful grip on me. How did I begin to unlearn them? The women's studies class I took in college helped a bit. However, I continued to consider feminism only in terms of situations outside of myself. I looked at my environment and catalogued the injustices, but did not look inside.

It wasn't until I was considering a relationship with a woman that I began to see the relevance of the feminist theory I had read as a first-year college student to my own life. My perspective changed dramatically. For example, in my first relationship with a woman, it became quickly apparent that in many ways I fit quite neatly into the passive "femme" role of the butch/femme stereotype. I was behaving as I had always behaved in relationships, but for the first time, now that my lover was a woman, my "normal" behavior appeared to me (and probably to her as well) strange and unbalanced. Why were my lover and I behaving so differently? Suddenly our roles appeared constructed rather than natural. I won't pretend that I woke up one day and found myself suddenly freed of my conditioning. Rather, I spent several years unfolding and unraveling the layers of misinformation I had internalized, learning more with each subsequent relationship or incident.

My body image began to change. Through the firsthand experience of my own attractions, I learned that women, and their bodies, are beautiful, though I did not immediately apply this knowledge to my opinion of my own body. There was one woman friend on whom I had a crush for more than two years. I thought she was beautiful, with her solid, powerful angles and healthy fullness. One day, with a sense of shock, I realized that her body was not so very different from mine and that I had been holding myself to a different, unattainable standard than I had been holding her and other women to. It was this experience of seeing my image reflected in another woman that finally allowed me to begin developing a positive relationship with my own body.

I learned from firsthand experience about the privilege differential that results when the gender of your partner changes. Before I had experienced some of society's disapproval and disregard, I had no sense of the privileges I had experienced in heterosexual relationships. In subsequent years, each time I changed partners I was painfully aware of this absurd double standard and began to strategize ways to live in such a way that I could challenge rather than collaborate with these injustices. I have made a personal commitment to be "out" as bisexual at every possible opportunity and to avoid taking privileges with a male lover that I would not have with my female lover. For these reasons, I have chosen not to marry, though I hope someday to establish a "domestic partnership" and have a "commitment ceremony." If I feel someone would be unwilling to hear me talk about a same-sex lover, I disclose nothing about *any* of my relationships, even if my current partner is of the opposite sex. This is not very easy, and occasionally I backslide, but I am rewarded with the knowledge that I am not contributing to the oppression of lesbian, gay, and bisexual people when I am in an opposite-sex relationship.

It was empowering to realize that men as romantic partners were optional, not required. I no longer felt pressured to lower my relationship standards in light of the shortage of good men. Yes, I might get involved with and spend the rest of my life with one, but then again I might choose to spend my life with a woman. Or perhaps simply with myself. This was to be my choice.

I realized how I had been performing my designated gender role. It's amazing how being in a same-sex relationship can make you realize just how much

of most heterosexual relationships is scripted from the first date to the bedroom to the dishes. In relationships with women, I learned how to lead and learned that I like to lead sometimes. As sometimes I like to follow. And as sometimes I prefer to negotiate every step with my partner, or to dance alone.

Finally, I made a personal commitment to hold men and women to the same standards in relationships. I realized that in our society women are grateful when a man behaves in a sensitive manner, but expect sensitivity of a woman as a matter of course. I decided that I would not settle for less from men, realizing that it means that I may be categorically eliminating most men as potential partners. So be it.

My experience with being in relationships with women has been in a way like a trip abroad. I learned that many of the things I had accepted as natural truths were socially constructed, and the first time I returned to a heterosexual relationship things felt different. I hadn't yet learned how to construct a relationship on my own terms, but I was aware that things were not quite right. As time passed, my self-awareness and self-confidence increased. I gathered more experience in lesbian relationships and began to apply my knowledge to subsequent heterosexual relationships.

It is not possible to know who or where I would be today had I remained heterosexual in my attractions and in my self-identity. Perhaps other events in my life would have triggered a feminist consciousness. At any rate, it is entirely clear to me that it was loving a woman that made me realize I had fallen outside my "script," which in turn forced me to realize there *was* a script. From there, I moved toward a critical self-awareness and the realization that I could shape and write my own life.　　[1992]

### NOTES

Thanks to Marti Hohmann, Rebecca Kaplan and Annie Senghas for their feedback and support while I was writing this essay.

1. Adrienne Rich, "Compulsory Heterosexuality and Lesbian Existence," *Signs: Journal of Women in Culture and Society* 5, no. 4, (1980), pp. 631–60.

## PART IV

# Institutions That Shape Women's Lives

We have examined the ways that sexist attitudes about women's potential, abilities, and social roles have limited our sense of self, impeded our growth, and damaged our self-confidence. Sexism, however, is more than a set of attitudes; it is firmly entrenched in the structure of society. Part IV examines the position of women in five of the major institutions that shape women's lives: the legal system, the economy, the family, the health care system, and religion. Together they have reinforced women's subordination in all areas of social life. Although we are accustomed to thinking of relationships such as family and motherhood as emotional and biological, they serve social and political purposes as well.

Feminist analysis has revealed that institutions tend to allocate power and resources in complex and subtle ways that systematically support patriarchy or male domination. While overt personal prejudice is apparent to most people, institutionalized sexism is so deeply embedded in our social life that it appears to be the natural order. Much of it remained unnoticed until the feminist movement called attention to it, revealing layer upon layer of discriminatory patterns. The deeper we look, the more patterns emerge. For example, women's analysis of the workforce first revealed much outright discrimination. Employers paid women less and excluded them from jobs because they were women. But when the Equal Pay Act of 1963 and Title Seven of the Civil Rights Act of 1967 made such discrimination illegal, women remained in a disadvantaged position in the workforce not only because of discrimination that eluded the law but as a result of occupational segregation, the clustering of women into female-dominated occupations that pay less and offer fewer opportunities for advancement than male-dominated occupations.

Our society has been organized around the notion that the public arenas of work, politics, and education are the province of men and the private world of home and family is female terrain. Although this division of activities and resources is powerful as ideology, it has never been an accurate description of the lives of all women. As Patricia Hill Collins argues, for example, most black women have occupied both public and private worlds, bearing both economic and nurturing responsibility for families.[1] Today a large proportion of women of all races and ethnic groups work outside the home. Despite these facts, the belief that women's natural role is in the family and man's in the public world shapes the primary institutions of social life. The contradiction between the realities of many women's lives and the social institutions structured by the belief in this division of labor is one of the major sources of tension in contemporary American life.

One of the most powerful vehicles for enforcing the subordination of women has been the legal system. As recently as 1961, the Supreme Court upheld a law exempting women from jury service because "woman is still regarded as the center of home and family life"[2] and therefore not subject to the same public obligations as men are. Laws have changed in the last 35 years, and the courts now recognize women's right to equal protection, but the legal system remains male-dominated and biased against women in many ways. At the same time, women have used the judicial system to challenge sexism and to fight for reproductive freedom, child support, domestic safety, and workplace justice, among others.

Women have always played crucial economic roles both inside and outside the family. The work that women do in the home is absolutely essential to economic life. Because it is unpaid, however, it is invisible and difficult to measure. Women have also been working outside the home for centuries. Female slaves worked in the fields, and young women factory workers were the first employees of the American textile industry. Until the middle of the twentieth century, most white women left their jobs when they married, but African-American women continued to work outside the home while caring for homes and children. In the past several decades women of all racial and ethnic groups have entered the workforce in increasing numbers. In 1995 women constituted 46% of the total workforce. Nevertheless, the belief that women's primary role is in the home continues to shape women's workplace experience, restricting opportunities, creating pay inequity, and preserving women's responsibility for child care and housework even while we hold full-time jobs.

Affirmative action policies have increased the hiring, promotion, job stability, and wages of women. Between 1970 and 1990 the proportion of women physicians more than doubled from 7.6% to 16.9%. From 1973 to 1993 the percentage of women lawyers and judges grew from 5.8% to 22.7%. By 1990 women were increasingly represented in high-graded civil service positions as a result of affirmative action programs. Women also experience psychological benefits from affirmative action. According to a 1990 study, for example, African-American women whose employers practiced affirmative action showed greater occupational ambition.[3]

Although sex discrimination is against the law, women continue to earn only 73% of what men earn. While there has been progress in the labor market position of women, this reduction in the wage gap in the past 15 years is more a result of declining earnings for men than significant increases for women. Women continue to encounter sexual harassment, sexual double standards, and what has been described as the glass ceiling, an invisible barrier of discrimination that has prevented women from advancing beyond a certain level. Recognizing that the clustering of women in low-paid, low-status jobs has been a major source of the wage inequities between women and men, some women have begun to enter occupations that have been historically male-dominated. Another approach to this problem is the demand for comparable worth or pay equity—the reevaluation of male- and female-dominated jobs on the basis of the required skill, effort, responsibility, and working conditions.

Women's responsibility for child care remains one of the biggest obstacles to economic equality for women. The United States lags behind other countries in providing child care facilities, parental leave, and other features that make the workplace compatible with parenting. It is one of a few countries without a national maternity leave policy and one of the few industrialized countries that does not provide universal health care or income supports to families with children. Without a fundamental restructuring of the workplace to accommodate workers with family responsibilities—both male and female—women will continue to be in a disadvantaged position.

The Family and Medical Leave Act of 1993 requires employers to give workers up to 12 weeks of unpaid leave during a 12-month period for birth or adoption; to care for a seriously ill parent, spouse, or child; or to undergo medical treatment for their own serious illness. Though helpful to some women workers, the law has restrictions, among them that it covers only employers with 50 or more employees. It is estimated that the act affects 5% of U.S. employers and 40% of all employees. Since the leave is unpaid, it is difficult for women in low-paying jobs to take advantage of the leave.

Because of the absence of affordable child care and the low pay of most women's jobs, many single women with children are consigned to poverty. Prior to 1996 these poor women were assured some cash assistance through welfare, Aid to Families with Dependent Children (AFDC). The Personal Responsibility and Work Opportunity Act (1996) eliminated AFDC and replaced it with the Temporary Assistance for Needy Families (TANF), a block grant program that removes any guarantee of assistance. It mandates states to force poor mothers into the low-wage labor market. However, there is not sufficient funding to create jobs, increase child care, or provide job training and health coverage to low-wage workers. Early evidence indicates that women are not finding the employment they are mandated to find.

Women, however, have a long history of organizing for better working conditions for themselves and others. Recently associations of working women such as 9to5, organizations for union women such as the Congress of Labor Union Women, and renewed commitments by the AFL-CIO to organize low-wage women workers have resulted in both economic gains for women and solidarity among women workers who often felt isolated.

The position of women in the workforce is inextricably connected with the position of women in the family. The division of power and resources in the patriarchal family has often subordinated the needs of married women to those of their spouses. The sentimental rhetoric that surrounds the family not only obscures the unequal power relations but also conveys the impression that only the patriarchal family is legitimate. In fact, the family, a group of people who are committed to each other and share resources, can take a variety of forms. The African-American family for example, often sustained by mothers, aunts, and grandmothers, has proved remarkably durable in the face of almost insurmountable odds.

Feminist theorists have found it useful to view motherhood as an institution as well as a relationship betwen mother and child. As an institution, motherhood was for a long time assumed to be women's primary function, one that made women unfit for full participation in other realms. The sentimentalization of motherhood obscures the realities of mothers' experience in a number of ways. While most mothers love and enjoy their children, motherhood can be lonely and sometimes painful in a society in which few social supports are available. When motherhood takes place outside the patriarchal family, the mantle of sentimentality disappears. Lesbian mothers have lost custody of their children, and single mothers face social censure. Sentimentalized motherhood also obscures the fact that not all women enjoy motherhood and that mothers who have no other sources of identity and satisfaction can become disoriented when children grow up. Some essays in this section tell the stories of real women whose lives belie the myths. They demonstrate the need to see motherhood as a more varied experience and to envision social supports that enable women to experience motherhood while participating fully in other aspects of human life.

Our society glorifies the nuclear family and disparages people, particularly women, who live outside it. Feminists believe that women should be able to choose how and with whom we live. Since one can choose freely only if a variety of lifestyles are considered legitimate, feminists seek to expand women's options, recognizing that different women will choose different ways to live and love.

Feminists insist that the nuclear family is not the only viable form in which to build lasting relationships and raise children. For feminists, a broadened definition of family includes any living arrangement in which people share time and space, contribute to the physical and psychological tasks of making a household function, share common history and ritual, and make a commitment to stay together over time. Members are not necessarily tied by biology or by the sanction of the state or church or by living in the same house all the time. Feminists work toward building families in which all members both give and receive support and love and have space to grow as autonomous individuals.

By supporting their families and maintaining nurturing homes, single mothers are defying the notion that children don't stand a chance in life because their father isn't present. Lesbian parents have struggled to affirm the validity of their families, even though they are different from others. Some women have created cooperative living arrangements in which they share household and parenting responsibilities.

The struggle for public recognition of one alternative family form, lesbian and gay marriage, has caused considerable controversy in the 1990s. In 1998 lesbians and gays can legally marry only in Hawaii, a situation that has fostered little change and caused considerable backlash. The Defense of Marriage Act, proposed in Congress and supported by President Clinton, affirms that states are not required to recognize marriages that were performed in other states.

Nevertheless, feminists still struggle to defend various forms of families that are democratic, cooperative living arrangements in which responsibility and power are shared and women can find both freedom and love. Our personal experiences in equitable communities and relationships will help us envision and create similar communities of care in our society at large.

One of the consequences of women's subordinate status in the workplace and family is the male domination of the health care system. Although women are the majority of health care consumers and do a great deal of the direct service work, most doctors, researchers, and managers of clinics and hospitals are men. As a result, women's health needs have not been adequately addressed. One particularly grievous example of this failure has been the slowness of the medical community to acknowledge the experience of women with AIDS.

For the past several decades women in the United States have been systematically excluded from the vast majority of research to develop new drugs, medical treatments, and surgical techniques. In 1990 the General Accounting Office released a report of an audit of the National Institutes of Health (NIH) that found that women were underrepresented in studies of diseases affecting both men and women. Some of the largest and most important medical studies of recent years had failed to enroll a single woman.[4]

Studies show that the doctor-patient relationship for many women exudes sexism. Professor Ann Turkel reports, "Women are patronized and treated like little girls. They are even referred to as girls. Male physicians will call female patients by their first names but they are always called doctor. They don't do that with men." Often women's symptoms are not taken seriously because physicians erroneously believe that they have no physical basis and are just "in their heads."[5]

The women's health movement has been a vital part of the rebirth of feminism. Through books such as *Our Bodies, Ourselves for the New Century* (Simon & Schuster, 1998), organizations such as the National Black Women's Health Project, and self-help groups, women have reclaimed their bodies, challenged the priorities of the medical establishment, and made women's experiences and needs visible. In 1991, for example, the National Breast Cancer Coalition united over 180 advocacy groups to push for more money for research on the causes of breast cancer.

The final institution that this part considers is institutionalized religion. Like health care institutions, women have been the members, men the decision makers. "It has been said that women are the 'backbone' of the church," writes Jacquelyn Grant, who studies black women and the church. "On the surface, this may appear to be a compliment, considering the function of the backbone in the human anatomy. . . . The telling part of the word 'backbone' is 'back'. It has become apparent to me that most of the ministers who use this term are referring to location rather than function. What they really mean is that women are in the 'background' and should be kept there; they are merely support workers."[6]

Patriarchal religion has had a powerful effect on women's lives not only by systematically excluding them from many leadership positions in most organized religions but by justifying subordination and enveloping it in divine sanction. Women who have spoken and acted on behalf of women's freedom have often found themselves colliding with church dogma.

In the 1990s religious fundamentalism has become more influential in the United States. In all of fundamentalism's forms, women are confined to a traditional, secondary status in the family and in society. In their efforts to influence governmental policy, fundamentalists have spearheaded efforts to challenge women's reproductive rights and right to sexual choice and freedom.

Women's struggle for equality in institutional religion has recently contributed to the decision of some religious groups to ordain women ministers and rabbis. This presence of women clergy may help change many people's vision of God as masculine. Women are doing some of the most challenging and innovative work in theology and ministry by infusing religious traditions with an emphasis on female experience. Other women have taken their quest for spirituality beyond organized religion and are developing their own forms of feminist spirituality that often have links both to historic female-centered religious practices and to the natural world.

All these institutions are intimately connected to each other. Women's experience in one reinforces our position in another, indicating that change in women's position in our society needs to take place on many fronts. The selections in this part show that within our social institutions, gender, class, and race work together to shape female experience. While our culture teaches us to believe that hard work and talent will be rewarded, institutions place white men in advantageous social positions. Understanding these institutional barriers enables us to see that all people do not have equal opportunity in our society and that to create it, we must make fundamental changes in our social institutions. Unless we recognize the historic advantages of white men, it is impossible to move toward a more equitable society. Affirmative action programs, which commit organizations to give preferences to women and members of other historically disadvantaged groups, recognize that in many ways a "white male affirmative action program" has been in place for centuries.

Finally, the selections in Part IV testify to the durability of patriarchy. Although women have made significant advances in the past 30 years, sexism is proving to be a stubborn adversary. As women occupy new territory in our society, new problems emerge or come into view. We are just beginning to understand, for example, the extent to which sexual harassment of women has crippled us in the workplace, particularly in nontraditional occupations. When barriers to women's equality are toppled, they often reappear in different forms, requiring us to develop new strategies.

*NOTES*

1. Patricia Hill Collins, *Black Feminist Thought* (New York: Routledge, 1990).
2. *Hoyt v. Florida,* 1969.
3. Affirmative Action: Expanding Employment Opportunities for Women, 10/1997, http://www.feminist.org/other/ccri/aafact2.html.
4. Leslie Laurence and Beth Weinhouse, "Outrageous Practices: The Alarming Truth About How Medicine Mistreats Women," in *Clashing Views on Abnormal Psychology.* Susan Nolen-Hoeksema, Guilford, Ct.: Dushkin/McGraw Hill, 1998.
5. Laurence and Weinhouse, op. cit.
6. Jacquelyn Grant, "Black Women and the Church," in *Some of Us Are Brave.* Gloria Hull, Patricia Bell Scott, and Beverly Smith, eds. (New York: Feminist Press, 1982).

# The Legal System

Laws shape women's experience of all institutions in our society. Although women have entered the legal profession in record numbers in the last decade, sexism continues to permeate the legal system.

In the first article, attorney Kristian Miccio paints both a historical and a contemporary picture of women's secondary status under the law. She describes the ways the legal system has constrained women and the ways feminists have used the law to fight for civil rights in the areas of work, reproductive rights, and violence against women. Despite feminists' efforts, reforms have been slow to take effect because of the sexist attitudes that still shape police and attorney practices, judicial rulings, and jury verdicts. Miccio concludes that systemic change will "require the infusion of feminist politics at every level of the justice system from the police to the courts."

"On Identity and Law" offers a case study that challenges the supposed objectivity of the law. Rather, we see how who you are can determine the justice you receive. A jury or judge's stereotypical views of whom a woman should be can undermine the truth. In Valerie Malcom's case, the verdict is understandable "only through lenses clouded by prejudice and misogyny."

Women have also used the law to struggle for equity. In "Women Versus Connecticut" Amy Kesselman describes an effort in the early 1970s to challenge Connecticut's anti-abortion statute that made a woman herself guilty of a felony for soliciting an abortion or permitting one to be performed on her. Women's liberation activists used the lawsuit in a grass-roots campaign to educate the public about the traumatic effects of the abortion laws on the lives of real women, and ultimately they had a significant impact on the judicial process.

---

 50

# *Women and the Law*

KRISTIAN MICCIO

America prides itself on the notion that we are a society of laws. The legal system provides a framework upon which we as a society define ourselves. It is a statement of our collective values and traditions. Within the American context, law has an additional function. It is a compact between equals: A self-governance contract between the governed and the governors. Yet women have been conspicuously missing from the fabric of our legal traditions. In fact, women were at one time specifically excluded from the body politic.[1]

---

[1] The Fourteenth Amendment to the Constitution, which enfranchised black men, specifically referred to males over the age of 21 as citizens with the right to vote. This excluded all women, regardless of race, class, or creed.

The framers of the Constitution believed that the public sphere and the exercise of citizenship were the domain of men. As Jefferson wrote, "Were the state a pure democracy there would still be excluded from our deliberation women, who, to prevent deprivation of morals and ambiguity of issues should not mix promiscuously in gatherings of men."[2] Clearly, Jefferson believed that the presence of women would pollute and corrupt not only the morals of men but the system itself. Jefferson's position echoed the prevailing view that women's social and political identity should be restricted and that her sexuality should be controlled.

The legal concept that women and men are equal before the law was not the original understanding of the Constitution's framers. Indeed, women's exclusion from the body politic was a direct consequence of our sex. Our body of law and our legal traditions restricted and confined women to that of the private sphere, and, in setting up this gilded cage, women's legal identity was shaped by and dependent on the men within the home.

In the eyes of the law, women were neither separate nor distinct legal beings. Simply put, because a woman derived her legal identity from men, she had no claim to rights commonly associated with citizenship. She could not vote, and her acquisition and control of private property was severely restricted.[3] Consequently, women's social status was defined by her ability to reproduce, and her legal status was shaped by her relationship to men within the family—as one's wife or as one's daughter. Women's legal identity, then, was subsumed into that of the husband or father. She had no separate legal character.

The British common-law tradition of "covered woman," which defined married women's legal status, was incorporated into American jurisprudence. William Blackstone, an eighteenth-century British legal theorist, summarized the doctrine of "femme couverte" in his Commentaries on the Law of England:

> By marriage, the husband and wife are one person in the law: that is, the very being or legal existence of the woman is suspended during the marriage, or at least is incorporated and consolidated into that of the husband; under whose wing, protection, and cover, she performs everything. . . . Upon this principle, of a union of person in husband and wife depend almost all the legal rights, duties and disabilities, that either of them acquire by the marriage. . . . a man can not grant anything to his wife, or enter into covenant with her: for the grant would be to suppose her separate existence; and to covenant with her would be only to covenant with himself and therefore it is also generally true that all compacts made between husband and wife, when single, are voided by the intermarriage. A woman indeed may be attorney for her husband, for that implies no separation from, but is rather a representation of her lord.[4]

This tradition guided our law until the mid-nineteenth century. With the passage of the Married Women's Property Act of 1848, many of the civil disabilities consistent with the acquisition of private property were lifted. Women as the sexual property of men and restrictions on their participation in public life remained intact until the late twentieth century.[5]

Upon marriage, a woman experienced a legal death. The first step in this process was the surrender of her name. This loss was more than a symbolic act; it was the initial step toward utter suspension of her legal existence.

Since married women were invisible in the eyes of the law, they could not take part in civil life.

---

[2] Quoted in Kay, Herma Hill, *Sex Discrimination and the Law* (West Publications, 1988, p. 1).

[3] In *Minor v. Happersett*, 88 U.S. 162, 22 L.Ed. 627 (1874), Virginia Minor attempted to vote in the elections of 1872. The U.S. Supreme Court ruled that the right to vote was not among the "privileges and immunities" of United States or federal citizenship. Therefore, the States were not prohibited by the Constitution from inhibiting this right and restricting it, "[the] important trust to men alone." The Court did state, however, that women, like children, were "persons" and may be citizens within the meaning of the Fourteenth Amendment. Women received the right to vote with passage of the Nineteenth Amendment in 1920. This followed a century of struggle by the first wave of feminists (suffragists).

[4] *Blackstone's Commentaries* [1966 ed.], t. 430, as quoted in Kay, Herma Hill, *Sex Discrimination and the Law* (West Publications, 1988, p. 913).

[5] Marital rape exemptions fell in many states in the late 1980s; however, a limited number of jurisdictions still cling to this vestige of women as chattel.

And the effects of such a civil death were profound. Women could not sue; they could not keep wages; they could not own property; they could not seek employment without spousal consent; they could not exercise any control over their children; and, finally, they had no control over their reproductive and sexual lives.

The doctrine of covered women transformed married women into the sexual property of their husbands. And because they were property, women could not exercise free will. Husbands, then, had complete control over their wives' bodies. Rape within marriage was not only a legal fiction, it was socially sanctioned and legally condoned. For women, the concept of a right to (bodily) privacy was alien.

A further consequence of "civil death" was economic dependency. Women could not work without the consent of their husbands. And if a woman was permitted to work outside the home, she was not entitled to keep her wages. This forced dependency kept women economically subservient and tied to hearth and home.

## WOMEN AND WORK

In 1873, Myra Bradwell's application for a license to practice law was denied by the Illinois Supreme Court. This denial was due solely to her sex—she was born female. Bradwell's case was heard by the U.S. Supreme Court, and it upheld the lower state court's decision to deny her access to the legal profession. Justice Bradley, in a concurring opinion, written for himself and his brethren Justices Swayne and Field, stated:

> The civil law, as well as nature herself, has always recognized a wide difference in the respective spheres and destinies of man and woman. Man is or should be woman's protector and defender. The natural and proper timidity and delicacy which belongs to the female sex evidently unfits it [sic] for many of the occupations of civil life. The constitution of the family organization, which is founded in divine ordinance, as well as in the nature of things, indicates the domestic sphere as that which properly belongs to the domain and function of womanhood. The harmony, not to say identity, of interests and views which belong, or should belong, to

the family institution is repugnant to the idea of a woman adopting a distinct and independent career from that of her husband.[6]

Critical to Bradley's concurrence in *Bradwell* is his reliance on "divine ordinance" in upholding an arbitrary denial of admission to the Illinois bar. Once invoked, it is difficult to rebut the notion of the "divine ordinance," and in so doing, Justice Bradley couched a misogynist assumption in rather lofty and untouchable rhetoric.[7]

Such reliance on "divinity" formed the basis for Constitutional interpretations that denied women access to occupations and restricted the scope of their labor. By invoking "divine ordinance," the Court placed its imprimatur on a set of social values that defined women as reproductive instruments of the state.

In *Muller v. Oregon*, a decision that followed *Bradwell*, the Court clearly outlined its view of women in relationship to the state. Oregon had prohibited women from working in any mechanical establishment, factory, or laundry for more than 10 hours per day. Not less than three years before *Muller*, the Supreme Court in *Lochner* had declared restricting the hours of bakers as unconstitutional since such regulations violated the workers' liberty interest—the right to contract. The Court resolved this obvious conflict by focusing on the unique function of women's reproductive ability and its value to the state.

The *Muller* Court held that

> As healthy mothers are essential to vigorous offspring, the physical well-being of woman becomes an object of public interest in order to preserve the strength and vigor of the race. . . . The limitations which this statute places upon her contractual powers, upon her right to agree with her employer as to

---

[6] 83 U.S. (16 Wall) 130, 141–142, 21 L.Ed. 442 (1873).

[7] Notwithstanding reference to a "divine ordinance," the doctrine of separation of church and state was not violated. The Court's decision and Bradley's concurrence did not establish a state religion. Rather, it put into perspective the values and mores of society at the time the decision was written. It is important to note, however, that the Court has explicitly relied on Judeo-Christian doctrine to deny protections afforded by the Fourteenth Amendment to such groups as gay men and lesbians (*Hardwick v. Bowers*).

the time she shall labor are not imposed solely for her benefit, but also largely for the benefit of all. Many words cannot make this plainer. The two sexes differ in structure of body, in the functions to be performed by each, in the amount of physical strength . . . the influence of vigorous health upon the future well-being of the race, the self-reliance which enables one to assert full rights, and in the capacity to maintain the struggle for subsistence. This difference justifies a difference in legislation and upholds that which is designed to compensate for some of the burdens which rest upon her.[8]

By viewing women's reproductive ability as a tool for the state, the Court was comfortable in restricting women's ability to contract freely. Yet in the nineteenth century, the right to contract was considered a fundamental right. Restrictions on this right were rare and only in those instances where the Court believed that the state had a strong or compelling interest. Limiting women's right to contract was premised solely on the state's interest in protecting the reproductive functions of women. Clearly, fundamental rights were premised on gender, and women did not hold this right in the same manner as men. And such "protection" carried with it a profound price—the eradication of a fundamental right.

Although much has changed concerning women's participation in the "public sphere," equality for women remains an ongoing struggle. It is important to recognize that the modern improvements women experience in the workplace were won through women's tireless campaign to ensure equality and to improve the quality of life for workers.

In 1963, women won a critical battle with the passage of the Equal Pay Act. Prior to its passage, employers were permitted to discriminate in pay, based on sex, notwithstanding similar work. With the EPA, employers were barred from paying women less as long as the work performed was of essentially the same nature as that performed by their male counterparts.

When issues of comparable worth are raised, EPA analysis is of little benefit. The EPA does not require that men and women be paid the same. Rather, it requires that workers who perform the same job must be paid the same wage. Therefore, a woman firefighter could not be paid less than her male counterparts as long as she performed the same tasks. Sex alone was not sufficient to warrant a difference in pay. Where a wage differential is predicated on a "factor other than sex," e.g., market factors, this difference is permissible. Comparable worth cases have failed because litigants have been unable to demonstrate that pay differences are based on sex and the devaluation of women's work, rather than as a consequence of "market factors."

In the mid-1960s, the advent of the civil rights and women's movements brought substantial changes in employment opportunities for male members of the ethnic minority communities and for women. In 1964, the Civil Rights Acts were passed, and at the eleventh hour, at the behest of Rep. Martha Griffin, "sex" was added to Title VII of the Civil Rights Act. Title VII, in combination with various executive orders signed by President Johnson, paved the way for a sustained attack on gender asymmetry in the workplace.

Following passage of Title VII, it was unlawful to discriminate "against any individual with respect to . . . compensation, terms, conditions or privileges of employment because of that individual's race, color, religion, sex or national origin."[9] Additionally, with Johnson's executive orders in 1967, federal contractors were mandated to establish goals and timetables to eradicate past and/or continuing discrimination. The latter orders, commonly referred to as affirmative action programs, placed an affirmative burden on all recipients of federal moneys not only to hire qualified women and minorities but to construct a plan to compensate for past discrimination.

It was the affirmative action laws of the 1960s that opened up "nontraditional" job classifications for women and minorities. Women were finding both job training and employment in such industries as the building trades, uniform occupations (police,

---

[8] It is important to note that the control of women's procreative ability served two functions: Women of "Yankee stock" should reproduce to propagate the (white) race, while immigrant and black women's reproductive ability was useful only in so much as their reproductive capabilities delivered future workers. *Muller v. Oregon;* 208 U.S. 412, 28 S. Ct. 324, 52 L.Ed 551 (1908).

---

[9] Title VII, Civil Rights Act, 1964.

fire, and sanitation), and "white-collar" professions. These laws, in conjunction with Title IX of the Educational Amendments which prohibited sexism in educational programs, did much to open doors previously closed to women.

With the election of Ronald Reagan in 1980 and his subsequent appointments to the Supreme Court and the federal bench, the gains made by women in employment were systematically eroded. Various Supreme Court decisions weakened the affirmative action laws of the 1960s, and the promise of the Civil Rights Act was broken. In the next century, women will have to recapture lost ground, while helping construct a legal theory that attacks the root cause of gender asymmetry in the workplace. This is a difficult task because it raises issues concerning biologic difference and challenges long-held notions concerning equal protection.

## REPRODUCTIVE RIGHTS

Prior to 1965, women's control over their reproductive lives was tenuous at best. It was virtually impossible for any woman, irrespective of marital status, to receive information concerning birth control and abortion. In most states it was a criminal offense for doctors to give any information about birth control. Clearly, if the states could criminalize information, the actual procedures themselves should be legally proscribed.

Women, then, could not learn appropriate methods to stop unwanted pregnancies, nor could they terminate such pregnancies. Their reproductive lives fell outside their control, and implicit in the criminalization of birth control and abortion was the heavy hand of state regulation and control.

The state's position concerning birth control and abortion has been nothing short of schizophrenic. According to the common law, abortions in the U.S. were permitted before "quickening," the period at which the fetus became ensouled. Prior to this point, the fetus was viewed as part of the mother's body, and abortions were not proscribed. In the mid-nineteenth century, this common-law distinction was eradicated as state after state passed new laws criminalizing abortion. By the end of the nineteenth century, abortion was illegal at any stage of pregnancy throughout the U.S.

During the mid-1960s and early 1970s, challenges to the states' restrictive birth control and abortion laws were undertaken. Where legislative reform seemed hopeless, feminists turned to the courts to identify and protect women's right to reproductive freedom.[10]

Central to a feminist politic was the belief that women's control over their bodies was a fundamental right. To deny women the right to decide when and if to procreate was a denial of a basic civil liberty. Overturning restrictive abortion and birth control laws became a primary political goal of the feminist civil rights struggles of this era.

### Birth Control

In 1965, the Supreme Court struck down a Connecticut law that criminalized counseling for and using contraceptives. The director of Planned Parenthood was convicted of providing a married couple with birth control information. She faced a possible fine and imprisonment of not less than 60 days and a maximum of one year. The case was appealed, and, after exhausting the state appellate process, the Supreme Court was petitioned to review the matter. In the now famous case of *Griswold v. Connecticut,* the Supreme Court ruled that the Connecticut statute was unconstitutional.

Writing for the majority, Justice William O. Douglas recognized that specific guarantees in the Bill of Rights "have penumbras, formed by emanations from those guarantees that help give them [the first ten amendments to the Constitution] life and substance . . . various guarantees create zones of privacy."[11] Douglas found that these zones of privacy

---

[10] In 1970, New York state reformed its abortion laws. New York's new law was one of the most liberal abortion statutes, and it foreshadowed the *Roe* decision handed down by the U.S. Supreme Court in 1973.

[11] Since the Constitution does not specifically enumerate a right of privacy, the Court located this right in existing amendments and provisions. In doing this, the Court recognized that the Constitution is a living, breathing document, and that the already existing provisions, if understood historically and contextually, could accommodate a privacy right analysis. The Court did not create a "new right"; rather, it interpreted existing law as incorporating this right. See, by way of contrast, articles on original intent and strict constructionist theory.

included a marital right of privacy that was protected from intrusion by the state.

Central to the Court's analysis in *Griswold* was the belief that the decision to procreate is at the heart of a cluster of constitutionally protected choices. No doubt the Court was repulsed by the idea that the state could intrude into a married couple's bedroom to regulate sexual practices and behavior,[12] but it was the nature of the decision (procreation) that the Court found worthy of privacy protection.

Following *Griswold*, the Court expanded the right of privacy to unmarried individuals. In *Eisenstadt v. Baird*, the Court struck down as unconstitutional a law that prohibited the distribution of contraceptives to unmarried persons. In *Eisenstadt*, the Court held that the liberty interest found in the Fourteenth Amendment involved a right of privacy, and "if the right of privacy [meant] anything, it [was] the right of the individual, married or single, to be free of unwarranted governmental intrusion into matters so fundamentally affecting a person as the decision whether to bear or beget a child."[13]

To the Court, marital status was irrelevant. What was critical and worthy of Constitutional protection was the decision to procreate. Such decisions, then, fell under the scope of Fourteenth Amendment protection.

Five years later, in *Carey v. Population Services*, the Supreme Court invalidated a New York law that regulated the availability of nonprescription contraceptives to minors.[14] Carey was a critical decision because it reaffirmed that women have a fundamental right not only to decide whether or not to procreate, but also to exercise that choice. Relying on *Roe v. Wade*, the abortion decision decided only four years earlier, the Court recognized that the right to

decide or choose is meaningless without the right to access. In *Carey*, the Court strengthened the principle that women's reproductive freedom was more than a theoretical right. Rather, the exercise of this right was an inherent part of the "right to choose." In the context of human existence, anything less would make it meaningless.

### Abortion Decisions

In 1973, the Supreme Court expanded fundamental rights protection to the right to decide to terminate a pregnancy. In *Roe v. Wade*, the majority held that the Fourteenth Amendment liberty interest involved a right of privacy concerning a woman's decision to terminate a pregnancy. The state could only intrude on that decision if there existed a compelling state interest, and the means chosen (regulatory plan) was narrowly drawn and closely tailored to the governmental objective. The burden, then, was on the state to justify its position and its methodology if they restricted access to abortion.

In *Roe*, and its companion case *Doe v. Bolton*, the Court did not vest women with an absolute right to terminate a pregnancy. Rather, it recognized that the state has a compelling interest to regulate abortion in order to protect the right of the fetus and maternal health.[15] The Court, then, did not view the issue through the prism of a woman's right to exercise control over her body; rather, the Court recognized competing rights and interests of the state and that of the fetus. In doing so, it set the stage for the erosion of the original premise that the fundamental right to decide when and if to procreate was at the center of a "cluster" of constitutionally protected choices located in the Fourteenth Amendment.

Finally, by recognizing fetal rights at the point of viability, the Court not only compromised women's

---

[12] This repulsion was dissipated when the Court was faced with the question of whether a right of privacy extends to homosexuality. In *Hardwick v. Bowers*, the Court upheld a Georgia statute that criminalized sodomy (a sex act anything other than intercourse) even if the acts were between consenting adults. The majority was quite clear that the right of privacy did not extend to the homosexual bedroom. Lurking behind the *Hardwick* decision was the majority's reliance on Judeo-Christian dogma. See *Hardwick v. Bowers*, specifically the Burger concurring opinion and Blackmun's dissent.
[13] *Eisenstadt v. Baird, supra*, 405 U.S. at 453.
[14] *Carey v. Population Services*, 431 U.S. 678 (1977).

[15] The Court set up an intricate system to accommodate what it viewed as conflicting rights and interests. During the first trimester, a woman's right to terminate a pregnancy was paramount; therefore, the state could not proscribe abortion. During the second trimester, the state's interest in protecting maternal health was compelling; therefore, the state could regulate the procedure as long as accessibility to abortion was not restricted. In the third trimester (viability), the combined interest of the state in protecting fetal life and the fetus's right to life were sufficiently compelling as to permit proscription of abortion unless maternal life was at issue.

bodily integrity, it subordinated her right to that of the fetus and the state. Under the scheme articulated by the Court, the state could proscribe abortions at the point of fetal viability. At this time in the pregnancy, set at the third trimester, the state can prohibit all abortions unless this procedure is necessary to save the life of the mother. The woman's fundamental right to decide (which included accessibility), then, is now lessened in relation to that of the fetus's right to life and the state's interest in protecting fetal life. At the point of viability, the rights and interests of the woman, the fetus, and the state all converge, and it is the woman's right that is subordinated.

From 1976 to 1992, there was a series of abortion decisions that chipped away at the fundamental right articulated in *Roe.* These decisions were the consequence of two important factors. First, with the election of Ronald Reagan in 1980 and of George Bush in 1988, an anti-women's rights political attitude was reflected in the federal appointments made by both presidents. Five Supreme Court Justices were appointed during this 8-year period.[16] The Supreme Court was being filled with jurists who were hostile to women's reproductive freedom.

Second, following *Roe,* the Right-to-Life (RTL) Movement went on the political offensive. Through a combination of direct political action (such as the Operation Rescue blockade of abortion clinics), election politics, and community-based politics, the abortion issue was cast from the perspective of the anti-women's rights activists.

During this period, Medicaid funds for abortion were cut off (*McRae v. Harris*), minors' rights were subordinated to parents' rights (*Webster* and *Casey*), mandatory waiting periods were imposed (*Webster* and *Casey*), and the state's interest in promoting childbirth was recognized and elevated to a compelling interest.

The combined effects of these decisions resulted in weakening women's fundamental right. Access was no longer an inherent part of the right to decide. Unlike the birth control decisions, the right to decide was construed in its literal form—the mental process of reaching a decision in a social vacuum. The Court then permitted a cutoff of Medicaid funds to poor women who wished to exercise their right to terminate a pregnancy. The Court believed that the state's cutoff did not place an affirmative burden on the decision-making process since the state did not create poverty.

The Court decision in *Harris* was sinister for two reasons. First, it removed access from contemplation of what constitutes a right, thereby creating an abstract right. Second, it placed the state's interest in promoting childbirth on a par with a woman's right to reproductive freedom.[17] *Harris,* then, severely weakened *Roe* and women's right to choose.

In July of 1992, in *Planned Parenthood v. Casey,* the Court changed the compelling interest test to one of undue burden. This shifted the burden to women to prove that the state's actions were "unduly burdensome" before strict scrutiny could be triggered. This was a severe deviation from *Roe,* which had placed the onus on the state, thereby invoking strict scrutiny at the outset.

Although reaffirming *Roe, Casey* weakened the fundamental character of woman's right to terminate her pregnancy. Indeed, it is questionable at best if what remains of *Roe* is mere form over substance,

---

[16] Justices O'Connor, Kennedy, Scalia, Souter, and Thomas. Following the newest decision, *Casey,* it is clear that Thomas and Scalia are aligned with Chief Justice Rehnquist in his opposition to the right of privacy and the protections that this right affords women in deciding to terminate a pregnancy. O'Connor, Kennedy, and Souter are on the record in support of the right but would permit more extensive compromise of that right.

[17] At issue in *Harris* was the Hyde Amendment, which restricted Medicaid funds for pregnant poor women. Under Hyde, the federal government would reimburse states only for prenatal care and birthing. If a poor woman wanted to exercise her right to terminate her pregnancy, no federal funds could be used. In effect, due to the cost of hospitalization, poor women would have no other choice but to carry to term or revert to back-alley abortions. The framers of Hyde justified this total ban on poor women's right to abort in the state's right to promote and favor childbirth. The Court recognized this interest. Moreover, it held that since the state did not create poverty, it was under no affirmative duty to ensure that poor women could actualize their decision to abort. The dissent in *Harris* understood the effects of the majority decision. Characterizing the majority decision as callous, the dissenters recognized that *Harris* obliterated the access component of a right—but only for poor women.

since a woman's right to choose is no longer treated as a fundamental right.[18]

## Conclusion

The Court's decisions in the abortion and birth control cases are dissimilar in one striking aspect. The birth control cases did not exorcise access from fundamental rights analysis. The fundamental character of an *individual's* right to decide to use contraceptives remains undisturbed. In contrast, in the abortion cases, a woman's fundamental right of privacy has been severely compromised. This is due in large part to who holds the right (women) with the convergence of "rights" now vested in the fetus and the state. Abortion, unlike birth control, implicates the fundamental right only of the woman. In birth control, the Court protected the right of women and men to decide (and act). It is no coincidence, then, that the right to terminate a pregnancy has been circumscribed according to the sex of the person who is vested with it.

## VIOLENCE AGAINST WOMEN

The problem of violence against women is at once simple and quite complex. It is simple because it is so obvious—indeed, such violence is everywhere. Women are beaten, abused, raped, and tortured on the streets, in the boardroom, and in the bedroom. Statistics tell us that violence against women is the leading cause of injury to women—more than car accidents, more than office-related accidents, and more than drug-related incidents.[19] Women are beaten, shot, and stabbed to death, not at the hands of strangers but by the men closest to them. In New York City in 1988, over 20,000 petitions for orders of protection were filed in New York County Family Court. Nationwide, 40% of all homicide victims are female; of that number, over 90% were killed by their husbands or boyfriends. Women are killed by intimates at a rate six times higher than men.[20]

The question is: Why are women killed and beaten at epidemic proportions?[21] Simply put, violence against women has been legally sanctioned and socially condoned. Wife-beating was legal, and marital rape is still sanctioned in some jurisdictions. This privilege extended to males was a direct outgrowth of the legal doctrine of "femme couverte," or "covered woman." Under this doctrine, women's legal existence was suspended or subsumed in that of the males. In the eyes of the law, women were invisible and, within the home, subject to the tyranny of the husband. Husbands could offer "subtle chastisement" or beat their wives as they beat their children.[22]

This cultural position vis-à-vis women's relationship to men in the family influenced American jurisprudence. The states codified this misogyny. Indeed, the decriminalization of assaults in the family and the marital rape exemption were a direct result of such misogyny in the law.

Prior to 1962 in New York state, assaults in the family that were low-level felonies if committed by strangers were routinely handled in family court. If a case managed to find its way into criminal court, it was automatically transferred because the criminal courts lacked "subject matter" jurisdiction.[23] Following hearings in the State Capitol, hearings that detailed the horrific violence experienced by women, New York modified its laws, and cases previously barred from prosecution were, theoretically, prosecutable under existing penal law statutes.

During the 1960s and 1970s, feminists were challenging the gender asymmetry of the laws involving "domestic violence." One such challenge called into question police-arrest avoidance in domestic violence cases. In *Bruno v. Codd,* the New York City Police Department (NYPD) was sued because line officers were refusing to arrest boyfriends and husbands accused of beating their girlfriends and wives. The plaintiffs in *Bruno* proved that the police were mediating cases even where

---

[18] It is important to note that the Court is *one* vote away from overturning *Roe*. As Justice Blackmun, the architect of *Roe*, commented: "I am 83 years old. I shall not be on this Court much longer."

[19] FBI Statistics, 1989.

[20] Department of Justice Statistics, 1990.

[21] Indeed, the U.S. Surgeon General has stated that domestic violence is the chief health risk faced by women.

[22] See *Blackstone's Commentaries, supra.*

[23] See NYS Family Court Act Section 813 and Besharov's Commentaries.

the woman was beaten with a weapon. Clearly, the doctrine of "subtle chastisement" affected police performance.

A settlement agreement flowed from *Bruno*, and the NYPD assured battered women and their advocates that they would, at the very least, exercise discretion. Therefore, when responding to domestic violence incidents, the police would assess whether an arrest was warranted rather than engage in a *de facto* refusal to arrest in cases where the victim and assailant were known to each other.

In *Sorichetti v. NYPD*, all discretion was removed from police where violations of a court order of protection were at issue. In *Sorichetti*, the police refused to enforce an order of protection which mandated that the noncustodial father return the minor child at 5:00 p.m. following visitation and that he refrain from harassing and assaultive conduct.

The father in this case has been adjudicated an abuser in the New York Family Court, and he was known to the police as a "wife beater." When Ms. Sorichetti appealed to the police to look for her daughter and her ex-husband, she was rebuffed. Yet her fear was well grounded. After Ms. Sorichetti had dropped her daughter off for a visit with the father, he had made a death threat. In addition, he had failed to return the child at the time prescribed by the Court. The death threat and the failure to adhere to the time schedule constituted two separate violations of the order. Yet, notwithstanding a valid court order, two violations of the order, and a state law which said that the police should arrest where there has been a violation of an order of protection, the police refused to act.

Following repeated requests for assistance to enforce the order, the police searched for and found young Dina Sorichetti. Her father had carried through on his threat by attempting to dismember the child. In this case, the Court awarded Ms. Sorichetti and her daughter $2.3 million for the police's failure to enforce the order, which resulted in a failure to protect her and her daughter. As a result of this damage award, the NYPD changed its police procedures, mandating a must-arrest policy where there is probable cause to believe that an order of protection has been violated.

Such New York cases illustrate that the gender asymmetry in law has resulted in unequal protection for female citizens.[24]

## *Rape*

**Marital Rape Exemption**    The marital rape exemption was a vestige of the common-law system that viewed women as inferior to men and as subjects of their husbands. At the core of this system was the view that a woman is the property of either her husband or her father. The purpose of rape law generally was to preserve the "value" of the sexual object.[25] Under Mosaic law, the rapist of a virgin was penalized by forcing him to pay the bride price to the father to marry the woman.[26] Under ancient Babylonian law, criminal rape was the "theft of virginity, an embezzlement of the woman's fair price on the market."[27] These ancient laws found themselves in Western jurisprudence. According to common law, the female victim could save her attacker from death by marriage.[28]

Within the family and against a third party, the husband had a property interest in the body and a right to the "personal enjoyment of his wife."[29] Moreover, since the person of the married woman merged into that of the husband, it was a legal impossibility to hold the husband accountable for rape because it would be as if he were charged with raping himself.

Finally, based on the marital contract, because a woman was incapable of withholding consent, rape of one's wife was a legal nullity. As Lord Matthew Hale stated in the seventeenth century:

> But the husband cannot be guilty of rape committed by himself upon his lawful wife, for by their mutual matrimonial consent and contract, the wife

---

[24] See also *Thurman v. Torrington*. Here, the police did nothing while Tracy Thurman's husband stomped on her face, threw her to the ground, and choked her. The police claimed that their refusal to arrest was premised on the fact that this was a domestic dispute.

[25] See S. Brownmiller, *Against Our Will: Men, Women, and Rape* (New York: Simon & Schuster, 1975, p. 9).

[26] Deuteronomy 22:13–29.

[27] Brownmiller, p. 9.

[28] Rape and Battery Between Husband and Wife, 6 Stan. L.Rev. 719 724 & n. 269 1954.

[29] *Oppenheim v. Krindel*, 140 N.E. 227, 228 (1923).

hath given up *herself in this kind unto her husband which she cannot retract* [emphasis added].[30]

Jurisdictions accepted Hale's notion without any question and codified this exemption into their statutes.[31] States then willingly constructed a system of unequal justice based on marital status and gender. Indeed, the laws were allowed to stand in the face of the Fourteenth Amendment and various state constitutions, which incorporated equal protection standards from the federal constitution into their own. Woman as sexual property of the husband superseded the right of female citizens to be secure in their persons.

The marital rape exemptions of most jurisdictions did not fall until the 1980s. With the re-emergence of the battered women's and anti-rape movements, the states were confronted with legal challenges to these exemptions. Based on federal and state equal protection laws, the highest courts in the various states struck these provisions as constitutionally offensive.[32]

**Rape: A Category of Crime Unto Itself**   Cultural misogyny found its way into the rules of evidence as well as into the states' penal laws. Rape, therefore, was treated unlike any other crime. Up until recently, women's testimony was considered incredible as a matter of law. States, therefore, enacted strict corroboration requirements in sexual assault (rape) and sodomy cases.[33]

Under the independent corroboration rule, the testimony of the victim was insufficient to sustain an indictment for rape. The state needed evidence of a "different character" to make out every element of the crime. Therefore, to prove that the sex act had occurred, one would need either physical trauma to the vaginal or anal area, or evidence of semen. To prove the identity of the defendant, if unknown to the victim, one would need a witness. To meet the sufficiency burden concerning consent, evidence of bodily injury was critical. Rape is the only crime that required its victim to be victimized again—via assault (physical injury).

In addition, because most states required that force be viewed through the eyes of the defendant, where he interposed a reasonable belief that the victim consented, this operated as a complete defense. The level of fear, actual or perceived by the victim, was irrelevant in these jurisdictions.

Finally, women's character was under attack at trials involving rape charges. The prevailing defense theory was that if the complainant consented to sex once, this operated as a blanket consent and was relevant to the issue of "force" in current prosecution. It was not uncommon for a victim's past sexual history to be paraded before the Court.

Feminists systematically challenged the independent corroboration rules and the evidentiary "fishing expeditions" into the victim's prior sexual history. As a result, states passed rape shield laws and repealed the independent corroboration rule.

Nevertheless, because misogynist attitudes die hard, rape convictions are difficult to achieve where the victim has had a sexual life or has had a dating relationship with the defendant. The underlying premise is that a woman is not empowered to refuse sexual advances, especially when she has either socialized or had an intimate relationship with the defendant. Hence, marital rape, date rape, and acquaintance rape cases are still very difficult to prosecute. Juries are loathe to convict under these circumstances: They will do everything in their power to discredit the victim while crediting the defendant.

\* \* \*

Although the law has been reformed to, theoretically, treat women as full human beings, these reforms are slow to take effect. This is because the justice system is still influenced by attitudes that view women as sexual property, reproductive instruments of the state, and unworthy of belief. Such

---

[30] I. Hale, *History of Pleas of the Crown;* pp. 6–9, as quoted in Kay, Herma Hill, *Sex Discrimination and the Law* (West Publications, 1992, p. 911).

[31] See *People v. Meli,* 19 NYS 365 (1922).

[32] See *People v. Liberta,* 64 NY 2d 152 [1984].

[33] Usually, such corroboration requirements exist when the victim (complainant) is either a minor or mentally incompetent. Under these circumstances, minors and mental incompetents could not normally testify under oath. Therefore, to sustain a conviction, the state needed independent corroboration to support the uncorroborated testimony of the victim. Such complainants were viewed, due to age and mental status, as legally incompetent.

attitudes shape police practices, prosecutorial discretion, judicial rulings, and jury verdicts.[34]

Creating systemic change will require the infusion of feminist politics at every level of the justice system, from the police to the courts. We will also need to evaluate the feminist theory and practice that has developed during the past decade to make sure that they adequately represent women's lives and defend women's rights. For example, the idea of the battered woman's syndrome was first developed by Lenore Walker to explain to juries why women who killed their assailants felt they had no choice even though there was a break in the violence. Further research and analysis has shown, however, that such situations often are, in fact, life-threatening to the woman. It does a disservice to the woman to refer to a psychological state rather than to see her as someone who has reasonably appraised her choices. Perhaps the real challenge of the twenty-first century will be to transform a legal system crafted to protect male power into one that brings women to the center of human discourse. *We* can then create a new legal tradition in which women's experience is no longer marginal.                    [1992]

 51

# *On Identity and Law*[1]

KRISTIAN MICCIO

Justice in the American legal system is often subverted by sexism, and in the process, women's identities are constructed in distorted ways. Nothing illustrates this better than the case of Valerie Malcom, a West Indian woman macheted by her former intimate partner and business associate who the defense attorney characterized as "a black widow spider."[2]

Malcom was a rare woman in the world of business, finance, and city contracts. At a time when the economy of New York City was precarious at best, she garnered millions in city contracts aimed at increasing minority hiring in the construction business. Malcom combined business acumen with ethnic pride and created a minority-owned and run subcontracting firm that linked minority construction teams with major building projects. Malcom could create matter out of nothing. And for this, she would pay dearly.

In 1990, Malcom formed a partnership with R, a Jamaican national. She discovered too late that their professional and personal relationship was a mistake. In the fall of 1991, because R was "skimming off the top," Malcom dissolved the business partnership. Within weeks of terminating their partnership, Malcom also ended their personal relationship because R was becoming threatening. Faced with losing social and political status within the Jamaican community, R left messages on Malcom's machine with not-so-veiled threats of bodily harm if she did not reinstate the partnership. Malcom took the case to the local police precinct in an attempt to obtain assistance. Her efforts were fruitless.[3]

In late winter, Malcom was visited by R in her office. He was convinced that Malcom owed him money. Although R had contributed neither capital nor services to the start-up of the business, Malcolm was willing to give him $150,000. The only caveat was that R would have to wait until some assets were liquidated. Enraged at hearing this, R drew a machete that he had hidden under his overcoat. He struck Malcom in the head and hand, causing a deep gash in the skull and amputation of the fingers.

Malcom's screams brought her co-workers into her office. In an attempt to deflect R's blows, the co-worker's heavy construction jacket was shredded wherever R's machete landed. The attack ended

---

[34] See New York State Task Force Report on Women in the Courts (1985), in which a judicial commission documented the misogyny in the justice system. It found that women litigants, rape victims, domestic violence victims, as well as female attorneys, were all treated with disrespect and in many cases with outright contempt. In New York, as in most states, women still await the full benefits of legal personage before the law.
[1] The original title of this subsection was "On Identity, Intersectionality, and the Law."

[2] Conversation with Valerie Malcom and "Assault Victim Called Black Widow Spider," *New York Post,* March 3, 1992.
[3] See, generally, *Twice Abused: Report of Battered Women and the Criminal Justice System* (1993).

only when local firefighters, called by Malcom's neighbors, came onto the scene. Malcom was taken to the hospital. She had lost five pints of blood and sustained a fractured skull and severed fingers. Since R's voice-activated tape recorder was in his coat pocket at the time of the attack, the entire event was recorded—Malcom's screams and R's frenzied rampage. The tape was introduced at trial along with pictures of Malcom's injuries, medical reports, the machete, the shredded jackets of both the victim and the eye witness, and Malcom's torn and blood-drenched clothing.[4]

R was subsequently acquitted of all charges; the jury returned a not guilty verdict because they believed that Malcom had "lured" R and "provoked" the attack.

I decide to use the Malcom case in my class on violence against women by intimate partners, in spite of the risks inherent in using such a graphic example of individual and systemic misogyny and racism. I use this case because it teaches about the power of the law to construct identities. During the trial, Valerie Malcom's persona is reconstructed— her very being suspended and reconstituted to conform to the dominant cultural definition of the "masculine woman," the annihilator of men. The defense casts her as the black widow spider, an ironic designation, given that R was never in danger of being maimed or killed—quite the contrary. Ultimately, Malcom is left indelibly transformed, forever changed, unrecognizable even to herself.[5]

I remember that as a woman and a lesbian, my reality is altered by what others perceive me to be: intimidating, aloof, masculine, a male basher, "dyke," "lezzie." I am lost in their interpretation of what I am not. I, like Valerie Malcom, have a self apart from what is perceived; and, like Valerie, I must carry a cultural passport in this land. For Valerie, for women, for gays and lesbians, for sister soulja, justice is illusory and the property of others. And knowing this, I will teach this class.

I assign articles that report on the trial and on the jury's reaction to Malcom. I assign critical portions of the transcript that record both direct and cross examination of Malcom and the closing arguments of the prosecutor and the defense counsel. In addition to these documents, students pour over transcripts of the audiotape. Finally, I ask them to read accounts of the Rodney King Simi Valley trial.

As a class we attempt to draw out the similarities between the cases: black victims, differently gendered/raced defendants, eyewitnesses, severe injuries, events memorialized on tape, and not guilty verdicts. Although students are troubled by the outcomes in both cases, they understand how the King verdict evolved. As E, a young African-American male reminds us, "If the verdict had come back for King, now that would have been shocking."

To be black in America is to be an outsider. E knows this; he has lived it every day of his young life in a way that I can only imagine—like a bad dream. My skin has shielded me from what he has experienced. Yet, I am not grateful, I am angry—it is merely a reprieve.

Many of my students have grown up with the realization that there are two forms of justice, one for whites and one for blacks. For the former, the police serve to protect. The latter too often experience the police as "occupying army."[6] These students know we are not all equal. E, Rodney King, and at least two-thirds of my class fear what I have been raised to respect. Yet, today we meet on common ground, brought together by two cases—by what Valerie Malcom and Rodney King can teach us.

---

[4] Malcom lost two-thirds of her body's blood volume. She was unconscious for three days and remained in the intensive care unit for two weeks. Although her fingers were reattached, she cannot use her hand without experiencing searing pain.

[5] Since 1989, I have recast the term *domestic violence* because it fails to adequately describe the nature of the violence or the relationship between survivor and assailant. Use of the term *violence against women by intimate partners* is my attempt to contextualize both the conduct and the status—it distinguishes intimate violence from acts initiated against women by strangers or by the state. Because one of three women will experience either physical or sexual abuse, it was a high probability that of the 25 women in the class over a third were directly affected by intrafamilial violence. *See, generally,* Lenore Walker, *The Battered Woman* (1993); Evan Stark, "*Violence Against Women as Coercive Control,*" 58 *Alb. L. Rev.* 1030 (1995); G. K. Miccio's "*Deconstructing the Myth of the Passive Battered Woman and the Protected Child in Neglect Proceedings,*" 58 *Alb. L. Rev.* 187 (1995).

---

[6] The Kerner Commission Report on the Watts Riots (1965).

None of the students can understand the jury's verdict in the Malcom case. It is a case that, on the surface, appears to be a sure conviction. The victim is a prosecutor's dream—articulate, well educated, a business woman, and self-possssed. Surely, her testimony alone will convict the defendant. And as C, a Latina student observes, "This isn't about race since both the victim and the defendant were people of color."

So the outcome is difficult to comprehend especially once the composition of the jury is revealed: seven women, five men, two African-Americans, five Latinos, and five people of European descent. Unlike the King case, in Malcom, the complainant, the defendant, and a majority of the jury share an identity—but not a common set of experiences. The defense creates an insuperable chasm between Malcom and the jury—particularly the women jurors.[7] Malcom is what they are not: she is the enemy—unfeminine, anti-male and anti-black. In the words of the defense, she is a woman who "brings Kings down."[8]

Students learn that in dispensing justice, who you are perceived to be is as important as what you've done. They come to understand that race and gender intersect in the construction of Malcom as the Black Widow Spider.

This is also a case involving intimate violence, in which male privilege is manifested in its most base form. And, in the lexicon of defense tactics, the very being of the woman—her self—is attacked and contorted, she is *too* strong, *too* articulate, *too* self-possessed, *too* independent. And in a world of gendered polar opposites, she is a threat to "the Man"—a "castrating bitch."

Once this image is projected, the jury can, as in the King case, discount what they heard and what they saw: her story is rewritten—now, her screams are manufactured, his rampage justifiable. The

shredded coat, her injuries, his fully intact clothing and body are invisible, so as to prepare the way for a verdict understandable only through lenses clouded by prejudice and misogyny.

While preparing to teach this class, I cannot help but remember the first time I met Valerie Malcom. She came to me for help, tormented by how the defense characterized her. She wanted Justice. She wanted to reclaim her self—uncompromised and unconcealed.

Malcom could live with the physical pain, the reattached fingers, and the physical disfigurement. She could also live with the fact that R walked the city streets and often stood—just stood—in front of her house and stared at the brick and glass that separated him from Malcom and her teenage daughter. She could live with all of this. What she could not live with was the image crafted by counsel that she ensnared innocent men—used and then disposed of them. Valerie Malcom could not accept that she was the sum of the defenses' parts, laid out before this jury of seven women and five men—dismembered and reassembled with the glue of cultural Other. And it was this memory that made her pain palpable.

And I knew that there was nothing I could do to help. In communications established with personnel at the Justice Department, it became clear early on that they were not interested in pursuing a federal civil rights claim action.[9] In their eyes, there was no state action even when they accepted the fact that

---

[7] Much has been said concerning why women do not make good jurors in rape and intimate violence cases. The prevailing wisdom is that women identify closely with the survivor, and in an attempt to distance themselves from the victim/survivor, they impose on her characteristics that are alien to affirm that this could not, would not, happen to them.

[8] Conversation with Valerie Malcom.

[9] Federal civil rights claims are usually brought under 43 USC 1983. It was this tool that held the murderers of Schwerner, Goodman, and Chaney accountable in the 1960s when the state acquitted the white defendants. In the 1990s, a federal civil rights action was brought by the federal government against Lemrick Nelson, an African American, for the murder of Yankel Rosenberg, a Jewish scholar killed in Crown Heights Brooklyn because he was Jewish. And it was a 1983 action in federal court that held the white police officers criminally liable for violating Rodney King's civil rights after the Simi Valley jury acquitted in state court. Under 1983, if an individual's civil rights are violated by a group of persons or by the state (failure of the state to protect and prosecute, and such failure is based on the victim's race, creed, sex or sexual origin), the federal government is empowered to prosecute, even when the defendants have been acquitted in state court.

the police failed to adequately investigate the case and preserve evidence. Malcom's claim that police inaction was predicated on her race and gender was rejected out of hand—even when the department was presented with letters that documented statements by the police that supported Malcom's contention. This was not the type of case for which the department would risk either resources or reputation—Malcom as black woman survivor of intimate violence remained invisible.

As I teach Malcom, I am flooded by the memories and the anger that had been tucked away for a year. I struggle with presenting the material in a way that acknowledges balance. Balance between emotion and logic, between fact and law, between self and others, between the individual and the collective "we." But I also recognize that cases such as Malcom trigger emotions and memories that do not know artificial boundaries. And yet, if I am to teach this case, an internal balance must be struck so that I can hear the voices of my students as they struggle to find themselves.

I do not see acts of violence against women by intimate partners as mere abstractions. They are everyday occurrences that mirror an anti-woman culture that annihilates the self.[10] Whether physical or psychological, such violence forever changes the survivor's self-conception and her view of the world.[11] The violence is gendered—an explosion of misogynistic rage. And it is personal.

I see myself in Valerie Malcom and in the words inscribed in the decisions, and it is this recognition that shapes how I teach my students empathy as well as legal discourse. And in doing this our souls are laid bare.[12]                    [1997]

---

[10] See, generally, Elizabeth Schneider, "Particularity and Generality," 57 *N.Y.U. L. Rev.* 34 (1992).
[11] See, generally, Evan Stark, "Violence Against Women as Coercive Control," 58 *Alb. L. Rev.* 1030 (1995); Susan Herman, "Intimate Violence" (Sage Publ., 1993); Rhonda Coplen, "Domestic Violence As Torture," in *International Human Rights As Women's Rights* (University of Chicago Press, 1993).
[12] It is no coincidence that this class produces individual disclosure concerning victimization and being victimizer. I have learned that my students can work through their pain and if properly directed can use their personal experience to inform their work as law students and lawyers.

 52

# Women Versus Connecticut: Conducting a Statewide Hearing on Abortion[1]

AMY KESSELMAN

Writing in 1989, shortly after the Supreme Court heard oral arguments in *Webster v. Reproductive Rights Services,* Nancy Stearns recalled her involvement in the courtroom battles to legalize abortion before *Roe v. Wade* and urged proponents of reproductive freedom to become politically active again. "We must never forget," she cautioned, "that *Roe v. Wade* did not just 'happen.' That decision came only after the short but intense political and legal efforts of women across the country."[2]

A sea change in attitudes toward abortion occurred during the five years before *Roe v. Wade.* Over half the people questioned in opinion polls in 1971 favored legalizing abortion; lawyers challenging abortion statutes, who had previously emphasized the interests of doctors, began in the early 1970s to argue on behalf of women's right to decide when to have a child; organizations that had been working to reform abortion laws changed their goals, strategies, and often their names to reflect the new movement for repeal of all state abortion statutes; and, after 1970, state courts began ruling in favor of women's right to an abortion.[3]

While many factors contributed to these rapid changes, the energy, passion, and politics of women's liberation activists were crucial. Transforming an abortion reform effort led by doctors and population controllers into a movement that argued for abortion as an essential ingredient of women's freedom, women's liberation activists brought the devastating effects of the abortion statutes on women's lives into the public consciousness and legal discourse. In addition to pressuring legislatures, participating in referenda, and organizing marches, demonstrations, and speak-outs throughout the country, women's liberation activists turned their attention to the courts. Teaming up with feminist lawyers and law students, they coupled litigation with grass-roots organizing in a creative strategy that both stimulated public discussion of reproductive rights and brought women's experiences of the abortion laws to bear on what went on in the courtroom. A cluster of the cases that were on their way to the Supreme Court when *Roe v. Wade* was decided were suits brought by large groups of women who claimed that their constitutional rights were being violated by their states' anti-abortion statutes. Recovering the stories of the campaigns that shaped these lawsuits will enable us to better understand how *Roe v. Wade* did happen.

The first of these cases was filed in New York in 1969 by a group of feminist activists and lawyers, but because the New York state legislature legalized abortion in 1970, their case, *Abramowicz v. Lefkowitz,* was never argued in court.[4] The New York suit, however, became the model for lawsuits filed by groups of women in several other states. The Connecticut case, *Abele v. Markle,* was particularly influential in framing the judicial opinions in *Roe v. Wade.* The story of this lawsuit and the organization that brought it demonstrates that judicial opinions do not occur in a vacuum; they are profoundly affected by the political movements of their time.

The Connecticut anti-abortion statute enacted in 1860 was one of the strictest in the country—the woman herself was guilty of a felony for soliciting an abortion, permitting one to be performed on her, or attempting to perform one on herself. When a reform bill exempting women who had been raped was introduced in the Connecticut legislature in 1967, it received little support and never emerged from committee. In April 1969 the legislature considered a bill promoted by the Connecticut Medical Society that would "allow a doctor, after consultation with two other physicians, to perform an abortion" that he or she felt was medically indicated.[5]

A group of women's liberation activists who had been engaged in consciousness raising began to follow the progress of the bill. Although they were not particularly enthusiastic about a bill that would give decision-making power to the doctor alone, a few members did attend the judiciary committee hearing, which was dominated by male experts on both sides of the issue. The women's liberation people did not get an opportunity to speak until the end of the day, and their testimony was not even recorded by the stenographer. "We were at the hearings—but we were invisible," recalled Ann Hill, one of the women who attended the hearing. "We were not 'experts' or 'professionals.' We had no credentials, no degrees, and the lawmakers did not want to hear us."[6]

This expedition squelched any lingering thoughts among women's liberation activists about using legislative action to repeal Connecticut's abortion law. "The legislature," they concluded "was completely beholden . . . to the Catholic church" and solidly against any reform in abortion laws, let alone their repeal.[7] The reform bill died in the judiciary committee.

Meanwhile, the women's liberation group had been getting calls from desperate pregnant women who thought women's liberation activists would know how to find an abortionist. Realizing that reproductive rights were crucial to the freedom they were beginning to envision, a group of activists decided to focus their efforts on the question of abortion.

The 15 women who began meeting in 1970 were all white, mostly in their mid-twenties and college educated. Several were students at Yale Law School, and one was a graduate student in biology. They set up a "make-shift referral" system, took turns answering the ever increasing calls from women seeking abortions, and began having "long free-floating discussions about what having the capacity to make babies meant to us." After discovering that, highly educated though they were, they "didn't know diddly about their bodies," they began to educate themselves about female anatomy.[8] Because most of them were political activists, they looked for ways to involve other women and divided into two project groups. While one group offered courses on "women and their bodies," the other began to consider ways to challenge Connecticut's abortion law.

Convinced that "courts were no less dominated by men and no more receptive to women than the legislature," the abortion work group approached the idea of a law suit with caution.[9] The activities of the New York Women's Health Collective—taking depositions at well-publicized open meetings, holding rallies, speak-outs, and meetings around the city and stimulating discussions about abortion in a wide variety of organizaitons—made it clear to the New Haven women that a lawsuit could be a "wonderful organizing vehicle." The goal, according to Betsy Gilbertson, "was not to change the law per se. The objective was to use the process of changing the law, which would be a good thing to do, to further the goals of the women's movement over all." [10]

As women's liberation activists, the members of the abortion work group brought into the campaign against Connecticut's abortion law several ideas that shaped their strategy and tactics. Two central tenets were the belief that abortion was inextricably connected with other dimensions of an oppressive social system and the conviction that collective political activity on their own behalf would strengthen women's sense of their own power to challenge this system. The lawsuit was to be a vehicle for stimulating discussion about abortion and its connection with other aspects of women's lives and bringing women together into political action. Central to this process would be women talking about their lives, since it was women, they believed, who were the experts about the effects of the abortion laws. Women speaking about their own experience would reveal the political nature of private life.

These ideas generated two crucial tactical decisions about the campaign to challenge the abortion law. First, instead of a traditional class action suit with one plaintiff representing a class, the lawsuit would involve as many plaintiffs as they could recruit, each claiming that her life was harmed by the anti-abortion statute. The organizers felt that "the mere act of putting your name down and saying 'I want to be a plaintiff, I want to take this position,' was very important politically for the individual women who signed up as plaintiffs." [11] Second, the abortion group rejected the help of male experts. Unlike many of the cases that were being filed against state abortion laws, only women could be plaintiffs in the Connecticut suit. Plaintiffs represented three groups of women who claimed to be injured by Connecticut's abortion law: women of childbearing age, women who were in a position to counsel other women about abortion, and women in the health care professions.

Even more controversial was the decision that only women could be lawyers and organizers. "The exclusion of men was necessary," they felt, "to ensure free participation by all women and to build our own self confidence as a group of people capable of winning our own struggles." [12] There "was a sense of unity and purpose," remembered Katie Roraback, "that could never have been achieved if there had been both men and women involved." [13] They did include some affidavits of male physicians as supporting evidence, but the actors in the suit were all women, a fact reflected in the name they chose for their organization: Women Versus Connecticut.

In all the Women Versus Connecticut literature in this early period, arguments for the legalization of abortion were embedded in a multifaceted analysis of women's oppression and a critique of capitalism. "We want control of our bodies," the plaintiff recruitment pamphlet declared.

> We are tired of being pressured to have children or not to have children. It is our decision. But control over our bodies is meaningless without control over our lives. Women must not be forced into personal and economic dependence on men or on degrading jobs in order to assure adequate care for the children they bear. Our decisions to bear children cannot be freely made if we know that aid in child care is not forthcoming and that we will be solely responsible for the daily care of our children.

The pamphlet argued against a society that put the needs of corporations before human needs, that exploited workers and polluted the environment. Its authors took pains to distinguish themselves from the population controllers by asserting, "We think the issue is not control of the world's population but control of the world's resources." [14]

Recognizing that making abortion legal would not guarantee that it was available and affordable for all women, Women Versus Connecticut activists committed themselves to both goals. "We think that we must get rid of the law," Sasha Harmon told a reporter in October 1970, when Women Versus Connecticut announced their plans to file the suit. "That's the necessary first step toward winning cheap and available legal abortions. Then we'll try to make sure that doctors and hospitals begin serving our needs, once the law doesn't stand in their way." [15]

By the time Women Versus Connecticut was recruiting plaintiffs and preparing legal arguments, the legislatures of New York state and Hawaii had legalized abortion, and federal courts in Wisconsin and Washington, D.C., had found anti-abortion laws unconstitutional. The Connecticut women felt that they had a good chance of winning their suit and believed that winning would strengthen the women's movement and give them a "voice to reckon with" as they mobilized women to work for "a health care system that was responsive to women." [16] They chose as their symbol the female silhouette that had decorated a popular women's liberation poster. To make the logo "proud and hopeful," they raised the woman's right hand in a gesture of defiance. [17]

After announcing their plans for a lawsuit, Women Versus Connecticut distributed their bright yellow pamphlet, with its carefully developed arguments and plaintiff coupon on the back, to women's groups throughout the state, asking to make presentations about their lawsuit. They began each group meeting by telling personal stories about their own lives and elicited stories from women in the audience. "We broke down our feelings of isolation," recalled Ann Hill. "Everybody had either had an abortion or had a friend who had an abortion or went to school with somebody who suddenly wasn't in school any more and they'd heard they were in some home for pregnant teens and banished from the society. . . . It was secret sharing and experience sharing." [18]

The process of transforming personal secrets into resources for a political and legal campaign continued for the organizers as well as the women they recruited. A woman in the organizers' group talked for the first time in her life about having given her child up for adoption, after the group had looked for months for someone to testify about this in court. The shame and anguish surrounding what had been a common practice for young white unmarried women who became pregnant in the 1950s and 1960s was so profound that most women never talked about that chapter of their lives. [19]

Despite the fact that New Haven, where the group was based, had a sizable African-American and growing Puerto Rican population, the movement that Women Versus Connecticut built, like the national abortion rights movement in the 1970s, was almost entirely white. While there were a few African-American plaintiffs, the organizing group remained all white and almost all the women involved in activities were white, a fact that probably contributed to the difficulty organizers had in mobilizing support for Medicaid abortions in the mid-1970s.

There were a number of interlocking reasons that Women Versus Connecticut remained a white organization. The separatist direction that black organizations were moving during the late 1960s and early 1970s generated a conviction among many white radicals that white people were their logical constituency. Furthermore, the idea of connecting with women of color about reproductive rights raised particular problems. In Connecticut, as in the rest of the country, the racist policies and practices of population control groups had left a bitter legacy in communities of color. [20] Most nationalist groups were hostile to both abortion and birth control, and white women were hesitant to talk with women of color about abortion. [21] According to Gail Falk, who had worked on the Black Panther defense as well as Women Versus Connecticut, "the prevailing black male idea" was that abortion, like forced sterilization, was seen as part of the genocidal war on African-American communities, and "we wouldn't have asked a woman at that time to cross over and take on her black brothers on that issue. . . . It would have felt like undermining black solidarity to go try to talk about something that was so clearly labeled. So it was more hands off out of respect." [22]

As Loretta Rosse has pointed out, many African-American women were reluctant to speak out about abortion because they did not want to "highlight abortion over other aspects of our struggle to achieve reproductive freedom." [23] While there were women of color who argued for women's right to an abortion, their voices were muted in the public discourse of the 1970s, and the white women in Women Versus Connecticut had few social connections that would allow them to reach these women. [24]

The Women Versus Connecticut message moved quickly throughout white communities in the state, and women joined the suit in numbers that astounded even the organizers. Between October 1970 and February 1971 they recruited 800 plaintiffs. The women who signed up to be plaintiffs brought a wide variety of experience to the lawsuit. Some had illegal or "therapeutic" abortions, some had carried a pregnancy to term against their will, and still others had no direct experience with abortion but nevertheless felt profoundly affected by the absence of legal abortion.[25]

As they developed their legal arguments, the lawyers and law students drew on the New York case and other suits that had been filed against state abortion laws, but they reworked them in close cooperation with the organizers in order to "integrate the legal arguments with the organizing effort and with the vision that infused the suit."[26] The primary arguments in their brief were that the abortion laws violated women's "right to privacy" and "right to life and liberty," denied poor women "equal protection of the law," and constituted a form of sex discrimination and cruel and unusual punishment.[27]

Women Versus Connecticut organizers were determined that their case, rather than emphasizing constitutional rights, would speak to the effects of the abortion laws on the lives of real women. Nancy Stearns argued that the lawsuit must make it clear to the judges "that it's flesh and blood people that they're talking about. . . . One of these days they'll even realize that it's their daughters and wives that we're talking about as well as all the other women they may or may not know."[28]

For these reasons the brief was constructed as a vehicle for describing the devastating emotional, physical, and economic effects of the abortion laws on women's lives. Combining constitutional arguments with a vivid panorama of the suffering caused by laws that criminalized abortion, the brief stated clearly that it was women whose cause they were defending—not members of the medical profession.

On March 2, 1971, Women Versus Connecticut filed their lawsuit. *Abele* (for Janice Abele, the first plaintiff on the lists) *v. Markle* (the Connecticut district attorney), with 858 plaintiffs. They turned the filing into a public event by demonstrating on the steps of the post office with posters and banners sporting their defiant logo and leaflets explaining the suit.

Significant breakthroughs for the proponents of abortion rights occurred in 1970 and 1971, and the Connecticut court participated in the shift of public attitude and practices. On December 13, 1971, an appeals court ruled that *Abele v. Markle* should be heard by a three-judge court. The court, however, ruled that nonpregnant women of childbearing age did not face sufficient personal harm to give them standing as plaintiffs. Only pregnant women, medical personnel, and counselors were judged to face sufficient harm to have standing in the case.

In February 1972, Women Versus Connecticut found a pregnant plaintiff and filed an affidavit asking for a temporary restraining order to allow her to have an abortion. Although only the pregnant plaintiff, counselors, and medical personnel were the official plaintiffs, the lawyers pursued their strategy of involving women of childbearing age in the lawsuit.

To the disappointment of Women Versus Connecticut, who wanted very much to have women talk about their lives in the courtroom, the court decided to make its decision on the basis of oral arguments and the written complaint. The affidavits submitted with the complaint, however, did describe the variety of hardships created by the abortion statutes. Women were also present in massive members for every public court event.

At a time when only 4% of lawyers and less than 1% of judges were women, the sight of a team of women lawyers and crowds of women in the courtroom lives vividly in the memory of the participants. According to Katie Roraback:

> It was a wonderful scene. I mean . . . you can't even imagine what the scene was like back then. . . . When you practiced law, you go into court, the judges were men, the bailiffs, the marshals, the sheriffs . . . ; they were all male. The court reporters were men; the . . . clerks were men; . . . it was a very masculine courtroom. There were all these male attorneys, and they tended to have male witnesses. I used to laugh and say, "We're friends of the bride" because the right-to-life movement was a male movement.[29]

On April 18, 1972, the three-judge district court consisting of Judges Edward Lumbard, Jon O. Newman, and Emmet Clarie declared Connecticut's abortion law unconstitutional. The majority opinion, written by Judge Lumbard, was, according to Katie Roraback, "one of the best that was written." Developing the liberty argument more fully than any previous decision, the opinion declared that the Connecticut law "trespasses unjustifiably on the personal privacy and liberty of its female citizenry." "Women," said Judge Lumbard, were "the equal to men" and "the appropriate decision-makers over matters regarding their fundamental concerns."[30]

The women of Women Versus Connecticut were jubilant, not only because they had won but because Judge Lumbard's opinion used stronger language than any rulings that had been rendered before and grounded his opinion "strongly in women's rights." Marilyn Seichter told the *Hartford Courant* that the "ruling was even more than she had expected of the court," and another spokesperson for Women Versus Connecticut commented, "[T]he decision recognized the right of women to the privacy of their bodies in clear unequivocal language."[31]

Judge Newman's concurring opinion, according to his own appraisal, "covered less ground" than Judge Lumbard's. However, it was Newman's words that played a crucial role in the events that unfolded in Connecticut after the decision was announced. After examining the history of abortion statutes in Connecticut, Newman concluded that the main state interest that lay behind the 1860 statute was concern for the health and morals of the mother. Since the *Griswold* decision had indicated that protecting a woman's morals was not a sufficient justification for intruding on her privacy, and recent medical developments had rendered abortion safer than childbirth, these state interests were no longer compelling. It was clear, according to Judge Newman, that the legislature had not intended to protect the life of the unborn child in framing the abortion statute. If it had, he reasoned, the constitutionality of the law would be a more complex issue.[32]

The state immediately appealed the ruling, which Governor Meskill called "an amazing decision," and requested a stay of execution to allow the abortion statutes to remain in effect pending the appeal. When on May 14 Justice Thurgood Marshall denied the state's request, Connecticut's abortion statute was off the books.[33]

Governor Meskill sprang into action, calling the legislature into a special session to enact a new abortion law and supporting a bill that was essentially the same as the law that had been declared unconstitutional. The only new features were a preamble proclaiming that the intent of the law was to "protect and preserve human life from the moment of conception" and stiffer penalties for violators. Invoking Judge Newman's comment in the concurring opinion, Meskill insisted that this new language would render the measure constitutional.

The atmosphere at the hearing held by the Joint Committee on Public Health and Safety on May 19, 1972, was light-years away from the hearings held three years earlier. Three hundred people packed the hearing room, most of whom were women, and feelings ran high. Women Versus Connecticut was present in force, displaying signs and banners and performing a play before the hearing began. There was frequent applause by both sides, and the chair repeatedly inveighed against "uncalled-for demonstrations," reminding the audience at one point, "It's not a ball game; it's a public hearing."[34]

The rhetoric had also changed on both sides. The many doctors who spoke in favor of the liberal bills spoke less about their own professional prerogatives and more about the needs of their women patients. Even some of the anti-abortion speakers also felt it necessary to declare their respect for women's rights before speaking against abortion.

After the eight hours of public testimony, the General Assembly's Public Health and Safety Committee met for an hour in closed session. Despite the fact that their vote, in the opinion of one of its members, went "completely contrary to the sentiments of the day-long hearing," the committee voted to present the Meskill bill to the assembly. On Sunday, petitions supporting the bill appeared at Catholic churches around the state and were presented to the legislature the next day. When the House debated the bill on May 22, spectators from both sides watched from the gallery, booing, hissing, and applauding with such vigor that the speaker repeatedly threatened to clear the gallery. After considering several amendments that would have softened the bill, both houses of the legislature approved the

Meskill bill with no qualifications.[35] The vote vividly illustrated the power of the Catholic church over Connecticut politics and the power of the governor over the state legislature.

The events in Hartford, which Lawrence Lader has called a "unique travesty of Federal court authority," brought abortion to the center of public debate in Connecticut, and, while it polarized many communities, it broadened support for the abortion rights movement.[36] As Women Versus Connecticut lawyers prepared their suit against the new law, more plaintiffs signed up, bringing the number to 2,000 in June when the case was filed. Women Versus Connecticut filed a memorandum asking for an injunction against the new law, and to support this motion they brought two pregnant women who had been denied abortions by medical committees of a hospital. "Women from all over the state," read their press release, "have expressed their outrage at the Governor and the Legislature for their preoccupation with the unborn."[37]

In addition to arguing that the new law was unconstitutional for the same reasons that the old law was, the memo discussed at length the influence of the Catholic church and argued that the preamble establishing the law as a means for protecting human life constituted "an enshrinement of religious doctrine in the law."[38]

On June 9, the court granted a temporary restraining order for one of the pregnant plaintiffs; the other, unable to wait, had obtained an abortion in New York. Instead of granting the request for a continued injunction against the new law, it decided, to the delight of Women Versus Connecticut lawyers, who were pleased to finally be able to present live testimony, to hold a hearing on the new law.

While the state brought photos and films to the hearing supporting its claims that the fetus was alive, the witnesses from Women Versus Connecticut testified about their lives. Interrupted repeatedly by attorneys encouraging them to speak up, three women described the experience of giving birth to children they could not afford to care for, the difficulties of finding work when they were pregnant or caring for young children, the terror of becoming pregnant when they knew it would be physically

hazardous, and the doomed marriage that resulted from one unwanted pregnancy and was haunted by the prospect of another. A fourth woman testified about her experience as an unwanted child who moved among various foster parents throughout her childhood. Marilyn Seichter, who gave the concluding argument for Women Versus Connecticut, observed that "this court (made up of three men) can never understand what the fear of pregnancy means to women" but urged the judges to try.[39]

On September 20, 1972, the court announced the majority decision, this time written by Judge Newman. "The fetus," he concluded, "is not a person within the meaning of the fourteenth amendment," and therefore the state had no compelling interest that could justify unconstitutionally abridging women's "right to privacy and personal choice in matters of sex and family life."[40]

The state's appeal reached the Supreme Court as it was deciding *Roe v. Wade.* Both of the decisions made in *Abele v. Markle* played a significant role in the opinion that Justice Blackmun framed that fall. As Nancy Stearns has noted, "Blackmun's description of the physical and emotional harm to women of an unwanted pregnancy, the stigma of an out-of-wedlock pregnancy, and the problems with bearing an unwanted child bears a striking resemblance to the language used by the Connecticut court" in the first *Abele v. Markle* decision.[41] In addition, Judge Newman's opinion on the status of the fetus vis-à-vis women's constitutional rights was influential as well.[42] "We won (again)," proclaimed the Women Versus Connecticut newsletter after *Roe v. Wade* was decided. Although the state continued its appeal, the case was returned to a lower court that voided the Connecticut statute (unanimously this time) in April 1973.[43]

The story of Women Versus Connecticut illustrates the powerful contribution of women's liberation ideas to the pre-*Roe* abortion rights movement. Their insistence on inserting the painful stories of women's thwarted attempts to control their reproductive lives into the public discourse gave vibrant meaning to that cardinal women's liberation notion "the personal is political." By bringing women's experiences into the courtroom and organizing a movement that made itself felt throughout the state, Women Versus Connecticut had a significant impact on the judicial process.

For three years a handful of women's liberation activists brought the subject of abortion into households throughout the state, forced the conservative politics of the state government into the public spotlight, and involved thousands of women in political action on behalf of reproductive freedom. The combination of litigation and grass-roots mobilization that they and women of other states engaged in was a crucial element in the making of *Roe v. Wade.*

## NOTES

1. I would like to thank Betsy Gilbertson for introducing me to Women Versus Connecticut, spending hours copying legal material and critically reading several drafts of this article. The article has also benefited enormously from Virginia Blaisdell's editorial assistance and the comments of Katie Roraback, Rickie Solinger, and Nancy Stearns.
2. Nancy Stearns, "*Roe v. Wade:* Our Struggle Continues," *Berkeley Women's Law Journal, 4,* (1988–89), 5.
3. See David Garrow, *Liberty and Sexuality: The Right to Privacy and the Making of Roe v. Wade* (New York: Macmillan, 1994), chapt. 8 for full descriptions of these changes.
4. Nancy Stearns, interview with author, February 11, 1995. For a fuller description of the New York case, see Diane Schulder and Florynce Kennedy, *Abortion Rap* (New York: McGraw-Hill, 1971).
5. Hartford, Connecticut, hearing of Judiciary Committee of the State Legislature, April 14, 1969, p. 39.
6. Ann Hill, "Abortion, Self Determination and the Political Process," unpublished paper, May 22, 1971.
7. Ann Hill, interview with author, December 1992.
8. Betsy Gilbertson, interview with author, August 6, 1991.
9. Ann Hill, unpublished speech at the Women and Power Conference, New Haven, Connecticut, June 1973.
10. Betsy Gilbertson, interview with author.
11. Nancy Stearns, interview.
12. Hill, "Abortion."
13. Catherine Roraback, interview with author, January 20, 1992.
14. Plaintiff Recruitment pamphlet.
15. *Modern Times,* October 1970, p. 5.
16. Ann Hill, unpublished speech.
17. Gail Falk, interview with author, October 10, 1992.
18. Ann Hill, interview.
19. Judy Robison, interview with author, October 9, 1992. See Rickie Solinger, *Wake Up Little Suzie: Single Pregnancy and Race Before Roe v. Wade* (New York: Routledge, 1992).
20. Planned Parenthood still called themselves "Planned Parenthood World Population," and in 1969 at their national convention a caucus of African-American workers organized against any statement on abortion as well as sterilization; papers of Planned Parenthood New Haven Chapter, Box 41, folder G, New Haven Historical Society. See also Thomas Littlewood, *The Politics of Population Control* (Notre Dame, IN: University of Notre Dame Press, 1977). Connecticut Planned Parenthood had been criticized because all six of their outreach workers in the Hartford area were African-American. Papers of Planned Parenthood, New Haven Chapter, board meeting, box 41, folder G.
21. The Black Panther Party, who were the black nationalist voices in New Haven were most familiar with in the late 1960s and 1970s, were divided on the question of abortion and birth control. According to Loretta Ross, the Black Panther Party supported legalized abortion ("Abortion: 1800–1970," in *Theorizing Black Feminisms: The Visionary Pragmatism of Black Women,* ed. Stanlie James and Abena Busia [New York: Routledge, 1993]). Black Panther literature, however, often condemned it. See, for example, Brenda Hyson, "New York Passed New Abortion Law Effective July, 1970," *Black Panther,* July 4, 1970.
22. Gail Falk, interview with author.
23. Loretta Ross, "African American Women and Abortion," in *Abortion Wars: A Half Century of Struggle 1950–2000,* ed. Rickie Solinger (Berkeley: University of California Press, 1998), p. 165.
24. Shirley Chisholm, Frances Beale, Patricia Robinson, and Florynce Kennedy were among the African-American activists who spoke out publicly for abortion in the late 1960s and early 1970s. See Ross, "Abortion," and Rev Polatnik, "Poor Black Sisters Decided for Themselves: A Case Study of Women's Liberation Activism," in *Black Women in America,* ed. Kim Marie Vaz (Thousand Oaks, CA: Sage, 1995).
25. "Report to Plaintiffs," February 1971; information about plaintiffs is from a chart constructed by Women Versus Connecticut organizers in the summer of 1971 giving details about 848 plaintiffs.
26. Betsy Gilbertson, interview with author.
27. "Complaint in Motion for a Declaratory Judgment in *Abele v. Markle,*" p. 5.
28. Quoted in Hill, "Abortion," from a plaintiff meeting at Yale Law School on April 22, 1971.
29. Catherine Roraback, interview with author.
30. *Federal Supplement,* Vol. 342, pp. 800–802. Lumbard's opinion built on the Supreme Court's decision one month earlier in *Eisenstadt v. Baird,* the Massachusetts case against Bill Baird, who had been arrested for distributing birth control and abortion information to a college audience. Garrow, *Liberty and Sexuality,* p. 542.
31. *Hartford Courant,* April 19, 1972; *New Haven Register,* April 19, 1972.
32. *Federal Supplement,* Vol. 342, p. 805.
33. *Hartford Courant,* May 14, 1972.
34. Transcript of the Hearings of Joint Committee on Public Health and Safety, May 19, 1972.
35. *New Haven Register,* May 20, 1972; *New York Times,* May 24, 1972.
36. Lawrence Lader, *Abortion II: Making the Revolution* (Boston: Beacon, 1973), p. 194.

37. Press Release, Women Versus Connecticut, May 26, 1972.
38. Memorandum in support of motion for contempt, to enforce injunction and for other relief, May 25, 1972; press release, Women Versus Connecticut, May 26, 1972.
39. Transcript of the hearing of *Abele v. Markle*, June 30, 1972.
40. Vol. 351 of *Federal Supplement to Cases Argued and Determined in U.S. District Courts*, pp. 224, 228.
41. Stearns, "*Roe v. Wade*," p. 5.
42. *New York Times*, January 23, 1973; *Time*, January 29, 1973.
43. Women Versus Connecticut Newsletter, February 1973.

[1998]

# Women and Work

The selections in this section consider the ways sexism shapes women's work both within and outside the home and suggest approaches to change.

While the media give the impression that women have unlimited opportunities and have made unprecedented career advances, the reality of the workplace is much more discouraging. Although women have made significant progress in a few areas, the majority of women face a sex-segregated labor market that devalues the work that most women do. Ellen Bravo and Gloria Santa Anna, co-directors of 9to5, National Association of Working Women, detail the problems women face at work and suggest policy changes needed to bring gender equity to the workplace. Data about the wage gap between men and women and a plan for eliminating sex and race discrimination in wages through a system of pay equity follow. Since most women and people of color are still segregated into a small number of jobs that are underpaid, a system of pay equity would ensure that the criteria employers use to set wages would consider sex and race neutral.

The work that women do in the home—housework, child care, and nurturing—is work that is extremely demanding, in time, energy, and skill. Women still do most work in the home despite their increasing participation in the labor force. "The Politics of Housework" is a classic piece from the early days of the women's liberation movement that points to the struggle involved in getting men to take responsibility for housework. Because it is associated with women, housework is seen as demeaning and lacking in value. Like many of the writings from this period, it demonstrates that an activity that has been treated as private is indeed political; that is, it involves the allocation of power and resources.

The daily struggle of women to balance the often competing demands of work and home responsibilities is described by Ellen Bravo in "The Job/Family Challenge Today." She writes, "While the workforce has changed drastically . . . most workplaces have changed very little to accommodate the realities of women's lives."

The dual role women workers are expected to take on combined with inequities in the workplace trap many women in poverty. When women have children and cannot find work that pays enough to support their families and pay for child care, they often have to turn to welfare. A former welfare recipient, Rita Henley Jensen, describes the realities of being a woman on welfare. She shows how in the early 1970s that system provided her a way out and how and why it doesn't now. In "Farewell to Welfare, but Not to Poverty," Randy Albelda and Chris Tilly describe the welfare "reform" legislation of 1996, point out the ways this will worsen the lives of poor women, and conclude with suggestions for reforms that would work.

In both the past and present women have challenged the discrimination they face in the workplace. Blanca Vázquez's interviews with Puerto Rican garment workers depict how the perseverance and combativeness of women can be a source of inspiration to all who "fight in countless ways to resist the lack of dignity in our lives."

Collective efforts by women make a significant difference in gaining equity in the workplace. "What Do Unions Do for Women?" shows that union membership under a collective bargaining agreement is associated with higher wages and longer job tenure, as well as a smaller pay gap between women and men. The selections about 9to5 describe the history of an association for working women that for over 25 years has organized low-wage women to fight for equity at work. In the process of doing so, it has helped women see that their struggles are not personal but based on the need to redistribute power in the workplace.

This section ends with two poems. Alice Walker's poem pays tribute to the strength and resourcefulness of her mother and the many black women whose labors of love and creativity made possible a future for their daughters. Marge Piercy celebrates people who work with purpose and vigor toward common goals.

---

## 🌿 53

# *An Overview of Women and Work*

ELLEN BRAVO AND
GLORIA SANTA ANNA

Any commentator reviewing progress in the United States during the twentieth century will list prominently the gains of working women. Swept away were laws and customs that prevailed for centuries—allowing lower pay for women doing the same work as men, permitting women to be fired for being pregnant, considering women fair game for harassment on the job. From doctor to drill sergeant, carpenter to CEO, women changed the face of the nation's workforce. The notion that women had been absent from certain jobs because they weren't capable was dealt a significant blow.

And yet, women in this country still earn less than men for equivalent jobs. Many women today lose their jobs when they give birth. Sexual harassment remains a persistent problem in the workplace. While women appear in almost every occupational category, they are woefully underrepresented in higher-paying positions.

In fact, the picture for working women is decidedly mixed. Gains have been real and important, but many women have not been significantly affected by them. A close look at three areas—pay, work/family balance, and welfare—helps illustrate the problems and their impact on women and their families. If women as a whole are to benefit, concern for equality must be joined with fundamental change in the way this society does business.

### WHO'S WORKING

A quick look at the numbers shows how greatly the workforce has changed. By 1995, women accounted for 46% of the total U.S. labor force, compared with 37.7% in 1960. Nearly six out of every ten women—58.9%—age 16 and over were now working or looking for work. Women are expected to make up 48% of the workforce by 2005.

While marriage and childbirth had never spelled the end of employment for certain groups of women, especially African Americans and immigrants, the majority of women in the past left the workforce to care for their families. That reality has changed drastically, as a result of shrinking real wages and growing expectations. Debate about whether women should work has become moot. Most women—including most married mothers—are in the labor force. More than half of all mothers with infants return to work before the baby's first birthday. Employment, however, has brought women neither equality nor an end to poverty.

## PAY

Despite dramatic increases in pay for some, earnings for women as a group remain not just lower than men's but often very low indeed:

- 21% of women working full-time in 1994 earned less than $13,800 for the year. For Latinas, the figure is 36%; for African Americans, 26%.
- 27% of employed mothers are in a household with income less than $23,500/year.

Why do women make so little money? Because their employers pay them so little. And why is that? Aside from the continuation of blatant discrimination, the reasons include the following factors:

1. Although there have been huge changes in jobs formerly closed to women, most women do the same jobs they've always done, and those jobs pay less than comparable jobs done by men.

- 60% of women workers are employed in service, sales, and clerical jobs.
- Even within certain occupations, women are clustered in the lower-paying jobs. In retail trades, for instance, women in 1994 constituted 82% of employees in gift and novelty shops but only 19% of those employed in higher-paying car dealerships.[1] More women work as physicians and lawyers but tend to be found disproportionately in family practices that pay less than other areas of medicine and law.
- More women are in professional and managerial positions, but they've made little headway in skilled construction trades and other traditionally male, blue-collar occupations or at the top of the corporate ladder. Women account for only 2% of skilled trades, 8% of police, and 5% of senior managers.
- Women of color are concentrated in the lowest-paying jobs, including domestic workers, nurses' aides, and child-care workers.[2]

Many people talk about the need to increase the number of women in science and math. While those efforts are needed, they ignore the underlying question: why does society value accountants more than social workers? Embedded in the market value of jobs in the legacy of past discrimination, based on gender and on race.

2. Women disproportionately are employed in part-time and temporary jobs. No law says these jobs have to pay the same as full-time and permanent positions or give any, much less equivalent, benefits.

Peggie has been a temp for more than 10 years because she cannot find permanent employment. During those years she worked stints of three years each at IBM and Coca-Cola. Her annual income is less than $12,000, and she has no benefits. To pay medical and dental bills, Peggie went without a car for two years. She lives in a one-bedroom apartment. "Even though I'm always working," said Peggie, "I live in poverty."

When Linda's marriage fell apart, she tried to find full-time employment but had to make do with three part-time jobs. None of her jobs provided health insurance, including the one at a nursing home. At age 38, Linda had a serious heart attack. She eventually found a doctor and hospital willing to do the surgery and was able to have hospital bills waived. Still, she owed $20,000 to 16 different health care professionals. After she recovered, Linda found a full-time job and a second, part-time position to pay something every month on those bills. She suffered another heart attack and died on that job the day before her 42nd birthday.

Part-time or temporary positions can be beneficial for women, as long as they are voluntary and equitable. Increasingly, these positions are neither. In 1992, close to one-third of those working part-time did so *involuntarily*.[3] Being paid less than full-time and permanent workers often means poverty wages. According to a recent report by the Economic Policy Institute, 28.1% of women employed by temporary help agencies earn less than $5.95 an hour.[4] So do 36.7% of female part-timers. Fewer than one of ten women temps, and two in ten part-timers receive health insurance from their employer.

3. Women are still largely responsible for family. The penalty for that is significant—and most

women never make it up. One study of professional women who took an average of 8.8 months per leave showed them earning 17% less than women who hadn't taken leave.[5] For lower-wage women, taking a leave may also mean losing a job and having to sart over, often having to go on welfare.

In a 1980 speech, Clarence Thomas spoke with disdain of his sister who had gone on welfare. He neglected to mention that she'd done so in order to care for an aunt who had a stroke.

4.   The globalization of the economy has affected women's pay in several ways. Large numbers of women from Asia, Central America, and elsewhere find themselves in the United States, their native economies turned upside-down by transnational corporations. Here they fill jobs U.S.-born workers try to avoid, sewing garments and assembling products in old-fashioned sweatshops, picking crops, not uncommonly with their children by their side. The most basic employment protections often elude them. Globalization has costs for U.S. workers as well, as the same transnationals move jobs overseas in the quest for ever cheaper labor. Decent-paying manufacturing jobs disappear, replaced by lower-paying industries or low-wage service jobs.

5.   Women are disproportionately represented among minimum-wage earners, accounting for two-thirds of all workers in this category. Of these women in 1993, 18% were married, and 8% were women maintaining families.

6.   Unionized women earn 30% more than non-union women. Despite talk of "supply and demand," wage levels depend above all on *bargaining power*. Being able to bargain collectively for pay and benefits helps diminish the under-evaluation of women's work and to create more opportunities for women to move into higher-paying jobs. A contract also ensures greater protection against arbitrary firing and a greater likelihood of paid maternity leave—with the longer job tenure ensuring higher pay. However, only 13% of all women are unionized. Although women have increased their percentage of all union members, up to 40% in 1994 from 34% a decade earlier, that gain also reflects the loss of union jobs for men—only 18% are in unions, down from 23% in 1984.

Clearly, the solution to women's low pay must be much more far-reaching than elevating greater numbers of women into jobs traditionally performed by men. To end poverty among women and their families will require fundamental restructuring of the economy.

## WORK/FAMILY ISSUES

Today 55% of working women provide half or more of their families' income. Only 8% of families with children fit the stereotype of Dad as breadwinner, Mom full-time at home. Yet the workplace has not kept pace with these changes in the workforce. Passage of the Family and Medical Leave Act in 1993 was an important step forward. This law allows women and men to take up to 12 weeks unpaid leave to care for a new child, a seriously ill child, spouse, or parent, or for a personal illness. But the impact of the bill remains unacceptably narrow. Consider these findings from the bipartisan Commission on Leave:[6]

•   Only 54.9% of U.S. workers—46.5% of private sector workers—both work for covered employers (those with 50 or more employees) and meet the eligibility requirements (12 months, 1,250 hours).

•   Only 10.8% of private-sector work sites are covered.

•   Noncovered employers are *not* taking care of the problem on their own. Only 32.3% offer parental leave, only 41.7% offer leave to care for a seriously ill child, spouse, or parent.

•   Only 58.2% of employees working at covered firms have heard of the act.

•   Women, younger workers, workers with low family incomes, and those not protected by collective bargaining are most likely to be ineligible or unable to afford leave. Of all ethnic groups, Latino workers are least likely to be protected.

• Of those who needed leave but didn't take it, 64% said they couldn't afford to lose their wages. Hourly workers and African Americans are most likely to be among those who need but didn't take leave.

• 11.6% of women leave-takers use public assistance to deal with lost income during leave. Of those with family incomes of $20,000 or less, more than 20% rely on public assistance during leave.

The law's narrow definitions of family and of reasons for taking leave ignore the realities of many families and the need to deal with routine illnesses or school matters. No provisions are made for same-sex couples, not to mention those who want to care for a sibling or another relative. We hear a lot about the importance of parental involvement in the schools. Yet 28% of employed parents report facing problems at work when they want to attend school activities, 23% when they need to attend parent-teacher conferences.[7] According to a study reported in *Pediatrics* magazine, 60% of the working poor do not have sick leave they can use to care for sick family members.

> Teresa works for an agency in Milwaukee that allows her to stay home if schools are closed unexpectedly because of snow or cold. One morning when the temperature reached 41 degrees below zero with the wind chill, the decision to close the schools was announced at 5:30 A.M. At 6:30 a neighbor knocked on Teresa's door. "You look like a nice person," she said. "Will you watch my children? I'll be fired if I don't get to work."

To meet the needs of today's workforce, both family leave and dependent care must be made more accessible and more affordable. That means challenging the view that these are private problems to be solved by individual employees.

## WELFARE

In 1997 we saw the passage of national welfare reform legislation—the stunning reversal of U.S. policy that for decades had guaranteed assistance to poor women and children. Unfortunately, the new policy is based on faulty assumptions and an unrealistic view of where women will work.

Many architects of welfare reform start with the premise that the majority of women are on welfare because they *won't work*. Their strategy is to *force them to work*—any job will do. They design extensive punishments for those who don't comply. Since women can't work without some assistance, they provide some help with insurance and child care. The measure of success is reduction in the welfare rolls.

In fact, 70% of women on welfare during a two-year period are working or looking for work.[9] They're *cyclers* (on and off welfare) or *combiners* (combine work and welfare). According to a study of six midwest states by Northern Illinois University, only 6.3% of Aid to Families with Dependent Children (AFDC) recipients never worked; only 3.4% of adults were under 18.[10]

The most serious problem with current plans is they're missing the key component: jobs. There aren't enough jobs, the ones that are available don't pay enough, and there's a mismatch between the job seekers and where good jobs are located and the skills they require.

We need to understand that most women are on welfare because of *problems with work* or with some other system in their lives, such as marriage or education. The strategy must be to *find solutions* for those problems—job training, creation of living wage jobs with affordable leave, adequate quality child care, health insurance, along with efforts to eliminate domestic violence, reach equity and quality in all schools, and so forth. Since the problems affect more people than those on welfare, the solutions need to be universal. The measure of sucess is *reduction in poverty and rise in self-sufficiency for families.*

## CONCLUSION

Often policy makers and advocates for women's rights speak of "women" as if one size fits all. But women exist in splendid diversity. Only a thorough understanding of specific conditions of various groups, an understanding that looks through the lens of class, race and ethnicity, and sexual orientation, can lead us to the range of solutions that women need. Progress for women cannot be mea-

## Office Double Standards

A businessman is aggressive, a businesswoman is pushy.
He's careful about details, she's picky.
He follows through, she doesn't know when to quit.
He's firm, she's stubborn.
He makes judgments, she reveals her prejudices.
He's a man of the world, she's "been around."
He exercises authority, she's bossy.
He's discreet, she's secretive.
He says what he thinks, she's opinionated.

(original sources, unfortunately, unknown)

sured only by what happens to women in professional and managerial jobs. In order for women as a whole to benefit, the fight for gender equality must go hand in hand with the struggle against all forms of oppression.

### NOTES

1. Cynthia Costello and Barbara Kivimac Kringold, eds., *The American Woman 1996–97* (New York: Norton, 1996).
2. See, "The Wage Gap: Myths and Facts," the next essay in this volume, for occupational concentrations by race, ethnicity, and gender.
3. Chris Tilly, *Half a Job* (Philadelphia: Temple University Press, 1996).
4. Anne Kalleberg et al., *Nonstandard Work, Substandard Jobs* (Washington, D.C.: Economic Policy Institute, 1997).
5. This 1994 study by business professors Joy Schneer and Frieda Reiton compared 128 women MBAs who had never taken a break with 63 who had taken some leave and gone back full time by 1987.
6. Commission on Leave, *A Workable Balance: Report to Congress on Family and Medical Leave Policies*, Washington, D.C.: U.S. Department of Labor (1996).
7. "The PTA/Newsweek National Education Survey," *Newsweek*, May 17, 1993.
8. *Pediatrics* magazine, August 1996.
9. Roberta Spalter-Roth et al., *Welfare That Works: The Working Lives of AFDC Recipients* (Washington, D.C.: Institute for Women's Policy Research, 1995).
10. Paul Kleppner and Nikolas Theodore, *Work After Welfare: Is the Midwest's Booming Economy Creating Enough Jobs?* (Chicago: Northern Illinois University, 1997).                                          [1998]

 **54**

# The Wage Gap: Myths and Facts

NATIONAL COMMITTEE ON PAY EQUITY

### WHAT IS PAY EQUITY?

Pay equity is a means of eliminating sex and race discrimination in the wage-setting system. Most women and people of color are still segregated into a small number of jobs—such as clericals, service workers, nurses and teachers. These jobs have historically been undervalued and continue to be underpaid because of the gender and race of the people who hold them. Pay equity means that the criteria employers use to set wages must be sex and race neutral.

### IS PAY EQUITY THE LAW?

Yes, two laws protect workers against wage discrimination. The Equal Pay Act of 1963 prohibits unequal pay for equal or "substantially equal" work performed by men and women. Title VII of the Civil Rights Act of 1964 prohibits wage discrimination on the basis of color, sex, religion, national origin or disability. In 1981, the Supreme Court made it clear that Title VII is broader than the Equal Pay Act, and prohibits wage discrimination even when the jobs are not identical. However, wage discrimination laws are poorly enforced and cases are extremely difficult to prove and win. Stronger legislation is needed to ease the burden of filing claims and to clarify the right to pay equity.

## THE WAGE GAP: 1996

**Women Earn 73.8% of Men's Earnings
Median Annual Wages by Race
and Gender, 1996**

|          | Men      | Women    |
|----------|----------|----------|
| White    | $32,966  | $24,160  |
| Black    | $26,404  | $21,473  |
| Hispanic | $21,056  | $18,665  |
| All      | $32,144  | $23,710  |

*Source:* U.S. Census Bureau, Money Income in the United States, 1996 Current Population Reports, Consumer Income, P60–197.

### WHY IS THERE A WAGE GAP?

The wage gap exists because most women and people of color are still segregated into a few low-paying occupations. More than half (61 percent) of all women workers hold jobs in sales, clerical and service jobs. Studies show that the more an occupation is dominated by women or people of color, the less it pays. Part of the wage gap results from differences in education, experience or time in the workforce. But a significant portion can not be explained by any of those factors; it is attributable to wage discrimination. In other words, certain jobs pay less because they are held by women or people of color.

### HASN'T THE WAGE GAP CLOSED CONSIDERABLY IN RECENT YEARS?

The wage gap has narrowed by about ten percentage points during the last ten years, from 61.7 percent in 1982 to 71.4 percent in 1995. However, about 60 percent in the change in the wage gap is due to the fall in men's real earnings. Approximately 40 percent of the change in the wage gap is due to the increase in women's wages. The ratio of women's to men's wages has fluctuated often, ranging from a low of 57 percent in the mid 1970's, and peaking at 72 percent in 1990 and again in 1993 and 1994. In 1995, the ratio dipped again as a result of a 1.5 percent decline in women's real earnings. In 1946, the ratio gap reached a high of 66 percent, but fell again to 64 percent in the 1950's.

### IS IT POSSIBLE TO COMPARE DIFFERENT JOBS?

Yes, employers have used job evaluations for nearly a century to set pay and rank for different occupations within a company or organization. Today, two out of three workers are employed by firms that use some form of job evaluation. The federal government, the nation's largest employer, has a 70 year old job evaluation system that covers nearly 2 million employees.

### WHO REALLY NEEDS PAY EQUITY?

Women, people of color, and white men who work in jobs that have been undervalued due to race or sex bias need pay equity. Many are the sole support for their families. Two out of three women workers are single, divorced, widowed, separated or have husbands who earn less than $15,000 per year. Discriminatory pay has consequences as people mature and across generations—it affects retirement security. Everyone in society is harmed by wage discrimination. Everyone needs pay equity.

### IS PAY EQUITY AN EFFECTIVE ANTI-POVERTY STRATEGY?

Yes, pay equity helps workers become self-sufficient and reduces their reliance on government assistance programs. A recent study found that nearly 40 percent of working poor women could leave welfare programs if they were to receive pay equity wage increases. Pay equity can bring great savings to tax payers at a minimal cost to business; adjustments would cost no more than 3.7 percent of hourly wage costs.

## WILL WHITE MEN'S WAGES BE REDUCED IF PAY EQUITY IS IMPLEMENTED?

No. Federal law prohibits reducing pay for any employee to remedy discrimination. Furthermore, male workers in female-dominated jobs benefit when sex discrimination is eliminated, as do white workers in minority-dominated jobs. Pay equity means equal treatment for all workers.

## WILL PAY EQUITY REQUIRE A NATIONAL WAGE SETTING SYSTEM?

No. Pay equity does not mandate across-the-board salaries for any occupation or tamper with supply and demand. It merely means that wages must be based on job requirements like skill, effort, responsibility and working conditions without consideration of race, sex or ethnicity.

## DOESN'T PAY EQUITY COST EMPLOYERS TOO MUCH?

In Minnesota, where pay equity legislation meant raises for 30,000 state employees, the cost was only 3.7 percent of the state's payroll budget over a four year period—less than 1 percent of the budget each year. In Washington State, pay equity was achieved at a cost of 2.6 percent of the state's personnel costs and was implemented over an eight year period. Voluntary implementation of pay equity is cost effective. Court-ordered pay equity adjustments can lead to greater costs. Discrimination is costly and illegal.

## WILL PAY EQUITY DISRUPT THE ECONOMY?

No. The Equal Pay Act, minimum wage, and child labor laws all provoked the same concerns, and all were implemented without major disruption. What disrupts the economy and penalizes families is the systematic underpayment of some people because of their sex or race. When wages for women and people of color are raised, their purchasing power will increase, strengthening the economy. One survey found that a growing number of businesses support the elimination of wage discrimination between

different jobs as "good business" and not inconsistent with remaining competitive.

## WHAT IS THE STATUS OF PAY EQUITY?

Pay equity is a growing national movement. Twenty states have made some adjustment of payrolls to correct sex or race bias. Seven of these states had successfully completed full implementation of a pay equity plan. Twenty-four states (including Washington, D.C.) have conducted studies to determine if sex was a wage determinant. Four states have examined their compensation systems to correct race bias as well.

## 1. THE UNITED STATES LABOR FORCE IS OCCUPATIONALLY SEGREGATED BY RACE AND SEX.

• In 1992, women constituted 45.7 percent of all workers in the civilian labor force (over 57 million women).[1]

• People of color constituted 14.5 percent of all workers.[2]

• Labor force participation is almost equal among white women, Black women, and women of Hispanic origin. In 1992, 57.2 percent (7.1 million) of Black women, 61.3 percent (52.7 million) of white women, and 52.8 percent (4.2 million of Hispanic women were in the paid labor force.[3]

• In 1992, women were:
   99.0 percent of all secretaries
   93.5 percent of all registered nurses
   98.8 percent of all pre-school and kindergarten teachers
   89.0 percent of all telephone operators
   73.2 percent of all teachers (excluding colleges and universities)
   86.6 percent of all data entry keyers
   Women were only:
    8.7 percent of all engineers
   30.3 percent of all lawyers and judges
   15.1 percent of all police and detectives
    8.2 percent of all precision, production, craft, and repair workers
   26.2 percent of all physicians[4]

The U.S. labor force is segregated by sex and race.

## Occupations with the Highest Concentration by Race/Ethnicity/Sex [5]

| | |
|---|---|
| Black women: | Social workers; postal clerks; dieticians; child-care workers and teacher's aides; private household cooks and cleaners; nursing aides, orderlies, and attendants |
| Black men: | Vehicle washers and equipment cleaners; bus drivers; concrete and terrazzo workers; guards; sheriffs, bailiffs, and other law enforcement |
| Hispanic women: | Private household cleaners and servants; child-care workers; janitors and cleaners; health service occupations; sewing machine operators; graders and sorters |
| Hispanic men: | Janitors and cleaners; construction trades; machine operators and tenders; cooks; drivers-sales workers; handlers, laborers, and helpers; roofers; groundskeepers, gardeners, farm and agricultural workers |
| White women: | Physical therapists; dental hygienists; secretaries and stenographers; bookkeepers, accounting and auditing clerks |
| White men: | Marketing, advertising, and public relations managers; engineers, architects, and surveyors; dentists; firefighters; construction supervisors; tool and die makers |
| Asian women: | Marine life workers; electrical assemblers; dressmakers; launderers |
| Asian men: | Physicians; engineers; professors; technicians; baggage porters; cooks; launderers; long shore equipment operators |
| Native American women: | Welfare aides; child-care workers; teacher's aides; forestry (except logging) |
| Native American men: | Marine life workers; hunters; forestry (except logging); fishers |

## 2. ECONOMIC STATUS.

• In 1992, 58 percent of all women were either the sole supporter of their families or their husbands earned less than $15,000.[6]

• Over 8.8 million women work full time in jobs that pay wages below the poverty line (in 1992 for a family of three the poverty line was $11,186 per year). They work in jobs such as day care, food counter, and many service jobs. Many more women than men are part of the working poor (125 percent of the poverty level) and work in jobs such as clerical, blue collar, and sales.[7]

• In 1992, married couple families with two children present had a median income of $43,818 while female headed households with two children present had a median income of only $11,591.[8]

• Women of color are in the lowest paid jobs.

• The majority of women, just as the majority of men, work out of economic necessity to support their families. Women do not work for "pin money."

### Occupations and Average Salaries of Occupations with a High Percentage of Women of Color [9]

| Occupation | Annual Weekly Salary | Percentage of Women of Color |
|---|---|---|
| Social workers | $489 | 16 |
| Health aides | 309 | 22 |
| Nursing aides | 266 | 31 |
| Food preparation workers | 236 | 10 |
| Sewing machine operators | 217 | 28 |
| Cleaners and servants | 191 | 26 |
| Child-care workers | 154 | 14 |

In 1992 median weekly salaries for all men were $505 and $381 for all women. Women of color represented approximately 7 percent of all workers.

## 3. THE WAGE GAP IS ONE OF THE MAJOR CAUSES OF ECONOMIC INEQUALITY IN THE UNITED STATES TODAY.

• In 1992, all men, working year-round full-time, were paid a median salary of $30,358.
• All women, working year-round full-time, were paid a median salary of $21,440.
• Therefore, women were paid 70.6 cents compared to each dollar paid to men.

The breakdown by race shows the double burden that women of color face because of race and sex discrimination.

### Year-Round Full-Time Earnings for 1992 [10]

| Race/Sex | Earnings | Earnings as a Percentage of White Men's |
|---|---|---|
| White men | $31,012 | 100.0 |
| Black men | 22,369 | 72.1 |
| Hispanic men | 20,049 | 64.6 |
| White women | $21,659 | 69.8 |
| Black women | 19,819 | 63.9 |
| Hispanic women | 17,138 | 55.3 |

Data for Asian/Pacific Islanders and native Americans is not available.

## 4. THE WAGE GAP HAS FLUCTUATED, BUT HAS NOT DISAPPEARED IN THE LAST SEVERAL DECADES.

Over the last decade, the wage gap has narrowed by about ten cents, from 60.2 percent in 1980 to 70.6 percent in 1992. However, a significant portion of the change is due to the fact that men's real earnings have fallen over the last several years. 38 percent of the change in the wage ratio can be attributed to the drop in men's earnings, while 62 percent is due to the increase in women's earnings over the decade.

## 5. THE CAUSE OF THE WAGE GAP IS DISCRIMINATION.

Differences in education, labor force experience, and commitment (years in the labor force) do not account for the entire wage gap.

• In 1992, women with college degrees earned $11,721 less per year than their white male colleagues, and only $1,916 more per year than white men with only a high-school diploma.
• College educated Hispanic women actually earned less than white men who had never taken a college course. [12]

### Changes in the Wage Gap, 1970–1995
Median Annual Earnings of Black Men and Women, Hispanic Men and Women, and White Men and Women as a Percentage of White Men's Median Annual Earnings

| Year | White Men | Black Men | Hispanic Men | White Women | Black Women | Hispanic Women |
|---|---|---|---|---|---|---|
| 1970 | 100% | 69.0% | N/A | 58.7% | 48.2% | N/A |
| 1975 | 100% | 74.3% | 72.1% | 57.5% | 55.4% | 49.3% |
| 1980 | 100% | 70.7% | 70.8% | 58.9% | 55.7% | 50.5% |
| 1985 | 100% | 69.7% | 68.0% | 63.0% | 57.1% | 52.1% |
| 1990 | 100% | 73.1% | 66.3% | 69.4% | 62.5% | 54.3% |
| 1992 | 100% | 72.6% | 63.3% | 70.0% | 64.0% | 55.4% |
| 1994 | 100% | 75.1% | 64.3% | 71.6% | 63.0% | 55.6% |
| 1995 | 100% | 75.9% | 63.3% | 71.2% | 64.2% | 53.4% |

• The National Academy of Sciences (NAS) found in 1981 that usually less than a quarter (25 percent) of the wage gap is due to differences in education, labor force experience, and commitment.

• According to the 1986 NAS study, *Women's Work, Men's Work,* "each additional percentage point female in an occupation was associated with $42 less in median annual earnings."

### 1995 Median Annual Earnings by Race and Sex

| Race/Gender | Earnings | Wage Ratio |
|---|---|---|
| White men | $32,172 | 100% |
| White women | $22,911 | 71.2% |
| Black men | $24,428 | 75.9% |
| Black women | $20,665 | 64.2% |
| Hispanic men | $20,379 | 63.3% |
| Hispanic women | $17,178 | 53.4% |

*Source:* U.S. Census Bureau, Money Income in the United States, 1996 Current Population Reports, Consumer Income, P60–197.

• According to the 1987 National Committee on Pay Equity (NCPE) study, in New York State, for every 5 to 6 percent increase in Black and Hispanic representation in a job there is one salary grade decrease. (One salary grade decrease amounts to a 5 percent salary decrease.)

• A 1985 U.S. Census Bureau study reported that differences in education, labor force experience, and commitment account for only 14.6 percent of the wage gap between men and women.

### 6. EMPLOYERS ARE ALWAYS COMPARING DIFFERENT JOBS IN ORDER TO SET WAGES.

• Two-thirds of employees are paid according to a formal job evaluation system.

### 7. THE COST OF IMPLEMENTING PAY EQUITY.

• Achieving pay equity usually costs about 2 to 5 percent of an employer's payroll budget.

For example, in the State of Minnesota, after conducting a job evaluation study, it was determined

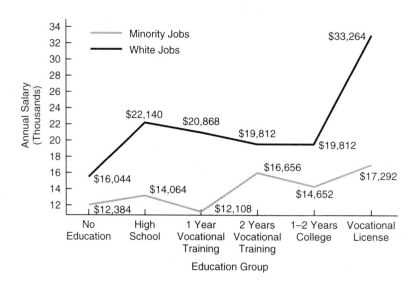

*Figure 1   White vs. Minority Wage Inequity by Education for Entry-Level Jobs*

that there was a 20 percent gap between comparable male-dominated and female-dominated jobs. It costs the state 3.7 percent of the payroll budget to eliminate this inequity. The adjustments were phased-in over a four-year period and have resulted in a narrowing of the wage gap by nine percentage points, without affecting overall employment for women in the state.

## 8. PAY EQUITY IS BEING ADDRESSED ALL OVER THE COUNTRY.

- All but five states (Alaska, Arkansas, Delaware, Georgia, and Idaho) have addressed the issue of pay equity.
- Twenty-four states and the District of Columbia have conducted job evaluation studies to determine if their wage setting systems are discriminatory.
- Twenty states have actually adjusted wages for women in jobs that have been found to be underpaid because of wage bias.
- Four states (New York, New Jersey, Florida, and Wisconsin) and Washington, D.C., have addressed race in addition to sex discrimination.[13]

## 9. EVERYONE IN SOCIETY BENEFITS FROM PAY EQUITY.

- Men's wages will not be lowered. Employers cannot remedy discrimination by penalizing another group. Men who are working in predominantly female jobs will also be paid more if pay equity adjustments are made. Everyone benefits from women and people of color being paid fairly. Whether it is your mother, sister, wife, or daughter, wage discrimination hurts the entire family. Men of color will benefit in additional ways to those listed for all men: elimination of race from the wage setting system will boost their wages and men of color are more likely to be found in undervalued "women's" occupations.
- Employers benefit because the employees' productivity will increase if there is a sense of fairness in how wages are set. Also, pay equity helps employers recruit and retain the best workers.
- Society benefits because if wage discrimina-

tion is eliminated, the need for government subsidies for food stamps, health care, etc., will not be as great. In addition, when workers whose wages were lowered by discrimination are paid fairly, their pensions will be greater upon retirement and they will need less government assistance in their senior years.

## WHERE WE GET THE STATISTICS

The U.S. Department of Commerce, Census Bureau, collects wage data every ten years. This data provides in-depth information for Blacks, whites, Hispanics, Asian/Pacific Islanders, and Native Americans. The 1990 decennial census figures of the national work force and occupational data sorted by gender and race had not been released as of January 1994.

The Census Bureau also provides annual salary data for Blacks, whites, and Hispanics. They gather this information in March of the following year and release it in September. Therefore, the annual salary data for 1993 will not have been released until September of 1994.

The U.S. Department of Labor, Bureau of Labor Statistics (BLS), provides quarterly reports each year on weekly salaries for Blacks, whites, and Hispanics. They also provide an annual average of weekly wages.

## NOTES

1. U.S. Department of Labor, Bureau of Labor Statistics, 1992 Annual Average Tables from *Employment and Earnings*, Jan., 1993.
2. Ibid.
3. U.S. Department of Commerce, Census Bureau, Current Population Reports, Consumer Income. Series P-60, No. 184, Table No. 31.
4. U.S. Department of Labor, Bureau of Labor Statistics, 1992 Annual Average Tables, Table 5.
5. Data for Black, Hispanic, and white men and women from the U.S. Department of Labor Bureau of Labor Statistics, 1992 Annual Averages, unpublished tables. Data for Asian and Native American men and women from U.S. Department of Commerce, 1980 Decennial Census.
6. U.S. Department of Commerce, Census Bureau, Current Population Reports, Consumer Income, Series P-60, No. 184, Table No. 28.
7. U.S. Department of Commerce, Census Bureau, Current Population Reports, Consumer Income, Series P-60, No. 185, Table A.

8. U.S. Department of Commerce, Census Bureau, Current Population Reports, Consumer Income, Series P-60, No. 184, Table No. 18.

9. U.S. Department of Labor, Bureau of Labor Statistics, 1992 Annual Averages, unpublished data.

10. U.S. Department of Commerce, Census Bureau, Current Population Reports, Consumer Income, Series P-60, No. 184, Table No. 31.

11. *Background on the Wage Gap,* National Committee on Pay Equity, 1126 Sixteenth Street, NW, Suite 411, Washington, D.C., 20036.

12. U.S. Department of Commerce, Census Bureau, Current Population Reports, Consumer Income, Series P-60, No. 184, Table No. 30.

13. *Pay Equity in the Public Sector,* 1993 Addendum, National Committee on Pay Equity, 1126 Sixteenth Street, NW, Suite 411, Washington, D.C., 20036.

[1994 and 1997]

# 🌿 55

# *The Politics of Housework*

### PAT MAINARDI OF REDSTOCKINGS

*Though women do not complain of the power of husbands, each complains of her own husband, or of the husbands of her friends. It is the same in all other cases of servitude; at least in the commencement of the emancipatory movement. The serfs did not at first complain of the power of the lords, but only of their tyranny.*

—John Stuart Mill
*On the Subjection of Women*

Liberated women—very different from Women's Liberation! The first signals all kinds of goodies, to warm the hearts (not to mention other parts) of the most radical men. The other signals—HOUSEWORK. The first brings sex without marriage, sex before marriage, cozy housekeeping arrangements ("I'm living with this chick") and the self-content of knowing that you're not the kind of man who wants a doormat instead of a woman. That will come later. After all, who wants that old commodity anymore, the Standard American Housewife, all husband, home and kids? The New Commodity, the Liberated Woman, has sex a lot and has a Career, preferably something that can be fitted in

with the household chores—like dancing, pottery, or painting.

On the other hand is Women's Liberation—and housework. What? You say this is all trivial? Wonderful! That's what I thought. It seemed perfectly reasonable. We both had careers, both had to work a couple of days a week to earn enough to live on, so why shouldn't we share the housework? So I suggested it to my mate and he agreed—most men are too hip to turn you down flat. You're right, he said. It's only fair.

Then an interesting thing happened. I can only explain it by stating that we women have been brainwashed more than even we can imagine. Probably too many years of seeing television women in ecstasy over their shiny waxed floors or breaking down over their dirty shirt collars. Men have no such conditioning. They recognize the essential fact of housework right from the very beginning. Which is that it stinks.

Here's my list of dirty chores: buying groceries, carting them home and putting them away; cooking meals and washing dishes and pots; doing the laundry, digging out the place when things get out of control; washing floors. The list could go on but the sheer necessities are bad enough. All of us have to do these things, or get someone else to do them for us. The longer my husband contemplated these chores, the more repulsed he became, and so proceeded the change from the normally sweet, considerate Dr. Jekyll into the crafty Mr. Hyde who would stop at nothing to avoid the horrors of—housework. As he felt himself backed into a corner laden with dirty dishes, brooms, mops and reeking garbage, his front teeth grew longer and pointier, his fingernails haggled and his eyes grew wild. Housework trivial? Not on your life! Just try to share the burden.

So ensued a dialogue that's been going on for several years. Here are some of the high points:

• "I don't mind sharing the housework, but I don't do it very well. We should each do the things we're best at." MEANING: Unfortunately I'm no good at things like washing dishes or cooking. What I do best is a little light carpentry, changing light bulbs, moving furniture (how often do *you* move furniture?). ALSO MEANING: Historically the lower classes (black men and us) have had hundreds of years experience doing menial jobs. It would be a waste of manpower to train someone else to do them now. ALSO MEANING: I don't like the dull, stupid, boring jobs, so you should do them.

• "I don't mind sharing the work, but you'll have to show me how to do it." MEANING: I ask a lot of questions and you'll have to show me everything every time I do it because I don't remember so good. Also don't try to sit down and read while I'M doing my jobs because I'm going to annoy hell out of you until it's easier to do them yourself.

• "We used to be so happy!" (Said whenever it was his turn to do something.) MEANING: I used to be so happy. MEANING: Life without housework is bliss. No quarrel here. Perfect Agreement.

• "We have different standards, and why should I have to work to your standards? That's unfair." MEANING: If I begin to get bugged by the dirt and crap I will say, "This place sure is a sty" or "How can anyone live like this?" and wait for your reaction. I know that all women have a sore called "Guilt over a messy house" or "Household work is ultimately my responsibility." I know that men have caused that sore—if anyone visits and the place *is* a sty, they're not going to leave and say, "He sure is a lousy housekeeper." You'll take the rap in any case. I can outwait you. ALSO MEANING: I can provoke innumerable scenes over the housework issue. Eventually doing all the housework yourself will be less painful to you than trying to get me to do half. Or I'll suggest we get a maid. She will do my share of the work. You will do yours. It's women's work.

• "I've got nothing against sharing the housework, but you can't make me do it on your schedule." MEANING: Passive resistance. I'll do it when I damned well please, if at all. If my job is doing dishes, it's easier to do them once a week. If taking out laundry, once a month. If washing the floors, once a year. If you don't like it, do it yourself oftener, and then I won't do it at all.

• "I hate it more than you. You don't mind it so much." MEANING: Housework is garbage work. It's the worst crap I've ever done. It's degrading and humiliating for someone of *my* intelligence to do it. But for someone of *your* intelligence. . . .

• "Housework is too trivial to even talk about."

MEANING: It's even more trivial to do. Housework is beneath my status. My purpose in life is to deal with matters of significance. Yours is to deal with matters of insignificance. You should do the housework.

• "This problem of housework is not a man-woman problem. In any relationship between two people one is going to have a stronger personality and dominate." MEANING: That stronger personality had better be *me*.

• "In animal societies, wolves, for example, the top animal is usually a male even where he is not chosen for brute strength but on the basis of cunning and intelligence. Isn't that interesting? MEANING: I have historical, psychological, anthropological and biological justification for keeping you down. How can you ask the top wolf to be equal?

• "Women's liberation isn't really a political movement." MEANING: The revolution is coming too close to home. ALSO MEANING: I am only interested in how I am oppressed, not how I oppress others. Therefore the war, the draft and the university are political. Women's liberation is not.

• "Man's accomplishments have always depended on getting help from other people, mostly women. What great man would have accomplished what he did if he had to do his own housework?" MEANING: Oppression is built into the system and I, as the white American male, receive the benefits of this system. I don't want to give them up.

Participatory democracy begins at home. If you are planning to implement your politics, there are certain things to remember.

1. He *is* feeling it more than you. He's losing some leisure and you're gaining it. The measure of your oppression is his resistance.

2. A great many American men are not accustomed to doing monotonous, repetitive work which never issues in any lasting, let alone important, achievement. This is why they would rather repair a cabinet than wash dishes. If human endeavors are like a pyramid with man's highest achievements at the top, then keeping oneself alive is at the bottom. Men have always had servants (us) to take care of this bottom stratum of life while they have confined their efforts to the rarefied upper regions. It is thus

ironic when they ask of women—Where are your great painters, statesmen, etc.? Mme. Matisse ran a military shop so he could paint. Mrs. Martin Luther King kept his house and raised his babies.

3. It is a traumatizing experience for someone who has always thought of himself as being against any oppression or exploitation of one human being by another to realize that in his daily life he has been accepting and implementing (and benefiting from) this exploitation; that his rationalization is little different from that of the racist who says, "Black people don't feel pain" (women don't mind doing the shitwork); and that the oldest form of oppression in history has been the oppression of 50 percent of the population by the other 50 percent.

4. Arm yourself with some knowledge of the psychology of oppressed peoples everywhere, and a few facts about the animal kingdom. I admit playing top wolf or who runs the gorillas is silly but as a last resort men bring it up all the time. Talk about bees. If you feel really hostile bring up the sex life of spiders. They have sex. She bites off his head.

The psychology of oppressed peoples is not silly. Jews, immigrants, black men and all women have employed the same psychological mechanisms to survive: admiring the oppressor, glorifying the oppressor, wanting to be like the oppressor, wanting the oppressor to like them, mostly because the oppressor held all the power.

5. In a sense, all men everywhere are slightly schizoid—divorced from the reality of maintaining life. This makes it easier for them to play games with it. It is almost a cliché that women feel greater grief at sending a son off to a war or losing him to that war because they bore him, suckled him, and raised him. The men who foment those wars did none of those things and have a more superficial estimate of the worth of human life. One hour a day is a low estimate of the amount of time one has to spend "keeping" oneself. By foisting this off on others, man has seven hours a week—one working day more to play with his mind and not his human needs. Over the course of generations it is easy to see whence evolved the horrifying abstractions of modern life.

6. With the death of each form of oppression, life changes and new forms evolve. English aristo-

crats at the turn of the century were horrified at the idea of enfranchising working men—were sure that it signaled the death of civilization and a return to barbarism. Some working men were even deceived by this line. Similarly with the minimum wage, abolition of slavery, and female suffrage. Life changes but it goes on. Don't fall for any line about the death of everything if men take a turn at the dishes. They will imply that you are holding back the revolution (their revolution). But you are advancing it (your revolution).

7. Keep checking up. Periodically consider who's actually *doing* the jobs. These things have a way of backsliding so that a year later once again the woman is doing everything. After a year make a list of jobs the man has rarely if ever done. You will find cleaning pots, toilets, refrigerators and ovens high on the list. Use time sheets if necessary. He will accuse you of being petty. He is above that sort of thing (housework). Bear in mind what the worst jobs are, namely the ones that have to be done every day or several times a day. Also the ones that are dirty—it's more pleasant to pick up books, newspapers, etc., than to wash dishes. Alternate the bad jobs. It's the daily grind that gets you down. Also make sure that you don't have the responsibility for the housework with occasional help from him. "I'll cook dinner for you tonight" implies it's really your job and isn't he a nice guy to do some of it for you.

8. Most men had a rich and rewarding bachelor life during which they did not starve or become encrusted with crud or buried under the litter. There is a taboo that says women mustn't strain themselves in the presence of men—we haul around 50 pounds of groceries if we have to but aren't allowed to open a jar if there is someone around to do it for us. The reverse side of the coin is that men aren't supposed to be able to take care of themselves without a woman. Both are excuses for making women do the housework.

9. Beware of the double whammy. He won't do the little things he always did because you're now a "Liberated Woman," right? Of course he won't do anything else either. . . .

I was just finishing this when my husband came in and asked what I was doing. Writing a paper on housework. Housework? he said. *Housework? Oh my god how trivial can you get? A paper on housework.*                            [1970]

## 🌿 56

## *The Job/Family Challenge Today*

ELLEN BRAVO

*"You mean I have to quit my job to spend time with my newborn?" Andrea asks. "Don't be silly," her boss responds. "You can quit. You can be fired. You can go broke hiring baby-sitters. Or you can collapse from exhaustion trying to do it all." Later, Andrea confides in a friend: "We have options our mothers never dreamed of."*
—Conversation from a "Cathy" cartoon by
Cathy Guisewite

The job/family challenge—if you have a job and children or have to care for an elderly relative or a partner who's ill, you know what the challenge is. It's the daily struggle to balance the often competing demands of your work and home lives, without putting either one at risk. Most of us can identify with the exhaustion of "trying to do it all." While the *work-force* has changed drastically—more than our mothers imagined—the *workplace* has not.

The most dramatic change in the workforce in recent years has been the growing number of women, including mothers of young children, employed outside the home. This transformation has affected not only the workforce but the American family as well. Yet if you're responsible for both a family and a job, you know that most workplaces have changed very little to accommodate the realities of their workers' lives.

These statistics show the extent of the changes:

• For the first time in history, most families don't have a wife/mother at home full time. From 1950 to 1991, the number of married women with paying jobs more than tripled. Wives now account for nearly three-fifths of all employed women, up

from one-quarter in 1950. The dual-earner couple is now the norm among families with children.

• Not only are most wives working, so are the majority of married mothers. Theirs has been the largest increase of any group of women. And more moms are taking paid jobs *before* their children start school. In 1950, only 12 percent of women with children under the age of six were in the paid labor force. In 1990, that figure had skyrocketed to 57 percent—due in part to the increasing need of families for the wives' income[1] and to the growing number of families dependent on women's income alone.[2]

• Perhaps the most striking change has been the number of mothers of *infants* who work outside the home. In 1970, the number was so small that the Bureau of Labor Statistics didn't even track it; today, more than half of mothers of children under the age of one year are in the workforce.

Many businesses say they've responded to the changing workforce with "family policies" but mean only that they provide leave for new mothers. Yet workers' needs extend far beyond time off for birth. Almost half of the U.S. labor force has responsibilities for young children or elderly relatives. A surprising number of these caregivers are men. While women spend much more time than men giving direct care to elderly relatives, males make up 44 percent of those with elder-care responsibilities.[3] As the Families and Work Institute points out, "benefits, policies, and programs designed to help workers balance their work, personal, and family lives shouldn't be viewed as special assistance for a small group of workers, but as general assistance for virtually all workers."[4]

The daily struggles of working families mainly involve family leave, dependent care, and flexible work schedules. Take a look at how these affect your own job/family challenge and how the failure to address these issues is hurting business as well as families.

### *FAMILY LEAVE*

Until 1993, the United States had no nationwide family leave policy. Leave was left up to states or, more often, individual companies. While all the Fortune 100 companies had maternity leave, most of these companies gave leave only to women during the time they were physically disabled by childbirth rather than offering both men and women time to care for a newborn. Only 28 percent gave postdisability or parenting leave to mothers; 22 percent to fathers; and 23 percent to adoptive parents.[5] And these large companies, employing only 5 percent of the nation's workers, were providing the most generous benefits. Small and middle-sized businesses tended to offer even less family leave.[6]

At that time, the only relevant law was the 1978 Pregnancy Discrimination Act, which said simply that companies couldn't treat pregnant women *differently* than other workers. Stories like these weren't uncommon:

> Brenda worked in the office of a downtown hotel. When she returned from her six-week maternity leave, she was told her job had been filled by someone else. Another position was waiting for her— but that one paid a dollar an hour less and was evening shift. Brenda had no car; the bus to her neighborhood stopped running before the evening shift ended. Brenda was forced to quit her job and go on welfare until she could find a job comparable to her old one.

> Denise was a plainclothes police officer in child abuse and neglect cases, a position she had worked hard to win. When her third child was born, Denise was entitled to take several months of unpaid leave in addition to her disability leave and vacation. She took only thirty unpaid days. When she returned to her job, however, Denise found that she would no longer be working in her specialty area; there was no requirement that she be returned to the same or equivalent job. She appealed the reassignment and was labeled a "troublemaker." Soon afterwards, Denise left the force. She went from earning $13 an hour to minimum wage.

### The Family and Medical Leave Act

With passage of the Family and Medical Leave Act (FMLA), the federal government for the first time established the principle that having a family shouldn't cost you your job. The FMLA, which went into effect in August 1993, guarantees workers a twelve-week unpaid leave—with no risk to their job—to take care of a newborn or newly adopted child or a sick family member or to deal with a personal illness. The law was a victory for working families, but it has serious shortcomings.

Even with the FMLA, you may run into problems taking a family leave. Because the Act covers only firms with 50 or more employees and only those who work at least 25 hours a week and have been on their job for at least a year, it leaves out 95 percent of all businesses and more than half of all workers. And some employers who are covered violate this law or the 1978 Pregnancy Discrimination Act. Enforcement agencies have been greatly weakened over the years, so little monitoring is done to see if businesses are complying. In 1993, pregnancy discrimination claims reached a six-year high, up 17 percent over the previous two years.[7] Donna's story is far from unusual:

> Donna Bovell worked at American Laboratories Associates in Fort Lauderdale, Florida. With good performance appraisals and two raises behind her, Donna's future with the company looked bright— until she told them she was pregnant. "Are you getting an abortion?" was her supervisor's response. A concerned co-worker warned Donna that her job was in danger as a result of the pregnancy. Since she'd done nothing wrong, Donna felt she couldn't lose her job. Then she discovered her personnel file was full of written complaints she'd never seen before. Donna was fired in May 1992, six months before her daughter was born. She still hasn't found another job. "We're a few feet from under," said Donna.[8]

Critics of the FMLA may say women have to be more accommodating in scheduling maternity leave. But some women find themselves out the door even when they go way beyond the call of duty:

> A sales rep had a phone installed in the maternity ward. She took literally no leave other than the time for delivery, and a few weeks later, she closed "the biggest deal of her career." Nevertheless, her boss claimed her performance had suffered and let her go.[9]

The number of pregnancy-related discrimination claims doesn't even tell the whole story. Many employees don't know their rights or lack funds to pursue a claim. Loretta was one of these:

Like Donna, Loretta felt her firing was a result of pregnancy discrimination. Unlike many women, she knew her rights. She went to the Equal Employment Opportunity Commission and to an attorney. But funds were a problem. "You don't have money. You have doctor bills." Loretta dropped her charge.[10]

If you are covered by the FMLA, you may still find the amount of time for leave too limited:

Linda had to go on maternity leave six weeks early because of a complication with her pregnancy. The time was applied to her FMLA leave, so she had only six weeks off after the delivery. "The law should give twelve weeks off [for birth]," said Linda, "regardless of how much time you may have taken off for other reasons. The pregnancy and postpartum should have separate leaves."

Even if you're allowed to take as much time as you need, most people can't afford to. One of the few things opponents and supporters of the FMLA agreed on was that many workers wouldn't be able to take leave if that time were unpaid. A special report issued by the Bureau of National Affairs in 1987 stated that passage of the FMLA would have "very limited practical effect: . . . About 77 percent of women work in lower paying, nonprofessional jobs, and likely would not be able to take [10 to 18] weeks without pay."[11] Many parents who long to stay home with a new or sick child are wrenched back to work by the necessity to pay the bills and to put food on the table.

The Families and Work Institutes' 1991 study of four states with parental leave laws (Minnesota, Wisconsin, Oregon, and Rhode Island) showed women from low-income households take less time off after childbirth than women from middle- and upper-income households; poor women often take less than the medically advised minimum of six weeks.[12] According to Sheila Kammerman and Alfred Kahn, fewer than 40 percent of working women have enough income to allow them to take a six-week leave without severe financial penalty.[13] This can cause serious problems, as in Leila's case:

Leila's boss allowed her to take off as long as she needed when her second baby was born. But be-

cause the leave was unpaid, Leila couldn't afford to stay home. She returned to work after one month. Six weeks later, Leila ruptured a disc in her back. Not only did she miss a considerable amount of time, she sustained an injury that will plague her for the rest of her life.

Some people refuse to make the tradeoff and find themselves out of a job at a time of greater demand on family finances. The costs of unemployment are high, both for workers and taxpayers. One study put the price tag at $607 million annually in lost earnings, plus an additional $108 million to taxpayers from increased public assistance.[14] Kerryn saw no other choice:

When Patricia was diagnosed with terminal ovarian cancer, her daughter Kerryn promised Patricia she wouldn't have to go through the ordeal alone. Even if her employer had agreed to let her take a leave, Kerryn couldn't afford to be without income. So she wound up on welfare. Two years after her mother's death, Kerryn is still trying to find a permanent, full-time job with benefits.

What makes this situation even more serious is the importance of women's income to families. According to 1993 Census Bureau data, approximately 25 percent of American families live on $20,000 or less; they can't afford to have a parent out of work. Far from working for "pin money," women contribute one-third to one-half of the total income in dual-earner households and are the sole source of support in most female-headed households and in some families with two adults. Since median income for African-American and Latino families is significantly lower than that for whites, these families are even more dependent on women's income—and more at risk when that income is cut off.

Finally, those women who are entitled to leave and can afford to take it still have to contend with a corporate culture that sees them as deficient for missing any work. One MBA banker, whose image among colleagues changed drastically after a three-month maternity leave, gave this description of the attitude toward women like herself: "That's not what people expect from a dedicated, high-performing employee. They want your soul."[15]

## Men and Leave

Most fathers do take some time off when their children are born—but not all, and not for long. Even in the four states with parental leave laws studied by the Families and Work Institute, not many more dads took leave to be with a new child. On average, the men missed one work week, and most used vacation rather than leave time to avoid loss of income. But pay wasn't the only thing holding them back. The Families and Work Institute reported that men are also affected by "persistent expectations in the workplace and in the larger society that men should—or at least will—give higher priority to their jobs than to parenting."[16] Lew's story is typical:

> Lew, who worked in the highly competitive field of broadcasting, opted to take his two-week vacation when his son was born. After one week, he got a call from his boss. "What are you doing, breast-feeding that baby yourself?" Lew was asked. "We could really use you here." Lew went back to the job—much to the chagrin of his wife.

In short, while the FMLA is a step in the right direction, the challenge of family leave is just as great if your company is too small to qualify, if you can't afford extended unpaid leave, if you're a man facing the still-prevalent notion that men don't have family responsibilities or if you're a woman shouldering a disproportionate share of the work.

## CHILD CARE

Time off isn't the only form of help working families need, of course. Time and money for good, dependable child and elder care remain a big hurdle for many.

Most people are familiar with the image that sociologist Arlie Hochschild, author of *The Second Shift*, calls "the woman with the flying hair":[17] She strides confidently through a commercial, briefcase in one hand, baby in another. Her body leans forward; her hair flows out behind her (she's white). This woman is confident and happy. Her choices include generous leave, flextime, and an on-site child-care center.

"The woman with the flying hair" does exist. Unfortunately, however, she's the exception. Consider these statistics:

- Less than 1 percent of the nation's 6 million private firms offer on-site child-care facilities.[18]
- Only 10 percent of private firms with ten or more employees offer any child-care assistance; 55 percent of large companies offer assistance, but, rather than direct aid, it usually takes the form of allowing employees to earmark pretax dollars for child care—a program that saves the company money as well, since it pays fewer payroll taxes as a result.[19]
- Only 29 percent of American workers have flexible work schedules.[20]
- Twenty years ago, relatives cared for more than 60 percent of kids whose mothers were employed; by 1988, that figure was down to 40 percent, a trend that is expected to continue even as the need for child care goes up.[21]

Family support systems, once a mainstay for working parents, are less and less available. In the past, most people worked close to where they lived and had relatives nearby. Children were under the surveillance of a whole neighborhood. With a more mobile society and fewer neighbors at home, most working parents now face the challenge of job and family alone.

This reality presents a catch-22 for women on welfare. On the one hand, recipients are called lazy, dependent, and a bad example to their children for wanting to be with them full time. Yet the mother's moving into the workforce may literally jeopardize her children by forcing them into inadequate day care or by taking away medical insurance.

Parents' difficulties with child care are having a direct effect on business. According to the Families and Work Institute's *National Study on the Changing Workforce*, 26 percent of employed parents with children under age thirteen had experienced a breakdown in their usual child care arrangements in the preceding three months. The Child Care Action Campaign estimates that such breakdowns cost American businesses $3 billion a year. A study by the Los Angeles Department of Water and Power showed that the company paid $1 million in wages over a one-year period to people who were absent because of child care problems.

Lack of help with elder care also takes a toll. An

estimated 11 percent of all caregivers, most of them female, have lost a job because of difficulty balancing work responsibilities with caring for an elderly relative.

## FLEXIBLE SCHEDULES

One of the greatest sources of stress for working families is lack of flexibility. A study conducted by Bank Street College for Merck, a pharmaceutical company, found that nearly one-third of respondents—the largest group—said the single change in the workplace that would most improve their work and family lives was a change in work schedules.[22] Consider Shawn's dilemma:

> When her son woke up with an ear infection, Shawn called the office to say she had to take him to the doctor. She wasn't allowed to make up the time because she hadn't notified her supervisor in advance. "Sorry," said Shawn, "my children just aren't considerate enough to warn me when they're coming down with something."

More companies are adding flexible scheduling, but we lack a precise picture. Many employers hire part-timers and call that flexibility. But the employees may *prefer* full-time work; 22.8 percent of part-time jobs are involuntary.[23] A 1990 study of 521 large corporations found an increase in flexible work arrangements; yet only 50 percent of these businesses offered flextime, and only 22 percent allowed job-sharing.[24] The majority of workers are in medium and small firms where flexibility is rare. Even in large companies, many workers complain about an increase in inflexibility—the use of mandatory overtime by their employers.[25]

## THE STRAIN OF THE CHALLENGE

Families are feeling the strain. If you're facing the challenge, this news won't surprise you. One woman interviewed by Lifetime Cable TV in February 1994 described the feeling of "working undercover. . . . I had to hide the fact not that I had kids, but that they had an impact on my life. I was shocked at the lack of options." A male lawyer put it this way: "[The way things are,] you can be a good father or you can be a good lawyer. You can't be both."

When the Families and Work Institute surveyed working families to see how they were managing, this is what they found:

- 42 percent say they feel "used up" by the end of the day.
- 66 percent say they don't spend enough time with their kids.
- What workers give up most is time for self; they want more flexibility, more time for personal and family life.
- A sizable proportion of workers, including men, say they would be willing to make substantial trade-offs to get flexible time, leave programs, and dependent-care assistance.

You should be able to have a family *and* a job—and keep your sanity in the bargain. Yet balancing work and family responsibilities was the number one issue women said they would raise to President Clinton in the 1994 "Working Women Count!" survey sponsored by the Women's Bureau.[26] This respondent's comment to the president was typical: "There are no breaks—the attitude is: have children and support them. How you do it is *your* problem!"

## ARE COMPANIES ADDRESSING THE CHALLENGE?

Some argue that businesses are adopting family-friendly policies on their own, even if they're not obliged by law. Surveys do show that a high percentage of large businesses offered maternity leave even before the FMLA. But most of those firms also have policies providing short-term disability; since 1978, they have been required by law to treat pregnancy the same as any other short-term disability. Far from being generous to working mothers, these companies may simply have been complying with *another* law.

In 1990, Buck Consultants surveyed 253 U.S. corporations about parental leave. Only 27 percent had such programs in place. When the remainder were asked if they would offer parental leave without a mandate, 62 percent said they would not.[27]

### Little Help for Most Needy

Though companies have been expanding job/family benefits and some have made great strides, a big disparity exists in benefits and support at large and

# The Job/Family Challenge

Almost half the workforce has responsibilities for young or elderly relatives. Passage of the FMLA has helped, but leave is still difficult because:

- Most workers can't afford to take much unpaid leave.
- The corporate culture discourages most men from sharing family responsibilities.
- Smaller firms are not covered by the FMLA.

Parents' problems with child care are taking a toll on family life and on business.

Working families need flexible schedules—and most don't have them.

small companies and at different wage levels. Those earning lower wages have much less access to health insurance, pension, flexible schedules, leave programs, and dependent-care assistance.[28] In short, parents who need the most help with their responsibilities for children are the least likely to receive that help at work.

## Are Family-Friendly Policies Unfair?

Some critics think job/family programs unfairly benefit women with children over other workers. But the Families and Work Institute's study showed dependent care benefits are clearly as important to men as women—and good for business as well. Those with access to a range of family benefits were much more likely to commit to the success of the company, to work hard to achieve that success, and to be happier in the process.

These findings are not brand new.

- In 1980, a Gallup Poll for the White House Conference on Families showed 54 percent of those surveyed identified flexible hours, including job-sharing, as their first priority.
- A 1981 national study by General Mills, entitled "Families at Work: Strengths and Strains," reported "Part-time work with full benefits emerged as the benefit with the greatest breadth and depth of support."
- In 1983, *Better Homes and Gardens* did a readers' survey: 66 percent of 21,500 respondents wanted more flexible hours, 29 percent specifically mentioned job-sharing.

## ARE FAMILIES ADDRESSING THE CHALLENGE?

Studies show that more men in dual-income families say they're doing an equal share, but their wives disagree. In *The Second Shift*, Arlie Hochschild reported that only 18 percent of husbands share equally; 61 percent of men do little or nothing.[29] Over the last two decades, women worked on household chores an average of 15 hours a week more than men. That comes to an extra month each year. University of Akron sociologist Patricia Ulbrich came up with an even more dismal picture when she analyzed data from a national study of 1,246 couples. Whether or not they're employed, American women average 32.3 hours of housework a week (not including child care), compared to 8.7 hours for men.[30]

"When I asked one man what he did to share the work of the home, he answered, 'I make all the pies,'" said Hochschild. "Another man grilled fish. Another baked bread. In their pies, their fish, and their bread, such men converted a single act into a substitute for a multitude of chores in the second shift—a token. [One guy] took care of the dog."[31]

The extra load is taking its toll on women, who are exhausted and frustrated—and angry. Columnist Donna Britt quoted one working mother's description of her weekend: "I got groceries, did at least sixteen loads of laundry, cleaned the grout, swept up plaster dust, put a coat of primer on a wall, changed the sheets, cleaned the basement, and changed the litter box. My husband took a nap. I can't talk about this . . ." [32]

All of these issues—more parents working, problems with leave, the expense and difficulty of dependent care, lack of flexible schedules, and outdated notions that men should not be concerned with family and housework—add up to the job/family challenge. [1995]

## NOTES

1. Joint Economic Committee, "Families on a Treadmill: Work and Income in the 1980s" (Washington, DC: U.S. Congress, January 1992). In the last 15 years, wives' income have kept families above water. On average, wives worked 32 percent more hours in 1989 than in 1979. Without the increased hours and wages of wives, incomes for 60 percent of American families would have been lower in 1989 than in 1979.
2. According to the Bureau of Labor Statistics, families headed by women accounted for 18.1 percent of all families in 1993, compared to 13.6 percent in 1975.
3. Ellen Galinsky, James T. Bond, and Dana E. Friedman, *The Changing Workforce: Highlights of the National Study* (New York: Families and Work Institute, 1993), 44.
4. Ibid., 58. According to the study, women spend a total of 19.9 hours a week taking care of elderly relatives; men spend 11.8 hours. Among caregivers of the elderly, 23 percent have responsibility for two or more elders, most of whom live near the person with caregiving responsibility.
5. Ellen Galinsky and James T. Bond, "Parental Leave Benefits for American Families" (New York: Families and Work Institute, 1993), 3.
6. Eileen Trezinski, "Employers' Parental Leave Policies: Does the Labor Market Provide Parental Leave?" in Janet Shibley Hyde and Marilyn J. Essex, eds., *Parental Leave and Child Care: Setting a Research and Policy Agenda* (Philadelphia: Temple University Press, 1991), 215–16. Trezinski analyzed two surveys, one conducted in Minnesota and one in Connecticut, covering firms of all sizes. Overall, the survey found that fewer than 10 percent of Minnesota firms provided time off to new parents to care for newborn children, as opposed to disability leave. The Connecticut survey echoed these findings. Even among the largest firms, only 13.9 percent offer job-protected infant-care leave. This figure decreases with firm size: only 7.2 percent for companies of 50 to 99 employees, 3.6 percent for the smallest firms.
7. "Pregnancy Discrimination," *Lifetime Magazine,* Lifetime Cable TV, February 22, 1994.
8. Ibid.
9. Harriet Brown, "Beyond the Mommy Track," *Vogue,* September 1991, 506.
10. "Pregnancy Discrimination."
11. Bureau of National Affairs, *Pregnancy and Employment Handbook* (Washington, DC: BNA, 1987), 5.
12. James T. Bond, Ellen Galinsky, et al., *Beyond the Parental Leave Debate: The Impact of Laws in Four States* (New York: Families and Work Institute, 1991), vi. In Rhode Island, which has a statewide Temporary Disability Insurance program, none of the low-income mothers took fewer than six weeks leave. This compared with up to 19 percent of low-income mothers in the other three states studied who went back to work before six weeks.
13. Sheila Kammerman, "Parental Leave and Infant Care," in Hyde and Essex, *Parental Leave and Child Care,* 15–16. Private group insurance policies are more likely to include maternity leave, but fewer workers—and fewer women workers in particular—are included under those policies today than in 1980. Women are also concentrated in smaller firms, which are less likely to provide sick leave. And women make up two-thirds of part-time workers, who often have no benefits at all. Kammerman and Kahn concluded that there's been no meaningful increase in the percentage of women workers with paid maternity disability leaves since 1981. Vacation and personal leave policies also haven't increased during that time.
14. Roberta Spalter-Roth and Heidi Hartmann, *Unnecessary Losses: Costs to Americans of the Lack of Family and Medical Leave* (Washington, DC: Institute for Women's Policy Research, 1990), 25, 30.
15. Deborah J. Swiss and Judith P. Walker, *Women and the Work/Family Dilemma* (New York: John Wiley & Sons, Inc., 1993), 197. This book was based on an in-depth survey of 902 women who had graduated from Harvard professional schools over a 10-year period. The authors found that the vast majority of the women ran into a "maternal wall." The women felt virtually no recognition in the workplace for their role as parents.
16. Galinsky and Bond, "Parental Leave Benefits for American Families," 5.
17. Ford Foundation Women's Program Forum, "Men and Women: At Home and in the Workplace" (New York: Ford Foundation, May 1991), 5.
18. 9to5 National Association of Working Women, "1994–95 Profile of Working Women" (Cleveland: 9to5 NAWW, 1994), 3.
19. Ibid.
20. Galinsky, Bond, and Friedman, *The Changing Workforce,* 79.
21. Jonathan R. Veum and Philip M. Gleason, "Child care: Arrangements and costs." *Monthly Labor Review,* October 1991, 10–11.
22. Ellen Galinsky et al., *Work and Family Life Study Pinpoints Sources of Stress for Corporate Workers,* 5 Family Resource Coalition Rep. 7, No. 2 (1986).
23. Economic Policy Institute, Washington, DC.
24. The Conference Board, *Flexible Staffing and Scheduling in U.S. Corporations* (New York: The Conference Board, 1990), 12. A 1994 study by Linda K. Stroh and Karen S. Kush (which they summarize in "Flextime: The Imaginary Innovation," *The New York Times,* November 27, 1994) asked how many companies have "formal, permanent flextime programs that are available to a significant portion of the work force." Only 14 percent of responding companies answered yes. Of the remainder, 92 percent said it was "unlikely" or "very unlikely" that they would ever adopt flextime.
25. Barbara Presley Noble, "The Work-Family Bottom Line," *The New York Times,* November 20, 1994, F25.

According to a survey by Massachusetts Mutual released in mid-November 1994, 41 percent of employees say their employers expect them to perform an unreasonable amount of overtime.

26.  Robert Reich, Secretary, U.S. Department of Labor, and Karen Nussbaum, Director, Women's Bureau, "Working Women Count! A Report to the Nation" (Washington, DC: U.S. Department of Labor, 1994), 3.
27.  Women's Legal Defense Fund, "Most Employers Do Not Currently Have Job-Guaranteed Family and Medical Leave" (Washington, DC: Women's Legal Defense Fund, 1991).
28.  Galinsky, Bond, and Friedman, *The Changing Workforce*, 90. Of those who earn less than $7 an hour, 32 percent have no health insurance, even for themselves; 36 percent in that wage group lack pensions.
29.  Arlie Hochschild with Anne Machung, *The Second Shift: Working Parents and the Revolution at Home* (New York: Viking Penguin, Inc., 1989), 1.
30.  Donna Britt, "So women can 'have it all'? Don't bet on it." *Milwaukee Journal*, September 26, 1994, A7.
31.  Hochschild, *The Second Shift*, 40.
32.  Britt, "So women can 'have it all'?"

## 🦎 57

# *Exploding the Stereotypes: Welfare*

RITA HENLEY JENSEN

I am a woman. A white woman, once poor but no longer. I am not lazy, never was. I am a middle-aged woman, with two grown daughters. I was a welfare mother, one of those women society considers less than nothing.

I should have applied for Aid to Families with Dependent Children when I was 18 years old, pregnant with my first child, and living with a boyfriend who slapped me around. But I didn't.

I remember talking it over at the time with a friend. I lived in the neighborhood that surrounds the vast Columbus campus of Ohio State University. Students, faculty, hangers-on, hippies, runaways, and recent émigrés from Kentucky lived side by side in the area's relatively inexpensive housing. I was a runaway.

On a particularly warm midsummer's day, I stood on High Street, directly across from the campus' main entrance, with an older, more sophisticated friend, wondering what to do with my life. With my swollen belly, all hope of my being able to cross the street and enroll in the university had evaporated. Now, I was seeking advice about how merely to survive, to escape the assaults and still be able to care for my child.

My friend knew of no place I could go, nowhere I could turn, no one else I could ask. I remember saying in a tone of resignation, "I can't apply for welfare." Instead of disagreeing with me, she nodded, acknowledging our mutual belief that taking beatings was better than taking handouts. Being "on the dole" meant you deserved only contempt.

In August 1965, I married my attacker.

Six years later, I left him and applied for assistance. My children were 18 months and five and a half years old. I had waited much too long. Within a year, I crossed High Street to go to Ohio State. I graduated in four years and moved to New York City to attend Columbia University's Graduate School of Journalism. I have worked as a journalist for 18 years now. My life on welfare was very hard—there were times when I didn't have enough food for the three of us. But I was able to get an education while on welfare. It is hardly likely that a woman on AFDC today would be allowed to do what I did, to go to school and develop the kind of skills that enabled me to make a better life for myself and my children.

This part summer, I attended a conference in Chicago on feminist legal theory. During the presentation of a paper related to gender and property rights, the speaker mentioned as an aside that when one says "welfare mother" the listener hears "black welfare mother." A discussion ensued about the underlying racism until someone declared that the solution was easy: all that had to be done was have the women in the room bring to the attention of the media the fact that white women make up the largest percentage of welfare recipients. At this point, I stood, took a deep breath, stepped out of my professional guise, and informed the crowd that I was a former welfare mother. Looking at my white hair, blue eyes, and freckled Irish skin, some laughed; others gasped—despite having just acknowledged that someone like me was, in fact, a "typical" welfare mother.

Occasionally I do this. Speak up. Identify myself as one of "them." I do so reluctantly because welfare mothers are a lightning rod for race hatred, class prejudice, and misogyny. Yet I am aware that as long as welfare is viewed as an *African American* woman's issue, instead of a *woman's* issue—whether that woman be white, African American, Asian, Latina, or Native American—those in power can continue to exploit our country's racism to weaken and even eliminate public support for the programs that help low-income mothers and their children.

I didn't have the guts to stand up during a 1974 reception for Ohio state legislators. The party's hostess was a leader of the Columbus chapter of the National Organization for Women and she had opened up her suburban home so that representatives of many of the state's progressive organizations could lobby in an informal setting for an increase in the state's welfare allotment for families. I was invited as a representative of the campus area's single mothers' support group. In the living room, I came across a state senator in a just-slightly-too-warm-and-friendly state induced by the potent combination of free booze and a crowd of women. He quickly decided I looked like a good person to amuse with one of his favorite jokes. "You want to know how a welfare mother can prevent getting pregnant?" he asked, giggling. "She can just take two aspirin—and put them between her knees," he roared, as he bent down to place his Scotch glass between his own, by way of demonstration. I drifted away.

I finally did gather up my courage to speak out. It was in a classroom during my junior year. I was enrolled in a course on the economics of public policy because I wanted to understand why the state of Ohio thought it desirable to provide me and my two kids with only $204 per month—59 percent of what even the state itself said a family of three needed to live.

For my required oral presentation, I chose "Aid to Families with Dependent Children." I cited the fact that approximately two thirds of all the poor families in the country were white; I noted that most welfare families consisted of one parent and two children. As an audiovisual aid, I brought my own two kids along. My voice quavered a bit as I delivered my intro: I stood with my arms around my children and said, "We are a typical AFDC family."

My classmates had not one question when I finished. I don't believe anyone even bothered to ask the kids' names or ages.

If I were giving this talk today, I would hold up a picture of us back then and say we still represent typical welfare recipients. The statistics I would cite to back up that statement have been refined since the 1970s and now include "Hispanic" as a category. In 1992, 38.9 percent of all welfare mothers were white, 37.2 percent were black, 17.8 percent were "Hispanic," 2.8 percent were Asian, and 1.4 percent were Native American.

My report, however, would focus on the dramatic and unrelenting reduction in resources available to low-income mothers in the last two decades.

Fact: In 1970, the average monthly benefit for a family of three was $178. Not much, but consider that as a result of inflation, that $178 would be approximately $680 today. And then consider that the average monthly payment today is only about $414. That's the way it's been for more than two decades: the cost of living goes up (by the states' own accounting, the cost of rent, food, and utilities for a family of three has doubled), but the real value of welfare payments keeps going down.

Fact: The 1968 Work Incentive Program (the government called it WIN; we called it WIP) required that all unemployed adult recipients sign up for job training or employment once their children turned six. The age has now been lowered to three, and states may go as low as age one. What that means is you won't be able to attend and finish college while on welfare. (In most states a college education isn't considered job training, even though experts claim most of us will need college degrees to compete in the workplace of the twenty-first century.)

Fact: Forty-two percent of welfare recipients will be on welfare less than two years during their entire lifetime, and an additional 33 percent will spend between two and eight years on welfare. The statistics haven't changed much over the years: women still use welfare to support their families when their children are small.

In 1974, I ended my talk with this joke: A welfare

mother went into the drugstore and bought a can of deodorant. I explained that it was funny because everyone knew that welfare mothers could not afford "extras" like personal hygiene products. My joke today would be: A welfare mother believed that if elected public officials understood these facts, they would not campaign to cut her family's benefits.

The idea that government representatives care about welfare mothers is as ridiculous to me now as the idea back then that I would waste my limited funds on deodorant. It is much clearer to me today what the basic functions of welfare public policy are at this moment in U.S. history.

By making war on welfare recipients, political leaders can turn the public's attention away from the government's redistribution of wealth to the wealthy. Recent studies show that the United States has become the most economically stratified of industrial nations. In fact, Federal Reserve figures reveal that the richest 1 percent of American households—each with a minimum net worth of $2.3 million—control nearly 40 percent of the wealth, while in Britain, the richest 1 percent of the population controls about 18 percent of the wealth. In the mid-1970s, both countries were on a par: the richest 1 percent controlled 20 percent of the wealth. President Reagan was the master of this verbal shell game. He told stories of welfare queens and then presided over the looting of the nation's savings and loans by wealthy white men.

Without a doubt, the current urgency for tax cuts and spending reductions can be explained by the fact that President Clinton tried to shift the balance slightly in 1992 and the wealthy ended up paying 16 percent more in taxes the following year, by one estimate.

The purpose of this antiwelfare oratory and the campaigns against sex education, abortion rights, and aid to teenage mothers is to ensure a constant supply of young women as desperate and ashamed as I was. Young women willing to take a job at any wage rate, willing to tolerate the most abusive relationships with men, and unable to enter the gates leading to higher education.

To accomplish their goals, political leaders continually call for reforms that include demands that welfare recipients work, that teenagers don't have sex, and that welfare mothers stop giving birth (but don't have abortions). Each "reform" addresses the nation's racial and sexual stereotypes: taking care of one's own children is not work; welfare mothers are unemployed, promiscuous, and poorly motivated; and unless the government holds their feet to the fire, these women will live on welfare for years, as will their children and their children's children.

This type of demagoguery has been common throughout our history. What sets the present era apart is the nearly across-the-board cooperation of the media. The national news magazines, the most prestigious daily newspapers, the highly regarded broadcast news outlets, as well as the supermarket tabloids and talk-radio hosts, have generally abandoned the notion that one of their missions is to sometimes comfort the afflicted and afflict the comfortable. Instead, they too often reprint politicians' statements unchallenged, provide charts comparing one party's recommendations to another's without really questioning those recommendations, and illustrate story after story, newscast after newscast, with a visual of an African American woman (because we all know they're the only ones on welfare) living in an urban housing project (because that's where all welfare recipients live) who has been on welfare for years.

When *U.S. News & World Report* did a major story on welfare reform this year, it featured large photographs of eight welfare recipients, seven of whom were women of color: six African Americans and one Latina or Native American (the text does not state her ethnicity). Describing the inability of welfare mothers to hold jobs (they are "hobbled not only by their lack of experience but also by their casual attitudes toward punctuality, dress, and co-workers"), the article offers the "excuse" given by one mother for not taking a 3 P.M. to 11 P.M. shift: "'I wouldn't get to see my kids,'" she told the reporter. You can't win for losing—should she take that 3-to-11 job and her unsupervised kids get in trouble, you can be sure some conservative would happily leap on her as an example of one of those poor women who are bad mothers and whose kids should be in orphanages.

Why don't the media ever find a white woman from Ohio or Iowa or Wisconsin, a victim of domestic violence, leaving the father of her two children to make a new start? Or a Latina mother like the one living in my current neighborhood, who has one child and does not make enough as a home health care attendant to pay for her family's health insurance? Or a Native American woman living on a reservation, creating crafts for pennies that will be sold by others for dollars?

Besides reinforcing stereotypes about the personal failings of welfare recipients, when my colleagues write in-depth pieces about life on welfare they invariably concentrate on describing welfare mothers' difficulties with the world at large: addictions, lack of transportation, dangerous neighbors, and, most recently, shiftless boyfriends who begin beating them when they do get jobs—as if this phenomenon were limited to relationships between couples with low incomes.

I wonder why no journalist I have stumbled across, no matter how well meaning, has communicated what I believe is the central reality of most women's lives on welfare: they believe all the stereotypes too and they are ashamed of being on welfare. They eat, breathe, sleep, and clothe themselves with shame.

Most reporting on welfare never penetrates the surface, and the nature of the relationship between the welfare system and the woman receiving help is never explored. Like me, many women fleeing physical abuse must make the welfare department their first stop after seeking an order of protection. Studies are scarce, but some recent ones of women in welfare-to-work programs across the U.S. estimate that anywhere from half to three fourths of participants are, or have been, in abusive relationships. And surveys of some homeless shelters indicate that half of the women living in them are on the run from a violent mate.

But if welfare is the means of escape, it is also the institutionalization of the dynamic of battering. My husband was the source of my and my children's daily bread and of daily physical and psychological attacks. On welfare, I was free of the beatings, but the assaults on my self-esteem were still frequent and powerful, mimicking the behavior of a typical batterer.

As he pounds away, threatening to kill the woman and children he claims to love, the abuser often accuses his victims of lying, laziness, and infidelity. Many times, he threatens to snatch the children away from their mother in order to protect them from her supposed incompetence, her laziness, dishonesty, and sexual escapades.

On welfare, just as with my husband, I had to prove every statement was not a lie. Everything had to be documented: how many children I had, how much I paid for rent, fuel, transportation, electricity, child care, and so forth. It went so far as to require that at every "redetermination of need" interview (every six months), I had to produce the originals of my children's birth certificates, which were duly photocopied over and over again. Since birth certificates do not change, the procedure was a subtle and constant reminder that nothing I said was accepted as truth. Ever.

But this is a petty example. The more significant one was the suspicion that my attendance at Ohio State University was probably a crime. Throughout my college years, I regularly reported that I was attending OSU. Since the WIN limit at that time was age six and my youngest daughter was two when I started, I was allowed to finish my undergraduate years without having to report to some job-training program that would have prepared me for a minimum-wage job. However, my caseworker and I shared an intuitive belief that something just had to be wrong about this. How could I be living on welfare and going to college? Outrageous! Each day I awoke feeling as if I were in a race, that I had to complete my degree before I was charged with a felony.

As a matter of fact, I remember hearing, a short time after I graduated, that a group of welfare mothers attending college in Ohio were charged with food stamp fraud, apparently for not reporting their scholarships as additional income.

Batterers frequently lie to their victims—it's a power thing. Caseworkers do too. For example, when I moved to New York to attend graduate school and applied for assistance, I asked my intake worker whether I could apply for emergency food stamps. She told me there was no emergency food program. The kids and I scraped by, but that statement was false. I was unaware of it until welfare rights advocates successfully sued the agency for

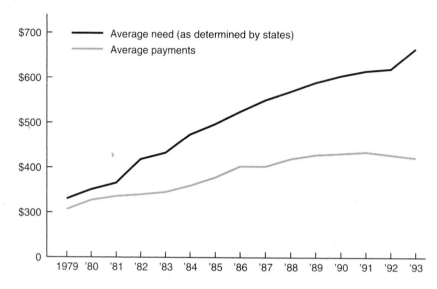

*Figure 2    Monthly AFDC Payments vs. Cost of Living for a Family of Three*

Source: U.S. Department of Health and Human Services

denying applicants emergency food assistance. In another case, when someone gave me a ten-year-old Opel so I could keep my first (very low paying) reporting job, my caseworker informed me in writing that mere possession of a car made me ineligible for welfare. (I appealed and won. The caseworker was apparently confused by the fact that although I was not allowed to have any assets, I did need the car to get to work. She also assumed a used car had to have some value. Not this one.)

Then there's the issue of sexual possessiveness: states rarely grant assistance to families with fathers still in the home. And as for feeling threatened about losing custody, throughout the time I was on welfare, I knew that if I stumbled at all, my children could be taken away from me. It is widely understood that any neighbor can call the authorities about a welfare mother, making a charge of neglect, and that mother, since she is less than nothing, might not be able to prove her competency. I had a close call once. I had been hospitalized for ten days and a friend took care of my children. After my return home, however, I was still weak. I would doze off on the sofa while the kids were awake—one time it happened when they were outside playing on

the sidewalk. A neighbor, seeing them there unattended, immediately called the child welfare agency, which sent someone out to question me and to look inside my refrigerator to see if I had any food. Luckily, that day I did.

Ultimately, leaving an abusive relationship and applying for welfare is a little like leaving solitary confinement to become part of a prison's general population. It's better, but you are still incarcerated.

None of this is ever discussed in the context of welfare reform. The idiot state legislator, the prosecutor in Ohio who brought the charges against welfare mothers years ago, Bill Clinton, and Newt Gingrich all continue to play the race and sex card by hollering for welfare reform. They continue to exploit and feed the public's ignorance about and antipathy toward welfare mothers to propel their own careers. Sadly, journalists permit them to do so, perhaps for the same reason.

Lost in all this are the lives of thousands of women impoverished by virtue of their willingness to assume the responsibility of raising their children. An ex-boyfriend used to say that observing my struggle was a little like watching someone standing in a room, with arms upraised to prevent the ceiling from pressing in on her. He wondered just how long I could prevent the collapse.

Today, welfare mothers have even less opportunity than I did. Their talent, brains, luck, and resourcefulness are ignored. Each new rule, regulation, and reform makes it even more unlikely that they can use the time they are on welfare to do as I did: cross the High Streets in their cities and towns, and realize their ambitions. Each new rule makes it more likely that they will only be able to train for a minimum-wage job that will never allow them to support their families.

So no, I don't think all we have to do is get the facts to the media. I think we have to raise hell any way we can.

Our goal is simple: never again should there be a young women, standing in front of the gates that lead to a better future, afraid to enter because she believes she must instead choose poverty and battery.                                              [1995]

 58

# *Farewell to Welfare but Not to Poverty*

RANDY ALBELDA AND CHRIS TILLY,
EDITED BY AMY KESSELMAN

Welfare as we knew it is gone.

What is in its place? A federal mandate to states to force poor mothers into the low-wage labor market any way they see fit. What is not in place, however, is sufficient funding, guarantees or even incentives to create the jobs or work supports that might make this poverty-fighting strategy possible. There are no federal requirements to increase the supply or funding of child care, little is being done to create jobs for women that pay living wages, there are no plans to expand health care to low wage workers, and there is no talk of boosting the educational and training opportunities for single mothers.

Welfare as we knew it—AFDC (Aid to Families with Dependent Children)—was no one's dream program, but it did guarantee cash assistance to very poor families, mainly single women and their children. Welfare as we have it—TANF (Temporary Assistance to Needy Families)—does more than remove the guarantee that needy families will receive assistance. It provides incentives for the states to spend less than they did under AFDC, includes a 60-month lifetime limit for assistance, and requires states to put a substantial percentage of all adult recipients into paid or unpaid jobs almost immediately.

Besides further eroding the safety net and fracturing an already ill-funded program, TANF provisions make it more difficult for states to help low-income mothers support their families through their own earnings. TANF's financial incentives are to place recipients directly into jobs—any jobs—making states less likely to provide education or meaningful job training. And while the new legislation will reduce welfare rolls, unless there are creative state initiatives and some federal changes to the law, poverty as we know it will increase.

## *EVERY MOTHER A WORKING MOTHER*

Jobs have always been promoted as this country's best solution to poverty, but this has never worked well for women, since women's wages alone are too low to support families. Yet work has never before been so explicitly forced on mothers, especially those with young children. The 1988 Family Support Act required states to turn AFDC into a jobs and training program for single parents. But more than half of them fulfilled the requirement by going to school. The 1980s emphasis on making recipients work-ready has turned into a 1990s mandate that mothers work. What happened?

Close to 70% of mothers are in the paid labor force. Public sentiment appears to say that if other mothers must work, why not single mothers? This rationale has been used to push poor women into an unrelenting labor market, but it won't work—and not just for poor single mothers. Our economy depends on women for free care of children and for doing low-wage jobs, yet there is an increasing expectation that every adult earn wages sufficient to support a family. For mothers, this is virtually impossible—you can't both provide free care and work enough hours to earn a family wage.

While many families fare poorly under society's new work expectations for women, single-mother families fare the worst for three simple reasons. First, like all women, single-mothers earn less, on average, than men do when they work. Second, raising children is time-consuming work, and children increase the cost of family life (they need food, clothing, shelter and care). Finally, in single-mother families, there is only one adult to both earn income and take care of children.

The difficulties single mothers face are borne out in the poverty statistics. In 1994, half of single-mother families were poor, compared to one out of every 20 married couples with no children. While only 8% of all people in the United States live in single mother families, they make up 28% of all poor persons.

## ENDING WELFARE

In August 1996, President Clinton signed the Personal Responsibility and Work Opportunity Act. Along with 22% cuts to Food Stamps and Supplemental Security Income (SSI) over the next six years, the bill eliminates AFDC. In its place is the Temporary Assistance for Needy Families (TANF) block grant.

The Republican Congress takes credit for this bill, but it is a scaled-down version of previous efforts to reform welfare. They also hoped to eliminate the Medicaid entitlement and severely reduce Food Stamps for all, but were repeatedly stymied because the political stakes were too high. State medical establishments receive too much Medicaid money to let it be discarded. Agribusiness made it clear they didn't intend to lose their best customer—the federal government—by cutting Food Stamps.

AFDC, on the other hand, didn't have strong enough "interest groups" protecting it. Two-thirds of the 13 million people receiving AFDC in 1966 were children. The Catholic church and women's groups—the two most active groups lobbying against passage of this bill—clearly did not hold much sway among these Republican legislators. Once the Republicans were able to isolate AFDC from Medicaid and drastic Food Stamps cuts, the President (running as an un-Democrat for reelec-

tion), couldn't resist signing a bill that assured him of much coveted suburban votes.

## THE TERMS OF TANF

There are four main components to TANF:

- ending the guarantee of cash assistance to poor families.
- establishing a new fiscal relationship, under which the federal government will provide fixed block grants to states, while no longer providing them with a financial incentive to spend additional money on low-income families.
- establishing a lifetime time limit of 60 months (not necessarily consecutive) on receiving assistance from federal TANF funds.
- penalizing states which do not force a substantial percentage of their adult recipients into narrowly defined work programs.

While the first change has received the most attention, all four drastically change the nature of poverty programs. Relying on the rhetoric that states know best and dependency bad, the Republican Congress eliminated the federal promise of cash assistance to needy families. The hard-earned struggles of the welfare rights movements of the 1960's and 1970's to assure that those eligible to receive AFDC (particularly African Americans) know their rights and receive their assistance were erased with a stroke of the pen.

With federal eligibility requirements eliminated, states may now define "needy" any way they want. They don't even have to use the same definition of needy across their state: needy in the city can be defined differently than needy in the suburbs.

States no longer have to provide cash assistance if they don't want to and can completely privatize their welfare system. The lack of uniform eligibility provisions opens the door to the systematic disentitlement of groups of people that was prevalent before the welfare rights movement. Anyone convicted of a drug-related felony cannot receive TANF funds, and immigrants who come to the United States are denied benefits until they have been here for five years (unless a state changes its own law).

## FIXED FEDERAL FUNDING

TANF also profoundly alters the fiscal relationship between states and the feds. The new law requires the Federal government to provide each state with the highest of their 1995, 1994 or average of 1992–1994 federal allocation of AFDC during every year from 1997–2002. There are no automatic adjustments for inflation or for need. This represents a dramatic change from AFDC, which was a matching grant: for every dollar a state spent on the program, it received a dollar (or more than a dollar for poor states). Although many states did not take full advantage of the match, this funding mechanism intentionally provided a strong incentive to increase spending.

Under the new block grant structure, states can spend as much as they please, but will not receive an extra penny from the feds. And once the money is gone, there is no more. With a recession and an increase in poor families, states will not necessarily have more resources to help out than they did in the past. There are several pools of money that states may tap into in case of deep recession, or if they reduce their TANF rolls, or if they reduce the number of out-of-wedlock births. But these are small bundles of cash and are set at fixed amounts to be split by all qualifying states.

Further, TANF actually permits states to spend less money. As long as states meet federal work participation requirements, they can cut up to a quarter of their 1994 spending levels without penalty (although to qualify for additional assistance in a recession, states must maintain full funding). One aspect of the bill that helped assure its passage was that most states will actually see a windfall for the first year or so of TANF, provided there is no recession. Because national AFDC rolls have fallen since 1994, federal and state spending levels were higher than in 1996. But, as inflation erodes the grant and as the business cycle turns, states will find themselves with less money from the feds and permission to spend less of their own money.

A particularly cruel aspect of the new law is the time limit. States are not allowed to allocate TANF money to any adult who has received TANF money for 60 months—regardless of how much assistance was received in any month or how long it took to accrue 60 months of aid. When AFDC was in place, the average amount of time any recipient receives aid over her lifetime was seven years. Sixty months is an arbitrary number and it will not serve the needs of many poor families. If fully enforced, this provision will throw many families into the street.

The time limit also works against the most positive reform already implemented by many states: allowing employed AFDC recipients to keep more of their cash assistance, even though it may be a small amount. Given the difficulties that single mothers face juggling jobs and kids, and given their relatively low average wages, most will need some form of support until their children are old enough to take care of themselves. That usually is more than 60 months.

The 60-month time limit pushes states concerned about families hitting the limit to avoid giving aid in small monthly amounts, even though this is precisely what some families need in order to make holding a job possible. While states can use their own funds to extend the limit or boost other programs that supplement work, the current political climate makes that unlikely. The only good thing about the time limit provision is that the federal government did not set up or fund a national registry for TANF recipients, so implementing time limits will be difficult.

## WORK, WORK, WORK

The final major piece of TANF is the federal requirement that states put recipients to work. The new law requires recipients whose youngest child is more than one year old to do some form of paid or unpaid work after 24 months of receiving benefits. Most schooling and job training will not count as "work." Further, unless states specifically opt out, adult recipients with children older than one must perform community service (meaning workfare) after only two months of obtaining benefits.

Although previous federal provisions also had work requirements, the 1988 law exempted women with a disabled child or whose youngest child was less than three, and most education qualified as being part of a work program. Plus, it provided day care and transportation costs for mothers, neither of which is required under the new law.

In addition to the work requirements, states must meet work participation rates or risk losing some of their federal grant. Every year a certain percentage of all adult recipients (whose youngest child is older than one) must be in a work program for a certain number of hours a week. In 1997, 20% of single mother families had to be at "work" for at least 20 hours a week, gradually increasing to 50% working for at least 30 hours during the year 2002.

The work requirements are structured in such a way to discourage states from providing education and training that would allow at least some women to move into decent paying jobs. States can provide education and training if they want, but most of the programs cannot count toward the work participation requirement. For states to hit their "quotas" they will want to place women into the labor market immediately.

The bottom line? The new law is designed to encourage states to reduce funding and welfare rolls by pushing women into an unrelenting low-wage labor market without the vital supports that make employment possible.

## WHY MANY SINGLE MOTHERS CAN'T WORK THEIR WAY OUT OF POVERTY

The clear message of TANF is "work your way out of poverty." And states are saddled with the responsibility of making mothers work. But they will find that for women, especially those with low educational attainment and little job experience, this is not possible without the supports necessary for mothers to work.

It's not for want of trying that single mothers have not been able to make ends meet. They work for pay about as many hours per year, on average, as other mothers about 1,000 hours a year (a year-round, full-time job logs 2,000 hours). But less than full-time work for most women in this country just doesn't pay enough to feed mouths, make rent payments, and provide care for children while at work.

Not all single mothers are poor—but half of them are (compared to a 5% poverty rate for married couples). For poor single mothers, the labor market usually doesn't provide a ticket off of welfare

or out of poverty. That's why AFDC (Aid to Families with Dependent Children, the program known as welfare) worked like a revolving door for so many of them.

Heidi Hartmann and Roberta Spalter-Roth of the Institute for Women's Policy Research (IWPR) report that half of single mothers who spend any time on welfare during a two-year period also work for pay. But that work only generates about one-third of their families' incomes. In short, work is not enough; like other members, they "package" their income from three sources; work in the labor market, support from men or other family members, and government aid. "Mothers typically need at least two of those sources to survive," says Spalter-Roth.

## THE TRIPLE WHAMMY

While all women, especially numbers, face barriers to employment with good wages and benefits, single mothers face a "triple whammy" that sharply limits what they can earn. Three factors—job discrimination against women, the time and money it takes to care for children, and the presence of only one adult—combine to make it nearly impossible for women to move off of welfare through work alone, without sufficient and stable supplemental income supports.

First, the average woman earns about two-thirds as much per hour as her male counterpart. Women who need to rely on welfare earn even less, since they often have lower skills, less work experience and more physical disabilities than other women. Between 1984 and 1988, IWPR researchers found, welfare mothers who worked for pay averaged a disastrous $4.18 per hour. Welfare mothers with jobs received employer-provided health benefits only one quarter of the time. Mothers on welfare are three times as likely as other women to work as maids, cashiers, nursing aides, child care workers, and waitresses—the lowest of the low-paid women's jobs.

Second, these families include kids. Like all mothers, single mothers have to deal with both greater demands on their time and larger financial demands—more "mouths to feed." A 1987 time-budget study found that the average time spent in household work for employed women with two or more children was 51 hours a week. Child care demands limit the time women can cut into their jobs, and interrupt them with periodic crises, ranging from a sick child to a school's summer break. This takes its toll on both the amount and the quality of work many mothers can obtain. "There's a sad match between women's needs for a little flexibility and time, and the growth in contingent jobs, part-time jobs, jobs that don't last all year," comments Spalter-Roth. "That's the kind of jobs they're getting."

Finally, and unlike other mothers, single mothers have only one adult in the family to juggle child care and a job. Fewer adults means fewer opportunities for paid work. And while a single mother may receive child care—that a resident father can provide.

What kind of prospects will welfare recipients face when they have been pushed into the workforce by TANF regulations? Two-thirds of welfare recipients hold no more than a high school diploma. The best way to tell how work requirements will work is to look at the women who already have the jobs that welfare recipients will be compelled to seek.

The news is not good. An unforgiving labor market, in recession and recovery alike, has hammered young, less-educated women, according to economists Jared Bernstein and Lawrence Mishel of the Economic Policy Institute, a Washington, D.C. think tank. Between 1979 and 1989, hourly wages plummeted for these women, falling most rapidly for African American women who didn't finish high school. This group's hourly wages, adjusted for inflation, fell 20% in that ten year period. Most young high school-or-less women continued to lose during 1989–93. At the end of this losing streak, average hourly wages ranged from $5 an hour for younger high school dropouts to $8 an hour for older women with high school diplomas.

Unemployment rates in 1993 for most of these young women are stunning: 42% for black female high school dropouts aged 16–25, and 26% for their Latina counterparts.

But young women don't have a monopoly on labor market distress: workforce-wide hourly wages fell 14% between 1973 and 1993, after controlling for inflation. Given the collapse of wage rates, work simply is not enough to lift many families out of poverty. Two-thirds of all people living in poor families with children—15 million Americans—live in families *with a worker* in 1991, report Isaac Shapiro and Robert Greenstein of the Center on Budget and Policy Priorities. And 5.5 million of these people in poverty had a family member who worked *year-round, full-time.*

## REFORMS THAT WOULD WORK

The problems of insufficient pay and time to raise children that face single-mother families—and indeed many families—go far beyond the welfare system. So the solution must be much more comprehensive than simply reforming that system. What we need is a set of thorough changes in the relations among work, family, and income.

- *Provide supports for low-wage workers.* The two most important supports are universal health coverage—going down in flames in Congress at the time of this writing—and a universal child care plan. Two-thirds of welfare recipients leave the rolls within two years, but lack of health insurance and child care drive many of them back: over half of the women who left welfare to work went back to AFDC. A society that expects all able-bodied adults to work—regardless of the age of their children—should also be a society that socializes the costs of going to work, by offering programs to care for children of all ages.
- *Create jobs.* This item seems to have dropped off the national policy agenda. Deficit-probing has hogtied any attempt at fiscal stimulus, and the Federal Reserve seems bent on stamping out growth in the name of preventing inflation. Government spending could be used to boost job growth, and even invest in creating public service jobs.
- *Make work pay by changing taxes and government assistance.* Make it not only for women working their way off welfare, but for everybody at the low end of the labor market. Clinton's preferred tool for this has been the Earned Income Tax Credit (EITC)—which gives tax credits to low-wage workers with children (this tax provision now outspends AFDC). Although they get the EITC, women on welfare who work suffer a penalty that takes away nearly a dollar of the AFDC grant for every dollar

earned. Making work pay would mean reducing or eliminating this penalty.

- *Make work pay by shoring up wages and benefits.* To ensure that the private sector does its part, raise the minimum wage. A full-time, year-round minimum wage job pays less than the poverty income threshold for a family of one. Conservatives and the small business lobby will trot out the bogeyman of job destruction, but studies on the last minimum wage increase showed a zero or even positive effect on employment. Hiking the minimum wage does eliminate lousy jobs, but the greater purchasing power crated by a higher wage floor generates roughly the same number of *better* jobs. In addition, mandate benefit parity for part-time, temporary, and subcontracted workers. This would close a loophole that a growing number of employers use to dodge fringe benefits.

- *Make a serious commitment to life-long education and training.* Education and training do help welfare recipients and other disadvantaged workers. But significant impacts depend on longer-term, intensive—and expensive—programs. We also need to expand training to a broader constituency, since training targeted only to the worst-off workers helps neither these workers, who get stigmatized in the eyes of employers, nor the remainder of the workforce, who get excluded. In Sweden, half the workforce takes some time off work for education in any given year.

- *Build flexibility into work.* "Increasingly," says Spalter-Roth, "all men and all women are workers *and* nurturers." Some unions have begun to bargain for the ability to move between full-time and part-time work, but in most work places changing hours means quitting a job and finding a new one. And though employees now have the right to unpaid family or medical leave, many can't afford to take time off. *Paid* leave would, of course, solve this problem. Failing that, temporary disability insurance (TDI) that is extended beyond disability situations to those facing a wide range of family needs could help. Five states (California, New York, New Jersey, Rhode Island, and Hawaii) currently run TDI systems funded by payroll taxes.

- *Mend the safety net, for times when earnings aren't enough.* Unemployment insurance has important gaps: low-wage earners receive even lower unemployment benefits, the long-term unemployed get cut off, new labor market entrants and re-entrants have no access to benefits, and in many states people seeking part-time work cannot collect. Closing these gaps would help welfare "packagers," as well as others at the low end of the labor market, to make ends meet. But even with all of these policies in place, there will be times when single mothers will either choose or be compelled to set aside paid work, sometimes for extended periods, to care for their families.

So welcome to reality. Most single mothers *cannot* work their way out of poverty—definitely not without supplemental support. There are many possible policy steps that could be taken to help them and other low-wage workers get the most out of an inhospitable labor market. But ultimately, old-fashioned welfare must remain part of the formula.

Resources: Heidi Hartmann and Robert Spalter-Roth, "The real employment opportunities of women participating in AFDC: What the market can provide" (1993) and "Welfare that works: An assessment of the administration's welfare reform proposal" (1994), Institute for Women's Policy Research; Jared Bernstein and Lawrence Mishel, "Trends in the low-wage labor market and welfare reform: The constraints on making work pay," Economic Policy Institute (1994); Isaac Shapiro and Robert Greenstein, *Making Work Pay: The Unfinished Agenda,* Center on Budget and Policy Priorities 1993; Randy Albelda and Chris Tilly, *Glass Ceilings and Bottomless Pits: Women, Income, and Poverty in Massachusetts,* Women's Statewide Legislative Network (Massachusetts) 1994.    [1994 and 1996]

 59

# The Stories Our Mothers Tell: Projections of Self in the Stories of Puerto Rican Women Garment Workers

BLANCA VÁZQUEZ

This excerpt is part of a larger manuscript entitled "Stories to Live By: Continuity and Change in Three Generations of Puerto Rican Women Garment Workers," written by Celia Alvarez, Rina Ben-mayor, Ana Juarbe and Blanca Vázquez, Center for Puerto Rican Studies, Hunter College, City University of New York. Founded as a result of the student and community movements of the 1960s and 70s, the Center has been documenting the Puerto Rican migration and the development of Puerto Rican community life in the U.S. since 1973. This work was undertaken in the mid-1980s as part of the Centro's "Voices of the Migration Project, An Oral History of the Puerto Rican Migration." We turned to oral histories because much of the history of Puerto Ricans in the United States resided in the memories and lived experiences of the overwhelmingly working-class Puerto Rican migrants. In the first phase of the project, we gathered the life histories of *pioneros*, pioneer migrants who had migrated in the 1920s and 30s. Many of those whom we interviewed had been active in creating organizations such as the Liga Puertorriqueña e Hispana (1926) and hometown clubs.

Because women were central to the world of work, family and the re-creation of community life, in the second phase of the project, we concentrated on the experiences of Puerto Rican women within the migration. We chose garment production as the most representative work experience of Puerto Rican women. For the most part, the research team was composed of first generation daughters of garment workers, and this close affinity to the work conditioned our interpretation of the life stories, as well as the *telling*. The stories contained accounts of hard work and pain as well as laughter, celebration and joy. In relaying their life experiences to a younger generation of listeners, the women were imparting lessons to us about perseverance, survival and success against the constraints imposed by the class, racial and gender discrimination they faced in the new environment.

The women whose life histories I am examining are now in their fifties and sixties. They grew up in Puerto Rico, for the most part, . . . in the midst of the Great Depression, a time of tremendous social upheaval and economic reorganization in Puerto Rico. They came from rural areas, still tied to declining agricultural sectors such as tobacco or coffee, or to wage labor in the cities and towns. My mother, for example, was born in Mayagüez to a very poor family. At the age of eight she helped her mother do home needlework. Shortly afterwards her mother died and she was then raised by her grandmother who took in laundry for a living and was also a midwife. My great-grandmother started her own life story by saying that she had been born in 1875, two years after slavery was abolished in Puerto Rico. The significance of this is that her mother had been a slave and that she herself had escaped this fate. Thus, the lives of these . . . women reflect the changes in Puerto Rico's social, political and economic reorganization under Spanish and U.S. rule.

Poverty and hardship characterize the early lives of the women. By the 1930s, the world-wide crises in capitalism had left the Puerto Rican economy in shambles. All the women worked as children to help support their families. They were also pulled from school because of this economic necessity. Education was out of the question for most of the poor, and especially for female children who in addition to being paid and most often unpaid workers, also helped cook, clean and care for their brothers and sisters while their mothers worked. . . . The women recount the experience of being pulled from school as a lost opportunity in their lives, the pain still evident in the *telling*. Out of this longing came the commitment to give to their children the education they had so missed in their lives. Education was the only escape from poverty, the only way to get off the land and out of the kitchens and *talleres*.

In looking across the board at the stories Puerto Rican women were telling, convergences began to emerge in the self-images of the women. These projections-of-self were powerful and offer an alternative view of working-class women: they convey a sense of women as strong, resourceful, ingenious and determined to overcome the obstacles they face day to day in the world of work. These images resonate from women I knew personally as well as from women I had had no prior contact with. The ways in which the women project themselves and what they have struggled against is indicative of a common historical experience and speaks to a convergence of individual and collective history.

The stories of María R., drawn from the world of

work, the arena in which she has been able to assert her selfhood despite oppressive conditions, illustrate these self-images. [At the time, María was] a 55-year-old garment worker and mother of seven children who migrated to New York from a rural area of Puerto Rico in 1948. Married at a very young age, she had two daughters when she and her husband decided they could not raise a family on the land and "progress." First her husband, then María and finally her two small daughters migrated to New York. The first story explains how María learned to sew on a machine.

Well, I continued working with the intention of looking for something better, but every time I went out to find a job, all the jobs available were for sewing machine operators and I said to myself, "My God, I have to learn to sew." I told [my husband] that we had to find a school so I could learn to sew. Then I went to a school on 14th Street and Union Square and I signed up for three classes. They charged $25 and the only thing they really taught us was to sew a straight seam.

But I took the classes . . . and I went to look for work as an operator. I didn't really know how to sew. I only knew how to start the machine although I had some knowledge of the machine because my mother had a small manual one in Puerto Rico. I used to watch my grandmother sew on that machine and I thought I could do it.

Well, I went to look for work, and oh, my God, wherever I went, whenever I sat down at the machine and touched the pedal, the machine seemed to run by itself! I was thrown out of a number of factories but five minutes here, fifteen minutes there, I kept getting more and more practice.

Then, I said to myself, "I'm going to see what kind of machines they have and if I see a Singer machine I'm going to say that I don't know how to sew on that particular machine." I went to a factory at 380 Broome Street and I noticed that they had Mero machines and no Singer machines. Now, since I had failed so many times I told the man that I knew how to sew but not on the machine they had. I told him I knew how to sew on a Singer. Blanca, because of that lie they showed me how to sew on the Mero. The man said to me, "If you can sew on a Singer, this one is easier." Then I said to him, "How is that possible with all those spools of thread?" He

said, "Well, I'll show you." He sat me down and calmly showed me how to thread the machine, how to tie up the thread when a spool ran low, not to let it run out, and that's where I started working on chenille robes.

This first story María tells in her animated way of speaking illustrates her ingenuity and resourcefulness. First she goes to school to learn to sew on a machine, then after repeated rejections at various factories because she doesn't sew well enough, María strategizes to get the job. She takes advantage of these "trial" periods to improve her sewing skills, then she tells one foreman that she knows how to sew but not on that particular machine. The foreman assures her that if she can sew on a Singer, she can learn to sew on a Mero and proceeds to give her the orientation she needs.

This story is typical of other stories María tells. She conveys that she has never been one to give up regardless of the objective problems she encounters. She doesn't downplay the disadvantages she faces, her lack of sewing skills or ability to speak English. In fact, she highlights these things in her stories, setting us up for a sort of punch line. The obstacles she faces are precisely the things she will operate against and overcome. The constraints are clear and that she will find a way around them, through them or over them is an inevitable outcome of her stories. In this first story it is her determination, willingness to face rejection and ultimately a clever little lie that will see her through to her goal—a better paying job so she can help to educate and feed her children.

The second story María tells takes place a few years later. Here we begin to see a change in her strategy, a different sense of her value as a worker and of her options in life. She starts the story by saying, "I was very important on the job."

I went to another place making panties. Then I learned another machine, the zig zag machine. At that time I was earning about $40 a week. Only two people know how to work on that machine, an American guy and I. We used to start the garment and then we would give it to the other operators. So that meant that any day that we missed these other people doesn't have no work to do and they had to send them home. So I was very important on the job.

Every time that a garment was new and it took me longer, I had to fight for the price. So at one point [a new garment] came in and this work was very hard. I cannot make enough money for the hours . . . and I said, "No, I am not doing this." He gave me a little more money but I said, "No, no, I can't do this job at this price," and so he fired me. I never was fired in my life from no job. He told me if you don't want to do the work just go home, but at this time I had the protection of the union. So I said, "O.K., I go home." I got up, took my pocketbook, then my coat and left but I [didn't] come here. I went to the union place and I report him. [The agent] said, "Don't worry about it. I'll be there tomorrow." I'll never forget, it was a Friday. On Monday he came up with me and . . . he talked to the boss and said, "You're going to time her with a clock and you are going to see how long she takes with the garment and you're going to pay her accordingly."

He did that and it came out to be more money. So he paid me but inside of me I was mad because he had fired me, *embarrassed* me in front of 50 people. And I say, "You are going to pay me one of these days." I was very rebellious in that.

And I waited . . . that particular day, the work was piled up to the ceiling, work that only I and this man we have to work first. I waited for that moment [when] this fellow was sick. I worked two days, I'll never forget. I worked Monday and Tuesday and on Wednesday I didn't report to work. I went next door and I [found] another job, this time in bathing suits. They paid me about 75 cents a garment which at that time, this was in 1956, was good money.

So on Friday when I was supposed to collect my money for the days I worked, the secretary told me that Al [wanted] to talk to me. So he came over and he told me, "María, you can't do this to me. You know that we don't have nobody to operate that machine. How much you want?" I said, "I don't want nothing. I don't want to work for you no more." He said, "You can't do that to me, you know I was paying good money." I said, "I don't care for your money." He said, "You don't find no job." I said, "I already have another job and I'll give you the address. I now work in Julia Sportswear." He knew that place paid good money.

Now María displays a different set of skills and strategies. At the beginning of the story she defines her status and worth as a worker with marketable skills. As the story progresses, she makes clear that being a union member confers rights that she will exercise and she can now fight in English as well as in Spanish. Not only does María still not fear rejection, she invites it by challenging her boss on what she feels is an unjust and exploitative price. He fires her for her defiance and she gets even by leaving the job precisely at a time when he needs her. Because of the relative ease of finding work in the boom era of the 1950s and 60s, María had the option as other women did—to go from factory to factory, to "shop" for better salaries and working conditions. Ultimately, it is this structural reality of garment production that allows María a wider range of strategies. In a subsequent story, María collectivizes her combativeness when as a chairlady in another factory, she stops the machines over an unfair piecework rate and calls in the union representative to back up the workers.

What then are the features of these stories? In the first place, they tell us that María is a very resourceful person and that she relies on her own ingenuity to overcome the obstacles in her life. This resourcefulness is a constant feature of her stories and appears in the narrations of other garment workers. As María's life story unfolds, she returns to school in order to enroll in a Manpower Training program in the 1970s and becomes a clerical worker in a public hospital.

The most striking pattern in María's stories and that of other garment workers I interviewed was one of omission. Missing from these stories was a sense of victimization. In spite of the hardships and discrimination these women have faced, there was little sense of resignation or defeat.

The women were projecting to us images of strength and combat in the face of the obstacles and constraints in their lives. The constraints are real and shared as a community, as measured by all the indices of poverty and disadvantage. The constraints are also ideological, and herein is the strength of these stories. In telling us these stories, the women impart values to us that will guide younger generations in what we have to do to survive in this country. In that sense, these stories can be said to have real intended meaning; they contain purpose and plan. Embedded in the stories are positive images and real strategies for women, for their children and for all who would listen.

The fact that these are stories of struggle and "success" is significant. I believe that on a symbolic level, these stories are the key to how we have survived as a people. We may not know the historical "facts," what really happened in those factory exchanges with the boss, how it would play back if we could recapture what actually happened. We are not looking at behavior which can be measured objectively. We are listening to how people relate their lives—*what is of value to them*. What we do know is that these stories "as is" and on face value have meaning for us as insiders; that they reveal a felt need to convey to younger generations what kind of people we are and need to be. The images and projections we get *as* women *from* women is that women struggle, wheel and deal, maneuver and confront and do whatever they have to do to accomplish their goals. The message we get from these stories is that if we are to survive, we need to be like our mothers in fundamental ways.

The lessons embedded in the stories differ and change over time. At times the confrontation with those who have power over us is direct; at times it is necessary to circumvent. At times the mechanism to cope is simply humor, to be able to take a difficult situation and put it into perspective by making it lighter for ourselves. . . .

The stories of garment workers . . . do what the larger society does not: they validate our experience and affirm our worth. The Centro's Oral History project has provided a space for our common experiences to be recognized. The stories we have collected allow us to give our mothers credit for being garment workers, for taking care of our families, for struggling in the community and at the workplace and for doing that with courage and commitment and at times, at great personal cost. Ultimately, underlying what our parents are saying is that they have not wholly internalized or accepted the terms of class and race that are meted out in this country. The underlying message we get, then, is one of resistance and rebellion.

We have learned a renewed respect for the struggles of garment workers, for their steadfastness, ingenuity and resolve in the midst of an alienating, oppressive and often hostile environment. If these stories prepare us, a younger generation of listeners, for anything, it is to understand how we survive as a people: through persistence, perseverance, combativeness, creativity and hard work. If we are to go further collectively we must internalize these lessons, drawn from the everyday lives of common people, and struggle together across ethnic, racial, language and national lines to create true opportunity and equality. To ensure that better future for our children that compelled our mothers and fathers to go to work each day, we, too, must fight in countless ways to resist the lack of dignity in our lives. For me, that is the value and the legacy contained in these stories. [1987]

# 60

# *What Do Unions Do for Women?*

JILL BRAUNSTEIN, LOIS SHAW, AND ROBIN DENNIS

At a time when union membership has been declining overall, a new report by IWPR [Institute for Women's Policy Research], *What Do Unions Do for Women,* shows that the number of women who are union members has continued to increase. As a result, women are currently 37 percent of organized labor's membership—a higher percentage than at any time in the U.S. labor movement's history. Thus the face of unionism in the U.S. is changing, even though much of the research on unions continues to focus on men. IWPR research shows that union membership is important for women because membership or coverage under a collective bargaining agreement is associated with higher wages and

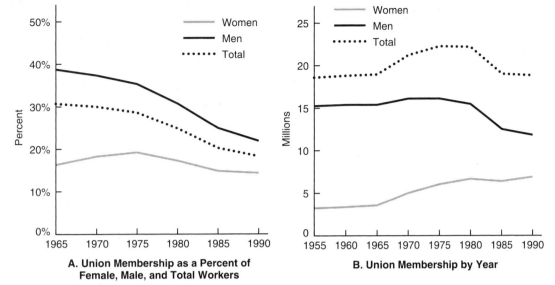

*Figure 1*   *Trends in Union Membership*

longer job tenure, as well as a smaller pay gap between women and men.

### TRENDS IN UNION MEMBERSHIP

Overall, since 1980, both the absolute number of union workers and the proportion of the U.S. workforce that is unionized has fallen. Among women, however, union membership has nearly kept pace with the rapidly growing female labor force, and the absolute number of women union members has continued to grow. The proportion of women workers who are union members increased from 16.3 percent in 1965 to 19.3 percent in 1975 and then fell to 14 percent in 1990 (see Figure 1). Approximately 7.4 million women were union members or represented by unions in 1992.

In contrast the proportion of male workers in unions fell from 39 percent in 1965 to 22 percent in 1990. About 11 million men had union representation in 1992.

### WHO ARE THE UNION WOMEN?

The number of union women is growing as unionization has shifted to areas such as teaching, nursing, and the public sector where women work in disproportionate numbers. IWPR's research also shows that unionization has increased among better educated and higher-wage women.

### Industry and Occupation

While male union members are predominately blue collar workers in manufacturing, construction, and public utilities, women in unions are predominately white collar workers in service industries (see Table 1). Professional and technical workers are the largest single group of women union members.

### Education

Among union members, women are more likely than men to be college educated, while men are more likely to be high school graduates (see Table 1).

This mapping illustrates the changing face of unions as women become a higher proportion of membership. It shows the movement of union membership from blue collar to white collar occupations, from manufacturing to professional specialty industries, and from high school to college-educated workers.

TABLE 1   Where Are the Union Workers?
(Union Members Working at Least Seven
Months), 1987

| Location | Women (in %) | Men (in %) |
|---|---|---|
| *By Occupation* | 100 | 100 |
| Administrative Support | 27 | 9 |
| Blue Collar | 18 | 59 |
| Professional/Technical | 39 | 18 |
| Sales | 5 | 3 |
| Service | 11 | 11 |
| *By Industry* | 100* | 100 |
| Finance/Trade | 8 | 10 |
| Manufacturing | 17 | 34 |
| Mining/Construction | 0 | 12 |
| Public Administration | 9 | 10 |
| Public Utilities | 12 | 18 |
| Service | 53 | 16 |
| *By Firm Size* | 100 | 100 |
| Less than 25 Employees | 3 | 6 |
| Between 25 & 99 Employees | 8 | 10 |
| At least 100 Employees | 89 | 84 |
| *By Education Level* | 100 | 100 |
| Less than High School | 12 | 17 |
| High School Diploma | 33 | 44 |
| Some College | 22 | 24 |
| College or More | 32 | 15 |

*May not add to 100 because of rounding.

*Source:* IWPR calculations based on the 1986 and 1987
panels of the Survey of Income and Program Participation.

## IMPACTS OF UNIONIZATION

### Increased Wages

Union membership or coverage by a collective bargaining agreement is associated with higher wages
for women. Unionized women earned an average of
$2.50 more per hour than non-unionized women.
This was equivalent to a union wage premium of
38 percent. When differences between unionized
and non-unionized women workers, such as education, are taken into account, the union wage premium is 90 cents or about 12 percent (see Figure 2).
This wage difference is reasonably certain to be due
to unionization alone.

### Relative Benefits for Women of Color

Unions benefit minority women, particularly African-Americans and Hispanics, at least as much as
white women. The union wage premium, slightly
more than the $2.50 gained by white women, rep-
resents a premium of about 45 percent for women
of color. Controlling for all other factors, women
of color who are unionized earn 87 cents or 13 percent more than non-unionized women. Although all
workers benefit from union representation, unions
increase wages more at the low end than at the high
end of the income distribution.

### Decreased Pay Gap

There is a smaller pay gap between male and female
workers in a unionized workforce ($2.77 per hour)
than in a non-unionized workforce ($3.45 per hour,
see Figure 2). Unionized women earned 75 cents for
every dollar earned by unionized men, while non-
unionized women earned 68 cents for every dollar
earned by non-unionized men.

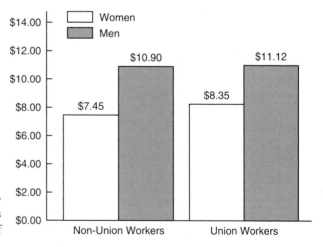

*Figure 2   What Unions Do For Sex Equity, 1987*

### Increased Job Tenure

Unionization is also associated with greater job tenure. Unionized women workers have twice as many years on the job as non-union workers. Among low-wage workers, union women have three more years of job tenure than non-union women. When the effect of union membership on years of job tenure is controlled statistically for differences in other factors that might affect tenure, unions increase job tenure by about one year or 20 percent, and increase tenure more (in percentage terms) for low-wage women workers than for high-wage women workers.

Labor law reform that increases women's ability to organize and to bargain collectively as well as increased voice for women within unions are necessary if the current 86 percent of women who are not organized or represented by collective bargaining agreements are to benefit from the increased wages, pay equity, and job security that unionization can bring.                                    [1994]

## ✢ 61

## *9to5: Organizing Low-Wage Women*

ELLEN BRAVO AND
GLORIA SANTA ANNA

When 9to5 was founded in Boston in 1973, the terms "sexual harassment," "pay equity," and "family leave" did not yet exist. But experiences with sexual degradation on the job, undervaluation of women's work, and lack of consideration for family responsibilities were common. So were the consequences, both financially and emotionally, for women workers.

The women who started 9to5 worked as secretaries in Boston's prestigious colleges. Karen Nussbaum and Ellen Cassedy were angry over the daily reminders from those with power that support staff had none. They attended a weekend workshop for office workers at the YWCA where women listed the problems: low pay, limited advancement opportunity, little say over working conditions. A teller said she didn't make enough to get a loan from the bank she worked for. A clerk in a hospital couldn't afford to get sick; a university secretary couldn't afford to send her children to college. For the most part, workshop participants were proud of their skills and their work. Their goal was not so much to get out of office work as to upgrade it—to change the way they were treated and paid.

Ten women got together after the workshop and printed a short newsletter about their key concerns. In the mornings on the way to work they passed out the newsletters in front of subway stops and large office complexes. The response was overwhelming. The group called a meeting and 300 women showed up, bursting with grievances about their work situations. In November 1973, they formed an association of working women and called it "9to5" after the usual hours of the business day.

The organization's early focus was on clericals, who represented the sphere of traditionally female jobs. Through research, the founders learned that one-third of all working women were employed in administrative support positions, the largest and fastest-growing sector of the workforce. Many of the women in these jobs lived near or in poverty— yet they were not being reached by anti-poverty groups, nor were they the focus of feminist organizations. At the time, most unions ignored them.

The movement began to grow. Women in other cities formed similar groups. In the mid 1970s, they joined together to make 9to5 a national association. Staff and volunteers answered questions about job problems and held workshops on how to ask for a raise, plan for retirement, and organize to win better treatment. And many began to celebrate actual victories. Women reported asking for raises for the first time in their lives—and getting them. Groups of clericals met with managers to demand policy changes, including accurate job descriptions and job postings. Women in the publishing, insurance, and banking industries filed discrimination charges and won millions of dollars in back pay as well as new promotion and training programs. A few corporations, pressured by 9to5 activists, set aside money to help pay for child care.

Inspired by the organization, Jane Fonda decided to make a movie about the concerns of office workers and called it *Nine to Five*, greatly increasing the group's visibility. (The original plot involved murdering the boss. "That's not really on our agenda," 9to5 activists persuaded Fonda, who changed the story to a kidnapping and fantasies of murder—all based on interviews with actual 9to5 members.)

Some actions brought quick results. When a bank in Milwaukee told its employees they would have to take over payments for dependent health coverage—the equivalent of a week's take-home pay—9to5 organized a demonstration outside the bank, with flyers that read, "Should banks care about kids?" Within days the bank gave the women a raise equivalent to the health premium. Other campaigns dragged on for years, such as the successful efforts by the Delta 9to5 Network to gain recognition for their class action lawsuit against the employer. Workers for the airline had numerous complaints of discrimination against employees with physical disabilities, including the practice of identifying and firing employees with HIV.

From the early days of organizing in Boston, 9to5 leaders were interested in the intersection between the women's movement and the labor movement. Would unionization be appropriate for clerical workers? Would union drives be successful? After some early local efforts in Boston, 9to5 began exploring a relationship with an international union. In 1981, District 925 was born as an affiliate of Service Employees International Union. Today that group, which functions as a separate organization from 9to5, has organized women office workers across the country to bargain collectively. Union women overall make higher wages than nonunion employees and often have greater benefits. In addition, a union contract can give protection from arbitrary firing and recognition for seniority. 9to5 found that working as a citywide nonprofit association had advantages as well, particularly in involving women for whom unionization wasn't an immediate

option and in attracting media visibility for working women's issues.

In addition to empowering women individually and in groups, 9to5 helped change the policy environment. Issues that were trivialized or laughed at when the group started—sexual harassment, family leave, pay equity, child care, and ergonomics—became part of the public agenda. Using interviews with the media, actions, testimony, and educational programs, 9to5 members also influenced the laws. They watched years of hard work result in passage of the 1978 Pregnancy Discrimination Act, the 1991 Civil Rights Act, and the 1993 Family and Medical Leave Act on the federal level, as well as numerous state pay equity and family leave laws, and some state statutes establishing protections for computer users.

The group's victories didn't escape the notice of management. In one midwestern city, the start of a 9to5 chapter was greeted with a seminar called "9to5: Not Just a Movie—How to Keep 9to5 Out of Your Office." The planners made one miscalculation: they'd forgotten who opens the mail. Several secretaries mailed the notice to the fledgling chapter, who sent someone to the seminar and called a press conference immediately afterward to denounce the tactics of trying to prevent employees from organizing in the workplace.

In the late 1980s, 9to5's agenda expanded to address the needs of those who work at the margins of the economy: part-time and temporary workers, women who cycle on and off welfare. 9to5 activists with direct experience of welfare drew attention to the connections between women's problems in the workforce and their need to rely on public assistance. What happens to all the women who lose their job because of discrimination or lack of family leave, they asked? If you really want to reform welfare, they told policy makers, start by taking a good look at the need to reform *work*.

Technological developments added another issue: electronic surveillance. In 1989, 9to5 started a hotline to track computer users who were being monitored on the job, often without their awareness. Workers resented being spied on. Spying, one woman said, is what you do to the enemy. She and her co-workers didn't want to be treated as the enemy.

Electronic surveillance wasn't the only reason people dialed the hotline. They called with every type of job problem, eager to find out if they had any rights. After the Clarence Thomas hearings in 1991, the line was deluged with calls about sexual harassment. Many of the callers had experienced the harassment years earlier. As one woman put it, "I've never told anyone before. I thought that's just what you had to put up with."

9to5 has worked hard to make visible the problems working women face and to identify solutions. The vehicle at times is humorous, such as the annual contest to "Rate Your Job: The Good, the Bad and the Downright Unbelievable." Winners have included the manager who sent his secretary to bars on Saturday nights with a beeper to save him the trouble of scoping out women he might like; the doctor who demanded his nurse return to the office after she found her children's baby-sitter had died in her home; and a chain store in California who cut a 15-year employee's hours to part-time, ending all her medical and dental benefits and her sick days. While working for short-term improvements, 9to5 also points to the root causes of

## Going Public

ELLEN BRAVO

Every April, in honor of Secretaries Week, 9 to 5 sponsors a national contest called "Nominate Your Boss: The Good, the Bad and the Downright Unbelievable." We use Public Service Announcements to attract entries to the contest. Subsequent publicity about the "winners" helps draw attention to sexual harassment, keeps the spotlight on offenders, calls attention to positive steps taken by employers, and honors the courageous women who are turning their private pain into public action. The winners:

### THE GOOD

In Canada, the United Steelworkers Union begins every conference and convention, whatever its topic, with a presentation defining what sexual harassment is and stating that it will not be tolerated at that meeting. Anyone violating this rule, it is announced, will be sent home with a letter to the local Executive Board detailing the offense.

### THE BAD

Louette Colombano was one of the first female police officers in her San Francisco district. While listening to the watch commander, she and the other officers stood at attention with their hands behind their backs. The officer behind her unzipped his fly and rubbed his penis against her hands.

### THE DOWNRIGHT UNBELIEVABLE

Katherine Young, who worked for a hotel chain, claimed her boss had fired her for refusing his advances. Alabama Judge E. B. Haltom ruled against her. The boss couldn't possibly have been interested in harassing Young, the judge noted, because unlike the boss's wife, Young "wore little or no makeup, and her hair was not colored in any way."

[1992]

poverty and discrimination and the need for lasting solutions.

Over the years 9to5 helped raise the *expectations* of low-wage women. Most women were already aware of problems on the job. As a popular 9to5 button put it, "My consciousness is fine—it's my *pay* that needs raising." Thanks to 9to5, women workers have gained greater awareness that they deserve better treatment. Yet most still *lack the belief that change is possible*—or the concept that they themselves are the real agents of change. 9to5 tries to address this gap by helping members recognize and expand their leadership skills and above all by showing the difference collective action can make. The organization popularizes success stories to demystify the change process, revealing the many small steps that lead to a victory.

Twenty-five years after its founding, 9to5 is still transforming itself. The group has always been multiracial and multicultural, with an emphasis on fighting all forms of discrimination. But for many years the highest-level staff were all or predominantly white. With leadership from many parts of the organization, 9to5 set about examining how to become a genuinely anti-oppression organization. The process included structural changes such as adding caucuses to create safe space for women of color, lesbian/bisexual women, and women in poverty to come together and expand their role in the organization. Board and staff reviewed everything from mission to program to methods of resolving conflict in order to make sure that the group consistently "walked its talk." A five-person management team developed a more collaborative structure for itself and welcomed flattening of the organization overall.

Above all, 9to5 strives to be a vehicle in which working women can see that the particular pain they've experienced isn't personal—it's not about one bad manager or one set of policies or one election but about power. Rather than striving simply to put more women into power, 9to5 aims to put more power in the hands of all women and all other groups who've been denied it.                    [1998]

## 62

# Women

ALICE WALKER

They were women then
My mama's generation
Husky of voice—Stout of
Step
With fists as well as
Hands
How they battered down
Doors
And ironed
Starched white
Shirts
How they led
Armies
Headragged Generals
Across mined
Fields
Booby-trapped
Kitchens
To discover books
Desks
A place for us
How they knew what we
*Must* know
Without knowing a page
Of it
Themselves                    [1974]

## 63

## *To Be of Use*

MARGE PIERCY

The people I love the best
jump into work head first
without dallying in the shallows
and swim off with sure strokes almost out of sight.
They seem to become natives of that element,
the black sleek heads of seals
bouncing like half-submerged balls.

I love people who harness themselves, an ox to a
     heavy cart,
who pull like water buffalo, with massive patience,
who strain in the mud and the muck to move things
     forward,
who do what has to be done, again and again.

I want to be with people who submerge
in the task, who go into the fields to harvest
and work in a row and pass the bags along,
who are not parlor generals and field deserters
but move in a common rhythm
when the food must come in or the fire be put out.

The work of the world is common as mud.
Botched, it smears the hands, crumbles to dust.
But the thing worth doing well done          [1982]

---

# Women and the Family

The family and motherhood are often thought of as "natural" entities rather than institutions that, in traditional forms, reinforce sexism and maintain women's subordinated status. The selections in this section first explore women's situation in the family and then some of their varied experiences with motherhood. The fictional pieces serve to highlight the emotional realities of some women's lives in the family, realities that are often obscured by rosy cultural images of family life.

While families can be a source of support for some women, sexism in families can hurt us in various ways. Women no longer lose their legal identity and right to contract as they did in earlier centuries, yet, as Susan Lehrer points out, "the nuclear family is a different place for women and men." The family offers women the hope of love but also the potential of entrapment, as Rosie learns in Hisaye Yamamoto's short story.

As discussed in the introduction to Part IV, feminists distinguish the experience of mothering from the institution of motherhood. "A Long Story" depicts the pain experienced by mothers when the state's prerogatives, rather than women's relationship with their children, define motherhood.

At the same time that women are limited by the institutions of the family and motherhood, they are sometimes blamed for its problems. June Jordan points to the way that black single mothers in particular are blamed for black poverty. Rather than eliminating the racism and sexism in our society that undermines black families and praising black women for their success in keeping families together, the media "experts" and government officials "talk about our mamas." Writing in 1987, she compares the "crisis of the black family" to what she saw as the truly significant crises of the day that the U.S. government was perpetuating through its international policy. Jordan points to the governmental, institutional, and social changes necessary to support all women and families.

The ability to make conscious choices about personal relationships is central to women's freedom. Because choice is integral to feminism, this section also presents alternatives to the traditional family. Women who are single or celibate are often stigmatized in our society. Yet some women have found the experience of living with oneself to be satisfying and liberating. Mary Helen Washington speaks to the strength she finds in living on her own.

Including children in a male-female relationship brings challenges as well as rewards. Alix Kates Shulman describes the agreement that she and her husband made in their attempt to bring equity to parenting. Although it may appear mechanical and extreme, it reflects the resolve and intentionality many parents find necessary to change gendered social roles and patterns in the family. For Ellen Davidson, living collectively brings benefits to both adults and children.

## 🌿 64

# *Family and Women's Lives*

SUSAN LEHRER

We tend to think about the family as a natural, biological unit. After all, everyone knows it takes two to make a baby. What is meant by family is more than biological relations, of course. In current debates, one specific form of family is referred to as "traditional": the nuclear family—mother, father, and their children, living together, with the father the main breadwinner and the mother responsible for the home. It is maintained and reinforced by law and the state, and forms the basis for social policy toward women and children. Yet only about 25% of American households are married couples and their children; the "traditional" version, in which the father is the sole family breadwinner, accounts for only 8.2% of American households and certainly does not reflect the realities of most of us (U.S. Bureau of the Census, 1991, p. 145).

Overwhelmingly, women's family life includes responsibility for children and the home (called "women's work"). But women also work outside the home in the paid labor force—including over half of women with children under one year of age. Using the outdated, inaccurate picture of "family," however, prevents the needs of women and real-life families from being recognized. This essay explores some of the broad historical changes that have changed the family, and the way in which family structure defines the opportunities, economic situation, and social position of women.

### *HISTORICAL OVERVIEW*

Before industrialization, the family was a working, productive unit, with women producing goods for family consumption, as well as maintaining the family's health and material well-being. For example, in *Little House on the Prairie*, Laura Ingalls Wilder describes her childhood frontier family in which Ma's contribution was clear and valued, and Pa's work took place within the family setting as well. This continued into the late nineteenth and early twentieth centuries in rural areas.

With the beginnings of industrialization, a major shift occurred, as "work" became something done outside the home, for pay, by men. "Women's work" within the home (called housework) was not paid labor and hence not seen as "real work." Thus, the roles of breadwinner and homemaker that are often taken for granted as "natural" are the result of specific historical changes like industrialization, and are, as Jesse Bernard (1981) put it, specific to a very short period in human history. The household itself changed from a unit of production to one primarily of consumption.

Although men were the main workers (for pay), right from the beginning of industrialization, women also worked outside their homes. For example, in making cloth (which was one of the first industries affected by the Industrial Revolution), young women were the main source for factory workers, because men's labor was needed in agricultural production and therefore scarce. Women received wages that were one-quarter to one-half those of men. From the beginning of wage labor and capitalist production for profit, the wage structure itself has been different (and lower) for female workers than for male workers. Although male workers were not well paid, their wages were expected to support a family; women were not expected to be self-supporting, let alone able to support anyone else. This meant women were dependent upon men for support, even when they did work outside the home.

The "power of the purse" reinforced the husband's control over his family. Under English common law, which our legal system is based on, when a woman married, she lost her own legal identity and her legal right to contract. For instance, her husband had control over all money and property of the family, including her wages. Marriage represented a legal contract in which women's status was subordinate to her husband's. Women's current subordination in marriage is rooted in legal tradition as well as in economic arrangements.

As commercial and industrial development expanded and a national economy emerged in the later 1800s, women's world was still supposed to be centered within the household—she was the "angel of the hearth," available to provide material and emotional comfort for the man, who braved the world of commercial competition. This idealized version of family was never quite accurate even in the nineteenth century. For middle-class women, it meant complete economic dependence on the goodwill of their husbands and fathers. Less well-off women worked in factories and sweatshops as young women or whenever they were not supported by a man's income. Women also added to the household income by taking in boarders or doing washing—usually ignored by official counts of family income and employment (Bose, 1987:113).

Enslaved African-American women were expected to perform similar tasks as men, and in the United States, unlike other countries, even slave marriage was not recognized by white law. African-American women worked in the fields as well as in the slave master's household. Nonetheless, studies indicate that many enslaved families sought to maintain strong ties (which amounted to an act of subversion under slavery), and after emancipation, large-scale relocations of African Americans were often an attempt to reunite families broken apart by slavery (Gutman, 1983). After slavery, whites still expected African-American wives to work for them; they were considered lazy if they presumed to stay home and act like ladies (Jones, 1985:59). Thus we see that the "traditional" family was only expected to apply to certain groups and not others—white, middle-class families primarily.

From this brief historical background, it is clear that the family is not a natural, unchanging entity, but it changes along with social and economic shifts in the larger social world. We are again in a time when these larger social forces are visibly changing the way families function. Although the number of women working outside the home has been slowly increasing since the early 1900s, the increase in the past two decades has been astounding. The vast majority of women now combine outside work and family life, and in addition, the proportion of women who are heads of households, never married, and working has also increased dramatically.

## THE NUCLEAR FAMILY: IT'S A DIFFERENT PLACE FOR WOMEN THAN MEN

The idealized image of family relationships is that they are warm, loving, and occasionally quarrelsome but, in the long run, supportive. As the saying goes, family is where, when you go there, they have to take you in. The image of the nuclear family—with the father the main money-maker and responsible for making the important decisions in the family—continues to be a very strong influence on family lifestyles. Choices made within the family setting that appear to be simply logical or natural are, in fact, the consequence of the nuclear family structure. For instance, since the man's job is considered the mainstay of the family, his occupational shifts take first place over other family concerns. Because his earnings are likely to be greater than his wife's if she works, her job is considered the logically expendable one. If they have children, the wife is the one who is going to quit work and "stay home with the baby." If his career plans favor relocating to a different city, hers are likely to suffer. This, in turn, reinforces the disparity in their earnings, making it seem natural that his job is the one that is really important, while hers is secondary. Many women's reluctance to plan a career (as distinguished from a job to earn money) reflects the reality that they are expected to fit it in around everything else in the family. Many men agree that their wife's education, job, and career plans are worthwhile, as long as dinner is still on the table, the house in order, and the kids taken care of when he walks in the door. Some men still talk about taking responsibility for their own child as "baby-sitting."

The reality is that different family members experience the "same" family very differently. Where money is short, it is women who "bridge the gap between what a household's resources really are and what a family's position is supposed to be" (Rapp, 1982:175). They stretch the available food, clothing, and resources to make ends meet. Where a family consistently comes up short at the end of the paycheck, it is the woman who eats less and does without, in order that the kids and husband can have enough. To talk about a family's standard of living as if all family members shared the same level of well-being or poverty is misleading. Yet social scientists typically use the husband's occupation in defining social class and just assume that the rest of the family is included. And defining a family's class by the husband's occupation does not provide a basis for understanding the very different life chances that men and women face within the "same" family, given the realities of divorce and single parenthood.

## FAMILIES: A MULTITUDE OF POSSIBILITIES

Probably the most talked-about change in American families in recent years has been the increase in family households headed by women. Women heading families face a series of obstacles that reflect the unwillingness of policy makers to recognize and address their condition. In order to work and support their families, women must have child care; then they must earn enough to provide for their families. Women's earnings are still less than 70% of men's. The good news is that this is a greater proportion than it has been in the recent past; the bad news is that this is because of the relative *decline* in men's earnings rather than an increase in women's overall income. This means that women heading households are more likely to be poor, not only because there is only one earner in the family but because that earner is a woman. It also means that the lack of affordable child care hits women who are heads of family especially hard. Yet American social policy has not recognized that child care is just as much a social necessity as educating children. The United States is far behind most European countries, which train child-care specialists and provide care for children from the youngest ages.

For many women, the descent to poverty occurs as a result of divorce. This is more likely to happen for white women than for black women, partly because of the overall lower earnings of black men relative to white men. Despite all the jokes about men paying their life fortune in alimony to ex-wives, the reality is that men's standard of living goes *up* following divorce, while women's drops precipitously. For example, the Working Women's Defense Fund calculated that mothers' standard of living de-

clined an average of 26%, while fathers' improved by 34% (Masnerus, 1995).

The transition from Mrs. to ex-Mrs. is especially difficult for older, long-married women, who often do not have marketable skills to support themselves. The tragic irony is that it is precisely those women who acceded to cultural expectations to stay at home and be good wives and mothers who suffer the most, both economically and emotionally. Women whose whole sense of identity centers around being a wife and mother must cope with profound loss of meaning as well as the economic shock of divorce. These older women are the ones more likely to get alimony (as distinguished from child support). Younger women from shorter-term marriages are unlikely to be awarded alimony and often are unable to even collect child support. In 1990, there were 10 million women living with children whose fathers were not in the home; only half were awarded child support at all, and only half of those received the full amount (U.S. Bureau of the Census, Feb. 1992, p. 2). Despite all the movies depicting the hilarious, heart-warming adventures of men raising children, responsibility for children following divorce still rests overwhelmingly with the mother. However, in situations in which both parents do want custody of the child, the woman stands a good chance of losing, because judges tend to be critical of her for spending time apart from her child for any reason, even to go to work or school. Since work is the normal life pattern for the child's father, he in turn is rewarded with custody for any devotion he does show to the kids. The mother is caught in a double bind: she is expected to work, at least when the children are in school, yet penalized for not being a full-time mother when she does.

The reasons for the increase in families headed by women are complex and cannot be reduced to a simple explanation. Young women are more likely to have worked. Shotgun weddings are less common now than in the past (judging by the fact that many fewer pregnant women marry before their first child is born (U.S. Bureau of the Census, 1992, p. 2). The options of abortion, and refusing to marry someone you don't like, are more acceptable now. Other explanations look at economic factors affecting couples' financial prospects as they consider marriage. There is extensive urban unemployment and poverty among young people, for whom education is less likely to lead to jobs that pay enough to support a family. The reality is, over 25% of families with children were headed by women in 1995, compared with less than 12% in 1970. Single-parent families are 31% of families with children under 18; less than 16% of them are headed by the father. Many African-American families are headed by women—58%, compared with 21% for white families and 31% for Hispanic-American families. And remember, not all families involve children—they also include elders or other relatives in the household (U.S. Bureau of the Census, Statistical Abstracts, 1996, p. 62).

Married couples with children still depend upon the wife to do the "second shift"—the housework. Even when both husband and wife work full-time, throughout the 1980s, two-thirds of working wives reported that they did most or all of the housework. The time women spent on housework remained about the same whether they worked or not. This may be beginning to change—partly because women have simply stopped doing so much of it, but also because couples believe in sharing household work (Schor, 1991:103).

Despite the variety of social arrangements in which people live their lives, social policy and law penalize those who do not live in nuclear family settings. One of the ways this happens is by excluding non-legally married family members from health insurance plans—without which Americans cannot afford to be sick. The high cost of medical coverage has now reached crisis proportions nationally. The United States is the only major industrial nation that does not have national health coverage for everybody. Hospitals frequently restrict visits for very ill people to "immediate family," meaning legal spouses, and also deny information and decision making to non-legally married couples of any sort. This exclusion especially affects gay couples (Thompson and Andrzejewski, 1988). The increasing numbers of people affected by these exclusions are being encouraged to declare so-called "living wills" and powers of attorney so that the person

they designate will be accorded the rights and responsibilities that a legal spouse would be without question.

### MOM AND APPLE PIE?

The conservatives who attack the women's movement for being anti-family have a specific form of the family in mind—one that certainly does not correspond to what real families are like. These fundamentalist doctrines of the political far right rigidly interpret the Bible to justify the patriarchal family, attack women's rights, and use the power of the laws to support their views. It is interesting that in times of social change—like the mid-1800s in the throes of industrialization, and our own time—ideologies advocating a return to an earlier, past "golden age" surface.

Now, even the basic, biological fact that it takes two to make a baby seems to be blurring at the edges with the advances of reproductive technologies. A woman may be pregnant and give birth to a child to whom she is not genetically related, from an ovum that was fertilized in vitro (outside the woman's body). The child then may potentially have two completely different sets of parents. What is the legal status of the woman who was pregnant with the child? What "rights," if any, has she to be considered the "mother"? Is a "contract" to give up the child after birth enforceable if she changes her mind? These are unresolved questions. Typically, the couple wishing to become parents is wealthy enough to pay large medical and legal fees, while the woman having the child has much lower income and less to spend on lawyers. Our thinking about women, pregnancy, parenting, and family will need to take these issues into account.

Another possibility is that a woman who wants to become pregnant but is having difficulties can opt for series of fertility treatments or implanting of fertilized eggs—procedures that are experimental and extremely expensive, uncomfortable, and uncertain. Others want to be parents but not within a male-female household, either gay/lesbian couples or single persons. All of these can also become families with parents who raise children, wipe sniffly noses, and clap at school plays. The challenge is to creatively respond to changed conditions, and to help shape that change in ways that will enhance rather than stifle peoples' lives.                    [1992]

## REFERENCES

Bernard, Jessie. "The Good Provider Role: Its Rise and Fall," *American Psychologist* vol. 36, No. 1, Jan. 1981, pp. 1–12.

Bose, Christine, "Devaluing Women's Work: The Undercount of Women's Employment in 1900 and 1980," in Christine Bose, Roslyn Feldberg, and Natalie Sokoloff, eds. *Hidden Aspects of Women's Work.* New York: Praeger, 1987, pp. 95–115.

Gutman, Herbert, "Persistent Myths About the Afro-American Family," in Michael Gordon, ed. *The American Family in Social-Historical Perspective,* 3rd ed. New York: St. Martin's Press, 1983, pp. 459–481.

Jones, Jacqueline. *Labor of Love, Labor of Sorrow: Black Women, Work and the Family from Slavery to the Present.* New York: Vintage, 1985.

Masnerus, Laura. "The Divorce Backlash: For Professional Women, the Price of Getting Out of a Marriage—and Keeping the Children—Is Getting Higher." *Working Woman,* 20(2) (Feb. 1995), 40 (7).

Rapp, Rayna. "Family and Class in Contemporary America: Notes Toward an Understanding of Ideology," in Barrie Thorne and Marilyn Yalom, eds. *Rethinking the Family: Some Feminist Questions.* New York: Longman, 1982.

Schor, Juliet. *The Overworked American: The Unexpected Decline of Leisure.* New York: Basic Books, 1991.

Thompson, Karen, and Andrzejewski, Julie. *Why Can't Sharon Kowalski Come Home?* San Francisco: Spinster/ Aunt Lute Book Company, 1988.

U.S. Bureau of the Census, U. S. Department of Commerce, "Household and Family Characteristics: March 1990 and 1989," *Current Population Reports,* Population Characteristics, Series P-20, No. 447, 1991.

U.S. Bureau of the Census, U.S. Department of Commerce, "How We're Changing, Demographic State of the Nation: 1991," *Current Population Reports,* Special Studies Series P-23, No. 177, February 1992.

U.S. Bureau of the Census, U.S. Department of Commerce, *Statistical Abstracts of the U.S.* (Washington, D.C.: U.S. Government Printing Office, 1996).

## 🌿 65

# *Seventeen Syllables*

HISAYE YAMAMOTO

The first Rosie knew that her mother had taken to writing poems was one evening when she finished one and read it aloud for her daughter's approval. It was about cats, and Rosie pretended to understand it thoroughly and appreciate it no end, partly because she hesitated to disillusion her mother about the quantity and quality of Japanese she had learned in all the years now that she had been going to Japanese school every Saturday (and Wednesday, too, in the summer). Even so, her mother must have been skeptical about the depth of Rosie's understanding, because she explained afterwards about the kind of poem she was trying to write.

See, Rosie, she said, it was a *haiku,* a poem in which she must pack all her meaning into seventeen syllables only, which were divided into three lines of five, seven, and five syllables. In the one she had just read, she had tried to capture the charm of a kitten, as well as comment on the superstition that owning a cat of three colors meant good luck.

"Yes, yes, I understand. How utterly lovely," Rosie said, and her mother, either satisfied or seeing through the deception and resigned, went back to composing.

The truth was that Rosie was lazy; English lay ready on the tongue but Japanese had to be searched for and examined, and even then put forth tentatively (probably to meet with laughter). It was so much easier to say yes, yes, even when one meant no, no. Besides, this was what was in her mind to say: I was looking through one of your magazines from Japan last night, Mother, and towards the back I found some *haiku* in English that delighted me. There was one that made me giggle off and on until I fell asleep—

It is morning, and lo!
I lie awake, *comme il faut,*
sighing for some dough.

Now, how to reach her mother, how to communicate the melancholy song? Rosie knew formal Japanese by fits and starts, her mother had even less English, no French. It was much more possible to say yes, yes.

It developed that her mother was writing the *haiku* for a daily newspaper, the *Mainichi Shimbun,* that was published in San Francisco. Los Angeles, to be sure, was closer to the farming community in which the Hayashi family lived and several Japanese vernaculars were printed there, but Rosie's parents said they preferred the tone of the northern paper. Once a week, the *Mainichi* would have a section devoted to *haiku,* and her mother became an extravagant contributor, taking for herself the blossoming pen name, Ume Hanazono.

So Rosie and her father lived for awhile with two women, her mother and Ume Hanazono. Her mother (Tome Hayashi by name) kept house, cooked, washed, and, along with her husband and the Carrascos, the Mexican family hired for the harvest, did her ample share of picking tomatoes out in the sweltering fields and boxing them in tidy strata in the cool packing shed. Ume Hanazono, who came to life after the dinner dishes were done, was an earnest, muttering stranger who often neglected speaking when spoken to and stayed busy at the parlor table as late as midnight scribbling with pencil on scratch paper or carefully copying characters on good paper with her fat, pale green Parker.

The new interest had some repercussions on the household routine. Before, Rosie had been accustomed to her parents and herself taking their hot baths early and going to bed almost immediately afterwards, unless her parents challenged each other to a game of flower cards or unless company dropped in. Now if her father wanted to play cards, he had to resort to solitaire (at which he always cheated fearlessly), and if a group of friends came over, it was bound to contain someone who was also writing *haiku,* and the small assemblage would be split in two, her father entertaining the non-literary members and her mother comparing ecstatic notes with the visiting poet.

If they went out, it was more of the same thing. But Ume Hanazono's life span, even for a poet's, was very brief—perhaps three months at most.

One night they went over to see the Hayano family in the neighboring town to the west, an adventure both painful and attractive to Rosie. It was attractive because there were four Hayano girls, all lovely and each one named after a season of the year (Haru, Natsu, Aki, Fuyu), painful because something had been wrong with Mrs. Hayano ever since the birth of her first child. Rosie would sometimes watch

Mrs. Hayano, reputed to have been the belle of her native village, making her way about a room, stooped, slowly shuffling, violently trembling (*always* trembling), and she would be reminded that this woman, in this same condition, had carried and given issue to three babies. She would look wonderingly at Mr. Hayano, handsome, tall, and strong, and she would look at her four pretty friends. But it was not a matter she could come to any decision about.

On this visit, however, Mrs. Hayano sat all evening in the rocker, as motionless and unobtrusive as it was possible for her to be, and Rosie found the greater part of the evening practically anaesthetic. Too, Rosie spent most of it in the girls' room, because Haru, the garrulous one, said almost as soon as the bows and other greetings were over, "Oh, you must see my new coat!"

It was a pale plaid of grey, sand, and blue, with an enormous collar, and Rosie, seeing nothing special in it, said, "Gee, how nice."

"Nice?" said Haru, indignantly. "Is that all you can say about it? It's gorgeous! And so cheap, too. Only seventeen-ninety-eight, because it was a sale. The saleslady said it was twenty-five dollars regular."

"Gee," said Rosie. Natsu, who never said much and when she said anything said it shyly, fingered the coat covetously and Haru pulled it away.

"Mine," she said, putting it on. She minced in the aisle between the two large beds and smiled happily. "Let's see how your mother likes it."

She broke into the front room and the adult conversation and went to stand in front of Rosie's mother, while the rest watched from the door. Rosie's mother was properly envious. "May I inherit it when you're through with it?"

Haru, pleased, giggled and said yes, she could, but Natsu reminded gravely from the door, "You promised me, Haru."

Everyone laughed but Natsu, who shamefacedly retreated into the bedroom. Haru came in laughing, taking off the coat. "We were only kidding, Natsu," she said. "Here, you try it on now."

After Natsu buttoned herself into the coat, inspected herself solemnly in the bureau mirror, and reluctantly shed it, Rosie, Aki, and Fuyu got their turns, and Fuyu, who was eight, drowned in it while her sisters and Rosie doubled up in amusement. They all went into the front room later, because Haru's mother quaveringly called to her to fix the tea and rice cakes and open a can of sliced peaches for everybody. Rosie noticed that her mother and Mr. Hayano were talking together at the little table—they were discussing a *haiku* that Mr. Hayano was planning to send to the *Mainichi*, while her father was sitting at one end of the sofa looking through a copy of *Life*, the new picture magazine. Occasionally, her father would comment on a photograph, holding it toward Mrs. Hayano and speaking to her as he always did—loudly, as though he thought someone such as she must surely be at least a trifle deaf also.

The five girls had their refreshments at the kitchen table, and it was while Rosie was showing the sisters her trick of swallowing peach slices without chewing (she chased each slippery crescent down with a swig of tea) that her father brought his empty teacup and untouched saucer to the sink and said, "Come on, Rosie, we're going home now."

"Already?" asked Rosie.

"Work tomorrow," he said.

He sounded irritated, and Rosie, puzzled, gulped one last yellow slice and stood up to go, while the sisters began protesting, as was their wont.

"We have to get up at five-thirty," he told them, going into the front room quickly, so that they did not have their usual chance to hang onto his hands and plead for an extension of time.

Rosie, following, saw that her mother and Mr. Hayano were sipping tea and still talking together, while Mrs. Hayano concentrated, quivering, on raising the handleless Japanese cup to her lips with both her hands and lowering it back to her lap. Her father, saying nothing, went out the door, onto the bright porch, and down the steps. Her mother looked up and asked, "Where is he going?"

"Where is he going?" Rosie said. "He said we were going home now."

"Going home?" Her mother looked with embarrassment at Mr. Hayano and his absorbed wife and then forced a smile. "He must be tired," she said.

Haru was not giving up yet. "May Rosie stay overnight?" she asked, and Natsu, Aki, and Fuyu

came to reinforce their sister's plea by helping her make a circle around Rosie's mother. Rosie, for once having no desire to stay, was relieved when her mother, apologizing to the perturbed Mr. and Mrs. Hayano for her father's abruptness at the same time, managed to shake her head no at the quartet, kindly but adamant, so that they broke their circle and let her go.

Rosie's father looked ahead into the windshield as the two joined him. "I'm sorry," her mother said. "You must be tired." Her father, stepping on the starter, said nothing. "You know how I get when it's *haiku*," she continued, "I forget what time it is." He only grunted.

As they rode homeward silently, Rosie, sitting between, felt a rush of hate for both—for her mother for begging, for her father for denying her mother. I wish this old Ford would crash, right now, she thought, then immediately, no, no, I wish my father would laugh, but it was too late: already the vision had passed through her mind of the green pick-up crumpled in the dark against one of the mighty eucalyptus trees they were just riding past, of the three contorted, bleeding bodies, one of them hers.

Rosie ran between two patches of tomatoes, her heart working more rambunctiously than she had ever known it to. How lucky it was that Aunt Taka and Uncle Gimpachi had come tonight, though, how very lucky. Otherwise she might not have really kept her half-promise to meet Jesus Carrasco. Jesus was going to be a senior in September at the same school she went to, and his parents were the ones helping with the tomatoes this year. She and Jesus, who hardly remembered seeing each other at Cleveland High where there were so many other people and two whole grades between them, had become great friends this summer—he always had a joke for her when he periodically drove the loaded pick-up up from the fields to the shed where she was usually sorting while her mother and father did the packing, and they laughed a great deal together over infinitesimal repartee during the afternoon break for chilled watermelon or ice cream in the shade of the shed.

What she enjoyed most was racing him to see which could finish picking a double row first. He, who could work faster, would tease her by slowing down until she thought she would surely pass him this time, then speeding up furiously to leave her several sprawling vines behind. Once he had made her screech hideously by crossing over, while her back was turned, to place atop the tomatoes in her green-stained bucket a truly monstrous, pale green worm (it had looked more like an infant snake). And it was when they had finished a contest this morning, after she had pantingly pointed a green finger at the immature tomatoes evident in the lugs at the end of his row and he had returned the accusation (with justice), that he had startlingly brought up the matter of their possibly meeting outside the range of both their parents' dubious eyes.

"What for?" she had asked.

"I've got a secret I want to tell you," he said.

"Tell me now," she demanded.

"It won't be ready till tonight," he said.

She laughed. "Tell me tomorrow then."

"It'll be gone tomorrow," he threatened.

"Well, for seven hakes, what is it?" she asked, more than twice, and when he had suggested that the packing shed would be an appropriate place to find out, she had cautiously answered maybe. She had not been certain she was going to keep the appointment until the arrival of her mother's sister and her husband. Their coming seemed a sort of signal of permission, of grace, and she had definitely made up her mind to lie and leave as she was bowing them welcome.

So as soon as everyone appeared settled back for the evening, she announced loudly that she was going to the privy outside, "I'm going to the *benjo!*" and slipped out the door. And now that she was actually on her way, her heart pumped in such an undisciplined way that she could hear it with her ears. It's because I'm running, she told herself, slowing to a walk. The shed was up ahead, one more patch away, in the middle of the fields. Its bulk, looming in the dimness, took on a sinisterness that was funny when Rosie reminded herself that it was only a wooden frame with a canvas roof and three canvas walls that made a slapping noise on breezy days.

Jesus was sitting on the narrow plank that was the sorting platform and she went around to the other side and jumped backwards to seat herself on the rim of a packing stand. "Well, tell me," she said without greeting, thinking her voice sounded reassuringly familiar.

"I saw you coming out the door," Jesus said. "I heard you running part of the way, too."

"Uh-huh," Rosie said. "Now tell me the secret."

"I was afraid you wouldn't come," he said.

Rosie delved around on the chicken-wire bottom of the stall for number two tomatoes, ripe, which she was sitting beside, and came up with a left-over that felt edible. She bit into it and began sucking out the pulp and seeds. "I'm here," she pointed out.

"Rosie, are you sorry you came?"

"Sorry? What for?" she said. "You said you were going to tell me something."

"I will, I will," Jesus said, but his voice contained disappointment, and Rosie fleetingly felt the older of the two, realizing a brand-new power which vanished without category under her recognition.

"I have to go back in a minute," she said. "My aunt and uncle are here from Wintersburg. I told them I was going to the privy."

Jesus laughed. "You funny thing," he said. "You slay me!"

"Just because you have a bathroom *inside*," Rosie said. "Come on, tell me."

Chuckling, Jesus came around to lean on the stand facing her. They still could not see each other very clearly, but Rosie noticed that Jesus became very sober again as he took the hollow tomato from her hand and dropped it back into the stall. When he took hold of her empty hand, she could find no words to protest; her vocabulary had become distressingly constricted and she thought desperately that all that remained intact now was yes and no and oh, and even these few sounds would not easily come out. Thus, kissed by Jesus, Rosie fell for the first time entirely victim to a helplessness delectable beyond speech. But the terrible, beautiful sensation lasted no more than a second, and the reality of Jesus' lips and tongue and teeth and hands made her pull away with such strength that she nearly tumbled.

Rosie stopped running as she approached the lights from the windows of home. How long since she had left? She could not guess, but gasping yet, she went to the privy in back and locked herself in. Her own breathing deafened her in the dark, close space, and she sat and waited until she could hear at last the nightly calling of the frogs and crickets. Even then, all she could think to say was oh, my, and the pressure of Jesus' face against her face would not leave.

No one had missed her in the parlor, however, and Rosie walked in and through quickly, announcing that she was next going to take a bath. "Your father's in the bathhouse," her mother said, and Rosie, in her room, recalled that she had not seen him when she entered. There had been only Aunt Taka and Uncle Gimpachi with her mother at the table, drinking tea. She got her robe and straw sandals and crossed the parlor again to go outside. Her mother was telling them about the *haiku* competition in the *Mainichi* and the poem she had entered.

Rosie met her father coming out of the bathhouse. "Are you through, Father?" she asked. "I was going to ask you to scrub my back."

"Scrub your own back," he said shortly, going toward the main house.

"What have I done now?" she yelled after him. She suddenly felt like doing a lot of yelling. But he did not answer, and she went into the bathhouse. Turning on the dangling light, she removed her denims and T-shirt and threw them in the big carton for dirty clothes standing next to the washing machine. Her other things she took with her into the bath compartment to wash after her bath. After she had scooped a basin of hot water from the square wooden tub, she sat on the grey cement of the floor and soaped herself at exaggerated leisure, singing "Red Sails in the Sunset" at the top of her voice and using da-da-da where she suspected her words. Then, standing up, still singing, for she was possessed by the notion that any attempt now to analyze would result in spoilage and she believed that the larger her volume the less she would be able to hear herself think, she obtained more hot water and poured it on until she was free of lather. Only then did she allow herself to step into the steaming vat, one leg first, then the remainder of her body inch by inch until the water no longer stung and she could move around at will.

She took a long time soaking, afterwards remembering to go around outside to stoke the embers of the tin-lined fireplace beneath the tub and to throw on a few more sticks so that the water might keep its heat for her mother, and when she finally returned to the parlor, she found her mother still talking *haiku* with her aunt and uncle, the three of them on another round of tea. Her father was nowhere in sight.

At Japanese school the next day (Wednesday, it was), Rosie was grave and giddy by turns. Preoccupied at her desk in the row for students on Book Eight, she made up for it at recess by performing wild mimicry for the benefit of her friend Chizuko. She held her nose and whined a witticism or two in what she considered was the manner of Fred Allen; she assumed intoxication and a British accent to go over the climax of the Rudy Vallee recording of the pub conversation about William Ewart Gladstone; she was the child Shirley Temple piping, "On the Good Ship Lollipop"; she was the gentleman soprano of the Four Inkspots trilling, "If I Didn't Care." And she felt reasonably satisfied when Chizuko wept and gasped, "Oh, Rosie, you ought to be in the movies!"

Her father came after her at noon, bringing her sandwiches of minced ham and two nectarines to eat while she rode, so that she could pitch right into the sorting when they got home. The lugs were piling up, he said, and the ripe tomatoes in them would probably have to be taken to the cannery tomorrow if they were not ready for the produce haulers tonight. "This heat's not doing them any good. And we've got no time for a break today."

It *was* hot, probably the hottest day of the year, and Rosie's blouse stuck damply to her back even under the protection of the canvas. But she worked as efficiently as a flawless machine and kept the stalls heaped, with one part of her mind listening in to the parental murmuring about the heat and the tomatoes and with another part planning the exact words she would say to Jesus when he drove up with the first load of the afternoon. But when at last she saw that the pick-up was coming, her hands went berserk and the tomatoes started falling in the wrong stalls, and her father said, "Hey, hey! Rosie, watch what you're doing!"

"Well, I have to go to the *benjo*," she said, hiding panic.

"Go in the weeds over there," he said, only half-joking.

"Oh, Father!" she protested.

"Oh, go on home," her mother said. "We'll make out for awhile."

In the privy Rosie peered through a knothole toward the fields, watching as much as she could of Jesus. Happily she thought she saw him look in the direction of the house from time to time before he finished unloading and went back toward the patch where his mother and father worked. As she was heading for the shed, a very presentable black car purred up the dirt driveway to the house and its driver motioned to her. Was this the Hayashi home, he wanted to know. She nodded. Was she a Hayashi? Yes, she said, thinking that he was a good-looking man. He got out of the car with a huge, flat package and she saw that he warmly wore a business suit. "I have something here for your mother then," he said, in a more elegant Japanese than she was used to.

She told him where her mother was and he came along with her, patting his face with an immaculate white handkerchief and saying something about the coolness of San Francisco. To her surprised mother and father, he bowed and introduced himself as, among other things, the *haiku* editor of the *Mainichi Shimbun*, saying that since he had been coming as far as Los Angeles anyway, he had decided to bring her the first prize she had won in the recent contest.

"First prize?" her mother echoed, believing and not believing, pleased and overwhelmed. Handed the package with a bow, she bobbed her head up and down numerous times to express her utter gratitude.

"It is nothing much," he added, "but I hope it will serve as a token of our great appreciation for your contributions and our great admiration of your considerable talent."

"I am not worthy," she said, falling easily into his style. "It is I who should make some sign of my humble thanks for being permitted to contribute."

"No, no, to the contrary," he said, bowing again.

But Rosie's mother insisted, and then saying that she knew she was being unorthodox, she asked if she might open the package because her curiosity was so great. Certainly she might. In fact, he would like her reaction to it, for personally, it was one of his favorite Hiroshiges.

Rosie thought it was a pleasant picture, which looked to have been sketched with delicate quickness. There were pink clouds, containing some graceful calligraphy, and a sea that was a pale blue except at the edges, containing four sampans with indications of people in them. Pines edged the water and on the far-off beach there was a cluster of thatched huts towered over by pine-dotted mountains of grey and blue. The frame was scalloped and gilt.

After Rosie's mother pronounced it without peer and somewhat prodded her father into nodding agreement, she said Mr. Kuroda must at least have a cup of tea after coming all this way, and although Mr. Kuroda did not want to impose, he soon agreed that a cup of tea would be refreshing and went along with her to the house, carrying the picture for her.

"Ha, your mother's crazy!" Rosie's father said, and Rosie laughed uneasily as she resumed judgment on the tomatoes. She had emptied six lugs when he broke into an imaginary conversation with Jesus to tell her to go and remind her mother of the tomatoes, and she went slowly.

Mr. Kuroda was in his shirtsleeves expounding some *haiku* theory as he munched a rice cake, and her mother was rapt. Abashed in the great man's presence, Rosie stood next to her mother's chair until her mother looked up inquiringly, and then she started to whisper the message, but her mother pushed her gently away and reproached, "You are not being very polite to our guest."

"Father says the tomatoes. . . ." Rosie said aloud, smiling foolishly.

"Tell him I shall only be a minute," her mother said, speaking the language of Mr. Kuroda.

When Rosie carried the reply to her father, he did not seem to hear and she said again, "Mother says she'll be back in a minute."

"All right, all right," he nodded, and they worked again in silence. But suddenly, her father uttered an incredible noise, exactly like the cork of a bottle popping, and the next Rosie knew, he was stalking angrily toward the house, almost running in fact, and she chased after him crying, "Father! Father! What are you going to do?"

He stopped long enough to order her back to the shed. "Never mind!" he shouted. "Get on with the sorting!"

And from the place in the fields where she stood, frightened and vacillating, Rosie saw her father enter the house. Soon Mr. Kuroda came out alone, putting on his coat. Mr. Kuroda got into his car and backed out down the driveway onto the highway. Next her father emerged, also alone, something in his arms (it was the picture, she realized), and, going over to the bathhouse woodpile, he threw the picture on the ground and picked up the axe. Smashing the picture, glass and all (she heard the explosion faintly), he reached over for the kerosene that was used to encourage the bath fire and poured it over the wreckage. I am dreaming, Rosie said to herself, I am dreaming, but her father, having made sure that his act of cremation was irrevocable, was even then returning to the fields.

Rosie ran past him and toward the house. What had become of her mother? She burst into the parlor and found her mother at the back window watching the dying fire. They watched together until there remained only a feeble smoke under the blazing sun. Her mother was very calm.

"Do you know why I married your father?" she said without turning.

"No," said Rosie. It was the most frightening question she had ever been called upon to answer. Don't tell me now, she wanted to say, tell me tomorrow, tell me next week, don't tell me today. But she knew she would be told now, that the telling would combine with the other violence of the hot afternoon to level her life, her world to the very ground.

It was like a story out of the magazines illustrated in sepia, which she had consumed so greedily for a period until the information had somehow reached her that those wretchedly unhappy autobiographies, offered to her as the testimonials of living men and women, were largely inventions: Her mother, at nineteen, had come to America and married her father as an alternative to suicide.

At eighteen she had been in love with the first son of one of the well-to-do families in her village. The two had met whenever and wherever they could, secretly, because it would not have done for his family to see him favor her—her father had no money; he was a drunkard and a gambler besides. She had learned she was with child; an excellent match had already been arranged for her lover. Despised by her family, she had given premature birth to a stillborn son, who would be seventeen now. Her family did not turn her out, but she could no longer project herself in any direction without refreshing in them the memory of her indiscretion. She wrote to Aunt Taka, her favorite sister in America, threatening to kill herself if Aunt Taka would not send for her. Aunt Taka hastily arranged a marriage with a young man of whom she knew, but lately arrived from Japan, a young man of simple mind, it was said, but of kindly heart. The young man was never told why his unseen betrothed was so eager to hasten the day of meeting.

The story was told perfectly, with neither groping for words nor untoward passion. It was as though her mother had memorized it by heart, reciting it to herself so many times over that its nagging vileness had long since gone.

"I had a brother then?" Rosie asked, for this was what seemed to matter now; she would think about the other later, she assured herself, pushing back the illumination which threatened all that darkness that had hitherto been merely mysterious or even glamorous. "A half-brother?"

"Yes."

"I would have liked a brother," she said.

Suddenly, her mother knelt on the floor and took her by the wrists. "Rosie," she said urgently, "Promise me you will never marry!" Shocked more by the request than the revelation, Rosie stared at her mother's face. Jesus, Jesus, she called silently, not certain whether she was invoking the help of the son of the Carrascos or of God, until there returned sweetly the memory of Jesus' hand, how it had touched her and where. Still her mother waited for an answer, holding her wrists so tightly that her hands were going numb. She tried to pull free. Promise, her mother whispered fiercely, promise. Yes, yes, I promise, Rosie said. But for an instant she turned away, and her mother, hearing the familiar glib agreement, released her. Oh, you, you, you, her eyes and twisted mouth said, you fool. Rosie, covering her face, began at last to cry, and the embrace and consoling hand came much later than she expected. [1988]

## 🦎 66

# *A Long Story*

BETH BRANT

*Dedicated to my Great-Grandmothers*
*Eliza Powless and Catherine Brant*

*"About 40 Indian children took the train at this depot for the Philadelphia Indian School last Friday. They were accompanied by the government agent, and seemed a bright looking lot."*
—*The Northern Observer*
(Massena, New York, July 20, 1892)

*"I am only beginning to understand what it means for a mother to lose a child."*
—Anna Demeter, *Legal Kidnapping*
(Beacon Press, Boston, 1977)

### *1890*

It has been two days since they came and took the children away. My body is greatly chilled. All our blankets have been used to bring me warmth. The women keep the fire blazing. The men sit. They talk among themselves. We are frightened by this sudden child-stealing. We signed papers, the agent said. This gave them rights to take our babies. It is good for them, the agent said. It will make them civilized, the agent said. I do not know *civilized.*

I hold myself tight in fear of flying apart in the air. The others try to feed me. Can they feed a dead woman? I have stopped talking. When my mouth opens, only air escapes. I have used up my sound screaming their names—She Sees Deer! He Catches The Leaves! My eyes stare at the room, the walls of scrubbed wood, the floor of dirt. I know there are people here, but I cannot see them. I see a darkness, like the lake at New Moon. Black, unmoving. In the center, a picture of my son and daughter being lifted onto the train. My daughter wearing the

dark blue, heavy dress. All of the girls dressed alike. Never have I seen such eyes! They burn into my head even now. My son. His hair cut. Dressed as the white men, his arms and legs covered by cloth that made him sweat. His face, streaked with tears. So many children crying, screaming. The sun on our bodies, our heads. The train screeching like a crow, sounding like laughter. Smoke and dirt pumping out the insides of the train. So many people. So many children. The women, standing as if in prayer, our hands lifted, reaching. The dust sifting down on our palms. Our palms making motions at the sky. Our fingers closing like the claws of the bear.

I see this now. The hair of my son held in my hands. I rub the strands, the heavy braids coming alive as the fire flares and casts a bright light on the black hair. They slip from my fingers and lie coiled on the ground. I see this. My husband picks up the braids, wraps them in cloth; he takes the pieces of our son away. He walks outside, the eyes of the people on him. I see this. He will find a bottle and drink with the men. Some of the women will join him. They will end the night by singing or crying. It is all the same. I see this. No sounds of children playing games and laughing. Even the dogs have ceased their noise. They lay outside each doorway, waiting. I hear this. The voices of children. They cry. They pray. They call me. *Nisten ha.* I hear this. *Nisten ha.**

### *1978*

I am wakened by the dream. In the dream my daughter is dead. Her father is returning her body to me in pieces. He keeps her heart. I thought I screamed . . . *Patricia!* I sit up in bed, swallowing air as if for nourishment. The dream remains in the air. I rise to go to her room. Ellen tries to lead me back to bed, but I have to see once again. I open her door. She is gone. The room empty, lonely. They said it was in her best interests. How can that be? She is only six, a baby who needs her mothers. She loves us. This has not happened. I will not believe this. Oh god, I think I have died.

Night after night, Ellen holds me as I shake. Our

---

*Mother.

sobs stifling the air in our room. We lie in our bed and try to give comfort. My mind can't think beyond last week when she left. I would have killed him if I'd had the chance! He took her hand and pulled her to the car. The look in his eyes of triumph. It was a contest to him, Patricia the prize. He will teach her to hate us. He will! I see her dear face. That face looking out the back window of his car. Her mouth forming the words *Mommy, Mama*. Her dark braids tied with red yarn. Her front teeth missing. Her overalls with the yellow flower on the pocket, embroidered by Ellen's hands. So lovingly she sewed the yellow wool. Patricia waiting quietly until she was finished. Ellen promising to teach her designs — chain stitch, french knot, split stitch. How Patricia told everyone that Ellen made the flower just for her. So proud of her overalls.

I open the closet door. Almost everything is gone. A few things hang there limp, abandoned. I pull a blue dress from the hanger and take it back to my room. Ellen tries to take it from me, but I hold on, the soft blue cotton smelling of my daughter. How is it possible to feel such pain and live? "Ellen?!" She croons my name. "Mary, Mary, I love you." She sings me to sleep.

## 1890

The agent was here to deliver a letter. I screamed at him and sent curses his way. I threw dirt in his face as he mounted his horse. He thinks I'm a crazy woman and warns me, "You better settle down Annie." What can they do to me? I am a crazy woman. This letter hurts my hand. It is written in their hateful language. It is evil, but there is a message for me.

I start the walk up the road to my brother. He works for the whites and understands their meanings. I think about my brother as I pull the shawl closer to my body. It is cold now. Soon there will be snow. The corn has been dried and hangs from our cabin, waiting to be used. The corn never changes. My brother is changed. He says that *I* have changed and bring shame to our clan. He says I should accept the fate. But I do not believe in the fate of child-stealing. There is evil here. There is much wrong in our village. My brother says I am a crazy woman because I howl at the sky every evening. He is a fool.

I am calling the children. He says the people are becoming afraid of me because I talk to the air and laugh like the raven overhead. But I am talking to the children. They need to hear the sound of me. I laugh to cheer them. They cry for us.

This letter burns my hands. I hurry to my brother. He has taken the sign of the wolf from over the doorway. He pretends to be like those who hate us. He gets more and more like the child-stealers. His eyes move away from mine. He takes the letter from me and begins the reading of it. I am confused. This letter is from two strangers with the names Martha and Daniel. They say they are learning civilized ways. Daniel works in the fields, growing food for the school. Martha cooks and is being taught to sew aprons. She will be going to live with the schoolmaster's wife. She will be a live-in girl. What is a *live-in girl?* I shake my head. The words sound the same to me. I am afraid of Martha and Daniel, these strangers who know my name. My hands and arms are becoming numb.

I tear the letter from my brother's fingers. He stares at me, his eyes traitors in his face. He calls after me, "Annie! Annie!" That is not my name! I run to the road. That is not my name! There is no Martha! There is no Daniel! This is witch work. The paper burns and burns. At my cabin, I quickly dig a hole in the field. The earth is hard and cold, but I dig with my nails. I dig, my hands feeling weaker. I tear the paper and bury the scraps. As the earth drifts and settles, the names Martha and Daniel are covered. I look to the sky and find nothing but endless blue. My eyes are blinded by the color. I begin the howling.

## 1978

When I get home from work, there is a letter from Patricia. I make coffee and wait for Ellen, pacing the rooms of our apartment. My back is sore from the line, bending over and over, screwing the handles on the doors of the flashy cars moving by. My work protects me from questions, the guys making jokes at my expense. But some of them touch my shoulder lightly and briefly as a sign of understanding. The few women, eyes averted or smiling in sympathy. No one talks. There is no time to talk. No room to talk, the noise taking up all space and breath.

I carry the letter with me as I move from room to room. Finally I sit at the kitchen table, turning the paper around in my hands. Patricia's printing is large and uneven. The stamp has been glued on halfheartedly and is coming loose. Each time a letter arrives, I dread it, even as I long to hear from my child. I hear Ellen's key in the door. She walks into the kitchen, bringing the smell of the hospital with her. She comes toward me, her face set in new lines, her uniform crumpled and stained, her brown hair pulled back in an imitation of a french twist. She knows there is a letter. I kiss her and bring mugs of coffee to the table. We look at each other. She reaches for my hand, bringing it to her lips. Her hazel eyes are steady in her round face.

I open the letter. *Dear Mommy. I am fine. Daddy got me a new bike. My big teeth are coming in. We are going to see Grandma for my birthday. Daddy got me new shoes. Love, Patricia.* She doesn't ask about Ellen. I imagine her father standing over her, coaxing her, coaching her. The letter becomes ugly. I tear it in bits and scatter them out the window. The wind scoops the pieces into a tight fist before strewing them in the street. A car drives over the paper, shredding it to garbage and mud.

Ellen makes a garbled sound. "I'll leave. If it will make it better, I'll leave." I quickly hold her as the dusk moves into the room and covers us. "Don't leave. Don't leave." I feel her sturdy back shiver against my hands. She kisses my throat, and her arms tighten as we move closer. "Ah Mary, I love you so much." As the tears threaten our eyes, the taste of salt is on our lips and tongues. We stare into ourselves, touching the place of pain, reaching past the fear, the guilt, the anger, the loneliness.

We go to our room. It is beautiful again. I am seeing it new. The sun is barely there. The colors of cream, brown, green mixing with the wood floor. The rug with its design of wild birds. The black ash basket glowing on the dresser, holding a bouquet of dried flowers bought at a vendor's stand. I remember the old woman, laughing and speaking rapidly in Polish as she wrapped the blossoms in newspaper. Ellen undresses me as I cry. My desire for her breaking through the heartbreak we share. She pulls the covers back, smoothing the white sheets, her hands repeating the gestures done at work. She

guides me onto the cool material. I watch her remove the uniform of work. An aide to nurses. A healer of spirit.

She comes to me in full flesh. My hands are taken with the curves and soft roundness of her. She covers me with the beating of her heart. The rhythm steadies me. Her heat is centering me. I am grounded by the peace between us. I smile at her face above me, round like a moon, her long hair loose and touching my breasts. I take her breast in my hand, bring it to my mouth, suck her as a woman—in desire, in faith. Our bodies join. Our hair braids together on the pillow. Brown, black, silver, catching the last light of the sun. We kiss, touch, move to our place of power. Her mouth, moving over my body, stopping at curves and swells of skin, kissing, removing pain. Closer, close, together, woven, my legs are heat, the center of my soul is speaking to her, I am sliding into her, her mouth is medicine, her heart is the earth, we are dancing with flying arms, I shout, I sing, I weep salty liquid, sweet and warm it coats her throat. This is my life. I love you Ellen, I love you Mary, I love, we love.

## 1891

The moon is full. The air is cold. This cold strikes at my flesh as I remove my clothes and set them on fire in the withered corn field. I cut my hair, the knife sawing through the heavy mass. I bring the sharp blade to my arms, legs, and breasts. The blood trickles like small red rivers down my body. I feel nothing. I throw the tangled webs of my hair into the flames. The smell, like a burning animal, fills my nostrils. As the fire stretches to touch the stars, the people come out to watch me—the crazy woman. The ice in the air touches me.

They caught me as I tried to board the train and search for my babies. The white men tell my husband to watch me. I am dangerous. I laugh and laugh. My husband is good only for tipping bottles and swallowing anger. He looks at me, opening his mouth and making no sound. His eyes are dead. He wanders from the cabin and looks out on the corn. He whispers our names. He calls after the children. He is a dead man.

Where have they taken the children? I ask the question of each one who travels the road past our door. The women come and we talk. We ask and ask. They say there is nothing we can do. The white man is like a ghost. He slips in and out where we cannot see. Even in our dreams he comes to take away our questions. He works magic that resists our medicine. This magic has made us weak. What is the secret about them? Why do they want our children? They sent the Blackrobes many years ago to teach us new magic. It was evil! They lied and tricked us. They spoke of gods who would forgive us if we believed as they do. They brought the rum with the cross. This god is ugly! He killed our masks. He killed our men. He sends the women screaming at the moon in terror. They want our power. They take our children to remove the inside of them. Our power. They steal our food, our sacred rattle, the stories, our names. What is left?

I am a crazy woman. I look to the fire that consumes my hair and see their faces. My daughter. My son. They still cry for me, though the sound grows fainter. The wind picks up their keening and brings it to me. The sound has bored into my brain. I begin howling. At night I dare not sleep. I fear the dreams. It is too terrible, the things that happen there. In my dream there is wind and blood moving as a stream. Red, dark blood in my dream. Rushing for our village. The blood moves faster. There are screams of wounded people. Animals are dead, thrown in the blood stream. There is nothing left. Only the air echoing nothing. Only the earth soaking up blood, spreading it in the four directions, becoming a thing there is no name for. I stand in the field watching the fire, The People watching me. We are waiting, but the answer is not clear yet. A crazy woman. That is what they call me.

*1979*

After taking a morning off work to see my lawyer, I come home, not caring if I call in. Not caring, for once, at the loss in pay. Not caring. My lawyer says there is nothing more we can do. I must wait. As if there has been something other than waiting. He has custody and calls the shots. We must wait and see how long it takes for him to get tired of being a mommy and a daddy. So, I wait.

I open the door to Patricia's room. Ellen and I keep it dusted and cleaned in case my baby will be

allowed to visit us. The yellow and blue walls feel like a mockery. I walk to the windows, begin to systematically tear down the curtains. I slowly start to ripe the cloth apart. I enjoy hearing the sounds of destruction. Faster, I tear the material into strips. What won't come apart with my hands, I pull at with my teeth. Looking for more to destroy, I gather the sheets and bedspread in my arms and wildly shred them to pieces. Grunting and sweating, I am pushed by rage and the searing wound in my soul. Like a wolf, caught in a trap, gnawing at her own leg to set herself free, I begin to beat my breasts to deaden the pain inside. A noise gathers in my throat and finds the way out. I begin a scream that turns to howling, then becomes hoarse choking. I want to take my fists, my strong fists, my brown fists, and smash the world until it bleeds. Bleeds! And all the judges in their flapping robes, and the fathers who look for revenge, are ground, ground into dust and disappear with the wind.

The word *lesbian*. Lesbian. The word that makes them panic, makes them afraid, makes them destroy children. The word that dares them. Lesbian. *I am one*. Even for Patricia, even for her, *I will not cease to be!* As I kneel amidst the colorful scraps, Raggedy Anns smiling up at me, my chest gives a sigh. My heart slows to its normal speech. I feel the blood pumping outward to my veins, carrying nourishment and life. I strip the room naked. I close the door.                                    [1985]

## 🌿 67

## *"Don't You Talk About My Mama!"*

JUNE JORDAN

I got up that morning, with malice toward no one. Drank my coffee and scanned the front page of *The New York Times*. And there it was. I remember, even now, the effrontery of that headline four years ago: "Breakup of Black Family Imperils Gains of Decades." I could hardly believe it. Here were these clowns dumping on us yet again. That was 1983, three years into the shameless Real Deal of Ronald Reagan. He'd taken or he'd shaken everything we Black folks needed just to hang in here, breathing in and out. And yet the headline absolutely failed to give credit where it was due. Instead, "politicians and scholars—black and white" dared to identify the *victims*—the Black single mothers raising 55 percent of all of our Black children *with no help from anybody anywhere*—as the cause of Black poverty! These expense-account professionals presumed to identify "the family crisis" of Black folks as "a threat to the future of Black people without equal." And this was not somebody's weird idea about how to say "thank you." (I could relate to that: somebody finally saying thank you to Black women!) No: This was just another dumb, bold insult to my mother.

Now when I was growing up, the one sure trigger to a down-and-out fight was to say something—anything—about somebody's mother. As a matter of fact, we refined things eventually to the point where you didn't have to get specific. All you had to do was push into the face of another girl or boy, close as you could, almost nose to nose, and just spit out the two words: "Your mother!" This item of our code of honor was not negotiable, and clearly we took it pretty seriously: Even daring to refer to someone's mother put you off-limits. From the time you learned how to talk, everybody's mama remained the holiest of holies. And we did not ever forget it, this fact, that the first, the last and the most, that the number-one persevering, resourceful, resilient and devoted person in our lives was, and would always be, your mother and my mother.

But sometimes, as you know, we grow up without growing wise. Sometimes we become so sophisticated we have to read *The New York Times* in order to figure out whether it's a hot or a rainy day. We read the fine print in order to find out the names of our so-called leaders. But what truly surprises me is Black folks listening to a whole lot of white blasphemy against Black feats of survival, Black folks paying attention to people who never even notice us except to describe us as "female-headed" or something equally weird. (I would like to know, for a fact,

has anybody ever seen a female-headed anything at all? What did it look like? What did it do?)

Now I am not opposed to sophistication per se, but when you lose touch with your mama, when you take the word of an absolute, hostile stranger over and above the unarguable truth of your own miraculous, hard-won history, and when you don't remember to ask, again and again, "Compared to what?" I think you don't need to worry about enemies anymore. You'd better just worry about yourself.

Back in 1965, Daniel P. Moynihan (now a U.S. senator from New York) issued a broadside insult to the national Black community. With the full support of a Democratic administration that was tired of Negroes carrying on about citizenship rights and integration and white racist violence, Moynihan came through with the theory that we, Black folks, and we, Black women in particular, constituted "the problem." And now there are Black voices joining the choruses of the absurd. There are national Black organizations and purported Black theoreticians who have become indistinguishable from the verified enemies of Black folks in this country. These sophisticated Black voices jump to the forefront of delighted mass-media exposure because they are willing to lament and to defame the incredible triumph of Black women, the victory of Black mothers that is the victory of our continuation as a people in America.

Archly delivering jargon phrases about "the collapse of Black family structure" and "the destructive culture of poverty in the ghetto" and, of course, "the crisis of female-headedness," with an additional screaming reference to "the shame of teenage pregnancy," these Black voices come to us as the disembodied blatherings of peculiar offspring: Black men and women who wish to deny the Black mother of their origins and who wish to adopt white Daniel P. Moynihan as their father. I happen to lack the imagination necessary to forgive, or understand, this phenomenon. But the possible consequences of this oddball public outcry demand our calm examination.

According to these new Black voices fathered by Mr. Moynihan, it would seem that the Black family subsists in a terrible, deteriorating state. That's the problem. The source of the problem is The Black Family (that is, it is not white; it suffers from "female-headedness"). The solution to The Black Family Problem is—you guessed it—The Black Family. It must become more white—more patriarchal, less "female-headed," more employed more steadily at better and better-paying jobs.

Now I would agree that the Black family is not white. I do not agree that the problem is "female-headedness." I would rather suggest that the problem is that women in general and that Black women in particular cannot raise our children and secure adequately paying jobs because this is a society that hates women and that believes we are replaceable, that we are dispensable, ridiculous, irksome facts of life. American social and economic hatred of women means that any work primarily identified as women's work will be poorly paid, if at all. Any work open to women will be poorly paid, at best, in comparison to work open to men. Any work done by women will receive a maximum of 64 cents on the dollar compared with wages for the same work done by men. Prenatal, well-baby care, day care for children, children's allowances, housing allowances for parents, paid maternity leave—all of the elemental provisions for the equally entitled citizenship of women and children are ordinary attributes of industrialized nations, except for one: the United States.

The problem, clearly, does not originate with women in general or Black women specifically, who, whether it's hard or whether it's virtually impossible, nevertheless keep things together. Our hardships follow from the uncivilized political and economic status enjoined upon women and children in our country, which has the highest infant mortality rate among its industrial peers. And, evidently, feels fine, thank you, about that. (Not incidentally, Black infant-mortality rates hold at levels twice that for whites.)

The Black Family persists *despite* the terrible deteriorating state of affairs prevailing in the United States. This is a nation unwilling and progressively unable to provide for the well-being of most of its citizens: Our economic system increasingly concentrates our national wealth in the hands of fewer and fewer interest groups. Our economic system increasingly augments the wealth of the richest sector of the citizenry, while it diminishes the real wages and the available livelihood of the poor. Our economic system refuses responsibility for the equitable sharing of national services and monies among its various peoples. Our economic system remains insensitive to the political demands of a democracy, and therefore it does not yield to the requirements of equal entitlement of all women and all children and Black, Hispanic and Native American men, the elderly and the disabled. If you total the American people you have an obvious majority of Americans squeezed outside the putative benefits of "free enterprise."

Our economic system continues its trillion-dollar commitment *not* to the betterment of the lives of its citizens but, rather, to the development and lunatic replication of a military-industrial complex. In this context, then, the Black family persists, yes, in a terrible deteriorating state. But we did not create this state. Nor do we control it. And we are not suffering "collapse." Change does not signify collapse. The nuclear, patriarchal family structure of white America was never our own; it was not *African*. And when we arrived to slavery here, why or how should we have emulated the overseer and the master? We who were counted in the Constitution as three-fifths of a human being? We who could by law neither marry nor retain our children against the predations of the slave economy? Nonetheless, from under the whip through underpaid underemployment and worse, Black folks have formulated our own family, our own home base for nurture and for pride. We have done this through extended kinship methods. And even Black teenage parents are trying, in their own way, to perpetuate the Black family.

The bizarre analysis of the Black family that blames the Black family for being not white and not patriarchal, not endowed with steadily employed Black husbands and fathers who enjoy access to middle-income occupations is just that: a bizarre analysis, a heartless joke. If Black men and Black women *wanted* Black men to become patriarchs of their families, if Black men wanted to function as head of the house—shouldn't they probably have some kind of a job? Can anyone truly dare to suggest that the catastrophic 46-percent unemployment rate now crippling working-age Black men is something that either Black men or Black women view as positive or desirable? Forty-six percent! What is the meaning of a man in the house if he cannot hold out his hand to help his family make it through the month, and if he cannot hold up his head with the pride and authority that regular, satisfying work for good pay provides? How or whom shall he marry and on what basis? Is it honestly puzzling to anyone that the 46-percent, Depression-era rate of unemployment that imprisons Black men almost exactly mirrors the 50 percent of Black households now maintained by Black women? Our Black families persist despite a racist arrangement of rewards such as the fact that the median Black family has only about 56 cents to spend for every dollar that white families have to spend. And a Black college graduate still cannot realistically expect to earn more than a white high-school graduate.

We, children and parents of Black families, neither created nor do we control the terrible, deteriorating state of our unjust and meanly discriminating national affairs. In its structure, the traditional Black family has always reflected our particular jeopardy within these unwelcome circumstances. We have never been "standard" or predictable or stabilized in any normative sense, even as our Black lives have never been standard or predictable or stabilized in a benign national environment. We have been flexible, ingenious and innovative or we have perished. And we have not perished. We remain and we remain different, and we have become necessarily deft at distinguishing between the negative differences—those imposed upon us—and the positive differences—those that joyously attest to our distinctive, survivalist attributes as a people.

Today we must distinguish between responsibility and consequence. We are not responsible for the systematic underemployment and unemployment of Black men or women. We are not responsible for racist hatred of us, and we are not responsible for the American contempt for women per se. We are not responsible for a dominant value system that quibbles over welfare benefits for chil-

dren and squanders deficit billions of dollars on American pie in the sky. But we must outlive the consequences of this inhumane, disposable-life ideology. We have no choice. And because this ideology underpins our economic system and the political system that supports our economy, we no longer constitute a minority inside America. We are joined in our precarious quandary here by all women and by children, Hispanic Americans and Native Americans and the quickly expanding population of the aged, as well as the temporarily or permanently disabled.

At issue now is the "universal entitlement" of American citizens (as author Ruth Sidel terms it in her important book *Women and Children Last: The Plight of Poor Women in Affluent America* [Viking Press, 1986]): What should American citizenship confer? What are the duties of the state in relation to the citizens it presumes to tax and to govern?

It is not the Black family in crisis but American democracy in crisis when the majority of our people oppose U.S. intervention in Central America and, nevertheless, the President proceeds to intervene. It is not the Black family in crisis but American democracy at stake when the majority of our people abhor South African apartheid and, nonetheless, the President proceeds to collaborate with the leadership of that evil. It is not the Black family in crisis but American democracy at risk when a majority of American citizens may no longer assume that social programs beneficial to them will be preserved and/or developed.

But if we, Black children and parents, have been joined by so many others in our precarious quandary here, may we not also now actively join with these other jeopardized Americans to redefine and to finally secure universal entitlement of citizenship that will at last conclude the shameful American history of our oppression? And what should these universal entitlements—our new American Bill of Rights—include?

1. Guaranteed jobs and/or guaranteed income to ensure each and every American in each and every one of the 50 states an existence *above* the poverty line.

2. Higher domestic minimum wages and, for the sake of both our narrowest and broadest self-interests, a coordinated, international minimum wage so that exhausted economic exploitation in Detroit can no longer be replaced by economic exploitation in Taiwan or Soweto or Manila.

3. Government guarantees of an adequate minimum allowance for every child regardless of the marital status of the parents.

4. Equal pay for equal work.

5. Affirmative action to ensure broadly democratic access to higher-paying occupations.

6. Compensation for "women's work" equal to compensation for "men's work."

7. Housing allowances and/or state commitments to build and/or to subsidize acceptable, safe and affordable housing for every citizen.

8. Comprehensive, national health insurance from prenatal through geriatric care.

9. Availability of state education and perpetual reeducation through graduate levels of study on the basis of student interest and aptitude rather than financial capacity.

10. A national budget that will invariably commit the main portion of our collective monies to our collective domestic needs for a good life.

11. Comprehensive provision for the well-being of all our children commensurate with the kind of future we are hoping to help construct. These provisions must include paid maternity and paternity leave and universal, state-controlled, public child-care programs for working parents.

12. Nationalization of vital industries to protect citizen consumers and citizen workers alike from the greed-driven vagaries of a "free market."

13. Aggressive nuclear-disarmament policies and, concurrently, aggressive state protection of what's left of the life-supportive elements of our global environment.

I do not believe that a just, a civilized nation can properly regard any one of these 13 entitlements as optional. And yet not one of them is legally in place in the United States. And why not? I think that, as a people, we have yet to learn how to say thank you in real ways to those who have loved us enough to keep us alive despite inhumane and unforgivable opposition to our well-being. For myself, I do not need any super-sophisticated charts and magical graphs to tell me my own mama done better than she could, and my mama's mama, *she* done better than I could. And *everybody's mama* done better than anybody had any right to expect she would. And that's the truth!

And I hope you've been able to follow my meaning. And a word to the wise, they say, should be sufficient. So, I'm telling you real nice: Don't you talk about my mama! [1987]

 68

# *Working at Single Bliss*

MARY HELEN WASHINGTON

*I*

*Apart from the forest*
*have you seen*
*that a tree alone*
*will often take inventive form . . .*
—Paulette Childress White
"A Tree Alone"

*She who has chosen her Self, who defines her Self, by choice, neither in relation to children nor men; who is Self-identified, is a Spinster, a whirling dervish spinning in a new time/space.* —Mary Daly
*Gyn/Ecology* (Beacon Press)

Last year I was asked to be on the "Tom Cottle Show," a syndicated television program that originates here in Boston. The psychiatrist-host wanted to interview six single women about their singleness. I hesitated only a moment before refusing. Six single women discussing the significance of their lives? No, I instinctively knew that the interview would end up being an interrogation of six unmarrieds (a pejorative, like coloreds)—women trying to rationalize lives of loss. Losers at the marriage game. *Les femmes manqués.*

I watched the program they put together without me, and sure enough, Cottle asked a few perfunctory questions about singleness and freedom, and then moved on rapidly to the real killer questions. I found it painful to watch these very fine women trapped in the net he'd laid. "Don't you ever come home from these glamorous lives of freedom [read selfishness] and sit down to dinner alone and just cry?" "What about sex?" "What about children?" The women struggled to answer these insulting questions with dignity and humor, but clearly the game was rigged against them. Imagine the interviewer lining up six couples and asking them the same kinds of questions: "Well, what about your sex lives?" "Why don't you have any children?" (or "Why do you have so many?") "Don't you ever come home at night, sit down to dinner, and wonder why you ever married the person on the other side of the table?" Of course, this interview would never take place—the normal restraint and politeness that are reserved for people whose positions are socially acceptable assure married folks some measure of protection and, at least, common decency.

"You're so lucky, footloose and fancy-free, with no responsibilities," a friend with two children once said to me. Ostensibly that's a compliment, or at least, it's supposed to be. But underneath it is really a critique of single people, implying that their lives do not have the moral stature of a life with "responsibilities." It's a comment that used to leave me feeling a little like a kid, a failed adult; for what's an adult with no responsibilities? A kid. I have had to learn to recognize and reject the veiled contempt in this statement because, of course, single people do have responsibilities.

At age 40, I have been a single adult for 20 years. No, I am neither widowed nor divorced. I am single in the pristine sense of that word—which unleashes that basic fear in all of us, "What will I do if I'm left by myself?" As I have more or less successfully dealt with that fear over the years, I am somewhat indignant at being cast as an irresponsible gadfly, unencumbered by the problems of Big People. I have earned a living and "kept myself," and I have done that without being either male or white in a world dominated by men and corroded by racism. I've sat up nights with students' papers and even later with their problems. Without any of the social props married people have, I have given many memorable parties. Like my aunts before me, I've celebrated the births, birthdays, first communions, graduations, football games, and track meets of my 10 nephews. And not a hair on my mother's head changes color without my noticing it.

As Zora Hurston's Janie says, "Two things everybody's got tuh do fuh theyselves. They got tuh go tuh God, and they got tuh find out about livin' fuh theyselves." If anything, a single person may be more aware of the responsibility to discover and create meaning in her life, to find community, to honor her creativity, to live out her values, than the person whose life is circumferenced by an immediate and intimate family life.

## II

*To be single and busy—nothing bad in that. Such people do much good.*

—Elizabeth Hardwick
*Sleepless Nights* (Random House)

To some extent my adolescent imagination was bewitched by the myth that marriage is *the* vertical choice in a woman's life—one that raises her status, completes her life, fulfills her dreams, and makes her a valid person in society. In the 1950s, all the movies, all the songs directed us to this one choice: to find our worldly prince and go two by two into the ark. Nothing else was supposed to matter quite as much and it was a surprise to discover that something else matters just as much, sometimes more.

But in spite of the romance-marriage-motherhood bombardment, I grew up in a kind of war-free zone where I heard the bombs and artillery all around me but was spared from a direct attack. I was raised in two very separate but mutually supportive communities—one black, one Catholic, both of which taught me that a woman could be her own person in the world.

In the all-women's Catholic high school and college in Cleveland, Ohio, where I put in eight formative years, we were required to think of ourselves as women with destinies, women whose achievements mattered—whether we chose marriage or religious life or, as it was called then, a life of "single blessedness." In fact, marriage and the single life seemed to my convent-honed ninth-grade mind to have a clearly equal status: they were both inferior to the intrinsically superior religious life.

The program of spiritual, intellectual, social, and physical development the nuns demanded of us allowed an involvement with myself I craved even in the ninth grade. *Some* dating was encouraged at Notre Dame Academy (ninth through twelfth grades)—not as a consuming emotional involvement but as part of a "normal social development." Boys had their place—on the periphery of one's life. (A girl who came to school with her boyfriend's taped class ring on her finger was subject to expulsion.) You were expected to be the central, dominant figure in the fabric of your own life.

The nuns themselves were vivid illustrations of that principle. For me they were the most powerful images of women imaginable—not ladies-in-waiting, not submissive homebodies, not domestic drudges, not deviants. They ran these women-dominated universes with aplomb and authority. Even if "Father" appeared on Monday morning for our weekly religious lesson, his appearance was tolerated as a kind of necessary token of the male hierarchy, and, when he left, the waters ran back together, leaving no noticeable trace of his presence.

Nuns were the busiest people I knew then. No matter how graceful and dignified the pace, they always seemed to be hurrying up and down the corridors of Notre Dame planning something important and exciting. Sister Wilbur directed dramatics and went to New York occasionally to see the latest Off-Broadway productions. Sister Kathryn Ann wrote poetry and went to teach in Africa. Another sister coached debate and took our winning teams to state championships in Columbus. Though technically nuns are not single, they do not have that affiliation with a male figure to establish their status. (After Mary Daly it should not be necessary to point out that God is not a man.) They also have to ward off the same stigma of being different from the norm as single people do. So it's only a little ironic that I got some of my sense of how a woman could be complete and autonomous and comfortable in the world—*sans* marriage—from the Sisters of Notre Dame.

The message I got from the black community about single life was equally forceful. So many black girls heard these words, they might have been programmed tapes: "Girl, get yourself an education, you can't count on a man to take care of you." "An education is something no one can take from you." "Any fool can get married, but not everyone can go to school."

I didn't know it then, but this was my feminist primer. Aim high, they said, because that is the only way a black girl can claim a place in this world. Marriage was a chancy thing, not dependable like diplomas: my mother and aunts and uncles said that even if you married a Somebody—a doctor or a lawyer—there was no assurance that he'd have a good heart or treat you right. They thought that the worst thing a woman could do was to get into financial dependency with a man—and it was not that they hated or distrusted men so much as they distrusted any situation that made an already vulnerable woman more powerless.

There was such reverence in my mother's voice for women of achievement that I never connected their social status with anything as mundane as marriage. The first black woman with a Ph.D., the first black woman school principal, the first woman doctor—I knew their names by heart and wanted to be one of them and do important things.

My third-grade teacher, the first black teacher at Parkwood Elementary in Cleveland, Ohio, was a single woman in her thirties. At age nine, I saw her as a tall, majestic creature who wore earrings, drove her own car, and made school pure joy. To my family and the neighborhood, Miss Hilliard was like a totem of our tribe's good fortune: an independent, self-sufficient, educated woman bringing her treasures back to their children. She was a part of that tradition of 19th-century black women whose desire for "race uplift" sent them to teach in the South and to schools like Dunbar High in Washington, D.C., and the School for Colored Youth in Philadelphia. Though many of these women were married, the majority of them were widowed for a great many years and those were often the years of achievement for them.

One of these 19th-century stellar examples, Anna Julia Cooper, dismissed the question of marriage as a false issue. The question should not be "How shall I so cramp, stunt, simplify, and nullify myself as to make me eligible for the horror of being swallowed up into some little man," but how shall a generation of women demand of themselves and of men "the noblest, the grandest and the best" in their capacities.

### III

*In the places of their childhoods, the*
*troubles they had getting grown,*
*the tales of men they told among*
*themselves as we sat unnoted*
*at their feet, we saw some image*
*of a past and future self.*
*The world had loved them even*
*less than their men but this did*
*not keep them from scheming*
*on its favor.*

—Sherley Anne Williams
*Some One Sweet Angel Chile* (William Morrow)

I learned early about being single from my five aunts. By the time I was old enough to notice, four were widowed and one divorced, so from my 12-year-old perspective, they were single women for a good part of their lives. They ran their own households, cooked, entertained, searched for spirituality, helped my mother to raise eight children, traveled some, went to work, cared for the sick, planned picnics. In short, they made up their lives by themselves, inventing the forms that satisfied them. And in the course of their "scheming" they passed on to me something about the rituals and liturgy of single life.

The eldest of these aunts, Aunt Bessie, lived as a single woman for 26 years. Her husband of 40 years died when she was 60 and she began to live alone for the first time since she was 18. She bought a huge old house, painted, decorated, and furnished every room with Oriental rugs and secondhand furniture purchased at estate sales. (Black people discovered this bonanza in the 1940s long before it became a middle-class fad.) She put in a new lawn, grew African violets, and started a whole new life for herself on Ashbury Avenue.

Aunt Bessie was secretly proud of how well she was doing on her own, and she used to tell me slyly how many of these changes she could not have made as a married woman: "Uncle wouldn't have bought this house, baby; he wouldn't have wanted this much space. He wouldn't have changed neighborhoods." She was finally doing exactly what pleased her, and the shape of her life as she had designed it in her singularity was much more varied, dynamic, and daring. What I learned from her is symbolized by that multilevel house on Ashbury Avenue. She had three bedrooms—she needed them for guests; on the third floor she made hats, which she sold for a living; the huge old basement was for her tools and lawn work. All this room was essential to the amount of living she planned to do.

Since she willed all of her furniture to me, my own flat resembles that house in many ways, and her spirit came with the furnishings: I have the sense of inhabiting every corner of my life just as she lived in all 10 rooms of her house. Even my overstocked refrigerator is a reflection of something I learned from her about taking care of your life. Another aunt, Hazel, died only a few years after she was widowed, and I remember Aunt Bessie's explanation of her untimely death as a warning about the perils of not taking your life seriously. "Hazel stopped cooking for herself after her husband died, just ate snacks and junk food instead of making a proper dinner for herself. And she got that cancer and died." The message was clear to me—even at age 12—that single life could be difficult at times and that living it well required some effort, but you were not supposed to let it kill you.

### IV

*[Friendship] is a profound experience which calls forth*
*our humanness and shapes our being. . . . This is true for*
*all persons, but it has a special significance for single per-*
*sons. For it is in the context of friendship that most single*
*persons experience the intimacy and immediacy of others.*

—Francine Cardman
"On Being Single"

Girded up with all of this psychological armament from my past, I still entered adult life without the powerful and sustaining myths and rituals that could provide respect and support for single life. Terms like "old maid" and "spinster," not yet redefined by a feminist consciousness, could still be used to belittle and oppress single women. By the time I was 35, I had participated in scores of marriage ceremonies, and even had begun sending anniversary cards to my married friends. But never once did I think of celebrating the anniversary of a friendship—even one that was by then 25 years old. (Aren't you entitled to gifts of silver at that milestone?)

Once, about 10 years ago, five of us single women from Cleveland took a trip to Mexico together. (Actually only four of the group were single; the fifth, Ernestine, was married and three months pregnant.) I remember that trip as seven days and eight nights of adventure, laughter, discovery, and closeness.

We were such typical tourists—taking snapshots of ancient ruins, posing in front of cathedrals, paying exorbitant sums to see the cliff divers (whose entire act took about 20 seconds), floating down debris-filled waterways to see some totally unnoteworthy sights, learning the hard way that in the hot Acapulco sun even us "killer browns" could get a sunburn. We stayed up at night talking about our lives, our dreams, our careers, our men, and laughing so hard in these late-night sessions that we hardly had the energy for the next morning's tour.

It was the laughter and the good talk (remember Toni Cade Bambara's short story "The Johnson Girls"?) that made the trip seem so complete. It was so perfect that even in the midst of the experience I knew it was to be a precious memory. Years later I asked my friend, Ponchita, why she thought the five of us never planned another trip like that, why we let such good times drift out of our lives without an attempt to recapture them. "Because," she said, "it wasn't enough. It was fun, stimulating, warm, exciting, but it wasn't 'The Thing That Made Life Complete,' and it wasn't leading us in that direction; I guess it was a little like 'recess.'" We wanted nests, not excitement. We wanted domestic bliss, not lives lived at random, no matter how thrilling, how wonderful. So there was the potential—those "dependable and immediate supports" existed. But without the dependable myths to accompany them, we couldn't seriously invest ourselves in those experiences.

When my friend Meg suggested we celebrate Mother's Day this year with a brunch for all our single, childless women friends, and bring pictures of the nieces and nephews we dote on, I recognized immediately the psychic value in honoring our own form of caretaking. We were establishing rituals by which we could ceremonially acknowledge our particular social identities.

My oldest friend Ponchita and I did exchange gifts last year on the twenty-fifth anniversary of our friendship, and never again will the form "anniversary" mean only a rite (right) of the married. My journey through the single life was beginning to have its own milestones and to be guided by its own cartography.

### V

*A life of pure decision, of thoughtful calculations, every inclination honored. They go about on their own, nicely accompanied in their singularity by the companion of possibility.*

—Elizabeth Hardwick
*Sleepless Nights*

Our Mexico trip was in 1971. In the next 10 years, I earned a Ph.D., became director of black studies at the University of Detroit, edited two anthologies, threw out my makeshift bricks-and-board furniture, began to think about buying a house and adopting a child, and in the process, decided that my life was no longer "on hold." These deliberate choices made me begin to regard my single status as an honorable estate. But you know, when I look back at that checklist of accomplishments and serious life plans, I feel resentful that I had to work so hard for the honor that naturally accompanies the married state. Overcompensation, however, sometimes has its rewards: I had established a reputation in my profession that brought the prospect of a fellowship year at Radcliffe and a new job in Boston.

When I was leaving Detroit, I was acutely aware of my single status. What kind of life was it, I wondered, if you could start all over again in a new city with nothing to show for your past except your furniture and your diplomas? I didn't even have a cat. Where were the signs and symbols of a coherent, meaningful life that others could recognize? What was I doing living at *random* like this? I had made this "pure" decision and was honoring my inclination to live in another city, to take a job that offered excitement and challenge. As I packed boxes alone, signed contracts with moving companies, and said good-bye at numerous dinners and going-away parties to all the friends I had made over 10 years, I felt not so very different from a friend who was moving after separating from his wife: "like a rhinoceros being cut loose from the herd."

I think it was the wide-open, netless freedom of it all that scared me, because I was truly *not* alone. I moved into a triple-decker in Cambridge where I live in a kind of semi-cooperative with two other families. Here, I feel secure, but independent and private. The journalist on the second floor and I read each other's work, and I exchange ideas about teaching methods with the three other professors in the house. We all share meals occasionally; we've met one another's extended families; and we celebrate one another's assorted triumphs. I have put together another network of friends whose lives I feel intimately involved in, and who, like me, are interested in making single life work—not disappear.

But I do not yet have the solid sense of belonging to a community that I had in Cleveland and Detroit, and sometimes I am unsettled by the variousness and unpredictableness of my single life. This simply means that I still have some choices to make—about deepening friendships, about having children (possibly adopting them), about establishing closer ties with the black community in Boston. If and when I do adopt a child, she or he will have a selection of godparents and aunts and uncles as large and varied as I had. That is one of the surest signs of the richness of my single life.

## VI

*You're wondering if I'm lonely:*
*OK then, yes, I'm lonely*
*as a plane rides lonely and level*
*on its radio beam, aiming*
*across the Rockies*
*for the blue-strung aisles*
*of an airfield on the ocean*

—Adrienne Rich
"Song" from *Diving into the Wreck* (Norton)

Last year Elizabeth Stone wrote an article in the *Village Voice* called "A Married Woman" in which she discussed how much her life had changed since she married at the age of 33. Somewhat boastfully, she remarked at the end that she had hardly made any reference in the whole article to her husband. But if a single woman describes her life without reference to romance—no matter how rich and satisfying her life may be, no matter what she says about wonderful friends, exciting work, cultural and intellectual accomplishments—in fact, the *more* she says about these things—the more skeptical people's reactions will be. That one fact—her romantic involvement—if it is not acceptable can cancel out all the rest. This is how society keeps the single woman feeling perilous about her sense of personal success.

Still, everybody wants and needs some kind of special alliance(s) in her life. Some people have alliances called marriage. (I like that word alliance: it keeps marriage in its proper—horizontal—place.) I'd like an alliance with a man who could be a comrade and kindred spirit, and I've had such alliances in the past. Even with the hassles, they were enriching and enjoyable experiences for me, but I have never wanted to forsake my singularity for this kind of emotional involvement. Whatever psychic forces drive me have always steered me toward autonomy and independence, out toward the ocean's expanse and away from the shore.

I don't want to sound so smooth and glib and clear-eyed about it all, because it has taken me more than a decade to get this sense of balance and control. A lot of rosaries and perpetual candles and expensive long-distance calls have gotten me through the hard times when I would have chosen the holy cloister over another day of "single blessedness." The truth is that those hard times were not caused by being single. They were part of every woman's struggle to find commitment and contentment for herself. Singleness does not define me, is not an essential characteristic of me. I simply wish to have it acknowledged as a legitimate way to be in the world. After all, we started using Ms. instead of Mrs. or Miss because *none* of us wanted to be defined by the presence or absence of a man.

*VII*

*Apart from the forest*
*a single tree will sometimes grow awry*
*in brave and extraordinary search*
*for its own shape*

—Paulette Childress White
"A Tree Alone"

When I first started running in 1972, I ran regularly with a man. As long as I had this male companion, the other men passing by either ignored me or gave me slight nods to show their approval of my supervised state. Eventually I got up the nerve to run alone around Detroit's Palmer Park, and then the men came out of the trees to make comments—usually to tell me what I was doing wrong ("Lift your legs higher" or "Stop waving your arms"), or to flirt ("Can I run with you, baby?" was by far the most common remark, though others were nastier).

Once a carload of black teenagers who were parked in the lot at the end of my run started making comments about my physical anatomy, which I started to dismiss as just a dumb teenage ritual. But on this particular day, something made me stop my run, walk over to the car, and say, "You know, when you see a sister out trying to get some exercise, as hard as that is for us, you ought to be trying to support her, because she needs all the help she can get." I didn't know how they would respond, so I was surprised when they apologized, and somewhat shamefaced, one of them said: "Go on, sister; we're with you."

Now, that incident occurred because I was alone, and the image has become part of my self-definition: I am a woman in the world—single and powerful and astonished at my ability to create my own security, "in brave and extraordinary search for my own shape." [1982]

# 69

# *A Marriage Agreement*

ALIX KATES SHULMAN

When my husband and I were first married, a decade ago, keeping house was less a burden than a game. We both worked full-time in New York City, so our small apartment stayed empty most of the day and taking care of it was very little trouble. Twice a month we'd spend Saturday cleaning and doing our laundry at the laundromat. We shopped for food together after work, and though I usually did the cooking, my husband was happy to help. Since our meals were simple and casual, there were few dishes to wash. We occasionally had dinner out and usually ate breakfast at a diner near our offices. We spent most of our free time doing things we enjoyed together, such as taking long walks in the evenings and spending weekends in Central Park. Our domestic life was beautifully uncomplicated.

When our son was born, our domestic life suddenly became *quite* complicated; and two years later, when our daughter was born, it became impossible. We automatically accepted the traditional sex roles that society assigns. My husband worked all day in an office; I left my job and stayed at home, taking on almost all the burdens of housekeeping and child raising.

When I was working I had grown used to seeing people during the day, to having a life outside the home. But now I was restricted to the company of two demanding preschoolers and to the four walls of an apartment. It seemed unfair that while my husband's life had changed little when the children were born, domestic life had become the only life I had.

I tried to cope with the demands of my new situation, assuming that other women were able to handle even larger families with ease and still find time for themselves. I couldn't seem to do that.

We had to move to another apartment to accommodate our larger family, and because of the children, keeping it reasonably neat took several hours a day. I prepared half a dozen meals every day for from one to four people at a time—and everyone ate different food. Shopping for this brood—or even just running out for a quart of milk—meant putting on snowsuits, boots and mittens; getting strollers or carriages up and down the stairs; and scheduling the trip so it would not interfere with one of the children's feeding or nap or illness or some other domestic job. Laundry was now a daily chore. I seemed to be working every minute of the day—and still there were dishes in the sink; still there wasn't time enough to do everything.

Even more burdensome than the physical work of housekeeping was the relentless responsibility I had for my children. I loved them, but they seemed to be taking over my life. There was nothing I could do, or even contemplate, without first considering how they would be affected. As they grew older, just answering their constant questions ruled out even a private mental life. I had once enjoyed reading, but now if there was a moment free, instead of reading for myself, I read to them. I wanted to work on my own writing, but there simply weren't enough hours in the day. I had no time for myself; the children were always *there.*

As my husband's job began keeping him at work later and later—and sometimes taking him out of town—I missed his help and companionship. I wished he would come home at six o'clock and spend time with the children so they could know him better. I continued to buy food with him in mind and dutifully set his place at the table. Yet sometimes whole weeks would go by without his having dinner with us. When he did get home the children often were asleep, and we both were too tired ourselves to do anything but sleep.

We accepted the demands of his work as unavoidable. Like most couples, we assumed that the wife must accommodate to the husband's schedule, since it is his work that brings in the money.

As the children grew older I began free-lance editing at home. I felt I had to squeeze it into my "free" time and not allow it to interfere with my domestic duties or the time I owed my husband—just as he felt he had to squeeze in time for the children during weekends. We were both chronically dissatisfied, but we knew no solutions.

After I had been home with the children for six years I began to attend meetings of the newly formed Women's Liberation Movement in New York City. At these meetings I began to see that my situation was not uncommon; other women too felt drained and frustrated as housewives and mothers. When we started to talk about how we would have chosen to arrange our lives, most of us agreed that even though we might have preferred something

different, we had never felt we had a choice in the matter. We realized that we had slipped into full domestic responsibility simply as a matter of course, and it seemed unfair.

When I added them up, the chores I was responsible for amounted to a hectic 6 A.M.–9 P.M. (often later) job, without salary, breaks or vacation. No employer would be able to demand these hours legally, but most mothers take them for granted—as I did until I became a feminist.

For years mothers like me have acquiesced to the strain of the preschool years and endless household maintenance without any real choice. Why, I asked myself, should a couple's decision to have a family mean that the woman must immerse years of her life in their children? And why should men like my husband miss caring for and knowing their children?

Eventually, after an arduous examination of our situation, my husband and I decided that we no longer had to accept the sex roles that had turned us into a lame family. Out of equal parts love for each other and desperation at our situation, we decided to re-examine the patterns we had been living by, and starting again from scratch, to define our roles for ourselves.

We began by agreeing to share completely all responsibility for raising our children (by then aged five and seven) and caring for our household. If this new arrangement meant that my husband would have to change his job or that I would have to do more free-lance work or that we would have to live on a different scale, then we would. It would be worth it if it could make us once again equal, independent and loving as we had been when we were first married.

Simply agreeing verbally to share domestic duties didn't work, despite our best intentions. And when we tried to divide them "spontaneously," we ended up following the traditional patterns. Our old habits were too deep-rooted. So we sat down and drew up a formal agreement, acceptable to both of us, that clearly defined the responsibilities we each had.

It may sound a bit formal, but it has worked for us. Here it is:

## MARRIAGE AGREEMENT

### I. Principles

We reject the notion that the work which brings in more money is more valuable. The ability to earn more money is a privilege which must not be compounded by enabling the larger earner to buy out of his/her duties and put the burden either on the partner who earns less or on another person hired from outside.

We believe that each partner has an equal right to his/her own time, work, value, choices. As long as all duties are performed, each of us may use his/her extra time any way he/she chooses. If he/she wants to use it making money, fine. If he/she wants to spend it with spouse, fine. If not, fine.

As parents we believe we must share all responsibility for taking care of our children and home— not only the work but also the responsibility. At least during the first year of this agreement, *sharing responsibility* shall mean dividing the *jobs* and dividing the *time.*

In principle, jobs should be shared equally, 50-50, but deals may be made by mutual agreement. If jobs and schedule are divided on any other than a 50-50 basis, then at any time either party may call for a re-examination and redistribution of jobs or a revision of the schedule. Any deviation from 50-50 must be for the convenience of both parties. If one party works overtime in any domestic job, he/she must be compensated by equal extra work by the other. The schedule may be flexible, but changes must be formally agreed upon. The terms of this agreement are rights and duties, not privileges and favors.

### II. Job Breakdown and Schedule

#### (A) Children

1. Mornings: Waking children; getting their clothes out; making their lunches; seeing that they have notes, homework, money, bus passes, books; brushing their hair; giving them breakfast (making coffee for us). Every other week each parent does all.

2. Transportation: Getting children to and from lessons, doctors, dentists (including making appointments), friends' houses, park, parties, movies, libraries. Parts occurring between 3 and 6 P.M. fall to wife. She must be compensated by extra work from husband (see 10 below). Husband does all weekend transportation and pick-ups after 6.

3. Help: Helping with homework, personal problems, projects like cooking, making gifts, experiments, planting; answering questions; explaining things. Parts occurring between 3 and 6 P.M. fall to wife. After 6 P.M. husband does Tuesday, Thursday and Sunday; wife does Monday, Wednesday and Saturday. Friday is free for whoever has done extra work during the week.

4. Nighttime (after 6 P.M.): Getting children to take baths, brush their teeth, put away their toys and clothes, go to bed; reading with them; tucking them in and having nighttime talks; handling if they wake or call in the night. Husband does Tuesday, Thursday and Sunday. Wife does Monday, Wednesday and Saturday. Friday is split according to who has done extra work during the week.

5. Baby sitters: Getting baby sitters (which sometimes takes an hour of phoning). Baby sitters must be called by the parent the sitter is to replace. If no sitter turns up, that parent must stay home.

6. Sick care: Calling doctors; checking symptoms; getting prescriptions filled; remembering to give medicine; taking days off to stay home with sick child; providing special activities. This must still be worked out equally, since now wife seems to do it all. (The same goes for the now frequently declared school closings for so-called political protests, whereby the mayor gets credit at the expense of the mothers of young children. The mayor closes only the schools, not the places of business or the government offices.) In any case, wife must be compensated (see 10 below).

7. Weekends: All usual child care, plus special activities (beach, park, zoo). Split equally. Husband is free all Saturday, wife is free all Sunday.

#### (B) Housework

8. Cooking: Breakfast; dinner (children, parents, guests). Breakfasts during the week are divided

equally; husband does all weekend breakfasts (including shopping for them and dishes). Wife does all dinners except Sunday nights. Husband does Sunday dinner and any other dinners on his nights of responsibility if wife isn't home. Whoever invites guests does shopping, cooking and dishes; if both invite them, split work.

9. Shopping: Food for all meals, housewares, clothing and supplies for children. Divide by convenience. Generally, wife does local daily food shopping; husband does special shopping for supplies and children's things.

10. Cleaning: Dishes daily; apartment weekly, biweekly or monthly. Husband does dishes Tuesday, Thursday and Sunday. Wife does Monday, Wednesday and Saturday. Friday is split according to who has done extra work during week. Husband does all the house cleaning in exchange for wife's extra child care (3 to 6 daily) and sick care.

11. Laundry: Home laundry, making beds, dry cleaning (take and pick up). Wife does home laundry. Husband does dry-cleaning delivery and pickup. Wife strips beds, husband remakes them.

Our agreement changed our lives. Surprisingly, once we had written it down, we had to refer to it only two or three times. But we still had to work to keep the old habits from intruding. If it was my husband's night to take care of the children, I had to be careful not to check up on how he was managing. And if the baby sitter didn't show up for him, I would have to remember it was *his* problem.

Eventually the agreement entered our heads, and now, after two successful years of following it, we find that our new roles come to us as readily as the old ones had. I willingly help my husband clean the apartment (knowing it is his responsibility) and he often helps me with the laundry or the meals. We work together and trade off duties with ease now that the responsibilities are truly shared. We each have less work, more hours together and less resentment.

Before we made our agreement I had never been able to find the time to finish even one book. Over the past two years I've written three children's books, a biography and a novel and edited a collection of writings (all will have been published by spring of 1972). Without our agreement I would never have been able to do this.

At present my husband works a regular 40-hour week, and I write at home during the six hours the children are in school. He earns more money now than I do, so his salary covers more of our expenses than the money I make with my free-lance work. But if either of us should change jobs, working hours or income, we would probably adjust our agreement.

Perhaps the best testimonial of all to our marriage agreement is the change that has taken place in our family life. One day after it had been in effect for only four months our daughter said to my husband, "You know, Daddy, I used to love Mommy more than you, but now I love you both the same."

[1971]

 70

# *Communal Living*

ELLEN DAVIDSON

As I write this, Alan is sitting on my lap. He's typing with great determination and delight, adding his own thoughts to this piece. My 1½-year-old daughter is at a sitter's house in order to let me write in peace, and here I am working with my 1½-year-old housemate as my helper. While this makes writing difficult, it also embodies a piece of the essence of communal living, a perfect example to keep in mind as I write.

Living in a communal house is unpredictable. You can't have an orderly life in which you control what happens. It's hard to find the salad servers when you want them. The measuring cup is never in the place that seems obvious. You can finally get your laundry sorted, and, when you head down to the basement, someone else is doing laundry and has four loads piled up and waiting. When you're in a hurry, there are inevitably two cars behind yours in the driveway. Communal living can also mean coming home and smelling homemade warm brownies, available right then and there for an afternoon snack. Or coming home and finding a housemate has made cedar plant shelves for the backyard. Or finding our 4-year-old in our housemates' bed for a morning cuddle because we were out of ours when she came looking. Or having fascinating conversations at all hours, conversations that stretch my thinking and imagination. There is something wonderfully companionable about brushing your teeth with another four or five people at the sink.

My husband and I have lived communally for 5½ years. For several years, there were eight adults and two children living here. For a while, there were four women and four men and then, for several years, five women and three men. When two of the adults moved out at the time two babies were being born, we decided space was tight and didn't replace those two adults. For the last year and a half, we have had the same group of two women, four men, and four children. We are two couples with two children each and two single people.

What does it mean to be a feminist living communally? It means that, in many ways, I can live out my values more easily and raise my children in an environment that is richer and more diverse.

For me, one of the most important values of feminism is affirmation of diversity. In a house with many other adults and children, we all experience, in deep and immediate personal ways, a range of values, beliefs, and lifestyles. My daughters are part of the lives of women and men who stay home and women and men who have jobs outside the home. Our housemates have friends in many circles. Our children meet people of different races and different values as extended family members rather than strangers. "Looking different" is not something our children will have to learn to understand later. For four years we had housemates who were actively involved in a New England dance community. There were meetings at our house. Dancing and music surrounded us. Now one of our housemates is active in the local Haitian community and in Haitian politics. There is a ten-foot cardboard boat in our basement from a demonstration against the deportation of Haitian refugees. Watching and participating in its creation on our front porch allowed all of us to learn more about Haiti and more about sails.

To me, being a feminist also means working toward a society that allows access to and affirmation for a wide range of work choices. Linda, the only other woman in the house, chooses to stay home full-time with her toddler while her husband works full-time. Both Jim and I work part-time and take care of our children part-time. One of the other two men in the house works full-time and the other part-time.

Our house is in a very diverse neighborhood. At the foot of our hill, you can go to a series of small markets: Haitian, Indian, Japanese/Korean, Guatemalan. At our neighborhood school, 50% of the children come from non-English-speaking homes. Hannah, our daughter, plays with a group of friends ranging in age from 3 to 8, consisting of both girls and boys and containing a mix of ethnicities and races. This is easy in a multiethnic neighborhood. We bring Channukah cookies, in the shapes of dreidels, menorahs, or six-pointed stars, to our Chinese neighbors, and they invite us over to celebrate the Chinese New Year. Every day, we have to work much harder to live in a house with diverse values and beliefs. At holidays, it is delightful to experience each other's customs and traditions. The older children love having more celebrations, doing more projects, hearing more stories. But it also creates tension with my husband's parents who, as Jews, have struggled to fight societal forces of assimilation and find it difficult to visit our house when Christian holidays are celebrated as part of our children's home lives.

As parents we aren't responsible for all of the daily modeling for our daughters. All of the men in our house cook comfortably and regularly. They are not Sunday morning brunch chefs. One of our male roommates could as frequently be found making his own clothes as replacing our bathroom floor, making eggroll filling in a five-gallon bucket as building recycling bins for the back porch—all with great enjoyment and expertise. More importantly than the way chores are divided, gender is rarely the determinant of how people think or feel—of nurturance, of emotional expression, of political perspective. In many ways, the gender roles in our house are so nontraditional that I can't fully keep in my consciousness what is daily life for so many people in this country.

In weighing life choices and making decisions to continue or not with this lifestyle, I find myself thinking about the advantages and disadvantages for our family. There is a very clear financial advantage. Living communally is much less expensive. On our income we couldn't possibly own a home in the Boston area any other way. Living communally means that we have enough money so that daily expenses are not a problem. It means that Jim and I can each work part-time and thus have more time together, more time with our children, and more time for other activities. We can have jobs we love and work at them a reasonable, rather than an excessive, amount of time.

It also means that less time is devoted to daily chores. We share these in a rather haphazard way, which works more or less efficiently depending on people's standards and how busy we each are. It does, however, consistently mean less work and more time to spend in other ways. Each of us is responsible for cooking less than one night a week, but we get full, delicious home-cooked meals five nights a week. We eat together at a table with cloth napkins and lit candles.

This time saving is one of the ways that makes it easier to live more ecologically—an important feminist value in my mind. The saving of time and energy from daily chores can go toward growing a prolific vegetable garden and doing complex recycling. Weather-proofing the house and buying energy-efficient light bulbs are chores that are chosen by interested people. We have the advantage of having the convenience of appliances but not having to own as many of them: a washing machine among all of us rather than having a washing machine for a family of four, two refrigerators, and two phones. We don't use a dishwasher because we all help clean up after dinner, carrying dinnertime conversations into the kitchen. In fact, those are often the best conversations, as it's hard to focus at the dinner table with three children all under 5 years old. But after

dinner, during cleanup, the children have drifted off to jump on the sofa, draw pictures, climb on their climbing structure . . . so we can talk more peacefully and often in more depth.

In spite of the chaos at dinner, dinnertime is still one of the best advantages of living communally, offering time to think and learn more about the world. Usually at least a few people have read the newspaper or heard some interesting tidbit on National Public Radio they want to discuss. We share ideas from conversations with other friends and colleagues. Often someone has been to a rally or picked up flyers around town. Dinnertime is when I learn more about the world, challenge my assumptions, get answers to my questions.

A big piece of my work is to supervise student teachers, and I need to be well informed about whatever they are teaching so I can ask useful questions and understand their lessons. At home, I have easy access to much of this information. I can describe lessons to my scientist housemates and check them for accuracy. I can learn more myself about whatever topic is being taught and thus ask better questions. So, while I never expected to learn about the metabolic activity of Haitian pigs, I am quite fascinated to have this information. When thermometers in different temperatures of water didn't behave as I, or my student, expected, I can go home and improve my own understanding of this situation.

Aaron, Jim, and I worked on a major curriculum project last spring; we wrote the teachers' guide for the PBS children's geography quiz show, "Where in the World Is Carmen Sandiego?" While we could have done a collaborative writing project even when not living communally, doing it this way meant we could work in small spurts as well as large chunks, have inspirations and discuss them at 11 P.M. or 7 A.M., and share resources easily. Elizabeth, now 12, has been our curriculum consultant for years. She plays all the games designed by my mathematics methods students and helps me critique them. We interview her to demonstrate understanding children's thinking. She gives us feedback on lessons we design.

There are many ways in which living communally makes child care easier. For regular weekly child care, we hire a sitter. But for time to talk on the phone, have conferences, run out to the store, put in a load of laundry, go to meetings, or go out to dinner, we can exchange with each other. We don't keep track. We don't trade hours. We simply ask if someone is home and willing to take care of our children. We are sensitive to each other's needs and may well hire a sitter for an evening out if our housemates have been doing a lot of child care for us lately. But this certainly gives us more mobility—it is easier, faster, cheaper, and more convenient than relying only on paid babysitters.

Our children have special relationships with different adults. Aaron is a wonderful companion for walks, a lover of plants, fish, and bugs. When Jim and I were called to be substitutes at Hannah's nursery school and were both busy working, Patrick went in for us. The children were thrilled to have a real veterinarian to talk with. When I am gone late at work, Aviva is perfectly delighted to nurse from Linda. Before dinner, Glen sometimes takes the three younger children out to a nearby park to run.

Our house is named Tkanye, the Russian word for weaving, a name we chose as we are weaving our lives together. A few years ago Jim and I wove bags for all of our housemates. We had the same warp for all the bags and varied the weft according to each person's style and our sense of their preferences in color and texture.

When Hannah was born 4½ years ago, she came into the world as our first child but with a doting big sister. Elizabeth, at 7 years old, was delighted to have a new baby in the house. For her, Hannah provided all the benefits of a baby sister with few of the disadvantages. Hannah giggled and bounced when Elizabeth entered a room, followed her around, tried to do everything she did—but Elizabeth didn't have to share her parents' love or attention. What a deal! When Elizabeth decided we were being too lackadaisical about toilet training Hannah, she took over putting Hannah on the potty. Hannah was thrilled to be becoming a big girl and to be wearing Elizabeth's old panties. Hannah and her friends play dress-up for hours with Elizabeth's outgrown party clothes. Last summer, Elizabeth went on a five-day vacation with us to a farm. Jim and I and the girls loved her company; having an older child along enriched the whole experience. Elizabeth loved getting to go on an extra vacation when her parents weren't available.

For Aviva, living communally has provided her a twin without the total exhaustion I would expect must be the case for parents of twins. Three weeks after she was born, Linda and Glen had Alan. Aviva wakes up in the morning looking for Alan. They share toys and fight over toys. They chase each other around the house. Occasionally they wear matching outfits.

Sometimes this feels to me like being back in a college dormitory or a sleepaway summer camp, both experiences I loved. Linda and I can share clothes with each other, something many of us give up if we get married to a man and live just as a couple. We both like reading feminist mysteries and trade these back and forth. As I go about my day and have experiences at work or in the community, I'm aware of thinking about what stories to tell Linda when I get home, stories she will enjoy because she is a woman. Linda is home during the day and reads the newspaper much more diligently than I do. I can count on her to point out articles I shouldn't miss. She and I often do small shopping errands for each other, not keeping track or charging the other, assuming it will all even out. When one of us finds a wonderfully cute baby outfit in a catalogue or in a store, we sometimes buy two of them, one for each baby. We give these for no occasion and with no record keeping.

This summer the house participated in a city-wide community circus, one of whose most impressive events is stilting. Hannah, at 4½, was originally considered too young to stilt. However, she insisted, so Jim and Elizabeth made her some stilts and, with both their help, was able to learn. The rest of us became intrigued with stilting. Soon, the whole house had stilts, courtesy of our master stilt-maker, Glen. I made stilting dresses for Hannah and me, and worked with Jim to make stilting pants for him. Elizabeth and I worked together to make her a stilting kimono, 2½ feet taller than her actual height. Linda rigged up a bridal dress for Hannah and a neighbor friend of Elizabeth's for the stilting fashion show. Since Alan and Aviva thought they were in the circus and often wandered across the stage, I made them both clown costumes to formalize their roles.

Jim and Elizabeth worked on pompons and trim. Patrick, our 6-foot 4-inch housemate, looked particularly impressive on Jim's 2½-foot stilts. A real community effort.

Communal living also has disadvantages. I'm not sure how these disadvantages relate to feminism, but they are decidedly central to my thinking about this choice. In many ways, Jim and I end up feeling like we are "married" to a whole group of people, a group we don't necessarily love and didn't know very well before living with them. This is true for others we talk with who live communally, for many of the same reasons. Because people's life situations change, there are times when housemates move on. For economic reasons, it is usually necessary to fill the spots. For us, on one occasion, Aaron, an old, close friend of ours, was eager to move in. However, on other occasions, we have had to look farther afield, choosing among strangers and friends of friends.

But even when you do know someone well, you can't necessarily know what they'll be like to live with. While we usually know much about our life-partner's style and habits from having spent nights and extensive time together before committing ourselves to a long-term arrangement, it is highly unlikely to know all that about even close friends before deciding to live together. Many of the issues that you have to work out in a marriage—money, housekeeping, child raising—come up again and again living in a group. These are both easier and harder to resolve with people you don't love and with whom you don't have a long-term commitment. On the one hand, differences may not matter so much—a housemate's choices still don't affect us as deeply as our partner's choices. But in spite of having a baseline agreement of "generosity of spirit," housemates sometimes still make judgments about each other's daily choices, and this can lead to tension.

There are daily adjustments to be made in what we can do. Every time there is hope for a thunderstorm, Hannah has been desperately wanting to make "Thunder Cake," a recipe in a book we often read aloud. If we lived just as a nuclear family, we could stop cooking dinner at the first sound of a storm, get out all those ingredients, and bake. When living with others, it's not as easy or fair to disrupt the dinner process. Living communally you have to choose your issues. One of our housemates insisted, for several months, on keeping his nonfunctioning car in the driveway. This took away space that the children could have used for biking, stilting, and roller skating. This was an issue worth raising, worth talking about, but not one to get into a major fight about. Other issues we choose to ignore rather than live with constant negotiation.

Maintaining outside friendships is different when you live communally. Sometimes our friends don't like or enjoy all of our housemates. That makes it less fun to have them over to visit. Sometimes our friends like our housemates but find that visiting, when the house starts with ten people at the dinner table, is overwhelming. Sometimes we try to have company on weekends when there are no official house meals, but that may or may not mean the kitchen and dining room are all ours.

There is a level of chaos inherent in having so many people in one house. The noise and activity feel never-ending. When Alan and Aviva are fighting, it is hard to determine how to discipline a child who isn't yours.

Though these problems are real, in balance, this choice seems right for us for now.

I'm aware how fascinating our house is to my colleagues, students, and others who visit us. When I had one of my classes over for classwork and dinner, I told them the rooms they could work in for their small groups. I made a comment that people who wanted to get a look at the whole house should choose the guest room on the third floor, as they could then peek in all the other rooms on the way. Four people immediately said, "We'll go up there," and ran off.

A friend of Patrick's from Kenya was here visiting with a friend of his. He explained to his friend how the men in this house were all brothers living here with their wives and children. He seemed delighted that we had made a choice so like the choices made in his country. Our next-door neighbors are Chinese. We have spent several years figuring out their relationship with each other, as they seem to have done with us. They, too, seem to have decided on one of the men as their "head of household" and all the rest of them as family.

For me, an important part of feminism is modeling alternative choices. As people visit and talk with us, they can begin to think more freely and broadly about options for living arrangements other than a traditional nuclear family. There are days when I think of this lifestyle as being completely different from what life would be like if Jim, Hannah, Aviva, and I had our own house. I envision that choice as making my daily life feel altogether different. Then there are other times when I can't even imagine why people ask so many questions because it doesn't feel different at all. We simply live together, as more than just roommates, in a loosely bonded extended family.                    [1992]

# Women and the Health Care System

Historically, women have been healers and have supported each other with skill and understanding when experiencing physical pain. The legacy of midwives in this country is one example. Yet beginning in the late eighteenth century, male physicians in the United States led a successful campaign to eliminate midwives. In the mid–nineteenth century, they also mounted an assault against the many women medical practitioners who were trained outside the male-dominated medical establishment.

Some of you may also be reading *Our Bodies, Ourselves for the New Century* (Simon and Schuster, 1998) in your course along with *Women: Images and Realities*. *Our Bodies, Ourselves* was written by a group of women who, impelled by the lack of available information about women's bodies, began meeting in 1969 to share information and experiences and publish what became the first of many editions of *Our Bodies, Ourselves*. Women of varied racial and class backgrounds from different parts of the country organized similarly to spawn the now extensive women's health movement.

Despite the strength of this movement, sexism in the medical system is wide-ranging. Women's health activists report patterns of the many types of abuse. Personnel in medical settings have not listened to women or believed what they said. They have withheld knowledge or lied; treated women without their consent; failed to warn them of risks; experimented on them; discriminated against them because of race, sexual preference, age, or disability; offered tranquilizers or moral advice instead of medical care or useful referrals to community resources; administered treatments that were unnecessarily mutilating; performed unnecessary operations; or sexually abused them. Carol Stevens's piece, "How Women Get Bad Medicine," describes some of these types of abuse in more detail.

Women of color are particularly vulnerable in the health care system. Suffering from AIDS, Elizabeth Ramos describes how doctors initially misdiagnosed and mistreated her and how this led to her current educational work with Latino teenagers. Evelynn Hammonds's article depicts the stereotypical way the media portray African-American women with AIDS, as well as the reality of their lives.

Breast cancer has become a very serious health threat for women. Rita Arditti and Tatiana Schreiber present evidence concerning the environmental causes of breast cancer. They point to the minimal research monies being spent on preventative approaches that address environmental causes and to the cancer establishment's emphasis on drug treatment.

Finally, Byllye Avery writes about the birth of the National Black Women's Health Network, one of the many grass-roots women's health projects that has advocated for women. This account represents the way many women nationwide have begun to provide for their own health care needs.

# 71

## How Women Get Bad Medicine

CAROL STEVENS *

By the time Sara and Bernie Blumenthal pulled up to the Washington Hospital Center, the emergency-room staff was waiting. They had been told to expect someone having a heart attack. When the Blumenthals arrived, they rushed toward Bernie. But Sara was the one having the heart attack.

It was a continuation of what Sara had been through for two days, ever since waking up in the middle of the night with a stabbing pain between her shoulder blades. She had gone to the hospital, only to be diagnosed with back spasms. But the pain didn't go away, and after repeated injections of muscle relaxants, her doctor gave her an electrocardiogram.

His face turned pale as he watched the needle jump. Sara Blumenthal had been having a heart attack—one that had destroyed one fifth of her heart muscle. The doctor sent Sara and her husband rushing to the hospital.

The failure to detect Sara's heart attack was understandable, considering that she was only 41, not overweight, and a nonsmoker for the past year. Also, as a woman, she was less likely than a man to have a heart attack. Still, her experience reflected a troubling side of modern medicine: that for all its progress, all its sophistication, it does not treat women and men the same.

It is true of patient care, with no less a source than the National Institute of Health's director, Dr. Bernadine Healy, contending that "women's medical complaints aren't taken seriously" and that women with "men's diseases"—such as coronary heart disease—aren't treated as aggressively as male patients. And it's true of medical research, in which studies traditionally have been done with only male subjects. Even when medical technology has been

geared to women, the results have been rife with problems.

When that happens, as it has most recently with breast implants, the calls come pouring into places like the National Women's Health Network here. The "what" questions—What health problems can be blamed on implants?—are easy to answer. The "whys" are harder. Why weren't women told about the serious health risks before getting implants? Why did federal agencies allow implants to be marketed in spite of safety questions? Why was this allowed to happen to women?

"You can hear it in their voices," says Toni Young of the Women's Health Network. "They're feeling helpless."

In the nineteen years since the Boston Women's Health Collective published the first edition of *Our Bodies, Ourselves,* one health crisis after another has seemed to justify the book's distrust of and dissatisfaction with the medical system. First it was the Dalkon Shield, an intrauterine contraceptive device (IUD) that was linked with high rates of pelvic infection, miscarriages, hysterectomies, and seventeen deaths before it was pulled from the market in 1974. Eight years later toxic shock syndrome, a life-threatening illness, was tied to the use of high-absorbency tampons. Tampon manufacturers were required to place warning labels on packages in 1982, but it wasn't until 1989 that the Food and Drug Administration, under court order, required manufacturers to standardize tampon absorbency levels.

Other studies discovered problems with estrogen. At the high levels found in some birth-control pills, researchers discovered a link with strokes, blood clots, and heart attacks. When prescribed in supplements for post-menopausal women, estrogen appeared to increase the risk of breast cancer.

All of these examples had one thing in common: women who had been healthy were put at risk by their exposure to medical technology.

Would these health-care crises have occurred if it were men's bodies being subjected to the same drugs and devices? "It's kind of like wondering how men would handle pregnancy," says Cindy Pearson, program director for the National Women's Health Network. "We'll never know, because men have never been put in that position."

---

*Leslie Milk contributed to this article.

The fact is that women have more contact with physicians than men. According to government estimates, 81 percent of women visit the doctor at least once a year, compared to 67 percent of men. "Women receive more examinations, lab tests, blood-pressure checks, drug prescriptions, and return appointments than men," says the American Medical Association.

Thanks to the reproductive process alone, millions of healthy women visit doctors' offices, clinics, and hospitals each year. "Women interact with the health-care system for contraceptives to avoid getting pregnant. They get involved again each time they get pregnant. And when they go back again during menopause," Pearson says.

This close contact with the medical field has its benefits. Regular gynecological checkups have allowed more and more women to detect cervical and breast cancer at an early stage, resulting in rising survival rates. But there are those who feel that too much medicine also has its costs, that because of their biology women are more likely to be exposed to the risk of infections, unnecessary procedures, and medical errors.

The truth is that in a society that rewards doctors for treating diseases, many physicians find it hard to leave well-enough women alone. "[The] inexhaustible capacity to cut and medicate women in this country comes, in part, from a cultural view that women's natural biological processes are treatable illnesses," writes Dr. Sidney Wolfe, director of the Public Citizen Health Research Group, in *Women's Health Alert*. "Menstruation, pregnancy, childbirth, and lactation are all normal female reproductive functions. But a series of paths, paved initially with good and legitimate intentions, have led to the commercialization of treatment for each of these normal female functions."

The inequality between health care for men and women exists on another level, too: Women who are sick don't often get the same quality of treatment. An AMA study confirms that women are less likely than men to receive kidney transplants, undergo coronary bypass surgery, or have their lung cancer diagnosed.

NIH's Bernadine Healy goes even further, contending that a "Yentl syndrome" exists, in which heart disease is too often considered a "man's disease in disguise" when, in fact, it is the leading cause of death among American women.

"Women who have chest pains are not treated the same as men unless tests show they are having a heart attack," Healy says. "This suggests that women are being treated by different standards and, at a broader level, that women have to act like men to be taken seriously."

Women's dissatisfaction with the medical system is based on the widely held belief that their doctors don't always take their complaints seriously. "If you scratch the surface of any woman's experience, you're likely to hear at least one example of how she believes she was treated inappropriately," says National Women's Health Network's Cindy Pearson.

Such as the Oakton teacher whose HMO blamed a bad drug reaction on "postpartum blues." Or the DC writer whose doctor wouldn't take her high fever seriously until her irate husband got on the phone. Or the 22-year-old Arlington woman whose doctor recommended surgery to treat her menstrual cramps.

Says a 28-year-old Annandale woman, "I kept asking my doctor whether the pains in my elbows were somehow related to my breast implants. But he told me I was being silly. When I finally changed doctors, my new physician found pools of silicone in the joints of my arms and legs. I'll always resent the first doctor for belittling me."

For years, women have treated these anecdotes as veterans do their war stories: harrowing tales to tell in private. But research has begun to confirm that these stories are not isolated incidents but part of a pattern. A 1979 study in the *Journal of the American Medical Association* found that doctors treat men and women complaining of the same symptoms differently. Researcher Karen Armitage found that doctors were more likely to refer male patients for diagnostic tests and to attribute women's complaints to stress or hypochondria.

In its own analysis of gender disparities, the AMA discovered that female heart patients were twice as likely as males to have the abnormal results of an exercise test blamed on "psychiatric or other non-cardiac causes."

"There is evidence that physicians are more

likely to perceive women's maladies than men's as the result of emotionality," the AMA concluded.

Another example: As recently as six years ago, the nation's leading urology textbook was rewritten after it was discovered that interstitial cystitis, an illness that afflicts 450,000 people nationwide—90 percent of them women—was not a psychosomatic condition that manifests itself in urinary problems—as doctors had been taught for nearly 100 years. Better diagnostic equipment showed that the bladder disorder, which does not respond to antibiotics, is the result of ulcers and bladder adhesions.

"When doctors couldn't see anything wrong with the women who came to them crying in pain, they'd conclude they were crazy," says Judith Heller, director of Affiliate Affairs for the Interstitial Cystitis Association. "They'd advise them to get married, to have a baby, or to get psychiatric help."

It would be simplistic to suggest that all doctors are sexist. But it would be fair to say that medical tradition has been often sexist. As part of their training, all doctors are taught to rely on generalizations and stereotypes to make diagnoses. "As physicians we are overwhelmed with information," says Dr. Jean Hamilton, an associate professor of psychiatry at the University of Texas's Southwestern Medical School. "Doctors use stereotypes to help them process some of this information."

Conventional medical wisdom, for instance, holds that heart disease is primarily a male disease. Yet for the last two years more American women have died of heart disease than men. The medical community also considers lung cancer a man's health problem. Yet the death rate for lung cancer has increased more than 100 percent in the last twenty years—virtually all due to the growing number of women who smoke.

Even doctors who try hard to provide equal health care are hampered by the fact that they often don't know if what works for men will work for women. Should, for instance, women join men in taking an aspirin a day to prevent heart attacks? It's hard to say. The frequently cited study touting the benefits of aspirin involved 22,071 men and no women. Will the same oat-bran recipes recommended for men with high cholesterol also cut a woman's risk of heart attack? Not necessarily. Early

studies excluding women showed that low-fat diets helped men ward off heart attacks by lowering their levels of LDL, or bad cholesterol. Yet subsequent studies of women have shown that they are at greater risk when their HDL, or good cholesterol, is too low. A diet that cuts a woman's good cholesterol along with her bad could be dangerous.

It's not surprising that most research into heart and lung disease has focused on men. Men die of heart disease at a younger age than women. And until women started smoking in numbers equal to men, they weren't at the same risk of developing lung cancer. It's not as easy to explain the medical-research community's fixation on men when it comes to studying diseases of primary concern to women.

Clinical depression is a case in point. Women are twice as likely as men to suffer from it. Yet initial research on antidepressants was conducted exclusively on men.

"I plan on having a second child, and I worry about how the antidepressants I'm on will affect my pregnancy," says a 35-year-old Maryland lawyer. "My doctor gives me an educated guess, but no one can tell me for sure because the research has never been done."

Diseases of the aging are another example. Women live an average of seven years longer than men, and often are plagued with arthritis and osteoporosis as they age. Yet women were excluded from a National Institute on Aging long-term study for its first twenty years.

The exclusion of women from medical research was a deliberate policy. Women were excluded for two reasons: Their bodies are more complicated. And they can have babies.

Women's changing hormone levels during their menstrual cycles were thought to skew test results. Researchers also feared that experimental treatments and drugs might harm women's reproductive systems or damage the fetuses of women who didn't know they were pregnant.

These are legitimate concerns. Unfortunately, once drugs and medical treatments are approved, they end up being prescribed for women despite women's fluctuating hormone levels and ability to reproduce and despite the fact that they have never been proven safe or effective for women.

"First the medical system excludes women from research, then it wants to turn around and extrapolate its findings to women. But you can't have it both ways," says Joanne Howes, a partner with Bass and Howes, a DC consulting firm specializing in women's health.

That proved true in the case of the antidepressants tested only on men. Only after they were prescribed for women was it discovered that changing female hormone levels limited their effectiveness. Subsequent studies showed that when women received the same doses as men, they were inappropriately medicated for parts of each month.

The pattern holds true in analyzing early warning signs for diseases. The assumption has been that symptoms of illnesses for women are the same as for men. But there is growing evidence that life-threatening illnesses manifest themselves differently in men and women.

The same treadmill tests that can identify men at risk for heart disease are not as accurate when used on women. Chest pains and angina also are more likely to be early warning signals of heart disease in men than in women. The result is that women are less likely to survive bypass surgery and heart attacks because their heart problems are more advanced by the time they are diagnosed.

Medicine's reliance on the male model also is causing problems for women with AIDS. Opportunistic infections and diseases such as Kaposi's sarcoma are common among gay men with the virus, but not among infected women. Instead, HIV-positive women are more likely to suffer from gynecological problems. But because the Centers for Disease Control's official definition of AIDS focuses on the symptoms that manifest themselves most frequently in men, infected women are excluded from taking part in clinical trials, receiving experimental drugs and, to some extent, qualifying for Social Security disability payments. At a hearing of the House human resources subcommittee last year, it was estimated that because of the CDC's limited definition, the number of women with AIDS is under-counted by at least one third.

Who's to blame for medical science that treats men better than women?

Some critics say the National Institutes of Health, the government's primary source of medical research, is the prime offender. Five years after the Public Health Service first concluded that the nation's research policies put women at a disadvantage, the General Accounting Office released a 1990 report criticizing NIH for failing to do anything about it. "The GAO report showed that when it came to women's health, no one was home at NIH," says Howes. The publicity that followed turned up other gender bias at NIH. For instance, only 3 of NIH's 2,000 researchers specialized in obstetrics and gynecology. Also, not one of the divisions within NIH is dedicated exclusively to obstetrics and gynecology. Plus, the research center was spending less than 14 percent of its annual budget on women's-health research.

The revelations were enough to prompt women scientists and researchers to form groups such as the Institute for Research in Women's Health, and the Society for the Advancement of Women's Health Research. One of their first stops was Capitol Hill, where their cause was adopted by the Congressional Caucus for Women's Issues. The women researchers formed their own political-action committee and began awarding research grants.

The pressure was effective. In 1990 Healy was named NIH's first woman director, and last October she unveiled the first step in her plan for correcting the medical system's gender bias: a $500-million Women's Health Initiative to track diseases including cancer, heart disease, and osteoporosis in some 140,000 women over the next decade. In the meantime, a newly created NIH Office of Research on Women's Health will identify other gaps in medical knowledge about women. The office is headed by Dr. Vivian W. Pinn, the former chairman of pathology at Howard University's College of Medicine.

"All of a sudden the issue has taken off . . . there is all this interest in increasing the budget for women's health," NIH's Center for Population Research and the president of the board of directors of the Society for Advancement of Women's Health Research. "Part of it is that the issue is so clear-cut. It is obvious to everyone that women weren't being treated fairly."

Earlier this year, the Bush administration's budget request included $89 million for its women's- and minority-health initiatives. This included a 40-percent increase in its funding for breast- and cervical-cancer research. In 1991, twenty grants were awarded by the Office of Research on Women's Health. Some $2.5 million has been earmarked for the study of interstitial cystitis, including funding for a data bank to track women with the disease.

As part of NIH's new focus, the University of Texas's Jean Hamilton and Sheryle Gallant, an associate professor at the Bethesda-based Uniformed Services University of the Health Sciences, have received a grant for nearly $600,000 to study the same subject Hamilton was told to stay away from as an NIH researcher more than a decade ago: the differences in the way men and women respond to drugs. "Now the idea that men and women will react differently to drugs seems so obvious it is embarrassing," Hamilton says. "But at the time, I was told there couldn't possibly be differences. The subject was very low priority."

One sign of the success of the women's medical movement is the eagerness of some men's health groups to imitate it. Chicago resident Edward Kaps co-founded an international support group for survivors of prostate cancer named Us Too after hearing a talk from Sharon Green, the executive director of Y-Me?, a support group for breast-cancer survivors.

"The men's movement is gradually growing, but it's still far behind where women are with diseases like breast cancer," says Dr. Mark Soloway, chairman of the urology department at the University of Miami. "Men are rapidly learning that it can be very productive to talk about their health problems."

That's especially true if the men are powerful politicians such as Republican Senators Bob Dole and Ted Stevens, and Democrat Alan Cranston, all of whom were treated for prostate cancer last year. "Now with senators who have had the disease, there's no doubt more money will be available for research," Soloway says.

Such predictions make leaders of the women's-health movement uneasy. Men have the same odds of developing prostate cancer as women face for breast cancer, about one in nine. If medical research becomes dependent on first-person testimonials, men have many more potential advocates in positions of power.

That's one more reason the promotion of women scientists and doctors to higher positions in the medical establishment has become a key issue. "Now that we have women in medical studies we need to have women doing medical studies. That's next," says Florence Haseltine.

The AMA says the number of women physicians has quadrupled in the last twenty years, with women now accounting for 34 percent of medical school graduates and nearly 17 percent of all practicing physicians. This year, for the first time, women made up more than 54 percent of the doctors in the first year of residency for obstetrics and gynecology.

Yet women are not well represented in the upper echelons of the medical establishment. Only 14 percent of NIH's top positions are held by women. The AMA's latest count shows no women serving as deans at U.S. medical schools and less than 10 percent female medical-school faculty. Women also are underrepresented outside of the primary-care specialties. Women doctors now account for almost 19 percent of all pediatricians, 15 percent of all internists, but less than 3 percent of all surgeons.

Medical research can be a particularly lonely field for women. "At NIH, women scientists are not valued. The prevailing attitude is, 'You're a girl. You should be taking care of patients because that's what girl doctors do,'" says Jean Hamilton, who filed a 1980s administrative complaint against the institutes, charging that they provided a hostile workplace for women scientists. Under the terms of her settlement, she cannot talk about its resolution.

There's also ongoing debate about the merits of women's-health research, with critics pointing out that it will result in an expensive and time-consuming replication of studies that have already been conducted on men.

"Sure, a lot of it is catch-up work. But there's nothing the matter with catch-up work if there is something that can be learned from it," says Haseltine.

More troubling to women scientists is the political climate surrounding research into the female reproductive process. They see a growing need for investigating such problems as the nation's high infant-mortality rate, the 22-year increase in the incidence of ectopic pregnancies, and the epidemic of sexually transmitted disease. But that raises issues of sexuality and birth control and, for some politicians, questions of morality. And that can become a stumbling block for research funding.

In recent years, the federal government has discouraged scientists from pursuing several areas of reproductive health. Responding to pressures from anti-abortion groups, the FDA in 1989 placed an import ban on RU-486, the so-called French abortion pill. As a result, scientists have had trouble obtaining the drug for study, even though it has shown promise as a treatment for infertility, fibroid tumors, breast cancer, and Cushing's syndrome, a disease caused by excessive cortisone. Similarly, a ban on federal funding of placental-tissue research has jeopardized research into its uses to help diabetics and patients suffering from Parkinson's, Alzheimer's and Huntington's diseases.

Some scientists have decided to stay away from reproductive health until the political climate changes. Instead they are focusing their research proposals on other areas of women's health.

Also, a push is on to make the health-care system more responsive to women. The Society for the Advancement of Women's Health Research has spent the last year talking to women at a series of roundtable meetings around the country.

What the group is hearing is that women are frustrated that no one specialty exists to handle all their medical needs, that they are still more likely than men to be shuffled from one specialist to another. Women would like to see the development of a "women's health" specialty, one that is broader than ob/gyn in that it would also address the effects of drugs and diseases on women. The researchers also are hearing that doctors still place a low priority on preventive medicine and are not very well trained in dealing with matters that aren't strictly medical, such as the issue of battered women.

Such complaints come at a time when the nation's health-care system has become a major campaign issue and is ripe for an overhaul. More than any time before, women are in a position to have a say in how the country approaches health care—

from the kind of research it does to the priorities of doctor-patient relationships.

Leaders of the women's-health movement are optimistic. They say it's only a matter of time before the traditional male model of medical care is replaced by a system more user-friendly to women.

"There's been an awakening to the fact that women are treated unfairly in medical research and patient care," says Bernadine Healy. "Now we have to make sure people stay awake and make women a part of mainstream medicine. We can't let people go back to sleep."                                                    [1992]

 72

# Elizabeth Ramos

BEBE NIXON

*Elizabeth was the mother of two hyperactive young sons, Christopher and Matthew. After her husband left her, she raised them alone while working full-time at the John Hancock Insurance Company. In April 1985 she started to have trouble breathing. Her doctor treated her for bronchitis, but she didn't get better. The doctor didn't test or treat her for anything else. Oddly, in May, she received notification from the Red Cross that blood she had routinely donated in February had tested positive for HIV infection. She didn't even know what that meant. When she asked the doctor if it could have anything to do with what was wrong with her, he said no. As her illness worsened, the doctor treated her again for bronchitis, then for stress, and finally, for hysteria.*

*In late September she developed pneumonia; frantic, she went on her own to the emergency room at Boston City Hospital. There, on October 1, she was diagnosed with PCP, the signature pneumonia of AIDS. She was in intensive care for nearly five weeks, being kept alive on a respirator. Her lungs were severely damaged.*

*When she got out of the hospital, she did two uncharacteristic and drastic things. First, she went public with her illness. She decided to devote all her time to speaking out against AIDS ignorance, to reaching the Hispanic community, especially teenagers, to making them know what AIDS was and how to avoid it. Second, she and two lawyers drew up a malpractice suit against the doctor who had so badly misdiagnosed and mistreated her illness. She wanted people to know what had happened to her, to highlight the price she had paid, and, if she won, to provide money for her sons after she was gone.*

## FALL 1987

Because of my condition, I can't have many goals in life. I could go to school again, but I never could use it in any professional way. Talking about AIDS, reaching out to people in the community, this is my joy right now. I have to use all my time to spread my message. I believe there's a mission for me to accomplish. If people see me and hear me, and even touch me, they'll know this is for real. It can happen to women, it can happen to men. Then maybe they'll start doing something about it.

I got AIDS from my boyfriend, José. I never used drugs. I wasn't promiscuous. But he had the virus, and I got it from him. He was an IV drug user. For the longest time, he denied that I got it from him. He said some bad things about me, about how *he* thought I got it. Then he got sick. He said it was this, he said it was that, he said it was skin cancer. Finally I asked him straight out. "Do you think I got it from you?" And he said yes. And yes, he had been sharing needles with different people around here, around the apartment complex. Clean needles are very hard to find here: once somebody has one, everybody uses it. I asked him, "I wonder if their wives know?" I talked to them. They don't know anything. And they don't believe me when I tell them what's happening, and what happened to me. The neighborhood is so congested, so close, everyone ends up living with everyone else. And I'm worried that if these men are infected, they will infect these women, and the women will infect other men, and they will infect their unborn babies. I want to do something to stop it. AIDS is one of the facts of life now, like the birds and the bees. We just have to add it on to everything else.

I'm an ordinary person. I got AIDS. It can happen to anyone. Anyone at all. If people know that, if they see me and really know that, then I will have made a difference. That's my goal. I know about people and places that a lot of the organized outreach can't reach out to. I know about drug users. I know about teenage girls in the projects. I know how they tell you anything they think you want to hear, and then go do exactly as they please. It takes a special kind of knowing, a having been there, to talk to them so they *listen*.

The teenagers I talk to, they're mostly girls. And usually by the time they come to hear me, they've already had some sexual experience. That's why

they come. They're scared. And I tell them, "You make sure that guy puts a condom *on* before he puts that thing *in*. You just make him. It won't be easy, because a lot of them are goin' to say, 'Bye, baby,' if you make them. But it does down to this: are you willing to *die* for this dude? Because if he has the virus, and he won't wear a condom, that's just what you'll do. Is it worth it?" They listen.

My kids are afraid that when they come home from school, they'll find me gone. Gone to the hospital, gone to heaven, just gone. It's hard to prepare them for my death. They hate this illness. Christopher once told me he wanted to be back inside my stomach. I asked him, "Why?" He said, "So I could fight the virus from inside you." They know, even my Chris, and he's only eight years old, they know there's no cure. They are very scared.

When I die, I want everyone to know why I died. And I want people to know that I tried very hard to get them to understand.

*In January 1988 a jury awarded Elizabeth $750,000 in her lawsuit against the doctor who had misdiagnosed her illness. Her greatest satisfaction was in knowing that her children could be taken care of after her death, that they would not be a financial burden to anyone.*

*She also had two dreams that could now come true. One was to buy a real house for her and the boys to live in. After much searching, she found one that she thought was just right for her, and she bought it, even though the price was way too high. She was ready to move in, but there was something she wanted to do first: Her other dream was to take the boys to Disney World. The trip was a prize she'd been given by the top fundraiser in the AAC's annual Walk for Life in June. With much fanfare and a great public send-off, Elizabeth, Matthew, and Christopher all went to Florida in mid-October. They did everything at Disney World; the boys went on every ride. But Elizabeth was exhausted by it, and she was getting sick again. After five days in Florida, she came home.*

*By this time, she had been hospitalized more than a dozen times. The disease was wearing her down. The day after she came back to Boston, she went into the hospital again. Within three days she had slipped into a coma. Less than ten days later, on November 4, 1988,*

*Elizabeth Ramos died. She never spent a single night in her new house.*

*The boys now live in New York with their Aunt Lucy. The dream house is on the market.*        [1991]

 73

# Missing Persons: African American Women, AIDS, and the History of Disease

EVELYNN HAMMONDS

*Nobody is ever in to see me or hear my complaints. They are never there when I try to make an appointment to get anything done. Nobody cares. I continue to get sick over and over again, and nobody listens to what I have to say. I don't think that's fair, because I feel I deserve better, because not only am I a woman, I am also a human being; and it's hard enough for me to deal with the issue of having AIDS, dying a day at a time and to have to live under the circumstances that I am under.[1]*

## WHY DO AFRICAN AMERICAN WOMEN DISPROPORTIONATELY GET AIDS?

In spite of the fact that the majority of women with AIDS are African American, the devastating toll that AIDS is taking on the lives of these women has yet to be perceived as a national crisis. Neither scientific, epidemiological, nor historical or cultural studies about AIDS have addressed the question of why African American women are at such greater risk for HIV infection and why their survival rates are so abysmally low. Now that the percentages for women with AIDS have more than doubled in the last two years (in some cities women make up twenty-five percent of the AIDS cases), research on women is in process. One might wonder, however, whether the government's recent focus on women is not mainly directed at their reproductive lives, that is, women become the risk factor for HIV in children. In this essay I want to look at a number of factors that have supported the invisibility of African American women with AIDS. First, I look at examples of the representation of these women in the media, in particular focusing on how media reports shape and reflect the social context of the epi-

demic with regard to African American women with AIDS. Secondly, I discuss how AIDs is affecting the lives of poor, African American women. In sum, I argue that African American women are disproportionately vulnerable to the ravages of AIDS in part because of the long-term and persistent failure of public health practices to control sexually transmitted diseases in the African American community.

It goes without saying that gender has not been at the center of discussions or research about AIDS. The way in which AIDS was first conceptualized as a disease of gay men, then a disease of various "risk groups," e.g., intravenous drug users, foreclosed the recognition of women as potentially a significant proportion of the AIDS caseload.[2] This is even more apparent when examining gender within racial categories. In the broadest sense, little attention has been paid to the plight of African American women with AIDS because they are women. Overall, the medical establishment and most activist groups have focused on men, who make up the larger numbers of people with AIDS.[3] And as feminists and other activists have documented, women have historically received unequal treatment in the United States health care system. African American women, as evidenced by their higher rates of many diseases, have long been among the least served by the health care system. AIDS appears in African American communities at the end of a long trail of neglect in the Reagan-Bush years—including the cut-off of federal funds for abortion, jobs, housing, and the failure to control *sexually transmitted diseases*. The conditions that African American women live under in their communities, their roles as mothers, wives, workers, and lovers, all shape their responses to AIDS.

## MEDIA IMAGES: "MOST ARE POOR, MANY ARE RECKLESS"

The impact of HIV infection on African American women and other women of color has received an odd sort of coverage in the media. On the one hand when the threat of AIDS to women is discussed, no mention is made of African American women. When African American women are discussed, they are relegated to the drug abuser category or partners of drug abusers or bad mother category for passing

AIDS on to their children. A good example of this appeared in August 1987 in an article by Jane Gross, which appeared on the front page of the *New York Times*. The headline read: "Bleak Lives: Women Carrying AIDS," followed by "Women Who Carry the AIDS Virus: Most Are Poor, Many are Reckless."[4] I refer to this article in part to underline how little has changed since it appeared in 1987 and because it so clearly lays out the assumptions about women who become infected with HIV.

First, the article stated the grim statistics; in New York City in August 1987 there were 50,000 women infected with HIV; eighty percent were black and Hispanic. The first paragraph of the article announced:

> They are the primary carriers of the disease from the world of drug abuse to the larger community, making their education an increasingly urgent task.

The identification of women as "carriers" was stated without supporting scientific data. Perhaps the writer was unaware of the scientific data but, by 1987, studies showed that women were at greater risk of infection from infected men than the other way around. Or, in the rhetoric of the medical literature, female to male transmission of HIV is "less efficient."[5] The women in this article are portrayed as passive victims in abusive relationships with men who are most often drug abusers. Their lives are described as "unruly," "chaotic," "despairing." The most demeaning attack is made on African American women who, though HIV positive, become pregnant and choose to continue their pregnancies rather than have an abortion. Gross reported that

> . . . Women explain that they want to have another child to leave something behind in the face of dearth, that they view a fifty-fifty chance of having a healthy baby acceptable odds. But counselors say these explanations usually do not surface until a pregnancy has proceeded past the point when abortion is possible. They wind up having babies more by default than intent.[6]

The behaviors highlighted by these experts' comments, suggest that these African American women are not responsible to themselves or to the children they bear. The prevalence of such attitudes is attested to by reports from women of color who are

HIV positive, who are, in many cities, being subjected to hostility from hospital staff and counselors because they want to have their babies. Gross, like other writers, portrays African American women largely from the perspective of neonatal infection, which implies that the women themselves are not patients but only vectors of disease, or put another way, the risk factor for their children.

The article goes on to quote a social worker who commented that from her experience running a counseling group, only the middle-class women in her group expressed concern about their health. "Among the poorest women, who are often indifferent or ignorant about health care, there is no demonstrated concern about their physical well-being. . . ." The sense of powerlessness that African American women who are HIV positive experience is used to emphasize their irresponsibility. Such comments leave unexamined the personal and economic difficulties that these women face in their attempts to get access to good health care and counseling. Gross does not present a portrait of women who are fighting a disease, and the reader is not drawn to be sympathetic toward them. Instead, it is a portrait of the by now classic stereotype of black women who are unstable and irresponsible, even more so because they now carry a deadly disease. They are blamed for not having control over their lives.

The article does not report that these women are being diagnosed at later stages in the disease. We are not told about the different opportunistic infections in women that could possibly mask early diagnosis. We are not told how many of these women have lost their homes and custody of children when their HIV status is made known, nor that their opportunities for anonymous testing, good counseling, or access to drug treatment programs are severely limited. There have now been recommendations to implement testing of all pregnant women. African American women are likely to become the first nonincarcerated, civilian United States citizens to confront mass screening for HIV. And I would suggest, in the wake of this recommendation, there is also the possibility that some might call for mandatory abortions or, given that Medicaid monies are not allowed to cover abortion in most states, preemptive sterilization for these same HIV-infected pregnant women.

## QUICK: NAME ONE BLACK WOMAN WITH AIDS

Gross's article is not atypical. I have read few stories in the mainstream media detailing the emotional trauma that HIV infection causes for African American women; nothing about survival strategies; no stories of daily life—how living with AIDS affects jobs, family relationships, or friendships. On Sunday, June 17, 1990, the *New York Times* ran a full page of profiles of black and white gay people living with AIDS. One woman was interviewed though no picture of her was printed. She said, "You want so much for someone to hold you, and no one wants to touch you." Her response only hints at the emotional trauma such women are facing. So many questions remain unasked in such accounts—how are these women dealing with the stigma associated with a disease that is perceived to be associated largely with white gay males? How are they dealing with the loss of their children or how are they preparing their children for their own impending deaths? What is happening to women who don't have children or extended families? Perhaps the problem is that, to date, no "famous" black woman has died of AIDS for the media to create a symbol that would garner support for African American women with the disease.

The tactics used by the media to make the American public aware of the various dimensions of the AIDS epidemic have been troubling. One tactic has been to take one person's story and transform it into a symbol for some particular aspect of the epidemic that needs to be addressed. For example, Ryan White epitomized the "innocent" child, made a victim of the bigoted attitudes of parents who barred him from his local school and town. White's story became the vehicle to educate the public about the small risk of AIDS being transmitted casually and the plight of "innocent" children who are stigmatized because of their infection. Similarly, the story of Kimberly Bergalis, alleged to have been infected by her dentist, has been the centerpiece of the debate over whether there should be restrictions on dentists, physicians, and health care workers who are HIV positive. White gay male artists, entertainers, and writers suffering and dying from AIDS are featured in articles that eloquently reveal to the larger heterosexual world the emotional toll that AIDS has taken in gay communities while breaking down stereotypes about gay life. These articles serve to reveal the junctures and disjunctures in our beliefs about sexuality and sexual practices as well as the anxieties in American life about sex and morality.

In each of these cases, in some way the media has used such symbols to subtly urge the public to embrace people with AIDS. African American women with AIDS are constantly represented with respect to drug use—either their own or their partner's. They are largely poor or working class. They are single mothers. Media portrayals of these people with AIDS allude to the spectre of drug abuse and uncontrolled sexuality coupled with welfare "dependency" and irresponsibility. Such allusions undermine any representations of African American women with AIDS that would allow them to be embraced by the larger public.

Public health educators have been challenged to deal with the issue of cultural sensitivity in AIDS prevention and education material, and thus have created advertising campaigns displaying African American women in a positive light. This advertising often presents nameless figures who may look more like the average black woman, and thus encourage other African American women to identify with the ads' message on AIDS prevention; but these ads may not be able to elevate the threat AIDS poses to African American women, or the plight of those already infected, to the levels of recognition that could dethrone the more prevalent negative imagery.

## THE FACE OF AIDS FOR AFRICAN AMERICAN WOMEN

The average age of African American women with AIDS at the time of diagnosis is thirty-six years. A significant number of the women were diagnosed when they were in their twenties and thus would have been infected as adolescents.[7] Most of these young women live in urban areas in the Northeast. The fact that many of the African American women with AIDS are so young is a startling statistic. It suggests that they were infected at an age when they had the least control over their sexual lives. They were at an age when they were vulnerable to the demands not just of partners of their own age, but older men as well. In contrast to a picture of women in their twenties aware of the consequences of their actions, instead some number of African American women contracted AIDS at an age when their ideas about sex were just being formed. Many of these young women also live in urban communities where few support systems exist to protect them and allow them to grow unmolested to adulthood. Additionally, it is reported that few HIV-infected individuals in communities of color with high rates of infection, such as in sections of New York City, know their infection status.[8] Many African American women and men simply do not know that they are in danger. Far too many are only found to have AIDS upon autopsy.

Though fifty-one percent of women with AIDS were infected through intravenous (IV) drug use, twenty-nine percent were infected through heterosexual contact.[9] As Ernest Drucker notes, in New York City, ". . . even those women who did have histories of IV drug use were, almost universally, *also* the sexual partners of men (sometimes many men) who were IV drug users. . . . Thus, it becomes extremely difficult to attribute these women's infection to one exposure or the other, since they were dually exposed for sustained periods of time to both risks of infection."[10] It is obvious then that African American women in such contexts are both dually exposed and dually victimized in a social setting now being ravaged by an incurable disease.

Every aspect of family life is touched by the presence of AIDS. "As AIDS cuts a swath through family after family, some have four or five members already sick with the disease and more infected."[11] Few people are aware of what these families face. Suki Ports, of the Minority Task Force on Aids, reported the following story:

> Frances worked. She had difficulty after the birth of her six-year-old and needed many transfusions. She had a second child, who is fourteen months old. This baby was diagnosed with AIDS, so Frances quit work to take care of her . . . She then had to make a choice. She could move into an SRO, with two children, one sick, no cooking facilities except a hot plate, and get full benefits, or move in with her mother and receive no benefits, because her mother works . . . Her choice was made. It is difficult, and it's straining the mothers' resources and good nature. Family benefits to assist the whole family are not available without creating a new precedent for payments in an already strained financial outlook.[12]

Many women are also hiding the fact that members of their family have AIDS. Long-practiced and familiar cultural beliefs are breaking down in the face of AIDS in African American communities. There is little evidence that fear or stigma is decreasing. Anecdotal reports suggest that some families who have relatives die of AIDS are refusing to have public funerals or indicate the cause of death in obituary notices. I found Frances's story as the debate was being waged in Congress on the bill that would mandate that businesses protect the jobs of workers who had to take leave to care for family members who are ill. I heard no one speak to the need for this bill because of the spread of the AIDS epidemic.

## CONCLUSION

I believe that the invisibility and objectification of African American women in the AIDS epidemic is tied to the historical treatment of African American women with respect to sexually transmitted disease. The Tuskegee syphilis experiment is just one example of the legacy of danger and death that sexually transmitted diseases represent for African American communities. For a black woman to expose that she had a sexually transmitted disease was, for much of this century, to render herself multiply stigmatized, bringing up older images of immorality and uncontrolled sexuality that neither class nor educational privilege could protect her from. It possibly meant that pregnancy carried more risks; it often precipitated long-term health problems and even early death. That physicians and public health experts have long accepted higher rates of sexually transmitted diseases among African American women is a sign that somehow this had quietly become a norm. That overt racial comments from white health care providers on the cause of this higher incidence of sexually transmitted disease and the attendant problems for fetal and maternal health are less evident today than in the 1920s is not necessarily a sign that attitudes have changed or that the stigma associated with these diseases has diminished.

Current public health efforts must address the long term stigma that African American women continue to experience with respect to sexually transmitted diseases. As the uninterrupted disparity in the incidence of these diseases within this community over the last fifty years indicates, those efforts have largely failed. Bringing to the fore the historical treatment and experience of African American women, their children, and their partners with respect to sexually transmitted diseases in the past is a necessary step.

In addition, most of all, what is needed is a viable black feminist movement. African American feminists need to intervene in the public and scientific debates about AIDS, making plain the impact that medical and public health policy will have on African American women. An analysis of gender is desperately needed to frame the discussion of sexual relations in the black community. Sexism lies behind the disempowerment and lack of control that African American women experience in the face of AIDS. African American women are multiply stigmatized in the AIDS epidemic—only a multifaceted African American feminist analysis attentive to issues of race, sex, gender, and power can adequately expose the impact of AIDS on our communities and formulate just policies to save women's lives.                                    [1995]

### NOTES

1. Testimony of Margaret Rivera, Report of the Public Hearing, "AIDS: Its Impact on Women, Children and Families." (New York State Division for Women, 12 June 1987), 21.
2. IV drug users were constructed as male in the mass media before the spectacle of "crack babies." Moreover, drug treatment models and facilities continue to favor male clients while the despair of women's addiction to crack disappears quickly behind our image of them as monsters for "delivering drugs" to their babies.
3. By using the term "attention," it is not my intent in this essay to disparage or belittle the heroic efforts of the many health care workers, activists, and others who *have* labored to bring the plight of African American women and other women with AIDS to light. By using the term "attention," I only mean to address the fact that the deaths of African American women with AIDS have not garnered the kind of front-page headlines or other prominent popular media attention given to other people with AIDS, as will be discussed more fully later in the essay.
4. Jane Gross, "Bleak Lives, Women Carrying AIDS," *New York Times,* 27 August 1987.
5. N. S. Padian, "Heterosexual Transmission of Acquired Immunodeficiency Syndrome: International Perspectives and National Projections," *Review of Infectious Diseases* 9 (1987): 947–960.
6. Gross, "Bleak Lives."
7. Ellerbrock, "Epidemiology," 2973.
8. Ernest Drucker, "Epidemic in the War Zone: AIDS and Community Survival in New York City," *International Journal of Health Services* 20, no. 4 (1990): 605. Drucker notes that fewer than ten percent of the estimated 150 to 250 thousand people infected with HIV in New York City know their HIV status.
9. Ellerbrock, "Epidemiology," 2974.
10. Drucker, "Epidemic," 609.
11. Drucker, "Epidemic," 613.
12. "AIDS: Its Impact on Women, Children and Families," 51.

 74

# *Breast Cancer: The Environmental Connection*

RITA ARDITTI AND
TATIANA SCHREIBER

Today in the United States, we live in the midst of a cancer epidemic. One out of every three people will get some form of cancer and one out of four will die from it. Cancer is currently the second leading cause of death; by the year 2000, it will likely have become the primary cause of death. It is now more than two decades since the National Cancer Act was signed, yet the treatments offered to cancer patients are the same as those offered 50 years ago: surgery, radiation, and chemotherapy (or slash, burn, and poison, as they are called bitterly by both patients and increasingly disappointed professionals). And in spite of sporadic optimistic pronouncements from the cancer establishment, survival rates for the three main cancer killers—lung, breast, and colo-rectal cancer—have remained virtually unchanged.

In the '60s and '70s, environmental activists and a few scientists emphasized that cancer was linked to environmental contamination, and their concerns began to have an impact on public understanding of the disease. In the '80s and '90s, however, with an increasingly conservative political climate and concerted efforts on the part of industry to play down the importance of chemicals as a cause of cancer, we are presented with a new image of cancer. Now it is portrayed as an individual problem that can only be overcome with the help of experts and, then, only if one has the money and know-how to recruit them for one's personal survival efforts. This emphasis on personal responsibility and lifestyle factors has reached absurd proportions. People with cancer are asked why they "brought this disease on themselves" and why they don't work harder at "getting well."

While people with cancer should be encouraged not to fall into victim roles and to do everything possible to strengthen their immune systems (our primary line of defense against cancer), it seems that the sociopolitical and economic dimensions of cancer have been pushed completely out of the picture. "Blaming the victim" is a convenient way to avoid looking at the larger environmental and social issues that form individual experiences. Here we want to talk about environmental links to cancer in general and to breast cancer in particular, the kinds of research that should be going on, why they're not happening, and the political strategies needed to turn things around.

Extensive evidence exists to indicate that cancer *is* an environmental disease. Even the most conservative scientists agree that approximately 80 percent of all cancers are in some way related to environmental factors. Support for this view relies on four lines of evidence: (1) dramatic differences in the incidences of cancer between communities—incidences of cancer among people of a given age in different parts of the world can vary by a factor of ten to a hundred; (2) changes in the incidence of cancer (either lower or higher rates) in groups that migrate to a new country; (3) changes in the incidence of particular types of cancer with the passage of time; and (4) the actual identification of the specific causes of certain cancers (such as the case of beta-naphthylamine, responsible for an epidemic of bladder cancer among dye workers employed at Du Pont factories). Other well-known environmentally linked cancers are lung cancer, linked to as-

bestos, arsenic, chromium, bischloromethyl ether, mustard gas, ionizing radiation, nickel, polycyclic hydrocarbons in soot, tar, oil, and of course, smoking; edometrial cancer, linked to estrogen use; thyroid cancer, often the result of childhood irradiation; and liver cancer, linked to exposure to vinyl chloride.

The inescapable conclusion is that if cancer is largely environmental in origin, it is largely preventable.

## OUR ENVIRONMENT IS A HEALTH HAZARD

"Environment" as we use it here includes not only air, water, and soil, but also our diets, medical procedures, and living and working conditions. That means that the food we eat, the water we drink, the air we breathe, the radiation to which we are exposed, where we live, what kind of work we do, and the stress that we suffer—these are responsible for at least 80 percent of all cancers. For instance, under current EPA regulations as many as 60 cancer-causing pesticides can legally be used to grow the most commonly eaten foods. Some of these foods are allowed to contain 20 or more carcinogens, making it impossible to measure how much of each substance a person actually consumes. As Rachel Carson wrote in *Silent Spring* in 1962, "This piling up of chemicals from many different sources creates a total exposure that cannot be measured. It is meaningless, therefore, to talk about the 'safety' of any specific amount of residues." In other words, our everyday food is an environmental hazard to our health.

Recently, a study on the trends in cancer mortality in industrialized countries has revealed that while stomach cancer has been steadily declining, brain and other central-nervous-system cancers, breast cancer, multiple myeloma, kidney cancer, non-Hodgkin's lymphoma, and melanoma have increased in persons aged 55 and older. Given this context, it is not extreme to suspect that breast cancer, which has reached epidemic proportions in the United States, may be linked to environmental ills. This year, estimates are that 180,000 women will develop breast cancer and 46,000 will die from it. In other words, in the coming year, nearly as many women will die from breast cancer as there were American lives lost in the entire Vietnam War. Cancer is the leading cause of death among women aged 35 to 54, with about a third of these deaths due to breast cancer. Breast cancer incidence data meet three of the four lines of reasoning linking it to the environment: (1) the incidence of breast cancer between communities can vary by a factor of seven; (2) the risk for breast cancer among populations that have migrated becomes that of their new residence within a generation, as is the case for Japanese women who have migrated to the United States; and (3) the incidence of breast cancer in the United States has swelled from one in twenty in 1940 to one in eight in the '90s.

A number of factors have been linked to breast cancer; a first blood relative with the disease, early onset of menstruation, late age at first full-term pregnancy, higher socioeconomic status, late menopause, being Jewish, etc. However, for the overwhelming majority (70 to 80 percent) of breast cancer patients, their illness is not clearly linked to any of these factors. Research suggests that the development of breast cancer probably depends on a complex interplay among environmental exposures, genetic predisposition to the disease, and hormonal activity.

Research on the actual identification of causal factors, however, is given low priority and proceeds at a snail's pace. We still don't know, for example, the effects of birth control pills and the hormone replacement therapy routinely offered to menopausal women. Hormonal treatments are fast becoming the method of choice for the treatment of infertility, while we know nothing about their long-range effects. And the standard addition of hormones in animal feed means that all women (and men) are exposed to hormone residues in meat. Since there is general consensus that estrogen somehow plays a role in the development of breast cancer, hormonal interventions (through food or drugs) are particularly worrisome.

We still don't know about the high fat-cancer link, but even if the high fat-breast cancer correlation is established, it is unlikely to fully explain how breast cancer develops. The breast is rich in adipose cells, and carcinogens that accumulate in these fat tissues may be responsible for inducing cancer rather than the fat itself or the fat alone. Environmental contamination of human breast milk with PCBs, PBBs and DDE (a metabolite of the pesticide DDT) is a widely acknowledged phenomenon. These fat-soluble substances are poorly metabolized and have a long half-life in human tissue.

Serious concerns have been raised about the risks that this contamination entails for infants who are breast-fed. But what is outrageous in the discussion about human breast milk poisoning is that little or no mention is made of the possible effects on the women themselves, particularly since it is known that most of these substances have *estrogenic* properties (that is, they behave like estrogen in the body). It is as if the women, whose breasts contain these carcinogens, do not exist. We witness the paradox of women being made invisible, even while their toxic breasts are put under the microscope.

## THE PESTICIDE STUDIES

Very recently, some scientists have at last begun to look at the chemical-breast cancer connection. In 1990, two Israeli scientists from Hebrew University's Hadassah School of Medicine, Elihu Richter and Jerry Westin, reported a surprising statistic. They found that Israel was the only country among 28 countries surveyed that registered a real drop in breast cancer mortality in the decade 1976 to 1986. This happened in the face of a worsening of all known risk factors, such as fat intake and age at first pregnancy. As Westin noted, "All and all, we expected a rise in breast cancer mortality of approximately 20 percent overall, and what we found was that there was an 8 percent drop, and in the youngest age group, the drop was 34 percent, as opposed to an expected 20 percent rise, so, if we put those two together, we are talking about a difference of about 50 percent, which is enormous."

Westin and Richter could not account for the drop solely in terms of demographic changes or improved medical intervention. Instead, they suspected it might have been related to a 1978 ban on three carcinogenic pesticides (benzene hexachloride, lindane, and DDT) that heavily contaminated milk and milk products in Israel. Prior to 1978, Westin said, "at least one of them [the three pesticides] was found in the milk here at a rate 100 times greater than it was in the U.S. in the same period, and in the worst case, nearly a thousand times greater." This observation led Westin and Richter to hypothesize that there might be a connection between the decrease in exposure following the ban and the decrease in breast cancer mortality. They believed the pesticides could have promoted enzymes that in turn increased the virulence of breast cancer in women. When the pesticides were removed from the diet, Westin and Richter speculated, there was a situation of much less virulent cancer and the mortality from breast cancer fell.

Westin and Richter are convinced that there is a critical need to increase awareness about environmental conditions and cancer. Health care clinicians, for example, could play an important role in the detection of potential exposures to toxic chemicals that might be missed in large studies. This is a refreshing view since it encourages individual physicians to ask questions about work environments, living quarters, and diet, the answers to which could provide important clues about the cancer–environment connection.

In the United States, levels of pesticide residues in adipose tissue have been decreasing since the 1970s (following the banning of DDT and decreased use of other carcinogenic pesticides) while the breast cancer rate continues to rise. This observation would seem to contradict the pesticide hypothesis. However, it is important to remember that the chemicals could act differently at different exposure levels, they are unlikely to act alone, and the time of exposure may be important. For example, if a child is exposed during early adolescence, when breast tissue is growing rapidly, the result may be different than exposure later in life.

### RADIATION AND MAMMOGRAPHY

Another area that demands urgent investigation is the role of radiation in the development of breast cancer. It is widely accepted that ionizing radiation at high doses causes breast cancer, but low doses are generally regarded as safe. Questions remain, however, regarding the shape of the dose-response curve, the length of the latency period, and the importance of age at time of exposure. These ques-

tions are of great importance to women because of the emphasis on mammography for early detection. There is evidence that mammography screening reduces death from breast cancer in women aged 50 or older. However, Dr. Rosalie Bertell (director of the International Institute of Concern for Public Health, author of *No Immediate Danger: Prognosis for a Radioactive World* [1985] and well-known critic of the nuclear establishment) raises serious questions about mammography screening. In a paper entitled "Comments on Ontario Mammography Program," Bertell criticized a breast cancer screening program planned by the Ontario Health Minister in 1989. Bertell argued that the program, which would potentially screen 300,000 women, was a plan to "reduce breast cancer death by increasing breast cancer incidence."

According to Bertell, the present breast cancer epidemic is a direct result of "above ground weapons testing" done in Nevada between 1951 and 1963, when 200 nuclear bombs were set off and the fallout dispersed across the country. Because the latency period for breast cancer peaks at about 40 years, this is an entirely reasonable hypothesis.

### THE SURVEILLANCE THEORY

Current theory supports the concept that cancerous mutations are a common phenomenon in the body of normal individuals and that the immune system intervenes before mutated cells can multiply. Known as the "surveillance" theory of cancer, the basic premise is that cancer can develop when the immune system fails to eliminate mutant cells. Carcinogenic mutations can be induced by radiation or chemicals, for instance, and if immunological competence is reduced at a critical time, the mutated cells can thrive and grow.

Given the apparent importance of the immune system in protecting us from cancer, we ought to be concerned not only with eliminating carcinogens in our environment but also with making certain that our immune systems are not under attack. Recent evidence that ultraviolet radiation depresses the immune system is therefore particularly ominous. At a hearing on "Global Change Research: Ozone Depletion and Its Impact," held in November 1991 by the Senate Committee on Commerce, Science, and

Transportation, a panel of scientists reported that ozone depletion is even more serious than previously thought. According to the data, the ozone layer over the United States is thinning at a rate of 3 to 5 percent per decade, resulting in increased ultraviolet radiation that "will reduce the quantity and quality of crops, increase skin cancer, *suppress the immune system,* and disrupt marine ecosystems" [our emphasis]. (The report also states that a 10 percent decrease in ozone will lead to approximately 1.7 million additional cases of cataracts world-wide per year and at least 250,000 additional cases of skin cancer.) As the writers make chillingly clear, since this is happening literally over our heads, there is no place for us to run.

In addition, dioxin (an extremely toxic substance that has been building up steadily in the environment since the growth of the chlorinated-chemical industry following World War II) can produce alterations that disrupt the immune system. "Free radicals" created by exposure to low-level radiation can cause immune system abnormalities. In other words, our basic mechanisms of defense against cancer are being weakened by the chemical soup in which we are immersed.

It follows that an intelligent and long-range cancer-prevention-strategy would make a clean environment its number one priority. Prevention, however, is given low priority in our national cancer agenda. In 1992, out of an almost $2 billion National Cancer Institute (NCI) budget, $132.7 million was spent on breast cancer research but only about 15 percent of that was for preventive research. Moreover, research on the cellular mechanism of cancer development, toward which much of the "prevention" effort goes, does not easily get translated into actual prevention strategies.

In his 1989 exposé of the cancer establishment, *The Cancer Industry,* Ralph Moss writes that until the late '60s, the cancer establishment presented the view that "cancer is . . . widely believed to consist of a hereditable, and therefore genetic," problem. That line of thinking is still with us but with added emphasis on the personal responsibility we each have for our cancers (smoking and diet) and little or no acknowledgement of the larger environmental context. In a chapter appropriately titled "Preventing Prevention," Moss provides an inkling of why this is so.

The close ties between industry and two of the most influential groups determining our national cancer agenda—the National Cancer Advisory Board and the President's Cancer Panel—are revealing. The chair of the President's Cancer Panel throughout most of the '80s, for example, was Armand Hammer, head of Occidental International Corporation. Among its subsidiaries is Hooker Chemical Company, implicated in the environmental disaster in Love Canal. In addition, Moss, formerly assistant director of public affairs at Memorial Sloan-Kettering Cancer Center (MSKCC), outlines the structure and affiliation of that institution's leadership. MSKCC is the world's largest private cancer center, and the picture that emerges borders on the surreal: in 1988, 32.7 percent of its board of overseers were tied to the oil, chemical and automobile industries; 34.6 percent were professional investors (bankers, stockbrokers, venture capitalists). Board members included top officials of drug companies—Squibb, Bristol-Myers, Merck—and influential members of the media—CBS, the *New York Times,* Warner's Communications, and *Reader's Digest*—as well as leaders of the $55-billion cigarette industry.

Moss's research leaves little doubt about the allegiances of the cancer establishment. Actual cancer prevention would require a massive reorganization of industry, hardly in the interest of the industrial and financial elites. Instead of preventing the generation of chemical and toxic waste, the strategy adopted by industry and government has been one of "management." But as Barry Commoner, director of the Center for the Biology of Natural Systems at Queens College in Brooklyn, New York, put it rather succinctly, "The best way to stop toxic chemicals from entering the environment is to not produce them."

Instead, the latest "prevention" strategy for breast cancer moves in a completely different direction. A trial has been approved that will test the effect of a breast cancer drug (an antiestrogen, tamoxifen) in a healthy population, with the hope that it will have a preventive effect. The trial will involve 16,000 women considered at high risk for breast cancer and will be divided into a control group and a tamoxifen group. The National Women's Health Network (a national public-interest organization dedicated solely to women and health) is unequivocal in its criticism of the trial. Adriane Fugh-Berman, a member of the Network board, wrote in its September/October 1991 newsletter, "In our view the trial is premature in its assumptions, weak in its hypothesis, questionable in its ethics and misguided in its public health ramifications." The criticisms center on the fact that tamoxifen causes liver cancer in rats and liver changes in all species tested and that a number of endometrial cancers have been reported among tamoxifen users. Fugh-Berman points out that approving the testing of a potent, hormonal drug in healthy women and calling that "prevention" sets a dangerous precedent. This drug-oriented trial symbolizes, in a nutshell, the paradoxes of short-sighted cancer-prevention strategies: more drugs are used to counteract the effect of previous exposures to drugs, chemicals or other carcinogenic agents. It is a vicious circle and one that will not be easily broken.

## CANCER, POVERTY, POLITICS

Though it is often said that affluent women are at higher risk for breast cancer, this disease is actually on the rise (both incidence and mortality) among African-American women, hardly an "affluent" population overall. The African-American Breast Cancer Alliance of Minnesota, organized in October 1990, has noted this steady increase and the limited efforts that have been made to reach African-Americans with information and prevention strategies. People of color often live in the most polluted areas of this country, where factories, incinerators, garbage, and toxic waster are part of the landscape. Native American nations are particularly targeted by waste-management companies that try to take advantage of the fact that "because of the sovereign relationship many reservations have with the federal government, they are not bound by the same environmental laws as the states around them."

Poverty and pollution go hand in hand. The 1988 Greenpeace report *Mortality and Toxics Along the Mississippi River* showed that the "total mortality rates and cancer mortality rates in the counties along the Mississippi River were significantly higher than in the rest of the nation's counties" and that "the areas of the river in which public health statistics are most troubling have populations which are disproportionately poor and black." These are also the areas that have the greatest number of toxic discharges. Louisiana has the dubious distinction of being the state with the most reported toxic releases—741.2 million pounds a year. Cancer rates in the Louisians section of the "Chemical Corridor" (the highly industrialized stretch of river between Baton Rouge and New Orleans) are among the highest in the nation. Use of the Mississippi River as a drinking-water source has been linked to higher than average rates of cancer in Louisiana. The rates of cancer of the colon, bladder, kidney, rectum, and lung all exceed national averages. Louisiana Attorney General William J. Guste, Jr., has criticized state officials who claimed that people of color and the poor *naturally* have higher cancer rates. You can't "point out race and poverty as cancer factors," said Guste, "without asking if poor people or blacks . . . reside in less desirable areas more heavily impacted by industrial emissions."

It follows that African-American women, living in the most contaminated areas of this country, would indeed be showing a disproportionate increase in breast cancer incidence. However, widespread epidemiological studies to chart such a correlation have not been undertaken. For instance, given the evidence implicating pesticides in the development of breast cancer, studies of migrant (and other) farm workers who have been exposed to such chemicals would seem imperative.

Women's groups around the country have started organizing to fight the breast cancer epidemic. A National Breast Cancer Coalition was founded in 1991. Its agenda is threefold: to increase the funding for research, to organize, and to educate. All of the recently organized groups consider prevention a priority, and one of their tasts will undoubtedly entail defining what effective prevention really means.

Cancer *is* and needs to be seen as a political issue. The women's health movement of the '70s made that strikingly clear and gave us a road map to the politics of women's health. In the '80s, AIDS activists have shown the power of direct action to influence research priorities and treatment deliveries. In the '90s, an effective cancer-prevention strategy demands that we challenge the present industrial practices of the corporate world, based solely on economic gains for the already powerful, and that we insist on an end to the toxic discharges that the government sanctions under the guise of "protecting our security." According to Lenny Siegel, research director of the Military Toxic Network, the Pentagon has produced more toxic waste in recent years—between 400,000 tons and 500,000 tons annually—than the five largest multinational chemical companies combined.

Indeed, if we want to stop not only breast cancer but all cancers, we need to think in global terms and to build a movement that will link together groups that previously worked at a respectful distance. At a worldwide level, the Women's World Congress for a Healthy Planet (attended by over 1500 women from 92 countries from many different backgrounds and perspectives) presented a position paper, Agenda 21, at the 1992 United Nations Earth Summit conference in Brazil. The paper articulates women's position on the environment and sustainable development that stresses pollution prevention, economic justice, and an end to conflict resolution through war and weapons production, probably the greatest force in destroying the environment.

On February 4, 1992, a group of 65 scientists released a statement at a press conference in Washington, D.C., entitled "Losing the 'War against Cancer'—Need for Public Policy Reforms," which calls for an amendment to the National Cancer Act that would "re-orient the mission and priorities of the NCI to cancer causes and prevention." The seeds of this movement have been sown. It is now our challenge to nourish this movement with grass-roots research, with demonstrations, and with demands that our society as a whole take responsibility for the environmental contamination that is killing us. [1992]

### NOTE

*Author's note:* Many thanks to the women of the Women's Community Cancer Project in Cambridge, Massachusetts, for their help and support. A longer version of this article with complete footnotes and references appeared in the *Resist* newsletter (May/June 1992).

## 🦎 75

# *Breathing Life Into Ourselves: The Evolution of the National Black Women's Health Project*

BYLLYE Y. AVERY

An important thing had happened for me in 1979. I began looking at myself as a black woman. Before that I had been looking at myself as a woman. When I left the birthing center, I went to work in a Comprehensive Employment Training Program (CETA) job at a community college and it brought me face-to-face with my sisters and face-to-face with myself. Just by the nature of the program and the population that I worked with, I had, for the first time in my life, a chance to ask a nineteen-year-old why—please give me the reason why—you have four babies and you're only nineteen years old. And I was able to listen, and bring these sisters together to talk about their lives. It was there that I started to understand the lives of black women and to realize that we live in a conspiracy of silence. It was hearing these women's stories that led me to start conceptualizing the National Black Women's Health Project.

First I wanted to do an hour-long presentation on black women's health issues, so I started doing research. I got all the books, and I was shocked at what I saw. I was angry—angry that the people who wrote these books didn't put it into a format that made sense to us, angry that nobody was saying anything to black women or to black men. I was so angry I threw one book across the room and it stayed there for three or four days, because I knew I had just seen the tip of the iceberg, but I also knew enough to know that I couldn't go back. I had opened my eyes, and I had to go on and look.

Instead of an hour-long presentation we had a conference. It didn't happen until 1983, but when it did, 2,000 women came. But I knew we couldn't just have a conference. From the health statistics I saw, I knew that there was a deeper problem. People needed to be able to work individually, and on a daily basis. So we got the idea of self-help groups. The first group we formed was in a rural area outside of Gainesville, with twenty-one women who were severely obese. I thought, "Oh this is a piece of cake. Obviously these sisters don't have any information. I'll go in there and talk to them about losing weight, talk to them about high blood pressure, talk to them about diabetes—it'll be easy."

Little did I know that when I got there, they would be able to tell me everything that went into a 1200-calorie-a-day diet. They all had been to Weight Watchers at least five or six times; they all had blood-pressure-reading machines in their homes as well as medications they were on. And when we sat down to talk, they said, "We know all that information, but what we also know is that living in the world that we are in, we feel like we are absolutely nothing." One woman said to me, "I work for General Electric making batteries, and, from the stuff they suit me up in, I know it's killing me." She said, "My home life is not working. My old man is an alcoholic. My kids got babies. Things are not well with me. And the one thing I know I can do when I come home is cook me a pot of food and sit down in front of the TV and eat it. And you can't take that away from me until you're ready to give me something in its place."

So that made me start to think that there was some other piece to this health puzzle that had been missing, that it's not just about giving information; people need something else. We just spent a lot of time talking. And while we were talking, we were planning the 1983 conference, so I took the information back to the planning committee. Lillie Allen (a trainer who works with NBWHP) was there. We worked with her to understand that we are dying inside. That unless we are able to go inside of ourselves and touch and breathe fire, breathe life into ourselves, that, of course, we couldn't be healthy. Lillie started working on a workshop that we named "Black and Female: What is the Reality?" This is a workshop that terrifies us all. And we are also terrified not to have it, because the conspiracy of silence is killing us.

## STOPPING VIOLENCE

As we started to talk, I looked at those health statistics in a new way. Now, I'm not saying that we

are not suffering from the things we die from— that's what the statistics give us. But what causes all this sickness? Like cardiovascular disease—it's the number one killer. What causes all that heart pain? When sisters take their shoes off and start talking about what's happening, the first thing we cry about is violence. The violence in our lives. And if you look in statistics books, they mention violence in one paragraph. They don't even give numbers, because they can't count it: the violence is too pervasive.

The number one issue for most of our sisters is violence—battering, sexual abuse. Same thing for their daughters, whether they are twelve or four. We have to look at how violence is used, how violence and sexism go hand in hand, and how it affects the sexual response of females. We have to stop it, because violence is the training ground for us.

When you talk to young people about being pregnant, you find out a lot of things. Number one is that most of these girls did not get pregnant by teenage boys; most of them got pregnant by their mother's boyfriends or their brothers or their daddies. We've been sitting on that. We can't just tell our daughters, "just say no." What do they do about all those feelings running around their bodies? And we need to talk to our brothers. We need to tell them, the incest makes us crazy. It's something that stays on our minds all the time. We need the men to know that. And they need to know that when they hurt us, they hurt themselves. Because we are their mothers, their sisters, their wives; we are their allies on this planet. They can't just damage one part of it without damaging themselves. We need men to stop giving consent, by their silence, to rape, to sexual abuse, to violence. You need to talk to your boyfriends, your husbands, your sons, whatever males you have around you—talk to them about talking to other men. When they are sitting around womanizing, talking bad about women, make sure you have somebody stand up and be your ally and help stop this. For future generations, this has got to stop somewhere.

## MOTHERS AND DAUGHTERS

If violence is the number one thing women talk about, the next is being mothers too early and too long. We've developed a documentary called "On Becoming a Woman: Mothers and Daughters Talking Together." It's eight mothers and eight daughters—sixteen ordinary people talking about extraordinary things.

The idea of the film came out of my own experience with my daughter. When Sonja turned eleven, I started bemoaning that there were no rituals left; there was nothing to let a girl know that once you get your period your life can totally change, nothing to celebrate that something wonderful is happening. So I got a cake that said, "Happy Birthday! Happy Menstruation!" It had white icing with red writing. I talked about the importance of becoming a woman, and, out of that, I developed a workshop for mothers and daughters for the public schools. I did the workshops in Gainesville, and, when we came to Atlanta, I started doing them there. The film took ten years, from the first glimmer of an idea to completion.

The film is in three parts. In the first part all the mothers talk about when we got our periods. Then the daughters who have their periods talk about getting theirs, and the ones who are still waiting talk about that. The second part of the film deals with contraception, birth control, anatomy and physiology. This part of the film is animated, so it keeps the kids' attention. It's funny. It shows all the anxiety: passing around condoms, hating it, saying, "Oh no, we don't want to do this."

The third part of the film is the hardest. We worked on communication with the mothers and daughters. We feel that the key to birth control and to controlling reproduction is the nature of the relationship between the parents and their young people. And what's happening is that everybody is willing to beat up on the young kids, asking, "Why did you get pregnant? Why did you do this?" No one is saying to the parents, "Do you need some help with learning how to talk to your young person? Do you want someone to sit with you? Do you want to see what it feels like?" We don't have all the answers. In this film, you see us struggling.

What we created, which was hard for the parents, is a safe space where everybody can say anything they need to say. And if you think about that, as parents, we have that relationship with our kids: we can ask them anything. But when we talk about sex, it's special to be in a space where the kids can ask *us*, "Mama, what do you do when you start feeling funny all in your body?" What the kids want to know is, what about lust? What do we do about it? And that's the very information that we don't want to give us. That's "our business." But they want to hear it from us, because they can trust us. And we have to struggle with how we do that: How do we share that information? How do we deal with our feelings?

### REALIZING THE DREAM

The National Black Women's Health Project has ninety-six self-help groups in twenty-two states, six groups in Kenya, and a group in Barbados and in Belize. In addition, we were just funded by the W. K. Kellogg Foundation to do some work in three housing projects in Atlanta. We received $1,032,000 for a three-year period to set up three community centers. Our plan is to do health screening and referral for adolescents and women, and in addition to hook them up with whatever social services they need—to help cut through the red tape. There will be computerized learning programs and individualized tutorial programs to help young women get their General Equivalency Degrees (GED), along with a panel from the community who will be working on job readiness skills. And we'll be doing our self-help groups—talking about who we are, examining, looking at ourselves.

We hope this will be a model program that can be duplicated anywhere. And we're excited about it. Folks in Atlanta thought it was a big deal for a group of black women to get a million dollars. We thought it was pretty good, too. Our time is coming. [1994]

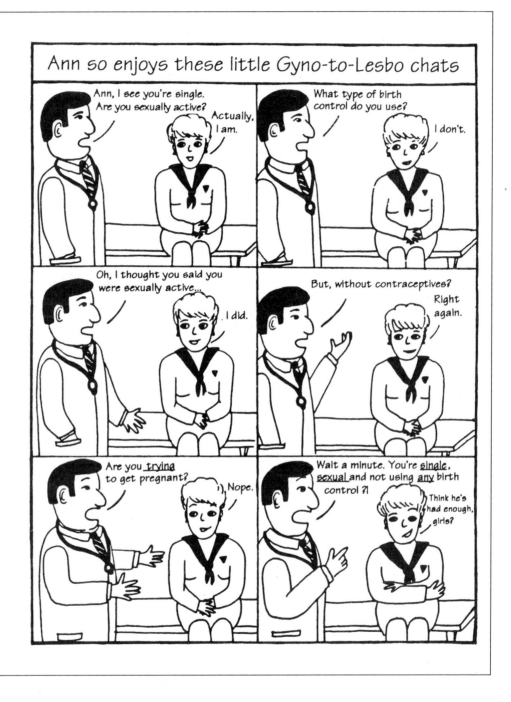

# Women and Religion

The values and policies of institutionalized religion have had a powerful impact on our life choices and views of ourselves. Many women appreciate the spiritual aspects of their religious traditions but find the discriminatory practices and policies of religious institutions confining and unjust.

A Catholic, Mary Ann Sorrentino writes about her experience of being publicly excommunicated for helping other women obtain abortions. She describes the pain imposed on her family when the church refused to confirm her daughter unless she repudiated what her mother believed.

While throughout most of Jewish history the synagogue has primarily been the domain of men, recently women have been ordained as rabbis. Laura Geller discusses some of the implications of women having this position of power in Judaism. Because social distance between the congregant and the clergy is diminished when the rabbi is a woman, she foresees a breakdown of religious hierarchy, leading Jews to see their rabbi not as a "priest" but as a teacher and enabling congregants to become more active participants in the life of the synagogue.

"In Her Own Image" describes the work of Christian women of various denominations who have entered the clergy. In addition to their feminist theological ideas, their very presence in churches challenges tradition. For example, Episcopal priest Carter Heyward, a lesbian, argues that it is important for gay and lesbian priests to be as "visible as we can be just to show that we are already here. It is not like the Church has a choice. We are in it already." These women's voices make visible and legitimate female experiences in churches and synagogues of the 1990s.

---

# 76

# *My Church Threw Me Out*

MARY ANN SORRENTINO

I have never had an abortion myself, nor have I ever performed one. But my Church has told me that because I believe that women should be able to have abortions if they so desire, I have automatically excommunicated myself. I still believe that I am a Catholic; I will always be a Catholic—whether or not I can take communion or be buried with the Church's rites. I intend to keep my faith and to fight to change my Church.

I had no idea that I was excommunicated until last May, two days before my daughter's confirmation. Her religion teacher called me that Friday morning and asked me to bring Luisa, who was then 15, to an afternoon meeting with Father Egan, our pastor. Although the teacher was not allowed to tell me why, she said that Luisa's confirmation hung in the balance. I was stunned. Luisa had passed all her tests, and another parish priest had already interviewed her once. I was expecting 20 guests on Sunday to celebrate. I called Father Egan immediately. He told me that Luisa could not be confirmed until he had interrogated her about her views on abortion.

His message was clear: I was the problem. For the last nine years I have been executive director of Planned Parenthood of Rhode Island. As far as the Catholic Church was concerned, my only child could not be confirmed until she had repudiated what her mother stood for.

No one had told Luisa why she was being dismissed from school early, so when I picked her up, she was in tears. She said, "I thought Daddy or Grandma died and that's why you came to get me." When I told her the reason, she began to sob.

I was so outraged at the idea of this ordeal Luisa had to go through that I decided to tape the meeting, in case we needed a record later. My husband, Al, who is a lawyer, accompanied Luisa and me, even though Father Egan had not invited him. When the priest arrived, Al told him he didn't understand why his daughter had to be singled out for questioning from a class of 75. "Because she lives in a particular atmosphere," Father Egan said. "Her mother is an advocate of abortion. I have to ascertain whether Luisa believes in abortion. That's all." Then Father Egan said to me, "You're the one who ties my hands. I *want* your daughter to be confirmed. But if she believes in a doctrine that conflicts with that confirmation, then one thing contradicts another."

I said, "Father, I want to go on record that I don't advocate abortion. What I advocate is that every women who is pregnant should be allowed to exercise her own conscience and her own choice."

"Well," Luisa spoke up, "I don't have any opinion of abortion. What my mother does for a living is her business."

"If you feel abortion is right, then we can't administer the sacrament," Father Egan replied.

Finally Luisa stated that she herself wouldn't have an abortion.

"But do you believe in abortion?" Father Egan persisted.

"I don't know," Luisa replied.

I felt I had to intervene. I asked Luisa, "But you wouldn't have one, right?"

"No," Luisa answered.

"Then you don't believe in it," Father Egan told her. He added to Al and me, "All I want her to say is that she doesn't advocate abortion." Luisa, by now very upset, left the room, tears running down her cheeks.

Then Father Egan said that he could not give me communion at the confirmation "because you're excommunicated. You should know that already."

I was stunned. Every now and again a "Right-to-Lifer" would accuse me of being excommunicated, but to hear this from a member of the Catholic clergy shocked me.

"I haven't been formally notified," I answered. "And I've taken communion as recently as Christmas." If I, a lifelong Catholic, were indeed excommunicated, I could no longer receive the sacraments of my faith, including communion and the last rites. Excommunication is a formal, official procedure: canon law requires that the local bishop, not a parish priest, inform a church member of excommunication. I knew that no American has been publicly excommunicated for more than 20 years. And I now know that church policy states that those who perform abortions and those who undergo them can be excommunicated. But I didn't know this last spring, and I don't fit either category.

"Your excommunication is automatic because abortion is a sin," said Father Egan. "When you publicly advocate abortion, you become what is known as a public sinner, and you cannot receive the sacraments."

"I don't believe this," I said. I was deeply hurt. But I was also very angry. The Church was trying to blackmail me through my child. The only reason we had allowed Luisa to be interrogated was that she had worked so hard to prepare for confirmation. The Church had us over a barrel.

For six months I did not discuss publicly what had happened to me because Al and I wanted to protect Luisa. On January 21, the eve of the anniversary of *Roe* v. *Wade,* the Supreme Court decision legalizing abortion, a "Right-to-Life" priest in my hometown of Providence, Rhode Island, placed a newspaper ad for a cable TV program he had produced. The ad asked whether Rhode Island's leading abortion advocate was really a Catholic.

The next day I watched with horrified fascination

as he went on the air and called me the state's "public enemy number one of babies in the womb." Then he gave his own answer to the question he had posed in his ad: He said that I wasn't really a Catholic because I had been excommunicated.

Many times during the past nine years, I've been quoted in newspapers and have appeared on radio and television shows in my state—the most Catholic in the union—where Catholics comprise 65 percent of the state's population. I can't count the number of times I've called, not for abortion, but for a pregnant woman's right to exercise her own conscience. Until Luisa's interrogation, no Church authority had ever contacted me or challenged my views. And to this day, the bishop of Providence has never addressed a word to me directly.

For second-generation Italian-Americans like me, excommunication seems like something that could just never happen. Catholicism is part of who I am. For me and for many Italians, Church dogma is closely interwoven with our ethnic and cultural fabric. We want our children to be initiated with God, so we make a big deal out of baptism. We're romantic—we love marriages, so the wedding ceremony has particular meaning for us. We mourn very deeply, so the last rites, the funeral and burial in holy ground are very much a part of our lives. But we tend to be flexible about Church rules. When I was growing up, I remember hearing my uncle say, "It doesn't matter what the Church says about birth control; no one is going to tell me what to do in my own bedroom."

I was raised to be a traditional Italian wife and mother; still, I've always had a history of fighting back. My father, who died when I was nine, was very proud that he could send me to an exclusive Catholic school, the Convent of the Sacred Heart, in Providence. But I felt the nuns there treated us Italians as second-class citizens, compared with the Irish girls. Once, when one of my Italian girlfriends didn't know an answer during an oral exam, the nuns pressed her so hard that she wet her pants. I got into a lot of trouble because I told them to stop picking on her.

Al and I got married right after my graduation. He still had a year of college to go, so I became a social worker. I soon found that I would have to take on the state government. My clients were welfare mothers who asked me for birth-control information. I gave it to them. My superior called me in and told me that the taxpayers of Rhode Island weren't paying my salary to have me discuss something they didn't believe in. So I complained to the head of the state welfare department and got other social workers to back me up. The policy eventually changed.

After his graduation, Al announced his plans to attend law school in Boston. This meant I had to keep on working and that we had to move. I was sad to leave my mother—I was extremely close to her—and all the rest of my family.

I cried a lot in those years—I wasn't very independent. I was still a typical Italian wife. Every night I made a three- or four-course gourmet meal. All Al did was study and work, not because he was lazy, but because I would't let him do anything else. Even though I kept getting promoted at work, I continued to take care of everything at home. I discovered my talent for administration and became a unit manager at a local hospital.

I always knew I wanted to have children, but we couldn't afford a baby then. I was taking the Pill, and that's how I first got into trouble with the Church.

During confession, when the priest heard I was practicing birth control, he refused to give me absolution. "I want you to go to Catholic Social Services to learn about the rhythm method," he said. "Father," I replied, "I'm a social worker. Do you know how many rhythm babies are born every year?" Friends told me I should confess to other priests who didn't think the Pill was a sin. I said no. It didn't make any sense to me to have to shop around for absolution. I stopped going to Mass regularly—but I never abandoned the Church.

I was pregnant at Al's law school graduation, which was exactly what I had wanted. When Luisa was born, she became the job of our lives, and she still is. Yet I have often wondered what I would do if I found myself pregnant today, at 42. I think the only honest answer is that I don't know. A fertilized egg that grows into a fetus is the beginning of human life, but I don't think of a fertilized egg as a person.

I do know that for the last nine years, the proudest work I've done has been holding the hands of women who needed someone with them during an abortion. And by helping these women, I have never considered myself any different from the hundreds of Catholic administrators of hospitals across this country where birth-control techniques are distributed, where sterilizations and abortions are performed. That's our work. I've never thought of myself as being any different from a Catholic lawyer who handles divorces. That's your work and you help people who come to you.

What I resent is the way I've been singled out and punished, considering what else is going on today in the diocese of Providence. Two priests are awaiting trial for the alleged sexual abuse of children. Another priest has been charged with perjury in the Von Bulow case. And the headmaster of a Catholic prep school here was recently arrested for transporting a male minor for immoral purposes. These men are passing out communion on one side of the altar rail while trying to keep me away on the other. I want my Church to explain.

Luisa's confirmation took place on a beautiful sunny Sunday, but as far as I was concerned, it was a funeral. I felt a terrible sense of helplessness because our child would be hurt no matter what I did. If I talked openly about the interrogation, she would be denied the sacrament. If I said nothing, we seemed to be accepting the Church's judgment. I felt as if my hands were tied. The guests all came to the party afterward, but Al, Luisa and I were just going through the motions.

I still cry when I think I might not be buried with my parents. I've told my husband that if I go first and the Church will not allow me to be buried alongside them at our Catholic cemetery, he should have my body cremated and scatter my ashes over their graves. That way I can be with them.

Part of my faith is a strong belief that nothing happens without a reason. I'm not a mystic, but I think there is some reason God singled me out for this trial. If the Catholic Church thinks it has embarrassed me or that I will go quietly and give up, the Church is mistaken. As God, Al and Luisa know, I am and will die a Catholic.                    [1986]

## 🌿 77

# *Reactions to a Woman Rabbi*

LAURA GELLER

At the conclusion of High Holiday services during my first year as an ordained rabbi, two congregants rushed up to talk to me. The first, a middle-aged woman, blurted out, "Rabbi, I can't tell you how different I felt about services because you are a woman. I found myself feeling that if you can be a rabbi, then maybe I could be a rabbi too. For the first time in my life I felt as though I could learn those prayers, I could study Torah, I could lead this service, I could do anything you could do. Knowing that made me feel much more involved in the service—much more involved with Judaism! Also, the service made me think about God in a different way. I'm not sure why." The second congregant had something very similar to tell me, but with a slightly different emphasis. He was a man, in his late twenties. "Rabbi, I realized that if you could be a rabbi, then certainly I could be a rabbi. Knowing that made the service somehow more accessible for me. I didn't need you to 'do it' for me. I could 'do it,' be involved with Jewish tradition, without depending on you."

It has taken me five years to begin to understand the significance of what these people told me.

Throughout most of Jewish history the synagogue has primarily been the domain of men. It has also been a very important communal institution. Was the synagogue so important because it was the domain of men, or was it the domain of men because it was so important? Perhaps the question becomes more relevant if we ask it in another way. If women become leaders in the synagogue, will the synagogue become less important? This concern was clearly expressed in 1955 by Sanders Tofield of the Conservative Movement's Rabbinical Assembly, when he acknowledged that one reason women are encouraged to remain within the private sphere of religious life is the fear that if women were to be completely integrated into all aspects of Jewish ritual, then men might relegate religious life to women and cease being active in the synagogue.[1] The fear connected with the "feminization" of Judaism is, largely, that once women achieve positions of power within the synagogue, men will feel that the synagogue is no longer sufficiently important to occupy their attention. The other side of the question is also being asked. Is the fact that women are becoming leaders in synagogues a sign that the synagogue is no longer an important institution?

The fact that these questions are posed increasingly suggests to me that the synagogue is not very healthy. Are synagogues so marginal in the life of American Jews that men really would limit their involvement because women are active participants?

The participation of women as leaders and especially as rabbis raises another concern for synagogues. Those two congregants on Rosh Hashanah expressed a feeling that has been echoed many times since then. When women function as clergy, the traditional American division between clergy and lay people begins to break down. Let me give an example from another religious tradition. A woman who is an Episcopal priest told me that when she offers the Eucharist people take it from her differently from the way they would take it from a male priest, even though she follows the identical ritual. People experience her as less foreign, and so the experience is more natural, less mysterious.

People don't attribute to women the power and prestige that they often attribute to men. Therefore, when women become rabbis or priests, there is often less social distance between the congregant and the clergy. The lessening of social distance and the reduction of the attribution of power and status leads to the breakdown of hierarchy within a religious institution. "If you can be a rabbi, then certainly I can be a rabbi!"

Clearly some would argue that the breakdown of traditional religious hierarchy is bad. However, in my view this change could bring about a profound and welcome change in American Judaism. It could lead to synagogues that see their rabbi not as "priest" but as teacher, and that see the congregations not as passive consumers of the rabbi's wisdom but as active participants in their own Jewish lives.

The ordination of women will lead to change in another important area of Judaism: the way Jews think about God. On a basic, perhaps subconscious, level, many Jews project the image of their rabbi onto their image of God. As Dr. Mortimer Ostow has pointed out, "While it is true that no officiant in the service actually represents God, to the average congregant God is psychologically represented by the rabbi, since he is the leader and the teacher and preacher of God's word."[2]

Most adult Jews know that it is inappropriate to envisage God as a male. But given the constant references in Jewish prayer to God as "Father" and "King," and given our childhood memories of imaging God as an old man with a long white beard, it is no surprise that to the extent Jews do conceptualize God in human terms, they often think of God as male or masculine.

Jewish tradition recognizes that God is not male. To limit God in this or any way is idolatrous; God is understood by tradition to encompass both masculinity and femininity and to transcend masculinity and femininity. Unfortunately, many Jews have never incorporated this complex image of God into their theology.

As long as the rabbi is a man, a Jew can project the image of the rabbi onto God. But when Jews encounter a rabbi who is a woman, it forces them to think about God as more than male or female. It provokes them to raise questions that most Jews don't like to confront: What or who is God? What do I believe about God? That primary religious question leads to others. How can we speak about God? What are the appropriate words, images and symbols to describe our relationship to God? Does the English rendering of Hebrew prayers convey the complexity of God? How can we change language, images, and symbols so they can convey this complexity?

All of these questions could lead to a more authentic relationship to Jewish tradition and to God. Once Jews begin to explore their image of God, they will also reevaluate their image of themselves. Because all of us are created in God's image, how we think about God shapes how we think about ourselves. That thinking leads to a reevaluation of men's and women's roles within our tradition and our world.

The ordination of women has brought Judaism to the edge of an important religious revolution. I pray we have the faith to push it over the edge.

[1983]

*NOTES*

1. Sanders Tofield, Proceedings of the Rabbinical Assembly 19 (1955), p. 190 as cited in Ellen M. Umansky, "Women and Rabbinical Ordination: A Viable Option? *Ohio Journal of Religious Studies*, vol. 4, Number 1 (March 1976), p. 63.
2. Dr. Mortimer Ostow, "Women and Change in Jewish Law," *Conservative Judaism* (Fall 1974), p. 7.

 78

# In Her Own Image

ROSE SOLARI

For as long as she can remember, Vienna Cobb Anderson wanted to be a priest. "I played priest when I was a child," she recalls. "I dressed up in my choir robes and performed marriage ceremonies. I held funerals for the neighborhood pets." Anderson, now rector of St. Margaret's Episcopal Church in Washington, D.C., gave up a career as an actress to enter the seminary in 1964, 12 years before the Episcopal Church approved the ordination of women. As far as she was concerned, her calling took precedence over the Church politics of the time.

"The men in seminary kept telling me not to rock the boat," she says of her early questions about sexism in the Church, "but I couldn't keep quiet. Once in class, the professor—who was, of course, also a priest—became so angry with me that he said, 'You must realize that there is a difference between a priest and other Christians.'" when Anderson pushed him to clarify his point, he blurted out, "I can celebrate the Eucharist, and you can't!"

Three decades later, Anderson celebrates the Eucharist every Sunday, proving her former teacher wrong.

She is not alone. Over the last 35 years, scores of Christian women of all denominations have brought feminism into their churches, re-examining everything from scripture to sexuality. Today, some of the most challenging and innovative work in both theology and ministry is being done by women professors and preachers who combine their religious traditions with a powerful emphasis on female identity and experience. This work is not limited to Christianity alone, nor to the United States: Feminists have formulated critiques and prescriptions for change in Jewish, Buddhist, and Islamic traditions, and feminist theologians have emerged in Asia, Africa, and Latin America. But even if one limits one's gaze to this country and to Christianity, it is clear that—whether their primary identification is as ethicists, womanists, or ecofeminists, whether they lead congregations or classes—women are breaking open the traditional definitions of what it means to be a disciple of Christ.

Their work is not without negative consequences. As the organizers of 1993's ecumenical Re-Imagining Conference discovered, many churches are willing to go only so far to accommodate the demands of these increasingly vocal and well-educated women. According to its planners, the aim of the conference was to provide a forum in which women from a variety of denominations could come together to explore feminist issues in the Church, as well as to celebrate their faith. However, the backlash experienced by the participants extended from ridicule in the press to punishment by their church hierarchies.

Yet they are undaunted. "I am just going on with my work," says Delores S. Williams, a pioneer in the African American, or "womanist," branch of feminist theology, who was singled out for some of the strongest criticism in the Christian press following the Re-Imagining Conference. "We all got backlash in one way or another. I'm not paying a bit of attention to it."

Williams has company in her fearlessness. Books and articles exploring a feminist approach to Christianity continue to proliferate, with more and more conferences, newsletters, and organizations springing up every year. Before 1960, one could find little literature on the role of women in the Church; with the emergence of feminism, however, women across the country began to turn a critical eye on all of the systems that might be contributing to their oppression. One of those systems was religion.

"I am a student of theology; I am also a woman." With these words, Valerie Saiving began her essay "The Human Situation: A Feminine View," which appeared in the April 1960 issue of the *Journal of Religion* and ushered in the opening decade of feminist theology. Saiving, then a doctoral student, discussed the ways in which her experiences as a woman seemed disconnected from the theology she was studying. She wrote, "I am no longer as certain as I once was that, when theologians speak of 'man,' they are using the word in its generic sense."

For the next three decades, women would echo Saiving's statement, both in conversation and in print. Beginning in academic journals and presses, then moving into the mainstream on a growing tide of feminist literature, women were discovering that, both on paper and in practice, Christian denominations had as a part of their foundation certain sexist assumptions that were damaging not only to the psyches of individual Christian women but also to the structure of the Church as a whole. Women writers and thinkers began to note such problematic elements of Christianity as the emphasis on Eve as the bringer of sin, the concept of God as father and son, and the theological writing of such thinkers as Thomas Aquinas, whose statements on the inferior nature of women were taught in theological seminaries all over the world.

Since the 1960s, feminist theologians have not simply been looking to make space for the feminine in a male hierarchy. Noting that the history of Christianity was shaped by a male bias that precluded women from participation in the formation of theology, teaching, and preaching, they have been demanding something much more radical. For most of them, the goal has been not to renovate the existing structure but to tear the whole building down and start over, creating something that they believe to be much closer to the roots of Christ's actual teachings and intentions.

## FOUNDING MOTHERS

Although the list of writers and thinkers in this field continues to grow—and new approaches are being developed every day—many women cite three early, key figures who helped make their work pos-

sible: Mary Daly, now a professor of philosophy at Yale University, whose first book, *The Church and the Second Sex*, was an impassioned critique of sexism in Christianity and who has now abandoned that tradition; Rosemary Radford Ruether, a professor at Garrett-Evangelical Theological Seminary in Illinois and the author or editor of over 25 books, including groundbreaking work on the cultural and historical roots of sexism in Christianity; and Beverly Wildung Harrison, a professor of Christian ethics at Union Theological Seminary in New York City, who works on some of the most controversial and difficult ethical subjects facing Christians today—such as the ethics of abortion rights and the obligation that Christians have to the poor—while encouraging and mentoring countless students in the field.

Unlike those whom they have inspired and guided, these women began their research and writing with relatively few sources and no guideposts. What they had was their own well-schooled intellects, which combined with the political climate of the 1960s to create a new way of looking at religion.

Mary Daly, who grew up a Roman Catholic and obtained doctorates in both philosophy and theology in Europe in the 1960s, was the first to bring the battle cry for feminist theology to a mainstream audience. Combining a thorough academic background with fiery prose, Daly, in her 1968 book, *The Church and the Second Sex*, blasted Christianity for providing women with images of themselves as inherently sinful and inferior. In a subsequent volume, *Beyond God the Father*, published in 1975, her critique gained momentum, and by her third book, *Gyn/Ecology*, published in 1978, she had left Christianity behind, positing that it was beyond hope of feminist reform. Unlike feminist theologians who work to separate what they see as Christianity's original, egalitarian message from subsequent patriarchal interpretations, Daly felt that such a task was impossible and unnecessary; to be a truly radical feminist, she asserted, one must part with Christianity altogether.

While Daly was working on her first two books, Rosemary Radford Ruether, then a young member of the Theology Department at Garrett-Evangelical Theological Seminary, began publishing articles that pushed the critique of Christianity in a different direction. Scholarly and reserved where Daly was impassioned and personal, Ruether theorized that the oppression of women stemmed from the dualistic thinking—placing, for example, the soul in opposition to the body, and spirit in opposition to nature—that has come to be a central aspect of Christian thought. This dualism, she maintained, resulted in a hierarchical structure wherein men are placed above nature and believe that it is their right to dominate it.

But while Ruether emphasizes the intellectual nature of her enterprise, a rare personal revelation can be found in her essay "The Question of Feminism," published in the early '70s. Having devoted herself early on to the pursuit of an academic career, Ruether was astonished when, just after her marriage, the monsignor of her husband's parish informed the young couple that if Rosemary was not pregnant within a year, he would know that they were "living in sin." Noting that she was fortunate in choosing a husband who did not share these expectations, Ruether says that it nonetheless seemed to her that her culture and religion were "bent on destroying the entire identity and future that I had constructed for myself."

If her own struggle seemed hard, she soon had an example of what might happen to a non-white, uneducated woman of the same religion. Ruether writes that in 1963, having just given birth to her third child, she met in the maternity ward a Mexican American woman named Assumptione, who had just delivered her ninth child and who tearfully described to Ruether and the attending physician the circumstances of her life. "The house was without central heating," Ruether writes. "She had to turn on the stove to keep the place warm and was always in danger of being asphyxiated by the fumes. There was little food. Her husband beat her." When the doctor suggested that the woman should avail herself of some form of birth control, "she could only reply that her priest did not allow her." This incident catalyzed Ruether's critique of sexism in the Church, ". . . not just for my own sake, but for those millions of Assumptiones weeping in maternity beds around the world."

## FROM FEMINIST TO WOMANIST

Among the rewards reaped by Ruether and Daly—both of them white and traditionally educated—is seeing their work inspire and instruct other groups of women across the country. One such group is African American women, who have developed their own approach to the role of feminism in Christianity, an approach that takes into account their experiences of oppression in a predominantly white culture.

For Delores S. Williams, an ordained Presbyterian minister who studied theology at Union Theological Seminary and is now on the faculty there, being in graduate school during the early days of feminist theology provided her with inspiration but also with some questions.

"Many of us [African Americans] were favorably disposed to the kinds of claims that theologians like Rosemary Ruether and Beverly Harrison were making," Williams says, "but we did understand that the women's experiences described in these texts did not fit the facts of our lives. So we were looking for a kind of anthropological understanding of womanhood that took seriously what our cultural context had been about. Then Alice Walker came out with this definition of 'womanist,' and right away we recognized that this was it."

Writer Alice Walker coined and defined "womanist" in a kind of preface to her 1974 collection of essays, *In Search of Our Mothers' Gardens*. The definition is composed of four parts that have since been claimed and explored by various womanist writers and theologians. The passage begins with such definitions as "a black feminist or feminist of color. . . . Responsible. In charge. *Serious*," and moves on to "A woman who loves other women, sexually and/or nonsexually," and concludes with "womanist is to feminist as purple is to lavender."

Walker, like Daly, opened a door that other women could step through. Whereas feminist theologians at that time were working to uncover and analyze the ways in which male bias had precluded them from participation in their religious traditions, the woman who would come to call themselves womanists noted that their oppression had been

perpetuated by all of white society. A womanist analyzing sexism in religion takes into account not only
race but also such interrelated factors as class, economic background, and culture. Over the next 20
years, Williams and many other African American
women—notably Katie Geneva Cannon, Renita
Weems, Toinette Eugene, Cheryl Townsend Gilkes,
and Emilie M. Townes—would bring womanist
perspectives to the study of theology, ethics, sociology, and literature, as well as the ministry.

Another distinctive element of womanist thought
is an emphasis on taking its dialogue out into the
public arena, or building bridges between the academy and people's everyday lives. A large number
of womanist professors are also ordained ministers,
who speak to their congregations about such issues as feeding and maintaining the self-image of
black women, or of the importance of encouraging
a younger generation to stay in school. Both from
the pulpit and in print, womanists pay particular attention to issues of oppression and violence. Gilkes,
for instance, is currently at work on a book about
how African American slaves interpreted the English Bible to help them survive their exploitation
and envision the possibility of future empowerment;
Townes recently edited the collection *A Troubling in
My Soul: Womanist Perspectives on Evil & Suffering,*
in which a variety of voices speak to such subjects as
the psychological violence that racist standards of
beauty inflict on black women and the history of
black Christian theological definitions of sin.

Williams has done some of her most controversial work on the link between biblical images of
atonement, such as the crucifixion, and violence in
contemporary society, and she is currently concerned with bringing womanist voices into political
issues, such as the welfare debate. "We need to be
in there as Christians," she says, "describing what
kind of reform ought to take place, a reform without stereotyping, that helps prople to discover dignity in work, and that provides supplements that
will help families stay together and establish themselves." Williams believes that by bringing discussion of such issues into church congregations as
well as academia, womanists can help reshape public policy along more humane lines.

## ORDINATION AND CELEBRATION

One area where women theologians have had to
fight a number of disparate battles is in the area of
ordination. The subject of how women worship,
and the question of who, if anyone, should be designated to lead, is one of the most imaginative and
diverse areas of contemporary feminist thought.
Currently, of the major denominations in the United
States, the Roman Catholic Church is alone in not
allowing the ordination of women at all. Many
Catholic women have switched their focus from the
battle for ordination to the pursuit of new, nonhierarchical models of worship. Meanwhile, in some
Protestant denominations, there are arguments over
a variety of issues that women have brought to the
ministry, including the ordination of openly gay and
lesbian priests.

The history of women's ordination in Protestant
churches in the U.S. is not easy to track, in part
because so many denominations are split into individual conferences or bodies with their own autonomous powers. In the Methodist Church, for
example, Anna Howard Shaw—suffragist and pro-
tégée of Susan B. Anthony—seems to have been
the first woman minister in the U.S., ordained by
the Methodist Episcopal Church, North, in 1880;
however, other Methodist churches did not grant
women the right to ordination until 1968. Mary Kay
Sauter, cofounder of the Re-Imagining Community and a candidate for ordination by the United
Church of Christ, says that her denomination ordained its first woman minister in 1850; it would
take the two mainstream Presbyterian bodies in this
country—divided between the northern and southern United States and called, respectively, "the Presbyterian Church in the U.S.A." and "the Presbyterian Church in the U.S."—another century to make
the same move, with the northern body approving
ordination in 1955 and the southern in 1964.

Overall, change seems to come earlier to local
chapters than to national associations, partly because in some denominations, church leaders who
approve women's ordination resist the idea that
women should be able to move into positions of
higher authority, such as that of bishop. Addition-

ally, as Episcopal priest Carter Heyward points out, "Any real, deep social change is not going to occur because a majority votes in favor of it. It takes some kind of prophetic voice or prophetic action, and then the people come along, sometimes many years later, and say, 'Oh, yes, that's right.'"

Heyward should know: Now a professor of theology at Episcopal Divinity School in Boston and the author of a number of books on feminist theology, including *Speaking of Christ: A Lesbian Feminist Voice* and *Staying Power*, she is one of 11 women ordained by the Episcopal Church in 1974—two years before that church officially sanctioned women's ordination.

"The Church had voted down ordination twice," she remembers, "so 11 of us, 4 bishops, and several thousand people said, 'Well, the time has come to really push the question.'" On July 29 of that year, Heyward and 10 other women were ordained in a ceremony in Philadelphia. For the next two years, issues raised by these "irregular" ordinations—from how to deal with the bishops involved to ways to respond to the new women priests—dominated Episcopal Church dialogue. Finally, in 1976, the Church retroactively recognized the ordination of those first women priests; the following year would see the first "regular" women's ordination in that tradition.

Now, according to Heyward, a different question rocks her denomination—whether or not to endorse the ordination of openly gay and lesbian priests. Although members of both groups have already been ordained, there is a movement in the Episcopal Church to bring charges against the bishops who ordained them.

Heyward, who came out as a lesbian in 1979, says that it is important for gay and lesbian priests to be "as visible as we can be just to show that we are already here. It is not like the Church has a choice. We are in it already." Heyward, who has written often on the subject of sexuality and spirituality, sees the linking of those two areas—for so long kept apart by institionalized Christianity—as a particular gift that gay and lesbian theologians can bring to the Church. "Everybody, regardless of sexual identity, needs to look at issues of what it means to be respon-

sible adults sexually and spiritually. Gays and lesbians are bringing an enormous gift to the Church, simply by raising these questions."

It is a gift that many churches find hard to accept. In 1993, the Presbyterian Church's General Assembly passed a resolution "to be engaged in the discipline of open, diligent, prayerful study and dialogue on the issues of human sexual behavior and orientation as they relate to membership, ministry, and ordination." The Assembly also agreed that the results of this study and dialogue would be discussed at their annual meeting in 1996. But Lisa Larges, a candidate for the ministry and an out lesbian, worries that this three-year period of reflection and study could become "a stalling tactic." So she founded her own organization, the Witness for Reconciliation Project, to help Presbyterian churches in the San Francisco Bay Area, where she lives, further their examination of the subject of gay and lesbian ordination. The organization has sponsored discussion groups and even a play based on the topic.

For Roman Catholic women, however, the ordination question has turned into an entirely new approach to worship. As early as the 1950s, Catholic nuns and laywomen were re-examining liturgy and their role in it. For example, at Grailville, a community of Catholic women based in rural Ohio, members were celebrating Mass with gender-inclusive language in the 1950s. Such events, followed by the changes established by the Second Vatican Council in the 1960s—including allowing priests to celebrate the Mass in the language of the congregation rather than in Latin and to face the congregation during the Eucharistic prayer rather than away from it—and by the 1975 formation of the Women's Ordination Conference, seemed to indicate that the ordination of women might come to Catholicism within the century. But while such optimism was extinguished with the selection in 1978 of the current pope, the conservative John Paul II, Catholic women have pursued a new approach to worship, one that does not require a priest at all.

Based on the work of New Testament scholar Elisabeth Schüssler Fiorenza, whose research maintains that early Christianity was a countercultural movement that smashed hierarchical patterns altogether, many Catholic feminists are now active in a movement called "Women-Church," an approach to church as a community in which all Christians are engaged in equal ministry to one another. While Women-Church communities are springing up all over the country, it is hard to say just how many women are currently involved. Mary Hunt, one of the leading proponents of Women-Church, says that there are over a hundred such communities in the Washington, D.C., area alone and that national conferences on the subject attract an audience of several thousand.

## WHY THEY STAY

The diversity of approaches and the liveliness of the dialogue that are hallmarks of feminist theology will no doubt continue to flourish in the 21st century. But while the women involved have made progress in changing the face of Christianity—both in academia and in the ministry—feminist theologians in the United States are also aware that an increasingly conservative political climate here may make their work harder. Yet few of the women interviewed for this article seem interested in following Mary Daly's path out of the Church. Rather, many are invigorated by the fight itself, while others find more pragmatic or personal reasons for continuing to rework Christian ground.

For many women, their inspiration to continue the fight for a church free of sexism derives from something closer to home—the influence, perhaps, of a loving mother or a kind aunt who embodied the particular gifts that women can bring to the ministry. Vienna Cobb Anderson, the first woman rector called to a major urban Episcopal parish, grew up in an old and powerful Episcopal family. Their family Bible dated back to 1607, and her grandfather was the senior warden of the parish where she grew up. Nonetheless, it was her grandmother who had the greatest effect on her future calling.

"Her concern for the whole community, and her desire to offer them something real, had a powerful effect on me," the rector says. "In many ways, she is my role model in the priesthood."

As feminist theologians in this country continue to work on issues ranging from ordination to birth control, from liturgy to world hunger, the image of Anderson's grandmother seems a telling one. In their emphasis on bringing the truth of women's experiences to their churches, what these scholars and ministers are offering may be, in a sense, the real bread of daily life, offered with a commitment to the principles of love and justice that are for them the basis of Christianity. Whether or not their church hierarchies ultimately accept this gesture seems to these women beside the point. What concerns them is the wholeness of their vision and the persistence of their calling to equality.                    [1995]

PART V

# The Differences Among Us:
# Divisions and Connections

We are encouraged, in our society, to see ourselves as individuals, whose progress in the world is determined by our own merits and efforts. As we have seen, however, the deeply rooted gender bias that shapes our institutions and culture stunts our possibilities as women. As Lee Bell has pointed out:

> One of the privileges of dominant group status is the luxury to see oneself as an individual. A white man, for example, is rarely defined by whiteness or maleness. If he does well on his job, he is acknowledged as a highly qualified individual. If he does poorly, the blame is attributed to him alone. Those in subordinated groups, however, can never fully escape being defined by their social group memberships. A Puerto Rican woman in the U.S. mainland, for example, may wish to be viewed as an individual and acknowledged for her personal talents and abilities. Yet she can never fully escape the dominant society's assumptions about her racial/ethnic group, language and gender. If she excels in her work, she may be seen as atypical or exceptional. If she does poorly, she may be seen as representative of the limitations of the group. In either case, she rises or falls not on the basis of individual qualities alone, but always also partly as a member of her group(s).[1]

As we can see from this example, being a woman who is also a member of another subordinate group means that one is affected simultaneously by multiple identities that interact with each other. One's race or ethnicity affects the way one experiences sexism, just as one's sex affects one's experience of racism. To address the needs of all women and to develop an inclusive feminist vision, it is important to understand the interlocking forms of oppression as they affect women's lives and relationships among different groups of women. Without eradicating all forms of domination, we will not be able to create a world in which all women can be free to determine their lives.

Why, many people ask, is it necessary to focus on difference? Why can't we focus on our common humanity or our common experiences as women? In a society in which some group's interests, norms, and values are dominant, suppressing difference means that the experience of people who are not among the dominant group is rendered invisible. In the United States, white, heterosexual, middle-class norms have been dominant and other people's experience is marginalized.

Part V focuses particularly on the effects of race, class, and sexual orientation on women's experience and relationships among women. It will examine the ways institutional discrimination as well as pervasive prejudice can prevent us from understanding the experiences we have in common and appreciating the differences among us as a resource. Some of the articles in this part make these divisions visible by focusing on the often painful dynamics in our daily lives that reinforce them. Because the barriers between women are strengthened by ignorance of each other's experience, Part V includes a large number of first-person and fictional accounts that

---

[1] Lee Anne Bell, "Theoretical Perspectives for Social Justice Education," in *Teaching Diversity and Social Justice: A Sourcebook* edited by Maurianne Adams, Lee Anne Bell, and Pat Griffin (New York: Routledge, 1997).

present women's experiences through their own eyes. In these stories and essays, the divisions among women emerge in different forms and play a variety of roles in women's lives. While you read these accounts, look for ways in which institutional and cultural racism, class bias, and discrimination against lesbians affect relations among individual women.

While individual prejudice serves to perpetuate divisions among people, discriminatory structures are deeply embedded in the workplace, schools, health care institutions, and political and legal systems. Just as sexism, which accords men power and privilege, is embedded in social institutions that shape our lives, racism, which accords white people power and privilege, is similarly entrenched in our social, economic, and political systems and the norms of our culture. Racism pervades our society, excluding people of color from resources and power, subjecting them to acts of violence and hatred, and rendering them marginal in academia, media, the law, and the business world.

Racism affects all of us, influencing the way we relate to each other and the way we see the world. Because our society marginalizes people of color, white people often think their experience is universal and don't recognize or value other people's activities, needs, or contributions. Adrienne Rich, in an essay called "Disloyal to Civilization," describes what she calls white "solipsism." This, she argues, is "not the consciously held *belief* that one race is inherently superior to all others, but a tunnel-vision which simply does not see non-white experience or existence as precious or significant, unless in spasmodic, impotent guilt reflexes." She argues that to get beyond this, white women need to listen closely to what the "politics of skin color" has meant to women of color.[2] This would involve understanding the ways that racism has kept women from working effectively against sexism, such as the exclusion of African-American women from the early twentieth-century suffrage organizations led by white women in order to avoid alienating white racist Southerners.

The class system has functioned in similar ways. Economic inequality is reinforced by social institutions and cultural values. As Holly Sklar has pointed out, in the United States today "public school budgets are heavily determined by private property taxes, allowing higher-income districts to spend much more than poor ones. In one large state in 1991–92, spending per pupil ranged from $2,337 in the poorest district to $56,791 in the wealthiest."[3] Women who have greater access to education, health care, employment opportunities, and other resources have sometimes worked for their own advancement, excluding and ignoring poor women. For example, middle- and upper-class women in Puerto Rico in the 1920s advanced a law that gave the right to vote only to literate women over 21, excluding thousands of illiterate women even though many of them had been working for decades to win

---

[2] Adrienne Rich, "Disloyal to Civilization," in *Lies, Secrets and Silence* (New York: Norton, 1979), pp. 306 and 307.
[3] Holly Sklar, "Imagine a Country," in *Race, Class and Gender in the United States,* edited by Paula Rothenberg (New York: St. Martins, 1995).

suffrage. Today, defending the legal right to abortion without also demanding *access* to abortion for women who depend on welfare and public health clinics would sacrifice the reproductive rights of thousands of women. In the past 20 years, increasing numbers of women in the United States have entered previously male-dominated professions such as business, law, and medicine, while large numbers of women continue to work in dead-end low-wage jobs, thus widening the class divisions among women.

Prejudice and discrimination against lesbians in our culture reflect what Adrienne Rich has called "compulsory heterosexuality," a complex web of laws, practices, and attitudes that enforce heterosexuality as a norm and render love relationships between people of the same sex "deviant."[4] As a result of institutional discrimination against lesbians and gay men, sometimes called heterosexism, lesbian mothers have been denied custody of their children, lesbian partners cannot get health coverage for each other, and lesbians have been fired from jobs because of their sexual orientation. Because of the heavy sanctions, many lesbians have hidden their sexual orientation from employers, family, and friends. Prejudice against lesbians thrives in an atmosphere in which lesbian lives and history are hidden. As a result, myths and misconceptions about lesbians are numerous in our culture.

Taboos against love between women have constrained the lives of all women. Fear of being labeled a lesbian often deters women from acting and speaking freely. For example, women have sometimes been afraid to develop close friendships because of the fear of being labeled a lesbian and have sometimes been hesitant to participate in activities that violate the norms of "femininity." As long as the accusation "What are you, some kind of dyke?" still has the power to scare women, no women can be free. Freedom to love whomever we choose is a central ingredient of feminism.

Becoming aware of the institutional inequities in our society encourages us to challenge what Peggy McIntosh has described as "the myth of meritocracy," the belief that permeates our culture that one's success is purely the result of one's own abilities and efforts, unaffected by the advantages or disadvantages that accrue to various social groups. Recognizing the ways that systems of power and privilege affect the lives of members of advantaged groups can help us better understand the way they affect people without these privileges.

The stories, essays, and poems in Part V address the many dimensions of prejudice and institutional discrimination as they affect women. They also reveal some of the attitudes that have prevented women from honestly addressing the differences among us, such as the assumptions that some people's experience is universal while others is marginal and deviant, the fear of conflict, and the desire to feel safe. By seeing differences from various women's points of view, we can begin to move beyond the distrust of difference that permeates our culture and use our varied experiences to enrich our analysis of society and understanding of human life.

---

[4] Adrienne Rich, "Compulsory Heterosexuality and Lesbian Existence," *Signs*, 5 (4), 631–60.

# Take a Closer Look: Racism in Women's Lives

Racism in our society operates on many levels and implicates all of us, whether we are conscious of it or not. Despite the advances of the civil rights movement, people of color continue to encounter racism both in institutions and among individuals. Because our society remains highly segregated by race and ethnicity, most of us grow up ignorant of the experiences and feelings of other groups of people. Beverly Tatum's article, which begins this section, explores the meaning of racism for all of us and makes useful distinctions between individual prejudice and racism, the system of advantages and disadvantages based on race that structures our social institutions. Understanding the ways that racism affects us requires us to recognize differences, despite pervasive pressure in our society to ignore them, as described in Adrienne Su's essay, "Codes of Conduct."

Many of the pieces in this section tell of the scars of racism through the eyes of its victims. They enable us to see both the enormously destructive power of racism and the will of the human spirit to resist it. They also reveal various forms that racism can take. The authors of the first two poems demonstrate the ways that racial stereotypes obliterate their individuality. "Take a Closer Look" and the excerpt from Angela Davis's *Autobiography* describe the agony of children trying to develop a sense of themselves in a racist world. While struggling to survive the daily hostility and contempt of white people in the South in the 1940s and 1950s, Davis developed methods of maintaining her dignity and self-respect. In her letter to Aunt Nanadine, Alexis De Veaux confronts the racism that people of color often internalize, proudly claiming her dark skin.

---

## 79

## *Defining Racism: "Can We Talk?"*

BEVERLY DANIEL TATUM

The impact of racism begins early. Even in our preschool years, we are exposed to misinformation about people different from ourselves. Many of us grew up in neighborhoods where we had limited opportunities to interact with people different from our own familes. When I ask my college students, "How many of you grew up in neighborhoods where most of the people were from the same racial group as your own?" almost every hand goes up. There is still a great deal of social segregation in our communities. Consequently, most of the early information we receive about "others"—people racially, religiously, or socioeconomically different from ourselves—does not come as the result of firsthand experience. The secondhand information we do receive has often been distorted, shaped by cultural stereotypes, and left incomplete.

Some examples will highlight this process. Several years ago one of my students conducted a research project investigating preschoolers' conceptions of Native Americans.[1] Using children at a local day care center as her participants, she asked these three- and four-year-olds to draw a picture of a Native American. Most children were stumped by her request. They didn't know what a Native American was. But when she rephrased the question and asked them to draw a picture of an Indian, they readily complied. Almost every picture included one central feature: feathers. In fact, many of them also included a weapon—a knife or tomahawk—and depicted the person in violent or aggressive terms. Though this group of children, almost all of whom were White, did not live near a large Native American population and probably had had little if any personal interaction with American Indians, they all had internalized an image of what Indians were like. How did they know? Cartoon images, in particular the Disney movie *Peter Pan,* were cited by the children as their number-one source of information. At the age of three, these children already had a set of stereotypes in place. Though I would not describe three-year-olds as prejudiced, the stereotypes to which they have been exposed become the foundation for the adult prejudices so many of us have.

Sometimes the assumptions we make about others come not from what we have been told or what we have seen on television or in books, but rather from what we have *not* been told. The distortion of historical information about people of color leads young people (and older people, too) to make assumptions that may go unchallenged for a long time. Consider this conversation between two White students following a discussion about the cultural transmission of racism:

"Yeah, I just found out that Cleopatra was actually a Black woman."

"What?"

The first student went on to explain her newly learned information. The second student exclaimed in disbelief, "That can't be true. Cleopatra was beautiful!"

What had this young woman learned about who in our society is considered beautiful and who is not? Had she conjured up images of Elizabeth Taylor when she thought of Cleopatra? The new information her classmate had shared and her own deeply ingrained assumptions about who is beautiful and who is not were too incongruous to allow her to assimilate the information at that moment.

Omitted information can have similar effects. For example, another young woman, preparing to be a high school English teacher, expressed her dismay that she had never learned about any Black authors in any of her English courses. How was she to teach about them to her future students when she hadn't learned about them herself? A White male student in the class responded to this discussion with frustration in his response journal, writing "It's not my fault that Blacks don't write books." Had one of his elementary, high school, or college teachers ever told him that there were no Black writers? Probably not. Yet because he had never been exposed to Black authors, he had drawn his own conclusions that there were none.

Stereotypes, omissions, and distortions all contribute to the development of prejudice. *Prejudice* is a preconceived judgment or opinion, usually based on limited information. I assume that we all have prejudices, not because we want them, but simply because we are so continually exposed to misinformation about others. Though I have often heard students or workshop participants describe someone as not having "a prejudiced bone in his body," I usually suggest they look again. Prejudice is one of the inescapable consequences of living in a racist society. Cultural racism—the cultural images and messages that affirm the assumed superiority of Whites and the assumed inferiority of people of color—is like smog in the air. Sometimes it is so thick it is visible, other times it is less apparent, but always, day in and day out, we are breathing it in. None of us would introduce ourselves as "smog-breathers" (and most of us don't want to be described as prejudiced), but if we live in a smoggy place, how can we avoid breathing the air? If we live in an environment in which we are bombarded with stereotypical images in the media, are frequently exposed to the ethnic jokes of friends and family members, and are rarely informed of the accomplishments of oppressed groups, we will develop the negative categorizations of those groups that form the basis of prejudice.

People of color as well as Whites develop these categorizations. Even a member of the stereotyped group may internalize the stereotypical categories about his or her own group to some degree. In fact, this process happens so frequently that it has a name, *internalized oppression.*

Certainly some people are more prejudiced than others, actively embracing and perpetuating negative and hateful images of those who are different from themselves. When we claim to be free of prejudice, perhaps what we are really saying is that we are not hatemongers. But none of us is completely innocent. Prejudice is an integral part of our socialization, and it is not our fault. Just as the preschoolers my student interviewed are not to blame for the negative messages they internalized, we are not at fault for the stereotypes, distortions, and omissions that shaped our thinking as we grew up.

To say that it is not our fault does not relieve us of responsibility, however. We may not have polluted the air, but we need to take responsibility, along with others, for cleaning it up. Each of us needs to look at our own behavior. Am I perpetuating and reinforcing the negative messages so pervasive in our culture, or am I seeking to challenge them? If I have not been exposed to positive images of marginalized groups, am I seeking them out, expanding my own knowledge base for myself and my children? Am I acknowledging and examining my own prejudices, my own rigid categorizations of others, thereby minimizing the adverse impact they might have on my interactions with those I have categorized? Unless we engage in these and other conscious acts of reflection and reeducation, we easily repeat the process with our children. We teach what we were taught. The unexamined prejudices of the parents are passed on to the children. It is not our fault, but it is our responsibility to interrupt this cycle.

### RACISM: A SYSTEM OF ADVANTAGE BASED ON RACE

Many people use the terms *prejudice* and *racism* interchangeably. I do not, and I think it is important to make a distinction. In his book *Portraits of White Racism,* David Wellman argues convincingly that limiting our understanding of racism to prejudice does not offer a sufficient explanation for the persistence of racism. He defines racism as a "system of advantage based on race."[2] In illustrating this definition, he provides example after example of how Whites defend their racial advantage—access to better schools, housing, jobs—even when they do not embrace overtly prejudicial thinking. Racism cannot be fully explained as an expression of prejudice alone.

This definition of racism is useful because it allows us to see that racism, like other forms of oppression, is not only a personal ideology based on racial prejudice, but a *system* involving cultural messages and institutional policies and practices as well as the beliefs and actions of individuals. In the context of the United States, this system clearly operates to the advantage of Whites and to the disadvantage of people of color. Another related definition of racism, commonly used by antiracist educators and consultants, is "prejudice plus power." Racial prejudice when combined with social power—access to social, cultural, and economic resources and decision-making—leads to the institutionalization of racist policies and practices. While I think this definition also captures the idea that racism is more than individual beliefs and attitudes, I prefer Wellman's definition because the idea of systematic advantage and disadvantage is critical to an understanding of how racism operates in American society.

In addition, I find that many of my White students and workshop participants do not feel powerful. Defining racism as prejudice plus power has little personal relevance. For some, their response to this definition is the following: "I'm not really prejudiced, and I have no power, so racism has nothing to do with me." However, most White people, if they are really being honest with themselves, can see that there are advantages to being White in the United States. Despite the current rhetoric about affirmative action and "reverse racism," every social indicator, from salary to life expectancy, reveals the advantages of being White.[3]

The systematic advantages of being White are often referred to as White privilege. In a now well-known article, "White Privilege: Unpacking the Invisible Knapsack," Peggy McIntosh, a White feminist scholar, identified a long list of societal privileges that she received simply because she was White.[4] She did not ask for them, and it is important to note that she hadn't always noticed that she was receiving them. They included major and minor advantages. Of course she enjoyed greater access to jobs and housing. But she also was able to shop in department stores without being followed by suspicious salespeople and could always find appropriate hair care products and makeup in any drugstore. She could send her child to school confident that the teacher would not discriminate against him on the basis of race. She could also be late for meetings, and talk with her mouth full, fairly confident that these behaviors would not be attributed to the fact that she was White. She could express an opinion in a meeting or in print and not have it labeled the "White" viewpoint. In other words, she was more often than not viewed as an individual, rather than as a member of a racial group.

The article rings true for most White readers, many of whom may have never considered the benefits of being White. It's one thing to have enough awareness of racism to describe the ways that people of color are disadvantaged by it. But this new understanding of racism is more elusive. In very concrete terms, it means that if a person of color is the victim of housing discrimination, the apartment that would otherwise have been rented to that person of color is still available for a White person. The White tenant is, knowingly or unknowingly, the beneficiary of racism, a system of advantage based on race. The unsuspecting tenant is not to blame for the prior discrimination, but she benefits from it anyway.

For many Whites, this new awareness of the benefits of a racist system elicits considerable pain, often accompanied by feelings of anger and guilt. These uncomfortable emotions can hinder further discussion. We all like to think that we deserve the good things we have received, and that others, too, get what they deserve. Social psychologists call this tendency a "belief in a just world."[5] Racism directly contradicts such notions of justice.

Understanding racism as a system of avantage based on race is antithetical to traditional notions of an American meritocracy. For those who have internalized this myth, this definition generates considerable discomfort. It is more comfortable simply to think of racism as a particular form of prejudice. Notions of power or privilege do not have to be addressed when our understanding of racism is constructed in that way.

The discomfort generated when a systemic definition of racism is introduced is usually quite visible in the workshops I lead. Someone in the group is usually quick to point out that this is not the definition you will find in most dictionaries. I reply, "Who wrote the dictionary?" I am not being facetious with this response. Whose interests are served by a "prejudice only" definition of racism? It is important to understand that the system of advantage is perpetuated when we do not acknowledge its existence.

## RACISM: FOR WHITES ONLY?

Frequently someone will say, "You keep talking about White people. People of color can be racist, too." I once asked a White teacher what it would mean to her if a student or parent of color accused her of being racist. She said she would feel as though she had been punched in the stomach or called a "low-life scum." She is not alone in this feeling. The word *racist* holds a lot of emotional power. For many White people, to be called racist is the ultimate insult. The idea that this term might only be applied to Whites becomes highly problematic for after all, can't people of color be "low-life scum" too?

Of course, people of any racial group can hold hateful attitudes and behave in racially discriminatory and bigoted ways. We can all cite examples of horrible hate crimes which have been perpetrated by people of color as well as Whites. Hateful behavior is hateful behavior no matter who does it. But when I am asked, "Can people of color be racist?" I reply, "The answer depends on your definition of racism." If one defines racism as racial prejudice, the answer is yes. People of color can and do have racial prejudices. However, if one defines racism as a system of advantage based on race, the answer is no. People of color are not racist because they do not systematically benefit from racism. And equally important, there is no systematic cultural and institutional support or sanction for the racial bigotry of people of color. In my view, reserving the term *racist* only for behaviors committed by Whites in the context of a White-dominated society is a way of acknowledging the ever-present power differential afforded Whites by the culture and institutions that make up the system of advantage and continue to reinforce notions of White superiority. (Using the same logic, I reserve the word *sexist* for men. Though women can and do have gender-based prejudices, only men systematically benefit from sexism.)

Despite my best efforts to explain my thinking on this point, there are some who will be troubled, perhaps even incensed, by my response. To call the racially motivated acts of a person of color acts of racial bigotry and to describe similar acts committed by Whites as racist will make no sense to some people, including some people of color. To those, I will respectfully say, "We can agree to disagree." At moments like these, it is not agreement that is essential, but clarity. Even if you don't like the definition of racism I am using, hopefully you are now clear about what it is. If I also understand how you are using the term, our conversation can continue—despite our disagreement.

Another provocative question I'm often asked is "Are you saying all Whites are racist?" When asked this question, I again remember that White teacher's response, and I am conscious that perhaps the question I am really being asked is, "Are you saying all Whites are bad people?" The answer to that question is of course not. However, all White people, intentionally or unintentionally, do benefit from racism. A more relevant question is what are White people as individuals doing to interrupt racism? For many White people, the image of a racist is a hood-wearing Klan member or a name-calling Archie Bunker figure. These images represent what might be called *active racism,* blatant, intentional acts of racial bigotry and discrimination. *Passive racism* is more subtle and can be seen in the collusion of laughing when a racist joke is told, of letting exclusionary hiring practices go unchallenged, of accept-

ing as appropriate the omissions of people of color from the curriculum, and of avoiding difficult race-related issues. Because racism is so ingrained in the fabric of American institutions, it is easily self-perpetuating.[6] All that is required to maintain it is business as usual.

I sometimes visualize the ongoing cycle of racism as a moving walkway at the airport. Active racist behavior is equivalent to walking fast on the conveyor belt. The person engaged in active racist behavior has identified with the ideology of White supremacy and is moving with it. Passive racist behavior is equivalent to standing still on the walkway. No overt effort is being made, but the conveyor belt moves the bystanders along to the same destination as those who are actively walking. Some of the bystanders may feel the motion of the conveyor belt, see the active racists ahead of them, and choose to turn around, unwilling to go to the same destination as the White supremacists. But unless they are walking actively in the opposite direction at a speed faster than the conveyor belt—unless they are actively antiracist—they will find themselves carried along with the others.

So, not all Whites are actively racist. Many are passively racist. Some, though not enough, are actively antiracist. The relevant question is not whether all Whites are racist, but how we can move more White people from a position of active or passive racism to one of active antiracism? The task of interrupting racism is obviously not the task of Whites alone. But the fact of White privilege means that Whites have greater access to the societal institutions in need of transformation. To whom much is given, much is required.

It is important to acknowledge that while all Whites benefit from racism, they do not all benefit equally. Other factors, such as socioeconomic status, gender, age, religious affiliation, sexual orientation, mental and physical ability, also play a role in our access to social influence and power. A White woman on welfare is not privileged to the same extent as a wealthy White heterosexual man. In her case, the systematic disadvantages of sexism and classism intersect with her White privilege, but the privilege is still there. This point was brought home to me in a 1994 study conducted by a Mount Holyoke graduate student, Phyllis Wentworth.[7] Wentworth interviewed a group of female college students, who were both older than their peers and were the first members of their families to attend college, about the pathways that led them to college. All of the women interviewed were White, from working-class backgrounds, from families where women were expected to graduate from high school and get maried or get a job. Several had experienced abusive relationships and other personal difficulties prior to coming to college. Yet their experiences were punctuated by "good luck" stories of apartments obtained without a deposit, good jobs offered without experience or extensive reference checks, and encouragement provided by willing mentors. While the women acknowledged their good fortune, none of them discussed their Whiteness. They had not considered the possibility that being White had worked in their favor and helped give them the benefit of the doubt at critical junctures. This study clearly showed that even under difficult circumstances, White privilege was still operating.

It is also true that not all people of color are equally targeted by racism. We all have multiple identities that shape our experience. I can describe myself as a light-skinned, well-educated, heterosexual, able-bodied, Christian African American woman raised in a middle-class suburb. As an African American woman, I am systematically disadvantaged by race and by gender, but I systematically receive benefits in the other categories, which then mediate my experience of racism and sexism. When one is targeted by multiple isms—racism, sexism, classism, heterosexism, ableism, anti-Semitism, ageism—in whatever combination, the effect is intensified. The particular combination of racism and classism in many communities of color is life-threatening. Nonetheless, when I, the middle-class Black mother of two sons, read another story about a Black man's unlucky encounter with a White police officer's deadly force, I am reminded that racism by itself can kill.                    [1997]

### NOTES

1.  Approximately 75 percent of all Black college students attend predominantly White colleges. For a discussion of Black college attendance and retention at White colleges in comparison to historically Black colleges, see W. R. Allen, "The color of success: African-American college student outcomes as predominantly White and historically Black public colleges and universities," *Harvard Educational Review* 62, no. 1 (1992): 26–44.
2.  For a detailed account and many more examples of campus racism, see J. R. Feagin and M. P. Sikes, *Living with racism: The Black middle-class experience* (Boston: Beacon Press, 1994), ch. 3.
3.  Many researchers have reported similar findings. For more information, see J. Fleming, *Blacks in college* (San Francisco: Jossey-Bass, 1984). See also W. R. Allen, E. G. Epp, and N. Z. Haniff (Eds.), *College in Black and White: African American students in predominantly White and historically Black public universities* (Albany: State University of New York Press, 1991).
4.  W. R. Allen, "The color of success," pp. 39–40. The National Study of Black College Students (NSBCS) surveyed more than twenty-five hundred Black college students attending a total of sixteen public universities (eight predominantly White and eight historically Black) about their college experiences and outcomes.
5.  For a discussion of White students' responses to learning about the racial identity development process of students of color, see B. D. Tatum, "Talking about race, learning about racism."
6.  Haley and Malcolm X, *The Autobiography of Malcolm X*, p. 174.
7.  M. E. Dyson, *Race rules: Navigating the color line* (Boston: Beacon Press, 1996), p. 151.

## 🌿 80

# *Codes of Conduct*

ADRIENNE SU

In the South, where I grew up, the people have an unspoken agreement. Reality is what everyone says it is. The agreement is meant to protect others from any perceived slight. It can be as innocuous as complimenting an ugly outfit, but among the truly polite, you could walk into church with a horse instead of your husband, and everyone would not only fail to notice anything wrong but also exclaim, "What a beautiful hat you have on! And Harry is looking so well! The two of you must come over for dinner sometime." By the end of the day, you'd actually believe that the horse was a man.

In the third grade, some friends and I often reenacted scenes from "Little House on the Prairie." My blonde friend played Mary because of the color of her hair. Another played Carrie, the youngest sister, because she was the youngest. I played Laura, "because you have dark hair," the others explained. Nobody ever pointed out that I did not in the slightest resemble a white Midwestern girl with freckles and brown pigtails. To suggest that perhaps I looked more like the long-lost daughter of a railroad worker of that time was to suggest that I looked different from my friends, and that simply was not done.

Not that the subject never came up—there might be a snack in my lunch that the other kids thought was strange, or a teacher might discreetly ask me about the trip my father took shortly after Nixon's visit opened China to the U.S. But most of the time, there was no language for addressing what made me different. No one asked me about Chinese culture or how to say things in Chinese, which I didn't know, anyway. Questions of the sort were considered rude, a way of pointing out that I looked Chinese, rather than like the Southern gal I was.

This doesn't sound too serious—just a form of Southern gentility. But imagine living your whole life in an environment where everyone says that a cat is a dog, all the time. Your perception of animals changes. You see a cat racing up a tree and remark, "My, that dog is a good climber." You hear a plaintive meow from outside and put a beef bone in the backyard. And when you yourself are a cat in this world, you grow to think you are a dog.

This is fine until you leave this world—and go to a land known as the North, were people not only recognize cathood but celebrate it. They form alliances to preserve feline culture, holding fish dinners and mouse-catching lectures. They hold cat networking activities and cat social events—even writers' conferences for cats who have a way with words. For the cat who's lived her whole life thinking she's a dog, this can come as a bit of a shock.

Up North, in college, I'd find myself in a group of Chinese Americans and think, Hey, I'm surrounded! before realizing that I blended in. I'd go to a gathering of Chinese students and wait to be discovered and thrown out. Talking with my Korean-American roommate, I found that I wasn't the only one whose lack of interest in math and science was seen as a possible birth defect.

One day, when I referred to myself as "Oriental," everyone in the room—white, Korean, Hispanic—pounced on me.

"It's Asian," they cried. "Oriental is offensive."

That was how I learned that there was a vocabulary for a long-unnamed aspect of my life. My visceral feelings of family obligation were known as filial piety, or, as my roommate and I described it, Asian guilt. My parents' unwillingness to contradict their friends was an act of saving face for all. And the melodramatic struggles to pay for dinner were not earnest fights but the desire to avoid guanxi, or obligation, to the other party.

I went home using not the big words of a kid home from college, but ordinary words for things that were familiar, in fact mundane, to my parents.

"I think we're making an unbalanced dinner," I said, peering into a beef stew. "Too many hot element ingredients, too few cold elements. Maybe—"

My mother, absorbed in The Wall Street Journal, waved a dismissive hand. My father, opening his mail, murmured, "Whatever." My brother, who was getting ready for hockey practice, was already out the door.

The next evening, I visited my best friend, the one who'd played Carrie, and sat down to my zillionth Southern dinner with her family.

"What classes are you taking?" her mother asked.

"I'm taking Chinese, so I can eavesdrop on my parents," I said, "and a course in East Asian religions—"

"What kind of job do you plan to get with that?" my friend's father joked.

"I just want to know enough to be able to talk to my relatives in China," I said. "To find out who I really am."

What happened next was very strange. You could hear a crumb of cornbread drop. My friend's house had always been a second home to me, as mine was to her, but on this topic, her family, unlike mine, was stuck. And it was my fault: I had carelessly dragged the conversation into never-never land, the land of what made me different.

During that frozen silence, I busied myself eating. Then I heard myself say:

"These mashed potatoes are wonderful! I've been so homesick for them. Up North, people just don't know how to cook."

My friend's mother urged me to have more. My friend's father passed the gravy and made a joke about Yankees. And instantly, my friend and I were eight years old again and digging into our plates, ravenous as puppies, because we were growing so fast.                                        [1997]

 81

# Salad

JANICE MIRIKITANI

The woman
did not mean to
offend me,

her blue eyes
blinking
at the glint
of my blade,

as I cut
precisely
like magic
the cucumber in
exact, even,
quick slices.

Do you orientals
do everything
so neatly?                                        [1982]

## 82

# I Am Not Your Princess

CHRYSTOS

*especially for Dee Johnson*

Sandpaper between two cultures which tear one
     another apart I'm not
a means by which you can reach spiritual
     understanding or even

learn to do beadwork
I'm only willing to tell you how to make fry bread
1 cup flour, spoon of salt, spoon of baking powder
Stir   Add milk or water or beer until it holds
     together
Slap each piece into rounds   Let rest
Fry in hot grease until golden
This is Indian food only if you know that Indian is
     a government word
which has nothing to do with our names for
     ourselves
I won't chant for you
I admit no spirituality to you
I will not sweat with you or ease your guilt with fine
     turtle tales
I will not wear dancing clothes to read poetry or
     explain hardly anything at all
I don't think your attempts to understand us are
     going to work so I'd rather
you left us in whatever peace we can still scramble
     up
after all you continue to do
If you send me one more damn flyer about how to
     heal myself for $300
with special feminist counseling I'll probably set
     fire to something
If you tell me one more time that I'm wise I'll throw
     up on you
Look at me
See my confusion   loneliness   fear   worrying
     about all our struggles to keep
what little is left for us
Look at my heart   not your fantasies
Please don't ever again tell me about your
     Cherokee great-great grandmother
Don't assume I know every other Native Activist in
     the world personally
That I even know the names of all the tribes
or can pronounce names I've never heard
or that I'm expert at the peyote stitch
If you ever
again tell me
how strong I am
I'll lay down on the ground & moan so you'll see
at last   my human weakness   like your own
I'm not strong   I'm scraped

I'm blessed with life while so many I've known are
    dead
I have work to do   dishes to wash   a house to
    clean   There is no magic
See my simple cracked hands which have washed
    the same things you wash
See my eyes dark with fear in a house by myself
    late at night
See that to pity me or to adore me are the same
1 cup flour, spoon of salt, spoon of baking powder
    & liquid to hold
remember this is only my recipe   There are many
    others
Let me rest
here
at least                                [1987]

 83

## *Take a Closer Look*

CARRIE CASTRO

Can you see as you
take a closer look
beyond how I appear
to be so self assured
of who I am.
My name alone
    morena
does not reveal
the inner thoughts
of uneasiness
I sometimes feel.

Let me take you
back
to a time
when I was young
and didn't understand
the significance
of colored skins
when I didn't realize
they made a difference.

Back
to a time
when I became
aware of the division
some say existed
between those born
here and those who
come from "over there,"
we made the difference.

Back
to a time
when I grew older
and longed to be
someone else
instead of "me"
because I didn't feel
that was good enough,
I made the difference.

Take a closer look
because inside
my insecurities
you will find
that the reasons
arise from the
cobwebbed minds
of those who cannot see
any beauty in faces
darker than their own.        [1980]

 84

## *An Autobiography* (excerpt)

ANGELA DAVIS

The big white house on top of the hill was not far
from our old neighborhood, but the distance could
not be measured in blocks. The government housing project on Eighth Avenue where we lived before
was a crowded street of little red brick structures—
no one of which was different from the other. Only
rarely did the cement surrounding these brick huts
break open and show patches of green. Without

space or earth, nothing could be planted to bear fruit or blossoms. But friends were there—and friendliness.

In 1948 we moved out of the projects in Birmingham, Alabama, to the large wooden house on Center Street. My parents still live there. Because of its steeples and gables and peeling paint, the house was said to be haunted. There were wild woods in back with fig trees, blackberry patches and great wild cherry trees. On one side of the house was a huge Cigar tree. There was space here and no cement. The street itself was a strip of orange-red Alabama clay. It was the most conspicuous house in the neighborhood—not only because of its curious architecture but because, for blocks around, it was the only house not teeming inside with white hostility. We were the first Black family to move into that area, and the white people believed that we were in the vanguard of a mass invasion.

At the age of four I was aware that the people across the street were different—without yet being able to trace their alien nature to the color of their skin. What made them different from our neighbors in the projects was the frown on their faces, the way they stood a hundred feet away and glared at us, their refusal to speak when we said "Good afternoon." An elderly couple across the street, the Montees, sat on their porch all the time, their eyes heavy with belligerence.

Almost immediately after we moved there the white people got together and decided on a border line between them and us. Center Street became the line of demarcation. Provided that we stayed on "our" side of the line (the east side) they let it be known we would be left in peace. If we ever crossed over to their side, war would be declared. Guns were hidden in our house and vigilance was constant.

Fifty or so yards from this hatred, we went about our daily lives. My mother, on leave from her teaching job, took care of my younger brother Benny, while waiting to give birth to another child, my sister Fania. My father drove his old orange van to the service station each morning after dropping me off at nursery school. It was next door to the Children's Home Hospital—an old wooden building where I was born and where, at two, I had my tonsils removed. I was fascinated by the people dressed in

white and tried to spend more time at the hospital than at the nursery. I had made up my mind that I was going to be a doctor—a children's doctor.

Shortly after we moved to the hill, white people began moving out of the neighborhood and Black families were moving in, buying old houses and building new ones. A Black minister and his wife, the Deyaberts, crossed into white territory, buying the house right next to the Montees, the people with the hateful eyes.

It was evening in the spring of 1949. I was in the bathroom washing my white shoelaces for Sunday School the next morning when an explosion a hundred times louder than the loudest, most frightening thunderclap I had ever heard shook our house. Medicine bottles fell off the shelves, shattering all around me. The floor seemed to slip away from my feet as I raced into the kitchen and my frightened mother's arms.

Crowds of angry Black people came up the hill and stood on "our" side, staring at the bombed-out ruins of the Deyaberts' house. Far into the night they spoke of death, of white hatred, death, white people, and more death. But of their own fear they said nothing. Apparently it did not exist, for Black families continued to move in. The bombings were such a constant response that soon our neighborhood became known as Dynamite Hill.

The more steeped in violence our environment became, the more determined my father and mother were that I, the first-born, learn that the battle of white against Black was not written into the nature of things. On the contrary, my mother always said, love had been ordained by God. White people's hatred of us was neither natural nor eternal. She knew that whenever I answered the telephone and called to her, "Mommy, a white lady wants to talk to you," I was doing more than describing the curious drawl. Every time I said "white lady" or "white man" anger clung to my words. My mother tried to erase the anger with reasonableness. Her experiences had included contacts with white people seriously committed to improving race relations. Though she had grown up in rural Alabama, she had become involved, as a college student, in anti-racist movements. She had worked to free the Scottsboro Boys and there had been whites—some of them Communists—in that struggle. Through her own political work, she had learned that it was possible for white people to walk out of their skin and respond with the integrity of human beings. She tried hard to make her little girl—so full of hatred and confusion—see white people not so much as what they were as in terms of their potential. She did not want me to think of the guns hidden in drawers or the weeping black woman who had come screaming to our door for help, but of a future world of harmony and equality. I didn't know what she was talking about.

When Black families had moved up on the hill in sufficient numbers for me to have a group of friends, we developed our own means of defending our egos. Our weapon was the word. We would gather on my front lawn, wait for a car of white people to pass by and shout the worst epithets for white people we knew: Cracker. Redneck. Then we would laugh hysterically at the startled expressions on their faces. I hid this pastime from my parents. They could not know how important it was for me, and for all of us who had just discovered racism, to find ways of maintaining our dignity.                    [1974]

# 🌿 85

# *Dear Aunt Nanadine*

ALEXIS DE VEAUX

Dear Aunt Nanadine,

As much as I love to write, I've never written you a letter. And "What do we need with letters?" you say. "We live in the same city, a bridge and a subway apart." Well, yesterday I took from the back of my closet that red three-piece walking suit you gave me. "Too fat to wear it now," you said, pushing it in a Macy's bag. "Take it."

So this letter is to say I used to admire you in that red suit; how it colored your light handsome beauty. And made you look so rich, so pockets full of freedom and loose change. Red, you instructed me, was a color *I* should *never ever* wear. I was absolutely "too dark." "Whose little black child are you?"

you'd tease. "Who knows who you belong to?" Did you know then that your teasing mirrored my own apprehension? *Who did I belong to?* Who does a dark-skinned child belong to in a family where lighter skin is predominant, in a society where dark can't mean anything positive? It's not supposed to. Who do you belong to and who do you trust?

Should I have not trusted you then when I was eight years old? Not listened when you advised me at ten that not only reds but certain bright pinks, yellows, blues and oranges were also off limits to me? And to other girls my color, like Cheryl Lynn Bruce, who grew up on the South Side of Chicago (grew up to become an actress). Cheryl was ten, and dark, and recalls: "I remember going to my grandmother's house one day (she taught piano). I put on a red outfit—red coat, red dress, red shoes, red everything. I was fascinated with the color red. And off I went to my grandmother's house. Well, my grandmother gasped when she saw me, and called my mother, and sent me back home. My mother opened the door, grabbed me inside and said, "Take off all that red. You are too dark to wear all that red." I hadn't understood there was a construct that decided what colors a dark girl could wear. I was ten at the time. Red is such a vibrant color. It calls attention, and it was calling attention to my skin. After the red incident, I felt there was a search to find a color I could wear that would not draw attention to my color. Mother dressed me in navy blue a lot because it was a neutral color. I became very conscious of how colors affected my skin.

Quite frankly, Aunt Nanadine, I was a little surprised when you gave me the suit. On the train, I wondered if you still thought I was "too dark." Was I lighter to you now? More acceptable? Had your feelings changed after some twenty years? At home, I stuck the suit in the closet of my writing room. I never wore it. It waited among my piles of complete and incomplete ideas, filed away, an unfinished draft of an old story. One day I would get back to it. But I could not sincerely thank you. And the next month, rummaging through some old notebooks, I came across this fragment of story: *I am a little girl. I am in the third grade. I come home from school. I run all the way today. My favorite dress—the navy one with tiny white polka dots—is torn at the sleeve and neck, with buttons missing and Lord, it's so dirty. There are dried tears on my face. My hair stands all over my head. I am pissed-as-shit. I know my mother is going to kill me. I bust through the apartment door.*

*"Girl, what happened to you?" she say.*

*"Had a fight."*

*"Fight 'bout what?"*

*"Livia and them keep calling me Blackie—"*

*"I send you outta here to go to school and learn something. Not to fight, miss."*

*"She started it. Callin' me Blackie and Lil Black Sambo."*

*"Well the next damn time she do, you tell her YOUR MOTHER say sticks 'n' stones might break your bones, but words will never harm you. Hear me?"*

*BULLSHIT, BLACKIE AIN'T MY NAME, I want to say. It hurts. It's painful. It's embarrassing, Momma. Livia is dark as me. Why everything Black got to be evil, everything dark got to be ugly? I say nothing. I learn the bravado of strike back. Incorporate the language of segregation: "inkspot," "your Momma come from Blackest Africa," "tar baby tar baby," "Black nigga." I say it in (great) anger to others on the block. This is a skill. It is a way to hurt another deeply. We all practice it. In 1956, nobody wants to be a "Blackie" or a "darkie" or no other kind of African nothing. Africa to (most of) us is Tarzan 'n' Jane: uncivilized life on the "Dark Continent," half-naked cannibals on TV. Africa was something to be ashamed of. The closer we are to that which symbolizes it, the greater our potential for shame.*

Reading and rereading the story, I wondered if anyone, any Black person, ever dared to call you Blackie, Aunt Nanadine, you with your elegant, light skin. And what would you have done to them if they had? What would you have done if *your* grandmother anointed elbows and knees religiously every Sunday with Pond's Vanishing Creme, to keep away the ashiness of "dark"?

I am not ungrateful for all the things you did teach me about my color: how to use Nadinola bleaching cream as a foundation under makeup; to buy my stockings in a shade of off-black; how to assimilate and integrate to survive; *fade in* as much as possible (however ridiculous, at times); to "act my age and not my color." All the ways you penetrated the interior of my feelings, where you and I

lived, I believed then, in a separation of shades; where our different colors wedged between us like a yoke. Separated and politically bound us to the psychological and psychic brutality that was American slavery. *That still binds us to generations of self-hatred,* a hatred of our darkness. Hatred for the overwhelming, monumental, lynching pain attached to it.

"Color has made extremely deep scars in Black people," says Sandra Ross, a good friend. (You might have seen some of her work, Aunt Nanadine. She's a freelance lighting designer in theaters around the city.) "It has affected what we do with our lives, what we *think* we can do or accomplish. It has shaped our self-esteem and sense of personal and group power. In my family, color wasn't mentioned. We talked about Black and white, but we didn't talk about light and dark." The neighbors did, though indirectly: "She's pretty for a Black child, smart for a Black child," they would say.

Is it just circumstantial that we are blood kin, women, products of America, descendants of heroines and slaves, that we have shared family crises and skeletons, but never talked intimately or honestly about skin tones and color? That I have never said to you: I like my color. I want to be even darker, blacker, still.

"I'm glad I'm as dark as I am because there is a certain point beyond which I can't compromise, beyond which I can't assimilate," Cheryl Lynn said to me over the phone. "I like to wear a lot of colors and bells and stuff to remind me that *I am different. I am an African.* And all the stares I get on the street and in the subway, even from my own people, are a healthy sign because we all need to be reminded that Black *is* beautiful, inherently beautiful, and we can enhance that beauty or twist it into something grotesque when we hide it."

When we deny it. When I am wrong *just because I am darker than you.* When my color *and* my sex are considered heavy deficits in the outside world. When, like Sandra, I cannot see myself as attractive for a long time, because I am, society says, repugnant and exotic: with my large breasts, my period, my pussy. "Just a dark, nappy girl." And as such, I must never call attention to myself. Never want it.

And never deserve it; because a dark girl was also unfeminine, unworthy, ignorant. *Neither ambition nor achievement was expected of me.* I could be propositioned by Black men, old enough to be my uncle. Rubbed against by a strange man in the subway on the way to school. I could be trespassed against in any number or variation of social ways, simply because, after all, I was only a Black girl. What a sad thing it was to learn that *a dark girl meant an ugly girl.* That my people had no standard for judging colored beauty. That within our race we judged ourselves by outside criteria. That there was no beauty underneath the nappy, unruly hair I was taught to fry and radically alter; no grace to my African buttocks squeezed into panty girdles at fifteen. Could I ask my mother if she thought I was beautiful? Could I demand to know if colored people had the *right* to be beautiful? If all the Sojourner Truth in me, all the Harriet Tubman, the Ida B. Wells-Barnett, all the Hatshepsut Queen of Egypt, all the dark, handsome history of my smell, talk, dreams, would not, indeed, one day rot inside the choking rope of

if you light you all right
if you brown stick around
if you Black git back

Can you see how your red suit in my closet would make me see red? That to open the closet door daily was to open a Pandora's box of racism between us? Because we are in the closet too. A color closet we cannot get out of. It is too personal, too much a knife in a never healing wound. There is nowhere inside my color, inside your color, to be objective. No way to fade in. No way not to be dark. *And what color is dark? Who is dark? Compared to what, compared to whom? Is a dark woman in a darker skinned family light or dark? Is a light woman in a high light/mulatto family dark? Will we end the racism or shall we perpetuate it?*

"What do you think?" I say to Cheryl Lynn, taking notes. She replies: "I've seen so many ranges of color since I became conscious of my own color that sometimes it seems pointless to make any distinctions between dark and dark. I've seen navy-blue people and dusty-gray ones and some a sandy, translucent black. Is an eggplant person darker than a maroon person? What does it mean, beyond that?" Some of us are darker than others but, Aunt Nanadine, we are all dark peoples.

That's what the sixties taught me. In the red, black, green artifacts of my African heritage, I could *learn to love* the dark me that was the Civil Rights movement here in America. The dark me that was the independence movement in Africa. That was an outside shade of brown. When I went on those marches and stood on those demonstration lines and chanted against our oppression, *I felt Black.* And the natural Black was beautiful to express. And it was as beautiful to express my anger as it was to express my natural, nappy hair; to express my skin by painting it. I celebrated every ritual that celebrated my darkness: Kwanzaa, nose piercing, braids, nationalism. I wanted American saturated with the henna on my lips. I wanted color: I wore reds and yellows and greens in provocative African combinations. *I wanted the freedom to be dark;* I could not get dark enough. In the summer, I disappeared on the beaches for days at a time. "Stay out the sun," you warned me. "It's just making you dark and oversensitive." "There's nothing wrong with being dark," I defended myself. Remember?

I remember *believing*, in the sixties. Many others do too. Like Carole Byard: "When we chanted 'Black is beautiful,' we were very assertive because we were *involved* in turning history around," she reminisced. "But some of the young people are not as aggressive as we were at their age. For many of them, it seems as if the sixties never happened. They are culturally embarrassed. There seems to be more of a willingness to merge, and not to assert cultural identity, particularly if it relates to Africa. Maybe they feel less threatened [than we did] by involvement with white cultural things."

I remember believing I wanted to judge myself from then on against *my own* darkness. And the darkness of my history. The sixties gave me a solid foundation, a bridewealth of "Africanity." Taught me to carry cultural beauty in my hair, my clothes, the words in my mouth. Taught me that while there was a "cultural Blackness" (artifacts), there is a "genetic dark," an *inside dark*, I must learn to love. *Learn to love the dark and trust it* because there are schools, clinics, governments, families, freedom, art to build between us.

But the sixties were only a beginning. And while it released some of our racial tension, it did not free us from our own color prejudices. When our slogans and anger no longer served us, when government and social backlash tested our spirit in the seventies, and Black was defined by Madison Avenue instead, some of us forgot that *our struggle did not begin in the sixties* and would not end there. Some of us mistook the invisibility of our darkness as the end of it.

Maybe that's not the stance to take at all, Carole disagrees, "Maybe the way we went about it is just no longer necessary. Maybe that's the difference between this decade and the last ones. Maybe we who were active in the sixties are like generals from another war. Maybe it's a *different* war, with different equipment for fighting it. Maybe it's not all gone, just different."

Different, but the same. Whether in Brooklyn, Baton Rouge, or Baltimore. Whether in Africa, the Caribbean, or America; at the core of our struggle lies an ugly pattern of color consciousness between family, strangers, friends. Lies deceptively, and hides, beneath our global view, like a pain. Or a journal entry:

*After dinner, Margo and I lay on her bed. Her quilt is a weave of cloth from the Ibo of Nigeria. We talk about her master's thesis topic: "The Impulse to Love in the Narratives of African American Slave Women." We smoked a good joint. Margo is a light-skinned Black woman. Her 'fro is big, but not kinky. Margo has African facial features. She's attractive. I am much darker. I have a short kinky 'fro. I have African facial features. I'm attractive. I was born in Harlem. Margo was born in Mississippi. She attends a prestigious Ivy League school. We live in Boston. Margo is very, very intelligent. Her mind is mercurial. When Margo smokes reefer she is aggressive. She sees how tall she is, how tall I am not. Wrestles me on the bed: "Let's play," she says. Punches me: "Let's fight." "No," I say. "Stop." When Margo's nose gets clobbered she cries, turns red. "You Black bitch," she spits. "I didn't mean to call you that," she says later. "Forget it," I say. Margo is my friend. We were lovers once. I quit her after that.*

Aunt Nanadine, it is the impulse to love that does not quit. To love my history sex skin. Not in spite of it but because of it. *To love myself.* As Carole says, "We must deal with the internal aspects of 'Black is beautiful.' Work on a stronger sense of self to make the whole group stronger by caring about our family histories, our health, our spirit, what kind of people we are. Our self-love. *If I love myself then I have to love you too.*"

And I have to love the visibility of mass protests that created the sixties, transformed lives forever, Africanized me. And still love it now, as it regroups underground; as today's fashions and the current national politics turn back the clock—turn our 'fros to Geri Curls and our cornrows to "extensions." "We have to evolve to a point of caring about contributing to the whole," Carole is quick to encourage. "It's a personal thing. Something each one of us has to do. In the sixties there was a lot of emphasis on mass health, mass healing, but now we have to strengthen the individual parts. We have to remember that the whole is equal to the sum of the parts."

Remember that in these ugly times, there *is* something to fall back on. Remember that it is the impulse to love that comes between the silence between aunt and niece. Comes in this letter saying I love you. Comes, as I write, struggling to internalize beauty, beause *color is still a critical issue between our people.* We still discriminate against our own. The darker ones against the lighter ones. The light ones against the dark. Little kids on the street today still call each other Blackie as a way to hurt each other deeply. And yet we cannot afford that "luxury." Or any other "luxury" of segregation that diminishes our numbers. We cannot afford to believe that we have been defeated; that "Black is beautiful" is dead. That dark is ugly. I am not dead and I am not defeated. I am beautiful. Black is in my heart, blood, work; in the eyes of my dreads, in the amber/cowrie of my tongue.

So Aunt Nanadine, I have taken the red suit out of my closet. I am going to the cleaners with it. Then to the mailbox to drop this letter. Please get in touch with me. I'd like to know how you feel about all this. Perhaps I can come see you soon. Next week I will give a talk on "Writing as Activist Art." I will wear our red suit. Thank you for giving it to me. I have always loved it.

Take care.

Moving forward to freedom: your niece,
Alexis
Brooklyn, 1982　　　　　　　　　　[1995]

# The Legacy of Class

In the United States, people don't talk about class very much. Nevertheless, most people are very aware of class differences as they manifest themselves in the way people look, talk, and move through the world, and this awareness affects the way we relate to each other. As Donna Langston explains in "Tired of Playing Monopoly?" our class backgrounds have a powerful effect on our values, the ways we see ourselves and the choices we have in our lives. For example, work outside the home has seemed to women who grew up in middle-class homes as a form of liberation, while women in poor and working-class families have always worked, often at alienating, dead-end jobs.

This section includes several stories and an essay that explore the meaning of class in women's lives. The first story is an excerpt from an autobiographical novel, *Daughter of Earth*, written by Agnes Smedley, a socialist activist in the early twentieth century. It describes a poor white child's anguish and confusion when treated with contempt and condescension by wealthier people. Such feelings linger in the consciousness of adult women such as Dorothy Allison and occasionally reemerge when interacting with people of different class backgrounds. For Bernice Mennis, being Jewish and working class are closely intertwined in her recollections of making sense of a world in which she often felt different.

The feminist ideal of sisterhood among women is often challenged by class divisions. In "Sisters," both women are African-American, united by the racism and sexism in their lives but divided by social class. Jealousy, competition, and the belief that one can make it on one's own if one is "tough enough" keep them from offering each other the support they each desperately need. In Toi Derricotte's poem, Grace Paley, a well-known North American writer, reaches across class differences with a small act of consideration.

---

## 86

# *Tired of Playing Monopoly?*

DONNA LANGSTON

I. Magnin, Nordstrom, The Bon, Sears, Penneys, K mart, Goodwill, Salvation Army. If the order of this list of stores makes any sense to you, then we've begun to deal with the first question which inevitably arises in any discussion of class here in the U.S.—huh? Unlike our European allies, we in the U.S. are reluctant to recognize class differences. This denial of class divisions functions to reinforce ruling class control and domination. America is, after all, the supposed land of equal opportunity where, if you just work hard enough, you can get ahead, pull yourself up by your bootstraps. What the old bootstraps theory overlooks is that some were born with silver shoe horns. Female-headed households, communities of color, the elderly, disabled and children find themselves, disproportionately, living in poverty. If hard work were the sole determinant of your ability to support yourself and your family, surely we'd have a different outcome for many in our society. We also, however, believe in luck and, on closer examination, it certainly is quite a coincidence that the "unlucky" come from certain race, gender and class backgrounds. In order to perpetuate racist, sexist and classist outcomes, we also have to believe that the current economic distribution is unchangeable, has always existed, and probably exists in this form throughout the known universe, i.e., it's "natural." Some people explain or try to account for poverty or class position by focusing on the personal and moral merits of an individual. If people are poor, then it's something they did or didn't do; they were lazy, unlucky, didn't try hard enough, etc. This has the familiar ring of blaming the victims. Alternative explanations focus on the ways in which poverty and class position are due to structural, systematic, institutionalized economic and political power relations. These power relations are based firmly on dynamics such as race, gender, and class.

In the myth of the classless society, ambition and intelligence alone are responsible for success. The myth conceals the existence of a class society, which serves many functions. One of the main ways it keeps the working-class and poor locked into a class-based system in a position of servitude is by cruelly creating false hope. It perpetuates the false hope among the working-class and poor that they can have different opportunities in life. The hope that they can escape the fate that awaits them due to the class position they were born into. Another way the rags-to-riches myth is perpetuated is by creating enough visible tokens so that oppressed persons believe they, too, can get ahead. The creation of hope through tokenism keeps a hierarchical structure in place and lays the blame for not succeeding on those who don't. This keeps us from resisting and changing the class-based system. Instead, we accept it as inevitable, something we just have to live with. If oppressed people believe in equality of opportunity, then they won't develop class consciousness and will internalize the blame for their economic position. If the working-class and poor do not recognize the way false hope is used to control them, they won't get a chance to control their lives by acknowledging their class position, by claiming that identity and taking action as a group.

The myth also keeps the middle class and upper class entrenched in the privileges awarded in a class-based system. It reinforces middle- and upper-class beliefs in their own superiority. If we believe that anyone in society really can get ahead, then middle- and upper-class status and privileges must be deserved, due to personal merits, and enjoyed—and defended at all costs. According to this viewpoint, poverty is regrettable but acceptable, just the outcome of a fair game: "There have always been poor people, and there always will be."

Class is more than just the amount of money you have; it's also the presence of economic security. For the working class and poor, working and eating are matters of survival, not taste. However, while one's class status can be defined in important ways in terms of monetary income, class is also a whole lot more—specifically, class is also culture. As a result of the class you are born into and raised in, class is your understanding of the world and where you fit in; it's composed of ideas, behavior, attitudes, values, and language; class is how you think, feel, act, look, dress, talk, move, walk; class is what stores you shop at, restaurants you eat in; class is the schools you attend, the education you attain; class is the very jobs you will work at throughout your adult life. Class even determines when we marry and become mothers. Working-class women become mothers long before middle-class women receive their bachelor's degrees. We experience class at every level of our lives; class is who our friends are, where we live and work even what kind of car we drive, if we own one, and what kind of health care we receive, if any. Have I left anything out? In other words, class is socially constructed and all-encompassing. When we experience classism, it will be because of our lack of money (i.e., choices and power in this society) and because of the way we talk, think, act, move—because of our culture.

Class affects what we perceive as and what we

have available to us as choices. Upon graduation from high school, I was awarded a scholarship to attend any college, private or public, in the state of California. Yet it never occurred to me or my family that it made any difference which college you went to. I ended up just going to a small college in my town. It never would have occurred to me to move away from my family for school, because no one ever had and no one would. I was the first person in my family to go to college. I had to figure out from reading college catalogs how to apply—no one in my family could have sat down and said, "Well, you take this test and then you really should think about . . ." Although tests and high school performance had shown I had the ability to pick up white middle-class lingo, I still had quite an adjustment to make—it was lonely and isolating in college. I lost my friends from high school—they were at the community college, vo-tech school, working, or married. I lasted a year and a half in this foreign environment before I quit college, married a factory worker, had a baby and resumed living in a community I knew. One middle-class friend in college had asked if I'd like to travel to Europe with her. Her father was a college professor and people in her family had actually travelled there. My family had seldom been able to take a vacation at all. A couple of times my parents were able—by saving all year—to take the family over to the coast on their annual two-week vacation. I'd seen the time and energy my parents invested in trying to take a family vacation to some place a few hours away; the idea of how anybody ever got to Europe was beyond me.

If class is more than simple economic status but one's cultural background, as well, what happens if you're born and raised middle-class, but spend some of your adult life with earnings below a middle-class income bracket—are you then working-class? Probably not. If your economic position changes, you still have the language, behavior, educational background, etc., of the middle class, which you can bank on. You will always have choices. Men who consciously try to refuse male privilege are still male; whites who want to challenge white privilege are still white. I think those who come from middle-class backgrounds need to recognize that their class privilege does not float out with the rinse water.

Middle-class people can exert incredible power just by being nice and polite. The middle-class way of doing things is the standard—they're always right, just by being themselves. Beware of middle-class people who deny their privilege. Many people have times when they struggle to get shoes for the kids, when budgets are tight, etc. This isn't the same as long-term economic conditions without choices. Being working-class is also generational. Examine your family's history of education, work, and standard of living. It may not be a coincidence that you share the same class status as your parents and grandparents. If your grandparents were professionals, or your parents were professionals, it's much more likely you'll be able to grow up to become a yuppie, if your heart so desires, or even if you don't think about it.

How about if you're born and raised poor or working-class, yet through struggle, usually through education, you manage to achieve a different economic level: do you become middle class? Can you pass? I think some working class people may successfully assimilate into the middle class by learning to dress, talk, and act middle-class—to accept and adopt the middle-class way of doing things. It all depends on how far they're able to go. To succeed in the middle-class world means facing great pressures to abandon working-class friends and ways.

Contrary to our stereotype of the working class—white guys in overalls—the working class is not homogeneous in terms of race or gender. If you are a person of color, if you live in a female-headed household, you are much more likely to be working-class or poor. The experience of Black, Latino, American Indian or Asian American working classes will differ significantly from the white working classes, which have traditionally been able to rely on white privilege to provide a more elite position within the working class. Working-class people are often grouped together and stereotyped, but distinctions can be made among the working-class, working-poor and poor. Many working-class families are supported by unionized workers who possess marketable skills. Most working-poor families are supported by non-unionized, unskilled men and women. Many poor families are dependent on welfare for their income.

Attacks on the welfare system and those who live on welfare are a good example of classism in action. We have a "dual welfare" system in this country whereby welfare for the rich in the form of tax-free capital gain, guaranteed loans, oil depletion allowances, etc., is not recognized as welfare. Almost everyone in America is on some type of welfare; but, if you're rich, it's in the form of tax deductions for "business" meals and entertainment, and if you're poor, it's in the form of food stamps. The difference is the stigma and humiliation connected to welfare for the poor, as compared to welfare for the rich, which is called "incentives." Ninety-three percent of welfare recipients are women. A common focal point for complaints about "welfare" is the belief that most welfare recipients are cheaters—goodness knows there are no middle-class income tax cheaters out there. Imagine focusing the same anger and energy on the way corporations and big business cheat on their tax revenues. Now, there would be some dollars worth quibbling about. The "dual welfare" system also assigns a different degree of stigma to programs that benefit women and children and programs whose recipients are primarily male, such as veterans' benefits. The implicit assumption is that mothers who raise children do not work and therefore are not deserving of their daily bread crumbs.

Working-class women's critiques have focused on the following issues:

*Education:* White middle-class professionals have used academic jargon to rationalize and justify classism. The whole structure of education is a classist system. Schools in every town reflect class divisions: like the store list at the beginning of this article, you can list schools in your town by what classes of kids attend, and in most cities you can also list by race. The classist system is perpetuated in schools with the tracking system, whereby the "dumbs" are tracked into homemaking, shop courses and vocational school futures, while the "smarts" end up in advanced math, science, literature, and college-prep courses. If we examine these groups carefully, the coincidence of poor and working-class backgrounds with "dumbs" is rather alarming. The standard measurement of supposed intelligence is white middle-class English. If you're other than white middle-

class, you have to become bilingual to succeed in the educational system. If you're white middle-class, you only need the language and writing skills you were raised with, since they're the standard. To do well in society presupposes middle-class background, experiences and learning for everyone. The tracking system separates those from the working class who can potentially assimilate to the middle class from all our friends, and labels us "college bound."

After high school, you go on to vocational school, community college, or college—public or private—according to your class position. Apart from the few who break into middle-class schools, the classist stereotyping of the working class as being dumb and inarticulate tracks most into vocational and low-skilled jobs. A few of us are allowed to slip through to reinforce the idea that equal opportunity exists. But for most, class position is destiny—determining our educational attainment and employment. Since we must overall abide by middle-class rules to succeed, the assumption is that we go to college in order to "better ourselves"—i.e., become more like them. I suppose it's assumed we have "yuppie envy" and desire nothing more than to be upwardly mobile individuals. It's assumed that we want to fit into their world. But many of us remain connected to our communities and families. Becoming college-educated doesn't mean we have to, or want to, erase our first and natural language and value system. It's important for many of us to remain in and return to our communities to work, live, and stay sane.

*Jobs:* Middle-class people have the privilege of choosing careers. They can decide which jobs they want to work, according to their moral or political commitments, needs for challenge or creativity. This is a privilege denied the working-class and poor, whose work is a means of survival, not choice. Working-class women have seldom had the luxury of choosing between work in the home or market. We've generally done both, with little ability to purchase services to help with this double burden. Middle- and upper-class women can often hire other women to clean their houses, take care of their children, and cook their meals. Guess what class and race those "other" women are? Working a double or triple day is common for working-class women. Only middle-class women have an array of choices such as: parents put you through school, then you choose a career, then you choose when and if to have babies, then you choose a support system of working-class women to take care of your kids and house if you choose to resume your career. After the birth of my second child, I was working two part-time jobs—one loading trucks at night—and going to school during the days. While I was quite privileged because I could take my colicky infant with me to classes and the day-time job, I was in a state of continuous semi-consciousness. I had to work to support my family; the only choice I had was between school or sleep: Sleep became a privilege. A white middle-class feminist instructor at the university suggested to me, all sympathetically, that I ought to hire someone to clean my house and watch the baby. Her suggestion was totally out of my reality, both economically and socially. I'd worked for years cleaning other peoples' houses. Hiring a working-class woman to do the shit work is a middle-class woman's solution to any dilemma which her privileges, such as a career, may present her.

*Individualism:* Preoccupation with one's self—one's body, looks, relationships—is a luxury working-class women can't afford. Making an occupation out of taking care of yourself through therapy, aerobics, jogging, dressing for success, gourmet meals and proper nutrition, etc., may be responses that are directly rooted in privilege. The middle-class have the leisure time to be preoccupied with their own problems, such as their waistlines, planning their vacations, coordinating their wardrobes, or dealing with what their mother said to them when they were five—my!

The white middle-class women's movement has been patronizing to working-class women. Its supporters think we don't understand sexism. The idea of women as passive, weak creatures totally discounts the strength, self-dependence and interdependence necessary to survive as working-class and poor women. My mother and her friends always had a less-than-passive, less-than-enamoured attitude toward their spouses, male bosses, and men in general. I know from listening to their conversa-

tions, jokes and what they passed on to us, their daughters, as folklore. When I was five years old, my mother told me about how Aunt Betty had hit Uncle Ernie over the head with a skillet and knocked him out because he was raising his hand to hit her, and how he's never even thought about doing it since. This story was told to me with a good amount of glee and laughter. All the men in the neighborhood were told of the event as an example of what was a very acceptable response in the women's community for that type of male behavior. We kids in the neighborhood grew up with these stories of women giving husbands, bosses, the welfare system, schools, unions and men in general—hell, whenever they deserved it. For me there were many role models of women taking action, control and resisting what was supposed to be their lot.          [1988]

## 🌱 87

# *The Birthday Party*

AGNES SMEDLEY

Then it was that the little white girl invited me to her birthday party. My mother objected to buying bananas as a present, but after I had cried and said everyone else was taking things, she grudgingly bought three.

"They are rich people," she protested bitterly, looking at the precious bananas, "an' there's no use givin' 'em any more."

When I arrived at the little girl's home I saw that other children had brought presents of books, silver pieces, handkerchiefs and lovely things such as I had never seen in my life. Fairy tales mentioned them but I never thought they really existed. They were all laid out on a table covered with a cloth shot through with gold. I had to walk up before them all and place my three bananas there, covertly touching the cloth shot through with gold. Then I made my way to a chair against the wall and sat down, trying to hide my feet and wishing that I had never come.

The other little girls and boys were quite at ease—

they had been at parties before. They were not afraid to talk or laugh and their throats didn't become whispery and hoarse when anyone asked them a question. I became more and more miserable with each passing moment. In my own world I could reply and even lead, and down beyond the tracks no boy dared touch me or my brother George. If he did he faced me with a jimpson weed as a weapon. But this was a new kind of hurt. In school I had not felt like this before the little white girl: there I had learned an invaluable lesson—that she was clean and orderly, but that I could *do* and learn things that she couldn't. Because of that and because of my teacher's protecting attitude toward me, she had been ashamed not to invite me to her party.

"Of course, if you're too busy to come, you must not feel that you ought, just because I've invited you," she had said. She was not much over ten, yet she had been well trained. I felt vaguely that something was wrong, yet I looked gratefully at her and replied:

"I'll come. I ain't got nothin' to do!"

Now here I was in a gorgeous party where I wasn't wanted. I had brought three bananas at a great sacrifice only to find that no other child would have dreamed of such a cheap present. My dress, that seemed so elegant when I left home, was shamefully shabby here. I was disturbed in my isolation by a number of mothers who called us into another room and seated us at a long table covered with a white tablecloth, marvelous cakes and fruit such as made my heart sink when I compared them with my three bananas. Only my desire to tell my mother all about it, and my desire to know everything in the world even if it hurt, kept me from slipping out of the door when no one was looking, and rushing home. I was seated next to a little boy at the table.

"What street do you live on?" he asked, trying to start a polite conversation.

"Beyond th' tracks."

He looked at me in surprise. "Beyond the tracks! Only tough kids live there!"

I stared back trying to think of something to say, but failed. He sought other avenues of conversation.

"My papa's a lawyer—what's yours?"

"Hauls bricks."

He again stared at me. That made me long to get him over beyond the tracks—he with his eye-glasses and store-made clothes! We used our sling-shots on such sissies. He was stuck-up, that was what he was! But what about I couldn't see.

"*My* papa don't haul bricks!" he informed me, as if to rub it in. Wherein the insult lay I couldn't see, yet I knew one was meant. So I insulted back.

"My papa can lick your papa I bet!" I informed him, just as a pleasant elegant mother bent over us with huge plates of yellow ice cream in her hands.

"Well, Clarence, and what are you talking about?" she asked affectionately.

"Her father hauls bricks and she lives beyond the tracks and she says her father can lick my father!" Clarence piped.

"That doesn't matter, dear, that doesn't matter! Now, now, just eat your ice cream." But I saw her eyes rest disapprovingly on me and I knew it did matter.

Clarence plunged his spoon into his ice cream and henceforth ignored me. I picked up my spoon, but it clattered against the plate. A dainty little girl in blue, with flaring white silk ribbons on her braid of hair, glanced at me primly. I did not touch the spoon again, but sat with my hands under me watching the others eating in perfect self-possession and without noise. I knew I could never eat like that and if I tried to swallow, the whole table would hear. The mother returned and urged me to eat, but I said I didn't like ice cream or cake! She offered me fruit and I took it, thinking I could eat it at home. But when the children left the table I saw that they carried no fruit. So I left mine beside the precious ice cream and cake.

In the next room little boys and girls were choosing partners for a game, and the little white girl was actually sitting at the piano ready to play. My eyes were glued on her—to think of being able to play the piano! Everyone was chosen for the game but me. No little boy bowed to me and asked:

"Will you be my partner, please?" I saw them avoid me deliberately . . . some of them the same little boys who were so stupid in school!

The mother of my little hostess tried to be kind:

"Are you sick, Marie?" she asked. "Would you like to go home?"

"Yes, mam." My voice was hoarse and whispery.

She took me to the door and smiled kindly, saying she hoped I had had a nice time.

"Yes, mam," my hoarse voice replied.

The door closed behind me. The game had started inside and voices of the children were shouting in laughter. In case anyone should be looking out of the window and think I cared, I turned my head and gazed sternly at a house across the street as I walked rapidly away.

And in case anyone I knew saw me with tears in my eyes I would say . . .                           [1929]

# ✿ 88

# *Context*

DOROTHY ALLISON

One summer, almost ten years ago, I brought my lover down to Greenville to visit my aunt Dot and the rest of my mama's family. We took our time getting there, spending one day in D.C. and another in Durham. I even thought about suggesting a side trip over to the Smoky Mountains, until I realized the reason I was thinking about that was that I was afraid. It was not my family I feared. It was my lover. I was afraid to take my lover home with me because of what I might see in her face once she had spent some time with my aunt, met a few of my uncles, and tried to talk to any of my cousins. I was afraid of the distance, the fear, or the contempt that I imagined could suddenly appear between us. I was afraid that she might see me though new eyes, hateful eyes, the eyes of someone who suddenly knew fully how different we were. My aunts' distance, my cousins' fear, or my uncles' contempt seemed much less threatening.

I was right to worry. My lover did indeed see me with new eyes, though it turned out that she was more afraid of my distancing myself from her than of her fear and discomfort coming between us. What I saw in her face after the first day in South Carolina was nothing I had expected. Her features were marked with a kind of tenuous awe, confusion, uncertainty, and shame. All she could say was

that she hadn't been prepared. My aunt Dot had welcomed her, served ice tea in a tall glass, and made her sit in the best seat at the kitchen table, the one near the window where my uncle's cigarette smoke wouldn't bother her. But my lover had barely spoken.

"It's a kind of a dialect, isn't it," she said to me in the motel that night. "I couldn't understand one word in four of anything your aunt said." I looked at her. Aunt Dot's accent was pronounced, but I had never thought of it as a dialect. It was just that she hadn't ever been out of Greenville County. She had a television, but it was for the kids in the living room. My aunt lived her life at that kitchen table.

My lover leaned into my shoulder so that her cheek rested against my collar bone. "I thought I knew what it would be like—your family, Greenville. You told me so many stories. But the words . . ." She lifted her hand palm up into the air and flexed the fingers as if she were reaching for an idea.

"I don't know," she said. "I thought I understood what you meant when you said 'working class' but I just didn't have a context."

I lay still. Although the motel air conditioner was working hard, I could smell the steamy moist heat from outside. It was slipping in around the edges of the door and windows, a swampy earth-rich smell that reminded me of being ten years old and climbing down to sleep on the floor with my sisters, hoping it would be a little cooler there. We had never owned an air conditioner, never stayed in a motel, never eaten in a restaurant where my mother did not work. Context. I breathed in the damp metallic air-conditioner smell and remembered Folly Beach.

When I was about eight my stepfather drove us there, down the road from Charleston, and all five of us stayed in one room that had been arranged for us by a friend of his at work. It wasn't a motel. It was a guesthouse, and the lady who managed it didn't seem too happy that we showed up for a room someone else had already paid for. I slept in a fold-up cot that kept threatening to collapse in the night. My sisters slept together in the bed across from the one my parents shared. My mama cooked on a two-burner stove to save us the cost of eating out, and our greatest treat was take-out food—fried fish my stepfather swore was bad and hamburgers from the same place that sold the fish. We were in awe of the outdoor shower under the stairs where we were expected to rinse off the sand we picked up on the beach. We longed to be able to rent one of the rafts, umbrellas, and bicycles you could get on the beach. But my stepfather insisted all that stuff was listed at robbery rates and cursed the men to who tried to tempt us with it. That didn't matter to us. We were overcome with the sheer freedom of being on a real vacation in a semi-public place all the time where my stepfather had to watch his temper, and of running everywhere in bathing suits and flip-flops.

We were there a week. Twice my stepfather sent us to the beach while he and Mama stayed in the room. We took the opportunity to follow other families around, to listen to fathers praising their sons and watch mothers blushing with pride at how people looked at their girls. We listened to accents and studied picnic menus. Everyone was strange and wonderful, on vacation.

My stepfather lost his temper only once on that trip. He was horrified at the prices in the souvenir shops and made us keep our hands in our pockets.

"Jew bastards will charge me if you break anything," he cursed.

I flinched at his words and then realized that the man behind the counter heard him. I saw his blush and outrage as his eyes followed my stepfather's movement toward the door. Then I saw his eyes flicker over to me and my sisters, registering the same contempt with which he had looked at my stepfather. Heat flamed in my neck and I wanted to apologize—to tell him we were not like our stepfather—but I could do nothing. I couldn't speak a word to him in front of my stepfather, and if I had, why would he have believed me? Remember this, I thought. Don't go deaf and blind to what this feels like, remember it. I gritted my teeth and kept my head up, looked that man in the face and mouthed, "I'm sorry," but I could not tell if he understood me.

What context did he have for people like us?

After my lover fell asleep that first night in Greenville, I lay awake a long time thinking. My lover was a Yankee girl from a good family, who had spent the summers of her childhood on the Jersey Shore. I had gone there with her, walked with her on the beaches of her memory, wide and flat and grey-white, so clear I felt intimidated. Seeing where she had grown up, meeting some of her family, I had understood her better, seen where some of her fear came from, and her pride. What had she understood about me today? I wondered.

I turned my head to the side to look at her sleep, her mouth soft against my skin. Her hair was dark and shiny, her teeth straight and white. I wondered what she would have thought of Folly Beach, the poor man's Jersey Shore, or of us if she could have seen us there. I burned with old shame and then stubbornly shook it off.

Context is so little to share, and so vital.   [1994]

## 🦎 89

# *Sisters*

BARBARA NEELY

*. . . and are we not one*
*daughter of the same dark mother's child*
*breathing one breath from a multitude of mouths . . .*
    —from the Sisterhood Song of the Yenga Nation

The offices of Carstairs and Carstairs Management Consultants had that hushed, forbidden air of after five o'clock. No light shone from beneath any of the office doors bordering the central typing pool which was also deserted, except for the new cleaning woman working her way among the desks. Lorisa was the last of the office staff to leave. She'd pushed the button for the elevator before she remembered the notes on Wider Housewares she wanted to look over before tomorrow morning's meeting. She turned and took a shortcut through the typing pool to her office.

"Good evening," she said to the grey uniform-clad back of the cleaning woman as the woman reached down to pick up a wastebasket. Lorisa automatically put on her polite, remote smile, the one that matched the distance in her tone, while she waited for the woman to move out of her way.

Jackie turned with the wastebasket still in her hand and let her eyes roam so slowly over the woman who'd spoken to her that she might have been looking for something in particular. Then she nodded, briefly, curtly, before turning, lifting the basket and dashing its contents into the rolling bin she pushed along ahead of her. Only then did she step aside.

Lorisa hurried into her office, careful not to slam the door and show her irritation. Where did they find the cleaning staff, the asylum for the criminally insane? The woman had given her a look cold enough to cut stone and barely acknowledged her greeting—as though she were not worth the time it took to be pleasant. She, who was always careful to speak to the gum-chewing black girls who worked in the mail room, the old man who shined shoes in the lobby, the newspaper man and any other of her people she met in the building who did menial work. None of them had ever been anything but equally polite to her. She had noticed the shoeshine man always had something pleasant to say to the mailroom girls and only a "Good day" to her. But considering the difference in their positions, his reticence with her seemed only natural and nothing like the attitude of the cleaning woman.

Although she'd only returned for her notes, she found herself moving papers from one side of her desk to the other, making a list of small tasks for tomorrow, staving off the moment when she would have to confront the cleaning woman once again. But Lorisa realized it wasn't the woman's curt nod or the slowness with which she'd moved aside that made her reluctant to leave her office. It was those eyes. Big, black, dense eyes with something knowing in them—something that had made her feel as though her loneliness and her fear of it, her growing uneasiness about her job, the disturbing hollowness where pleasure in her comfortable life should be, and all her other fears and flaws were as visible to the cleaning woman as so many wrinkles and smudges on her dress. When their eyes had met, the sense of secret knowledge already shared had filled her with an almost overwhelming desire to say something, to explain something about a part of herself she couldn't name. The woman's look of cold disdain had only corroborated her feeling of having been revealed and found wanting. "Your shit ain't so hot, honey, and you know it," the woman's eyes

seemed to say. It didn't occur to Lorisa that the way she'd spoken to the cleaning woman could have anything to do with the woman's response. She was tired, with too much work and too little rest. And she was always over-imaginative when her period was about to start. She forced herself to open the door to her office and was nearly lightheaded with relief to find the cleaning woman nowhere in sight.

In the descending elevator, she realized that the term "cleaning woman" rang false against the face and figure she'd just encountered. Cleaning women were fat and full of quiet kindness and mother wit. They were not women who looked to be in their late twenties—her own age—with faces strong and proud as her own. They didn't have lean, hard-muscled arms and eyes like onyx marbles. She remembered her grandmother, her father's squat, black, broad-nosed mother who had cooked and cleaned for white people all of her life. On those rare occasions when Lorisa's mother had consented to a visit from her mother-in-law, or, rarer still, when the family paid the older woman a visit in North Carolina, Grandmother would wait on everyone. She would slip into your room while you were in the bathroom in the morning and make your bed, hang up your clothes, and spirit away anything that looked the least bit in need of mending, washing, or pressing. But her dedication didn't earn her much praise.

"Young black girls learn enough about being mammies without your mother to set an example," Lorisa had once heard her mother say to her father. Her mother was explaining why it was impossible for Lorisa to spend part of her summer with her grandmother, despite Lorisa's and her grandmother's wishes. She'd been sent to camp instead, a camp at which, she remembered now, the white kids had called her and the three other black girls "niggers" and put spiders in their beds. As she crossed the lobby, it occurred to her that her grandmother had once been young, just like the woman cleaning the typing pool. Had there been fire in her grandmother's eyes, too, when she was young? Had she spit in the white folks soup, the way the slaves used to do? How long did it take to make a *real* cleaning woman?

\* \* \*

Jackie banged another wastebasket against her bin with such vigor she left a dent in the basket. What had made her act like that? She slammed the basket down beside the desk and moved on to the next one. The woman was only trying to be polite. But a mean, evil rage had risen up at the very sight of her—walking around like she owned the place, having her own office. And those shoes! She must have paid a hundred dollars for them shoes! Who'd she think she was? Jackie dumped the last basket and began dry mopping the floor with an over-sized dust-mop. A college education didn't give her the right to give nobody that uptight little greeting, like an icicle down somebody's back, she thought. She'd run into three or four other black women with really good jobs in other buildings where she cleaned. A couple of them had had that air of doing you a favor when they spoke to you, too. But they'd been light-skinned and looked like models, which somehow made their hinctiness less personal. This woman's smooth dark face and big round eyes reminded Jackie of a girl she'd hung out with in school; and she had a cousin with the same big legs and small waist. She didn't need for no plain ole everyday-looking black woman to speak to her because she thought she ought to. She got more than enough of being practically patted on her head, if not her behind, from the phony whites she worked for. She wasn't taking that stuff from one of her own, too!

She let her mind slip into a replay of her latest run-in with her snooty white supervisor in which she'd once again had to point out that she only gave respect when she got it. She was hoping to draw a parallel between the two situations and thereby relieve herself of the knowledge that in the moment when she'd first seen the woman standing there—as crisp and unused as a new dollar bill, as far removed from emptying other people's wastebaskets as a black woman was likely to get—she had been struck dumb by jealousy. She swung the mop in wide arcs, putting more energy into the chore than was called for.

She was just finishing up the Men's Room when she heard the elevator bell. When she left the bathroom no light showed from beneath the woman's door. Although she'd already cleaned the private offices, Jackie crossed the typing pool and tiptoed into the woman's office. She stood in the middle of the room. Light from the street below made turning on the overhead light unnecessary. A hint of some peppery perfume lingered in the air, like a shadow of the woman who worked there. It was a good-sized office, with a beige leather sofa under an abstract painting in shades of blues and brown; a glass and chrome coffee table with dried flowers in a bowl. A big, shiny, wooden desk.

Jackie ran her fingers along the edge of the desk as she walked slowly round it. She stood in front of the leather desk chair and placed the fingertips of both hands lightly on the desk. She leaned forward and looked toward the sofa as though addressing an invisible client or underling. Then she sat—not as she usually sat, with a sigh of relief at getting off her feet as she plopped solidly down. She sat slowly, her head held high, her back straight. In her imagination, she wore Lorisa's raw silk shirtwaist and turquoise beads. Gold glistened at her ears and on her small, manicured hands. Her hair was long and pulled back into a sleek chignon. The desk hid her suddenly corn-free feet, sporting one hundred dollar shoes. And she knew things—math, the meaning of big words, what to tell other people to do . . . things that meant you were closer to being the boss than to being bossed.

Once, so long ago it seemed like the beginning of time, she'd thought she might be something—nothing grand enough for an office like this. Being a secretary is what she'd dreamed about: dressing real neat, walking with her legs close together, in that switchy way secretaries always had on TV, typing and filing and so forth. She must have been about ten years old when she'd hoped for that, not old enough to know that chubby-butt, black-skinned, unwed mothers with GED diplomas and short, nappy hair didn't get jobs as downtown secretaries or very much else, besides floor-moppers or whores, unless they had a college education. She'd had to drop out of school to take care of her son. She'd never considered marrying Carl's father and he had never asked if she wanted to get married. They were both fifteen and had only had sex twice. Since then, it seemed she only met two kinds of men—those she didn't like who liked her and those she liked who weren't interested in her. Her marriage dream was no more real than any of her other dreams. She lifted a slim, black pen from its desk holder, shined it on the edge of the apron she wore over her uniform, and quickly replaced it.

But hadn't she at least suspected, even back when she was ten and still dreaming about secretarial school and happy-ever-after, that this was what her life was going to be—just what her mother's life had been and that of all her girlfriends who were not in jail or on dope or working themselves to death for some pimp or factory owner? Hadn't she known that questions like: "And what do you want to be when you grow up, little girl?" were only grown-ups' way of not talking to her, since they already knew the limits of her life?

A longing beyond words welled up from her core and threatened to escape into a moan so deep and so wrenching its gathering made her suddenly short of breath. She rose quickly from the chair and headed for the door.

What happened to the part of yourself that dreams and hopes, she wondered. Was it just a phase of growing up, to believe you might amount to something, might do something with your life besides have babies and be poor? And how come some people got to have their dreams come true and others didn't?

\* \* \*

Lorisa lay with her head thrown back against the edge of the high steel tub, droplets from the swirling water gently splashing her face, tightening the skin across her forehead. She stopped by the spa for a whirlpool bath and fifteen minutes in the steam room every day after work. As a reward, she told herself, without thinking about what there was about her work that warranted rewarding. She shifted her weight, careful to keep her feet from the sucking pipe that pulled the water in and forced it out to knead and pummel her muscles, dissolving the tension across her shoulders. But not quite.

Jim Daily's face rose behind her eyelids—a pale, oval moon altering the landscape of her leisure with its sickly light. She pressed her eyelids down as hard as possible, but Daily's face remained.

"You notice how much she looks like the maid in that cleanser commercial? You know the one I mean," he'd gone on to whoever was in earshot, to

whoever would listen, as he'd circled her, trapped her with his penetrating voice. "Go ahead," he told her, "Put your hand on your hip and say, 'Look, chile!'" He'd transformed his voice into a throaty falsetto. His pale blue gaze had pinned her to the spot where she stood, like a spotlight, as he'd waited for her to perform, to act like some nigger clown in some minstrel show. All in fun, of course; just joking, of course; no offense intended, of course. A hot flush of shame had warmed her cheeks. Is that how she looked to him, to them? she'd wondered, searching her mind for real similarities between herself and the commercial caricature of whom Daily spoke, even though she knew in her heart that he never saw her, that all black women's faces were most likely one to him.

Lorisa tried to let go of the memory, to give herself over to the soothing water, but her back was stiff now, her tongue pressed too firmly to the roof of her mouth behind tightly clenched teeth. All the rage she couldn't let herself release at the time came rolling to the surface in a flood of scenes in which she said all the things she might have said to him, if she'd had the luxury of saying and acting as she pleased—like the cleaning woman in her office. She saw herself putting her hand on her hip and telling Daily what an ignorant, racist dog he was. A stiletto-thin smile curved her lips at the thought of how he would have looked, standing there with his face gone purple and his whiny nasal voice finally silenced.

Of course, from Daily's point of view, from the firm's point of view, she would only have proved conclusively that all blacks were belligerent and had no sense of proportion, none of the civilizing ability to laugh at themselves. And, of course, she would have lost her job. Daily was slightly senior to her. He was also a white male in a white male firm where she, and the two white women consultants, did everything they could to distract attention from the fact that they were not biologically certified for the old boys' club. And Lorisa knew she was on even shakier ground than the white women on staff.

She was the one who got the smallest and most mundane clients with whom to work. It was her ideas that were always somehow attributed to someone else. She was invariably the last to know about changes in the firm's policies or procedures and office gossip was stone cold by the time she heard it. For a while, she'd been fairly successful at convincing herself all this was due to her being a very junior member of the staff, that race had nothing to do with it. Of course, she realized, with the seventh sense of a colored person in a white society, which members of the firm hated her silently and politely because of her color. Daily was not alone in his racism and he was probably less dangerous, with his overt ignorance, than the quiet haters. But they were individuals. The firm was different. The firm was only interested in making all the money it could. It didn't really care who did the work. Wasn't that what she'd been taught in her college economics courses? But more and more, as men with less seniority and skills than she were given serious responsibilities, she was increasingly unable to plaster over the cracks in the theory that the firm was somehow different from the individuals of which it is composed. More and more she was forced to accept the very good possibility that she'd been hired as a token and would be kept as a company pet, as long as she behaved herself . . . or until some other type of token/pet became more fashionable.

It seemed ironic that in college she'd been one of the black students most involved in trying to better race relations. She'd helped organize integrated retreats and participated in race workshops. She'd done her personal share by rooming with a white girl who became her best friend, costing her what few black girlfriends she'd had on campus. She could almost count the number of dates she'd had on one hand. There were only a few black boys on campus to begin with and a third of them were more interested in her white roommate or light-skinned colored girls than they'd been in the likes of her. Those who had dated her had done so only once and spread the word that she was "lame," and "cold." She quickly evaded the thought that her love life hadn't improved appreciably since college. Back then, there were times when she had felt more comfortable with some of the white kids than she had with some of the black ones, although she'd denied this vehemently when a black girl accused her of it. And she'd originally liked being the only black at Carstairs and Carstairs. She'd thought she'd have more of a chance to get ahead on her own, without

other blacks and their problems and claims to her allegiance.

"We're so proud of our Lorisa," her mother's prim school teacher's voice repeated inside Lorisa's head. The occasion had been a family dinner honoring Lorisa's completion of graduate school and the job offer from Carstairs. "Yes, indeed," her mother had gone on, "Lorisa is a fine example of what a young colored woman can do, if she just puts all this race and sex mess behind her and steps boldly, acts forcefully on her own behalf."

Lorisa wondered what her mother would say if she knew how often her daughter longed for just one pair of dark eyes in one brown face in which to see herself mirrored and know herself whole in moments when she was erased by her co-workers' assumptions about her ability or brains based on her color, not to mention her sex. It was only now that she, herself, realized how much she needed for that brown face to belong to a woman. How long had it been since she'd had one of those I-can-tell-you-cause-you're-just-like-me talks that she remembered from her late childhood and early teens? But that was before she and her girlfriends had been made to understand the ways in which they were destined to compete and to apprehend the generally accepted fact that women could not be trusted.

Still, she'd been smart to keep her mouth shut with Daily. The economy wasn't all that good and lots of companies were no longer interested in trying to incorporate blacks. She could have opened her mouth and ended up with nothing more than her pride. No job. No money. No future. She picked at the possibility like a worrisome scab, imagining herself unable to pay the rent on her newly furnished and decorated apartment or meet the payments on her new car, living a life of frozen fish sticks and cheap pantyhose in a roach-ridden apartment. She saw herself clerking in a supermarket or department store, waiting on people who had once waited on her. Or worse. The face of the cleaning woman from her office replaced Daily's in her mind's eye—the woman's scowl, her hands in cheap rubber gloves, her eyes showing something hot and unsettling, like the first glow of an eruption-bound volcano.

They said it wasn't like the old days. Nowadays, blacks could do anything whites could do. Hadn't a black man gone into space? Hadn't a black woman been named Miss America? Then why was it, she wondered, that the minute she began to contemplate being out of work and what would be available to her, it was only work near the bottom that she expected to find? It was as though her degrees, her experience and skills would amount to nothing, once she descended into the ranks of the black unemployed.

But she was not going to be unemployed. She was not going to be on the outside. She was from a family of achievers. Her father was the first black to get an engineering degree from his alma mater. Her mother had been named best teacher by the local parent-teacher's association for three years in a row. How could she ever explain getting fired to them? Or to members of the black business women's association she'd recently joined? No. She intended to stay right where she was and prove to Carstairs and Carstairs that she was just as dedicated to profit margins and sales, just as adept at sniffing out a rival's weakness and moving in for the kill, just as practiced in the fine art of kissing her superior's ass, as any white boy they could find. She rose quickly from the tub and snatched her towel off the rack, irritated that relaxation had once again eluded her.

\* \* \*

The room was starting to have that acrid, funky odor of people in danger of losing their last dime. Jackie looked around the card table. Light bounced off Big Red's freckled forehead; his belly was a half-submerged beach ball bobbing above the table. Mabel's lips were pressed near to disappearance. It was a look she'd wear as long as there were cards on the table. Her gambling mask, she called it. Bernice was half drunk. Jackie hated playing cards with drunks. They either knocked over a drink and soaked the cards, or started some shit with one of the other players. Bernice had already signified to Alma about the whereabouts and doings of Alma's old man, Rickie, a good-looking Puerto Rican with a Jones for blue-black thighs. Ramrod Slim sat just like his name. His color and the millions of tiny wrinkles on his face reminded Jackie of raisins and prunes.

Jackie riveted her eyes and attention on Slim's hands as he passed out the cards. The hand he dealt her was as indifferent as all the other hands she'd been dealt tonight. Sweat formed a film separating her fingers from the cards. Oh Jesus! If she could just win a couple of hands, win just enough to pay on Carl's dental bill so the dentist would adjust the child's braces. She gritted her teeth at the memory of the note Carl had brought home when he went for his last visit, a note saying he shouldn't return without at least a fifty-dollar payment. Bastard! Honky bastard! All they ever cared about was money. But, of course, it was more than the dentist's money she needed now.

When she'd decided to get in the game, she'd told herself she had twelve dollars' card-playing money. If she lost it, she would leave the game and not have lost anything other than the little bit of extra money she had left over from her bills and other necessities. If she won, there'd be money for the dentist and the shoes she needed so badly. She'd found a quarter on the way to work—a sure sign of luck.

But not only had she lost her twelve dollars, she'd also lost her light bill money, all of her carfare for next week and was now in danger of losing part of her grocery money. She gripped her cards and plucked. Damn! Shit on top of shit. She wasn't hardly in the way of winning this hand. She longed for a drink to take away the taste of defeat, to drown the knowledge of once again having made the wrong decision, taken the wrong risk. She would have to get some money from somewhere. She let her mind run over her list of friends in order of the likelihood of their being able to lend her something and was further disheartened. Almost everybody she knew was either laid off or about to be. Those who were working steady were in debt and had kids to feed, too. She didn't have a man at the moment. The last one had borrowed twenty-five dollars from her and disappeared. But she would have to find the money somewhere, somehow. She wondered what it would be like to be able to lose this little bit of cash—not much more than a pair of those alligator pumps that woman had worn in the building where she'd cleaned yesterday. She tried to make space in her anxious mind in which to imagine having enough money not to constantly be concerned about it.

"Girl! Is you gonna play cards or daydream?" Big Red grumbled.

Jackie made a desultory play, waited for her inevitable loss, indifferent to whom the winner might be.

\* \* \*

The Carstairs were consummate party givers. They liked entertaining. They liked the accolades providing lavish amounts of expensive food and drink brought them. It was what they did instead of donating to charity. Mr. Carstairs invariably invited all the professional members of the firm and made no secret of how much pleasure it gave him when they were all in attendance. As usual, on party nights, the front door of the Carstairs' twenty-room country place was wide open. A jumble of voices underscored the music that danced out to meet Lorisa as she walked slowly up the front steps.

She hoped it would be different this time. Perhaps, just this once, they would not all turn toward her when she first entered the room and leave her feeling blotted out by their blank, collective stare. She could have made it easier on herself by bringing a date, but she didn't know a man she disliked and trusted enough to subject to one of the Carstairs' parties, or a man who liked her well enough to make the sacrifice. Nevertheless, she attended all the Carstairs' parties, always leaving just as someone started banging out "Dixie" on the piano or telling the latest Jewish, Polish, or gay joke. She knew who would be the butt of the next go-round.

But tonight, she would do more than put in a respectful appearance. Tonight she would prove she was prepared to make whatever sacrifice necessary to play on the team. For she'd decided that it was her non-team player behavior—her inability to laugh at a good joke, no matter who was the butt of it; her momentary appearances at office social functions; her inability to make other staff accept that she was no different from them in any way that counted—that kept her from total acceptance into the firm. Tonight, she would break through the opaque bubble that seemed to keep her from being seen or heard, making her as murky to the whites on staff as they were to her.

After the usual genuflection before the Carstairs and the obligatory exchange of comments about how very glad they were she could come and how pleased she was to be there, Lorisa ordered a stiff drink from the barman and began to circulate with determination. She stopped at one small grouping after another, asking about wives and children, looking interested in golf scores, remaining noncommittal on the issues of busing and affirmative action until her tongue felt swollen, her lips parched and stretched beyond recovery. And still she pressed on: dancing with Bill Steele; laughing at Daily's tasteless joke about a crippled child; listening to Mrs. Carstairs reminisce about Annie Lee, the dear, dead, colored woman who had raised her, while her mama languished on a chaise lounge with a twenty-year-old migraine. And still she pressed on.

And she thought she made her point. She was sure she saw some of them, the ones who counted— the ones who watched the junior staff for signs of weakness or leadership—smile in her direction, nodding their heads as though dispensing a blessing when she caught their eye. Her success was clear in the gentle hug from Mrs. Carstairs, a sign of approval that all the women in the office had come to covet. It was this sense of having proved herself worthy that made her decide to speak to Jill Franklin.

She'd had no intention of trying to enlist anyone in the firm in her struggles with Daily. While she felt one or two of them—including Jill—might be sympathetic, none of them had ever attempted to intervene on her behalf or had even shown overt empathy for her. But the flush of acceptance made her feel as though she had a right to make requests of staff, just like any other member of the firm. She'd been talking to Jill and Ken Horton, whose offices bordered her own, about baseball, until Ken's wife dragged him away. For a few moments, both of the women were quiet. Lorisa gathered strength from the silence, then spoke.

"Listen, Jill, I need to ask you something. You've been working with Jim Daily for a while, now. And you seem to know him well, get along with him. Tell me, is there anything I can do to make him stop?"

"Stop what?" Jill's voice was full of innocent curiosity, her face bland as milk.

For the first time, since she'd arrived at the party, Lorisa looked someone directly in the eye. Jill's eyes had that same blue distance she saw in Daily's eyes.

"Stop . . ." she began, searching desperately for something safe to say to cover her error.

"Hey, you two! This is a party, come out of that corner!" Somebody Lorisa didn't recognize grabbed Jill's hand and pulled her out to the patio where some people were dancing. Lorisa went in search of the Carstairs and made her good-nights.

*　*　*

Jackie spotted Mr. Gus as soon as she pushed open the door. He was where she'd expected him to be this time of evening: on his favorite stool near the far end of the bar, away from the juke box in the front of the long room, but not too close to the bathrooms at the back.

"Hey, Miz Pretty." Harold rubbed his grungy bar cloth in a circle and gave her a wink. Cissy and her old man, Juice (so called for his love of it), sat in a booth opposite the bar and stared past each other. Miz Hazel, who ran the newspaper stand, nursed a mug of beer and half a shot of something while she and Harold watched a baseball game on the portable TV at their end of the bar. Jackie was glad for the game. Talking to Mr. Gus would be easier than if the juke box was going. And she did have to talk to Mr. Gus. She'd tried all her girlfriends, her mother and even her hairdresser. Everyone was broke as she was. Mr. Gus was her last hope. She stopped thinking about all the years she'd promised herself that no matter how broke she got, she wouldn't turn to this sly, old brown coot.

She slid onto a stool three up from Mr. Gus and told Harold to bring her a vodka and orange juice. She glanced at Mr. Gus in the long mirror hanging behind the rows of bottles in front of her. He was looking at the newspaper lying on the bar beside his glass. He didn't lean over the paper, the way most people would. He sat with his back straight, his head slightly inclined, his folded hands resting on the edge of the bar in front of his drink. The white of his shirt glistened in the blue bar light. She had never seen him without shirt and tie, despite the fact that he wore a uniform at work, just like her.

"How you doin', Mr. Gus?"

He looked up as though surprised to find her there, as though he hadn't seen her from the moment she stepped in the door, as though he hadn't been waiting for her since she was a little girl. Mr. Gus was a neighborhood institution. Being a man who understood the economic realities of most black women's lives, he'd cultivated two generations of little girls and was working on a third generation. He took them for rides in his car, gave them candy— all on the up and up, of course. He would never touch a child. He got a portion of his pleasure from waiting, anticipating. Many of Jackie's little play-mates had come to learn they could depend on their old friend, nice Mr. Gus, for treats in their adult lives, too. Only now the candy was cash and the price was higher than a "Thank you, Mr. Gus." But despite the fact that she made next-to-no salary and had a child to raise, Jackie had never come around. Until now. Mr. Gus smiled.

"Anything in the paper about that boy who got shot on Franklin Street, last night?" Jackie craned her neck in his direction, her eyes seeming to search the front page of the paper, her chest thrust forward, in her low-cut sweater. She skipped her behind over the barstools between them, still pretending to be intent upon the headlines. But she was mindful of the cat-with-cream smile on his face. It was a smile that made her sure he knew why she was there; that he had sensed, in that special way some men have, that she was vulnerable, could be run to ground like a wounded doe.

She hadn't meant to drink so much, but Mr. Gus was generous. And he was an excellent listener. There was something about his attitude, his stillness and sympathetic expression that allowed women to tell him things they wouldn't reveal to their best friends. They told their men's secrets, what they had dreamed about the night before and anything else that was on their minds, as though injected with a truth-inducing drug. To many women, what was a little sex for badly needed cash, after this kind of intimacy? It was a line of thinking Mr. Gus encouraged.

And so, Jackie had rattled on about her lousy job and what her supervisor had said to her and how hard it was trying to raise a boy alone. Mr. Gus nodded and tsked, asked a question or two to prime the pump when she hesitated, ordered more drinks and waited for the beg, the plea. And, of course, the payback.

But in the end, Jackie couldn't do it. She told him how badly Carl needed his braces adjusted and what a fool she'd been to lose her carfare and light bill money in a card game. But when it came to asking him could he see his way clear to let her have seventy-five or even fifty dollars, the same hard glint in his eye that had put her off as a child made her hold her tongue. She did try to get him to say his lines— to ask why she sighed so forlornly, or what she meant when she said, in that frightened voice, that she didn't know what she was going to do. But Mr. Gus refused to play. He wanted the beg. He'd been waiting for it for a long, long time.

They left the bar together. Jackie now a little rocky on her feet, Mr. Gus unwilling to lose when he was so very close. He took her up to his place for one last drink. The smell of old men's undershirts sobered her a bit.

"I sure hate to see you in such a bad way," he said as she sat at his kitchen table trying to adjust her breathing to the bad air.

"Course, you coulda had all I got." He poured another dollop of Seagrams in her jelly glass. Jackie quickly drank it down.

"I don't know why you always been so mean to me, Miz Jackie." He rose and walked to stand behind her chair, kneading her left shoulder with pudgy fingers that radiated damp heat, like a moist heat pad. She willed herself not to pull her shoulder away. He breathed like a cat purring.

"Why you so mean, Miz Jackie?" He spoke in a wheedling, whiny tone, as though he, not she, were on the beg.

"You know Mr. Gus ain't gon let you and little Carl go wanting. Don't you know that, now?" He crept closer to the back of her chair, still moving his fingers in damp slow circles.

"I got me a little piece of money, right here in the bedroom; and I want you to have it."

\* \* \*

At first, Lorisa had considered it a sign of her growing esteem among her superiors that she was chosen to take Stanley Wider, of Wider Housewares, to dinner for a preliminary discussion about his signing a contract with the firm. She was so grateful for any indication of growing favor that it hadn't occurred to her to wonder why she, a junior member of the firm, with no real experience with prestigious clients, should be given this plum. The Wider account

had the potential for being very big, very important to the career of whoever pulled him in. Now that dinner with Wider was nearly over, Lorisa understood why she'd been chosen.

Mr. Wider was what the women in the office called "a lunch man"—a client who turned into a sex fiend after dark and could, therefore, only be talked to over lunch. Looking at him, anyone would think he was a kindly, trustworthy genteel man— like Walter Cronkite. Only his eyes and his words told the truth about him. She smiled up from her Peach Melba into his lean, clean-shaven face to find his eyes once again caressing her breasts. He smiled sheepishly, boyishly, when he realized he'd been caught. But his eyes remained cold and hard.

Ralph Wider was a serious pursuer of young corporate women on the rise. In the sixties, when women began pressuring for more room at the top, he'd been bitterly against the idea. But a chance encounter with an extremely ambitious female sales representative had shown him the benefits of affirmative active. In his analysis, women in business fell into two categories: those who were confident and competent enough to know they didn't need to take their panties down to do business; and those who could be convinced that in at least his case, a little sex would get them more business than a lot of facts. He didn't meet many black ones and the ones he met were always smart. He figured they had to be to get high enough to deal with him. But he had a fairly good record of convincing category-one women to slip down a notch. The challenge added spice to his business dealings.

"We're very excited about the possibility of working with your people," Lorisa began, trying once again to introduce the reason for their having dinner together. "We think we can . . ."

"You know, I've always admired black women. You all are so . . . so uninhibited." He stretched the last word out into an obscenity. "I bet you can be a very friendly young lady, when you want to be."

*This man is important, not just to the firm, but to my career,* Lorisa reminded herself before she spoke.

"I'm afraid I've never been particularly famous for my friendliness, Mr. Wider, but I am a first rate efficiency specialist and I've got some ideas about how to increase . . ."

He lifted his glass in a toast as she spoke. "To freedom" he said with a sly grin.

Twice more she tried to raise the subject of business. Each time he countered with another invitation to spend a weekend on his boat or take a ride in his plane, or have dinner with him in his hotel room the following night.

She knew what she should say to him. She'd practiced gently and firmly explaining that she did not appreciate passes as a part of her work. But she'd never had occasion to use that speech, before. And this man had the power to greatly improve her position in the firm, simply by what he said about their evening together.

"Excuse me," she said between dessert and cognac. She could feel his eyes poking at her behind as she headed for the Ladies Room.

She wrapped wet paper towels around her neck, careful not to dampen her blouse and held her wrists under the cold water tap to calm herself. Tears quickened in her eyes at the sudden desire to tell some woman her woes; to explain about *him* being out there waiting for her and what ought she to do. Somebody deep inside urged her to go out there, pour a glass of ice water in his lap and run like hell— the same someone who'd urged her to talk to Daily as though he had a tail; the same someone who'd urged her to major in archeology instead of business and to stop smiling at white people, at least on weekends. But she was no fool. She wanted the Wider account and the prestige of getting it. She wanted her salary, her vacations, her car. She wanted to prove she was just as good as anybody else in the firm. At the moment, she just didn't know why she needed to prove it.

Lorisa dried her hands, checked her make-up and straightened her shoulders. She couldn't come apart now. She couldn't let them think she was incapable of handling any task the firm gave her. For all she knew, she was being tested. She brushed at her hair and willed that frightened look out of her eyes. I have a contract to get, she told herself as she opened the door.

She stared at his slim, distinguished figure as she crossed the room. So deceiving, she thought, like a bright shiny apple turned to maggotty mush on the inside. But if she could just get him to agree to look at the prospectus. He rose as she returned to her seat.

"I mean it, little lady," he said as he sat down, "I think you're really something special. I'm sure I can do business with you!" he added with a smile as his leg brushed hers beneath the table.

*   *   *

If there'd been any way for Lorisa to avoid getting on the elevator with Jackie, she'd have done so. If there'd been other people she'd have had no hesitation about getting on. Other people would have kept her from speaking, as she now feared she might. She didn't look at the woman as she entered the elevator, but she didn't need to. She remembered those eyes. The elevator doors hissed shut before her. The lobby button was already lit so she had only to stand there. She kept her eyes straight ahead and wondered if the elevator always moved this slowly or if the damned thing was going to stall, leaving them alone together for the rest of the night.

Jackie studied Lorisa's back and tried to get up the courage to say something. This was the first time she'd seen the woman since their encounter a couple of evenings ago. She still felt bad about how she'd responded. She wanted to apologize, maybe even change her luck by doing so.

"I'm real sorry for the way I acted the other day. Let me buy you a drink to make up for it," she practiced in her head, even though she didn't have enough money to buy herself a drink. She saw the two of them walking down the street to Libby's Place where she knew she could buy a round or two on credit. They would sit in a booth near the back. The juke box would be off, so the place would be quiet enough for talk. The woman would buy her a drink in return and they would talk about what they needed to talk about. Wasn't no black woman's life without something that needed talking about. But none of that was really going to happen. She could tell from the way the woman stood that she didn't want to be bothered.

As the elevator reached the lower floors, Lorisa reached in her pocket, pulled out her leather driving gloves and smoothed them on over long, slim fingers. She tried to keep her attention focused on what she was doing and away from her urge to somehow make herself acceptable to the woman standing behind her.

"Girl, you sure are evil!" she heard herself saying in a way that smacked of respect for the woman's willingness to give her economic betters hell. She saw them walking out of the building together. She would tell the woman her name and offer her a lift. Their talk in the car would be slow but easy. They might discover they liked one another.

But, of course, that whole scene was irrational. Why should she take a chance on being insulted again? Why should it make any difference to her whether this woman considered her somebody worth being pleasant to? She pressed her lips firmly together as the elevator finally slid to a stop. She stepped quickly forward and brisk-stepped her way to the other door, trying to put as much distance between herself and the cleaning woman as possible, before she did something she would regret.

After all, it wasn't as though they had anything in common.                                                    [1985]

# 🌿 90

# *Jewish and Working Class*

BERNICE MENNIS

When I was called to speak at this conference about working-class experience, my immediate reaction was: "No, get someone else." One voice said: "I have nothing worthwhile to say." A second voice said: "I was not born poor. I always ate well. I never felt deprived. I have not suffered enough to be on this panel." Both voices silenced me. The first came from my class background—a diminished sense of competence, ability, control, power. ("Who are you anyway? You have nothing to say. No one cares or will listen.") The second, the guilt voice, comes from a strange combination of my Jewishness, my fear of anti-Semitism, my own psychological reaction to my own deprivations: a denial of my own pain if someone else seems to suffer more.

Economic class has been a matter of both shame and pride for me, depending on the value judgments of the community with which I identified. The economic class reality has always remained the same: My father had a very small outdoor tomato and banana stand and a small cellar for ripening the fruit. Until he was 68, he worked twelve hours a day, six days a week, with one week vacation. Although he worked hard and supported our family well, my father did not feel proud of his work, did not affirm his strength. Instead, he was ashamed to have me visit his fruit stand; he saw his work as dirty, himself as an "ignorant greenhorn." The legacy of class.

And I accepted and echoed back his shame. In elementary school, when we had to go around and say what work our parents did, I repeated my father's euphemistic words: "My father sells wholesale and retail fruits and vegetables." It's interesting that later, when I was involved in political actions, my shame turned to pride of that same class background. The poorer one was born, the better, the more credit.

Both reactions—shame and pride—are based on a false assumption that one has control and responsibility for what one is born into. (Society—those in power, institutions—is responsible for people being born into conditions of economic limitation and suffering, for racism and classism. But as individuals we do not choose our birth.) That blame/credit often prevents us from seeing clearly the actual effects of growing up in a certain class: what it allows, what it inhibits, blocks, destroys. Also, if we take credit for what is out of our control, we sometimes do not take sufficient credit and responsibility for what is in our control: our consciousness, our actions, how we shape our lives.

What becomes difficult immediately in trying to understand class background is how it becomes hopelessly entangled with other issues: the fact that my father was an immigrant who spoke with a strong accent, never felt competent to write in English, always felt a great sense of self-shame that he projected onto his children; that my father had witnessed pogroms and daily anti-Semitism in his tiny *shtetl* in Russia, that we were Jewish, that the Holocaust occurred; that neither of my parents went to school beyond junior high school; that I was the younger daughter, the "good" child who accepted almost everything without complaining or acknowledging pain; that my sister and I experienced our worlds very differently and responded in almost opposite ways. It's difficult to sort out class, to see clearly. . . .

Feelings of poverty or wealth are based on one's experiences and where one falls on the economic spectrum. The economic class and the conditions we grow up under are very real, objective, but how we label and see those circumstances is relative, shaped by what we see outside ourselves. Growing up in the Pelham Parkway–Lydig Avenue area of the Bronx, I heard my circumstances echoed everywhere: Everyone's parents spoke Yiddish and had accents; they all spoke loudly and with their hands; few were educated beyond junior high school; no one dressed stylishly or went to restaurants (except for special occasions) or had fancy cars or dishwashers or clothes washers. (Our apartment building had, and still has, only one washing machine for 48 apartments. The lineup of baskets began early in the morning. My mother and I hung the clothes on the roof.) We ate good kosher food and fresh fruits and vegetables (from my uncle's stand). My mother sewed our clothes or we would shop in Alexander's and look for bargains (clothes with the manufacturers' tags removed). Clothes were passed between sisters, cousins, neighbors. I never felt poor or deprived. I had no other perspective, no other reality from which to judge our life.

When I went to the World's Fair and watched the G.E. exhibit of "Our Changing World," I remember being surprised that what I believed was a modern-day kitchen—an exact duplicate of our kitchen at home—was the kitchen of the '40s. When I received a fellowship for graduate school, I was surprised to discover I was eligible for the maximum grant because my parents' income fell in the lowest income category. I was surprised when I met friends whose parents talked about books and psychology and art, when I met people who noticed labels and brand names and talked about clothes and cars (but never mentioned costs and money).

What I also didn't see or appreciate was all the work and struggle of my parents to maintain and nourish us, work done silently and without any credit for many years. A few years ago I wrote a poem called "The Miracle" about my mother and her skilled unacknowledged work.

Clearly our assumptions, expectations, and hopes are unconsciously shaped by our class backgrounds. At a very young age I learned to want only what my parents could afford. It was a good survival mechanism that allowed me never to feel deprived or denied. At a later age, when I would read in natural history books about the "immortal species," the lesson was reaffirmed: The key to survival was always to become smaller, to minimize needs. Those species that had become dependent on more luxuriant conditions perished during hard times. Those used to less survived.

There is something powerful about surviving by adapting to little. The power comes from an independence of need, an instinct that allows us to get by. But it is a defense, and, like any defense, its main fault was that it never allowed me to feel the edge of my own desires, pains, deprivations. I defined my needs by what was available. Even now I tend to minimize my needs, to never feel deprived—a legacy of my class background.

Class background reveals itself in little ways. Around food, for example. My family would sip their soup loudly, putting mouth close to bowl. We would put containers directly on the table and never use a butter dish. We would suck bone marrow with gusto, pick up chicken bones with our hands, crunch them with our teeth, and leave little slivers on our otherwise empty plates. We would talk loudly and argue politics over supper. Only later did I become conscious of the judgment of others about certain behavior, ways of eating, talking, walking, dressing, being. Polite etiquette struck me as a bit absurd, as if hunger were uncivilized: the delicate portions, the morsels left on the plate, the proper use of knife and fork, the spoon seeming to go in the opposite direction of the mouth. The more remote one was from basic needs, the higher one's class status. I usually was unconscious of the "proper be-havior": I did not notice. But if I ever felt the eye of judgment, my first tendency would be to exaggerate my "grossness" in order to show the absurdity of others' snobbish judgments. I would deny that that judgment had any effect other than anger. But I now realize that all judgment has effect. Some of my negative self-image as *klutz*, *nebbish*, ugly, unsophis-ticated is a direct result of the reflection I saw in the judging, sophisticated eye of the upper class.

Lack of education and lack of money made for an insecurity and fear of doing almost anything, a fear tremendously compounded by anti-Semitism and World War II. My parents were afraid to take any risks—from both a conviction of their own in-competence and a fear that doing anything big, hav-ing any visibility, would place them in danger. From them I inherited a fear that if I touched something, did anything, I would make matters worse. There was an incredible nervousness in my home around fixing anything, buying anything big, filling out any forms. My mother still calls me to complete forms for her. When my father was sick, my parents needed me to translate everything the doctor said, not because they did not understand him, but be-cause their fear stopped them from listening when anyone very educated or in authority spoke.

I did not inherit the fear of those in authority. In fact, my observation of people's condescension, use of authority, and misuse of power helped shape my politics at a young age. I identified with the under-dog, was angry at the bully, fought against the mis-use of power. But I did inherit their fear of taking risks, of doing anything big, of trying anything new. I have trouble with paper forms; I've never been able to write a grant proposal; I have no credit cards. I sometimes seek invisibility as a form of safety.

For poorer people, for people who experience prejudice, there is a strong feeling that one has no power, no ability to affect or control one's environ-ment. For nine years my family and I lived in a very small three-room apartment; my sister and I had no bedroom of our own. When we moved from the fifth floor to the sixth, we got a tiny room just big enough for two beds and a cabinet. I never thought to put up a picture, to choose a room color or a bedspread.

I had no notion of control over private space, of shaping my environment.

That feeling of lack of control over one's environ-ment, of no right to one's own space, was psycho-logically intensified by my parents' experiences of anti-Semitism and by the Holocaust. These fostered a deep sense of powerlessness and vulnerability and, on an even more basic level, a doubt whether we re-ally had a right to exist on this earth.

In college I took a modern dance class. A group of us began "dancing" by caving in on ourselves, slinking around the side walls of the gym. I remem-ber the teacher saying that to dance one needed to be able to open one's arms and declare the beauty of one's being, to take up one's space on the dance floor: to say "I am here." For many women who ex-perience poverty and prejudice this kind of self-assertion feels foreign, impossible, dangerous. One of the unconscious effects of being born wealthy is a natural sense of one's right to be here on this earth, an essential grace that comes from the feeling of be-longing. (The danger, of course, is that wealthier people often take up too much space. They do not see the others crushed under their wide flinging steps.) Where the poorer person's danger is the self-consciousness that shrinks us into invisibility, the wealthier one's is the unconscious arrogance that inflates.

But what happens when one feels self-conscious and small and is seen as large, wealthy, powerful, controlling? At a young age, I knew the anti-Semitic portrait of the wealthy, exploitative Jew. I also knew that I did not feel powerful or controlling. My par-ents and I felt powerless, fearful, vulnerable. We owned nothing. All my parents saved, after working fifty years, would not equal the cost of one year of college today. What does it mean to have others' definition of one's reality so vastly different from one's experience of it? The effects are confusion, anger, entrapment. I lost touch with what was real, what my own experiences really were.

As a political person I felt particularly vulnerable to the hated image of "the Jew." I knew it was a stereotype and not my experience or the experience of the Jews I grew up with—but it still made me feel guilt, not pride, for any success I did have, for any rise in status. If the stereotype said "Jews have everything," the only way I could avoid that stereotype would be to have nothing. If you are poor, you are not a Jew. If you are successful, you are a bad Jew. The trap.

The economic and professional success of many second-generation Jews became tinged for me, as if we had done something wrong. To feel bad about achievement, to hold back one's power, is very destructive. My aunts and uncles, my parents, my friends' parents all had little education and little money. Yet we—my cousins, my sister, my friends—not only went to college, but even to graduate school and law school. I was speaking the other day with my aunt, who was saying what a miracle it was that her four children were all professionals and she was poor and uneducated. But the miracle was not really a miracle at all. It was the result of parents who saw education as very, very important—as a way out of the entrapment of class and prejudice. It was the result of parents who worked desperately hard so that their children could have that way out. It was a City College system in New York City that provided completely free education while we worked and lived at home.

In one generation we created an incredible economic, class, professional, and educational distance between ourselves and our parents. The danger of this success is that we forget the material soil that nourished us, the hard work that propped us up;

that we lose our consciousness of the harm and evil of condescension, exploitation, oppression, the pain of being made to feel inferior and invisible. Anzia Yezierska, a Jewish immigrant writer, says "Education without a heart is a curse." But to keep that consciousness and that heart and to be able to step onto the dance floor of life and say "I am here," reflecting back to our parents the beauty and strength we inherited from them, that would be a very real "miracle" indeed.                              [1987]

## 🌿 91

# *Grace Paley Reading*

TOI DERRICOTTE

Finally, the audience gets
restless, & they send me
to hunt for Grace. I find her
backing out of the bathroom, bending
over, wiping up her footprints
as she goes with a little
sheet of toilet paper, explaining,
"In some places, after the lady mops, the bosses
    come to check on her.
I just don't want them to think
she didn't do her job."                              [1997]

# "Are You Some Kind of Dyke?"
# The Perils of Heterosexism

Attitudes toward lesbians vary across culture and have changed over time. In the United States, loving sensual relationships between women were not seen as deviant in the seventeenth through nineteenth centuries; it was women who passed as men who were punished. In the late nineteenth century medical experts began to define lesbianism as an illness, and close connections among women became suspect. After World War II the taboos against lesbianism became extremely powerful, resulting in the erasure of lesbian experience from history, discrimination against lesbians in social, political, and economic institutions, and the proliferation of prejudices, misconceptions, and myths about lesbian life.

The essays and short story in this section examine the consequences of heterosexism for all women, exploring the ways that heterosexuality is enforced through prejudice, fear, and the denial of resources to lesbian couples. Suzanne Pharr demonstates that homophobia, the fear of homosexuality, and heterosexism, the assumption that heterosexuality is a superior way of life, are used to prevent all women from challenging sexism. In "Cat," love between two young girls feels natural to them until the prejudice of adults destroys it. Carla Trujillo describes the ways that Chicana lesbians are threatening to the established power relations in the Chicano community and urges Chicanas to recognize the commonalities among lesbian and heterosexual women.

Because of the hostility and bigotry lesbians face, coming out is a difficult process for both lesbians and their children. In some situations, being open about being a lesbian would entail serious risks. For both Jewelle Gomez and Megan McGuire, however, relationships with friends and family were strengthened when they were open about their lives.

---

# 92

## *Homophobia and Sexism*

SUZANNE PHARR

Homophobia works effectively as a weapon of sexism because it is joined with a powerful arm, heterosexism. Heterosexism creates the climate for homophobia with its assumption that the world is and must be heterosexual and its display of power and privilege as the norm. Heterosexism is the systemic display of homophobia in the institutions of society. Heterosexism and homophobia work together to enforce compulsory heterosexuality and that bastion of patriarchal power, the nuclear family. The central focus of the rightwing attack against women's liberation is that women's equality, women's self-determination, women's control of our own bodies and lives will damage what they see as the crucial societal institution, the nuclear family. The attack has been led by fundamentalist ministers across the country. The two areas they have focused on most consistently are abortion and homosexuality, and their passion has led them to bomb women's clinics and to recommend deprogramming for homosexuals and establishing camps to quarantine people with AIDS. To resist marriage and/or heterosexuality is to risk severe punishment and loss.

It is not by chance that when children approach puberty and increased sexual awareness they begin to taunt each other by calling these names: "queer," "faggot," "pervert." It is at puberty that the full force of society's pressure to conform to heterosexuality and prepare for marriage is brought to bear. Children know what we have taught them, and we have given clear messages that those who deviate from standard expectations are to be made to get back in line. The best controlling tactic at puberty is to be treated as an outsider, to be ostracized at a time when it feels most vital to be accepted. Those who are different must be made to suffer loss. It is also at puberty that misogyny begins to be more apparent, and girls are pressured to conform to societal norms that do not permit them to realize their full potential. It is at this time that their academic achievements begin to decrease as they are coerced into compulsory heterosexuality and trained for dependency upon a man, that is, for economic survival.

There was a time when the two most condemning accusations against a woman meant to ostracize and disempower her were "whore" and "lesbian." The sexual revolution and changing attitudes about heterosexual behavior may have led to some lessening of the power of the word *whore,* though it still has strength as a threat to sexual property and prostitutes are stigmatized and abused. However, the word *lesbian* is still fully charged and carries with it the full threat of loss of power and privilege, the threat of being cut asunder, abandoned, and left outside society's protection.

To be a lesbian is to be *perceived* as someone who has stepped out of line, who has moved out of sexual/economic dependence on a male, who is woman-identified. A lesbian is perceived as someone who can live without a man, and who is therefore (however illogically) against men. A lesbian is perceived

as being outside the acceptable, routinized order of things. She is seen as someone who has no societal institutions to protect her and who is not privileged to the protection of individual males. Many heterosexual women see her as someone who stands in contradiction to the sacrifices they have made to conform to compulsory heterosexuality. A lesbian is perceived as a threat to the nuclear family, to male dominance and control, to the very heart of sexism.

Gay men are perceived also as a threat to male dominance and control, and the homophobia expressed against them has the same roots in sexism as does homophobia against lesbians. Visible gay men are the objects of extreme hatred and fear by heterosexual men because their breaking ranks with male heterosexual solidarity is seen as a damaging rent in the very fabric of sexism. They are seen as betrayers, as traitors who must be punished and eliminated. In the beating and killing of gay men we see clear evidence of this hatred. When we see the fierce homophobia expressed toward gay men, we can begin to understand the ways sexism also affects males through imposing rigid, dehumanizing gender roles on them. The two circumstances in which it is legitimate for men to openly physically affectionate with one another are in competitive sports and in the crisis of war. For many men, these two experiences are the highlights of their lives, and they think of them again and again with nostalgia. War and sports offer a cover of all-male safety and dominance to keep away the notion of affectionate openness being identified with homosexuality. When gay men break ranks with male roles through bonding and affection outside the arenas of war and sports, they are perceived as not being "real men," that is, as being identified with women, the weaker sex that must be dominated and that over the centuries has been the object of male hatred and abuse. Misogyny gets transferred to gay men with a vengeance and is increased by the fear that their sexual identity and behavior will bring down the entire system of male dominance and compulsory heterosexuality.

If lesbians are established as threats to the status quo, as outcasts who must be punished, homophobia can wield its power over all women through lesbian baiting. Lesbian baiting is an attempt to control women by labeling us as lesbians because our behavior is not acceptable, that is, when we are being independent, going our own way, living whole lives, fighting for our rights, demanding equal pay, saying no to violence, being self-assertive, bonding with and loving the company of women, assuming the right to our bodies, insisting upon our own authority, making changes that include us in society's decision-making; lesbian baiting occurs when women are called lesbians because we resist male dominance and control. And it has little or nothing to do with one's sexual identity.

To be named as lesbian threatens all women, not just lesbians, with great loss. And any woman who steps out of role risks being called a lesbian. To understand how this is a threat to all women, one must understand that any woman can be called a lesbian and there is no real way she can defend herself: there is no way to credential one's sexuality. ("The Children's Hour," a Lillian Hellman play, makes this point when a student asserts two teachers are lesbians and they have no way to disprove it.) She may be married or divorced, have children, dress in the most feminine manner, have sex with men, be celibate—but there are lesbians who do all those things. *Lesbians look like all women and all women look like lesbians.* There is no guaranteed method of identification, and as we all know, sexual identity can be kept hidden. (The same is true for men. There is no way to prove their sexual identity, though many go to extremes to prove heterosexuality.) Also, women are not necessarily born lesbian. Some seem to be, but others become lesbians later in life after having lived heterosexual lives. Lesbian baiting of heterosexual women would not work if there were a definitive way to identify lesbians (or heterosexuals).

We have yet to understand clearly how sexual identity develops. And this is disturbing to some people, especially those who are determined to discover how lesbian and gay identity is formed so that they will know where to start in eliminating it. (Isn't it odd that there is so little concern about discovering the causes of heterosexuality?) There are many theories: genetic makeup, hormones, socialization, environment, etc. But there is no conclusive evidence that indicates that heterosexuality comes from one process and homosexuality from another. We do know, however, that sexual identity can be

in flux, and we know that sexual identity means more than just the gender of people one is attracted to and has sex with. To be a lesbian has as many ramifications as for a woman to be heterosexual. It is more than sex, more than just the bedroom issue many would like to make it: it is a woman-centered life with all the social interconnections that entails. Some lesbians are in long-term relationships, some in short-term ones, some date, some are celibate, some are married to men, some remain as separate as possible from men, some have children by men, some by alternative insemination, some seem "feminine" by societal standards, some "masculine," some are doctors, lawyers and ministers, some laborers, housewives and writers: what all share in common is a sexual/affectional identity that focuses on women in its attractions and social relationships.

If lesbians are simply women with a particular sexual identity who look and act like all women, then the major difference in living out a lesbian sexual identity as opposed to a heterosexual identity is that as lesbians we live in a homophobic world that threatens and imposes damaging loss on us for being *who we are*, for choosing to live whole lives. Homophobic people often assert that homosexuals have the choice of not being homosexual; that is, we don't have to act out our sexual identity. In that case, I want to hear heterosexuals talk about their willingness not to act out their sexual identity, including not just sexual activity but heterosexual social interconnections and heterosexual privilege. It is a question of wholeness. It is very difficult for one to be denied the life of a sexual being, whether expressed in sex or in physical affection, and to feel complete, whole. For our loving relationships with humans feed the life of the spirit and enable us to overcome our basic isolation and to be interconnected with humankind.

If, then, any woman can be named a lesbian and be threatened with terrible losses, what is it she fears? Are these fears real? Being vulnerable to a homophobic world can lead to these losses:

• *Employment.* The loss of job leads us right back to the economic connection to sexism. This fear of job loss exists for almost every lesbian except perhaps those who are self-employed or in a business that does not require societal approval.

Consider how many businesses or organizations you know that will hire and protect people who are openly gay or lesbian.

• *Family.* Their approval, acceptance, love.

• *Children.* Many lesbians and gay men have children, but very, very few gain custody in court challenges, even if the other parent is a known abuser. Other children may be kept away from us as though gays and lesbians are abusers. There are written and unwritten laws prohibiting lesbians and gays from being foster parents or from adopting children. There is an irrational fear that children in contact with lesbians and gays will become homosexual through influence or that they will be sexually abused. Despite our knowing that 95 percent of those who sexually abuse children are heterosexual men, there are no policies keeping heterosexual men from teaching or working with children, yet in almost every school system in America, visible gay men and lesbians are not hired through either written or unwritten laws.

• *Heterosexual privilege and protection.* No institutions, other than those created by lesbians and gays—such as the Metropolitan Community Church, some counseling centers, political organizations such as the National Gay and Lesbian Task Force, the National Coalition of Black Lesbians and Gays, the Lambda Legal Defense and Education Fund, etc.,—affirm homosexuality and offer protection. Affirmation and protection cannot be gained from the criminal justice system, mainstream churches, educational institutions, the government.

• *Safety.* There is nowhere to turn for safety from physical and verbal attacks because the norm presently in this country is that it is acceptable to be overtly homophobic. Gay men are beaten on the streets; lesbians are kidnapped and "deprogrammed." The National Gay and Lesbian Task Force, in an extended study, has documented violence against lesbians and gay men and noted the inadequate response of the criminal justice system. One of the major differences between homophobia/ heterosexism and racism and sexism is that because of the Civil Rights Movement and the women's movement racism and sexism are expressed more covertly (though with great harm); because there has not been a major, visible lesbian and gay movement, it is permissible to be overtly homophobic in any institution or public forum. Churches spew forth homophobia in the same way they did racism prior to the Civil Rights Movement. Few laws are in place to protect lesbians and gay men, and the criminal justice system is wracked with homophobia.

• *Mental health.* An overtly homophobic world in which there is full permission to treat lesbians and gay men with cruelty makes it difficult for lesbians and gay men to maintain a strong sense of well-being and self-esteem. Many lesbians and gay men are beaten, raped, killed, subjected to aversion therapy, or put in mental institutions. The impact of such hatred and negativity can lead one to depression and, in some cases, to suicide. The toll on the gay and lesbian community is devastating.

• *Community.* There is rejection by those who live in homophobic fear, those who are afraid of association with lesbians and gay men. For many in the gay and lesbian community, there is a loss of public acceptance, a loss of allies, a loss of place and belonging.

• *Credibility.* This fear is large for many people: the fear that they will no longer be respected, listened to, honored, believed. They fear they will be social outcasts.

The list goes on and on. But any one of these essential components of a full life is large enough to make one deeply fear its loss. A black woman once said to me in a workshop, "When I fought for Civil Rights, I always had my family and community to fall back on even when they didn't fully understand or accept what I was doing. I don't know if I could have borne losing them. And you people don't have either with you. It takes my breath away."

What does a woman have to do to get called a lesbian? Almost anything, sometimes nothing at all, but certainly anything that threatens the status quo, anything that steps out of role, anything that asserts the rights of women, anything that doesn't indicate submission and subordination. Assertiveness, standing up for oneself, asking for more pay, better working conditions, training for and accepting a nontraditional (you mean a man's?) job, enjoying the company of women, being financially independent, being in control of one's life, depending first and foremost upon oneself, thinking that one can do whatever needs to be done, but above all, working for the rights and equality of women.

In the backlash to the gains of the women's liberation movement, there has been an increased effort to keep definitions man-centered. Therefore, to work on behalf of women must mean to work against men. To love women must mean that one hates men. A very effective attack has been made against the word *feminist* to make it a derogatory word. In current backlash usage, *feminist* equals *man-hater* which equals *lesbian*. This formula is created in the hope that women will be frightened away from their work on behalf of women. Consequently, we now have women who believe in the rights of women and work for those rights while from fear deny that they are feminists, or refuse to use the word because it is so "abrasive."

So what does one do in an effort to keep from being called a lesbian? She steps back into line, into the role that is demanded of her, tries to behave in such a way that doesn't threaten the status of men, and if she works for women's rights, she begins modifying that work. When women's organizations begin doing significant social change work, they inevitably are lesbian-baited; that is, funders or institutions or community members tell us that they can't work with us because of our "man-hating attitudes" or the presence of lesbians. We are called too strident, told we are making enemies, not doing good.

The battered women's movement has seen this kind of attack: the pressure has been to provide services only, without analysis of the causes of violence against women and strategies for ending it. To provide only services without political analysis or direct action is to be in an approved "helping" role; to analyze the causes of violence against women is to begin the work toward changing an entire system of power and control. It is when we do the latter that we are threatened with the label of man-hater or lesbian. For my politics, if a women's social change organization has not been labeled lesbian or communist, it is probably not doing significant work; it is only "making nice."

Women in many of these organizations, out of fear of all the losses we are threatened with, begin to modify our work to make it more acceptable and less threatening to the male-dominated society which we originally set out to change. The work can no longer be radical (going to the root cause of the problem) but instead must be reforming, working only on the symptoms and not the cause. Real change for women becomes thwarted and stopped. The word *lesbian* is instilled with the power to halt our work and control our lives. And we give it its power with our fear.                              [1988]

 93

# Cat

JULIE CARTER

It is three days after my twelfth birthday and my mother is sitting beside me on the edge of my bed. She is holding a box of sanitary napkins and a little booklet that reads "What Every Young Girl Should Know" and telling me for the third straight year that I am to read the book and keep the pads hidden from the sight of Daddy and Leroy. I am hardly listening. I am sneaking furtive glances out the window and patiently waiting for her to finish so I can meet the boys out on the lot for our softball game.

My mother is saying, "Look, you've thrown your pretty dress on the floor." She is bending down to pick it up. It is a white flared dress with large yellow flowers. Daddy bought it for my birthday. I am remembering the party, the coconut cake with the twelve ballerinas holding twelve pink candles. Momma had straightened my hair but refused to wave it tight to my head so it would look like a process, the way I usually wear it. Instead she has fluffed up the curls like she does my sister Dee Dee's hair. Momma is serving punch in a white apron or just standing around with her hands in the pockets. When she catches my eye she motions with her head for me to go over and talk with the other girls who are standing in a cluster around the record player. I smile nervously back at her, but remain where I am. My friends are all acting strange. Leroy, my brother and very best friend, has been stuck up under Diedra Young all evening and Raymond and Zip-Zip are out on the back steps giggling with Peggy and Sharon. Jeffrey teases me about my knobby black knees under my new dress until I threaten to punch him in the mouth. I wander out to the kitchen to play with Fluffy, our cat, until Momma misses me and comes to drag me back to the party.

Now, sitting on my bed with Momma, she is saying she will have to get me a training bra. I self-consciously reach up and touch my breasts then jerk my hands down again. I hate them. I'm always hurting them when I bump into things and now when I fight I not only have to protect my face and head I have to worry about getting hit in the breast too.

"Momma, can I go now? I gotta pitch today," I say. Momma puts her arm around my shoulder and pulls me closer to her. "Sugar, you've got to stop playing with those boys all the time; why don't you go play with Sheila, that nice young girl who's staying with the Jenkins?"

"But I don't know her."

"Well, you can get to know her. She's a nice girl and she doesn't know anybody. You can introduce her to the rest of the girls."

"But Dee Dee know them better than I do."

"Yeah, sugar, but Sheila doesn't have any girlfriends and you don't either, so you could be friends with each other."

I pull away from her. "I got friends," I say. I'm getting annoyed with the conversation, I want to go out and play. I get up and walk over to the window and stand there with my back to her.

"O.K.," Momma says finally, "but I've invited the Jenkins over for lunch Sunday and if you want to be friends with Sheila fine, if not . . ." She shrugs her shoulders.

"You gonna make Dee Dee be there too?"

"Yup."

"Can we invite Zip-Zip and Jeffrey?"

She hesitates a moment. ". . . Maybe next time."

"O.K., can I go now?" I am inching towards the door.

"All right, scoot." She pats me on the butt as I pass her. I am running down the steps, jumping over the last two. Dee Dee, who has been listening at the door, says, "Can I go with you, Cat?"

"No."

"Why not?"

"'Cause you can't."

I reach the vacant lot where we play ball. There is no game today. The boys are busy gathering ammunition—dirt clods, rocks, bottles—for the fight with the white boys from across the tracks.

Dee Dee whines to Leroy: "Leroy, I wanna go."

"You can't," Leroy says.

"How come?"

"'Cause you're too young."

"I'm just as old as Jeffrey!"

"You can't go," Leroy says, ". . . besides you're a girl."

"Cat's a girl," she says indignantly.

We all ignore her. We are gathering sticks and rocks and throwing them into an empty milk crate.

"How come I can't go? Huh? How come?" Nobody answers her. We are all walking across the lot. Raymond and Leroy are carrying the ammunition; Dee Dee is standing where we left her, yelling, "I'm gonna tell Momma what you're up to! I'm gonna tell you going cross the tracks to fight with those white boys." Then, after a moment or two: ". . . And Cat's got Kotex in her dresser drawer!" My neck burns but I keep walking.


I am sixteen years old and sitting in Sheila's dining room. We are playing checkers and I am losing and not minding at all. Her cousin Bob comes in. He is stationed in Georgia and on leave from the army. He says hi to Sheila, ignores me completely and walks through to the back with his green duffel bag in his left hand. His voice drifts in from the kitchen, "Where'd the little bulldagger come from?" Sheila springs back from the table so fast her chair overturns. She yells in the kitchen doorway, "You shut your nasty mouth, Bob Jenkins!" The next day we are supposed to make cookies for her aunt's birthday but she calls to suggest we do it over my house instead. I do not go back over Sheila's again unless Dee Dee is with me, or there is no one home.


We are in Fairmount Park within some semi-enclosed shrubbery. Sheila and I are lying on our backs on an old army blanket. We look like Siamese twins joined together at the head. The sky is blue above us and I am chewing on the straw that came with my coke.

"Cat, tell me again how you used to almost be late for school all the time 'cause you used to be waiting for me to come out of my house so we could walk to school together," Sheila says.

"I've told you three thousand times already."

"Well, tell me again, I like to hear it."

"If you hadn't been peeping from behind the curtains yourself and waiting for *me* to come out we'd both have gotten to school on time."

She laughs softly then turns over on her stomach.

"I want a kiss," she says.

I lean up on my elbow, check around to make sure nobody's peeping through the bushes then turn and press my lips to hers. After a few seconds she pulls away. "Man, Cat, I never felt this way about anybody before."

"Me neither." I reach over and touch her hand. We kiss again, briefly, our lips just touching. Then we turn and lie as we were before but continue holding hands.

"Cat?"

"Yeah?"

"I think I'm in love."

"Me too."

She squeezes my hand. I squeeze hers back.

"What would you do if Bob came by and saw us now?" Sheila asks.

"What would you do?"

"I don't know. I'd just say hi, I guess."

"Then I would too," I say.

The sun has moved and is now shining directly over us. I cover my eyes with my arm.

"Bob would say we're both bulldaggers," Sheila says after a while.

"Yeah, I guess he would," I say.

"We aren't bulldaggers, are we, Cat?"

"No, bulldaggers want to be men and we don't want to be men, right?"

"Right, we just love each other and there's nothing wrong with loving someone."

"Yeah and nobody can choose who you fall in love with."

"Right."

Sheila and I are in her bedroom; her uncle is standing over the bed shouting, "What the hell's going on here?" He is home from work early. Sheila and I scramble for the sheet and clutch it across our bodies. I am waiting for her uncle to leave so I can get up and dressed, but he just stands there staring, thunder in his face. Finally I release my end of the sheet and scramble to the foot of the bed. Sheila's stockings are entwined in my blouse. I cram panties into my pocket and pull blue jeans over naked, ashen legs. I am trembling. Her uncle's eyes follow me around the room like harsh spotlights.

Later at my house, Momma, Daddy and I are in the dining room. Leroy and Dee Dee are in their rooms, the doors are shut tight; they've been ordered not to open them. My mother sits on the couch wringing her hands. I sit stiffly forward on the edge of a straight backed chair. My head down. My teeth clenched. My father stomps back and forth across the floor, his hands first behind him, holding each other at the butt, then gesturing out in front of him. He is asking, "What's this I hear about you being in bed with the Jenkins girl?" I sit still on the edge of my chair, looking straight ahead.

"I'm talking to you, Catherine!" His voice is booming to the rafters, I'm sure the neighbors hear. It is dark outside and a slight breeze puffs out the window curtains. I am holding a spool of thread that had been on the table. I am squeezing it in my hands, the round edges intrude into my palms. I continue to squeeze.

"You hear me talking to you, girl?" He is standing directly over me now, his voice reverberates in my ear. I squeeze the spool of thread and stare at a spider-shaped crack in the wall above the light switch. There is an itch on my left leg, below my knee. I do not scratch. Dogs bark in the backyards and one of the Williams kids is getting a spanking. I hear the strap fall, a child wailing, and an angry female voice.

My father is saying, "Look, you'd better say something, you brazen heifer!" He jerks my head around to face him. I yank it back to stare at the crack in the wall.

"You're lucky Tom Jenkins didn't have you arrested—forcing yourself on that girl like that. . . ."

"What? What? What force? Sheila didn't say I forced her to do anything!"

"If you didn't force her, then what happened?"

"Sheila didn't say that! She didn't say it! Mr. Jenkins must have said it!" I am on my feet and trembling, and screaming at the top of my lungs.

"Then what did happen?" my father screams back at me. I sit back down in the chair and again stare at the crack in the wall over the light switch. Trying to concentrate on it, blot out my father's voice. I cannot. I get up and run to the chair where my mother sits. I am pulling on her arm. "Momma, Sheila didn't say that, did she? She didn't say I forced her?"

Momma sits there biting on her bottom lip and wringing her hands. She does not look at me. She lays her hand on my head and does not speak. My father grabs my arm and yanks me away. I am enveloped in his sour breath as he shouts, "Look, I'm a man of God and don't you dare doubt my word!" I yank my arm from his grip and run towards the steps, toward the safety of my bedroom.

"I haven't dismissed you!" I hear my father's footsteps behind me. He grabs me by my tee shirt and swings me around. I lose my footing and fall at the bottom of the steps.

"Arthur, Arthur!" My mother is running behind us. My father's knee is in my chest; he is yelling in a hoarse angry voice, "Catherine Johnson, I have one more thing to say to you, then we needn't discuss it anymore, but you listen carefully because I mean every word I say: There will be no bulldaggers in my house, do you understand me? THERE WILL BE NO BULLDAGGERS IN MY HOUSE!"

I am sitting beside Sheila on a bench in Fairmount Park; we are within walking distance of the spot where we used to meet with our lunch on Daddy's old army blanket. The grass is completely green except for one long crooked brown streak where the boys trampled a short cut to the basketball court. The leaves are green too, save for one or two brown and yellow ones beneath the bench at our feet. Sheila's head is bent.

"I'm sorry," she is saying. She is picking minute pieces of lint from a black skirt. "I'm really sorry but

you don't know how my uncle is when he gets mad." I am silent. I am watching three boys play basketball on the court about twenty yards away. A tall white kid leaps up and dunks the ball.

"I just didn't know what else to do," Sheila continues. "I was scared and Uncle Jim kept saying, 'She made you do it, didn't she? She made you do it, didn't she?' And before I knew it, I'd said 'yes'." A short black kid knocks the ball out of bounds and a fat boy in a green shirt darts out to retrieve it.

"Cathy?" Her hand is on my forearm and I turn to look her full in the face. "I'm sorry, Cat, I just didn't know what else to do." I turn again towards the basketball court. The tall white boy is holding the ball under his arm and shaking the hand of a short kid. The fat boy in the green sweat shirt is pulling a navy blue poncho on over his head.

"Cathy, please?" Sheila is saying. I turn to look her full in the face. "It's all right, Sheila, it's all right." It is getting windy. The basketball court empties and Sheila asks if I'll meet her at our spot next Saturday. I lie and say yes. She checks to make sure no one's looking, pecks me on the cheek, then gets up to leave. I sit watching the empty basketball court for a long time, then I get up and take the long way home.                                         [1983]

 94

# Chicana Lesbians: Fear and Loathing in the Chicano Community

CARLA TRUJILLO

The vast majority of Chicano heterosexuals perceive Chicana lesbians as a threat to the community. Homophobia, that is, irrational fear of gay or lesbian people and/or behaviors, accounts, in part, for the heterosexist response to the lesbian community. However, I argue that Chicana lesbians are perceived as a greater threat to the Chicano community because their existence disrupts the established order of male dominance, and raises the consciousness of many Chicanas regarding their own independence and control. Some writers have addressed these topics,[1] however, an analysis of the complexities of lesbian existence alongside this perceived threat has not been undertaken. While this essay is by no means complete, it attempts to elucidate the underlying basis of these fears which, in the very act of the lesbian existence, disrupt the established norm of patriarchal oppression.

## SEXUALITY

As lesbians, our sexuality becomes the focal issue of dissent. The majority of Chicanas, both lesbian and heterosexual, are taught that our sexuality must conform to certain modes of behavior. Our culture voices shame upon us if we go beyond the criteria of passivity and repression, or doubts in our virtue if we refuse.[2] We, as women, are taught to suppress our sexual desires and needs by conceding all pleasure to the male. As Chicanas, we are commonly led to believe that even talking about our participation and satisfaction in sex is taboo. Moreover, we (as well as most women in the United States) learn to hate our bodies, and usually possess little knowledge of them. Lourdes Arguelles did a survey on the sexuality of 373 immigrant Latinas and found that over half of the women possessed little knowledge of their reproductive systems or their own physiology. Most remarked they "just didn't look down there."[3]

Not loving our bodies affects how we perceive ourselves as sexual beings. As lesbians, however, we have no choice but to confront our sexuality before we can confront our lesbianism. Thus the commonly held viewpoint among heterosexuals that we are "defined by our sexuality" is, in a way, partially true. If we did not bring our sexuality into consciousness, we would not be able to confront ourselves and come out.

After confronting and then acknowledging our attraction, we must, in turn, learn to reclaim that what we're told is bad, wrong, dirty, and taboo— namely our bodies, and our freedom to express ourselves in them. Too often we internalize the homophobia and sexism of the larger society, as well as that of our own culture, which attempts to keep us from loving ourselves. As Norma Alarcón states,

"[Chicana lesbians] must act to negate the negation."[4] A Chicana lesbian must learn to love herself, both as a woman and a sexual being, before she can love another. Loving another woman not only validates one's own sexuality, but also that of the other woman, by the very act of loving. Understanding this, a student in a workshop Cherríe Moraga and I conducted on lesbian sexuality stated, "Now I get it. Not only do you have to learn to love your own vagina, but someone else's too."[5] It is only then that the subsequent experiences of love and commitment, passion and remorse can also become our dilemmas, much like those of everyone else. The effort to consciously reclaim our sexual selves forces Chicanas to either confront their own sexuality or, in refusing, castigate lesbians as *vendidas*\* to the race, blasphemers to the church, atrocities against nature, or some combination.

## IDENTIFICATION

For many Chicanas, our identification as women, that is, as complete women, comes from the belief that we need to be connected to a man.[6] Ridding ourselves of this parasitic identification is not always easy, for we grow up, as my Chicana students have pointed out, defined in a male context: daddy's girl, some guy's girlfriend, wife, or mother. Vying for a man's attention compromises our own personal and intellectual development. We exist in a patriarchal society that undervalues women.[7] We are socialized to undervalue ourselves, as well as anything associated with the concept of self. Our voice is considered less significant, our needs and desires secondary. As the Chicanas in the MALCS workshop indicated,[8] our toleration of unjust behavior from men, the church, the established order, is considered an attribute. How much pain can we bear in the here-and-now so that we may be better served in the afterlife? Martyrdom, the cloth of denial, transposes itself into a gown of cultural beauty.

Yet, an alliance with a man grants a woman heterosexual privileges, many of which are reified by the law, the church, our families and, of course, "la causa." Women who partake in the privileges of

---

\*traitors.

male sexual alliance may often do so at the cost of their own sense of self, since they must often subvert their needs, voice, intellect, and personal development in these alliances. These are the conditional contradictions commonly prescribed for women by the patriarchy in our culture and in the larger society. Historically, women have been viewed as property.[9] Though some laws have changed, ideologically little else has. Upon marriage, a father feels he can relinquish "ownership" and "responsibility" of his daughter to her husband. The Chicana feminist who confronts this subversion, and critiques the sexism of the Chicano community, will be called *vendida* if she finds the "male defined and often anti-feminist" values of the community difficult to accept.[10]

The behaviors necessary in the "act of pursuing a man" often generate competition among women, leading to betrayal of one another.[11] When a woman's sense of identity is tied to that of a man, she is dependent on this relationship for her own self-worth. Thus, she must compete with other women for his attention. When the attention is then acknowledged and returned, she must work to ensure that it is maintained. Ensuring the protection of this precious commodity generates suspicion among women, particularly single, unattached women. Since we're all taught to vie for a man's attention, we become, in a sense, sexual suspects to one another. The responsibility is placed entirely upon the woman with little thought given to the suspected infidelity of the man.

We should ask what role the man places himself in regarding his support of these behaviors. After all, the woman is commonly viewed as his possession. Hence, in the typical heterosexual relationship both parties are abetting the other, each in a quest that does not improve the status of the woman (nor, in my view, that of the man), nor the consciousness of either of them.

How does the Chicana lesbian fit into this picture? Realistically, she doesn't. As a lesbian she does many things simultaneously: she rejects "compulsory heterosexuality";[12] she refuses to partake in the "game" of competition for men; she confronts her own sexuality; and she challenges the norms placed upon her by culture and society, whose desire is to subvert her into proper roles and places. This is done, whether consciously or unconsciously, by the very aspect of her existence. In the course of conducting many workshops on lesbian sexuality, Chicana heterosexuals have often indicated to me that they do not associate with lesbians, since it could be assumed that either (1) they, too, must be lesbians, or (2) if they're not, they must be selling out to Anglo culture, since it is implied that Chicana lesbians do and thus any association with lesbians implicates them as well. This equivocation of sexual practice and cultural alliance is a retrograde ideology, quite possibly originating from the point of view that the only way to uplift the species is to propagate it. Thus, homosexuality is seen as "counter-revolutionary."

Heterosexual Chicanas need not be passive victims of the cultural onslaught of social control. If anything, Chicanas are usually the backbone of every *familia*, for it is their strength and self-sacrifice which often keeps the family going. While heterosexual Chicanas have a choice about how they want to live their lives (read: how they choose to form their identities[13]), Chicana lesbians have very little choice, because their quest for self-identification comes with the territory. This is why "coming out" can be a major source of pain for Chicana lesbians, since the basic fear of rejection by family and community is paramount.[14] For our own survival, Chicana lesbians must continually embark on the creation or modification of our own *familia*, since this institution, as traditionally constructed, may be non-supportive of the Chicana lesbian existence.[15]

## MOTHERHOOD

The point of view that we are not complete human beings unless we are attached to a male is further promoted by the attitude that we are incomplete as women unless we become mothers. Many Chicanas are socialized to believe that our chief purpose in life is raising children.[16] Not denying the fact that motherhood can be a beautiful experience, it becomes, rather, one of the few experiences not only supported [by] but expected in a traditional Chicano community. Historically, in dual-headed households, Chicanas (as well as other women) were relegated to the tasks of home care and child rearing, while the men took on the task of earning the family's income.[17] Economic need, rather than feminist consciousness, has been the primary reason for the change to two-income households. Nevertheless, for many Chicanas, motherhood is still seen by our culture as the final act in establishing our "womanhood."

Motherhood among Chicana lesbians does exist. Many lesbians are mothers as by-products of divorce, earlier liaisons with men, or through artificial insemination. Anecdotal evidence I have obtained from many Chicana lesbians in the community indicates that lesbians who choose to become mothers in our culture are seen as aberrations of the traditional concept of motherhood, which stresses male-female partnership. Choosing to become a mother via alternative methods of insemination, or even adopting children, radically departs from society's view that lesbians and gay men cannot "successfully" raise children. Therefore, this poses another threat to the Chicano community, since Chicana lesbians are perceived as failing to partake in one of their chief obligations in life.

## RELIGION

Religion, based on the tradition of patriarchal control and sexual, emotional, and psychological repression, has historically been a dual means of hope for a better afterlife and social control in the present one. Personified by the Virgen de Guadalupe, the concept of motherhood and martyrdom go hand in hand in the Catholic religion. Nevertheless, as we are all aware, religion powerfully affects our belief systems concerning life and living. Since the Pope does not advocate a homosexual lifestyle,[18] lesbians and gay men are not given sanction by the largely Catholic Chicano community—hence, fulfilling our final threat to the established order. Chicana lesbians who confront their homosexuality must, in turn, confront (for those raised in religious households) religion, bringing to resolution some compromise of religious doctrine and personal lifestyle. Many choose to alter, modify, or abandon religion, since it is difficult to advocate something which condemns our existence. This exacerbates a sense of alienation for Chicana lesbians who feel they cannot wholly participate in a traditional religion.

In sum, Chicana lesbians pose a threat to the Chicano community for a variety of reasons, primarily because they threaten the established social hierarchy of patriarchal control. In order to "come-out," Chicana lesbians must confront their sexuality, therefore bringing a taboo subject to consciousness. By necessity, they must learn to love their bodies, for it is also another woman's body which becomes the object of love. Their identities as people alter and become independent of men, hence there is no need to submit to, or perform the necessary behaviors that cater to wooing, the male ego. Lesbians (and other feminist women) would expect to treat and be treated by men as equals. Men who have traditionally interacted with women on the basis of their gender (read: femininity) first, and their brains second, are commonly left confused when the lesbian (or feminist) fails to respond to the established pecking order.

Motherhood, seen as exemplifying the final act of our existence as women, is practiced by lesbians, but usually without societal or cultural permission. Not only is it believed that lesbians cannot become mothers (hence, not fulfilling our established purpose as women), but if we do, we morally threaten the concept of motherhood as a sanctified entity, since lesbianism doesn't fit into its religious or cultural confines. Lastly, religion, which does not support the homosexual lifestyle, seeks to repudiate us as sinners if we are "practicing," and only tolerable if not. For her personal and psychological survival, the Chicana lesbian must confront and bring to resolution these established cultural and societal conflicts. These "confrontations" go against many of the values of the Chicano community, since they pose a threat to the established order of male control. Our very existence challenges this order, and in some cases challenges the oftentimes ideologically oppressive attitudes toward women.

It is widely assumed that lesbians and heterosexual women are in two completely different enclaves in regard to the type and manner of the oppression they must contend with. As illustrated earlier in this essay, this indeed, may be true. There do exist, however, different levels of patriarchal oppression which affect all of us as women, and when combined inhibit our collective liberation. If we, as lesbian and heterosexual Chicanas, can open our eyes and look at all that we share as women, we might find commonalities even among our differences. First and foremost among them is the status of *woman*. Uttered under any breath, it implies subservience; cast to a lower position not only in society, but in our own culture as well.

Secondly, the universal of the body. We are all female and subject to the same violations as any woman in society. We must contend with the daily threat of rape, molestation, and harassment—violations which affect all of us as women, lesbian or not.

As indicated earlier, our sexuality is suppressed by our culture—relegated to secrecy or embarrassment, implicating us as wrongful women if we profess to fulfill ourselves sexually. Most of us still grow up inculcated with the dichotomy of the "good girl-bad girl" syndrome. With virtue considered as the most admirable quality, it's easy to understand which we choose to partake. This generates a cloud of secrecy around any sexual activity, and leads, I am convinced, to our extremely high teenage pregnancy rate, simply because our families refuse to acknowledge the possibility that young women may be sexually active before marriage.

We are taught to undervalue our needs and voices. Our opinions, viewpoints, and expertise are considered secondary to those of males—even if we are more highly trained. Time and again, I have seen otherwise sensible men insult the character of a woman when they are unable to belittle her intellectual capacities.[19] Character assassinations are commonly disguised in the familiar "*vendida* to the race" format. Common it seems, because it functions as the ultimate insult to any conscientious *política*. Because many of us are taught that our opinions matter little, we have difficulty at times, raising them. We don't trust what we think, or believe in our merits. Unless we are encouraged to do so, we have difficulty thinking independently of male opinion. Chicanas must be constantly encouraged to speak up, to voice their opinions, particularly in areas where no encouragement has ever been provided.

As Chicanas (and Chicanos), most of us are subject to the effects of growing up in a culture besieged by poverty and all the consequences of it: lack of education, insufficient political power and health care, disease and drugs. We are all subject to the effects of a society that is racist, classist and homophobic, as well as sexist, and patriarchally dominant. Colonization has imposed itself and affected the disbursement of status and the collective rights of us as individuals. Chicanas are placed in this order at a lower position, ensconced within a tight boundary which limits our voices, our bodies, and our brains. In classic dissonant fashion, many of us become complicit in this (since our survival often depends on it) and end up rationalizing our very own limitations.

The collective liberation of people begins with the collective liberation of half its constituency—namely women. The view that our hierarchical society places Chicanos at a lower point, and they in turn must place Chicanas lower still, is outmoded and politically destructive. Women can no longer be relegated to supporting roles. Assuaging delicate male egos as a means of establishing our identities is retrograde and subversive to our own identities as women. Chicanas, both lesbian and heterosexual, have a dual purpose ahead of us. We must fight for our own voices as women, since this will ultimately serve to uplift us as a people.

*NOTES*

1. Cherríe Moraga, *Loving in the War Years: Lo que nunca pasó por sus labios* (Boston: South End Press, 1983), 103, 105, 111, 112, 117.
2. See Ana Castillo's essay on sexuality: "La Macha: Toward a Beautiful Whole Self" in *Chicana Lesbians: The Girls Our Mothers Warned Us About,* ed. Carla Trujillo (Berkeley: Third Woman Press, 1991). Also see *The Sexuality of Latinas, Third Woman* 4 (1989).
3. Lourdes Arguelles, "A Survey of Latina Immigrant Sexuality," presented at the National Association for Chicano Studies Conference, Albuquerque, New Mexico, March 29–April 1, 1990.
4. Norma Alarcón, personal communication, MALCS (Mujeres Activas en Letras y Cambio Social) Summer Research Institute, University of California, Los Angeles, August 3–6, 1990.
5. Chicana Leadership Conference, Workshop on Chicana lesbians, University of California, Berkeley, Feb. 8–10, 1990.
6. This was spoken of in great detail in a workshop on Chicana Empowerment and Oppression by Yvette Flores Ortiz at the MALCS, 1990.
7. There are multitudes of feminist books and periodicals which attest to the subordinate position of women in society. Listing them is beyond the scope of this essay.

8. Yvette Flores Ortiz, MALCS, 1990.

9. Peggy R. Sanday, "Female Status in the Public Domain," in *Women, Culture & Society*, eds. Michelle Rosaldo and Louise Lamphere (Stanford: Stanford University Press, 1974), 189–206.

10. *Loving in the War Years*, 113.

11. See Ana Castillo's "La Macha: Toward a Beautiful Whole Self." See also *Loving in the War Years*, 136.

12. Adrienne Rich, "Compulsory Heterosexuality and Lesbian Existence," in *Women: Sex and Sexuality*, eds. Catharine R. Stimpson and Ethel Spector Person (Chicago: University of Chicago Press, 1980), 62–91.

13. As Moraga states, "only the woman intent on the approval can be affected by the disapproval," *Loving in the War Years*, 103.

14. Rejection by family and community is also an issue for gay men; however, their situation is muddied by the concomitant loss of power.

15. Cherríe Moraga attests to the necessity of Chicanas needing to "make *familia* from scratch" in *Giving Up the Ghost* (Los Angeles: West End Press, 1986), 58.

16. *Loving in the War Years*, 113.

17. Karen Sacks, "Engels Revisited: Women, the Organization of Production and Private Property" in *Women, Culture & Society*, 207–222.

18. Joseph Cardinal Ratzinger, Prefect, and Alberto Bouone, Titular Archbishop of Caesarea in Numedia, Secretary, "Letter to the Bishops of the Catholic Church in the Pastoral Care of Homosexual Persons," October 1, 1986. Approved by Pope John Paul II, adopted in an ordinary session of the Congregation for the Doctrine of Faith and ordered published. Reprinted in *The Vatican and Homosexuality*, eds. Jeannine Gramick and Pat Furey (New York: Crossroad Publishing Co., 1988), 1–10.

19. This occurred often to the women MeChA (Movimiento Estudiantil Chicano de Aztlán) leaders who were on the Berkeley campus between 1985 and 1989. It also occurred to a Chicana panel member during a 1990 National Association for Chicano Studies presentation, when a Chicano discussant disagreed with the recommendations based on her research.                    [1991]

# 🌿 95

# *Livin' in a Gay Family*

MEGAN MCGUIRE

Homosexuality first entered my life when I was twelve years old. The words fag, queer, dyke, and homo were used all around me. I even used them. These words were used to disrespect someone. If you were a fag, you were an outcast or someone others didn't like. In the fall of my seventh-grade year, I began to fear those words and hate people who identified with those words.

And then my mother told me she was gay. She came out. She was a dyke, a fag, a queer. My mother was one of "those" people. I couldn't let any of my friends know. I was afraid they would not like me or that my classmates would beat me up. I wouldn't let anyone know that the other woman, Barb, who was living in my house, was my other mother. I hadn't known about my mom's sexuality until one day when I went into her bedroom and asked "Mom, are you gay?" She told me that she was gay. I became really upset and decided for myself that she was straight. I never gave myself time to think, what if my mom was in fact gay? Then it sunk in. My mom was gay. I cried and got really angry. I wanted to know why she was putting my brother and me into a situation where we had to be secretive about our family. For five years I lived with the secret. It caused me to lie, be angry, and be sad. No one I knew could know that I was living in a gay family.

The first four years my mom was "out" was a very lonely time for me. When I moved up to Boston from Washington, DC, in 1990, I was in a new city, a new school, and a new life. I made friends. I wanted to be liked, so all I could do was laugh at the jokes my friends made about gays. The people I called my "friends" were not people I wanted to be my friends. I hadn't figured out how to make real friends whom I could trust with the secret. I wasn't ready to tell anybody about my family because I wasn't ready to deal with it myself. I was very lonely and depressed, so I occupied myself playing soccer and sitting in front of the TV.

When I entered high school, I played three sports and joined several clubs. I didn't make time to find a group of people who would give me support. Because I was participating in all of these activities, people got to know me and my face became well recognized. I was an active student who pushed for change in student government and played in almost every female volleyball, basketball, and softball game. I felt the pressure to keep the secret a secret. I thought that all the popularity I had gained and the friends I had made would end if people knew my mom was gay.

Despite my social success, I spent most of the

Once I had the knowledge of a word and a sense of its importance to me, I didn't feel the need to explain, confess, or define my identity as a lesbian. The process of reclaiming my ethnic identity in this country was already all-consuming. Later, of course, in moments of glorious self-righteousness, I did make declarations. But they were not usually ones I had to make. Mostly they were a testing of the waters. A preparation for the rest of the world which, unlike my grandmother, might not have a grounding in what true love is about. My first lover, the woman who'd been in my bed once a week most of our high school years, finally married. I told her with my poems that I was a lesbian. She was not afraid to ask if what she'd read was about her, about my love for her. So there, amidst her growing children, errant husband, and bowling trophies I said yes, the poems were about her and my love for her, a love I'd always regret relinquishing to her reflexive obeisance to tradition. She did not flinch either. We still get drunk together when I go home to Boston.

During the 1970s I focused less on career than on how to eat and be creative at the same time. Graduate school and a string of non-traditional jobs (stage manager, mid-town messenger, etc.) left me so busy I had no time to think about my identity. It was a long time before I made the connection between my desire, my isolation, and the difficulty I had with my writing. I thought of myself as a lesbian between girlfriends—except the between had lasted five years. After some anxiety and frustration I deliberately set about meeting women. Actually, I knew many women, including my closest friend at the time, another black woman also in the theatre. She became uncharacteristically obtuse when I tried to open up and explain my frustration at going to the many parties we attended and being too afraid to approach women I was attracted to, certain I would be rejected either because the women were straight and horrified or gay and terrified of being exposed. For my friend theoretical homosexuality was acceptable, even trendy. Any uncomfortable experience was irrelevant to her. She was impatient and unsympathetic. I drifted away from her in pursuit of the women's community, a phrase that was not in my vocabulary yet, but I knew it was something more than just "women." I fell into that community by connecting with other women writers, and that helped me to focus on my writing and on my social life as a lesbian.

Still, none of my experiences demanded that I bare my soul. I remained honest but not explicit. Expediency, diplomacy, discretion, are all words that come to mind now. At that time I knew no political framework through which to filter my experience. I was more preoccupied with the Attica riots than with Stonewall. The media helped to focus our attentions within a proscribed spectrum and obscure the connections between the issues. I worried about who would shelter Angela Davis, but the concept of sexual politics was remote and theoretical.

I'm not certain exactly when and where the theory and reality converged.

Being a black woman and a lesbian unexpectedly blended like that famous scene in Ingmar Bergman's film *Persona*. The different faces came together as one, and my desire became part of my heritage, my skin, my perspective, my politics, and my future. And I felt sure that it had been my past that helped make the future possible. The women in my family had acted as if their lives were meaningful. Their lives were art. To be a lesbian among them was to be an artist. Perhaps the convergence came when I saw the faces of my great-grandmother, grandmother, and mother in those of the community of women I finally connected with. There was the same adventurous glint in their eyes; the same determined step; the penchant for breaking into song and for not waiting for anyone to take care of them.

I need not pretend to be other than who I was with any of these women. But did I need to declare it? During the holidays when I brought home best friends or lovers my family always welcomed us warmly, clasping us to their magnificent bosoms. Yet there was always an element of silence in our neighborhood, and surprisingly enough in our family, that was disturbing to me. Among the regulars in my father, Duke's, bar, was Maurice. He was eccentric, flamboyant, and still ordinary. He was accorded the same respect by neighborhood children as every other adult. His indiscretions took their place comfortably among the cyclical, Saturday night, man/woman scandals of our neighborhood. I regret never having asked my father how Maurice and he had become friends.

Soon I felt the discomforting silence pressing against my life more persistently. During visits home to Boston it no longer sufficed that Lydia and Dolores were loving and kind to the "friend" I brought home. Maybe it was just my getting older. Living in New York City at the age of thirty in 1980, there was little I kept deliberately hidden from anyone. The genteel silence that hovered around me when I entered our home was palpable but I was unsure whether it was already there when I arrived or if I carried it home within myself. It cut me off from what I knew was a kind of fulfillment available only from my family. The lifeline from Grace, to Lydia, to Dolores, to Jewelle was a strong one. We were bound by so many things, not the least of which was looking so much alike. I was not willing to be orphaned by silence.

If the idea of cathedral weddings and station wagons held no appeal for me, the concept of an extended family was certainly important. But my efforts were stunted by our inability to talk about the life I was creating for myself, for all of us. It felt all the more foolish because I thought I knew how my family would react. I was confident they would respond with their customary aplomb just as they had when I'd first had my hair cut as an Afro (which they hated) or when I brought home friends who were vegetarians (which they found curious). While we had disagreed over some issues, like the fight my mother and I had over Vietnam when I was nineteen, always when the deal went down we sided with each other. Somewhere deep inside I think I believed that neither my grandmother nor my mother would ever censure my choices. Neither had actually raised me; my great-grandmother had done that, and she had been a steely barricade against any encroachment on our personal freedoms and she'd never disapproved out loud of anything I'd done.

But it was not enough to have an unabashed admiration for these women. It is one thing to have pride in how they'd so graciously survived in spite of the odds against them. It was something else to be standing in a Times Square movie theater faced with the chance to say "it" out loud and risk the loss of their brilliant and benevolent smiles.

My mother had started reading the graffiti written on the wall of the bathroom stall. We hooted at each of her dramatic renderings. Then she said (not breaking her rhythm since we all know timing is everything), "Here's one I haven't seen before— 'DYKES UNITE'." There was that profound silence again, as if the frames of my life had ground to a halt. We were in a freeze-frame and options played themselves out in my head in rapid succession: Say nothing? Say something? Say what?

I laughed and said, "Yeah, but have you seen the rubber stamp on my desk at home?"

"No," said my mother with a slight bit of puzzlement. "What does it say?"

"I saw it," my grandmother called out from her stall. "It says: 'Lesbian Money!'"

"What?"

"*Lesbian Money,*" Lydia repeated.

"I just stamp it on my big bills," I said tentatively, and we all screamed with laughter. The other woman at the sinks tried to pretend we didn't exist.

Since then there has been little discussion. There have been some moments of awkwardness, usually in social situations where they feel uncertain. Although we have not explored the "it," the shift in our relationship is clear. When I go home it is with my lover and she is received as such. I was lucky. My family was as relieved as I to finally know who I was. [1990]

# Understanding and Valuing Difference

The first step to bridging the differences among us is to broaden our view of female experience so that we can understand the complex ways in which various forms of discrimination and prejudice affect the lives of different women. In an effort to deepen their understanding of divisions among women, women in positions of relative privilege have also found it useful to reexamine their own experience with a view to understanding how it has been affected by various systems of domination. Minnie Bruce Pratt, a white southern woman, reaches back to her childhood to remember the exclusiveness and narrowness of the world that she inherited. As a woman, however, her relationship to the privilege and power of the white men of her class was always ambivalent. Peggy McIntosh, recognizing that being white has given her unearned advantages in a racist society, struggles to look at these advantages from the point of view of people who do not share them. Understanding these advantages can enable those of us who benefit from them to better support the struggles of people who are disadvantaged by systems of unequal power and privilege.

In her influential essay "Age, Race, Class, and Sex: Women Redefining Difference," Audre Lorde, a black writer who died of cancer in 1993, warns us of the dangers of ignoring difference, urging us to work harder with ourselves and each other to ensure that our differences, rather than dividing us, will enrich our struggle and our vision. In "Friday Night," one woman reaches out to another, conscious both of what they share and of the different cultures they each bring to their friendship.

---

## 97

## *"Who Am I If I'm Not My Father's Daughter?"*

MINNIE BRUCE PRATT

As a white woman, raised small-town middle-class, Christian, in the Deep South, I was taught to be a *judge,* of moral responsibility and punishment only in relation to *my* ethical system; was taught to be a *preacher,* to point out wrongs and tell others what to do; was taught to be a *martyr,* to take all the responsibility for change and the glory, to expect others to do nothing; was taught to be a *peacemaker,* to mediate, negotiate between opposing sides because *I* knew the right way. When I speak, or speak up, about anti-Semitism and racism, I struggle not to speak with intonations, the gestures, the assumption of these roles, and not to speak out of any role of ought-to; I ask that you try not to place me in that role. I am trying to speak today to women like myself, out of need: as a woman who loves other women passionately and wants us to be able to be together as friends in this unjust world.

But where does the need come from, if by skin color, ethnicity, birth culture, we are women who are in a position of material advantage, where we gain at the expense of others, of other women? A place where *we* can have a degree of safety, comfort, familiarity, just by staying put. Where is our *need* to change what we were born into? What do we have to gain?

When I try to think of this, I think of my father, of how, when I was about eight years old, he took me up the front marble steps of the courthouse in my town. He took me inside, up the worn wooden steps, stooped under the feet of the folks who had gone up and down to be judged, or to gawk at others being judged, up past the courtroom where my grandfather had leaned back his chair and judged for more than 40 years, up to the attic, to some narrow steps that went to the roof, to the clock tower with a walled ledge.

What I would have seen at the top: on the streets around the courthouse square: the Methodist church, the limestone building with the county health department, board of education, welfare department (my mother worked there), the yellow brick Baptist church, the Gulf station, the pool hall (no women allowed), Cleveland's grocery, Ward's shoe store; then all in a line, connected: the bank, the post office, Dr. Nicholson's office, one door for whites, one for blacks, then separate: the Presbyterian church, the newspaper office, the yellow brick jail, same brick as the Baptist church, and as the courthouse.

What I could not have seen from the top: the sawmill, or Four Points where the white mill folks lived, or the houses of blacks in Veneer Mill quarters.

This is what I would and would not have seen, or so I think, for I never got to the top. When he told me to go up the steps in front of him, I tried to, crawling on hands and knees, but I was terribly afraid. I couldn't—or wouldn't—do it. He let me crawl down: he was disgusted with me, I thought. I think now that he wanted to show me a place he had climbed to as a boy, a view that had been his father's, and his, and would be mine. But I was *not* him. I had not learned to take that height, that being set apart as my own: a white girl, not a boy.

And yet I know I have been shaped by my relation to those buildings, and to the people in the buildings, by ideas of who should be working in the board of education, of who should be in the bank handling money, of who should have the guns and the keys to the jail, of who should be *in* the jail; I have been shaped by what I didn't see, or didn't notice, on those streets.

Each of us carries around with us those growing-up places, the institutions, a sort of backdrop, a stage-set. So often we act out the present against a backdrop of the past, within a frame of perception that is so familiar, so safe that it is terrifying to risk changing it even when we know our perceptions are distorted, limited, constricted by that old view.

So this is one gain for me as I change: I learn a way of looking at the world that is more accurate, complex, multilayered, multidimensioned, more truthful: to see the world of overlapping circles, like movement on the millpond after a fish has jumped, instead of the courthouse square with me in the middle. I feel the *need* to look differently because I've learned that what is presented to me as an accurate view of the world is frequently a lie: so that to look through an anthology of women's studies that has little or no work by women of color is to be up on that ledge above the town and be thinking that I see the town, without realizing how many lives have been pushed out of sight, beside unpaved roads. I'm learning that what I think that I *know* is an accurate view of the world is frequently a lie: as when I was in a discussion about the Women's Pentagon Action with several women, four of us Christian-raised, one Jewish. In describing the march through Arlington Cemetery, one of the four mentioned the rows of crosses. I had marched for a long time through that cemetery; I nodded to myself, visualized rows of crosses. No, said the Jewish woman, they were headstones, with crosses or Stars of David engraved above the names. We four objected; we had all seen crosses. The Jewish woman had some photographs of the march through the cemetery, laid them on the table. We saw rows and rows of rectangular gravestones, and in the foreground, clearly visible, one inscribed with a name and a Star of David.

So I gain truth when I expand my constricted eye, an eye that has only let in what I have been taught to see. But there have been other constrictions: the fear around my heart when I must deal with the *fact* of folk who exist, with their own lives, in other places besides the narrow circle I was raised in. I have learned that my fear of these folks is kin to a terror that has been in my birth culture for years, for centuries, the terror of people who have set themselves apart and *above,* who have wronged others and feel they are about to be found out and punished. It is the terror that in my culture has been expressed in lies about dirty Jews who kill for blood, sly Arab hordes who murder, brutal Indians who massacre, animal blacks who rise in rebellion in the middle of the night and slaughter. It is the terror that has *caused* the slaughter of all these peoples. It is the terror that was my father with his stack of John Birch newspapers, his belief in a Communist-Jewish-Black conspiracy. It is the desperate terror, the knowledge that something is *wrong,* and tries to end fear by attack.

I get afraid when I am trying to understand myself in relation to folks different from me, when there are discussions, conflicts about anti-Semitism and racism among women, criticisms, criticisms of *me;* when, for instance, in a group discussion about race and class, I say I feel we have talked too much about race, not enough about class, and a woman of color asks me in anger and pain if I don't think her skin has something to do with class; when, for instance, I say carelessly to a Jewish friend that there were no Jews where I grew up, she begins to ask me: How do I know? Do I hear what I'm saying? and I get afraid; when I feel my racing heart, breath, the tightening of my skin around me, literally defenses to protect my narrow circle, I try to say to myself: yes, that fear is there, but I will try to be at the edge between my fear and the outside, on the edge at my skin, listening, asking what new thing will I hear, will I see, will I let myself feel, beyond the fear. I try to say to myself: that to acknowledge the complexity of another's existence is not to deny my own. I try to say: when I acknowledge what my people, what those who are like me, have done to people with less power and less safety in the world, I can make a place for things to be different, a place where I can feel grief, sorrow, not to be sorry *for* the others, but to mourn, to expand my circle of self, follow my need to loosen the constrictions of fear, be a break in the cycle of fear and attack.

To be caught within the narrow circle of the self is not just a fearful thing, it is a *lonely* thing. When I could not climb the steps that day with my father, maybe I knew on some level that my place was with women, not with men, that I did not want his view of the world. Certainly, I have felt this more and more strongly since my coming out as a lesbian. Yet so much has separated me from other women, ways in which my culture set me apart by race, by ethnicity, by class. I understood abruptly one day how lonely this made me when a friend, a black woman, spoke to me casually in our shared office: and I heard how she said my name: the lingering accent, so much like how my name is said at home. Yet I knew enough of her history and mine to know how much separated us: the chasm of murders, rapes, lynchings, the years of daily humiliations done by my people to hers. I went and stood in the hallway and cried, thinking of how she said my name like home, and how divided our lives were.

It is a pain I come to over and over again when, for instance, I realize how *habitually* I think of my culture, my ethics, my morality, as the culmination of history, as the logical extension of what has gone before; the kind of thinking represented by my use, in the past, of the word *Judeo-Christian,* as if Jewish history and lives have existed only to culminate in Christian culture, the kind of thinking that the U.S. government is using now to promote Armageddon in the Middle East; the kind of thinking that I did until recently about Indian lives and culture in my region, as if Indian peoples have existed only in museums since white folks came in the 1500s; the kind of thinking that separates me from women in cultures different from mine, makes their experience less central, less important than mine. It is painful to keep understanding this separation, within myself and in the world. Yet I have felt that the need to be with other women can be the breaking through the shell around me, painful, but a coming through into a new place, where with understanding and change, the loneliness won't be necessary.

If we have these things to gain, and more, by struggling against racism and anti-Semitism in ourselves, what keeps us from doing so, at any one moment, what keeps us from action? In part, I know I hesitate because I have struggled painfully, for years, to make this new place for myself with other women, and I hesitate to disrupt it.

In part I hesitate because the process of uncovering my complicity is so painful: it is the stripping down, layer after layer, of my identity: skin, blood, heart: to find out how much of what I am has been shaped by my skin and family, to find out which of my thoughts and actions I need to change, which I need to keep as my own. Sometimes I fear that stripping away the layers will bring me to nothing, that the only values that I and my culture have are based on negativity, exclusion, fear.

Often I have thought: *what* of who I am is worth saving? worth taking into the future? But I have learned that as the process of shaping identity was long, so the process of change is long. I know that change speeds up the more able I am to put into material shape what I have learned from struggling with anti-Semitism and racism, to begin to act for change can widen perception, loosen fear, ease loneliness. I know that we can choose to act in ways that get us closer to the longed-for but unrealized world, a world where we each are able to live, but not by trying to make someone less than us, not by someone else's blood or pain.                    [1984]

 98

# White Privilege: Unpacking the Invisible Knapsack

PEGGY MCINTOSH

Through work to bring materials from Women's Studies into the rest of the curriculum, I have often noticed men's unwillingness to grant that they are over-privileged, even though they may grant that women are disadvantaged. They may say they will work to improve women's status, in the society, the university, or the curriculum, but they can't or won't support the idea of lessening men's. Denials which amount to taboos surround the subject of advantages which men gain from women's disadvantages. These denials protect male privilege from being fully acknowledged, lessened or ended.

Thinking through unacknowledged male privilege as a phenomenon, I realized that since hierarchies in our society are interlocking, there was most likely a phenomenon of white privilege which was similarly denied and protected. As a white person, I realized I had been taught about racism as something which puts others at a disadvantage, but had been taught not to see one of its corollary aspects, white privilege, which puts me at an advantage.

I think whites are carefully taught not to recognize white privilege, as males are taught not to recognize male privilege. So I have begun in an untutored way to ask what it is like to have white privilege. I have come to see white privilege as an invisible package of unearned assets which I can count on cashing in each day, but about which I was 'meant' to remain oblivious. White privilege is like an invisible weightless knapsack of special provisions, maps, passports, codebooks, visas, clothes, tools and blank checks.

Describing white privilege makes one newly accountable. As we in Women's Studies work to reveal male privilege and ask men to give up some of their power, so one who writes about having white privilege must ask, "Having described it, what will I do to lessen or end it?"

After I realized the extent to which men work from a base of unacknowledged privilege, I understood that much of their oppressiveness was unconscious. Then I remembered the frequent charges from women of color that white women whom they encounter are oppressive. I began to understand why we are justly seen as oppressive, even when we don't see ourselves that way. I began to count the ways in which I enjoy unearned skin privilege and have been conditioned into oblivion about its existence.

My schooling gave me no training in seeing myself as an oppressor, as an unfairly advantaged person, or as a participant in a damaged culture. I was taught to see myself as an individual whose moral state depended on her individual moral will. My schooling followed the pattern my colleague Elizabeth Minnich has pointed out: whites are taught to think of their lives as morally neutral, normative, and average, and also ideal, so that when we work to benefit others, this is seen as work which will allow "them" to be more like "us."

I decided to try to work on myself at least by identifying some of the daily effects of white privilege in my life. I have chosen those conditions which I think in my case *attach somewhat more to skin-color privilege* than to class, religion, ethnic status, or geographical location, though of course all these other factors are intricately intertwined. As far as I can see, my African American co-workers, friends and acquaintances with whom I come into daily or frequent contact in this particular time, place, and line of work cannot count on most of these conditions.

1. I can if I wish arrange to be in the company of people of my race most of the time.
2. If I should need to move, I can be pretty sure of renting or purchasing housing in an area which I can afford and in which I would want to live.
3. I can be pretty sure that my neighbors in such a location will be neutral or pleasant to me.
4. I can go shopping alone most of the time, pretty well assured that I will not be followed or harassed.
5. I can turn on the television or open to the front page of the paper and see people of my race widely represented.
6. When I am told about our national heritage or about "civilization," I am shown that people of my color made it what it is.
7. I can be sure that my children will be given curricular materials that testify to the existence of their race.
8. If I want to, I can be pretty sure of finding a publisher for this piece on white privilege.
9. I can go into a music shop and count on finding the music of my race represented, into a supermarket and find the staple foods which fit with my cultural traditions, into a hairdresser's shop and find someone who can cut my hair.
10. Whether I use checks, credit cards, or cash, I can count on my skin color not to work against the appearance of financial reliability.
11. I can arrange to protect my children most of the time from people who might not like them.
12. I can swear, or dress in second hand clothes, or not answer letters, without having people

attribute these choices to the bad morals, the poverty, or the illiteracy of my race.
13. I can speak in public to a powerful male group without putting my race on trial.
14. I can do well in a challenging situation without being called a credit to my race.
15. I am never asked to speak for all the people of my racial group.
16. I can remain oblivious of the language and customs of persons of color who constitute the world's majority without feeling in my culture any penalty for such oblivion.
17. I can criticize our government and talk about how much I fear its policies and behavior without being seen as a cultural outsider.
18. I can be pretty sure that if I ask to talk to "the person in charge," I will be facing a person of my race.
19. If a traffic cop pulls me over or if the IRS audits my tax return, I can be sure I haven't been singled out because of my race.
20. I can easily buy posters, postcards, picture books, greeting cards, dolls, toys, and children's magazines featuring people of my race.
21. I can go home from most meetings of organizations I belong to feeling somewhat tied in, rather than isolated, out-of-place, outnumbered, unheard, held at a distance, or feared.
22. I can take a job with an affirmative action employer without having co-workers on the job suspect that I got it because of race.
23. I can choose public accommodation without fearing that people of my race cannot get in or will be mistreated in the places I have chosen.
24. I can be sure that if I need legal or medical help, my race will not work against me.
25. If my day, week, or year is going badly, I need not ask of each negative episode or situation whether it has racial overtones.
26. I can choose blemish cover or bandages in "flesh" color and have them more or less match my skin.

I repeatedly forgot each of the realizations on this list until I wrote it down. For me white privilege has turned out to be an elusive and fugitive subject. The pressure to avoid it is great, for in facing it I must give up the myth of meritocracy. If these things are true, this is not such a free country; one's life is not what one makes it; many doors open for certain people through no virtues of their own.

In unpacking this invisible backpack of white privilege, I have listed conditions of daily experience which I once took for granted. Nor did I think of any of these perquisites as bad for the holder. I now think that we need a more finely differentiated taxonomy of privilege, for some of these varieties are only what one would want for everyone in a just society, and others give licence to be ignorant, oblivious, arrogant and destructive.

I see a pattern running through the matrix of white privilege, a pattern of assumptions which were passed on to me as a white person. There was one main piece of cultural turf; it was my own turf, and I was among those who could control the turf. *My skin color was an asset for any move I was educated to want to make.* I could think of myself as belonging in major ways, and of making social systems work for me. I could freely disparage, fear, neglect, or be oblivious to anything outside of the dominant cultural forms. Being of the main culture, I could also criticize it fairly freely.

In proportion as my racial group was being made confident, comfortable, and oblivious, other groups were likely being made inconfident, uncomfortable, and alienated. Whiteness protected me from many kinds of hostility, distress, and violence, which I was being subtly trained to visit in turn upon people of color.

For this reason, the word "privilege" now seems to me misleading. We usually think of privilege as being a favored state, whether earned or conferred by birth or luck. Yet some of the conditions I have described here work to systematically overempower certain groups. Such privilege simply *confers dominance* because of one's race or sex.

I want, then, to distinguish between earned strength and unearned power conferred systematically. Power from unearned privilege can look like strength when it is in fact permission to escape or to dominate. But not all of the privileges on my list are inevitably damaging. Some, like the expectation that neighbors will be decent to you, or that your race will not count against you in court, should be the norm in a just society. Others, like the privilege to ignore less powerful people, distort the humanity of the holders as well as the ignored groups.

We might at least start by distinguishing between positive advantages which we can work to spread, and negative types of advantages which unless rejected will always reinforce our present hierarchies. For example, the feeling that one belongs within the human circle, as Native Americans say, should not be seen as privilege for a few. Ideally it is an *unearned entitlement.* At present, since only a few have it, it is an *unearned advantage* for them. This paper results from a process of coming to see that some of the power which I originally saw as attendant on being a human being in the U.S. consisted in *unearned advantage* and *conferred dominance.*

I have met very few men who are truly distressed about systemic, unearned male advantage and conferred dominance. And so one question for me and others like me is whether we will be like them, or whether we will get truly distressed, even outraged, about unearned race advantage and conferred dominance and if so, what we will do to lessen them. In any case, we need to do more work in identifying how they actually affect our daily lives. Many, perhaps most, of our white students in the U.S. think that racism doesn't affect them because they are not people of color; they do not see "whiteness" as a racial identity. In addition, since race and sex are not the only advantaging systems at work, we need similarly to examine the daily experience of having age advantage, or ethnic advantage, or physical ability, or advantage related to nationality, religion, or sexual orientation.

Difficulties and dangers surrounding the task of finding parallels are many. Since racism, sexism, and heterosexism are not the same, the advantaging associated with them should not be seen as the same. In addition, it is hard to disentangle aspects of unearned advantage which rest more on social class, economic class, race, religion, sex and ethnic identity than on other factors. Still, all of the oppressions are interlocking, as the Combahee River Collective Statement of 1977 continues to remind us eloquently.

One factor seems clear about all of the interlocking oppressions. They take both active forms which we can see and embedded forms which as a member of the dominant group one is taught not to see. In my class and place, I did not see myself as a racist because I was taught to recognize racism only in individual acts of meanness by members of my group, never in invisible systems conferring unsought racial dominance on my group from birth.

Disapproving of the systems won't be enough to change them. I was taught to think that racism could end if white individuals changed their attitudes. [But] a "white" skin in the United States opens many doors for whites whether or not we approve of the way dominance has been conferred on us. Individual acts can palliate, but cannot end, these problems.

To redesign social systems we need first to acknowledge their colossal unseen dimensions. The silences and denials surrounding privilege are the key political tool here. They keep the thinking about equality or equity incomplete, protecting unearned advantage and conferred dominance by making these taboo subjects. Most talk by whites about equal opportunity seems to me now to be about equal opportunity to try to get into a position of dominance while denying that *systems* of dominance exist.

It seems to me that obliviousness about white advantage, like obliviousness about male advantage, is kept strongly inculturated in the United States so as to maintain the myth of meritocracy, the myth that democratic choice is equally available to all. Keeping most people unaware that freedom of confident action is there for just a small number of people props up those in power, and serves to keep power in the hands of the same groups that have most of it already.

Though systematic change takes many decades, there are pressing questions for me and I imagine for some others like me if we raise our daily consciousness on the perquisites of being light-skinned. What will we do with such knowledge? As we know from watching men, it is an open question whether we will choose to use unearned advantage to weaken hidden systems of advantage, and whether we will use any of our arbitrarily-awarded power to try to reconstruct power systems on a broader base.

[1989]

## ❦ 99

# *Age, Race, Class, and Sex: Women Redefining Difference**

AUDRE LORDE

Much of Western European history conditions us to see human differences in simplistic opposition to each other: dominant/subordinate, good/bad, up/down, superior/inferior. In a society where the good is defined in terms of profit rather than in terms of human need, there must always be some group of people who, through systematized oppression, can be made to feel surplus, to occupy the place of dehumanized inferior. Within this society, that group is made up of Black and Third World people, working-class people, older people, and women.

As a forty-nine-year-old Black lesbian feminist socialist mother of two, including one boy, and a member of an interracial couple, I usually find myself a part of some group defined as other, deviant, inferior, or just plain wrong. Traditionally, in american society, it is the members of oppressed, objectified groups who are expected to stretch out and bridge the gap between the actualities of our lives and the consciousness of our oppressor. For in order to survive, those of us for whom oppression is as american as apple pie have always had to be watchers, to become familiar with the language and manners of the oppressor, even sometimes adopting them for some illusion of protection. Whenever the need for some pretense of communication arises, those who profit from our oppression call upon us to share our knowledge with them. In other words, it is the responsibility of the oppressed to teach the oppressors their mistakes. I am responsible for educating teachers who dismiss my children's culture in school. Black and Third World people are expected to educate white people as to our humanity. Women

---

*Paper delivered at the Copeland Colloquium, Amherst College, April 1980.

are expected to educate men. Lesbians and gay men are expected to educate the heterosexual world. The oppressors maintain their position and evade responsibility for their own actions. There is a constant drain of energy which might be better used in redefining ourselves and devising realistic scenarios for altering the present and constructing the future.

Institutionalized rejection of difference is an absolute necessity in a profit economy which needs outsiders as surplus people. As members of such an economy, we have *all* been programmed to respond to the human differences between us with fear and loathing and to handle that difference in one of three ways: ignore it, and if that is not possible, copy it if we think it is dominant, or destroy it if we think it is subordinate. But we have no patterns for relating across our human differences as equals. As a result, those differences have been misnamed and misused in the service of separation and confusion.

Certainly there are very real differences between us of race, age, and sex. But it is not those differences between us that are separating us. It is rather our refusal to recognize those differences, and to examine the distortions which result from our misnaming them and their effects upon human behavior and expectation.

*Racism, the belief in the inherent superiority of one race over all others and thereby the right to dominance. Sexism, the belief in the inherent superiority of one sex over the other and thereby the right to dominance. Ageism. Heterosexism. Elitism. Classism.*

It is a lifetime pursuit for each one of us to extract these distortions from our living at the same time as we recognize, reclaim, and define those differences upon which they are imposed. For we have all been raised in a society where those distortions were endemic within our living. Too often, we pour the energy needed for recognizing and exploring difference into pretending those differences are insurmountable barriers, or that they do not exist at all. This results in a voluntary isolation, or false and treacherous connections. Either way, we do not develop tools for using human difference as a springboard for creative change within our lives. We speak not of human difference, but of human deviance.

Somewhere, on the edge of consciousness, there is what I call a *mythical norm*, which each one of us within our hearts knows "that is not me." In america, this norm is usually defined as white, thin, male, young, heterosexual, christian, and financially secure. It is with this mythical norm that the trappings of power reside within this society. Those of us who stand outside that power often identify one way in which we are different, and we assume that to be the primary cause of all oppression, forgetting other distortions around difference, some of which we ourselves may be practicing. By and large within the women's movement today, white women focus upon their oppression as women and ignore differences of race, sexual preference, class, and age. There is a pretense to a homogeneity of experience covered by the word *sisterhood* that does not in fact exist.

Unacknowledged class differences rob women of each others' energy and creative insight. Recently a women's magazine collective made the decision for one issue to print only prose, saying poetry was a less "rigorous" or "serious" art form. Yet even the form our creativity takes is often a class issue. Of all the art forms, poetry is the most economical. It is the one which is the most secret, which requires the least physical labor, the least material, and the one which can be done between shifts, in the hospital pantry, on the subway, and on scraps of surplus paper. Over the last few years, writing a novel on tight finances, I came to appreciate the enormous differences in the material demands between poetry and prose. As we reclaim our literature, poetry has been the major voice of poor, working class, and Colored women. A room of one's own may be a necessity for writing prose, but so are reams of paper, a typewriter, and plenty of time. The actual requirements to produce the visual arts also help determine, along class lines, whose art is whose. In this day of inflated prices for material, who are our sculptors, our painters, our photographers? When we speak of a broadly based women's culture, we need to be aware of the effect of class and economic differences on the supplies available for producing art.

As we move toward creating a society within which we can each flourish, ageism is another distortion of relationship which interferes without vision. By ignoring the past, we are encouraged to repeat its mistakes. The "generation gap" is an important social tool for any repressive society. If the younger members of a community view the older members as contemptible or suspect or excess, they will never be able to join hands and examine the living memories of the community, nor ask the all important question, "Why?" This gives rise to a historical amnesia that keeps us working to invent the wheel every time we have to go to the store for bread.

We find ourselves having to repeat and relearn the same old lessons over and over that our mothers did because we do not pass on what we have learned, or because we are unable to listen. For instance, how many times has this all been said before? For another, who would have believed that once again our daughters are allowing their bodies to be hampered and purgatoried by girdles and high heels and hobble skirts?

Ignoring the differences of race between women and the implications of those differences presents the most serious threat to the mobilization of women's joint power.

As white women ignore their built-in privilege of whiteness and define *woman* in terms of their own experience alone, then women of Color become "other," the outsider whose experience and tradition is too "alien" to comprehend. An example of this is the signal absence of the experience of women of Color as a resource for women's studies courses. The literature of women of Color is seldom included in women's literature courses and almost never in other literature courses, nor in women's studies as a whole. All too often, the excuse given is that the literatures of women of Color can only be taught by Colored women, or that they are too difficult to understand, or that classes cannot "get into" them because they come out of experiences that are "too different." I have heard this argument presented by white women of otherwise quite clear intelligence, women who seem to have no trouble at all teaching and reviewing work that comes out of the vastly different experiences of Shakespeare, Molière, Dostoyefsky, and Aristophanes. Surely there must be some other explanation.

This is a very complex question, but I believe one of the reasons white women have such difficulty reading Black women's work is because of their reluctance to see Black women as women and different from themselves. To examine Black women's literature effectively requires that we be seen as whole people in our actual complexities—as individuals, as women, as human—rather than as one of those problematic but familiar stereotypes provided in this society in place of genuine images of Black women. And I believe this holds true for the literatures of other women of Color who are not Black.

The literatures of all women of Color recreate the textures of our lives, and many white women are heavily invested in ignoring the real differences. For as long as any difference between us means one of us must be inferior, then the recognition of any difference must be fraught with guilt. To allow women of Color to step out of stereotypes is too guilt provoking, for it threatens the complacency of those women who view oppression only in terms of sex.

Refusing to recognize difference makes it impossible to see the different problems and pitfalls facing us as women.

Thus, in a patriarchal power system where white-skin privilege is a major prop, the entrapments used to neutralize Black women and white women are not the same. For example, it is easy for Black women to be used by the power structure against Black men, not because they are men, but because they are Black. Therefore, for Black women, it is necessary at all times to separate the needs of the oppressor from our own legitimate conflicts within our communities. This same problem does not exist for white women. Black women and men have shared racist oppression and still share it, although in different ways. Out of that shared oppression we have developed joint defenses and joint vulnerabilities to each other that are not duplicated in the white community, with the exception of the relationship between Jewish women and Jewish men.

On the other hand, white women face the pitfall of being seduced into joining the oppressor under the pretense of sharing power. This possibility does not exist in the same way for women of Color. The tokenism that is sometimes extended to us is not an invitation to join power; our racial "otherness" is a visible reality that makes that quite clear. For white women there is a wider range of pretended choices and rewards for identifying with patriarchal power and its tools.

Today, with the defeat of ERA, the tightening economy, and increased conservatism, it is easier once again for white women to believe the dangerous fantasy that if you are good enough, pretty enough, sweet enough, quiet enough, teach the children to behave, hate the right people, and marry the right men, then you will be allowed to co-exist with patriarchy in relative peace, at least until a man needs your job or the neighborhood rapist happens along. And true, unless one lives and loves in the trenches it is difficult to remember that the war against dehumanization is ceaseless.

But Black women and our children know the fabric of our lives is stitched with violence and with hatred, that there is no rest. We do not deal with it only on the picket lines, or in dark midnight alleys, or in the places where we dare to verbalize our resistance. For us, increasingly, violence weaves through the daily tissues of our living—in the supermarket, in the classroom, in the elevator, in the clinic and the schoolyard, from the plumber, the baker, the saleswoman, the bus driver, the bank teller, the waitress who does not serve us.

Some problems we share as women, some we do not. You fear your children will grow up to join the patriarchy and testify against you, we fear our children will be dragged from a car and shot down in the street, and you will turn your backs upon the reasons they are dying.

The threat of difference has been no less blinding to people of Color. Those of us who are Black must see that the reality of our lives and our struggle does not make us immune to the errors of ignoring and misnaming difference. Within Black communities where racism is a living reality, differences among us often seem dangerous and suspect. The need for unity is often misnamed as a need for homogeneity, and a Black feminist vision mistaken for betrayal of our common interests as a people. Because of the continuous battle against racial erasure that Black women and Black men share, some Black women still refuse to recognize that we are also oppressed as women, and that sexual hostility against Black women is practiced not only by the white racist society, but implemented within our Black communities as well. It is a disease striking the heart of Black

nationhood, and silence will not make it disappear. Exacerbated by racism and the pressures of powerlessness, violence against Black women and children often becomes a standard within our communities, one by which manliness can be measured. But these women-hating acts are rarely discussed as crimes against Black women.

As a group, women of Color are the lowest paid wage earners in America. We are the primary targets of abortion and sterilization abuse, here and abroad. In certain parts of Africa, small girls are still being sewed shut between their legs to keep them docile and for men's pleasure. This is known as female circumcision, and it is not a cultural affair as the late Jomo Kenyatta insisted, it is a crime against Black women.

Black women's literature is full of the pain of frequent assault, not only by a racist patriarchy, but also by Black men. Yet the necessity for and history of shared battle have made us, Black women, particularly vulnerable to the false accusation that antisexist is anti-Black. Meanwhile, womanhating as a recourse of the powerless is sapping strength from Black communities, and our very lives. Rape is on the increase, reported and unreported, and rape is not aggressive sexuality, it is sexualized aggression. As Kalamu ya Salaam, a Black male writer points out, "As long as male domination exists, rape will exist. Only women revolting and men made conscious of their responsibility to fight sexism can collectively stop rape." *

Differences between ourselves as Black women are also being misnamed and used to separate us from one another. As a Black lesbian feminist comfortable with the many different ingredients of my identity, and a woman committed to racial and sexual freedom from oppression, I find I am constantly being encouraged to pluck out some one aspect of myself and present this as the meaningful whole, eclipsing or denying the other parts of self. But this is a destructive and fragmenting way to live. My fullest concentration of energy is available to

---

*From "Rape: A Radical Analysis, An African-American Perspective" by Kalamu y Salaam in *Black Books Bulletin*, vol. 6, no. 4 (1980).

me only when I integrate all the parts of who I am, openly, allowing power from particular sources of my living to flow back and forth freely through all my different selves, without the restrictions of externally imposed definition. Only then can I bring myself and my energies as a whole to the service of those struggles which I embrace as part of my living.

A fear of lesbians, or of being accused of being a lesbian, has led many Black women into testifying against themselves. It has led some of us into destructive alliances, and others into despair and isolation. In the white women's communities, heterosexism is sometimes a result of identifying with the white patriarchy, a rejection of that interdependence between women-identified women which allows the self to be, rather than to be used in the service of men. Sometimes it reflects a die-hard belief in the protective coloration of heterosexual relationships, sometimes a self-hate which all women have to fight against, taught us from birth.

Although elements of these attitudes exist for all women, there are particular resonances of heterosexism and homophobia among Black women. Despite the fact that woman-bonding has a long and honorable history in the African and African-american communities, and despite the knowledge and accomplishments of many strong and creative women-identified Black women in the political, social and cultural fields, heterosexual Black women often tend to ignore or discount the existence and work of Black lesbians. Part of this attitude has come from an understandable terror of Black male attack within the close confines of Black society, where the punishment for any female self-assertion is still to be accused of being a lesbian and therefore unworthy of the attention or support of the scarce Black male. But part of this need to misname and ignore Black lesbians comes from a very real fear that openly women-identified Black women who are no longer dependent upon men for their self-definition may well reorder our whole concept of social relationships.

Black women who once insisted that lesbianism was a white woman's problem now insist that Black lesbians are a threat to Black nationhood, are consorting with the enemy, are basically un-Black.

These accusations, coming from the very women to whom we look for deep and real understanding, have served to keep many Black lesbians in hiding, caught between the racism of white women and the homophobia of their sisters. Often, their work has been ignored, trivialized, or misnamed, as with the work of Angelina Grimke, Alice Dunbar-Nelson, Lorraine Hansberry. Yet women-bonded women have always been some part of the power of Black communities, from our unmarried aunts to the amazons of Dahomey.

And it is certainly not Black lesbians who are assaulting women and raping children and grandmothers on the streets of our communities.

Across this country, as in Boston during the spring of 1979 following the unsolved murders of twelve Black women, Black lesbians are spearheading movements against violence against Black women.

What are the particular details within each of our lives that can be scrutinized and altered to help bring about change? How do we redefine difference for all women? It is not our differences which separate women, but our reluctance to recognize those differences and to deal effectively with the distortions which have resulted from the ignoring and misnaming of those differences.

As a tool of social control, women have been encouraged to recognize only one area of human difference as legitimate, those differences which exist between women and men. And we have learned to deal across those differences with the urgency of all oppressed subordinates. All of us have had to learn to live or work or coexist with men, from our fathers on. We have recognized and negotiated these differences, even when this recognition only continued the old dominant/subordinate mode of human relationship, where the oppressed must recognize the masters' difference in order to survive.

But our future survival is predicated upon our ability to relate within equality. As women, we must root out internalized patterns of oppression within ourselves if we are to move beyond the most superficial aspects of social change. Now we must recognize differences among women who are our equals, neither inferior nor superior, and devise ways to use each other's difference to enrich our visions and our joint struggles.

The future of our earth may depend upon the ability of all women to identify and develop new definitions of power and new patterns of relating across difference. The old definitions have not served us, nor the earth that supports us. The old patterns, no matter how cleverly rearranged to imitate progress, still condemn us to cosmetically altered repetitions of the same old exchanges, the same old guilt, hatred, recrimination, lamentation, and suspicion.

For we have, built into all of us, old blueprints of expectations and response, old structures of oppression, and these must be altered at the same time as we alter the living conditions which are a result of those structures. For the master's tools will never dismantle the master's house.

As Paulo Freire shows so well in *The Pedagogy of the Oppressed,** the true focus of revolutionary change is never merely the oppressive situations which we seek to escape, but that piece of the oppressor which is planted deep within each of us, and which knows only the oppressors' tactics, the oppressors' relationships.

Change means growth, and growth can be painful. But we sharpen self-definition by exposing the self in work and struggle together with those whom we define as different from ourselves, although sharing the same goals. For Black and white, old and young, lesbian and heterosexual women alike, this can mean new paths to our survival.

We have chosen each other
and the edge of each others battles
the war is the same
if we lose
someday women's blood will congeal
upon a dead planet
if we win
there is no telling
we seek beyond history
for a new and more possible meeting.†        [1980]

---

* Seabury Press, New York, 1970.
† From "Outlines," unpublished poem.

## ✺ 100

## *Friday Night*

LINDA HOGAN

Sometimes I see a light in her kitchen
that almost touches mine,
and her shadow falls straight
through trees and peppermint
and lies down at my door
like it wants to come in.

Never mind that on Friday nights
she slumps out her own torn screen
and lies down crying on the stoop.
And don't ask about the reasons;
she pays her penalties for weeping.
Emergency Room:
Eighty dollars to knock a woman out.
And there are laughing red-faced neighbor men
who put down their hammers
to phone the county.
Her crying tries them all.
Don't ask for reasons
why they do not collapse
outside their own tight jawbones
or the rooms they build
a tooth and nail at a time.

Never mind she's Mexican
and I'm Indian
and we have both replaced the words
to the national anthem with our own.
Or that her house smells of fried tortillas
and mine of Itchko and sassafras.

Tonight she was weeping in the safety of moonlight
and red maples.
I took her a cup of peppermint tea,
and honey,
it was fine blue china
with marigolds growing inside the curves.
In the dark, under the praying mimosa
we sat smoking little caves of tobacco light,
me and the *Señora of Hysteria*, who said
Peppermint is every bit as good as the ambulance.
And I said, Yes. It is home grown.        [1985]

PART VI

# The Consequences of Sexism:
# Current Issues

The previous parts have demonstrated that the subordination of women is embedded in social institutions and sustained by culture. They demonstrate the ways that the unequal gender relations in combination with the other unequal power relations in society structure social life and shape our experiences. By examining three particular issues that women face today—the meaning of aging for women; the violence women face in their homes, the streets, and the workplace; and women's continuing battle to control their reproductive lives—Part VI will illuminate the implications of the attitudes, policies, and practices that we have studied in earlier parts.

For example, the disadvantaged position of women in the work force and the lack of financial compensation for women's work in the home results in far more women over 65 living in poverty than their male contemporaries. Women living alone are disproportionately represented among the elderly poor, and their poverty often results in inadequate health care. Old women who live alone are often the victims of criminals and indifferent, paternalistic social service and health care agencies. Improving the position of all women in the work force will address some of these problems, but changes in social policy are required to provide adequate health care and pensions for people who have spent much of their lives outside the work force and to ensure that affordable housing is available for the thousands of old women living alone.

The emphasis on physical beauty as a measure of female worth and the popular equation of female beauty with youthfulness contribute to the marginalization of old women. While aging men are often considered "distinguished," women are offered a panoply of cosmetics, surgery, and hair products to camouflage their age. As Cynthia Rich points out, even language trivializes old women's actions. While usually not meant maliciously, phrases such as "little old lady" demean and belittle old women.

As Margaret Sanger said in 1914, "enforced motherhood is the most complete denial of a woman's right to life and liberty." [1] Women have tried to control their reproductive lives throughout history, sharing contraceptive and abortion information among themselves. In the early twentieth century Margaret Sanger led the crusade to legalize birth control and improve the contraceptive technology available to women. Undeterred by arrests and harassment, she and other crusaders succeeded in establishing birth control clinics throughout the country and legalizing the distribution of birth control information and devices.

Although birth control was widely used by the 1960s, some states still restricted its use until the Supreme Court declared such restrictions unconstitutional in 1965 (*Griswold v. Connecticut*). As we have shown in the discussion of women and the law, the Supreme Court in *Roe v. Wade* in 1973 drew on the "right to privacy" ideas articulated in the *Griswold* decision to declare unconstitutional state laws that criminalized abortion. Since 1973, women's reproductive rights have been under fierce attack, and the Supreme Court has retreated from its support of all women's right to choose.

---

[1] *The Woman Rebel*, June 1914, p. 25.

The activities of the anti-abortion movement have brought reproductive rights to the center of the political stage in the last decade. Opponents of abortion have harassed abortion clinics and doctors who perform abortion, pressured legislatures to limit abortions, and succeeded in getting the Republican Party to adopt an anti-abortion platform. In recent years several staff members of abortion clinics were murdered or wounded by anti-abortion terrorists.

The advocates of women's reproductive rights have called themselves the "pro-choice" movement, emphasizing a woman's right to choose whether or when she has a child. The anti-choice forces have called themselves "the right to life" movement, contending that human life exists from the moment of conception. Beneath this argument lie conflicting views of sexuality, women's role in society, and individual liberty. As Kristin Luker has shown in *Abortion and the Politics of Motherhood,* most activists in the "right to life" movement adhere to traditional views about women's role, believe that sexuality should be confined to the family, and feel that women's most important role is motherhood.[2] Advocates of women's right to choose believe that these decisions should be made by individual women and that all women have a right to choose how they live, with whom they have sex, and when and whether they have children. Whereas some anti-abortion activists have argued that we should work for more social supports for parenting rather than working for abortion, pro-choice advocates have maintained that, although these are worthwhile goals, we should pursue them at the same time that we work to preserve individual women's control over their reproductive lives. The debate about abortion is inextricably entangled with the broader debate about women's position in society.

Although the majority of the American people favor legal abortion, the "right to life" movement has succeeded in severely curtailing women's access to abortion on both a federal and state level. Since the Hyde Amendment, passed in 1976, women on welfare have been denied federal funding for abortion, and most states also prohibit the use of state funds for abortion. As a result of congressional action in 1996, women in the U.S. armed services can no longer obtain abortions in overseas military hospitals, women who work for the federal government can no longer choose a health plan that covers abortion, and the funding for international family planning clinics has been radically reduced.[3] Many states have restricted women's rights to abortion in various ways, including parental consent requirements for minors, waiting periods and restrictions on late-term abortions. Abortion services are becoming harder to obtain, since the threat of violence has resulted in fewer doctors who will perform abortions. Rural women have less access to abortion because providers are concentrated in metropolitan areas. According to Marlene Fried, "Ninety-four percent of nonmetropolitan counties have no services."[4] Without access to abortion

---

[2] Kristin Luker, *Abortion and the Politics of Motherhood* (Berkeley: University of California Press, 1984).
[3] National Abortion Rights Action League, "Who Decides? A State-by-State Review of Abortion and Reproductive Rights," www.NARAL.org, 1977.
[4] Marlene Fried, "Legal and Inaccessible," in *Abortion Wars: A Half Century of Struggle, 1950–2000,* Rickie Solinger, ed. (Berkeley: University of California Press, 1998), p. 214.

services, the legal right is meaningless. For this reason, Billye Avery, the founder of the National Black Woman's Health Project, has urged feminists to speak of reproductive health, which includes both the right to make decisions about one's reproductive life and access to the services required to make that right a reality.

As the selections in Part VI make clear, returning to the days of illegal abortion would not eliminate abortion; women would continue to try to control their reproductive lives and would find illegal and sometimes unsafe ways to do it. Because they would have even less access to safe abortions than they do today, it is poor women who would suffer. In addition, studies of women suggest that in many areas, a majority of the women who died as a result of unsafe illegal abortions before *Roe v. Wade* were women of color.[5] Women of color have also been denied control of their reproductive lives through involuntary sterilization. Believing that poor women of color were having too many babies, doctors in poor communities, often supported by federal funds, have sterilized thousands of childbearing women without their informed consent. Latina, African-American, and Native American women pressured government agencies to enact guidelines to protect women from being deprived of their rights through sterilization abuse.

The anti-choice forces in the United States, in asserting the right of the state to control the behavior of pregnant women, are not only elevating the fetus to the status of human life but relegating the woman to the status of carrier or, as the writer Katha Pollitt has put it, "potting soil."[6] As Ruth Hubbard points out, however, the concern for fetal life that allegedly motivates the regulation of pregnant women's behavior appears hypocritical when little is being done to improve the social and economic conditions of poverty that endanger so many babies.

Violence against women, although it has existed for centuries, has been hidden behind the cloak of privacy that has surrounded the family. The feminist insistence on the political nature of private life enabled women to talk about the experience of violence, revealing how widespread it was and shattering the myths that have surrounded it. As the readings in this part make clear, women of all backgrounds have experienced violence, often at the hands of men they love.

Perhaps the most pervasive form of violence toward women is sexual harassment. For centuries women and girls have endured various forms of harassment, from ogling on the street to demands for sex in return for rewards or with threat of reprisal. Recent reports have revealed widespread harassment of girls and women in grade school and high school as well as in college, the workplace, and the street. Sexual harassment has been the subject of fierce debate in the media as our culture, accustomed to viewing women as sexual objects, grapples with the distinction between consensual and nonconsensual sexual activity. As women struggle for equality in previously male terrains such as the military, pervasive sexual harassment reinforces their alien and marginalized status.

The roots of domestic violence lie in the soil of the patriarchal family. The be-

[5] Loretta J. Ross, "African-American Women and Abortion," in Solinger, *Abortion Wars*, p. 161.
[6] Katha Pollitt, "The New Assault on Feminism," *The Nation*, March 26, 1990, p. 418.

lief that wives are the possessions of a male head of household who should control the behavior of all other family members is deeply embedded in social traditions. Women's disadvantaged position in the work force and their continued responsibility for child raising reinforces their economic dependence on their husbands, making it difficult for women to leave abusive relationships. For years, domestic violence eluded the criminal justice system because police were reluctant to interfere in family life. Women who have been trained all their lives to believe that they should adjust to men's needs and fix any problems that arise in their relationships are often trapped in violent relationships by their own feelings of guilt and shame.

In the past two decades, women have organized to make the criminal justice system more effective in dealing with domestic violence by educating police and changing laws to ensure that women get the protection they need from law enforcement agencies. Women have also organized a network of shelters for women who are fleeing abusive relationships, but these shelters can only house a fraction of those who need them. In 1996, the trial of O. J. Simpson, a star football player, charged with the murder of his wife Nicole Simpson, focused the country's attention on the prevalence of domestic violence as evidence of Simpson's violent treatment of Nicole surfaced during the trial. Violence against women is more openly discussed than it has been in the recent past, and victims today are more likely to know where to turn for help. Despite these advances, however, violence remains a part of the lives of thousands of women.

Sexual violence affects the lives of all women. Fear of rape shapes women's behavior from girlhood, restricting our movements and limiting our freedom. But despite the precautions women learn to take, thousands of women and girls are raped and molested each year. In 1996, 97,464 rapes were reported to the FBI, averaging one rape every 5 minutes.[7] Rape, however, is a grossly underreported crime; the FBI estimates that only about 16% of all rapes are reported. Researchers have suggested that depending on how rape is defined, somewhere between 15% and 40% of women are victims of rape or attempted rape during their lifetime.[8]

Despite its pervasiveness, women's experience of sexual violence was, until recently, rarely discussed in public. In 1979 Susan Griffen's article, "Rape: The All-American Crime," broke the silence about rape and called attention to the ways that images of sexual violence pervade Western culture. Susan Brownmiller's comprehensive study, *Against Our Will,* continued this investigation, tracing the history of rape in Western culture and demonstrating that, far from being a problem of individual psychopaths, sexual violence against women has been reinforced by our legal and criminal justice system and prevailing ideas about gender and sexuality.[9] The belief that women are the sexual property of men is still alive today, embodied in the legal statutes of the thirty-one states in which it is legal for a man to rape his wife in some

[7] U.S. Department of Justice, Bureau of Justice Statistics, *Criminal Victimization 1996* (Washington, D.C.: Government Printing Office, November 1997).
[8] National Victim's Center and Crime Victims Research and Treatment Center, *Rape in America: A Report to the Nation* (Columbia: University of South Carolina, 1992).
[9] Susan Brownmiller, *Against Our Will: Men, Women and Rape* (New York: Simon and Schuster, 1975).

situations.[10] The notion that women are responsible for male sexual behavior is reflected in the humiliating questions rape victims are often asked about their sexual histories and contributes to the low rate of conviction in rape trials.

Racism has shaped the experience of rape in this culture, from the systematic rape of enslaved African-American women to the false charges of rape that were used as a pretext for lynching African-American men in the South in the early twentieth century. African-American rape victims are less frequently believed by white juries, and African-American men are more frequently convicted. The popular myth of the black rapist clouds the reality that most rapes are committed by men who are of the same race as their victims.

Among the myriad misconceptions that surround the subject of rape is the notion that most rapes are committed by strangers. In fact, researchers estimate that between 60% and 80% of all rapes are acquaintance rapes, many of them in dating situations. The traditions of sexual conquest in which women are seen as sexual objects and male sexuality is assumed to be uncontrollable make it particularly difficult for the victims of date rape to speak out and be taken seriously. Male culture on college campuses, particularly in fraternities, has encouraged the treatment of women as sexual prey and celebrated male lust and conquest. Wherever it occurs, rape is an expression of women's subordinate status. To combat it we must assert women's right to say no to unwanted sex and to be seen as sexual actors, not objects.

The sexual abuse of young girls by a trusted adult is another form of sexual violence that has surfaced in horrifying proportions in recent years. Researchers estimate that one in four girls is a victim of sexual abuse. Girls are often painfully confused when molested by an adult from whom they crave affection and approval. Feelings of betrayal often follow women into adulthood. Like the other forms of sexual violence, the molestation of girl children is a violation of female bodily integrity and a cruel exercise of power.

Because they confront us with some of the most horrifying consequences of sexism, the essays and stories in this chapter are upsetting. However, acknowledging the contempt with which women have often been treated enables us to take action against it, as the women described in the next part of this book have done.

---

[10] *Fact Sheet* (Berkeley, CA: National Clearinghouse on Marital Rape, 1993).

# Aging

Aging is a painful process for many midlife and older women whose lives are marked by vulnerability to poverty, crime, poor health, and inadequate housing. The selections in this section address these realities, focusing on the general living conditions of many older women, as well as the personal experiences of older women who are struggling on their own.

We begin with an overview of the economic, social, and health concerns of older women. These data, collected by the Older Women's League, document the realities of many older women's lives. A national membership organization in Washington, D.C., the Older Women's League is dedicated to achieving economic, political, and social equity for midlife and older women through education, research, and public advocacy. The Older Women's League advocates for a national, universal health care system, reform of the Social Security system, and government policies to end discrimination at work and to provide affordable housing for older women.

Another aspect of older women's vulnerability is depicted in "The Women in the Tower," which recounts the struggles of older black women to obtain adequate security in their apartment building. As these women make their needs and rights known to the housing authority, the media present them in stereotypically negative terms, casting them as insignificant and diminishing their efforts.

Old women are often caught between their desire for independence and their physical fragility. Anna Marie Quevedo describes the vulnerability of her nana in a large urban area without an effective and genuine support system. At the same time, other women have joined together to live collectively and stand up for their rights as women. The experiences of the group, Wonderful Older Women, speak to the potential empowerment of wise and seasoned women.

---

## 101

## *The Realities of Older Women's Lives*

OLDER WOMEN'S LEAGUE

The discrimination many women face as young women becomes magnified as they age. The image portrayed in the media today of older women as financially secure and enjoying the benefits of good health are largely untrue. The Older Women's League (OWL), the only national organization representing the 56 million American women 40 years of age and older, has a commitment to spotlighting the realities of most older women's lives, making it clear to policy makers and society that they cannot ignore the needs of this vulnerable group of citizens.

Growing old in America is very different for women and men. Race and ethnicity, family, and economic resources are primary influences in the quality of older women's lives. The economic status of older women reflects their past lives, education, employment history, and marital status, and it is far too often an extension of the problems and choices they dealt with earlier in their lives. Older women are far more likely than men to be living in poverty and isolation. Rather than being cared for, they are likely to sacrifice their health and their livelihood to care for others.

The economic chasm that is evident between women and men during their work lives continues to widen when they retire. Women working full-time earn 75% of what men earn, and the wage gap widens with age; women 55 years and older working full-time earned only 66% of the wages of men in the same age range. Forty-two percent of women 65 and older live at 25% of federal poverty levels or less. In 1995, they had a median income of $9,335—62% of the $14,983 annual median income of older men. In 1995, older women were over twice as likely (13.5%) to be living in poverty as men (6.2%). In fact, almost three-fourths of the four million older poor people in the United States are women.

Older African-American and Latina women are especially vulnerable to a life of poverty. In 1995, 31% of African-American women age 65 and over and 28.9% of older Latinas were living in poverty, compared with 14% of white women and 13.6% of all older women.

The most vulnerable segment of the female population is composed of women who have been single their entire lives. Totally dependent on their own resources, they are the most likely cohort of the population to live out their days in poverty. In 1994, among unmarried women 65 years and over, 64% of those getting monthly checks would have been poor without Social Security; 95% of these women depend on Social Security for 90% or more of their income, and 22% have no other source of income.

It is important to note that women living as couples with other women are doubly disadvantaged. Considered single in their eligibility for government programs, they not only are unable to take advantage of any tax and other benefits to which married partners are entitled but also are not eligible for any benefits that may accrue to widows after their partners' death.

Many women are only a man away from poverty. Half of all poor widows were not poor before the death of their husbands. Almost four times more widows live in poverty than do wives the same age. Some projections suggest that Social Security and increased access to pensions will effectively end poverty among older men and married couples by 2020. But poverty will remain widespread among older women living alone, who are separated, divorced, widowed, or never married.

Separated and divorced women are substantially poorer than widows, and all are poorer than wives. Approximately 37% of women over 61 years old who were separated from their husbands in 1994 lived below the poverty line. Thirty-three percent of divorced women over 65 lived in poverty, compared with 27% of widowed women.

The decisions that women make when they enter the work force about what kind of work they will do and how long they will work have serious consequences for their economic well-being in their old age. Simply put, nonentry or late entry into the job market, job interruptions, and temporary or part-time employment characterize most women's employment history when they are the primary caregiver in the family. Such an employment record has a devastating impact on a woman's employment, health, and retirement benefits.

Over the past 25 years, women have been steadily increasing their labor force participation. In 1960, 37.5% of women were in the labor force; by 1996, that number had grown to 59.4%. However, women move in and out of jobs more rapidly than men do (women stay with an employer an average of 4.8 years, compared with an average for men of 6.6 years), making it more likely that they will not vest in employer pensions or other benefits.

The average woman now spends 11.5 years out of the work force, usually for caregiving—about six years more than her male counterpart, and time she is not vesting in a pension or paying into Social Security. Today, many women in midlife are part of the "sandwich generation"—sandwiched between caring simultaneously for small children and aging parents. And, because the fastest-growing segment of the population today is the 85 and older group, the "sandwich" is increasingly a triple decker, for those caring for grandmothers, mothers, and small children, all at the same time.

Many younger women believe that this is a problem of the past, and as more women enter the work force and have greater access to pensions and other benefits, their lives in old age will be different. But three in five women today have the same kinds of jobs that women have traditionally held: sales, clerical, and retail—low-wage positions that frequently offer no benefits. And they hold those jobs for the same reasons: the need to move in and out of the work force to care for their families.

OWL believes that the legacy of poverty in older age does not need to be passed from others to daughters and granddaughters. We understand the faults and biases in the structure of the U.S. retirement system, which is based on male work and life patterns. We believe that women have the power to make changes to that structure. In addition, it is possible for some women to break the cycle of poverty that assails older women by understanding the impact of the decisions they make during their work lives.

## SOCIAL SECURITY

Social Security is supposed to be a gender-neutral program. But lifestyles were very different in 1935 when the program was instituted, and retirement plans, both Social Security and private pensions, were designed on male work and life patterns. The Social Security system has not kept up with the changes in women's lives.

In 1993, men at birth had a life expectancy of 72.1 years, women 78.9. At age 65, the life expectancy for women is an additional 19.2 years, while for men it is only 15.4 years. By 2070, according to Social Security Administration projections, a 65-year-old woman can expect to live to 87, another 22 years, while a man will live to 83, only 18 years. Because of their greater longevity, most American women will live out their lives as widows. Currently, half of all women age 65 and over are widows, and about 100,000 women become widowed annually.

The Social Security system still best serves the traditional family: a paid worker (usually the husband), an unpaid homemaker (usually the wife), and children. Today, however, most American families do not fit that profile, and even fewer will in the future. For one example, we have the dilemma of dual entitlement and single benefit—a woman in a two-earner couple who is entitled to both a worker benefit on her earnings and a spousal benefit on her husband's can receive only the greater of the two, which is usually the spouse benefit.

Millions of widowed older women depend exclusively on Social Security for adequate income during retirement. This is particularly true for women of color. However, the Social Security benefits they receive are not adequate for their needs. Black women are more likely than white women to take the reduced benefits associated with early retirement: almost 66% begin drawing Social Security before age 65, in part because of the stress of a lifetime of low wages and physical work, and because women experience age discrimination earlier than men. The incidence of poverty is dramatically higher among elderly women of color who live alone—43% for blacks and other women of color and 35% for Latinas—compared with a poverty rate of 16% for white elderly women living alone.

According to the General Accounting Office, approximately 80% of widows become poor only upon the death of their husbands. Their husbands tended to retire early because of poor health. The resulting loss of earnings, as well as medical expenses, deplete the resources available to the widows. The husband's death may also ultimately mean the loss of his pension income.

The increase in the divorce rate also has contributed to the growing diversity of family roles and work patterns, since many divorced women must work to support themselves or their families. Today, the number of women between the ages of 45 and 64 who are separated, divorced, or widowed is twice that of men. Most of these women are the sole support of their families.

Since 1960, the percentage of women drawing a benefit based on their own work records has remained virtually constant—36%—even though the percentage of women dually entitled to benefits on both their and their husband's has jumped from 5% in 1960 to 25% in 1993. Despite the increased participation of women in the work force, most working women receive exactly the same benefit as if they had never worked outside the home. In addition, so-called "zero years"—those years when a woman has left the work force for caregiving purposes—are averaged in when the amount of a woman's benefit amount is calculated, resulting inevitably in lowered benefits.

Sixty times more women than men are dependent on their divorced spouse's earnings for Social Security benefits. And while a divorced person age 62 and over can receive Social Security upon divorce if the former spouse is drawing Social Security, she must wait two years if the former spouse is still in the work force. For many women without other options, this waiting period can be a time of great deprivation and may be regarded as imposing a penalty on divorce.

Many similar inequities exist in the system for widows and divorced spouses. As the discussions about keeping the Social Security system solvent for succeeding generations of recipients move forward, OWL believes they must be accompanied by a discussion about correcting the structural inequities in this fundamental piece of women's economic security.

## PENSIONS

Today, with more and more women entering the work force, and with the numbers of women receiving pensions growing, many people predict that younger women will be able to look forward to a more secure old age. OWL's 1998 Mother's Day Report, *Women, Work and Money: Increasing the Chances for a Secure Retirement,* points out that the old axiom that a secure retirement is dependent on a sturdy "three-legged stool" of Social Security, savings, and pensions does not work for older women.

As noted earlier, women's labor force participation has been steadily increasing over the past 25 years, but their work patterns have not changed. Women move more rapidly in and out of jobs than men do—women stay with an employer an average of 4.8 years, compared with an average for men of 6.6 years—making it more likely that they will not vest in employer pensions. In 1996, employed women (26.3%) were more likely than employed men (10.7%) to work part-time. The industries in which many of these women work—health care, hospitality, education, and child care—are much less likely to offer employer-provided pensions. Only 14.9% of women employed part time in 1995 were covered by employer pensions.

In this context, it bears repeating that in 1996, median weekly earnings for women working full-time were $418 compared with the median weekly earnings for full-time men of $557. Lower-waged workers save less, are adding less to their Social Security accounts, and can contribute less to their pension funds—if they have the opportunity. As stated earlier, lower-wage workers are less likely to be covered by employer-provided pensions.

In 1995, women were only slightly less likely than men (38.9% vs. 43.3%) to be covered by an employer pension plan. However, that means that more than 60% of working women were not covered by an employer pension plan. Some surveys indicate that, as more women have access to pensions, they are achieving parity with men. However, one reason that this, in fact, is happening is that, with downsizing and other work force dynamics, fewer men are now covered by employer pensions.

Half of working women whose employers do not offer a pension plan work for small businesses with fewer than 25 employees. Importantly, many working women who participate in pension plans will never receive an income from these plans because they will leave the employer before they are able to vest in the plan. In fact, fully 25% of women age 40 and over who formerly participated in an employer pension plan do not expect to receive retirement benefits from that plan.

One indication of the adequacy of retirement income from an employer pension plan is the extent to which the retirement income from that plan replaces the worker's preretirement wages. For women age 55 and over, the wage replacement rates from pensions have been declining: prior to 1975, private pensions replaced 30% of the wages received during the year prior to retirement for those women age 55 and older receiving pensions. By 1990–1994, private pension annuities were replacing only 21% of women's preretirement wages.

The amount of lump sum distributions being paid to workers as they approach retirement provides an indicator of the extent to which these payments are adequate to provide a secure retirement income. The median payout for men in 1994 ($11,373) was over twice as much as the median payout ($5,005) received by women.

Among men and women with account balances in defined contribution plans sponsored by former employers, the median account balance for men ($20,000) is four times as great as the median account balance for women ($5,000). Among new pensioners in 1993–1994, men received median annual benefits of $9,600, whereas women received median annual benefits of $4,800. The percentage of new female private annuity recipients decreased from 35% in 1989 to 31% in 1994, largely as a result of the shift to defined contribution plans at large firms where male employees predominate.

It is clear that women need good pension coverage more than men, because (1) they have to pay for one-third more retirement years than men, (2) they start retirement with a smaller base of savings and Social Security, and (3) they are six times more likely than men to end their lives single.

## HEALTH CARE

In the past decade, a major change has occurred in our nation's health care system. Managed care is rapidly replacing traditional fee-for-service insurance plans with systems that combine delivery and financing of health care into one package. While traditional fee-for-service medicine is still an option for some Americans, more and more Medicare— and particularly Medicaid—recipients are being required to receive their health care through some form of managed care plan.

Women have unique health care needs that must be considered when assessing the impact of managed care. Women live longer than men—seven years, on average—and the income gap widens with age, creating increasing financial barriers to health care for women, who have a higher rate of chronic conditions such as arthritis, osteoporosis, diabetes, multiple sclerosis, lupus, thyroid problems, and reproductive cancers. Managed care has been successful in providing access to preventive services such as mammography, Pap smears, and bone mass testing—crucial to long-term good health for women as they age. Additionally, while men experience acute illness, the chronic nature of older women's health

problems places long-term limitations on their everyday activities.

According to OWL's 1997 Mother's Day report, *Managed Care: Risks and Opportunities for Midlife and Older Women*, managed care contains built-in incentives to underuse services, particularly specialty care, and older women are likely to have complex health conditions requiring care from a number of specialists. In a prepaid plan, the provider is at risk if the cost of treating the patient exceeds the rate at which the provider is reimbursed. Additionally, a common cost containment strategy in managed care is the restriction of access to more expensive drugs through formularies—a limited list of reimbursable medications from which doctors can prescribe. Formularies usually list multisource, often generic, drugs containing the same active ingredients in the same dosage as the original patented drugs, but generally costing less.

A study of almost 13,000 HMO patients completed for the OWL report shows that, for women, increased formulary restrictions mean more visits to physicians, emergency room visits, hospitalizations, and prescriptions. They also saw a greater number of different providers. In another example of the ways in which managed care does not meet the unique needs of women, the Congressional Budget Office reports that primary care physicians in HMOs were less likely to diagnose or appropriately treat patients with depression, primarily women. Additionally, mental health professionals in plans may not be trained in geriatric mental health, and limitations to appropriate drugs frequently prevent access to appropriate treatment for older women.

Concerns raised about managed care have heightened importance for the rapidly growing number of women in Medicare managed care: disruption of patient-provider relationships, dissatisfaction with delivery of services, difficulties gaining access to specialists, pharmaceuticals and costly treatments, and shortened hospital stays after surgery.

If not already poor, an older woman's health care costs can push her over the brink into poverty. Despite Medicare, women over 65 spend, even after paying their Medicare Part B premium, an average of $1,200 out-of-pocket annually on health care costs. Women are the primary users of long-term care, yet Medicare provides minimal assistance for home care and requires a family to spend down to near poverty to be reimbursed for institutionalized care. Spouses of institutionalized patients can also experience financial hardship, if not impoverishment.

Additionally, new Medicare "choices" recently enacted by Congress are designed for healthier and wealthier patients, and OWL believes that women receiving Medicare must not only become particularly careful consumers but work to make certain that their existing benefits are not reduced in the name of cost containment.

Women must become educated health care consumers, learning all they can about HMO plan rules, options for specialty care and grievance and appeal mechanisms when they receive inappropriate or inadequate services, and asserting their rights when necessary. More importantly, they must advocate for comprehensive reforms.

This essay has only begun to delineate and define the problems facing our nation's older women. A national agenda that includes OWL's positions can mean a healthier and more secure future for the 56 million American women 40 years of age and older.                                    [1998]

## 🦎 102

# *The Women in the Tower*

CYNTHIA RICH

In April 1982 a group of Black women demand a meeting with the Boston Housing Authority. They are women between the ages of sixty-six and eighty-one. Their lives, in the "housing tower for the elderly" where they live, are in continual danger. "You're afraid to get on the elevator and you're afraid to get off," says Mamie Buggs, sixty-six. Odella Keenan, sixty-nine, is wakened in the nights by men pounding on her apartment door. Katherine Jefferson, eighty-one, put three locks on her door,

but "I've come back to my apartment and found a group of men there eating my food."

The menace, the violence, is nothing new, they say. They have reported it before, but lately it has become intolerable. There are pictures in the *Boston Globe* of three of the women, and their eyes flash with anger. "We pay our rent, and we're entitled to some security," says Mamie Buggs. Two weeks ago, a man attacked and beat up Ida Burres, seventy-five, in the recreation room. Her head wound required forty stitches.

"I understand your desire for permanent security," says Lewis Spence, the BHA representative. "But I can't figure out any way that the BHA is going to be offering 24-hour security in an elderly development." He is a white man, probably in his thirties. His picture is much larger than the pictures of the women.

The headline in the *Boston Globe* reads, "Elderly in Roxbury building plead with BHA for 24-hour security." Ida Burres is described in the story as "a feisty, sparrow-like woman with well-cared for gray hair, cafe au lait skin and a lilting voice." The byline reads "Viola Osgood."

I feel that in my lifetime I will not get to the bottom of this story, of these pictures, of these words.

*Feisty, sparrow-like, well-cared for gray hair, cafe au lait skin, lilting voice.*

*Feisty.* Touchy, excitable, quarrelsome, like a mongrel dog. "Feisty" is the standard word in newspaper speak for an old person who says what she thinks. As you grow older, the younger person sees your strongly felt convictions or your protest against an intolerable life situation as an amusing overreaction, a defect of personality common to mongrels and old people. To insist that you are a person deepens the stigma of your Otherness. Your protest is not a specific, legitimate response to an outside threat. It is a generic and arbitrary quirkiness, coming from the queer stuff within yourself—sometimes annoying, sometimes quaint or even endearing, never, never to be responded to seriously.

*Sparrow-like.* Imagine for a moment that you have confronted those who have power over you, demanding that they do something to end the terror of your days and nights. You and other women have organized a meeting of protest. You have called the press. Imagine then opening the newspaper and seeing yourself described as "sparrow-like." That is no simple indignity, no mere humiliation. The fact that you can be described as "sparrow-like" is in part why you live in the tower, why nobody attends. Because you do not look like a natural person—that is, a young or middle-aged person—you look like a sparrow. The real sparrow is, after all, a sparrow and is seen merely as homely, but a woman who is sparrow-like is unnatural and ugly.

A white widow tells of smiling at a group of small children on the street and one of them saying, "You're ugly, ugly, ugly." It is what society has imprinted on that child's mind: to be old, and to look old, is to be ugly, so ugly that you do not deserve to live. Crow's feet. Liver spots. The media: "I'm going to wash that gray right out of my hair and wash in my 'natural' color." "Get rid of those unsightly spots." And if you were raised to believe that old is ugly, you play strange tricks in your own head. An upper middle class white woman, a woman with courage and zest for life, writes in 1982: "When we love we do not see our mates as the young view us— wrinkled, misshapen, unattractive." But then she continues: "We still retain, somewhere, the *memory* of one another as beautiful and lustful, and we see each other at our *once-best*."

Old is ugly and unnatural in a society where power is male-defined, powerlessness disgraceful. A society where natural death is dreaded and concealed, while unnatural death is courted and glorified. But old is ugliest for women. A white woman newscaster in her forties remarks to a sportscaster who is celebrating his sixtieth birthday: "What women really resent about men is that *you* get more attractive as you get older." A man is as old as he feels, a woman as old as she looks. You're ugly, ugly, ugly.

Aging has a special stigma for women. When our wombs are no longer ready for procreation, when our vaginas are no longer tight, when we no longer serve men, we are unnatural and ugly. In medical school terminology, we are a "crock"; in the language of the street, we are an "old bag." The Sanskrit word for widow is "empty." But there is more than that.

*Sparrow-like.* The association of the old woman with a bird runs deep in the male unconscious. Apparently, it flows back to a time when men acknowledged their awe of what they were outsiders to—the interconnected, inseparable mysteries of life and death, self and other, darkness and light. Life begins in genital darkness, comes into light, and returns to darkness as death. The child in the woman's body is both self and other. The power to offer the breast is the power to withhold it. The Yes and the No are inextricable. In the beginning was the Great Mother, mysteriously, powerfully connected to the wholeness of Nature and her indivisible Yeses and Nos. But for those outside the process, the oneness was baffling and intolerable, and the Great Mother was split. Men attempted to divide what they could not control—nature and women's relationship to it. The Great Mother was polarized into separate goddesses or into diametrically opposed aspects of a single goddess. The Good Mother and the Terrible Mother. The Good Mother created life, spread her bounty outward, fertilized the crops, nourished and protected, created healing potions. The Terrible Mother, the original old Witch, dealt in danger and destruction, devoured children as food for herself, concocted poisons. Wombs ≠ tomb, light ≠ darkness, other ≠ self. A world of connectedness was split down the middle.

The Terrible Mother was identified with the winged creatures that feed on mammals: vultures, ravens, owls, crows, bats. Her images in the earliest known culture of India show her as old, birdlike, hideous: "Hooded with a coif or shawl, they have high, smooth foreheads above their staring circular eye holes, their owl-beak nose and grim slit mouth. The result is terrifying . . . the face is a grinning skull."

Unable to partake of the mystery of wholeness represented by the Great Mother, men first divided her, then wrested more and more control of her divided powers. The powerful Good Mother— bounteous life-giver, creator and nurturer of others—became the custodian of children who "belong" to the man or the male state. She can no longer even bear "his" child without the guiding forceps or scalpel of a man. She is the quotidian cook (men are the great chefs) who eats only after she has served others. She is the passive dispenser—as nurse, mother, wife—of the "miracles" of modern medicine created by the brilliance of man.

The Terrible Mother—the "old Woman of the West," guardian of the dead—represented men's fear of the powerful aspect of woman as intimate not only with the mysteries of birth but also of death. Today men are the specialists of death—despite a recent study that suggests that men face natural death with much more anxiety than women do. Today male doctors oversee dying, male priests and rabbis perform the rituals of death, and even the active role of laying out the dead no longer belongs to woman (now the work of male undertakers). Woman is only the passive mourner, the helpless griever. And it is men who vie with each other to invent technologies that can bring about total death and destruction.

The Terrible Mother—the vulture or owl feeding on others—represented the fear of death, but also the fear of woman as existing not only to create and nurture others but to create and nurture her Self. Indeed, the aging woman's body is a clear reminder that women have a self that exists not only for others; it descends into her pelvis as if to claim the womb-space for its own. Woman's Self—her meeting of her own needs, seen by men as destructive and threatening—has been punished and repressed, branded "unnatural" and "unwomanly."

In this century, in rural China, they had a practice called "sunning the jinx." If a child died, or there was some similar misfortune, it was seen as the work of a jinx. The jinx was always an old, poor woman, and she was exposed to the searing heat of the summer sun until she confessed. Like the witches burned throughout Europe in the fifteenth to seventeenth centuries, she was tortured by double-think. If she died without confessing, they had eliminated the jinx. If she confessed her evil powers, she was left in the sun for three more days to "cure her." In Bali today, the Terrible Mother lingers on in magic plays, as Ranga, the witch who eats children, "a huge old woman with drooping breasts and a mat of white hair that comes down to her feet." It is a man who plays her part, and he must be old since only an old man can avoid the evil spirit of the Terrible Mother.

In present-day white culture, men's fear of the Terrible Mother is managed by denial: by insisting on the powerlessness of the old woman, her harmless absurdity and irrelevance. The dread of her power lingers, reduced to farce—as in the Hansel and Gretel story of the old witch about to devour the children until the boy destroys her, or in the comic juxtaposition of Arsenic and Old Lace. The image of her winged power persists, totally trivialized, in the silly witch flying on her broomstick, and in "old bat," "old biddy," "old hen," "old crow," "crow's feet," "old harpy." Until, in April of 1982, an old woman's self-affirmation, her rage at her disempowerment, her determination to die naturally and not at the hands of men, can be diminished to feistiness, and she can be perceived as sparrow-like.

*Sparrow-like.* Writing for white men, did Viola Osgood unconsciously wish to say, "Ida Burres is not a selfish vulture—even though she is doing what old women are not meant to do, speak for their own interests (not their children's or grandchildren's but their own). She is an innocent sparrow, frail and helpless"? Or had she herself so incorporated that demeaning image—sparrow-like—that she saw Ida Burres through those eyes? Or both?

*Well-cared for gray hair.* Is that about race? About class? An attempt to dispel the notion that a poor Black woman is unkempt? Would Viola Osgood describe a Black welfare mother in terms of her "well-groomed afro"? Or does she mean to dispel the notion that this *old* woman is unkempt? Only the young can afford to be careless about their hair, their dress. The care that the old woman takes with her appearance is not merely to reduce the stigma of ugly; often it is her most essential tactic for survival: it signals to the person who sees her, I am old, but I am not senile. My hair is gray but it is well-cared for. Because to be old is to be guilty of craziness and incapacity unless proven otherwise.

*Cafe au lait skin.* Race? Class? Age? Not dark black like Katherine Jefferson, but blackness mitigated. White male reader, who has the power to save these women's lives, you can't dismiss her as Black, poor, old. She is almost all right, she is almost white. She is Black and old, but she has something in common with the young mulatto woman whose skin you have sometimes found exotic and sensual. And she is not the power of darkness that you fear in the Terrible Mother.

*A lilting voice.* I try to read these words in a lilting voice: "I almost got my eyes knocked out. A crazy guy just came in here and knocked me down and hit me in the face. We need security." These words do not lilt to me. A woman is making a demand, speaking truth to power, affirming her right to live—Black, Old, Poor, Woman. Is the "lilting" to say, "Although her words are strong, although she is bonding with other women, she is not tough and dykey"? Is the "lilting" to say, "Although she is sparrowlike, although she is gray-haired, something of the mannerisms you find pleasing in young women remain, so do not ignore her as you routinely do old women"?

I write this not knowing whether Viola Osgood is Black or white. I know that she is a woman. And I know that it matters whether she is Black or white, that this is not a case of one size fits all. But I know that Black or white, any woman who writes news articles for the *Globe*, or for any mainstream newspaper, is mandated to write to white men, in white men's language. That any messages to women, Black or white, which challenge white men's thinking can at best only be conveyed covertly, subversively. That any messages of appeal to those white men must be phrased in ways that do not seriously threaten their assumptions, and that such language itself perpetuates the power men have assumed for themselves. And I know that Black or white, ageism blows in the wind around us and certainly through the offices of the *Globe*. I write this guessing that Viola Osgood is Black, because she has known that the story is important, cared enough to make sure the photographer was there. I write this guessing that the story might never have found its way into the *Globe* unless through a Black reporter. Later, I find out that she is Black, thirty-five.

And I think that Viola Osgood has her own story to tell. I think that I, white Jewish woman of fifty, still sorting through to find the realities beneath the lies, denials and ignorance of my lifetime of segregations, cannot write this essay. I think that even

when we try to cross the lines meant to separate us as women—old and young, Black and white, Jew and non-Jew—the seeds of division cling to our clothes. And I think this must be true of what I write now. But we cannot stop crossing, we cannot stop writing.

*Elderly in Roxbury building plead with BHA for 24-hour security.* Doubtless, Viola Osgood did not write the headline. Ten words and it contains two lies—lies that routinely obscure the struggles of old women. *Elderly.* This is not a story of elderly people, it is the story of old women, Black old women. Three-fifths of the "elderly" are women; almost all of the residents of this tower are women. An old woman has half the income of an old man. One out of three widows—women without the immediate presence of a man—lives below the official poverty line, and most women live one third of their lives as widows. In the United States, as throughout the world, old women are the poorest of the poor. Seven percent of old white men live in poverty, forty-seven percent of old Black women. "The Elderly," "Old People," "Senior Citizens," are inclusive words that blot out these differences. Old women are twice unseen—unseen because they are old, unseen because they are women. Black old women are thrice unseen. "Elderly" conveniently clouds the realities of power and economics. It clouds the convergence of racial hatred and fear, hatred and fear of the aged, hatred and fear of women. It also clouds the power of female bonding, of these women in the tower who are acting together as women for women.

*Plead.* Nothing that these women say, nothing in their photographs, suggests pleading. These women are angry, and if one can demand where there is no leverage—and one can—they are demanding. They are demanding their lives, to which they know full well they have a right. Their anger is clear, direct, unwavering. "Pleading" erases the force of their confrontation. It allows us to continue to think of old women, if we think of them at all, as meek, cowed, to be pitied, occasionally as amusingly "feisty," but not as outraged, outrageous women. Old women's anger is denied, tamed, drugged, infantilized, trivialized. And yet anger in an old woman is a remarkable act of bravery, so dangerous is her world, and her status in that world so marginal, precarious. Her anger is an act of insubordination—the refusal to accept her subordinate status even when everyone, children, men, younger women, and often other older women, assumes it. "We pay our rent, and we're entitled to some security." When will a headline tell the truth: Old, Black, poor women confront the BHA demanding 24-hour security?

*The housing tower for the elderly.* A tall building filled with women, courageous women who bond together, but who with every year are less able to defend themselves against male attack. A tower of women under siege. A ghetto within a ghetto. The white male solution to the "problem of the elderly" is to isolate the Terrible Mother.

That tower, however, is not simply architectural. Nor is the male violence an "inner city problem." Ten days later, in nearby Stoughton, a man will have beaten to death an eighty-seven-year-old white woman, leaving her body with "multiple blunt injuries around her face, head, and shoulders." This woman was not living in a housing tower for the elderly. She lived in the house where she was born. "She was very, very spry. She worked in her garden a lot and she drove her own car," reports a neighbor. She had the advantages of race, class, a small home of her own, a car of her own. Nor did she turn away from a world that rejects and demeans old women ("spry," like "feisty," is a segregating and demeaning word). At the time of her murder, she was involved in planning the anniversary celebration at her parish.

Yet she was dead for a week before anyone found her body. Why? The reporter finds it perfectly natural. "She outlived her contemporaries and her circle of immediate relatives." Of course. How natural. Unless we remember de Beauvoir: "One of the ruses of oppression is to camouflage itself behind a natural situation since, after all, one cannot revolt against nature." * How natural that young people, or even the middle aged, should have nothing in common with an old woman. Unthinkable that she should have formed friendships with anyone who was not in her or his seventies or eighties or nineties. It is

natural that without family, who must tolerate the stigma, or other old people who share the stigma, she would have no close ties. And it is natural that no woman, old or young, anywhere in the world, should be safe from male violence.

But it is not natural. It is not natural, and it is dangerous, for younger women to be divided as by a taboo from old women—to live in our own shaky towers of youth. It is intended, but it is not natural that we be ashamed of, dissociated from, our future selves, sharing men's loathing for the women we are daily becoming. It is intended, but it is not natural that we be kept ignorant of our deep bonds with old women. And it is not natural that today, as we reconnect with each other, old women are still an absence for younger women.

As a child—a golden-haired Jew in the segregated South while the barbed wire was going up around the Warsaw ghetto—I was given fairy tales to read. Among them, the story of Rapunzel, the golden-haired young woman confined to a tower by an old witch until she was rescued by a young prince. My hair darkened and now it is light again with gray. I know that I have been made to live unnaturally in a tower for most of my fifty years. My knowledge of my history—as a woman, as a lesbian, as a light-skinned woman in a world of dark-skinned women, as the Other in a Jew-hating world— shut out. My knowledge of my future—as an old woman—shut out.

Today I reject those mythic opposites: young/ old, light/darkness, life/death, other/self, Rapunzel/ Witch, Good Mother/Terrible Mother. As I listen to the voices of the old women of Warren Tower, and of my aging self, I know that I have always been aging, always been dying. Those voices speak of wholeness: To nurture Self = to defy those who endanger that Self. To declare the I of my unique existence = to assert the We of my connections with other women. To accept the absolute rightness of my natural death = to defend the absolute value of my life. To affirm the mystery of my daily dying and the mystery of my daily living = to challenge men's violent cheapening of both.

But I cannot hear these voices clearly if I am still afraid of the old witch, the Terrible Mother in myself, or if I am estranged from the real old women of

---

*Simone de Beauvoir, *The Ethics of Ambiguity* (New York: Citadel, 1948), p. 83.

this world. For it is not the wicked witch who keeps Rapunzel in her tower. It is the prince and our divided selves.

Note: There was no follow-up article on the women of the tower, but Ida Burres, Mamie Buggs, Mary Gordon, Katherine Jefferson, Odella Keenan, and the other women of Warren Tower, did win what they consider to be adequate security—"of course, it is never all that you could wish," said Vallie Burton, President of the Warren Tower Association. They won because of their own bonding, their demands, and also, no doubt, because of Viola Osgood.                                                      [1983]

## 🌿 103

## *The Day Nani Fell and I Wasn't There to Catch Her*

ANNA MARIE QUEVEDO

Nana
lives alone in Echo Park
   Allison Street
one block above the Sunset

Sundays
before glaucoma clouded eyes
ruined her independence
she went to mass

sometimes at La Placita
once in awhile Saint Vibiana's
occasionally Saint Anthony's
every single Sunday
every novena Friday

my nana
at the bus stop
waiting patiently for the #10 going downtown
arriving amid clouds of stinking gasoline fumes

   (she'd complain to me
    "Los Angeles is an ugly city"
     she wished she'd never left Silver.)

after church
shopping at the Grand Central
another walk to the bus stop
#28 going home

suddenly she stumbled!
hand stretched out to break the fall
too late
collarbone snapped, shoulder blade broken
downtown L.A. strangers hardly noticed

Nana
went to a medi-cal hungry doctor
told her it was only a sprain and didn't set it
now her shoulder is slumped
her arm permanently crippled

in Silver City someone would have softened the fall
                                                      [1982]

## 🌿 104

## *Wonderful Older Women*

RUTH DREAMDIGGER

*Wonderful, Wonderful Older Women*
(To the tune, "Wonderful, Wonderful Copenhagen")

Wonderful, wonderful older women,
Wonderful women are we.
And we're here to say that we're on our way
Breaking chains and flying free.

We are the women who've borne the children,
Cooked and cleaned and cried.
But we're learning how to be changing now,
And we're wonderful women, wonderful women,
Wonderful women, we're WOW!!

   The young person yells, "Go to it, grandma!" as I ride my bicycle along the city street. "But you're too old to wear your hair that way," says the precocious four-year-old, squinting at my straight, grey hair, cut in a buster-brown style. "You look so young," says the well-meaning friend.

   To all of them I feel like shouting, "No! No! No! Stop the stereotyping! Stop the categorizing! Stop the patronizing! And stop devaluing the years of my life!" For these are some of the ways in which people, confused by societal myths, try to smother me in my 57 years.

With 28 years of mothering behind me (loving, thinking, planning for others), I figure that I have about 28 years of dream-digging ahead of me. (I chose the name Dreamdigger because it tells me who I am, just as names were originally meant to do. I am a dreamer in two ways: I try to understand my sleeping dreams, and I also have a life-long dream of a loving society. I am a digger into my own personality, into whatever work I do, and also into the earth.) I don't relish society dragging me down by loading old patterns on me. Realistically I know that the fight to be myself—not "grandma," not "mother," not "little old lady in tennis shoes" will take up much of the energy of those 28 years.

History (or herstory, as I say now) is powerfully against me. Down through the centuries older women have been stereotyped and persecuted just as have been Blacks and Jews. As termagants, gossips, witches, they have been dunked, burned, stoned. As mothers to grown men, grandmas to young people, ancient aunts, sweet old ladies, they have been deposited in rocking chairs, kept in up-stairs rooms, patronized and driven to depression and alcoholism. (I heard on the radio just today: "Grandmothers don't have to do anything. They just have to be there.") They have been feared for their power and ridiculed for their ineptitude. Occasionally they have been revered as Wise Old Women.

The rising tide of expectations has caught up older women just as it has caught up other oppressed groups. A mind-boggling thought has entered our heads: "*We don't have to take the roles assigned to us!*" Freed from the straight-jacket in which motherhood held many of us, we are looking warily at the new garment which society holds out to us. No, thank you kindly, we are not going to be little old ladies!

So, what are we going to be then? We are going to be artists, workers, musicians, scholars, revolutionaries, speakers, organizers, travelers, lovers, gardeners, writers. In short, we will do everything that everybody else does (except that maybe we won't do quite so much laundry, house-cleaning, and child-care!).

How will we do it? First of all, we will search for ourselves beneath the layers that have been laid upon us as children, as adolescents, as wives and mothers, as single women. We will use for that purpose every tool that seems right for us—consciousness raising, professional counseling (warily), peer counseling, dream groups, and whatever else our fertile brains discover.

Secondly, we will band together for support, for the exchange of ideas, and for **empowerment.** I write that in bold letters because it is hard for me to think of having power—in my own life, in the world of ideas, in the effort to shake up the patriarchal structure—but **empowerment** is what I work toward, not *in spite of* being an older woman, but *because* I am an older woman with the variety of strengths I have acquired in my life struggle.

In the Movement for a New Society,* that banding together has come about through a collective known as WOW (Wonderful Older Women). As I think back to those first rather sporadic meetings, I am amazed at the number of ways in which we showed our lack of confidence in ourselves and in each other. But we persevered, knowing that we did have it within ourselves to be supportive of each other. As we taped our herstories in those early days, I noted that one woman spoke only about her fam-

---

*The Movement for a New Society (1971–1988) was a nationwide network of small groups working for basic social change. Although non-religious, it had a strong Quaker influence.

MNS members believed that the process of achieving a goal was as important as the goal itself, and that the personal and the political were closely entwined. Most members lived communally and did their political work in small groups known as collectives. Although many non-violent actions were carried out (e.g., blockade of arms shipments to Pakistan; opposition to Limerick nuclear plant), MNS was best known for its training sessions, which were attended by people from all over the world. Several people who were MNS members continue to focus on that activity.

MNS members tended to be prolific writers. Probably the most widely read book is *Resource Manual for a Living Revolution* (fondly nicknamed *The Monster Manual*). A spin-off of MNS, New Society Publishers, P.O. Box 582, Santa Cruz, CA 95061-0582, continues to publish books related to non-violent social change.

ily, not one word about herself. We brainstormed the negative ideas that we feel other people have of us, and then we brainstormed the qualities that we know we have as vibrant, caring, thoughtful human beings. We discussed papers that had been written by other members of the MNS community. We planned a picnic together.

But I think the event that either marked or evoked the change in us from a collection of frightened and frustrated individuals to a collective of women who saw themselves as a potential force in the community was a weekend retreat after we had been meeting for several months. Here was a group of women who had spent almost all of their lives nourishing and supporting other people. Here we were all together, without any children to nourish and support, without any men to nourish and support, and we did an amazing job of nourishing and supporting each other. When we drove back together, we knew that a change had occurred. Although we didn't become *officially* an MNS collective until many months later, we ourselves knew from that weekend that we were indeed a collective of Wonderful Older Women.

We decided to set ourselves the task of writing. Most of us have tremendous blocks about seeing ourselves as writers. But by using a process of group writing developed by some people within the MNS community, we are getting over that hurdle. Our paper will be about social change from our felt needs as older women. We have brainstormed our herstories, our struggles, our oppressions, and we have started to talk and listen in small groups, which will then give us encouragement as each puts together the thoughts that have emerged. When we have completed the writing on these three sections, we will work together on strategy.

In the fall the Continental Walk for Disarmament and Social Justice came through Philadelphia. One of our members was on the organizing committee and asked WOW to lead the singing. We felt a little uneasy, but not undone, to find that we were preceded by professional singers! But it was soon apparent that we were a hit. With our arms around each other, supporting each other both physically and psychologically, we sang with such thorough enjoyment of this new experience that everyone caught our enthusiasm. It was our vitality that carried the occasion, vitality that has much more to do with lack of fear than with age.

Our most recent challenge was a speak-out to MNS women about the ways in which we have to deal with discrimination even in this revolutionary community. (In a speak-out, the members of an oppressed group speak their feelings freely without response by the listeners. After the speak-out, the listeners can meet in small groups to express their feelings out of hearing of the speak-out members.) We often feel invisible, are not taken seriously. We have difficulty in joining communal households. The struggles of our lives are not acknowledged, our efforts to rid ourselves of old survival patterns are unappreciated, our achievements are unrecognized. And in ways more subtle than in the world at large, we are still stereotyped, categorized, patronized, and the years of our lives treated like a disease. But the younger MNS women did hear us and did begin to understand the importance of coming to terms with us, with their own mothers, and with the fact that they, too, will sometime be older. (The MNS community has been the best growing place we have seen for older women, but, in the words of the feminist song, "We still ain't satisfied.")

Our next effort will be responsibility for the Orientation Weekend, which Philadelphia MNS schedules every month. People who share in this experience learn a little about MNS analysis, vision and strategy, living in community, macro-analysis, training and action. It is the first time that we have worked together as organizers of more than an evening meeting.

These are the visible actions we are taking, but the psychological strength we have received from each other since the retreat is most important of all. Older women often support and comfort each other in times of trial. It is less often that they have supported each other to be assertive in getting what they want, need and deserve. We remain individuals and rejoice in our individuality. This is important because society tends to lump all older women together in one big blob of a stereotype. We encourage each other to stand up for our rights, to be different when we want to be, to try new jobs, to travel, to lead workshops.

We constantly remind each other that the phrase "personal is political" is particularly relevant for us. Each time we show that our old age is a fine time of life, we give a younger woman hope and energy. Each time we disprove a myth about older women, we are performing a political act. For myths about the way groups of people *should* be are glue that holds together society when it is not truly functional. Each time we refuse to be "mother" to a grown person, we are undermining the structure that imprisons women and maintains men in false responsibility patterns. Mothers can be considered one of the classes of people on whom capitalism depends. Men who carry huge amounts of responsibility (and in a patriarchal system, almost every man feels that he does) must have someone to take care of them, someone with whom they can be little boys. Each time we refuse to absorb the tensions of dog-eat-dog economy, we throw a monkey wrench into the capitalist society, which, with its emphasis on competition, is certain to create tremendous pressures. When women refuse to take the mother role, the system will have to change to accommodate reasonable sharing of responsibility. The secretary on the job and the wife or mother at home are the ones who soften life for those who function within it, whether they be a busy executive, ambitious young man, or worker bedevilled by his foreman. It is hard for us as older women to stop being absorbers because we have done it for so long, and because it is so closely

associated with love. But as we see more clearly how we are used, we can say "No."

Today while I waited for the trolley, I sang this little ditty to myself. Maybe it will feel good to you, as it did to me.

I'm gonna free myself to sing about myself
Sing about myself, sing about myself,
I'm gonna free myself to sing about myself,
For singing is what I need for me.

I also decided that I needed to cry, dance, think, shout and laugh about myself. How about you?

### SUGGESTIONS FOR OURSELVES AS OLDER WOMEN

Affirm our past and plan our future.
Take care of our bodies.
Respect our capacity for clear thinking.
Recognize the unique beauty of older women.
Form a support-action group with older women, but form friendships in a wide age spectrum.
Expect to be taken seriously.
Be ready for new ideas and new loyalties.
Expect sexual and sensual pleasure.
Undertake some structure or discipline in which personal growth will take place.
Look for new areas of competence.
Please ourselves in clothing, habits and life styles even if (especially if) our choices do not fit the usual image of the older woman.          [1977]

# Rights and Choices: Reproductive Health

The *Roe v. Wade* decision of 1973 legalized abortion in the United States, guaranteeing for the first time a woman's right to choose between pregnancy and abortion. Since this landmark decision, however, women's right to a safe and legal abortion has been steadily eroded, as documented in the introduction to this part.

The controversy about abortion reflects an often simplistic attempt to pit the rights of women against the rights of the fetus. Ellen Willis argues that the "right to life" position is flawed because it is based on the assumption that fetal rights are separate from women's rights. Commenting on college students' positions on this issue, Laura Wells observes that many students have been influenced by anti-choice positions, even when they support general feminist ideals. These two pieces convey the complex nature of the abortion rights controversy.

Anti-abortion legislation, particularly parental consent and notification laws that require teenage women to obtain a parent's approval for abortion, have limited women's right to abortion. Mike Males compares the assumptions about the lives of adolescent females on which some of these laws are based with the reality of their lives. The devastating effects of such legislation on young women are explored in "Abortion Denied." William Bell provides a personal narrative of the tragic consequences of Indiana's parental consent laws. His daughter, Becky, was 18 years old when she died from an infection resulting from an illegal abortion. Rather than risk her parents' disappointment by telling them about her pregnancy, Becky had chosen to obtain an abortion on her own.

The concept of reproductive rights extends beyond the right to safe, legal abortions and includes women's choices and rights regarding all aspects of reproductive health. Ruth Hubbard shows that pregnant women's rights are often subordinated to those of the fetus and argues for meeting the economic, social, and educational needs of women and their children. Iris Lopez focuses on the social, historical, and personal conditions that shape, influence, and constrain Puerto Rican women's fertility decisions with respect to sterilization.

Feminists have proposed reproductive rights agendas that address the needs of all women. The agenda designed by Kathryn Kolbert, a lawyer active in defense of women's rights to choose, conceives of reproductive rights broadly. She emphasizes not only the legality of abortion but access to abortion, birth control, and other reproductive health services. Kolbert's agenda also recognizes that for women to make reproductive choices, we must have economic equality and sexual freedom.

## ❧ 105

# *Abortion:*
# *Is a Woman a Person?*

ELLEN WILLIS

If propaganda is as central to politics as I think, the opponents of legal abortion have been winning a psychological victory as important as their tangible gains. Two years ago, abortion was almost always discussed in feminist terms—as a political issue affecting the condition of women. Since then, the grounds of the debate have shifted drastically; more and more, the right-to-life movement has succeeded in getting the public and the media to see abortion as an abstract moral issue having solely to do with the rights of fetuses. Though every poll shows that most Americans favor legal abortion, it is evident that many are confused and disarmed, if not convinced, by the antiabortionists' absolutist fervor. No one likes to be accused of advocating murder. Yet the "pro-life" position is based on a crucial fallacy—that the question of fetal rights can be isolated from the question of women's rights.

Recently, Garry Wills wrote a piece suggesting that liberals who defended the snail-darter's right to life and opposed the killing in Vietnam should condemn abortion as murder. I found this notion breathtaking in its illogic. Environmentalists were protesting not the "murder" of individual snail-darters but the practice of wiping out entire species of organisms to gain a short-term economic benefit; most people who opposed our involvement in Vietnam did so because they believed the United States was waging an aggressive, unjust and/or futile war. There was no inconsistency in holding such positions and defending abortion on the grounds that women's welfare should take precedence over fetal life. To claim that three very different issues, each with its own complicated social and political context, all came down to a simple matter of preserving life was to say that all killing was alike and equally indefensible regardless of circumstance. (Why, I wondered, had Wills left out the destruction of hap-

less bacteria by penicillin?) But aside from the general mushiness of the argument, I was struck by one peculiar fact: Wills had written an entire article about abortion without mentioning women, feminism, sex, or pregnancy.

Since the feminist argument for abortion rights still carries a good deal of moral and political weight, part of the antiabortionists' strategy has been to make an end run around it. Although the mainstream of the right-to-life movement is openly opposed to women's liberation, it has chosen to make its stand on the abstract "pro-life" argument. That emphasis has been reinforced by the movement's tiny left wing, which opposes abortion on pacifist grounds and includes women who call themselves "feminists for life." A minority among pacifists as well as right-to-lifers, this group nevertheless serves the crucial function of making opposition to abortion respectable among liberals, leftists, and moderates disinclined to sympathize with a right-wing crusade. Unlike most right-to-lifers, who are vulnerable to charges that their reverence for life does not apply to convicted criminals or Vietnamese peasants, antiabortion leftists are in a position to appeal to social conscience—to make analogies, however facile, between abortion and napalm. They disclaim any opposition to women's rights, insisting rather that the end cannot justify the means—murder is murder.

Well, isn't there a genuine moral issue here? If abortion *is* murder, how can a woman have the right to it? Feminists are often accused of evading this question, but in fact an evasion is built into the question itself. Most people understand "Is abortion murder?" to mean "Is the fetus a person?" But fetal personhood is ultimately as inarguable as the existence of God; either you believe in it or you don't. Putting the debate on this plane inevitably leads to the nonconclusion that it is a matter of one person's conscience against another's. From there, the discussion generally moves on to broader issues: whether laws defining the fetus as a person violate the separation of church and state; or conversely, whether people who believe an act is murder have not only the right but the obligation to prevent it. Unfortunately, amid all this lofty philosophizing, the concrete, human reality of the pregnant woman's dilemma gets lost, and with it an essential ingredient of the moral question.

Murder, as commonly defined, is killing that is unjustified, willful, and malicious. Most people would agree, for example, that killing in defense of one's life or safety is not murder. And most would accept a concept of self-defense that includes the right to fight a defensive war or revolution in behalf of one's independence or freedom from oppression. Even pacifists make moral distinctions between defensive violence, however deplorable, and murder; no thoughtful pacifist would equate Hitler's murder of the Jews with the Warsaw Ghetto rebels' killing of Nazi troops. The point is that it's impossible to judge whether an act is murder simply by looking at the act, without considering its context. Which is to say that it makes no sense to discuss whether abortion is murder without considering why women have abortions and what it means to force women to bear children they don't want.

We live in a society that defines child rearing as the mother's job; a society in which most women are denied access to work that pays enough to support a family, child-care facilities they can afford, or any relief from the constant, daily burdens of motherhood; a society that forces mothers into dependence on marriage or welfare and often into permanent poverty; a society that is actively hostile to women's ambitions for a better life. Under these conditions the unwillingly pregnant woman faces a terrifying loss of control over her fate. Even if she chooses to give up the baby, unwanted pregnancy is in itself a serious trauma. There is no way a pregnant woman can passively let the fetus live; she must create and nurture it with her own body, in a symbiosis that is often difficult, sometimes dangerous, always uniquely intimate. However gratifying pregnancy may be to a woman who desires it, for the unwilling it is literally an invasion—the closest analogy is to the difference between lovemaking and rape. Nor is there such a thing as foolproof contraception. Clearly, abortion is by normal standards an act of self-defense.

Whenever I make this case to a right-to-lifer, the exchange that follows is always substantially the same:

*RTL:* If a woman chooses to have sex, she should be willing to take the consequences. We must all be responsible for our actions.

*EW:* Men have sex, without having to "take the consequences."

*RTL:* You can't help that—it's biology.

*EW:* You don't think a woman has as much right as a man to enjoy sex? Without living in fear that one slip will transform her life?

*RTL:* She has no right to selfish pleasure at the expense of the unborn.

It would seem, then, that the nitty-gritty issue in the abortion debate is not life but sex. If the fetus is sacrosanct, it follows that women must be continually vulnerable to the invasion of their bodies and loss of their freedom and independence—unless they are willing to resort to the only perfectly reliable contraceptive, abstinence. This is precisely the "solution" right-to-lifers suggest, usually with a touch of glee; as Representative Elwood Rudd once put it, "If a woman has a right to control her own body, let her exercise control before she gets pregnant." A common ploy is to compare fucking to overeating or overdrinking, the idea being that pregnancy is a just punishment, like obesity or cirrhosis.

In 1979 it is depressing to have to insist that sex is not an unnecessary, morally dubious self-indulgence but a basic human need, no less for women than for men. Of course, for heterosexual women giving up sex also means doing without the love and companionship of a mate. (Presumably, married women who have had all the children they want are supposed to divorce their husbands or convince them that celibacy is the only moral alternative.) "Freedom" bought at such a cost is hardly freedom at all and certainly not equality—no one tells men that if they aspire to some measure of control over their lives, they are welcome to neuter themselves and become social isolates. The don't-have-sex argument is really another version of the familiar antifeminist dictum that autonomy and femaleness—that is, female sexuality—are incompatible; if you choose the first, you lose the second. But to pose this choice is not only inhumane; it is as deeply disingenuous as "Let them eat cake." No one, least of all the antiabortion movement, expects or wants significant numbers of women to give up sex and marriage. Nor are most right-to-lifers willing to allow abortion for rape victims. When all the cant about "responsibility" is stripped away, what the right-to-life position comes down to is, if the effect of prohibiting abortion is to keep women slaves to their biology, so be it.

 In their zeal to preserve fetal life at all costs, antiabortionists are ready to grant fetuses more legal protection than people. If a man attacks me and I kill him, I can plead self-defense without having to prove that I was in danger of being killed rather than injured, raped, or kidnapped. But in the annual congressional battle over what if any exceptions to make to the Medicaid abortion ban, the House of Representatives has bitterly opposed the funding of abortions for any reason but to save the pregnant woman's life. Some right-to-lifers argue that even the danger of death does not justify abortion; others have suggested "safeguards" like requiring two or more doctors to certify that the woman's life is at least 50 percent threatened. Antiabortionists are forever worrying that any exception to a total ban on abortion will be used as a "loophole": better that any number of women should ruin their health or even die than that one woman should get away with not having a child "merely" because she doesn't want one. Clearly this mentality does not reflect equal concern for all life. Rather, antiabortionists value the lives of fetuses above the lives and welfare of women, because at bottom they do not concede women the right to an active human existence that transcends their reproductive function. Years ago, in an interview with Paul Krassner in *The Realist*, Ken Kesey declared himself against abortion. When Krassner asked if his objection applied to victims of rape, Kesey replied—I may not be remembering the exact words, but I will never forget the substance—"Just because another man planted the seed, that's no reason to destroy the crop." * To this

day I have not heard a more eloquent or chilling metaphor for the essential premise of the right-to-life movement: that a woman's excuse for being is her womb. It is an outrageous irony that antiabortionists are managing to pass off this profoundly immoral idea as a noble moral cause.

The conservatives who dominate the right-to-life movement have no real problem with the antifeminism inherent in their stand; their evasion of the issue is a matter of public relations. But the politics of antiabortion leftists are a study in self-contradiction: in attacking what they see as the violence of abortion, they condone and encourage violence against women. Forced childbearing does violence to a woman's body and spirit, and it contributes to other kinds of violence: deaths from illegal abortion; the systematic oppression of mothers and women in general; the poverty, neglect, and battering of unwanted children; sterilization abuse.

Radicals supposedly believe in attacking a problem at its roots. Yet surely it is obvious that restrictive laws do not keep women from seeking abortions; they just create an illicit, dangerous industry. The only way to drastically reduce the number of abortions is to invent safer, more reliable contraceptives, ensure universal access to all birth control methods, eliminate sexual ignorance and guilt, and change the social and economic conditions that make motherhood a trap. Anyone who is truly committed to fostering life should be fighting for women's liberation instead of harassing and disrupting abortion clinics (hardly a nonviolent tactic, since it threatens the safety of patients). The "feminists for life" do talk a lot about ending the oppression that drives so many women to abortion; in practice, however, they are devoting all their energy to increasing it.

Despite its numerical insignificance, the antiabortion left epitomizes the hypocrisy of the right-to-life crusade. Its need to wrap misogyny in the rhetoric of social conscience and even feminism is actually a perverse tribute to the women's movement; it is no longer acceptable to declare openly that women deserve to suffer for the sin of Eve. I suppose that's progress—not that it does the victims of the Hyde Amendment much good.        [1981]

---

*A reader later sent me a copy of the Kesey interview. The correct quotation is "You don't plow under the corn because the seed was planted with a neighbor's shovel."

# 🌿 106

# *In Response to a "Moderate" View of Abortion*

LAURA WELLS

As a teacher of an introductory women's studies course at a public, four-year college for nearly five years, I have been impressed by students' overall enthusiasm and receptivity to feminist principles. Many students embrace feminist perspectives on work and family, health, law, and the media. In discussions of abortion, however, I can detect the success of the anti-abortion movement in blurring the issues and putting advocates for choice on the defensive. This is evident when meaningful abortion discussion is derailed by a statement that is offered as if it is a reasonable compromise between two extremist positions: "I think abortion should be legal, but I'm against it when women use it for birth control."

One glaring problem with the statement is, of course, that abortion *is* a means of birth control. For what other purpose might women "use" abortion? Recreation? Political gain? Social status? Personal enrichment? Obviously not. Because our reproductive capabilities cannot be separated from other aspects of our lives, women sometimes terminate unwanted pregnancies. Studies show that this has been true throughout history, and worldwide. We are fortunate when we have contraceptive options as well. However, there are virtually *no* circumstances under which women have absolute control over contraception/conception. The "compromise" argument suggests that any woman who wants to avoid pregnancy can do so if only her will is great enough. To see the fallacy in this view, one has only to consider the many familiar problems with contraceptive methods.

To be effective, all contraceptive methods require that users understand human reproduction and the functions of the various contraceptive methods. Further, women need to know which methods are appropriate and how to use them. Our class discussions reveal that this information is by no means universally accessible to women, either in schools or in their communities. When they do gain access to contraception, cost often affects whether it is used reliably.

There are few methods over which women have absolute control. Most require some degree of co-operation by sexual partners. Inequality and abuses of power, in forms ranging from rape to ridicule, threats to promises, readily affect contraceptive use. And sometimes contraceptives simply fail, even under the best of circumstances. In *Taking Chances: Abortion and the Decision Not to Contracept*, Kristin Luker demonstrates that in our culture, where motherhood is idealized and sex romanticized, women don't always think clearly about long-term effects and take risks they may later regret.[1] For all of these reasons, unwanted pregnancies do occur in women's lives, sometimes more than once.

Students who maintain that abortion should be legal, but oppose abortion when it's "used for birth control," reveal their ignorance of the various conditions that contribute to unwanted pregnancies. Fortunately, education can replace existing myths and misconceptions with an understanding of these issues.

However, these students' view also reflects a terrible assumption: that someone can determine whether women are *deserving* of abortion alternatives based on their (presumed) actions/conditions at the time of impregnation. Does this mean that a woman could be excused from a "the-condom-broke" kind of unwanted pregnancy, although another is punished for pregnancy that results from "he'd leave me if I made him use one"? Is a first abortion tolerable on the basis that "we all make mistakes," while subsequent abortions are judged to be evidence of a woman's utter negligence? Are we really willing to return to the old notion that pregnancy is a suitable punishment for "bad girls"?

Contempt for women who "use abortion as birth control" is not only deeply woman-blaming, but

---

[1] Kristin Luker, *Taking Chances: Abortion and the Decision Not to Contracept* (Berkeley: University of California Press, 1975).

also falsely self-righteous. Isn't it really a thinly veiled justification for rejecting another woman's need for an abortion, while preserving the right for oneself?

For all of these reasons, the students' statement is not a compromise position. It is neither reasonable nor logical, but disguises age-old misogyny as moderation, and deceives the speaker into thinking that her statement is pro-choice when, in fact, it is profoundly threatening to the reproductive rights of all women.                                    [1992]

## 🌿 107

# Parental Consent Laws: Are They a "Reasonable Compromise"?

MIKE MALES

Laws requiring parental consent before a girl under age 18 can obtain an abortion have won endorsement by the U.S. Supreme Court, the U.S. Senate, all three presidential candidates, 20 state legislatures and 80 percent of the American public—and are even seen by many pro-abortion choice adults as a "reasonable compromise."

Yet reaffirmation of parental consent laws is by far the most disturbing and intrusive element of the Supreme Court's June 30 [1992] ruling allowing new curbs on abortion, one that demonstrates the mechanism by which abortion rights can be summarily removed from vulnerable populations.

Parental consent laws authorize an outside party—a parent, or a judge if the girl goes to court to obtain an abortion without telling her parents—to force a teenage girl to bear a child against her will. Once another person can decide when a female must bear a child, the 1973 *Roe vs. Wade* decision guaranteeing access to abortion is abrogated. It becomes simply a matter of how many barriers can be raised to deny abortion to the only women who stand to lose the right in any case—the young and the poor.

Parental consent is already the most popular restriction enacted by states and Congress. In upholding such laws, justices again swept aside monumental realities regarding abortion patterns among teenagers, the family conditions of girls who cannot inform their parents, and the miserable experiences of states with such laws.

The court's ruling embodies diametrically opposing views of family life. In striking down spousal notice laws, justices recognized America's epidemic of domestic abuse and the plight of wives who cannot reveal abortion plans to their husbands for fear of violence and alienation. In upholding parental notice and consent, justices painted an idyllic portrait of loving family concern, ignoring that these same violent, disowning husbands can also be violent, disowning fathers.

Thus seven wealthy justices, averaging well over age 60, ignored the day-to-day realities of millions of girls such as L.V., a 16-year-old Montanan with abusive, alcoholic, estranged parents; impoverished, a prior victim of incest, pregnant by a 24-year-old man she planned to marry in an effort to escape harsh conditions but who had left town.

Montana has no parental consent law. Had such law been in effect, L.V. would have risked violent abuse by her parents when told of her pregnancy. The local judge, an anti-abortion fundamentalist, almost certainly would have refused any petition for her to obtain an abortion without parental consent. Thus her choices: self-abort, obtain an illegal abortion, have the child or leave school on a weekday to drive hours to seek an amenable judge.

The gasoline industry has been the chief beneficiary of parental consent laws. After Massachusetts passed such a law in 1981, Brandeis University researchers found 1,000 Massachusetts girls traveling to nearby states for abortions every year. Minnesota's similar law drove hundreds of girls to clinics in Fargo, N.D., and Wisconsin.

Parental consent laws highlight the cruelty of anti-abortion regulation; the rich and mobile retain the ability to go to other states or countries; the young and the poor are forced into untenable positions. The effect of such laws is to demand a useless, stressful judicial runaround for girls already facing difficult situations.

## POVERTY, RAPE, ABUSE

Supporters of parental consent laws ignore the grim conditions of millions of youth. Six million children do not live with parents, according to the Casey Foundation. Four million children and adolescents were added to poverty rolls during the '80s. Three million children are physically abused, sexually abused or neglected every year. The National Women's Study indicates 500,000 to 1 million children and adolescents were raped in 1990; offender profiles show 90 percent of all rapists are adults. A recent Washington study shows two-thirds of all pregnant teenagers were sexually abused during childhood or adolescence, many by parents.

Impoverished, abused girls are by far the most likely to become pregnant. Having ignored worsening childhood poverty, abuse and health care which contribute to adolescent pregnancy and abortion, politicians now back harsh restrictive substitutes for genuine initiatives to help the young.

Surveys of Montana abortion clinics show that three-fourths of all minor girls voluntarily choose to include a parent in abortion decisions. Those who do not (nearly all of whom involve another trusted adult—an aunt, older sister, family friend) are overwhelmingly from homes where parents are violent or rigidly judgmental. Parental consent laws function to further traumatize that population of girls already subjected to childhood's worst abuses.

Parental involvement laws do not promote parental involvement. In Massachusetts and Minnesota, 40 to 45 percent of all girls (many after judge-shopping) obtain abortions without parental notice, a level higher than in Montana (24 percent), which has no law. "The law has, more than anything, disrupted and harmed families" and "can provoke violence," U.S. District Judge Donald Alsop wrote in a compelling opinion ignored by the Supreme Court.

In briefs filed in Judge Alsop's court reviewing parental consent and notification laws, Minnesota and Massachusetts judges recounted harassed, terrified, angry girls forced to reveal intimate details of their lives in intimidating court proceedings. "They find it a very nerve-racking experience," wrote one judge; another described "incredible amounts of stress" shown in "tone of voice, tenor of voice, shaking, wringing of hands," even physical illness. Judges, some personally opposed to abortion, unanimously agreed parental consent laws are useless and punitive.

While the Supreme Court upheld parental and judicial "rights" to decide that a minor girl must have a baby, there is no mandate that parents or the court pay her pregnancy expenses and the 18-year, $200,000 cost of raising a child she did not want to have—one an adult woman would have been allowed to abort. Bizarrely, a judge who finds a girl too immature for an abortion may force her to be a mother.

## ADULT-TEEN SEX

There is, further, no requirement that the male partner in "teenage" abortions face similar sanctions. The reason: It is *adult men*, not teenage boys, who cause or collaborate in the vast majority of all "teenage" pregnancies and abortions, including the 5 percent of all "teen" pregnancies that result from rape. Vital and health statistics records indicate 90 percent of all pregnancies among girls under age 18 are caused by adult men over age 18, and more than half by men over age 20. The "adult-teen" pregnancy and abortion reality is one lawmakers and justices refuse to face.

Thus the only ones left to punish are young girls. And yet, minor girls are hardly the cause of the prevalence of abortion that anti-abortion forces find so offensive. Only one out of 10 abortions is performed on a girl under age 18; less than 2 percent of all abortions in the country involve a pregnancy caused by a couple in which *both* partners are under age 18. The young, like the poor, are targeted for oppressive restrictions because they can't fight back.

Punishment appears, in the end, both the motive and result of parental consent laws. In a . . . *Dateline* NBC report, the legislative sponsor of Ohio's parental notification law equated a pregnant teenage girl with a criminal who commits theft or vandalism. The laws' chief effects are delay, fear, stress, expense, hazard, forced motherhood and—now that the Supreme Court has invited states to experiment with harsher restrictions against teenagers and other vulnerable women—a return to dangerous illicit and self-induced measures.                [1992]

## ✸ 108

# *Testimony of William Bell (on Raised Bill #5447)*

CONNECTICUT STATE LEGISLATURE

My name is Bill Bell and I reside in Indianapolis, Indiana, with my wife Karen and my 20 year old son Bill.

I submit this testimony with mixed emotions: dreading to relive the death of my daughter but also realizing a responsibility to others, that the punitive and restrictive laws that are being heard before this committee are understood by all. In writing and in theory these laws appear reasonable and safe. But in practice they are punishing.

My daughter Becky made a mistake and became pregnant. Parental consent laws, very similar to those you are considering today, dictated that in order to terminate her pregnancy she must obtain approval of her parents, petition the courts, or travel to another state that would allow her a safe clinical abortion, *or* seek back-alley assistance. She died [from] an illegal abortion.

In confiding with her best friend she said, "I don't want to disappoint my mother and dad, I love them so much."

Knowing my daughter, I believe that the judicial option would have been too intimidating, given her desperate emotional state. She would also have been faced with the prospect of appearing before a pro-life judge. Hardly a reasonable option considering the fact that she had decided to terminate her pregnancy. She chose the last option available to her, an illegal abortion.

Unfortunately, we have been unable to piece together all the circumstances and today we struggle with the question, why did our daughter have to endure such mental torture in making what turned out to be her final decision?

She was intelligent enough to pursue her options, yet we live with the pain of knowing our daughter was desperate and alone, and because of these punishing and restrictive laws, she further compounded her initial mistake with another, and paid for it with her life.

My daughter was a quality child. She was raised in a functional family environment and was encouraged to develop her own thinking and reasoning skills. Yet, in her time of crisis, others had dictated how she must react, thus denying her a legitimate option that all women should enjoy, the right of self-determination.

Had our daughter come to us, her mother and I would have counseled her, made her aware of all her options, the circumstances and the consequences, to the best of our ability. But I can state emphatically that the final decision would have been hers.

As it stands today, legislators, judges, self-appointed moralists, and parents are making the decisions for these young women, allowing little or no input from them. Decisions that are clearly along the lines of their own political, moral or religious beliefs. How can we legislate or dictate that families communicate? How can we dictate to people how they must act or react in a time of crisis?

I realize a great number of young women are going to their parents for counsel and for this I am grateful. Since the death of our daughter, my wife and I have counseled several young women and have been fortunate to get the parents involved. But what about the young woman who doesn't want to disappoint her family?

If I understand correctly, the legislation before you offers no accommodation for a real life situation like that of a Becky Bell. Nor does it consider the young lady from a dysfunctional home who may fear her physical well-being. These laws speak to theories and hypotheticals, they do not address the real life issues taking place today. I submit to you, these punitive and restrictive laws being considered, if enacted, will serve to further isolate the young women of this state. They will serve as a punishment to those who have made a mistake. In the interest of political gain and in the name of God, my daughter was punished.

Others took it upon themselves to decide my daughter's fate, thus denying her a safe option, the best care. Their theories and political stance were placed ahead of and valued more than the life of my daughter.

These laws clearly denied her a safe and reasonable option. And because she had decided to terminate her pregnancy, forced her into making a fatal mistake. My beautiful Becky Bell died on September 16th, 1988.

My daughter's death *will* count for something. She was somebody, somebody beautiful. I will not sit idly by and not speak out to others that could face the same torment that the Bell family now lives with. Not as long as there are those who will go to any length to take away basic human rights.

I am not promoting abortion, far from it. But I am speaking out against those who want to punish, who suggest that we can reduce teenage pregnancy through legislation. I am speaking out against those who will simply not address the needs of birth control and sex education.

Sex among teenagers will not be regulated by legislation, nor will it be eliminated.

I am a man with a broken heart, and it is my desire that speaking out will in some way prevent others from living this same nightmare.

I urge you to consider real life situations and not punish the young women of this state and uphold the rights of all the people of Connecticut, not just the parents.

Rebecca Suzanne Bell was not a theory, she was a beautiful human being. She was my daughter, taken away because others *thought* they had all of the answers. The bill before you doesn't have all of the answers either and I urge you to defeat this legislation. [1990]

# 🌿 109

# *Using Pregnancy to Control Women*

RUTH HUBBARD

Strange things have been happening to this culture's ideas about pregnancy. More and more, physicians, judges, legislators, and the media are presenting pregnancy as a contest in which pregnant women and the embryos and fetuses we nourish in our bodies are represented as lined up on opposing sides.

But construing the "interests" of embryos and fetuses as opposed to those of the women whose bodies sustain them makes no sense biologically or socially. A pregnant woman's body is an organic unit, of which the fetus is a part. She shares with her fetus one blood supply as well as other essential functions. Any foods or digestive products, hormones or drugs, or anything else that involves either can have an impact on the other.

This does not mean that pregnant women should scan all their feelings, thoughts, and actions for possible ill effects on the fetus within them. It is probably true that stresses they experience will be transmitted to the fetus, but that includes the stresses and anxieties that would arise from trying to live a life free of stress and anxiety. What it does mean, however, is that it is counterproductive to heap needless stress on pregnant women by worrying them about possible sources of harm to their fetus and by subjecting them to often still-experimental tests and procedures to detect fetal disabilities for which they or the fetus are not specifically predicted to be at risk. Some of today's stresses of pregnancy are evoked by exaggerated concerns and watchfulness intended to avert relatively unlikely risks.

Precisely because anything that is done to a pregnant woman or to her fetus has an impact on both, pregnant women must be the ones to decide whether to carry their pregnancy to term. Only they can know whether they are prepared to sustain the pregnancy as well as the future relationship to their child.

As part of this trend of looking upon embryos and fetuses as though their "interests" could be separated from those of the women whose bodies sustain them, we have been witnessing: (1) prosecutions of pregnant women or of women who have recently given birth for so-called fetal abuse; (2) court-mandated Caesarean sections; and (3) so-called fetal protection practices in which employers bar women of child-bearing age (defined in one instance as 16 to 54 years) from certain kinds of jobs that are said to put a potential fetus at risk, in case these women become pregnant.

I want to look at these three situations and then speculate about why this is happening now and why only in the United States.

## "DISTRIBUTING DRUGS TO A MINOR"

Across the nation in the last few years women have been charged with the crime of "distributing drugs to a minor via the umbilical cord" or similarly Orwellian accusations. Since the legal status of the fetus is uncertain, most of these have not stood up in court. Presumably for this reason, in Florida, Jennifer Johnson, a woman who had just birthed her baby, so that it was now legally a born child, was charged with delivering an illicit drug to a minor via the umbilical cord while it was still attached to the cord. Despite the absurdity of this construct, she was convicted.

It seems reasonable to assume that drug use during pregnancy can harm the fetus, though it is not at all clear how dangerous it is. The designation "crack baby" usually is not the result of health-care workers noting behavioral abnormalities in a newborn. It came on the scene because a test was devised that can detect metabolic products resulting from women's drug use close to the time of birth. As a result, babies of mothers who fall into certain "suspect" categories—young, unmarried, poor, of color—are tested more or less routinely and especially in public hospitals. (In one recent instance where the test result was challenged by the young woman and her mother—though not until after the young woman and her baby had been forcibly separated—it turned out that the drugs the test detected were medically administered to the woman during labor.)

A recent article in the medical journal *The Lancet* explains that there are no accurate assessments of the dangers to the fetus of drug use by pregnant women. Its authors show that Canada's Society of Pediatric Research between 1980 and 1989 much more frequently accepted papers for presentation at its annual meeting that documented adverse effects of drug use during pregnancy than papers of the same, or superior, scientific quality that failed to detect any harm. As the authors point out, this kind of bias in publication of research reports makes it impossible to know how great the risk actually is. But even if we go with the common wisdom that drugs taken by pregnant women are likely to harm

the fetus, the problem is that very few drug-treatment programs accept women, fewer yet pregnant women, and even fewer, women on Medicaid. In fact, Jennifer Johnson's sentence in Florida included as a condition of her fifteen-year probation that she enter a drug-treatment program, something she had tried, but been unable, to do while pregnant. Another was that she be gainfully employed, something she had also tried, but been unable, to achieve. In other words, she was first victimized by an unresponsive system and then blamed for not availing herself of the remedies she had tried, but been unable, to obtain. She ended up convicted for the government's negligence and neglect.

It is important to realize that just about all the women who have been prosecuted for prenatal injuries to their babies have been poor and of color. Most of them have had little or no prenatal care and have given birth in public or teaching hospitals. None has been a white, suburban drug user, in the care of a private obstetrician. The so-called war on drugs requires public hospitals to report instances of suspected drug use, while private physicians can avoid doing so. Obviously, this policy is counterproductive, since it will make women who could benefit from medical and social services avoid them for fear of being declared unfit to care for their children.

## COURT-MANDATED CAESAREANS

In most cases, a woman submits to a Caesarean section when a physician warns that giving birth vaginally would endanger her baby. This is true in this country, as elsewhere, despite the fact that the incidence of Caesarean sections in the United States is higher (about one in four) than in any other industrialized country (it is one in ten in the Netherlands, which has one of the lowest infant mortality rates in the world). But occasionally, a woman refuses on religious grounds, out of fear of surgery, or for other reasons. Whereas physicians and attorneys argued in print as late as 1979 that physicians have it in their power to cajole or threaten, but that cutting someone open against her will constitutes battery, since 1980 obstetricians have been granted court orders for performing Caesarean sections against the explicit will of the pregnant woman. In a number of instances pregnant women have escaped the operation by going underground or by giving birth vaginally before the court order could be implemented. In all of them the babies have been born unharmed, despite the obstetrician's direst predictions. In one case, the physician had testified that without a Caesarean there was a 99 percent risk that the baby would die and a 50 percent risk of death to the woman if she gave birth vaginally. She did, and both she and the baby were fine, which just shows that birth outcomes are notoriously unpredictable, except to say that most births end well. These situations, too, have involved mostly poor women—many of them of color, and whose primary language is not English—presumably because of the range of power imbalances between obstetricians and pregnant women. The prevalent differences in class, race, sex, and education that interfere with communication even in the best of circumstances are exacerbated when the women have unusual religious convictions or are young or unmarried or don't speak the same language as the doctor.

There is hope that a recent decision handed down by the District of Columbia Court of Appeals may make courts more reluctant to order Caesareans against the wishes of pregnant women. On April 26, 1990, this court ruled on the case of Angela Carder, a woman who was pregnant and dying of cancer. After 26 weeks of gestation, when it became clear that she would not survive until the end of her pregnancy, Georgetown Hospital in Washington, D.C., got a court order to perform a Caesarean section against her wishes as well as those of her parents, her husband, and her attending physicians. Both she and the baby died within 24 hours of surgery. The American Public Health Association, the American Medical Association, the American College of Obstetricians and Gynecologists, and other health and civil liberties organizations joined, as friends of the court, in a suit brought against the hospital. The majority of the D.C. Court of Appeals held that "in virtually all cases, the question of what is to be done is to be decided by the patient—the pregnant woman—on behalf of herself and the fetus." Though this decision governs only in the District of Columbia, we can hope that it will lend weight to refusals of surgery by pregnant women in other jurisdictions.

## FETAL ENDANGERMENT IN THE WORKPLACE

Reproductive hazards in the workplace were cited in 1977 as grounds for requiring five women at the American Cyanamid plant in Willow Island, West Virginia, to be sterilized, if they wanted to retain jobs paying $225 per week plus substantial overtime instead of being transferred to janitorial jobs at $175 per week with no extras. None of these women was pregnant or planning a pregnancy, yet without the operation, they were considered "potentially pregnant." A number of such situations have arisen since, and currently the U.S. Supreme Court has agreed to hear an appeal against a lower court decision supporting Johnson Controls' "fetal protection" policy. . . .*

The grounds for barring the women have been that the work involves exposure to lead or other chemicals or radiation that could endanger a fetus, despite the fact that these agents also put men's reproductive processes, and specifically sperm, at risk. And these situations have only occurred relative to higher-paying jobs, traditionally occupied by men, to which women have been newcomers. Comparable concerns have not been raised about women employed in traditionally female jobs in which they are routinely exposed to hazardous chemicals or radiation, such as surgical operating room or x-ray technician, nurse, beautician, or indeed, clerical or domestic worker. Whether the women are planning to have children appears to be irrelevant. Rather, fertile women, as a class, are always considered "potentially pregnant." This is just one more way to keep women out of higher-paying jobs by dressing up sex discrimination as fetal protection. Of course, it also enhances the status of the fetus as a person,

---

*Editor's note: In March, 1991 in *UAW v. Johnson Controls, Inc.,* the Supreme Court unanimously declared unconstitutional Johnson Controls' policy of excluding women of childbearing capacity from jobs in which they would be exposed to lead.

while relegating all women, pregnant or not, to the status of fetal carriers.

These kinds of "protections" make no sense from the viewpoint of health, because any substance that endangers a fetus is also dangerous for workers—female *and* male. But it is cheaper for companies to fire "potentially pregnant" workers (which means any woman who cannot prove she is infertile) than to clean up the workplace so that it becomes safe for everyone. Employers claim they are barring women because they are afraid of lawsuits should a worker whose baby is born with a disability, claim that disability was brought on by workplace exposure. But, in fact, no such suit has ever been filed and, considering the problems Vietnam veterans have experienced in suits claiming reproductive damages from exposure to Agent Orange and farm workers from exposure to toxic pesticides, such a suit is not likely to present a major risk to employers.

## WHY?

So, why are these various fetal protection activities happening and why only in the United States? Indeed, why do many cities and states post warnings in bars and subways, now also appearing on liquor bottles, that read: "Warning! Drinking alcoholic beverages during pregnancy can cause birth defects"? (Note: any alcoholic beverage, no specification of how much or of alcohol content, and no mention of possible detrimental effects on sperm.)

No doubt, the antiabortion movement has helped raise "the fetus" to mythic proportions. Perhaps also prenatal technologies, especially ultrasound imaging, have made fetuses seem more real than before. Not so long ago, physicians could find out about a fetus' health only by touching or listening to a pregnant woman's distended belly. Now, in the minds of many people, fetuses have an identity separate from that of the woman whose body harbors them, since it is not unusual for their future parents to know their sex and expected health status.

But that doesn't explain why these activities are peculiar to the United States. Europeans often assume that anything that is accepted in the United States today will be accepted in Europe tomorrow—or, if not tomorrow, the next day. But pregnancy is not like Coca-Cola. It is embedded in culture and framed by a network of economic and social policies. We cannot understand the profound differences between the ways pregnant women are regarded here and in other Western countries unless we face the fact that this country alone among industrialized nations has no coherent programs of health insurance, social and economic supports for pregnant women, maternal and child care, and protection of workers' rights. This has been true since the beginning of this century, but the situation has been aggravated since the dismemberment of the, however meager, social policies that existed before the Reagan era. Recent pronouncements by "drug czar" William Bennett and Secretary of Health and Human Services Louis Sullivan, urging that drug use during pregnancy be taken as prima facie evidence of child abuse, are among the ways the administration is shifting blame for the disastrous economic and social policies that have resulted in huge increases in poverty, homelessness, and unprecedented levels of drug use onto the victims of these policies.

While the economic circumstances of women and children, and especially those of color, are deteriorating and disparities in access to services and in infant mortality rates are increasing, what a fine trick it is to individualize these conditions and blame women for selfishly putting their fetuses at risk. Yet taking women to court for fetal endangerment creates more low-income women and more babies that will be warehoused in hospitals or shuttled among an insufficient number of adequate foster homes by overloaded social-service systems. These are not solutions. They are merely ways of diverting attention from the enormous systemic problems that have been aggravated by the Reagan-Bush years and of shifting blame for the consequences onto the most vulnerable people.

The editorial in the June [1990] issue of the *American Journal of Public Health* (Vol. 80, No. 6) calls attention to the longstanding correlation of birthweight with parental income and living environment, regardless of maternal age, education, or marital status. The author points out that although U.S. infant mortality has declined since the 1940s, the overall decline slowed during the conservative Eisenhower and Reagan-Bush years. He also shows that, though infant mortality has gone down overall since 1947, Black/white infant mortality *ratios* have risen from 1.61 in 1947 to 2.08 in 1987 (where race, as usual, is to be interpreted as an indicator of the range of disadvantages that result from racism and not as a biological signifier).

Again and again, studies have documented the deleterious effects of adverse economic and social conditions on maternal and infant health. But it continues to be far easier to get money for yet another study than for the policies and programs that could ameliorate or, indeed, eliminate the dismal conditions that jeopardize the health and welfare of women and children.

### *WHAT TO DO?*

We have to take whatever political actions we can to support the efforts of various community organizations and to pressure government agencies at all levels to provide the economic, social, and educational supports that will let women and children live *above* the poverty level, not below it. We need what other industrialized nations have: adequate education, job security, proper nutrition, subsidized housing, universal health care, accessible drug-treatment programs, and so on. The lack of these is responsible for the disproportionate U.S. infant mortality and disability rates, not women's neglectful behavior during pregnancy.

A friend recently suggested that, rather than being sued, pregnant women should sue in the name of "the fetus" for access to the economic, social, and health measures that are necessary for successful pregnancy outcomes. Of course, this concept suffers from the fact that it, too, makes the fetus a person. Furthermore, such suits probably would not hold up in court, since, while the U.S. Constitution guarantees certain freedoms and rights, it does not guarantee the economic and social conditions necessary for every one to be able to exercise them. Despite this, a well-orchestrated campaign of this sort could educate and politicize people about the shallowness and hypocrisy of the government's supposed efforts at fetal protection, and so could be used to rally support for the kinds of measures that can improve the needlessly dismal economic and social circumstances in which large sectors of the U.S. population live. [1990]

# 110

# *Agency and Constraint: Sterilization and Reproductive Freedom Among Puerto Rican Women in New York City*

IRIS LOPEZ

This article focuses on the social, historical and personal conditions that shape, influence and constrain Puerto Rican women's fertility decisions with respect to sterilization.[1] It examines the reasons why Puerto Rican women have one of the highest documented rates of sterilization in the world by concentrating on the interplay between resistance and constraints and by teasing out some of the contradictions in their reproductive decisions about sterilization.[2] It also highlights the diversity of experiences that sterilized Puerto Rican women have with *la operación,* the colloquial term used to refer to sterilization among Puerto Rican women.

With the exception of cases of sterilization abuse, this ethnographic study demonstrates that Puerto Rican women make decisions about sterilization that are limited by their sociopolitical conditions. Their reproductive decisions are based on a lack of options circumscribed by a myriad of personal, social and historical forces that operate simultaneously to shape and constrain Puerto Rican women's fertility options. Presenting women as active agents of their reproductive decisions does not suggest that they are exercising free will or that they are not oppressed but that they make decisions within the limits of their constraints. As their oral histories reveal, women do actively seek to transform and improve their lives, and controlling their reproduction is one of the primary means of which they avail themselves to do so. Yet, as their oral histories also show, the constraints of their lives play an equally significant role in shaping their reproductive decisions and experiences. Consequently, this study takes into account the role that class, race and gender play in determining the range of options that individuals have available and how much control they have over them. While it is undeniable that all women have had their fertility options limited by the types of contraceptives developed and because they have had to bear much of the burden of population control, it is imperative to recognize that poor women are even more constrained.

## MIGRATION AND STERILIZATION: TWO SIDES OF THE POPULATION COIN

In order to understand the reasons why Puerto Rican women in Puerto Rico as well as in the United States have such a high rate of sterilization, it is essential to examine the sociopolitical and ideological framework in which sterilization developed in the island. Puerto Rico became a colony of the United States in 1898. As early as 1901 government officials attributed Puerto Rico's poverty and underdevelopment to an "overpopulation problem." Though the "problem of overpopulation" in Puerto Rico was more the result of U.S. capitalist, policy and legislative interests than of uncontrollable growth in population, an ideology of population was developed and implemented as a rationale for encouraging the migration of Puerto Ricans along with the sterilization of over one-third of all Puerto Rican women (Bonilla and Campos 1983).[3] As a result of this ideology, migration was used as a temporary escape valve to the "overpopulation problem," while they experimented with more lasting and efficacious solutions, such as sterilization and diverse methods of fertility control.[4]

In New York City, sterilization became available for "birth control" purposes in the decade of the sixties. Puerto Rican women migrating to New York City in the fifties were already familiar with *la operación* because of its extensive use in Puerto Rico. By the decade of the seventies sterilization abuse in New York City had become a pervasive theme

among, though not exclusively, poor women of color (CARASA 1979; Rodriguez-Trias 1978; Velez 1978; Davis 1981). Sterilization abuse takes place when an individual submits to a tubal ligation or vasectomy without their knowledge and/or consent or because they are blatantly pressured to accept sterilization. In the seventies, many judicial cases were documented of poor women who had been threatened with having their welfare rights taken away if they did not accept sterilization, were not given consent forms at all, or were provided with consent forms to sign while they were in labor (Rodriguez-Trias 1978). In this study, I found a few cases of women who were interned in a hospital for a different kind of surgery and were sterilized without their knowledge or consent, and many cases of women who were sterilized but were not aware of the permanent nature of a tubal ligation. In 1975, after a long and harrowing struggle undertaken by women's groups, health and community activists, sterilization guidelines were implemented in New York City to protect women and men against sterilization abuse.[5]

One of the questions my work raises is how do we then talk about agency and/or freedom of reproductive choice among Puerto Rican women in the context of the historical legacy of coercion and sterilization abuse? Although sterilization abuse is an important part of Puerto Rican women's experiences, on the island as well as in the U.S., it is important to keep in mind that not all Puerto Rican women who have undergone the operation perceive themselves as having been coerced. Therefore, in examining Puerto Rican women's reproductive decisions, I take into account the diversity of their reproductive circumstances by considering the variation of their experiences, which range from sterilization abuse to those women who suggest that they have voluntarily made the decision to be sterilized. Rather than pose these experiences in opposition to each other, I contend that all decisions are socially constrained and mediated when individuals confront them as active social agents.

## REVISITING THE IDEOLOGY OF CHOICE

The ideology of choice is paramount in a discussion of sterilization among Puerto Rican women. At the heart of this research lies the question of what constitutes a "choice" and what the concept of "voluntary" means in the context of the lives of Puerto Rican women. The "ideology of choice" is based on the assumption that people have options, that we live in a "free" society and have infinite alternatives from which to choose. As individual agents, we are purportedly capable of making decisions through envisioning appropriate goals, in order to increase our options. Implicitly, the higher the social and class status the greater the options. Striving toward the middle or upper class is, in part, a striving toward a "freedom" of expanded choice, which is part of the reward of upward mobility. By focusing on individual choice, we overlook the fact that choices are primed by larger institutional structures and ideological messages.

Even though today's contraceptive technology is limited for all women, the options presented to these women were constrained by their lack of knowledge about the different forms of birth control technology as a result of limited resources and staff in the clinics/hospitals available to them. Therefore, reproductive freedom not only requires the ability to choose from a series of safe, effective, convenient and affordable methods of birth control developed for men and women, but also a context of equitable social, political and economic conditions that allows women to decide whether or not to have children, how many and when (Colon et al. 1992; Hartman 1987; Petchesky 1984). Consequently, I have deliberately avoided framing the fertility decisions of Puerto Rican women within a paradigm of choice because it obfuscates the reality of their fertility histories and experiences as colonial/neo-colonial women.

## BIRTH CONTROL VERSUS POPULATION CONTROL

Although sterilization is technically considered birth control, a distinction needs to be made between sterilization and birth control on an analytical level as a result of the way it is used and its consequences for women's lives. For my purposes, birth control is defined as the ability to space children while sterilization entirely eliminates the management of birth control. In fact it renders the need to control fertility irrelevant. In most cases, sterilization marks the end of a woman's ability to reproduce. It is a method of population control which I have termed "fertility control" rather than "conception control." *The important distinction is between population control as a state imposition and birth control as a personal right.* It is not between sterilization and other forms of controlling births. Population control may be achieved through other methods. Norplant and abortion, for example, are presently considered. Population control is when a population policy imposes the control of fertility, as opposed to the individual right to control their own fertility, and even be sterilized if that is their desire. Fertility control can be defined as a population policy that imposes the curtailment of population growth on women, eliminating the individual's right to control her own fertility.

In addition to the technical differences between sterilization and birth control, sterilization also functions as fertility control when population policy is defined and implemented by health care providers to curtail the rate of population growth among a particular class or ethnic group because they are considered, in eugenic terms, a social burden, and therefore should not procreate (Hartman 1987). Consequently, the important issue here is not sterilization technology per se, but the way population policy is defined, translated and implemented.

## DIVERSITY OF EXPERIENCES

In addition to becoming sterilized for a series of reasons, Puerto Rican women experience sterilization in a host of different ways. For example, while sterilization may give one woman a great deal of freedom, it may be oppressive to another. Moreover, at one point, a woman may perceive sterilization as independence, yet at a different point in her life she may perceive it as oppressive. For example, a woman who is glad she is sterilized may regret it later if her child dies or if she remarries and is not able to have any more children. Sometimes resistance and oppression occupy different spaces and other times they occupy the same space because different realities can, and often do, coexist within a particular content. For example, a Puerto Rican woman may decide to get sterilized because she does not want any more children. This is a vital decision for her because it gives her more control over her body, therefore giving her more self-determination over her life. In contrast, the state's motivation for encouraging her sterilization is due to her dependency on welfare, where she is considered a burden on the state. By attempting to control her fertility, motivated by considerations of economy and politics, the state imposes its double standard of "choice" and "freedom" which is potent oppression. Consequently, women and the state's interests intersect on the level that there is consensus between the woman and the state—to control her fertility. Sterilization becomes simultaneously oppressive while it offers elements of empowerment, because both the state and women's motivation for wanting to limit their own fertility are at once synchronized as well as diametrically opposed. Therefore, on this level, there is both consensus as well as conflict and oppression (Lopez 1994).

Finally, it is also important to consider that voluntary sterilization must be available as a means of "birth control" for women to exert their reproductive freedom. Some women seek sterilization because they have achieved their desired family ties and they either decide independently or with their companion/husband that they do not desire, and/or cannot afford, to have any more children. Those women tend to use sterilization as fertility control because of their social and historical predisposition towards this technology and due to the lack of viable options. Given women's conditions, in some cases, sterilization may be the most reasonable decision they can make. There is also the possibility that even if these women had viable alternatives and their conditions were different, they still might elect sterilization. However, for the majority of women in this study, this is not the case.

## SOCIOECONOMIC CONSIDERATIONS

While most lower-income women experience difficult socioeconomic situations, households headed by female single parents fare even worse. Sixty-six percent of the women in this study are heads of households. Almost all of the women in this study stated that they had been married at least once, though 53.1 percent said that they were separated, divorced or widowed. Almost three-quarters (70 percent) received either supplementary or full assistance from Aid to Dependent Children. The mean annual income in 1981 was $7,000 or less. This income supports a mean of 3.4 children and two adults. With this money, women support themselves and their children, buy food and clothing and also pay the rent.[6]

The employed Puerto Rican women in this neighborhood are low-wage workers with little job stability, generally working in tedious jobs and often under difficult conditions. Eighty percent of the women in this study claimed that their economic circumstances directly or indirectly strongly influenced their decisions to become sterilized. Forty-four percent felt that if their economic conditions had been better, they would not have undergone surgery.

Although their socioeconomic position permeates every aspect of these women's lives, many of them did not reduce their reasons for becoming sterilized to strictly economic considerations because this was not how most of them expressed their views about sterilization and their lives. Instead they talked about the burglaries, the lack of hot water in the winter and the dilapidated environment in which they live. Additionally, mothers are constantly worried about the adverse effect that the environment might have on their children. Their neighborhoods are poor with high rates of visible crime and substance abuse. Often women claimed that they were sterilized because they could not tolerate having children in such an adverse environment and/or because they simply could not handle more children than they already had under the conditions in which they lived. However, rarely did anyone say that they were sterilized because their annual income was only $7,000. They mostly talked indirectly about the conditions that led them to get sterilized.

## PROBLEMS WITH BIRTH CONTROL

The quality of health care services a woman has access to significantly influences her knowledge of contraceptives and attitudes about them. *The lack of safe and effective temporary methods of birth control prompted many women in this sample to get sterilized.* Although 76 percent of the women used temporary methods of birth control before getting sterilized, they expressed dissatisfaction with the contraceptives available, especially the pill and the IUD. As one woman stated:

> The pill made me swell up. After three years, I had an IUD inserted. It made me bleed a lot so I had it removed. I was sterilized at the age of twenty-five because I couldn't use the pill or the IUD. I tried using Norforms and the withdrawal method before I was sterilized but neither method worked very well.

Thus, because women are cognizant of the constraints that their economic resources, domestic responsibilities and problems with contraceptives place on their fertility options, many of them feel that sterilization is the only feasible "choice." In addition to the combination of social and historical factors previously mentioned that limit and constrain Puerto Rican women's fertility decisions, such as socioeconomic considerations, these women's fear to allow their children to play outdoors because of the high rate of crime in their neighborhood, their lack of access to quality health care services and many of the domestic difficulties that stem from poverty, personal and familial issues also influence their fertility decisions.

### WOMEN MARRY YOUNG AND ARE PRIMARILY RESPONSIBLE FOR THEIR FERTILITY AND CHILD REARING

The tendency to either marry or have their children while they are still relatively young precipitates their decision to get sterilized at a younger age: 66 percent of these women were sterilized between the ages of twenty-five and twenty-nine as compared to Euro-American and Afro-American women at the age ranges of thirty to thirty-four (New York City Health and Hospital Corporation 1982). Moreover, most of the women in this study married and had their children before the age of twenty-five.

Therefore, by their mid-twenties, they had already achieved their desired family size but still had approximately twenty years of fecundity left. Since the most effective method available to curtail fertility is sterilization, their "choice" was to accept it or continue using temporary methods of birth control for the next twenty years.

The average woman in this study had between two and three children, their perception of the ideal family size. More than half (56.7 percent) claimed that they were completely responsible for their fertility and child rearing. While this may appear as an issue of individual choice, it is part and parcel of the construction of the nuclear family in a patriarchal society in which the brunt of the responsibility of child rearing and birth control is relegated to women. This is accomplished by providing birth control mainly to women and few if any contraceptives for men.

### WOMEN'S RELIGIOUS VIEWS AND FAMILIARITY WITH LA OPERACIÓN

Although Puerto Rico is a Catholic country, Catholicism does not appear to have a direct effect on most women's decisions to be sterilized. Eighty-seven percent of the women in this sample were raised as Catholics. Of these women only 32 percent felt that sterilization goes against their religious beliefs. In contrast, however, women's familiarity with *la operación* has had a profound effect on predisposing them towards sterilization.

The prolonged use of tubal ligation has transformed it into part of the cultural repertoire for a large segment of the Puerto Rican population. Women's perceptions about *la operación* are also strongly influenced by the large number of females within their own families who have been sterilized. The effect that almost six decades of exposure to this operation has had on predisposing Puerto Rican women to sterilization cannot be underestimated.

To acknowledge that sterilization has a cultural dimension to it does not, however, make the decision to become sterilized one based on free will since free will does not exist in a vacuum. Nor does such a decision suggest that it originates from women's "folk" culture, as some scholars have implied through the language that they have used to describe this phenomenon (Presser 1973).[7]

Although the cultural beliefs of Puerto Rican women play an important role in their fertility decisions, particularly because of their misinformation about this procedure, this approach, like the culture of poverty thesis, blames the individual (Lewis 1976). For Puerto Rican women sterilization became part of their cultural repertoire because of the political, social and economic conditions that favored it, creating the conditions for their predisposition towards sterilization through the use of population control policies and initiatives.

## CONCLUSION

In order to accentuate the interplay between elements of resistance and constraints/oppression, this study has highlighted the complex, contradictory and multidimensional nature of Puerto Rican women's experiences with sterilization. The issue of sterilization among Puerto Rican women is a complicated one indeed. On the one hand, with the exception of victims of sterilization abuse, the majority of Puerto Rican women suggest that they made a decision between getting sterilized or continuing to have children under adverse conditions. Because of the limited nature of this "choice," however, many women feel they had no other viable alternative but to opt for, or to accept, sterilization.

In attempting to exercise control over their lives, Puerto Rican women may use sterilization as an element of resistance to forge some social space for themselves by refusing to have more children than they desire, and/or by attempting to exert some control over their socioeconomic situation, female subordination and/or problematic relationships. This forces us to reevaluate the culture of poverty thesis of Puerto Rican complacency, passivity and lack of planning.

At the same time, it is necessary to frame their reproductive decisions within the context of the constraints that they face. Despite women's desire to plan their lives, in addition to having children there are other forces operating simultaneously to shape, frame and limit their fertility choices. Puerto Rican women's "individual choice" has been substantively circumscribed by the United States/Puerto Rican colonial population policy as well as by women's poverty, race and gender oppression. The problem with sterilization is, of course, not the technology itself but the way it has been used to solve Puerto Rico's economic problem of underdevelopment and poverty by sterilizing Puerto Rican women. Then, moreover, given the social and economic constraints discussed, sterilization appears to them as the only viable alternative.

After four decades of residence in the United States, Puerto Rican women are still living in poverty, and they are still faced with the same dilemma of how to control their fertility. Although there are certainly more contraceptives today than there were in the past, after using and experiencing health problems with the pill and IUD, a large number of Puerto Rican women turn to sterilization, a method of fertility control they have now been practicing for approximately six decades. Aside from their predisposition to *la operación*, sterilization is also frequently recommended to them in municipal hospitals. Although public attention in New York City is not directed at an overpopulation problem, as it is in Puerto Rico, the "welfare problem" is an item of considerable debate since it is the poor who are considered to have too many children.

By not offering women alternatives such as quality health care services, safe and effective temporary methods of birth control for both men and women, abortion services, quality and affordable day care centers and opportunities for a better standard of living (Hartman 1987), women's fertility options have been effectively narrowed, at times making sterilization the only viable alternative. Until Puerto Rican women achieve a more equitable status in society and are able to improve their socioeconomic situation, they will continue to have one of the highest documented rates of sterilization in the world. Reproductive freedom means having all the alternatives and the conditions in order to decide whether or not to have children. As long as women continue to have children under these inequitable conditions we cannot talk about reproductive freedom.

## NOTES

I would like to thank my good friends, Alice Colon and Caridad Souza, for reading and discussing my paper and for their insightful and editorial recommendations.

1. Sterilization consists of cutting and suturing the fallopian tubes in the female to permanently block the flow of the sperm to the egg cell and to prevent the egg cell from entering the uterus. In its broadest meaning, sterilization includes hysterectomies and vasectomies. The latter is the method used to sterilize men. Female sterilization is also referred to as tubal ligation.

2. In 1982, a study by a Puerto Rican demographer, Vas-

quez-Calzada, showed that 39 percent of Puerto Rico's female population between the ages of fifteen and forty-five were surgically sterilized (Vasquez-Calzada 1982). A similar situation can be found for Puerto Rican women and other minorities in the United States. In New York City, where this research took place, Latinas have a rate of sterilization seven times greater than that of Euro-American women and almost twice that of Afro-American women (New York City Health and Hospital Corporation 1982). Although information is scarce for most cities, my study of Puerto Rican women in one neighborhood in New York found that in 47 percent of the households one or more Puerto Rican women over age twenty were surgically sterilized. Moreover, another study reveals that in Hartford, Connecticut, 51 percent of Puerto Rican females of reproductive age were sterilized (Gangalez et al. 1980).

3. After World War II, Puerto Rico became a model for the strategy of development known as Operation Bootstrap and a testing laboratory for the pill, IUD, EMKO contraceptive cream and the development of sterilization technology. By 1937 sterilization was implemented in Puerto Rico as a method of "birth control." The legislation grew out of the Eugenics Movement that developed in the United States to sterilize people considered socially or intellectually inferior. Finally, it is also important to keep in mind that for 31 years in Puerto Rico sterilization is systematically available while temporary methods of birth control were only haphazardly available. For a complete history of Puerto Rico's birth control movement see Ramirez de Arellano and Scheipp's (1983) work.

4. Interestingly, sterilization was never official government policy in Puerto Rico (Presser 1973; Henderson 1976; Ramirez de Arellano and Sheipp 1993). It took place unoffically and became a common practice condoned by the Puerto Rican government and many of its health officials, frequently filling the gap for the systematic lack of temporary methods of birth control. Albeit many birth control clinics opened and closed throughout Puerto Rico's history, it was not until 1968 that federally funded contraceptives were made avilable thoughout the island. It is within this context of a policy prompting population control, particularly for poor women, that decisions regarding sterilization must be analyzed.

5. The legislation mandated that a thirty-day period of time be observed between the time an individual signs a consent form to the day she is operated on. It also stipulates that women under the age of twenty-one could not be sterilized with federal funds, and that a consent form must be provided in a person's native language, and administered in written and oral form.

6. In 1981, more than three-quarters of the women in this study were not working outside the home, although 12.5 percent were actively looking for jobs. Of the women who have spouses, 31.3 percent had husbands who were employed and 15.6 percent had husbands who were not working at the time this study took place.

7. The language that Presser used to describe this phenomenon is problematic. In reference to sterilization she states: "Its widespread practice represents a 'grass roots' response among Puerto Rican women who sought an effective means of limiting their family size" (Presser 1973: 1). The difficulty is not with the acknowledgment that there is a cultural dimension to sterilization but that she dissociates culture from the social, political and historical content.

## WORKS CITED

Bonilla, Frank, and Ricardo Campos (1983). Evolving Patterns of Puerto Rican Migration. In *The Americas in the New International Division of Labor*, Steve Sanderson (ed.). New York: Holms and Meir, pp. 172–205.

Colon, Alice, Ana Luisa Davila, Maria Dolores Fernos, Ruth Silva Bonilla, and Ester Vicente (1992). Salud y Derechos Reproductivos. Tercer Encuentro de Investigadoras Auspiciado Por el Proyecto de Intercambio CUNY-UPR.

Committee for Abortion Rights and Against Sterilization Abuse (1979). Women under Attack: Abortion, Sterilization Abuse, and Reproductive Freedom. New York: Committee against Sterilization Abuse.

Davis, Angela (1981). Women, Race, and Class. New York: Random House.

Gangalez, Maria V. Barrera, P. Guanaccia, and S. Schensul (1980). The Impact of Sterilization on Puerto Rican Women, the Family, and the Community, Unpublished Report. Connecticut: Hispanic Health Council.

Hartman, Betsy (1987). Reproductive Rights and Wrongs: The Global Politics of Population Control and Contraceptive Choice. New York: HarperCollins.

Henderson, Peta (1976). Population Policy, Social Structure, and the Health System in Puerto Rico: The Case of Female Sterilization. Ph.D. dissertation, University of Connecticut.

Lewis, Oscar (1976, 1966c). La Vida: A Puerto Rican Family in the Culture of Poverty. San Juan and New York: Vintage Books.

Lopez, Iris (1994). A Question of Choice. An Ethnographic Study of the Reproduction of Sterilization among Puerto Rican Women (forthcoming).

New York City Health and Hospital Corporation (1982). Sterilizations Reported in New York City, Unpublished Data, Department of Biostatistics.

Petchesky, Rosalind. (1984). Abortion and Woman's Choice: The State, Sexuality, and Reproductive Freedom. New York: Longman Series in Feminist Theory.

Presser, Harriet (1973). Sterilization and Fertility Decline in Puerto Rico. Population Monograph No. 13. Berkeley: University of California Press.

Ramirez de Arellano, Annette and Conrad Scheipp (1983). Colonialism, Catholicism, and Contraception: A History of Birth Control in Puerto Rico. Chapel Hill: University of North Carolina Press.

Rodriguez-Trias, Helen (1978). Women and the Health Care System: Committee against Sterilization Abuse. New York: Barnard College.

Vasquez-Calzada, Jose (1982). La Población de Puerto Rico Y Su Trajectoria Historica. Edcuela de Salud Publica, Reciento de Ciencias Médicas. Puerto Rico: Universidad de Puerto Rico.

Velez, Carlos (1978). Se Me Acabo la Canción. Paper presented at the International Congress of Anthropological and Ethnological Sciences, New Delhi, India, December.

## 🦎 111

# *Developing a Reproductive Rights Agenda for the Next Century*

KATHRYN KOLBERT

This is a call for a reproductive rights agenda for the next century. It suggests a process for developing a comprehensive approach to reproductive rights issues and outlines an agenda that can serve as a starting point for further discussions. Defining our goals is essential to achieving them. By taking the time now to articulate our vision of the future and grapple with the many hard questions that surround reproduction—questions about sexuality, childbearing, and parenting—we can develop and build a consensus about the basic premises of our work. We will then be better able to set priorities and develop collective strategies to achieve our goals.

## 1. FREEDOM AND LEGAL RIGHTS TO MAKE VOLUNTARY DECISIONS

Our law[s] and social institutions must enable women to make voluntary, thoughtful, and deliberate choices about their own sexuality, childbearing, and parenting and must respect the decisions that women make for themselves and their families.

All persons must have the legal right to make voluntary and informed decisions. Our legal system cannot be used to deprive women of equal access to a full range of reproductive options. Nor can it be used to coerce women's reproductive behavior or choices, regardless of age, ancestry, creed, disability, economic status, marital status, national origin, parental status, race, sex, or sexual orientation.

## 2. COMPREHENSIVE, QUALITY, AND AFFORDABLE HEALTH CARE AND HUMAN SERVICES

### A. A Full Range of Reproductive Options

Women must have access to the full range of safe, effective, and affordable birth control methods, and medical research must develop better, safer methods. Men as well as women must assume responsibility for birth control, and technologies must be developed that will enable them to do so.

Women who find themselves pregnant must have access to quality counseling to determine their reproductive choices. If they choose to terminate their pregnancies, they must have access to all safe and affordable abortion methods and related health services at or near their homes or jobs.

Women who choose to carry a pregnancy to term must have access to quality prenatal care, genetic screening and counseling, childbirth and postpartum care, and pediatric care for their children.

Pregnant women, especially poor women and women in Black, Hispanic, and Native American communities who are experiencing a crisis of drug and alcohol abuse, must be provided reproductive health, maternity and addiction services in an environment that is supportive and free of stigma. They must be fully informed of the risks to themselves and their infants in a way that is caring and nonpunitive and that helps them to deal with additional problems of poverty, poor housing, and male violence.

All women must have access to confidential and quality care for sexually transmitted diseases. Women who are HIV positive or at risk for AIDS who are or may become pregnant have the same right to noncoercive counseling and choice as women with other disabilities or possible fetal impairments. AIDS testing, like prenatal diagnosis, should be offered on an anonymous or confidential and voluntary basis and within a program of counseling and education that respects all persons' rights to express their sexuality.

### B. Comprehensive Care

Because reproductive choice includes the ability to care for as well as bear children, comprehensive health care and human services must be available to all families. Whether offered through public or private health programs, the services must be physically accessible—to disabled and rural women, to those dependent on public transportation, to those who work nights—and must be affordable to all.

## C. Safe and Quality Care

Health and human services including all reproductive health services should focus on health, wellness, and the prevention of problems, as well as on the cure and amelioration of problems, and should be provided in a culturally supportive manner, in an environment that is free from violence, deception, and fraud. Women should define their own needs and be enabled through the use of these services to make positive changes in their lives.

Medical practitioners must not adopt unnecessary or invasive practices that endanger women's lives or health and must not use their power or authority to coerce reproductive decisions. For example, procedures such as sterilization, hysterectomy, amniocentesis, ultrasound, Caesarean section, or electronic fetal monitoring should be used only when medically appropriate. To prevent further medical abuse, the crisis in malpractice and liability insurance which has forced medical practitioners to adopt unnecessary or invasive practices in order to protect against legal liability must be addressed without leaving women unprotected.

## D. Informed Consent and Informed Refusal

Principles of informed consent and informed refusal must be an intrinsic part of the decision making process and must be backed up by supportive counseling. Only when women have full knowledge about the ramifications of accepting or rejecting a particular health option, including explanations of medical procedures and their risks and benefits in understandable terms in the woman's own language, can decisions be voluntary. At the same time, women must have the option of refusing particular types of information—e.g., the sex of the child after amniocentesis. In addition, informed consent must not become a pretext for harassment or discouragement of a particular reproductive choice, such as abortion or sterilization.

## 3. SEXUALITY, REPRODUCTIVE, AND LIFE SKILL EDUCATION

Women, particularly teenage women, often become pregnant because they lack essential knowledge about sex, pregnancy, and contraception. Persons of all ages must have sufficient information about their sexuality and reproductive health to make intelligent decisions about sexuality, childbearing, and parenting. Information about how their bodies work, varied forms of sexuality, contraceptives, and sexually transmitted diseases must be provided to all persons at accessible locations, in a manner that is understandable and age-appropriate. Men as well as women must be taught that they have equal responsibility to be well informed about and to participate fully in choices related to sexual behavior, reproduction, and parenting.

It is especially important that women and men should be fully informed about the risks and pathology of AIDS and the necessity of using condoms or other "safe sex" practices. Public education campaigns to prevent the spread of HIV should be administered in a context that respects all persons' needs to express their sexuality, both inside and outside the traditional framework of marriage and heterosexuality.

But education about sexuality and reproduction is only a part of the solution. Women, especially young women, often choose to become mothers because they have no realistic possibilities of advancement in society. Our educational system must provide women with the opportunity to set ambitious goals for their future, and the background to make these goals a reality, enabling women to choose motherhood when it is the best choice for them.

## 4. FREEDOM TO EXPRESS ONE'S SEXUALITY, AND TO ADOPT VARIED FAMILY ARRANGEMENTS OR LIFESTYLES

If women and men are coerced or socialized into heterosexual relationships, or if childbearing or childrearing is permissible only within heterosexual relationships, then people's ability to make intimate decisions about reproduction, as well as about sexuality and parenting, is constrained. Society must not discriminate against, stigmatize, or penalize persons on the basis of their sexuality or sexual preference. Moreover, varied forms of sexual expression including heterosexuality, bisexuality, and homosexuality must be accepted as normal human responses, with positive meaning and value.

Women must be free to say no to sexuality, child-bearing, and parenting as they are to choose these options. Women must be free to express their sexuality in whatever noncoercive forms they choose, without recriminations, without effect on their value in our society or their self-esteem, and without fear of becoming pregnant if they do not wish to be so.

Varied forms of family and living arrangements must be acceptable choices. When women choose to parent outside of marriage, or to live collectively or inter-generationally, these choices must be respected. The legal barriers to and social stigma of unwed parenthood, inter-racial childbearing, or lesbian motherhood must be eliminated if true reproductive choice for all women is to be an option. Moreover, since pressure to have children is often brought about because there are few other acceptable adult-child relationships, we must encourage alternative forms of adult-child interaction.

## 5. ECONOMIC EQUITY AND REPRODUCTION

In order that all persons have equal opportunity to become parents, they must have the means to do so. The economic barriers to alternative forms of reproduction, such as the cost of adoption, donor insemination, in vitro fertilization, or embryo transfer must be lessened for low-income women through fee reduction or subsidies.

If we want a society in which children are truly an option, women must have the economic means to raise their children—to provide adequate food, clothing, and shelter and quality child care and education. We must work to eliminate the feminization of poverty that today so limits women's reproductive options and work to create jobs and a welfare system that afford dignity to all and which is free from coercive childbearing policies. Without an economy and social services that support women, women are unable to support their children and families; responsible parenting is possible only in a society that provides the necessary resources for parents.

Public policies must be enacted that will ease the burdens of working parents, caught between responsibilities of job and home. In addition to quality, affordable child care services, a reproductive rights agenda requires gender-neutral pregnancy and child care leave provisions and flexible work schedules available without penalty to fathers as well as mothers. To make these provisions available to all working parents and not just the most privileged, leave time must be paid. Corporate and governmental employers should be encouraged to initiate internal education programs, similar to those currently underway regarding sexual harassment, to change employee attitudes about male and same-sex partner participation in prenatal and child care tasks.

## 6. FREEDOM FROM VIOLENCE

Because fear of violence by a spouse or partner and fear of sexual assault limit everyone's ability to make intimate decisions, all persons must be free to choose whether, when, and with whom they have sex and have children, and to raise their children without fear of sexual assault, abuse, violence, or harassment in their homes, on the streets, or at their jobs.

## 7. FREEDOM FROM REPRODUCTIVE HAZARDS

All persons must be free from reproductive hazards within the environment, in their homes, and at their workplaces. Rather than attempting to repair the effects of reproductive hazards by treating infertility or disease or by banning fertile women from hazardous worksites (and consequently from higher paying jobs), we must eliminate the hazards.

## 8. FAMILY LAW AND SERVICES

In order to enable all persons to freely form the arrangements in which they parent, they must be able to establish and terminate these arrangements without economic and social penalty. Fair and equitable marriage, domestic partnership, divorce, child support, and child custody laws must be available and enforceable by women whose marriage or other family arrangements have dissolved or proven inadequate. In the event of the death or disability of both of a child's parents, governmental and community resources must provide for the well-being of the child. In the event of child abuse or neglect, governmental and community resources must provide necessary medical, social, and legal services to keep families together.

## 9. POLITICAL PARTICIPATION

All persons must have the full right to express their views and, through organized, collective, and non-violent action, to work actively for positive, systematic changes that will guarantee reproductive choice. Women must have the opportunity to be involved at all levels of the political process and within all political parties and be encouraged to take positions of leadership.                                    [1998]

# Sexual Harassment

Although we often associate it with the workplace, sexual harrassment can occur in diverse settings, from the classroom to the boardroom to the doctor's office. Women who are sexually harrassed come from all walks of life, reflecting our shared vulnerability to unwanted sexual attention. In fact, recent studies show that throughout grade school and middle school, girls are subject to sexual teasing and taunting that often make the schoolyard a hostile environment. Julia Whealin provides an overview of recent research on sexual harassment in the United States. She shows us the extent of this problem, describing some of the effects of sexual harassment on women.

Diane Hugs's description of her sexually abusive doctor reminds us of how institutional practices reinforce the continued maltreatment and abuse of women. Her story encourages patients not to accept sexual actions on the part of physicians and suggests steps to take if it does occur.

Another common experience of unwanted sexual attention for many women is addressed in "Construction Workers, Subway Creeps, and Other Daily Hazards: Confronting Harassers in the Community." Women are vulnerable to harassment just by walking down the street past men who make sexual comments and gestures and leer at women. This behavior is, unfortunately, extremely common and often intimidates women who feel they have no recourse but to "take it." Rather than trying to ignore street harassment, this essay provides concrete examples of ways that women can actively counter such behavior.

We also include in this section a guide for women students who have experienced sexual harassment in their college or university. Because sexual harassment of women students is about power and control, many women victims feel unable to confront their harasser. This article provides clear, concise information about strategies for dealing with harassment so that we can reclaim our dignity and stand up for our rights.

This section concludes with another example of resistance. In "style no. 1," Sonia Sanchez describes how an African-American woman draws on her own ingenuity and traditions of female assertiveness to avert a stranger's sexual harassment. In so doing, she mantains her self-respect and is able to keep on walking, "with the wind singing in her veins."

## 112

# *Sexual Harassment: An Overview of Its Impact for Women*

JULIA WHEALIN

A growing awareness of exploitation and oppression has developed in the wake of the civil rights and women's movements. With this, our conception of violence and exploitation has expanded from that of "the criminal on the street" to encompass interpersonal behavior among acquaintances, such as sexual harassment. The awareness of such exploitation has encouraged people to stand up legally for their rights both to strangers and to those with whom they may have a close relationship, such as an employer, teacher, physician, or peer.

In 1980, the Equal Employment Opportunities Commission used the following definition to describe sexual harassment:

> Unwelcome sexual advances, requests for sexual favors, and other verbal or physical conduct of a sexual nature constitute sexual harassment when 1) submission to such conduct is made either explicitly or implicitly a term or condition of an individual's employment, 2) submission to or rejection of such conduct by an individual is used as a basis for employment decisions affecting such individual, or 3) such conduct has the purpose or effect of unreasonably interfering with an individual's work performance or creating an intimidating, hostile, or offensive working environment.

Sexual harassment therefore differs from flirtation, flattery, or requests for a date to the extent that it lacks mutuality. Two types of sexual harassment are currently recognized by the law. The first, "*quid pro quo,*" occurs when sexual favors are requested in exchange for an employment or academic opportunity. The second type of sexual harassment has come to be known as the "hostile environment." It occurs when unwelcome, severe, and pervasive sexual conduct interferes with the target individual's performance or otherwise creates an intimidating or hostile environment (Lewis, Hastings, & Morgan, 1992).

### EXTENT OF THE PROBLEM

The extent of sexual harassment among adults has been documented in the past two decades. The first study to investigate the prevalence of sexual harassment was a readers' poll conducted by *Redbook* magazine (Safran, 1976). Ninety percent of the 9,000 women who responded to this survey reported that they had been sexually harassed at some point in their lives. Although this prevalence is probably biased by the fact that a random sampling research design was not used. the response rate made it apparent that sexual harassment was a widespread problem for women.

In 1981, a carefully designed, random-sample survey of 24,000 U.S. government workers revealed that 42% of women and 15% of men experienced sexual harassment on the job in the prior two years (U.S. Merit Systems Protection Board, 1981). The consequences of the harassment were often extensive. For instance, of those who had experienced harassment, 52% reported that they had quit because of it or were fired. Furthermore, the survey showed that most of those who were harassed did not take formal action against the harasser: only 5% filed complaints. This widely publicized study was replicated in 1988 with similar results. Comparable rates of sexual harassment are also reported in smaller studies of specific professions, such as airline personnel, social workers, and female lawyers. Moreover, similar rates of sexual harassment have been reported by white-collar as well as blue-collar workers (Kissman, 1990). However, workers in settings composed predominantly of the opposite sex tend to report higher rates of harassment than workers in occupations traditional for their sex (Mansfield, Koch, Henderson, & Vicary, 1991; U.S. Merit Systems Protection Board, 1988).

Surveys in college settings reveal that sexual harassment is also a problem there, although less than that reported by studies of other settings (Charney & Russell, 1994). For instance, about one-fourth of female students surveyed at three large Northeastern universities said that they had been harassed by a professor. In another study, 16% of female university counseling center clients reported experiencing sexual harassment while at the university. Rates are reportedly higher for graduate students and medical students than for undergraduates. In addition to educational and occupational settings, individuals are sexually harassed by various other perpetrators, from physicians to strangers on the street.

## HARASSERS AND HARASSEES

One commonality among various settings is that women are often the victims of sexual harassment. Furthermore, those who experience sexual harassment in occupational settings are more likely in lower-level positions in the organization, nonwhite, and young (U.S. Merit Systems Protection Board, 1988). Those who report harassment often hold lower-income occupations and are the sole supporters of families (Crull, 1979). Conversely, perpetrators of sexual harassment are more likely to be men. For example, in a sample of medical residents, 96% of female victims and 55% of male victims reported sexually harassing behaviors by a male (Komaromy, Bindman, Haber, & Sande, 1993).

Understanding the reported characteristics of harassers, based on reports of those harassed, helps to explain some of the dynamics of the behavior. The U.S. Merit Systems Protection Board study (1981) found, for example, that most harassers were married. Furthermore, most harassers of women were older than their victims, whereas most harassers of men were younger than the victims. Harassers of both women and men tended to act alone rather than with another person. Moreover, both women and men reported that their harasser had bothered others at work. Perpetrators of harassment were more likely to be co-workers, while supervisors were harassers in 40% of the cases. Women in this study, however, were more likely than men to be harassed by a supervisor. This result is consistent with that of another study (Crull, 1979) in which 70% of women reported that their harassers had "the power to fire or promote" them. Thus, much of the time, harassers target women who in some way are less powerful than they.

To obtain information about men who harass, Pryor (1987) developed the Likelihood to Sexually Harass Scale. This scale is a self-report inventory in which men are asked to imagine themselves in ten situations in which they control an important reward or punishment for an attractive woman. They are then asked to rate the likelihood of using this power to sexually exploit the woman (and thus engage in quid pro quo sexual harassment). Several attitudes were evidenced among men who admitted to harassing behaviors. Specifically, men who were high on the Likelihood to Sexually Harass Scale (1) held adversarial sexual beliefs, (2) found it difficult to assume another's perspective, (3) endorsed traditional male sex role stereotypes, (4) were high in authoritarianism, and (5) reported a higher likelihood to rape a woman, assuming that they would not be held responsible for their actions. In another study using the scale, men who scored high on the scale showed significantly more thoughts associating themes of sexuality with social power (Pryor & Stoller, 1992, cited in Pryor, Lavite, & Stoller, 1993).

## RESPONSE TO SEXUAL HARASSMENT

The victim's response to sexual harassment varies from ignoring the behavior to filing a grievance complaint. In the U.S. Merit Systems Protection Board (1981, 1988) studies, about 11% of victims responded by reporting the harassment to a higher authority. As few as 2.5% of those harassed initiated an official grievance procedure. Of those who responded actively by filing a formal complaint, 47% reported that the action "made things better," regardless of whether the complaint was successful. Thirty-three percent, however, felt that their filing a complaint "made things worse" because of retaliation by the harasser or social stigmatization.

In another investigation, which surveyed 304 women and 205 men by telephone, 17% of those reporting harassment in a work situation reported that they had quit their jobs or asked for a transfer as a result of the harassment. Additionally, about one-third of victims in this study chose to ignore the harassment, while almost 40% said something themselves to the harasser. Only 8% said something to their boss regarding the harassment, and 3% of those harassed actually reported the behavior (Loy & Stewart, 1984). Respondents in this study were also asked about the organization's response to their experiences of harassment. Many of those harassed reported negative outcomes at their place of employment. Social stigmatization among co-workers was the most common negative outcome, reported by one-third of the victims. Other negative responses reported included being ignored by the harasser, being given lower performance evaluations, or being denied a promotion. Moreover, a negative response was reported more often when those harassed responded by saying something to the harasser. Fewer negative responses were reported, however, when those harassed ignored the behavior or went to their supervisors with complaints.

Organizational effects linked with sexual harassment can be quite profound. For example, harassment in an occupational setting can result in the deterioration of interpersonal work relationships and can strain working alliances with the opposite sex. Often, those harassed leave their jobs as a result of sexual harassment (Loy & Stewart, 1984; U.S. Merit Systems Protection Board, 1988). The effects of harassment in universities have also been substantial, as they has led students to drop courses, change majors, as well as give up career intentions (Fitzgerald et al., 1990). In summary, the research performed to date suggests that sexual harassment can have a serious, detrimental effect on one's interpersonal relationships with co-workers, on the career path one feels able to choose, and on one's evaluation and promotion in that career.

## EFFECTS OF SEXUAL HARASSMENT ON WOMEN

In addition to direct work- or school-related consequences, sexual harassment can lead to negative personal ramifications. For example, difficulties with work relationships decrease access to work-related information and support from others (DiTomasio, 1989) that is needed for women to advance in their careers. Lowered self-esteem and self-confidence may follow the realization that rewards were due to one's sexual attraction rather than one's work ability. Furthermore, work performance has been purported to decline owing to a loss of motivation, feelings of anxiety, and the distracting nature of the harassment (Woody & Perry, 1993).

Physical and psychological symptoms are another personal ramification of sexual harassment. For instance, physical ailments such as headaches, decreased appetite, weight loss, sleep problems, and an increase in respiratory or urinary tract infections are reported by victims of harassment. Psychological difficulties associated with harassment include anger, fear, sadness, anxiety, irritability, loss of self-esteem, feelings of humiliation and alienation, and a sense of helplessness and vulnerability (Jenson & Gutek, 1992).

Gender-based abuse, such as sexual harassment, may be related to the increased depression rates seen in women (Hamilton, Alagna, King, & Lloyd, 1987). Indeed, substantial depressive symptoms reportedly resulted from sexual harassment in one sample of women in a community (Loy & Stewart, 1984). Furthermore, 84 professional women experienced feelings of depression and self-blame after simply listening to an audio simulation of sexual harassment in which they were asked to imagine themselves as the victim (Samoluk & Pretty, 1994).

In some cases, the stress induced by the victimization may result in a posttraumatic stress reaction (Hamilton et al., 1987). Flashbacks, shock, emotional numbing, sleep disturbance, anxiety, and constriction of affect have accompanied the symptoms of depression seen in those who have been harassed. Sexual harassment can reinforce the internalization of social stereotypes and prejudice that define women as a devalued group. When such a stereotype is internalized, reactions such as isolation, extreme irrationality, and the tendency to minimize or deny harassment may result.

## GENDER DIFFERENCES AND SEXUAL HARASSMENT

Research has demonstrated that men and women tend to perceive sexual harassment differently. For instance, women generally perceive a greater number of behaviors to be harassing than men (Baker, Terpstra, & Cutler, 1990; Gutek, Morasch, & Cohen, 1983). In particular, women are more likely than men to perceive harassing incidents as actual harassment when they include touching, when they are accompanied by a negative comment about their work, and when they are initiated by a man or a higher-status person (Gutek et al., 1983). Findings additionally show that women are less likely than men to blame women for being sexually harassed (Jensen & Gutek, 1982).

Studies of the effects of sexual harassment show that similar behaviors may have a different impact on women than on men. Women view behavior such as sexual propositions as inappropriate and likely to cause discomfort, while men more often do not see them as inappropriate or as causing as much discomfort (Garlick, 1994; Roscoe, Strouse, & Goodwin, 1994). In one study, approximately half of working men said they would respond positively to unsolicited sexual attention (Berdahl, Magley, & Waldo, 1996). Written descriptions of the men's view of the situations included comments that the sexual harassment "doesn't bother me" or that it "makes the job more fun." A second viewpoint that emerged was that the men felt as though they had control over the situation. Men's responses indicated that, when they did not like the behavior, they would confront the perpetrator or report that person to a supervisor. This reaction is in contrast to women's responses, which more often included perceived threat and lack of control, as well as passive responding (Fitzgerald et al., 1990).

In general, the same behaviors women may experience as sexually harassing may be more often experienced by men as nonthreatening social-sexual behavior. However, the term *harassment* implies that the behavior must be stressful to the victim (Fitzgerald, Swan, & Fischer, 1995). Although males may like or dislike the unsolicited sexual attention, the behaviors do not tend to have the strong impact on men that they do on women. Thus, research suggests that the sexual advances of women toward men often do not result in a perceived hostile or offensive environment that may interfere with one's ability to perform.

## SUMMARY OF SEXUAL HARASSMENT

To review the current findings regarding sexual harassment of adults, the most extensive and carefully designed studies to date suggest that approximately 42% of women and 15% of men report that they have been sexually harassed in their workplaces in the preceding two years. About one-fourth of female students experience harassment while at college. Perpetrators of sexual harassment are most often men, and victims are more often women. Sexual harassment frequently has negative ramifications for the victim. Victims report negative workplace responses, such as poor performance evaluations. In colleges, women have changed majors and dropped courses because of harassment. Additionally, the stress resulting from harassment can have significant physical and psychological consequences on the victim.

Despite the negative impact of harassment, research performed to date suggests that much can be done to address its perpetration. As sexual harassers often bother several victims, a woman can realize that she is not singled out by the harasser. Other women have likely come before her, and if nothing is done, more women will be harassed in the future. Most women report that going to supervisors with complaints helps end the harassment. While few women report filing formal grievances, those who do usually find that it helps end the harassment. Unfortunately, women who address harassment can suffer personal and occupational stresses as a result. It therefore may be important to gain aid from others. Peers likely will assist and support their friends. When peers are not able to provide the help that is needed, supervisors, friends, women's organizations, and therapists are available to lend needed advice.

Finally, while investigations have helped to identify the victims and perpetrators of sexual harassment, research is necessary that explores ways to prevent the behavior. Interventions are much needed at the organizational level to teach employers and educators about the legal and personal ramifications of harassment. Women are demanding the right they deserve to have harassment-free work and school environments, and institutions must respond by making sexual harassment a serious offense.

## REFERENCES

Baker, D. D., Terpstra, D. E., & Cutler, B. D. (1990). Perceptions of sexual harassment: A re-examination of gender differences. *Journal of Psychology, 124,* 409–416.

Berdahl, J. L., Magley, V. J., & Waldo, C. R. (1996). The sexual harassment of men? Exploring the concept with theory and data. *Psychology of Women Quarterly, 20,* 527–547.

Charney, D. A., & Russell, R. C. (1994). An overview of sexual harassment. *American Journal of Psychiatry, 151,* 10–17.

Crull, P. (1979). The impact of sexual harassment on the job: A profile of the experiences of 92 women. *Working Women's Institute Research Series Report, 3,* 1–7.

DiTomasio, N. (1989). Sexuality in the workplace: Discrimination and harassment. In J. Hearn, D. L. Sheppard, P. Tancred-Sherriff, & G. Burrell (Eds.), *The sexuality of the organization* (pp. 71–90). Newbury Park, CA: Sage.

Fitzgerald, L. F., Swan, S., & Fischer, K. (1995). Why didn't she just report him? The psychological and legal implications of women's responses to sexual harassment. *Journal of Social Issues, 51,* 117–138.

Fitzgerald, L. F., Shullman, S. L., Bailey, N., Richards, M., Swecker, J., Gold, Y., Ormerod, A. J., & Weitzman, L. M. (1990). The incidence and dimensions of sexual harassment in academia and the workplace. *Journal of Vocational Behavior, 32,* 152–175.

Garlick, R. (1994). Male and female responses to ambiguous instructor behaviors. *Sex Roles, 30,* 124–158.

Gutek, B. A., Morasch, B., & Cohen, A. G. (1983). Interpreting social-sexual behavior in a work setting. *Journal of Vocational Behavior, 22,* 30–48.

Hamilton, J. A., Alagna, S. W., King, L. S., & Lloyd, C. (1987). The emotional consequences of gender-based abuse in the workplace: New counseling programs for sexual discrimination. *Women and Therapy, 14,* 155–182.

Jensen, I. W., & Gutek, B. A. (1982). Attributions and assignment of responsibility in sexual harassment. *Journal of Social Issues, 38,* 121–138.

Kissman, K. (1990). Women in blue-collar occupations: An exploration of constraints and facilitators. *Journal of Sociology and Social Welfare, 17,* 139–149.

Komaromy, M., Bindman, A. B., Haber, R. J., & Sande, M. A. (1993). Sexual harassment in medical training. *New England Journal of Medicine, 328,* 322–326.

Lewis, J. F., Hastings, S. C., & Morgan, A. C. (1992). *Sexual harassment in education.* Topeka, KS: National Organization on Legal Problems in Education.

Loy, P. H., & Stewart, L. P. (1984). The extent and effects of sexual harassment of working women. *Sociological Focus, 17,* 31–43.

Mansfield, P. K., Koch, P. B., Henderson, J., Vicary, J. R., Cohen, M., & Young, E. W. (1991). The job climate for women in traditionally male blue-collar occupations. *Sex Roles, 25,* 63–75.

Pryor, J. B. (1987). Sexual harassment proclivities in men. *Sex Roles, 17,* 269–290.

Pryor, J. B., Lavite, C. M., & Stoller, L. M. (1993). A social psychological analysis of sexual harassment: The person/situation interaction. *Journal of Vocational Behavior, 42,* 68–83.

Roscoe, B., Strouse, J. S., & Goodwin, M. P. (1994). Sexual harassment: Early adolescents' self-reports of experiences and acceptance. *Adolescence, 29,* 515–523.

Safran, C. (1976). Sexual harassment: A view from the top. *Redbook, 156,* 1–7.

Samoluk, S. B., & Pretty, G. M. H. (1994). The impact of sexual harassment simulations on women's thoughts and feelings. *Sex Roles, 30,* 679–697.

U.S. Merit Systems Protection Board Office of Merit Systems Review. (1981). *Sexual Harassment in the Federal Government: Is it a problem?* Washington, D.C.: U.S. Government Printing Office.

U.S. Merit Systems Protection Board. (1988). *Sexual harassment in the Federal government: An update.* Washington, D.C.: U.S. Government Printing Office.

Woody, R. H., & Perry, N. W. (1993). Sexual harassment victims: Psycholegal and family therapy considerations. *American Journal of Family Therapy, 21,* 136–144.

# 🌿 113

# *Mandatory Doctor's Visit*

DIANE HUGS

Being a disabled woman with a progressive disability requires that I document some of that disability through Social Security. Knowing that my primary physician documented what she saw on my visits, it surprised me a little when Social Security sent me a letter stating that I must see their doctor or I might no longer be considered disabled. This was funny because the small progression of my disability was not even the reason I was on Social Security and could no longer work. But they set up an appointment for me with a doctor I had never heard of and assigned the day and time of this appointment, and they stipulated that I had to go to that appointment.

As usual I took along a friend to the doctor's office; I've found it useful to have someone with me as a patient advocate and to help me remember what I wanted to ask. The doctor's office was in an old building with many rooms in his suite. When we got there it was unusually quiet for an office. We checked around and could not find anyone there. So we picked out what we thought might be the waiting room and waited for the doctor to show up.

The exam was routine and did not require that I remove my clothing. During the exam the doctor started by stroking my thigh as he looked over my chart sent by Social Security. He then asked me about my level of sensation since I am a paraplegic and cannot feel below the point of my paralysis. I held out my hands in front of me indicating that my sensation ended about the same level as my breasts. The doctor stroked my breast and asked me if I could feel that. Since he was below where I can feel

I told him no, biting my lip so I wouldn't scream at him. Then he moved up to my level of sensation and touched my breast again with a stroking motion. I said, "Yes I can feel that. But is this necessary?" The reason I wondered was because he was checking neurological data and he was not a neurologist. He answered. "Actually it isn't, I was just curious."

During the exam he rubbed my shoulders and even kissed me; in fact he tried to kiss me on the lips but I turned away. There was no safe way I could think of to stop him; after all, his report would affect my Social Security status, and that is all the income I have in the world. Even though he could not deny I was disabled, he could have messed with my case to stop my checks at least temporarily. This was a psychological weapon which I felt was held over me the entire time I was there. So I kept my mouth shut and held myself back from hitting him during the exam.

As soon as I made it out of the office I burst into tears. My friend felt terrible for not having stood up for me but she was afraid of making more trouble for me. I was numb as I waited for the accessible van to pick me up and drive me home. Once inside the van I broke into tears again and told the driver what had happened. She was furious and told me to call the Center for Independent Living to get some advice. That was very helpful because at that time I could barely think at all.

Upon returning home I called the Center and the first person I talked to told me to call the rape crisis line. At first I was surprised at this suggestion; I had not been raped, just molested. But then I remembered that the local rape crisis center did more than counsel women who had been raped. They also gave information about what you can do or who you can contact in situations like this. So I called the crisis line and talked to one of their counselors. She told me to file a complaint with the police, that this was a crime and I should prosecute. It took me by surprise to have my feelings validated so strongly. Keeping the momentum up I called the police immediately after speaking with the counselor. During the hour and a half that it took before the officer arrived I went through a tornado of feelings. Was I taking this all too seriously? Would the officer think I was paranoid to be making such a charge? Were my perceptions accurate or was I blowing this out of proportion?

While the officer was not the most understanding or sensitive person, he did take what I was saying seriously. He wrote out the complaint and told me they would be back in touch with me for more information and that the medical ethics board would be notified. A few days later my friend was asked to meet with the police and an investigator from the Board of Medical Quality Assurance. She told me the investigator was a really nice guy who seemed seriously interested in seeing this case prosecuted. The next day the investigator came by to take my statement. He was disgusted by the story and hoped they would be able to do something to stop this doctor. It made me feel stronger to be taken so seriously and the investigator thanked me for filing the charges. He had two similar cases with physicians he was working on but it had taken the women years to come forward, making it a lot more difficult to prosecute. Because I had reported the event so quickly, there was a better chance of the investigator being able to prosecute. He first contacted Social Security to obtain a list of others who had been sent to this particular doctor. He needed to know if there were other women who had been similarly mistreated but who had not had the courage to report it. Although he went through every channel including the police, Social Security would not release any information. They claimed it would violate rights to privacy of Social Security recipients. He even asked if they would have their own people contact other patients they had sent to this doctor to see if anyone else had been abused, but they simply refused his requests. I was so angry—it was a lame excuse for Social Security to say it was a violation of our rights to privacy when they were the ones that made me (and how many other women) go to see this doctor.

Finally the investigator came up with a plan that Social Security would go along with. An undercover policewoman was to be sent in to see the doctor as if she were a disabled woman being sent in by Social Security. She sat in a wheelchair and had all the same forms as I had from Social Security. The exam went the same, the doctor did almost exactly the same things to her. When I learned of this, I realized this must be routine for him to mistreat and abuse

Social Security or disabled patients during the exam. And although the undercover policewoman felt horrible and powerless when he kissed her and fondled her breasts, she wrote in her report that she wasn't sure if his actions were criminal. What I think she and the system did not understand was that he had power over my life through what he could do to my Social Security payments. I know it wasn't a weapon he could hold over the undercover policewoman, but I wished she had understood that he had no way of stopping her income. She could have fought back without risking her livelihood.

The district attorney did not see grounds to prosecute. This same D.A. was known for not prosecuting sex-related crimes; in fact later that year he was required by the City Council to prosecute over seventy rape cases he had passed by. Knowing that he did not take sex crimes very seriously, I checked to see if there was any other way to get this into court. But the sad fact is that the D.A. has the final call on whether or not to prosecute a case, and nothing I could do or say could change that fact. My next hope was the Board of Medical Quality Assurance. They brought him up before the discipline board and asked him to explain himself. The doctor admitted to everything that had happened; he just didn't think there was anything wrong with it. The Board warned him to keep his hands to himself and left it at that. Even though I wrote the Board an impassioned plea to reconsider on the grounds that his position of working for Social Security was a weapon against disabled women, they would not hear me.

This was more than I could take. On one hand I was told that I was right, that he had no right to fondle and kiss me, that in fact it was criminal; on the other hand no one would do anything to stop him from doing it to every woman he came into contact with. It really bothered me that he was not only going to get away with what he had done, but there was also no way for my testimony to keep other women safe. I told Social Security that his report on me was invalid since I was a victim, not a client; they told me they didn't want to hear about my personal problems. No way could I make them stop sending people to this doctor. It was driving me crazy to feel so helpless.

Having exhausted all means of legal prosecution, I decided to take him into civil court. There was a lawyer, Leslie Levy, with an outstanding reputation, so I decided to call her. She took the case even though I didn't have a dime and went right to work on it. The malpractice insurance company jumped into defending him even though they said they were in no way liable, because there is an exclusion for the insurance companies for any act that may be deemed criminal rather than a malpractice claim. So we had to battle these high-priced lawyers even though their company assumed no responsibility. There were two years of foot dragging and legal manipulation which my lawyer had to fight while the doctor continued to practice. He said he would settle for five hundred dollars. I rejected this because I could see no indication that he had the slightest clue that he had done something wrong.

Two years after filing this case and having every legal trick in the book thrown at us, we finally got around to doing court depositions. I was unable to sit upright at the time so not only was I unable to go to his deposition, I had to give mine from my bed. Instead of having all these strangers in my bedroom I used the bed in the living room. That was a very good thing because the doctor decided to show up and listen to my statement. A deposition requires the presence of lawyers from both sides along with a court reporter, and that felt like a huge invasion in itself. The deposition lasted about three hours and I was very lucky to have such a brilliant lawyer on my side. She did not let them get away with asking anything that was not relevant. She jumped up and down a lot, screaming at the other lawyer to back off. Since Leslie was familiar with abusive lawyers and litigants, she protected me from unnecessary harassment and abuse, for which I am eternally grateful to her.

That deposition did the job. The doctor seemed to realize I had been hurt. For the first time he understood that he had done damage, though he was not willing to pay for it. So onwards towards court we went. It was finished four months later and while I cannot divulge the outcome, I can say that the judge was understanding and resolved the case so I didn't have to go before a whole courtroom with it. The terms of the settlement prohibit me from saying anything.

I am still left with feelings of rage and sadness about what he did to me and how the system let him get away with it. If it had not been for the interest of Leslie Levy I would have been left out in the cold. There are not enough lawyers like her.

The legal system is still predominately male and does not take women seriously. It is not a lucrative business for lawyers to take on such cases since there's not that much money in these cases even if you get the court system to see the damage done. For me that was the hardest part, being asked, "Describe how this hurt you" in front of strangers who were not sensitive to my feelings. How to explain what having this uncaring authority figure run his hands all over me did to me, how he made me feel like a whore.

I used to trust doctors, but not anymore. I lost trust not only in the system which ignored my pain, but also I lost trust in people in general. It took over four years for me to let a stranger touch me at all. I had to explain to the doctor's lawyer that this lack of trust, not wanting to be touched, was damage in itself. He tried to downplay it by asking me if I would ever let anyone touch me again. I told him I had every intention of healing from this and hoped to be able to regain my trust. I fought hard. I fought long. It was worth the effort. The doctor knows he was wrong now. I just wish I had been able to stop him from continuing to practice. But I did everything I could and I can live with that.

What I would like to say to other women, disabled or not, is that a doctor does not have the right to touch you in any inappropriate way. We all have the right to fight back. More women need to fight the doctors who don't know the limits of conduct. If you are not sure whether your doctor went too far, but you do not feel good about what happened, follow it through. Contact the Board of Medical Quality Assurance, rape crisis centers and please, if you think there is even a possibility of a criminal case, call the police. The more women who call doctors on misconduct, the fewer doctors will continue to do harm to their women patients. If you cannot do this for yourself, please consider doing it for the next woman. Even though your doctor may not have taken you seriously, having to answer to all the different authorities will make

him think twice before he treats another patient the same way again.                    [1992]

## ❧ 114

# *Construction Workers, Subway Creeps, and Other Daily Hazards: Confronting Harassers in the Community*

MARTHA LANGELAN

Harassment on the job is frequent enough, but most women face an even greater probability of being harassed out in the community, everywhere from bus stops and bars to cafés and art museums. All three categories of harassment (sexual predation, dominance, and territorial harassment) happen regularly in public areas.

Community harassment of all kinds appears to be committed more often by strangers than acquaintances, although both occur. Casual, male-dominance harassment is the most common form of harassment on the street and in public facilities; it seems to be most prevalent in downtown areas where the population is highly mobile and the protection of anonymity is readily available for the harassers. All harassers take advantage of opportunity to some extent, but one type of anonymous community assailant—the groper, a sexual-pastime harasser who gets his thrills from fondling women in public—is highly opportunistic, specifically striking in crowded buses, subways, and elevators full of strangers.

Harassment in the community has real economic repercussions, both for women and for merchants. Women lose the right to use large areas of the public space that their own taxes support; they pay for many public facilities that they cannot freely enjoy. The risk of harassment strongly influences women's decisions about where and when their own towns are safe: which parks are a pleasant place for lunch and which are battle zones; which public streets offer an uninterrupted walk and which are hostile male territory; which stores, restaurants, and shopping centers to patronize or to avoid. Merchants who are oblivious to harassment can lose a large share of potential business. Allowing even a few harassers to operate in the shopping center, in the parking lot, or on the street out front (never mind in the store itself) drives women away even more efficiently than having a pornography/sex-paraphernalia shop next door. Sexual harassment (including the use of crude sexist advertising, the public equivalent of pornography in the workplace) very efficiently defines which parts of the public environment are accessible and which are off limits to women.

As the writer Katha Pollitt has noted, "Many women act—and are treated—as if the urban outdoors were alien ground. . . . A city in which women claimed their share of public space would look rather different and feel even more so." Pollitt cites the "constant low-level aggravation" of harassment, the fact that a bus stop is a "stage for female vulnerability," not just a place to wait for a bus, and half a dozen other examples. She describes the simple experience of walking through a small New York City park on an autumn afternoon: Within moments, two men harassed her; one "invited me to take my clothes off and [the other] wanted to know why I wasn't smiling." The park was unacknowledged but undeniable male territory: "[There] were perhaps 50 men, strolling, ambling, striding along eating hot dogs, sitting on benches and reading the paper or trading illegal substances as though they had all the time in the world—and 3 women, all walking quickly and grimly, as I was now doing, as though late for an appointment with the dentist." When a male friend later objected that the problem wasn't the men but the petty criminals in the park, Pollitt noted how interesting it was that he still felt comfortable enough to eat his lunch there, but the women he worked with did not. Pollitt concluded, "A great deal of what we call public space is, in fact, male turf."[1]

Sexual harassment transforms the urban landscape into a very different kind of terrain for women. Activities that seem perfectly unremarkable to men turn into steep, uphill battles for women. For example, when a national health and environmental magazine suggested a few years ago that running in the city was a delight and hikers should jog through downtown parks and streets to stay in shape, many women in Washington hooted with scorn. The article was, of course, written by a man, who assumed that *his* pleasant experience of running in the city was universal. The author never bothered to ask women what their runs were like, and had no idea of the barrage of interruptions, sexual comments, and verbal threats women receive every time they put on their running shorts.

As Katha Pollitt noted, bus stops, like parks, can be havens for harassers. For economic reasons, women are by far the majority of bus riders in most cities, but at bus stops they are a captive audience for harassers; most women will just endure the abuse, since leaving the vicinity to escape the harasser means missing the bus. However, women are not waiting for the bus companies to take action—they are now reclaiming this public space for themselves. Here's a classic success story from Martina in Philadelphia:

### THE BUS STOP

It was about 5:15 on a Wednesday afternoon. I came around the corner to catch the bus and saw seven or eight women and one man in the bus shelter. I could tell that something was going on. I saw him lurching up to one woman, then another, and I noticed that the women were standing very close together, looking uneasy. Then I got close enough to hear what he was saying. It was a steady stream of "Hey, mama, hey, bitch, you look good, I sure would like to lick you, hey, bitch, watsamatter, you don't like it that way, you uptight, how about you, honey. . . ." He was moving in on one woman after another in the group; they kept shifting closer to each other, looking the other way, trying to ignore him. It was really nasty—he was right up against them, in their faces.

I thought, "Boy, is this miserable—can't even catch the bus in our own neighborhood in peace!" So I took a deep breath and marched into the bus

---

[1] Katha Pollitt, "Hers," *New York Times,* December 12, 1985.

shelter. I said to the women, "Is this guy bothering you?" They nodded. I put my hands on my hips, stood there like I owned the pavement, and said, "Stop harassing women! I don't like it, no woman likes it! You get out of here!"

He turned on me, with a surprised look on his face. "Hey, bitch," he growled at me, "what you talking about I'm waiting for the bus!"

I took a half step toward him. I said, in my best voice-of-command tone, "This is OUR bus stop. You're harassing women. I heard what you were saying, bitch this and bitch that, you want to lick us. Stop harassing women! You want to catch the bus, you go wait down there by the stop sign. GO ON, MOVE!"

He hesitated. The women watched. Nobody breathed. I stood my ground, kept looking him straight in the eye, and repeated. "I SAID STOP HARASSING WOMEN! YOU HEARD ME! GO STAND BY THAT STOP SIGN!" Still no movement. Dead silence. Then he started to say something—it began with the word "bitch" but I didn't give him a chance to get the rest out. I kept going, just rolled right over him: "NONE OF US ARE GOING TO PUT UP WITH YOUR UGLY BEHAVIOR. THAT'S HARASSMENT AND WE ALL WANT YOU OUT OF THIS BUS SHELTER!"

And without another word he walked out of the shelter and over to the stop sign, fifteen feet away.

The women burst into cheers. Some actually clapped. I felt great. We talked about harassment; I told them how I'd learned to confront in the rape crisis center self-defense class. We were all still talking and laughing when the bus came, a few minutes later.

He stood there by the stop sign, looking kind of stunned—didn't say another word, and never did get on the bus.

Martina demonstrated how one woman can turn even a tough harassment situation around, if she knows what to do. She named the behavior, refused to let him off the hook, ordered him to stop, and kept control of the interaction by interrupting his efforts to intimidate her. It was touch and go for a few minutes. What finally defeated the harasser was her explicit statement on behalf of women in general— she redefined his victims as her allies and multiplied the power of her confrontation when she said that

*all* of the women wanted him out of their bus stop. When Martina emphasized their collective strength, she finally demolished his assumptions about his power to control the situation.           [1993]

## 115

# *In Case of Sexual Harassment: A Guide for Women Students*

BERNICE SANDLER

### *MYTHS ABOUT SEXUAL HARASSMENT*

Myth: Sexual harassment only happens to women who are provocatively dressed.

Fact: Sexual harassment can happen to anyone, no matter how she dresses.

Myth: If the women has only said "NO" to the harasser, he would have stopped immediately.

Fact: Many harassers are told "NO" repeatedly and it does no good. NO is too often heard as YES.

Myth: If a woman ignores sexual harassment, it will go away.

Fact: No, it won't. Generally, the harasser is a repeat offender who will not stop on his own. Ignoring it may be seen as assent or encouragement.

Myth: All men are harassers.

Fact: No, only a few men harass. Usually there is a pattern of harassment: one man harasses a number of women either sequentially or simultaneously, or both.

Myth: Sexual harassment is harmless. Women who object have no sense of humor.

Fact: Harassment is humiliating and degrading. It undermines school careers and often threatens economic livelihood. No one should have to endure humiliation with a smile.

Myth: Sexual harassment affects only a few people.

Fact: Surveys on campus shows that up to 30 percent of all female college students experience some form of sexual harassment. Some surveys of women in the working world have shown that as many as 70 percent have been sexually harassed in some way.

## WHAT YOU CAN DO ABOUT SEXUAL HARASSMENT

Ignoring sexual harassment does not make it go away. Indeed, it may make it worse because the harasser may misinterpret no response as approval of his behavior. However, there are things you can do, from informal strategies to formal ones. Here are some of your options.

• Know your rights. Sexual harassment is illegal in many instances. Your college or university may also have specific policies prohibiting faculty and staff from sexually harassing students and employees. Familiarize yourself with these policies. (For example, you can ask the Dean of Students if there is a policy.)

• Speak up at the time. Be sure to say "NO" clearly, firmly and without smiling. This is not a time to be polite or vague. (For example, you can say, "I don't like what you are doing," or "Please stop—you are making me very uncomfortable.") There is a chance—albeit small—that the harasser did not realize that his behavior was offensive to you. Additionally, if you decide to file charges at a later date, it is sometimes helpful, but not essential, to have objected to the behavior.

• Keep records, such as a journal and any letters or notes received. Note the dates, places, times, witnesses and the nature of the harassment—what he said and did and how you responded.

• Tell someone, such as fellow students or co-workers. Find out if others have been harassed by the same person and if they will support you should you decide to take action. Sharing your concern helps to avoid isolation and the tendency to blame yourself. Sexual harassment incidents are usually not isolated; most sexual harassers have typically harassed several or many people.

• Identify an advocate, perhaps a counselor, who can give you emotional support as well as help and information about both informal and formal institutional procedures.

• Write a letter. Many people have successfully stopped sexual harassment by writing a special kind of letter to the harasser. This letter should be polite, low-key and detailed, and consists of three parts:

• Part I is a factual account of what has happened, without any evaluation, as seen by the writer. It should be as detailed as possible with dates, places and a description of the incident(s). (For example, "Last week at the department party you asked me to go to bed with you." Or "On Oct. 21, when I came to you for advice on my test, you patted my knee and tried to touch my breast.")

• Part II describes how the writer feels about the events described in Part I, such as misery, dismay, distrust, and revulsion. (For example, "My stomach turns to knots when I come to class," or "I'm disgusted when I look at you.")

• Part III consists of what the writer wants to happen next. This part may be very short, since most writers usually just want the behavior to stop. (For example, "I don't even want you to touch me again or to make remarks about my sexuality," or "Please withdraw my last evaluation until we can work out a fair one.")

The letter should be delivered either in person or be registered or certified mail. Copies are not sent to campus officers or the press. The writer should keep at least one copy of the letter. (In the unlikely event that it fails to achieve its purpose, the letter can later be used to document retaliation or in support of a formal complaint or lawsuit.)

In most cases, the harasser is often astonished that his behavior is viewed in the way the writer sees it. He may also be fearful of a formal charge, and worry about who else has seen the letter. The letter also seems to be far more powerful than a verbal request—even those who may have ignored verbal requests to stop, often respond differently when the request is put into writing. The recipient of the letter rarely writes back; usually he just stops the sexual harassment immediately, and typically does not harass anyone else either.

Occasionally the harasser may want to apologize or discuss the situation. You don't need to discuss it if you don't want to—you can simply reiterate that you want the behavior to stop and it's not necessary to discuss it.

There are many advantages to writing a letter:

- It helps the victim regain a sense of being in control of the situation;
- it often avoids formal charges and a public confrontation;
- it keeps the incident(s) confidential;
- it provides the harasser with a new perspective on his behavior;
- it may minimize or prevent retaliation against the writer;
- it is not necessary to address questions such as legality, confidentiality, evidence and due process; and
- it usually works.                                        [1992]

# 116

## *style no. 1*

SONIA SANCHEZ

i come from a long line of rough mamas.

so here i was walking down market street. coming out of a city hall meeting. night wind at my back, dressed in my finest. black cashmere coat caressing the rim of my gray suede boots. hat sitting acey duecy. anointing the avenue with my black smell.

and this old dude. red as his car inching its way on the sidewalk. honked his horn. slid his body al-most out of his skin. toward me. psst. psst. hey. let's you and me have some fun. psst. psst. c'mon babe. don't you want some of this?

and he pulled his penis out of his pants. held the temporal wonder of men in his hands.

i stopped. looked at him. a memory from deep in the eye. a memory of saturday afternoon movie-houses where knowledge comes with a tremulous cry. old white men. spiderlike. spinning their webs towards young girls legs and out budabbot and lou-costello smiles melted. and we moved in the high noon walk of black girls. smelling the breath of an old undertow.

and i saw mama Dixon, dancing on his head. mama Dixon. big loud friend of the family. who stunned us with her curses and liquor. being herself. whose skin breathed hilarious breaths. and i greased my words on her tongue. and she gave them back to me like newly tasted wine.

motha fucka. you even offend the night i said. you look like an old mole coming out of its hole. take yo slimy sat ole ass home. fo you get what's coming to you. and yo generation. ask yo mama to skin you. that is if you have had one cuz anybody ugly as you couldna been born.

and i turned my eyes eastward. toward the ga-rage. waking up the incipient night with my steps. ready for the short days. the wind singing in my veins.                                                   [1987]

# Violence Against Women in Intimate Relationships

Physical violence directed at women by their intimate partners has made the home a frightening and dangerous place for the millions of women who are abused each year. For many of these women, fear of social judgment and shame often prevent them from speaking out about their lives, thereby gaining support and possibly changing their relationships. This section begins with the voices of two women who have found the courage to expose their abuse. Del Martin's friend and Mitsuye Yamada come from different cultural backgrounds yet share the terror of living with their abuser. The risks these women take in breaking their silence reveal that all too often, society tacitly condones violence against women in intimate relationships.

Myths and misconceptions prevent many people from understanding the experiences of battered women and the reasons that they stay in abusive relationships. Many assume that if "it was really that bad" abused women would leave the relationship. Others think that if "she learns to stay out of his way, she wouldn't get hurt." These myths are dangerous, setting the stage for social acceptance of this violence against women. The reality is that social and economic realities deter battered women from picking up and leaving abusive relationships. Ann Jones provides an overview of violence against women in the home, as well as in dating relationships, and suggests steps that our society must take to end this violence. She sees the connection between making political, social, and economic changes that address sexism and reducing violence against women.

Margaretta Wan Ling and Cheng Imm Tan discuss the experiences of Asian-American women who face numerous obstacles experienced at shelters for battered women and law enforcement agencies and imposed by the traditions of their own cultures. While these examples highlight the interaction of racism and sexism in the lives of women of color, they also demonstrate how all battered women confront similar issues and share common experiences.

# ❧ 117

# *A Letter From a Battered Wife*

DEL MARTIN

*A friend of mine received the following letter after discussing wife-beating at a public meeting.*

I am in my thirties and so is my husband. I have a high school diploma and am presently attending a local college, trying to obtain the additional education I need. My husband is a college graduate and a professional in his field. We are both attractive and, for the most part, respected and well-liked. We have four children and live in a middle-class home with all the comforts we could possibly want.

I have everything, except life without fear.

For most of my married life I have been periodically beaten by my husband. What do I mean by "beaten"? I mean that parts of my body have been hit violently and repeatedly, and that painful bruises, swelling, bleeding wounds, unconsciousness, and combinations of these things have resulted.

Beating should be distinguished from all other kinds of physical abuse—including being hit and shoved around. When I say my husband threatens me with abuse I do not mean he warns me that he may lose control. I mean that he shakes a fist against my face or nose, makes punching-bag jabs at my shoulder, or makes similar gestures which may quickly turn into a full-fledged beating.

I have had glasses thrown at me. I have been kicked in the abdomen when I was visibly pregnant. I have been kicked off the bed and hit while lying on the floor—again, while I was pregnant. I have been whipped, kicked and thrown, picked up again and thrown down again. I have been punched and kicked in the head, chest, face, and abdomen more times than I can count.

I have been slapped for saying something about politics, for having a different view about religion, for swearing, for crying, for wanting to have intercourse. I have been threatened when I wouldn't do something he told me to do. I have been threatened when he's had a bad day and when he's had a good day.

I have been threatened, slapped, and beaten after stating bitterly that I didn't like what he was doing with another woman.

After each beating my husband has left the house and remained away for a few days.

Few people have ever seen my black and blue face or swollen lips because I have always stayed indoors afterwards, feeling ashamed. I was never able to drive following one of these beatings, so I could not get myself to a hospital for care. I could never have left my young children alone, even if I could have driven a car.

Hysteria inevitably sets in after a beating. This hysteria—the shaking and crying and mumbling—is not accepted by anyone, so there has never been anyone to call.

My husband on a few occasions did phone a day or so later so we could agree on an excuse I would use for returning to work, the grocery store, the dentist appointment, and so on. I used the excuses—a car accident, oral surgery, things like that.

Now, the first response to this story, which I myself think of, will be "Why didn't you seek help?"

I did. Early on in our marriage I went to a clergyman who, after a few visits, told me that my husband meant no real harm, that he was just confused and felt insecure. I was encouraged to be more tolerant and understanding. Most important, I was told to forgive him the beatings just as Christ had forgiven me from the cross. I did that, too.

Things continued. Next time I turned to the doctor. I was given little pills to relax me and told to take things a little easier. I was just too nervous.

I turned to a friend, and when her husband found out, he accused me of either making things up or exaggerating the situation. She didn't, but she could no longer really help me. Just by believing me she was made to feel disloyal.

I turned to a professional family guidance agency. I was told there that my husband needed help and that I should find a way to control the incidents. I couldn't control the beatings—that was the whole point of my seeking help. At the agency I found I had to defend myself against the suspicion that I wanted to be hit, that I invited the beatings. Good God! Did the Jews invite themselves to be slaughtered in Germany?

I did go to two more doctors. One asked me what

I had done to provoke my husband. The other asked if we had made up yet.

I called the police one time. They not only did not respond to the call, they called several hours later to ask if things had "settled down." I could have been dead by then!

I have nowhere to go if it happens again. No one wants to take in a woman with four children. Even if there were someone kind enough to care, no one wants to become involved in what is commonly referred to as a "domestic situation."

Everyone I have gone to for help has somehow wanted to blame me and vindicate my husband. I can see it lying there between their words and at the end of their sentences. The clergyman, the doctor, the counselor, my friend's husband, the police—all of them have found a way to vindicate my husband.

No one has to "provoke" a wife-beater. He will strike out when he's ready and for whatever reason he has at the moment.

I may be his excuse, but I have never been the reason.

I know that I do not want to be hit. I know, too, that I will be beaten again unless I can find a way out for myself and my children. I am terrified for them also.

As a married woman I have no recourse but to remain in the situation which is causing me to be painfully abused. I have suffered physical and emotional battering and spiritual rape because the social structure of my world says I cannot do anything about a man who wants to beat me. . . . But staying with my husband means that my children must be subjected to the emotional battering caused when they see their mother's beaten face or hear her screams in the middle of the night.

I know that I have to get out. But when you have nowhere to go, you know that you must go on your own and expect no support. I have to be ready for that. I have to be ready to support myself and the children completely, and still provide a decent environment for them. I pray that I can do that before I am murdered in my own home.

I have learned that no one believes me and that I cannot depend upon any outside help. All I have left is the hope that I can get away before it is too late.

I have learned also that the doctors, the police, the clergy, and my friends will excuse my husband

for distorting my face, but won't forgive me for looking bruised and broken. The greatest tragedy is that I am still praying, and there is not a human person to listen.

Being beaten is a terrible thing; it is most terrible of all if you are not equipped to fight back. I recall an occasion when I tried to defend myself and actually tore my husband's shirt. Later, he showed it to a relative as proof that I had done something terribly wrong. The fact that at that moment I had several raised spots on my head hidden by my hair, a swollen lip that was bleeding, and a severely damaged cheek with a blood clot that caused a permanent dimple didn't matter to him. What mattered was that I tore his shirt! That I tore it in self-defense didn't mean anything to him.

My situation is so untenable I would guess that anyone who has not experienced one like it would find it incomprehensible. I find it difficult to believe myself.

It must be pointed out that while a husband can beat, slap, or threaten his wife, there are "good days." These days tend to wear away the effects of the beating. They tend to cause the wife to put aside the traumas and look to the good—first, because there is nothing else to do; second, because there is nowhere and no one to turn to; and third, because the defeat is the beating and the hope is that it will not happen again. A loving woman like myself always hopes that it will not happen again. When it does, she simply hopes again, until it becomes obvious after a third beating that there is no hope. That is when she turns outward for help to find an answer. When that help is denied, she either resigns herself to the situation she is in or pulls herself together and starts making plans for a future life that includes only herself and her children.

For many the third beating may be too late. Several of the times I have been abused I have been amazed that I have remained alive. Imagine that I have been thrown to a very hard slate floor several times, kicked in the abdomen, the head, and the chest, and still remained alive!

What determines who is lucky and who isn't? I could have been dead a long time ago had I been hit the wrong way. My baby could have been killed or deformed had I been kicked the wrong way. What saved me?

I don't know. I only know that it has happened and that each night I dread the final blow that will kill me and leave my children motherless. I hope I can hang on until I complete my education, get a good job, and become self-sufficient enough to care for my children on my own. [1983]

## 🌿 118

## *The Club*

MITSUYE YAMADA

He beat me with the hem of a kimono
worn by a Japanese woman
this prized
painted
wooden statue
carved to perfection
in Japan or maybe Hong Kong.

She was usually on display
in our living room atop his bookshelf
among his other overseas treasures
I was never to touch.
She posed there most of the day
her head tilted
her chin resting lightly
on the white pointed fingertips
of her right hand
her black hair
piled high on her head
her long slim neck bared
to her shoulders.
An invisible hand
under the full sleeve
clasped her kimono
close to her body
its hem flared
gracefully around her feet.

That hem
made fluted red marks
on these freckled arms
my shoulders
my back.

That head
inside his fist
made camel
bumps
on his knuckles.
I prayed for her
that her pencil thin neck
would not snap
or his rage would be unendurable.
She held fast for me
didn't even chip or crack.

One day, we were talking
as we often did the morning after.
Well, my sloe-eyed beauty, I said
have you served him enough?
I dared to pick her up with one hand
I held her gently by the flowing robe
around her slender legs.
She felt lighter than I had imagined.
I stroked her cold thighs
with the tips of my fingers
and felt a slight tremor.

I carried her into the kitchen and wrapped her
in two sheets of paper towels
We're leaving
I whispered
you and I
together.

I placed her
between my clothes in my packed suitcase.
That is how we left him
forever. [1989]

## 🌿 119

## *Battering: Who's Going to Stop It?*

ANN JONES

"He's fucking going nuts . . . ," Nicole Brown Simpson told a police dispatcher on October 25, 1993. Eight months later, after O. J. Simpson was arrested for the murder of his ex-wife and her friend Ronald Goldman, that 911-call was played and replayed on television and radio, plunging startled Americans into the midst of a typical terrifying incident of what we lamely call "domestic" violence. Previously, both O. J. Simpson and Jon Russo, vice president of the Hertz Corporation, which retained Simpson as its spokesman even after he pleaded no contest to assaulting Nicole in 1989, had described O. J.'s wife beating as a private "family matter" of no significance.

The press calls O. J. Simpson the most famous American ever charged with murder, but he's certainly not the first celebrity to be a batterer, or even to be implicated in homicide. In fact, the list of celebrity batterers from the sports world alone is a long one which includes boxer Sugar Ray Leonard, baseball star Daryl Strawberry, former University of Alabama basketball coach Wimp Sanderson, former heavyweight champ Mike Tyson (cited by then-wife Robin Givens and subsequently convicted of raping Miss Black Rhode Island), California Angels pitcher Donnie Moore (who shot and wounded his estranged wife, Tonya, before killing himself in 1989), and Philadelphia Eagles defensive lineman Blenda Gay (stabbed to death in 1976 by his battered wife, Roxanne, who said she acted in self-defense).

The list of entertainers named as batterers is also lengthy and star-studded. Tina Turner reported in her autobiography that husband Ike abused her for years. Ali MacGraw described the violent assaults of Steve McQueen. Sheila Ryan sued her thenhusband James Caan in 1980, alleging that he'd beaten her. Madonna accused Sean Penn, and Daryl Hannah named Jackson Browne. Such incidents make titillating copy for scandal sheets and tabloid TV.

And such incidents continue to be commonplace—as all-American as football—precisely because so many people still think of battering as, in O. J.'s words, "no big deal." But when America listened last June to that 911-tape, eavesdropping on the private, violent raging of the man publicly known as the cool, affable Juice, anyone could hear that what Nicole Brown was up against was a very big deal indeed. For the first time, Americans could hear for themselves the terror that millions of American women live with every day.

That terror begins with small, private, seemingly ordinary offenses. Take this list of complaints logged in a single week by the security office of one small institution. One woman harassed by "unwanted attention" from a man. One woman "annoyed" at finding "obscene photographs" in her desk. Two women "annoyed" by obscene phone calls from men. One woman sexually assaulted in her living quarters by a male acquaintance. One woman stalked by a man in violation of a restraining order.

Routine offenses? You bet. And they're increasingly common—not just because women are fed up with such behavior and reporting it more often, but because these days there's more and worse to report.

What makes this particular list of complaints noteworthy is that it comes from the security office at a small New England college—the sort of place where old stone buildings surround a quadrangle shaded by ancient trees. The sort of place where parents who can afford it send their daughters to be *safe* from the dangers of the "real" world, safe from violence and violent men.

These days, however, there seems to be no safe haven. Not in exclusive Brentwood. Not even on the picture-perfect college campus. Violence, which has always struck women of every social class and race, seems to be aimed increasingly at the young.

Last year, at Mount Holyoke College—the oldest women's college in the country—the student newspaper carried the front page headline: "Domestic Violence on the Rise." Reported cases of "domestic" violence were increasing all across the country, according to student reporter Gretchen Hitchner—and on the Mount Holyoke campus as well. "There are five or six students on campus who have obtained stay-away orders," Hitchner reported.

Beyond the boundaries of the campus, the statistics grew much worse. Statewide, in Massachusetts in 1991, a woman was murdered by a current or former husband or boyfriend every twenty days. By 1993, such a murder occurred once every eight days. Among the dead: Tara Hartnett, a twenty-one-year-old senior psychology major at the nearby University of Massachusetts at Amherst. In February 1993, Tara Hartnett had obtained a restraining order against James Cyr, Jr., her former boyfriend and the father of her eleven-month-old daughter. In March, when Hartnett's roommates were away on spring break, Cyr broke in, stabbed Hartnett, set the house on fire, and left her to die of smoke inhalation.

"Incidents" like the murder of Tara Hartnett happen all the time. Every day, in fact, four or five women die in the United States at the hands of their current or former husbands or boyfriends. But recently feminists (like me) who call attention to these crimes have been taking a lot of heat for perpetuating the image of women as "victims." Critics charge that "victim feminists" exaggerate the dangers women face in male violence. Katie Roiphe, for example, suggests in her book *The Morning After* that most alleged cases of date rape involve nothing more than second thoughts by daylight after bad sex the night before. Battering, according to the critics, is nothing that any woman with moderate self-esteem and a bus token can't escape. What prevents women from exercising our full female power and strength, some say, is not male violence but the *fear* of violence induced by fuddy-duddy feminists who see all women as victims.

Could it be true that the apparent crime wave against women, on campus and off, is only a delusion of paranoid radical feminists? Is it real violence that keeps women down, or only feminists' hysterical perceptions that hamper us?

In Canada, where the same questions were raised, Statistics Canada attempted to find out by interviewing 12,300 women nationwide in the most comprehensive study of violence against women ever undertaken. The results were worse than expected. They showed violence against women to be far more common than earlier, smaller scale studies had indicated. They revealed that more than half of Canadian women (51 percent) have been physically or sexually assaulted at least once in their adult lives. And more than half of those women said they'd been attacked by dates, boyfriends, husbands, friends, family members, or other men familiar to them. One in ten Canadian women, or one million, had been attacked in the past year.

These figures apply only to Canada, but considering that the United States is a more violent culture all around, it's unlikely that women in the United States are any safer from attack. In fact, battering alone is now the single leading cause of injury to women in the United States. A million women every year visit physicians and hospital emergency rooms for treatment of battering injuries. The National Centers for Disease Control identify battering as a leading cause of the spread of HIV and AIDS, as countless batterers force "their" women into unprotected sex. The American Medical Association reports that 38 percent of obstetric patients are battered during pregnancy, and studies name battering during pregnancy a cause of birth defects and infant mortality.

Survivors confirm that a man often begins to batter during a woman's first pregnancy, when she is most vulnerable and least able to pack up and move. Marie's husband, a lawyer, beat her so severely during her seventh month that she went into labor. He then ripped out the phone, locked her in a second-floor bedroom, and left the house. She barely survived, and the little boy she bore that day has always been small and frail. Carol miscarried after her husband knocked her down and kicked her repeatedly in the belly. He threatened to kill her if she tried to leave. When she became pregnant again, he beat her again, saying "I'm going to kill that baby and you, too." Instead, she killed him with his own gun and was sentenced to twenty years in prison, where she bore her child and gave it up for adoption. Jean left her husband after he repeatedly punched her in the belly while she was pregnant. Later, when a doctor told Jean that her daughter had epilepsy, he asked if Jean had suffered a fall or an "accident" of any kind during pregnancy. Now that her daughter is in college and still suffering seizures, Jean says, "I only lived with that man for a year, but he casts his shadow over every day of my life, and my daughter's, too."

Millions of women live with such consequences of male violence, but it's not surprising that many choose another way out. Battering is cited as a contributing factor in a quarter of all suicide attempts by women, and half of all suicide attempts by black women. At least 50 percent of homeless women and children in the United States are in flight from male violence. Only a few years ago the FBI reported that in the United States a man beats a woman every eighteen seconds. By 1989, the figure was fifteen seconds. Now it's twelve.

Some people take those facts and statistics at face value to mean that male violence is on the rise; while others argue that what's increasing is merely the *reporting* of violence. But no matter how you interpret the numbers, it's clear that male violence is not going *down*.

As crime statistics go, homicide figures are most likely to be accurate, for the simple reason that homicides produce corpses—hard to hide and easy to count. Homicide figures all across the country—like those in Massachusetts—indicate so clearly that violence against women is on the rise that some sociologists have coined a new term for a common crime: "femicide." The FBI estimates that every year men murder about three thousand wives and girlfriends. The conclusion is inescapable: male violence against women is *real*. And it is widespread.

Such violence was once thought of as the plague of married women, but battering, like date rape, affects young, single women as well. In its recent study, Statistics Canada found that a disproportionate number of women reporting physical or sexual assault were young. Women ages eighteen to twenty-four were more than twice as likely as older women to report violence in the year preceding the study; 27 percent of them had been attacked in the past year. In the United States, the first study of "premarital abuse," conduced in 1985, reported that one in five college students was the victim of "physical aggression," ranging from slapping and hitting to "more life threatening violence." When a guy who'd had too much to drink offered Sarah a ride home from a fraternity party, she turned him down and advised him not to drive. He waited for her outside and beat her up—to "teach the bitch a lesson," he said. Susan went home for her first break from college and told her hometown boyfriend that she wanted to date at school. In response, he deliberately pulled out clumps of her hair, broke her arm, and drove her car into a tree. After Bonnie broke up with a possessive guy she'd been dating at college, he sneaked into her home at night and smashed in

her head with a hatchet. Typically, guys like this think they're *entitled* to get their way, by any means necessary. Resorting to violence seems justified to them. They think they've done nothing wrong—or at least no more than she *asked* for.

Even high school boys are acting out the macho myth. A study of white middle-class high school juniors and seniors found that roughly one in four had some experience of dating violence, either as victim or perpetrator. In another study one in three teenage girls reported being subjected to physical violence by a date. After reviewing many such studies of high school and college students, Barrie Levy, author of *In Love and In Danger: A Teen's Guide to Breaking Free of Abusive Relationships*, reports that "an average of twenty-eight percent of the students experienced violence in a dating relationship. That is more than one in every four students." Male counselors who work with wife beaters confirm that many older batterers first began to use violence as teenagers, against their dates.

That doesn't mean that violence against young women is just "kid's stuff." According to the FBI, 20 percent of women murdered in the United States are between the ages of fifteen and twenty-four. Recently a high school boy in Texas shot his girlfriend for being "unfaithful," and for good measure he killed her best friend, too. Former police officer Barbara Arrighi, who has witnessed increased date rape, battering, and stalking among college students as assistant director for public safety at Mount Holyoke College, bluntly sums up the situation: "Anyone who doesn't believe America has a serious problem with violence against young women," she says, "is living in Lalaland."

Some who've studied dating violence say young women may be more vulnerable to male aggression because they believe so innocently in "true love." Schooled by romance novels and rock videos, which typically mingle sex and violence, they're more likely to mistake jealousy, possessiveness, control, and even physical or sexual assault for passion and commitment. In fact, in some surveys of college dating, about one-third of students interviewed reported that their relationships *improved* after violence—although most of the students who said so were men.

Consider the case of Kristin Lardner who was twenty-one in 1992 when her ex-boyfriend Michael Cartier gunned her down on a Boston street, then later shot himself. Kristin Lardner herself was scared to death of Michael Cartier, a man she had dated for only two months; and she did just what abused women are supposed to do. She stopped dating Cartier the first time he hit her; and when he followed her, knocked her down in the street, and kicked her unconscious, she got a restraining order against him. But even after she was murdered, Lardner's roommate and best friend still bought the "romantic" view of Michael Cartier's violence. She told reporters that Lardner had "cared" about Cartier, and "she was the only one who ever did. That's what pushed him over the edge . . . when he lost her."

Young men, too, buy into this romantic scenario. One of Michael Cartier's male friends commented after the murder: "He loved her a lot and it was probably a crime of passion. He didn't do it because he's nuts," the friend said. "He was in love."

But Cartier's former girlfriend, Rose Ryan, also talked to reporters, and what she had to say put Michael Cartier's "love" in a new light. She had cared about Cartier, too, she said, and for months she had tried to make him happy with love and kindness and Christmas presents, even after he started to abuse her. It didn't work. Finally, after he attacked her with scissors, she brought assault charges against him and got him jailed for six months. Then, after Cartier murdered Kristin Lardner, Rose Ryan spoke about his "lovemaking." "After he hit me several times in the head," she said, "he started to cry." He would say, "I'm so sorry. I always hit people I love." And the clincher: "My mother, she never loved me. You're the only one."

It's a familiar part of the batterer's control technique, that message. And it often works because it appeals at once to a woman's compassion and her power, snaring her in a web of "love" and "violence" as two contradictory concepts become inextricably entwined. It leads some women to reinterpret a boyfriend's violent behavior as passion. It leads some—like Rose Ryan for a while—to forgive and try to help a batterer to change. Attorney Lynne Gold-Birkin, founder of the American Bar Association's Committee on Domestic Violence and chair of the ABA's family law section, recently pointed out on ABC's *This Week with David Brinkley* that many married women subjected to abuse don't walk out at once "because they don't want the marriage to end; they want him to stop beating them." But in the end, as the story of Kristin Lardner shows, even a woman who tolerates no violence at all is not safe from it.

To find an explanation for the high rate of male violence against young women, we have to look to the source: to men. Many people still mistakenly believe that batterers are somehow different from ordinary men—that they are "crazy" men with short fuses who "lose control" of themselves and blow up, especially when under the influence of drink or drugs. But those who counsel batterers say that just the reverse is true: the battering man is perfectly in control of himself—and of the woman he batters. That, after all, is the purpose of battering. A man—of any age—threatens, intimidates, abuses, and batters a woman to make her do what he wants. It works. He gets his way, and as a bonus he gets a heady rush of experiencing his own power. As one reformed eighteen-year-old guy put it: "I enjoyed intimidating people." David Adams, director of Emerge, a Boston counseling program for batterers, points out that the same man who says he "loses control" of his temper with "his" woman will be perfectly calm when the police arrive. "Clearly he knows what he's doing," Adams says. "He's making rational choices about how to act with whom—on the basis of what he can get away with."

It's likely, then, that young women—even young women "in love"—get battered for the same reason older women get battered. Namely, they have minds of their own. They want to do what *they* want. Battered women are often mistakenly thought of as "passive" or "helpless" because some of them look that way *after* they've been beaten into submission and made hostage to terror. Their inability to escape is the *result* of battering, not its cause. According to one study, three out of four battering victims are actually single or separated women trying to get free of men who won't let them go. They are not merely victims; they are the resistance. But they are almost entirely on their own.

How can we help women get free of this violence? That's the question that survivors of battering and their advocates have been grappling with for twenty years. And they've done a phenomenal job. Never before in history has there been such an organization of crime victims united to rescue other victims and prevent further crimes. Although battered women's shelters are still so overburdened that they must turn away more women than they take in, they have provided safe haven over the years for millions of women and their children. Undoubtedly, they have saved thousands of lives.

In addition, the battered women's movement has brought battering out of the private household and into the spotlight of public debate. There it has raised a much harder question: how can we make men stop their violence? To that end, the battered women's movement has pushed for—and achieved—big changes in legislation, public policy, and law enforcement. The Violence against Women Act, passed by Congress in 1994, is only one recent example. This bill correctly considers male violence against women as a violation of women's civil rights and provides a wide range of legal remedies for women.

But what's needed is a national campaign to go after the men at fault. Experts such as Susan Schechter, author of *Women and Male Violence*, say that men continue to use violence to get their way *because they can*. Nobody stops them. There's no reason for a man who uses violence to change his behavior unless he begins to suffer some real consequences, some punishment that drives home strong social and legal prohibitions against battering. In the short run, the most effective way to protect women and children, save lives, and cut down violence is to treat assault as the crime it is: to arrest batterers and send them to jail.

Usually, that's not what happens. Right now, most batterers suffer *no* social or legal consequences at all for their criminal behavior. Although police in most states and localities are now authorized to arrest batterers, many police departments still don't enforce the law. If police do make arrests, prosecutors commonly fail to prosecute. And if batterers are convicted, judges often release them—or worse, order them into marital counseling *with* the women they've assaulted. Many men are required to attend a few weekly sessions of a therapeutic support group where they shoot the breeze with other batterers, after which their crime is erased from the record books. (Counselors like David Adams who lead such groups are the first to say that the groups don't work.) One 1991 study found that among assaultive men arrested, prosecuted, convicted, and sentenced, less than 1 percent (0.9 percent) served any time in jail. The average batterer taken into custody by police is held less than two hours. He walks away laughing at his victim and at the police as well.

Even men convicted of near-fatal attacks upon their girlfriends or wives are likely to draw light sentences or be released on probation with plenty of opportunity to finish the job. The husband of Burnadette Barnes, for example, shot her in the head while she slept, served three months in prison for the offense, and was released to threaten her again. Desperate, Burnadette Barnes hired a man to kill her husband. She was convicted of murder and conspiracy to murder and sentenced to life in prison.

In Michigan, police officer Clarence Ratliff shot and killed his estranged wife, Carol Irons, who incidentally was the youngest woman ever appointed to the Michigan bench. (As a judge she was known to treat domestic violence cases seriously.) When the police tried to arrest Ratliff, he squeezed off a few wild shots before he surrendered. For killing his wife, Ratliff got ten to fifteen years; for shooting at the cops, two life terms plus some additional shorter terms for using a firearm.

Such cases make clear that in the scales of American justice men weigh more than women. Assaulting a man is a serious crime, but assaulting a woman or even killing her—well, that's not so bad.

We can do better. Thanks to the battered women's movement, we now know that any social, economic, or political development that counteracts sexism and promotes sex equality helps in the long run to eliminate violence by reducing the power men hold, individually and institutionally, over women. We now know that all the institutions to which battered women and children are likely to turn for help—hospitals, mental health facilities, social welfare services, child protective services, police departments, civil and criminal courts, schools, churches—must join a *concerted* effort to prevent violence before it occurs and stop it when it does. They must stand ready to defend the constitutional right that belongs to all women—(though no one ever speaks of it): the right to be free from bodily harm.

That's where college can set a good example for the rest of society. While public officials often seem to accept violence against women as an inevitable social problem, colleges can't afford to. They're obliged to keep their students safe. Mount Holyoke's Barbara Arrighi says,

> We've had to work at safety, but as a closed, self-contained system we have advantages over the big world. If one of our students is victimized, she finds a whole slew of helpers available right away—campus and city police, medical services, housing authorities, counselors, chaplains, academic deans. We'll ban offenders from the campus under trespass orders. We'll make arrests. We'll connect her to the county prosecutor's victim/witness assistance program. We'll go to court with her. We'll help her get a protective order or file a civil complaint. We take these things seriously, we don't try to pin the blame on her, and we don't fool around.

What Arrighi describes is the way the system ought to work in every community.

As things stand now, it's still up to women to make the system respond—and too often, on a case-by-case basis. It takes time, money, courage, and determination to get a result that looks like justice. Take the case of Stephanie Cain, for example. A college student, she had dated Elton "Tony" Ekstrom III for nine months. Then, during the course of one hour on the night of April 28, 1992, he beat her up. He punched and kicked her repeatedly, leaving her with a fractured nose and a face nearly unrecognizable to those who saw her immediately following the attack. Afterward, she said, she lost confidence and mistrusted people. She suffered seizures and had to drop out of college. Major surgery to reconstruct her nose permanently altered her appearance.

Ekstrom was arrested and charged with assault and battery with a dangerous weapon: his foot. But Stephanie Cain wasn't permitted to tell her story in court, for Ekstrom never went to trial. Instead he was allowed to plead guilty to a reduced charge of assault and battery. The judge gave him a two-year suspended sentence, and Ekstrom walked away—still thinking he'd done nothing wrong.

That result upset Stephanie Cain. Worried that Ekstrom might do the same thing to another woman, she decided to sue him for the damage he'd done. In December 1992, when she was back in college finishing her degree, she finally got her day in court. "The best part," she said, "was looking right at him, knowing I wasn't afraid of him anymore." After hearing her story, the jury awarded Cain and her parents $153,000 in damages for her injuries, medical expenses, and emotional distress. At last Ekstrom was to pay a price for his criminal act, as a civil court jury compensated Stephanie Cain for a crime the criminal court had failed to punish. "Every time I look in the mirror," Cain said, "I'm reminded of what happened. There's no reason he should just forget it."

The victory she won was a victory for all women. But it shouldn't have been that hard. And she shouldn't have had to fight for justice all by herself.

[1996]

# 120

# *Holding Up More Than Half the Heavens*

MARGARETTA WAN LING AND CHENG IMM TAN

Because of the barriers of language, culture, and economic disparities and the vagaries of racism and sexism, Asian Pacific American (APA) victims of domestic violence suffer revictimization at the hands of institutions designed to serve battered women. According to the 1990 U.S. Census, Asians and Pacific Islanders are the fastest growing minority group, totalling nearly seven million. And yet, in the entire United States only two shelters exist for APA women, one safe-home network and one advocacy group that provides culturally sensitive programs and counseling.[1] Of the domestic violence resources available—police, shelters, hotlines, human services programs—few have staff who speak Asian Pacific languages. Given the highly sensitive nature of addressing domestic violence, it is unacceptable not to have linguistically accessible resources. The language barrier, in effect, shuts out most refugee and immigrant women. In addition, many battered women's shelters turn away APA women because of language and cultural difficulties or sheer racism. Economic concerns present yet another obstacle. Most women who are victims of domestic violence do not have control of the family's money. Many leave their homes with little besides the clothes on their backs. This means that many battered APA women who have gathered up the strength and courage to flee the violence in their homes must then return there because they have no other viable options. Legal protection is also often both inaccessible because of cultural and linguistic barriers and unavailable because of institutionalized racism and sexism. There are too many examples of the revictimization of battered APA women by institutionalized forces; it would require another whole book just to document the abuses we have seen. Consider the story of Ling.

One evening as Ling was cleaning some fish for dinner her husband, who had beaten her repeatedly for the past eight years, and had given her concussions, a broken hip, and a broken jaw, began to pick a fight. Ling did not answer any of his accusations and her enduring silence made him even angrier. He picked up a chair to strike her. She sidestepped the impending blow and screamed at him to stop. The chair broke against the door and he lunged at her, more enraged than before. Ling tried to ward him off by waving the knife that she had been using to clean the fish for dinner that evening. He continued to lunge at her and in attempting to get the knife, fell upon the knife and cut himself. He continued to strike out at Ling.

Terrified, Ling ran to a nearby store to call the police. When the police came, her husband who spoke good English, accused Ling of attacking him. Ling's English was not enough to defend herself. The police whom she called arrested Ling and put her in jail. They set her bond at $2,500. The case against Ling is still pending. This is how our justice system works to protect battered women.

### THE PRIMACY OF FEAR OF RACIST ATTACKS, THE SACRIFICE OF OUR SISTERS

Within each ethnic group, male control and domestic violence take on culturally specific expressions. APA communities have tolerated and overlooked domestic violence for some of the same reasons that mainstream society has tolerated and overlooked it for so long—the unquestioning acceptance of patriarchy, of male control and privilege. Some APA activists worry that bringing domestic violence into the open will confirm negative stereotypes about the community, and further fuel the fires of anti-Asian sentiment. To expose the problem within APA communities is not a statement about the greater violence or misogyny in Asian Pacific culture. Instead, the sad reality is that Asian men, like all other men, live in a male-dominated culture that views women as property, objects they must control and possess. Compounding this reality, or underlying it, are cultures that view violence as an acceptable solution to problems.

As a reaction to the pervasive racism and cultural imperialism that threaten to undermine our cultural integrity, APA activists and community leaders have been reluctant to look self-critically at traditional misogynistic attitudes and practices for fear that it would reinforce racist stereotypes about Asian Pacific Americans. This attitude of denial, however, does not keep racism at bay. Instead, it is at odds with cherished notions of our rights as humans and citizens.

The same reasons that inspire the unequivocal and emphatic support of APA activists to identify crimes motivated by race, color, and/or national origin as hate crimes hold for crimes motivated by gender. As with crimes of racist hate, statistics on domestic violence are inadequate; elected officials will not fund programs until we fully document the violence; keeping such statistics would encourage more public awareness and debate on the crimes.

While there is an emerging effort on the part of APA women activists to include domestic violence as a hate crime, APA civil rights and advocacy groups have not supported their work. We believe that along with sexist motivations, fear of betraying our brothers, of adding to their oppression, plays a role in the glaring absence of their support. Such fear causes APA activists to overlook and ignore domestic violence. It has meant sacrificing the lives of our sisters.

A heinous example of this is Dong Lu Chen's murder of his wife, Jian Wan Chen, and his successful use of the cultural defense. On September 7, 1987, Jian Wan Chen's husband smashed her skull in with a claw hammer after she allegedly admitted to having an affair. Chen's teenage son discovered her body in the family's Brooklyn apartment. The trial judge sentenced Dong to five years probation on a reduced manslaughter charge after concluding, based on the testimony of an anthropologist, that Dong was driven to violence by traditional Chinese values about adultery and loss of manhood. APA activists came out in support of the cultural defense as a necessary tool to protect immigrants in U.S. courtrooms.

Does this mean that Jian Wan Chen's immigrant status is negligible, or that such activists believe that Asian men are traditionally more violent and misogynistic than their white counterparts? Does it mean that the status of Jian Wan Chen as an Asian sister, as a human being, is negligible when weighed against the crime of her husband? And what are the repercussions of such outrage? Domestic violence counselors have reported that the case has convinced many battered APA women that they have no protection, period. As for the lawyers, they feel "empowered" to use the cultural defense at any opportunity.[2] What does this say about our society, about our value of human life, about our perception of justice?

The fear of racist attacks on our cultures and communities is so pervasive and deep that it has frustrated our attempts at addressing domestic violence in APA communities. When we first started addressing such issues in the Boston area, we re-

ceived harassing calls, our tires were slashed, threats and accusations were made that we were family-wreckers. This fear and anger from the APA community have also compromised our strategies in responding to domestic violence. Activists and community leaders have advocated treatments that do not threaten traditional beliefs and practices, such as mediation, family counseling, and elder intervention. Such measures, however, do not address the underlying attitudes and institutions that uphold violence against APA women and children.

## OUR STRUGGLE TOGETHER

Domestic violence demeans and destroys our communities more than any other violence perpetuated on us. It is not an isolated issue. It is not a private family affair protected by the rights of privacy. It is a violent crime of hate that attacks the very fiber of our collective health and we should treat it as such. Symptoms of the sickness spill beyond the confines of the home and taint our participation in the community, our performances in jobs and schools, our personal relationships. It harms every aspect of our lives and the lives that we touch. Because it is premised on unequal relationships and because of its destructive and often fatal impact, domestic violence is not suitable for internal solutions nor should the rights of privacy protect it.

The power to define domestic violence, to give credence to its reality, means much more than validating the experiences of battered women and children. Recognizing the critical dimensions of domestic violence in APA communities translates into accessing resources for dealing with the symptoms, such as making local community health clinics and doctors aware of and able to treat the problems, providing multilingual and multicultural services, and making outside funding sources available to shelters and programs. It means community pressure—saying that domestic violence is unacceptable, that we can no longer sweep it under the proverbial rug or sanction it with patriarchal/misogynist sayings. It means, most of all, empowering victims: stopping the internalization of blame, recognizing their agency to leave, and reaching the empowerment to heal and realize their potentials as humans.

We Asian Pacific Americans in control of our

destinies, who are concerned about the well-being of our families and our communities, we must be the ones to break the silence.

Our challenge as leaders and activists in our communities is to strategize ways we can work together to address domestic violence in our own communities. We need to examine and change the underlying attitudes and structures within our communities that maintain violence against women and children. We need to focus on both intervention and prevention. We need to work together on outreach and education to make our communities aware of domestic violence issues and to create intolerance to violence against women and children.

Those of us who work in community health and social services agencies must make information on domestic violence available. We need to have in-house training sessions for our staff so they will understand the seriousness of the problem and know, at the very least, how to approach suspected victims of domestic violence to offer information and resources. We need to take on the responsibility and be the vehicle for change. We need to begin to collect data on domestic violence. As long as no data exist, government agencies at all levels can deny the problem and we will continue to lack the political leverage to advocate for appropriate services.

We need to push for multilingual and multicultural services in the human service, legal, and law enforcement systems so that they do not overlook or underserve the needs of Asian Pacific Americans. We need ethnically specific services like Asian women's shelters and resources that are culturally sensitive and appropriate but also connected to the larger resources. Lack of access to services places the lives of Asian Pacific American women and children at unnecessary risk.

Most of all, we need to go inward, deep within, to examine the effects of domestic violence on our persons, to get rid of the shame and blame we feel as victims, to recognize our responsibility and agency for change if we are perpetrators of the violence, to heal the wounds that keep us silent and complicit.                                    [1994]

### NOTES

1. Centers in San Francisco, Los Angeles, and New York City provide programs for Chinese, Korean, Philippine, Japanese, Indonesian, Laotian, Vietnamese, and Cambodian women, and are staffed with multilingual abuse-hotlines. A program in Boston provides counseling and advocacy services for Vietnamese, Cambodian, and Chinese women. Bilingual hotlines are available for Koreans in Honolulu and Chicago and for Indians in New Brunswick, New Jersey.
2. Alexis Jetter, "Fear is Legacy of Wife Killing in Chinatown," *Newsday*, November 26, 1989.

# Sexual Violence and Rape

Sexual violence against women and girls, like battering, is surrounded by images and myths that mask the realities of assaulted women's lives. Whether or not we have personally experienced sexual assault, the threat of violence shadows all women's lives.

Recently many young women have begun to speak out about the climate of sexual intimidation that pervades high school social life. Athena Devlin and Pamela Fletcher write about the sexual assault and coercion of girls, pointing out the ways that "the silence between them" perpetuated their powerlessness. After describing the many instances in her life in which no one challenged the sexual assault of girls and young women, Fletcher invites us to envision a time when women are "connected to each other, when we no longer feel the need and desire to conspire with men against each other in order to survive in a misogynist, violent culture."

Susan Griffin's 1971, article drew rape out of the realm of inexplicable atrocities and placed it squarely in the context of a patriarchal society. It generated a good deal of analysis about the connection between rape and prevailing ideas about women, men, and sexuality. This analysis has led more recently to a movement against marital and acquaintance rape.

Rape is an abuse of power that is expressed through sexual violence. Many misconceptions about rape suggest that assaulted women somehow "provoked" their attackers into raping them, either verbally or by seductive dress and demeanor. However, as Ntozake Shange's poem shows, the irrational violence of rape occurs "with no immediate cause."

While stranger rape and acquaintance rape are similar, they differ in significant ways. Perhaps the most notable characteristic of acquaintance rape is the betrayal of trust experienced by a woman when someone she knows, and may care about, rapes her. Peggy Reeves Sanday surveys studies of acquaintance rape on college campuses and its impact on women. In doing so, she confronts the myths about acquaintance rape that prevent many women from naming coercive sexual experiences as rape.

# The Shame of Silence

ATHENA DEVLIN

As in every high school, there was in mine a set of especially powerful boys who were "popular." At my school in Texas, they were all football stars. When I was a freshman, and dying to make a good impression, I was invited by one of them to come over to his house to watch television. I don't think I will ever be able to forget (much to my embarrassment these days) how excited I was. By the time I left my house, my room looked like a clothes bomb had exploded in it. I was smiling from ear to ear, probably having visions of becoming a cheerleader. I forgot to ask myself *why* he had called me. I forgot to remember that I was *not* what you would call a popular girl. I rang his doorbell with a pounding heart and ridiculous aspirations. Bill let me in and led me into the living room. There, sitting on couches, were about eight boys. They were all watching a porno film on the VCR. They looked at me with open dislike and said "hi" pretty much in unison. I just stood there, frozen with disappointment while a blond woman acted out ecstasy on the television screen. No one spoke. After what seemed like a very long time, I turned away and walked into the kitchen just off the living room and sat at the table. I was embarrassed by my expectations. I felt like I had forgotten my "place." Now I remembered. I knew why I had been invited over. Bill let me stay in the kitchen by myself for about 20 minutes. When he finally walked in he just looked at me and said "You wanna go outside?" I said yes because it felt like the only way out. We went out to his back yard; to reclining deck chairs by a lit pool. We started making out. His hands were everywhere, his breath stank. I felt worthless and just let it happen. Then, when he leaned over to get to the hook of my bra, I looked up and there they all were, all eight of them standing on the second floor balcony watching us. I started yelling. Bill didn't say anything. He didn't tell them to go away, he didn't offer me an explanation. I sud-

denly got the feeling that it had all been planned this way. I was trying to stand and get my shirt back on when Bill took my hand and pulled me behind a fence at the back of the yard. When we got there, he turned and told me he wanted a hand job. I gave him one and left. I felt only one thing, and it wasn't anger; it was shame.

To be a "successful" girl in Highland Park was to be successful with boys. So, undeniably the girls that I grew up with viewed each other as less important than the boys they dated and more often than not, as would-be enemies. Nothing was ever as important as being accepted by men. And this, quite effectively, alienated us from one another. The key to success with boys in my high school was having the right kind of reputation, and reputation for a girl was for the most part focused narrowly on her looks and her sexual life. Importantly, it was the boys who decided what "type" a girl was sexually—which, in a social setting like this one, gave them a lot of power. What put them in this position was exactly that thing the girls lacked: each other. Maybe it was from all those hours of football practice where they had to depend on one another that did it, or maybe it was just because they felt important enough not to seek female approval as desperately as we sought theirs that made some sort of solidarity among them more possible. But in any event, it was to their distinct advantage. For girls, trying to please the powers that be was very confusing because we were supposed to be attractive and sexually exciting in order to be accepted, while simultaneously prudish and innocent. We were supposed to be sweet and deferential towards them but we were also supposed to be able to stop them when they went too far. I suppose I never got that delicate balance down. I got one side of the equation but not the other.

Not surprisingly, then, the shame I felt by having been treated as worthless by boys was something I desperately wanted to *hide*. I had failed, it seemed in the most important way. I never told any of my girl friends about that night and, because of my shame, which covered everything, I wasn't even really aware of my anger, and it certainly did not occur to me to *show* any anger towards these boys. I had never heard a girl publicly denounce a boy for his behavior towards her, though I had seen many a girl be thoroughly disgraced in those hallways of Highland Park High. So, when the story of my night with the football stars got passed along by the boys, the girls who heard about it never tried to comfort me. They whispered about me instead, often to the very boys that had been involved. They were gaining points by disassociating themselves from me, because I was the one at fault. Boys will be boys after all. It's the girls who say yes that were held accountable at my high school—by both sexes.

About six months later when my reputation as a "slut" had been firmly established, I began hanging out with a girl named Cindy who had a similar public identity. Some of the boys from the group that participated in that horrible night often asked us out when their regular girl friends were away or safely tucked behind curfews. I usually said no, although I occasionally agreed because going out with them still felt like a form of acceptance. At least they thought I was pretty enough to make out with. But Cindy went out with them a lot. One Friday night something happened. To this day I do not know what actually went on (no surprise). I just knew she was upset and the following Monday, Will, one of the boys she went out with, started hassling her in the hall. She began to cry in the middle of passing period with everyone staring. Suddenly, and for the first time, I felt incredibly angry and before fear held me back, I began to yell at Will. I don't remember what I said exactly, but it was something to the effect of who did he think he was, and that I thought he was an asshole. I don't think he had ever been so surprised. He stared at me in complete amazement. And so did Cindy. Unfortunately, it didn't take him too long to recover and he told me in a voice loud enough for everyone in the building to hear, that I was a whore and everyone knew it, that I would sleep with anyone (I was still a virgin at the time), and that I was completely disgusting. The contempt in his voice was incredible. I started to feel ashamed again. One did not have scenes like this at Highland Park. But the surprise was Cindy hated me for it. In her opinion I had done an unforgivable thing in sticking up for her. And, what I learned was that

girls didn't want each other's protection because it made them less attractive to boys. They feared focusing on each other too much.

For me, however, this incident was a turning point because afterwards these boys left me alone completely. I was released from the painful confusion of boys wanting me and disliking me at the same time—ignoring me or talking about me behind my back and then calling me up late on Friday night. I had yelled at a football star in front of everyone. That made me completely unacceptable as opposed to only marginally so. People began to make sure they didn't cross my path. I was left alone. Moreover, I was feared. It was then that I began to realize just how much the boys depended on the girls not do anything to defend themselves, that they depended heavily on our passivity. I saw that they lived in fear of us taking action. Any action. And I began to suspect that the isolation I noticed so many of the girls at my high school in Dallas feeling served a purpose useful enough to be a consequence of deliberateness. Still, I never made another scene.

But that was not really the greatest tragedy. Rather it was, and is, that girls grow up not knowing each other very well. And that while going through the same things, they are without both the benefit of each other's comfort and understanding, and more vulnerable to abuse. I am close to only one girl who went to high school with me, and that is probably only because we ended up at the same college. When I told her about writing this essay she told me, for the first time, some of her experiences at Highland Park. They were as tortured and humiliating as mine, but I had never heard her stories before and she had never heard mine. High school obviously wasn't a great experience for either of us, and while we sat there tracing the damage through to our present lives, I desperately wished it had been different. And it could have been if we could have shaken off the terrible trap of shame and talked about our lives and found ways to support each other. It seems clear to me now that not only were the boys protecting each other, but we girls were protecting the boys through the silence that existed between us.                    [1992]

🌿 122

# Whose Body Is It, Anyway?

PAMELA FLETCHER

## RAPE

I never heard the word while growing up. Or, if I had, I blocked it out because its meaning was too horrific for my young mind: a stranger, a weapon, a dark place, blood, pain, even death. But I do remember other people's responses to it, especially those of women. I specifically remember hearing about Rachel when I was in high school in the '70s. The story was that she "let" a group of boys "pull a train" on her in the football field one night. I remember the snickers and the looks of disgust of both the girls and the boys around campus. It was common knowledge that nobody with eyes would want to fuck Rachel; she had a face marred by acne and glasses. But, she had *some* body.

While I am writing this essay, I remember the stark sadness and confusion I felt then. This same sadness returns to me now, but I am no longer confused. Then I wondered how she could "do" so many guys and actually like it (!). Then I thought maybe she didn't like it after all, and maybe, just maybe, they made her do it. But the word rape never entered my mind. After all, she knew them, didn't she? There was no weapon, no blood. She survived, didn't she? And, just what was she doing there all by herself, anyway? Now, I know what "pulling a train" is. Now I know they committed a violent crime against her body and her soul. Now I know why she walked around campus with that wounded face, a face that none of us girls wanted to look into because we knew intuitively that we would see a reflection of our own wounded selves. So the other girls did not look into her eyes. They avoided her and talked about her like she was "a bitch in heat." Why else would such a thing have happened to her?

I tried to look into Rachel's eyes because I wanted to know something—what, I didn't know. But she looked down or looked away or laughed like a lunatic, you know, in that eerie, loud, nervous manner

that irritated and frightened me because it didn't ring true. Now I wonder if she thought such laughter would mask her pain. It didn't.

## PAINFUL SILENCE AND DEEP-SEATED RAGE

I remember another story I heard while I was in college. Larry told me that his close friend, Brenda, let Danny stay over one night in her summer apartment after they had smoked some dope, and he raped her. Larry actually said that word.

"Don't tell anyone," Brenda begged him. "I never should have let him spend the night. I thought he was my friend."

Larry told me not to ever repeat it to anyone else. And, trying to be a loyal girlfriend to him and a loyal friend to Brenda, I didn't say anything. When we saw Danny later at another friend's place, we neither confronted nor ignored him. *We acted as though everything was normal.* I felt agitated and angry. I wondered why Larry didn't say anything to Danny, you know, man-to-man, like: "That shit was not cool, man. Why you go and do somethin' like that to the sista?"

It never occurred to me to say anything to Brenda, because I wasn't supposed to know, or I was supposed to act as though I didn't know, stupid stuff like that. I sat there, disconnected from her, watching her interact with people, Danny among them, acting as though everything was normal.

## DENIAL

Since I began writing this essay two months ago, I have had such difficulty thinking about my own related experiences. I hadn't experienced rape. Or, had I? For months, in the hard drive of my subconscious mind, I searched for files that would yield any incidence of sexual violence or sexual terrorism. When certain memories surfaced, I questioned whether those experiences were "real rapes."

I have some very early recollections that challenge me. Max, my first boyfriend, my childhood sweetheart, tried to pressure me into having sex with him when we were in junior high. Two of my friends, who were the girlfriends of his two closest friends, also tried to pressure me because they were already "doing it" for their "men."

"Don't be a baby," they teased. "Everybody's doing it."

But I wouldn't cave in, and I broke up with Max because he wasn't a decent boy.

A year later, when we reached high school, I went crawling back to Max because I "loved" him and couldn't stand his ignoring me. He stopped ignoring me long enough to pin me up against the locker to kiss me roughly and to suck on my neck long and hard until he produced sore, purple bruises, what we called hickies. I had to hide those hideous marks from my parents by wearing turtleneck sweaters. Those hickies marked me as his property and gave his friends the impression that he had "done" me, even though we hadn't gotten that far yet. We still had to work out the logistics.

I hated when he gave me hickies, and I didn't like his exploring my private places as he emotionally and verbally abused me, telling me I wasn't pretty like Susan: "Why can't you look like her?" And I remember saying something like, "Why don't you go be with her, if that's what you want?" He answered me with a piercing "don't-you-ever-talk-to-me-like-that-again" look, and I never asked again. He continued, however, to ask me the same question.

In my heart, I realized that the way he treated me was wrong because I felt violated; I felt separated from my body, as if it did not belong to me. But at sixteen I didn't know how or what to feel, except that I felt confused and desperately wanted to make sense out of what it meant to be a girl trapped inside a woman's body. Yes, I felt trapped, because I understood that we girls had so much to lose now that we could get pregnant. Life sagged with seriousness. Now everybody kept an eye on us: our parents, the churches, the schools, and the boys. Confusion prevailed. While we were encouraged to have a slight interest in boys (lest we turn out "funny") so that ultimately we could be trained to become good wives, we were instructed directly and indirectly to keep a safe distance away from them.

We liked boys and we thought we wanted love, but what we really wanted as youth was to have some fun, some clean, innocent fun until we got married and gave our virtuous selves to our husbands just as our mothers had done. We female children had inherited this lovely vision from our mothers and from fairy tales. Yet now we know that those visions were not so much what our mothers had experienced, but what they wished they had experienced, and what they wanted for us.

We thought "going with a boy" in the early '70s would be romance-filled fun that involved holding hands, stealing kisses, exchanging class rings, and wearing big lettered sweaters. Maybe it was, for some of us. But I know that many of us suffered at the hands of love.

I soon learned in high school that it was normal to be mistreated by our boyfriends. Why else would none of us admit to each other the abuse we tolerated? These boys "loved" us, so we believed that they were entitled to treat us in any way they chose. We believed that somehow we belonged to them, body and soul. Isn't that what many of the songs on the radio said? And we just knew somehow that if we did give into to them, we deserved whatever happened, and if we didn't give in, we still deserved whatever happened. Such abuse was rampant because we became and remained isolated from each other by hoisting our romances above our friendships.

We didn't define what they did to us as rape, molestation, or sexual abuse. We called it love. We called it love if it happened with our boyfriends, and we called other girls whores and sluts if it happened with someone else's boyfriend or boyfriends, as in the case of Rachel and "the train."

We called it love because we had tasted that sweet taste of pain. Weren't they one and the same?

### REALIZATION

One sharp slap from Max one day delivered the good sense I had somehow lost when I got to high school. After that point I refused to be his woman, his property. When I left home for college, I left with the keen awareness that I had better take good care of myself. In my involvement with Max, I had allowed a split to occur between my body and my soul, and I had to work on becoming whole again.

I knew that I was growing stronger (though in silent isolation from other young women and through intense struggle) when I was able to successfully resist being seduced (read: molested) by several college classmates and when I successfully fought off the violent advances and the verbal abuse (what I now recognize as an attempted rape) of someone with whom I had once been sexually intimate.

But how does a woman become strong and whole in a society in which women are not permitted (as if we need permission!) to possess ourselves, to own our very bodies? We females often think we are not entitled to ourselves, and many times we give ourselves away for less than a song. The sad truth of the matter is that this is how we have managed to survive in our male-dominated culture. Yet, in the wise words of the late Audre Lorde, "the Master's tools will never dismantle the Master's house." In other words, as long as we remain disconnected from ourselves and each other and dependent on abusive males, we will remain weak, powerless, and fragmented.

Just imagine how different our lives would be today if we were not injured by internalized misogyny and sexism. Imagine how different our lives would be if we would only open our mouths wide and collectively and loudly confront males and *really* hold them accountable for the violent crimes they perpetrate against females. Imagine how our lives would be if all mothers tell their daughters the truth about romantic love and teach them to love themselves as females, to value and claim their bodies, and to protect themselves against violent and disrespectful males.

What if we girls in junior high and high school believed we deserve respect rather than verbal and sexual abuse from our male classmates? What if we girls in my high school had confronted the gang of boys who raped Rachel that night in the football field twenty years ago, rather than perpetuated that cycle of abuse and shame she suffered? What if Larry and I had confronted Danny for raping Brenda that summer night in her apartment? What if Brenda had felt safe enough to tell Larry, me, and the police? What if we females believed ourselves and each other to be as important and deserving of our selfhood as we believe males to be? Just imagine.

Envision a time when we women are connected to ourselves and each other, when we no longer feel the need and desire to conspire with men against each other in order to survive in a misogynist, violent culture. We must alter our destructive thinking about being female so that we can begin to accept, love, and cherish our femaleness. It is the essence of our lives.

Readjusting our lens so we can begin to see ourselves and each other as full, capable, and mighty human beings will take as much work as reconstructing our violent society. Neither job is easy, but the conditions and the tasks go hand in hand. Two ways to begin our own transformation are to become physically active in whatever manner we choose so we can take pleasure in fully connecting to ourselves and in growing physically stronger, and to respect, protect, support, and comfort each other. Once we stop denying that our very lives are endangered, we will soon discover that these steps are not only necessary but viable in empowering ourselves and claiming our right to exist as whole human beings in a peaceful, humane world.           [1993]

## ❧ 123

# *Rape:*
# *The All-American Crime*

SUSAN GRIFFEN

### I

I have never been free of the fear of rape. From a very early age I, like most women, have thought of rape as part of my natural environment—something to be feared and prayed against like fire or lightning. I never asked why men raped; I simply thought it one of the many mysteries of human nature.

I was, however, curious enough about the violent side of humanity to read every crime magazine I was able to ferret away from my grandfather. Each issue featured at least one "sex crime," with pictures of a victim, usually in a pearl necklace, and of the ditch or the orchard where her body was found. I was never certain why the victims were always women, nor what the motives of the murderer were, but I did guess that the world was not a safe place for women. I observed that my grandmother was meticulous about locks, and quick to draw the shades before anyone removed so much as a shoe. I sensed that danger lurked outside.

At the age of eight, my suspicions were confirmed. My grandmother took me to the back of the house where the men wouldn't hear, and told me that strange men wanted to do harm to little girls. I learned not to walk on dark streets, not to talk to strangers, or get into strange cars, to lock doors, and to be modest. She never explained why a man would want to harm a little girl, and I never asked.

If I thought for a while that my grandmother's fears were imaginary, the illusion was brief. That year, on the way home from school, a schoolmate a few years older than I tried to rape me. Later, in an obscure aisle of the local library (while I was reading *Freddy the Pig*) I turned to discover a man exposing himself. Then, the friendly man around the corner was arrested for child molesting.

My initiation to sexuality was typical. Every woman has similar stories to tell—the first man who attacked her may have been a neighbor, a family friend, an uncle, her doctor, or perhaps her own father. And women who grow up in New York City always have tales about the subway. . . .

When I was very young, my image of the "sexual offender" was a nightmarish amalgamation of the bogey man and Captain Hook: he wore a black cape, and he cackled. As I matured, so did my image of the rapist. Born into the psychoanalytic age, I tried to "understand" the rapist. Rape, I came to believe, was only one of many unfortunate evils produced by sexual repression. Reasoning by tautology, I concluded that any man who would rape a woman must be out of his mind.

Yet, though the theory that rapists are insane is a popular one, this belief has no basis in fact. According to Professor Menachem Amir's study of 646 rape cases in Philadelphia, *Patterns in Forcible*

*Rape*, men who rape are not abnormal. Amir writes, "Studies indicate that sex offenders do not constitute a unique or psychopathological type; nor are they as a group invariably more disturbed than the control groups to which they are compared." Alan Taylor, a parole officer who has worked with rapists in the prison facilities at San Luis Obispo, California, stated the question in plainer language, "Those men were the most normal men there. They had a lot of hang-ups, but they were the same hang-ups as men walking out on the street."

Another canon in the apologetics of rape is that, if it were not for learned social controls, all men would rape. Rape is held to be natural behavior, and not to rape must be learned. But in truth rape is not universal to the human species. Moreover, studies of rape in our culture reveal that far from being impulsive behavior, most rape is planned. Professor Amir's study reveals that in cases of group rape (the "gangbang" of masculine slang), 90 percent of the rapes were planned; in pair rapes, 83 percent of the rapes were planned; and in single rapes, 58 percent were planned. These figures should significantly discredit the image of the rapist as a man who is suddenly overcome by sexual needs society does not allow him to fulfill.

Far from the social control of rape being learned, comparisons with other cultures lead one to suspect that, in our society, it is rape itself that is learned. (The fact that rape is against the law should not be considered proof that rape is not in fact encouraged as part of our culture.)

This culture's concept of rape as an illegal, but still understandable, form of behavior is not a universal one. In her study *Sex and Temperament*, Margaret Mead describes a society that does not share our views. The Arapesh do not ". . . have any conception of the male nature that might make rape understandable to them." Indeed our interpretation of rape is a product of our conception of the nature of male sexuality. A common retort to the question, why don't women rape men, is the myth that men have greater sexual needs, that their sexuality is more urgent than women's. And it is the nature of human beings to want to live up to what is expected of them.

And this same culture which expects aggression from the male expects passivity from the female. Conveniently, the companion myth about the nature of female sexuality is that all women secretly want to be raped. Lurking beneath her modest female exterior is a subconscious desire to be ravished. The following description of a stag movie, written by Brenda Starr in Los Angeles' underground paper, *Everywoman,* typifies this male fantasy. The movie "showed a woman in her underclothes reading on her bed. She is interrupted by a rapist with a knife. He immediately wins her over with his charm and they get busy sucking and fucking." An advertisement in the *Berkeley Barb* reads, "Now as all women know from their daydreams, rape has a lot of advantages. Best of all it's so simple. No preparation necessary, no planning ahead of time, no wondering if you should or shouldn't; just whang! bang!" Thanks to Masters and Johnson even the scientific canon recognizes that for the female, "whang! bang!" can scarcely be described as pleasurable.

Still, the male psyche persists in believing that, protestations and struggles to the contrary, deep inside her mysterious feminine soul, the female victim has wished for her own fate. A young woman who was raped by the husband of a friend said that days after the incident the man returned to her home, pounded on the door and screamed to her, "Jane, Jane. You loved it. You know you loved it."

The theory that women like being raped extends itself by deduction into the proposition that most or much of rape is provoked by the victim. But this too is only myth. Though provocation, considered a mitigating factor in a court of law, may consist of only "a gesture," according to the Federal Commission on Crimes of Violence, only 4 percent of reported rapes involved any precipitative behavior by the woman.

The notion that rape is enjoyed by the victim is also convenient for the man who, though he would not commit forcible rape, enjoys the idea of its existence, as if rape confirms that enormous sexual potency which he secretly knows to be his own. It is for the pleasure of the armchair rapist that detailed accounts of violent rapes exist in the media.

Indeed, many men appear to take sexual pleasure from nearly all forms of violence. Whatever the motivation, male sexuality and violence in our culture seem to be inseparable. James Bond alternately whips out his revolver and his cock, and though there is no known connection between the skills of gun-fighting and love-making, pacifism seems suspiciously effeminate. . . .

In the spectrum of male behavior, rape, the perfect combination of sex and violence, is the penultimate act. Erotic pleasure cannot be separated from culture, and in our culture male eroticism is wedded to power. Not only should a man be taller and stronger than a female in the perfect love-match, but he must also demonstrate his superior strength in gestures of dominance which are perceived as amorous. Though the law attempts to make a clear division between rape and sexual intercourse, in fact the courts find it difficult to distinguish between a case where the decision to copulate was mutual and one where a man forced himself upon his partner.

The scenario is even further complicated by the expectation that, not only does a woman mean "yes" when she says "no," but that a really decent woman ought to begin by saying "no," and then be led down the primrose path to acquiescence. Ovid, the author of Western Civilization's most celebrated sex-manual, makes this expectation perfectly clear:

> . . . and when I beg you to say "yes," say "no." Then let me lie outside your bolted door. . . . So Love grows strong. . . .

That the basic elements of rape are involved in all heterosexual relationships may explain why men often identify with the offender in this crime. But to regard the rapist as the victim, a man driven by his inherent sexual needs to take what will not be given him, reveals a basic ignorance of sexual politics. For in our culture heterosexual love finds an erotic expression through male dominance and female submission. A man who derives pleasure from raping a woman clearly must enjoy force and dominance as much or more than the simple pleasures of the flesh. Coitus cannot be experienced in isolation. The weather, the state of the nation, the level of sugar in the blood—all will affect a man's ability to achieve orgasm. If a man can achieve sexual pleasure after terrorizing and humiliating the object of his passion, and in fact while inflicting pain upon her, one must assume he derives pleasure directly from terrorizing, humiliating and harming a woman. According to Amir's study of forcible rape, on a statistical average the man who has been convicted of rape was found to have a normal sexual personality, tending to be different from the normal, well-adjusted male only in having a greater tendency to express violence and rage.

And if the professional rapist is to be separated from the average dominant heterosexual, it may be mainly a quantitative difference. For the existence of rape as an index to masculinity is not entirely metaphorical. Though this measure of masculinity seems to be more publicly exhibited among "bad boys" or aging bikers who practice sexual initiation through group rape, in fact, "good boys" engage in the same rites to prove their manhood. In Stockton, a small town in California which epitomizes silent-majority America, a bachelor party was given last summer for a young man about to be married. A woman was hired to dance "topless" for the amusement of the guests. At the high point of the evening the bridegroom-to-be dragged the woman into a bedroom. No move was made by any of his companions to stop what was clearly going to be an attempted rape. Far from it. As the woman described, "I tried to keep him away—told him of my *herpes genitalis,* et cetera, but he couldn't face the guys if he didn't screw me." After the bridegroom had finished raping the woman and returned with her to the party, far from chastising him, his friends heckled the woman and covered her with wine.

It was fortunate for the dancer that the bridegroom's friends did not follow him into the bedroom for, though one might suppose that in group rape, since the victim is outnumbered, less force would be inflicted on her, in fact, Amir's studies indicate, "the most excessive degrees of violence occurred in group rape." Far from discouraging violence, the presence of other men may in fact encourage sadism, and even cause the behavior. In an unpublished study of group rape by Gilbert Geis and Duncan Chappell, the authors refer to a study by

W. H. Blanchard which relates, "The leader of the male group . . . apparently precipitated and maintained the activity, despite misgivings, because of a need to fulfill the role that the other two men had assigned to him. 'I was scared when it began to happen,' he says. 'I wanted to leave but I didn't want to say it to the other guys—you know—that I was scared.'"

Thus it becomes clear that not only does our culture teach men the rudiments of rape, but society, or more specifically other men, encourage the practice of it.

## II

*Every man I meet wants to protect me. Can't figure out what from.*
                                                    —*Mae West*

. . . According to the male mythology which defines and perpetuates rape, it is an animal instinct inherent in the male. The story goes that sometime in our pre-historical past, the male, more hirsute and burly than today's counterparts, roamed about an uncivilized landscape until he found a desirable female. (Oddly enough, this female is *not* pictured as more muscular than the modern woman.) Her mate does not bother with courtship. He simply grabs her by the hair and drags her to the closest cave. Presumably, one of the major advantages of modern civilization for the female has been the civilizing of the male. We call it chivalry.

But women do not get chivalry for free. According to the logic of sexual politics, we too have to civilize our behavior. (Enter chastity. Enter virginity. Enter monogamy.) For the female, civilized behavior means chastity before marriage and faithfulness within it. Chivalrous behavior in the male is supposed to protect that chastity from involuntary defilement. The fly in the ointment of this otherwise peaceful system is the fallen woman. She does not behave. And therefore she does not deserve protection. Or, to use another argument, a major tenet of the same value system: what has once been defiled cannot again be violated. One begins to suspect that it is the behavior of the fallen woman, and not that of the male, that civilization aims to control.

The assumption that a woman who does not respect the double standard deserves whatever she gets (or at the very least "asks for it") operates in the courts today. While in some states a man's previous rape convictions are not considered admissible evidence, the sexual reputation of the rape victim is considered a crucial element of the facts upon which the court must decide innocence or guilt. . . .

According to the double standard, a woman who has had sexual intercourse out of wedlock cannot be raped. Rape is not only a crime of aggression against the body; it is a transgression against chastity as defined by men. When a woman is forced into a sexual relationship, she has, according to the male ethos, been violated. But she is also defiled if she does not behave according to the double standard, by maintaining her chastity, or confining her sexual activities to a monogamous relationship.

One should not assume, however, that a woman can avoid the possibility of rape simply by behaving. Though myth would have it that mainly "bad girls" are raped, this theory has no basis in fact. Available statistics would lead one to believe that a safer course is promiscuity. In a study of rape done in the District of Columbia, it was found that 82 percent of the rape victims had a "good reputation." Even the Police Inspector's advice to stay off the streets is rather useless, for almost half of reported rapes occur in the home of the victim and are committed by a man she has never before seen. Like indiscriminate terrorism, rape can happen to any woman, and few women are ever without this knowledge.

But the courts and the police, both dominated by white males, continue to suspect the rape victim, *sui generis*, of provoking or asking for her own assault. According to Amir's study, the police tend to believe that a woman without a good reputation cannot be raped. The rape victim is usually submitted to countless questions about her own sexual mores and behavior by the police investigator. This preoccupation is partially justified by the legal requirements for prosecution in a rape case. The rape victim must have been penetrated, and she must have made it clear to her assailant that she did not want penetration (unless of course she is unconscious). A refusal to accompany a man to some isolated place to allow him to touch her does not in the eyes of the court, constitute rape. She must have said "no" at the crucial genital moment. And the rape victim, to qualify as such, must also have put up a physical struggle—unless she can prove that to do so would have been to endanger her life.

But the zealous interest the police frequently exhibit in the physical details of a rape case is only partially explained by the requirements of the court. A woman who was raped in Berkeley was asked to tell the story of her rape four different times "right out in the street," while her assailant was escaping. She was then required to submit to a pelvic examination to prove that penetration had taken place. Later, she was taken to the police station where she was asked the same questions again: "Were you forced?" "Did he penetrate?" "Are you sure your life was in danger and you had no other choice?" This woman had been pulled off the street by a man who held a 10-inch knife at her throat and forcibly raped her. She was raped at midnight and was not able to return to her home until five in the morning. Police contacted her twice again in the next week, once by telephone at two in the morning and once at four in the morning. In her words, "The rape was probably the least traumatic incident of the whole evening. If I'm ever raped again, . . . I wouldn't report it to the police because of all the degradation. . . ."

If white women are subjected to unnecessary and often hostile questioning after having been raped, third world women* are often not believed at all. According to the white male ethos (which is not only sexist but racist), third world women are defined from birth as "impure." Thus the white male is provided with a pool of women who are fair game for sexual imperialism. Third world women frequently do not report rape and for good reason. When blues singer Billie Holliday was 10 years old, she was taken off to a local house by a neighbor and raped. Her mother brought the police to rescue her, and she was taken to the local station crying and bleeding:

> When we got there, instead of treating me and Mom like somebody who called the cops for help, they

---

*Editor's note: "Third World" was used to describe women of color in the U.S. at the time this article was written.

treated me like I'd killed somebody. . . . I guess they had me figured for having enticed this old goat into the whorehouse. . . . All I know for sure is they threw me into a cell . . . a fat white matron . . . saw I was still bleeding, she felt sorry for me and gave me a couple glasses of milk. But nobody else did anything for me except give me filthy looks and snicker to themselves.

After a couple of days in a cell they dragged me into a court. Mr. Dick got sentenced to five years. They sentenced me to a Catholic institution.

Clearly the white man's chivalry is aimed only to protect the chastity of "his" women.

As a final irony, that same system of sexual values from which chivalry is derived has also provided womankind with an unwritten code of behavior, called femininity, which makes a feminine woman the perfect victim of sexual aggression. If being chaste does not ward off the possibility of assault, being feminine certainly increases the chances that it will succeed. To be submissive is to defer to masculine strength; is to lack muscular development or any interest in defending oneself; is to let doors be opened, to have one's arm held when crossing the street. To be feminine is to wear shoes which make it difficult to run; skirts which inhibit one's stride; underclothes which inhibit the circulation. Is it not an intriguing observation that those very clothes which are thought to be flattering to the female and attractive to the male are those which make it impossible for a woman to defend herself against aggression?

Each girl as she grows into womanhood is taught fear. Fear is the form in which the female internalizes both chivalry and the double standard. Since, biologically speaking, women in fact have the same if not greater potential for sexual expression as do men, the woman who is taught that she must behave differently from a man must also learn to distrust her own carnality. She must deny her own feelings and learn not to act from them. She fears herself. This is the essence of passivity, and of course, a woman's passivity is not simply sexual but functions to cripple her from self-expression in every area of her life.

Passivity itself prevents a woman from ever considering her own potential for self-defense and forces her to look to men for protection. The woman is taught fear, but this time fear of the other; and yet her only relief from this fear is to seek out the other. Moreover, the passive woman is taught to regard herself as impotent, unable to act, unable even to perceive, in no way self-sufficient, and, finally, as the object and not the subject of human behavior. It is in this sense that a woman is deprived of the status of a human being. She is not free to be. . . .

## III

If the basic social unit is the family, in which the woman is a possession of her husband, the superstructure of society is a male hierarchy, in which men dominate other men (or patriarchal families dominate other patriarchal families). And it is no small irony that, while the very social fabric of our male-dominated culture denies women equal access to political, economic and legal power, the literature, myth and humor of our culture depicts women not only as the power behind the throne, but the real source of the oppression of men. The religious version of this fairy tale blames Eve for both carnality and eating of the tree of knowledge, at the same time making her gullible to the obvious devices of a serpent. Adam, of course, is merely the trusting victim of love. Certainly this is a biased story. But no more biased than the one television audiences receive today from the latest slick comedians. Through a media which is owned by men, censored by a State dominated by men, all the evils of this social system which make a man's life unpleasant are blamed upon "the wife." The theory is: were it not for the female who waits and plots to "trap" the male into marriage, modern man would be able to achieve Olympian freedom. She is made the scapegoat for a system which is in fact run by men.

Nowhere is this more clear than in the white racist use of the concept of white womanhood. The white male's open rape of black women, coupled with his overweening concern for the chastity and protection of his wife and daughters, represents an extreme of sexist and racist hypocrisy. While on the one hand she was held up as the standard for purity and virtue, on the other the Southern white woman was never asked if she wanted to be on a pedestal, and in fact any deviance from the male-defined standards for white womanhood was treated severely. (It is a powerful commentary on American racism that the historical role of Blacks as slaves, and thus possessions without power, has robbed black women of legal and economic protection through marriage. Thus black women in Southern society and in the ghettoes of the North have long been easy game for white rapists.) The fear that black men would rape white women was, and is, classic paranoia. Quoting from Ann Breen's unpublished study of racism and sexism in the South "*The New South: White Man's Country*," Frederick Douglass legitimately points out that, had the black man wished to rape white women, he had ample opportunity to do so during the civil war when white women, the wives, sisters, daughters and mothers of the rebels, were left in the care of Blacks. But yet not a single act of rape was committed during this time. The Ku Klux Klan, who tarred and feathered black men and lynched them in the honor of the purity of white womanhood, also applied tar and feathers to a Southern white woman accused of bigamy, which leads one to suspect that Southern white men were not so much outraged at the violation of the woman as a person, in the few instances where rape was actually committed by black men, but at the violation of his property rights." In the situation where a black man was found to be having sexual relations with a white woman, the white woman could exercise skin-privilege, and claim that she had been raped, in which case the black man was lynched. But if she did not claim rape, she herself was subject to lynching.

In constructing the myth of white womanhood so as to justify the lynching and oppression of black men and women, the white male has created a convenient symbol of his own power which has resulted in black hostility toward the white "bitch," accompanied by an unreasonable fear on the part of many white women of the black rapist. Moreover, it is not surprising that after being told for two centuries that he wants to rape white women, occasionally a black man does actually commit that act. But it is crucial

to note that the frequency of this practice is outrageously exaggerated in the white mythos. Ninety percent of reported rape is intra- not inter-racial. . . .

Indeed, the existence of rape in any form is beneficial to the ruling class of white males. For rape is a kind of terrorism which severely limits the freedom of women and makes women dependent on men. Moreover, in the act of rape, the rage that one man may harbor toward another higher in the male hierarchy can be deflected toward a female scapegoat. For every man there is always someone lower on the social scale on whom he can take out his aggressions. And that is any woman alive.

This oppressive attitude towards women finds its institutionalization in the traditional family. For it is assumed that a man "wears the pants" in his family—he exercises the option of rule whenever he so chooses. Not that he makes all the decisions— clearly women make most of the important day-to-day decisions in a family. But when a conflict of interest arises, it is the man's interest which will prevail. His word, in itself, is more powerful. He lords it over his wife in the same way his boss lords it over him, so that the very process of exercising his power becomes as important an act as obtaining whatever it is his power can get for him. This notion of power is key to the male ego in this culture, for the two acceptable measures of masculinity are a man's power over women and his power over other men. A man may boast to his friends that "I have 20 men working for me." It is also aggrandizement of his ego if he has the financial power to clothe his wife in furs and jewels. And, if a man lacks the wherewithal to acquire such power, he can always express his rage through equally masculine activities—rape and theft. Since male society defines the female as a possession, it is not surprising that the felony most often committed together with rape is theft. . . .

\* \* \*

Rape is an act of aggression in which the victim is denied her self-determination. It is an act of violence which, if not actually followed by beatings or murder, nevertheless always carries with it the threat of death. And finally, rape is a form of mass terrorism, for the victims of rape are chosen indiscriminately, but the propagandists for male supremacy broadcast that it is women who cause rape by being unchaste or in the wrong place at the wrong time—in essence, by behaving as though they were free.

The threat of rape is used to deny women employment. (In California, the Berkeley Public Library, until pushed by the Federal Employment Practices Commission, refused to hire female shelvers because of perverted men in the stacks.) The fear of rape keeps women off the streets at night. Keeps women at home. Keeps women passive and modest for fear that they be thought provocative.

It is part of human dignity to be able to defend oneself, and women are learning. Some women have learned karate; some to shoot guns. And yet we will not be free until the threat of rape and the atmosphere of violence is ended, and to end that the nature of male behavior must change.

But rape is not an isolated act that can be rooted out from patriarchy without ending patriarchy itself. The same men and power structure who victimize women are engaged in the act of raping Vietnam, raping Black people and the very earth we live upon. Rape is a classic act of domination where, in the words of Kate Millett, "the emotions of hatred, contempt, and the desire to break or violate personality," take place. This breaking of the personality characterizes modern life itself. No simple reforms can eliminate rape. As the symbolic expression of the white male hierarchy, rape is the quintessential act of our civilization, one which, Valerie Solanis warns, is in danger of "humping itself to death."

[1971]

# ❧ 124

# *With No Immediate Cause*

NTOZAKE SHANGE

every 3 minutes a woman is beaten
every five minutes a
woman is raped/every ten minutes

a lil girl is molested
yet i rode the subway today
i sat next to an old man who
may have beaten his old wife
3 minutes ago or 3 days/30 years ago
he might have sodomized his
daughter but i sat there
cuz the young men on the train
might beat some young women
later in the day or tomorrow
i might not shut my door fast
enuf/push hard enuf
every 3 minutes it happens
some woman's innocence
rushes to her cheeks/pours from her mouth
like the betsy wetsy dolls have been torn
apart/their mouths
mensis red & split/every
three minutes a shoulder
is jammed through plaster & the oven door/
chairs push thru the rib cage/hot water or
boiling sperm decorate her body
i rode the subway today
& bought a paper from a
man who might
have held his old lady onto
a hot pressing iron/i dont know
maybe he catches lil girls in the
park & rips open their behinds
with steel rods/i cdnt decide
what he might have done i only
know every 3 minutes
every 5 minutes every 10 minutes/so
i bought the paper
looking for the announcement
there has to be an announcement
of the women's bodies found
yesterday/the missing little girl
i sat in a restaurant with my
paper looking for the announcement
a yng man served me coffee
i wondered did he pour the boiling
coffee/on the woman cuz she waz stupid/
did he put the infant girl/in
the coffee pot/with the boiling coffee/cuz she cried
    too much

what exactly did he do with hot coffee
i looked for the announcement
the discovery/of the dismembered
woman's body/the
victims have not all been
identified/today they are
naked & dead/refuse to
testify/one girl out of 10's not
coherent/i took the coffee
& spit it up/i found an
announcement/not the woman's
bloated body in the river/floating
not the child bleeding in the
59th street corridor/not the baby
broken on the floor/
    "there is some concern
    that alleged battered women
    might start to murder their
    husbands & lovers with no
    immediate cause"
i spit up    i vomit    i am screaming
we all have immediate cause
every 3 minutes
every 5 minutes
every 10 minutes
every day
women's bodies are found
in alleys & bedrooms/at the top of the stairs
before i ride the subway/buy a paper/drink
coffee/i must know/
have you hurt a woman today
did you beat a woman today
throw a child cross a room
    are the lil girl's panties
    in yr pocket
did you hurt a woman today

i have to ask these obscene questions
the authorities require me to
establish
immediate cause

every three minutes
every five minutes
every ten minutes
every day          [1970]

## ✿ 125

# *Naming and Studying Acquaintance Rape*

PEGGY REEVES SANDAY

*When it comes to my masculinity I get very defensive. Because I know that men are admired for having many partners, I set quotas—so many girls in one month. The joy of sex for me is the feeling of acceptance and approval which always goes with having sex with a new person.* —Male college student [1]

Martha McCluskey went to college during a time when feminist activism for rape reform was well under way, however not yet widely publicized outside scholarly and legal circles. In 1977 she was sexually abused by a group of fraternity brothers while a student at Colby College. At the time, however, Martha thought that being assaulted by "normal white college men . . . was not significant" and she didn't understand it as "real violence." It wasn't until after graduating from Yale Law School that she wrote about the assault in an article in the *Maine Law Review* on "privileged violence in college fraternities."

It happened at the beginning of vacation, when her dorm was nearly empty. As she described it:

> I am standing in the hallway looking out the window for my ride home. I turn around and my suitcase is gone; Joe and Bill from down the hall are laughing as they carry it away. I follow them. I hear a door lock behind me. They let go of my suitcase and grab me.
>
> I am lying on the bare linoleum floor of Joe's bedroom. In the room are a group of Lambda Chi and KDR pledges who live on my hall; several of them are football players. Some are sitting on the bed, laughing. Two others are pinning my arms and my legs to the floor. Joe is touching me while the others cheer.
>
> I am a friendly fellow-classmate as I reasonably explain that I'm in a rush to catch a ride, that I'm not in the mood to joke around; that I'd really like them to please cut it out. It takes a few long upside-down seconds before things look different. As I start to scream and fight I feel like I am shattering a world that will not get put back together. They let me go.
>
> Later I don't talk about this, not even to myself.

I sit near Joe and Bill in sociology and English classes. I don't talk in class.[2]

Starting in the 1970s, research on acquaintance rape conducted by psychologists, sociologists, and medical researchers began, and by the 1990s a significant body of knowledge on all aspects of sexual assault and abuse had been established. At first the research focused on the annual incidence and lifetime prevalence of acquaintance rape in order to establish the scope of the problem, but soon expanded to include causes, consequences, social and psychological costs, and prevention. The studies operated within the legal definition of rape as sexual intercourse, including oral or anal penetration, due to force, the threat of force, or by taking advantage of a person's incapacity to consent. Most studies focused on the heterosexual rape of females. However, in recent years attention has turned also to the heterosexual and same-sex rape of male victims. Least attention has been given same-sex rape of women.[3]

## THE EARLY STUDIES

Studies making a distinction between jump-from-the-bushes stranger rape and rape involving people who know one another go back at least to the 1950s. In 1952 the *Yale Law Journal* recognized that rape ranges from "brutal attacks familiar to tabloid readers to half won arguments of couples in parked cars." Kalven and Zeisel's distinction between "aggravated" and "simple" rape in their national study of fifties trials was the first to demonstrate that a significant proportion (40 percent) of rape cases going to trial involved acquaintances. Both of these acknowledged that when the parties know one another a conviction is much more difficult. Kalven and Zeisel were able to attribute the difficulty to juror prejudice by showing that judges were much more likely than jurors to believe that the evidence warranted a conviction in cases of simple rape.[4]

The most well-known of the early studies acknowledging the scope of acquaintance rape was authored by sociologist Menachem Amir. Based on an examination of police files of rapes occurring in 1958 and 1960, Amir concluded that rapists are generally "normal" men. About half of all the rapes were committed by men who knew their victims. Only 42 percent of the rapists were complete strangers to their victims, and not all of the victims resisted to the utmost.[5] More than half of the victims were submissive during the rape; about one fifth of the victims put up a strong physical fight; and another quarter actively resisted in some other way, like screaming. Twenty percent of the victims were between the ages of ten and fourteen, and 25 percent between fifteen and nineteen. The younger the victim the less likely she was to resist.[6]

The first widely read feminist studies mentioning acquaintance or date rape were authored by Susan Brownmiller and Diana Russell in the mid-1970s. In her landmark study, *Against Our Will*, Brownmiller is the first to use the term "date rape." The kind of interaction Brownmiller labeled date rape was typical of men and women caught in the double bind of the sexual revolution. Men pressed their advantage thinking that all women now "wanted it," but nice girls hadn't yet learned to make a no stick. Brownmiller phrased the problem as follows:

> In a dating situation an aggressor may press his advantage to the point where pleasantness quickly turns to unpleasantness and more than the woman bargained for, yet social propriety and the strictures of conventional female behavior that dictate politeness and femininity demand that the female gracefully endure, or wriggle away if she can, but a direct confrontation falls outside of the behavioral norms. These are the cases about which the police are wont to say, "She changed her mind afterward," with no recognition that it was only afterward that she dared pull herself together and face up to the fact that she had truly been raped.[7]

Brownmiller's historic contribution to the anti-rape movement is in her valuable analysis of the cultural forces shaping female passivity when confronted with male sexual aggression and her conceptualization of rape as violence. Brownmiller urged a generation of young women to learn to say no and overcome their historical training to be nice. She recognized that date rapes hardly ever get to court and don't look good on paper because the "intangibles of victim behavior . . . present a poor case."[8] These are the kinds of cases that Kalven and Zeisel found usually ended in acquittals. Brownmiller admits that even with her feminist awareness she often feels like shouting, "Idiot, why didn't you see the warning signs earlier?" upon hearing such cases.

Before she began researching rape in the early 1970s, Diana Russell held the "crazed stranger" theory of rape, believing that rape was "an extremely sadistic and deviant act, which could be performed only by crazy or psychopathic people." The idea had never occurred to her that rape by a lover, friend, or colleague was possible. She learned differently in 1971 while she was attending the highly publicized rape trial of Jerry Plotkin in San Francisco. Plotkin was a jeweler accused of abducting a young woman at gunpoint to his swank apartment, where he and three other men raped and forced her to commit various sexual acts.[9]

During the trial, which drew many feminist protestors, Russell began hearing stories from other women who had been raped but who had not reported the rape, fearing the treatment they would probably receive in the courtroom. The outcome of the Plotkin trial was a grim reminder of why so few were willing to report. The jury acquitted Plotkin because of the complainant's prior sex life, which was gone over in minute detail in the courtroom.[10] Convinced of the injustice of the verdict and aware of the need for further education, Russell embarked on a program of research that would produce two of the most important early studies of acquaintance rape.

Russell's first book, *The Politics of Rape*, was based on interviews with ninety women. In chapters titled "Lovers Rape, Too," "Some of Our Best Friends Are Rapists," and "Fathers, Husbands, and Other Rapists," to name just a few, Russell records women's experiences which demonstrate that rape is just as likely to occur between acquaintances as between strangers. The level of force employed during rape ranged from intimidation in some instances to extreme force in others. A typical case is reflected in one woman's statement that she put up as much struggle as she could, but he "used all of his strength, and he was very forceful and kept [her] down."[11] Another woman, who was raped by a fraternity brother, said she didn't scream because she was afraid he would call his frat brothers and "run a train" on her.[12]

The reasons these women gave for not reporting their experiences reflect the dominant belief that to do so would be embarrassing and useless. The first woman thought about going to the police but decided against it, believing that her accusation of rape would be impossible to prove. The woman who was raped by the frat brother told a close friend but remained silent otherwise, due to depression.[13] Another woman, who had been gang raped after getting into a car, told her brother, who called her a whore. When she told her husband many years later, he started punching her in the head. She never thought of going to the police, for fear of how her parents would react. One by one the women Russell interviewed gave similar reasons for not reporting.[14]

In 1978, Russell conducted a survey in San Francisco of 930 randomly selected women ranging in age from eighteen to eighty. Her results provided a statistical profile of acquaintance-versus-stranger rape in a diverse population of all social classes and racial/ethnic groups. The study followed the legal definition of rape in California and most other states at that time. Questions were asked about experiences of forced, nonconsensual intercourse as well as about experiences of "unwanted" sexual intercourse while asleep, unconscious, drugged, or otherwise helpless. The inclusion of the question about physical helplessness due to alcohol or drugs also was in keeping with the legal definition of rape in California. Russell was very careful to exclude from the rape category any experiences in which women reported *feeling* rather than *being* forced.[15]

Of the 930 women, 24 percent reported at least one completed rape, and 31 percent reported at least one attempted rape.[16] Russell used the term acquaintance rape as an umbrella term to distinguish rapes involving people who know one another from rapes involving strangers. Thirty-five percent of the women in her study experienced rape or attempted rape by an acquaintance (ranging in degrees of intimacy from casual acquaintances to lovers) as compared with 11 percent raped by strangers and 3 percent by relatives (other than husbands or ex-husbands).[17] Only 8 percent of all incidents of rape and attempted rape were reported to the police.[18] These incidents were much more likely to involve strangers than men known to the victim.[19]

Another important early survey was conducted in 1978 by psychologist Mary Koss of nearly four thousand college students at Kent State University, where she taught. As a young psychology professor just starting out in the mid-seventies, Koss had read Susan Brownmiller's book on rape and felt that the next step should be a scientific study of the epidemiology of rape. When she first designed the Kent State study, Koss preferred the label "hidden rape" to "acquaintance rape" because of the growing recognition in law enforcement circles that rape was "the most underreported of major crimes." She chose to study "unacknowledged victims of rape," women who have experienced forced sexual intercourse but do not call it rape.

In criminology terms, the unacknowledged victim is the "safe victim." For law enforcement purposes it is always important to identify the kinds of people most likely to be safe victims in any class of crime so that they can be protected through educational programs informing them of their rights. At the time Koss embarked on the Kent State survey, government estimates suggested that "only 40–50 percent of the rapes that occur each year are reported to the police." [20]

Koss's goal was to determine the prevalence of hidden rape. For the survey, she identified four degrees of sexual aggression ranging from what she called "low sexual victimization" to "high sexual victimization" in order to separate gradations of sexual abuse. [21] The category labeled "high sexual victimization" was the category that Koss defined as rape. It included women who said they had experienced unwanted intercourse or penetration of the mouth or anus from a man or men who used or threatened to use physical force. Koss separated this category of rape victims into two types: women who acknowledged they had been raped and those who did not name what happened to them as rape. Koss found that 13 percent of the women interviewed answered yes to at least one of three questions asking them whether they had experienced forced penetration at any time since the age of fourteen. Only 6 percent of the women interviewed, however, answered yes to the question "Have you ever been raped?" [22]

Less than 5 percent of the men in the study admitted to using force. Those who admitted to using force were remarkably similar to the sexually aggressive men described in Kirkendall's 1961 study of college men. For example, like their 1950s counterparts, the Kent State males expressed attitudes illustrative of the double standard. They were more approving of sexual relationships with prostitutes and more disapproving of sexual freedom for women than the less aggressive men in the study. They preferred traditional women, who were dependent, attention-seeking, and suggestible. Their first experiences with sexual intercourse tended to be unsatisfactory, but they expressed more pride in these experiences than the less aggressive men. When asked if they had sex the first time because it was socially expected, nearly half of the men in the sexually aggressive groups answered yes, as compared with only a quarter of the nonsexually aggressive men.

There were other differences between the types of men in Koss's study reminiscent of Kirkendall's findings. The highly sexually aggressive men were more likely to identify with a male peer culture. More were likely to be in fraternities than those reporting no or low sexual aggression. They were more insensitive to the woman's resistance and more likely to think that sexual aggression was normal sexual behavior, part of the game that had to be played with women. They believed that a woman would be only moderately offended if a man forced his way into her house after a date or forced his attentions in other ways. [23]

## RECENT STUDIES

To see whether she could replicate her Kent State findings in a nationwide sample, Koss joined with *Ms.* magazine in a 1985 survey of 6,159 students on thirty-two college campuses. The results of this survey would play a significant role in stepping up anti-rape activism on college campuses, and in inspiring the campus section of the Violence Against Women Act, which would be introduced into Congress five years later.

The survey questions were similar to those Koss used in the Kent State study. This time, however, she included a question about unwanted sexual intercourse that occurred because of the effects of alcohol or drugs. The results showed the extent to which sexual behavior in a college population had changed since Kinsey's male and female studies in the 1940s and 1950s. For example, the percentages of college-age males who were having sexual intercourse rose from 44 percent, reported by Kinsey, to 75 percent, reported by Koss in the 1980s. For college-age females, the percentages changed from 20 percent, reported by Kinsey, to 69 percent, reported by Koss.[24] Morton Hunt, who conducted a survey of the sexual behavior of two thousand individuals in twenty-four cities in 1972, found a similar increase for college men, but a less marked increase for college women.[25]

The results of Koss's national study were widely disseminated and quoted after publication in the *Journal of Consulting and Clinical Psychology* in 1987.[26] Robin Warshaw's *I Never Called It Rape*, the first major book on acquaintance rape, was based on Koss's study. Warshaw reported that one in four women surveyed were victims of rape or attempted rape, 84 percent of those raped knew their attacker, and that 57 percent of the rapes happened on dates.[27] The women thought that most of their offenders (73 percent) were drinking or using drugs at the time of the assault, and 55 percent admitted to using intoxicants themselves. Most of the women thought that they had made their nonconsent "quite" clear and that the offender used "quite a bit" of force. They resisted by using reasoning (84 percent) and physical struggle (70 percent).[28] Only one quarter (27 percent) of the rape victims acknowledged themselves as such. Five percent reported their rapes to the police. Although many women did not call it rape, Koss reported that "the great majority of rape victims conceptualized their experience in highly negative terms and felt victimized whether or not they realized that legal standards for rape had been met."[29]

The results for the men were similar to what Koss had found at Kent State. One quarter of the men reported involvement in some form of sexual aggression, ranging from unwanted touching to rape. Three percent admitted to attempted rape and 4.4 percent to rape.[30] A high percentage of the males did not name their use of force as rape. Eighty-eight percent said it was definitely *not* rape. Forty-seven percent said they would do the same thing again.[31]

Koss's findings that men viewed the use of force as normal were corroborated by other surveys conducted on college campuses. For example, one study cited by Russell found that 35 percent of the males questioned about the likelihood that they would rape said they might if they could get away with it. When asked whether they would force a female to do something sexual she really did not want to do, 60 percent of the males indicated in a third college study that they might, "given the right circumstances."[32]

Convicted rapists hold similar beliefs. In a study of 114 rapists, Diana Scully found that many either denied that the sexual activity for which they were convicted was rape, or they claimed it hadn't happened. One told her the sexual activity for which he was convicted was "just fucking." Other rapists told her that men rape because they have learned that in America they can get away with it because victims don't report. Almost none of the convicts she interviewed thought they would go to prison. Most of them perceived rape as a rewarding, low-risk act.[33]

Since the early studies conducted by Koss and Russell, a number of additional scientifically designed research studies conducted on campuses in various states and in various communities reveal that an average of between 13 percent and 25 percent of the participating females respond affirmatively to questions asking if they had ever been penetrated against their consent by a male who used force, threatened to use force, or took advantage of them when they were incapacitated with alcohol or other drugs.[34] A more recent national study, published in 1992 by the National Victim Center, defined rape more narrowly by leaving alcohol and drugs out of the picture. Thirteen percent of this national sample of a cross-section of women reported having been victims of at least one completed rape in their lifetimes. Most of these women had been raped by someone they knew.[35]

## ACQUAINTANCE GANG RAPE

In the 1980s quite a few cases of acquaintance gang rape were reported around the country. In the *Ms.* article announcing the results of Koss's Kent State study, Karen Barrett describes an incident that took place at Duke University in the Beta Phi Zeta fraternity. A woman had gotten very drunk and passed out. Men lined up outside the door yelling, "Train!" Although the woman did not press charges, saying that she had been a willing participant, Duke moved against the fraternity after it was discovered that senior members had assigned a pledge the task of "finding a drunk woman for a gang bang." [36]

In Koss's national study she found that 16 percent of the male students who admitted rape, and 10 percent of those who admitted attempting a rape, took part in episodes involving more than one attacker. [37] In 1985 Julie Ehrhart and Bernice Sandler wrote a report for the Association of American Colleges describing such incidents. They found a common pattern. When a vulnerable young woman is high on drugs, drunk, or too weak to protest, she becomes a target for a train. In some cases her drinks might have been spiked with alcohol without her knowledge. When she is approached by several men in a locked room, she reacts with confusion and panic. As many as two to eleven or more men might have sex with her. [38]

In a survey of twenty-four documented cases of alleged college gang rape reported during the 1980s, psychologist Chris O'Sullivan found that thirteen were perpetrated by fraternity men, nine by groups of athletes, and two by men unaffiliated with any group. Nineteen of the cases were reported to the police. In eleven cases, the men pleaded guilty to lesser charges. In five of the six cases that went to trial, all of the men were acquitted. The only finding of "guilty" in the twenty-four cases she studied involved black defendants on football scholarships. [39]

In 1983, I began hearing stories describing gang rape on college campuses in several parts of the country. One such incident became the focus of my book *Fraternity Gang Rape*. The incident was brought to my attention by a student, whom I called Laurel in the book. Laurel alleged that she was raped at a fraternity party when she was drunk and too high on LSD to know what was happening. The local district attorney for sex crimes, William Heinman, concluded that a gang rape had occurred because from his investigation of Laurel's state during the party, "there was no evidence that she was lucid" and able to give consent. When her behavior was described to Judge Lois Forer, she also concluded that Laurel was "incapable of giving consent." [40]

The brothers claimed that Laurel had lured them into what they called an "express." Reporting the party activities that night, they posted the following statement on their bulletin board a few days later:

> Things are looking up for the [name of fraternity] sisters program. A prospective leader for the group spent some time interviewing several [brothers] this past Thursday and Friday. Possible names for the little sisters include [the] "little wenches" and "the [name of fraternity] express." [41]

One of the boys involved in the act, who lost his virginity that night, said that he thought what happened was normal sexual behavior, even though the trauma experienced by Laurel sent her to a hospital for a long period of recovery and kept her out of school for two years. He explained his behavior by referring to the pornography he and his brothers watched together at the house. "Pulling train," as they called it, didn't seem odd to him because "it's something that you see and hear about all the time." [42]

Another brother talked at length with me about what he thought happened. Tom [pseudonym] was adamant that it was not rape because Laurel did not name it rape at first. It was only later that she called it rape after talking to campus feminists, he said. He suggested that the real problem was "her sexual identity confusion" and that both men and women who are sexually confused indulge in casual sex. According to Tom, a lot of guys "engage in promiscuous sex to establish their sexuality," because male sexual identity is based on sexual performance. The male ego is built on sexual conquests as a way of gaining respect from other men. For men, he said, there was lots of peer pressure to be sexually successful. [43]

When I asked Tom about Laurel's bruises, he admitted that she had been bruised that night because she had taken acid and was dancing wildly. He added that sex always involves some degree of force, which also explained the bruises. He went on to say that "subconsciously women are mad that they are subordinate in sex and are the objects of force." [44]

### NOTES

1.  Interview with anonymous college student, spring 1984.
2.  McCluskey (1992:261–62).
3.  For an excellent summary of studies of the heterosexual

and homosexual assault of male victims, see Struckman-Johnson (1991:192–213).

For another source see Hickson et al. (1994), which describes a study of 930 homosexually active men living in England and Wales in which 27.6 percent said they had been sexually assaulted or had had sex against their will. Some of these men reported being abused by women assailants. Another source on male-male acquaintance rape is Mezey and King (1992).

For a study of partner abuse in lesbian relationships see Renzetti (1992).

4. Kalven and Zeisel (1966:254).
5. Amir (1971). See LeGrand (1973:922–23) on Amir and for other studies on proportion of stranger to acquaintance rape cases.

  For still another study see Prentky, Burgess, and Carter (1986:73–98). These authors state that a sample of sixteen studies showed that the incidence of stranger rape ranged from 26 percent to 91 percent.
6. Amir (1971:245) and LeGrand (1973:922–24).
7. Brownmiller (1975:257).
8. Ibid.
9. Russell (1984a:11). First published in 1974.
10. Ibid., p. 12.
11. Ibid., p. 102.
12. Ibid., p. 136. A "train" is a sexual ritual in which a number of men line up to rape a women in succession. See Sanday (1990) for a discussion of trains.
13. Ibid., pp. 107; 137.
14. Ibid., pp. 31–34.
15. Russell (1984b:34; 37–38).
16. Ibid., p. 35.
17. Ibid., p. 59.
18. Ibid., pp. 35–36.
19. Ibid., pp. 96–97; 284.
20. Koss (1985:194).
21. The kind of behavior Brownmiller (1975:257) called date rape (see discussion in the text) corresponded to Koss's (1985:196) "low sexual victimization" category, which Koss does not label rape.
22. Two of the three questions used to determine the 13 percent asked whether actual or threatened physical force had been used in nonconsensual intercourse. The third question asked whether oral or anal intercourse or penetration with an object through the use of force or threat of force had been used in nonconsensual intercourse. Koss (1981: Table 4, p. 51). See also Koss and Oros (1982:455–57).
23. Koss (1981:21–27).
24. For Kinsey data see Kinsey (1953:330–31; 1948:348). From Koss's data, which she supplied to me, I calculated results from the responses to the question: "Have you ever willingly had sexual intercourse with a member of the opposite sex?" The percentages refer to those answering yes.
25. Hunt (1974:149–53).
26. For the first published version see Koss, Gidycz, and Wisniewski (1987:162–70).
27. Warshaw (1988:11). See also Koss (1988:15–16).
28. Koss (1988:15–16).
29. Koss (1992a:122–26). For more discussion of these statistics and how they were used in the backlash against Koss, see Chapter 11.
30. One and a half percent of the men said they had forced a woman into intercourse, oral or anal penetration, or penetration with objects by using threats or physical force, 4 percent of the men said they had intercourse with an unwilling woman by giving her drugs or alcohol. See Koss (1988:8).
31. Koss (1988:18–19).
32. Malamuth study summarized by Russell (1984b:159); Briere study in Russell (1984b:64). See also Malamuth (1981:138–157).
33. Scully (1990:27–28; 159; 163).
34. For a summary of these studies and others, see Koss and Cook (1993:110). For further discussion of acquaintance rape statistics, see Chapter 11.
35. For a summary of many studies, see Koss (1993:1,062–9). For the 1992 national study on rape, see National Victim Center (1992). Koss found that 16 percent of the women in her national sample said they had experienced nonconsensual sex due to a man's force, threat of force, or use of alcohol. When Koss excluded the question about alcohol, this figure was reduced to 11 percent; see Koss and Cook (1993:106).
36. Barrett (1982:50–51).
37. Warshaw (1988:101).
38. See discussion in Sanday (1990:1–2). See also Ehrhart and Sandler (1985).
39. O'Sullivan (1991:144; 151).
40. Sanday (1990:74–75).
41. Ibid., pp. 5–7.
42. Ibid., p. 34.
43. Ibid., pp. 71–72.
44. Ibid., p. 72.

# Incestuous Sexual Abuse

The sexual abuse of a girl by a relative or close family friend has been shrouded in secrecy, even though it occurs to approximately one out of four girls. Incestuous sexual abuse challenges the assumption that safety, love, and trust can be found in the family. The pieces in this section address this issue from several different perspectives. Melba Wilson considers reactions to incestuous sexual abuse in the African-American community, calling attention to misinformed attempts to blame mothers for the occurrence of incest. Wilson presents a black feminist framework for understanding incest, thereby placing it in a sociopolitical, as opposed to individual, context. Although Wilson's work focuses on African-American families, her analysis is appropriate for all groups, as she indicates that incest occurs in all races and economic groups.

Peri Rainbow provides a compelling personal account of recovering from childhood incest. Recovering the long-buried memories and learning about their effects on her enabled Rainbow to understand and change her own destructive emotional patterns.

Women who are surviving incest have found different ways of dealing with their abuse. While Peri Rainbow's story is one of surviving and recovering, Emilie Morgan asserts, "Don't Call Me a Survivor." Having been raped several times by the age of 18, Morgan does not yet feel like a survivor, since she is just beginning to tell her story. She reminds us that each of us heals at a different pace, struggling with the self-doubts and pain associated with assault.

In "Silver," Deborah Miranda remembers being raped by her mother's boyfriend, when she was 7 years old. It is not until many years later, when her own daughter is turning 7 years old, that Miranda begins to remember the horror of her rape. By confiding in friends and writing poetry to express her feelings and reactions, Miranda is able to start healing.

# 126

## *Toward a Black Feminist Understanding of Child Sexual Abuse*

MELBA WILSON

Sexual harassment, violence and exploitation of women transcends class and race boundaries. Black and white men, regardless of their class position, align with each other on the basis of shared sexism. The consequences of this for black communities are that black men who are victimised by racism in common with black women also collude, as males, to oppress black women in a sexist way.

This belies a failure to understand the dynamics of class structures which seek to undermine the cohesion of black communities. Some black men (and it is my argument that it is mainly these men who sexually abuse black girls and women) fail to make the connection between racism and sexism. They play out their sexist and sexualised aggression with black girls/women as the losers. Black men who commit sexual abuse against children devalue us as a community of people and undermine attempts to throw off stereotypes and work towards shared and equitable solutions for all.

The sexism of some black men and the racism of white society results in a reluctance by some black women survivors of incest and CSA to name their abusers and therein take control of their lives. If a woman does take action, and goes to the police for example, she is likely to be condemned by her own community for betrayal and to have her own sexuality called into question by the wider community, thus reinforcing the stereotypes. If she doesn't, she is left with maintaining the silence which gives tacit approval to the abuse, and thus undervalues her own worth as a participating and *equal* member of the community.

I view the task of black feminists as being to work towards overcoming this compulsion to blame black women for their own abuse. It is a struggle which must make us question any knee-jerk tendency to treat women as mindless objects or body parts. As black women, we should be arguing for a respect which recognises the mutual right of black women and black men to break free of the confines laid down by others; confines which have conspired to keep us all victims, by dividing one from the other. My argument is for the right to live our lives unfettered, and on our own terms; with the roles we occupy being roles that are defined by ourselves.

### FAMILY DYSFUNCTION AND BLAMING BLACK WOMEN

One reason why it is important to advance a black and feminist perspective in the field of child sexual abuse is because it challenges the view of the black family as dysfunctional: that it has inherent problems which are a result of its make-up and/or the dynamics within it. The dysfunction theory states that sexual abuse occurs in families with problems; problems, the theory holds, which can be caused by inadequate or unavailable mothers. It is, however, an erroneous premise (and one which should be countered) to say that CSA occurs only or even mainly in "problem families." One of the things we know for certain is that it occurs across the socioeconomic spectrum. It is also important to recognise that this theory represents another assault on black women and roles prescribed for us, which often do not jibe with how we see ourselves.

The main point to be made with regard to this theory and black people is that the criteria against which black families are judged by some professionals who contribute to the incest industry is based firmly within a Eurocentric framework; a framework which fails to understand or even attempt to understand the complexities or the dimensions of black family life.

Patricia Hill Collins, a Black American feminist and scholar, discusses the tendency to impose Eurocentric values on non-European cultures in her essay, "The Meaning of Motherhood in Black Culture and Black Mother/Daughter Relationships." She refers to research by a West African sociologist, Christine Oppong, which "suggests that the Western notion of equating household with family be abandoned because it obscures women's family roles in African cultures." Collins notes:

While the archetypal white, middle-class nuclear family conceptualizes family life as being divided into two oppositional spheres—the "male" sphere of economic providing and the "female" sphere of affective nurturing—this type of rigid sex role segregation was not part of the West African tradition. Mothering was not a privatized nurturing "occupation" reserved for biological mothers, and the economic support of children was not the exclusive responsibility of men. Instead, for African women, emotional care for children and providing for their physical survival were interwoven as interdependent, complementary dimensions of motherhood.[1]

Collins points to recent research which shows that more of this traditional, African-based concept of mothering has been retained by African-Americans than had previously been thought; and that a workable variation of this West African perspective has developed in response to the pressures and changes wrought by the dominant Eurocentric American culture, to produce an Afrocentric ideology of motherhood. Similarly, in Britain, this concept holds up. Black women, upon marriage, have not expected, or been expected, to remain within the home. The economic realities of life for black people in this country, as elsewhere, has historically and to the present day made this an impracticality.

This does not suggest that the black family is harmed by, or becomes (or indeed is) dysfunctional because of this fact. Black women and black families have traditionally had to develop other means to ensure their survival in response to the pressures engendered by racism and economic disadvantage. Collins notes that one response to this was the development of "women-centred" networks which have the responsibility of nurturing and care for children within a community-wide ethos:

In African-American communities, the boundaries distinguishing biological mothers of children from other women who care for children are often fluid and changing. Biological mothers or bloodmothers are expected to care for their children. But African and African-American communities have also recognized that vesting one person with full responsibility for mothering a child may not be wise or possible. As a result, "othermothers," women who assist bloodmothers by sharing mothering respon-

sibilities, traditionally have been central to the institution of Black motherhood.

Blaming women for the occurrence of child sexual abuse is not a new phenomenon. The gender twist associated with the blame of black women for its occurrence in black communities, however, cannot go unchallenged. Despite rumblings about the tip of the iceberg of female sexual abuse of children (discussed later), overwhelming evidence points to men as the primary perpetrators. No amount of theorising about its causes can escape that fact.

The issue to be addressed, instead, is that of why CSA is to be found in every stratum of society. Contained within this should be a critical discussion of why it is equally widespread in so-called "normal" families. The questions to be asked are: "What is normal?" and "Whose normality?"

No doubt there are many women who have been sexually abused as children who do indeed hold their mothers responsible for what has happened to them. "I think there are some mothers who never knew," said one survivor, "but *this* mother [her mother] knew. She beat me. The way she beat me told me so. Her tears told me so. It was then that I knew that she knew that I knew."

Another mother colluded upon learning of her daughter's incest, because of the precarious nature of the family's economic circumstances, and because she could not face the prospect of life without her man. I am convinced that my own mother did not know of my abuse. This is due in part to the fact that she was not around for long periods of my childhood—being a working black woman who had to provide for her own and her children's welfare in the face of a crumbling marriage.

A cursory viewing of the situation would suggest that we fit the Western scenario ascribed to the dysfunctional family: that is, one that does not function normally because of an absent or collusive mother. But a wider view reveals, as Collins notes, the presence of "othermothers" in our lives. The presence of such women is not unusual in black communities. Rather, they are an integral and expected part of our cultural tradition. In my case, there was my grandmother, who also was not aware of the abuse, but who provided the stability that I needed in an otherwise precarious world. Other survivors have spoken of aunts or mother's friends or other women who took them under their wing.

The starting point for why sexual abuse occurs, however, should not be where the mother *was*, but what the father or male *did*. Cultural considerations which should more appropriately be taken into account include the effects of poverty and economic circumstances. Though it is no defence for the perpetration of CSA it is important to note the part played by poverty.

## CULTURAL DIFFERENCES

Another reason for developing a black and feminist perspective about CSA concerns the need to look at cultural differences in how sexual abuse is manifested in black communities. This involves an examination of our experiences of abuse (what actually happens) and in how we choose to deal with them as black people (for example, there is often a reluctance to go to the authorities). We need to look at life experiences: for example, growing up poor and black in Texas, instead of white and middle class in wherever; or at specific instances: for example, at who perpetrates sexual abuse. Research has shown that a significant proportion of black girls are abused by their mother's men friends.[2] What are the implications of *that* in our communities?

In "A Comparison of Afro-American and White American Victims," Russell et al. note:

> That the experiences of white victims are assumed to be the norm for all minority victims is evident in the lack of ethnicity-based child sexual abuse research. But the assumption that data on Whites accurately reflect the experiences of the members of all other groups denies the role of cultural differences in people's lives, denies the fact that racism has an impact, and reflects the White bias of most researchers in this field.[3]

In practice, it has meant that child sexual abuse has come to be regarded, as Marlene Bogle and others have pointed out, as the norm by some within and many outside black communities. In addition, ignorance of or a refusal to accept the existence of sexual abuse as an issue in non-white communities has had

the effect of obstructing or limiting access to treatment for many black children who are abused.

The following account from a 1984 New York Women Against Rape conference was related by Julia Perez, a black, Puerto Rican social worker and organiser. It illustrates the pitfalls inherent in adhering to stereotypes. The incident, she said, involved "four white men, a white feminist and a Jewish woman":

> I walked into the room . . . One of the young men, because he knows I work with men in prison, said to me, "I am doing a survey to see what kind of a sentence you would give a man who raped, and has been sexually molesting his six-year-old daughter." I said: "I would put his ass in jail, for life." This woman looked up at me and said, "Well honey, you might as well put all your Black brothers down South in prison because this is a socially acceptable mode of behavior among Blacks there." I just looked at her and said, "Where did you get your statistics?" I didn't drag her out because I didn't have the energy to do that.
>
> I walked out into the hall with this knot in my stomach and pain that you could not believe. Then, the feminist walked out and said, "That's really terrible she did that to you, because we all know that Black families are female-headed anyway."[4]

The message of black feminists must be twofold. First, to make clear that black women and children do not expect to be sexually abused as a matter of course. We must stress that, if we are to survive as whole and healthy communities, we cannot allow some of our men to continue to carry out this abuse, and remain silent about it. It is a position based on the inalienable right we have as women to complete and undisputed control over our bodies.

The black feminist position as regards sexual abuse is one of challenging aggressive and oppressive male behaviour on the basis that it violates our rights as women and as black people. There's a line in the film, *The Color Purple*, in which Celie, when freeing herself from the oppressive presence of Mister tells him, "Whatever you've done to me has already been done to you." Black men (and black women) who view feminism as a "white girl's thing" and who regard the struggle of black feminists as secondary and far to the back of the black struggle would do well to remember that it is only when we all "reach the promised land" as whole, healthy human beings, that our people really will be free. We cannot continue to trash one half of the body politic and expect the repercussions not to rebound on all of us as people of colour.

Black feminism must also speak to those outside our communities, about their stereotypes of black women and black men. For it is only by gaining an understanding of the ways in which we as black people and as women are oppressed by existing power structures (which an exploration of feminism affords), that we can begin to change our destinies and take control of our lives.

### NOTES

1. P. H. Collins, "The Meaning of Motherhood in Black Culture and Black Mother/Daughter Relationships," *Sage*, 4 (2), Fall, 1987.
2. See D. Russell, *The Secret Trauma: Incest in the Lives of Girls and Women*, Basic Books, New York, 1986.
3. D. Russell et al., "The Long-term Effects of Incestuous Abuse. A Comparison of Afro-American and White American Victims," in G. E. Wyatt and G. J. Powell (eds), *The Lasting Effects of Child Sexual Abuse*, Sage, London, 1988.
4. J. Perez, "A Step towards Multiculturalism," panel discussion, Women Against Rape Fifth Annual Conference, New York, 1984.                    [1994]

## 🦎 127

# *Making Sense of the Experience of Incest Survivors*

PERI L. RAINBOW

I grew into adulthood with lingering questions about my past. Mostly, I wondered why I couldn't remember anything that happened to me before my parents' divorce, when I was twelve. I wasn't quite sure what I was supposed to remember, and I cautiously asked friends about their childhood memories. "Do you remember when you were seven years old, or eight, or six?" I'd listen to the details my friends re-

membered, not just special occasions like birthdays or holidays, but daily occurrences and what it felt like to be a child, and I'd wonder why I didn't know this about my life. I never let anyone know why I was asking and never revealed my own gaps. I didn't understand why, but I felt ashamed about not remembering. I did have what I call "Kodak memories." I would look at a childhood picture and repeat stories that were told to me about those times, vaguely sensing familiarity. But I felt no real connection with the child in the photograph. It was as if I was looking into the eyes of a stranger. Some unknown child stared back at me. Although I knew intellectually that the child was me, I felt deep inside that I was someone different. I didn't know then that the sexual abuse I had suffered was too painful to remember and that by blocking it out, I had also blocked out the memories of my childhood. I couldn't remember what being a child actually felt like. Feeling and knowing were to remain separate and distinct experiences for me for a long time to come.

I was a daring and promiscuous adolescent. At age fourteen, I had my first consensual sexual experience, and I also began to experiment with drugs. The fear and anticipation I felt when taking risks were uncannily familiar. So was sexual stimulation, and I found some comfort in this familiarity. Something about these experiences, though, while familiar and therefore comforting, also felt unsatisfying and vaguely frightening.

I spent my adolescence escaping life and my feelings about it, through chemicals, sex, and music. I was fortunate to connect with people (friends my own age and older) who were able to keep me relatively safe, despite my muted awareness. I was, however, raped by a "friend" at age fifteen and molested by my mother's (male) partner at around the same time. I dismissed these incidents as insignificant and my fault. Actually, I didn't think about these incidents or define them as sexual assaults until my first college women's studies course. Instead of attending to the life my mother provided, I created my own "family" and spent a lot of time away from home. I was introduced to Gerry Garcia and the Grateful Dead at age fourteen, and their world —concert touring, LSD, marijuana, and sex—became my own. My friends and acquaintances became my family. They kept me distant from the pain buried inside, and perhaps in some ways they gave me the love that I needed to survive. I found solace in my head, using drugs to stay there, and found love through sex, using my body to feel wanted. I didn't understand then how significant this separation was and how I was doing exactly what I had learned to do as a child to survive the incest. I survived without feeling very much for many years. I was blessed with a fair amount of intelligence, and that, coupled with charm and an air of aloofness possible for one who rarely feels, enabled me to do well in high school.

I took these patterns (survival skills) with me to college and spent the first two years experimenting with drugs and men. I barely passed my classes, as I was rarely if ever fully present at any point during that time. Toward the end of my sophomore year, an incident occurred that I was absolutely unprepared for. I was working at a vacation resort to support myself through college. One day, as I was working by the swimming pool giving out sporting equipment, I looked up and saw Bill, my father's best friend. He had been my music teacher, my caretaker, my "uncle"; he was family. A flood of physical and emotional feelings engulfed me when I recognized him. I was repulsed and terrified, and I was confused, as I could not explain any of this. My body reacted to these feelings as if it were a completely separate entity. I choked. I couldn't breathe and gasped for air, immediately hyperventilating. I felt excruciating pain in my stomach and in my vagina. I doubled over, vomited, and began to cry uncontrollably. It was as if something horrible was happening to my body, only right then and there, nothing was. As soon as I could, I locked myself in the equipment hut and rocked myself to safety. Although my mind had no memory of the sexual abuse, my body remembered.

That first flashback set in motion a process in which I have been involved, both consciously and subconsciously, ever since. In the many flashbacks that followed, remnants of the past would surface, sometimes like torn pieces of still photos stored in my brain, other times like a flood. With each flashback I was thrown into the past, and I felt the terror

and the pain I must have known as a little girl. I was fortunate that these experiences lasted only seconds or moments, but from each one I emerged frightened and confused. Memories would also surface, not only of the abuse but also of happy times in my childhood, times I had not previously recalled. During flashbacks, I felt as if I were occupying the past. I was fully conscious of the present during the memories and simply took a mental note of their surfacing. I am still aware when new memories surface and always declared it out loud. At one point I wrote down everything I remembered, good and bad, as I feared that I would forget again. I now know that once the mind releases thee things, they are back forever. Survivors remember when our minds are convinced that our bodies can tolerate the pain of knowing. Once we know, we know. It's interesting to me that the memories of the abuse, although confusing, did not surprise me. Somewhere inside I had always known. Knowing and believing, however, are two very different things.

What happened for me next further confused me and made it difficult for me to trust my judgment. I told my mother. I said, "I think Bill did something to me." She said, "Oh, don't be ridiculous—you just never liked him." It felt like my head was about to pop off my shoulders. I felt invisible, and for a moment I believed her. "I must be crazy" was what went through my mind, but then quickly, perhaps because of the vividness of my recent emotions, I thought, "No way." I did not, however, try to convince my mother of what I barely knew myself. It wasn't until four years later, when Bill's picture appeared in a local paper as he was being led away by police for molesting a little girl, that my mother believed me. Interestingly, that arrest cracked my mother's own wall of denial, and she remembered that Bill had been arrested at least once before, when I was about seven years old. He had exposed himself to a group of young campers near the place where our families spent our summers. It is the place where my most severe memories of abuse are from.

Once I began to believe that something actually did happen to me, the memories and flashbacks, as vague and disjointed as they were, became more disturbing. Now that my body was mine, it felt like it was betraying me. I felt crazy. I had difficulty being alone and difficulty being with others. Drugs helped to numb the pain but also interfered with my ability to function as a college student. I took a leave from school and left the state for several months, most of which was spent in a marijuana fog.

I returned to college believing more than ever that I had experienced something horrible involving Bill but ready to focus on something outside myself. My memories were still vague, and perhaps shifting my focus was a much needed distraction. I also believed that because of my own suffering, my college education, and my newly recognized class privilege that I could and ought to help others. I had always wanted to work in human services. I felt comfortable with pain and suffering and, as I could not touch my own, felt passionate about the suffering of others. I had declared a sociology major early on in my college career. After my hiatus, I stumbled upon an elective that was cross-listed with the Women's Studies Program. The course, entitled "Violence Against Women in the U.S.," was taught by a soft-spoken, even-tempered, radical feminist named Alice Fix. In this class, I realized that it was not my fault that a "friend" forced me to have intercourse against my will, despite the fact that I had invited him to my room. Redefining and clarifying that experience from my adolescence helped me to better understand my connection to suffering. Although I still didn't really know what had happened to me as a child, I did know that at age fifteen, Greg's behavior was not unfamiliar. The more I learned about other women's experiences, with sexual violence in particular and life in general, the more I felt a bond with other women. Like the survivors I work with in group therapy, I began to experience women's power. I learned about resistance and survival and became aware of my own.

It would be wonderful to say that my healing began there and progressed upwardly thereafter; however, healing from trauma does not work that way. Survivors take "baby steps" and often pace themselves so as not to be overwhelmed. I slowed down the process of recognizing my childhood abuse by doing what I had always done so skillfully: I split myself in two. I separated my mind (knowledge) from my body (feelings) as a child. I reentered a familiar dissociated state of being. Intellectually, I be-

came passionate about feminism and learning about women's lives. I became politically active, joining organizations, demonstrating, educating others about violence against women. I worked at a shelter for battered women and became the director of a women's crisis center. I was a leader, using my head to guide me. My body, however, stayed in what was familiar and unsafe.

I struggled for two years to maintain this dichotomy. Feminism tugged at my body. The personal, after all, is the political, and I had difficulty keeping my body, my heart, distant from the lives of other women. I had, throughout my life, often found my body at risk from others and even tried on several occasions to take my own life as well. Now, I was meeting other women who did so too, and as we learned more about and valued each other, it didn't seem to make much sense. It took nearly dying at the hands of my partner, however, and a radical intervention by a women's studies professor to move me to take action on my own behalf. I left the abusive relationship and began therapy. I also pursued my professional development in a more focused way.

Through my study of sexual abuse I learned about the dissociative process and became determined to share this knowledge with others. I wanted survivors and those who care about us to know that the residual effects, those "crazy" thoughts and behaviors, make perfect sense and that there is hope for recovery. It was knowledge and feelings together, perhaps in sync for me for the first time, that convinced me to continue on this path. The emotions I felt were connected not only to my own experience as a victim but to the courage of millions of survivors, who have struggled to understand and improve the quality of their lives. My feminist beliefs gave me faith in the possibility of change and appreciation for passion as a wonderfully powerful force.

As a budding feminist therapist, I recognized the misogyny inherent in men's abuse of women and children. I believe that the sexist socialization of men plays an important role in this. I also believe that as a feminist, it is my responsibility to take action. And so, I have proceeded to learn and to share, helping others to understand and heal.

Bennett Braun's work on traumatic memory helped me to understand what I and millions of trauma survivors have experienced. He uses the levels of the "BASK" Model of Dissociation (behavior, affect, sensation, and knowledge) to explain that when a traumatic event occurs, it is often fragmented by the brain and stored separately on each of these levels. One level—for example, knowledge of an event—may be accessible to one's consciousness.[1] I knew that those childhood pictures were of me; however, sensation, feelings related to the event, were not available. I could not recall what it felt like to be her. The process by which one's brain separates these levels is called dissociation. A person may dissociate from the past, such as I did regarding my experience with childhood. or may dissociate in the present, such as not feeling events currently occurring. I, like many survivors, incorporated dissociation into my functioning as a child, so that I could avoid feeling and reliving painful events. As they were happening, the sensations were stored in one place and the knowledge in another. Both levels remained distant from my consciousness; the knowledge, however, was closer to the surface. Also like many survivors, I experience current dissociation. When a trauma survivor is in what is perceived to be an unsafe situation, she or he may describe feeling nothing or numb or might lose conscious knowledge and therefore not recall what she or he did during that particular time period. Dissociation is a common protective mechanism that shields the survivor from events or memories of events too painful to feel. When controlled, it is a remarkable tool a survivor might use to get through uncomfortable situations. Taking control, learning to ground oneself to the present, is an important part of the healing process. It is initially a difficult concept to internalize, since dissociation first occurred automatically.

I also learned that seeing the man who abused me triggered the instant recall that occurred in my body and that my response was a common reaction to the surfacing of a traumatic memory. Since I was still so psychologically defended, so unsafe, and therefore not ready to access the memory cognitively, my mind kept part of it buried. After seeing my perpetrator, however, my body no longer could do so. Un-

like a typical memory, though, in which you know that this thing happened in the past, an abreaction or flashback feels as if it's occurring in the present. I felt like I was back there, and my body was responding to an assault. I felt the physical pain, the terror, and the disgust. I was, for those moments, approximately six years old.

Survivors of trauma experience many forms of dissociation when memories of the past are triggered; a smell, a sound, a color, a person, a type of food—anything can trigger a memory. Flashbacks can be as dangerous as any form of dissociation, since one loses consciousness of the present while it's happening. For a few seconds, a few minutes, perhaps a few days, a survivor might be responding to the past, not the present. This is a confusing state of consciousness and easy to mistrust. It mimics the state of mind of an incest victim, who is often disbelieved and made to feel that her true reality is not possible.

As I reflect on my own healing process and the healing of the hundreds of survivors I have known, I find it perfectly understandable that so many deny that the abuse ever really happened. The survivors I have known are not anxious to identify as such. Why would anyone want to believe that the person or persons who were supposed to love and protect them brutalized them instead? And because our society has denied the existence of incest from the time of the subject's first public appearance, denial is institutionally supported. In her invaluable book entitled *Trauma and Recovery*, Judith Herman explains how Sigmund Freud, the "father" of psychoanalysis, identified childhood sexual abuse at the root of the hysterical symptoms of his adult female patients.[2] Freud, however, ensconced as he was in the upper-middle-class life of Vienna, was unwilling to confront what Herman calls the "radical social implications" of his theory about the origins of female hysteria—that incestuous abuse was widespread even among the middle class. Unwilling to risk the derision of his colleagues and the possible loss of financial support for his work, Freud reinterpreted his patients' stories as fantasies resulting from an

---

[1] B. G. Braun, "The BASK Model of Dissociation," *Dissociation* 1 (1) (1988), 5.

[2] J. L. Herman, *Trauma and Recovery* (New York: HarperCollins, 1992), pp. 13–14.

unsatisfied and immature desire to have sex with their fathers. By defining his female patients as hysterical liars, Freud laid the foundation for the future of medical and psychiatric treatment of women and the pervasive belief in the dishonest, immature, and pathologically sexual nature of women and children. With this one decision, Freud laid the groundwork for the institutional denial of the abuse of female children by adult men.

Survivors of sexual abuse also learn to mistrust their own judgments and perceptions and often have difficulty trusting other people. In addition survivors often have difficultly expressing anger and engaging in sexual intimacy. As survivors often associate anger with violence (a logical connection for many), the notion of expressing anger is terrifying. Some survivors cannot imagine expressing anger without hurting themselves or someone else, and many often do. For some, getting in touch with their anger means allowing years of rage to surface, and that kind of explosion seems deadly. It is as if one has been sitting on top of an active volcano, and moving from that spot will result in a cascade of hot lava that could carry anyone in its path very far away. Learning to own one's anger, understand one's rage, and express these emotions safety are important parts of the healing process. With guidance, survivors have developed quite remarkable ways of safely releasing rage and finding support from the people they love to deal with the frightening intensity of these emotions.

Sexual intimacy, understandably, is also problematic for many survivors. When control of one's body was taken and exploited for another's pleasure, it is difficult to find physical closeness with another person pleasurable. Sometimes survivors feel betrayed by their own bodies because they remember feeing pleasurable sensations stimulated by an abuser. Survivors frequently avoid sexual intimacy. Some dissociate, so as to maintain a relationship without actually feeling anything. Others equate sex with love and, as they have been taught and as I did, use their bodies to feel a sense of self-worth. Unfortunately, each of these scenarios can have negative and often dangerous consequences. Survivors need to find safe consensual situations in which to experience sexual pleasure and to develop boundaries. This work, like the rest, involves trust and time.

Survivors who have experienced healing and worked to move beyond their victimization have chosen to live life with full awareness. Moving on means accepting what has happened and its effects and living life to its fullest despite the difficulties. It means using newly identified skills to improve the quality of one's life and acknowledging the support of others. Although some would argue that forgiveness is essential to healing, I believe that some things are simply unforgivable. I do not forgive the man who forced himself on me again and again, throughout my childhood. For me, forgiveness came in forgiving myself, for not being good enough, pretty enough, smart enough, to have the kind of love I had always wanted. It also came for me in forgiving my mother who, although not the perfect parent, did all she knew how to do. I believe she did the best she could, and I have been truly blessed with the opportunity to build a solid relationship with her. I have also been blessed with the chance to make a contribution to the lives of incest survivors. I am committed to sharing my knowledge with others and to working for change. As a psychotherapist, a teacher, a friend, and a lover, I use my skills every day. I believe, however, that real change—an end to sexual violence—will only come through transforming the institutions of our society that support and perpetuate it: the media, which surround us with objectified female bodies; the medical system, which denies and pathologizes women's pain; the legal system, which claims to seek truth while ignoring women's realities; the institutions of family and religion, which are traditionally organized to repress women and every other place in society where women are devalued and men are taught that true masculinity, an ideal to strive for, is defined by one's ability to gain power over others, by any means possible. My abuser no longer controls my life, but I am bombarded with messages daily that reinforce my vulnerability as a woman. I am determined to control my own life, in spite of these messages, and to use my power to promote change. I know that this work is not easy. I know that I am not alone. I honor each day as an accomplishment.

# 🌿 128

## *Don't Call Me a Survivor*

EMILIE MORGAN

I was sixteen the next time I was raped. I was sexually active at that point, and the rape occurred on a date. He didn't overpower me like the man who had raped me three years earlier. He simply didn't stop when I told him to.

Despite the fact that I was three years older and the rape itself was far less momentous, I was much more affected by it this time. In those three years, I had fully internalized the view that a woman is somehow to blame if she is raped, and this experience wasn't as clear-cut as the first one. Although I held him ultimately responsible, I couldn't help scrutinizing my own behavior. I had consented to everything up until that point. I knew what my limits were, but it's possible I didn't make myself clear to him. Maybe the word no wasn't enough.

This time I didn't go to the police. I knew it was rape, but I felt partially to blame. Why bother trying to explain it to anyone just so they could vindicate him and put me to shame?

What made the experience even worse was having to see him at school every single day. The way he looked at me made me realize that he knew what he had gotten away with. I know he told all of his friends. One day some guy walked up to me at my locker and asked how much I charged.

Later that year I switched schools. He graduated with honors and is a pre-law student right now.

I was raped again two years later, the summer before I was to go off to college. I don't remember everything about that night, but I do remember what I was feeling; I remember my thoughts. I am not sure which was harder: being gang-raped, or having the sudden realization that this is what it means to be a woman.

There was a clock, a digital clock on the shelf by the table. Having the clock there was very important to me. It was my only reminder that the world was continuing as usual, despite what was happening to me. It became a symbol, a tie to life. In many ways it represented the hope that my life would also continue, in time. . . .

I was at a party. I was playing cards with several men in one of the side rooms. One of them said to the others, "Does anyone feel like going on a train ride tonight?" They all exchanged glances and kind of nodded in agreement. Before I had a chance to realize what was happening, someone grabbed me from behind and threw me against the wall. One of them held me down while a couple of the others took off my clothes. They each proceeded to rape me, several times, and then invited their friends to do the same.

I didn't know when I would be able to leave—how long it would last. It was six hours and twenty-six minutes. I started to believe it was never going to end. It hasn't. It happens again every night in my dreams. Every night I see their faces, I feel the pain, the powerlessness. Every night I realize the control they have over my life, and I cry. This has been the longest six and a half hours of my life.

There was something else, something I will never forget. I couldn't escape it then, and it still continues today. The music. It was constant. It wasn't so much the act that was occurring, but the music that was playing that made me realize my status as a woman. The lyrics, from NWAs *Niggaz 4 Life,* told me who I was in their eyes:

> In reality, a fool is one who believes that all women are ladies.
>     A nigga is one who believes all ladies are bitches and all bitches are created equal.
>     To me, all bitches are the same. . . .
>     To me, all bitches ain't shit.

I couldn't escape the music. I tried to imagine other things, anything besides what was happening to me. Sometimes I could almost forget the physical pain I was in, but I couldn't escape the music. The volume was turned up just loud enough so that no one could hear me scream. The tape player was set on automatic reverse so that it would play over and over again. The sound penetrated my ears. The words fractured my soul. And the message shattered my life.

So, fellas, next time they try to tell a lie, that they never would suck a dick, punch the bitch in the eye and then the ho will fall to the ground and you open up her mouth put your dick in it and move the shit around.

When I was finally able to leave, I didn't have all of my clothes. I gathered together what I could and just ran. I got to my car and drove straight to the hospital. The waiting room was full of people, and everyone just stared at me. Children commented on my lack of clothing, which revealed the fist marks and scratches that marked my body. In that moment, I was transformed back to that thirteen-year-old child being watched in the shower. On no other occasion have I experienced that kind of vulnerability. I spent the night in the emergency room, telling my story over and over again to doctors, cops and social workers.

The next morning, I hardly recognized myself. I went home and looked at myself in the bathroom mirror. My face was swollen. My arms and legs were black and blue with bruises. My chest and back were burned from where they put out their cigarettes. I will always have those scars.

While I was standing there, I noticed that for the first time since the rape began, I was all alone, and there was no more music. Yet neither was there silence. I still felt the pain. I fell to the floor and cried. I knew my screams would never be heard, and the music would never fade away. . . .

It was four months later that I found myself at a Take Back the Night march. I was eighteen years old and in my first semester of college. That night I found myself surrounded by women, most of whom I hardly knew. Yet we all knew each other's story as if it were our own. It was. We were all there for the same reason. Our lives had all been affected by sexual violence, and we were ready to heal.

With candles in our hands and tears in our eyes, we listened to story after story of women just like me. We held hands and closed our eyes and asked for the healing to begin. . . .

We have heard the stories, the pain, the silence of women, who are all different, and who are just like you and me. We all need healing. We need healing of our memories, of our silence, we need healing of our bodies, of our minds.

I couldn't hold back the tears, tears I had held inside for so many years. When it came time to name the names of those who had been hurt by sexual violence, I remained silent. But I knew the healing had already begun. I listened as the names of countless women were shouted out as if it was roll call and I was back in elementary school. I was not alone. I was surrounded by strong women who were all surviving. The energy in that room could not be contained. We marched throughout the campus, releasing the years of pain and anger that we had held inside for far too long. We shouted into the air of the city and the ears of those who would listen, demanding that our voices be heard. I screamed the night I was raped, but nobody heard me.

Please don't call me a survivor. I really don't feel like one. Not yet anyway. I have a lot more healing to do, and it's going to take time. I am just a woman who has a story to tell, and I am learning how to make it heard.                                    [1995]

## 🌿 129

# *Silver*

DEBORAH A. MIRANDA

### *I. FORGE*

It's my earliest memory. A man presses a woman into a stucco wall, holds a knife to her throat. A small child in a white cotton dress and white leather shoes sits in a corner and cries. She needs to be picked up. Maybe she's wet or hungry or tired. There is a fourth presence in the room. It's fear.

The man is my father, the woman is my mother. I am the screaming child. The knife—a kitchen knife, silver and bright—is my fear.

I remember a little more. Now I'm three years old. We are still living in the barrio, my mother, father, and me; we are like Stone Age people giving way to Bronze. My father will soon be sent to prison. My mother, always on the edge of some bottomless place, will disappear for almost a year. But for this little time we were a family. Daddy builds LA's skyscrapers, coming home to shower, slicking back his black hair with Tres Flores, face and tattooed arms almost black against his clean T-shirt and chinos. Mama tends our little apartment, watering the avocado tree crucified on toothpicks and suspended in the water of a highball glass, speaking broken Spanish to neighborhood women when she hangs out our laundry on the communal clothesline in back. And me, in sunsuit and sandals, short "pixie" haircut, darting in and out of the ground-floor apartment from coolness to perpetual summer.

On this day I am playing with a boy from another apartment—his name might be Tony—who offends me deeply. To prove how seriously I take this—whatever it is—I run into our apartment to ask my mother for a butter knife. I know, of course, that she'd never give me a sharp knife, but I use butter knives in my play often enough that it isn't an unusual request. Prying rocks from the hard earth, making mud pies, chopping up spiky yucca leaves for my doll's dinner . . .

I find my mother in the kitchen. She is slender, her skin luminous in the dark air, humming with that inner peace she sometimes attains when the delicate details of shopping, housekeeping, and errands have gone smoothly. Her hair is in pin curls, crisscrossed all over her head, under a gold silky scarf that hangs down her back. She smells bright, like cold purple wine in a clean glass. Her eyes are deep blue and have a familiar far-away focus. She hands me the knife absentmindedly; she is doing dishes, cooking. Maybe my father will be home from work soon. Maybe the apartment smells of tomatoes soaking into fried onions, green peppers; rice grains slowly swelling into plumpness. Maybe, like the other mamas, my mother has a pile of tortillas, made early that morning, wrapped in a damp clean dish towel and warming in the small gas oven, while chops or hamburgers grill on the stove.

I take the shiny stainless silver blade and walk outside into the sun, to the boy in white T-shirt and shorts. I back him up to the cream-colored wall of the apartment building with its sharp nubbly swirls of texture, and I hold the knife to the boy's thin brown throat. I tell him, "Don't say that again!"

I remember his eyes, dark as mine, wide and defiant, but beginning to be scared. Maybe he hollers. Maybe my mother follows me out to see what use I have for the butter knife. "What's going on?" she cries, "What are you doing?"

Maybe he called me a name, said I was white; or, worse, Indian. Maybe he was repeating something the barrio women said about my pale mother. I don't know for certain, but I still remember the long cool butter knife in my hand: hard, smooth, a kind of silver that will last.

It stays there, hidden in the shadows of my hair as it grows. Every once in a while I test the edge—every year, the blade cuts a little deeper. I break crayons, smash soft wax into the imperfect letters of my name. I kick my way through the crowd of older kids at the playground who say I can't use the swings. My father says I should hit those kids. I see how he fights for what he wants; how his fists work for him. I hear my mother crying that she's leaving for good. I am afraid, afraid of what I might do with this anger against people who don't understand that my whole body feels as if it is wrapped around a bright and soul-less blade.

## II. SHEATH

By the time I am six I have a reputation. Not what you think: I am not a bully. Too much has happened to me for that easy solution. My father has disappeared. My mother has disappeared and come back; remarried. We are in Washington State now. Instead of an apartment, we live in a trailer, in a trailer court tucked into the wet, rural lands of south Puget Sound. On Sundays when we visit my stepfather's relatives, I hide behind Mama's chair.

The aunts think I'm adorable, try to bribe me out of the corner with Rice Krispie squares and kind voices. One of them tells me, "I wish I had a permanent tan like yours." The uncles don't know I exist, and I don't, not in their rec room world, feet propped up, a game on television, TV trays loaded with chips and sandwiches and beer in short fat brown bottles.

It's all new to me: thick gray and red wool socks, bright orange hunting caps, plaid shirts, boots heavy with mud tracking across Aunt Carole's clean kitchen floor while she yells at the men, "Get out, out!"

I stay close to Mama, watch the cousins slam in and out of the house, grabbing handfuls of chips to eat outdoors, where their domain begins and the adult world ends.

For a long time I am too shy to explore. But I guess kinds are attracted to kids; it's normal to want to play blind man's bluff and sing B-I-N-G-O. For a moment I forget that I'm not normal. When Pete darts inside the house, my aunt grabs her son, nudges him toward me, prods him to ask, "You wanna play too?" I can hear voices chanting a familiar rhyme in the front yard. I slide from behind the chair, follow Pete through the door.

Outside CeeCee and Betty exchange looks; Pete mutters, "My mom made me ask her." The way he says *her* sets me apart, makes it okay for the cousins to trip me during a game of tag. I play anyway. I'll show them I'm not a baby. They know I won't complain; they wallop my skinny chest with interlocked arms when we play red rover out on the asphalt streets of their subdivision, or snatch an ice-cream bar out of my hand.

What they don't know is how sharp I am inside. I can stand there without tears, watch one of them lick my Creamsicle down to the clean wooden stick, and not say a word. I can stand there because inside I am slashing them to ribbons.

"Say you're ugly," Pete demands, holding my ice cream above CeeCee's wide-open mouth. "Say you look like an old brown piece of dog turd."

My lips are pressed so tightly together, they sting. CeeCee lunges up at the now-dripping orange and vanilla ice-cream slab, and misses. Pete hoists in higher, his small blue-gray eyes easily estimating the distance. "I'm gonna let Cee have it, Mexican. Come on, Brownie, just say it. Say, *I'm ugly....*"

"Geez, Pete," Betty is whining, chin sticky with her own ice cream, "It's melting, it's gonna fall off the stick. Hurry up! Give it to us!"

I feel the scratchy branches of my aunt's huge juniper bushes at the back of my knees, smell their unmistakable heat stench rising up behind me. Pete leans closer and I have to step back. I don't want to, but his milky face looms up. . . .

For a second our eyes click level. Pete sees my usual scared-of-her-own-shadow self; I see deep into his happy lust. How glad he is that I am terrified! But close up, his pleasure strikes me like a flint, and he sees something unexpected—defiance—spark in me. He narrows his eyes.

"Take your stupid ice cream," he sneers, slams the wet gooey mess into my face, laughs as I gasp, fall backward into the junipers, into the stinking warm green branches that break under me and release still more acrid oil. Then I cry.

My cousins think I'm not tough; but Mama strokes my hair and says to Aunt Carole, "If she has Ed's blood, she can take care of herself. You just wait." I wonder if she knows. I'm so careful not to let it show; clench my jaw, my tongue pressed into the roof of my mouth. If she knows the bad things I think, she might leave again. Or I might be the one to disappear. At night I grind my teeth. Nobody says anything about the sharp hungry part of me.

### III.  WHETSTONE

Except Buddy. Buddy must know. Buddy is a friend of my mama's. I'm seven years old now. My stepfather isn't home much, drives trucks to places with names like Tiger Mountain, Woodinville, North Bend. Buddy, who lives close to our neighborhood, is at our little trailer almost every day bringing beer, cigarettes, candy. There's always something for everyone, and a few minutes of that special attention, that tenderness human beings crave and do not get. I want some of it, too. I like the way he listens when I read out loud, how he says I'm the smartest girl he knows; I take the candy and the hugs eagerly, guiltily.

But Buddy kisses my mama in a way that I don't like. I glare at him. Mama laughs and tells Buddy, "Let's go for a ride." "What about . . . ?" Buddy asks, nodding at me. "Bring her," Mama nods, Pall Mall in one hand, beer in the other. She slurs words in the way that makes my stomach knot. "Put her in the backseat and drive around for a while. She'll drift off."

She always tells people what a good traveler I am.

It's true. I can't fight the dark sky, the warmth of the heater coming on, tires against the asphalt. I am betrayed by my mother's intimate knowledge of me. Even as I see my mother's shadow sliding across the front seat closer to Buddy, I fall asleep.

It doesn't take long for Buddy to get me, and Helen, too. Helen is a year younger than me, but we are best friends. Helen is a red-headed, freckle-faced white girl, but when we stand together in our matching green dresses, matching socks and shoes, we think we are twins. I'm better at reading, she's better at math, so we help each other with homework. But I'm older, I watch out for Helen on the playground or at the park. I let her play with my special doll, the one that has a real horse tail for hair. Buddy teaches us to braid it, and it's glossy, thick. There's a lake where Helen and I love to swim. He takes us for the whole day, and we have fun; but I don't like spending what seems an hour changing into my swimming suit because Buddy won't stop peeking. And there's an orchard near his house where we can pick apples for free, if we spend the night. His wife loves kids, he says. Our mothers say it's okay.

But Buddy's wife sleeps hard, goes shopping the next day. It is here, in his house that night, and in the orchard the next morning, that Buddy finally rapes me. I don't know this is rape; I do know I can't tell. Does he say that to me, "Don't tell"? No, he doesn't need threats. I can't tell because at seven years old I don't have words to describe the pain thrusting into my vagina—a hand around my throat—sound of a man's ragged breath next to my ear. I can't tell because I never said *no* to anything Buddy ever gave me. I can't tell because I didn't stop him when he did it to Helen, too. Most of all, I can't tell because there is nobody who wants to hear.

There are some things I can never do without thinking of Buddy. Braid my hair. Put on a swimming suit. See apple orchards, hear the buzz of bees and yellow jackets when the fruit falls to the earth, bruised. And after my family moves away, I never have a best friend again. I hate that he is still in me, that cells in my brain hold his image. Some people forget being molested. Some people don't even know it happened to them. My problem is that I

can't forget. Instead of growing dull and faint, my anger gets sharper and sharper. Like a knife. Like a big silver knife.

## IV. UNSHEATHED

I am fifteen years old. We are in yet another trailer, this time on an isolated five acres of land. My step-father has left us; my father has returned. He brought a son with him, conceived the moment he stepped out of San Quentin. Eddie is five years old now, and I have raised him for the past two years, losing my heart to the dark skin, arched eyebrows, brown eyes wide with curiosity, pain, life. He is the first person I have ever met who looks like me. He is my only family. Eddie is sleeping at this moment, exhausted, on his stomach, in the next room. He can't sleep on his back because of the welts left by my father's belt.

I am standing over my father as he lies passed out on his bed. I don't know where my mother is. The smell of spilt beer and sweat is strong on the sheets, the pillowcases, in the thick curtains of the window above his husky, muscular form. It's very late at night, or else early in the morning, and all around our tin trailer one-hundred-foot pines sway shaggy and green in the winter rain. There are no stars, no moon. There are no lights anywhere but in this room, the overhead light striking what is in my hand, reflecting a false silver aura to the walls, furniture, linoleum.

I am holding the little handgun my father keeps in the trailer. It is gray metal, with a black handle. I want to put it to my father's temple and pull the trigger.

Yes, it's loaded. Yes, here is the safety, here is the way he taught me to take the safety off. My hand is not even trembling. My teeth are clenched. I list the reasons: he would never hit Eddie again; he would never cause Mom to drink, to cry, ask me to call in sick for her again; he would never read my journals, break into my locked file cabinet, my secrets, again.

I try to think of consequences. Blood. Police. Remann Hall, where they send the bad kids, the place I have been threatened with forever, by grown-ups, by the whispers of schoolmates.

*What if it doesn't kill him, what if he wakes up? Am I more afraid of failure than success? What about*

*Eddie? What about his life, tortured by this man? Can't I do it for him?*

Maybe this is a movie. Someone else's movie. If this moment were captured on time machine film and examined frame by frame, would I see dozens upon dozens of angels flitting in and out of the picture, holding my hand down? Keeping my hand from lifting the gun to my father's head, to my own head?

The gun butt hefts in my hand. Why do I think it feels like a big butcher knife? Why do I feel as though I have stood here before with this weapon in my hands? I put it back on the shelf. I go to bed, cold. The rains comes down all night without stopping.

## V.  CUTTING EDGE

I'm a grown woman. I'm married. We have two children, two years apart. Sometimes, when they have been sick a lot, or up all night for too many nights, or both, I scream at my children, enraged over dirty clothes, writing on walls, toys never put away. For a long time, I can hold in these explosions, clean the house or eat, instead. Then I begin to write poetry again, the first time I have considered being a writer since I was fifteen. The writing seems to help at first; it's a relief to capture my daughter's temper tantrum in a poem, create something whole from the destruction of a day. The deeper I go, the less patience I have. My life—carefully constructed to include husband, children, solid old house—is no longer moving forward in time. The more I write, the further backward my words take me. I don't go easily or willingly. But I need to write too badly to let it take the blame for my mood swings. It's easier to blame the kids.

Around the summer my daughter turns seven years old, I begin to have bad dreams. Knives. Bees. Screams that are unheard. I feel something coming unwrapped, coming loose, unleashed inside me. My children have never seen me so uncontrolled; they laugh. In order to be taken seriously, I begin to throw things. At them. One day I take my daughter by the wrists and squeeze. I, who have only ever swatted behinds gently, spank hard. I scream into their faces. My son, the one with my little brother's face, is terrified, learns to hide when he hears me

lose my temper, come stomping up the stairs. He promises me he'll "be good." My daughter is defiant without apology. She screams right back. This happens several times a week, then several times a day. I know I am losing her. My husband asks what's wrong. I don't have words to tell him.

I confide in two friends what is happening. These women live two thousand miles away, and the written words we exchange are safe. Like older sisters, they share their own stories of lost families, abuse, and healing. Yet even on paper I am ashamed of many things: the rape, the silence, my anger. Slowly, our letters to each other become more specific. Finally I write a poem about my being raped at seven years old. I cannot show it to my husband. I send it to my friends, apologize for anything that might upset them. What happens next saves me.

One woman writes back, "Your letter and poem make me want to cry with rage." The second woman tells me not to apologize for the ugliness of what I've written. She says, "Let it out."

I can see there has been no forgetting of the events—only the emotions. Terror, loneliness, terrible anger. Anger is cutting a way out of layers of scar tissue, slashing a path through anything standing too close to me—even my daughter, my son. It is a knife that has been sheathed too long, never disposed of properly, left out where a child could find it. I decide I won't let that happen. I must tell. I give the poem to my husband.

When he reads it, we both cry.

Other poems follow this one, written in safe moments at the beach, in the sun, while cleaning the house. I cry a lot; this scares me. I want to stop hiding from these emotions, but I want to survive them, too. One night I dream that I take a knife—a kitchen knife—from my house, ride through town on my bike. I hold the knife pressed between my right hand and the handlebar as I pedal through dusk, blade pointing out. This is dangerous; I could accidentally stab someone. I must get rid of the knife. But where? The streets are crowded, full of after-work shoppers and pre-dinner strollers. Finally I drop the knife into a dishpan full of dirty silverware at an outdoor café and ride on into a cool evening, full of relief and pleasure at finding a solution. No one will ever look there; and the café will quickly absorb the extra blade as part of its inventory. Out of my reach, it will not harm anyone.

## VI. RE-FORGED

Right now it's early morning, almost dawn. I sit in my study. The door I hung by myself is closed. The cedar paneling on the walls and ceiling glows warm, almost cinnamon. Hanging here and there are paintings, postcards from friends, announcements for poetry publications. There is a desk, a file cabinet that stands unlocked. A white cat stretches out on the braided rug, bathing delicately. Upstairs, my husband and two children sleep heavily, peacefully. They are not afraid of the dark or the tall lilac bushes blowing against the windows.

My daughter always wakes first, comes drifting downstairs with her brown hair flopped to one side, rubbing her eyes, heading for my lap. Summer is finally over, hanging on with hot weather and clear skies through September; now October, the month I was born in, announces itself with fog and cold winds. My daughter burrows into my arms and I wrap a big sweater around us both. We don't speak for a long time. When we do discuss the day ahead, Miranda whispers, "Will you braid my hair for school?" She doesn't ask lightly. Behind her question are years of frustrating tangles, slippery baby-hair fiascoes. I have never been able to braid her hair. My fingers don't know the right moves somehow; or, I tell myself, Miranda didn't inherit the thick Indian hair that falls to my waist. We've kept her hair short for a long time. But over the spring and summer, it has grown out stronger, darker, past her shoulders. I say, "I think we can manage a little braid today," and Miranda smiles. That sharpness between us is gone; what remains is like old silver, smooth and warm, just a little bit polished by time. Like most pure metals, it gives to the touch.   [1996]

PART VII

# Changing Our World

Although changing the position of women in our society can seem like an overwhelming task, women have in fact made significant progress when they have organized. By articulating a critique of male domination and demanding the inclusion of women in social and political life, feminist movements have been crucial to accomplishing these changes. By thus changing the environment, organized feminism has supported and inspired women's efforts to work on their own behalf wherever they are. This part, therefore, begins with a brief survey of what historians often refer to as the first and second waves of feminism in the United States. Both these movements had profound effects on society and culture. In this discussion, we examine both the strengths and weaknesses of the movement, so that knowledge of the past can inform our efforts to improve the position of women in the present.

The first wave of feminism, which emerged in the 1840s, began with a broad-ranging critique of women's social, political, and economic position in society as expressed by the Resolutions of the Seneca Falls Convention. Much of this initial breadth, however, was lost as the movement narrowed to focus on achieving the right to vote. The second wave of feminism that emerged in the 1960s reengaged many of these issues, developing a critique of the politics of personal life through a process that came to be called consciousness raising. Elizabeth Gilbertson, a member of a consciousness-raising group remembers:

> We would take some piece of experience, that it had never occurred to me at least to think about differently, and talk about it. Like . . . high school, and the importance of having boobs, and what it was like to be smart, and . . . whether you could major in math or science. The things which are now canons of the faith. . . . So we would look at one another and say, "Well, I remember" and kind of piece it together like that. "The way that I felt about this was. . . ." The experience that captured that best for me was one day looking at the front page of the newspaper and there was not a single woman's name on it—and I had been reading the newspaper all my life and I had never noticed that. It was like that. And this light—I mean it was literally like someone had screwed in a lightbulb. And all of a sudden I had a set of lenses for looking at the world that I hadn't had before, and the whole world looked different through them.[1]

While the analysis that emerged from these discussions was often presented as applicable to all women, it reflected the experience of the white middle-class women who dominated most of the early consciousness-raising groups. Women within the black, Latino, Asian, and American Indian movements of the late 1960s and 1970s were questioning the sexism within their own movements, often encountering resistance from movement men. While some of the ideas being articulated by white feminists resonated in the lives of women of color, others were alien to their experience. In groups of their own, women of color broke traditional silences and generated a feminist analysis that spoke to their experience and recognized the interaction of racism and sexism in their lives. In an Asian women's group in the early 1970s, for example, Miya Iwataki remembers:

---

[1] Interview by Amy Kesselman with Elizabeth Gilbertson, July 6, 1991.

Women began talking about years of scotch-taping eyelids to create a double eyelid fold and then carefully painting in over with Maybelline eyeliner. Women began to break through years of checking out each other as competition for Asian men; of fearing being found out that one was not a virgin; or having to be anything but a "natural woman."[2]

For the women who were reinventing feminism, the rediscovery of a history of feminist thought and practice was enormously exhilarating; it reconfirmed their belief in the necessity and possibility of changing women's position at a time when women's liberation activists were being ridiculed and discounted. Members of a Chicana women's group in 1971, for example, were delighted to discover a women's organization that published a newspaper called *Hijas de Cuahtemac* during the 1910 Mexican revolution, and they decided to use the same name for their own group. Anna Nieto-Gomez, one of the members, remembers that

> it was like I had been in a cave and someone has just lit the candle. I [suddenly] real-ized how important it was to read about your own kind, the women of your own culture, or your own historical heritage, doing the things that you were doing. [It] reaffirmed and validated that you're not a strange, alien person, that what you're doing is not only normal but a part of your history.[3]

Throughout the 1970s and 1980s, the movement grew and challenged the subordination of women in a wide variety of arenas. Although the achievements of the feminist movement have been impressive, the goal of creating a society in which women are able to participate fully in all aspects of social and political life is still unrealized. In the midst of the process of approaching this goal, however, a multilayered assault against feminism was launched. In the 1980s the "New Right," a coalition of conservative and religious organizations, mounted an offensive against women's rights and has succeeded in restricting women's reproductive freedom, diluting affirmative action programs, and preventing the passage of the Equal Rights Amendment. Most people in our country favor equal rights and reproductive freedom for women, but they have not been sufficiently organized to prevent the erosion of many of the accomplishments of the previous decades. While there was still a great deal of support for the general goals of feminism, many women hesitated to identify themselves with the feminist movement. "I'm not a feminist but . . . ," a refrain of the 1980s, represented the success of a media attack on feminism that Susan Faludi exposed in her best-selling book *Backlash*.

Nevertheless, feminism has not disappeared but continues to grow, taking new forms as it tackles new problems. Women throughout the world are organizing on their own behalf, and in the last 15 years a global feminist movement has developed, bringing women together from all parts of the world. Western feminists meeting with

---

[2] Interview with Miya Iwataki as quoted in Sherna Gluck, "Whose Feminism, Whose History," in *Community Activism and Feminist Politics: Organizing Across Race, Class and Gender,* Nancy A. Naples, ed. (New York: Routledge, 1998), p. 40.
[3] Interview with Anna Nieto-Gomez, quoted in Gluck, *Community Activism.*

women in Africa, Asia, and Latin America have realized that feminism must encompass survival issues, such as access to food and water, in order to support women's struggles for self-determination. This expanding global consciousness raises challenging issues for feminists in the United States.

In the past fifteen years, feminists seeking to connect women of various countries have established organizations, sponsored international conferences, and promoted education about women's issues in various parts of the world. Such networks increase the possibility of cooperative action across national boundaries. A global feminist movement can challenge what Charlotte Bunch calls the "dynamic of domination embedded in male violence" by working against militarism, racism, and sexism wherever it exists.

In the 1990s, signs are emerging of another revival of feminist energy in the United States. The massive increase in wage-earning mothers in the last two decades is heightening awareness of the need for public policy changes that will support women and their families; the reproductive rights movement has been reinvigorated in response to the anti-abortion decisions of the Supreme Court, and women are running for office with money raised by feminist fund-raising efforts.

A third wave of American feminism is beginning to take shape. Leslie Heywood and Jennifer Drake, two women who describe themselves as third wave feminists, see their movement as combining "elements of second wave critique of beauty and culture, sexual abuse, and power structures, while it also acknowledges and makes use of the pleasure, danger, and defining power of those structures."[4] Women singers are introducing passionate feminist lyrics into popular music, and young women are producing "zines" that express anger at the pressures on young girls to conform to media-inspired images of femininity and outrage at violence against women. Reclaiming the word "girl," which second wave feminists found demeaning, young feminists are infusing it with a new spirit of independence, defiance, and female solidarity.

One of the strengths of contemporary feminism is its multi-issue approach. As women confront sexism in different situations, new issues emerge and our understanding of women's experience deepens. The final section of this part includes descriptions of women organizing in various contexts from the 1970s to the 1990s. The writers tell stories of women who, inspired by growing legitimacy of feminist concerns, refused to accept unfair treatment or who perceived a problem and decided to do something about it. In all of these organizing efforts, consciousness raising was a crucial ingredient since women needed to talk to each other about their experience in order to develop strategy. In some situations, such as women dealing with AIDS in prison, breaking the silence in itself makes an enormous difference. These stories demonstrate that, despite the media proclamations, feminism did not die in the

---

[4]Leslie Heywood and Jennifer Drake, "Introduction," in *Third Wave Agenda: Being Feminist, Doing Feminism,* Leslie Heywood and Jennifer Drake, eds. (Minneapolis: University of Minnesota Press, 1997), p. 3.

1980s; it lived in the many efforts of women organizing around specific issues on both national and local levels.

The final selections address the activism of the 1990s. As women develop strategy and tactics to address current issues, they are reviving methods such as civil disobedience and developing new approaches to change. Young women bring a fresh perspective to feminism as they grew up in a world in which feminist ideas and language were an integral part of our culture.

# Feminism as a Social Movement

We have discussed feminist *ideas* earlier in this book, but we turn in this section to a consideration of feminism as a *social movement*, beginning with a brief history of feminism in the United States from 1848 to 1990 and documents from the first and second wave of feminism. The first document was signed by the people who gathered at the first women's rights convention in Seneca Falls, New York, in 1848 and describes the wide range of issues they discussed. It is useful to think about the extent to which the goals of the Seneca Falls convention have been achieved and what issues seem most resistant to change.

Three years later, Sojourner Truth addressed a women's rights convention in Akron, Ohio. The speech that she made was popularized by Frances Gage, who wrote it down 12 years after it was given, and differed significantly from the version that was reported at the time. The Gage version, featuring the refrain "Ain't I a Woman," became a rallying cry for the feminist movement, but historians believe that the newspaper version was closer to her actual words. We present first the speech reported in the *Salem Anti-Slavery Bugle* in 1851 that historian Nell Painter has recovered in her biographical work on Sojourner Truth; we follow this with Frances Gage's version.

The third document was written in the early days of the second wave of feminism. It describes the evolution of consciousness raising as a technique for understanding women's oppression, an important source of insight for women's liberation activists in the 1960s and 1970s. The insights that emerged in consciousness raising often laid the foundation for action projects. As women talked about their bodies, for example, they confronted their own woeful ignorance, a legacy of years of secrecy and shame. Convinced that knowledge was an essential ingredient of controlling one's own body, they determined to teach themselves and each other about women's physiology. Susan Brownmiller tells the story of the Boston Women's Health Book Collective, which emerged from this process and produced a book that was on the best-seller list for years, was translated into many languages, and has become a valuable resource for women throughout the world.

In the next three essays, women of color discuss the analysis that emerged from their discussion of the inseparable, multiple oppression that they encounter. Their writing speaks to the necessity of working against all forms of oppression simultaneously, which involves working with men against racism while challenging their sexism, an often painful process.

The feminism of women of color draws on the day-to-day heroism of mothers and grandmothers, which is embodied for Barbara Smith in Alice Walker's definition of "womanist." Chicana feminists, Alma Garcia explains, have had to struggle against sexist traditions deeply embedded in their culture. In an essay written after attending the founding convention of Ohoyo, a national organization of American

Indian women in 1979, Kate Shanley points out that American Indian feminists seek to retain the alternative family forms and communal values of tribal life. As all these selections point out, coalitions among different groups of women can only be meaningful if each group has had a chance to develop its own agenda.

Like any movement that challenges established hierarchies and cherished beliefs, the feminist movement has encountered ridicule and opposition. In her best-selling book *Backlash: The Undeclared War on American Women,* Susan Faludi exposed the media assault on feminism during the 1980s. Faludi argues that the press, TV, movies, and the fashion industry have endeavored to convince women to relinquish the struggle for equality and respect by proclaiming that although women have won all the rights they need, it only makes them miserable. In fact, equality has not been achieved, and women are struggling to combine work and family without institutional supports.

Despite the backlash, women throughout the world continue to organize against violence, discrimination, and exploitation. One of the most exciting developments of the 1980s was the networking among women from around the world. Many international organizations have emerged that address violence against women, the role of women in development, the effect of war on women's lives, and an increase in women's political and economic power around the world. The 1995 conference in Beijing was a watershed event for the emerging global feminist movement, strengthening the international connections among women's groups and laying the groundwork for future activities. One of the major challenges to women around the world is the growth of multinational corporations that move around the world in search of cheap female labor. The athletic footwear industry in particular has become highly profitable by moving its factories to Asia where young women who had been trained to sacrifice themselves for their families' well-being are hired at extremely low wages. In the final essay in this section, Cynthia Enloe describes the resistance of some of these women workers suggesting ways that women in the United States can support their efforts.

---

# 🌿 130

# *A History of Feminist Movements in the U.S.*

AMY KESSELMAN

The history of feminism is a story of ebb and flow. There have been periods when women's issues were on everyone's lips. Laws changed, barriers toppled, and a world where women and men participated equally in all aspects of life seemed to be around the corner. Such periods were often followed by periods of reaction in which feminism was labeled evil and socially destructive, and efforts to achieve equality for women stagnated.

While women have worked to improve their lives throughout history in a variety of ways, historians often describe the organized women's movements of the United States as two waves of feminism. These waves pushed women's issues to the forefront of national politics. The first and second waves of U.S. feminism were both born in periods of cultural upheaval, when many people were engaged in questioning social, cultural, and political norms. The first wave of feminism emerged among women who were active in the reform movements of the 1840s and 1850s. In particular, the antislavery movement nurtured female organizing efforts and stimulated thinking about the meaning of human rights for women. In 1848, a group of women who had been involved in Quaker and antislavery activities organized a convention at Seneca Falls, New York, to "discuss the social, civil and religious rights of women" (Flexner, 1970, p. 74). About 300 people gathered and adopted a series of resolutions drafted by Elizabeth Cady Stanton, calling for an end to the subordination of women in all areas of life. While both women and men attended this convention, the speeches and resolutions made it clear, in the words of Stanton, "that woman herself must do this work; for woman alone can understand the height, the depth, the length and the breadth of her degradation" (Flexner, 1970, p. 77). After the Seneca Falls convention, women's rights conventions were held yearly, and women all over the country engaged in efforts to change unjust laws, improve the education of women, and eliminate the barriers to women's participation in public life.

While the leadership of the women's rights movement was predominantly white, there were several prominent African-American women who worked for the emancipation of both African Americans and women. Maria Stewart of Boston was one of the first women to speak in public to groups of women and men, urging African-American women to become economically independent. Sojourner Truth, a spell-binding orator, spoke at women's rights and antislavery meetings of the connection between freedom for women and emancipation of enslaved African Americans. After the Civil War, Mary Ann Shadd Cary argued that black women were eligible to vote under the Fourteenth Amendment, and she successfully registered to vote in 1871. Frances Ellen Watkins Harpur, a poet and lecturer, spoke frequently at women's rights conventions as a voice for black women (Giddings, 1984).

Obtaining the right to vote was just one of the many goals of the women's rights movement at first, but by the end of the Civil War, it became the primary focus of the movement. Women's rights activists believed that winning suffrage was a necessary tool for achieving all other aspects of women's emancipation. Women worked state by state to obtain the right to vote, and by 1900, they had gained suffrage in several western states. After the turn of the century, a new generation of women suffragists renewed the effort to pass an amendment to the Constitution granting women the right to vote.

The focus on suffrage had advantages and disadvantages. It was a concrete reform that could be used to mobilize women, and it symbolized, perhaps more than anything else, the participation of women as individuals in public life (Du Bois, 1978). On the other hand, winning the right to vote required gaining the approval of male voters and politicians. Women suffragists often adopted whatever arguments they felt were necessary to persuade those in power that it was in their interest to grant women the right to vote. They often invoked traditional gender roles as they campaigned for the vote, urging, for example, that women would "sew the seams and cook the meals; to vote won't take us long" (Knight & Julty, 1958).

Suffragist pragmatism also intensified the racism, nativism, and class bias of the white, native-born leadership of the major suffrage organizations (Kraditor, 1981). In the late nineteenth and early twentieth centuries, immigrants poured into the United States, radically changing the social, economic, and political landscape. The rhetoric of women's suffrage leadership often reflected the bias of white, native-born citizens against these new Americans. Carrie Chapman Catt, for example, who became president of the National American Woman's Suffrage Association, warned against the danger of "the ignorant foreign vote which was sought to be brought up by each party . . ." (Catt, 1894, p. 125). Urging literacy requirements, she concluded that the best solution would be to "cut off the vote of the slums and give it to the women . . ." (Catt, 1894, p. 125).

Similarly, southern white suffragists were willing to invoke racism to further their cause, arguing that the enfranchisement of white women would help sustain white supremacy in the South. When the NAWSA voted in 1903 to allow state chapters to determine their own membership, it gave tacit approval to southern racism. Southern clubs excluded African-American women and often argued that suffrage be granted only to those who met property or literacy requirements.

Despite the racism of white women's suffrage organizations, African-American women were actively involved in efforts to gain the right to vote in the early twentieth century by organizing black women's suffrage clubs throughout the U.S. "If white women needed the vote to acquire advantages and protection of their rights, then black women needed the vote even more so" argued Adella Hunt Logan, a member of the Tuskegee Woman's Club (Giddings, 1984, p. 121). The NAWSA, however, was engaged in efforts to get the women's suffrage amendment passed by a U.S. Senate dominated by white southern men. As a result, they were less than hospitable to African-American women's groups who wanted to affiliate, arguing that they should resubmit their application after the vote was won.

While the women's suffrage movement focused on the single issue of winning the right to vote, the late nineteenth and early twentieth centuries saw the flowering of many different efforts by women to improve their lives and the lives of others. A movement to make birth control legal and available to all women was led by Margaret Sanger, Emma Goldman, and others. A crusade against lynching was initiated by Ida B. Wells. Black and white women educators worked to improve women's educational opportunities, and women labor activists organized to improve the wages and working conditions of the wage-earning women who worked in factories, stores, and offices.

Attitudes toward women's capabilities began to shift, and the image of the "new woman" of the early twentieth century embodied self-reliance and involvement with the world. During this period, the word "feminism" was introduced by women who believed women's emancipation required deeper changes than the right to vote. They argued for the full integration of women into social, political, and economic life. While suffragists often argued for the right to vote in the name of women's traditional roles, claiming that women's propensity for nurturance and housekeeping would be useful in the

public world, feminists renounced self-sacrifice in favor of self-development (Cott, 1987). African-American activists like Anna Cooper argued for a women's movement that challenged all forms of domination and made alliances with all oppressed peoples. Socialists like Charlotte Perkins Gilman suggested that women's emancipation required the elimination of private housekeeping in favor of community kitchens and child-care centers.

After 72 years of work, the women's suffrage amendment was ratified by the states in 1920. In the decades that followed, the women's movement shrank in numbers and influence, and those women who remained active were divided about the best way to improve women's lives. While the Constitution now gave all citizens the right to vote, African Americans of both sexes had been disenfranchised in the South by racist violence and state laws. While magazines and newspapers often proclaimed that women's equality had been achieved, the barriers to their full participation in the workplace, in politics, and in cultural and social life remained intact. Feminism fell into disrepute, conjuring up images of fanatic women out to spoil men's fun. When the Great Depression of the 1930s created massive unemployment, female wage earners were regarded with suspicion, further intensifying antifeminist sentiment. By the post–World War II era, a resurgence of the cult of domesticity denigrated female ambition, even though large numbers of women were working for wages. In the 1960s, when women again began to rebel against their subordinate status, the first wave of feminism was a distant memory, and recovering its history was an important ingredient in developing a new movement.

What lessons can we learn from the rise and fall of the first wave of American feminism? Winning the right to vote, a seemingly basic democratic right, took almost a century to accomplish and required an enormous amount of brilliant organizing, writing, and speaking. The benefit of hindsight, however, enables us to see that a great deal was sacrificed to achieve this goal. The capitulation of the suffrage movement to racism and prejudice against immigrants meant that it spoke for a narrow segment of women. Its failure to challenge the division between men's and women's worlds meant that when it won the right to vote, many forms of sexism remained. The suffrage movement demonstrates the perils of focusing exclusively on one goal, deferring others until it is achieved.

The second wave of feminism developed among different groups of women whose combined resources and insights augmented its power. The equal rights segment of the movement originated among women working within government agencies who were frustrated with the slow pace of change. They founded the National Organization for Women (NOW) in 1966 to work for equality in work, education, and politics. One of NOW's founders, Betty Friedan, wrote the influential best seller, *The Feminine Mystique.* This book described the frustrations of college-educated suburban housewives and argued that women should be encouraged to pursue careers as well as motherhood (Friedan, 1964).

The tensions that were building in the lives of women during the 1950s and 1960s, however, went beyond the need for work outside the home; they had to do with the devaluation of women in everyday life, sexual objectification, the violence against women that permeated society, and the socialization of women to meet the needs of men (Evans, 1979). These aspects of sexism were so tightly woven into the fabric of American culture that they were taken for granted and rarely discussed. Young women who had been involved in the social movements for peace and justice in the 1960s were able to bring these issues into the open. Accustomed to being on the fringes of respectability, they were willing to talk about subjects that were previously hidden and analyze their own lives for insights about the nature of women's oppression. "Consciousness raising," the reexamination of one's life through feminist lenses, was a tool for understanding women's experience. As women began to talk about their childhoods, their sexual lives, their feelings about being female, their work and school experiences, and their experience of male violence, the contours of feminist theory emerged. These young women called their movement "women's liberation," and argued for radical changes in the political, social, and economic institutions of our country.

The interaction between these two groups strengthened the feminist movement. NOW broadened its agenda to include the issues raised by women's liberation, recognizing that the achievement of equality would require deep systemic changes in the relationship between home and family, the concepts of "femininity" and "masculinity," and the educational and political systems. While women's liberation groups were generating analysis and challenging long-held assumptions, NOW provided concrete strategies for implementing these ideas, such as litigation against discriminatory corporations and efforts to change laws governing rape, violence, and divorce.

As different groups of women developed feminist analysis to address their experience, feminism grew deeper and broader. The process was not always without friction, as groups who felt their needs were being ignored confronted the leaders of feminist organizations. After several stormy meetings, NOW included the protection of lesbian rights in its agenda. Women of color reshaped feminist analysis to address their experience, and challenged feminist organizations to work against racism and develop an "all-inclusive sisterhood" (Dill, 1983).

Feminists accomplished a great deal in a short period of time. Ridiculed at first by the media, they quickly changed public consciousness about a host of issues, from rape to employment discrimination. Feminists worked in a variety of ways to change laws, attitudes, practices, and institutions. NOW and other equal rights groups challenged sex-segregated want ads, sued hundreds of major corporations for sex discrimination, and lobbied in state legislatures to change laws about rape, domestic violence, divorce, and employment. Women working outside the system established battered women's shelters, rape crisis centers, and feminist health clinics. Feminists inside universities created women's studies programs and engaged in research about women in various disciplines. Throughout the 1970s and 1980s, countless women made changes in their individual lives: going back to school or to a job, leaving oppressive marriages, developing emotional and sexual relationships with other women, working to develop relationships of mutuality and respect with men.

Because reproductive freedom was clearly central to women's efforts to participate fully and equally in society, feminists throughout the country united in efforts to repeal abortion laws, reinvigorating an abortion reform movement that had been active throughout the 1960s. While a few states legalized abortion in the early 1970s, most state legislatures were resistant to efforts to decriminalize abortion, so women throughout the country filed suits against state laws that made abortion illegal. The suit against the Texas laws, *Roe v. Wade,* made its way to the Supreme Court, which legalized abortion in its landmark decision in 1973.

Many feminists felt that the effort to end sex discrimination would be substantially enhanced by a federal amendment guaranteeing equal rights to women. In 1972, an Equal Rights Amendment was passed by the U.S. Congress, proclaiming that "equality of rights under the laws shall not be denied or abridged by the U.S. or by any State on account of sex" (Hoff-Wilson, 1986, p. 125). The amendment was then sent on to be ratified by the states and was quickly approved in the legislatures of 34 of the 38 states required for final passage. It stalled, however, in 14 states in which a new coalition of conservative organizations had mobilized to defeat it. Charging that the Equal Rights Amendment and the feminist revolution that it came to symbolize would undermine traditional values and deprive women of the protections they have as wives and mothers, opponents of the ERA enlisted women in their anti-ERA campaign. Mormon and evangelical religious organizations poured resources into efforts to defeat the ERA. Their rhetoric tapped into anxiety about changes in the division of labor, sexuality, and the family and galvanized a new antifeminist coalition that opposed the ERA, the legalization of abortion, and other feminist reforms. When the deadline arrived in 1982, the ERA had not passed in enough states for ratification.

The ascendancy of the right wing in the Republican Party in the 1980s further enhanced the power of the new right assault, and many of the gains of the 1970s were seriously threatened. The second wave of feminism, however, left an indelible imprint on American society. While the momentum may have slowed, millions of women's lives have been changed, and cherished assumptions about gender, sexuality, work, and family have been deeply shaken. Although women remain a minority in positions of political power, their voices are being heard more clearly on public policy issues. Integrating feminist approaches to these issues into public policy will require continued pressure on the centers of political power.                                      [1992]

## REFERENCES

Catt, C. C. (1894). *The Woman's Journal,* Dec. 15, as quoted in A. Kraditor, *The Ideas of the Woman's Suffrage Movement, 1890–1920.* New York: Norton, 1981, p. 125.

Cott, N. F. (1987). *Grounding of Modern Feminism.* New Haven, CT: Yale University Press.

Dill, B. T. (1983). "Race, Class, and Gender: Prospects for an All-Inclusive Sisterhood." *Feminist Studies* 9(1), pp. 131–50.

Du Bois, E. C. (1978). *Feminism and Suffrage: The Emergence of an Independent Women's Movement in America 1848–69.* Ithaca, NY: Cornell University Press.

Evans, S. M. (1979). *Personal Politics: The Roots of Women's Liberation in the Civil Rights Movement and the New Left.* New York: Knopf.

Flexner, E. (1970). *Century of Struggle.* Cambridge, MA: Harvard University Press.

Friedan, B. (1964). *The Feminine Mystique.* New York: Dell.

Giddings, P. (1984). *When and Where I Enter.* New York: Morrow.

Hoff-Wilson, J. (Ed.) (1986). *Rights of Passage: The Past and Future of the Equal Rights Amendment.* Bloomington, IN: Indiana University Press, p. 125.

Knight, E., & Julty, S. (1958). "Getting Out the Vote," in *Songs of the Suffragettes* (Phonograph Record No. FH5281), Folkways.

Kraditor, A. (1981). *The Ideas of the Women's Suffrage Movement, 1890–1920.* New York: Norton.

# 131

# *The Seneca Falls Women's Rights Convention, 1848*

### *"DECLARATION OF SENTIMENTS"*

When, in the course of human events, it becomes necessary for one portion of the family of man to assume among the people of the earth a position different from that which they have hitherto occupied, but one to which the laws of nature and of nature's God entitle them, a decent respect to the opinions of mankind requires that they should declare the causes that impel them to such a course.

We hold these truths to be self-evident: that all men and women are created equal; that they are endowed by their Creator with certain inalienable rights; that among these are life, liberty, and the pursuit of happiness; that to secure these rights governments are instituted, deriving their just powers from the consent of the governed. Whenever any form of government becomes destructive of these ends, it is the right of those who suffer from it to refuse allegiance to it, and to insist upon the institution of a new government, laying its foundation on such principles, and organizing its powers in such form, as to them shall seem most likely to effect their safety and happiness. Prudence indeed, will dictate that governments long established should not be changed for light and transient causes; and accordingly all experience hath shown that mankind are more disposed to suffer, while evils are sufferable, than to right themselves by abolishing the forms to which they were accustomed. But when a long train of abuses and usurpations, pursuing invariably the same object evinces a design to reduce them under absolute despotism, it is their duty to throw off such government, and to provide new guards for their future security. Such has been the patient sufferance of the women under this government, and such is now the necessity which constrains them to demand the equal station to which they are entitled.

The history of mankind is a history of repeated injuries and usurpations on the part of man toward woman, having in direct object the establishment of an absolute tyranny over her. To prove this, let facts be submitted to a candid world.

He has never permitted her to exercise her inalienable right to the elective franchise.

He has compelled her to submit to laws, in the formation of which she had no voice.

He has withheld from her rights which are given to the most ignorant and degraded men—both natives and foreigners.

Having deprived her of this first right of a citizen, the elective franchise, thereby leaving her without representation in the halls of legislation, he has oppressed her on all sides.

He has made her, if married, in the eye of the law, civilly dead.

He has taken from her all right in property, even to the wages she earns.

He has made her, morally, an irresponsible being, as she can commit many crimes with impunity, provided they be done in the presence of her husband. In the covenant of marriage, she is compelled to promise obedience to her husband, he becoming, to all intents and purposes, her master—the law giving him power to deprive her of her liberty, and to administer chastisement.

He has so framed the laws of divorce, as to what shall be the proper causes, and in case of separation, to whom the guardianship of the children shall be given, as to be wholly regardless of the happiness of women—the law, in all cases, going upon a false supposition of the supremacy of man, and giving all power into his hands.

After depriving her of all rights as a married woman, if single, and the owner of property, he has taxed her to support a government which recognizes her only when her property can be made profitable to it.

He has monopolized nearly all the profitable employments, and from those she is permitted to follow, she receives but a scanty remuneration. He closes against her all the avenues to wealth and distinction which he considers most honorable to himself. As a teacher of theology, medicine, or law, she is not known.

He has denied her the facilities for obtaining a thorough education, all colleges being closed against her.

He allows her in Church, as well as State, but a subordinate position, claiming Apostolic authority for her exclusion from the ministry, and, with some exceptions, from any public participation in the affairs of the Church.

He has created a false public sentiment by giving to the world a different code of morals for men and women, by which moral delinquencies which exclude women from society, are not only tolerated, but deemed of little account in man.

He has usurped the prerogative of Jehovah himself, claiming it as his right to assign for her a sphere of action, when that belongs to her conscience and to her God.

He has endeavored, in every way that he could,

to destroy her confidence in her own powers, to lessen her self-respect, and to make her willing to lead a dependent and abject life.

Now, in view of this entire disfranchisement of one-half the people of this country, their social and religious degradation—in view of the unjust laws above mentioned, and because women do feel themselves aggrieved, oppressed, and fraudulently deprived of their most sacred rights, we insist that they have immediate admission to all the rights and privileges which belong to them as citizens of the United States.

In entering upon the great work before us, we anticipate no small amount of misconception, misrepresentation, and ridicule; but we shall use every instrumentality within our power to effect our object. We shall employ agents, circulate tracts, petition the State and National legislatures, and endeavor to enlist the pulpit and the press in our behalf. We hope this Convention will be followed by a series of Conventions embracing every part of the country.

## SENECA FALLS RESOLUTIONS

Whereas, The great precept of nature is conceded to be, that "man shall pursue his own true and substantial happiness." Blackstone in his Commentaries remarks, that this law of Nature being coeval with mankind, and dictated by God himself, is of course superior in obligation to any other. It is binding over all the globe, in all countries and at all times; no human laws are of any validity if contrary to this, and such of them as are valid, derive all their force, and all their validity, and all their authority, mediately and immediately, from this original; therefore,

*Resolved,* That such laws as conflict, in any way, with the true and substantial happiness of woman, are contrary to the great precept of nature and of no validity, for this is "superior in obligation to any other."

*Resolved,* That all laws which prevent woman from occupying such a station in society as her conscience shall dictate, or which place her in a position inferior to that of man, are contrary to the great precept of nature, and therefore of no force or authority.

*Resolved,* That woman is man's equal—was intended to be so by the Creator, and the highest good of the race demands that she should be recognized as such.

*Resolved,* That the women of this country ought to be enlightened in regard to the laws under which they live, that they may no longer publish their degradation by declaring themselves satisfied with their present position, nor their ignorance, by asserting that they have all the rights they want.

*Resolved,* That inasmuch as man, while claiming for himself intellectual superiority, does accord to woman moral superiority, it is pre-eminently his duty to encourage her to speak and teach, as she has an opportunity, in all religious assemblies.

*Resolved,* That the same amount of virtue, delicacy, and refinement of behavior that is required of woman in the social state, should also be required of man, and the same transgressions should be visited with equal severity on both man and woman.

*Resolved,* That the objection of indelicacy and impropriety, which is so often brought against woman when she addresses a public audience, comes with a very ill-grace from those who encourage, by their attendance, her appearance on the stage, in the concert, or in feats of the circus.

*Resolved,* That woman has too long rested satisfied in the circumscribed limits which corrupt customs and a perverted application of the Scriptures have marked out for her, and that it is time she should move in the enlarged sphere which her great Creator has assigned her.

*Resolved,* That it is the duty of the women of this country to secure to themselves their sacred right to the elective franchise.

*Resolved,* That the equality of human rights results necessarily from the fact of the identity of the race in capabilities and responsibilities.

*Resolved, therefore,* That, being invested by the Creator with the same capabilities, and the same consciousness of responsibility for their exercise, it is demonstrably the right and duty of woman, equally with man, to promote every righteous cause by every righteous means; and especially in regard to the great subjects of morals and religion, it is self-evidently her right to participate with her brother in teaching them, both in private and in public, by writing and by speaking, by any instrumentalities proper to be used, and in any assemblies proper to be held; and this being a self-evident truth growing out of the divinely implanted principles of human nature, any custom or authority adverse to it, whether modern or wearing the hoary sanction of antiquity, is to be regarded as a self-evident falsehood, and at war with mankind.

*Resolved*, That the speedy success of our cause depends upon the zealous and untiring efforts of both men and women, for the overthrow of the monopoly of the pulpit, and for the securing to women an equal participation with men in the various trades, professions, and commerce.          [1848]

## 🌿 132

# *Sojourner Truth's Speech*

*Sojourner Truth was born into slavery in Ulster County, New York in about 1797 (the exact date of her birth is uncertain). After her escape from slavery she became involved in several of the religious and political movements of her day. Changing her name from Isabella to Sojourner Truth, she traveled widely, speaking eloquently against slavery, for women's rights and about her vision of a kind and loving God. She died in Battle Creek, Michigan in 1883.*

*At the 1851 Women's Rights Convention in Akron, Ohio, Sojourner Truth gave a stirring speech on women's rights. Below are two versions: a contemporary newspaper account and the reminiscences of Frances Gage, a prominent white suffragist. (We have dropped the dialect Gage used to record Sojourner Truth's words.)*

### THE ANTI-SLAVERY BUGLE

One of the most unique and interesting speeches of the Convention was made by Sojourner Truth, an emancipated slave. It is impossible to transfer it to paper, or convey any adequate idea of the effect it produced upon the audience. Those only can appreciate it who saw her powerful form, her whole-souled, earnest gestures, and listened to her strong and truthful tones. She came forward to the platform and addressing the President said with great simplicity:

May I say a few words? Receiving an affirmative answer, she proceeded; I want to say a few words about this matter. I am a woman's rights. [*sic*] I have as much muscle as any man, and can do as much work as any man. I have plowed and reaped and husked and chopped and mowed, and can any man do more than that? I have heard much about the sexes being equal; I can carry as much as any man, and can eat as much too, if I can get it. I am as strong as any man that is now. As for intellect, all I can say is, if a woman have a pint and man a quart—why cant she have her little pint full? You need not be afraid to give us our rights for fear we will take too much,—for we cant take more than our pint'll hold. The poor men seem to be all in confusion, and dont know what to do. Why children, if you have woman's rights give it to her and you will feel better. You will have your own rights, and they wont be so much trouble. I cant read, but I can hear. I have heard the bible and have learned that Eve caused man to sin. Well if woman upset the world, do give her a chance to set it right side up again. The Lady has spoken about Jesus, how he never spurned woman from him, and she was right. When Lazarus died, Mary and Martha came to him with faith and love and besought him to raise their brother. And Jesus wept—and Lazarus came forth. And how came Jesus into the world? Through God who created him and woman who bore him. Man, where is your part? But the women are coming up blessed be God and a few of the man are coming up with them. But man is in a tight place, the poor slave is on him, woman is coming on him, and he is surely between a hawk and a buzzard.          [1851]

### FRANCES GAGE'S REMINISCENCES

The second day the work waxed warm. Methodist, Baptist, Episcopal, Presbyterian, and Universalist ministers came in to hear and discuss the resolutions presented. One claimed superior rights and privileges for man, on the ground of "superior intellect"; another, because of the "manhood of Christ; if God had desired the equality of woman, He would have given some token of His will through the birth, life, and death of the Saviour." Another gave us a theological view of the "sin of our first mother."

There were very few women in those days who dared to "speak in meeting"; and the august teachers of the people were seemingly getting the better of us, while the boys in the galleries, and the sneerers among the pews, were hugely enjoying the discomfiture, as they supposed, of the "strong-minded." Some of the tender-skinned friends were on the point of losing dignity, and the atmosphere betokened a storm. When, slowly from her seat in the corner rose Sojourner Truth, who, till now, had scarcely lifted her head. "Don't let her speak!" gasped half a dozen in my ear. She moved slowly and solemnly to the front, laid her old bonnet at her feet, and turned her great speaking eyes to me. There was a hissing sound of disapprobation above and below. I rose and announced "Sojourner Truth," and begged the audience to keep silence for a few moments. The tumult subsided at once, and every eye was fixed on this almost Amazon form, which stood nearly six feet high, head erect, and eyes piercing the upper air like one in a dream. At her first word there was a profound hush. She spoke in deep tones, which, though not loud, reached every ear in the house, and away through the throng at the doors and windows.

"Well, children, where there is so much racket there must be something out of kilter. I think that 'twixt the Negroes of the South and the women at the north all talking about rights, the white men will be in a fix pretty soon. But what's all this here talking about?

"That man over there says that women need to be helped into carriages, and lifted over ditches and to have the best place everywhere. Nobody ever helps me into carriages, or over mudpuddles, or gives me any best place!" And raising herself to her full height, and her voice to a pitch like rolling thunder, she asked, "And ar'n't I a woman? I could work as much and eat as much as a man—when I could get it—and bear the lash as well! And ar'n't I a woman? I have borne thirteen children, and seen them almost all sold off to slavery, and when I cried out with my mother's grief, none but Jesus heard me! And ar'n't I a woman?

"Then they talk about this thing in the head; what this they call it?" ("Intellect" whispered some one near.) "That's it, honey. What's that got to do with women's rights or Negroes? If my cup won't hold but a pint, and your holds a quart, wouldn't you be mean not to let me have my little half-measure full?" And she pointed her significant finger, and sent a keen glance at the minister who had made the argument. The cheering was long and loud.

"Then that little man in black there, he says women can't have as much rights as men, 'cause Christ wasn't a woman! Where did your Christ come from?" Rolling thunder couldn't have stilled that crowd, as did those deep, wonderful tones, as she stood there with outstretched arms and eyes of fire. Raising her voice still louder, she repeated, "Where did your Christ come from? From God and a woman! Man had nothing to do with him." Oh, what a rebuke that was to that little man.

Turning again to another objector, she took up the defense of Mother Eve, I cannot follow her through it all. It was pointed, and witty and solemn; eliciting at almost every sentence deafening applause; and she ended by asserting: "If the first woman God ever made was strong enough to turn the world upside down all alone, these women together" (and she glanced her eye over the platform) "ought to be able to turn it back, and get it right side up again! And now they are asking to do it, the men better let them. Obliged to you for hearing me, and now old Sojourner has got nothing more to say."

Amid roars of applause, she returned to her corner, leaving more than one of us with streaming eyes, and hearts beating with gratitude. She had taken us up in her strong arms and carried us safely over the slough of difficulty turning the whole tide in our favor.                                    [1863]

## 133

# *Consciousness Raising: A Radical Weapon*

KATHIE SARACHILD

*From a talk given to the First National Conference of Stewardesses for Women's Rights in New York City, March 12, 1973.*

To be able to understand what feminist consciousness-raising is all about, it is important to remember that it began as a program among women who all considered themselves radicals.

Before we go any further, let's examine the word "radical." It is a word that is often used to suggest extremist, but actually it doesn't mean that. The dictionary says radical means root, coming from the Latin word for root. And that is what we meant by calling ourselves radicals. We were interested in getting to the roots of problems in society. You might say we wanted to pull up weeds in the garden by their roots, not just pick off the leaves at the top to make things momentarily look good. Women's Liberation was started by women who considered themselves radicals in this sense.

Our aim in forming a women's liberation group was to start a *mass movement of women* to put an end to the barriers of segregation and discrimination based on sex. We knew radical thinking and radical action would be necessary to do this. We also believed it necessary to form Women's Liberation groups which excluded men from their meetings.

In order to have a radical approach, to get to the root, it seemed logical that we had to study the situation of women, not just take random action. How best to do this came up in the women's liberation group I was in—New York Radical Women, one of the first in the country—shortly after the group had formed. We were planning our first public action and wandered into a discussion about what to do next. One woman in the group, Ann Forer, spoke up: "I think we have a lot more to do just in the area of raising our consciousness," she said. "Raising consciousness?" I wondered what she meant by that. I'd never heard it applied to women before.

"I've only begun thinking about women as an oppressed group," she continued, "and each day, I'm still learning more about it—my consciousness gets higher."

Now I didn't consider that I had just started thinking about the oppression of women. In fact, I thought of myself as having done lots of thinking about it for quite a while, and lots of reading, too. But then Ann went on to give an example of something she'd noticed that turned out to be a deeper way of seeing it for me, too.

"I think a lot about being attractive," Ann said. "People don't find the real self of a woman attractive." And then she went on to give some examples. And I just sat there listening to her describe all the false ways women have to act: playing dumb, always being agreeable, always being nice, not to mention what we had to do to our bodies with the clothes and shoes we wore, the diets we had to go through, going blind not wearing glasses, all because men didn't find our real selves, our human freedom, our basic humanity "attractive." And I realized I still could learn a lot about how to understand and describe the particular oppression of women in ways that could reach other women in the way this had just reached me. The whole group was moved as I was, and we decided on the spot that what we needed—in the words Ann used—was to "raise our consciousness some more."

At the next meeting there was an argument in the group about how to do this. One woman—Peggy Dobbins—said that what she wanted to do was make a very intensive study of all the literature on the question of whether there really were any biological differences between men and women. I found myself angered by that idea.

"I think it would be a waste of time," I said. "For every scientific study we quote, the opposition can find their scientific studies to quote. Besides, the question is what *we* want to be, what we think we are, not what some authorities in the name of science are arguing over what we are. It is scientifically impossible to tell what the biological differences are between men and women—if there are any besides the obvious physical ones—until all the social and political factors applying to men and women are equal. Everything we have to know, have to prove, we can get from the realities of our own lives. For instance, on the subject of women's intelligence. We know from our own experience that women play dumb for men because, if we're too smart, men won't like us. I know, because I've done it. We've all done it. Therefore, we can simply deduce that women are smarter than men are aware of, and smarter than all those people who make studies are aware of, and that there are a lot of women around who are a lot smarter than they look and smarter than anybody but themselves and maybe a few of their friends know."

In the end the group decided to raise its consciousness by studying women's lives by topics like childhood, jobs, motherhood, etc. We'd do any outside reading we wanted to and thought was important. But our starting point for discussion, as well as our test of the accuracy of what any of the books said, would be the actual experience we had in these areas. One of the questions, suggested by Ann Forer, we would bring at all times to our studies would be—who and what has an *interest* in maintaining the oppression in our lives. The kind of actions the group should engage in, at this point, we decided—acting on an idea of Carol Hanisch, another woman in the group—would be consciousness-raising actions . . . actions brought to the public for the specific purpose of challenging old ideas and raising new ones, the very same issues of feminism we were studying ourselves. Our role was not to be a "service organization," we decided, nor a large "membership organization." What we were talking about being was, in effect, Carol explained, a "zap" action, political agitation and education group something like what the Student Non-Violent Coordinating Committee (S.N.C.C.) had been. We would be the first to dare to say and do the undareable, what women really felt and wanted. The first job now was to raise awareness and understanding, our own and others—awareness that would prompt people to organize and to act on a mass scale.

The decision to emphasize our own feelings and experiences as women and to test all generalizations and reading we did by our own experience was actually the scientific method of research. We were in effect repeating the 17th century challenge of science to scholasticism: "study nature, not books," and put all theories to the test of living practice and action. It was also a method of radical organizing tested by other revolutions. We were applying to women and to ourselves as women's liberation organizers the practice a number of us had learned as organizers in the civil rights movement in the South in the early 1960's.

Consciousness-raising—studying the whole gamut of women's lives, starting with the full reality of one's own—would also be a way of keeping the movement radical by preventing it from getting sidetracked into single issue reforms and single issue organizing. It would be a way of carrying theory about women further than it had ever been carried before,

as the groundwork for achieving a radical solution for women as yet attained nowhere.

It seemed clear that knowing how our own lives related to the general condition of women would make us better fighters on behalf of women as a whole. We felt that all women would have to see the fight of women as their own, not as something just to help "other women," that they would have to see this truth about their own lives before they would fight in a radical way for anyone. "Go fight your own oppressors," Stokely Carmichael had said to the white civil rights workers when the black power movement began. "You don't get radicalized fighting other people's battles," as Beverly Jones, author of the pioneering essay, "Toward a Female Liberation Movement," put it. [1973]

 134

# The Boston Women's Health Book Collective

SUSAN BROWNMILLER

*Collective* was always a word with variable meanings in women's liberation. The utopian desire to submerge individual ego for the greater political good led to a range of experiments in the sixties and seventies such as fitful stabs at group writing and the founding of communal houses where personal lives intermingled at every conceivable level and food, clothes, and money were shared. Of all the experiments, foolish and grand, that marked the era, I can say without fear of contradiction that the Boston Women's Health Book Collective stands as an unqualified success. It became the heroic lifetime achievement for the twelve relatively unknown women who wrote and edited the feminist classic *Our Bodies, Ourselves.*

Nancy Hawley had grown up in radical politics. Her mother had been in the Communist Party, and Nancy herself was a charter member of the Students for a Democratic Society at the University of Michigan. After an inspiring conversation in 1968 with her old chum Kathie Amatniek, she started one of the first consciousness-raising groups in Cambridge, enlisting the young mothers in her child's cooperative play group. Happily pregnant again, she attended the stormy Thanksgiving conference in Lake Villa, Illinois, but unlike Amatniek, Charlotte Bunch, and many others, Hawley came away from it euphoric. A heated discussion on motherhood led by Shulamith Firestone, who said that pregnancy was barbaric and women would be equal only when science offered technological alternatives to biological reproduction, left her convinced that the movement needed her input.

In May 1969, a month after giving birth, Hawley chaired an overflowing workshop called "Women and Their Bodies" at a New England regional conference on women's liberation. (This was the Mother's Day weekend conference at Emmanuel College in Boston, which led to the founding of the socialist-feminist Bread and Roses and where Cell Sixteen gave a rousing karate demonstration.) Summoning an incident fresh in her mind, Hawley opened her workshop by reporting a glib, sexist remark by her obstetrician. "He said," she recalls, "that he was going to sew me up real tight so there would be more sexual pleasure for my husband." Hawley's report, and her outrage, unleashed a freewheeling exchange on patronizing male doctors, childbirth, orgasm, contraception, and abortion that was so voluble and intense nobody wanted to go home.

"Everybody had a doctor story," exclaims Paula Doress, who was scheduled to give birth two weeks later. "We put aside our prepared papers and did consciousness raising."

Vilunya Diskin, in another workshop, received an excited report from Hawley that night. Diskin had survived the Holocaust by being placed with a Polish family. As a young married woman in Boston, she had undergone two traumatic childbirths with severe complications. Her first baby lived, but she had lost her second to hyaline membrane, a lung disease that the hospital had failed to monitor in time. "I was solidly middle-class and well educated, and my health care had been appalling," she says. "So I could imagine what it was like for others without my resources."

A fluid core of activists from the Emmanuel conference agreed to continue meeting in order to compile a list of doctors they felt they could trust. They resolved as well to take the "Women and Their Bodies" workshop into the community, wherever they could find free space in church basements and nursery schools. "Our idea," says Diskin, "was to go out in pairs. We hoped that the women who attended the workshop would then go on and give it themselves."

To the core group's bewilderment, the doctors list kept dwindling. Every time it got up to four seemingly solid, unimpeachable names, somebody new showed up to exclaim, "Oh, do I have a story about *him*!" But the workshop project soared. As the summer turned into fall, the women amassed enough hard medical information and the confidence to borrow a lounge at MIT for a 12-session course. Venereal disease and "Women, Medicine and Capitalism" were added to the program.

Ruth Bell, a stranger to Boston, went to the course at MIT in an oversized pair of "Oshkosh, by Gosh" denim overalls, her maternity outfit. "Fifty women were talking about their lives, their sexuality, their feelings," she remembers. "I raised my hand and said, 'I'm pregnant for the first time and I don't know much about this and I'm having nightmares.' Three or four other women got up and said 'That happened to me, too. Let's meet after and talk about it and maybe we can figure something out.' That's how it was. Somebody had a concern, she raised her hand, and three or four others said, 'Boy, that happened to me, too.'"

Joan Ditzion, married to a Harvard medical student and debating whether to have kids, was transfixed by a large, detailed drawing of a vagina with labia and clitoris that the women had placed on an easel. "I'd only seen pictures like that in my husband's textbooks. These women were speaking so easily, without shame. I got my first sense that women could own our own anatomy."

Wendy Sanford, born into an upper-class Republican family, was battling depression after her son's birth. Her friend Esther Rome, a follower of Jewish Orthodox traditions, dragged her to the second MIT session. Previously Wendy had kept her distance from political groups. "I walked into the lounge," she recalls, "and they were talking about masturbation. I didn't say a word. I was shocked; I was fascinated. At a later session someone gave a breastfeeding demonstration. That didn't shock me—I'd been doing it—but then we broke down into small groups. I had never 'broken down into a small group' in my life. In my group people started talking about postpartum depression. In that one 45-minute period I realized that what I'd been blaming myself for, and what my husband had blamed me for, wasn't my personal deficiency. It was a combination of physiological things and a real societal thing, isolation. That realization was one of those moments that makes you a feminist forever."

Ruth Bell gave birth to her daughter in the middle of the course and returned to become "a second-stage original member" of the amorphous collective, along with Joan Ditzion and a renewed, reenergized Wendy Sanford. "There was an open invitation to anyone who wanted to help revise the course notes into a more formal packet," Bell remembers. "If you wanted to work on writing, you'd pair or triple up with people who could do research."

"We had to get hold of good medical texts," says Paula Doress, "so we borrowed student cards to get into Countway, the Harvard Medical School library. It was very eye-opening to realize that we could understand the latinized words."

"Then we'd stand up at a meeting and read what we had written," Ruth Bell continues. "People would make notes. Somebody would raise a hand and say, 'I think you should add this sentence' or 'You need a comma here.' This was how the first editing got done."

Duplicated packets of the course material were making their way around the country. Closer to home, somebody contacted the New England Free Press, a leftist mail-order collective in downtown Boston. "Basically they were a bunch of men, conventionally Marxist, who printed and sold pamphlets at 10 to 25 cents," Jane Pincus sums up. "They didn't see us as political." The mail-order collective grudgingly agreed to publish and distribute the health course papers if the women paid their own printing costs. "So we raised $1,500 from our parents and friends," Pincus relates. "And then we

had to hire somebody to send out the orders because the demand was so great."

Five thousand stapled copies of "Women and Their Bodies" on newsprint paper with amateur photos and homey line drawings rolled off the press in December 1970 bearing a cover price of 75 cents. The blunt 136-page assault on the paternalism of the medical establishment that juxtaposed personal narratives with plainspoken prescriptives immediately sold out. A second edition of 15,000 copies, with the price lowered to 35 cents, bore an important change. In one of those Eureka moments, somebody had exclaimed, "Hey, it isn't women and *their* bodies—it's us and our bodies. *Our Bodies, Ourselves.*"

Women's centers in big cities and college towns were thirsting for practical information and new ways to organize. The Boston collective's handbook with its simple directive, "You can substitute the experience in your city or state here," fit the bill. Subsequent press runs for *Our Bodies, Ourselves* were upped to 25,000 in an attempt to satisfy the demand. Three printings in 1971 were followed by six printings in 1972.

"We are working on revisions," the collective declared. "We want to add chapters on menopause and getting older and attitudes toward children, etc., etc., but we haven't had time." There was no shortage of feedback. "The first edition was weak on the dangers of high-dose estrogen oral contraceptives," Barbara Seaman remembers. She mailed the women a copy of her book, *The Doctors' Case Against the Pill,* and was gratified to see that the next edition reflected her concern. "A woman in Iowa wrote in and said, 'You didn't mention ectopic pregnancy,'" remembers Jane Pincus. "And we said 'Great, write about it and we'll put it in.' This is really how the book evolved."

It was only a matter of time before the big guns in New York publishing got wind of the phenomenal underground success. In the fall of 1972 they came courting with offers of a modest advance. Jonathan Dolger at Simon & Schuster had roomed with Jane Pincus's husband at college, but Charlotte Mayerson at Random House possessed what looked like an insurmountable advantage. "Charlotte was a she, and I was not," says Dolger. "They wanted a woman to edit their book and in truth, we didn't have many women at S & S in those days." Dolger asked Alice Mayhew, a recent arrival, to accompany him to Boston.

Dressed in army fatigues and work boots, the collective grilled the two editors about their intentions. While Dolger quaked in his business suit, Mayhew brusquely got down to business. "I got the impression they were all married to professors at MIT and Harvard," she remembers, not far off the mark. The following evening it was Mayerson's turn to present her case.

For the first time in their experience as a working collective, the women were unable to reach a consensus. They felt a sisterly bond with Mayerson, and indeed they would work with her on later projects, but she would not get the best-selling *Our Bodies, Ourselves*. Random House was owned at the time by RCA, a conglomerate with huge government defense contracts, rendering it complicitous in the war machine. An independent company and seemingly purer, Simon & Schuster won the agonizing vote by a narrow margin.

Freezing their ranks, the women incorporated as a nonprofit foundation. One member, suddenly desirous of a change in lifestyle, split for Toronto. The last to come aboard were Judy Norsigian, their "baby" at 23, and Norma Swenson, their "old lady" at 40. Norsigian and Swenson were to become the public face of the collective over the years.

When news of the commercial sale appeared in the penultimate *New England Free Press*, the mail-order leftists commandeered a page of their own to cry foul, warning that a capitalist publisher would impede the building of socialist consciousness. The women dodged the ideological brickbats as best they could while they readied their beloved creation for its aboveground debut. "Everything had to be decided by consensus," Mayhew remembers. "It took a long time. But we knew they were in touch with a generation of young women who wanted to be talked to straightforwardly. We would have been dopey to interfere."

Rape, an emerging issue for feminists, became a chapter in the handsome, large-format 1973 Si-mon & Schuster *Our Bodies, Ourselves*. Judy Norsigian, a veteran of the commune movement, wrote a chapter on nutrition. Mindful of the rising tide of lesbian consciousness, the women sent out a call for the appropriate expertise. A Boston gay women's collective produced "In Amerika They Call Us Dykes," insisting on anonymity and complete editorial control of the pages. Continuing the policy started in the first newsprint edition, the illustrations for the aboveground *Our Bodies, Ourselves* included many line drawings and photographs of African-American women. A sharp dig at the U.S. military presence in Vietnam survived in the aboveground edition (the context was venereal disease), but the proviso "Don't forget that Ortho and Tampax are capitalist organizations pushing their own products for profits" got axed. "Women, Medicine and Capitalism," a lengthy polemic, shrank to an unrecognizable paragraph in "Women and Health Care" amid the nitty-gritty on yeast infections, cystitis, and crabs. Softer rhetoric was a collective decision, in line with the women's desires to reach the mainstream and include more facts, but they resisted the ladylike language a copy editor they nicknamed Blue Pencil wished to impose. "Where we wrote *pee*," says Jane Pincus, "Blue Pencil changed it to *urinate*. We changed it right back."

*Our Bodies, Ourselves* sold more than a million copies and earned more than a half million dollars in royalties for the collective in its first five years of commercial distribution. More important, it became the premier sourcebook for a generation of sexually active young women across all lines of race and class. It was deeply discounted or given out free at birth control clinics, and it found an audience among hard-to-reach teenagers when it was adopted as a teaching tool in hundreds of high school sex education programs. The royalty money was dispersed to movement projects except for the pittance paid to the staff people, chiefly Norsigian, Swenson, and Rome. By the latter part of the 1970s, the collective, which convened periodically to work on updated editions, had witnessed four divorces and three second marriages. A few members left the Boston area with their husbands, and one discovered her lesbian identity. All told, the women reared nearly two dozen children. "People used to come from overseas and ask to the see the house where the collective lived," says Norma Swenson. "I think they were disappointed to find that we led individual lives."                                                    [1998]

 135

# *Introduction to* Home Girls: A Black Feminist Anthology

BARBARA SMITH

Black women as a group have never been fools. We couldn't afford to be. Yet in the last two decades many of us have been deterred from identifying with a liberation struggle which might say significant things to women like ourselves, women who believe that we were put here for a purpose in our own right, women who are usually not afraid to struggle.

Although our involvement has increased considerably in recent years, there are countless reasons why Black and other Third World women have not identified with contemporary feminism in large numbers.[1] The racism of white women in the women's movement has certainly been a major factor. The powers-that-be are also aware that a movement of progressive Third World women in this country would alter life as we know it. As a result there has been a concerted effort to keep women of color from organizing autonomously and from organizing with other women around women's political issues. Third World men, desiring to maintain power over "their women" at all costs, have been among the most willing reinforcers of the fears and myths about the women's movement, attempting to scare us away from figuring things out for ourselves.

It is fascinating to look at various kinds of media from the late 1960s and early 1970s, when feminism was making its great initial impact, in order to see what Black men, Native American men, Asian American men, Latino men, and white men were saying about the irrelevance of "women's lib" to women of color. White men and Third World men, ranging from conservatives to radicals, pointed to the seeming lack of participation of women of color in the movement in order to discredit it and to undermine the efforts of the movement as a whole. All kinds of men were running scared because they knew that if the women in their midst were changing, they were going to have to change too. In 1976 I wrote:

> Feminism is potentially the most threatening of movements to Black and other Third World people because it makes it absolutely essential that we examine the way we live, how we treat each other, and what we believe. It calls into question the most basic assumption about our existence and this is the idea that biological, i.e., sexual identity determines all, that it is the rationale for power relationships as well as for all other levels of human identity and action. An irony is that among Third World people biological determinism is rejected and fought against when it is applied to race, but generally unquestioned when it applies to sex.[2]

In reaction to the "threat" of such change, Black men, with the collaboration of some Black women, developed a set of myths to divert Black women from our own freedom.

## *MYTHS*

*Myth No. 1: The Black woman is already liberated.* This myth confuses liberation with the fact that Black women have had to take on responsibilities that our oppression gives us no choice but to handle. This is an insidious, but widespread myth that many Black women have believed themselves. Heading families, working outside the home, not building lives or expectations dependent on males, seldom being sheltered or pampered as women, Black women have known that their lives in some ways incorporated goals that white middle-class women were striving for, but race and class privilege, of course, reshaped the meaning of those goals profoundly. As W.E.B. DuBois said so long ago about Black women: ". . . our women in black had freedom contemptuously thrust upon them."[3] Of all the people here, women of color generally have the fewest choices about the circumstances of their lives. An ability to cope under the worst conditions is not liberation, although our spiritual capacities have often made it look like a life. Black men didn't say anything about how poverty, unequal pay, no childcare, violence of every kind including battering, rape, and sterilization abuse, translated into "liberation."

Underlying this myth is the assumption that Black women are towers of strength who neither feel nor need what other human beings do, either emotionally or materially. White male social scientists, particularly Daniel P. Moynihan with his "matriarchy theory," further reinforce distortions concerning Black women's actual status. A song inspired by their mothers and sung by Sweet Honey in the Rock, "Oughta Be A Woman," lyrics by June Jordan and music by Bernice Johnson Reagon, responds succinctly to the insensitivity of the myth that Black women are already liberated and illustrates the home-based concerns of Black feminism:

## Oughta Be A Woman

Washing the floors to send you to college
Staying at home so you can feel safe
What do you think is the soul of her knowledge
What do you think that makes her feel safe

Biting her lips and lowering her eyes
To make sure there's food on the table
What do you think would be her surprise
If the world was as willing as she's able

Hugging herself in an old kitchen chair
She listens to your hurt and your rage
What do you think she knows of despair
What is the aching of age

The fathers, the children, the brothers
Turn to her and everybody white turns to her
What about her turning around
Alone in the everyday light

There oughta be a woman can break
Down, sit down, break down, sit down
Like everybody else call it quits on Mondays
Blues on Tuesdays, sleep until Sunday
Down, sit down, break down, sit down

A way outa no way is flesh outa flesh
Courage that cries out at night
A way outa no way is flesh outa flesh

Bravery kept outa sight
A way outa no way is too much to ask
Too much of a task for any one woman[4]

*Myth No. 2: Racism is the primary (or only) oppression Black women have to confront.* (Once we get that taken care of, then Black women, men, and children will all flourish. Or as Ms. Luisah Teish writes, we can look forward to being "the property of powerful men.")[5]

This myth goes hand in hand with the one that the Black woman is already liberated. The notion that struggling against or eliminating racism will completely alleviate Black women's problems does not take into account the way that sexual oppression cuts across all racial, nationality, age, religious, ethnic, and class groupings. Afro-Americans are no exception.

It also does not take into account how oppression operates. Every generation of Black people, up until now, has had to face the reality that no matter how hard we work we will probably not see the end of racism in our lifetimes. Yet many of us keep faith and try to do all we can to make change now. If we have to wait for racism to be obliterated *before* we can begin to address sexism, we will be waiting for a long time. Denying that sexual oppression exists or requiring that we wait to bring it up until racism, or in some cases capitalism, is toppled, is a bankrupt position. A Black feminist perspective has no use for ranking oppressions, but instead demonstrates the simultaneity of oppressions as they affect Third World women's lives.

*Myth No. 3: Feminism is nothing but man-hating.* (And men have never done anything that would legitimately inspire hatred.)

It is important to make a distinction between attacking institutionalized, systematic oppression (the goal of any serious progressive movement) and attacking men as individuals. Unfortunately, some of the most widely distributed writing about Black women's issues has not made this distinction sufficiently clear. Our issues have not been concisely defined in these writings, causing much adverse reaction and confusion about what Black feminism really is.[6]

This myth is one of the silliest and at the same

time one of the most dangerous. Anti-feminists are incapable of making a distinction between being critically opposed to sexual oppression and simply hating men. Women's desire for fairness and safety in our lives does not necessitate hating men. Trying to educate and inform men about how their feet are planted on our necks doesn't translate into hatred either. Centuries of anti-racist struggle by various people of color are not reduced, except by racists, to our merely hating white people. If anything it seems that the opposite is true. People of color know that white people have abused us unmercifully and it is only sane for us to try to change that treatment by every means possible.

Likewise the bodies of murdered women are strewn across the landscape of this country. Rape is a national pastime, a form of torture visited upon all girls and women, from babies to the aged. One out of three women in the U.S. will be raped during her lifetime. Battering and incest, those home-based crimes, are pandemic. Murder, of course, is men's ultimate violent "solution." And if you're thinking as you read this that I'm exaggerating, please go get today's newspaper and verify the facts. If anything is going down here it's woman-hatred, not man-hatred, a war against women. But wanting to end this war still doesn't equal man-hating. The feminist movement and the anti-racist movement have in common trying to ensure decent human life. Opposition to either movement aligns one with the most reactionary elements in American society.

*Myth No. 4: Women's issues are narrow, apolitical concerns. People of color need to deal with the "larger struggle."* This myth once again characterizes women's oppression as not particularly serious, and by no means a matter of life and death. I have often wished I could spread the word that a movement committed to fighting sexual, racial, economic, and heterosexist oppression, not to mention one which opposes imperialism, anti-Semitism, the oppressions visited upon the physically disabled, the old and the young, at the same time that it challenges militarism and imminent nuclear destruction is the very opposite of narrow. All segments of the women's movement have not dealt with all of these issues, but neither have all segments of Black

people. This myth is plausible when the women's movement is equated only with its most bourgeois and reformist elements. The most progressive sectors of the feminist movement, which includes some radical white women, have taken the above issues, and many more, quite seriously. Third World women have been the most consistent in defining our politics broadly. Why is it that feminism is considered "white-minded" and "narrow" while socialism or Marxism, from verifiably white origins, is legitimately embraced by Third World male politicos, without their having their identity credentials questioned for a minute?

*Myth No. 5: Those feminists are nothing but Lesbians.* This may be the most pernicious myth of all and it is essential to understand that the distortion lies in the phrase "nothing but" and not in the identification Lesbian. "Nothing but" reduces Lesbians to a category of beings deserving of only the most violent attack, a category totally alien from "decent" Black folks, i.e., not your sisters, mothers, daughters, aunts, and cousins, but bizarre outsiders like no one you know or *ever* knew.

Many of the most committed and outspoken feminists of color have been and are Lesbians. Since many of us are also radicals, our politics, as indicated by the issues merely outlined above, encompass all people. We're also as Black as we ever were. (I always find it fascinating, for example, that many of the Black Lesbian-feminists I know still wear their hair natural, indicating that for us it was more than a "style.") Black feminism and Black Lesbianism are not interchangeable. Feminism is a political movement and many Lesbians are not feminists. Although it is also true that many Black feminists are not Lesbians, this myth has acted as an accusation and a deterrent to keep non-Lesbian Black feminists from manifesting themselves, for fear it will be hurled against them.

Fortunately this is changing. Personally, I have seen increasing evidence that many Black women of whatever sexual preference are more concerned with exploring and ending our oppression than they are committed to being either homophobic or sexually separatist. Direct historical precedent exists for such commitments. In 1957, Black playwright and activist Lorraine Hansberry wrote the following in a letter to *The Ladder,* an early Lesbian periodical:

> I think it is about time that equipped women began to take on some of the ethical questions which a male-dominated culture has produced and dissect and analyze them quite to pieces in a serious fashion. It is time that "half the human race" had something to say about the nature of its existence. Otherwise—without revised basic thinking—the woman intellectual is likely to find herself trying to draw conclusions—moral conclusions—based on acceptance of a social moral superstructure which has never admitted to the equality of women and is therefore immoral itself. As per marriage, as per sexual practices, as per the rearing of children, etc. In this kind of work there may be women to emerge who will be able to formulate a new and possible concept that homosexual persecution and condemnation has at its roots not only social ignorance, but a philosophically active anti-feminist dogma.[7]

I would like a lot more people to be aware that Lorraine Hansberry, one of our most respected artists and thinkers, was asking in a Lesbian context some of the same questions we are asking today, and for which we have been so maligned.

Black heterosexuals' panic about the existence of both Black Lesbians and Black gay men is a problem that they have to deal with themselves. A first step would be for them to better understand their own heterosexuality, which need not be defined by attacking everybody who is not heterosexual.

## HOME TRUTHS

Above are some of the myths that have plagued Black feminism. The truth is that there is a vital movement of women of color in this country. Despite continual resistance to women of color defining our specific issues and organizing around them, it is safe to say in 1982 that we have a movement of our own. I have been involved in building that movement since 1973. It has been a struggle every step of the way and I feel we are still in just the beginning stages of developing a workable politics and practice. Yet the feminism of women of color, particularly of Afro-American women, has wrought many changes during these years, has had both obvious and unrecognized impact upon the development of other political groupings and upon the lives and hopes of countless women.

The very nature of radical thought and action is that it has exponentially far-reaching results. But because all forms of media ignore Black women, in particular Black feminists, and because we have no widely distributed communication mechanisms of our own, few know the details of what we have accomplished. One of the purposes of *Home Girls* is to get the word out about Black feminism to the people who need it most: Black people in the U.S., the Caribbean, Latin America, Africa—everywhere. It is not possible for a single introduction or a single book to encompass all of what Black feminism is, but there is basic information I want every reader to have about the meaning of Black feminism as I have lived and understood it.

In 1977, a Black feminist organization in Boston of which I was a member from its founding in 1974, the Combahee River Collective, drafted a political statement for our own use and for inclusion in Zillah Eisenstein's anthology, *Capitalist Patriarchy and the Case for Socialist Feminism.* In our opening paragraph we wrote:

> The most general statement of our politics at the present time would be that we are actively committed to struggling against racial, sexual, heterosexual, and class oppression and see as our particular task the development of integrated analysis and practice based upon the fact that the major systems of oppression are interlocking. The synthesis of these oppressions creates the conditions of our lives. As Black women we see Black feminism as the logical political movement to combat the manifold and simultaneous oppressions that all women of color face.

The concept of the simultaneity of oppression is still the crux of a Black feminist understanding of political reality and, I believe, one of the most significant ideological contributions of Black feminist thought.

We examined our own lives and found that everything out there was kicking our behinds—race, class, sex, and homophobia. We saw no reason to rank oppressions, or, as many forces in the Black community would have us do, to pretend that sexism, among all the "isms," was not happening to us. Black feminists' efforts to comprehend the complexity of our situation as it was actually occurring, almost immediately began to deflate some of the cherished myths about Black womanhood, for example, that we are "castrating matriarchs" or that we are more economically privileged than Black men. Although we made use of the insights of other political ideologies, such as socialism, we added an element that has often been missing from the theory of others: what oppression is comprised of on a day-to-day basis, or as Black feminist musician Linda Tillery sings, ". . . what it's really like/To live this life of triple jeopardy." [8]

This multi-issued approach to politics has probably been most often used by other women of color who face very similar dynamics, at least as far as institutionalized oppression is concerned. It has also altered the women's movement as a whole. As a result of Third World feminist organizing, the women's movement now takes much more seriously the necessity for a multi-issued strategy for challenging women's oppression. The more progressive elements of the left have also begun to recognize that the promotion of sexism and homophobia within their ranks, besides being ethically unconscionable, ultimately undermines their ability to organize. Even a few Third World organizations have begun to include the challenging of women's and gay oppression on their public agendas.

Approaching politics with a comprehension of the simultaneity of oppressions has helped to create a political atmosphere particularly conducive to coalition building. Among all feminists, Third World women have undoubtedly felt most viscerally the need for linking struggles and have also been most capable of forging such coalitions. A commitment to principled coalitions, based not upon expediency, but upon our actual need for each other is a second major contribution of Black feminist struggle. Many contributors to *Home Girls* write out of a sense of our ultimate interdependence. Bernice Johnson Reagon's essay, "Coalition Politics: Turning the Century," should be particularly noted. She writes:

You don't go into coalition because you just *like* it. The only reason you would consider trying to team up with somebody who could possibly kill you, is because that's the only way you can figure you can stay alive. . . . Most of the time you feel threatened to the core and if you don't you're not really doing no coalescing.

The necessity for coalitions has pushed many groups to rigorously examine the attitudes and ignorance within themselves which prevent coalitions from succeeding. Most notably, there has been the commitment of some white feminists to make racism a priority issue within the women's movement, to take responsibility for their racism as individuals, and to do antiracist organizing in coalition with other groups. Because I have written and spoken about racism during my entire involvement as a feminist and have also presented workshops on racism for white women's organizations for several years during the 1970s, I have not only seen that there are white women who are fully committed to eradicating racism, but that new understandings of racial politics have evolved from feminism, which other progressive people would do well to comprehend. [9]

Having begun my political life in the Civil Rights movement and having seen the Black liberation movement virtually destroyed by the white power structure, I have been encouraged in recent years that women can be a significant force for bringing about racial change in a way that unites oppressions instead of isolating them. At the same time the percentage of white feminists who are concerned about racism is still a minority of the movement, and even within this minority those who are personally sensitive and completely serious about formulating an *activist* challenge to racism are fewer still. Because I have usually worked with politically radical feminists, I know that there are indeed white women worth building coalitions with, at the same time that there are apolitical, even reactionary, women who take the name of feminism in vain.

One of the greatest gifts of Black feminism to ourselves has been to make it a little easier simply to *be* Black and female. A Black feminist analysis has enabled us to understand that we are not hated and abused because there is something wrong with us, but because our status and treatment is absolutely prescribed by the racist, misogynistic system under which we live. There is not a Black woman in this country who has not, at some time, internalized and been deeply scarred by the hateful propaganda about us. There is not a Black woman in America who has not felt, at least once, like "the mule of the world," to use Zora Neale Hurston's still apt phrase.[10] Until Black feminism, very few people besides Black women actually cared about or took seriously the demoralization of being female *and* colored *and* poor *and* hated.

When I was growing up, despite my family's efforts to explain, or at least describe, attitudes prevalent in the outside world, I often thought that there was something fundamentally wrong with me because it was obvious that me and everybody like me was held in such contempt. The cold eyes of certain white teachers in school, the Black men who yelled from cars as Beverly and I stood waiting for the bus, convinced me that I must have done something horrible. How was I to know that racism and sexism had formed a blueprint for my mistreatment long before I had ever arrived here? As with most Black women, others' hatred of me became self-hatred, which has diminished over the years, but has by no means disappeared. Black feminism has, for me and for so many others, given us the tools to finally comprehend that it is not something we have done that has heaped this psychic violence and material abuse upon us, but the very fact that, because of who we are, we are multiply oppressed. Unlike any other movement, Black feminism provides the theory that clarifies the nature of Black women's experience, makes possible positive support from other Black women, and encourages political action that will change the very system that has put us down.

*NOTES*

1. The terms Third World women and women of color are used here to designate Native American, Asian American, Latina, and Afro-American women in the U.S. and the indigenous peoples of Third World countries wherever they may live. Both the terms Third World women and women of color apply to Black American women. At times in the introduction Black women are specifically designated as Black or Afro-American and at other times the terms women of color and Third World women are used to refer to women of color as a whole.
2. Smith, Barbara. "Notes for Yet Another Paper on Black Feminism, Or Will the Real Enemy Please Stand Up?" in *Conditions: Five, The Black Women's Issue*, eds. Bethel & Smith. Vol. 2, No. 2 (Autumn, 1979), p. 124.

3. DuBois, W.E.B. *Darkwater, Voices from Within the Veil,* New York: AMS Press, 1969, p. 185.
4. Jordan, June & Bernice Johnson Reagon. "Oughta Be A Woman," *Good News,* Chicago: Flying Fish Records, 1981, Songtalk Publishing Co. Quoted by permission.
5. Teish, Luisah. "Women's Spirituality: A Household Act," in *Home Girls,* ed. Smith. Watertown: Persephone Press, Inc., 1983. All subsequent references to work in *Home Girls* will not be cited.
6. See Linda C. Powell's review of Michele Wallace's *Black Macho and the Myth of the Super Woman* ("Black Macho and Black Feminism") in this volume and my review of Bell Hooks' (Gloria Watkins) *Ain't I A Woman: Black Women and Feminism* in *The New Women's Times Feminist Review,* Vol. 9, no. 24 (November, 1982), pp. 10, 11, 18, 19 & 20 and in *The Black Scholar,* Vol. 14, No. 1 (January/February 1983), pp. 38–45.
7. Quoted from *Gay American History: Lesbians and Gay Men in the U.S.A.,* ed. Jonathan Katz. New York: T. Y. Crowell, 1976, p. 425. Also see Adrienne Rich's "The Problem with Lorraine Hansberry," in "Lorraine Hansberry: Art of Thunder, Vision of Light," *Freedomways,* Vol. 19, No. 4, 1979, pp. 247–255 for more material about her woman-identification.
8. Tillery, Linda. "Freedom Time," *Linda Tillery,* Oakland: Olivia Records, 1977, Tuizer Music.
9. Some useful articles on racism by white feminists are Elly Bulkin's "Racism and Writing: Some Implications for White Lesbian Critics." *Sinister Wisdom* 13 (Spring, 1980), pp. 3–22; Minnie Bruce Pratt's "Rebellion." *Feminary,* Vol. 11, Nos. 1 & 2 (1980), pp. 6–20; and Adrienne Rich's "Disloyal to Civilization: Feminism, Racism, Gynephobia." *On Lies, Secrets and Silence: Selected Prose 1966–1978.* New York: W. W. Norton, 1979, pp. 275–310.
10. Hurston, Zora Neale. *Their Eyes Were Watching God.* Urbana: University of Illinois, 1937, 1978, p. 29.    [1983]

## 136

# *The Development of Chicana Feminist Discourse*

ALMA M. GARCIA

Between 1970 and 1980, a Chicana feminist movement developed in the United States that addressed the specific issues that affected Chicanas as women of color. During the 1960s, the Chicano movement, characterized by a politics of protest, came into being, and focused on a wide range of issues: social justice, equality, educational reforms, and political and economic self-determination for Chicano communities in the United States.[1] Various struggles evolved within the Chicano movement: the United Farmworkers' unionization efforts;[2] the New Mexico Land Grant movement;[3] the Colorado-based Crusade for Justice;[4] the Chicano student movement;[5] and the Raza Unida Party.[6]

## ORIGINS OF CHICANA FEMINISM

Rowbotham argues that women may develop a feminist consciousness as a result of their experiences with sexism in revolutionary struggles or mass social movements.[7] Chicana feminists began the search for a "room of their own" by assessing their participation within the Chicano movement. Their feminist consciousness emerged from a struggle for equality with Chicano men and from a reassessment of the role of the family as a means of resistance to oppressive societal conditions.

Historically, as well as during the 1960s and 1970s, the Chicano family represented a source of cultural and political resistance to the various types of discrimination experienced in the American society.[8] At the cultural level, the movement emphasized the need to safeguard the value of family loyalty. At the political level, the Chicano movement used the family as a strategic organizational tool for protest activities.

As women began to question their traditional female roles,[9] dramatic changes in the structure of Chicano families occurred. Thus, a Chicana feminist movement originated from the nationalist Chicano struggle: Rowbotham refers to such a feminist movement as "a colony within a colony."[10] But as the Chicano movement developed during the 1970s, Chicana feminists began to draw up their own political agenda and entered into a dialogue with the movement that explicitly reflected their struggles to secure a room of their own within it.

## CHICANA FEMINISM AND CULTURAL NATIONALISM

During the 1960s and 1970s, Chicana feminists responded to the criticism that Chicano cultural nationalism and feminism were irreconcilable. Cultural nationalism represented a major, but not monolithic, component of the Chicano movement. It emphasized cultural pride, resistance, and survival within an Anglo-dominated nation-state. Thus, cultural nationalism shaped the political direction of the Chicano social protest movement. Sharing ideological roots with Black cultural nationalism, Chicanismo, as Chicano cultural nationalism became known, advocated a movement of cultural renaissance and resistance within Chicano communities throughout the United States. Chicanismo emphasized Mexican cultural pride as a source of political unity and strength capable of mobilizing Chicanos as an oppositional political group within the dominant American political landscape. Thus, Chicanismo provided a framework for the development of a collective ethnic consciousness—the essence of any nationalist ideology—that challenged the ideological hegemony of Anglo America. Moreover, Chicano cultural nationalism situated the sociohistorical experiences of Chicanos within a theoretical model of internal colonialism. Chicano communities were analyzed as ethnic "nations" existing under direct exploitation by the dominant society. "Nationalism, therefore, was to be the common denominator for uniting all Mexican Americans and making possible effective political mobilization."[11]

One source of ideological disagreement between Chicana feminism and this cultural nationalist ideology was cultural survival. Many Chicana feminists believed that a focus on cultural survival did not acknowledge the need to alter male-female relations within Chicano communities. For example, Chicana feminists criticized the notion of the "ideal Chicana" that glorified Chicanas as strong, long-suffering women who had endured and kept Chicano culture and the family intact. To Chicana feminists, this concept represented an obstacle to the redefinition of gender roles. Nieto Gomez stated:

> Some Chicanas are praised as they emulate the sanctified example set by [the Virgin] Mary. The woman par excellence is mother and wife. She is to love and support her husband and to nurture and teach her children. Thus, may she gain fulfillment as a woman. For a Chicana bent upon fulfillment of her personhood, this restricted perspective of her role as a woman is not only inadequate but crippling.[12]

Chicana feminists were also skeptical about the cultural nationalist interpretation of machismo. Such an interpretation viewed machismo as an ideological tool used by the dominant Anglo society to justify the inequalities experienced by Chicanos. According to this interpretation, the relationship between Chicanos and the larger society was that of an internal colony dominated and exploited by the capitalist economy.[13] Machismo, like other cultural traits, was blamed by Anglos for blocking Chicanos from succeeding in the American society. In reality, the economic structure and colony-like exploitation were to blame.

Some Chicana feminists agreed with this analysis of machismo, asserting that a mutually reinforcing relationship existed between internal colonialism and the development of the myth of machismo. According to Sosa Riddell, machismo was a myth "propagated by subjugators and colonizers, which created damaging stereotypes of Mexican/Chicano males."[14] As a type of social control imposed by the dominant society the myth of machismo distorted gender relations within Chicano communities, creating stereotypes of Chicanas as passive and docile women. As Nieto concluded: "Although the term 'machismo' is correctly denounced by all because it stereotypes the Latin man . . . it does a great disservice to both men and women. Chicano and Chicana alike must be free to seek their own individual fulfillment."[15]

Some Chicana feminists criticized the myth of machismo used by the dominant society to legitimate racial inequality, but others moved beyond this level of analysis to distinguish between the machismo that oppressed both men and women and the sexism in Chicano communities in general, and the Chicano movement in particular, that oppressed Chicana women.[16] According to Vidal, the origins of a Chicana feminist consciousness were prompted by the sexist attitudes and behavior of Chicano males, which constituted a "serious obstacle to women anxious to play a role in the struggle for Chicana liberation."[17]

Furthermore, many Chicana feminists disagreed with the cultural nationalist view that machismo could be a positive value within a Chicano cultural value system. They challenged the notion that machismo was a source of masculine pride for Chicanos and therefore a defense mechanism against the dominant society's racism. Chicana feminists called for changes in the ideologies responsible for distorting relations between women and men. One such change was to modify the cultural nationalist position that looked upon machismo as a source of cultural pride.

Chicana feminists called for a focus on the universal aspects of sexism that shape gender relations in both Anglo and Chicano culture. Although they acknowledged the economic exploitation of all Chicanos, they outlined the double exploitation experienced by Chicanas. Sosa Riddell concluded: "It was when Chicanas began to seek work outside of the family groups that sexism became a key factor of oppression along with racism."[18] Francisca Flores summarized some of the consequences of sexism:

> It is not surprising that more and more Chicanas are forced to go to work in order to supplement the family income. The children are farmed out to a relative to baby-sit with them, and since these women are employed in the lower income jobs, the extra pressure placed on them can become unbearable.[19]

## CHICANA FEMINISM AND FEMINIST BAITING

The systematic analysis by Chicana feminists of the impact of racism and sexism on Chicanas within American society and, above all, within the Chicano movement was often misunderstood as a threat to the political unity of the Chicano movement. But Marta Cotera, a leading voice of Chicana feminism, pointed out:

> The aggregate cultural values we [Chicanas] share can also work to our benefit if we choose to scrutinize our cultural traditions, isolate the positive attributes and interpret them for the benefit of women. It's unreal that Hispanas have been browbeaten for so long about our so-called conservative (meaning reactionary) culture. It's also unreal that we have let men interpret culture only as those practices and attitudes that determine who does the dishes around the house. We as women also have the right to interpret and define the philosophical and religious traditions beneficial to us within our culture, and which we have inherited as

our tradition. To do this, we must become both conversant with our history and philosophical evolution, and analytical about the institutional and behavioral manifestations of the same.[20]

Such Chicana feminists were attacked for developing a "divisive ideology"—a feminist ideology that was frequently viewed as a threat to the Chicano movement as a whole. As Chicana feminists examined their roles as women activists within the Chicano movement, an ideological split developed. One group saw itself as "loyalists" who believed that the Chicano movement did not have to deal with sexual inequities because Chicano men as well as Chicano women experienced racial oppression. According to Nieto Gomez, who was not a loyalist, their belief was that if men oppress women, it is not the men's fault but rather that of the system.[21]

Even if such a problem existed, and they did not believe that it did, the loyalists maintained that such a matter would best be resolved internally, within the Chicano movement. They denounced the formation of a separate Chicana feminist movement on the grounds that it was a politically dangerous strategy, perhaps Anglo-inspired. Such a movement would undermine the unity of the Chicano movement by raising an issue that was not seen as central. Loyalists viewed racism as the most important issue within the Chicano movement. Nieto Gomez quotes one such loyalist:

> I am concerned with the direction that the Chicanas are taking in the movement. The words such as liberation, sexism, male chauvinism, etc., were prevalent. The terms mentioned above plus the theme of individualism is a concept of the Anglo society; terms prevalent in the Anglo women's movement. The familia has always been our strength in our culture. But it seems evident . . . that you [Chicana feminists] are not concerned with the familia, but are influenced by the Anglo woman's movement.[22]

Chicana feminists were also accused of undermining the values associated with Chicano culture. Loyalists saw the Chicana feminist movement as an "anti-family, anti-cultural, anti-man and therefore an anti-Chicano movement."[23] Feminism was, above all, believed to be an individualistic search for identity that detracted from the Chicano move-

ment's "real" issues, such as racism. Nieto Gomez quotes a loyalist: "And since when does a Chicana need identity? If you are a real Chicana then no one regardless of the degrees needs to tell you about it. The only ones who need identity are the vendidas, the falsas, and the opportunists."[24]

The ideological conflicts between Chicana feminists and loyalists persisted throughout the 1970s, exacerbated during various Chicana conferences. At times, such confrontations served to increase Chicana feminist activity that challenged the loyalists' attacks, yet these attacks also served to suppress feminist activities.

Chicana feminists as well as Chicana feminist lesbians continued to be labeled *vendidas*, or "sellouts." Chicana loyalists continued to view Chicana feminism as associated not only with melting into white society but, more seriously, with dividing the Chicano movement. Similarly, many Chicano males were convinced that Chicana feminism was a divisive ideology incompatible with Chicano cultural nationalism. Nieto Gomez said that "[with] respect to [the] Chicana feminist, their credibility is reduced when they are associated with [feminism] and white women." She added that as a result, Chicana feminists often faced harassment and ostracism within the Chicano movement.[25] Similarly, Cotera stated that Chicanas "are suspected of assimilating into the feminist ideology of an alien [white] culture that actively seeks our cultural domination."[26]

Chicana feminists responded quickly and often vehemently to such charges. Flores answered, in an editorial, that birth control, abortion, and sex education are not merely "white issues." Reacting to the accusation that feminists were responsible for the "betrayal of [Chicano] culture and heritage," Flores said, "Our culture hell"—a phrase that became a dramatic slogan of the Chicana feminist movement.[27]

Chicana feminists' defense throughout the 1970s against those declaring that a feminist movement was divisive for the Chicano movement was to reassess their roles within the Chicano movement and to call for an end to male domination. Their challenges of traditional gender roles represented a means to achieve equality.[28] To increase the participation of and opportunities for women in the Chicano movement, feminists agreed that both Chicanos and Chicanas had to address the issue of gender inequality.[29] Furthermore, Chicana feminists argued that the resistance that they encountered reflected the existence of sexism on the part of Chicano males and the antifeminist attitudes of the Chicana loyalists. Nieto Gomez, in reviewing the experiences of Chicana feminists in the Chicano movement, concluded that Chicanas "involved in discussing and applying the women's question have been ostracized, isolated and ignored." She argued that "in organizations where cultural nationalism is extremely strong, Chicana feminists experience intense harassment and ostracism."[30] Black and Asian American women also faced severe criticism as they pursued feminist issues in their own communities. Indeed, as their participation in collective efforts to end racial oppression increased, so did their confrontations with sexism.[31]

## CHICANA FEMINISTS AND
## WHITE FEMINISTS

The historical relationship between Chicana feminists and white feminists developed along problematic, if not contentious, lines. A major ideological tension between them involved the analysis by Chicana feminists of their experiences as both women and members of an ethnic community. Although Chicana feminists were critical of the patriarchal tendencies within the Chicano cultural nationalist movement, their feminist writings reveal a constant focus on the nature and consequences of racism on their daily lives, as well as on the role of a modified nationalist response as a form of resistance against the pernicious effects of racism.

Chicana feminists struggled to develop a feminist ideology that would successfully integrate race and gender as analytical tools. Feminism and nationalism were seen as political ideologies that could complement each other and, therefore, provide a more sharply focused view of the structural conditions of inequality experienced by Chicanas in American society. To the extent that Chicana feminists viewed the white feminist movement as incapable of integrating women of color and their nationalist struggles, political coalitions between the

two groups appeared impossible. Nevertheless, Chicana feminists engaged in an ideological dialogue with white feminists.

Several issues made coalition-building difficult. First, Chicana feminists criticized what they considered to be a cornerstone of white feminist thought: an emphasis on gender oppression to explain the life circumstances of women. Chicana feminists believed that the white feminist movement overlooked the effects of racial oppression experienced by Chicanas and other women of color. Thus, Del Castillo maintained that the Chicana feminist movement was "different primarily because we are [racially] oppressed people."[32] In addition, Chicana feminists criticized white feminists who believed that a general women's movement would be able to overcome racial differences among women. Chicanas interpreted this as a failure by the white feminist movement to deal with racism. Without the incorporation of an analysis of racial oppression to explain the experiences of Chicanas as well as other women of color, a coalition with white feminists would be highly unlikely.[33] Longeaux y Vasquez concluded: "We must have a clearer vision of our plight and certainly we cannot blame our men for the oppression of the women."[34]

Chicana feminists adopted an analysis that began with race as a critical variable in interpreting the experiences of Chicano communities in the United States. They expanded this analysis by identifying gender as a variable interconnected with race in analyzing the specific daily life circumstances of Chicanas in Chicano communities. They did not view women's struggles as secondary to the nationalist movement but argued instead for an analysis of race and gender as multiple sources of oppression.[35] Thus, Chicana feminism went beyond the limits of an exclusively racial theory of oppression that tended to overlook gender and also beyond the limits of a theory of oppression based exclusively on gender that tended to overlook race.

A second factor preventing an alliance between Chicana feminists and white feminists was the middle-class orientation of white feminists. Throughout the 1970s Chicana feminists viewed the white feminist movement as a middle-class movement.[36] In contrast, they viewed the Chicano movement in general as a working-class movement. They repeatedly made reference to the difference, and many began their works with a section dissociating themselves from the "women's liberation movement." Chicana feminists as activists in the broader Chicano movement identified as major struggles the farmworkers' movement, welfare rights, undocumented workers, and prisoners' rights. Such issues were seen as far removed from the demands of the white feminist movement, and Chicana feminists could not get white feminist organizations to deal with them.[37]

White feminist organizations were also accused of being exclusionary, patronizing, or racist in their dealings with Chicanas and other women of color. Cotera states:

> Minority women could fill volumes with examples of put-downs, put-ons, and out-and-out racism shown to them by the leadership in the [white feminist] movement. There are three major problem areas in the minority-majority relationship in the movement: (1) paternalism or maternalism, (2) extremely limited opportunities for minority women . . . , (3) outright discrimination against minority women in the movement.[38]

Chicana feminists continued to stress the importance of developing autonomous feminist organizations that would address the struggles of Chicanas as members of an ethnic minority and as women. Rather than attempt to overcome the obstacles to coalition-building between Chicana feminists and white feminists, Chicanas called for autonomous feminist organizations for all women of color.[39] Chicana feminists believed that sisterhood was indeed powerful but only to the extent that racial and class differences were understood and, above all, respected. Nieto concludes: "The Chicana must demand that dignity and respect within the women's rights movement which allows her to practice feminism within the context of her own culture. . . . Her approaches to feminism must be drawn from her own world."[40]

## CHICANA FEMINISM: AN EVOLVING FUTURE

Chicana feminists, like Black, Asian American, and Native American feminists, experience specific life conditions that are distinct from those of white feminists. Socioeconomic and cultural differences in Chicano communities directly shaped the development of Chicana feminism and the relationship between Chicana feminists and feminists of other racial and ethnic groups, including white feminists. Future dialogue among all feminists will require a shared understanding of the existing differences as well as of the similarities. Like other women of color, Chicana feminists must address issues that specifically affect them as women of color. In addition, Chicana feminists must address issues that have particular impact on Chicano communities, such as poverty, limited opportunities for higher education, high school dropouts, health care, bilingual education, immigration reform, prison reform, welfare, and recently, United States policies in Central America.

At the academic level, an increasing number of Chicana feminists continue to join in a collective effort to carry on the feminist legacy inherited from the 1970s. In June 1982 a group of Chicana academics organized the national feminist organization Mujeres Activas en Letras y Cambio Social (MALCS) in order to build a support network for Chicana professors, undergraduates, and graduate students. The organization's major goal is to fight the race, class, and gender oppression facing Chicanas in institutions of higher education. In addition, MALCS aim to bridge the gap between academic work and the Chicano community.

In 1984 the national conference of the National Association for Chicano Studies (NACS), held in Austin, Texas, adopted the theme *"Voces de la Mujer"* in response to demands from the Chicana Caucus. As a result, for the first time since its founding in 1972, the NACS national conference addressed the issue of women. Compared with past conferences, a large number of Chicanas participated by presenting their research and chairing and moderating panels. A plenary session addressed the gender inequality in higher education and within NACS. And at the business meeting, sexism within NACS was again seriously debated because it continues to be one of the "unsettled issues" of concern to Chicana feminists. A significant outcome of the conference was that its published proceedings that year were the first to be devoted to Chicanas and Mexicanas.[41]

Chicana feminists continue to raise critical issues concerning the nature of the oppression experienced by Chicanas and other women of color. They, like African American, Asian American, and Native American feminists, focus on the consequences of the intersection of race, class, and gender in the daily lives of women in American society. Chicana feminists have adopted a theoretical perspective that emphasizes the simultaneous impact of these critical variables for women of color.[42]

Chicana feminists have emphasized that Chicanas have made few gains in comparison to white men and women, as well as Chicano men, in terms of labor-force participation, income, education levels, rates of poverty, and other socioeconomic status indicators. Over the past forty years, Chicanas have made only small occupational moves from low-pay unskilled jobs to higher-pay skilled and semiprofessional employment. Studies indicate that about 66 percent remain occupationally segregated in such low-paying jobs as sales, clerical, service, and factory work. Further, Chicanas experience major social-structural constraints that limit their upward social mobility.[43] Less than 15 percent of all Chicanas have entered the occupational ranks of professionals, educational administrators, and business managers. In addition, Chicano families had approximately two-thirds of the family income of non-Hispanic families—approximately the same as ten years ago—and about 46 percent of families headed by Chicanas had incomes below the poverty level.

Chicana feminists are also concerned about Chicano schooling; the persistently low levels of educational attainment are deemed to be evidence of the role of race, class, and gender stratification in reinforcing and perpetuating inequalities. Chicanas, as well as all Latinas, have shockingly high dropout rates, with the not surprising consequence that Chicanas are scarce in the halls of academe.[44] According to one of the few studies on Chicanas in higher education, "of all the major population groups, Mexican American females are the poorest and the most underrepresented in higher education."[45]

Despite the limited numbers of Chicana aca-

demics, Chicana feminist discourse has developed within the academy as Chicana feminists have entered into specific dialogues with other feminists. Chicanas have criticized feminist scholarship for the exclusionary practices that have resulted from the discipline's limited attention to differences among women relating to race, ethnicity, class, and sexual preference.[46] Interestingly, Chicana feminists are also critical of Chicano studies and ethnic studies scholarship, which have too often lacked a systematic gender analysis.[47] As a result, Chicana feminist discourse is integrating the experiences of Chicanas within these academic disciplines. Chicana feminist scholars advocate restructuring the academy in order to integrate the "new knowledge" about women,[48] in this case, Chicanas. Indeed, Chicana feminist scholarship "came of age" in the 1990s, with publication of a variety of anthologies written by and about Chicanas.[49]

Chicana feminist scholars are revitalizing the fields of Chicano studies, ethnic studies, and women's studies. Indeed, many of them argue that their writings are creating a separate, interdisciplinary field: Chicana studies.

Sociologist Denise Segura reflects on the different approaches found among Chicana feminist scholars:

> There are several types of Chicana scholarship. One type tries to connect research on Chicanas to mainstream frameworks in the respective fields; another type tries to develop an understanding of the status and oppression of Chicanas, using feminist frameworks as points of departure; another type, connected to postmodernist frameworks, tries to get away from all mainstream thought. It begins with Chicanas as a point of departure and builds from there an understanding of their uniqueness as well as their commonalities with other oppressed peoples in this society.[50]

In their study of Chicana feminism among Chicanas in higher education and Chicana white-collar workers, Pesquera and Segura found that Chicana feminism is not ideologically monolithic. Pesquera and Segura documented the emergence of ideologically divergent strands of Chicana feminism based on the social positioning of specific groups of Chicanas.[51] A future task for Chicana feminist scholars will be to explore further the dynamic interaction of cross-cutting memberships based on class, education, sexual orientation, and other critical variables in order to understand better the continued development of Chicana feminist discourse in the twenty-first century.

Chicana scholars are truly moving in new directions. Chicana feminist writings represent the accumulated maturity of an intellectual tradition rooted in the political activism of the 1960s. Nevertheless, Chicana feminists, like other feminist women of color, continue to join their intellectual discourse with their political activism. Indeed, each informs the other. Pesquera and Segura succinctly characterize the major underlying force of Chicana feminist discourse as a

> Chicana critique of cultural, political and economic conditions in the United States. It is influenced by the tradition of advocacy scholarship, which challenges the claims of objectivity and links research to community concerns and social change. It is driven by a passion to place the Chicana, as speaking subject, at the center of intellectual discourse.[52]

The voices of Chicana feminists will continue to resonate as the next century approaches. Their struggles and triumphs will continue to shape the ideological direction of American feminism and future generations of feminists.

## NOTES

1. Mario Barrera, "The Study of Politics and the Chicano," *Aztlan* 5 (1976): 9–26; Carlos Munoz, Jr., "The Politics of Protest and Liberation: A Case Study of Repression and Cooptation," *Aztlan* 5 (1974): 119–141; Armando Navarro, "The Evolution of Chicano Politics," *Aztlan* 5 (1974): 57–84.
2. John Dunne, *Delano: The Story of the California Grape Strike* (New York: Straus, 1967); Sam Kushner, *Long Road to Delano* (New York: International, 1975); Eugene Nelson, *Huelga: The First 100 Days* (Delano, CA: Farm Workers Press, 1966).
3. Peter Nabokov, *Tijerina and the Courthouse Raid* (Albuquerque: University of New Mexico Press, 1969).
4. Tony Castro, *Chicano Power* (New York: Saturday Review Press, 1974): Matt Meier and Feliciano Rivera, *The Chicanos* (New York: Hill & Wang, 1972).
5. F. Chris Garcia and Rudolpho O. de la Garza, *The Chicano Political Experience* (North Scituate, MA: Duxbury, 1977).
6. John Shockley, *Chicano Revolt in a Texas Town* (South Bend: University of Notre Dame Press, 1974).
7. Sheila Rowbotham, *Women, Resistance and Revolution:*

*A History of Women and Revolution in the Modern World* (New York: Vintage, 1974).
8. Maxine Baca Zinn, "Political Familism: Toward Sex Role Equality in Chicano Families," *Aztlan* 6 (1977): 13–27.
9. Ibid.
10. Rowbotham, *Women, Resistance and Revolution*, p. 206.
11. Carlos Munoz, Jr., *Youth, Identity, Power: The Chicano Movement* (New York: Verso, 1989), p. 77.
12. Ibid., p. 4.
13. Tomas Almaguer, "Historical Notes on Chicano Oppression," *Aztlan* 5 (1974): 27–56; Mario Barrera, *Race and Class in the Southwest* (Notre Dame: University of Notre Dame Press, 1979).
14. Adaljiza Sosa Riddell, "Chicanas en el Movimiento," *Aztlan* 5 (1974): 159.
15. Nieto Gomez, "Chicanas Identify," p. 4.
16. Henri Chavez, "The Chicanas," *Regeneracion* 1 (1971): 14; Marta Cotera, *The Chicana Feminist* (Austin, TX: Austin Information Systems Development, 1977); Marta Cotera, "Feminism: the Chicana and Anglo Versions: An Historical Analysis," in *Twice a Minority: Mexican American Women*, ed. Margarita Melville (St. Louis, MO: C. V. Mosby, 1980), pp. 217–234; Adelaida Del Castillo, "La Vision Chicana," *La Gente* 8 (1974): p. 8; Evelina Marquez and Margarita Ramirez, "Women's Task Is to Gain Liberation," in *Essays on La Mujer*, ed. Rosaura Sanchez and Rosa Martinez Cruz (Los Angeles: UCLA Chicano Studies Center, 1977), pp. 188–194; Riddell, "Chicanas en el Movimiento"; Maxine Baca Zinn, "Chicanas: Power and Control in the Domestic Sphere," *De Colores* 2 no. 3, (1975): 19–31.
17. Mirta Vidal, "New Voice of La Raza: Chicanas Speak Out," *International Socialist Review* 32 (1971): 8.
18. Riddell, "Chicanas en el Movimiento," p. 159.
19. Francisca Flores, "Conference of Mexican Women: Un Remolina," *Regeneracion*, no. 1 (1971): 4.
20. Cotera, *The Chicana Feminist*, p. 9.
21. Anna Gomez Nieto, "La Feminista," *Encuentro Remenil* 1 (1973): 34–47, lt p. 35.
22. Ibid.
23. Ibid.
24. Ibid.
25. Anna Gomez Nieto, "Sexism in the Movement," *La Gente* 6, no. 4 (1976): 10.
26. Cotera 1977, p. 30.
27. Flores, "Conference of Mexican Women," p. 1.
28. Enriqueta Longeaux y Vasquez, "The Woman of La Raza," *El Grito del Norte* (November 1969): 12. Also, Enriqueta Longeaux y Vasquez, "La Chicana: Let's Build a New Life," *El Grito del Norte* 2 (November 1969): 11.
29. Evey Chapa, "Report from the National Women's Political Caucus," *Magazin* 11 (1973); 37–39; Chavez, "The Chicanas"; Del Castillo, "La Vision Chicana"; Cotera, *The Chicana Feminist*; Dorinda Moreno, "The Image of the Chicana and the La Raza Woman," *Caracol* 2 (1979): 14–15.
30. Nieto, "La Feminista," p. 31.
31. Chow, "The Development of Feminist Consciousness," p. 288; hooks, *Ain't I a Woman*; White, "Listening to the Voices of Black Feminism."

32. Del Castillo, "La Vision Chicana," p. 8.
33. Chapa, "Report from the National Women's Political Caucus"; Cotera, *The Chicana Feminist*; Nieto Gomez, "La Feminista"; Longeaux y Vasquez, "Soy Chicana Primera."
34. Longeaux y Vasquez, "Soy Chicana Primera."
35. Cotera, *The Chicana Feminist*.
36. Chapa, "Report from the National Women's Political Caucus"; Cotera, *The Chicana Feminist*; Longeaux y Vasquez, "Soy Chicana Primero"; Martinez, "The Chicana"; Nieto, "The Chicana and the Women's Rights Movement"; Orozco, "La Chicana and 'Women's Liberation.'"
37. Cotera, *The Chicana Feminist*.
38. Cotera, "Feminism," p. 227.
39. Cotera, *The Chicana Feminist*; Sylvia Gonzalez, "Toward a Feminist Pedagogy for Chicana Self-Actualization," *Frontiers* 5 (1980): 48–51; Consuelo Nieto, "Consuelo Nieto on the Women's Movement," *Interracial Books for Children*," Bulletin 5, no. 4 (1975).
40. Consuelo Nieto, "The Chicana and the Women's Rights Movement"; *La Luz,* September 3, 1974, p. 4.
41. Cordova et al., *Chicana Voices*.
42. Moraga and Anzaldua, *This Bridge Called My Back;* Moraga, "La Guera"; hooks, *Feminist Theory;* Alma Garcia, "Studying Chicanas" in *Chicana Voices,* Teresa Cordova et al. (Austin, Texas; Center for Mexican American Studies, 1986); Gloria Anzaldua, *Borderlands/ La Frontera: The New Mestiza* (San Francisco: Aunt Lute Press, 1987); Gloria Anzaldua, *Making Face, Making Sant—Haciendo Caras: Creative and Critical Perspectives by Feminists of Color* (San Francisco: Aunt Lute Press, 1990).
43. Denise Segura, "Chicana and Mexican Immigrant Women at Work: Impact of Class, Race, and Gender on Occupational Mobility," *Gender and Society* 3 (1989): 37–52; Mary Romero, *Maid in the U.S.A.* (New York: Routledge, 1992).
44. Christine Marie Sierra, "The University Setting Reinforces Inequality," in Cordova et al., *Chicana Voices,* pp. 5–7; Orozco, "La Chicana and 'Women's Liberation'"; Denise Segura, "Chicanas and Triple Oppression in the Labor Force," in Cordova et al., *Chicana Voices,* pp. 47–65; Denise Segura, "Slipping Through the Cracks: Dilemmas in Chicana Education," in *Building with Our Hands,* ed. Adeala de la Torre and Beatrice Pesquera (Berkeley: University of California Press, 1993).
45. Maria Chacon, *Chicanas in Post-Secondary Education* (Stanford: Stanford University Press, 1982).
46. Maxine Baca Zinn, Lynn Weber Cannon, Elizabeth Higginbotham, and Bonnie Thornton Dill, "The Cost of Exclusionary Practices in Women's Studies," *Signs* 11 (1986): 290–302.
47. Mujeres en Marcha, *Chicanas in the 80s: Unsettled Issues* (Berkeley: Chicano Studies Publication Unit, 1983); Orozco, "La Chicana and 'Women's Liberation'"; Norma Alarcon, "The Theoretical Subject(s) of This Bridge Called My Back and Anglo American Feminism," in *Criticism in the Borderlands: Studies in Chicano Literature, Culture and Ideology,* ed. Hector Calderon and Jose David Saldivar (Durham: Duke University Press,

1991); Alma Garcia, "Chicano Studies and 'La Chicana' Courses: Curriculum Options and Reforms," in *Community Empowerment and Chicano Scholarship: Selected Proceedings of National Association of Chicano Studies, 1992.*
48. Joan Wallach Scott, *Gender and Politics in History* (New York: Columbia University Press, 1988).
49. Adeala de la Torre and Beatrice Pesquera, eds., *Building with Our Hands* (Berkeley: University of California Press, 1993); Tey Diana Rebolledo and Eliana S. Rivero, *Infinite Divisions: An Anthology of Chicana Literature* (Tucson: University of Arizona Press, 1993); Norma Alarcon et al., *Chicana Critical Issues* (Berkeley: Third World Press, 1993).
50. Segura, quoted in *Building With Our Hands,* p. 6.
51. Beatriz M. Pesquera and Denise M. Segura, "There Is No Going Back: Chicanas and Feminism," in *Chicana Critical Issues,* ed. Norma Alarcon (Berkeley: Third Woman Press, 1993), pp. 95–115.
52. Ibid., p. 1.                                      [1997]

 137

# Thoughts on Indian Feminism

KATE SHANLEY

Attending the Ohoyo conference in Grand Forks, North Dakota was a returning home for me in a spiritual sense—taking my place beside other Indian women, and an actual sense—being with my relatives and loved ones after finally finishing my pre-doctoral requirements at the university. Although I have been a full-time student for the past six years, I brought to the academic experience many years in the workaday world as a mother, registered nurse, volunteer tutor, social worker aide, and high school outreach worker. What I am offering in this article are my thoughts as an Indian woman on feminism. Mine is a political perspective that seeks to re-view the real-life positions of women in relation to the theories that attempt to address the needs of those women.

Issues such as equal pay for equal work, child health and welfare, and a woman's right to make her own choices regarding contraceptive use, sterilization and abortion—key issues to the majority women's movement—affect Indian women as well; however, equality *per se,* may have a different meaning for Indian women and Indian people. That difference begins with personal and tribal sovereignty—the right to be legally recognized as peoples empowered to determine our own destinies. Thus, the Indian women's movement seeks equality in two ways that do not concern mainstream women: (1) on the individual level, the Indian woman struggles to promote the survival of a social structure whose organizational principles represent notions of family different from those of the mainstream; and (2) on the societal level, the People seek sovereignty as a people in order to maintain a vital legal and spiritual connection to the land, in order to *survive* as a people.

The nuclear family has little relevance to Indian women; in fact, in many ways, mainstream feminists now are striving to redefine family and community in a way that Indian women have long known. The American lifestyle from which white middle-class women are fighting to free themselves, has not taken hold in Indian communities. Tribal and communal values have survived after four hundred years of colonial oppression.

It may be that the desire on the part of mainstream feminists to include Indian women, however sincere, represents tokenism just now, because too often Indian people, by being thought of as spiritual "mascots" to the American endeavor, are seen more as artifacts than a real people able to speak for ourselves. Given the public's general ignorance about Indian people, in other words, it is possible that Indian people's real-life concerns are not relevant to the mainstream feminist movement in a way that constitutes anything more than a "representative" facade. Charges against the women's movement of heterosexism and racism abound these days; it is not my intention to add to them except to stress that we must all be vigilant in examining the underlying assumptions that motivate us. Internalization of negative (that is, sexist and racist) attitudes towards ourselves and others can and quite often does result from colonialist (white patriarchal) oppression. It is more useful to attack the systems that keep us ignorant of each other's histories.

The other way in which the Indian women's movement differs in emphasis from the majority women's movement, lies in the importance Indian people place on tribal sovereignty—it is the single most pressing political issue in Indian country today. For Indian people to survive culturally as well as materially, many battles must be fought and won in the courts of law, precisely because it is the legal recognition that enables Indian people to govern ourselves according to our own world view—a world view that is antithetical to the *wasicu* (the Lakota term for "takers of the fat") definition of progress. Equality for Indian women within tribal communities, therefore, holds more significance than equality in terms of the general rubric "American."

Up to now I have been referring to the women's movement as though it were a single, well-defined organization. It is not. Perhaps in many ways socialist feminists hold views similar to the views of many Indian people regarding private property and the nuclear family. Certainly, there are some Indian people who are capitalistic. The point I would like to stress, however, is that rather than seeing differences according to a hierarchy of oppressions (white over Indian, male over female), we must practice a politics that allows for diversity in cultural identity as well as in sexual identity.

The word "feminism" has special meanings to Indian women, including the idea of promoting the continuity of tradition, and consequently, pursuing the recognition of tribal sovereignty. Even so, Indian feminists are united with mainstream feminists in outrage against woman and child battering, sexist employment and educational practices, and in many other social concerns. Just as sovereignty cannot be granted but *must be recognized* as an inherent right to self-determination, so Indian feminism must also be recognized as powerful in its own terms, in its own right.

Feminism becomes an incredibly powerful term when it incorporates diversity—not as a superficial political position, but as a practice. The women's movement and the Indian movement for sovereignty suffer similar trivialization, because narrow factions turn ignorance to their own benefit so that they can exploit human beings and the lands they live on for corporate profit. The time has come for Indian women and Indian people to be known on our own terms. This nuclear age demands new terms of communication for all people. Our survival depends on it. Peace.                    [1984]

## 🌿 138

# *Blame It on Feminism*

SUSAN FALUDI

To be a woman in America at the close of the 20th century—what good fortune. That's what we keep hearing, anyway. The barricades have fallen, politicians assure us. Women have "made it," Madison Avenue cheers. Women's fight for equality has "largely been won," *Time* magazine announces. Enroll at any university, join any law firm, apply for credit at any bank. Women have so many opportunities now, corporate leaders say, that we don't really need equal opportunity policies. Women are so equal now, lawmakers say, that we no longer need an Equal Rights Amendment. Women have "so much," former President Ronald Reagan says, that the White House no longer needs to appoint them to higher office. Even American Express ads are saluting a woman's freedom to charge it. At last, women have received their full citizenship papers.

And yet . . .

Behind this celebration of the American woman's victory, behind the news, cheerfully and endlessly repeated, that the struggle for women's rights is won, another message flashes. You may be free and equal now, it says to women, but you have never been more miserable.

This bulletin of despair is posted everywhere— at the newsstand, on the TV set, at the movies, in advertisements and doctors' offices and academic journals. Professional women are suffering "burnout" and succumbing to an "infertility epidemic." Single women are grieving from a "man shortage." The *New York Times* reports: Childless women are "depressed and confused" and their ranks are swelling. *Newsweek* says: Unwed women are "hysterical" and crumbling under a "profound crisis of confidence." The health advice manuals inform: High-powered career women are stricken with unprecedented outbreaks of "stress-induced disorders," hair loss, bad nerves, alcoholism, and even heart attacks. The psychology books advise: Independent women's loneliness represents "a major mental health problem today." Even founding feminist Betty Friedan has been spreading the word: she warns that women now suffer from a new identity crisis and "new 'problems that have no name.'"

How can American women be in so much trouble at the same time that they are supposed to be so blessed? If the status of women has never been higher, why is their emotional state so low? If women got what they asked for, what could possibly be the matter now?

The prevailing wisdom of the past decade has supported one, and only one, answer to this riddle: it must be all that equality that's causing all that pain. Women are unhappy precisely *because* they are free. Women are enslaved by their own liberation. They have grabbed at the gold ring of independence, only to miss the one ring that really matters. They have gained control of their fertility, only to destroy it. They have pursued their own professional dreams—and lost out on the greatest female adventure. The women's movement, as we are told time and again, has proved women's own worst enemy.

"In dispensing its spoils, women's liberation has given my generation high incomes, our own cigarette, the option of single parenthood, rape crisis centers, personal lines of credit, free love, and female gynecologists," Mona Charen, a young law student, writes in the *National Review*, in an article titled "The Feminist Mistake." "In return it has effectively robbed us of one thing upon which the happiness of most women rests—men." The *National Review* is a conservative publication, but such charges against the women's movement are not confined to its pages. "Our generation was the human sacrifice" to the women's movement, *Los Angeles Times* feature writer Elizabeth Mehren contends in a *Time* cover story. Baby-boom women like her, she says, have been duped by feminism: "We believed the rhetoric." In *Newsweek*, writer Kay Ebeling dubs feminism "the Great Experiment That Failed" and asserts "women in my generation, its perpetrators, are the casualties." Even the beauty magazines are saying it: *Harper's Bazaar* accuses the women's movement of having "lost us [women] ground instead of gaining it."

In the last decade, publications from the *New York Times* to *Vanity Fair* to the *Nation* have issued a steady stream of indictments against the women's movement, with such headlines as WHEN FEMINISM FAILED or THE AWFUL TRUTH ABOUT WOMEN'S LIB. They hold the campaign for women's equality responsible for nearly every woe besetting women, from mental depression to meager savings accounts, from teenage suicides to eating disorders to bad complexions. The "Today" show says women's liberation is to blame for bag ladies. A guest columnist in the *Baltimore Sun* even proposes that feminists produced the rise in slasher movies. By making the "violence" of abortion more acceptable, the author reasons, women's rights activists made it all right to show graphic murders on screen.

At the same time, other outlets of popular culture have been forging the same connection: in Hollywood films, of which *Fatal Attraction* is only the most famous, emancipated women with condominiums of their own slink wild-eyed between bare walls, paying for their liberty with an empty bed, a barren womb. "My biological clock is ticking so loud it keeps me awake at night," Sally Field cries in the film *Surrender*, as, in an all too common transformation in the cinema of the '80s, an actress who once played scrappy working heroines is now showcased groveling for a groom. In prime-time television shows, from "thirtysomething" to "Family Man," single, professional, and feminist women are humiliated, turned into harpies, or hit by nervous breakdowns; the wise ones recant their independent ways by the closing sequence. In popular novels, from Gail Parent's *A Sign of the Eighties* to Stephen King's *Misery*, unwed women shrink to sniveling spinsters or inflate to fire-breathing she-devils; renouncing all aspirations but marriage, they beg for wedding bands from strangers or swing axes at reluctant bachelors. We "blew it by waiting," a typically remorseful careerist sobs in Freda Bright's *Singular Women;* she and her sister professionals are "condemned to be childless forever." Even Erica Jong's high-flying independent heroine liter-

ally crashes by the end of the decade, as the author supplants *Fear of Flying*'s saucy Isadora Wing, a symbol of female sexual emancipation in the '70s, with an embittered careerist-turned-recovering-"codependent" in *Any Woman's Blues*—a book that is intended, as the narrator bluntly states, "to demonstrate what a deadend the so-called sexual revolution had become, and how desperate so-called free women were in the last few years of our decadent epoch."

Popular psychology manuals peddle the same diagnosis for contemporary female distress. "Feminism, having promised her a stronger sense of her own identity, has given her little more than an identity *crisis,*" the best-selling advice manual *Being a Woman* asserts. The authors of the era's self-help classic *Smart Women/Foolish Choices* proclaim that women's distress was "an unfortunate consequence of feminism," because "it created a myth among women that the apex of self-realization could be achieved only through autonomy, independence, and career."

Finally, some "liberated" women themselves have joined the lamentations. In confessional accounts, works that invariably receive a hearty greeting from the publishing industry, "recovering Superwomen" tell all. In *The Cost of Loving: Women and the New Fear of Intimacy,* Megan Marshall, a Harvard-pedigreed writer, asserts that the feminist "Myth of Independence" has turned her generation into unloved and unhappy fast-trackers, "dehumanized" by careers and "uncertain of their gender identity." Other diaries of mad Superwomen charge that "the hard-core feminist viewpoint," as one of them puts it, has relegated educated executive achievers to solitary nights of frozen dinners and closet drinking. The triumph of equality, they report, has merely given women hives, stomach cramps, eye-twitching disorders, even comas.

But what "equality" are all these authorities talking about?

If American women are so equal, why do they represent two-thirds of all poor adults? Why are more than 80 percent of full-time working women making less than $20,000 a year, nearly double the male rate? Why are they still far more likely than men to live in poor housing and receive no health insurance, and twice as likely to draw no pension? Why does the average working woman's salary still lag as far behind the average man's as it did twenty years ago? Why does the average female college graduate today earn less than a man with no more than a high school diploma (just as she did in the '50s)—and why does the average female high school graduate today earn less than a male high school dropout? Why do American women, in fact, face the worst gender-based pay gap in the developed world?

If women have "made it," then why are nearly 80 percent of working women still stuck in traditional "female" jobs—as secretaries, administrative "support" workers and salesclerks? And, conversely, why are they less than 8 percent of all federal and state judges, less than 6 percent of all law partners, and less than one half of 1 percent of top corporate managers? Why are there only three female state governors, two female U.S. senators, and two Fortune 500 chief executives? Why are only nineteen of the four thousand corporate officers and directors women—and why do more than half the boards of Fortune companies still lack even one female member?

If women "have it all," then why don't they have the most basic requirements to achieve equality in the work force? Unlike virtually all other industrialized nations, the U.S. government still has no family-leave and child care programs—and more than 99 percent of American private employers don't offer child care either. Though business leaders say they are aware of and deplore sex discrimination, corporate America has yet to make an honest effort toward eradicating it. In a 1990 national poll of chief executives at Fortune 1000 companies, more than 80 percent acknowledged that discrimination impedes female employees' progress—yet, less than 1 percent of these same companies regarded *remedying* sex discrimination as a goal that their personnel departments should pursue. In fact, when the companies' human resource officers were asked to rate their department's priorities, women's advancement ranked last.

If women are so "free," why are their reproductive freedoms in greater jeopardy today than a decade earlier? Why do women who want to postpone childbearing now have fewer options than ten years ago? The availability of different forms of contraception has declined, research for new birth control has virtually halted, new laws restricting abortion—or even *information* about abortion—for young and poor women have been passed, and the U.S. Supreme Court has shown little ardor in defending the right it granted in 1973.

The word may be that women have been "liberated," but women themselves seem to feel otherwise. Repeatedly in national surveys, majorities of women say they are still far from equality. Nearly 70 percent of women polled by the *New York Times* in 1989 said the movement for women's rights had only just begun. Most women in the 1990 Virginia Slims opinion poll agreed with the statement that conditions for their sex in American society had improved "a little, not a lot." In poll after poll in the decade, overwhelming majorities of women said they needed equal pay and equal job opportunities, they needed an Equal Rights Amendment, they needed the right to an abortion without government interference, they needed a federal law guaranteeing maternity leave, they needed decent child care services. They have none of these. So how exactly have we "won" the war for women's rights?

Seen against this background, the much ballyhooed claim that feminism is responsible for making women miserable becomes absurd—and irrelevant. The afflictions ascribed to feminism are all myths. From "the man shortage" to "the infertility epidemic" to "female burnout" to "toxic day care," these so-called female crises have had their origins not in the actual conditions of women's lives but rather in a closed system that starts and ends in the media, popular culture, and advertising—an endless feedback loop that perpetuates and exaggerates its own false images of womanhood.

Women themselves don't single out the women's movement as the source of their misery. To the contrary, in national surveys 75 to 95 percent of women credit the feminist campaign with *improving* their lives, and a similar proportion say that the women's movement should keep pushing for change. Less than 8 percent think the women's movement might have actually made their lot worse.

\* \* \*

What actually is troubling the American female population, then? If the many ponderers of the Woman Question really wanted to know, they might have asked their subjects. In public opinion surveys, women consistently rank their own *inequality,* at work and at home, among their most urgent concerns. Over and over, women complain to pollsters about a lack of economic, not marital, opportunities; they protest that working men, not working women, fail to spend time in the nursery and the kitchen. The Roper Organization's survey analysts find that men's opposition to equality is "a major cause of resentment and stress" and "a major irritant for most women today." It is justice for their gender, not wedding rings and bassinets, that women believe to be in desperately short supply. When the *New York Times* polled women in 1989 about "the most important problem facing women today," job discrimination was the overwhelming winner; none of the crises the media and popular culture had so assiduously promoted even made the charts. In the 1990 Virginia Slims poll, women were most upset by their lack of money, followed by the refusal of their men to shoulder child care and domestic duties. By contrast, when the women were asked where the quest for a husband or the desire to hold a "less pressured" job or to stay at home ranked on their list of concerns, they placed them at the bottom.

As the last decade ran its course, women's unhappiness with inequality only mounted. In national polls, the ranks of women protesting discriminatory treatment in business, political, and personal life climbed sharply. The proportion of women complaining of unequal employment opportunities jumped more than ten points from the '70s, and the number of women complaining of unequal barriers to job advancement climbed even higher. By the end of the decade, 80 percent to 95 percent of women said they suffered from job discrimination and unequal pay. Sex discrimination charges filed with the Equal Employment Opportunity Commission rose nearly 25 percent in the Reagan years, and charges of general harassment directed at working women climbed 208 percent. In the decade, complaints of sexual harassment jumped 70 percent. At home, a much increased proportion of women complained

to pollsters of male mistreatment, unequal relationships, and male efforts to, in the words of the Virginia Slims poll, "keep women down." The share of women in the Roper surveys who agreed that men were "basically kind, gentle, and thoughtful" fell from almost 70 percent in 1970 to 50 percent by 1990. And outside their homes, women felt more threatened, too: in the 1990 Virginia Slims poll, 72 percent of women said they felt "more afraid and uneasy on the streets today" than they did a few years ago. Lest this be attributed only to a general rise in criminal activity, by contrast only 49 percent of men felt this way.

The truth is that the 1980s saw a powerful counter-assault on women's rights, a backlash, an attempt to retract the handful of small and hard-won victories that the feminist movement did manage to win for women. This counterassault is largely insidious: in a kind of pop-culture version of the Big Lie, it stands the truth boldly on its head and proclaims that the very steps that have elevated women's position have actually led to their downfall.

The backlash is at once sophisticated and banal, deceptively "progressive" and proudly backward. It deploys both the "new" findings of "scientific research" and the dime-store moralism of yesteryear; it turns into media sound bites both the glib pronouncements of pop-psych trend-watchers and the frenzied rhetoric of New Right preachers. The backlash has succeeded in framing virtually the whole issue of women's rights in its own language. Just as Reaganism shifted political discourse far to the right and demonized liberalism, so the backlash convinced the public that women's "liberation" was the true contemporary American scourge—the source of an endless laundry list of personal, social, and economic problems.

But what has made women unhappy in the last decade is not their "equality"—which they don't yet have—but the rising pressure to halt, and even reverse, women's quest for that equality. The "man shortage" and the "infertility epidemic" are not the price of liberation; in fact, they do not even exist. But these chimeras are the chisels of a society-wide backlash. They are part of a relentless whittling-down process—much of it amounting to outright propaganda—that has served to stir women's private anxieties and break their political wills. Identifying feminism as women's enemy only furthers the ends of a backlash against women's equality, simultaneously deflecting attention from the backlash's central role and recruiting women to attack their own cause.

Some social observers may well ask whether the current pressures on women actually constitute a backlash—or just a continuation of American society's long-standing resistance to women's rights. Certainly hostility to female independence has always been with us. But if fear and loathing of feminism is a sort of perpetual viral condition in our culture, it is not always in an acute stage; its symptoms subside and resurface periodically. And it is these episodes of resurgence, such as the one we face now, that can accurately be termed "backlashes" to women's advancement. If we trace these occurrences in American history, we find such flare-ups are hardly random; they have always been triggered by the perception—accurate or not—that women are making great strides. These outbreaks are backlashes because they have always arisen in reaction to women's "progress," caused not simply by a bedrock of misogyny but by the specific efforts of contemporary women to improve their status, efforts that have been interpreted time and again by men—especially men grappling with real threats to their economic and social well-being on other fronts—as spelling their own masculine doom.

The most recent round of backlash first surfaced in the late '70s on the fringes, among the evangelical right. By the early '80s, the fundamentalist ideology had shouldered its way into the White House. By the mid-'80s, as resistance to women's rights acquired political and social acceptability, it passed into the popular culture. And in every case, the timing coincided with signs that women were believed to be on the verge of breakthrough.

Just when women's quest for equal rights seemed closest to achieving its objectives, the backlash struck it down. Just when a "gender gap" at the voting booth surfaced in 1980, and women in politics began to talk of capitalizing on it, the Republican party elevated Ronald Reagan and both political parties began to shunt women's rights off their platforms. Just when support for feminism and the Equal Rights Amendment reached a record high in 1981, the amendment was defeated the following year. Just when women were starting to mobilize against battering and sexual assaults, the federal government stalled funding for battered-women's programs, defeated bills to fund shelters, and shut down its Office of Domestic Violence—only two years after opening it in 1979. Just when record numbers of younger women were supporting feminist goals in the mid-'80s (more of them, in fact, than older women) and a majority of all women were calling themselves feminists, the media declared the advent of a younger "postfeminist generation" that supposedly reviled the women's movement. Just when women racked up their largest percentage ever supporting the right to abortion, the U.S. Supreme Court moved toward reconsidering it.

In other words, the antifeminist backlash has been set off not by women's achievement of full equality but by the increased possibility that they might win it. It is a preemptive strike that stops women long before they reach the finish line. "A backlash may be an indication that women really have had an effect," feminist psychiatrist Dr. Jean Baker Miller has written, "but backlashes occur when advances have been small, before changes are sufficient to help many people. . . . It is almost as if the leaders of backlashes use the fear of change as a threat before major change has occurred." In the last decade, some women did make substantial advances before the backlash hit, but millions of others were left behind, stranded. Some women now enjoy the right to legal abortion—but not the 44 million women, from the indigent to the military work force, who depend on the federal government for their medical care. Some women can now walk into high-paying professional careers—but not the more than 19 million still in the typing pools or behind the department store sales counters. (Contrary to popular myth about the "have-it-all" baby-boom women, the largest percentage of women in this generation remain typists and clerks.)

As the backlash has gathered force, it has cut off the few from the many—and the few women who have advanced seek to prove, as a social survival tactic, that they aren't so interested in advancement after all. Some of them parade their defection from the women's movement, while their working-class peers founder and cling to the splintered remains of the feminist cause. While a very few affluent and celebrity women who are showcased in news articles boast about having "found my niche as Mrs. Andy Mill" and going home to "bake bread," the many working-class women appeal for their economic rights—flocking to unions in record numbers, striking on their own for pay equity and establishing their own fledgling groups for working women's rights. In 1986, while 41 percent of upper-income women were claiming in the Gallup poll that they were not feminists, only 26 percent of low-income women were making the same claim.

*    *    *

*Backlash* happens to be the title of a 1947 Hollywood movie in which a man frames his wife for a murder he's committed. The backlash against women's rights works in much the same way: its rhetoric charges feminists with all the crimes it perpetrates. The backlash line blames the women's movement for the "feminization of poverty"—while the backlash's own instigators in Washington pushed through the budget cuts that helped impoverish millions of women, fought pay equity proposals, and undermined equal opportunity laws. The backlash line claims the women's movement cares nothing for children's rights—while its own representatives in the capital and state legislatures have blocked one bill after another to improve child care, slashed billions of dollars in federal aid for children, and relaxed state licensing standards for day care centers. The backlash line accuses the women's movement of creating a generation of unhappy single and childless women—but its purveyors in the media are the ones guilty of making single and childless women feel like circus freaks.

To blame feminism for women's "lesser life" is to miss entirely the point of feminism, which is to win women a wider range of experience. Feminism remains a pretty simple concept, despite repeated—and enormously effective—efforts to dress it up in greasepaint and turn its proponents into gargoyles. As Rebecca West wrote sardonically in 1913, "I my-

self have never been able to find out precisely what feminism is: I only know that people call me a feminist whenever I express sentiments that differentiate me from a doormat."

The meaning of the word "feminist" has not really changed since it first appeared in a book review in the *Athenaeum* of April 27, 1895, describing a woman who "has in her the capacity of fighting her way back to independence." It is the basic proposition that, as Nora put it in Ibsen's *A Doll's House* a century ago, "Before everything else I'm a human being." It is the simply worded sign hoisted by a little girl in the 1970 Women's Strike for Equality: I AM NOT A BARBIE DOLL. Feminism asks the world to recognize at long last that women aren't decorative ornaments, worthy vessels, members of a "special-interest group." They are half (in fact, now more than half) of the national population, and just as deserving of rights and opportunities, just as capable of participating in the world's events, as the other half. Feminism's agenda is basic: It asks that women not be forced to "choose" between public justice and private happiness. It asks that women be free to define themselves—instead of having their identity defined for them, time and again, by their culture and their men.

The fact that these are still such incendiary notions should tell us that American women have a way to go before they enter the promised land of equality.

*NOTES*

509    Women's fight for . . . : Nancy Gibbs, "The Dreams of Youth," *Time*, Special Issue: "Women: The Road Ahead," Fall 1990, p. 12.

509    Women have "so much" . . . : Eleanor Smeal, *Why and How Women Will Elect the Next President* (New York: Harper & Row, 1984), p. 56.

509    The *New York Times* reports . . . : Georgia Dullea, "Women Reconsider Childbearing Over 30," *New York Times*, Feb. 25, 1982, p. C1.

509    *Newsweek* says: Unwed women . . . : Eloise Salholz, "The Marriage Crunch," *Newsweek*, June 2, 1986, p. 55.

509    The health advice manuals . . . : See, for example, Dr. Herbert J. Freudenberger and Gail North, *Women's Burnout* (New York: Viking Penguin, 1985); Marjorie Hansen Shaevitz, *The Superwoman Syndrome* (New York: Warner Books, 1984); Harriet Braiker, *The Type E Woman* (New York: Dodd, Mead, 1986); Donald Morse and M. Lawrence Furst, *Women Under Stress* (New York: Van Nostrand Reinhold Co., 1982); Geor-

gia Witkin-Lanoil, *The Female Stress Syndrome* (New York: Newmarket Press, 1984).

509 The psychology books . . . : Dr. Stephen and Susan Price, *No More Lonely Nights: Overcoming the Hidden Fears That Keep You from Getting Married* (New York: G. P. Putnam's Sons, 1988), p. 19.

509 Even founding feminist Betty Friedan . . . : Betty Friedan, *The Second Stage* (New York: Summit Books, 1981), p. 9.

509 "In dispensing its spoils . . .": Mona Charen, "The Feminist Mistake," *National Review,* March 23, 1984, p. 24.

509 "Our generation was the human sacrifice . . .": Claudia Wallis, "Women Face the '90s," *Time,* Dec. 4, 1989, p. 82.

509 In *Newsweek,* writer . . . : Kay Ebeling, "The Failure of Feminism," *Newsweek,* Nov. 19, 1990, p. 9.

510 Even the beauty magazines . . . : Marilyn Webb, "His Fault Divorce," *Harper's Bazaar,* Aug. 1988, p. 156.

510 In the last decade . . . : Mary Anne Dolan, "When Feminism Failed," *The New York Times Magazine,* June 26, 1988, p. 21; Erica Jong, "The Awful Truth About Women's Liberation," *Vanity Fair,* April 1986, p. 92.

510 The "Today" show . . . : Jane Birnbaum, "The Dark Side of Women's Liberation," *Los Angeles Herald Examiner,* May 24, 1986.

510 A guest columnist . . . : Robert J. Hooper, "Slasher Movies Owe Success to Abortion" (originally printed in the *Baltimore Sun*), *Minneapolis Star Tribune,* Feb. 1, 1990, p. 17A.

510 In popular novels . . . : Gail Parent, *A Sign of the Eighties* (New York: G. P. Putnam's Sons, 1987); Stephen King, *Misery* (New York: Viking, 1987).

510 We "blew it by . . .": Freda Bright, *Singular Women* (New York: Bantam Books, 1988), p. 12.

510 Even Erica Jong's . . . : Erica Jong, *Any Woman's Blues* (New York: Harper & Row, 1989) pp. 2–3. A new generation of young "post-feminist" female writers, such as Mary Gaitskill and Susan Minot, also produced a bumper crop of grim-faced unwed heroines. These passive and masochistic "girls" wandered the city zombie-like; they came alive and took action only in seeking out male abuse. For a good analysis of this genre, see James Wolcott, "The Good-Bad Girls," *Vanity Fair,* Dec. 1988, p. 43.

510 "Feminism, having promised her . . .": Dr. Toni Grant, *Being a Woman: Fulfilling Your Femininity and Finding Love* (New York: Random House, 1988), p. 25.

510 The authors of . . . : Dr. Connell Cowan and Dr. Melvyn Kinder, *Smart Women/Foolish Choices* (New York: New American Library, 1985) p. 16.

510 In *The Cost of Loving* . . . : Megan Marshall, *The Cost of Loving: Women and the New Fear of Intimacy* (New York: G. P. Putnam's Sons, 1984), p. 218.

510 Other diaries of . . . : Hilary Cosell, *Woman on a Seesaw: The Ups and Downs of Making It* (New York: G. P. Putnam's Sons, 1985); Deborah Fallows, *A Mother's Work* (Boston: Houghton Mifflin, 1985); Carol Orsborn, *Enough is Enough* (New York: Pocket Books, 1986); Susan Bakos, *This Wasn't Supposed to Happen* (New York: Continuum, 1985). Even when the women aren't really renouncing their liberation, their publishers pro-

mote the texts as if they were. Mary Kay Blakely's *Wake Me When It's Over* (New York: Random House, 1989), an account of the author's diabetes-induced coma, is billed on the dust jacket as "a chilling memoir in which a working supermom exceeds her limit and discovers the thin line between sanity and lunacy and between life and death."

510 If American women are so equal . . . : "Money, Income and Poverty Status in the U.S.," 1989, Current Population Reports, U.S. Bureau of the Census, Department of Commerce, Series P-60, #168.

510 Why are nearly 75 percent . . . : Margaret W. Newton, "Women and Pension Coverage," *The American Woman 1988–89: A Status Report,* ed. by Sara E. Rix (New York: W. W. Norton & Co., 1989) p. 268.

510 Why are they still . . . : Cushing N. Dolbeare and Anne J. Stone, "Women and Affordable Housing," *The American Woman 1990–91: A Status Report,* ed. by Sara E. Rix (W. W. Norton & Co., 1990) p. 106; Newton, "Pension Coverage," p. 268; "1990 Profile," 9 to 5/National Association of Working Women; Salaried and Professional Women's Commission Report, 1989, p. 2.

511 Why does the average . . . : "Briefing Paper on the Wage Gap," National Committee on Pay Equity, p. 3; "Average Earnings of Year-Round, Full-Time Workers by Sex and Educational Attainment," 1987, U.S. Bureau of the Census, February 1989, cited in *The American Woman 1990–91,* p. 392.

511 If women have "made it," then . . . : Susanna Downie, "Decade of Achievement, 1977–1987," The National Women's Conference Center, May 1988, p. 35; statistics from 9 to 5/National Association of Working Women.

511 And, conversely . . . : Statistics from Women's Research & Education Institute, U.S. Bureau of the Census, U.S. Bureau of Labor Statistics, Catalyst, Center for the American Woman and Politics. See also *The American Woman 1990–91,* p. 359; Deborah L. Rhode, "Perspectives on Professional Women," *Stanford Law Review,* 40, no. 5 (May 1988): 1178–79; Anne Jardim and Margaret Hennig, "The Last Barrier," *Working Woman,* Nov. 1990, p. 130; Jaclyn Fierman, "Why Women Still Don't Hit the Top," *Fortune,* July 30, 1990, p. 40.

511 Unlike virtually . . . : "1990 Profile," 9 to 5/National Association of Working Women; Bureau of Labor Statistics, 1987 survey of nation's employers. See also "Who Gives and Who Gets," *American Demographics,* May 1988, p. 16; "Children and Families: Public Policies and Outcomes, A Fact Sheet of International Comparisons," U.S. House of Representatives, Select Committee on Children, Youth and Families.

511 In a 1990 national poll . . . : "Women in Corporate Management," national poll of Fortune 1000 companies by Catalyst, 1990.

511 Why do women who want . . . : Data from Alan Guttmacher Institute.

511 Nearly 70 percent . . . : E. J. Dionne, Jr., "Struggle for Work and Family Fueling Women's Movement," *New York Times,* Aug. 22, 1989, p. A1. The Yankelovich Clancy Shulman poll (Oct. 23–25, 1989, for *Time/*

CNN) and the 1990 Virginia Slims Opinion Poll (The Roper Organization Inc., 1990) found similarly large majorities of women who said that they needed a strong women's movement to keep pushing for change.

511 Most women in the . . . : The 1990 Virginia Slims Opinion Poll, The Roper Organization, Inc., pp. 8, 18.

511 In poll after . . . : The Louis Harris poll, 1984, found 64 percent of women wanted the Equal Rights Amendment and 65 percent favored affirmative action. Similar results emerged from the national *Woman's Day* poll (Feb. 17, 1984) by *Woman's Day* and Wellesley College Center for Research on Women, which emphasized middle-American conventional women (80 percent were mothers and 30 percent were full-time homemakers). The *Woman's Day* poll found a majority of women, from all economic classes, seeking a wide range of women's rights. For instance, 68 percent of the women said they wanted the ERA, 79 percent supported a woman's right to choose an abortion, and 61 percent favored a federally subsidized national childcare program. Mark Clements Research Inc.'s Annual Study of Women's Attitudes found in 1987 that 87 percent of women wanted a federal law guaranteeing maternity leave and about 94 percent said that more child care should be available. (In addition, 86 percent wanted a federal law enforcing the payment of child support.) The Louis Harris Poll found 80 percent of women calling for the creation of more day-care centers. See *The Eleanor Smeal Report*, June 28, 1984, p. 3; Warren T. Brookes, "Day Care: Is It a Real Crisis or a War Over Political Turf?" *San Francisco Chronicle*, April 27, 1988, p. 6; Louis Harris, *Inside America* (New York: Vintage Books, 1987), p. 96.

511 To the contrary . . . : In the 1989 *Time*/CNN poll, 94 percent of women polled said the movement made them more independent; 82 percent said it is still improving women's lives. Only 8 percent said it may have made their lives worse. A 1986 *Newsweek* Gallup poll found that 56 percent of women identified themselves as "feminists," and only 4 percent described themselves as "anti-feminists."

512 In public opinion . . . : In the Annual Study of Women's Attitudes (1988, Mark Clements Research), when women were asked, "What makes you angry?" they picked three items as their top concerns: poverty, crime, and their own inequality. In the 1989 *New York Times* Poll, when women were asked what was the most important problem facing women today, job inequality ranked first.

512 The Roper Organization's . . . : Bickley Townsend and Kathleen O'Neil, "American Women Get Mad," *American Demographics*, Aug. 1990, p. 26.

512 When the *New York Times* . . . : Dionne, "Struggle for Work and Family," p. A14.

512 In the 1990 . . . : 1990 Virginia Slims Opinion Poll, pp. 29–30, 32.

512 In national polls . . . : Data from Roper Organization and Louis Harris polls. The 1990 Roper survey found most women reporting that things had "gotten worse" in the home and that men were more eager "to keep women down": See 1990 Virginia Slims Opinion Poll, pp. 18, 21, 54. The Gallup Organization polls charted

an 8 percent increase in job discrimination complaints from women between 1975 and 1982. Mark Clements Research's 1987 Women's Views Survey (commissioned by *Glamour* magazine) found that on the matter of women's inequality, "more women feel there is a problem today." Reports of wage discrimination, the survey noted, had jumped from 76 percent in 1982 to 85 percent in 1988. (See "How Women's Minds Have Changed in the Last Five Years," *Glamour*, Jan. 1987, p. 168.) The annual surveys by Mark Clements Research also find huge and increasing majorities of women complaining of unequal treatment in hiring, advancement, and opportunities in both corporate and political life. (In 1987, only 30 percent of women believed they got equal treatment with men when being considered for financial credit.) A *Time* 1989 poll found 94 percent of women complaining of unequal pay, 82 percent of job discrimination.

512 Sex discrimination charges . . . : Statistics from U.S. Equal Employment Opportunity Commission, "National Database: Charge Receipt Listing," 1982–88; "Sexual Harassment," 1981–89.

512 At home, a much increased . . . : Townsend and O'Neil, "American Women Get Mad," p. 28.

512 And outside their . . . : 1990 Virginia Slims Opinion Poll, p. 38.

513 Just when women . . . : "Inequality of Sacrifice," p. 23.

513 Just when record numbers . . . : A 1986 Gallup poll conducted for *Newsweek* found a majority of women described themselves as feminists and only 4 percent said they were "antifeminists." While large majorities of women throughout the '80s kept on favoring the full feminist agenda (from the ERA to legal abortion), the proportion of women who were willing publicly to call themselves feminists dropped off suddenly in the late '80s, after the mass media declared feminism the "F-word." By 1989, only one in three women were calling themselves feminists in the polls. Nonetheless, the pattern of younger women espousing the most pro-feminist sentiments continued throughout the decade. In the 1989 Yankelovich poll for *Time*/CNN, for example, 76 percent of women in their teens and 71 percent of women in their twenties said they believed feminists spoke for the average American woman, compared with 59 percent of women in their thirties. Asked the same question about the National Organization for Women, the gap appeared again: 83 percent of women in their teens and 72 percent of women in their twenties said NOW was in touch with the average woman, compared with 65 percent of women in their thirties. See Downie, "Decade of Achievement," p. 1; 1986 Gallup/*Newsweek* poll; 1989 Yankelovich/*Time*/CNN poll.

513 "A backlash may be an indication that . . .": Dr. Jean Baker Miller, *Toward a New Psychology of Women* (Boston: Beacon Press, 1976), pp. xv–xvi.

513 Some women now . . . : Kate Michelman, "20 Years Defending Choice, 1969–1988," National Abortion Rights Action League, p. 4.

513 Some women can now . . . : "Employment and Earnings," Current Population Survey, Table 22, Bureau of Labor Statistics, U.S. Department of Labor.

513 (Contrary to popular myth . . . ): Cheryl Russell, *100 Predictions for the Baby Boom* (New York: Plenum Press, 1987), p. 64.

514 While a very few . . . : "A New Kind of Love Match," *Newsweek,* Sept. 4, 1989, p. 73; Barbara Hetzer, "Superwoman Goes Home," *Fortune,* Aug. 18, 1986, p. 20; "Facts on Working Women," Aug. 1989, Women's Bureau, U.S. Department of Labor, no. 89—2; and data from the Coalition of Labor Union Women and Amalgamated Clothing and Textile Workers Union. The surge of women joining unions in the late '80s was so great that it single-handedly halted the ten-year decline in union membership. Black women joined unions at the greatest rate. Women led strikes around the country, from the Yale University administrative staffs to the Daughters of Mother Jones in Virginia (who were instrumental in the Pittston coal labor battle) to the Delta Pride catfish plant processors in Mississippi (where women organized the largest strike by black workers ever in the state, lodging a protest against a plant that paid its mostly female employees poverty wages, punished them if they skinned less than 24,000 fish a day, and limited them to six timed bathroom breaks a week). See Tony Freemantle, "Weary Strikers Hold Out in Battle of Pay Principle," *Houston Chronicle,* Dec. 2, 1990, p. 1A; Peter T. Kilborn, "Labor Fight on a Catfish 'Plantation,'" *The News and Observer,* Dec. 16, 1990, p. J2.

514 In 1986, while . . . : 1986 Gallup Poll; Barbara Ehrenreich, "The Next Wave," *Ms.,* July/August 1987, p. 166; Sarah Harder, "Flourishing in the Mainstream: The U.S. Women's Movement Today," *The American Woman 1990–91,* p. 281. Also see 1989 Yankelovich Poll: 71 percent of black women said feminists have been helpful to women, compared with 61 percent of white women. A 1987 poll by the National Women's Conference Commission found that 65 percent of black women called themselves feminists, compared with 56 percent of white women.

514 The backlash line claims . . . : Data from Children's Defense Fund. See also Ellen Wojahm, "Who's Minding the Kids?" *Savvy,* Oct. 1987, p. 16; "Child Care: The Time is Now," Children's Defense Fund, 1987, pp. 8–10.

514 "I myself . . .": Rebecca West, *The Clarion,* Nov. 14, 1913, cited in Cheris Kramarae and Paula A. Treichler, *A Feminist Dictionary* (London: Pandora Press, 1985) p. 160.

514 The meaning of the word "feminist" . . . : *The Feminist Papers: From Adams to de Beauvoir,* ed. by Alice S. Rossi (New York: Bantam Books, 1973), p. xiii. For discussion of historical origins of term feminism, see Karen Offen, "Defining Feminism: A Comparative Historical Approach," in *Signs: Journal of Women in Culture and Society,* 1988, 14, no. 1, pp. 119–57.

514 I AM NOT A BARBIE DOLL . . . : Carol Hymowitz and Michaele Weissman, *A History of Women in America* (New York: Bantam Books, 1978), p. 341.          [1991]

## ⚹ 139

# *Bringing the Global Home*

CHARLOTTE BUNCH

One of the most exciting world developments today is the emergence of feminism all over the globe. Women of almost every culture, color, and class are claiming feminism for themselves. Indigenous movements are developing that address the specific regional concerns of women's lives and that expand the definition of what feminism means and can do in the future.

This growth of feminism provides both the challenge and the opportunity for a truly global women's movement to emerge in the 1980s. But a global movement involves more than just the separate development of feminism in each region, as exciting and important as that is. Global feminism also requires that we learn from each other and develop a global perspective within each of our movements. It means expansion of our understandings of feminism and changes in our work, as we respond to the ideas and challenges of women with different perspectives. It means discovering what other perspectives and movements mean to our own local setting. Any struggle for change in the late-twentieth century must have a global consciousness since the world operates and controls our lives internationally already. The strength of feminism has been and still is in its decentralized grass-roots nature, but for that strength to be most effective, we must base our local and national actions on a world view that incorporates the global context of our lives. This is the challenge of bringing the global home.

A global feminist perspective on patriarchy worldwide also illustrates how issues are interconnected, not separate isolated phenomena competing for our attention. This involves connections among each aspect of women's oppression and of that subordination to the socioeconomic conditions of society, as well as between local problems and global realities.

To develop global feminism today is not a luxury—it requires going to the heart of the problems in our world and looking at nothing less than the threats to the very survival of the planet. We are standing on a precipice facing such possibilities as nuclear destruction, worldwide famine and depletion of our natural resources, industrial contamination, and death in many forms. These are the fruits of a world ruled by the patriarchal mode—of what I call the "dynamic of domination," in which profits and property have priority over people, and where fear and hatred of differences have prevented a celebration of and learning from our diversity.

Feminists are part of a world struggle that is taking place today over the direction that the future will take. Crucial choices are being made about the very possibilities for life in the twenty-first century—from macro-level decisions about control over resources and weapons to micro-level decisions about control over individual reproduction and sexuality. At this juncture in history, feminism is perhaps the most important force for change that can begin to reverse the dynamic of patriarchal domination by challenging and transforming the way in which humans look at ourselves in relation to each other and to the world.

## A GLOBAL VIEW OF FEMINISM

The excitement and urgency of issues of global feminism were brought home to me at a Workshop on Feminist Ideology and Structures sponsored by the Asian and Pacific Centre for Women and Development in Bangkok in 1979. Women from each region presented what they were doing in relation to the themes of the UN Decade for Women. In doing this, we realized the importance of the international male-dominated media in influencing what we knew and thought about each other before we came to Bangkok.

We saw how the media has made the women's movement and feminism appear trivial, silly, selfish, naïve, and/or crazy in the industrialized countries while practically denying its existence in the Third World. Western feminists have been portrayed as concerned only with burning bras, having sex, hating men, and/or getting to be head of General Motors. Such stereotypes ignore the work of most feminists and distort even the few activities the media do

report. So, for example, basic political points that women have tried to communicate—about what it means to love ourselves in a woman-hating society—get twisted into a focus on "hating" men. Or those demonstrations that did discard high-heeled shoes, makeup, or bras, as symbolic of male control over women's self-definition and mobility, have been stripped of their political content.

Thus, women who feel that their priorities are survival issues of food or housing are led to think that Western feminists are not concerned with these matters. Similarly, media attempts to portray all feminists as a privileged elite within each country seek to isolate us from other women. The real strength of feminism can be seen best in the fact that more and more women come to embrace it in spite of the overwhelming effort that has gone into distorting it and trying to keep women away.

By acknowledging the power of the media's distortion of feminism at the Bangkok workshop, we were able to see the importance of defining it clearly for ourselves. Our definition brought together the right of every woman to equity, dignity, and freedom of choice through the power to control her own life and the removal of all forms of inequalities and oppression in society. We saw feminism as a world view that has an impact on all aspects of life, and affirmed the broad context of the assertion that the "personal is political." This is to say that the individual aspects of oppression and change are not separate from the need for political and institutional change.

Through our discussion, we were able to agree on the use of this concept of feminism to describe women's struggles. While some had reservations about using the word "feminism," we chose not to allow media or government distortions to scare us away from it. As one Asian pointed out, if we shied away from the term, we would simply be attacked or ridiculed for other actions or words, since those who opposed us were against what we sought for women and the world and not really concerned with our language.

In Copenhagen at the 1980 NGO Forum, the conference newspaper came out with a quote-of-the-day from a Western feminist that read: "To talk feminism to a woman who has no water, no home, and no food is to talk nonsense." Many of us felt that the quote posed a crucial challenge to feminists. We passed out a leaflet, "What Is Feminism?," describing it as a perspective on the world that would address such issues, and we invited women to a special session on the topic. Over three hundred women from diverse regions gathered to debate what feminism really means to us and how that has been distorted by the media and even within our own movements.

The second challenge we saw in the quote was that if it were true and feminists did not speak to such issues, then we would indeed be irrelevant to many women. We therefore discussed the importance of a feminist approach to development—one that both addresses how to make home, food, and water available to all and extends beyond equating "development" with industrialization. Terms like "developing nations" are suspect and patronizing. While we need to look at the real material needs of all people from a feminist perspective, we can hardly call any countries "developed." For this reason, while I find all labels that generalize about diverse parts of the world problematic, I use "Western" or "industrialized" and "Third World," rather than "developing" and "developed."

Recently at a meeting in New York, I saw another example of confusion about the meaning of feminism. Two women who had just engaged in civil disobedience against nuclear weapons were discussing feminism as the motivating force behind their actions, when a man jumped up impatiently objecting, "But I thought this meeting was about disarmament, not feminism." It was the equivalent of "to talk feminism in the face of nuclear destruction is to talk nonsense." Such attitudes portray feminism as a luxury of secondary concern and thus both dismiss female experience as unimportant and limit our politics. They fundamentally misconstrue feminism as about "women's issues" rather than as a political perspective on life.

Seeing feminism as a transformational view is crucial to a global perspective. But to adopt a global outlook does not mean, as some feminists fear and male politicos often demand, that we abandon

working on the "women's issues" that we fought to put on the political agenda. Nor does it imply setting aside our analysis of sexual politics. Rather it requires that we take what we have learned about sexual politics and use feminist theory to expose the connections between the "women's issues" and other world questions. In this way, we demonstrate our point that all issues are women's issues and need feminist analysis. For example, we must show how a society that tacitly sanctions male violence against women and children, whether incest and battery at home, rape on the streets, or sexual harassment on the job, is bound to produce people who are militaristic and believe in their right to dominate others on the basis of other differences such as skin color or nationality. Or we can point out how the heterosexist assumption that every "good" woman wants to and eventually will be supported by a man fuels the economic policies that have produced the feminization of poverty worldwide. This refusal to accept a woman who lives without a man as fully human thus allows policy makers to propose such ideas as keeping welfare payments or even job opportunities for single mothers limited since they "contribute to the destruction of the family."

The examples are endless. The task is not one of changing our issues but of expanding the frameworks from which we understand our work. It means taking what we have learned in working on "women's issues" and relating that to other areas, demanding that these not be seen as competing but as enabling us to bring about more profound change. To use the illustration above, to seek to end militarism without also ending the dynamic of domination embedded in male violence at home would be futile. And so, too, the reverse: we will never fully end male violence against individual women unless we also stop celebrating the organized violence of war as manly and appropriate behavior.

## MAKING CONNECTIONS

The interconnectedness of the economic and sexual exploitation of women with militarism and racism is well illustrated in the area of forced prostitution and female sexual slavery. It is impossible to work on one aspect of this issue without confronting the whole socioeconomic context of women's lives. For example, females in India who are forced into prostitution are often either sold by poverty-stricken families for whom a girl child is considered a liability, or they have sought to escape arranged marriages they find intolerable. In the United States, many girls led into forced prostitution are teenage runaways who were victims of sexual or physical abuse at home, and for whom there are no jobs, services, or safe places to live.

In parts of Southeast Asia, many women face the limited economic options of rural poverty; joining assembly lines that pay poorly, destroy eyesight, and often discard workers over thirty; or of entering the "entertainment industry." In Thailand and the Philippines, national economies dependent on prostitution resulted from U.S. military brothels during the Vietnam War. When that demand decreased, prostitution was channeled into sex tourism—the organized multimillion-dollar transnational business of systematically selling women's bodies as part of packaged tours, which feeds numerous middlemen and brings foreign capital into the country. In all these situations, the patriarchal beliefs that men have the right to women's bodies, and that "other" races or "lower" classes are subhuman, underlie the abuse women endure.

Feminists organizing against these practices must link their various aspects. Thus, for example, women have simultaneously protested against sex tourism and militarism, created refuges for individual victims who escape, and sought to help women develop skills in order to gain more control over their lives. Japanese businesses pioneered the development of sex tourism. Feminists in Japan pioneered the opposition to this traffic. They work with Southeast Asian women to expose and shame the Japanese government and the businesses involved in an effort to cut down on the trade from their end.

On the international level, it is clear that female sexual slavery, forced prostitution, and violence against women operate across national boundaries and are political and human rights abuses of great magnitude. Yet, the male-defined human rights community by-and-large refuses to see any but the most narrowly defined cases of slavery or "political"

torture as their domain. We must ask what is it when a woman faces death at the hands of her family to save its honor because she was raped? What is it when two young lesbians commit suicide together rather than be forced into unwanted marriages? What is it when a woman trafficked out of her country does not try to escape because she knows she will be returned by the police and beaten or deported? An understanding of sexual politics reveals all these and many more situations to be political human-rights violations deserving asylum, refugee status, and the help that other political victims are granted. As limited as human rights are in our world, we must demand at least that basic recognition for such women, while we seek to expand concern for human rights generally.

In these areas as well as others, feminists are creating new interpretations and approaches—to human rights, to development, to community and family, to conflict resolution, and so on. From local to global interaction, we must create alternative visions of how we can live in the world based on women's experiences and needs in the here-and-now.

## *LEARNING FROM DIVERSITY*

In sharing experiences and visions across national and cultural lines, feminists are inspired by what others are doing. But we are also confronted with the real differences among us. On the one hand, our diversity is our strength. It makes it possible for us to imagine more possibilities and to draw upon a wider range of women's experiences. On the other hand, differences can also divide us if we do not take seriously the variations on female oppression that women suffer according to race, class, ethnicity, religion, sexual preference, age, nationality, physical disability, and so on. These are not simply added onto the oppression of women by sex, but shape the forms by which we experience that subordination. Thus, we cannot simply add up the types of oppression that a woman suffers one-by-one as independent factors but must look at how they are interrelated.

If we take this approach, we should be more capable of breaking down the ways in which difference itself separates people. Patriarchal society is constructed on a model of domination by which each group is assigned a place in the hierarchy according to various differences, and then allocated power or privileges based on that position. In this way, difference becomes threatening because it involves winning or losing one's position/privileges. If we eliminated the assignment of power and privilege according to difference, we could perhaps begin to enjoy real choices of style and variations of culture as offering more creative possibilities in life.

The world has been torn apart by various male divisions and conflicts for thousands of years and we should not assume that women can overcome and solve in a short time what patriarchy has so intricately conceived. The oppressions, resentments, fears, and patterns of behavior that have developed due to racism, classism, nationalism, and sexism, are very deep. We cannot just wish them away with our desire for women to transcend differences. Above all, we do not overcome differences by denying them or downplaying their effects on us—especially when the one denying is in the position of privilege.

A white woman can only legitimately talk about overcoming differences of race if she struggles to understand racism both as it affects her personally and as she affects it politically. A heterosexual can get beyond the divisions of sexual preference only by learning about both the oppression of lesbians and by acknowledging the insights that come from that orientation. A U.S. American must understand the effects of colonialism before she can hope for unity with women beyond national boundaries. Too often the call to transcend differences has been a call to ignore them at the expense of the oppressed. This cannot be the route of global feminism. We can only hope to chart a path beyond male divisions by walking through them and taking seriously their detrimental effects on us as women. This examination of and effort to eliminate other aspects of oppression does not come before or after working on sexism—it is simultaneous.

A crucial part of this process is understanding that reality does not look the same from different people's perspectives. It is not surprising that one way that feminists have come to understand about differences has been through the love of a person from another culture or race. It takes persistence

and motivation—which love often engenders—to get beyond one's ethnocentric assumptions and really learn about other perspectives. In this process and while seeking to eliminate oppression, we also discover new possibilities and insights that come from the experience and survival of other peoples.

In considering what diversity means for a global movement, one of the most difficult areas for feminists is culture. In general, we affirm cultural diversity and the variety it brings to our lives. Yet, almost all existing cultures today are male-dominated. We know the horrors male powers have wrought over the centuries in imposing one cultural standard over another. Popular opposition to such imposition has often included affirmation of traditional cultures. Certainly none of our cultures can claim to have the answers to women's liberation since we are oppressed in all of them.

We must face the fact that in some instances male powers are justifying the continuation or advocating the adoption of practices oppressive to women by labeling them "cultural" and/or "resistance to Western influence." Feminists must refuse to accept *any* forms of domination of women—whether in the name of tradition or in the name of modernization. This is just the same as refusing to accept racial discrimination in the name of "culture," whether in the South of the USA or in South Africa. Feminists are seeking new models for society that allow for diversity while not accepting the domination of any group. For this, women in each culture must sort out what is best from their own culture and what is oppressive. Through our contact with each other, we can then challenge ethnocentric biases and move beyond the unconscious cultural assumptions inherent in our thinking.

In taking into account and challenging the various forms of domination in the world, we do not necessarily accept existing male theories about or solutions to them. We must always have a woman-identified approach—that is, one of seeking to identify with women's situations rather than accepting male definitions of reality. Such a process enables us to distinguish what is useful from male theories and to see where feminist approaches are being or need to be applied to issues such as race, class, and culture. Further, in a world so saturated with woman-hating, it is through woman-identification, which involves profoundly learning to love women and to listen for women's authentic perspectives, that we can make breakthroughs in these areas.

We confront a similar dilemma when examining nationalism. From a feminist perspective, I see nationalism as the ultimate expression of the patriarchal dynamic of domination—where groups battle for control over geographic territory, and justify violence and aggression in the name of national security. Therefore I prefer the term "global" to "international" because I see feminism as a movement among peoples beyond national boundaries and not among nation-states. Yet, nationalism has also symbolized the struggle of oppressed peoples against the control of other nations. And many attempts to go beyond nationalism have simply been supranational empire-building, such as the idea of turning Africans into "Frenchmen." Further, in the context of increasing global control over us all by transnational corporations, many see nationalism as a form of resistance. In seeking to be global, feminists must therefore find ways to transcend patriarchal nationalism without demanding sameness, and while still preserving means of identity and culture that are not based on domination.

### THINK GLOBALLY, ACT LOCALLY

A major obstacle that feminists face in seeking to be global is our lack of control over the resources necessary for maintaining greater contact worldwide. It takes time and money as well as energy and commitment to overcome the problems of distance, language, and culture. Feminists have little control over existing institutions with global networks, such as the media, churches, universities, and the state, but sometimes we must utilize such networks even as we try to set up our own.

Since feminists have limited resources for global travel and communication, it is vital that we learn how to be global in consciousness while taking action locally. For this, we must resist the tendency to separate "international" work into a specialized category of political activity that is often viewed as inaccessible to most women. This tendency reflects a hierarchical mode in which the "world level" is

viewed as above the "local level." For those whose work focuses primarily on the global aspects of issues, the challenge is not to lose touch with the local arena on which any effective movement is based. For those whose work is focused locally, the challenge is to develop a global perspective that informs local work. For all of us, the central question is to understand how the issues of women all over the world are interrelated and to discern what that means specifically in each setting.

Global interaction is not something that we choose to do or not to do. It is something in which we are already participating. All we choose is whether to be aware of it or not, whether to try to understand it and how that affects our actions. For citizens of the U.S., we begin our global consciousness with awareness of the impact that our country's policies have on other people's daily lives. I learned in the antiwar movement that often the most useful thing that we can do for people elsewhere is to make changes in the U.S. and in how it exercises power in the world.

There are many well-known issues such as military aggression, foreign aid and trade policies, or the possibility of worldwide destruction through nuclear weapons or chemical contamination that we see as global. But there are numerous less obvious illustrations of global interrelatedness, from the present world economy where women are manipulated as an international cheap labor pool to the traffic in women's bodies for forced prostitution. Therefore, any attempt we make to deal with the needs of women in the U.S., such as employment, must examine the global context of the problem. In this instance, that means understanding how multinational corporations move their plants from country to country or state to state, exploiting female poverty and discouraging unionization by threatening to move again. We must use global strategies, such as that proposed by one group on the Texas-Mexico border advocating an international bill of rights for women workers as a way to organize together for basic standards for all. In a world where global forces affect us daily, it is neither possible nor conscionable to achieve a feminist utopia in one country alone. . . .

## A MATTER OF PERSPECTIVE

Beyond techniques and information, the primary task remains one of attitude, approach, and perspective. The point is not that we necessarily change the focus of our work but that we make connections that help to bring its global aspects to consciousness—in our programs, our slogans, our publications, and our conversations with other women. It is when we try to make a hierarchy of issues, keeping them separate and denying the importance of some in order to address others, that we are all defeated.

To use a previous example, if I cannot develop an analysis and discuss openly the ways in which heterosexism supports the international feminization of poverty, without having some women's homophobia prevent them from utilizing this insight, or without having some lesbians fear that I have abandoned "their issue" by working more on global poverty, then work in both areas is diminished. I believe that the path to effective global feminist theory and action is not through denial of any issue or analysis but through listening, questioning, struggling, and seeking to make connections among them.

To work locally with a global perspective does require stretching feminism, not to abandon its insights but to shed its cultural biases, and thus to expand its capacity to reach all people. In this process, we risk what seems certain at home by taking it into the world and having it change through interaction with other realities and perceptions. It can be frightening. But if we have confidence in ourselves and in the feminist process, it can also be exciting. It can mean the growth of a more effective feminism with a greater ability to address the world and to bring change. If we fail to take these risks and ignore the global dimensions of our lives, we lose possibilities for individual growth and we doom feminism to a less effective role in the world struggle over the direction of the twenty-first century.

My visions of global feminism are grand, perhaps even grandiose. But the state of the world today demands that women become less modest and dream/plan/act/risk on a larger scale. At the same time, the realization of global visions can only be achieved through the everyday lives and action of women locally. It depends on women deciding to shape their own destiny, claiming their right to the world, and exercising their responsibility to make it in some way, large or small, a better place for all. As more women do this with a growing world perspective and sense of connection to others, we can say that feminism is meeting the challenge of bringing the global home.                [1987]

## 140

# Beijing '95: Moving Women's Human Rights from Margin to Center

CHARLOTTE BUNCH AND
SUSANA FRIED

The Fourth World Conference on Women in Beijing established clearly that women are a global force for the twenty-first century and that women's human rights are central to women's leadership for the future. Women's rights as human rights permeated debates and delegates' speeches at the official UN intergovernmental conference as well as at the parallel Non-Governmental Organization (NGO) Forum held some thirty miles away in Huairou, where it was a palpable presence in many sessions. The combined effect of these activities was a groundswell of support for making the entire Platform an affirmation of the human rights of women, including women's rights to education, health, and freedom from violence, as well as to the exercise of citizenship in all its manifestations. Previous UN women's conferences were seen as primarily about women and development or even women's rights, but not about the concept of human rights as it applies to women.

This report assesses the Beijing Declaration and Platform for Action, which came out of the governmental conference, focusing on its implications for women's human rights advocacy. The conference was mandated to produce a consensus "platform" that would implement the goals set forth in the "Forward-Looking Strategies" from the 1985 Nairobi World Conference on Women and advance the 1995 conference theme of "Action for Equality, Development, and Peace." More than four thousand NGO delegates accredited to the governmental conference worked to influence the document's articulation of the conditions faced by women worldwide as well as the content of the strategies proposed.

In the context of such international UN meetings, controversies over language are debates about the direction of governmental policy. If the agreements that result from these meetings are to be meaningful beyond the moment, attention must be paid to the details of the compromises, as well as to the subtextual disputes they represent. These documents address several aspects of international debates over gender roles, including (1) ways in which feminist language and concepts are beginning to inform public policy, (2) instances in which these concepts are deployed to undermine feminist goals, (3) cases in which the links between feminist theoretical analyses and political practices are weak, and (4) spaces where the political attention of women's movements must be focused in a more concerted fashion.

An important caveat to be made about documents that come out of UN conferences is that they are consensus based, which means that often the lowest common denominator prevails, and, therefore, weak language may emerge from the most contentious and passionate debates. Nevertheless, getting reluctant governments even to agree to weak text when it represents an advancement over their prior positions can be important. Further, these documents and programs of action do not have the status of international law. Instead, they carry political and moral weight as policy guidelines for the UN, governments, and other international organizations. To use these documents effectively, they must be approached as statements of best intentions and commitments to which organized groups can seek to hold governments and the UN accountable.

Overall, the Beijing Platform for Action is a positive affirmation of women's human rights in many areas. It demands the economic and political empowerment of women and calls for more active intervention by governments on behalf of women's equality. The successes that women achieved in this process have been long in the making. They grow out of many decades of women's organizing generally, and specifically out of twenty years of attention to women at the UN, and four years of women's explicit and increasing participation as an organized force in UN intergovernmental conferences addressing major global concerns, such as the environment (Rio de Janeiro, 1992), human rights (Vienna, 1993), population and development (Cairo, 1994), and social development (Copenhagen, 1995). This has resulted in increasingly sophisticated lobbying of governmental delegates by women whose efforts are based on years of working to build international feminist strategies around common concerns, such as reproductive rights and violence against women. Networking among women prior to the Beijing conference produced effective cross-cultural alliances and led to significant collaboration between women on government delegations, in the UN and in NGO caucuses.

The Platform for Action outlines action for the human rights of women in twelve interrelated critical areas, from poverty and education to violence and the media. In spite of concerted attempts by religious fundamentalists and secular conservatives to narrow the reach of human rights, women's rights are framed throughout the Platform as indivisible, universal, and inalienable human rights. Such an understanding can be transformed into human rights practices—reaffirming women's rights to literacy, food, and housing, along with their rights to freedom of association and speech and to live free of violence, enslavement, or torture.

Yet, while the Platform clearly moves in the direction of advancing women's rights as human rights, it also reflects contentious debate about women's role in society and the construction of gender. The subtext to the Platform was the ongoing controversy about feminism and gender roles. For instance, one of the hottest debates in the final preparatory meeting was over the use of the term *gender* in the draft Platform. The Vatican and a few states argued against using *gender* at all unless it was explicitly tied to the "natural" biological roles of the sexes. When its efforts failed, the Holy See noted in its final statement to the conference that its members understood the term *gender* to be "grounded in biological sexual identity, male or female. . . . The Holy See thus excludes dubious interpretations based on world views which assert that sexual identity can be adapted indefinitely to suit new and different purposes."[1]

Some major controversies illustrate what women gained and the limitations of the Platform for Action. For example, in the contested area of sexual rights, many thought governments would not accept this language, and the phrase *sexual rights* per se was rejected. However, these boundaries were expanded in the health section of the Platform, which states in paragraph 97 that "the human rights of women include their right to have control over and decide freely and responsibly on matters related to their sexuality, including sexual and reproductive health, free of coercion, discrimination and violence." Similarly, explicit support for the rights of lesbians and the term *sexual orientation* were excluded from the Platform in final late-night negotiations. Nevertheless, the door was opened with this first open discussion of the issue in the UN, which also exposed the virulence of homophobia among those who manipulate it to oppose women's rights generally. At least some governments in each region of the world supported the need to include sexual orientation as deserving of protection from discrimination, and a number stated that their interpretation of the prohibition against discrimination on the basis of "other" status in several human rights treaties applies to lesbians and gays.

Another major debate centered on the term *universal* and the use of religion and culture to limit women's human rights. Women sought to maintain the 1993 Vienna World Conference on Human Rights recognition that women's human rights are universal, inalienable, indivisible, and interdependent. The Vatican, some Islamist governments, and a few other states overtly attempted unsuccessfully to limit the extent of universal application of women's human rights. However, they used this debate to claim that there is a feminist imperialism that reflects

disrespect for religion and culture, an overzealous individualism, and an effort to impose Western values that destroy the family and local communities. Nineteen states entered reservations to text in the Platform that was not in conformity with Islamic law or traditional religious interpretations, particularly references to reproductive health and rights, inheritance, sexuality, and abortion. This is not a new debate, but women need to learn better how to argue for universality of rights without implying homogenization, especially around religion and culture, which can be positive for some women.

Human rights is not a static concept; it has varying meanings depending on a range of political, intellectual, and cultural traditions. Often in international organizing women speak of "culture" and national sovereignty in debates over human rights only as negative influences because they are so often used as excuses to deny women's rights. However, culture is constructed in many ways and exists not only as hegemonic culture but also as alternative cultures, oppositional cultures, and cultures of resistance. Women must create a more nuanced conversation that can address the tension between calls for recognizing the universality of women's human rights and the respect for and nurturance of local cultures and oppositional strategies. This entails women's defining the terms of debate and of culture themselves rather than letting the debate be defined by others.

The movement for women's human rights has sought to be a partial answer to this tension. In contrast to organizing that emphasizes categories of difference or identity, which were also well represented at the NGO Forum and government conference, efforts around women's human rights take as their reason for coming together the construction of a common political goal, based on a set of norms or justice, however problematic that may be, rather than a commonality of experience. The coalitions that emerge, then, are politically constructed, rather than determined on the basis of biology, geography, culture, ethnicity, and so on. The potential of such coalitions could be seen at the NGO Forum and in many of the global issue caucuses that lobbied together across geographical lines for more feminist language in the Platform for Action.

---

[1] United Nations, *UN Report of the Fourth World Conference on Women* (New York: United Nations, 1995), 165.

This incorporation of women's human rights language and concepts by governments and organizations from all parts of the world and in all manner of ways indicates more than a rhetorical gesture. It represents a shift in analysis that moves beyond single-issue politics or identity-based organizing and enhances women's capacity to build global alliances based on collective political goals and a common agenda. Moreover, because human rights is a language that has legitimacy among many individuals and governments, the appeal to human rights agreements and international norms can fortify women's organizing.

However, realization of the potential we viewed in Beijing requires vigorous leadership and a willingness to engage in open and often difficult political dialogue across many differences that tend to divide women. It also demands that women become politically active in local communities, in national political contests, and in international debates in the effort to reshape the terms of debate for the twenty-first century. The Beijing Platform for Action can be a vital tool in this process as it provides an affirmation of women's rights as human rights and outlines many of the actions necessary to realize women's empowerment. But how far the Platform and the concept of women's human rights will take women depends on whether women are able to use them to further their efforts to influence policy and action at all levels from the global to the local.      [1996]

# 🌿 141

## *The Globetrotting Sneaker*

CYNTHIA ENLOE

All the "New World Order" really means to corporate giants like athletic shoemakers is that they now have the green light to accelerate long-standing industry practices. In the early 1980s, the field marshals commanding Reebok and Nike, which are both U.S.-based, decided to manufacture most of their sneakers in South Korea and Taiwan, hiring local women. L.A. Gear, Adidas, Fila, and Asics

quickly followed their lead. In short time, the coastal city of Pusan, South Korea, became the "sneaker capital of the world." Between 1982 and 1989 the U.S. lost 58,500 footwear jobs to cities like Pusan, which attracted sneaker executives because its location facilitated international transport. More to the point, South Korea's military government had an interest in suppressing labor organizing, and it had a comfortable military alliance with the U.S. Korean women also seemed accepting of Confucian philosophy, which measured a woman's morality by her willingness to work hard for her family's well-being and to acquiesce to her father's and husband's dictates. With their sense of patriotic duty, Korean women seemed the ideal labor force for export-oriented factories.

U.S. and European sneaker company executives were also attracted by the ready supply of eager Korean male entrepreneurs with whom they could make profitable arrangements. This fact was central to Nike's strategy in particular. When they moved their production sites to Asia to lower labor costs, the executives of the Oregon-based company decided to reduce their corporate responsibilities further. Instead of owning factories outright, a more efficient strategy would be to subcontract the manufacturing to wholly foreign-owned—in this case, South Korean—companies. Let them be responsible for workers' health and safety. Let them negotiate with newly emergent unions. Nike would retain control over those parts of sneaker production that gave its officials the greatest professional satisfaction and the ultimate word on the product: design and marketing. Although Nike was following in the footsteps of garment and textile manufacturers, it set the trend for the rest of the athletic footwear industry.

But at the same time, women workers were developing their own strategies. As the South Korean pro-democracy movement grew throughout the 1980s, increasing numbers of women rejected traditional notions of feminine duty. Women began organizing in response to the dangerous working conditions, daily humiliations, and low pay built into their work. Such resistance was profoundly threatening to the government, given the fact that South Korea's emergence as an industrialized "tiger" had depended on women accepting their "role" in growing industries

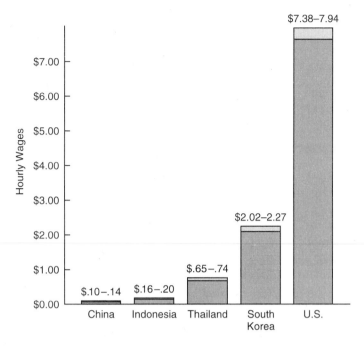

*Figure 1    Hourly Wages in Athletic Footwear Factories*

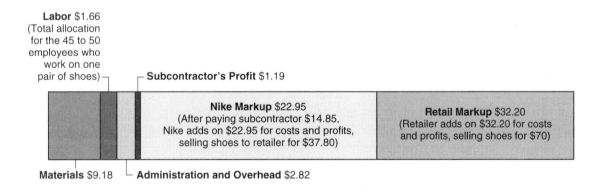

*Figure 2    A $70 Pair of Nike Pegasus: Where the Money Goes*

like sneaker manufacture. If women reimagined their lives as daughters, as wives, as workers, as citizens, it wouldn't just rattle their employers; it would shake the very foundations of the whole political system.

At the first sign of trouble, factory managers called in government riot police to break up employ-

ees' meetings. Troops sexually assaulted women workers, stripping, fondling, and raping them "as a control mechanism for suppressing women's engagement in the labor movement," reported Jeong-Lim Nam of Hyosung Women's University in Taegu. It didn't work. It didn't work because the feminist activists in groups like the Korean Women Workers

Association (KWWA) helped women understand and deal with the assaults. The KWWA held consciousness-raising sessions in which notions of feminine duty and respectability were tackled along with wages and benefits. They organized independently of the male-led labor unions to ensure that their issues would be taken seriously, in labor negotiations and in the pro-democracy movement as a whole.

The result was that women were at meetings with management, making sure that in addition to issues like long hours and low pay, sexual assault at the hands of managers and health care were on the table. Their activism paid off: in addition to winning the right to organize women's unions, their earnings grew. In 1980, South Korean women in manufacturing jobs earned 45 percent of the wages of their male counterparts; by 1990, they were earning more than 50 percent. Modest though it was, the pay increase was concrete progress, given that the gap between women's and men's manufacturing wages in Japan, Singapore, and Sri Lanka actually *widened* during the 1980s. Last but certainly not least, women's organizing was credited with playing a major role in toppling the country's military regime and forcing open elections in 1987.

Without that special kind of workplace control that only an authoritarian government could offer, sneaker executives knew that it was time to move. In Nike's case, its famous advertising slogan—"Just Do It"—proved truer to its corporate philosophy than its women's "empowerment" ad campaign, designed to rally women's athletic (and consumer) spirit. In response to South Korean women workers' newfound activist self-confidence, the sneaker company and its subcontractors began shutting down a number of their South Korean factories in the late 1980s and early 1990s. After bargaining with government officials in nearby China and Indonesia, many Nike subcontractors set up shop in those countries, while some went to Thailand. China's government remains nominally Communist; Indonesia's ruling generals are staunchly anti-Communist. But both are governed by authoritarian regimes who share the belief that if women can be kept hard at work, low paid, and unorganized, they can serve as a magnet for foreign investors.

Where does all this leave South Korean women—or any woman who is threatened with a factory closure if she demands decent working conditions and a fair wage? They face the dilemma confronted by thousands of women from dozens of countries. The risk of job loss is especially acute in relatively mobile industries; it's easier for a sneaker, garment, or electronics manufacturer to pick up and move than it is for an automaker or a steel producer. In the case of South Korea, poor women had moved from rural villages into the cities searching for jobs to support not only themselves, but parents and siblings. The exodus of manufacturing jobs has forced more women into the growing "entertainment" industry. The kinds of bars and massage parlors offering sexual services that had mushroomed around U.S. military bases during the Cold War have been opening up across the country.

But the reality is that women throughout Asia are organizing, knowing full well the risks involved. Theirs is a long-term view; they are taking direct aim at companies' nomadic advantage, by building links among workers in countries targeted for "development" by multinational corporations. Through sustained grassroots efforts, women are developing the skills and confidence that will make it increasingly difficult to keep their labor cheap. The United Nations conference on women in Beijing, China, was a rare opportunity to expand their cross-border strategizing.

The Beijing conference provided an important opportunity to call world attention to the hypocrisy of the governments and corporations doing business in China. Numerous athletic shoe companies followed Nike in setting up manufacturing sites throughout the country. This included Reebok—a company claiming its share of responsibility for ridding the world of "injustice, poverty, and other ills that gnaw away at the social fabric," according to a statement of corporate principles.

Since 1988, Reebok has been giving out annual human rights awards to dissidents from around the world. But it wasn't until 1992 that the company adopted its own "human rights production standards"—after labor advocates made it known that the quality of life in factories run by its subcontractors was just as dismal as that at most other athletic shoe suppliers in Asia. Reebok's code of conduct, for example, includes a pledge to "seek" those sub-contractors who respect workers' rights to organize. The only problem is that independent trade unions are banned in China. Reebok has chosen to ignore that fact, even though Chinese dissidents have been the recipients of the company's own human rights award. As for working conditions, Reebok now says it sends its own inspectors to production sites a couple of times a year. But they have easily "missed" what subcontractors are trying to hide—like 400 young women workers locked at night into an over-crowded dormitory near a Reebok-contracted factory in the town of Zhuhai, as reported last August in the *Asian Wall Street Journal Weekly*.

Nike's cofounder and CEO Philip Knight has said that he would like the world to think of Nike as "a company with a soul that recognizes the value of human beings." Nike, like Reebok, says it sends in inspectors from time to time to check up on work conditions at its factories; in Indonesia, those factories are run largely by South Korean subcontractors. But according to Donald Katz in a recent book on the company, Nike spokesman Dave Taylor told an in-house newsletter that the factories are "[the sub-contractors'] business to run." For the most part, the company relies on regular reports from sub-contractors regarding its "Memorandum of Under-standing," which managers must sign, promising to impose "local government standards" for wages, working conditions, treatment of workers, and ben-efits.

In April, the minimum wage in the Indonesian capital of Jakarta will be $1.89 *a day*—among the highest in a country where the minimum wage var-ies by region. And managers are required to pay only 75 percent of the wage directly; the remainder can be withheld for "benefits." By now, Nike has a well-honed response to growing criticisms of its low-cost labor strategy. Such wages should not be seen as exploitative, says Nike, but rather as the first rung on the ladder of economic opportunity that Nike has extended to workers with few options. Otherwise, they'd be out "harvesting coconut meat in the tropical sun," wrote Nike spokesman Dusty Kidd, in a letter to the *Utne Reader*. The all-is-relative response craftily shifts attention away from

reality: Nike didn't move to Indonesia to help Indo-nesians; it moved to ensure that its profit margin continues to grow. And that is pretty much guaran-teed in a country where "local standards" for wages rarely take a worker over the poverty line. A 1991 survey by the International Labor Organization (ILO) found that 88 percent of women working at the Jakarta minimum wage at the time—slightly less than a dollar a day—were malnourished.

A woman named Riyanti might have been among the workers surveyed by the ILO. Interviewed by the *Boston Globe* in 1991, she told the reporter who had asked about her long hours and low pay: "I'm happy working here. . . . I can make money and I can make friends." But in fact, the reporter discov-ered that Riyanti had already joined her coworkers in two strikes, the first to force one of Nike's Korean subcontractors to accept a new women's union and the second to compel managers to pay at least the minimum wage. That Riyanti appeared less than forthcoming about her activities isn't surprising. Many Indonesian factories have military men posted in their front offices who find no fault with managers who tape women's mouths shut to keep them from talking among themselves. They and their superiors have a political reach that extends far beyond the barracks. Indonesia has all the makings for a polit-ical explosion, especially since the gap between rich and poor is widening into a chasm. It is in this set-ting that the government has tried to crack down on any independent labor organizing—a policy that Nike has helped to implement. Referring to a re-cent strike in a Nike-contracted factory, Tony Nava, Nike representative in Indonesia, told the *Chicago Tribune* in November 1994 that the "troublemak-ers" had been fired. When asked about Nike policy on the issue, spokesman Keith Peters struck a con-ciliatory note: "If the government were to allow and encourage independent labor organizing, we would be happy to support it."

Indonesian workers' efforts to create unions in-dependent of governmental control were a surprise to shoe companies. Although their moves from South Korea have been immensely profitable [see chart], they do not have the sort of immunity from activism that they had expected. In May 1993, the murder of a female labor activist outside Surabaya set off a storm of local and international protest. Even the U.S. State Department was forced to take note in its 1993 worldwide human rights report, describing a system similar to that which generated South Korea's boom 20 years earlier: severely restricted union organizing, security forces used to break up strikes, low wages for men, lower wages for women—complete with government rhetoric celebrating women's contribution to national development.

Yet when President Clinton visited Indonesia he made only a token effort to address the country's human rights problem. Instead, he touted the benefits of free trade, sounding indeed more enlightened, more in tune with the spirit of the post–Cold War era than do those defenders of protectionist trading policies who coat their rhetoric with "America first" chauvinism. But "free trade" as actually being practiced today is hardly *free* for any workers—in the U.S. or abroad—who have to accept the Indonesian, Chinese, or Korean workplace model as the price of keeping their jobs.

The not-so-new plot of the international trade story has been "divide and rule." If women workers and their government in one country can see that a sneaker company will pick up and leave if their labor demands prove more costly than those in a neighbor country, then women workers will tend to see their neighbors not as regional sisters, but as competitors who can steal their precarious livelihoods. Playing women off against each other is, of course, old hat. Yet it is as essential to international trade politics as is the fine print in GATT.

But women workers allied through networks like the Hong Kong-based Committee for Asian Women are developing their own post–Cold War foreign policy, which means addressing women's needs: how to convince fathers and husbands that a woman going out to organizing meetings at night is not sexually promiscuous; how to develop workplace agendas that respond to family needs; how to work with male unionists who push women's demands to the bottom of their lists; how to build a global movement.

These women refuse to stand in awe of the corporate power of the Nike or Reebok or Adidas executive. Growing numbers of Asian women today have concluded that trade politics have to be understood by women on their own terms. If women in Russia and Eastern Europe can challenge Americanized consumerism, if Asian activists can solidify their alliances, and if U.S. women can join with them by taking on trade politics—the post-Cold War sneaker may be a less comfortable fit in the 1990s.                    [1997]

---

This article draws from the work of South Korean scholars Hyun Sook Kim, Seung-kyung Kim, Katherine Moon, Seungsook Moon, and Jeong-Lim Nam.

# Women Organizing: Many Issues, Many Voices

The ideas of feminism have influenced countless women, changing their ideas about themselves and expectations of their future. But ending women's subordination requires more than consciousness. It requires working together to challenge sexist practices and institutions and creating organizations that embody a vision of a more humane and just society. How do people move from a consciousness of injustice to political involvement? In the following essay, Rebecca Walker describes the process by which she commits herself to working politically for women's freedom. Written immediately after the Senate confirmation hearings of Clarence Thomas, the Supreme Court Justice, after he had been accused of sexual harassment by Anita Hill, a former employee, Walker's essay echoes the outrage of many women at what they saw as a vivid enactment of women's political powerlessness.

Women have always played important roles in community activism. Often women's involvement in local struggles leads them to discover their lack of political power and to challenge the limitations of their roles within the family. The women who organized against toxic waste dumps, for example, motivated by a desire to make their communities safe for their families, encountered a male-dominated power structure that fails to take the needs of the community seriously. Through their work against the toxic waste dump, they became more conscious of the political inequities in both their homes and their communities and of their own power as they organized together.

Feminism cannot be located in one central organization. Rather, it exists in the myriad groups and organizing projects that women form when they encounter injustice or seek to address unmet needs. We present here three examples of women organizing in various contexts. In each situation, the first step was breaking the silence about women's experience and naming the problems they faced. The ideas and activities of each group reflect their particular needs and perspectives. The Asian activists described by Sonia Shah have developed a political perspective that reflects their resistance to assimilation and their demand to become visible both as Asians and as women. The neighborhood women worked to translate their family- and community-based activism into political power, transforming their own consciousness in the process. The women in "Voices" created an organization for women with AIDS in prison in the late 1980s. Their organization was able to make institutional changes while engaged in meeting the needs of women prisoners.

The activism of the 1990s is taking a variety of forms. Barbara Yoshida describes the power of civil disobedience, a tactic used in the past by various oppressed groups and revived in response to the erosion of women's reproductive freedom. In the final essay, young women, impelled by anger at the negative influence of teen magazines, created their own multicultural, feminist magazine for young women.

# 142

# *Becoming the Third Wave*

REBECCA WALKER

I am not one of the people who sat transfixed before the television, watching the Senate hearings. I had classes to go to, papers to write, and frankly, the whole thing was too painful. A black man grilled by a panel of white men about his sexual deviance. A black woman claiming harassment and being discredited by other women. . . . I could not bring myself to watch that sensationalized assault [on] the human spirit.

To me, the hearings were not about determining whether or not Clarence Thomas did in fact harass Anita Hill. They were about checking and redefining the extent of women's credibility and power.

Can a woman's experience undermine a man's career? Can a woman's voice, a woman's sense of self-worth and injustice, challenge a structure predicated upon the subjugation of our gender? Anita Hill's testimony threatened to do that and more. If Thomas had not been confirmed, every man in the United States would be at risk. For how many senators never told a sexist joke? How many men have not used their protected male privilege to thwart in some way the influence or ideas of a woman colleague, friend, or relative?

For those whose sense of power is so obviously connected to the health and vigor of the penis, it would have been a metaphoric castration. Of course this is too great a threat.

While some may laud the whole spectacle for the consciousness it raised around sexual harassment, its very real outcome is more informative. He was promoted. She was repudiated. Men were assured of the inviolability of their penis/power. Women were admonished to keep their experiences to themselves.

The backlash against U.S. women is real. As the misconception of equality between the sexes becomes more ubiquitous, so does the attempt to restrict the boundaries of women's personal and political power. Thomas's confirmation, the ultimate rally of support for the male paradigm of harassment, sends a clear message to women: "Shut up! Even if you speak, we will not listen."

I will not be silenced.

I acknowledge the fact that we live under siege. I intend to fight back. I have uncovered and unleashed more repressed anger than I thought possible. For the umpteenth time in my 22 years, I have been radicalized, politicized, shaken awake. I have come to voice again, and this time my voice is not conciliatory.

The night after Thomas' confirmation I ask the man I am intimate with what he thinks of the whole mess. His concern is primarily with Thomas' propensity to demolish civil rights and opportunities for people of color. I launch into a tirade. "When will progressive black men prioritize my rights and well-being? When will they stop talking so damn much about 'the race' as if it revolved exclusively around them?" He tells me I wear my emotions on my sleeve. I scream "I need to know, are you with me or are you going to help them try to destroy me?"

A week later I am on a train to New York. A beautiful mother and daughter, both wearing green outfits, sit across the aisle from me. The little girl has tightly plaited braids. Her brown skin is glowing and smooth, her eyes bright as she chatters happily while looking out the window. Two men get on the train and sit directly behind me, shaking my seat as they thud into place. I bury myself in *The Sound and the Fury*. Loudly they begin to talk about women. "Man, I fucked that bitch all night and then I never called her again." "Man, there's lots of girlies over there, you know that ho, live over there by Tyrone? Well, I snatched that shit up."

The mother moves closer to her now quiet daughter. Looking at her small back I can see that she is listening to the men. I am thinking of how I can transform the situation, of all the people in the car whose silence makes us complicit.

Another large man gets on the train. After exchanging loud greetings with the two men, he sits next to me. He tells them he is going to Philadelphia to visit his wife and child. I am suckered into thinking that he is different. Then, "Man, there's a ton of females in Philly, just waitin' for you to give 'em some." I turn my head and allow the fire in my eyes to burn into him. He takes up two seats and has hands with huge swollen knuckles. I imagine the gold rings on his fingers slamming into my face. He senses something, "What's your name, sweetheart?" The other men lean forward over the seat.

A torrent explodes: "I ain't your sweetheart, I ain't your bitch, I ain't your baby. How dare you have the nerve to sit up here and talk about women that way, and then try to speak to me." The woman/ mother chimes in to the beat with claps of sister- hood. The men are momentarily stunned. Then the comeback: "Aw, bitch, don't play that woman shit over here 'cause that's bullshit." He slaps the back of one hand against the palm of the other. I refuse to back down. Words fly.

My instinct kicks in, telling me to get out. "Since I see you all are not going to move, I will." I move to the first car. I am so angry that thoughts of murder, of physically retaliating against them, of separatism, engulf me. I am almost out of body, just shy of being pure force. I am sick of the way women are negated, violated, devalued, ignored. I am livid, unrelenting in my anger at those who invade my space, who wish to take away my rights, who refuse to hear my voice.

As the days pass, I push myself to figure out what it means to be a part of the Third Wave of feminism. I begin to realize that I owe it to myself, to my little sister on the train, to all of the daughters yet to be born, to push beyond my rage and articulate an agenda. After battling with ideas of separatism and militancy, I connect with my own feelings of pow- erlessness. I realize that I must undergo a transfor- mation if I am truly committed to women's empow- erment. My involvement must reach beyond my own voice in discussion, beyond voting, beyond reading feminist theory. My anger and awareness must translate into tangible action.

I am ready to decide, as my mother decided be- fore me, to devote much of my energy to the history, health, and healing of women. Each of my choices will have to hold to my feminist standard of justice.

To be a feminist is to integrate an ideology of equality and female empowerment into the very fi- ber of my life. It is to search for personal clarity in the midst of systemic destruction, to join in sister- hood with women when often we are divided, to understand power structures with the intention of challenging them.

While this may sound simple, it is exactly the kind of stand that many of my peers are unwilling to take. So I write this as a plea to all women, especially the women of my generation: Let Thomas' confir- mation serve to remind you, as it did me, that the fight is far from over. Let this dismissal of a woman's experience move you to anger. Turn that outrage into political power. Do not vote for them unless they work for us. Do not have sex with them, do not break bread with them, do not nurture them if they don't prioritize our freedom to control our bodies and our lives.

I am not a postfeminism feminist. I am the Third Wave.                                      [1992]

## 🌿 143

# *Blue-Collar Women and Toxic-Waste Protests*
## *The Process of Politicization*

CELENE KRAUSS

### THE EXPERIENCE OF TOXIC-WASTE PROTESTERS: THE PROCESS OF POLITICIZATION

What I examine is the process by which blue-collar women, who were never involved in the political sys- tem, become politicized as they are forced to con- nbfront inequities of power in the political system, trivialization of their involvement on the part of middle-class, male governmental officials, and grow- ing conflicts with their spouses as a result of their in- volvement in protest activities. The analysis is based on interviews, conference presentations of activists, and writings of women involved with the Citizen's Clearinghouse for Hazardous Waste, a national or- ganization created by Lois Gibbs as a resource for community groups struggling with toxic-waste issues around the United States. Gibbs is best known for her successful campaign to relocate families in Love Canal, New York, when residents discovered that they lived adjacent to a hazardous toxic dump site that endangered their health and their lives.[1]

### Family and the Inequities of Public Power

Complicating women's involvement in toxic-waste issues is the exclusion of most people from the policy-making process. Generally, government makes toxic-waste policies without the knowledge of community residents. People may not know that they live near a toxic dump, or they assume that it is regulated by government.

Toxic-waste dump sites have been located primarily in blue-collar and people of color communities; hence, it is not surprising that blue-collar women have played a significant role in this movement. Because women are traditionally responsible for the health of their children, they are the most likely to make the link between toxic waste and their children's ill health. In communities around the United States, women are discovering numerous toxics-related health hazards (e.g., multiple miscarriages, birth defects, cancer deaths, and neurological symptoms). Their initial response to this discovery is to contact their government, because they assume that government will protect the health and welfare of their children. Said Gibbs:

> I grew up in a blue-collar community, it was very patriotic, into democracy . . . I believed in government . . . I believed that if you had a complaint, you went to the right person in government. If there was a way to solve the problem, they would be glad to do it.[2]

But Gibbs and others faced an indifferent government. At Love Canal, local governmental officials argued that toxic-waste pollution was insignificant, the equivalent of smoking just three cigarettes a day; in South Brunswick, New Jersey, local officials argued that living with pollution was "the price of a better way of life."[3] State officials often withheld information from residents because "they didn't want to panic the public," further undermining confidence in government. For example, at Stringfellow, California, where 800,000 gallons of toxic-waste chemicals pumped into the community flowed directly behind the elementary school and into the playground, children played in puddles contaminated by toxic wastes, yet officials withheld information for fear of panicking the public.

Faced with government's indifference to a dangerous toxic-waste situation and its impact on their families, many women became activists, turning to protest activities in order to protect their families. At Love Canal, for example, women vandalized a construction site, burned effigies of the governor, and were arrested during a baby-carriage blockade. Women justified their protests on the grounds that they were making the system do what it's supposed to do.

Women become involved in these issues because they are concerned about the health effects on their families. As they become involved, they must ultimately confront more than the issue of toxic wastes; they must confront a government indifferent to their needs. In doing so, they learn about a world of power usually hidden from them:

> All our lives we are taught to believe certain things about ourselves as women, about democracy and justice, and about people in positions of authority. Once we become involved with toxic waste problems, we need to confront some of our old beliefs and change the way we view things. . . . We take on government and polluters. . . . We are up against the largest corporations in the United States. They have lots of money to lobby, pay off, bribe, cajole and influence. They threaten us. Yet we challenge them with the only things we have—people and the truth. We learn that our government is not out to protect our rights. To protect our families we are now forced to picket, protest and shout.[4]

As a first step, blue-collar women are forced to examine their own assumptions about political power. As they become involved, they see the contradiction between a government that claims to act on behalf of the public interest, a government that holds the family sacrosanct, and the actual policies and actions that government pursues. They see the ways in which government policy often favors the wishes of powerful business interests over the health and welfare of children and their families. The result is a more critical political stance that informs the militancy of their activism.[5]

## Class, Gender and Resources of Power

As blue-collar women become involved in toxic-waste issues, they also come into conflict with a public world where policymakers are traditionally white, male and middle-class. As Zeff *et al.* have noted:

> Seventy to eighty per cent of local leaders are women. They are women leaders in a community run by men. Because of this, many of the obstacles that these women face as leaders stem from the conflicts between their traditional female role in the community and their new role as leader: conflicts with male officials and authorities who have not yet adjusted to these persistent, vocal, head-strong women challenging the system. . . . Women are frequently ignored by male politicians, male government officials and male corporate spokesmen. . . .[6]

Many women who become involved in grass-roots activism do not consider themselves activists and have rarely been involved in the political process. Initially they may be intimidated by the idea of entering the public arena. Male officials further exacerbate this intimidation by ignoring women, criticizing them for being overemotional, and especially by delegitimizing their authority by labeling them "hysterical housewives," a label widely used regardless of the professional status of the woman. As a source of empowerment, blue-collar women have appropriated the criticisms and used them against their critics. Notes Cora Tucker, who organized a toxic-waste fight in rural Halifax, Virginia:

> When they first called me a hysterical housewife I used to get very upset and go home and cry. . . . I've learned that's a tactic men use to keep us in our place. So when they started the stuff on toxic waste. . . . I went back and a guy gets up and says, "We have a whole room full of hysterical housewives today, so men we need to get prepared." I said, "You're exactly right. We're hysterical and when it comes to matters of life and death, especially mine, I get hysterical." And I said, "If men don't get hysterical, there's something wrong with them." From then on, they stopped calling us hysterical housewives. . . .[7]

The language of "hysterical housewives," "emotional women," and "mothers" has become a language of critique and empowerment that exposes

the limits of the public arena to address the importance of family, health, and community.

The traditional role of mother as protector of the family can empower blue-collar activists. Their view of this role provides the motivation for women to take risks in defense of their families. Lois Gibbs, for example, has written of her insecurity when she first went to her neighbors' homes to conduct a health survey of her community at Love Canal. When she approached the first house and no one answered, she ran home relieved. Then she thought about her son and his seizures, gathered up her courage and tried again and again. On another level, these women have learned to derive power from their emotionality, a quality valued in the private sphere of family and motherhood but scorned in the public arena:

> What's really so bad about showing your feelings? Emotions and intellect are not conflicting traits. In fact, emotions may well be the quality that makes women so effective in this movement. . . . They help us speak the truth.[8]

Grass-roots activists look to their experiences as organizers of family life as a further source of empowerment. Lois Gibbs notes that women organized at Love Canal by constantly analyzing how they would handle a situation in the family and then translating that analysis into political action. For example, says Gibbs,

> If our child wanted a pair of jeans, who would they go to? Well they might go to their father since their father had the money—that meant that we should go to Governor Carey.[9]

Gibbs notes that the Citizen's Clearinghouse for Hazardous Wastes conducts women's organizing conferences, which help them learn to translate their skills as family organizers into the political arena.

Finally, blue-collar women recognize the power they wield in bringing moral issues to the public, exposing the contradiction between a society that purports to value motherhood and family, yet creates social policies that undermine these values. As Gibbs notes:

> We bring the authority of mother—who can condemn mothers?—it is a tool we have. Our crying

brings the moral issues to the table. And when the public sees our children it brings a concrete, moral dimension to our experience—they are not an abstract statistic.[10]

The private world of family is a resource used as they struggle to protect their families in the public sphere. In the process of protest, blue-collar women come to see the ways in which class and gender shape inequities of traditional political power and the contradiction between the values of family and community espoused by those in power and the actual policies and actions that government pursues. This analysis informs their consciousness and the direction of their action and becomes a resource to empower them.

### Gender Conflicts in the Family

As blue-collar women become activists, they are also forced to confront power relations and highly traditional gender roles characteristic of the blue-collar family. They begin to see the ways in which relationships within the patriarchal family mirror larger power relations within the society.

> Women's involvement in grassroots activism may change their views about the world and their relations with their husbands. Some husbands are actively supportive. Some take no stand: "Go ahead and do what you want. Just make sure you have dinner on the table and my shirts washed." Others forbid time away from the family.[11]

For many women, their experience contradicts an assumption in the family that both husband and wife are equally concerned with the well-being of children. As Gibbs notes,

> The husband in a blue-collar community is saying get your ass home and cook me dinner, it's either me or the issue, make your choice. The woman says: how can I make a choice, you're telling me choose between the health of my children and your fucking dinner, how do I deal with that?[12]

When women are asked to make such a choice—between their children and their husbands' needs—they see the ways in which the children are their concern, not their husband's. This leads to tremendous conflict and sometimes results in more equal power relations within the family, a direction that

CCHW is trying to encourage by organizing family stress workshops. Generally, however, the families of activist women do not tolerate this stress well. Gibbs notes the very high divorce rate among activists and that, following protest activities, CCHW receives a higher number of reports of wife-battering. Thus, blue-collar women's involvement in grassroots protests may disrupt the traditional organization of family life, revealing inequities in underlying power relationships. Ironically, the traditional family itself often becomes a casualty of this process.

## IMPLICATIONS FOR PUBLIC POLICY AND SOCIAL CHANGE

For the most part, the formal policy-making process excludes the participation of those people most affected because they are seen as having only limited, particularistic self-interests. In contrast, grass-roots protests concerning toxic wastes show us an informal process of resistance for people ordinarily excluded. In order to realize their political goals, they develop an oppositional or critical consciousness that informs the direction of their actions and challenges the power of traditional policymakers. When they see how the system excludes them, they go outside the formal policy-making process. When they cannot get the government to protect them from corporations, they use protest to force the political system to act on their behalf. Involvement in protest activities concerning toxic-waste issues ultimately leads many blue-collar women to a redefinition of politics and policy making from below, in which policies begin with the lives of those most directly affected. Their experience exposes the false assumption that the traditional policy-making process will be democratic and responsive to their needs. Rooted in the particular, they transcend the particular as they uncover and confront a world of political power shaped by gender and class.

The theoretical perspectives provided by feminism and the new social historiography help to make visible this process of politicization. As blue-collar women fight to protect their children and communities from hazards posed by toxic wastes, they reevaluate the everyday world of their experience. This leads to a critical examination of traditional assumptions about relationships in the family, community, and society. Traditional beliefs in the working-class culture about home, family, and women's roles serve a crucial function in this process. These beliefs provide the initial impetus for women's involvement in issues of toxic wastes and ultimately become a rich source of empowerment, as women appropriate and reshape traditional language and meanings into an ideology of resistance. Ultimately they develop a broader analysis of power as it is shaped by gender and class. The inequities of power between blue-collar women and middle-class male public officials expose the contradiction between a government that claims to act on behalf of family and the actual policies and actions of that government, revealing traditional power relationships within the family. In these ways, blue-collar women come to reject the dominant ideology that separates the public and private arenas, rendering invisible and insignificant the private sphere of women's work. This enables them to act politically and, in some measure, challenge the social relationships of power. In so doing they implement an alternative view of policy making fundamentally more inclusive and democratic. Thus, their political activism has implications far beyond the visible single-issue policy concern of the toxic-waste dump site or the siting of a hazardous-waste incinerator. Fighting toxic wastes in defense of the family becomes the lever for the transformation of consciousness and the political action of blue-collar women.

*NOTES*

1. Many of the quotes in this analysis are drawn from an interview with Lois Gibbs, director of the Citizen's Clearinghouse for Hazardous Waste (May, 1989, Cherry Hill, N.J.), and presentations of community activists at a Women in Toxics Organizing Conference, November, 1987, which were published by the Citizens Clearinghouse for Hazardous Wastes, 1989, in a pamphlet called *Empowering Ourselves: Women and Toxics Organizing,* ed. Robbin Lee Zeff, Marsha Love, and Karen Stults.
2. Zeff et al., *Empowering Ourselves.*
3. Ibid.
4. Ibid., 31.
5. For a more in-depth analysis of the development of political consciousness, read Celene Krauss, "The Elusive Process of Citizen Activism," *Social Policy* 14 (1983): 50–55; and Celene Krauss, "Community Struggles and the Shaping of Democratic Consciousness," *Sociological Forum* 4 (1989): 227–238.
6. Zeff et al., *Empowering Ourselves,* 25.
7. Ibid., 4.

8. Gibbs interview.
9. Ibid.
10. Ibid.
11. Ibid., 33.
12. Ibid. [1991]

 144

# *Presenting the Blue Goddess: Toward a National Pan-Asian Feminist Agenda*

SONIA SHAH

We all laughed sheepishly about how we used to dismiss the South Asian women in our lives as doormats irrelevant to our feminist lives. For most of us in that fledgling South Asian American women's group in Boston, either white feminists or black feminists had inspired us to find our Asian feminist heritage. Yet neither movement had really prepared us for actually finding any. The way either group defined feminism did not, could not, define our South Asian feminist heritages. That, for most of us, consisted of feisty immigrant mothers, ball-breaking grandmothers, Kali-worship (Kali is the blue goddess who sprang whole from another woman and who symbolizes "shakti"—Hindi for womanpower), social activist aunts, freedom-fighting/Gandhian great-aunts. In many ways, white feminism, with its "personal is political" maxim and its emphasis on building sisterhood and consciousness raising, had brought us together. Black feminism, on the other hand, had taught us that we could expect more— that feminism can incorporate a race analysis. Yet, while both movements spurred us to organize, neither included our South Asian American agendas— battery of immigrant women, the ghettoization of the Indian community, cultural discrimination, and bicultural history and identity.

I felt we were starting anew, starting to define a South Asian American feminism that no one had articulated yet. As I began to reach out to other Asian

American women's groups over the years and for this chapter, however, that sense faded a bit. Asian American women have been organizing themselves for decades, with much to show for it.

Our shakti hasn't yet expressed itself on a national stage accessible to all our sisters. But we are entering a moment in our organizing when we will soon be able to create a distinctly Asian American feminism, one that will be able to cross the class and culture lines that currently divide us.

The first wave of Asian women's organizing, born of the women's liberation and civil rights movements of the 1960s, established groups like Asian Women United in San Francisco, Asian Sisters in Action in Boston, and other more informal networks of primarily professional, East Asian American women. They focused on empowering Asian women economically and socially and accessing political power. Asian Women United, for example, has produced videos like *Silk Wings*, which describes Asian women in nontraditional jobs, and books like *Making Waves*, an anthology of Asian American women's writing.

In contrast, the second wave of organizing, politicized by the 1980s multicultural movements, includes the many ethnically specific women's groups that tend to start out as support networks, some later becoming active in the battered women's movement (like Manavi in New Jersey, Sneha in Hartford, and the New York Asian Women's Center, which offer battery hotlines and shelter for Asian women) and others working in the women-of-color and lesbian/gay liberation movements. Culturally, these groups are Korean, Indian, Cambodian, Filipina, and from other more recently arrived immigrant groups who may not have felt part of the more established, primarily East Asian women's networks. These different groups are divided by generation, by culture, and by geographic location. Anna Rhee, a cofounder of the Washington Alliance of Korean American Women (WAKAW), a group of mostly 1.5 generation (those who emigrated to the United States in early adulthood) and second-generation Korean American women, with an average age of twenty-seven to twenty-eight, says she felt "we were starting anew, because of the focus on English speaking Korean women, which was different from any other group we had seen." WAKAW, like many

similar groups, started as a support group, but has since evolved into activism, with voter registration and other projects.

Talking to various Asian American women activists, I was inspired by the many projects they have undertaken, and impressed with the overwhelming sense women had that the Asian American women's community today stands at a crossroads and has great potential. The New York Asian Women's Center, which runs several programs fighting violence against Asian women, just celebrated its tenth birthday. The Pacific Asian American Women's Bay Area Coalition honors Asian American women with Woman Warrior (á la Maxine Hong Kingston's novel) leadership awards, catapulting their honorees on to other accolades. Indian Subcontinent Women's Alliance for Action (ISWAA) in Boston just assembled a grassroots arts exhibit of works by and for South Asian women. Asian Women United, in addition to several other videos, is working on a video of Asian American visual artists. The Washington Alliance for Korean American women is taking oral histories of Korean mothers and daughters. Everyone has a story of another group starting up, another exciting Asian American woman activist.

So far, Asian American women activists have used two general organizing models. The first is based on the fact that Asian women need each other to overcome the violence, isolation, and powerlessness of their lives; no one else can or will be able to help us but each other. The groups that come together on this basis focus on the immediate needs of the community: housing battered women, finding homes for abandoned women and children, providing legal advocacy for refugee women, and so forth.

The second model is based on shared identity and the realization that both Asian and U.S. mainstream cultures make Asian American women invisible. The groups that come together on this basis work on articulating anger about racism and sexism, like other women of color groups, but also on fighting the omnipresent and seductive pressure to assimilate, within ourselves and for our sisters.

Today, our numbers are exploding, in our immigrant communities and their children, and subsequently, in our activist communities. Our writers, poets, artists, and filmmakers are coming of age.

Our activist voices against anti-Asian violence, battery, and racism are gaining legal, political, and social notice. We still have much ground to cover in influencing mainstream culture: we must throw those exoticizing books about Asian women off the shelf and replace them with a slew of works on pan-Asian feminism; women of color putting together collections of radical essays must be able to "find" Asian American feminists; *Ms.* magazine must offer more than a colorful photo of an Indian mother and daughter with less than three lines about them in a related cover article; critics must stop touting Asian American women's fiction as "exotic treasures"; Fifth Avenue advertising executives must stop producing ads that exploit tired stereotypes of Asian female "exotic beauty" and "humble modesty" with images of silky black hair and Asian women demurely tucking tampons into their pockets.

Our movement faces crucial internal challenges as well. Longtime Asian American feminist activists, such as Helen Zia, a contributing editor to *Ms.*, wonder, "What makes us different from white feminists or black feminists? What can we bring to the table?" and complain that "these questions haven't really been developed yet." Others, such as Jackie Church, a Japanese American activist, state that "there just aren't enough Asian American feminists who aren't doing five different things at once."

On the one hand, our national Asian women's groups, while inclusive across Asian ethnicities, haven't yet developed an Asian feminism *different* from black or white feminism. On the other, our ethnically specific groups, while emotionally resonant and culturally specific, are still remote and inaccessible to many of our sisters.

The movements of the 1960s colluded with the mainstream in defining racism in black and white terms; racism is still defined as discrimination based on skin color, that is, race. They also, to some extent, elevated racism, defined in this way, to the top of layers of oppression. This narrow definition has distorted mainstream perception of anti-Asian racism and even our perception of ourselves—as either nonvictims of racism or victims of racism based on skin color. By these assumptions, an Indian assaulted because she "dresses weird" is not a victim of racism; a Chinese shopkeeper harassed because she has a "funny accent" is not a victim of racism. Mainstream culture finds neither of these incidents as disturbing, unacceptable, or even downright "evil" as racism. By this definition, one must be in either the black or white camp to even speak about racism, and we are expected to forget ourselves. Whites try to convince us we are really *more like them;* depending on our degree of sensitivity toward racist injustice, we try to persuade blacks that we are more like them.

For example, many Asian American women have described Asian women's experience of racism as a result of stereotypes about "exotica" and "china dolls," two stereotypes based on our looking different from white people. But our experiences of racism go far beyond that. Rather than subvert the definition of racism itself, or uncover new layers of oppression just as unacceptable and pernicious as racism but based on what I call cultural discrimination, we have attempted to fit our experience of discrimination into the given definition. We too assume that racism is the worst kind of oppression, by emphasizing that racism against us is based on skin color and racial differences. Indeed, when we forged our first wave of women's movement, solidarity with other people of color whose activism revolved around black/white paradigms of oppression was a matter of survival. And organizing around racially based oppressions served as common ground for all ethnic Asians.

Yet our experiences of oppression are, in many qualitative ways, different from those of black and white people. For me, the experience of "otherness," the formative discrimination in my life, has resulted from culturally different (not necessarily racially different) people thinking they were culturally central: thinking that *my* house smelled funny, that *my* mother talked weird, that *my* habits were strange. They were normal; I wasn't.

Today, a more sophisticated understanding of oppression is emanating from all people of color groups. The Los Angeles riots, among other ethnic conflicts, unmasked to belated national attention the reality of an ethnic conflict (between blacks and browns, as well as between the white power structure and oppressed people of color) impossible to explain away simply as white-against-black racism. Multicultural movements and growing internationalism have raised questions about our hierarchy of oppressions. Asian American men and women activists are beginning to create legal and social definitions of cultural discrimination. Our movement can march beyond black/white paradigms that were once useful, and start to highlight cultural discrimination—our peculair blend of cultural and sexist oppression based on our accents, our clothes, our foods, our values, and our commitments. When we do this successfully, we will have not just laid a common ground for all ethnic Asian women for the practical goal of gaining power, we will have taken an important political step toward understanding and, from there, struggling against the many layers of oppression.                                      [1997]

 145

# National Congress of Neighborhood Women

MARCIA NEWFIELD

*It started with a dream in 1974, a dream of having the efforts of local grassroots women, from various ethnic backgrounds, recognized and respected. We came to see that the enemy was isolation from others who are as committed as we are, discouragement, and a lack of attention to our own self-development. The complexity of community life today presents problems so difficult that we believe women need a special kind of network to empower and support us becoming strong, effective, and efficient leaders.*

*—Jan Peterson, Neighborhood Women founder; coordinator, Women, Home and Community Super Coalition*

*When we convene women across cultures, we lead them through a dialogue that ends in a strategic plan. We come together out of our strength. We are self-reliant, self-determining women working toward self-sufficiency. We're not looking for social workers or food baskets. We're looking for partners who will help us move toward our vision in a way that honors our strengths and our gifts.*

*—LaDoris Payne, Neighborhood Women Leadership Team, WomanSpirit, St. Louis*

*I got involved in the Tenants' Association to help the people meet their needs—like getting their due from Housing, getting the development up to par, getting educational programs in here. And to try to take away some of the fear of living in public housing. You wouldn't believe what I have been offered to sell this community out—jobs, $5,000, $10,000 at a time. But I'm unbuyable. Before this I was a private person.*

*—Hortense (Tessie) Smith, Neighborhood Women, Williamsburg/Greenpoint Board; president, Bushwick Houses, Brooklyn, NY*

## NEIGHBORHOOD WOMEN'S BEGINNINGS

In the early 1970s, educated middle-class women were fighting for professional access to what had been considered "male domains" in order to claim the full range of their hitherto repressed powers and to change the world in the process. The fact that they could do this while maintaining their personal and family obligations earned them the status (and problems) of "superwomen." However, there was no bridge consciously built between the women trying to storm the gates of male privilege and the women in lower-income neighborhoods whose sense of identity lay in strengthening their families and communities. In 1974, Barbara Milkulski, who later became a U.S. Senator from Maryland, Nancy Seifer, who later wrote *Nobody Speaks for Me*, and Jan Peterson, director of the Conselyea Block Association Education Action Center, an anti-poverty program in the Williamsburg/Greenpoint section of Brooklyn, prevailed on Monsignor Geno Baroni, then head of the National Center for Urban Ethnic Affairs, to call a conference of neighborhood women and community organizers in Washington, D.C. The small conference of 30 led to a larger assembly of 150. They voted to form an organization that would help them to improve their lives and neighborhoods and represent neighborhood women accurately to the world at large. It was decided that the national office should be located in a poor and working-class neighborhood, Williamsburg/Greenpoint in Brooklyn, New York. Peterson financed a national staff through the federal Comprehensive Education and Training Act (CETA), and a group of local women raised rent for a storefront office through cake sales. Monsignor gave his blessings, and the National Congress of Neighborhood Women was born as a not-for-profit organization dedicated to supporting women's leadership in efforts to improve their lives and neighborhoods.

One of Neighborhood Women's first projects was a neighborhood college program designed for mature women (and men) from the area, many of whom had never finished high school, lacked confidence, and didn't have an interest in colleges catering to young people. Working in affiliation with various universities, Neighborhood Women participated in the design of the curriculum for an associate's degree, the choice of texts, and the selection of faculty. The neighborhood college had a much higher than usual rate of student retention and became a model for similar community-based college programs throughout the country. Rather than use their education to leave the old neighborhood and be part of the "up and out" pattern, many graduates used their new degree to qualify for responsible staff positions in local community institutions, as well as serve on community planning boards.

"Like a midwife," writes psychologist Mary Belenky, "Neighborhood Women is always helping to give birth to new projects. The range has included the first shelter for battered woman, an experimental high school for students disaffected from the local public schools and many other job training and cultural programs. . . . Neighborhood Women even got involved in developing new housing in the neighborhood, a formidable undertaking for any citizens' group."[1] When they heard that an abandoned hospital complex in the neighborhood was going to be demolished, they could see that the four brick and stone buildings would provide a wonderful setting for the many families in the area who were in desperate need of decent and affordable housing. Neighborhood Women and five other community groups formed a coalition to block demolition of the hospital and then, later, to oversee its conversion to a warehouse for homeless men. Their 10-year effort resulted in an aesthetic renovation of three buildings into apartments for low-income people.

## A GRASSROOTS WOMEN'S PERSPECTIVE

Committed to partnering across race, class, culture, geography, and other differences, the National Congress of Neighborhood Women saw, as early as the 1970s, that neighborhood women do the work of holding communities together. Everywhere an army of women was the infrastructure of neighborhoods in cities, towns, and rural areas; they ran the block association, the church, the PTA, the day care board, the tenants' group. Nevertheless, these grassroots women leaders neither got the jobs their ad-

vocacy created nor had a voice in local, national, and international policies that affected them. A central premise of Neighborhood Women is that a grassroots women leaders' perspective is needed in order for significant changes to occur in the lives of low-income people.

The National Congress also saw that various progressive movements of the time were not inclusive. The civil rights movement did not have a gender perspective, the women's movement did not reach out to low-income neighborhood women, and the community development movement did not have a women's perspective. In its 24-year history, Neighborhood Women has had an impact on all these movements and is still working at full speed, on mostly volunteer energy, to facilitate grassroots women having a voice in articulating and discussing issues and getting a share of resources, including space. As an official United Nations nongovernmental organization (NGO), they have also fostered international links among community activists to strengthen women's capacity to plan, get resources, and maintain organizations in an era when the "reform" of welfare, public housing, education, and the economy is hurting the poor.

## LEARNING EXCHANGES

As Neighborhood Women traveled around the country, they came to see that most often women get involved at the grassroots level because of deeply felt convictions that the situations in their families, neighborhoods, workplaces, and nation have become intolerable and therefore must be confronted. Sandy Schilen, an economist and Neighborhood Women national organizer, has stated,

> In facilitating dialogue among grassroots women's organizations across the U.S. for the past 24 years, Neighborhood Women has collected ample evidence that women's engagement in holistic, comprehensive neighborhood development is critical because of the way women perceive turf, appreciate environment, situate neighborhood growth, care about sustainability, resist violence and abuse, and enhance the spirit of and quality of life. For the past two decades the national government has pursued public policy approaches which treat poverty as a problem best solved through the delivery of social services to individuals, and community develop-

---

[1] *A Tradition That Has No Name,* Mary Field Belenky, Lynne A. Bond, and Jacqueline S. Weinstock (New York: Basic Books, 1997), pp. 221–222.

ment as a process best accomplished by investing in development corporations which commonly are structured hierarchically and dominated by outside professions (predominantly male). Although anthropologists and sociologists agree that community organizing is one of the first steps to social development, there is virtually no commitment of government or foundation resources to support community organizing. Either we therapize or social-work low-income people or imprison them: criminal justice solutions or social welfare solutions.

## NEIGHBORHOOD WOMEN PRINCIPLES AND PRACTICES

Neighborhood Women's first decade was dedicated to establishing voice and visibility and refining their organizing principles as they tested their strength, found their power, and developed tools useful to grassroots women around the country. To speak and hear each other across a broad spectrum of issues, Neighborhood Women established a national dialogue to articulate the following principles:

• Honoring values of dignity, mutual respect and trust
• Honoring diversity in social identity and oppression issues
• Supporting women's leadership and initiatives
• Strengthening ties to local neighborhoods
• Strengthening families and communities in their many forms
• Fostering processes fostering dignity, mutual respect, and trust
• Organizing through support groups and networks
• Holding government accountable to assist self-help
• Working in principled partnerships, coalitions, and supercoalitions

Action strategies to manifest these principles were also arrived at and adopted by member consensus:

1. Encourage low-income women to participate and lead in the development of their communities.
2. Identify and share the creative projects and methods developed by urban and rural grassroots women's groups.
3. Increase the opportunities for grassroots women to network locally, nationally, and internationally.
4. Focus national attention on the capabilities and successes of low-income women.

## LEADERSHIP SUPPORT, NATIONAL NETWORKING, AND AFFILIATES

Along with developing networking strategies, Neighborhood Women realized they had to design a consciousness-raising tool to foster a critical analysis of community development. Lisel Burns, a longtime Neighborhood Women board member, synthesized the "Leadership Support Process," providing agreements and meeting formats in which women could express their feelings as leaders in their communities, be sensitive to diverse realities, deconstruct issues, and envision new solutions. To facilitate open communication and real listening, ground rules include equal time for all participants—no one speaks twice before each who wishes to speaks once; no putdowns of self or others are permitted; no advice is offered—"I" statements or questions are used to support someone, and voiced appreciations of self and others are made at all meetings. The process also includes "vision questions," a way of calling forth the dreams of a women's values–based community of support and inviting clear analyses of the social and economic contexts that must be altered to make those dreams reality.

As Neighborhood Women members traveled around the country, visiting and getting to know other grassroots women's groups, they started to see deep similarities. A 1987 Conference on Housing Options for Women brought together 300 women (from 36 states and 8 countries) who were actively engaged in grassroots housing development efforts involving public and community affordable housing. The consensus among the women reaffirmed the need for a national network to share strategies, provide mutual support, and strengthen women's capacity to plan. This inspired Neighborhood Women to separate their local and national programs. An independent, affiliated local organization—Neighborhood Women of Williamsburg/Greenpoint—was created. Responding to grassroots women's desire

## What Some Neighborhood Women Affiliates Are Doing

- Begun as a self-help response to poverty in rural Orland, Maine, the H.O.M.E. (Homemakers Organized for More Employment) cooperative offers affordable housing via its community land trust, employs 40 people, serves as an outlet for 300 home crafters, and offers day care to college students and shelters to people in greatest need.
- Tenant-led organizing at James Weldon John Public Housing Development in East Harlem, New York, led to tenant control of a $21 million renovation, community gardens, summer festivals, and recent rollbacks of Housing Authority control initiatives.
- Rural women who started Woodland Community Land Trust in Clairfield, Tennessee, created their own local currency, sustainable logging jobs, and affordable housing.
- Faith-based WomanSpirit, in St. Louis, Missouri, led by and serving women of color, created a "Circles of Hope" training model, combining values-based support groups and alternative economic popular education.
- In Portland, Oregon, Housing Our Families created a women's community development corporation, which builds family-friendly housing, managed by Neighborhood Women.

for training in leadership development and support to help them achieve recognition as agents of their own development versus being passive recipients of "help," Neighborhood Women also established an annual five-day Training Institute on Women and Community Development. This retreat has served as a unifying base and place to exchange and harvest experiences and insights. At the institute women learn from each other about projects and approaches that worked. They establish informal linkages and ongoing support networks and exchange experiences of success as well as strategies for solving problems, gaining public attention, and influencing policy.

Neighborhood Women affiliates range from rural land trusts to effective public and low-income housing associations—all led by, and largely composed of, women—in Appalachia, the Pacific Northwest, the Northeast, the Midwest, and Midsouth. Membership benefits include materials and access to trainers; hands-on help with local and regional community building events; an annual summer training retreat; access to grassroots developers from Africa,

Asia, Latin America, and other regions; plus ties to coalitions, allied networks, and UN conferences.

### GLOBAL CONNECTIONS

Grassroots leaders realized that the feminization of poverty in the United States and the growing deterioration of funding for communities (the Reagan administration had cut 60% of housing monies) was resembling more and more the situation of women in the developing countries. Moreover, grassroots women in the Southern and Eastern hemispheres had accomplished very successful organizing efforts that the U.S. media didn't extensively report, such as microcredit loan programs in Asia and land trusts in Africa.

In 1985, Neighborhood Women teamed up with representatives from women's grassroots organizations from India, Kenya, Philippines, Cameroon, and the United States, and Caroline Pezzullo, a longtime Catholic social movement leader and UN consultant. They formed GROOTS (Grassroots Organizations Operating Together in Sisterhood) International to support grassroots women leaders all over the world, gaining a voice in international forums. GROOTS network is now organized in nine world regions; Neighborhood Women is the Focal Point for North America.

At the Fourth World Women's Conference in Beijing in 1995, GROOTS successfully lobbied the NGO Forum organizers to provide space for a "Grassroots Tent," where grassroots women could share and inspire others to share in a nonhierarchical way. It was considered to be one of the most vital places at the conference of 30,000 women. Grassroots women's concerns—including land tenure, evictions, credit for livelihoods, and affordable housing and capacity building—were represented through the Grassroots Caucus and influenced the writing of the Beijing Platform for Action. Neighborhood Women also followed up on the UN 1987 Habitat International Coalition, a conference designed to focus on land and housing rights for the poor of the world, by hosting ten U.S. regional forums to show the female face and key elements of sustainability at the grassroots level as well as the commitments of national governments responding to the worldwide housing and human settlements movement.

### CONSTANCY AMID CONSTANT CHANGE

Neighborhood Women has changed with the times. The founding local, originally composed of Italian and Black women leaders, is now Latina, reflecting changes in the neighborhood. The national Neighborhood Women has set its sights higher and broader every year and continually attracts new affiliates and venues. Plans for the next decade include building their base, linking with others in diversity, gaining strength through principled partnerships, and preparing a five-year civic and popular education campaign to bring core themes and social issues directly to people at the local community level, bypassing local politicians and false policy debates on nightly television.

Neighborhood Women continues to invite projects and participation by "principled partners"— people from all sectors, including government, values/faith-based groups, concerned businesspeople, schools, colleges, and other nonprofits—who understand that coalition and support among all sectors of society are critical for community development to shift from agendas set by funders to visions determined by communities. Neighborhood Women invites members of the academic community to explore the bridge that the university can be to encouraging grassroots women's leadership and a healthy community life.                    [1998]

## 🌿 146

# *Voices*

WOMEN OF ACE (AIDS COUNSELING AND EDUCATION), BEDFORD HILLS CORRECTIONAL FACILITY

*The authors of this essay are Kathy Boudin, Judy Clark, "D," Katrina Haslip, Maria D. L. Hernandez, Suzanne Kessler, Sonia Perez, Deborah Plunkett, Aida Rivera, Doris Romeo, Carmen Royster, Cathy Salce, Renee Scott, Jenny Serrano, and Pearl Ward.*

### INTRODUCTION

We are writing about ACE because we feel that it has made a tremendous difference in this prison and could make a difference in other prisons. ACE stands for AIDS Counseling and Education. It is a collective effort by women in Bedford Hills Correctional Facility. This article will reflect that collectivity by being a patchwork quilt of many women's voices.

ACE was started by inmates in 1988 because of the crisis that AIDS was creating in our community. According to a blind study done in the Fall-Winter of 1987–88, almost 20 percent of the women entering the New York state prison system were HIV infected.[1] It is likely to be higher today. In addition, women here have family members who are sick and friends who are dying. People have intense fears of transmission through casual contact because we live so closely together. Women are worried about their children and about having safe sex. All this need and energy led to the creation of ACE.

### BEFORE ACE

Prior to the formation of ACE, Bedford was an environment of fear, stigma, lack of information, and evasion. AIDS was a word that was whispered. People had no forum in which to talk about their fears. The doctors and nurses showed their biases. They preferred to just give advice, and many wouldn't touch people because of their own fears. There were several deaths. This inflamed people's fear more. People didn't want to look at their own vulnerability—their IV drug use and unsafe sex.

> I felt very negative about people who I knew were sick. To save face, I spoke to them from afar. I felt that they all should be put into a building by themselves because I heard that people who were healthy could make them sick and so they should get specific care. I figured that I have more time (on my sentence); why should I be isolated? They should be. I felt very negative and it came a lot from fear.[2]

Women at Bedford who are sick are housed in a hospital unit called In Patient Care (IPC). ACE members remember what IPC was like before ACE:

> The IPC area—the infirmary—was horrible before, a place where nobody wanted to be. It was a place to go to die. Before ACE people started going there, it looked like a dungeon. It was unsanitary. Just the look of it made people feel like they were going to die. That was the end.

There was no support system for women who wanted to take the HIV-antibody test:

> I had a friend who tested positive. The doctor told her, you are HIV positive, but that doesn't mean you have AIDS. You shouldn't have sex, or have a baby, and you should avoid stress. Period. No information was given to her. No counseling and support. She freaked out.

## THE BEGINNING OF ACE: BREAKING THE SILENCE

Some of us sensed that people needed to talk, but no one would break the silence. Finally, five women got together, and made a proposal to the superintendent:

> We said that we ourselves had to help ourselves. We believed that as peers we would be the most effective in education, counseling, and building a community of support. We stated four main goals: to save lives through preventing the spread of HIV; to create more humane conditions for those who are HIV positive; to give support and education to

women with fears, questions, and needs related to AIDS; to act as a bridge to community groups to help women as they reenter the community.

The superintendent accepted the proposal. Each of the five women sought out other women in the population who they believed were sensitive and would be interested in breaking the silence. When they reached 35, they stopped and a meeting was called.

## BREAKING THE SILENCE CHANGED US: WE BEGAN TO BUILD A COMMUNITY

> At that first meeting a sigh of relief was felt and it rippled out. There was a need from so many directions. People went around the table and said why they were there. About the fourth or fifth woman said, "I'm here because I have AIDS." There was an intense silence. It was the first time anyone had said that aloud in a group. By the end of the meeting, several more women had said that they were HIV positive. Breaking the silence, the faith that it took, and the trust it built was really how ACE started.

## BREAKING THE SILENCE MEANT SOMETHING SPECIAL TO PWAS

> I often ask myself how it is that I came to be open about my status. For me, AIDS had been one of my best kept secrets. It took me approximately 15 months to discuss this issue openly. As if not saying it aloud would make it go away. I watched other people with AIDS (PWAs), who were much more open than I was at the time, reveal to audiences their status/their vulnerability, while sharing from a distance, from silence, every word that was being uttered by them. I wanted to be a part of what they were building, what they were doing, their statement, "I am a PWA," because I was. It was a relief when I said it. I could stop going on with the lie. I could be me. People were supportive and they didn't shun me. And now I can go anywhere and be myself.

## SUPPORTING PWAS

PWAs and HIV-positive women are at the heart of our work. ACE believes that everyone facing HIV-related illness is confronting issues of life and death and struggling to survive and thrive.

> We had to have some place for PWAs to share their experiences with each other. There have been

numerous support groups which allowed us to express things that hadn't been verbalized but that had been on our minds. It was interesting to see that we had similar issues: how to tell significant others, our own vulnerability about being open, living with AIDS. My first group was a mixture of people. Some were recently diagnosed and others had been diagnosed for two years. It was informative and it was emotional. Sometimes we would just come to a meeting and cry. Or we might come there and not even talk about the issue of AIDS and just have a humor session because we are just tired of AIDS.

One of the first things that ACE ever did was to work in IPC.

ACE started going to IPC. We painted, cleaned up, made it look so good that now the women want to stay there. We take care of the girls who are sick, making them feel comfortable and alive. Now, women there know they have a friend. They feel free, they talk, and look forward to visits. They know they're not there to die, not like before.

## BEING A BUDDY

I have been involved in ACE for about three years. About a year ago I started visiting the women in IPC. I was really afraid at first. Not afraid of getting sick, but of becoming emotionally involved and then have the women die. At first, I tried to keep my feelings and friendship at a minimum. The more I went, the more I lost this fear. There is one woman I have gotten closer to than the rest. She has been in IPC since I first started going there. We are buddies. For me to be her buddy means unconditionally loving her and accepting her decisions. I go almost every night to IPC. Some nights we just sit there and say nothing. But there is comfort in my presence. She had a stroke before I met her. So there is a lot she cannot do for herself. There are times when I bathe and dress her. Iron her clothes. I do not think of any of these things as chores. Soon she will be going home. I am overjoyed, but I'm also saddened knowing that I will not see her again. I will miss her hugs, her complaining, and her love. But I would do it all over again and I probably will with someone else.

## MEDICAL ADVOCACY

It is obviously a matter of life or death for anyone who is HIV infected to get good medical care and have a good relationship with her health providers. Medical facilities in prisons start out understaffed and ill equipped, and the AIDS crisis escalated these problems enormously. In the 1970s women prisoners here instituted a class action suit, *Todaro v. Ward,* to demand better medical care. Because of that case, the medical facilities and care at Bedford are monitored for the court by an outside expert. That expert issued a report criticizing all aspects of the medical department for being inadequately prepared to meet women's AIDS-related medical needs, and the prison faced a court hearing and possible contempt charges. Under that pressure the state agreed to numerous changes that brought new medical staff and resources, including a full-time medical director, a part-time infectious disease specialist, and more nurses. ACE was able to institute a medical advocacy plan that allowed ACE members to accompany women to their doctor's consultation visit to ensure that nothing was missed. Afterward, there can be a private discussion between the patient and the advocate to clarify matters for the woman, to explore possibilities of treatment, or just to allow the person to express whatever emotions she experienced when she received the news from the doctor.

## PEER EDUCATION

Our approach is *peer* education, which we believe is best suited for the task of enabling a community to mobilize itself to deal with AIDS. The people doing the training clearly have a personal stake in the community. The education is for all, in the interests of all. This is communicated from the beginning by the women doing the teaching.

Our peer education takes a problem-posing approach. We present issues as problems facing all of us, problems to be examined by drawing on the knowledge and experience of the women being trained. What are the issues between a man and a woman, for example, that make it hard for a woman to demand that her man use a condom? Will distributing free needles or advocating bleach kits stop the spread of AIDS among IV drug users?

Our educational work is holistic. Education is not solely a presentation of facts, although that is an important part of the trainers' responsibilities. But what impact do feelings and attitudes have on how people deal with facts? Why would a person who knows that you cannot get AIDS by eating from a PWA's plate still act occasionally as if you could? Why would a person who knows that sex without a condom could be inviting death, not use a condom? For education to be a deep process, it involves understanding the whole person; for education to take root within a community, it means thinking about things on a community, social level.

> Coming to prison, living under these conditions, was scary, and AIDS made it even scarier. I was part of a society that made judgments and had preconceived ideas about the women in prison.

## EDUCATING OURSELVES

### Workshops

To become members of ACE, women must be educated through a series of eight workshops. We look at how stigma and blame have been associated with diseases throughout history, and how the sexism of this society impacts on women in the AIDS epidemic. We teach about the nature of the virus, strategies for treatment, and holistic approaches. After the eight weeks, we ask who would like to become involved, and then there is a screening process. The Superintendent has final approval. The workshops are followed by more intensive training of women who become members.

### Orientation

When women enter the New York state prison system, they must come first to Bedford Hills, where they either stay or move on after several weeks to one of several other women's prisons. ACE members talk with the women when they first arrive.

> We do orientations of 10 to 35 women. We explain to them how you can and cannot get AIDS, about testing and about ACE. Sometimes the crowd is very boisterous and rude. I say "AIDS" and they don't want to hear about it. But those are the ones I try to reach. After orientation is over, the main ones that didn't want to hear about AIDS are the ones who want to talk more and I feel good about that. A lot of times, their loudness is a defense because they

are afraid of their own vulnerability. They know that they are at risk for HIV infection because of previous behaviors. After I finish doing orientation, I have a sense of warmth, because I know I made a difference in some of their lives.

### Seminars

One of the main ways we interact with our sisters is through seminars. We talk about AIDS issues with groups of women on living units, in classrooms, and in some of the other prison programs such as family violence, drug treatment, and Children's Center.

> The four back buildings are dormitories, each holding 100 women with double bunked beds. We from ACE gather right after count, with our easel and newsprint and magic markers and our three-by-five cards with the information on whatever presentation we're making. We move in twos and threes through the connecting tunnels to the building. When we arrive some of the women are sitting in the rec room, but many others are in their cubicles/cells. They ask why we're here. We look like a traveling troupe—and we've felt like it, not knowing what to expect. Some women are excited that we're going to talk about AIDS. Others say, "forget it," or "fuck you, I've heard enough about it, it's depressing."

But we begin, and people slowly gather.

> We ask the women to help us role-play a situation such as a woman going home from prison, trying to convince her man, who has been taking care of her while she's inside, to use a condom. Then the role-play is analyzed. What problems are encountered and how do we deal with those problems? We try to come up with suggestions that we can see ourselves using in that situation. We talk about the risk of violence.

One of the most immediate problems people have is whether or not to take the HIV-antibody test. We do not push testing. We explain what the test is and have a group discussion of things the women need to consider. A woman may be inclined to get tested, but she needs to know that she is likely to be transferred upstate before the results come back from the lab. The choice is up to her. Toward the end of the seminar, PWAs talk about their experiences living with AIDS.

When they speak, they bring together everything that we have said. Not only that, but they let people know that living with AIDS is not instant death. It makes people realize why the struggles, working together, and being as one are so important. When I hear the women who are PWAs speak, it makes me realize that I could have been in their shoes, or I could still be, if they hadn't been willing to talk about their risk behaviors and what has happened to them. It gives me the courage to realize that it's not all about me. It's actually about us.

We end each seminar with all the women standing with our arms around each other or holding hands—without any fear of casual contact—singing our theme song, "Sister."[3] We sing, having come to a new place where we are for each other, unified. We all feel some sense of relief and some sense of hope. Talking about AIDS openly has changed how we live. We leave the seminar with the knowledge that we can talk about AIDS and that we're going to be okay. . . .

## Counseling

When we conduct the seminars and orientation sessions, women come up to us afterward with personal questions and problems. It could be they are HIV positive, or they are thinking of taking the test, or they have a family member who is sick, or they are thinking about getting involved with someone in a relationship. Sometimes they raise one issue, but underlying it are a lot of other issues they're not yet ready to talk about. Because women know we're in ACE, we're approached in our housing units, at school, on the job, in the mess hall, as we walk from one place to another. Women stop us, needing to talk. We're a haven for women because they know ACE has a principle of confidentiality. Women can trust us not to abuse the information they are sharing with us.

Peer counseling. I'm just impressed that we can do it. I didn't know what kind of potential we'd have as peers. We talk the language that each of us understands. Even if it's silent, even if it's with our eyes, it's something that each of us seems to understand. I know I wouldn't want someone from the Department of Health who hasn't even taken a Valium to try to educate me about IV drug use. How could

they give me helpful hints? I would feel that they are so out of tune with reality that I wouldn't be able to hear them.

## A CRISIS AND OPPORTUNITY FOR OUR COMMUNITY

We are a small community and we are so isolated you can feel it—the suffering, the losses, the fears, the anxiety. Out in the street you don't have a community of women affected and living together facing a problem in this same way. We can draw on the particular strengths that women bring: nurturance, caring, and personal openness. So many women prisoners have worked in nursing and old age homes. Yet when they did, they were never given respect. Here these same activities are valued, and the women are told "thank you," and that creates initiative and feelings of self-worth. And ACE helps us to be more self-conscious about a culture of caring that as women we tend to create in our daily lives.

For the first time in prison I was part of a group that cared about other prisoners in prison. What did that feel like? It felt like I wasn't alone in caring about people, because in this type of setting I was beginning to wonder about people caring.

## OUR IMPACT ON WOMEN

We know that we have played a role in communicating information about what is safe and what is not safe in sexual behavior—both between a man and woman and between two women—and we have certainly been able to create open and relaxed discussions about all this. But we know that actually changing behaviors is another leap ahead of us. We are learning that it's not a one-shot deal, that information doesn't equal behavior change, and it's not just an individual thing. Social norms have to change, and this takes time. And when you talk about women having to initiate change you're up against the fact that women don't have that kind of empowerment in this society. Women who have been influenced by ACE have experienced a change in attitude, but it is unclear whether this will translate into behavior change once they leave the prison.

When I first started taking the workshops I was 100 percent against using condoms. And yet I like anal sex. But now my views are different. We're the bosses of our own bodies. You know, a lot of people say it's a man's world. Well, I can't completely agree.

## *OUR DIVERSITY IS A STRENGTH*

We are a diverse community of women: Black, Latin, and white, and also from countries throughout the world. In ACE there was at first a tendency to deny the differences, maybe out of fear of disunity. Now there is a more explicit consciousness growing that we can affirm our diversity and our commonality because both are important. In the last workshop on women, we broke for a while into three groups—Black, Latina, and white women—to explore the ways AIDS impacted on our particular culture and communities. We are doing more of those kinds of discussions and developing materials that address concerns of specific communities.

---

## *"Sister"*

CRIS WILLIAMSON

Born of the earth
Child of God
Just one among the family
And you can count on me
To share the load
And I will always help you
Hold burdens
And I will be the one
To help you ease your pain

Lean on me, I am your sister
Believe on me, I am your friend

I will fold you in my arms
Like a white wing dove
Shine in your soul
Your spirit is crying

Born of the earth
Child of God
Just one among the family
And you can count on me
To share the load
And I will always help you
Hold burdens
And I will be the one
To help you ease your pain

Lean on me, I am your sister
Believe on me, I am your friend
Lean on me, I am your sister
Believe on me, I am your friend

The Hispanic Sector of ACE is particularly active, conducting seminars in Spanish and holding open meetings for the population to foster Hispanic awareness of AIDS issues.

> The workshops didn't deal enough with different ethnic areas, and being Puerto Rican and half-Indian, some things seemed ridiculous in terms of the Hispanic family. Some of the ways people were talking about sex wouldn't work in a traditional Hispanic family. For example, you can't just tell your husband that he has to wear a condom. Or say to him, "You have to take responsibility." These approaches could lead to marital rape or abuse. The empowerment of Hispanic women means making sure that their children are brought up.

## WORKING IN A PRISON

We have a unique situation at Bedford Hills. We have a prison administration that is supportive of inmates developing a peer-based program to deal with AIDS. However, because we are in a prison there are a lot of constraints and frustrations. Before we had staff persons to supervise us, we could not work out of an office space. That meant that we couldn't see women who wanted to talk on an individual level unless we ran into them in the yard or rec room.

You could be helping someone in IPC take her daily shower; it's taking longer than usual because she is in a lot of pain or she needs to talk, but that's not taken into consideration when the officer tells you that you have to leave immediately because it's "count-time." You could be in the rec room, a large room with a bunch of card tables, loud music, and an officer overseeing groups of women sitting on broken-down chairs. You're talking to a woman in crisis who needs comforting. You reach out to give her a hug and the C.O. may come over to admonish you, "No physical contact, ladies." Or maybe a woman has just tested positive. She's taken her first tentative steps to reach out by talking to someone from ACE and joining a support group. Days after her first meeting, she is transferred to another prison.

It's been difficult to be able to call ourselves counselors and have our work formally acknowledged by the administration. Counseling is usually done by professionals in here because it carries such liability and responsibility. We're struggling for the legitimacy of peer counseling. The reality is that we've been doing it in our daily lives here through informal dialogue. We now have civilian staff to supervise us, and Columbia University will be conducting a certification training program to justify the title "peer counselor."

After working over two years on our own, we are now being funded by a grant from the New York State AIDS Institute, coordinated by Columbia University School of Public Health and by Women and AIDS Resource Network (WARN). The money has allowed hiring staff to work with ACE. ACE began as a totally volunteer inmate organization with no office or materials, operating on a shoestring and scrambling for every meeting. Now we have an office in a prime location of the prison, computers, and a civilian staff responsible for making certain that there is something to show for their salaries. Inmates who used to work whenever they could find the time are now paid 73 cents a day as staff officially assigned to the ACE Center. The crises are no longer centered around the problems of being inside a prison, but more on how to sustain momentum and a real grassroots initiative in the context of a prison. This is a problem faced by many other community organizations when they move past the initial momentum and become more established institutions.

## BUILDING A CULTURE OF SURVIVAL

When, in the spring of 1987, we said, "Let's make quilt squares for our sisters who have died," there were more than 15 names. Over the next year we made more and more quilt squares. The deaths took a toll not just on those who knew the women but on all of us. Too many women were dying among us. And, for those who were HIV positive or worried that they might be, each death heightened their own vulnerabilities and fears. We have had to develop ways to let people who are sick know that if they die, their lives will be remembered, they will be honored and celebrated, and they will stay in our hearts.

> I remember our first memorial. Several hundred women contributed money—25 cents, 50 cents,

a dollar—for flowers. Both Spanish and Black women sang and in the beginning everyone held hands and sang "That's What Friends Are For," and in the end we sang "Sister." People spoke about what Ro meant to them. Ro had died and we couldn't change that. But we didn't just feel terrible. We felt love and caring and that together we could survive the sadness and loss.

In the streets, funerals were so plastic, but here, people knew that it could be them. It's not just to pay respect. When we sang "Sister," there was a charge between us. Our hands were extended to each other. There was a need for ACE and we could feel it in the air.

It was out of that same need that ACE was formed. It will be out of that same need that ACE will continue to strive to build community and an environment of trust and support. We are all we have—ourselves. If we do not latch on to this hope that has strengthened us and this drive that has broken our silence, we too will suffer and we will remain stigmatized and isolated. Feel our drive in our determination to make changes, and think "community," and make a difference.

### NOTES

1. Perry F. Smith et al., *Infection Among Women Entering the New York State Correctional System* (1990), unpublished manuscript.
2. All quotations are from the authors' conversations with prisoners at Bedford Hills.
3. By Cris Williamson, from the album *The Changer and the Changed*, Olivia Records, 1975.                    [1990]

 147

# Taking It Lying Down . . . In the Street!

BARBARA YOSHIDA

It was 2:30 on a hot afternoon in July. The apartment was packed with people sitting on the floor, with barely enough room to move. If there was air conditioning, we couldn't feel it. Some of us were fanning ourselves, and we were all trying to keep

from talking. People wanted to talk because they were nervous, and some were just plain scared. The noise level would rise in a wave, someone would plead for quiet, and a few moments later another wave of voices would rise. We wanted to get moving. It was almost impossible to sit quietly. For several weeks now the tension has been building, and here we were, within a stone's throw of the Holland Tunnel. Only we weren't here to throw stones. All we wanted to do was sit down in the street.

For several weeks, in anticipation by the Supreme Court on the Casey decision, pro-choice activists had been planning a massive civil disobedience action: to shut down the Tunnel on the eve of the July 4th weekend. There was really never a doubt in my mind that I would participate. I did wonder about all those flyers, though. They were wheatpasted all over downtown Manhattan. Seemed risky to me, to flaunt the action publicly like that.

This was the perfect action for my first civil disobedience, though, because I feel more strongly about it than any other issue. It concerns women's rights, women's health, and civil rights in general. We knew that whatever decision the Supreme Court made, it would chip away at *Roe v. Wade*, and if they wanted us to take it lying down, we'd take it lying down in the street! They can't acknowledge our rights to make decisions about our own bodies and then take that right away—not even a little bit.

So on July 1st I left the WAC (Women's Action Coalition) meeting with Marilyn Minter and we headed over to the Gay & Lesbian Center on West 13th Street. We found out that we couldn't actually meet at the Center. The Court had slapped an injunction on us, a very widesweeping one: no one could walk down any street even *leading* to Port Authority property, from now 'til the end of time, and we couldn't meet at the Center. Because the Center was named in the injunction, we knew for sure that cops had been at our meetings. We grouped together down the street, were told to go to a second location, and from there went to a third address where we met on the roof.

It was a fine night for a bunch of bad girls to get together. OK, there were some bad boys, too. The thing that really impressed me was that the women were organizing this and the men were there to show support. I've never been to an Act-Up meeting. I've heard that the men pretty much run things. It seems to me, though, that a transference of knowledge has taken place there from men to women that has not occurred in the heterosexual world. Gay men have shared the power. Or maybe lesbian women have just taken it—they are even more marginalized in our society than gay men or heterosexual women, they have learned how the gay men take power, and they know they can do the same thing. Three or four women took the responsibility to organize this action and see it through, injunction and all. And it was extremely well organized. Our legal team was headed by three women: Mary Dorman, Lori Cohen, and Joan Gibbs. Many training sessions, conducted by women, had led to this rooftop meeting.

At first, the dark rooftop was only back-lit by the streetlights far below, which made it a bit romantic. We discussed the ramifications of violating the injunction—the possibility of more charges being given than the usual "dis con" (disorderly conduct) and "resisting arrest" charges, being kept in jail longer, more people being "put through the system," maybe even fines. People were urged to reconsider, and leave if they wanted. Some left. I am sure that the group would have been twice as large if it hadn't been for the injunction. Personally, it made me even more committed—it made my blood boil. Someone hooked up a light, and we put down the phone number of a person to be contacted if we were kept in jail too long, and any special information, such as medication we might need. This information would be kept at "Central." Before leaving, everyone received a slip of paper with an address and time on it for the next day, July 2nd. We were told to memorize it and talk to no one.

The next afternoon, the group found itself divided among several different locations within walking distance of the Tunnel. An hour later we left those locations in groups of three, each of us memorizing part of yet another address. We were not to stop anywhere along the way, ensuring that no one would make a phone call to tip off the police. Walking to this final destination, we felt the thrill of being part of a covert operation. The police were all over the place, and we were walking down Varick, right in the middle of them. There were plenty of paddy wagons, too.

Now we were packed in this space, two hundred hot, edgy people. Many of us were doing civil disobedience for the first time. Finally we got the word to start filing down the stairs, which would open right on Watts Street. It was relief to start moving. Within minutes we heard that the first people were already being arrested! We had to run down the stairs, still trying to hold hands. We rushed out to Varick Street and sat down. Another group ran up Varick to block a second entrance to the Tunnel. The first arrests were rougher than necessary. We all chanted "No violence!" I looked at a cop standing right in front of me, and his fists were clenched in anger. I looked right into his eyes and said "No violence!" until I saw his fists relax. Soon the arrests became slow-paced and methodical. We continued to chant, "Abortion is health care, health care is a right!" as each person's turn came to be arrested.

I must say that I took pride in being arrested for something that meant so much to me. I was never politically active before, and now that another wave of feminism is building, I have a chance to jump on that wave and hang ten! Women often have difficulty taking action, doing things for themselves. Becoming an activist is one of the most empowering things I've ever done for myself. Civil disobedience is a particularly effective tool for social change, and it's *especially* good for women.

I'll never forget that feeling. Forcing the police to lift me into the van because I would not help them, I felt in control, and I kept shouting "No choice, no peace!" It became a litany, a personal affirmation of everything I believed. The quality of my voice began to change. I felt a deep growl from somewhere down in my gut erupting into this rhythmic chant. I was speaking to the entire world, I was part of something much bigger than myself, bigger than this one action. I almost didn't recognize my own voice. I felt charged and powerful. I have never been more sure of myself, more sure that what I was doing was right.                                    [1992]

## 🌿 148

# HUES *Magazine:*
# *The Making of a Movement*

TALI EDUT, WITH DYANN LOGWOOD
AND OPHIRA EDUT

Hello, my name is Tali . . . and I was an addict. You see, once upon a time I had this problem. I just couldn't stop myself from subscribing to magazines for women and girls "just like me." I confess that I was a victim of the ill mainstream media; the glamorized trappings that amounted to just about every "ism" in the book. If a product was being pushed, in all its brightly colored wrapping, I was zealously tearing off the bow. Though I now publish a magazine that encourages intelligence and self-sufficiency "for women of all sizes, ethnic backgrounds, and lifestyles," it was my lifelong battle with the pressures and the standards of "successful" women's magazines that motivated me to collaborate with my girls to create *HUES* magazine.

While growing up, I learned a lot from women's magazines. I learned how to apply just the right shade of lipstick to get that "special guy" to (not) notice me. I learned that all the stretching, pulling, and lifting in the world couldn't make me pencil thin like the teenage models I was *supposed* to look like. Beauty, success, and coolness, they taught me, were reserved for an illusory circle of pale-skinned, prom-perfect ultrafemmes with tiny features and unchallenged minds. No matter how outstanding I was on my own, these glossies assured me that life was never really complete without a man by my side.

The saddest part about the image-obsession craze is that it keeps women so preoccupied with feeling bad about our appearances that our minds and souls become secondary. Instead of investing money in mutual funds or taking night classes, the only numbers we're interested in crunching are the ones on the scales at Jenny Craig. The struggle for self-esteem is ongoing for many women. It's undeniably easier for a woman to find outlets for self-hatred than to find ones that tell her to feel good about who

she is. All she has to do is pick up a magazine. If she doesn't know that airbrushing is the only real answer to cellulite, she might believe the hype.

When we were nineteen years old, [my twin sister] Ophi and I met Dyann Logwood. She had been sitting in the dorm room of a mutual friend when Ophi walked by, and Ophi (as she said later) was just drawn in. The two of them wound up having such an amazing conversation that they actually forgot about the guy they had each come to visit. I was introduced a couple of days later, and we soon became an inseparable trio. It was odd that we got along so well, because our backgrounds were really different. Dyann was African American, the daughter of a Pentecostal preacher. Her upbringing had been strict and somewhat conservative, in a religious sense. Although we all came from integrated schools, Dyann was among a significant population of African American students. Ophi and I were two of possibly twenty Jews in our school district, and the only Israelis. Although Jewish traditions such as holidays and seven years of Hebrew school were upheld, our family tended to be more liberal about daily life. In high school, Dyann was well known for her public speaking abilities and was nicknamed Jesse Jackson for her pro-Black speeches. Although Ophi and I were known for winning writing contests and making crazy, artistic clothes, we were more on the outside fringe. We tended to be more closeted about our Jewish heritage then, preferring to blend instead of making any grandiose political statements about ethnicity.

In spite of our differences, our friendship was both medicinal and educational. Our late-night talks over pizza and vending machine snacks were like group therapy sessions and basement political meetings. (And you wouldn't believe how good junk food tasted after years of oat bran and frozen yogurt.) It was from these talks that we gained a perspective into worlds beyond our own doorsteps.

Dyann was the first woman the two of us had ever met who didn't constantly put herself down. She wasn't afraid to take pride in the things she did well. In her mind, if you didn't believe you were "all that," no one else would, either. At sixteen, she had decided that she didn't want to go through life hating herself. She enlisted the help of a few daily affirmations, wherein she would look in the mirror and tell herself she was beautiful and strong. She swore by it as a confidence booster. That was such an odd concept for me and Ophi. We could hardly fathom looking in the mirror and saying, "You look okay, I guess." But beautiful? That was a whole new ball game. The three of us were all shaped similarly—short and thick. The difference was that in Dyann's community, being skinny was considered unattractive and "having some meat on your bones" was actually a sign of beauty. As a teen, Dyann had felt an uncomfortable urgency to sprout some curves, whereas Ophi and I had worked obsessively to diminish ours. Although Dyann had felt less impact from teen girls' magazines (the permanent absence of Black models and issues had dulled her interest), she had been unduly affected by the industry's by-product—what she referred to as "the Black Barbie syndrome." The Black woman with light skin, green eyes, and long hair (which, I learned from Dyann, is sometimes hard for Black women to grow)—essentially the Whitest-looking Black woman—was touted as the most beautiful. Whereas a lot of Jewish girls Ophi and I knew were constantly dieting, blow-drying the curl out of their hair, and occasionally spending spring break at the plastic surgeon's, Dyann was acquainted with Black women who spent hundreds of dollars getting their hair permed straight, popping colored contacts, even buying over-the-counter skin bleach.

Getting to the stage of believing she was a strong, beautiful woman wasn't easy for Dyann, though. In spite of Hollywood's portrayal of hard-core Black women who didn't take any shit, Dyann recalled regular sermons about a woman's role being to support her man at all times. She also remembered the girls at her church being commanded to "keep their legs closed." Although the women she grew up around had a strong presence, they rarely challenged the church-prescribed role of wife and mother. Similarly, although no one was directly insisting that Ophi and I become stereotypical, overbearing Jewish mothers, we always felt pressured to find that "nice Jewish boy" to make our lives complete. For all of us, growing beyond the prescribed definition of womanhood demanded a good deal of work.

While we were chowing down, we talked about a lot of things besides physical image. We'd all had interracial friendships prior to college, but they had tended to be more color-blind (you're aware of surface differences, for instance, but you choose to ignore them for fear of bringing up possibly unpleasant issues). Whether it was the self-actualizing aura of college life or the fact that we were suddenly awakening to the ills that surrounded us, the three of us couldn't seem to have a conversation that wasn't political. We talked about *everything:* How people in Dyann's classes often assumed she was there only because of affirmative action. How futile it was for Blacks and Jews to debate the significance of slavery versus the Holocaust. How sad it was that a man's influence could quash a woman's dreams. How our teachers had rarely encouraged us toward big-money careers. How hard it was to decide whether Judaism was a race or a religion. How annoying it was that our peers assumed we were sellouts or wanna-be's because we didn't hang exclusively with people inside our cultures.

From those talks a new cross-cultural guideline emerged: don't tiptoe around the issues, but also be prepared to shut up and listen. Initially we were all somewhat clueless about each other's cultures, and, I won't pretend that we disbelieved every stereotype. (We cracked up when Dyann revealed that someone had once told her that the word *Jew* came from *jewelry,* because Jewish people owned all the jewelry stores.) It took a little while before we were able to admit that we weren't always liberal ambassadors with innate understandings of every cultural truth and faux pas. After hanging out for a couple of weeks, we reached a comfortable understanding that if someone said something ignorant, another could correct her without ending the friendship, and that if someone asked a "stupid" question, we would try to answer it without jumping down the other's throat. Above all, we learned to listen and learn from each other's experiences. I had once believed that racism had been eradicated along with the Jim Crow laws. Dyann's life stories helped me and Ophi see that we still had a lot of privileges on the basis of our paler features. And, after the three of us decided to be roommates, we saw firsthand how many apartments suddenly became "unavailable" when Dyann walked into the rental office.

By the time we figured we knew *everything* there was to know about Black and Jewish cultures—as if—we got the idea that our talks might be a good basis for bringing more women together across cultural "boundaries." We knew we weren't the only three women in the world who had been affected by an era of heroin-addicted models and Martha Stewart-like supermoms. We were especially concerned with the impact on women like ourselves, who were considered "cultural others."

While we were waiting for inspiration on the perfect way to unite all women, I got my first behind-the-scenes look at women's magazines. I was back at home on summer break, thumbing through my little sister's *Sassy* magazine. At that time, *Sassy* was arguably the closest thing to a teenage feminist publication that existed. Of all the teen and women's magazines on the shelves, it was the one publication with a voice that I could sort of relate to. The writers were frank and opinionated, rather than prissy and NutraSweetish. So, when I arrived at the page announcing that *Sassy* was having a "Reader-Produced Issue Contest," my interest was stirred. Essentially, *Sassy* was offering teenagers the opportunity to "replace" its entire staff for one issue. I had always had an interest in both the media and New York City (where *Sassy* was located), so, with the technical skill I'd gained from a couple of computer graphics classes at the University of Michigan, I decided to try for the role of art director. A few weeks later, Neill, then the real art director of *Sassy*, phoned with the unbelievable news that I would be taking his place for the month of August.

At *Sassy* I joined the other contest winners—a small but amazing group of young women from all over the United States and Canada. After five minutes, I felt my transformation from a midwestern hopeful to a cosmopolitan diva begin. We were all hyped to try out a few revolutionary ideas, as we were under the impression that we could "recreate" this issue. I, for one, wanted to put some of my own political awakenings into action in this mag. Unfortunately, the reader model winners had already been instructed that to enter, they had to fit the standard dimensions (at least 5'8" tall, size seven clothes).

Still, amid the "goth" fashion shoots (heavy black eyeliner, dyed black hair), a few of the more political contestants and I managed to slip in a little consciousness. We included a basic piece about feminism and an article by the Filipina reader-editor about growing up as a "minority."

We learned our first big lesson when we chose a Black girl and a Filipina girl to model for the cover. When we met with the publishing board to discuss our potential cover design, we expected a briefing on basic concerns, such as which articles to make into headlines and the best ways to pose the models. Instead, talk turned, uh, political. We were told that if we wanted to use these two models, we also had to include a White girl in the picture. According to the publisher's supposed expertise and marketing data, a cover without a White girl would alienate a tremendous number of readers at the newsstand. The South, after all, was an important area, and they didn't want to lose any subscribers. Although the publishers never came right out and said it, the message was clear: *Sassy* was yet another magazine strictly concerned with the number of White people reading it.

Looking back, I realize that there were other tears in the fabric of *Sassy*. The hip editorial staff was constantly at odds with the number-crunching publishing board. Writers were not allowed to touch certain subjects, such as abortion and homosexuality, at the risk of losing lucrative makeup ads. The fashion department at *Sassy* was made up of beautiful and stylish women, but few had the anorexic proportions of the models they chose month after month. Gone were my notions of some insidious White man picking seven-foot-girls from an uber-waif lineup. I saw firsthand how easily the status quo image of female beauty was perpetuated—and by women, at that! Here were women who actually had the power to reduce the damaging pressures on teen girls—pressures that are directly linked to eating disorders and poor esteem among girls and women; yet they were unwilling to take the risk. Their claim was that fashion companies made sample clothing in size seven only. (Perhaps at the heart of this brainwash is a group of fashion designers giddy over the yards of fabric they have saved during the thin-is-in craze.) Still, I wondered, if *Sassy* was able to use its influence to bring offbeat fashions such as combat boots to American teen girls, then how hard could it really be to rustle up a pair of pants in a size fourteen? The old *Sassy was* an "alternative," in the sense that encouraged more independence than its boy-crazy competitors, such as *Teen* and *YM*. Nonetheless, it never dethroned the anglo beauty queen—even if she was wearing Doc Martens.

I returned from my *Sassy* summer to the University of Michigan feeling both jaded and inspired. On the one hand, I had acquired some incredible new knowledge. Not only had I peeped the inside track of the magazine industry, but I had also gained a fairly comprehensive understanding of what went into producing a national publication. On the other hand, I had learned that what goes on behind the scenes of the media is not nearly as glamorous as what's seen on the pages.

That semester, Dyann, Ophi, and I enrolled in an introductory women's studies class. Part of the curriculum included a semester-long "action project" that involved working with women's issues in some capacity. Inspiration struck while we were musing over ideas for the assignment: why not try to create our own women's magazine and distribute it on campus?

We were in unanimous agreement that we wanted this project to be not just a magazine but a movement that would bring women together across "boundaries." We envisioned a sort of sisterhood, which we defined partly in reference to our own friendship, being played out on the pages. We saw the need for greater loyalty among women. Among our peers it was often considered cooler to be "one of the guys" than "one of the girls." Sisterhood to us meant having a support network strong enough that a woman could stand up for herself without feeling crazy or alone. It also meant having a greater sense of loyalty between women, so that, for example, we would believe each other if we said we were raped, not go after our best friend's boyfriend, stand up for a girl who gets called a slut, not feel threatened by someone we think is "prettier," and so on. Beyond that, we wanted to encourage a new style of communication among women that was more direct than conflict-avoiding. The three of us were able to accept each other's differences without feeling hos-

tile or competitive because we had an in-your-face, no-holds-barred approach to communication. We wanted to see more women talk to each other instead of about each other when dissension arose, which we felt would diminish much of the hostility that often goes on between women.

Because a conscious magazine for young women hadn't been printed to date, we didn't have a model on which to base ours. Although this made our task a little harder, it also allowed for greater creativity. Our ideas definitely diverged from the mainstream periodical selection. The publication would have to be a women's magazine of a different kind, one that would include rather than exclude. It would speak to women's intelligence, promoting self-esteem and sisterhood. It would be fun and serious, intellectual and raw at the same time. It would highlight women's experiences and direct readers to resources. It would encourage solution-oriented positivity rather than hopeless frustration. Above all, it would give women a new, real standard to look to, rather than the unattainable gloss of other women's magazines.

One of our major concerns was to provide a movement that would include women who are traditionally excluded from the mainstream—not only as participants but also as cocreators. We'd had enough of the typical women's organizations that planned their agendas with a mostly White board and then wondered why they couldn't seem to get any "women of color" to participate in their struggles. I remember feeling disgusted after the three of us attended an open planning meeting for a women's conference. Under the presumption that the meeting was going to run democratically, we instead butted up against a "good old girls network"—a group of established self-proclaimed feminists who had a prescribed set of right and wrong answers for all women. Although the discussion participants insisted that they wanted to draw in "women of color," they were opposed to trying anything beyond setting up a special "women-of-color" booth in the waiting area and bringing in one Latina professor to speak. The meeting ended up being just another illustration of the constant marginalization of non-White women into the category of "other." (I mean, if non-White women get to be "women of color," then do White women have exclusive rights to the word "women"?) This happens so often among "well-meaning" feminist groups. They claim that they want to include all women, but they want to control the quantity and the quality of women's participation.

The three of us wanted to see multiculturalism finally done right in a women's movement. It wasn't about hand-holding and singing cheesy songs. And we weren't trying to pimp "diversity" as a cover-up for token representation or do some overhyped Benetton we-are-the-world thing. Rather, we were looking for a forum wherein women of different cultures and classes would come together without losing their identities. We envisioned a successful modern women's movement in terms of the old patchwork quilt cliché. Each square would represent its own identity, but the pieces would be inextricably sewn together.

It was important to us that women of all cultures and classes be properly represented in our magazine. We agreed that a code of self-representation was the best way to handle this. If a story was to be told, we wanted it straight from the source. So, there wouldn't be any term-paper-cum-news-story on an American woman's fourth-hand experience with female circumcision; but there might be a story by a woman who had undergone the process, or there might be three women's stories. The way we figured it, the truth was best when it was undiluted by an outsider's inferred understanding. It was also important to us that we illustrate the diversity that existed within a single culture. To break down the stereotypical notion that all Asians, lesbians, single moms, and so on, think in the same way, we wanted to highlight a variety of thoughts within each community.

After mych brainstorming, we decided to name our magazine *HUES*, which conveniently shaped itself into an acronym for "Hear Us Emerging Sisters." It seemed like a word that could translate into more than just the obvious multicultural innuendo. *HUES* represented to us the varying shades of womanhood. It was inclusive (rather than simply *HUE*), and, best of all, it wasn't some frou-frou beauty reference like "mirabelle" or "allure."

With the name decided upon, we posted flyers and E-mail across campus and soon assembled a small—but truly multicultural—group of women. The *HUES* collective—which included a bisexual Black TA, a Filipina political science major, a Nigerian-born art major from the South Bronx, a single mother attending community college, a White woman who worked with the mentally ill, a Puerto Rican–Chinese photographer, and a Jewish pre-law major—spanned an even broader range of experiences than we'd expected. Still, believe it or not, there was rarely any tension. The women who came to spend Wednesday evenings eating pizza in our living room were a lot like the three of us—open-minded and willing to listen and learn. It didn't hurt that we all seemed to have good senses of humor, too. There were plenty of laughs as we sat around planning the new world order.

Before the presses rolled, the *HUES* collective took time out to assess the status of our generation of women. Would they be receptive to a new women's movement? At the time we were planning our first issue, the movie *Disclosure* (in which a male exec has an extramarital encounter with his female boss, then wins a sexual harassment case against her) was on its way to the box office, and "politically correct" was fast becoming America's favorite dirty word. The trend seemed to be toward gender neutrality rather than separatism. Not only did many women seem to fear the idea of joining together with other women, but also a lot of them saw no practical need in it. Their lives had been only covertly touched by sexism, and they were uneasy with the idea of rocking the boat.

We decided that the general attitude of our generation could be summed by the catchphrase "fear of a feminist planet." A lot of poor and non-White women associated feminism with privileged, middle-, and upper-class Whites who wanted to control their struggles and mediate their issues. In many instances the absence of non-Whites from women's groups confirmed this suspicion. Then there were the countless clueless, who still believed that pro-woman equaled anti-man. In the end, a lot of these young women wound up being feminists by default.

So, we asked ourselves, how could we package feminist ideals such as sisterhood and empowerment in a way that would speak to more than just a small segment of the female population? We started with terminology. Instead of directly calling *HUES* a feminist magazine, we subtitled it *A Woman's Guide to Power and Attitude*. We felt this allowed women to choose how they wanted to define themselves in the realm of the women's movement, be it feminist, womanist, pro-woman, or something else. Meanwhile, we focused on what we felt were the most pertinent issues. Body image, self-esteem, sisterhood, cross-cultural relations, and education topped the list. To make these issues digestible, we felt it was important to write articles in a sisterly tone and to add some humor to the lineup. It was like spoon-feeding feminism to the fearful, as opposed to ramming it down people's throats. We preferred to show through personal anecdotes rather than preach from some political pulpit. And, to keep a good balance of heavy and lighter pieces, we decided that *HUES* should highlight various facets of pop culture, from conscious fashion to music reviews to interviews with well-known women. We saw these pieces as an opportunity to give important press coverage to talented women who might be overlooked in other magazines.

Because we knew Gen-Xers were used to sensory overload, articles would have to be complemented by appealing graphics and photos. We would use models of all sizes, looks, and ethnic backgrounds throughout the entire magazine, reinforcing the idea that *HUES* represented *all* women. Unlike the "concerned" women's magazines that, for example, printed a "shocking" exposé on anorexia, only to follow with a Kate Moss fashion spread, *HUES* had to have a nonhypocritical balance between content and image.

Our aim was to make *HUES* look as well designed as any other publication on the shelves. Of course, it took a few tries to get to that point. When we finally published the first issue of *HUES* in April 1992, it was actually a half-size, black-and-white 'zine. We had raised enough money to print one thousand copies through receiving a few donations from campus groups and by throwing a few hip-hop parties around town. Articles included a piece called "Why Feminists Need Men," a piece on female rappers, and the story of a Filipina rape survivor.

The response to the premier issue was overwhelmingly positive. We got E-mail and letters from women thanking us for producing something aimed at making women feel good about themselves. Of course, there were a couple of annoying responses along the way, such as the one from a man angry about our editorial "No Justice, No Piece . . . Down with John Wayne Bobbitt." But we remained unfazed by our critics. Over the next two years, we pumped out three more issues. With each magazine we improved the quality of our contents and upgraded the "look." Our fourth issue was full size and printed on glossy paper. We added more resource-oriented articles that would connect women with helpful and proactive organizations. We finally had a good set of regular one-page columns on which to structure future issues. And, through fund raisers and the sale of ads to local businesses, we had enough money to do our first color cover and eight inside color pages.

What amazed us most was how *HUES* seemed to travel on its own. Because a lot of students brought *HUES* home from school with them, the magazine crossed state lines. We started getting calls from people across the country who loved *HUES* and wanted to subscribe. During the summer of 1994, after our fourth issue, we got a call from *Ms.* magazine, which published a one-page article about our magazine. Soon after that, the *Chicago Tribune* called. We had no idea how either publication had found *HUES*, but we realized that with our "sisters" we had created something that obviously appealed to women beyond Ann Arbor, Michigan.

At that point Ophi and I had graduated from college, and the three of us figured that it was high time we took *HUES* to the next level. When we decided on our national launch in early 1995, we were pretty starry-eyed. We connected with a few national distributors who promised to shelve *HUES* in chain stores and newsstands from New York to California. We decided to complement sales with big promotional drop-offs at colleges across the country, which would also help get out the word about *HUES*. We were interested in selling ad space to companies that didn't objectify women or sensationalize culture. With the money from ad sales, we planned to make *HUES* more visible, create self-esteem workshops, and spread the message of sisterhood. Everyone— ourselves included—was *sure* that hordes of big corporations would be pouring their dollars into *HUES*. We approached companies that had advertised in other women's magazines. It seemed logical that companies would want to invest in a magazine that targeted *all* women instead of just a select handful. We boasted promising newsstand visibility, positive press write-ups, and piles of letters pouring in from women telling us that *HUES* was what they'd been waiting for all their lives.

Still, the big-money players weren't ready for us. Advertisers of universal women's products unabashedly told us that *HUES* "wasn't their audience." Even supposedly "alternative" companies such as charitable long-distance services gave us the same line. One ad agency actually told us that "ethnics don't sell." To another we were "spreading ourselves too thin with the multicultural, multisexual thing." Then we were informed that "college women don't spend enough to make them worth our ad dollars." To us, these rejections added up to one thing—society was still uncomfortable with the idea of an intelligent, self-empowered woman. Advertisers counted on women having low self-esteem in order to sell more "nighttime cellulite cream." A magazine that encouraged women to use their minds threatened the very premise many companies clung to. *What would happen if she figured out that our gym shoes aren't going to give her the body of an aerobics instructor? If she realized that our totally smudge-proof mascara won't bring her Prince Charming? Hmmm . . . let's keep her misinformed, guys.*

We also discovered that in big time publishing, a lot relies on who you know (and whether or not you are a Time, Inc., publication). Being an independently owned magazine was another strike against us. In many cases it prevented us from even getting a foot in the door. But getting rejected by everyone from Nike to Kotex was actually a blessing in disguise. It gave us an opportunity to reevaluate our goals. We had always been firm in our desire to keep *HUES* a resource for women, including women business owners. We decided to make *HUES* into an affordable network for more conscious companies to reach conscious consumers (i.e., *HUES* readers). And we had to learn a thing or two about creative financing. Although Dyann, Ophi, and I had honed the art of organizing young women into a produc-

tive unit, we had to start thinking like businesswomen as well. Dyann created a college marketing department from which college professors began ordering *HUES* for use in course curriculum, as well as an internal sales network for feminist bookstores.

We were also blessed to have families who believed in us enough to co-sign a start-up loan from a local bank. With that extra boost, along with revenues from some smaller advertisers, we launched our first national issue. It sold beautifully on the newsstand, and soon our 1-800 number was ringing with subscribers, the press, and people wanting a *HUES* woman to come speak at their conference. After that we did manage to sell a four-page ad to Levi's Jeans for Women for our second national issue, and we hoped that perhaps that would give us an edge with a few other clothing companies. Since then, we've connected with some awesome publications that share our mission, such as *New Moon: The Magazine for Girls and Their Dreams; Teen Voices;* and *Hip Mama.* In the spirit of true sisterhood, our four publications are forming an umbrella organization to support each other and share resources.

Today, Dyann, Ophi, and I are scrambling around trying to finalize the last-minute details of our eighth—and fourth national—issue, which is due to go on press in (aaaghh) only two weeks. There are articles that need to be dropped into layout, and filler columns to write and edit, not to mention that a few companies are still deciding what size ad to run. Even after five years of publishing, there is still the hectic buzz of uncertainty and instability. Still, we remain confident that *HUES* is what women need; we just may be a few years ahead of our time. In creating a publication that is not just a magazine but a movement, our goal remains to create a new standard of self-acceptance for women. And, whether or not *HUES* becomes the "femme-pire" of our dreams, we do hope the ideals—such as promoting sisterhood and including a diversity of women—will somehow translate into other women's magazines. A reporter recently asked me if I thought a magazine like *HUES* could ever move into the mainstream and be as big as, say, *Glamour.* I guess that one is up to the women of the world. For now, it still feels good to be a part of a new movement that truly includes *all* women.      [1997]

149

# *Like a Mountain*

NAOMI LITTLEBEAR

Nobody can push back an ocean
It's gonna rise back up in waves.
And nobody can stop the wind from blowin',
Stop a mind from growin'.

Somebody may stop my voice from singing
But the song will live on and on.

You can't kill the spirit
It's like a mountain,
Old and strong; it lives on and on.

Nobody can stop a woman from feelin'
That she has to rise up like the sun
Somebody may change the words we're sayin'
But the truth will live on and on.

You can't kill the spirit
It's like a mountain,
Old and strong; it lives on and on.      [ca. 1970]

We hope that the many different voices in *Women: Images and Realities* have spoken to you and deepened your understanding of women's experience. Although you may not have agreed with everything you read, we hope the book has stimulated your thinking. We have tried in this anthology to do several things: to demonstrate the commonalities and differences among women, to emphasize the power of women talking and working together, to stimulate your thinking about the ways women of different backgrounds can work together effectively, and to encourage you to participate in the process of improving women's lives. Although this book has concluded, we hope your involvement with feminism continues.

# Further Readings

*Part I: What Is Women's Studies*

*All the Women Are White, All the Blacks Are Men, But Some of Us Are Brave.* Gloria T. Hull, Patricia Bell-Scott, and Barbara Smith, eds. Feminist Press, Old Westbury, NY, 1982.

*The American Women's Almanac: An Inspiring and Irreverent Women's History.* Louise Bernikow. In association with the National Women's History Project. Berkley Books, New York, 1997.

*Changing Our Minds: Feminist Transformation of Knowledge.* Susan Aiken, Karen Anderson, Myra Dinnerstein, Judy Note Lensink, and Patricia MacCorquodale, eds. SUNY Press, Albany, NY, 1988.

*Feminism and Science.* Oxford Readings in Feminism. Evelyn Fox Keller and Helen E. Longino, eds. Oxford University Press, New York, 1996.

*Feminist Education: A Special Topic Issue of the Journal of Thought.* Barbara Hillyer Davis. College of Education, University of Oklahoma, Norman, 1985.

*Feminist Pedagogy: An Update.* Frinde Maher and Nancy Schniedewind, eds. *Women's Studies Quarterly,* Fall/Winter 1993.

*Feminist Thought. A Comprehensive Introduction* (2nd ed.). Rosemarie Tong. Westview, Boulder, CO, 1998.

*Generations: A Century of Women Speak About Their Lives.* Myriam Miedziant and Alisa Malinovich, eds. Atlantic Monthly Press, New York, 1997.

*The Impact of Feminist Research in the Academy.* Christie Farnham, ed. Indiana University Press, Indianapolis, 1987.

*Learning About Women: Gender, Politics, and Power.* Jill K. Conway, Susan C. Bourque, and Joan W. Scott, eds. University of Michigan Press, Ann Arbor, 1989.

*Lesbian Studies: Present and Future.* Margaret Cruikshank, ed. Feminist Press, Old Westbury, NY, 1982.

*Life Notes: Personal Writings by Contemporary Black Women.* Patricia Bell-Scott, ed. Norton, New York, 1994.

*Myths of Gender: Biological Theories of Women and Men.* Anne Fausto-Sterling. Basic Books, New York, 1992.

*On Lies, Secrets and Silence: Selected Prose.* Adrienne Rich. Norton, New York, 1979.

*Reflections on Gender and Science.* Evelyn Fox Keller. Yale University Press, New Haven, CT, 1985.

*Talking Back: Thinking Feminist, Thinking Black.* bell hooks. South End Press, Boston, 1989.

*Talking Gender: Public Images, Personal Journeys and Political Critiques.* Nancy Hewitt, Jean O'Barr, and Nancy Rosebaugh, eds. University of North Carolina Press, Chapel Hill, 1996.

*Thinking Feminist: Key Concepts in Women's Studies.* Diane Richardson and Victoria Robinson, eds. Guilford, New York, 1993.

*Transforming the Curriculum: Ethnic Studies and Women's Studies.* Johnella Butler and John Walter. SUNY Press, Albany, NY, 1991.

*Questions of Gender: Perspectives and Paradoxes.* Dina L. Anselmi and Anne L. Law. McGraw-Hill, New York, 1998.

*Women's Studies International.* Aruna Rao, ed. Feminist Press, New York, 1991.

*Women's Studies in the South.* Rhoda E. Barge Johnson, ed. Kendall/Hunt, Dubuque, IA, 1991.

PART II: BECOMING A WOMAN IN OUR SOCIETY

### Dominant Ideas About Women

*Allegra Maud Goldman.* Edith Konecky. Jewish Publication Society, Philadelphia, 1987.

*Cuentos: Stories by Latinas.* Alma Gomez, Cherrie Moraga, and Mariann Roma-Carmona, eds. Kitchen Table Press, New York, 1983.

*Daughters of Sorrow: Attitudes Towards Black Women 1880–1920.* Beverly Guy-Sheftall. Carlsen, Brooklyn, 1990.

*Disfigured Images: The Historical Assault on Afro-American Women.* Patricia Morton. Greenwood, New York, 1991.

*Gender Shock: Exploding the Myths of Male and Female.* Phyllis Burke. Anchor, New York, 1996.

*Gender: Stereotypes and Roles* (3rd ed.). Susan A. Basow. Wadsworth, Belmont, CA, 1992.

*Girls Speak Out: Finding Your True Self.* Andrea Johnston. Scholastic Press, New York, 1997.

*Our Feet Walk the Sky: Women of the South Asian Diaspora.* Women of South Asian Descent Collective, ed. Aunt Lute Books, San Francisco, 1993.

### Learning Sexism

*AAUW Report: How Schools Shortchange Girls.* American Association of University Women, Washington, D.C., 1993.

*Body Politics: Power, Sex and Non-Verbal Communication.* Nancy Henley. Prentice-Hall, Englewood Cliffs, NJ, 1977.

*Cecelia Reclaimed: Feminist Perspective on Gender and Music.* Susan Cook and Judy Tsou. University of Illinois Press, Urbana, 1994.

*The Chilly Classroom Climate: A Guide to Improve the Education of Women.* Bernice Sandler, Lisa Silverberg, and Roberta Hall. National Association for Women in Education, Washington, D.C., 1996.

*Educated in Romance: Women, Achievement and College Culture.* Dorothy Holland. University of Chicago Press, Chicago, 1990.

*Failing at Fairness: How America's Schools Cheat Girls.* Myra and David Sadker, Scribners, New York, 1994.

*From Reverence to Rape: The Treatment of Women in the Movies.* Molly Haskell. University of Chicago Press, Chicago, 1987.

*Gender and Non-Verbal Behavior.* Nancy Henley and Clara Mayo. Springer, New York, 1981.

*Gender, Race and Class in the Media.* Gail Dines and Jean Humez, eds. Sage, Thousand Oaks, CA, 1995.

*Gendered Lives: Communication, Gender and Culture.* Julia Wood. Wadsworth, Belmont, CA, 1994.

*Language, Gender, and Society.* Nancy Henley, Charise Kramarae, and Barrie Thorne. Newbury House, Rowley, MA, 1983.

*Man Made Language.* Dale Spender. Routledge, Kegan, Paul, Boston, 1985.

"Media Images, Feminist Issues." Deborah Rhode. *Signs: A Journal of Women and Culture,* vol. 20, no. 3, pp. 685–710, 1995.

*Media-tions: Forays into the Culture and Gender Wars.* Elayne Rapping. South End, Boston, 1994.

"Missing Voices: Women in the U.S. News Media." Special issue of *Extra,* New York, 1982.

*Prime Time Feminism: Television, Media Culture and the Women's Movement Since 1970.* Bonnie Dow. University of Pennsylvania Press, Philadelphia, 1996.

*Putting on Appearances: Gender and Advertising.* Diane Barthel. Temple University Press, Philadelphia, 1988.

"Redesigning Women." Special issue of *Media and Values,* no. 49, Winter 1989.

*Representing Women: Myths of Femininity in the Popular Media.* Myra McDonald. St. Martin's, New York, 1995.

*SchoolGirls: Young Women, Self-Esteem, and the Confidence Gap.* Peggy Orenstein. Doubleday, New York, 1994.

"Secrets in Public: Sexual Harassment in Our Schools." Nan Stein, Nancy Marshall, and Linda Tropp. Center for Research on Women, Wellesley, MA, 1993.

*What's Wrong with This Picture? The Status of Women on Screen and Behind the Camera in Entertainment TV.* Sally Steenland. National Commission on Working Women of Wider Opportunities for Women, Los Angeles, 1990.

*You Just Don't Understand: Women and Men in Conversation.* Deborah Tannen. Ballantine, New York, 1990.

## PART III:  GENDER AND WOMEN'S BODIES

### Female Beauty

*Am I Thin Enough Yet? The Cult of Thinness and the Commercialization of Identity.* Sharlene Hesse-Biber. Oxford University Press, New York, 1996.

*Beauty Bound.* Rita Freedman. Lexington Books, Lexington, MA, 1986.

*The Bluest Eye.* Toni Morrison. Random House, New York, 1970.

*Bodymakers: A Cultural Anthology of Women's Body Building.* Leslie Heywood. Rutgers University Press, Piscataway, NJ, 1998.

*Eating Our Hearts Out: Personal Accounts of Women's Relationship to Food.* Leslea Newman. Crossing Press, Freedom, CA, 1993.

*Generations: A Memoir.* Lucille Clifton. Random House, New York, 1976.

*The Power of Beauty.* Nancy Friday. HarperCollins, New York, 1996.

*In Search of Our Mothers' Gardens.* Alice Walker. Harcourt Brace Jovanovich, New York, 1983.

*The Third Woman.* Dexter Fisher, ed. Houghton Mifflin, Boston, 1980.

*The Tribe of Dina: A Jewish Women's Anthology.* Melanie Kaye Kantrowitz and Irena Klepfisz, eds. Sinister Wisdom, Montpelier, VT, 1986.

### Sexuality and Relationships

*Closer to Home: Bisexuality and Feminism.* Elizabeth Reba Weise, ed. Seal Press, Seattle, WA, 1992.

*Embracing the Fire: Sisters Talk About Sex and Relationships.* Julia Boyd. Dutton, New York, 1997.

*Gorilla My Love.* Toni Cade Bambara. Random House, New York, 1972.

*Frictions II: Stories by Women.* Rhea Tregebov, ed. Second Story Press, Toronto, 1993.

*The Hand I Fan With.* Tina McElroy Ansa. Anchor, New York, 1996.

*Gendered Relationships.* Julia T. Wood, ed. Mayfield, Mountain View, CA, 1996.

*Latina Realities: Essays on Healing, Migration, and Sexuality.* Olivia M. Espin. Westview, Boulder, CO, 1997.

*Men We Cherish: African American Women Praise the Men in Their Lives.* Brooke Stephens, ed. Anchor, New York, 1997.

*The Politics of Women's Bodies: Sexuality, Appearance, and Behavior.* Rose Weitz, ed. Oxford University Press, New York, 1998.

*Sex Is Not a Natural Act and Other Essays.* Leonore Tiefer. Westview, Boulder, CO, 1994.

*Stolen Women: Reclaiming Our Sexuality, Taking Back Our Lives.* Gail E. Wyatt. Wiley, New York, 1997.

*Troubling the Angels: Women Living with HIV/AIDS.* Patti Lather and Chris Smithies. Westview, Boulder, CO, 1997.

*With the Power of Each Breath: A Disabled Woman's Anthology.* Susan E. Browne, Debra Connors, and Nancy Stern, eds. Cleis, Pittsburgh, 1985.

*Women on Top.* Nancy Friday. Pocket Books, New York, 1991.

PART IV: INSTITUTIONS THAT SHAPE WOMEN'S LIVES

### The Legal System

*Alchemy of Race and Rights: Diary of a Law Professor.* Patricia Williams. Harvard University Press, Cambridge, MA, 1991.

*Black Women and the New World Order: Social Justice and the African American Female.* Willa Mae Hemmons. Praeger, Westport, CT, 1996.

*The Female Body and the Law.* Zillah R. Eisenstein. University of California Press, Berkeley, 1988.

*Feminism and the Power of Law.* Carol Smart. Routledge, New York, 1989.

*Feminist Legal Theory: Readings in Law and Gender.* Katharine T. Bartlett and Rosanne Kennedy, eds. Westview, Boulder, CO, 1991.

*Law, Gender, and Injustice: A Legal History of U.S. Women.* Joan Hoff. New York University Press, New York, 1991.

*Mothers in Law: Feminist Theory and the Legal Regulation of Motherhood.* Martha Fineman and Isabel Karpin, eds. Columbia University Press, New York, 1995.

*The Rights of Women: The Basic ACLU Guide to Women's Rights.* Susan Deller Ross. Southern Illinois University Press, Carbondale, 1993.

*Unequal Protection: Women, Children, and the Elderly in Court.* Lois G. Forer. Norton, New York, 1991.

*Women's Rights and the Law.* Laura Otten. Praeger, Westport, CT, 1993.

### Women and Work

*Between Feminism and Labor: The Significance of the Comparable Worth Movement.* Linda Blum. University of California Press, Berkeley, 1991.

*Black Women in the Labor Force.* Phyllis Wallace with Linda Datcher and Julianne Malveaux. MIT Press, Cambridge, MA, 1980.

*Black Women in the Workplace: Impacts of Structural Change in the Economy.* Bette Woody. Greenwood Press, New York, 1992.

*The Economic Emergence of Women.* Barbara Bergmann. Basic Books, New York, 1986.

*The Endless Day: The Political Economy of Women and Work.* Bettina Berch. Harcourt Brace Jovanovich, 1982.

*Fetal Rights: Women's Rights: Gender Equality in the Workplace.* Suzanne Uttaro Samuels. University of Wisconsin, Madison, 1995.

*For Crying Out Loud: Women's Poverty in the United States.* Diane Dujon and Ann Withorn, eds. South End, Boston, 1996.

*Glass Ceilings and Bottomless Pits: Women's Work, Women's Poverty.* Randy Abelda and Chris Tilly. South End Press, Boston, 1997.

*Keeping Women and Children Last: America's War on the Poor.* Ruth Sidel. Penguin, New York, 1996.

*Making Ends Meet: How Single Mothers Survive Welfare and Low Wage Work.* Kathryn Edin. Russell Sage Foundation, New York, 1997.

*Men and Women of the Corporation.* Rosabeth Moss Kanter. Basic Books, New York, 1977.

*Mexicanas at Work in the United States.* Margarita Melville, ed. Mexican American Studies Program, University of Houston, Houston, TX, 1988.

*Never Done: A History of American Housework.* Susan Strasser. Pantheon, New York, 1982.

*New Field Guide to the U.S. Economy.* Nancy Folbre. New Press, New York, 1995.

*Puerto Rican Women and Work: Bridges in Transnational Labor.* Altagracia Ortiz, ed. Temple University Press, Philadelphia, 1996.

*The Politics of Parenthood: Child Care, Women's Rights and the Myth of the Good Mother.* Mary Frances Berry. Viking, New York, 1993.

*Race, Gender and Work: A Multicultural Economic History of Women in the United States.* Theresa Amott and Julie Matthaei. South End, Boston, 1996.

*Tyranny of Kindness: Dismantling the Welfare System to End Poverty in America.* Theresa Funiciello. Atlantic Monthly Press, New York, 1993.

*Under Attack, Fighting Back: Women and Welfare in the United States.* Mimi Abramovitz. Monthly Review Press, New York, 1996.

*We'll Call You If We Need You: Experiences of Women Working Construction.* Susan Eisenberg. ILR, Ithaca, NY, 1998.

*With Silk Wings: Asian American Women at Work.* Elaine Kim and Janice Otani. Asian Women United of California, Oakland, CA, 1983.

*Women's Work, Women's Lives: A Comparative Economic Perspective.* Francine Blau. National Bureau of Economic Research, Cambridge, MA, 1990.

## Women and the Family

*All Our Families; New Policies for a New Century.* Mary Ann Mason, Arlene Skolnick, and Stephen Sugarman, eds. University of California Press, Berkeley, 1998.

*The Autobiography of My Mother.* Jamaica Kincaid. Plume, New York, 1997.

*Beyond the Traditional Family: Voices of Diversity.* Betty Polisar Reigot and Rita Spina, eds. Springer, New York, 1996.

*Black Mothers and Daughters: Their Roles and Functions in American Society.* Gloria Joseph. Doubleday, New York, 1981.

*Considering Parenthood: A Workbook for Lesbians.* Stacey Pes. Spinsters Ink, San Francisco, 1985.

*A Family Affair: The Real Lives of Black Single Mothers.* Barbara Omalade. Kitchen Table Press, Latham, NY, 1986.

*Families in Cultural Context: Strengths and Challenges in Diversity.* Mary Kay DeGenova, ed. Mayfield, Mountain View, CA, 1997.

*Farewell to Manzanar.* Jeann Wakatsuki Houston. Bantam, New York, 1974.

*I've Always Wanted to Tell You: Letters to Our Mothers: An Anthology of Contemporary Women Writers.* Constance Warloeed. Pocket Books, New York, 1997.

*The Job-Family Challenge.* Ellen Bravo. Wiley, New York, 1995.

*The Joy Luck Club.* Amy Tan. Putnam, New York, 1989.

*Lesbian Nuns: Breaking the Silence.* Rosemary Curba and Nancy Manahan. Naiad, Tallahassee, FL, 1985.

*Motherguilt: How Our Culture Blames Mothers for What's Wrong with Society.* Diane Eyer. Random House, New York, 1996.

*A Mother's Place: Taking the Debate About Motherhood Beyond Guilt and Blame.* Susan Chira. HarperCollins, New York, 1998.

*Politics of the Heart: A Lesbian Parenting Anthology.* Sandra Pollack and Jeanne Vaughn, eds. Firebrand, Ithaca, NY, 1987.

*Of Woman Born: Motherhood as Experience and Institution.* Adrienne Rich. Norton, New York, 1986.

*Women Living Single: Thirty Women Share Their Stories of Navigating Through a Married World.* Faber & Faber, Boston, 1996.

## Women and the Health Care System

*Alive and Well: A Lesbian Health Guide.* Circe Hepburn. Crossing Press, Freedom, CA, 1988.

*The Black Women's Health Book: Speaking for Ourselves.* Evelyn C. White, ed. Seal, Seattle, 1990.

*Body and Soul: The Black Women's Guide to Physical Health and Emotional Well-Being.* Linda Villarosa, ed. Harper Perennial, New York, 1994.

*The Cancer Journals.* Audre Lorde. Spinsters Ink, Argyles, NY, 1980.

*Double Exposure: Women's Health Hazards on the Job and at Home.* Wendy Chavkin. Monthly Review Press, New York, NY, 1984.

*Our Bodies, Ourselves for the New Century: A Book by and for Women.* The Boston Women's Health Book Collective. Simon & Schuster, New York, 1998.

*River of Tears: The Politics of Black Women's Health Care.* Delores S. Aldridge and La Frances Rodgers-Rose. Traces Publishing, Newark, NJ, 1993.

*Sisters of the Yam: Black Women and Self Recovery.* bell hooks. Boston, South End, 1993.

*Vamps, Virgins and Victims: How Can Women Fight AIDS?* Robin Gorna. Cassell, London, 1996.

*What Makes Women Sick: Gender and the Political Economy of Health.* Leslie Doyal, Rutgers University Press, New Brunswick, NJ, 1995.

*Women and AIDS: Negotiating Safer Practices, Care and Representation.* Nancy Roth and Linda Fuller, eds. Haworth, Binghamton, NY, 1998.

*Women and Madness.* Phyllis Chesler. Doubleday, Garden City, NY, 1972.

### Women and Religion

*Beyond God the Father: Toward a Philosophy of Women's Liberation.* Mary Daly. Beacon, Boston, 1973.

*The Church and the Second Sex.* Mary Daly. Beacon, Boston, 1985.

*Daughters of Thunder: Black Women Preachers and Their Sermons 1850–1979.* Betty Collier-Thomas. Jossey-Bass, San Francisco, 1998.

*Gender and Judaism: The Transformation of Tradition.* T. M. Rudavsky, ed. New York University Press, New York, 1995.

*Fundamentalism and Gender.* John Stratton Hawley. Oxford, University Press, New York, 1994.

*I Asked for Intimacy: Stories of Blessings, Betrayals and Birthings.* Renita J. Weems. Lura Media, San Diego, 1994.

*My Soul Is a Witness: African American Spirituality.* Gloria Wade-Gayles. Beacon, Boston, 1995.

*Religion and Women.* Arvind Sharma, ed. SUNY Press, Albany, NY, 1994.

*Sexism and God-Talk: Toward a Feminist Theology.* Rosemary Radford Ruether. Beacon, Boston, 1983.

*Wise Women: Over 2,000 Years of Spiritual Writing by Women.* Susan Cahill, ed. Norton, New York, 1996.

*Women and Fundamentalism: Islam and Christianity.* Shahin Gerami. Garland, New York, 1996.

*Women and Goddess Traditions, in Antiquity and Today.* Karen King, ed. Fortress, Minneapolis, 1997.

### PART V: THE DIFFERENCES AMONG US: DIVISIONS AND CONNECTIONS

*Afrikete, An Anthology of Black Lesbian Writing.* Catherine McKinley and Joyce DeLaney, eds. Doubleday, New York, 1995.

*All American Women: Lines That Divide, Ties That Bind.* Johnetta Cole, ed. Free Press, New York, 1986.

*American Indian Women: Telling Their Lives.* Gretchen M. Bataille and Kathleen Mullen Sand. University of Nebraska Press, Lincoln, 1984.

*Asian and Pacific American Experiences: Women's Perspectives.* Nobuya Tsuchida, Linda Mealey, and Gail Thoen, eds. Asian/Pacific American Learning Resource Center and General College, University of Minnesota, Minneapolis, 1982.

*Borderlands/La Frontera.* Gloria Anzaldua. Spinsters/Aunt Lute, San Francisco, 1987.

*Calling Home: Working Class Women's Writings: An Anthology.* Janet Zandy, ed. Rutgers University Press, New Brunswick, NJ, 1990.

*Daughter of Earth.* Agnes Smedley. Feminist Press, Old Westbury, NY, 1973.

*Farewell to Manzanar.* Jeanne Wakatsuki Houston. Bantam, New York, 1994.

*Food for Our Grandmothers.* Joanna Kadi. South End, Boston, 1994.

*The Forbidden Stitch: An Asian American Women's Anthology.* Shirley Geok-Lin Lim, Mauyumi Tsutakawa, and Margarita Donnely, eds. Calyx Books, Corvalis, OR, 1989.

*Homophobia: A Weapon of Sexism.* Suzanne Pharr. Chardon, Little Rock, AR, 1988.

*I Am Your Sister: Women Organizing Across Sexualities.* Audre Lourde. Kitchen Table Press, Latham, NY, 1986.

*Making Face, Making Soul, Creative and Critical Perspectives by Women of Color.* Gloria Anzaldua, ed. Aunt Lute, San Francisco, 1990.

*Making More Waves: An Anthology of Writings by and about Asian American Women.* Elaine Kim, ed. Beacon, Boston, 1997.

*Names We Call Home: Autobiography on Racial Identity.* Becky Thompson and Sangeeta Tyagi, eds. Routledge, New York, 1996.

*Nice Jewish Girls: A Lesbian Anthology.* Evelyn Torton Beck, ed. Beacon, Boston, 1989.

*Our Feet Walk the Sky: Women of the South Asian Diaspora.* Women of the South Asian Descent Collective. Aunt Lute Books, San Francisco, 1993.

*Race, Class and Gender: Common Bonds, Different Voices.* Esther Ngan-ling Chow, Doris Wilkinson, and Maxine Baca Zinn. Sage, Thousand Oaks, CA, 1996.

*The Sacred Hoop: Recovering the Feminine in American Indian Tradition.* Paula Gunn Allen. Beacon, Boston, 1986.

*Skin: Talking about Sex, Class and Literature.* Dorothy Allison. Firebrand, Ithaca, NY, 1994.

*Teaching for Diversity and Social Justice: A Sourcebook.* Maurianne Adams, Lee Anne Bell, and Pat Griffin, eds. Routledge, New York, 1997.

*That's What She Said: Contemporary Poetry and Fiction by Native American Women.* Rayna Green, ed. Indiana University Press, Bloomington, 1984.

*The Things That Divide Us.* Faith Conlon, ed. Seal, Seattle, 1985.

*The Tribe of Dina: A Jewish Women's Anthology.* Melanie Kay Kantrowitz and Irena Klepfisz, eds. Beacon, Boston, 1986.

*This Bridge Called My Back: Writings by Radical Women of Color.* Cherrie Moraga and Gloria Anzaldua. Peresephone, Watertown, MA, 1981.

*The Wedding.* Dorothy West. Anchor, New York, 1995.

*White Women, Race Matters: The Social Construction of Whiteness.* Ruth Frankenberg, University of Minnesota Press, Minneapolis, 1993.

*Why Are all the Black Kids Sitting Together in the Cafeteria and Other Conversations About Race.* Beverly Daniel Tatum. Basic Books, New York, 1997.

*With Wings: An Anthology of Literature by and About Women with Disabilities.* Marsha Saxton and Florence Howe, eds. Feminist Press, New York, 1987.

*Women of Color in U.S. Society.* Maxine Baca Zinn and Bonnie Thornton Dill, eds., Temple University Press, Philadelphia, 1995.

*Worlds of Pain: Life in the Working Class Family.* Lillian Breslow Rubin, Basic Books, New York, 1992.

## PART VI: THE CONSEQUENCES OF SEXISM: CURRENT ISSUES

### Aging

*Getting Over Getting Older.* Letty Cottin Pogrebin. Berkley, NY, 1996.

*Growing Older, Getting Better.* Jane Porcino. Addison-Wesley, Reading, MA, 1983.

*Look Me in the Eye: Old Women, Aging, and Ageism.* Barbara MacDonald and Cynthia Rich. Spinsters Ink, San Francisco, 1983.

*Midlife Women: Contemporary Issues.* Joan Matthews Jacobson. Jones & Bartlett, Boston, 1995.

*The Other Within Us: Feminist Explorations of Women and Aging.* Marilyn Pearsall, ed. Westview, Boulder, CO, 1997.

*Ourselves, Growing Older: Women Aging with Knowledge and Power.* Paula Doress, Diana Laskin Siegal, Midlife and Older Women Book Project, and Boston Women's Health Book Collective. Simon & Schuster, New York, 1987.

*Remembered Lives: The Work of Ritual, Storytelling and Growing Older.* Barbara Meyerhoff. University of Michigan Press, Ann Arbor, 1992.

*Tish Sommers, Activist, and the Founding of the Older Women's League.* Patricia Huckle and Tish Sommers. University of Tennessee Press, Knoxville, 1991.

*Wearing Purple: Four Longtime Friends Celebrate the Joys and Challenges of Growing Older.* Lydia Lewis Alexander, Marilyn Hill Harper, Otis Holloway Owens, and Mildred Lucas Peterson. Berkley, NY, 1996.

*When I Am an Old Woman I Shall Wear Purple.* Sandra Martz. Papier-Mache, Manhattan Beach, CA, 1987.

### Rights and Choices: Reproductive Health

*Abortion Wars: A Half Century of Struggle 1950–2000.* Rickie Solinger, ed. University of California Press, Berkeley, 1998.

*Abortion Without Apology: Radical History for the 1990s.* Ninia Baehr. South End Press, Boston, 1990.

*Abortion and the Politics of Motherhood.* Kristin Luker. University of California Press, Berkeley, 1984.

*Birth or Abortion? Private Struggles in a Political World.* Kate Maloy and Maggie Jones Patterson. Plenum, New York, 1992.

*The Choices We Made: 25 Women and Men Speak Out About Abortion.* Angela Bonavoglia. Random House, New York, 1991.

*Feminist Approaches to Bioethics: Theoretical Reflections and Practical Applications.* Rosemarie Tong. Westview, Boulder, CO, 1996.

*From Abortion to Reproductive Freedom.* Marlene Gerber Fried, ed. South End, Boston, 1990.

*Killing the Black Body: Race, Reproduction, and the Meaning of Liberty.* Dorothy Roberts. Pantheon, New York, 1997.

"La Mujer Puertorríquena, Su Cuerpo, y Su Lucha por la Vida: Experiences with Empowerment in Hartford Connecticut." Candida Flores, Lani Davison, Enid Mercedes Rey, Migdalia Rivera and Maria Serrano, in *From Abortion to Reproductive Freedom: Transforming a Movement.* Marlene Gerber Fried, ed. South End, Boston, 1990.

*Our Right to Choose: Toward a New Ethic of Abortion.* Beverly W. Harrison. Beacon, Boston, 1983.

*A Question of Choice.* Sarah Weddington. Putnam, New York, 1992.

*Reproductive Rights and Wrongs: The Global Politics of Population Control and Contraceptive Choice.* Betsy Hartmann. Harper & Row, New York, 1987.

*Roe v. Wade,* cite as 93 s.ct. 705 (1973). Jane Roe, et al., appellants, v. Henry Wade, no. 70-18. Argued Dec. 13, 1971. Reargued Oct. 11, 1972. Decided Jan. 22, 1973. Supreme Court reporter.

*Taking Chances: Abortion and the Decision Not to Contracept.* Kristin Luker. University of California Press, Berkeley, 1975.

### Sexual Harassment

*Back Off.* Martha Lanegelan, ed. Fireside, New York, 1993.

*Bearing Witness: Sexual Harassment and Beyond.* Celia Morris. Little, Brown, New York, 1994.

*The 9 to 5 Guide to Combatting Sexual Harassment: Candid Advice from 9 to 5.* Ellen Bravo and Ellen Cassedy. National Assocation of Working Women. Wiley, New York, 1992.

*No More "Nice Girl": Power, Sexuality, and Success in the Workplacex.* Rosemary Agonito. Adams, Holbrook, MA, 1993.

*Secrets in Public: Sexual Harassment in Our Schools.* Nan Stein, Nancy Marshall, and Linda Troop, eds. Center for Research on Women, Wellesley, MA, 1993.

*Sexual Harassment: Women Speak Out.* Amber Coverdale Sumrall and Dena Taylor, eds. Crossings, Freedom, CA, 1992.

*Sexual Harassment in Academe: The Ethical Issues.* Leslie Pickering Francis. Rowman & Littlefield, Lanham, MD, 1997.

*Sexual Harassment on Campus: A Guide for Administrators, Faculty and Students.* Bernice Sandler and Robert Shoop, eds. Allyn and Bacon, Boston, 1997.

## Violence Against Women in Intimate Relationships

*Battered Wives.* Del Martin. Glide, San Francisco, 1976.

*Chain, Chain, Change: For Black Women Dealing with Physical and Emotional Abuse.* Evelyn C. White. Seal, Seattle, 1985.

*For the Latina in an Abusive Relationship.* Myrna Zambrano. Seal, Seattle, 1983.

*Getting Away With Murder: Weapons for the War Against Domestic Violence.* Raoul Felder and Barbara Victor. Simon & Schuster, New York, 1996.

*Getting Free: A Handbook for Women in Abusive Relationships.* Ginny NiCarthy. Seal, Seattle, 1986.

*Heroes of Their Own Lives: The Politics and History of Family Violence, Boston, 1880–1960.* Linda Gordon. Viking, New York, 1988.

*No Safe Haven: Male Violence Against Women at Home, at Work, and in the Community.* Mary Koss. American Psychological Association, Washington, D.C., 1994.

*Women and Male Violence: The Visions and Struggles of the Battered Women's Movement.* Susan Schechter. South End, Boston, 1982.

*Women at Risk: Domestic Violence and Women's Health.* Evan Stark and Anne Flitcraft. Sage, Thousand Oaks, CA, 1996.

## Sexual Violence and Rape

*Acquaintance Rape: The Hidden Crime.* Andrea Parrot and Laurie Bechhofer. Wiley, New York, 1991.

*Against Our Will: Men, Women, and Rape.* Susan Brownmiller. Simon & Schuster, New York, 1975.

*Fraternity Gang Rape.* Peggy Sanday. New York University Press, New York, 1990.

*I Never Called It Rape.* Robin Warshaw and Mary P. Koss. Harper & Row, New York, 1988.

*Sexual Assault on Campus: The Problem and the Solution.* Carol Bohmer and Andrea Parrot. Lexington, New York, 1993.

*Transforming a Rape Culture.* Emelie Buchwald, Pamela Fletcher, and Martha Roth, eds. Milkweed, Minneapolis, 1993.

*Warrior Marks: Female Genital Mutilation and the Sexual Blinding of Women.* Alice Walker and Pratibha Parmar. Harcourt Brace, New York, 1993.

*A Woman Scorned: Acquaintance Rape on Trial.* Peggy Reeves Sanday, Doubleday, New York, 1996.

## Incestuous Sexual Abuse

*Bad Girls/Good Girls.* Nan Bauer Maglin and Donna Perry, eds. Rutgers University Press, New Brunswick, NJ, 1996.

*Betrayal Trauma: The Logic of Forgetting Childhood Abuse.* Jennifer Freyd. Harvard University Press, Cambridge, MA, 1996.

*The Courage to Heal.* Ellen Bass and Laura Davis. Harper & Row, New York, 1988.

*Crossing the Boundary: Black Women Survive Incest.* Melba Wilson. Seal, Seattle, 1994.

*Secret Survivors: Uncoving Incest and Its Aftereffects in Women.* Sue E. Blume. Wiley, New York, 1990.

*The Secret Trauma: Incest in the Lives of Girls and Women.* Diana E. H. Russell. Basic, New York, 1984.

*Voices in the Night: Women Speaking About Incest.* Toni A. H. McNaron and Yarrow Margan. Cleis, Minneapolis, 1982.

PART VII: CHANGING OUR WORLD

## *Feminism as a Social Movement*

*Ain't I a Woman: Black Women and Feminism.* bell hooks. South End, Boston, 1981.

*Black Feminist Thought: Knowledge, Consciousness and the Politics of Empowerment.* Patricia Hill Collins. Unwin Hyman, Boston, 1990.

*Century of Struggle.* Eleanor Flexner. Athenaeum, New York, 1972.

*The Challenge of Local Feminisms.* Amrita Basu, ed. Westview, Boulder, CO, 1995.

*Changing Our Lives: Lesbian Passions, Politics and Priorities.* Veronica Groocock. London, Cassell, 1995.

*Chicana Feminist Thought: The Basic Historical Writings.* Alma Garcia, ed. Routledge, New York, 1997.

*Dragon Ladies: Asian American Feminists Breathe Fire.* Sonia Shah, ed. South End, Boston, 1997.

*Faces of Feminism: An Activist's Reflections on the Women's Movement.* Sheila Tobias, Westview, Boulder, CO, 1997.

*Feminism in Our Time: The Essential Writings, WWII to the Present.* Miriam Schneir, ed. Random House, New York, 1994.

*The Feminist Papers: From Adams to De Beauvoir.* Alice Rossi. Northeastern University Press, Boston, 1988.

*Freedom from Violence: Women's Strategies From Around the World.* Margaret Schuler, ed. OEF International Unifem, New York, 1992.

*A Girl's Guide to Taking over the World: Writings From the Girl Zine Revolution.* Karen Green and Tristan Taormino, eds. St. Martin Griffin, New York, 1997.

*Home Girls: A Black Feminist Anthology.* Barbara Smith, ed. Kitchen Table Press, Latham, NY, 1983.

*Listen Up: Voices From the Next Feminist Generation.* Barbara Findlen. Seal, Seattle, 1995.

*Living Chicana Theory.* Carla Trujillo, ed. Third Woman Press, Berkeley, CA, 1998.

*Moving the Mountain: The Women's Movement in America Since 1960.* Flora Davis. Simon & Schuster, New York, 1991.

*Ours By Right: Women's Rights as Human Rights.* Joanna Kerr, ed. Zed, New York, 1993.

*Sisterhood Is Global: The First Anthology of Writings from the International Women's Movement.* Anchor Press/Doubleday, Garden City, NY, 1984.

*Third Wave Agenda: Being Feminist, Doing Feminism.* Leslie Heywood and Jennifer Drake, eds. University of Minnesota Press, Minneapolis, 1997.

*To Be Real: Telling the Truth and Changing the Face of Feminism.* Rebecca Walker. Doubleday, New York, 1995.

*When and Where I Enter: The Impact of Black Women on Race and Sex in America.* Paula Giddings. Morrow, New York, 1984.

*Words of Fire: An Anthology of African-American Feminist Thought.* Beverly Guy-Sheftall, ed. New Press, New York, 1995.

## *Women Organizing: Many Issues, Many Voices*

*Bridges of Power: Women's Multicultural Alliances.* Lisa Albrecht and Rose Brewer. New Society Publishers, Philadelphia, 1990.

*Community Activism and Feminist Politics: Organizing Across Race, Class and Gender.* Nancy Naples, ed. Routledge, New York, 1998.

*Earth Follies: Coming to Feminist Terms With the Global Environmental Crisis.* Joan Seager. Routledge, New York, 1993.

*Ecofeminism.* Maria Mies and Vandana Shiva. Zed Books, London, 1993.

*Feminist Fatale.* Paula Kamin. Fine, New York, 1991.

*Frontline Feminism 1975–1995: Essays from Sojourner's First Twenty Years.* Karen Cahn, ed. Aunt Lute Books, San Francisco, 1995.

*National Congress of Neighborhood Women Training Sourcebook*. Neighborhood Women, Brooklyn, 1993.

*No Middle Ground: Women and Radical Protest*. Kathleen M. Blee, ed. New York University Press, New York, 1998.

*Passionate Politics*. Charlotte Bunch, St. Martin's, New York, 1987.

*Peace as a Women's Issue: A History of the U.S. Movement for World Peace and Women's Rights*. Harriet Alonso. Syracuse University Press, Syracuse, NY, 1993.

*Rocking the Boat: Union Women's Voices, 1915–1975*. Brigid O'Farrell and Joyce L. Kornbluh. Rutgers University Press, New Brunswick, NJ, 1993.

*Rocking the Ship of State: Toward a Feminist Peace Politics*. Adrienne Harris and Ynestra King. Westview, Boulder, CO, 1989.

*A Tradition That Has No Name*. Mary Field Belenky, Lynne Bond, and Jacqueline Weinstock. Basic Books, New York, 1997.

*Toxic Struggles: The Theory and Practice of Environmental Justice*. Richard Hofrichter. New Society, Philadelphia, 1993.

*Voicing Power: Conversations with Visionary Women*. Gail Hanlon, ed. Westview, Boulder, CO, 1997.

*Women, AIDS, and Activism*. ACT UP/NY, Women and AIDS Book Group. South End Press, Boston, 1990.

*Women and Male Violence: The Visions and Struggles of the Battered Women's Movement*. Susan Schechter. South End, Boston, 1982.

*Women and the Politics of Empowerment*. Ann Bookman and Sandra Morgan. Temple University Press, Philadelphia, 1988.

*Women Transforming Politics: An Alternative Reader*. Cathy Cohen, Kathleen Jones, and Joan Tronto. New York University Press, New York, 1997.

*You Can't Kill the Spirit*. Pam McAllister. New Society Publishers, Philadelphia, 1992.

# Credits

*Article 71:* Reprinted by permission of Carol Stevens. Copyright © 1992 Carol Stevens.

*Article 72:* Reprinted by permission of David R. Godine, Publisher, Inc. Copyright © 1991 by Bebe Nixon.

*Article 73:* Reprinted with permission from Radical America.

*Article 74:* Reprinted with permission by Resist, Inc. Edited with permission of the author.

*Article 75:* First appeared in *Sojourner* Magazine, Boston, MA. From *Black Woman's Health Book: Speaking for Ourselves* by Evelyn White, ed. Reprinted with permission of Byllye Avery.

*Article 76:* From *Redbook,* June 1986. Used with permission from Redbook Magazine.

*Article 77:* From *On Being a Jewish Feminist* by Susannah Heschel, editor. Copyright © 1983 by Schocken Books, distributed by Pantheon Books, a division of Random House, Inc.

*Article 78:* Reprinted with permission from the July/August 1995 issue of *Common Boundary* magazine, 7005 Florida Street, Chevy Chase, MD 20815.

*Article 79:* Portions of Chapter 1 "Defining Racism" from *Why Are All the Black Kids Sitting Together in the Cafeteria?* by Beverly Daniel Tatum. Copyright © 1997 by Beverly Daniel Tatum. Reprinted by permission of Basic Books, a subsidiary of Perseus Books Group, LLC.

*Article 80:* From *Girls: An Anthology,* Edith Chevat, Laurie Piette, and Angie Angabrite, editors. Reprinted with permission of Edith Chevat.

*Article 81:* Reprinted from *Awake in the River,* Isthmus Press, 1978. Copyright © 1978 Janice Mirikitani, San Francisco, CA.

*Article 82:* Reprinted from *Not Vanishing,* Press Gang, Vancouver, Canada, 1988. Used with permission from the author.

*Article 83:* From *Morena,* Francisco A. Lomeli, editor. Reprinted with permission.

*Article 84:* From *An Autobiography* by Angela Davis, Random House, 1974. Reprinted with permission of the author.

*Article 85:* From *Afrikete, An Anthology of Black Lesbian Writing,* Catherine McKinley and Joyce Delancy, editors. Copyright © 1994, 1982 Alexis DeVeaux. Reprinted with permission of the author.

*Article 86:* From *Changing Our Power: An Introduction to Women's Studies.* Reprinted with permission of Donna Langston.

*Article 88:* Reprinted from *Skin: Talking About Sex, Class and Literature,* Firebrand Books, Ithaca, N.Y. Copyright © 1994 by Dorothy Allison. With permission from the publisher.

*Article 89:* From *The Things That Divide Us* by Faith Conlon, Rachel da Siva, and Barbara Wilson, editors, Seal Press, 1985. Reprinted with permission of the publisher.

*Article 90:* From *The Tribe of Dina* by Melanie Kaye/Kantrowitz. Copyright © 1989, 1986 by Melanie Kaye/Kantrowitz. Reprinted by permission of Beacon Press.

*Article 91:* "Grace Paley Reading" from *Tender* by Toi Derricotte. Copyright © 1997 by Toi Derricotte. Reprinted by permission of the University of Pittsburgh Press.

*Article 92:* From *Homophobia: A Weapon of Sexism* by Suzanne Pharr. Copyright © 1988 Chardon Press. Reprinted by permission of the publisher.

*Article 93:* From *Home Girls: A Black Feminist Anthology.* Copyright © 1983 by Julie Blackwommon aka Julie Carter. Used with permission of the author.

*Article 94:* From *Chicana Lesbians,* Carla Trujillo, editor, Third Woman Press, 1991. Reprinted by permission of the author.

*Article 95:* From *Harvard Educational Review,* 66:2 (Summer) 1996. Copyright © 1998 by the President and Fellows of Harvard College. All rights reserved.

*Article 96:* From *Forty-Three Septembers* by Jewelle Gomez, Firebrand Books, 1993. Copyright © 1993 by Jewelle Gomez. Reprinted by permission of the publisher.

*Article 97:* An earlier version of "Identity: Skin Blood Heart" by Minnie Bruce Pratt in *Rebellion, Essays 1980–1991,* Firebrand Books, 1991. Copyright © 1991 by Minnie Bruce Pratt. Reprinted by permission of the publisher.

*Article 98:* Copyright © 1988 by Peggy McIntosh. Excerpted from "White Privilege and Male Privilege: A Personal Account of Coming to See Correspondences Through Work in Women's Studies," Working Paper #189, Wellesley College Center for Research on Women, Wellesley, MA 02181. Longer version available. Permission to reprint must be obtained from Peggy McIntosh at (781) 283-2520; Fax (781) 283-2504.

*Article 99:* From *A Burst of Light* by Audre Lord, Firebrand Books, 1988. Copyright © 1988 by Audre Lorde. Used with permission from the publisher.

*Article 100:* From *Seeing Through the Sun* by Linda Hogan, Amherst: The University of Massachusetts Press, 1985. Copyright © 1985 by Linda Hogan. Reprinted with permission of the publisher.

*Article 101:* Reprinted with permission from Older Women's League.

*Article 102:* From *Look Me in the Eye: Old Women, Aging, and Ageism, Expanded Edition,* by Barbara Macdonald with Cynthia Rich, Spinsters Ink, 1983. Available from Spinsters Ink, P.O. Box 300170, Minneapolis, MN 55403.

*Article 103:* From *Every Other Path,* Arcadio Morales, Jr. and Brian Martinez, editors. Permission granted by Francisco A. Lomeli.

*Article 104:* Reprinted by permission of Christina Nannarone, eldest daughter of Ruth Dreamdigger, d. 6/18/97, and executor of her estate.

*Article 105:* From *Beginning to See the Light,* Wesleyan University Press, 1992. Copyright © 1992 by Ellen Willis. Reprinted by permission of University Press of New England.

*Article 106:* Copyright © 1992 by Laura Wells. By permission of the author.

*Article 107:* Reprinted from *In These Times,* a bi-weekly newsmagazine published in Chicago.

*Article 109:* First printed in *Sojourner: The Women's Forum,*